Foundations of Computer Science
C Edition

PRINCIPLES OF COMPUTER SCIENCE SERIES

Series Editors
Alfred V. Aho, Bellcore, Morristown, New Jersey
Jeffrey D. Ullman, Stanford University, Stanford California

Alfred V. Aho and Jeffrey D. Ullman
Foundations of Computer Science: Pascal Edition
Foundations of Computer Science: C Edition

Egon Börger, Editor
Trends in Theoretical Computer Science

Michael J. Clancy and Marcia C. Linn
Designing Pascal Solutions

A. K. Dewdney
The New Turing Omnibus: 66 Excursions in Computer Science

Vladimir Drobot
Formal Languages and Automata Theory

Robert Floyd and Richard Biegel
The Language of Machines

David Maier
The Theory of Relational Databases

Martti Mäntylä
An Introduction to Solid Modeling

Shamim Naqvi and Shalom Tsur
A Logical Language for Data and Knowledge Bases

Christos Papadimitriou
The Theory of Database Concurrency Control

Theo Pavlidis
Algorithms for Graphics and Image Processing

Gregory J. E. Rawlins
Compared to What? An Introduction to the Analysis of Algorithms

Stuart C. Shapiro
LISP: An Interactive Approach
COMMONLISP: An Interactive Approach

Wei-Min Shen
Autonomous Learning From the Environment

James A. Storer
Data Compression: Methods and Theory

Steven Tanimoto
Elements of Artificial Intelligence Using COMMONLISP, 2nd Edition

Jeffrey D. Ullman
Computational Aspects of VLSI
Principles of Database and Knowledge-Base Systems, Vol. I: Classical Database Systems
Principles of Database and Knowledge-Base Systems, Vol. II: The New Technologies

Foundations of
Computer
Science
C Edition

Alfred V. Aho

Jeffrey D. Ullman

Computer Science Press

An Imprint of W. H. Freeman and Company • New York

Library of Congress Cataloging-in-Publication Data

Aho, Alfred V.
 Foundations of Computer Science / Alfred V. Aho, Jeffrey D.
Ullman. — C ed.
     p.   cm. -— (Principles of Computer Science)
  Includes index.
ISBN 0-7167-8284-7
  1. Computer Science.   2. C (Computer program language)
I. Ullman, Jeffrey D., 1942-   II. Title.
QA76.A334   1995
004–dc20   94-35405
                                                          CIP

Computer Science Press

An imprint of W. H. Freeman and Company
41 Madison Avenue, New York, NY 10010
20 Beaumont Street, Oxford OX1 2NQ, England

Second printing 1996, RRD

❖ Table of Contents

Preface

This book was motivated by the desire we and others have had to further the evolution of the core course in computer science. Many departments across the country have revised their curriculum in response to the introductory course in the science of computing discussed in the "Denning Report," (Denning, P. J., D. E. Comer, D. Gries, M. C. Mulder, A. Tucker, J. Turner, and P. R. Young, "Computing as a Discipline," *Comm. ACM* **32**:1, pp. 9–23, January 1989.). That report draws attention to three working methodologies or processes — theory, abstraction, and design — as fundamental to all undergraduate programs in the discipline. More recently, the *Computing Curricula 1991* report of the joint ACM/IEEE-CS Curriculum Task Force echoes the Denning Report in identifying key recurring concepts which are fundamental to computing, especially: conceptual and formal models, efficiency, and levels of abstraction. The themes of these two reports summarize what we have tried to offer the student in this book.

This book developed from notes for a two-quarter course at Stanford — called CS109: *Introduction to Computer Science* — that serves a number of goals. The first goal is to give beginning computer science majors a solid foundation for further study. However, computing is becoming increasingly important in a much wider range of scientific and engineering disciplines. Therefore, a second goal is to give those students who will not take advanced courses in computer science the conceptual tools that the field provides. Finally, a more pervasive goal is to expose all students not only to programming concepts but also to the intellectually rich foundations of the field.

Our first version of this book was based on programming in Pascal and appeared in 1992. Our choice of Pascal as the language for example programs was motivated by that language's use in the Computer Science Advanced Placement Test as well as in a plurality of college introductions to programming. We were pleased to see that since 1992 there has been a significant trend toward C as the introductory programming language, and we accordingly developed a new version of the book using C for programming examples. Our emphasis on abstraction and encapsulation should provide a good foundation for subsequent courses covering object-oriented technology using C++.

At the same time, we decided to make two significant improvements in the content of the book. First, although it is useful to have a grounding in machine architecture to motivate how running time is measured, we found that almost all curricula separate architecture into a separate course, so the chapter on that subject was not useful. Second, many introductory courses in the theory of computing emphasize combinatorics and probability, so we decided to increase the coverage and cluster the material into a chapter of its own.

Foundations of Computer Science covers subjects that are often found split between a discrete mathematics course and a sophomore-level sequence in computer science in data structures. It has been our intention to select the mathematical foundations with an eye toward what the computer user really needs, rather than what a mathematician might choose. We have tried to integrate effectively the mathematical foundations with the computing. We thus hope to provide a better feel for the soul of computer science than might be found in a programming course, a discrete mathematics course, or a course in a computer science subspecialty. We believe that, as time goes on, all scientists and engineers will take a foundational course similar to the one offered at Stanford upon which this book is based. Such a course in computer science should become as standard as similar courses in calculus and physics.

Prerequisites

Students taking courses based on this book have ranged from first-year undergraduates to graduate students. We assume only that students have had a solid course in programming. They should be familiar with the programming language ANSI C to use this edition. In particular, we expect students to be comfortable with C constructs such as recursive functions, structures, pointers, and operators involving pointers and structures such as dot, ->, and &.

Suggested Outlines for Foundational Courses in CS

In terms of a traditional computer science curriculum, the book combines a first course in data structures — that is, a "CS2" course — with a course in discrete mathematics. We believe that the integration of these subjects is extremely desirable for two reasons:

1. It helps motivate the mathematics by relating it more closely to the computing.

2. Computing and mathematics can be mutually reinforcing. Some examples are the way recursive programming and mathematical induction are related in Chapter 2 and the way the free/bound variable distinction for logic is related to the scope of variables in programming languages in Chapter 14. Suggestions for instructive programming assignments are presented throughout the book.

There are a number of ways in which this book can be used.

A Two-Quarter or Two-Semester Course

The CS109A-B sequence at Stanford is typical of what might be done in two quarters, although these courses are rather intensive, being 4-unit, 10-week courses each. These two courses cover the entire book, the first seven chapters in CS109A and Chapters 8 through 14 in CS109B.

A One-Semester "CS2" Type Course

It is possible to use the book for a one-semester course covering a set of topics similar to what would appear in a "CS2" course. Naturally, there is too much material in the book to cover in one semester, and so we recommend the following:

1. *Recursive algorithms and programs* in Sections 2.7 and 2.8.

2. *Big-oh analysis and running time of programs*: all of Chapter 3 except for Section 3.11 on solving recurrence relations.

3. *Trees* in Sections 5.2 through 5.10.

4. *Lists*: all of Chapter 6. Some may wish to cover lists before trees, which is a more traditional treatment. We regard trees as the more fundamental notion, but there is little harm in switching the order. The only significant dependency is that Chapter 6 talks about the "dictionary" abstract data type (set with operations *insert*, *delete*, and *lookup*), which is introduced in Section 5.7 as a concept in connection with binary search trees.

5. *Sets and relations.* Data structures for sets and relations are emphasized in Sections 7.2 through 7.9 and 8.2 through 8.6.

6. *Graph algorithms* are covered in Sections 9.2 through 9.9.

A One-Semester Discrete Mathematics Course

For a one-semester course emphasizing mathematical foundations, the instructor could choose to cover:

1. *Mathematical induction and recursive programs* in Chapter 2.

2. *Big-oh analysis, running time, and recurrence relations* in Sections 3.4 through 3.11.

3. *Combinatorics* in Sections 4.2 through 4.8.

4. *Discrete probability* in Sections 4.9 through 4.13.

5. *Mathematical aspects of trees* in Sections 5.2 through 5.6.

6. *Mathematical aspects of sets* in Sections 7.2, 7.3, 7.7, 7.10, and 7.11.

7. *The algebra of relations* in Sections 8.2, 8.7, and 8.9.

8. *Graph algorithms and graph theory* in Chapter 9.

9. *Automata and regular expressions* in Chapter 10.

10. *Context-free grammars* in Sections 11.2 through 11.4.

11. *Propositional and predicate logic* in Chapters 12 and 14, respectively.

Features of This Book

To help the student assimilate the material, we have added the following study aids:

1. Each chapter has an outline section at the beginning and a summary section at the end highlighting the main points.

2. Marginal notes mark important concepts and definitions. However, items mentioned in section or subsection headlines are not repeated in the margin.

3. "Sidebars" are separated from the text by double lines. These short notes serve several purposes:

   ✦ Some are elaborations on the text or make some fine points about program or algorithm design.

   ✦ Others are for summary or emphasis of points made in the text nearby. These include outlines of important kinds of proofs, such as the various forms of proof by induction.

   ✦ A few are used to give examples of *fallacious* arguments, and we hope that the separation from the text in this way will eliminate possible misconstruction of the point.

◆   A few give very brief introductions to major topics like undecidability or the history of computers to which we wish we could devote a full section.

4.   Most of the sections end with exercises. There are more than 1000 exercises or parts spread among the sections. Of these roughly 30% are marked with a single star, which indicates that they require more thought than the unstarred exercises. Approximately another 10% of the exercises are doubly starred, and these are the most challenging.

5.   Chapters end with bibliographic notes. We have not attempted to be exhaustive, but offer suggestions for more advanced texts on the subject of the chapter and mention the relevant papers with the most historical significance.

About the Cover

It is a tradition for computer science texts to have a cover with a cartoon or drawing symbolizing the content of the book. Here, we have drawn on the myth of the world as the back of a turtle, but our world is populated with representatives of some of the other, more advanced texts in computer science that this book is intended to support. They are:

The teddy bear: R. Sethi, *Programming Languages: Concepts and Constructs*, Addison-Wesley, Reading, Mass., 1989.

The baseball player: J. D. Ullman, *Principles of Database and Knowledge-Base Systems*, Computer Science Press, New York, 1988.

The column: J. L. Hennessy and D. A. Patterson, *Computer Architecture: a Quantitative Approach*, Morgan-Kaufmann, San Mateo, Calif., 1990.

The dragon: A. V. Aho, R. Sethi, and J. D. Ullman, *Compiler Design: Principles, Techniques, and Tools*, Addison-Wesley, Reading, Mass., 1986.

The triceratops: J. L. Peterson and A. Silberschatz, *Operating Systems Concepts*, second edition, Addison-Wesley, Reading, Mass., 1985.

Acknowledgments

We are deeply indebted to a number of colleagues and students who have read this material and given us many valuable suggestions for improving the presentation. We owe a special debt of gratitude to Brian Kernighan, Don Knuth, Apostolos Lerios, and Bob Martin who read the original Pascal manuscript in detail and gave us many perceptive comments. We have received, and gratefully acknowledge, reports of course testing of the notes for the Pascal edition of this book by Michael Anderson, Margaret Johnson, Udi Manber, Joseph Naor, Prabhakar Ragde, Rocky Ross, and Shuky Sagiv.

There are a number of other people who found errors in earlier editions, both the original notes and the various printings of the Pascal edition. In this regard, we would like to thank: Susan Aho, Michael Anderson, Aaron Edsinger, Lonnie Eldridge, Todd Feldman, Steve Friedland, Christopher Fuselier, Mike Genstil, Paul Grubb III, Barry Hayes, John Hwang, Hakan Jakobsson, Arthur Keller, Dean Kelley, James Kuffner Jr., Steve Lindell, Richard Long, Mark MacDonald, Simone Martini, Hugh McGuire, Alan Morgan, Monnia Oropeza, Rodrigo Philander, Andrew Quan, Stuart Reges, John Stone, Keith Swanson, Steve Swenson, Sanjai Tiwari, Eric Traut, and Lynzi Ziegenhagen.

We acknowledge helpful advice from Geoff Clem, Jon Kettenring, and Brian Kernighan during the preparation of the C edition of *Foundations of Computer Science.*

Peter Ullman produced a number of the figures used in this book. We are grateful to Dan Clayton, Anthony Dayao, Mat Howard, and Ron Underwood for help with TEX fonts, and to Hester Glynn and Anne Smith for help with the manuscript preparation.

On-Line Access to Code, Errata, and Notes

You can obtain copies of the major programs in this book by anonymous ftp to host `ftp-cs.stanford.edu`. Login with user name `anonymous` and give your name and host as a password. You may then execute

```
cd fcsc
```

where you will find programs from this book. We also plan to keep in this directory information about errata and what course notes we can provide.

A. V. A.
Chatham, NJ

J. D. U.
Stanford, CA

July, 1994

1

❖

Computer Science: The Mechanization of Abstraction

Abstraction

Though it is a new field, computer science already touches virtually every aspect of human endeavor. Its impact on society is seen in the proliferation of computers, information systems, text editors, spreadsheets, and all of the wonderful application programs that have been developed to make computers easier to use and people more productive. An important part of the field deals with how to make programming easier and software more reliable. But fundamentally, computer science is a science of *abstraction* — creating the right model for thinking about a problem and devising the appropriate mechanizable techniques to solve it.

Every other science deals with the universe as it is. The physicist's job, for example, is to understand how the world works, not to invent a world in which physical laws would be simpler or more pleasant to follow. Computer scientists, on the other hand, must create abstractions of real-world problems that can be understood by computer users and, at the same time, that can be represented and manipulated inside a computer.

Sometimes the process of abstraction is simple. For example, we can model the behavior of the electronic circuits used to build computers quite well by an abstraction called "propositional logic." The modeling of circuits by logical expressions is not exact; it simplifies, or abstracts away, many details — such as the time it takes for electrons to flow through circuits and gates. Nevertheless, the propositional logic model is good enough to help us design computer circuits well. We shall have much more to say about propositional logic in Chapter 12.

Exam scheduling

As another example, suppose we are faced with the problem of scheduling final examinations for courses. That is, we must assign course exams to time slots so that two courses may have their exams scheduled in the same time slot only if there is no student taking both. At first, it may not be apparent how we should model this problem. One approach is to draw a circle called a *node* for each course and draw a line called an *edge* connecting two nodes if the corresponding courses have a student in common. Figure 1.1 suggests a possible picture for five courses; the picture is called a *course-conflict graph.*

Given the course-conflict graph, we can solve the exam-scheduling problem by repeatedly finding and removing "maximal independent sets" from the graph. An

1

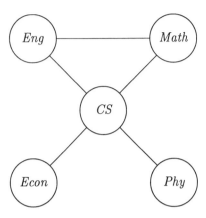

Fig. 1.1. Course-conflict graph for five courses. An edge between two courses indicates that at least one student is taking both courses.

Maximal independent set

independent set is a collection of nodes that have no connecting edges within the collection. An independent set is *maximal* if no other node from the graph can be added without including an edge between two nodes of the set. In terms of courses, a maximal independent set is any maximal set of courses with no common students. In Fig. 1.1, $\{Econ, Eng, Phy\}$ is one maximal independent set. The set of courses corresponding to the selected maximal independent set is assigned to the first time slot.

We remove from the graph the nodes in the first maximal independent set, along with all incident edges, and then find a maximal independent set among the remaining courses. One choice for the next maximal independent set is the singleton set $\{CS\}$. The course in this maximal independent set is assigned to the second time slot.

We repeat this process of finding and deleting maximal independent sets until no more nodes remain in the course-conflict graph. At this point, all courses will have been assigned to time slots. In our example, after two iterations, the only remaining node in the course-conflict graph is *Math*, and this forms the final maximal independent set, which is assigned to the third time slot. The resulting exam schedule is thus

TIME SLOT	COURSE EXAMS
1	*Econ, Eng, Phy*
2	*CS*
3	*Math*

This algorithm does not necessarily partition the courses among the smallest possible number of time slots, but it is simple and does tend to produce a schedule with close to the smallest number of time slots. It is also one that can be readily programmed using the techniques presented in Chapter 9.

Notice that this approach abstracts away some details of the problem that may be important. For example, it could cause one student to have five exams in five consecutive time slots. We could create a model that included limits on how many exams in a row one student could take, but then both the model and the solution

Abstraction: Not to Be Feared

The reader may cringe at the word "abstraction," because we all have the intuition that abstract things are hard to understand; for example, abstract algebra (the study of groups, rings, and the like) is generally considered harder than the algebra we learned in high school. However, abstraction in the sense we use it implies simplification, the replacement of a complex and detailed real-world situation by an understandable model within which we can solve a problem. That is, we "abstract away" the details whose effect on the solution to a problem is minimal or nonexistent, thereby creating a model that lets us deal with the essence of the problem.

to the exam-scheduling problem would be more complicated.

Often, finding a good abstraction can be quite difficult because we are forced to confront the fundamental limitations on the tasks computers can perform and the speed with which computers can perform those tasks. In the early days of computer science, some optimists believed that robots would soon have the prodigious capability and versatility of the *Star Wars* robot C3PO. Since then we have learned that in order to have "intelligent" behavior on the part of a computer (or robot), we need to provide that computer with a model of the world that is essentially as detailed as that possessed by humans, including not only facts ("Sally's phone number is 555-1234"), but principles and relationships ("If you drop something, it usually falls downward").

Knowledge representation

We have made much progress on this problem of "knowledge representation." We have devised abstractions that can be used to help build programs that do certain kinds of reasoning. One example of such an abstraction is the directed graph, in which nodes represent entities ("the species cat" or "Fluffy") and arrows (called *arcs*) from one node to another represent relationships ("Fluffy is a cat," "cats are animals," "Fluffy owns Fluffy's milk saucer"); Figure 1.2 suggests such a graph.

Another useful abstraction is formal logic, which allows us to manipulate facts by applying rules of inference, such as "If X is a cat and Y is the mother of X, then Y is a cat." Nevertheless, progress on modeling, or abstracting, the real world or significant pieces thereof remains a fundamental challenge of computer science, one that is not likely to be solved completely in the near future.

❖❖ 1.1   What This Book Is About

This book will introduce the reader, who is assumed to have a working knowledge of the programming language ANSI C, to the principal ideas and concerns of computer science. The book emphasizes three important problem-solving tools:

1. *Data models*, the abstractions used to describe problems. We have already mentioned two models: logic and graphs. We shall meet many others throughout this book.

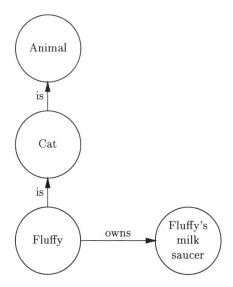

Fig. 1.2. A graph representing knowledge about Fluffy.

2. *Data structures*, the programming-language constructs used to represent data models. For example, C provides built-in abstractions, such as structures and pointers, that allow us to construct data structures to represent complex abstractions such as graphs.

3. *Algorithms*, the techniques used to obtain solutions by manipulating data as represented by the abstractions of a data model, by data structures, or by other means.

Data Models

We meet data models in two contexts. Data models such as the graphs discussed in the introduction to this chapter are abstractions frequently used to help formulate solutions to problems. We shall learn about several such data models in this book: trees in Chapter 5, lists in Chapter 6, sets in Chapter 7, relations in Chapter 8, graphs in Chapter 9, finite automata in Chapter 10, grammars in Chapter 11, and logic in Chapters 12 and 14.

Data models are also associated with programming languages and computers. For example, C has a data model that includes abstractions such as characters, integers of several sizes, and floating-point numbers. Integers and floating-point numbers in C are only approximations of integers and reals in mathematics because of the limited precision of arithmetic available in computers. The C data model also includes types such as structures, pointers, and functions, which we shall discuss in more detail in Section 1.4.

Data Structures

When the data model of the language in which we are writing a program lacks a built-in representation for the data model of the problem at hand, we must represent the needed data model using the abstractions supported by the language. For this purpose, we study *data structures*, which are methods for representing in the data model of a programming language abstractions that are not an explicit part of that language. Different programming languages may have strikingly different data models. For example, unlike C, the language Lisp supports trees directly, and the language Prolog has logic built into its data model.

Algorithms

An *algorithm* is a precise and unambiguous specification of a sequence of steps that can be carried out mechanically. The notation in which an algorithm is expressed can be any commonly understood language, but in computer science algorithms are most often expressed formally as programs in a programming language, or in an informal style as a sequence of programming language constructs intermingled with English language statements. Most likely, you have already encountered several important algorithms while studying programming. For example, there are a number of algorithms for *sorting* the elements of an array, that is, putting the elements in smallest-first order. There are clever searching algorithms such as *binary search*, which quickly finds a given element in a sorted array by repeatedly dividing in half the portion of the array in which the element could appear.

These, and many other "tricks" for solving common problems, are among the tools the computer scientist uses when designing programs. We shall study many such techniques in this book, including the important methods for sorting and searching. In addition, we shall learn what makes one algorithm better than another. Frequently, the *running time*, or time taken by an algorithm measured as a function of the size of its input, is one important aspect of the "quality" of the algorithm; we discuss running time in Chapter 3.

Other aspects of algorithms are also important, particularly their simplicity. Ideally, an algorithm should be easy to understand and easy to turn into a working program. Also, the resulting program should be understandable by a person reading the code that implements the algorithm. Unfortunately, our desires for a fast algorithm and a simple algorithm are often in conflict, and we must choose our algorithm wisely.

Underlying Threads

As we progress through this book, we shall encounter a number of important unifying principles. We alert the reader to two of these here:

1. *Design algebras.* In certain fields in which the underlying models have become well understood, we can develop notations in which design trade-offs can be expressed and evaluated. Through this understanding, we can develop a theory of design with which well-engineered systems can be constructed. Propositional logic, with the associated notation called *Boolean algebra* that we encounter in Chapter 12, is a good example of this kind of design algebra. With it, we can design efficient circuits for subsystems of the kind found in digital computers. Other examples of algebras found in this book are the algebra of sets in Chapter 7, the algebra of relations in Chapter 8, and the algebra of regular expressions in Chapter 10.

2. *Recursion* is such a useful technique for defining concepts and solving problems that it deserves special mention. We discuss recursion in detail in Chapter 2 and use it throughout the rest of the book. Whenever we need to define an object precisely or whenever we need to solve a problem, we should always ask, "What does the recursive solution look like?" Frequently that solution has a simplicity and efficiency that makes it the method of choice.

✦✦ 1.2   What This Chapter Is About

The remainder of this chapter sets the stage for the study of computer science. The primary concepts that will be covered are

✦   Data models (Section 1.3)

✦   The data model of the programming language C (Section 1.4)

✦   The principal steps in the software-creation process (Section 1.5)

We shall give examples of several different ways in which abstractions and models appear in computer systems. In particular, we mention the models found in programming languages, in certain kinds of systems programs, such as operating systems, and in the circuits from which computers are built. Since software is a vital component of today's computer systems, we need to understand the software-creation process, the role played by models and algorithms, and the aspects of software creation that computer science can address only in limited ways.

In Section 1.6 there are some conventional definitions that are used in C programs throughout this book.

✦✦ 1.3   Data Models

Any mathematical concept can be termed a data model. In computer science, a data model normally has two aspects:

1. The values that objects can assume. For example, many data models contain objects that have integer values. This aspect of the data model is *static*; it tells us what values objects may take. The static part of a programming language's
Type system
data model is often called the *type system*.

2. The operations on the data. For example, we normally apply operations such as addition to integers. This aspect of the model is *dynamic*; it tells us the ways in which we can change values and create new values.

Programming Language Data Models

Each programming language has its own data model, and these differ from one another, often in quite substantial ways. The basic principle under which most programming languages deal with data is that each program has access to "boxes," which we can think of as regions of storage. Each box has a type, such as `int` or `char`. We may store in a box any value of the correct type for that box. We often
Data object
refer to the values that can be stored in boxes as *data objects*.

Name

We may also name boxes. In general, a *name* for a box is any expression that denotes that box. Often, we think of the names of boxes as the variables of the program, but that is not quite right. For example, if x is a variable local to a recursive function F, then there may be many boxes named x, each associated with a different call to F. Then the true name of such a box is a combination of x and the particular call to F.

Most of the data types of C are familiar: integers, floating-point numbers, characters, arrays, structures, and pointers. These are all static notions.

Dereferencing

The operations permitted on data include the usual arithmetic operations on integers and floating-point numbers, accessing operations for elements of arrays or structures, and pointer *dereferencing*, that is, finding the element pointed to by a pointer. These operations are part of the dynamics of the C data model.

The list data model

In a programming course, we would see important data models that are not part of C, such as lists, trees, and graphs. In mathematical terms, a list is a sequence of n elements, which we shall write as $(a_1, a_2, \ldots, a_n)$, where a_1 is the first element, a_2 the second, and so on. Operations on lists include inserting new elements, deleting elements, and *concatenating* lists (that is, appending one list to the end of another).

✦ **Example 1.1.** In C, a list of integers can be represented by a data structure called a *linked list* in which list elements are stored in cells. Lists and their cells can be defined by a type declaration such as

```
typedef struct CELL *LIST;
struct CELL {
    int element;
    struct LIST next;
};
```

This declaration defines a self-referential structure CELL with two fields. The first is element, which holds the value of an element of the list and is of type int.

The second field of each CELL is next, which holds a pointer to a cell. Note that the type LIST is really a pointer to a CELL. Thus, structures of type CELL can be linked together by their next fields to form what we usually think of as a linked list, as suggested in Fig. 1.3. The next field can be thought of as either a pointer to the next cell or as representing the entire list that follows the cell in which it appears. Similarly, the entire list can be represented by a pointer, of type LIST, to the first cell on the list.

Fig. 1.3. A linked list representing the list $(a_1, a_2, \ldots, a_n)$.

Cells are represented by rectangles, the left part of which is the element, and the right part of which holds a pointer, shown as an arrow to the next cell pointed to. A dot in the box holding a pointer means that the pointer is NULL.[1] Lists will be covered in more detail in Chapter 6. ✦

---

[1] NULL is a symbolic constant defined in the standard header file stdio.h to be equal to a value that cannot be a pointer to anything. We shall use it to have this meaning throughout the book.

Data Models Versus Data Structures

Despite their similar names, a "list" and a "linked list" are very different concepts. A list is a mathematical abstraction, or data model. A linked list is a data structure. In particular, it is the data structure we normally use in C and many similar languages to represent abstract lists in programs. There are other languages in which it is not necessary to use a data structure to represent abstract lists. For example, the list $(a_1, a_2, \ldots, a_n)$ could be represented directly in the language Lisp and in the language Prolog similarly, as $[a_1, a_2, \ldots, a_n]$.

Data Models of System Software

Operating systems

Data models are found not only in programming languages but also in operating systems and applications programs. You are probably familiar with an operating system such as UNIX or MS-DOS (perhaps with Microsoft Windows).[2] The function of an operating system is to manage and schedule the resources of a computer. The data model for an operating system like UNIX has concepts such as files, directories, and processes.

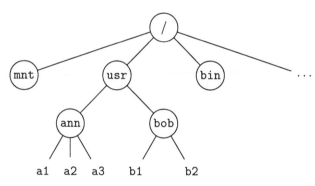

Fig. 1.4. A typical UNIX directory/file structure.

Files

1. The data itself is stored in *files*, which in the UNIX system are strings of characters.

Directories

2. Files are organized into *directories*, which are collections of files and/or other directories. The directories and files form a tree with the files at the leaves.[3] Figure 1.4 suggests the tree that might represent the directory structure of a typical UNIX operating system. Directories are indicated by circles. The root directory / contains directories called `mnt`, `usr`, `bin`, and so on. The directory `/usr` contains directories `ann` and `bob`; directory `ann` contains three files: `a1`, `a2`, and `a3`.

---

[2] If you are unfamiliar with operating systems, you can skip the next paragraphs. However, most readers have probably encountered an operating system, perhaps under another name. For example, the Macintosh "system" is an operating system, although different terminology is used. For example, a directory becomes a "folder" in Macintosh-ese.

[3] However, "links" in directories may make it appear that a file or directory is part of several different directories.

Processes

Pipes

3. *Processes* are individual executions of programs. Processes take zero or more streams as input and produce zero or more streams as output. In the UNIX system, processes can be combined by *pipes*, where the output from one process is fed as input into the next process. The resulting composition of processes can be viewed as a single process with its own input and output.

✦ **Example 1.2.** Consider the UNIX command line

```
bc | word | speak
```

The symbol | indicates a *pipe*, an operation that makes the output of the process on the left of this symbol be the input to the process on its right. The program bc is a desk calculator that takes arithmetic expressions, such as $2 + 3$, as input and produces the answer 5 as output. The program word translates numbers into words; speak translates words into phoneme sequences, which are then uttered over a loudspeaker by a voice synthesizer. Connecting these three programs together by pipes turns this UNIX command line into a single process that behaves like a "talking" desk calculator. It takes as input arithmetic expressions and produces as output the spoken answers. This example also suggests that a complex task may be implemented more easily as the composition of several simpler functions. ✦

There are many other aspects to an operating system, such as how it manages security of data and interaction with the user. However, even these few observations should make it apparent that the data model of an operating system is rather different from the data model of a programming language.

Text editors

Another type of data model is found in text editors. Every text editor's data model incorporates a notion of text strings and editing operations on text. The data model usually includes the notion of *lines*, which, like most files, are character strings. However, unlike files, lines may have associated line numbers. Lines may also be organized into larger units such as paragraphs, and operations on lines are normally applicable anywhere within the line — not just at the front, like the most common file operations. The typical editor supports a notion of a "current" line (where the cursor is) and probably a current position within that line. Operations performed by the editor include various modifications to lines, such as deletion or insertion of characters within the line, deletion of lines, and creation of new lines. It is also possible in typical editors to search for features, such as specific character strings, among the lines of the file being edited.

In fact, if you examine any other familiar piece of software, such as a spreadsheet or a video game, a pattern emerges. Each program that is designed to be used by others has its own data model, within which the user must work. The data models we meet are often radically different from one another, both in the primitives they use to represent data and in the operations on that data that are offered to the user. Yet each data model is implemented, via data structures and the programs that use them, in some programming language.

The Data Model of Circuits

We shall also meet in this book a data model for computer circuits. This model, called *propositional logic*, is most useful in the design of computers. Computers are composed of elementary components called *gates*. Each gate has one or more inputs and one output; the value of an input or output can be only 0 or 1. A gate performs a simple function — such as AND, where the output is 1 if all the inputs are 1 and the output is 0 if one or more of the inputs are 0. At one level of abstraction, computer design is the process of deciding how to connect gates to perform the basic operations of a computer. There are many other levels of abstraction associated with computer design as well.

Figure 1.5 shows the usual symbol for an AND-gate, together with its *truth table,* which indicates the output value of the gate for each pair of input values.[4] We discuss truth tables in Chapter 12 and gates and their interconnections in Chapter 13.

x	y	z
0	0	0
0	1	0
1	0	0
1	1	1

Fig. 1.5. An AND-gate and its truth table.

♦   **Example 1.3.** To execute the C assignment statement a = b+c, a computer performs the addition with an *adder* circuit. In the computer, all numbers are represented in binary notation using the two digits 0 and 1 (called *binary digits,* or *bits* for short). The familiar algorithm for adding decimal numbers, where we add the digits at the right end, generate a carry to the next place to the left, add that carry and the digits at that place, generate a carry to the next place to the left, and so on, works in binary as well.

Bit

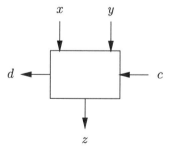

Fig. 1.6. A one-bit adder: dz is the sum $x + y + c$.

One-bit adder

Out of a few gates, we can build a *one-bit adder* circuit, as suggested in Fig. 1.6. Two input bits, x and y, and a *carry-in* bit c, are summed, resulting in a *sum* bit z and a *carry-out* bit d. To be precise, d is 1 if two or more of c, x, and y are 1,

---

[4] Note that if we think of 1 as "true" and 0 as "false," then the AND-gate performs the same logical operation as the && operator of C.

The Ripple-Carry Addition Algorithm

We all have used the ripple-carry algorithm to add numbers in decimal. To add $456 + 829$, for example, one performs the steps suggested below:

```
  1                 0
4 5 6             4 5 6             4 5 6
8 2 9             8 2 9             8 2 9
─────             ─────             ─────
    5               8 5           1 2 8 5
```

That is, at the first step, we add the rightmost digits, $6 + 9 = 15$. We write down the 5 and carry the 1 to the second column. At the second step, we add the carry-in, 1, and the two digits in the second place from the right, to get $1 + 5 + 2 = 8$. We write down the 8, and the carry is 0. In the third step, we add the carry-in, 0, and the digits in the third place from the right, to get $0 + 4 + 8 = 12$. We write down the 2, but since we are at the leftmost place, we do not carry the 1, but rather write it down as the leftmost digit of the answer.

Binary ripple-carry addition works the same way. However, at each place, the carry and the "digits" being added are all either 0 or 1. The one-bit adder thus describes completely the addition table for a single place. That is, if all three bits are 0, then the sum is 0, and so we write down 0 and carry 0. If one of the three is 1, the sum is 1; we write down 1 and carry 0. If two of the three are 1, the sum is 2, or 10 in binary; we write down 0 and carry 1. If all three are 1, then the sum is 3, or 11 in binary, and so we write down 1 and carry 1. For example, to add 101 to 111 using binary ripple-carry addition, the steps are

```
  1                 1
1 0 1             1 0 1             1 0 1
1 1 1             1 1 1             1 1 1
─────             ─────             ─────
    0               0 0           1 1 0 0
```

while z is 1 if an odd number (one or three) of c, x, and y are 1, as suggested by the table of Fig. 1.7. The carry-out bit followed by the sum bit — that is, dz — forms a two-bit binary number, which is the total number of x, y, and c that are 1. In this sense, the one-bit adder adds its inputs.

x	y	c	d	z
0	0	0	0	0
0	0	1	0	1
0	1	0	0	1
0	1	1	1	0
1	0	0	0	1
1	0	1	1	0
1	1	0	1	0
1	1	1	1	1

Fig. 1.7. Truth table for the one-bit adder.

Ripple-carry adder

Many computers represent integers as 32-bit numbers. An adder circuit can then be composed of 32 one-bit adders, as suggested in Fig. 1.8. This circuit is often called a *ripple-carry adder,* because the carry ripples from right to left, one bit at a time. Note that the carry into the rightmost (low-order bit) one-bit adder is always 0. The sequence of bits $x_{31}x_{30}\cdots x_0$ represents the bits of the first number being added, and $y_{31}y_{30}\cdots y_0$ is the second addend. The sum is $dz_{31}z_{30}\cdots z_0$; that is, the leading bit is the carry-out of the leftmost one-bit adder, and the following bits of the sum are the sum bits of the adders, from the left.

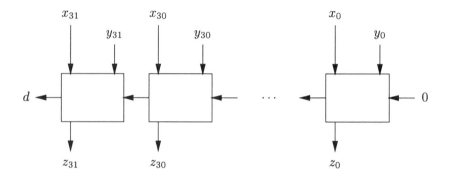

Fig. 1.8. A ripple-carry adder: $dz_{31}z_{30}\cdots z_0 = x_{31}x_{30}\cdots x_0 + y_{31}y_{30}\cdots y_0$.

The circuit of Fig. 1.8 is really an algorithm in the data model of bits and the primitive operations of gates. However, it is not a particularly good algorithm. The reason is that until we compute the carry-out of the rightmost place, we cannot compute z_1 or the carry-out of the second place. Until we compute the carry-out of the second place, we cannot compute z_2 or the carry-out of the third place, and so on. Thus, the time taken by the circuit is the length of the numbers being added — 32 in our case — multiplied by the time needed by a one-bit adder.

One might suspect that the need to "ripple" the carry through each of the one-bit adders, in turn, is inherent in the definition of addition. Thus, it may come as a surprise to the reader that computers have a much faster way of adding numbers. We shall cover such an improved algorithm for addition when we discuss the design of circuits in Chapter 13. ✦

EXERCISES

1.3.1: Explain the difference between the static and dynamic aspects of a data model.

1.3.2: Describe the data model of your favorite video game. Distinguish between static and dynamic aspects of the model. *Hint*: The static parts are not just the parts of the game board that do not move. For example, in Pac Man, the static part includes not only the map, but the "power pills," "monsters," and so on.

1.3.3: Describe the data model of your favorite text editor.

1.3.4: Describe the data model of a spreadsheet program.

✦✦ 1.4 The C Data Model

In this section we shall highlight important parts of the data model used by the C programming language. As an example of a C program, consider the program in Fig. 1.10 that uses the variable num to count the number of characters in its input.

```
#include <stdio.h>
main()
{
    int num;
    num = 0;
    while (getchar() != EOF)
        ++num; /* add 1 to num */
    printf("%d\n", num);
}
```

Fig. 1.10. C program to count number of input characters.

The first line tells the C preprocessor to include as part of the source the standard input/output file stdio.h, which contains the definitions of the functions getchar and printf, and the symbolic constant EOF, a value that represents the end of a file.

A C program itself consists of a sequence of definitions, which can be either function definitions or data definitions. One must be a definition of a function called main. The first statement in the function body of the program in Fig. 1.10 declares the variable num to be of type int. (All variables in a C program must be declared before their use.) The next statement initializes num to zero. The following while statement reads input characters one at a time using the library function getchar, incrementing num after each character read, until there are no more input characters. The end of file is signaled by the special value EOF on the input. The printf statement prints the value of num as a decimal integer, followed by a newline character.

EOF

The C Type System

We begin with the static part of the C data model, the type system, which describes the values that data may have. We then discuss the dynamics of the C data model, that is, the operations that may be performed on data.

In C, there is an infinite set of types, any of which could be the type associated with a particular variable. These types, and the rules by which they are constructed, form the *type system* of C. The type system contains basic types such as integers, and a collection of type-formation rules with which we can construct progressively more complex types from types we already know. The basic types of C are

1. Characters (char, signed char, unsigned char)
2. Integers (int, short int, long int, unsigned)
3. Floating-point numbers (float, double, long double)
4. Enumerations (enum)

Integers and floating-point numbers are considered to be *arithmetic types*.

The type-formation rules assume that we already have some types, which could be basic types or other types that we have already constructed using these rules. Here are some examples of the type formation rules in C:

1. *Array types.* We can form an array whose elements are type T with the declaration

   T `A[n]`

   This statement declares an array `A` of n elements, each of type T. In C, array subscripts begin at 0, so the first element is `A[0]` and the last element is `A[`$n-1$`]`. Arrays can be constructed from characters, arithmetic types, pointers, structures, unions, or other arrays.

Members of a structure

2. *Structure types.* In C, a structure is a grouping of variables called *members* or *fields*. Within a structure different members can have different types, but each member must have elements of a single type. If $T_1, T_2, \ldots, T_n$ are types and $M_1, M_2, \ldots, M_n$ are member names, then the declaration

   ```
   struct S {
       T₁ M₁;
       T₂ M₂;
           ...
       Tₙ Mₙ;
   }
   ```

   defines a structure whose *tag* (i.e., the name of its type) is S and that has n members. The ith member has the name M_i and a value of type T_i, for $i = 1, 2, \ldots, n$. Example 1.1 is an illustration of a structure. This structure has tag `CELL` and two members. The first member has name `element` and has integer type. The second has name `next` and its type is a pointer to a structure of the same type.

   The structure tag S is optional, but it provides a convenient shorthand for referring to the type in later declarations. For example, the declaration

   `struct` S `myRecord;`

   defines the variable `myRecord` to be a structure of type S.

3. *Union types.* A union type allows a variable to have different types at different times during the execution of a program. The declaration

   ```
   union {
       T₁ M₁;
       T₂ M₂;
           ...
       Tₙ Mₙ;
   } x;
   ```

   defines a variable `x` that can hold a value of any of the types $T_1, T_2, \ldots, T_n$. The member names $M_1, M_2, \ldots, M_n$ help indicate which type the value of `x` should be regarded as being. That is, `x.`M_i refers to the value of `x` treated as a value of type T_i.

4. *Pointer types.* C is distinctive for its reliance on pointers. A variable of type pointer contains the address of a region of storage. We can access the value of another variable indirectly through a pointer. The declaration

    T *p;

defines the variable p to be a pointer to a variable of type T. Thus p names a box of type pointer to T and the value in box p is a pointer. We often draw the value of p as an arrow, rather than as an object of type T itself, as shown in Fig. 1.11. What really appears in the box named p is the address, or location, at which an object of type T is stored in the computer.

Consider the declaration

    int x, *p;

In C, the unary operator & is used to obtain the address of an object, so the statement

    p = &x;

assigns the address of x to p; that is, it makes p point to x.

The unary operator * applied to p fetches the value of the box pointed to by p, so the statement

    y = *p;

assigns to y the contents of whatever box p points to. If y is a variable of type int, then

    p = &x;
    y = *p;

is equivalent to the assignment

    y = x;

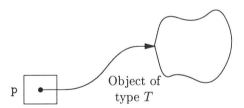

Fig. 1.11. Variable p is of type pointer to T.

◆ **Example 1.4.** C has the typedef construct to create synonyms for type names. The declaration

    typedef int Distance;

```
typedef int type1[10];

typedef type1 *type2;

typedef struct {
    int field1;
    type2 field2;
} type3;

typedef type3 type4[5];
```

Fig. 1.12. Some C `typedef` declarations.

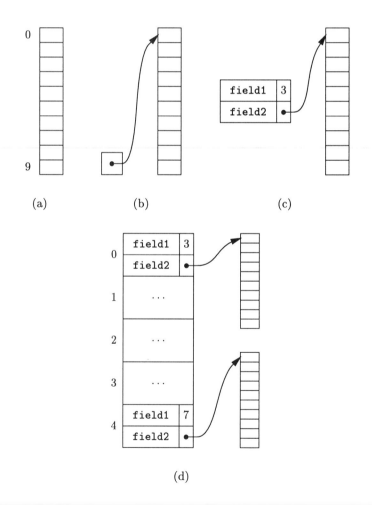

(a)   (b)   (c)

(d)

Fig. 1.13. Visualization of type declarations in Fig. 1.12.

Types, Names, Variables, and Identifiers

A number of terms associated with data objects have different meanings but are easy to confuse. First, a type describes a "shape" for data objects. In C, a new name T may be defined for an existing type using the typedef construct

typedef <type descriptor> T

Type descriptor

Here the *type descriptor* is an expression that tells us the shape of objects of the type T.

A typedef declaration for T does not actually create any objects of that type. An object of type T is created by a declaration of the form

T x;

Here, x is an *identifier,* or "variable name." Possibly, x is *static* (not local to any function), in which case the box for x is created when the program starts. If x is not static, then it is local to some function F. When F is called, a box whose name is "the x associated with this call to F" is created. More precisely, the name of the box is x, but only uses of the identifier x during the execution of this call to F refer to this box.

As mentioned in the text, there can be many boxes each of whose name involves the identifier x, since F may be recursive. There may even be other functions that also have used identifier x to name one of their variables. Moreover, names are more general than identifiers, since there are many kinds of expressions that could be used to name boxes. For instance, we mentioned that *p could be the name of an object pointed to by pointer p, and other names could be complex expressions such as (*p).f[2] or p->f[2]. The last two expressions are equivalent and refer to the array element number 2 of the field f of the structure pointed to by pointer p.

allows the name Distance to be used in place of the type int.

Consider the four typedef declarations in Fig. 1.12. In the conventional view of data in C, an object of type type1 is an array with 10 slots, each holding an integer, as suggested in Fig. 1.13(a). Likewise, objects of type type2 are pointers to such arrays, as in Fig. 1.13(b). Structures, like those of type3, are visualized as in Fig. 1.13(c), with a slot for each field; note that the name of the field (e.g., field1) does not actually appear with the value of the field. Finally, objects of the array type type4 would have five slots, each of which holds an object of type type3, a structure we suggest in Fig. 1.13(d). ✦

Functions

Functions also have associated types, even though we do not associate boxes or "values" with functions, as we do with program variables. For any list of types $T_1, T_2, \ldots, T_n$, we can define a function with n parameters consisting of those types, in order. This list of types followed by the type of the value returned by the function (the *return-value*) is the "type" of the function. If the function has no return value, its type is void.

Return-value

In general, we can build types by applying the type-construction rules arbitrarily, but there are a number of constraints. For example, we cannot construct an "array of functions," although we can construct an array of pointers to functions. The complete set of rules for constructing types in C can be found in the ANSI standard.

Operations in the C Data Model

The operations on data in the C data model can be divided into three categories:

1. Operations that create or destroy a data object.

2. Operations that access and modify parts of a data object.

3. Operations that combine the values of data objects to form a new value for a data object.

Data Object Creation and Disposal

For data creation, C provides several rudimentary mechanisms. When a function is called, boxes for each of its local arguments (parameters) are created; these serve to hold the values of the arguments.

Another mechanism for data creation is through the use of the library routine `malloc(n)`, which returns a pointer to n consecutive character positions of unused storage that can be used to store data by the caller of `malloc`. Data objects can then be created in this storage region.

C has the analogous methods for destroying data objects. Local parameters of a function call cease to exist when the function returns. The routine `free` releases the storage created by `malloc`. In particular, the effect of calling `free(p)` is to release the storage area pointed to by p. It is disastrous to use `free` to get rid of an object that was not created by calling `malloc`.

Data Access and Modification

C has mechanisms for accessing the components of objects. It uses `a[i]` to access the ith element of array a, `x.m` to access member m of a structure named x, and `*p` to access the object pointed to by pointer p.

Modifying, or *writing*, values in C is done principally by the assignment operators, which allow us to change the value of an object.

◆ **Example 1.5.** If a is a variable of type `type4` defined in Example 1.4, then

```
a[0].(*field2[3]) = 99;
```

assigns the value 99 to the fourth element of the array pointed to by `field2` in the structure that is the first element of the array a. ◆

Data Combination

C has a rich set of operators for manipulating and combining values. The principal operators are

1. *Arithmetic operators.* C provides:

a)   The customary binary arithmetic operators $+$, $-$, $*$, $/$ on integers and floating-point numbers. Integer division truncates (4/3 yields 1).

b)   There are the unary $+$ and $-$ operators.

c)   The modulus operator i % j produces the remainder when i is divided by j.

d)   The increment and decrement operators, ++ and --, applied to a single integer variable add or subtract 1 from that variable, respectively. These operators can appear before or after their operand, depending on whether we wish the value of the expression to be computed before or after the change in the variable's value.

2.   *Logical operators.* C does not have a Boolean type; it uses zero to represent the logical value false, and nonzero to represent true.[5] C uses:

a)   && to represent AND. For example, the expression x && y returns 1 if both operands are nonzero, 0 otherwise. However, y is not evaluated if x has the value 0.

b) || represents OR. The expression x || y returns 1 if either x or y is nonzero, and returns 0 otherwise. However, y is not evaluated if x is nonzero.

c)   The unary negation operator !x returns 0 if x is nonzero and returns 1 if $x = 0$.

d)   The conditional operator is a ternary (3-argument) operator represented by a question mark and a colon. The expression x?y:z returns the value of y if x is true (i.e., it is nonzero) and returns the value of z if x is false (i.e., 0).

3.   *Comparison operators.* The result of applying one of the six relational comparison operators (==, !=, <, >, <=, and >=) to integers or floating point numbers is 0 if the relation is false and 1 otherwise.

4.   *Bitwise manipulation operators.* C provides several useful bitwise logical operators, which treat integers as if they were bits strings equal to their binary representations. These include & for bitwise AND, | for bitwise inclusive-or, ^ for bitwise exclusive-or, << for left shift, >> for right shift, and a tilde for left shift.

5.   *Assignment operators.* C uses = as the assignment operator. In addition, C allows expressions such as

```
x = x + y;
```

to be written in a shortened form

```
x += y;
```

Similar forms apply to the other binary arithmetic operators.

---

[5]   We shall use TRUE and FALSE as defined constants 1 and 0, respectively, to represent Boolean values; see Section 1.6.

6.   *Coercion operators.* Coercion is the process of converting a value of one type into an equivalent value of another type. For example, if x is a floating-point number and i is an integer, then x = i causes the integer value of i to be converted to a floating-point number with the same value. Here, the coercion operator is not shown explicitly, but the C compiler can deduce that conversion from integer to float is necessary and inserts the required step.

EXERCISES

1.4.1: Explain the difference between an identifier of a C program and a name (for a "box" or data object).

1.4.2: Give an example of a C data object that has more than one name.

1.4.3: If you are familiar with another programming language besides C, describe its type system and operations.

✦✦ 1.5   Algorithms and the Design of Programs

The study of data models, their properties, and their appropriate use is one pillar of computer science. A second, equally important pillar is the study of algorithms and their associated data structures. We need to know the best ways to perform common tasks, and we need to learn the principal techniques for designing good algorithms. Further, we need to understand how the use of data structures and algorithms fits into the process of creating useful programs. The themes of data models, algorithms, data structures, and their implementation in programs are interdependent, and each appears many times throughout the book. In this section, we shall mention some generalities regarding the design and implementation of programs.

The Creation of Software

In a programming class, when you were given a programming problem, you probably designed an algorithm to solve the problem, implemented the algorithm in some language, compiled and ran the program on some sample data, and then submitted the program to be graded.

In a commercial setting, programs are written under rather different circumstances. Algorithms, at least those simple enough and common enough to have names, are usually small parts of a complete program. Programs, in turn, are usually components of a larger system, involving hardware as well as software. Both the programs and the complete systems in which they are embedded are developed by teams of programmers and engineers; there could be hundreds of people on such a team.

Software development process

The development of a software system typically spans several phases. Although these phases may superficially bear some resemblance to the steps involved in solving the classroom programming assignment, most of the effort in building a software system to solve a given problem is not concerned with programming. Here is an idealized scenario.

Problem definition and specification. The hardest, but most important, part of the task of creating a software system is defining what the problem really is and then specifying what is needed to solve it. Usually, problem definition begins by analyzing the users' requirements, but these requirements are often imprecise and hard to write down. The system architect may have to consult with the future users of the system and iterate the specification, until both the specifier and the users are satisfied that the specification defines and solves the problem at hand. In the specification stage, it may be helpful to build a simple prototype or model of the final system, to gain insight into its behavior and intended use. Data modeling is also an important tool in the problem-definition phase.

Prototyping

Design. Once the specification is complete, a high-level design of the system is created, with the major components identified. A document outlining the high-level design is prepared, and performance requirements for the system may be included. More detailed specifications of some of the major components may also be included during this phase. A cost-effective design often calls for the reuse or modification of previously constructed components. Various software methodologies such as object-oriented technology facilitate the reuse of components.

Software reuse

Implementation. Once the design is fixed, implementation of the components can proceed. Many of the algorithms discussed in this book are useful in the implementation of new components. Once a component has been implemented, it is subject to a series of tests to make sure that it behaves as specified.

Integration and system testing. When the components have been implemented and individually tested, the entire system is assembled and tested.

Installation and field testing. Once the developer is satisfied that the system will work to the customer's satisfaction, the system is installed on the customer's premises and the final field testing takes place.

Maintenance. At this point, we might think that the bulk of the work has been done. Maintenance remains, however, and in many situations maintenance can account for more than half the cost of system development. Maintenance may involve modifying components to eliminate unforeseen side-effects, to correct or improve system performance, or to add features. Because maintenance is such an important part of software systems design, it is important to write programs that are correct, rugged, efficient, modifiable, and — whenever possible — portable from one computer to another.

It is very important to catch errors as early as possible, preferably during the problem-definition phase. At each successive phase, the cost of fixing a design error or programming bug rises greatly. Independent reviews of requirements and designs are beneficial in reducing downstream errors.

Programming Style

An individual programmer can ease the maintenance burden greatly by writing programs that others can read and modify readily. Good programming style comes only with practice, and we recommend that you begin at once to try writing programs that are easy for others to understand. There is no magic formula that will guarantee readable programs, but there are several useful rules of thumb:

1. Modularize a program into coherent pieces.

2. Lay out a program so that its structure is clear.

3. Write intelligent comments to explain a program. Describe, clearly and precisely, the underlying data models, the data structures selected to represent them, and the operation performed by each procedure. When describing a procedure, state the assumptions made about its inputs, and tell how the output relates to the input.

4. Use meaningful names for procedures and variables.

Defined constants

5. Avoid explicit constants whenever possible. For example, do not use 7 for the number of dwarfs. Rather, use a defined constant such as `NumberOfDwarfs`, so that you can easily change all uses of this constant to 8, if you decide to add another dwarf.

Global variables

6. Avoid the use of "global variables" — that is, variables defined for the program as a whole — unless the data represented by that variable really is used by most of the procedures of the program.

Test suite

Another good programming practice is to maintain a test suite of inputs that will try to exercise every line of code while you are developing a program. Whenever new features are added to the program, the test suite can be run to make sure that the new program has the same behavior as the old on previously working inputs.

✦✦ 1.6 Some C Conventions Used Throughout the Book

There are several definitions and conventions that we shall find useful as we illustrate concepts with C programs. Some of these are common conventions found in the standard header file `stdio.h`, while others are defined specially for the purposes of this book and must be included with any C program that uses them.

NULL

1. The identifier `NULL` is a value that may appear anywhere a pointer can appear, but it is not a value that can ever point to anything. Thus, `NULL` in a field such as `next` in the cells of Example 1.1 can be used to indicate the end of a list. We shall see that `NULL` has a number of similar uses in other data structures. `NULL` is properly defined in `stdio.h`.

2. The identifiers `TRUE` and `FALSE` are defined by

```
#define TRUE 1
#define FALSE 0
```

TRUE and FALSE

Thus, `TRUE` can be used anywhere a condition with logical value true is wanted, and `FALSE` can be used for a condition whose value is false.

BOOLEAN

3. The type `BOOLEAN` is defined as

```
typedef int BOOLEAN;
```

We use `BOOLEAN` whenever we want to stress the fact that we are interested in the logical rather than the numeric value of an expression.

EOF

4. The identifier EOF is a value that is returned by file-reading functions such as getchar() when there are no more bytes left to be read from the file. An appropriate value for EOF is provided in stdio.h.

Cell definition

5. We shall define a macro that generates declarations of cells of the kind used in Example 1.1. An appropriate definition appears in Fig. 1.14. It declares cells with two fields: an element field whose type is given by the parameter Type and a next field to point to a cell with this structure. The macro provides two external definitions: CellName is the name of structures of this type, and ListName is a name for the type of pointers to these cells.

```
#define DefCell(EltType, CellType, ListType)          \
typedef struct CellType *ListType;                     \
struct CellType {                                       \
    EltType element;                                    \
    ListType next;                                      \
}
```

Fig. 1.14. A macro for defining list cells.

✦ **Example 1.6.** We can define cells of the type used in Example 1.1 by the macro use

```
DefCell(int, CELL, LIST);
```

The macro then expands into

```
typedef struct CELL, LIST;
struct CELL {
    int element;
    LIST next;
}
```

As a consequence, we can use CELL as the type of integer cells, and we can use LIST as the type of pointers to these cells. For example,

```
CELL c;
LIST L;
```

defines c to be a cell and L to be a pointer to a cell. Note that the representation of a list of cells is normally a pointer to the first cell on the list, or NULL if the list is empty. ✦

❖ 1.7 Summary of Chapter 1

At this point you should be aware of the following concepts:

✦ How data models, data structures, and algorithms are used to solve problems

✦ The distinction between a list as a data model and a linked list as a data structure

✦ The presence of some kind of data model in every software system, be it a programming language, an operating system, or an application program

✦ The key elements of the data model supported by the programming language C

✦ The major steps in the development of a large software system

✦✦ 1.8 Bibliographic Notes for Chapter 1

Kernighan and Ritchie [1988] is the classic reference for the C programming language. Roberts [1994] is a good introduction to programming using C.

Stroustrup [1991] has created an object-oriented extension of C called C++ that is now widely used for implementing systems. Sethi [1989] provides an introduction to the data models of several major programming languages.

Brooks [1974] eloquently describes the technical and managerial difficulties in developing large software systems. Kernighan and Plauger [1978] provide sound advice for improving your programming style.

American National Standards Institute (ANSI) [1990]. *Programming Language C*, American National Standards Institute, New York.

Brooks, F. P. [1974]. *The Mythical Man Month*, Addison-Wesley, Reading, Mass.

Kernighan, B. W., and P. J. Plauger [1978]. *The Elements of Programming Style*, *second edition*, McGraw-Hill, New York.

Kernighan, B. W., and D. M. Ritchie [1988]. *The C Programming Language*, second edition, Prentice-Hall, Englewood Cliffs, New Jersey.

Roberts, E. S. [1994]. *A C-Based Introduction to Computer Science*, Addison-Wesley, Reading, Mass.

Sethi, R. [1989]. *Programming Languages: Concepts and Constructs*, Addison-Wesley, Reading, Mass.

Stroustrup, B. [1991]. *The C++ Programming Language*, second edition, Addison-Wesley, Reading, Mass.

2

Iteration, Induction, and Recursion

The power of computers comes from their ability to execute the same task, or different versions of the same task, repeatedly. In computing, the theme of *iteration* is met in a number of guises. Many concepts in data models, such as lists, are forms of repetition, as "A list either is empty or is one element followed by another, then another, and so on." Programs and algorithms use iteration to perform repetitive jobs without requiring a large number of similar steps to be specified individually, as "Do the next step 1000 times." Programming languages use looping constructs, like the while- and for-statements of C, to implement iterative algorithms.

Closely related to repetition is *recursion,* a technique in which a concept is defined, directly or indirectly, in terms of itself. For example, we could have defined a list by saying "A list either is empty or is an element followed by a list." Recursion is supported by many programming languages. In C, a function F can call itself, either directly from within the body of F itself, or indirectly by calling some other function, which calls another, and another, and so on, until finally some function in the sequence calls F. Another important idea, *induction,* is closely related to "recursion" and is used in many mathematical proofs.

Iteration, induction, and recursion are fundamental concepts that appear in many forms in data models, data structures, and algorithms. The following list gives some examples of uses of these concepts; each will be covered in some detail in this book.

1. *Iterative techniques.* The simplest way to perform a sequence of operations repeatedly is to use an iterative construct such as the for-statement of C.

2. *Recursive programming.* C and many other languages permit recursive functions, which call themselves either directly or indirectly. Often, beginning programmers are more secure writing iterative programs than recursive ones, but an important goal of this book is to accustom the reader to thinking and programming recursively, when appropriate. Recursive programs can be simpler to write, analyze, and understand.

Notation: The Summation and Product Symbols

An oversized Greek capital letter sigma is often used to denote a summation, as in $\sum_{i=1}^{n} i$. This particular expression represents the sum of the integers from 1 to n; that is, it stands for the sum $1 + 2 + 3 + \cdots + n$. More generally, we can sum any function $f(i)$ of the summation index i. (Of course, the index could be some symbol other than i.) The expression $\sum_{i=a}^{b} f(i)$ stands for

$$f(a) + f(a+1) + f(a+2) + \cdots + f(b)$$

For example, $\sum_{j=2}^{m} j^2$ stands for the sum $4 + 9 + 16 + \cdots + m^2$. Here, the function f is "squaring," and we used index j instead of i.

As a special case, if $b < a$, then there are no terms in the sum $\sum_{i=a}^{b} f(i)$, and the value of the expression, by convention, is taken to be 0. If $b = a$, then there is exactly one term, that for $i = a$. Thus, the value of the sum $\sum_{i=a}^{a} f(i)$ is just $f(a)$.

The analogous notation for products uses an oversized capital pi. The expression $\prod_{i=a}^{b} f(i)$ stands for the product $f(a) \times f(a+1) \times f(a+2) \times \cdots \times f(b)$; if $b < a$, the product is taken to be 1.

---

3. *Proofs by induction.* An important technique for showing that a statement is true is "proof by induction." We shall cover inductive proofs extensively, starting in Section 2.3. The following is the simplest form of an inductive proof. We begin with a statement $S(n)$ involving a variable n; we wish to prove that $S(n)$ is true. We prove $S(n)$ by first proving a *basis*, that is, the **Basis** statement $S(n)$ for a particular value of n. For example, we could let $n = 0$ and **Inductive step** prove the statement $S(0)$. Second, we must prove an *inductive step,* in which we prove that the statement S, for one value of its argument, follows from the same statement S for the previous values of its argument; that is, $S(n)$ implies $S(n+1)$ for all $n \geq 0$. For example, $S(n)$ might be the familiar summation formula

$$\sum_{i=1}^{n} i = n(n+1)/2 \tag{2.1}$$

which says that the sum of the integers from 1 to n equals $n(n+1)/2$. The basis could be $S(1)$ — that is, Equation (2.1) with 1 in place of n — which is just the equality $1 = 1 \times 2/2$. The inductive step is to show that $\sum_{i=1}^{n} i = n(n+1)/2$ implies that $\sum_{i=1}^{n+1} i = (n+1)(n+2)/2$; the former is $S(n)$, which is Equation (2.1) itself, while the latter is $S(n+1)$, which is Equation (2.1) with $n+1$ replacing n everywhere n appears. Section 2.3 will show us how to construct proofs such as this.

4. *Proofs of program correctness.* In computer science, we often wish to prove, formally or informally, that a statement $S(n)$ about a program is true. The statement $S(n)$ might, for example, describe what is true on the nth iteration of some loop or what is true for the nth recursive call to some function. Proofs of this sort are generally inductive proofs.

5. *Inductive definitions.* Many important concepts of computer science, especially those involving data models, are best defined by an induction in which we give

a basis rule defining the simplest example or examples of the concept, and an inductive rule or rules, where we build larger instances of the concept from smaller ones. For instance, we noted that a list can be defined by a basis rule (an empty list is a list) together with an inductive rule (an element followed by a list is also a list).

6.   *Analysis of running time.* An important criterion for the "goodness" of an algorithm is how long it takes to run on inputs of various sizes (its "running time"). When the algorithm involves recursion, we use a formula called a *recurrence equation,* which is an inductive definition that predicts how long the algorithm takes to run on inputs of different sizes.

Each of these subjects, except the last, is introduced in this chapter; the running time of a program is the topic of Chapter 3.

✦✦ 2.1   What This Chapter Is About

In this chapter we meet the following major concepts.

✦   Iterative programming (Section 2.2)

✦   Inductive proofs (Sections 2.3 and 2.4)

✦   Inductive definitions (Section 2.6)

✦   Recursive programming (Sections 2.7 and 2.8)

✦   Proving the correctness of a program (Sections 2.5 and 2.9)

In addition, we spotlight, through examples of these concepts, several interesting and important ideas from computer science. Among these are

✦   Sorting algorithms, including selection sort (Section 2.2) and merge sort (Section 2.8)

✦   Parity checking and detection of errors in data (Section 2.3)

✦   Arithmetic expressions and their transformation using algebraic laws (Sections 2.4 and 2.6)

✦   Balanced parentheses (Section 2.6)

✦✦ 2.2   Iteration

Each beginning programmer learns to use iteration, employing some kind of looping construct such as the for- or while-statement of C. In this section, we present an example of an iterative algorithm, called "selection sort." In Section 2.5 we shall prove by induction that this algorithm does indeed sort, and we shall analyze its running time in Section 3.6. In Section 2.8, we shall show how recursion can help us devise a more efficient sorting algorithm using a technique called "divide and conquer."

Common Themes: Self-Definition and Basis-Induction

As you study this chapter, you should be alert to two themes that run through the various concepts. The first is self-definition, in which a concept is defined, or built, in terms of itself. For example, we mentioned that a list can be defined as being empty or as being an element followed by a list.

The second theme is basis-induction. Recursive functions usually have some sort of test for a "basis" case where no recursive calls are made and an "inductive" case where one or more recursive calls are made. Inductive proofs are well known to consist of a basis and an inductive step, as do inductive definitions. This basis-induction pairing is so important that these words are highlighted in the text to introduce each occurrence of a basis case or an inductive step.

There is no paradox or circularity involved in properly used self-definition, because the self-defined subparts are always "smaller" than the object being defined. Further, after a finite number of steps to smaller parts, we arrive at the basis case, at which the self-definition ends. For example, a list L is built from an element and a list that is one element shorter than L. When we reach a list with zero elements, we have the basis case of the definition of a list: "The empty list is a list."

As another example, if a recursive function works, the arguments of the call must, in some sense, be "smaller" than the arguments of the calling copy of the function. Moreover, after some number of recursive calls, we must get to arguments that are so "small" that the function does not make any more recursive calls.

Sorting

To sort a list of n elements we need to permute the elements of the list so that they appear in nondecreasing order.

✦ **Example 2.1.** Suppose we are given the list of integers $(3, 1, 4, 1, 5, 9, 2, 6, 5)$. We sort this list by permuting it into the sequence $(1, 1, 2, 3, 4, 5, 5, 6, 9)$. Note that sorting not only orders the values so that each is either less than or equal to the one that follows, but it also preserves the number of occurrences of each value. Thus, the sorted list has two 1's, two 5's, and one each of the numbers that appear once in the original list. ✦

We can sort a list of elements of any type as long as the elements have a "less-than" order defined on them, which we usually represent by the symbol $<$. For example, if the values are real numbers or integers, then the symbol $<$ stands for the usual less-than relation on reals or integers, and if the values are character strings, we would use the lexicographic order on strings. (See the box on "Lexicographic Order.") Sometimes when the elements are complex, such as structures, we might use only a part of each element, such as one particular field, for the comparison.

The comparison $a \leq b$ means, as always, that either $a < b$ or a and b are the same value. A list $(a_1, a_2, \ldots, a_n)$ is said to be *sorted* if $a_1 \leq a_2 \leq \cdots \leq a_n$; that is, if the values are in nondecreasing order. *Sorting* is the operation of taking an arbitrary list $(a_1, a_2, \ldots, a_n)$ and producing a list $(b_1, b_2, \ldots, b_n)$ such that

Sorted list

Lexicographic Order

The usual way in which two character strings are compared is according to their *lexicographic order*. Let $c_1c_2 \cdots c_k$ and $d_1d_2 \cdots d_m$ be two strings, where each of the c's and d's represents a single character. The lengths of the strings, k and m, need not be the same. We assume that there is a $<$ ordering on characters; for example, in C characters are small integers, so character constants and variables can be used as integers in arithmetic expressions. Thus we can use the conventional $<$ relation on integers to tell which of two characters is "less than" the other. This ordering includes the natural notion that lower-case letters appearing earlier in the alphabet are "less than" lower-case letters appearing later in the alphabet, and the same holds for upper-case letters.

We may then define the ordering on character strings called the *lexicographic, dictionary,* or *alphabetic* ordering, as follows. We say $c_1c_2 \cdots c_k < d_1d_2 \cdots d_m$ if either of the following holds:

Proper prefix

1. The first string is a *proper prefix* of the second, which means that $k < m$ and for $i = 1, 2, \ldots, k$ we have $c_i = d_i$. According to this rule, bat < batter. As a special case of this rule, we could have $k = 0$, in which case the first string has no characters in it. We shall use ϵ, the Greek letter epsilon, to denote the

Empty string

empty string, the string with zero characters. When $k = 0$, rule (1) says that $\epsilon < s$ for any nonempty string s.

2. For some value of $i > 0$, the first $i - 1$ characters of the two strings agree, but the ith character of the first string is less than the ith character of the second string. That is, $c_j = d_j$ for $j = 1, 2, \ldots, i - 1$, and $c_i < d_i$. According to this rule, ball < base, because the two words first differ at position 3, and at that position ball has an l, which precedes the character s found in the third position of base.

---

1. List $(b_1, b_2, \ldots, b_n)$ is sorted.

Permutation

2. List $(b_1, b_2, \ldots, b_n)$ is a *permutation* of the original list. That is, each value appears in list $(a_1, a_2, \ldots, a_n)$ exactly as many times as that value appears in list $(b_1, b_2, \ldots, b_n)$.

A *sorting algorithm* takes as input an arbitrary list and produces as output a sorted list that is a permutation of the input.

✦ **Example 2.2.** Consider the list of words

base, ball, mound, bat, glove, batter

Given this input, and using lexicographic order, a sorting algorithm would produce this output: ball, base, bat, batter, glove, mound. ✦

Selection Sort: An Iterative Sorting Algorithm

Suppose we have an array A of n integers that we wish to sort into nondecreasing

Convention Regarding Names and Values

We can think of a variable as a box with a name and a value. When we refer to a variable, such as abc, we use the constant-width, or "computer" font for its name, as we did in this sentence. When we refer to the value of the variable abc, we shall use italics, as *abc*. To summarize, abc refers to the name of the box, and *abc* to its contents.

order. We may do so by iterating a step in which a smallest element[1] not yet part of the sorted portion of the array is found and exchanged with the element in the first position of the unsorted part of the array. In the first iteration, we find ("select") a smallest element among the values found in the full array A[0..n-1] and exchange it with A[0].[2] In the second iteration, we find a smallest element in A[1..n-1] and exchange it with A[1]. We continue these iterations. At the start of the $i + 1$st iteration, A[0..i-1] contains the i smallest elements in A sorted in nondecreasing order, and the remaining elements of the array are in no particular order. A picture of A just before the $i + 1$st iteration is shown in Fig. 2.1.

Fig. 2.1. Picture of array just before the $i + 1$st iteration of selection sort.

In the $i + 1$st iteration, we find a smallest element in A[i..n-1] and exchange it with A[i]. Thus, after the $i + 1$st iteration, A[0..i] contains the $i + 1$ smallest elements sorted in nondecreasing order. After the $(n - 1)$st iteration, the entire array is sorted.

A C function for selection sort is shown in Fig. 2.2. This function, whose name is SelectionSort, takes an array A as the first argument. The second argument, n, is the length of array A.

Lines (2) through (5) select a smallest element in the unsorted part of the array, A[i..n-1]. We begin by setting the value of index small to i in line (2). The for-loop of lines (3) through (5) consider all higher indexes j in turn, and *small* is set to j if A[j] has a smaller value than any of the array elements in the range A[i..j-1]. As a result, we set the variable small to the index of the first occurrence of the smallest element in A[i..n-1].

After choosing a value for the index small, we exchange the element in that position with the element in A[i], in lines (6) to (8). If *small* = i, the exchange is performed, but has no effect on the array. Notice that in order to swap two elements, we need a temporary place to store one of them. Thus, we move the value

---

[1] We say "*a* smallest element" rather than "*the* smallest element" because there may be several occurrences of the smallest value. If so, we shall be happy with any of those occurrences.

[2] To describe a range of elements within an array, we adopt a convention from the language Pascal. If A is an array, then A[i..j] denotes those elements of A with indexes from i to j, inclusive.

```
        void SelectionSort(int A[], int n)
        {
            int i, j, small, temp;
(1)         for (i = 0; i < n-1; i++) {
                /* set small to the index of the first occur- */
                /* rence of the smallest element remaining */
(2)             small = i;
(3)             for (j = i+1; j < n; j++)
(4)                 if (A[j] < A[small])
(5)                     small = j;
                /* when we reach here, small is the index of */
                /* the first smallest element in A[i..n-1]; */
                /* we now exchange A[small] with A[i] */
(6)             temp = A[small];
(7)             A[small] = A[i];
(8)             A[i] = temp;
            }
        }
```

Fig. 2.2. Iterative selection sort.

in A[small] to temp at line (6), move the value in A[i] to A[small] at line (7), and finally move the value originally in A[small] from temp to A[i] at line (8).

✦ **Example 2.3.** Let us study the behavior of SelectionSort on various inputs. First, let us look at what happens when we run SelectionSort on an array with no elements. When $n = 0$, the body of the for-loop of line (1) is not executed, so SelectionSort does "nothing" gracefully.

Now let us consider the case in which the array has only one element. Again, the body of the for-loop of line (1) is not executed. That response is satisfactory, because an array consisting of a single element is always sorted. The cases in which n is 0 or 1 are important boundary conditions, on which it is important to check the performance of any algorithm or program.

Finally, let us run SelectionSort on a small array with four elements, where A[0] through A[3] are

$$
\begin{array}{c c c c c}
 & 0 & 1 & 2 & 3 \\
\text{A} & \boxed{40} & \boxed{30} & \boxed{20} & \boxed{10}
\end{array}
$$

We begin the outer loop with $i = 0$, and at line (2) we set small to 0. Lines (3) to (5) form an inner loop, in which j is set to 1, 2, and 3, in turn. With $j = 1$, the test of line (4) succeeds, since $A[1]$, which is 30, is less than $A[small]$, which is $A[0]$, or 40. Thus, we set small to 1 at line (5). At the second iteration of lines (3) to (5), with $j = 2$, the test of line (4) again succeeds, since $A[2] < A[1]$, and so we set small to 2 at line (5). At the last iteration of lines (3) to (5), with $j = 3$, the test of line (4) succeeds, since $A[3] < A[2]$, and we set small to 3 at line (5).

We now fall out of the inner loop to line (6). We set temp to 10, which is $A[small]$, then A[3] to $A[0]$, or 40, at line (7), and A[0] to 10 at line (8). Now, the

Sorting on Keys

When we sort, we apply a comparison operation to the values being sorted. Often the comparison is made only on specific parts of the values and the part used in the comparison is called the *key*.

For example, a course roster might be an array A of C structures of the form

```
struct STUDENT {
    int studentID;
    char *name;
    char grade;
} A[MAX];
```

We might want to sort by student ID, or name, or grade; each in turn would be the key. For example, if we wish to sort structures by student ID, we would use the comparison

```
A[j].studentID < A[small].studentID
```

at line (4) of SelectionSort. The type of array A and temporary temp used in the swap would be struct STUDENT, rather than integer. Note that entire structures are swapped, not just the key fields.

Since it is time-consuming to swap whole structures, a more efficient approach is to use a second array of pointers to STUDENT structures and sort only the pointers in the second array. The structures themselves remain stationary in the first array. We leave this version of selection sort as an exercise.

---

first iteration of the outer loop is complete, and array A appears as

$$
\begin{array}{cccc}
0 & 1 & 2 & 3
\end{array}
$$
A $\boxed{10\,|\,30\,|\,20\,|\,40}$

The second iteration of the outer loop, with $i = 1$, sets small to 1 at line (2). The inner loop sets j to 2 initially, and since $A[2] < A[1]$, line (5) sets small to 2. With $j = 3$, the test of line (4) fails, since $A[3] \geq A[2]$. Hence, $small = 2$ when we reach line (6). Lines (6) to (8) swap A[1] with A[2], leaving the array

$$
\begin{array}{cccc}
0 & 1 & 2 & 3
\end{array}
$$
A $\boxed{10\,|\,20\,|\,30\,|\,40}$

Although the array now happens to be sorted, we still iterate the outer loop once more, with $i = 2$. We set small to 2 at line (2), and the inner loop is executed only with $j = 3$. Since the test of line (4) fails, *small* remains 2, and at lines (6) through (8), we "swap" A[2] with itself. The reader should check that the swapping has no effect when $small = i$. ✦

Figure 2.3 shows how the function SelectionSort can be used in a complete program to sort a sequence of n integers, provided that $n \leq 100$. Line (1) reads and stores n integers in an array A. If the number of inputs exceeds MAX, only the first MAX integers are put into A. A message warning the user that the number of inputs is too large would be useful here, but we omit it.

Line (3) calls SelectionSort to sort the array. Lines (4) and (5) print the integers in sorted order.

```
        #include <stdio.h>

        #define MAX 100
        int A[MAX];
        void SelectionSort(int A[], int n);

        main()
        {
            int i, n;
            /* read and store input in A */
(1)         for (n = 0; n < MAX && scanf("%d", &A[n]) != EOF; n++)
(2)             ;
(3)         SelectionSort(A,n); /* sort A */
(4)         for (i = 0; i < n; i++)
(5)             printf("%d\n", A[i]); /* print A */
        }

        void SelectionSort(int A[], int n)
        {
            int i, j, small, temp;
            for (i = 0; i < n-1; i++) {
                small = i;
                for (j = i+1; j < n; j++)
                        if (A[j] < A[small])
                            small = j;
                temp = A[small];
                A[small] = A[i];
                A[i] = temp;
            }
        }
```

Fig. 2.3. A sorting program using selection sort.

EXERCISES

2.2.1: Simulate the function SelectionSort on an array containing the elements

a)   6, 8, 14, 17, 23
b)   17, 23, 14, 6, 8
c)   23, 17, 14, 8, 6

How many comparisons and swaps of elements are made in each case?

2.2.2**: What are the minimum and maximum number of (a) comparisons and (b) swaps that SelectionSort can make in sorting a sequence of n elements?

2.2.3: Write a C function that takes two linked lists of characters as arguments and returns TRUE if the first string precedes the second in lexicographic order. *Hint*: Implement the algorithm for comparing character strings that was described in this section. Use recursion by having the function call itself on the tails of the character strings when it finds that the first characters of both strings are the same. Alternatively, one can develop an iterative algorithm to do the same.

2.2.4*: Modify your program from Exercise 2.2.3 to ignore the case of letters in comparisons.

2.2.5: What does selection sort do if all elements are the same?

2.2.6: Modify Fig. 2.3 to perform selection sort when array elements are not integers, but rather structures of type struct STUDENT, as defined in the box "Sorting on Keys." Suppose that the key field is studentID.

2.2.7*: Further modify Fig. 2.3 so that it sorts elements of an arbitrary type T. You may assume, however, that there is a function *key* that takes an element of type T as argument and returns the key for that element, of some arbitrary type K. Also assume that there is a function *lt* that takes two elements of type K as arguments and returns TRUE if the first is "less than" the second, and FALSE otherwise.

2.2.8: Instead of using integer indexes into the array A, we could use pointers to integers to indicate positions in the array. Rewrite the selection sort algorithm of Fig. 2.3 using pointers.

2.2.9*: As mentioned in the box on "Sorting on Keys," if the elements to be sorted are large structures such as type STUDENT, it makes sense to leave them stationary in an array and sort pointers to these structures, found in a second array. Write this variation of selection sort.

2.2.10: Write an iterative program to print the distinct elements of an integer array.

2.2.11: Use the $\sum$ and $\prod$ notations described at the beginning of this chapter to express the following.

a)   The sum of the odd integers from 1 to 377

b)   The sum of the squares of the even integers from 2 to n (assume that n is even)

c)   The product of the powers of 2 from 8 to 2^k

2.2.12: Show that when $small = i$, lines (6) through (8) of Fig. 2.2 (the swapping steps) do not have any effect on array A.

✧✦ 2.3   Inductive Proofs

Mathematical induction is a useful technique for proving that a statement $S(n)$ is true for all nonnegative integers n, or, more generally, for all integers at or above some lower limit. For example, in the introduction to this chapter we suggested that the statement $\sum_{i=1}^{n} i = n(n+1)/2$ can be proved true for all $n \geq 1$ by an induction on n.

Now, let $S(n)$ be some arbitrary statement about an integer n. In the simplest form of an inductive proof of the statement $S(n)$, we prove two facts:

Naming the Induction Parameter

It is often useful to explain an induction by giving the intuitive meaning of the variable n in the statement $S(n)$ that we are proving. If n has no special meaning, as in Example 2.4, we simply say "The proof is by induction on n." In other cases, n may have a physical meaning, as in Example 2.6, where n is the number of bits in the code words. There we can say, "The proof is by induction on the number of bits in the code words."

Inductive hypothesis

1. The *basis* case, which is frequently taken to be $S(0)$. However, the basis can be $S(k)$ for any integer k, with the understanding that then the statement $S(n)$ is proved only for $n \geq k$.

2. The *inductive step*, where we prove that for all $n \geq 0$ [or for all $n \geq k$, if the basis is $S(k)$], $S(n)$ implies $S(n+1)$. In this part of the proof, we assume that the statement $S(n)$ is true. $S(n)$ is called the *inductive hypothesis*, and assuming it to be true, we must then prove that $S(n+1)$ is true.

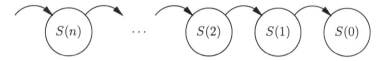

Fig. 2.4. In an inductive proof, each instance of the statement $S(n)$ is proved using the statement for the next lower value of n.

Figure 2.4 illustrates an induction starting at 0. For each integer n, there is a statement $S(n)$ to prove. The proof for $S(1)$ uses $S(0)$, the proof for $S(2)$ uses $S(1)$, and so on, as represented by the arrows. The way each statement depends on the previous one is uniform. That is, *by one proof of the inductive step, we prove each of the steps implied by the arrows in Fig. 2.4.*

✦ **Example 2.4.** As an example of mathematical induction, let us prove

STATEMENT $S(n)$: $\displaystyle\sum_{i=0}^{n} 2^i = 2^{n+1} - 1$ for any $n \geq 0$.

That is, the sum of the powers of 2, from the 0th power to the nth power, is 1 less than the $(n+1)$st power of 2.[3] For example, $1 + 2 + 4 + 8 = 16 - 1$. The proof proceeds as follows.

BASIS. To prove the basis, we substitute 0 for n in the equation $S(n)$. Then $S(n)$ becomes

---

[3] $S(n)$ can be proved without induction, using the formula for the sum of a geometric series. However, it will serve as a simple example of the technique of mathematical induction. Further, the proofs of the formulas for the sum of a geometric or arithmetic series that you have probably seen in high school are rather informal, and strictly speaking, mathematical induction should be used to prove those formulas.

$$\sum_{i=0}^{0} 2^i = 2^1 - 1 \tag{2.2}$$

There is only one term, for $i = 0$, in the summation on the left side of Equation (2.2), so that the left side of (2.2) sums to 2^0, or 1. The right side of Equation (2.2), which is $2^1 - 1$, or $2 - 1$, also has value 1. Thus we have proved the basis of $S(n)$; that is, we have shown that this equality is true for $n = 0$.

INDUCTION. Now we must prove the inductive step. We assume that $S(n)$ is true, and we prove the same equality with $n + 1$ substituted for n. The equation to be proved, $S(n + 1)$, is

$$\sum_{i=0}^{n+1} 2^i = 2^{n+2} - 1 \tag{2.3}$$

To prove Equation (2.3), we begin by considering the sum on the left side,

$$\sum_{i=0}^{n+1} 2^i$$

This sum is almost the same as the sum on the left side of $S(n)$, which is

$$\sum_{i=0}^{n} 2^i$$

except that (2.3) also has a term for $i = n + 1$, that is, the term 2^{n+1}.

Since we are allowed to assume that the inductive hypothesis $S(n)$ is true in our proof of Equation (2.3), we should contrive to use $S(n)$ to advantage. We do so by breaking the sum in (2.3) into two parts, one of which is the sum in $S(n)$. That is, we separate out the last term, where $i = n + 1$, and write

$$\sum_{i=0}^{n+1} 2^i = \sum_{i=0}^{n} 2^i + 2^{n+1} \tag{2.4}$$

Now we can make use of $S(n)$ by substituting its right side, $2^{n+1} - 1$, for $\sum_{i=0}^{n} 2^i$ in Equation (2.4):

$$\sum_{i=0}^{n+1} 2^i = 2^{n+1} - 1 + 2^{n+1} \tag{2.5}$$

When we simplify the right side of Equation (2.5), it becomes $2 \times 2^{n+1} - 1$, or $2^{n+2} - 1$. Now we see that the summation on the left side of (2.5) is the same as the left side of (2.3), and the right side of (2.5) is equal to the right side of (2.3). We have thus proved the validity of Equation (2.3) by using the equality $S(n)$; that proof is the inductive step. The conclusion we draw is that $S(n)$ holds for every nonnegative value of n. ✦

Why Does Proof by Induction Work?

In an inductive proof, we first prove that $S(0)$ is true. Next we show that if $S(n)$ is true, then $S(n + 1)$ holds. But why can we then conclude that $S(n)$ is true for all $n \geq 0$? We shall offer two "proofs." A mathematician would point out that

Substituting for Variables

People are often confused when they have to substitute for a variable such as n in $S(n)$, an expression involving the same variable. For example, we substituted $n + 1$ for n in $S(n)$ to get Equation (2.3). To make the substitution, we must first mark every occurrence of n in S. One useful way to do so is to replace n by some new variable — say m — that does not otherwise appear in S. For example, $S(n)$ would become

$$\sum_{i=0}^{m} 2^i = 2^{m+1} - 1$$

We then literally substitute the desired expression, $n + 1$ in this case, for each occurrence of m. That gives us

$$\sum_{i=0}^{n+1} 2^i = 2^{(n+1)+1} - 1$$

When we simplify $(n + 1) + 1$ to $n + 2$, we have (2.3).

Note that we should put parentheses around the expression substituted, to avoid accidentally changing the order of operations. For example, had we substituted $n + 1$ for m in the expression $2 \times m$, and not placed the parentheses around $n + 1$, we would have gotten $2 \times n + 1$, rather than the correct expression $2 \times (n + 1)$, which equals $2 \times n + 2$.

---

each of our "proofs" that induction works requires an inductive proof itself, and therefore is no proof at all. Technically, induction must be accepted as axiomatic. Nevertheless, many people find the following intuition useful.

In what follows, we assume that the basis value is $n = 0$. That is, we know that $S(0)$ is true and that for all n greater than 0, if $S(n)$ is true, then $S(n + 1)$ is true. Similar arguments work if the basis value is any other integer.

First "proof": *Iteration of the inductive step.* Suppose we want to show that $S(a)$ is true for a particular nonnegative integer a. If $a = 0$, we just invoke the truth of the basis, $S(0)$. If $a > 0$, then we argue as follows. We know that $S(0)$ is true, from the basis. The statement "$S(n)$ implies $S(n + 1)$," with 0 in place of n, says "$S(0)$ implies $S(1)$." Since we know that $S(0)$ is true, we now know that $S(1)$ is true. Similarly, if we substitute 1 for n, we get "$S(1)$ implies $S(2)$," and so we also know that $S(2)$ is true. Substituting 2 for n, we have "$S(2)$ implies $S(3)$," so that $S(3)$ is true, and so on. No matter what the value of a is, we eventually get to $S(a)$, and we are done.

Second "proof": *Least counterexample.* Suppose $S(n)$ were not true for at least one value of n. Let a be the least nonnegative integer for which $S(a)$ is false. If $a = 0$, then we contradict the basis, $S(0)$, and so a must be greater than 0. But if $a > 0$, and a is the least nonnegative integer for which $S(a)$ is false, then $S(a - 1)$ must be true. Now, the inductive step, with n replaced by $a - 1$, tells us that $S(a - 1)$ implies $S(a)$. Since $S(a - 1)$ is true, $S(a)$ must be true, another contradiction. Since we assumed there were nonnegative values of n for which $S(n)$ is false and derived a contradiction, $S(n)$ must therefore be true for any $n \geq 0$.

Error-Detecting Codes

We shall now begin an extended example of "error-detecting codes," a concept that is interesting in its own right and also leads to an interesting inductive proof. When we transmit information over a data network, we code characters (letters, digits, punctuation, and so on) into strings of bits, that is, 0's and 1's. For the moment let us assume that characters are represented by seven bits. However, it is normal to transmit more than seven bits per character, and an eighth bit can be used to help detect some simple errors in transmission. That is, occasionally, one of the 0's or 1's gets changed because of noise during transmission, and is received as the opposite bit; a 0 entering the transmission line emerges as a 1, or vice versa. It is useful if the communication system can tell when one of the eight bits has been changed, so that it can signal for a retransmission.

To detect changes in a single bit, we must be sure that no two characters are represented by sequences of bits that differ in only one position. For then, if that position were changed, the result would be the code for the other character, and we could not detect that an error had occurred. For example, if the code for one character is the sequence of bits 01010101, and the code for another is 01000101, then a change in the fourth position from the left turns the former into the latter.

One way to be sure that no characters have codes that differ in only one position is to precede the conventional 7-bit code for the character by a *parity bit*. If the total number of 1's in a group of bits is odd, the group is said to have *odd parity*. If the number of 1's in the group is even, then the group has *even parity*. The coding scheme we select is to represent each character by an 8-bit code with even parity; we could as well have chosen to use only the codes with odd parity. We force the parity to be even by selecting the parity bit judiciously.

Parity bit

ASCII ✦ **Example 2.5.** The conventional ASCII (pronounced "ask-ee"; it stands for "American Standard Code for Information Interchange") 7-bit code for the character A is 1000001. That sequence of seven bits already has an even number of 1's, and so we prefix it by 0 to get 01000001. The conventional code for C is 1000011, which differs from the 7-bit code for A only in the sixth position. However, this code has odd parity, and so we prefix a 1 to it, yielding the 8-bit code 11000011 with even parity. Note that after prefixing the parity bits to the codes for A and C, we have 01000001 and 11000011, which differ in two positions, namely the first and seventh, as seen in Fig. 2.5. ✦

A: 0 1 0 0 0 0 0 1

C: 1 1 0 0 0 0 1 1

Fig. 2.5. We can choose the initial parity bit so the 8-bit code always has even parity.

We can always pick a parity bit to attach to a 7-bit code so that the number of 1's in the 8-bit code is even. We pick parity bit 0 if the 7-bit code for the character at hand has even parity, and we pick parity bit 1 if the 7-bit code has odd parity. In either case, the number of 1's in the 8-bit code is even.

No two sequences of bits that each have even parity can differ in only one position. For if two such bit sequences differ in exactly one position, then one has exactly one more 1 than the other. Thus, one sequence must have odd parity and the other even parity, contradicting our assumption that both have even parity. We conclude that addition of a parity bit to make the number of 1's even serves to create an error-detecting code for characters.

The parity-bit scheme is quite "efficient," in the sense that it allows us to transmit many different characters. Note that there are 2^n different sequences of n bits, since we may choose either of two values (0 or 1) for the first position, either of two values for the second position, and so on, a total of $2 \times 2 \times \cdots \times 2$ (n factors) possible strings. Thus, we might expect to be able to represent up to $2^8 = 256$ characters with eight bits.

However, with the parity scheme, we can choose only seven of the bits; the eighth is then forced upon us. We can thus represent up to 2^7, or 128 characters, and still detect single errors. That is not so bad; we can use 128/256, or half, of the possible 8-bit codes as legal codes for characters, and still detect an error in one bit.

Similarly, if we use sequences of n bits, choosing one of them to be the parity bit, we can represent 2^{n-1} characters by taking sequences of $n-1$ bits and prefixing the suitable parity bit, whose value is determined by the other $n - 1$ bits. Since there are 2^n sequences of n bits, we can represent $2^{n-1}/2^n$, or half the possible number of characters, and still detect an error in any one of the bits of a sequence.

Is it possible to detect errors and use more than half the possible sequences of bits as legal codes? Our next example tells us we cannot. The inductive proof uses a statement that is not true for 0, and for which we must choose a larger basis, namely 1.

✦   **Example 2.6.** We shall prove the following by induction on n.

<table>
<tr><td>Error-detecting
code</td><td>**STATEMENT** $S(n)$: If C is any set of bit strings of length n that is *error detecting* (i.e., if there are no two strings that differ in exactly one position), then C contains at most 2^{n-1} strings.</td></tr>
</table>

This statement is not true for $n = 0$. $S(0)$ says that any error-detecting set of strings of length 0 has at most 2^{-1} strings, that is, half a string. Technically, the set C consisting of only the empty string (string with no positions) is an error-detecting set of length 0, since there are no two strings in C that differ in only one position. Set C has more than half a string; it has one string to be exact. Thus, $S(0)$ is false. However, for all $n \geq 1$, $S(n)$ is true, as we shall see.

BASIS. The basis is $S(1)$; that is, any error-detecting set of strings of length one has at most $2^{1-1} = 2^0 = 1$ string. There are only two bit strings of length one, the string 0 and the string 1. However, we cannot have both of them in an error-detecting set, because they differ in exactly one position. Thus, every error-detecting set for $n = 1$ must have at most one string.

INDUCTION. Let $n \geq 1$, and assume that the inductive hypothesis — an error-detecting set of strings of length n has at most 2^{n-1} strings — is true. We must show, using this assumption, that any error-detecting set C of strings with length $n + 1$ has at most 2^n strings. Thus, divide C into two sets, C_0, the set of strings in C that begin with 0, and C_1, the set of strings in C that begin with 1. For instance, suppose $n = 2$ and C is the code with strings of length $n + 1 = 3$ constructed using a parity bit. Then, as shown in Fig. 2.6, C consists of the strings 000, 101, 110, and 011; C_0 consists of the strings 000 and 011, and C_1 has the other two strings, 101 and 110.

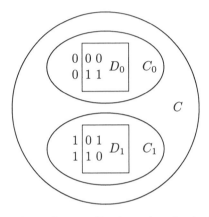

Fig. 2.6. The set C is split into C_0, the strings beginning with 0, and C_1, the strings beginning with 1. D_0 and D_1 are formed by deleting the leading 0's and 1's, respectively.

Consider the set D_0 consisting of those strings in C_0 with the leading 0 removed. In our example above, D_0 contains the strings 00 and 11. We claim that D_0 cannot have two strings differing in only one bit. The reason is that if there are two such strings — say $a_1 a_2 \cdots a_n$ and $b_1 b_2 \cdots b_n$ — then restoring their leading 0's gives us two strings in C_0, $0 a_1 a_2 \cdots a_n$ and $0 b_1 b_2 \cdots b_n$, and these strings would differ in only one position as well. But strings in C_0 are also in C, and we know that C does not have two strings that differ in only one position. Thus, neither does D_0, and so D_0 is an error detecting set.

Now we can apply the inductive hypothesis to conclude that D_0, being an error-detecting set with strings of length n, has at most 2^{n-1} strings. Thus, C_0 has at most 2^{n-1} strings.

We can reason similarly about the set C_1. Let D_1 be the set of strings in C_1, with their leading 1's deleted. D_1 is an error-detecting set with strings of length n, and by the inductive hypothesis, D_1 has at most 2^{n-1} strings. Thus, C_1 has at most 2^{n-1} strings. However, every string in C is in either C_0 or C_1. Therefore, C has at most $2^{n-1} + 2^{n-1}$, or 2^n strings.

We have proved that $S(n)$ implies $S(n + 1)$, and so we may conclude that $S(n)$ is true for all $n \geq 1$. We exclude $n = 0$ from the claim, because the basis is $n = 1$, not $n = 0$. We now see that the error-detecting sets constructed by parity check are as large as possible, since they have exactly 2^{n-1} strings when strings of n bits are used. ✦

How to Invent Inductive Proofs

There is no "crank to turn" that is guaranteed to give you an inductive proof of any (true) statement $S(n)$. Finding inductive proofs, like finding proofs of any kind, or like writing programs that work, is a task with intellectual challenge, and we can only offer a few words of advice. If you examine the inductive steps in Examples 2.4 and 2.6, you will notice that in each case we had to rework the statement $S(n+1)$ that we were trying to prove so that it incorporated the inductive hypothesis, $S(n)$, plus something extra. In Example 2.4, we expressed the sum

$$1 + 2 + 4 + \cdots + 2^n + 2^{n+1}$$

as the sum

$$1 + 2 + 4 + \cdots + 2^n$$

which the inductive hypothesis tells us something about, plus the extra term, 2^{n+1}.

In Example 2.6, we expressed the set C, with strings of length $n + 1$, in terms of two sets of strings (which we called D_0 and D_1) of length n, so that we could apply the inductive hypothesis to these sets and conclude that both of these sets were of limited size.

Of course, working with the statement $S(n + 1)$ so that we can apply the inductive hypothesis is just a special case of the more universal problem-solving adage "Use what is given." The hard part always comes when we must deal with the "extra" part of $S(n+1)$ and complete the proof of $S(n+1)$ from $S(n)$. However, the following is a universal rule:

✦   An inductive proof must at some point say "$\cdots$and by the inductive hypothesis we know that$\cdots$." If it doesn't, then it isn't a inductive proof.

EXERCISES

2.3.1: Show the following formulas by induction on n starting at $n = 1$.

a) $\sum_{i=1}^{n} i = n(n+1)/2$.

b) $\sum_{i=1}^{n} i^2 = n(n+1)(2n+1)/6$.

c) $\sum_{i=1}^{n} i^3 = n^2(n+1)^2/4$.

d) $\sum_{i=1}^{n} 1/i(i+1) = n/(n+1)$.

Triangular number

2.3.2: Numbers of the form $t_n = n(n+1)/2$ are called *triangular numbers,* because marbles arranged in an equilateral triangle, n on a side, will total $\sum_{i=1}^{n} i$ marbles, which we saw in Exercise 2.3.1(a) is t_n marbles. For example, bowling pins are arranged in a triangle 4 on a side and there are $t_4 = 4 \times 5/2 = 10$ pins. Show by induction on n that $\sum_{j=1}^{n} t_j = n(n+1)(n+2)/6$.

2.3.3: Identify the parity of each of the following bit sequences as even or odd:

a)   01101

b)   111000111

c)   010101

2.3.4: Suppose we use three digits — say 0, 1, and 2 — to code symbols. A set of strings C formed from 0's, 1's, and 2's is *error detecting* if no two strings in C differ in only one position. For example, $\{00, 11, 22\}$ is an error-detecting set with strings of length two, using the digits 0, 1, and 2. Show that for any $n \geq 1$, an error-detecting set of strings of length n using the digits 0, 1, and 2, cannot have more than 3^{n-1} strings.

2.3.5*: Show that for any $n \geq 1$, there is an error-detecting set of strings of length n, using the digits 0, 1, and 2, that has 3^{n-1} strings.

2.3.6*: Show that if we use k symbols, for any $k \geq 2$, then there is an error-detecting set of strings of length n, using k different symbols as "digits," with k^{n-1} strings, but no such set of strings with more than k^{n-1} strings.

2.3.7*: If $n \geq 1$, the number of strings using the digits 0, 1, and 2, with no two consecutive places holding the same digit, is $3 \times 2^{n-1}$. For example, there are 12 such strings of length three: 010, 012, 020, 021, 101, 102, 120, 121, 201, 202, 210, and 212. Prove this claim by induction on the length of the strings. Is the formula true for $n = 0$?

2.3.8*: Prove that the ripple-carry addition algorithm discussed in Section 1.3 produces the correct answer. *Hint*: Show by induction on i that after considering the first i places from the right end, the sum of the tails of length i for the two addends equals the number whose binary representation is the carry bit followed by the i bits of answer generated so far.

2.3.9*: The formula for the sum of n terms of a geometric series $a, ar, ar^2, \ldots, ar^{n-1}$ is

$$\sum_{i=0}^{n-1} ar^i = \frac{(ar^n - a)}{(r - 1)}$$

Prove this formula by induction on n. Note that you must assume $r \neq 1$ for the formula to hold. Where do you use that assumption in your proof?

2.3.10: The formula for the sum of an arithmetic series with first term a and increment b, that is, $a, (a + b), (a + 2b), \ldots, (a + (n - 1)b)$, is

$$\sum_{i=0}^{n-1} a + bi = n(2a + (n - 1)b)/2$$

a)   Prove this formula by induction on n.

b)   Show how Exercise 2.3.1(a) is an example of this formula.

2.3.11: Give two informal proofs that induction starting at 1 "works," although the statement $S(0)$ may be false.

2.3.12: Show by induction on the length of strings that the code consisting of the odd-parity strings detects errors.

Arithmetic and Geometric Sums

There are two formulas from high-school algebra that we shall use frequently. They each have interesting inductive proofs, which we ask the reader to provide in Exercises 2.3.9 and 2.3.10.

Arithmetic series

An *arithmetic series* is a sequence of n numbers of the form

$$a, (a + b), (a + 2b), \ldots, (a + (n - 1)b)$$

The first term is a, and each term is b larger than the one before. The sum of these n numbers is n times the average of the first and last terms; that is:

$$\sum_{i=0}^{n-1} a + bi = n(2a + (n - 1)b)/2$$

For example, consider the sum of $3 + 5 + 7 + 9 + 11$. There are $n = 5$ terms, the first is 3 and the last 11. Thus, the sum is $5 \times (3 + 11)/2 = 5 \times 7 = 35$. You can check that this sum is correct by adding the five integers.

Geometric series

A *geometric series* is a sequence of n numbers of the form

$$a, ar, ar^2, ar^3, \ldots, ar^{n-1}$$

That is, the first term is a, and each successive term is r times the previous term. The formula for the sum of n terms of a geometric series is

$$\sum_{i=0}^{n-1} ar^i = \frac{(ar^n - a)}{(r - 1)}$$

Here, r can be greater or less than 1. If $r = 1$, the above formula does not work, but all terms are a so the sum is obviously an.

As an example of a geometric series sum, consider $1 + 2 + 4 + 8 + 16$. Here, $n = 5$, the first term a is 1, and the ratio r is 2. Thus, the sum is

$$(1 \times 2^5 - 1)/(2 - 1) = (32 - 1)/1 = 31$$

as you may check. For another example, consider $1 + 1/2 + 1/4 + 1/8 + 1/16$. Again $n = 5$ and $a = 1$, but $r = 1/2$. The sum is

$$\left(1 \times (\tfrac{1}{2})^5 - 1\right)/(\tfrac{1}{2} - 1) = (-31/32)/(-1/2) = 1\tfrac{15}{16}$$

Error-correcting code

2.3.13**: If no two strings in a code differ in fewer than three positions, then we can actually correct a single error, by finding the unique string in the code that differs from the received string in only one position. It turns out that there is a code of 7-bit strings that corrects single errors and contains 16 strings. Find such a code. *Hint*: Reasoning it out is probably best, but if you get stuck, write a program that searches for such a code.

2.3.14*: Does the even parity code detect any "double errors," that is, changes in two different bits? Can it correct any single errors?

Template for Simple Inductions

Let us summarize Section 2.3 by giving a template into which the simple inductions of that section fit. Section 2.4 will cover a more general template.

1. Specify the statement $S(n)$ to be proved. Say you are going to prove $S(n)$ by induction on n, for all $n \geq i_0$. Here, i_0 is the constant of the basis; usually i_0 is 0 or 1, but it could be any integer. Explain intuitively what n means, e.g., the length of codewords.

2. State the basis case, $S(i_0)$.

3. Prove the basis case. That is, explain why $S(i_0)$ is true.

4. Set up the inductive step by stating that you are assuming $S(n)$ for some $n \geq i_0$, the "inductive hypothesis." Express $S(n+1)$ by substituting $n+1$ for n in the statement $S(n)$.

5. Prove $S(n+1)$, assuming the inductive hypothesis $S(n)$.

6. Conclude that $S(n)$ is true for all $n \geq i_0$ (but not necessarily for smaller n).

❖❖ 2.4 Complete Induction

In the examples seen so far, we have proved that $S(n+1)$ is true using only $S(n)$ as an inductive hypothesis. However, since we prove our statement S for values of its parameter starting at the basis value and proceeding upward, we are entitled to use $S(i)$ for all values of i, from the basis value up to n. This form of induction is called *complete* (or sometimes *perfect* or *strong*) *induction*, while the simple form of induction of Section 2.3, where we used only $S(n)$ to prove $S(n+1)$ is sometimes called *weak* induction.

Strong and weak induction

Let us begin by considering how to perform a complete induction starting with basis $n = 0$. We prove that $S(n)$ is true for all $n \geq 0$ in two steps:

1. We first prove the basis, $S(0)$.

2. As an inductive hypothesis, we assume all of $S(0), S(1), \ldots, S(n)$ to be true. From these statements we prove that $S(n+1)$ holds.

As for weak induction described in the previous section, we can also pick some value a other than 0 as the basis. Then, for the basis we prove $S(a)$, and in the inductive step we are entitled to assume only $S(a), S(a+1), \ldots, S(n)$. Note that weak induction is a special case of complete induction in which we elect not to use any of the previous statements except $S(n)$ to prove $S(n+1)$.

Figure 2.7 suggests how complete induction works. Each instance of the statement $S(n)$ can (optionally) use any of the lower-indexed instances to its right in its proof.

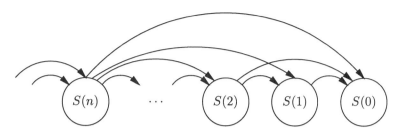

Fig. 2.7. Complete induction allows each instance to use one, some, or
all of the previous instances in its proof.

Inductions With More Than One Basis Case

When performing a complete induction, there are times when it is useful to have
more than one basis case. If we wish to prove a statement $S(n)$ for all $n \geq i_0$, then
we could treat not only i_0 as a basis case, but also some number of consecutive
integers above i_0, say $i_0, i_0 + 1, i_0 + 2, \ldots, j_0$. Then we must do the following two
steps:

1. Prove each of the basis cases, the statements $S(i_0), S(i_0 + 1), \ldots, S(j_0)$.

2. As an inductive hypothesis, assume all of $S(i_0), S(i_0 + 1), \ldots, S(n)$ hold, for
    some $n \geq j_0$, and prove $S(n + 1)$.

✦   **Example 2.7.** Our first example of a complete induction is a simple one that
uses multiple basis cases. As we shall see, it is only "complete" in a limited sense.
To prove $S(n + 1)$ we do not use $S(n)$ but we use $S(n - 1)$ only. In more general
complete inductions to follow, we use $S(n)$, $S(n - 1)$, and many other instances of
the statement S.

   Let us prove by induction on n the following statement for all $n \geq 0$.[4]

STATEMENT $S(n)$: There are integers a and b (positive, negative, or 0) such that
   $n = 2a + 3b$.

BASIS. We shall take both 0 and 1 as basis cases.

i)   For $n = 0$ we may pick $a = 0$ and $b = 0$. Surely $0 = 2 \times 0 + 3 \times 0$.

ii) For $n = 1$, pick $a = -1$ and $b = 1$. Then $1 = 2 \times (-1) + 3 \times 1$.

INDUCTION. Now, we may assume $S(n)$ and prove $S(n + 1)$, for any $n \geq 1$. Note
that we may assume n is at least the largest of the consecutive values for which we
have proved the basis: $n \geq 1$ here. Statement $S(n + 1)$ says that $n + 1 = 2a + 3b$
for some integers a and b.

   The inductive hypothesis says that all of $S(0), S(1), \ldots, S(n)$ are true. Note
that we begin the sequence at 0 because that was the lowest of the consecutive basis
cases. Since $n \geq 1$ can be assumed, we know that $n - 1 \geq 0$, and therefore, $S(n - 1)$
is true. This statement says that there are integers a and b such that $n - 1 = 2a + 3b$.

---

[4] Actually, this statement is true for all n, positive or negative, but the case of negative n
   requires a second induction which we leave as an exercise.

Since we need a in the statement $S(n+1)$, let us restate $S(n-1)$ to use different names for the integers and say there are integers a' and b' such that

$$n - 1 = 2a' + 3b' \qquad (2.6)$$

If we add 2 to both sides of (2.6), we have $n + 1 = 2(a' + 1) + 3b'$. If we then let $a = a' + 1$ and $b = b'$, we have the statement $n + 1 = 2a + 3b$ for some integers a and b. This statement is $S(n + 1)$, so we have proved the induction. Notice that in this proof, we did not use $S(n)$, but we did use $S(n - 1)$. ✦

Justifying Complete Induction

Like the ordinary or "weak" induction discussed in Section 2.3, complete induction can be justified intuitively as a proof technique by a "least counterexample" argument. Let the basis cases be $S(i_0), S(i_0 + 1), \ldots, S(j_0)$, and suppose we have shown that for any $n \geq j_0$, $S(i_0), S(i_0 + 1), \ldots, S(n)$ together imply $S(n+1)$. Now, suppose $S(n)$ were not true for at least one value of $n \geq i_0$, and let b be the smallest integer equal to or greater than i_0 for which $S(b)$ is false. Then b cannot be between i_0 and j_0, or the basis is contradicted. Further, b cannot be greater than j_0. If it were, all of $S(i_0), S(i_0 + 1), \ldots, S(b - 1)$ would be true. But the inductive step would then tell us that $S(b)$ is true, yielding the contradiction.

Normal Forms for Arithmetic Expressions

We shall now explore an extended example concerning the transformation of arithmetic expressions to equivalent forms. It offers an illustration of a complete induction that takes full advantage of the fact that the statement S to be proved may be assumed for all arguments from n downward.

By way of motivation, a compiler for a programming language may take advantage of the algebraic properties of arithmetic operators to rearrange the order in which the operands of an arithmetic expression are evaluated. The goal is of this rearrangement is to find a way for the computer to evaluate the expression using less time than the obvious evaluation order takes.

In this section we consider arithmetic expressions containing a single associative and commutative operator, like +, and examine what rearrangements of operands are possible. We shall prove that if we have any expression involving only the operator +, then the value of the expression is equal to the value of any other expression with + applied to the same operands, ordered and/or grouped in any arbitrary way. For example,

$$\big(a_3 + (a_4 + a_1)\big) + (a_2 + a_5) = a_1 + \Big(a_2 + \big(a_3 + (a_4 + a_5)\big)\Big)$$

We shall prove this claim by performing two separate inductions, the first of which is a complete induction.

✦   **Example 2.8.** We shall prove by complete induction on n (the number of operands in an expression) the statement

Associativity and Commutativity

Associative law

Recall that the *associative law* for addition says that we can add three values either by adding the first two and then adding the third to the result, or by adding the first to the result of adding the second and third; the result will be the same. Formally,

$$(E_1 + E_2) + E_3 = E_1 + (E_2 + E_3)$$

where E_1, E_2, and E_3 are any arithmetic expressions. For instance,

$$(1 + 2) + 3 = 1 + (2 + 3)$$

Here, $E_1 = 1$, $E_2 = 2$, and $E_3 = 3$. Also,

$$\big((xy) + (3z - 2)\big) + (y + z) = xy + \big((3z - 2) + (y + z)\big)$$

Here, $E_1 = xy$, $E_2 = 3z - 2$, and $E_3 = y + z$.

Commutative law

Also recall that the *commutative law* for addition says that we can sum two expressions in either order. Formally,

$$E_1 + E_2 = E_2 + E_1$$

For example, $1 + 2 = 2 + 1$, and $xy + (3z - 2) = (3z - 2) + xy$.

STATEMENT $S(n)$: If E is an expression involving the operator $+$ and n operands, and a is one of those operands, then E can be transformed, by using the associative and commutative laws, into an expression of the form $a + F$, where F is an expression involving all the operands of E except a, grouped in some order using the operator $+$.

Statement $S(n)$ only holds for $n \geq 2$, since there must be at least one occurrence of the operator $+$ in E. Thus, we shall use $n = 2$ as our basis.

BASIS. Let $n = 2$. Then E can be only $a + b$ or $b + a$, for some operand b other than a. In the first case, we let F be the expression b, and we are done. In the second case, we note that by the commutative law, $b + a$ can be transformed into $a + b$, and so we may again let $F = b$.

INDUCTION. Let E have $n + 1$ operands, and assume that $S(i)$ is true for $i = 2, 3, \ldots, n$. We need to prove the inductive step for $n \geq 2$, so we may assume that E has at least three operands and therefore at least two occurrences of $+$. We can write E as $E_1 + E_2$ for some expressions E_1 and E_2. Since E has exactly $n + 1$ operands, and E_1 and E_2 must each have at least one of these operands, it follows that neither E_1 nor E_2 can have more than n operands. Thus, the inductive hypothesis applies to E_1 and E_2, as long as they have more than one operand each (because we started with $n = 2$ as the basis). There are four cases we must consider, depending whether a is in E_1 or E_2, and on whether it is or is not the only operand in E_1 or E_2.

a) E_1 is a by itself. An example of this case occurs when E is $a + (b + c)$; here E_1 is a and E_2 is $b + c$. In this case, E_2 serves as F; that is, E is already of the form $a + F$.

b) E_1 has more than one operand, and a is among them. For instance,

$$E = \big(c + (d + a)\big) + (b + e)$$

where $E_1 = c + (d + a)$ and $E_2 = b + e$. Here, since E_1 has no more than
n operands but at least two operands, we can apply the inductive hypothesis
to tell us that E_1 can be transformed, using the commutative and associative
laws, into $a + E_3$. Thus, E can be transformed into $(a + E_3) + E_2$. We apply the
associative law and see that E can further be transformed into $a + (E_3 + E_2)$.
Thus, we may choose F to be $E_3 + E_2$, which proves the inductive step in
this case. For our example E above, we may suppose that $E_2 = c + (d + a)$
is transformed by the inductive hypothesis into $a + (c + d)$. Then E can be
regrouped into $a + \big((c + d) + (b + e)\big)$.

c) E_2 is a alone. For instance, $E = (b+c)+a$. In this case, we use the commutative
law to transform E into $a + E_1$, which is of the desired form if we let F be E_1.

d) E_2 has more than one operand, including a. An example is $E = b + (a + c)$.
Apply the commutative law to transform E into $E_2 + E_1$. Then proceed as
in case (b). If $E = b + (a + c)$, we transform E first into $(a + c) + b$. By the
inductive hypothesis, $a + c$ can be put in the desired form; in fact, it is already
there. The associative law then transforms E into $a + (c + b)$.

In all four cases, we have transformed E to the desired form. Thus, the inductive
step is proved, and we conclude that $S(n)$ for all $n \geq 2$. ✦

✦   **Example 2.9.** The inductive proof of Example 2.8 leads directly to an algorithm that puts an expression into the desired form. As an example, consider the
expression

$$E = \big(x + (z + v)\big) + (w + y)$$

and suppose that v is the operand we wish to "pull out," that is, to play the role of
a in the transformation of Example 2.8. Initially, we have an example of case (b),
with $E_1 = x + (z + v)$, and $E_2 = w + y$.

Next, we must work on the expression E_1 and "pull out" v. E_1 is an example of
case (d), and so we first apply the commutative law to transform it into $(z + v) + x$.
As an instance of case (b), we must work on the expression $z + v$, which is an
instance of case (c). We thus transform it by the commutative law into $v + z$.

Now E_1 has been transformed into $(v+z)+x$, and a further use of the associative
law transforms it to $v+(z+x)$. That, in turn, transforms E into $\big(v+(z+x)\big)+(w+y)$.
By the associative law, E can be transformed into $v + \big((z + x) + (w + y)\big)$. Thus,
$E = v + F$, where F is the expression $(z + x) + (w + y)$. The entire sequence of
transformations is summarized in Fig. 2.8. ✦

Now, we can use the statement proved in Example 2.8 to prove our original
contention, that any two expressions involving the operator $+$ and the same list
of distinct operands can be transformed one to the other by the associative and
commutative laws. This proof is by weak induction, as discussed in Section 2.3,
rather than complete induction.

$$\begin{aligned}
&\big(x + (z + v)\big) + (w + y)\\
&\big((z + v) + x\big) + (w + y)\\
&\big((v + z) + x\big) + (w + y)\\
&\big(v + (z + x)\big) + (w + y)\\
&v + \big((z + x) + (w + y)\big)
\end{aligned}$$

Fig. 2.8. Using the commutative and associative laws, we can "pull out" any operand, such as v.

✦ **Example 2.10.** Let us prove the following statement by induction on n, the number of operands in an expression.

STATEMENT $T(n)$: If E and F are expressions involving the operator $+$ and the same set of n distinct operands, then it is possible to transform E into F by a sequence of applications of the associative and commutative laws.

BASIS. If $n = 1$, then the two expressions must both be a single operand a. Since they are the same expression, surely E is "transformable" into F.

INDUCTION. Suppose $T(n)$ is true, for some $n \geq 1$. We shall now prove $T(n + 1)$. Let E and F be expressions involving the same set of $n+1$ operands, and let a be one of these operands. Since $n + 1 \geq 2$, $S(n + 1)$ — the statement from Example 2.8 — must hold. Thus, we can transform E into $a + E_1$ for some expression E_1 involving the other n operands of E. Similarly, we can transform F into $a + F_1$, for some expression F_1 involving the same n operands as E_1. What is more important, in this case, is that we can also perform the transformations in the opposite direction, transforming $a + F_1$ into F by use of the associative and commutative laws.

Now we invoke the inductive hypothesis $T(n)$ on the expressions E_1 and F_1. Each has the same n operands, and so the inductive hypothesis applies. That tells us we can transform E_1 into F_1, and therefore we can transform $a + E_1$ into $a + F_1$. We may thus perform the transformations

$$\begin{aligned}
E \;\; &\to \cdots \to a + E_1 \quad \text{Using } S(n + 1)\\
&\to \cdots \to a + F_1 \quad \text{Using } T(n)\\
&\to \cdots \to F \qquad\;\;\; \text{Using } S(n + 1) \text{ in reverse}
\end{aligned}$$

to turn E into F. ✦

✦ **Example 2.11.** Let us transform $E = (x+y)+(w+z)$ into $F = \big((w+z)+y\big)+x$. We begin by selecting an operand, say w, to "pull out." If we check the cases in Example 2.8, we see that for E we perform the sequence of transformations

$$(x + y) + (w + z) \to (w + z) + (x + y) \to w + \big(z + (x + y)\big) \tag{2.7}$$

while for F we do

$$\big((w + z) + y\big) + x \to \big(w + (z + y)\big) + x \to w + \big((z + y) + x\big) \tag{2.8}$$

We now have the subproblem of transforming $z + (x + y)$ into $(z + y) + x$. We shall do so by "pulling out" x. The sequences of transformations are

$$z + (x + y) \rightarrow (x + y) + z \rightarrow x + (y + z) \tag{2.9}$$

and

$$(z + y) + x \rightarrow x + (z + y) \tag{2.10}$$

That, in turn, gives us a subproblem of transforming $y + z$ into $z + y$. We do so by an application of the commutative law. Strictly speaking, we use the technique of Example 2.8 to "pull out" y for each, leaving $y + z$ for each expression. Then the basis case for Example 2.10 tells us that the expression z can be "transformed" into itself.

We can now transform $z + (x + y)$ into $(z + y) + x$ by the steps of line (2.9), then applying the commutative law to subexpression $y + z$, and finally using the transformation of line (2.10), in reverse. We use these transformations as the middle part of the transformation from $(x + y) + (w + z)$ to $\big((w + z) + y\big) + x$. First we apply the transformations of line (2.7), and then the transformations just discussed to change $z + (x + y)$ into $(z + y) + x$, and finally the transformations of line (2.8) in reverse. The entire sequence of transformations is summarized in Fig. 2.9. ✦

$(x + y) + (w + z)$	Expression E
$(w + z) + (x + y)$	Middle of (2.7)
$w + \big(z + (x + y)\big)$	End of (2.7)
$w + \big((x + y) + z\big)$	Middle of (2.9)
$w + \big(x + (y + z)\big)$	End of (2.9)
$w + \big(x + (z + y)\big)$	Commutative law
$w + \big((z + y) + x\big)$	(2.10) in reverse
$\big(w + (z + y)\big) + x$	Middle of (2.8) in reverse
$\big((w + z) + y\big) + x$	Expression F, end of (2.8) in reverse

Fig. 2.9. Transforming one expression into another using the commutative and associative laws.

EXERCISES

2.4.1: "Pull out" from the expression $E = (u + v) + \Big(\big(w + (x + y)\big) + z\Big)$ each of the operands in turn. That is, start from E in each of the six parts, and use the techniques of Example 2.8 to transform E into an expression of the form $u + E_1$. Then transform E_1 into an expression of the form $v + E_2$, and so on.

2.4.2: Use the technique of Example 2.10 to transform

a) $w + \big(x + (y + z)\big)$ into $\big((w + x) + y\big) + z$
b) $(v + w) + \big((x + y) + z\big)$ into $\big((y + w) + (v + z)\big) + x$

2.4.3*: Let E be an expression with operators $+$, $-$, $*$, and $/$; each operator is binary only; that is, it takes two operands. Show, using a complete induction on the number of occurrences of operators in E, that if E has n operator occurrences, then E has $n + 1$ operands.

Binary operator

A Template for All Inductions

The following organization of inductive proofs covers complete inductions with multiple basis cases. As a special case it includes the weak inductions of Section 2.3, and it includes the common situation where there is only one basis case.

1. Specify the statement $S(n)$ to be proved. Say that you are going to prove $S(n)$ by induction on n, for $n \geq i_0$. Specify what i_0 is; often it is 0 or 1, but i_0 could be any integer. Explain intuitively what n represents.

2. State the basis case(s). These will be all the integers from i_0 up to some integer j_0. Often $j_0 = i_0$, but j_0 could be larger.

3. Prove each of the basis cases $S(i_0), S(i_0 + 1), \ldots, S(j_0)$.

4. Set up the inductive step by stating that you are assuming

$$S(i_0), S(i_0 + 1), \ldots, S(n)$$

(the "inductive hypothesis") and that you want to prove $S(n + 1)$. State that you are assuming $n \geq j_0$; that is, n is at least as great as the highest basis case. Express $S(n + 1)$ by substituting $n + 1$ for n in the statement $S(n)$.

5. Prove $S(n + 1)$ under the assumptions mentioned in (4). If the induction is a weak, rather than complete, induction, then only $S(n)$ will be used in the proof, but you are free to use any or all of the statements of the inductive hypothesis.

6. Conclude that $S(n)$ is true for all $n \geq i_0$ (but not necessarily for smaller n).

2.4.4: Give an example of a binary operator that is commutative but not associative.

2.4.5: Give an example of a binary operator that is associative but not commutative.

2.4.6*: Consider an expression E whose operators are all binary. The *length* of E is the number of symbols in E, counting an operator or a left or right parenthesis as one symbol, and also counting any operand such as 123 or abc as one symbol. Prove that E must have an odd length. *Hint*: Prove the claim by complete induction on the length of the expression E.

2.4.7: Show that every negative integer can be written in the form $2a + 3b$ for some (not necessarily positive) integers a and b.

2.4.8*: Show that every integer (positive or negative) can be written in the form $5a + 7b$ for some (not necessarily positive) integers a and b.

2.4.9*: Is every proof by weak induction (as in Section 2.3) also a proof by complete induction? Is every proof by complete induction also a proof by weak induction?

2.4.10*: We showed in this section how to justify complete induction by a least counterexample argument. Show how complete induction can also be justified by an iteration.

Truth in Advertising

There are many difficulties, both theoretical and practical, in proving programs correct. An obvious question is "What does it mean for a program to be 'correct'?" As we mentioned in Chapter 1, most programs in practice are written to satisfy some informal specification. The specification itself may be incomplete or inconsistent. Even if there were a precise formal specification, we can show that no algorithm exists to prove that an arbitrary program is equivalent to a given specification.

However, in spite of these difficulties, it is beneficial to state and prove assertions about programs. The loop invariants of a program are often the most useful short explanation one can give of how the program works. Further, the programmer should have a loop invariant in mind while writing a piece of code. That is, there must be a reason why a program works, and this reason often has to do with an inductive hypothesis that holds each time the program goes around a loop or each time it performs a recursive call. The programmer should be able to envision a proof, even though it may be impractical to write out such a proof line by line.

✧✦ 2.5 Proving Properties of Programs

In this section we shall delve into an area where inductive proofs are essential: proving that a program does what it is claimed to do. We shall see a technique for explaining what an iterative program does as it goes around a loop. If we understand what the loops do, we generally understand what we need to know about an iterative program. In Section 2.9, we shall consider what is needed to prove properties of recursive programs.

Loop Invariants

Inductive assertion

The key to proving a property of a loop in a program is selecting a *loop invariant,* or *inductive assertion,* which is a statement S that is true each time we enter a particular point in the loop. The statement S is then proved by induction on a parameter that in some way measures the number of times we have gone around the loop. For example, the parameter could be the number of times we have reached the test of a while-loop, it could be the value of the loop index in a for-loop, or it could be some expression involving the program variables that is known to increase by 1 for each time around the loop.

✦   **Example 2.12.** As an example, let us consider the inner loop of `SelectionSort` from Section 2.2. These lines, with the original numbering from Fig. 2.2, are

```
(2)            small = i;
(3)            for (j = i+1; j < n; j++)
(4)                if (A[j] < A[small])
(5)                    small = j;
```

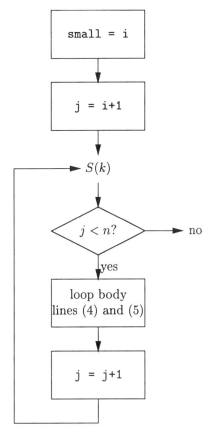

Fig. 2.10. Flowchart for the inner loop of `SelectionSort`.

Recall that the purpose of these lines is to make `small` equal to the index of an element of `A[i..n-1]` with the smallest value. To see why that claim is true, consider the flowchart for our loop shown in Fig. 2.10. This flowchart shows the five steps necessary to execute the program:

1. First, we need to initialize `small` to i, as we do in line (2).

2. At the beginning of the for-loop of line (3), we need to initialize j to $i + 1$.

3. Then, we need to test whether $j < n$.

4. If so, we execute the body of the loop, which consists of lines (4) and (5).

5. At the end of the body, we need to increment j and go back to the test.

In Fig. 2.10 we see a point just before the test that is labeled by a loop-invariant statement we have called $S(k)$; we shall discover momentarily what this statement must be. The first time we reach the test, j has the value $i + 1$ and `small` has the value i. The second time we reach the test, j has the value $i+2$, because j has been incremented once. Because the body (lines 4 and 5) sets `small` to $i + 1$ if $A[i + 1]$ is less than $A[i]$, we see that `small` is the index of whichever of $A[i]$ and $A[i + 1]$ is smaller.[5]

---

[5] In case of a tie, *small* will be i. In general, we shall pretend that no ties occur and talk about "the smallest element" when we really mean "the first occurrence of the smallest element."

Similarly, the third time we reach the test, the value of j is $i + 3$ and small is the index of the smallest of A[i..i+2]. We shall thus try to prove the following statement, which appears to be the general rule.

STATEMENT $S(k)$: If we reach the test for $j < n$ in the for-statement of line (3) with k as the value of loop index j, then the value of small is the index of the smallest of A[i..k-1].

Note that we are using the letter k to stand for one of the values that the variable j assumes, as we go around the loop. That is less cumbersome than trying to use j as the value of j, because we sometimes need to keep k fixed while the value of j changes. Also notice that $S(k)$ has the form "if we reach $\cdots$," because for some values of k we may never reach the loop test, as we broke out of the loop for a smaller value of the loop index j. If k is one of those values, then $S(k)$ is surely true, because any statement of the form "if A then B" is true when A is false.

BASIS. The basis case is $k = i + 1$, where i is the value of the variable i at line (3).[6] Now $j = i + 1$ when we begin the loop. That is, we have just executed line (2), which gives small the value i, and we have initialized j to $i + 1$ to begin the loop. $S(i + 1)$ says that small is the index of the smallest element in A[i..i], which means that the value of small must be i. But we just observed that line (2) causes small to have the value i. Technically, we must also show that j can never have value $i + 1$ except the first time we reach the test. The reason, intuitively, is that each time around the loop, we increment j, so it will never again be as low as $i + 1$. (To be perfectly precise, we should give an inductive proof of the assumption that $j > i + 1$ except the first time through the test.) Thus, the basis, $S(i + 1)$, has been shown to be true.

INDUCTION. Now let us assume as our inductive hypothesis that $S(k)$ holds, for some $k \geq i + 1$, and prove $S(k + 1)$. First, if $k \geq n$, then we break out of the loop when j has the value k, or earlier, and so we are sure never to reach the loop test with the value of j equal to $k + 1$. In that case, $S(k + 1)$ is surely true.

Thus, let us assume that $k < n$, so that we actually make the test with j equal to $k + 1$. $S(k)$ says that small indexes the smallest of A[i..k-1], and $S(k + 1)$ says that small indexes the smallest of A[i..k]. Consider what happens in the body of the loop (lines 4 and 5) when j has the value k; there are two cases, depending on whether the test of line (4) is true or not.

1. If $A[k]$ is not smaller than the smallest of A[i..k-1], then the value of small does not change. In that case, however, small also indexes the smallest of A[i..k], since $A[k]$ is not the smallest. Thus, the conclusion of $S(k + 1)$ is true in this case.

2. If $A[k]$ is smaller than the smallest of $A[i]$ through $A[k-1]$, then small is set to k. Again, the conclusion of $S(k + 1)$ now holds, because k is the index of the smallest of A[i..k].

---

[6] As far as the loop of lines (3) to (5) is concerned, i does not change. Thus, $i + 1$ is an appropriate constant to use as the basis value.

Thus, in either case, small is the index of the smallest of A[i..k]. We go around the for-loop by incrementing the variable j. Thus, just before the loop test, when j has the value $k + 1$, the conclusion of $S(k + 1)$ holds. We have now shown that $S(k)$ implies $S(k + 1)$. We have completed the induction and conclude that $S(k)$ holds for all values $k \geq i + 1$.

Next, we apply $S(k)$ to make our claim about the inner loop of lines (3) through (5). We exit the loop when the value of j reaches n. Since $S(n)$ says that small indexes the smallest of A[i..n-1], we have an important conclusion about the working of the inner loop. We shall see how it is used in the next example. ✦

```
(1)          for (i = 0; i < n-1; i++) {
(2)              small = i;
(3)              for (j = i+1; j < n; j++)
(4)                  if (A[j] < A[small])
(5)                      small = j;
(6)              temp = A[small];
(7)              A[small] = A[i];
(8)              A[i] = temp;
             }
```

Fig. 2.11. The body of the SelectionSort function.

✦   **Example 2.13.** Now, let us consider the entire SelectionSort function, the heart of which we reproduce in Fig. 2.11. A flowchart for this code is shown in Fig. 2.12, where "body" refers to lines (2) through (8) of Fig. 2.11. Our inductive assertion, which we refer to as $T(m)$, is again a statement about what must be true just before the test for termination of the loop. Informally, when i has the value m, we have selected m of the smallest elements and sorted them at the beginning of the array. More precisely, we prove the following statement $T(m)$ by induction on m.

STATEMENT $T(m)$: If we reach the loop test $i < n - 1$ of line (1) with the value of variable i equal to m, then

a)   A[0..m-1] are in sorted order; that is, $A[0] \leq A[1] \leq \cdots \leq A[m-1]$.

b)   All of A[m..n-1] are at least as great as any of A[0..m-1].

BASIS. The basis case is $m = 0$. The basis is true for trivial reasons. If we look at the statement $T(0)$, part (a) says that A[0..-1] are sorted. But there are no elements in the range $A[0], \ldots, A[-1]$, and so (a) must be true. Similarly, part (b) of $T(0)$ says that all of A[0..n-1] are at least as large as any of A[0..-1]. Since there are no elements of the latter description, part (b) is also true.

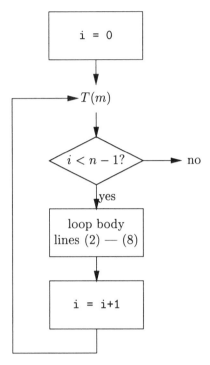

Fig. 2.12. Flow-chart for the entire selection sort function.

INDUCTION. For the inductive step, we assume that $T(m)$ is true for some $m \geq 0$, and we show that $T(m+1)$ holds. As in Example 2.12, we are trying to prove a statement of the form "if A then B," and such a statement is true whenever A is false. Thus, $T(m+1)$ is true if the assumption that we reach the for-loop test with i equal to $m+1$ is false. Thus, we may assume that we actually reach the test with i having the value $m+1$; that is, we may assume $m < n - 1$.

When i has the value m, the body of the loop finds a smallest element in A[m..n-1] (as proved by the statement $S(m)$ of Example 2.12). This element is swapped with $A[m]$ in lines (6) through (8). Part (b) of the inductive hypothesis, $T(m)$, tells us the element chosen must be at least as large as any of A[0..m-1]. Moreover, those elements were sorted, so now all of A[i..m] are sorted. That proves part (a) of statement $T(m+1)$.

To prove part (b) of $T(m+1)$, we see that $A[m]$ was just selected to be as small as any of A[m+1..n-1]. Part (a) of $T(m)$ tells us that A[0..m-1] were already as small as any of A[m+1..n-1]. Thus, after executing the body of lines (2) through (8) and incrementing i, we know that all of A[m+1..n-1] are at least as large as any of A[0..m]. Since now the value of i is $m+1$, we have shown the truth of the statement $T(m+1)$ and thus have proved the inductive step.

Now, let $m = n - 1$. We know that we exit the outer for-loop when i has the value $n-1$, so $T(n-1)$ will hold after we finish this loop. Part (a) of $T(n-1)$ says that all of A[0..n-2] are sorted, and part (b) says that $A[n-1]$ is as large as any of the other elements. Thus, after the program terminates the elements in A are in nonincreasing order; that is, they are sorted. ♦

Loop Invariants for While-Loops

When we have a while-loop of the form

> **while** (<condition>)
>   <body>

it usually makes sense to find the appropriate loop invariant for the point just before the test of the condition. Generally, we try to prove the loop invariant holds by induction on the number of times around the loop. Then, when the condition becomes false, we can use the loop invariant, together with the falsehood of the condition, to conclude something useful about what is true after the while-loop terminates.

While-loop termination

However, unlike for-loops, there may not be a variable whose value counts the number of times around the while-loop. Worse, while the for-loop is guaranteed to iterate only up to the limit of the loop (for example, up to $n - 1$ for the inner loop of the **SelectionSort** program), there is no reason to believe that the condition of the while-loop will ever become false. Thus, part of the proof of correctness for a while-loop is a proof that it eventually terminates. We usually prove termination by identifying some expression E, involving the variables of the program, such that

1. The value of E decreases by at least 1 each time around the loop, and

2. The loop condition is false if E is as low as some specified constant, such as 0.

Factorial

♦ **Example 2.14.** The factorial function, written $n!$, is defined as the product of the integers $1 \times 2 \times \cdots \times n$. For example, $1! = 1$, $2! = 1 \times 2 = 2$, and

$$5! = 1 \times 2 \times 3 \times 4 \times 5 = 120$$

Figure 2.13 shows a simple program fragment to compute $n!$ for integers $n \geq 1$.

```
(1)          scanf("%d", &n);
(2)          i = 2;
(3)          fact = 1;
(4)          while (i <= n) {
(5)              fact = fact*i;
(6)              i++;
             }
(7)          printf("%d\n", fact);
```

Fig. 2.13. Factorial program fragment.

To begin, let us prove that the while-loop of lines (4) to (6) in Fig. 2.13 must terminate. We shall choose E to be the expression $n - i$. Notice that each time around the while-loop, i is increased by 1 at line (6) and n remains unchanged. Therefore, E decreases by 1 each time around the loop. Moreover, when E is -1 or less, we have $n - i \leq -1$, or $i \geq n + 1$. Thus, when E becomes negative, the loop condition $i \leq n$ will be false and the loop will terminate. We don't know how large E is initially, since we don't know what value of n will be read. Whatever that value is, however, E will eventually reach as low as -1, and the loop will terminate.

Now we must prove that the program of Fig. 2.13 does what it is intended to do. The appropriate loop-invariant statement, which we prove by induction on the value of the variable i, is

STATEMENT $S(j)$: If we reach the loop test $i \leq n$ with the variable i having the value j, then the value of the variable fact is $(j - 1)!$.

BASIS. The basis is $S(2)$. We reach the test with i having value 2 only when we enter the loop from the outside. Prior to the loop, lines (2) and (3) of Fig. 2.13 set fact to 1 and i to 2. Since $1 = (2 - 1)!$, the basis is proved.

INDUCTION. Assume $S(j)$, and prove $S(j + 1)$. If $j > n$, then we break out of the while-loop when i has the value j or earlier, and thus we never reach the loop test with i having the value $j + 1$. In that case, $S(j + 1)$ is trivially true, because it is of the form "If we reach $\cdots$."

Thus, assume $j \leq n$, and consider what happens when we execute the body of the while-loop with i having the value j. By the inductive hypothesis, before line (5) is executed, fact has value $(j - 1)!$, and i has the value j. Thus, after line (5) is executed, fact has the value $j \times (j - 1)!$, which is $j!$.

At line (6), i is incremented by 1 and so attains the value $j + 1$. Thus, when we reach the loop test with i having value $j + 1$, the value of fact is $j!$. The statement $S(j + 1)$ says that when i equals $j + 1$, fact equals $((j + 1) - 1)!$, or $j!$. Thus, we have proved statement $S(j + 1)$, and completed the inductive step.

We already have shown that the while-loop will terminate. Evidently, it terminates when i first attains a value greater than n. Since i is an integer and is incremented by 1 each time around the loop, i must have the value $n + 1$ when the loop terminates. Thus, when we reach line (7), statement $S(n + 1)$ must hold. But that statement says that fact has the value $n!$. Thus, the program prints $n!$, as we wished to prove.

As a practical matter, we should point out that on any computer the factorial program in Fig. 2.13 will print $n!$ as an answer for very few values of n. The problem is that the factorial function grows so rapidly that the size of the answer quickly exceeds the maximum size of an integer on any real computer. ✦

EXERCISES

2.5.1: What is an appropriate loop invariant for the following program fragment, which sets sum equal to the sum of the integers from 1 to n?

```
scanf("%d",&n);
sum = 0;
for (i = 1; i <= n; i++)
    sum = sum + i;
```

Prove your loop invariant by induction on i, and use it to prove that the program works as intended.

2.5.2: The following fragment computes the sum of the integers in array A[0..n-1]:

```
sum = 0;
for (i = 0; i < n; i++)
    sum = sum + A[i];
```

What is an appropriate loop invariant? Use it to show that the fragment works as intended.

2.5.3*: Consider the following fragment:

```
scanf("%d", &n);
x = 2;
for (i = 1; i <= n; i++)
    x = x * x;
```

An appropriate loop invariant for the point just before the test for $i \leq n$ is that if we reach that point with the value k for variable i, then $x = 2^{2^{k-1}}$. Prove that this invariant holds, by induction on k. What is the value of x after the loop terminates?

```
sum = 0;
scanf("%d", &x);
while (x >= 0) {
    sum = sum + x;
    scanf("%d", &x);
}
```

Fig. 2.14. Summing a list of integers terminated by a negative integer.

2.5.4*: The fragment in Fig. 2.14 reads integers until it finds a negative integer, and then prints the accumulated sum. What is an appropriate loop invariant for the point just before the loop test? Use the invariant to show that the fragment performs as intended.

2.5.5: Find the largest value of n for which the program in Fig. 2.13 works on your computer. What are the implications of fixed-length integers for proving programs correct?

2.5.6: Show by induction on the number of times around the loop of Fig. 2.10 that $j > i + 1$ after the first time around.

✦✦ 2.6 Recursive Definitions

Inductive definition

In a *recursive*, or *inductive*, definition, we define one or more classes of closely related objects (or facts) in terms of the objects themselves. The definition must not be meaningless, like "a widget is a widget of some color," or paradoxical, like "something is a glotz if and only if it is not a glotz." Rather, a recursive definition involves

1.   One or more *basis rules*, in which some simple objects are defined, and

2.   One or more *inductive rules*, whereby larger objects are defined in terms of smaller ones in the collection.

✦   **Example 2.15.** In the previous section we defined the factorial function by an iterative algorithm: multiply $1 \times 2 \times \cdots \times n$ to get $n!$. However, we can also define the value of $n!$ recursively, as follows.

BASIS. $1! = 1$.

INDUCTION. $n! = n \times (n-1)!$.

For example, the basis tells us that $1! = 1$. We can use this fact in the inductive step with $n = 2$ to find

$$2! = 2 \times 1! = 2 \times 1 = 2$$

With $n = 3$, 4, and 5, we get

$$3! = 3 \times 2! = 3 \times 2 = 6$$
$$4! = 4 \times 3! = 4 \times 6 = 24$$
$$5! = 5 \times 4! = 5 \times 24 = 120$$

and so on. Notice that, although it appears that the term "factorial" is defined in terms of itself, in practice, we can get the value of $n!$ for progressively higher values of n in terms of the factorials for lower values of n only. Thus, we have a meaningful definition of "factorial."

Strictly speaking, we should prove that our recursive definition of $n!$ gives the same result as our original definition,

$$n! = 1 \times 2 \times \cdots \times n$$

To do so, we shall prove the following statement:

STATEMENT $S(n)$: $n!$, as defined recursively above, equals $1 \times 2 \times \cdots \times n$.

The proof will be by induction on n.

BASIS. $S(1)$ clearly holds. The basis of the recursive definition tells us that $1! = 1$, and the product $1 \times \cdots \times 1$ (i.e., the product of the integers "from 1 to 1") is evidently 1 as well.

INDUCTION. Assume that $S(n)$ holds; that is, $n!$, as given by the recursive definition, equals $1 \times 2 \times \cdots \times n$. Then the recursive definition tells us that

$$(n+1)! = (n+1) \times n!$$

If we use the commutative law for multiplication, we see that

$$(n+1)! = n! \times (n+1) \tag{2.11}$$

By the inductive hypothesis,

$$n! = 1 \times 2 \times \cdots \times n$$

Thus, we may substitute $1 \times 2 \times \cdots \times n$ for $n!$ in Equation (2.11) to get

$$(n+1)! = 1 \times 2 \times \cdots \times n \times (n+1)$$

which is the statement $S(n + 1)$. We have thereby proved the inductive hypothesis and shown that our recursive definition of $n!$ is the same as our iterative definition. ✦

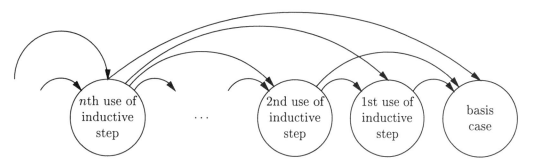

Fig. 2.15. In a recursive definition, we construct objects in rounds, where the objects constructed in one round may depend on objects constructed in all previous rounds.

Figure 2.15 suggests the general nature of a recursive definition. It is similar in structure to a complete induction, in that there is an infinite sequence of cases, each of which can depend on any or all of the previous cases. We start by applying the basis rule or rules. On the next round, we apply the inductive rule or rules to what we have already obtained, to construct new facts or objects. On the following round, we again apply the inductive rules to what we have, obtaining new facts or objects, and so on.

In Example 2.15, where we were defining the factorial, we discovered the value of 1! by the basis case, 2! by one application of the inductive step, 3! by two applications, and so on. Here, the induction had the form of an "ordinary" induction, where we used in each round only what we had discovered in the previous round.

✦ **Example 2.16.** In Section 2.2 we defined the notion of lexicographic order of
Lexicographic order
strings, and our definition was iterative in nature. Roughly, we test whether string $c_1 \cdots c_n$ precedes string $d_1 \cdots d_m$ by comparing corresponding symbols c_i and d_i from the left, until we either find an i for which $c_i \neq d_i$ or come to the end of one of the strings. The following recursive definition defines those pairs of strings w and x such that w precedes x in lexicographic order. Intuitively, the induction is on the number of pairs of equal characters at the beginnings of the two strings involved.

BASIS. The basis covers those pairs of strings for which we can immediately resolve the question of which comes first in lexicographic order. There are two parts of the basis.

1. $\epsilon < w$ for any string w other than ϵ itself. Recall that ϵ is the empty string, or the string with no characters.

2. If $c < d$, where c and d are characters, then for any strings w and x, we have $cw < dx$.

INDUCTION. If $w < x$ for strings w and x, then for any character c we have $cw < cx$.

For instance, we can use the above definition to show that base < batter. By rule (2) of the basis, with $c = $ s, $d = $ t, $w = $ e, and $x = $ ter, we have se < tter. If we apply the recursive rule once, with $c = $ a, $w = $ se, and $x = $ tter, we infer that ase < atter. Finally, applying the recursive rule a second time with $c = $ b, $w = $ ase, and $x = $ atter, we find base < batter. That is, the basis and inductive steps appear as follows:

$$
\begin{array}{ccc}
\text{se} & < & \text{tter} \\
\text{ase} & < & \text{atter} \\
\text{base} & < & \text{batter}
\end{array}
$$

We can also show that bat < batter as follows. Part (1) of the basis tells us that ϵ < ter. If we apply the recursive rule three times — with c equal to t, a, and b, in turn — we make the following sequence of inferences:

$$
\begin{array}{ccc}
\epsilon & < & \text{ter} \\
\text{t} & < & \text{tter} \\
\text{at} & < & \text{atter} \\
\text{bat} & < & \text{batter}
\end{array}
$$

Now we should prove, by induction on the number of characters that two strings have in common at their left ends, that one string precedes the other according to the definition in Section 2.2 if and only if it precedes according to the recursive definition just given. We leave these two inductive proofs as exercises. ✦

In Example 2.16, the groups of facts suggested by Fig. 2.15 are large. The basis case gives us all facts $w < x$ for which either $w = \epsilon$ or w and x begin with different letters. One use of the inductive step gives us all $w < x$ facts where w and x have exactly one initial letter in common, the second use covers those cases where w and x have exactly two initial letters in common, and so on.

Expressions

Arithmetic expressions of all kinds are naturally defined recursively. For the basis of the definition, we specify what the atomic operands can be. For example, in C, atomic operands are either variables or constants. Then, the induction tells us what operators may be applied, and to how many operands each is applied. For instance, in C, the operator < can be applied to two operands, the operator symbol − can be applied to one or two operands, and the function application operator, represented by a pair of parenthesis with as many commas inside as necessary, can be applied to one or more operands, as $f(a_1, \ldots, a_n)$.

✦ **Example 2.17.** It is common to refer to the following set of expressions as "arithmetic expressions."

BASIS. The following types of atomic operands are arithmetic expressions:

1. Variables
2. Integers
3. Real numbers

INDUCTION. If E_1 and E_2 are arithmetic expressions, then the following are also arithmetic expressions:

1. $(E_1 + E_2)$
2. $(E_1 - E_2)$
3. $(E_1 \times E_2)$
4. $(E_1 \; / \; E_2)$

Infix operator

The operators $+$, $-$, $\times$, and $/$ are said to be binary operators, because they take two arguments. They are also said to be *infix* operators, because they appear between their two arguments.

Additionally, we allow a minus sign to imply negation (change of sign), as well as subtraction. That possibility is reflected in the fifth and last recursive rule:

5. If E is an arithmetic expression, then so is $(-E)$.

Unary, prefix operator

An operator like $-$ in rule (5), which takes only one operand, is said to be a *unary* operator. It is also said to be a *prefix* operator, because it appears before its argument.

Figure 2.16 illustrates some arithmetic expressions and explains why each is an expression. Note that sometimes parentheses are not needed, and we can omit them. In the final expression (vi) of Fig. 2.16, the outer parentheses and the parentheses around $-(x + 10)$ can be omitted, and we could write $y \times -(x + 10)$. However, the remaining parentheses are essential, since $y \times -x + 10$ is conventionally interpreted as $(y \times -x) + 10$, which is not an equivalent expression (try $y = 1$ and $x = 0$, for instance).[7] ✦

$$
\begin{array}{lll}
i) & x & \text{Basis rule (1)} \\
ii) & 10 & \text{Basis rule (2)} \\
iii) & (x + 10) & \text{Recursive rule (1) on } (i) \text{ and } (ii) \\
iv) & \left(-(x + 10)\right) & \text{Recursive rule (5) on } (iii) \\
v) & y & \text{Basis rule (1)} \\
vi) & \left(y \times \left(-(x + 10)\right)\right) & \text{Recursive rule (3) on } (v) \text{ and } (iv)
\end{array}
$$

Fig. 2.16. Some sample arithmetic expressions.

---

[7] Parentheses are redundant when they are implied by the conventional precedences of operators (unary minus highest, then multiplication and division, then addition and subtraction) and by the convention of "left associativity," which says that we group operators at the same precedence level (e.g., a string of pluses and minuses) from the left. These conventions should be familiar from C, as well as from ordinary arithmetic.

More Operator Terminology

Postfix operator

A unary operator that appears after its argument, as does the factorial operator ! in expressions like $n!$, is said to be a *postfix* operator. Operators that take more than one operand can also be prefix or postfix operators, if they appear before or after all their arguments, respectively. There are no examples in C or ordinary arithmetic of operators of these types, although in Section 5.4 we shall discuss notations in which all operators are prefix or postfix operators.

Ternary operator

An operator that takes three arguments is a *ternary* operator. In C, ?: is a ternary operator, as in the expression c?x:y meaning "if c then x else y." In general, if an operator takes k arguments, it is said to be *k-ary*.

Balanced Parentheses

Strings of parentheses that can appear in expressions are called *balanced parentheses*. For example, the pattern ((())) appears in expression (*vi*) of Fig. 2.16, and the expression

$$\Big((a+b) \times \big((c+d)-e\big)\Big)$$

has the pattern (()(())). The empty string, ϵ, is also a string of balanced parentheses; it is the pattern of the expression x, for example. In general, what makes a string of parentheses balanced is that it is possible to match each left parenthesis with a right parenthesis that appears somewhere to its right. Thus, a common definition of "balanced parenthesis strings" consists of two rules:

1. A balanced string has an equal number of left and right parentheses.

Profile

2. As we move from left to right along the string, the profile of the string never becomes negative, where the *profile* is the running total of the number of left parentheses seen minus the number of right parentheses seen.

Note that the profile must begin and end at 0. For example, Fig. 2.17(a) shows the profile of (()(())), and Fig. 2.17(b) shows the profile of ()(())().

There are a number of recursive definitions for the notion of "balanced parentheses." The following is a bit subtle, but we shall prove that it is equivalent to the preceding, nonrecursive definition involving profiles.

BASIS. The empty string is a string of balanced parentheses.

INDUCTION. If x and y are strings of balanced parentheses, then $(x)y$ is also a string of balanced parentheses.

✦ **Example 2.18.** By the basis, ϵ is a balanced-parenthesis string. If we apply the recursive rule, with x and y both equal to ϵ, then we infer that () is balanced. Notice that when we substitute the empty string for a variable, such as x or y, that variable "disappears." Then we may apply the recursive rule with:

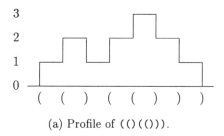

(a) Profile of $(()(()))$.

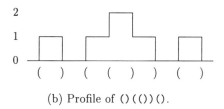

(b) Profile of $()(())()$.

Fig. 2.17. Profiles of two strings of parentheses.

1. $x = ()$ and $y = \epsilon$, to discover that $(())$ is balanced.

2. $x = \epsilon$ and $y = ()$, to find that $()()$ is balanced.

3. $x = y = ()$ to infer that $(())()$ is balanced.

As a final example, since we now know that $(())$ and $()()$ are balanced, we may let these be x and y in the recursive rule, respectively, and show that $((()))()()$ is balanced. ✦

We can show that the two definitions of "balanced" specify the same sets of strings. To make things clearer, let us refer to strings that are balanced according to the recursive definition simply as *balanced* and refer to those balanced according to
Profile-balanced the nonrecursive definition as *profile-balanced.* That is, the profile-balanced strings are those whose profile ends at 0 and never goes negative. We need to show two things:

1.   Every balanced string is profile-balanced.

2.   Every profile-balanced string is balanced.

These are the aims of the inductive proofs in the next two examples.

✦   **Example 2.19.** First, let us prove part (1), that every balanced string is profile-balanced. The proof is a complete induction that mirrors the induction by which the class of balanced strings is defined. That is, we prove

STATEMENT $S(n)$: If string w is defined to be balanced by n applications of the recursive rule, then w is profile-balanced.

BASIS. The basis is $n = 0$. The only string that can be shown to be balanced without any application of the recursive rule is ϵ, which is balanced according to the basis rule. Evidently, the profile of the empty string ends at 0 and does not go negative, so ϵ is profile-balanced.

INDUCTION. Assume that $S(i)$ is true for $i = 0, 1, \ldots, n$, and consider an instance of $S(n + 1)$, that is, a string w whose proof of balance requires $n + 1$ uses of the recursive rule. Consider the last such use, in which we took two strings x and y, already known to be balanced, and formed w as $(x)y$. We used the recursive rule $n + 1$ times to form w, and one use was the last step, which helped form neither x nor y. Thus, neither x nor y requires more than n uses of the recursive rule. Therefore, the inductive hypothesis applies to both x and y, and we can conclude that x and y are profile-balanced.

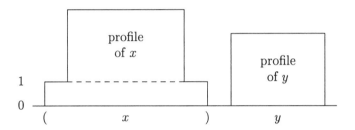

Fig. 2.18. Constructing the profile of $w = (x)y$.

The profile of w is as suggested in Fig. 2.18. It first goes up one level, in response to the first left parenthesis. Then comes the profile of x, raised one level, as indicated by the dashed line. We used the inductive hypothesis to conclude that x is profile-balanced; therefore, its profile begins and ends at level 0 and never goes negative. As the x portion of w's profile is raised one level in Fig. 2.18, that portion begins and ends at level 1 and never goes below level 1.

The explicitly shown right parenthesis between x and y lowers the profile of w to 0. Then comes the profile of y. By the inductive hypothesis, y is profile-balanced. Thus, the y portion of w's profile does not go below 0, and it ends the profile of w at 0.

We have now constructed the profile of w and see that it meets the condition for a profile-balanced string. That is, it begins and ends at 0, and it never becomes negative. Thus, we have proved that if a string is balanced, it is profile-balanced. ✦

Now we shall address the second direction of the equivalence between the two definitions of "balanced parentheses." We show in the next example that a profile-balanced string is balanced.

✦ **Example 2.20.** We prove part (2), that "profile-balanced" implies "balanced," by complete induction on the length of the string of parentheses. The formal statement is

Proofs About Recursive Definitions

Notice that Example 2.19 proves an assertion about a class of recursively defined objects (the balanced strings of parentheses) by induction on the number of times the recursive rule is used to establish that the object is in the defined class. That is a very common way to deal with recursively defined concepts; in fact, it is one of the reasons recursive definitions are useful. As another illustration, in Example 2.15, we showed a property of the recursively defined factorial values (that $n!$ is the product of the integers from 1 to n) by induction on n. But n is also 1 plus the number of times we used the recursive rule in the definition of $n!$, so the proof could also be considered an induction on the number of applications of the recursive rule.

STATEMENT $S(n)$: If a string w of length n is profile-balanced, then it is balanced.

BASIS. If $n = 0$, then the string must be ϵ. We know that ϵ is balanced by the basis rule of the recursive definition.

INDUCTION. Suppose that profile-balanced strings of length equal to or less than n are balanced. We must prove $S(n + 1)$, that profile-balanced strings of length $n + 1$ are also balanced.[8] Consider such a string w. Since w is profile-balanced, it cannot start with a right parenthesis, or its profile would immediately go negative. Thus, w begins with a left parenthesis.

Let us break w into two parts. The first part starts at the beginning of w and ends where the profile of w first becomes 0. The second part is the remainder of w. For example, the profile of Fig. 2.17(a) first becomes 0 at the end, so if $w = (()(()))$, then the first part is the entire string and the second part is ϵ. In Fig. 2.17(b), where $w = ()(())()$, the first part is $()$, and the second part is $(())()$.

The first part can never end in a left parenthesis, because then the profile would be negative at the position just before. Thus, the first part begins with a left parenthesis and ends with a right parenthesis. We can therefore write w as $(x)y$, where (x) is the first part and y is the second part. Both x and y are shorter than w, so if we can show they are profile-balanced, then we can use the inductive hypothesis to infer that they are balanced. Then we can use the recursive rule in the definition of "balanced" to show that $w = (x)y$ is balanced.

It is easy to see that y is profile-balanced. Figure 2.18 also illustrates the relationship between the profiles of w, x, and y here. That is, the profile of y is a tail of the profile of w, beginning and ending at height 0. Since w is profile-balanced, we can conclude that y is also. Showing that x is profile-balanced is almost the same. The profile of x is a part of the profile of w; it begins and ends at level 1 in the profile of w, but we can lower it by one level to get the profile of x. We know that the profile of w never reaches 0 during the extent of x, because we picked (x) to be the shortest prefix of w that ends with the profile of w at level 0. Hence, the profile of x within w never reaches level 0, and the profile of x itself never becomes negative.

We have now shown both x and y to be profile-balanced. Since they are each

---

[8] Note that all profile-balanced strings happen to be of even length, so if $n + 1$ is odd, we are not saying anything. However, we do not need the evenness of n for the proof.

shorter than w, the inductive hypothesis applies to them, and they are each balanced. The recursive rule defining "balanced" says that if x and y are balanced, then so is $(x)y$. But $w = (x)y$, and so w is balanced. We have now completed the inductive step and shown statement $S(n)$ to be true for all $n \geq 0$. ✦

EXERCISES

2.6.1*: Prove that the definitions of lexicographic order given in Example 2.16 and in Section 2.2 are the same. *Hint*: The proof consists of two parts, and each is an inductive proof. For the first part, suppose that $w < x$ according to the definition in Example 2.16. Prove the following statement $S(i)$ by induction on i: "If it is necessary to apply the recursive rule i times to show that $w < x$, then w precedes x according to the definition of 'lexicographic order' in Section 2.2." The basis is $i = 0$. The second part of the exercise is to show that if w precedes x in lexicographic order according to the definition in Section 2.2, then $w < x$ according to the definition in Example 2.16. Now the induction is on the number of initial positions that w and x have in common.

2.6.2: Draw the profiles of the following strings of parentheses:

a) (( ) (( ))
b) ( ) ( )) (( )
c) ((( ) ( )) ( ) ( ))
d) (( ) (( ) (( ))))

Which are profile-balanced? For those that are profile-balanced, use the recursive definition in Section 2.6 to show that they are balanced.

2.6.3*: Show that every string of balanced parentheses (according to the recursive definition in Section 2.6) is the string of parentheses in some arithmetic expression (see Example 2.17 for a definition of arithmetic expressions). *Hint*: Use a proof by induction on the number of times the recursive rule of the definition of "balanced parentheses" is used to construct the given string of balanced parentheses.

2.6.4: Tell whether each of the following C operators is prefix, postfix, or infix, and whether they are unary, binary, or k-ary for some $k > 2$:
a) <
b) &
c) %

2.6.5: If you are familiar with the UNIX file system or a similar system, give a recursive definition of the possible directory/file structures.

2.6.6*: A certain set S of integers is defined recursively by the following rules.

BASIS. 0 is in S.

INDUCTION. If i is in S, then $i + 5$ and $i + 7$ are in S.

a) What is the largest integer *not* in S?

b)   Let j be your answer to part (a). Prove that all integers $j + 1$ and greater are in S. *Hint*: Note the similarity to Exercise 2.4.8 (although here we are dealing with only nonnegative integers).

2.6.7*: Define recursively the set of even-parity strings, by induction on the length of the string. *Hint*: It helps to define two concepts simultaneously, both the even-parity strings and the odd-parity strings.

2.6.8*: We can define sorted lists of integers as follows.

BASIS. A list consisting of a single integer is sorted.

INDUCTION. If L is a sorted list in which the last element is a, and if $b \geq a$, then L followed by b is a sorted list.

Prove that this recursive definition of "sorted list" is equivalent to our original, nonrecursive definition, which is that the list consist of integers

$$a_1 \leq a_2 \leq \cdots \leq a_n$$

Remember, you need to prove two parts: (a) If a list is sorted by the recursive definition, then it is sorted by the nonrecursive definition, and (b) if a list is sorted by the nonrecursive definition, then it is sorted by the recursive definition. Part (a) can use induction on the number of times the recursive rule is used, and (b) can use induction on the length of the list.

2.6.9**: As suggested by Fig. 2.15, whenever we have a recursive definition, we can classify the objects defined according to the "round" on which each is generated, that is, the number of times the inductive step is applied before we obtain each object. In Examples 2.15 and 2.16, it was fairly easy to describe the results generated on each round. Sometimes it is more challenging to do so. How do you characterize the objects generated on the nth round for each of the following?

a)   Arithmetic expressions like those described in Example 2.17. *Hint*: If you are familiar with trees, which are the subject of Chapter 5, you might consider the tree representation of expressions.

b)   Balanced parenthesis strings. Note that the "number of applications used," as discussed in Example 2.19, is not the same as the round on which a string is discovered. For example, (())() uses the inductive rule three times but is discovered on round 2.

✦✦ 2.7   Recursive Functions

Direct and indirect recursion

A recursive function is one that is called from within its own body. Often, the call is *direct;* for example, a function F has a call to F within itself. Sometimes, however, the call is *indirect*: some function F_1 calls a function F_2 directly, which calls F_3 directly, and so on, until some function F_k in the sequence calls F_1.

There is a common belief that it is easier to learn to program iteratively, or to use nonrecursive function calls, than it is to learn to program recursively. While we cannot argue conclusively against that point of view, we do believe that recursive programming is easy once one has had the opportunity to practice the style.

More Truth in Advertising

A potential disadvantage of using recursion is that function calls on some machines are time-consuming, so that a recursive program may take more time to run than an iterative program for the same problem. However, on many modern machines function calls are quite efficient, and so this argument against using recursive programs is becoming less important.

Profiling

Even on machines with slow function-calling mechanisms, one can *profile* a program to find how much time is spent on each part of the program. One can then rewrite the parts of the program in which the bulk of its time is spent, replacing recursion by iteration if necessary. That way, one gets the advantages of recursion throughout most of the program, except for a small fraction of the code where speed is most critical.

Recursive programs are often more succinct or easier to understand than their iterative counterparts. More importantly, some problems are more easily attacked by recursive programs than by iterative programs.[9]

Often, we can develop a recursive algorithm by mimicking a recursive definition in the specification of a program we are trying to implement. A recursive function that implements a recursive definition will have a basis part and an inductive part. Frequently, the basis part checks for a simple kind of input that can be solved by the basis of the definition, with no recursive call needed. The inductive part of the function requires one or more recursive calls to itself and implements the inductive part of the definition. Some examples should clarify these points.

✦ **Example 2.21.** Figure 2.19 gives a recursive function that computes $n!$ given a positive integer n. This function is a direct transcription of the recursive definition of $n!$ in Example 2.15. That is, line (1) of Fig. 2.19 distinguishes the basis case from the inductive case. We assume that $n \geq 1$, so the test of line (1) is really asking whether $n = 1$. If so, we apply the basis rule, $1! = 1$, at line (2). If $n > 1$, then we apply the inductive rule, $n! = n \times (n-1)!$, at line (3).

```
          int fact(int n)
          {
(1)           if (n <= 1)
(2)               return 1; /* basis */
              else
(3)               return n*fact(n-1); /* induction */
          }
```

Fig. 2.19. Recursive function to compute $n!$ for $n \geq 1$.

For instance, if we call `fact(4)`, the result is a call to `fact(3)`, which calls

---

[9] Such problems often involve some kind of search. For instance, in Chapter 5 we shall see some recursive algorithms for searching trees, algorithms that have no convenient iterative analog (although there are equivalent iterative algorithms using stacks).

Defensive Programming

The program of Fig. 2.19 illustrates an important point about writing recursive programs so that they do not run off into infinite sequences of calls. We tacitly assumed that `fact` would never be called with an argument less than 1. Best, of course, is to begin `fact` with a test that $n \geq 1$, printing an error message and returning some particular value such as 0 if it is not. However, even if we believe very strongly that `fact` will never be called with $n < 1$, we shall be wise to include in the basis case all these "error cases." Then, the function `fact` called with erroneous input will simply return the value 1, which is wrong, but not a disaster (in fact, 1 is even correct for $n = 0$, since 0! is conventionally defined to be 1).

However, suppose we were to ignore the error cases and write line (1) of Fig. 2.19 as

```
if (n == 1)
```

Then if we called `fact(0)`, it would look like an instance of the inductive case, and we would next call `fact(-1)`, then `fact(-2)`, and so on, terminating with failure when the computer ran out of space to record the recursive calls.

`fact(2)`, which calls `fact(1)`. At that point, `fact(1)` applies the basis rule, because $n \leq 1$, and returns the value 1 to `fact(2)`. That call to `fact` completes line (3), returning 2 to `fact(3)`. In turn, `fact(3)` returns 6 to `fact(4)`, which completes line (3) by returning 24 as the answer. Figure 2.20 suggests the pattern of calls and returns. ✦

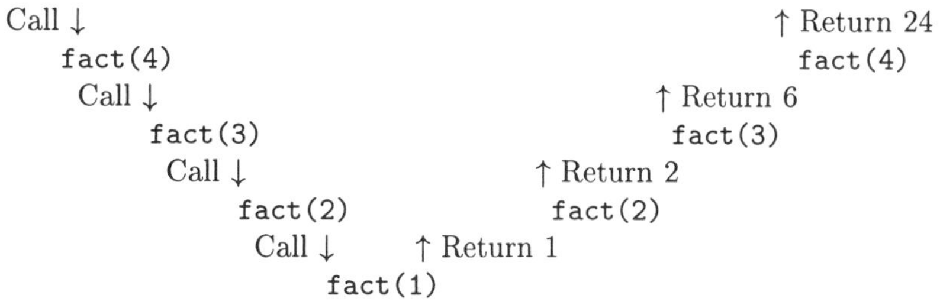

Call ↓   ↑ Return 24
     `fact(4)`   `fact(4)`
      Call ↓   ↑ Return 6
        `fact(3)`   `fact(3)`
         Call ↓   ↑ Return 2
           `fact(2)`   `fact(2)`
            Call ↓   ↑ Return 1
              `fact(1)`

Fig. 2.20. Calls and returns resulting from call to `fact(4)`.

Size of arguments

We can picture a recursion much as we have pictured inductive proofs and definitions. In Fig. 2.21 we have assumed that there is a notion of the "size" of arguments for a recursive function. For example, for the function *fact* in Example 2.21 the value of the argument n itself is the appropriate size. We shall say more about the matter of size in Section 2.9. However, let us note here that it is essential for a recursion to make only calls involving arguments of smaller size. Also, we must reach the basis case — that is, we must terminate the recursion — when we reach some particular size, which in Fig. 2.21 is size 0.

In the case of the function `fact`, the calls are not as general as suggested by Fig. 2.21. A call to `fact(n)` results in a direct call to `fact(n-1)`, but `fact(n)` does

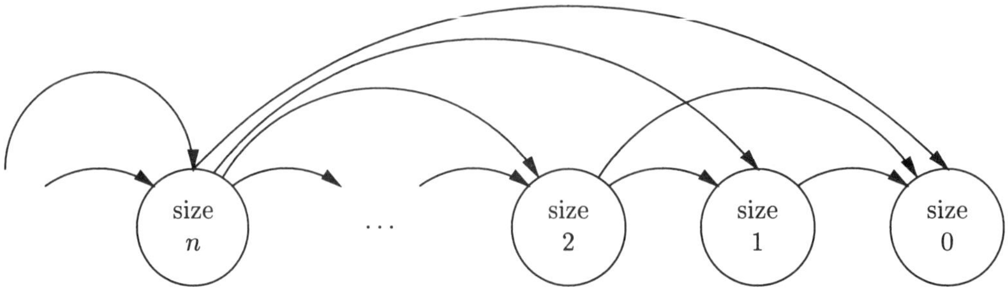

Fig. 2.21. A recursive function calls itself with arguments of smaller size.

not call `fact` with any smaller argument directly.

✦ **Example 2.22.** We can turn the function `SelectionSort` of Fig. 2.2 into a recursive function `recSS`, if we express the underlying algorithm as follows. Assume the data to be sorted is in `A[0..n-1]`.

1.   Pick a smallest element from the tail of the array `A`, that is, from `A[i..n-1]`.

2.   Swap the element selected in step (1) with `A[i]`.

3.   Sort the remainder of the array, `A[i+1..n-1]`.

We can express selection sort as the following recursive algorithm.

BASIS. If $i = n - 1$, then only the last element of the array remains to be sorted. Since any one element is already sorted, we need not do anything.

INDUCTION. If $i < n - 1$, then find the smallest element in `A[i..n-1]`, swap it with `A[i]`, and recursively sort `A[i+1..n-1]`.

The entire algorithm is to perform the above recursion starting with $i = 0$.

Backward induction

If we see i as the parameter in the preceding induction, it is a case of *backward induction,* where we start with a high basis and by the inductive rule solve instances with smaller values of the parameter in terms of instances with higher values. That is a perfectly good style of induction, although we have not previously mentioned its possibility. However, we can also see this induction as an ordinary, or "forward" induction on a parameter $k = n - i$ that represents the number of elements in the tail of the array waiting to be sorted.

In Fig. 2.22, we see the program for `recSS(A,i,n)`. The second parameter `i` is the index of the first element in the unsorted tail of the array `A`. The third parameter `n` is the total number of elements in the array `A` to be sorted. Presumably, n is less than or equal to the maximum size of `A`. Thus, a call to `recSS(A,0,n)` will sort the entire array `A[0..n-1]`.

In terms of Fig. 2.21, $s = n - i$ is the appropriate notion of "size" for arguments of the function `recSS`. The basis is $s = 1$ — that is, sorting one element, in which case no recursive calls occur. The inductive step tells us how to sort s elements by picking the smallest and then sorting the remaining $s - 1$ elements.

At line (1) we test for the basis case, in which there is only one element remaining to be sorted (again, we are being defensive, so that if we somehow make a

```
        void recSS(int A[], int i, int n)
        {
            int j, small, temp;
(1)         if (i < n-1) {/* basis is when i = n-1, in which case */
                          /* the function returns without changing A */
                          /* induction follows */
(2)             small = i;
(3)             for (j = i+1; j < n; j++)
(4)                 if (A[j] < A[small])
(5)                     small = j;
(6)             temp = A[small];
(7)             A[small] = A[i];
(8)             A[i] = temp;
(9)             recSS(A, i+1, n);
            }
        }
```

Fig. 2.22. Recursive selection sort.

call with $i \geq n$, we shall not go into an infinite sequence of calls). In the basis case, we have nothing to do, so we just return.

The remainder of the function is the inductive case. Lines (2) through (8) are copied directly from the iterative version of selection sort. Like that program, these lines set `small` to the index of the array `A[i..n-1]` that holds a smallest element and then swap this element with `A[i]`. Finally, line (9) is the recursive call, which sorts the remainder of the array. ✦

EXERCISES

2.7.1: We can define n^2 recursively as follows.

BASIS. For $n = 1$, $1^2 = 1$.

INDUCTION. If $n^2 = m$, then $(n+1)^2 = m + 2n + 1$.

a)   Write a recursive C function to implement this recursion.

b)   Prove by induction on n that this definition correctly computes n^2.

2.7.2: Suppose that we are given array `A[0..4]`, with elements 10, 13, 4, 7, 11, in that order. What are the contents of the array `A` just before each recursive call to `recSS`, according to the recursive function of Fig. 2.22?

2.7.3: Suppose we define cells for a linked list of integers, as discussed in Section 1.3, using the macro `DefCell(int, CELL, LIST)` of Section 1.6. Recall, this macro expands to be the following type definition:

Divide-and-Conquer

One way of attacking a problem is to try to break it into subproblems and then solve the subproblems and combine their solutions into a solution for the problem as a whole. The term *divide-and-conquer* is used to describe this problem-solving technique. If the subproblems are similar to the original, then we may be able to use the same function to solve the subproblems recursively.

There are two requirements for this technique to work. The first is that the subproblems must be simpler than the original problem. The second is that after a finite number of subdivisions, we must encounter a subproblem that can be solved outright. If these criteria are not met, a recursive algorithm will continue subdividing the problem forever, without finding a solution.

Note that the recursive function recSS in Fig. 2.22 satisfies both criteria. Each time it is invoked, it is on a subarray that has one fewer element, and when it is invoked on a subarray containing a single element, it returns without invoking itself again. Similarly, the factorial program of Fig. 2.19 involves calls with a smaller integer value at each call, and the recursion stops when the argument of the call reaches 1. Section 2.8 discusses a more powerful use of the divide-and-conquer technique, called "merge sort." There, the size of the arrays being sorted diminishes very rapidly, because merge sort works by dividing the size in half, rather than subtracting 1, at each recursive call.

```
typedef struct CELL *LIST;
struct CELL {
    int element;
    LIST next;
};
```

Write a recursive function find that takes an argument of type LIST and returns TRUE if some cell of the list contains the integer 1698 as its element and returns FALSE if not.

2.7.4: Write a recursive function add that takes an argument of type LIST, as defined in Exercise 2.7.3, and returns the sum of the elements on the list.

2.7.5: Write a version of recursive selection sort that takes as argument a list of integers, using the cells mentioned in Exercise 2.7.3.

2.7.6: In Exercise 2.2.8 we suggested that one could generalize selection sort to use arbitrary *key* and *lt* functions to compare elements. Rewrite the recursive selection sort algorithm to incorporate this generality.

2.7.7*: Give a recursive algorithm that takes an integer i and produces the binary representation of i as a sequence of 0's and 1's, low-order bit first.

GCD

2.7.8*: The *greatest common divisor* (GCD) of two integers i and j is the largest integer that divides both i and j evenly. For example, $gcd(24, 30) = 6$, and $gcd(24, 35) = 1$. Write a recursive function that takes two integers i and j, with $i > j$, and returns $gcd(i, j)$. *Hint*: You may use the following recursive definition of gcd. It assumes that $i > j$.

BASIS. If j divides i evenly, then j is the GCD of i and j.

INDUCTION. If j does not divide i evenly, let k be the remainder when i is divided by j. Then $gcd(i, j)$ is the same as $gcd(j, k)$.

2.7.9**: Prove that the recursive definition of GCD given in Exercise 2.7.8 gives the same result as the nonrecursive definition (largest integer dividing both i and j evenly).

2.7.10: Often, a recursive definition can be turned into an algorithm fairly directly. For example, consider the recursive definition of "less than" on strings given in Example 2.16. Write a recursive function that tests whether the first of two given strings is "less than" the other. Assume that strings are represented by linked lists of characters.

2.7.11*: From the recursive definition of a sorted list given in Exercise 2.6.8, create a recursive sorting algorithm. How does this algorithm compare with the recursive selection sort of Example 2.22?

✦✦ 2.8   Merge Sort: A Recursive Sorting Algorithm

Divide and conquer

We shall now consider a sorting algorithm, called *merge sort,* which is radically different from selection sort. Merge sort is best described recursively, and it illustrates a powerful use of the *divide-and-conquer* technique, in which we sort a list $(a_1, a_2, \ldots, a_n)$ by "dividing" the problem into two similar problems of half the size. In principle, we could begin by dividing the list into two arbitrarily chosen equal-sized lists, but in the program we develop, we shall make one list out of the odd-numbered elements, $(a_1, a_3, a_5, \ldots)$ and the other out of the even-numbered elements, $(a_2, a_4, a_6, \ldots)$.[10] We then sort each of the half-sized lists separately. To complete the sorting of the original list of n elements, we merge the two sorted, half-sized lists by an algorithm to be described in the next example.

In the next chapter, we shall see that the time required for merge sort grows much more slowly, as a function of the length n of the list to be sorted, than does the time required by selection sort. Thus, even if recursive calls take some extra time, merge sort is greatly preferable to selection sort when n is large. In Chapter 3 we shall examine the relative performance of these two sorting algorithms.

Merging

To "merge" means to produce from two sorted lists a single sorted list containing all the elements of the two given lists and no other elements. For example, given the lists $(1, 2, 7, 7, 9)$ and $(2, 4, 7, 8)$, the merger of these lists is $(1, 2, 2, 4, 7, 7, 7, 8, 9)$. Note that it does not make sense to talk about "merging" lists that are not already sorted.

One simple way to merge two lists is to examine them from the front. At each step, we find the smaller of the two elements at the current fronts of the lists, choose that element as the next element on the combined list, and remove the chosen element from its list, exposing a new "first" element on that list. Ties can be broken

---

[10] Remember that "odd-numbered" and "even-numbered" refer to the positions of the elements on the list, and not to the values of these elements.

L_1	L_2	M
$1, 2, 7, 7, 9$	$2, 4, 7, 8$	empty
$2, 7, 7, 9$	$2, 4, 7, 8$	1
$7, 7, 9$	$2, 4, 7, 8$	$1, 2$
$7, 7, 9$	$4, 7, 8$	$1, 2, 2$
$7, 7, 9$	$7, 8$	$1, 2, 2, 4$
$7, 9$	$7, 8$	$1, 2, 2, 4, 7$
9	$7, 8$	$1, 2, 2, 4, 7, 7$
9	8	$1, 2, 2, 4, 7, 7, 7$
9	empty	$1, 2, 2, 4, 7, 7, 7, 8$
empty	empty	$1, 2, 2, 4, 7, 7, 7, 8, 9$

Fig. 2.23. Example of merging.

arbitrarily, although we shall take from the first list when the leading elements of both lists are the same.

✦   **Example 2.23.** Consider merging the two lists

$$L_1 = (1, 2, 7, 7, 9) \text{ and } L_2 = (2, 4, 7, 8)$$

The first elements of the lists are 1 and 2, respectively. Since 1 is smaller, we choose it as the first element of the merged list M and remove 1 from L_1. The new L_1 is thus $(2, 7, 7, 9)$. Now, both L_1 and L_2 have 2 as their first elements. We can pick either. Suppose we adopt the policy that we always pick the element from L_1 in case of a tie. Then merged list M becomes $(1, 2)$, list L_1 becomes $(7, 7, 9)$, and L_2 remains $(2, 4, 7, 8)$. The table in Fig. 2.23 shows the merging steps until lists L_1 and L_2 are both exhausted. ✦

We shall find it easier to design a recursive merging algorithm if we represent lists in the linked form suggested in Section 1.3. Linked lists will be reviewed in more detail in Chapter 6. In what follows, we shall assume that list elements are integers. Thus, each element can be represented by a "cell," or structure of the type struct CELL, and the list by a type LIST, which is a pointer to a CELL. These definitions are provided by the macro DefCell(int, CELL, LIST), which we discussed in Section 1.6. This use of macro DefCell expands into:

```
typedef struct CELL *LIST;
struct CELL {
    int element;
    LIST next;
};
```

The element field of each cell contains an integer, and the next field contains a pointer to the next cell on the list. If the element at hand is the last on the list, then the next field contains the value NULL, which represents a null pointer. A list of integers is then represented by a pointer to the first cell on the list, that is, by a variable of type LIST. An empty list is represented by a variable with the value

```
        LIST merge(LIST list1, LIST list2)
        {
(1)         if (list1 == NULL) return list2;
(2)         else if (list2 == NULL) return list1;
(3)         else if (list1->element <= list2->element) {
                /* Here, neither list is empty, and the first list
                    has the smaller first element. The answer is the
                    first element of the first list followed by the
                    merge of the remaining elements. */
(4)             list1->next = merge(list1->next, list2);
(5)             return list1;
            }
            else { /* list2 has smaller first element */
(6)             list2->next = merge(list1, list2->next);
(7)             return list2;
            }
        }
```

Fig. 2.24. Recursive merge.

NULL, in place of a pointer to the first element.

Figure 2.24 is a C implementation of a recursive merging algorithm. The function merge takes two lists as arguments and returns the merged list. That is, the formal parameters list1 and list2 are pointers to the two given lists, and the return value is a pointer to the merged list. The recursive algorithm can be described as follows.

BASIS. If either list is empty, then the other list is the desired result. This rule is implemented by lines (1) and (2) of Fig. 2.24. Note that if both lists are empty, then list2 will be returned. But that is correct, since the value of list2 is then NULL and the merger of two empty lists is an empty list.

INDUCTION. If neither list is empty, then each has a first element. We can refer to the two first elements as list1->element and list2->element, that is, the element fields of the cells pointed to by list1 and list2, respectively. Fig 2.25 is a picture of the data structure. The list to be returned begins with the cell of the smallest element. The remainder of the list is formed by merging all but that element.

For example, lines (4) and (5) handle the case in which the first element of list 1 is smallest. Line (4) is a recursive call to merge. The first argument of this call is list1->next, that is, a pointer to the second element on the first list (or NULL if the first list only has one element). Thus, the recursive call is passed the list consisting of all but the first element of the first list. The second argument is the entire second list. As a consequence, the recursive call to merge at line (4) will return a pointer to the merged list of all the remaining elements and store a pointer to this merged list in the next field of the first cell on list 1. At line (5), we return a pointer to that cell, which is now the first cell on the merged list of all the elements.

Figure 2.25 illustrates the changes. Dotted arrows are present when merge is

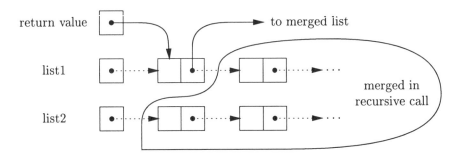

Fig. 2.25. Inductive step of merging algorithm.

called. Solid arrows are created by merge. Specifically, the return value of merge is a pointer to the cell of the smallest element, and the next field of that element is shown pointing to the list returned by the recursive call to merge at line (4).

Finally, lines (6) and (7) handle the case where the second list has the smallest element. The behavior of the algorithm is exactly as in lines (4) and (5), but the roles of the two lists are reversed.

✦ **Example 2.24.** Suppose we call merge on the lists $(1, 2, 7, 7, 9)$ and $(2, 4, 7, 8)$ of Example 2.23. Figure 2.26 illustrates the sequence of calls made to merge, if we read the first column downward. We omit the commas separating list elements, but commas are used to separate the arguments of merge.

CALL	RETURN
merge(12779, 2478)	122477789
merge(2779, 2478)	22477789
merge(779, 2478)	2477789
merge(779, 478)	477789
merge(779, 78)	77789
merge(79, 78)	7789
merge(9, 78)	789
merge(9, 8)	89
merge(9, NULL)	9

Fig. 2.26. Recursive calls to merge.

For instance, since the first element of list 1 is less than the first element of list 2, line (4) of Fig. 2.24 is executed and we recursively merge all but the first element of list 1. That is, the first argument is the tail of list 1, or $(2, 7, 7, 9)$, and the second argument is the full list 2, or $(2, 4, 7, 8)$. Now the leading elements of both lists are the same. Since the test of line (3) in Fig. 2.24 favors the first list, we remove the 2 from list 1, and our next call to merge has first argument $(7, 7, 9)$ and second argument $(2, 4, 7, 8)$.

The returned lists are indicated in the second column, read upward. Notice that, unlike the iterative description of merging suggested by Fig. 2.23, the recursive algorithm assembles the merged list from the rear, whereas the iterative algorithm assembles it from the front. ✦

Splitting Lists

Another important task required for merge sort is splitting a list into two equal parts, or into parts whose lengths differ by 1 if the original list is of odd length. One way to do this job is to count the number of elements on the list, divide by 2, and break the list at the midpoint. Instead, we shall give a simple recursive function split that "deals" the elements into two lists, one consisting of the first, third, and fifth elements, and so on, and the other consisting of the elements at the even positions. More precisely, the function split removes the even-numbered elements from the list it is given as an argument and returns a new list consisting of the even-numbered elements.

The C code for function split is shown in Fig. 2.27. Its argument is a list of the type LIST that was defined in connection with the merge function. Note that the local variable pSecondCell is defined to be of type LIST. We really use pSecondCell as a pointer to the second cell on a list, rather than as a list itself; but of course type LIST is, in fact, a pointer to a cell.

It is important to observe that split is a function with a side effect. It removes the cells in the even positions from the list it is given as an argument, and it assembles these cells into a new list, which becomes the return value of the function.

```
      LIST split(LIST list)
      {
          LIST pSecondCell;

(1)       if (list == NULL) return NULL;
(2)       else if (list->next == NULL) return NULL;
          else { /* there are at least two cells */
(3)           pSecondCell = list->next;
(4)           list->next = pSecondCell->next;
(5)           pSecondCell->next = split(pSecondCell->next);
(6)           return pSecondCell;
          }
      }
```

Fig. 2.27. Splitting a list into two equal pieces.

The splitting algorithm can be described inductively, as follows. It uses an induction on the length of a list; that induction has a multiple basis case.

BASIS. If the list is of length 0 or 1, then we do nothing. That is, an empty list is "split" into two empty lists, and a list of a single element is split by leaving the element on the given list and returning an empty list of the even-numbered elements, of which there are none. The basis is handled by lines (1) and (2) of Fig. 2.27. Line (1) handles the case where list is empty, and line (2) handles the case where it is a single element. Notice that we are careful not to examine list->next in line (2) unless we have previously determined, at line (1), that list is not NULL.

INDUCTION. The inductive step applies when there are at least two elements on `list`. At line (3), we keep a pointer to the second cell of the list in the local variable `pSecondCell`. Line (4) makes the `next` field of the first cell skip over the second cell and point to the third cell (or become NULL if there are only two cells on the list). At line (5), we call `split` recursively, on the list consisting of all but the first two elements. The value returned by that call is a pointer to the fourth element (or NULL if the list is shorter than four elements), and we place this pointer in the `next` field of the second cell, to complete the linking of the even-numbered elements. A pointer to the second cell is returned by `split` at line (6); that pointer gives us access to the linked list of all the even-numbered elements of the original list.

The changes made by `split` are suggested in Fig. 2.28. Original pointers are dotted, and new pointers are solid. We also indicate the number of the line that creates each of the new pointers.

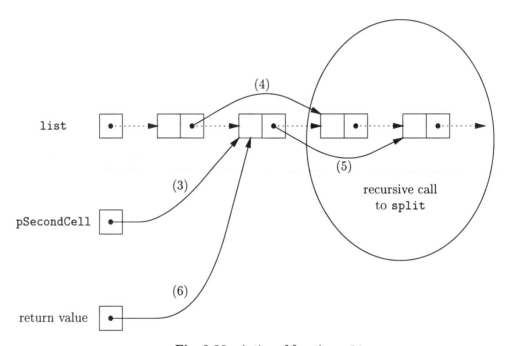

Fig. 2.28. Action of function `split`.

The Sorting Algorithm

The recursive sorting algorithm is shown in Fig. 2.29. The algorithm can be described by the following basis and inductive step.

BASIS. If the list to be sorted is empty or of length 1, just return the list; it is already sorted. The basis is taken care of by lines (1) and (2) of Fig. 2.29.

INDUCTION. If the list is of length at least 2, use the function `split` at line (3) to remove the even-numbered elements from `list` and use them to form another list, pointed to by local variable `SecondList`. Line (4) recursively sorts the half-sized lists, and returns the merger of the two lists.

```
      LIST MergeSort(LIST list)
      {
          LIST SecondList;

(1)       if (list == NULL) return NULL;
(2)       else if (list->next == NULL) return list;
          else {
              /* at least two elements on list */
(3)           SecondList = split(list);
              /* Note that as a side effect, half
                 the elements are removed from list */
(4)           return merge(MergeSort(list), MergeSort(SecondList));
          }
      }
```

Fig. 2.29. The merge sort algorithm.

✦   **Example 2.25.** Let us use merge sort on the list of single-digit numbers

742897721

We again omit commas between digits for succinctness. First, the list is split into two, by the call to split at line (3) of MergeSort. One of the resulting lists consists of the odd positions, and the other the evens; that is, list = 72971 and SecondList = 4872. At line (4), these lists are sorted, resulting in lists 12779 and 2478, and then merged to produce the sorted list 122477789.

However, the sorting of the two half-sized lists does not occur by magic, but rather by the methodical application of the recursive algorithm. Initially, MergeSort splits the list on which it is called, if the list has length greater than 1. Figure 2.30(a) shows the recursive splitting of the lists until each list is of length 1. Then the split lists are merged, in pairs, going up the tree, until the entire list is sorted. This process is suggested in Fig. 2.30(b). However, it is worth noting that the splits and merges occur in a mixed order; not all splits are followed by all merges. For example, the first half list, 72971, is completely split and merged before we begin on the second half list, 4872. ✦

The Complete Program

Figure 2.31 contains the complete merge sort program. It is analogous to the program in Fig. 2.3 that was based on selection sort. The function MakeList on line (1) reads each integer from the input and puts it into a linked list by a simple recursive algorithm, which we shall describe in detail in the next section. Line (2) of the main program contains the call to MergeSort, which returns a sorted list to PrintList. The function PrintList marches down the sorted list, printing each element.

EXERCISES

2.8.1: Show the result of applying the function merge to the lists $(1, 2, 3, 4, 5)$ and $(2, 4, 6, 8, 10)$.

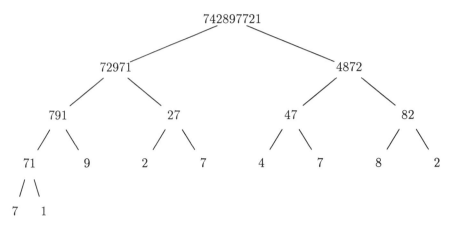

(a) Splitting.

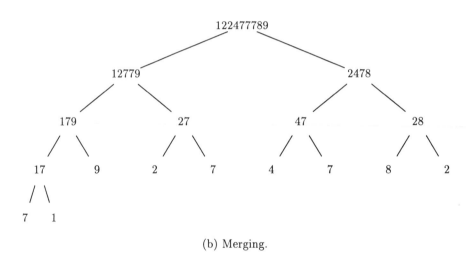

(b) Merging.

Fig. 2.30. Recursive splitting and merging.

2.8.2: Suppose we start with the list $(8, 7, 6, 5, 4, 3, 2, 1)$. Show the sequence of calls to merge, split, and MergeSort that result.

Multiway merge sort

2.8.3*: A *multiway* merge sort divides a list into k pieces of equal (or approximately equal) size, sorts them recursively, and then merges all k lists by comparing all their respective first elements and taking the smallest. The merge sort described in this section is for the case $k = 2$. Modify the program in Fig. 2.31 so that it becomes a multiway merge sort for the case $k = 3$.

2.8.4*: Rewrite the merge sort program to use the functions lt and key, described in Exercise 2.2.8, to compare elements of arbitrary type.

2.8.5: Relate each of the functions (a) merge (b) split (c) MakeList to Fig. 2.21. What is the appropriate notion of size for each of these functions?

```
      #include <stdio.h>
      #include <stdlib.h>

      typedef struct CELL *LIST;
      struct CELL {
          int element;
          LIST next;
      };

      LIST merge(LIST list1, LIST list2);
      LIST split(LIST list);
      LIST MergeSort(LIST list);
      LIST MakeList();
      void PrintList(LIST list);

      main()
      {
          LIST list;

(1)       list = MakeList();
(2)       PrintList(MergeSort(list));
      }

      LIST MakeList()
      {
          int x;
          LIST pNewCell;

(3)       if (scanf("%d", &x) == EOF) return NULL;
          else {
(4)           pNewCell = (LIST) malloc(sizeof(struct CELL));
(5)           pNewCell->next = MakeList();
(6)           pNewCell->element = x;
(7)           return pNewCell;
          }
      }

      void PrintList(LIST list)
      {
(8)       while (list != NULL) {
(9)           printf("%d\n", list->element);
(10)          list = list->next;
          }
      }
```

Fig. 2.31(a). A sorting program using merge sort (start).

```
LIST MergeSort(LIST list)
{
    LIST SecondList;

    if (list == NULL) return NULL;
    else if (list->next == NULL) return list;
    else {
        SecondList = split(list);
        return merge(MergeSort(list), MergeSort(SecondList));
    }
}

LIST merge(LIST list1, LIST list2)
{
    if (list1 == NULL) return list2;
    else if (list2 == NULL) return list1;
    else if (list1->element <= list2->element) {
        list1->next = merge(list1->next, list2);
        return list1;
    }
    else {
        list2->next = merge(list1, list2->next);
        return list2;
    }
}

LIST split(LIST list)
{
    LIST pSecondCell;

    if (list == NULL) return NULL;
    else if (list->next == NULL) return NULL;
    else {
        pSecondCell = list->next;
        list->next = pSecondCell->next;
        pSecondCell->next = split(pSecondCell->next);
        return pSecondCell;
    }
}
```

Fig. 2.31(b). A sorting program using merge sort (conclusion).

❖❖ 2.9 Proving Properties of Recursive Programs

If we want to prove a certain property of a recursive function, we generally need to prove a statement about the effect of one call to that function. For example, that effect might be a relationship between the arguments and the return value, such as "the function, called with argument i, returns $i!$." Frequently, we define a notion of the "size" of the arguments of a function and perform a proof by induction on this

size. Some of the many possible ways in which size of arguments could be defined
are

1. The value of some argument. For instance, for the recursive factorial program
    of Fig. 2.19, the appropriate size is the value of the argument n.

2. The length of a list pointed to by some argument. The recursive function split
    of Fig. 2.27 is an example where the length of the list is the appropriate size.

3. Some function of the arguments. For instance, we mentioned that the recursive
    selection sort of Fig. 2.22 performs an induction on the number of elements in
    the array that remain to be sorted. In terms of the arguments n and i, this
    function is $n - i + 1$. As another example, the appropriate size for the merge
    function of Fig. 2.24 is the sum of the lengths of the lists pointed to by the two
    arguments of the function.

Whatever notion of size we pick, it is essential that when a function is called
with arguments of size s, it makes only function calls with arguments of size $s - 1$ or
less. That requirement is so we can do an induction on the size to prove a property
of the program. Further, when the size falls to some fixed value — say 0 — the
function must make no recursive calls. This condition is so we can start off our
inductive proof with a basis case.

◆   **Example 2.26.** Consider the factorial program of Fig. 2.19 in Section 2.7. The
statement to prove by induction on i, for $i \geq 1$, is

STATEMENT $S(i)$: When called with the value i for the argument n, fact returns $i!$.

BASIS. For $i = 1$, the test at line (1) of Fig. 2.19 causes the basis, line (2), to be
executed. That results in the return value 1, which is $1!$.

INDUCTION. Assume $S(i)$ to be true, that is, when called with some argument
$i \geq 1$, fact returns $i!$. Now, consider what happens when fact is called with $i + 1$
as the value of variable n. If $i \geq 1$, then $i + 1$ is at least 2, so the inductive case, line
(3), applies. The return value is thus $n \times fact(n - 1)$; or, since the variable n has
the value $i + 1$, the result $(i + 1) \times fact(i)$ is returned. By the inductive hypothesis,
fact(i) returns $i!$. Since $(i + 1) \times i! = (i + 1)!$, we have proved the inductive step,
that fact, with argument $i + 1$, returns $(i + 1)!$. ◆

◆   **Example 2.27.** Now, let us examine the function MakeList, one of the auxiliary
routines in Fig. 2.31(a), in Section 2.8. This function creates a linked list to hold
the input elements and returns a pointer to this list. We shall prove the following
statement by induction on $n \geq 0$, the number of elements in the input sequence.

STATEMENT $S(n)$: If $x_1, x_2, ..., x_n$ is the sequence of input elements, `Makelist` creates a linked list that contains $x_1, x_2, ..., x_n$ and returns a pointer to this list.

BASIS. The basis is $n = 0$, that is, when the input sequence is empty. The test for `EOF` in line (3) of `MakeList` causes the return value to be set to `NULL`. Thus, `MakeList` correctly returns an empty list.

INDUCTION. Suppose that $S(n)$ is true for $n \geq 0$, and consider what happens when `MakeList` is called on an input sequence of $n + 1$ elements. Suppose we have just read the first element x_1.

Line (4) of `MakeList` creates a pointer to a new cell c. Line (5) recursively calls `Makelist` to create, by the inductive hypothesis, a pointer to a linked list for the remaining n elements, $x_2, x_3, \ldots, x_n$. This pointer is put into the next field of c at line (5). Line (6) puts x_1 into the element field of c. Line (7) returns the pointer created by line (4). This pointer points to a linked list for the $n + 1$ input elements, $x_1, x_2, \ldots, x_n$.

We have proved the inductive step and conclude that `MakeList` works correctly on all inputs. ✦

✦   **Example 2.28.** For our last example, let us prove the correctness of the merge-sort program of Fig. 2.29, assuming that the functions `split` and `merge` perform their respective tasks correctly. The induction will be on the length of the list that `MergeSort` is given as an argument. The statement to be proved by complete induction on $n \geq 0$ is

STATEMENT $S(n)$: If `list` is a list of length n when `MergeSort` is called, then `MergeSort` returns a sorted list of the same elements.

BASIS. We take the basis to be both $S(0)$ and $S(1)$. When `list` is of length 0, its value is `NULL`, and so the test of line (1) in Fig. 2.29 succeeds and the entire function returns `NULL`. Likewise, if `list` is of length 1, the test of line (2) succeeds, and the function returns `list`. Thus, `MergeSort` returns `list` when n is 0 or 1. This observation proves statements $S(0)$ and $S(1)$, because a list of length 0 or 1 is already sorted.

INDUCTION. Suppose $n \geq 1$ and $S(i)$ is true for all $i = 0, 1, \ldots, n$. We must prove $S(n + 1)$. Thus, consider a list of length $n + 1$. Since $n \geq 1$, this list is of length at least 2, so we reach line (3) in Fig. 2.29. There, `split` divides the list into two lists of length $(n + 1)/2$ if $n + 1$ is even, and of lengths $(n/2) + 1$ and $n/2$ if $n + 1$ is odd. Since $n \geq 1$, none of these lists can be as long as $n + 1$. Thus, the inductive hypothesis applies to them, and we can conclude that the half-sized lists are correctly sorted by the recursive calls to `MergeSort` at line (4). Finally, the two sorted lists are merged into one list, which becomes the return value. We have assumed that `merge` works correctly, and so the resulting returned list is sorted. ✦

```
DefCell(int, CELL, LIST);

int sum(LIST L)
{
    if (L == NULL) sum = 0;
    else sum = L->element + sum(L->next);
}

int find0(LIST L)
{
    if (L == NULL) find0 = FALSE;
    else if (L->element == 0) find0 = TRUE;
    else find0 = find0(L->next);
}
```

Fig. 2.32. Two recursive functions, sum and find0.

EXERCISES

2.9.1: Prove that the function PrintList in Fig. 2.31(b) prints the elements on the list that it is passed as an argument. What statement $S(i)$ do you prove inductively? What is the basis value for i?

2.9.2: The function sum in Fig. 2.32 computes the sum of the elements on its given list (whose cells are of the usual type as defined by the macro DefCell of Section 1.6 and used in the merge-sort program of Section 2.8) by adding the first element to the sum of the remaining elements; the latter sum is computed by a recursive call on the remainder of the list. Prove that sum correctly computes the sum of the list elements. What statement $S(i)$ do you prove inductively? What is the basis value for i?

2.9.3: The function find0 in Fig. 2.32 returns TRUE if at least one of the elements on its list is 0, and returns FALSE otherwise. It returns FALSE if the list is empty, returns TRUE if the first element is 0 and otherwise, makes a recursive call on the remainder of the list, and returns whatever answer is produced for the remainder. Prove that find0 correctly determines whether 0 is present on the list. What statement $S(i)$ do you prove inductively? What is the basis value for i?

2.9.4*: Prove that the functions (a) merge of Fig. 2.24 and (b) split of Fig. 2.27 perform as claimed in Section 2.8.

2.9.5: Give an intuitive "least counterexample" proof of why induction starting from a basis including both 0 and 1 is valid.

2.9.6**: Prove the correctness of (your C implementation of) the recursive GCD algorithm of Exercise 2.7.8.

✦✦ 2.10 Summary of Chapter 2

Here are the important ideas we should take from Chapter 2.

✦ Inductive proofs, recursive definitions, and recursive programs are closely related ideas. Each depends on a basis and an inductive step to "work."

✦ In "ordinary" or "weak" inductions, successive steps depend only on the previous step. We frequently need need to perform a proof by complete induction, in which each step depends on all the previous steps.

✦ There are several different ways to sort. Selection sort is a simple but slow sorting algorithm, and merge sort is a faster but more complex algorithm.

✦ Induction is essential to prove that a program or program fragment works correctly.

✦ Divide-and-conquer is a useful technique for designing some good algorithms, such as merge sort. It works by dividing the problem into independent subparts and then combining the results.

✦ Expressions are defined in a natural, recursive way in terms of their operands and operators. Operators can be classified by the number of arguments they take: unary (one argument), binary (two arguments), and k-ary (k arguments). Also, a binary operator appearing between its operands is infix, an operator appearing before its operands is prefix, and one appearing after its operands is postfix.

❖❖ 2.11   Bibliographic Notes for Chapter 2

An excellent treatment of recursion is Roberts [1986]. For more on sorting algorithms, the standard source is Knuth [1973]. Berlekamp [1968] tells about techniques — of which the error detection scheme in Section 2.3 is the simplest — for detecting and correcting errors in streams of bits.

Berlekamp, E. R. [1968]. *Algebraic Coding Theory*, McGraw-Hill, New York.

Knuth, D. E. [1973]. *The Art of Computer Programming*, Vol. III: *Sorting and Searching*, Addison-Wesley, Reading, Mass.

Roberts, E. [1986]. *Thinking Recursively*, Wiley, New York.

3

❖❖

The Running Time of Programs

In Chapter 2, we saw two radically different algorithms for sorting: selection sort and merge sort. There are, in fact, scores of algorithms for sorting. This situation is typical: every problem that can be solved at all can be solved by more than one algorithm.

How, then, should we choose an algorithm to solve a given problem? As a general rule, we should always pick an algorithm that is easy to understand, implement, and document. When performance is important, as it often is, we also need to choose an algorithm that runs quickly and uses the available computing resources efficiently. We are thus led to consider the often subtle matter of how we can measure the running time of a program or an algorithm, and what steps we can take to make a program run faster.

❖❖ 3.1 What This Chapter Is About

In this chapter we shall cover the following topics:

✦ The important performance measures for programs

✦ Methods for evaluating program performance

✦ "Big-oh" notation

✦ Estimating the running time of programs using the big-oh notation

✦ Using recurrence relations to evaluate the running time of recursive programs

The big-oh notation introduced in Sections 3.4 and 3.5 simplifies the process of estimating the running time of programs by allowing us to avoid dealing with constants that are almost impossible to determine, such as the number of machine instructions that will be generated by a typical C compiler for a given source program.

We introduce the techniques needed to estimate the running time of programs in stages. In Sections 3.6 and 3.7 we present the methods used to analyze programs with no function calls. Section 3.8 extends our capability to programs with calls to nonrecursive functions. Then in Sections 3.9 and 3.10 we show how to deal with recursive functions. Finally, Section 3.11 discusses solutions to recurrence relations, which are inductive definitions of functions that arise when we analyze the running time of recursive functions.

✦✦ 3.2   Choosing an Algorithm

If you need to write a program that will be used once on small amounts of data and then discarded, then you should select the easiest-to-implement algorithm you know, get the program written and debugged, and move on to something else. However, when you need to write a program that is to be used and maintained by many people over a long period of time, other issues arise. One is the understandability, or

Simplicity

simplicity, of the underlying algorithm. Simple algorithms are desirable for several reasons. Perhaps most important, a simple algorithm is easier to implement correctly than a complex one. The resulting program is also less likely to have subtle bugs that get exposed when the program encounters an unexpected input after it has been in use for a substantial period of time.

Clarity

Programs should be written clearly and documented carefully so that they can be maintained by others. If an algorithm is simple and understandable, it is easier to describe. With good documentation, modifications to the original program can readily be done by someone other than the original writer (who frequently will not be available to do them), or even by the original writer if the program was done some time earlier. There are numerous stories of programmers who wrote efficient and clever algorithms, then left the company, only to have their algorithms ripped out and replaced by something slower but more understandable by subsequent maintainers of the code.

Efficiency

When a program is to be run repeatedly, its efficiency and that of its underlying algorithm become important. Generally, we associate efficiency with the time it takes a program to run, although there are other resources that a program sometimes must conserve, such as

1.   The amount of storage space taken by its variables.

2.   The amount of traffic it generates on a network of computers.

3.   The amount of data that must be moved to and from disks.

For large problems, however, it is the running time that determines whether a given program can be used, and running time is the main topic of this chapter. We shall, in fact, take the efficiency of a program to mean the amount of time it takes, measured as a function of the size of its input.

Often, understandability and efficiency are conflicting aims. For example, the reader who compares the selection sort program of Fig. 2.3 with the merge sort program of Fig. 2.32 will surely agree that the latter is not only longer, but quite a bit harder to understand. That would still be true even if we summarized the explanation given in Sections 2.2 and 2.8 by placing well-thought-out comments in the programs. As we shall learn, however, merge sort is much more efficient than selection sort, as long as the number of elements to be sorted is a hundred or more. Unfortunately, this situation is quite typical: algorithms that are efficient for large amounts of data tend to be more complex to write and understand than are the relatively inefficient algorithms.

The understandability, or simplicity, of an algorithm is somewhat subjective. We can overcome lack of simplicity in an algorithm, to a certain extent, by explaining the algorithm well in comments and program documentation. The documentor should always consider the person who reads the code and its comments: Is a reasonably intelligent person likely to understand what is being said, or are further explanation, details, definitions, and examples needed?

On the other hand, program efficiency is an objective matter: a program takes what time it takes, and there is no room for dispute. Unfortunately, we cannot run the program on all possible inputs — which are typically infinite in number. Thus, we are forced to make measures of the running time of a program that summarize the program's performance on all inputs, usually as a single expression such as "n^2." How we can do so is the subject matter of the balance of this chapter.

✦✦ 3.3 Measuring Running Time

Once we have agreed that we can evaluate a program by measuring its running time, we face the problem of determining what the running time actually is. The two principal approaches to summarizing the running time are

1. Benchmarking

2. Analysis

We shall consider each in turn, but the primary emphasis of this chapter is on the techniques for analyzing a program or an algorithm.

Benchmarking

When comparing two or more programs designed to do the same set of tasks, it is customary to develop a small collection of typical inputs that can serve as *benchmarks*. That is, we agree to accept the benchmark inputs as representative of the job mix; a program that performs well on the benchmark inputs is assumed to perform well on all inputs.

For example, a benchmark to evaluate sorting programs might contain one small set of numbers, such as the first 20 digits of π; one medium set, such as the set of zip codes in Texas; and one large set, such as the set of phone numbers in the Brooklyn telephone directory. We might also want to check that a program works efficiently (and correctly) when given an empty set of elements to sort, a singleton set, and a list that is already in sorted order. Interestingly, some sorting algorithms perform poorly when given a list of elements that is already sorted.[1]

---

[1] Neither selection sort nor merge sort is among these; they take approximately the same time on a sorted list as they would on any other list of the same length.

The 90-10 Rule

Profiling

In conjunction with benchmarking, it is often useful to determine where the program under consideration is spending its time. This method of evaluating program performance is called *profiling* and most programming environments have tools called *profilers* that associate with each statement of a program a number that represents the fraction of the total time taken executing that particular statement. A related utility, called a *statement counter,* is a tool that determines for each statement of a source program the number of times that statement is executed on a given set of inputs.

Locality and hot spots

Many programs exhibit the property that most of their running time is spent in a small fraction of the source code. There is an informal rule that states 90% of the running time is spent in 10% of the code. While the exact percentage varies from program to program, the "90-10 rule" says that most programs exhibit significant locality in where the running time is spent. One of the easiest ways to speed up a program is to profile it and then apply code improvements to its "hot spots," which are the portions of the program in which most of the time is spent. For example, we mentioned in Chapter 2 that one might speed up a program by replacing a recursive function with an equivalent iterative one. However, it makes sense to do so only if the recursive function occurs in those parts of the program where most of the time is being spent.

As an extreme case, even if we reduce to zero the time taken by the 90% of the code in which only 10% of the time is spent, we will have reduced the overall running time of the program by only 10%. On the other hand, cutting in half the running time of the 10% of the program where 90% of the time is spent reduces the overall running time by 45%.

Analysis of a Program

To analyze a program, we begin by grouping inputs according to size. What we choose to call the size of an input can vary from program to program, as we discussed in Section 2.9 in connection with proving properties of recursive programs. For a sorting program, a good measure of the size is the number of elements to be sorted. For a program that solves n linear equations in n unknowns, it is normal to take n to be the size of the problem. Other programs might use the value of some particular input, or the length of a list that is an input to the program, or the size of an array that is an input, or some combination of quantities such as these.

Running Time

It is convenient to use a function $T(n)$ to represent the number of units of time taken by a program or an algorithm on any input of size n. We shall call $T(n)$ the *running time* of the program. For example, a program may have a running time $T(n) = cn$, where c is some constant. Put another way, the running time of this program is linearly proportional to the size of the input on which it is run. Such a program or algorithm is said to be *linear time*, or just *linear*.

Linear-time algorithm

We can think of the running time $T(n)$ as the number of C statements executed by the program or as the length of time taken to run the program on some standard computer. Most of the time we shall leave the units of $T(n)$ unspecified. In fact, as we shall see in the next section, it makes sense to talk of the running time of a program only as some (unknown) constant factor times $T(n)$.

Quite often, the running time of a program depends on a particular input, not just on the size of the input. In these cases, we define $T(n)$ to be the *worst-case* running time, that is, the maximum running time on any input among all inputs of size n.

Worst and average-case running time

Another common performance measure is $T_{avg}(n)$, the average running time of the program over all inputs of size n. The average running time is sometimes a more realistic measure of what performance one will see in practice, but it is often much harder to compute than the worst-case running time. The notion of an "average" running time also implies that all inputs of size n are equally likely, which may or may not be true in a given situation.

✦   **Example 3.1.** Let us estimate the running time of the `SelectionSort` fragment shown in Fig. 3.1. The statements have the original line numbers from Fig. 2.2. The purpose of the code is to set `small` to the index of the smallest of the elements found in the portion of the array `A` from `A[i]` through `A[n-1]`.

```
(2)              small = i;
(3)              for(j = i+1; j < n; j++)
(4)                  if (A[j] < A[small])
(5)                      small = j;
```

Fig. 3.1. Inner loop of selection sort.

To begin, we need to develop a simple notion of time units. We shall examine the issue in detail later, but for the moment, the following simple scheme is sufficient. We shall count one time unit each time we execute an assignment statement. At line (3), we count one unit for initializing j at the beginning of the for-loop, one unit for testing whether $j < n$, and one unit for incrementing j, each time we go around the loop. Finally, we charge one unit each time we perform the test of line (4).

First, let us consider the body of the inner loop, lines (4) and (5). The test of line (4) is always executed, but the assignment at line (5) is executed only if the test succeeds. Thus, the body takes either 1 or 2 time units, depending on the data in array `A`. If we want to take the worst case, then we can assume that the body takes 2 units. We go around the for-loop $n - i - 1$ times, and each time around we execute the body (2 units), then increment j and test whether $j < n$ (another 2 units). Thus, the number of time units spent going around the loop is $4(n - i - 1)$. To this number, we must add 1 for initializing `small` at line (2), 1 for initializing j at line (3), and 1 for the first test $j < n$ at line (3), which is not associated with the end of any iteration of the loop. Hence, the total time taken by the program fragment in Fig. 3.1 is $4(n - i) - 1$.

It is natural to regard the "size" m of the data on which Fig. 3.1 operates as $m = n - i$, since that is the length of the array `A[i..n-1]` on which it operates. Then the running time, which is $4(n - i) - 1$, equals $4m - 1$. Thus, the running time $T(m)$ for Fig. 3.1 is $4m - 1$. ✦

Comparing Different Running Times

Suppose that for some problem we have the choice of using a linear-time program A whose running time is $T_A(n) = 100n$ and a quadratic-time program B whose running time is $T_B(n) = 2n^2$. Let us suppose that both these running times are the number of milliseconds taken on a particular computer on an input of size n.[2] The graphs of the running times are shown in Fig. 3.2.

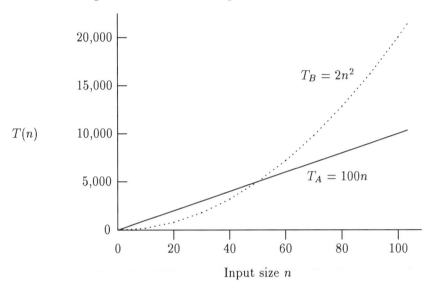

Fig. 3.2. Running times of a linear and a quadratic program.

From Fig. 3.2 we see that for inputs of size less than 50, program B is faster than program A. When the input becomes larger than 50, program A becomes faster, and from that point on, the larger the input, the bigger the advantage A has over B. For inputs of size 100, A is twice as fast as B, and for inputs of size 1000, A is 20 times as fast.

The functional form of a program's running time ultimately determines how big a problem we can solve with that program. As the speed of computers increases, we get bigger improvements in the sizes of problems that we can solve with programs whose running times grow slowly than with programs whose running times rise rapidly.

Again, assuming that the running times of the programs shown in Fig. 3.2 are in milliseconds, the table in Fig. 3.3 indicates how large a problem we can solve with each program on the same computer in various amounts of time given in seconds. For example, suppose we can afford 100 seconds of computer time. If computers become 10 times as fast, then in 100 seconds we can handle problems of the size that used to require 1000 seconds. With algorithm A, we can now solve problems 10 times as large, but with algorithm B we can only solve problems about 3 times as large. Thus, as computers continue to get faster, we gain an even more significant advantage by using algorithms and programs with lower growth rates.

---

[2] This situation is not too dissimilar to the situation where algorithm A is merge sort and algorithm B is selection sort. However, the running time of merge sort grows as $n \log n$, as we shall see in Section 3.10.

Never Mind Algorithm Efficiency; Just Wait a Few Years

Frequently, one hears the argument that there is no need to improve the running time of algorithms or to select efficient algorithms, because computer speeds are doubling every few years and it will not be long before any algorithm, however inefficient, will take so little time that one will not care. People have made this claim for many decades, yet there is no limit in sight to the demand for computational resources. Thus, we generally reject the view that hardware improvements will make the study of efficient algorithms superfluous.

There are situations, however, when we need not be overly concerned with efficiency. For example, a school may, at the end of each term, transcribe grades reported on electronically readable grade sheets to student transcripts, all of which are stored in a computer. The time this operation takes is probably linear in the number of grades reported, like the hypothetical algorithm A. If the school replaces its computer by one 10 times as fast, it can do the job in one-tenth the time. It is very unlikely, however, that the school will therefore enroll 10 times as many students, or require each student to take 10 times as many classes. The computer speedup will not affect the size of the input to the transcript program, because that size is limited by other factors.

On the other hand, there are some problems that we are beginning to find approachable with emerging computing resources, but whose "size" is too great to handle with existing technology. Some of these problems are natural language understanding, computer vision (understanding of digitized pictures), and "intelligent" interaction between computers and humans in all sorts of endeavors. Speedups, either through improved algorithms or from machine improvements, will enhance our ability to deal with these problems in the coming years. Moreover, when they become "simple" problems, a new generation of challenges, which we can now only barely imagine, will take their place on the frontier of what it is possible to do with computers.

TIME sec.	MAXIMUM PROBLEM SIZE SOLVABLE WITH PROGRAM A	MAXIMUM PROBLEM SIZE SOLVABLE WITH PROGRAM B
1	10	22
10	100	70
100	1000	223
1000	10000	707

Fig. 3.3. Problem size as a function of available time.

EXERCISES

3.3.1: Consider the factorial program fragment in Fig. 2.13, and let the input size be the value of n that is read. Counting one time unit for each assignment, read, and write statement, and one unit each time the condition of the while-statement is tested, compute the running time of the program.

3.3.2: For the program fragments of (a) Exercise 2.5.1 and (b) Fig. 2.14, give an appropriate size for the input. Using the counting rules of Exercise 3.3.1, determine the running times of the programs.

3.3.3: Suppose program A takes $2^n/1000$ units of time and program B takes $1000n^2$ units. For what values of n does program A take less time than program B?

3.3.4: For each of the programs of Exercise 3.3.3, how large a problem can be solved in (a) 10^6 time units, (b) 10^9 time units, and (c) 10^{12} time units?

3.3.5: Repeat Exercises 3.3.3 and 3.3.4 if program A takes $1000n^4$ time units and program B takes n^{10} time units.

❖❖ 3.4 Big-Oh and Approximate Running Time

Suppose we have written a C program and have selected the particular input on which we would like it to run. The running time of the program on this input still depends on two factors:

1. The computer on which the program is run. Some computers execute instructions more rapidly than others; the ratio between the speeds of the fastest supercomputers and the slowest personal computers is well over 1000 to 1.

2. The particular C compiler used to generate a program for the computer to execute. Different programs can take different amounts of time to execute on the same machine, even though the programs have the same effect.

As a result, we cannot look at a C program and its input and say, "This task will take 3.21 seconds," unless we know which machine and which compiler will be used. Moreover, even if we know the program, the input, the machine, and the compiler, it is usually far too complex a task to predict exactly the number of machine instructions that will be executed.

For these reasons, we usually express the running time of a program using "big-oh" notation, which is designed to let us hide constant factors such as

1. The average number of machine instructions a particular compiler generates.

2. The average number of machine instructions a particular machine executes per second.

For example, instead of saying, as we did in Example 3.1, that the `SelectionSort` fragment we studied takes time $4m - 1$ on an array of length m, we would say that it takes $O(m)$ time, which is read "big-oh of m" or just "oh of m," and which informally means "some constant times m."

The notion of "some constant times m" not only allows us to ignore unknown constants associated with the compiler and the machine, but also allows us to make some simplifying assumptions. In Example 3.1, for instance, we assumed that all assignment statements take the same amount of time, and that this amount of time was also taken by the test for termination in the for-loop, the incrementation of j around the loop, the initialization, and so on. Since none of these assumptions is valid in practice, the constants 4 and -1 in the running-time formula $T(m) = 4m - 1$ are at best approximations to the truth. It would be more appropriate to describe $T(m)$ as "some constant times m, plus or minus another constant" or even as "at most proportional to m." The notation $O(m)$ enables us to make these statements without getting involved in unknowable or meaningless constants.

On the other hand, representing the running time of the fragment as $O(m)$ does tell us something very important. It says that the time to execute the fragment on progressively larger arrays grows linearly, like the hypothetical Program A of Figs. 3.2 and 3.3 discussed at the end of Section 3.3. Thus, the algorithm embodied by this fragment will be superior to competing algorithms whose running time grows faster, such as the hypothetical Program B of that discussion.

Definition of Big-Oh

We shall now give a formal definition of the notion of one function being "big-oh" of another. Let $T(n)$ be a function, which typically is the running time of some program, measured as a function of the input size n. As befits a function that measures the running time of a program, we shall assume that

1. The argument n is restricted to be a nonnegative integer, and

2. The value $T(n)$ is nonnegative for all arguments n.

Let $f(n)$ be some function defined on the nonnegative integers n. We say that

   "$T(n)$ is $O\big(f(n)\big)$"

if $T(n)$ is at most a constant times $f(n)$, except possibly for some small values of n. Formally, we say that $T(n)$ is $O\big(f(n)\big)$ if there exists an integer n_0 and a constant $c > 0$ such that for all integers $n \geq n_0$, we have $T(n) \leq cf(n)$.

Witnesses   We call the pair n_0 and c *witnesses* to the fact that $T(n)$ is $O\big(f(n)\big)$. The witnesses "testify" to the big-oh relationship of $T(n)$ and $f(n)$ in a form of proof that we shall next demonstrate.

Proving Big-Oh Relationships

We can apply the definition of "big-oh" to prove that $T(n)$ is $O\big(f(n)\big)$ for particular functions T and f. We do so by exhibiting a particular choice of witnesses n_0 and c and then proving that $T(n) \leq cf(n)$. The proof must assume only that n is a nonnegative integer and that n is at least as large as our chosen n_0. Usually, the proof involves algebra and manipulation of inequalities.

✦ **Example 3.2.** Suppose we have a program whose running time is $T(0) = 1$, $T(1) = 4$, $T(2) = 9$, and in general $T(n) = (n+1)^2$. We can say that $T(n)$ is $O(n^2)$, **Quadratic running time** or that $T(n)$ is *quadratic*, because we can choose witnesses $n_0 = 1$ and $c = 4$. We then need to prove that $(n+1)^2 \leq 4n^2$, provided $n \geq 1$. In proof, expand $(n+1)^2$ as $n^2 + 2n + 1$. As long as $n \geq 1$, we know that $n \leq n^2$ and $1 \leq n^2$. Thus

$$n^2 + 2n + 1 \leq n^2 + 2n^2 + n^2 = 4n^2$$

Template for Big-Oh Proofs

Remember: all big-oh proofs follow essentially the same form. Only the algebraic manipulation varies. We need to do only two things to have a proof that $T(n)$ is $O(f(n))$.

1. State the witnesses n_0 and c. These witnesses must be specific constants, e.g., $n_0 = 47$ and $c = 12.5$. Also, n_0 must be a nonnegative integer, and c must be a positive real number.

2. By appropriate algebraic manipulation, show that if $n \geq n_0$ then $T(n) \leq cf(n)$, for the particular witnesses n_0 and c chosen.

Alternatively, we could pick witnesses $n_0 = 3$ and $c = 2$, because, as the reader may check, $(n + 1)^2 \leq 2n^2$, for all $n \geq 3$.

However, we cannot pick $n_0 = 0$ with any c, because with $n = 0$, we would have to show that $(0 + 1)^2 \leq c0^2$, that is, that 1 is less than or equal to c times 0. Since $c \times 0 = 0$ no matter what c we pick, and $1 \leq 0$ is false, we are doomed if we pick $n_0 = 0$. That doesn't matter, however, because in order to show that $(n + 1)^2$ is $O(n^2)$, we had only to find one choice of witnesses n_0 and c that works. ◆

It may seem odd that although $(n + 1)^2$ is larger than n^2, we can still say that $(n + 1)^2$ is $O(n^2)$. In fact, we can also say that $(n + 1)^2$ is big-oh of any fraction of n^2, for example, $O(n^2/100)$. To see why, choose witnesses $n_0 = 1$ and $c = 400$. Then if $n \geq 1$, we know that

$$(n + 1)^2 \leq 400(n^2/100) = 4n^2$$

by the same reasoning as was used in Example 3.2. The general principles underlying these observations are that

1. *Constant factors don't matter.* For any positive constant d and any function $T(n)$, $T(n)$ is $O(dT(n))$, regardless of whether d is a large number or a very small fraction, as long as $d > 0$. To see why, choose witnesses $n_0 = 0$ and $c = 1/d$.[3] Then $T(n) \leq c(dT(n))$, since $cd = 1$. Likewise, if we know that $T(n)$ is $O(f(n))$, then we also know that $T(n)$ is $O(df(n))$ for any $d > 0$, even a very small d. The reason is that we know that $T(n) \leq c_1 f(n)$ for some constant c_1 and all $n \geq n_0$. If we choose $c = c_1/d$, we can see that $T(n) \leq c(df(n))$ for $n \geq n_0$.

2. *Low-order terms don't matter.* Suppose $T(n)$ is a polynomial of the form

$$a_k n^k + a_{k-1} n^{k-1} + \cdots + a_2 n^2 + a_1 n + a_0$$

where the leading coefficient, a_k, is positive. Then we can throw away all terms but the first (the term with the highest exponent, k) and, by rule (1), ignore the constant a_k, replacing it by 1. That is, we can conclude $T(n)$ is $O(n^k)$. In proof, let $n_0 = 1$, and let c be the sum of all the positive coefficients among the a_i's, $0 \leq i \leq k$. If a coefficient a_j is 0 or negative, then surely $a_j n^j \leq 0$. If

---

[3] Note that although we are required to choose constants as witnesses, not functions, there is nothing wrong with choosing $c = 1/d$, because d itself is some constant.

Fallacious Arguments About Big-Oh

The definition of "big-oh" is tricky, in that it requires us, after examining $T(n)$ and $f(n)$, to pick witnesses n_0 and c once and for all, and then to show that $T(n) \leq cf(n)$ for all $n \geq n_0$. It is not permitted to pick c and/or n_0 anew for each value of n. For example, one occasionally sees the following fallacious "proof" that n^2 is $O(n)$. "Pick $n_0 = 0$, and for each n, pick $c = n$. Then $n^2 \leq cn$." This argument is invalid, because we are required to pick c once and for all, without knowing n.

a_j is positive, then $a_j n^j \leq a_j n^k$, for all $j < k$, as long as $n \geq 1$. Thus, $T(n)$ is no greater than n^k times the sum of the positive coefficients, or cn^k.

♦ **Example 3.3.** As an example of rule (1) ("constants don't matter"), we can see that $2n^3$ is $O(.001n^3)$. Let $n_0 = 0$ and $c = 2/.001 = 2000$. Then clearly $2n^3 \leq 2000(.001n^3) = 2n^3$, for all $n \geq 0$.

As an example of rule (2) ("low order terms don't matter"), consider the polynomial

$$T(n) = 3n^5 + 10n^4 - 4n^3 + n + 1$$

The highest-order term is n^5, and we claim that $T(n)$ is $O(n^5)$. To check the claim, let $n_0 = 1$ and let c be the sum of the positive coefficients. The terms with positive coefficients are those with exponents 5, 4, 1, and 0, whose coefficients are, respectively, 3, 10, 1, and 1. Thus, we let $c = 15$. We claim that for $n \geq 1$,

$$3n^5 + 10n^4 - 4n^3 + n + 1 \leq 3n^5 + 10n^5 + n^5 + n^5 = 15n^5 \qquad (3.1)$$

We can check that inequality (3.1) holds by matching the positive terms; that is, $3n^5 \leq 3n^5$, $10n^4 \leq 10n^5$, $n \leq n^5$, and $1 \leq n^5$. Also, the negative term on the left side of (3.1) can be ignored, since $-4n^3 \leq 0$. Thus, the left side of (3.1), which is $T(n)$, is less than or equal to the right side, which is $15n^5$, or cn^5. We can conclude that $T(n)$ is $O(n^5)$.

In fact, the principle that low-order terms can be deleted applies not only to polynomials, but to any sum of expressions. That is, if the ratio $h(n)/g(n)$ approaches 0 as n approaches infinity, then $h(n)$ "grows more slowly" than $g(n)$, or **Growth rate** "has a lower growth rate" than $g(n)$, and we may neglect $h(n)$. That is, $g(n) + h(n)$ is $O(g(n))$.

For example, let $T(n) = 2^n + n^3$. It is known that every polynomial, such as n^3, grows more slowly than every exponential, such as 2^n. Since $n^3/2^n$ approaches 0 as n increases, we can throw away the lower-order term and conclude that $T(n)$ is $O(2^n)$.

To prove formally that $2^n + n^3$ is $O(2^n)$, let $n_0 = 10$ and $c = 2$. We must show that for $n \geq 10$, we have

$$2^n + n^3 \leq 2 \times 2^n$$

If we subtract 2^n from both sides, we see it is sufficient to show that for $n \geq 10$, it is the case that $n^3 \leq 2^n$.

For $n = 10$ we have $2^{10} = 1024$ and $10^3 = 1000$, and so $n^3 \leq 2^n$ for $n = 10$. Each time we add 1 to n, 2^n doubles, while n^3 is multiplied by a quantity $(n+1)^3/n^3$

that is less than 2 when $n \geq 10$. Thus, as n increases beyond 10, n^3 becomes progressively less than 2^n. We conclude that $n^3 \leq 2^n$ for $n \geq 10$, and thus that $2^n + n^3$ is $O(2^n)$. ✦

Proofs That a Big-Oh Relationship Does Not Hold

If a big-oh relationship holds between two functions, then we can prove it by finding witnesses. However, what if some function $T(n)$ is *not* big-oh of some other function $f(n)$? Can we ever hope to be sure that there is not such a big-oh relationship? The answer is that quite frequently we can prove a particular function $T(n)$ is not $O(f(n))$. The method of proof is to assume that witnesses n_0 and c exist, and derive a contradiction. The following is an example of such a proof.

✦   **Example 3.4.** In the box on "Fallacious Arguments About Big-Oh," we claimed that n^2 is not $O(n)$. We can show this claim as follows. Suppose it were. Then there would be witnesses n_0 and c such that $n^2 \leq cn$ for all $n \geq n_0$. But if we pick n_1 equal to the larger of $2c$ and n_0, then the inequality

$$(n_1)^2 \leq cn_1 \tag{3.2}$$

must hold (because $n_1 \geq n_0$ and $n^2 \leq cn$ allegedly holds for all $n \geq n_0$).

If we divide both sides of (3.2) by n_1, we have $n_1 \leq c$. However, we also chose n_1 to be at least $2c$. Since witness c must be positive, n_1 cannot be both less than c and greater than $2c$. Thus, witnesses n_0 and c that would show n^2 to be $O(n)$ do not exist, and we conclude that n^2 is not $O(n)$. ✦

EXERCISES

3.4.1: Consider the four functions

f_1: n^2
f_2: n^3
f_3: n^2 if n is odd, and n^3 if n is even
f_4: n^2 if n is prime, and n^3 if n is composite

For each i and j equal to 1, 2, 3, 4, determine whether $f_i(n)$ is $O(f_j(n))$. Either give values n_0 and c that prove the big-oh relationship, or assume that there are such values n_0 and c, and then derive a contradiction to prove that $f_i(n)$ is not $O(f_j(n))$. *Hint*: Remember that all primes except 2 are odd. Also remember that there are an infinite number of primes and an infinite number of composite numbers (nonprimes).

3.4.2: Following are some big-oh relationships. For each, give witnesses n_0 and c that can be used to prove the relationship. Choose your witnesses to be minimal, in the sense that $n_0 - 1$ and c are not witnesses, and if $d < c$, then n_0 and d are not witnesses.

a) n^2 is $O(.001n^3)$
b) $25n^4 - 19n^3 + 13n^2 - 106n + 77$ is $O(n^4)$
c) 2^{n+10} is $O(2^n)$
d) n^{10} is $O(3^n)$
e)* $\log_2 n$ is $O(\sqrt{n})$

Template for Proofs That a Big-Oh Relationship Is False

The following is an outline of typical proofs that a function $T(n)$ is not $O(f(n))$. Example 3.4 illustrates such a proof.

1. Start by supposing that there were witnesses n_0 and c such that for all $n \geq n_0$, we have $f(n) \leq cg(n)$. Here, n_0 and c are symbols standing for unknown witnesses.

2. Define a particular integer n_1, expressed in terms of n_0 and c (for example, $n_1 = \max(n_0, 2c)$ was chosen in Example 3.4). This n_1 will be the value of n for which we show $T(n_1) \leq cf(n_1)$ is false.

3. Show that for the chosen n_1 we have $n_1 \geq n_0$. This part can be very easy, since we may choose n_1 to be at least n_0 in step (2).

4. Claim that because $n_1 \geq n_0$, we must have $T(n_1) \leq cf(n_1)$.

5. Derive a contradiction by showing that for the chosen n_1 we have $T(n_1) > cf(n_1)$. Choosing n_1 in terms of c can make this part easy, as it was in Example 3.4.

3.4.3*: Prove that if $f(n) \leq g(n)$ for all n, then $f(n) + g(n)$ is $O(g(n))$.

3.4.4**: Suppose that $f(n)$ is $O(g(n))$ and $g(n)$ is $O(f(n))$. What can you say about $f(n)$ and $g(n)$? Is it necessarily true that $f(n) = g(n)$? Does the limit $f(n)/g(n)$ as n goes to infinity necessarily exist?

❖❖ 3.5   Simplifying Big-Oh Expressions

As we saw in the previous section, it is possible to simplify big-oh expressions by dropping constant factors and low-order terms. We shall see how important it is to make such simplifications when we analyze programs. It is common for the running time of a program to be attributable to many different statements or program fragments, but it is also normal for a few of these pieces to account for the bulk of the running time (by the "90-10" rule). By dropping low-order terms, and by combining equal or approximately equal terms, we can often greatly simplify the expressions for running time.

The Transitive Law for Big-Oh Expressions

To begin, we shall take up a useful rule for thinking about big-oh expressions. A relationship like $\leq$ is said to be *transitive*, because it obeys the law "if $A \leq B$ and $B \leq C$, then $A \leq C$." For example, since $3 \leq 5$ and $5 \leq 10$, we can be sure that $3 \leq 10$.

The relationship "is big-oh of" is another example of a transitive relationship. That is, if $f(n)$ is $O(g(n))$ and $g(n)$ is $O(h(n))$, it follows that $f(n)$ is $O(h(n))$. To see why, first suppose that $f(n)$ is $O(g(n))$. Then there are witnesses n_1 and c_1 such that $f(n) \leq c_1 g(n)$ for all $n \geq n_1$. Similarly, if $g(n)$ is $O(h(n))$, then there are witnesses n_2 and c_2 such that $g(n) \leq c_2 h(n)$ for all $n \geq n_2$.

Polynomial and Exponential Big-Oh Expressions

The *degree* of a polynomial is the highest exponent found among its terms. For example, the degree of the polynomial $T(n)$ mentioned in Examples 3.3 and 3.5 is 5, because $3n^5$ is its highest-order term. From the two principles we have enunciated (constant factors don't matter, and low-order terms don't matter), plus the transitive law for big-oh expressions, we know the following:

1.   If $p(n)$ and $q(n)$ are polynomials and the degree of $q(n)$ is as high as or higher than the degree of $p(n)$, then $p(n)$ is $O\big(q(n)\big)$.

2.   If the degree of $q(n)$ is lower than the degree of $p(n)$, then $p(n)$ is *not* $O\big(q(n)\big)$.

Exponential   3.   *Exponentials* are expressions of the form a^n for $a > 1$. Every exponential grows faster than every polynomial. That is, we can show for any polynomial $p(n)$ that $p(n)$ is $O(a^n)$. For example, n^5 is $O\big((1.01)^n\big)$.

4.   Conversely, no exponential a^n, for $a > 1$, is $O\big(p(n)\big)$ for any polynomial $p(n)$.

Let n_0 be the larger of n_1 and n_2, and let $c = c_1 c_2$. We claim that n_0 and c are witnesses to the fact that $f(n)$ is $O\big(h(n)\big)$. For suppose $n \geq n_0$. Since $n_0 = \max(n_1, n_2)$, we know that $n \geq n_1$ and $n \geq n_2$. Therefore, $f(n) \leq c_1 g(n)$ and $g(n) \leq c_2 h(n)$.

Now substitute $c_2 h(n)$ for $g(n)$ in the inequality $f(n) \leq c_1 g(n)$, to prove $f(n) \leq c_1 c_2 h(n)$. This inequality shows $f(n)$ is $O\big(h(n)\big)$.

✦   **Example 3.5.** We know from Example 3.3 that

$$T(n) = 3n^5 + 10n^4 - 4n^3 + n + 1$$

is $O(n^5)$. We also know from the rule that "constant factors don't matter" that n^5 is $O(.01n^5)$. By the transitive law for big-oh, we know that $T(n)$ is $O(.01n^5)$. ✦

Describing the Running Time of a Program

We defined the running time $T(n)$ of a program to be the maximum number of time units taken on any input of size n. We also said that determining a precise formula for $T(n)$ is a difficult, if not impossible, task. Frequently, we can simplify matters considerably by using a big-oh expression $O(f(n))$ as an upper bound on $T(n)$.

For example, an upper bound on the running time $T(n)$ of `SelectionSort` is an^2, for some constant a and any $n \geq 1$; we shall demonstrate this fact in Section 3.6. Then we can say the running time of `SelectionSort` is $O(n^2)$. That statement is intuitively the most useful one to make, because n^2 is a very simple function, and stronger statements about other simple functions, like "$T(n)$ is $O(n)$," are false.

However, because of the nature of big-oh notation, we can also state that the running time $T(n)$ is $O(.01n^2)$, or $O(7n^2 - 4n + 26)$, or in fact big-oh of any quadratic polynomial. The reason is that n^2 is big-oh of any quadratic, and so the transitive law plus the fact that $T(n)$ is $O(n^2)$ tells us $T(n)$ is big-oh of any quadratic.

Worse, n^2 is big-oh of any polynomial of degree 3 or higher, or of any exponential. Thus, by transitivity again, $T(n)$ is $O(n^3)$, $O(2^n + n^4)$, and so on. However, we shall explain why $O(n^2)$ is the preferred way to express the running time of `SelectionSort`.

Tightness

First, we generally want the "tightest" big-oh upper bound we can prove. That is, if $T(n)$ is $O(n^2)$, we want to say so, rather than make the technically true but weaker statement that $T(n)$ is $O(n^3)$. On the other hand, this way lies madness, because if we like $O(n^2)$ as an expression of running time, we should like $O(0.5n^2)$ even better, because it is "tighter," and we should like $O(.01n^2)$ still more, and so on. However, since constant factors don't matter in big-oh expressions, there is really no point in trying to make the estimate of running time "tighter" by shrinking the constant factor. Thus, whenever possible, we try to use a big-oh expression that has a constant factor 1.

Figure 3.4 lists some of the more common running times for programs and their informal names. Note in particular that $O(1)$ is an idiomatic shorthand for "some constant," and we shall use $O(1)$ repeatedly for this purpose.

BIG-OH	INFORMAL NAME
$O(1)$	constant
$O(\log n)$	logarithmic
$O(n)$	linear
$O(n \log n)$	$n \log n$
$O(n^2)$	quadratic
$O(n^3)$	cubic
$O(2^n)$	exponential

Fig. 3.4. Informal names for some common big-oh running times.

Tight bound

More precisely, we shall say that $f(n)$ is a *tight* big-oh bound on $T(n)$ if

1. $T(n)$ is $O\big(f(n)\big)$, and

2.   If $T(n)$ is $O\big(g(n)\big)$, then it is also true that $f(n)$ is $O\big(g(n)\big)$. Informally, we cannot find a function $g(n)$ that grows at least as fast as $T(n)$ but grows slower than $f(n)$.

✦   **Example 3.6.** Let $T(n) = 2n^2 + 3n$ and $f(n) = n^2$. We claim that $f(n)$ is a tight bound on $T(n)$. To see why, suppose $T(n)$ is $O\big(g(n)\big)$. Then there are constants c and n_0 such that for all $n \geq n_0$, we have $T(n) = 2n^2 + 3n \leq cg(n)$. Then $g(n) \geq (2/c)n^2$ for $n \geq n_0$. Since $f(n)$ is n^2, we have $f(n) \leq (c/2)g(n)$ for $n \geq n_0$. Thus, $f(n)$ is $O\big(g(n)\big)$.

On the other hand, $f(n) = n^3$ is not a tight big-oh bound on $T(n)$. Now we can pick $g(n) = n^2$. We have seen that $T(n)$ is $O\big(g(n)\big)$, but we cannot show that $f(n)$ is $O\big(g(n)\big)$, since n^3 is not $O(n^2)$. Thus, n^3 is not a tight big-oh bound on $T(n)$. ✦

Simplicity

The other goal in our choice of a big-oh bound is simplicity in the expression of the function. Unlike tightness, simplicity can sometimes be a matter of taste. However, we shall generally regard a function $f(n)$ as *simple* if

Simple function

1.   It is a single term and

2.   The coefficient of that term is 1.

✦ **Example 3.7.** The function n^2 is simple; $2n^2$ is not simple because the coefficient is not 1, and $n^2 + n$ is not simple because there are two terms. ✦

Tightness and simplicity may conflict

There are some situations, however, where the tightness of a big-oh upper bound and simplicity of the bound are conflicting goals. The following is an example where the simple bound doesn't tell the whole story. Fortunately, such cases are rare in practice.

```
        int PowersOfTwo(int n)
        {
            int i;
(1)         i = 0;
(2)         while (n%2 == 0) {
(3)             n = n/2;
(4)             i++;
            }
(5)         return i;
        }
```

Fig. 3.5. Counting factors of 2 in a positive integer n.

✦ **Example 3.8.** Consider the function `PowersOfTwo` in Fig. 3.5, which takes a positive argument n and counts the number times 2 divides n. That is, the test of line (2) asks whether n is even and, if so, removes a factor of 2 at line (3) of the loop body. Also in the loop, we increment `i`, which counts the number of factors we have removed from the original value of `n`.

Let the size of the input be the value of n itself. The body of the while-loop consists of two C assignment statements, lines (3) and (4), and so we can say that the time to execute the body once is $O(1)$, that is, some constant amount of time, independent of n. If the loop is executed m times, then the total time spent going around the loop will be $O(m)$, or some amount of time that is proportional to m. To this quantity we must add $O(1)$, or some constant, for the single executions of lines (1) and (5), plus the first test of the while-condition, which is technically not part of any loop iteration. Thus, the time spent by the program is $O(m) + O(1)$. Following our rule that low-order terms can be neglected, the time is $O(m)$, unless $m = 0$, in which case it is $O(1)$. Put another way, the time spent on input n is proportional to 1 plus the number of times 2 divides n.

Using Big-Oh Notation in Mathematical Expressions

Strictly speaking, the only mathematically correct way to use a big-oh expression is after the word "is," as in "$2n^2$ is $O(n^3)$." However, in Example 3.8, and for the remainder of the chapter, we shall take a liberty and use big-oh expressions as operands of addition and other arithmetic operators, as in $O(n) + O(n^2)$. We should interpret a big-oh expression used this way as meaning "some function that is big-oh of." For example, $O(n) + O(n^2)$ means "the sum of some linear function and some quadratic function." Also, $O(n) + T(n)$ should be interpreted as the sum of some linear function and the particular function $T(n)$.

How many times does 2 divide n? For every odd n, the answer is 0, so the function `PowersOfTwo` takes time $O(1)$ on every odd n. However, when n is a power of 2 — that is, when $n = 2^k$ for some k — 2 divides n exactly k times. When $n = 2^k$, we may take logarithms to base 2 of both sides and conclude that $\log_2 n = k$. That is, m is at most logarithmic in n, or $m = O(\log n)$.[4]

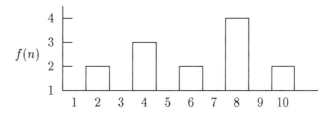

Fig. 3.6. The function $f(n) = m(n) + 1$, where $m(n)$ is the number of times 2 divides n.

We may thus say that the running time of `PowersOfTwo` is $O(\log n)$. This bound meets our definition of simplicity. However, there is another, more precise way of stating an upper bound on the running time of `PowersOfTwo`, which is to say that it is big-oh of the function $f(n) = m(n) + 1$, where $m(n)$ is the number of times 2 divides n. This function is hardly simple, as Fig. 3.6 shows. It oscillates wildly but never goes above $1 + \log_2 n$.

Since the running time of `PowersOfTwo` is $O\big(f(n)\big)$, but $\log n$ is not $O\big(f(n)\big)$, we claim that $\log n$ is not a tight bound on the running time. On the other hand, $f(n)$ is a tight bound, but it is not simple. ✦

The Summation Rule

Suppose a program consists of two parts, one of which takes $O(n^2)$ time and the other of which takes $O(n^3)$ time. We can "add" these two big-oh bounds to get the running time of the entire program. In many cases, such as this one, it is possible to "add" big-oh expressions by making use of the following *summation rule*:

---

[4] Note that when we speak of logarithms within a big-oh expression, there is no need to specify the base. The reason is that if a and b are bases, then $\log_a n = (\log_b n)(\log_a b)$. Since $\log_a b$ is a constant, we see that $\log_a n$ and $\log_b n$ differ by only a constant factor. Thus, the functions $\log_x n$ to different bases x are big-oh of each other, and we can, by the transitive law, replace within a big-oh expression any $\log_a n$ by $\log_b n$ where b is a base different from a.

Logarithms in Running Times

If you think of logarithms as something having to do with integral calculus ($\log_e a = \int_1^a \frac{1}{x} dx$), you may be surprised to find them appearing in analyses of algorithms. Computer scientists generally think of "$\log n$" as meaning $\log_2 n$, rather than $\log_e n$ or $\log_{10} n$. Notice that $\log_2 n$ is the number of times we have to divide n by 2 to get down to 1, or alternatively, the number of 2's we must multiply together to reach n. You may easily check that $n = 2^k$ is the same as saying $\log_2 n = k$; just take logarithms to the base 2 of both sides.

The function `PowersOfTwo` divides n by 2 as many times as it can, And when n is a power of 2, then the number of times n can be divided by 2 is $\log_2 n$. Logarithms arise quite frequently in the analysis of divide-and-conquer algorithms (e.g., merge sort) that divide their input into two equal, or nearly equal, parts at each stage. If we start with an input of size n, then the number of stages at which we can divide the input in half until pieces are of size 1 is $\log_2 n$, or, if n is not a power of 2, then the smallest integer greater than $\log_2 n$.

Suppose $T_1(n)$ is known to be $O(f_1(n))$, while $T_2(n)$ is known to be $O(f_2(n))$. Further, suppose that f_2 grows no faster than f_1; that is, $f_2(n)$ is $O(f_1(n))$. Then we can conclude that $T_1(n) + T_2(n)$ is $O(f_1(n))$.

In proof, we know that there are constants n_1, n_2, n_3, c_1, c_2, and c_3 such that

1. If $n \geq n_1$, then $T_1(n) \leq c_1 f_1(n)$.
2. If $n \geq n_2$, then $T_2(n) \leq c_2 f_2(n)$.
3. If $n \geq n_3$, then $f_2(n) \leq c_3 f_1(n)$.

Let n_0 be the largest of n_1, n_2, and n_3, so that (1), (2), and (3) hold when $n \geq n_0$. Thus, for $n \geq n_0$, we have

$$T_1(n) + T_2(n) \leq c_1 f_1(n) + c_2 f_2(n)$$

If we use (3) to provide an upper bound on $f_2(n)$, we can get rid of $f_2(n)$ altogether and conclude that

$$T_1(n) + T_2(n) \leq c_1 f_1(n) + c_2 c_3 f_1(n)$$

Therefore, for all $n \geq n_0$ we have

$$T_1(n) + T_2(n) \leq c f_1(n)$$

if we define c to be $c_1 + c_2 c_3$. This statement is exactly what we need to conclude that $T_1(n) + T_2(n)$ is $O(f_1(n))$.

✦   **Example 3.9.** Consider the program fragment in Fig. 3.7. This program makes A an $n \times n$ identity matrix. Lines (2) through (4) place 0 in every cell of the $n \times n$ array, and then lines (5) and (6) place 1's in all the diagonal positions from A[0][0] to A[n-1][n-1]. The result is an identity matrix A with the property that

$$\text{A} \times \text{M} = \text{M} \times \text{A} = \text{M}$$

```
(1)          scanf("%d",&n);
(2)          for (i = 0; i < n; i++)
(3)              for (j = 0; j < n; j++)
(4)                  A[i][j] = 0;
(5)          for (i = 0; i < n; i++)
(6)              A[i][i] = 1;
```

Fig. 3.7. Program fragment to make **A** an identity matrix.

for any $n \times n$ matrix **M**.

Line (1), which reads **n**, takes $O(1)$ time, that is, some constant amount of time, independent of the value n. The assignment statement in line (6) also takes $O(1)$ time, and we go around the loop of lines (5) and (6) exactly n times, for a total of $O(n)$ time spent in that loop. Similarly, the assignment of line (4) takes $O(1)$ time. We go around the loop of lines (3) and (4) n times, for a total of $O(n)$ time. We go around the outer loop, lines (2) to (4), n times, taking $O(n)$ time per iteration, for a total of $O(n^2)$ time.

Thus, the time taken by the program in Fig. 3.7 is $O(1) + O(n^2) + O(n)$, for the statement (1), the loop of lines (2) to (4), and the loop of lines (5) and (6), respectively. More formally, if

$T_1(n)$ is the time taken by line (1),
$T_2(n)$ is the time taken by lines (2) to (4), and
$T_3(n)$ is the time taken by lines (5) and (6),

then

$T_1(n)$ is $O(1)$,
$T_2(n)$ is $O(n^2)$, and
$T_3(n)$ is $O(n)$.

We thus need an upper bound on $T_1(n) + T_2(n) + T_3(n)$ to derive the running time of the entire program.

Since the constant 1 is certainly $O(n^2)$, we can apply the rule for sums to conclude that $T_1(n) + T_2(n)$ is $O(n^2)$. Then, since n is $O(n^2)$, we can apply the rule of sums to $(T_1(n) + T_2(n))$ and $T_3(n)$, to conclude that $T_1(n) + T_2(n) + T_3(n)$ is $O(n^2)$. That is, the entire program fragment of Fig. 3.7 has running time $O(n^2)$. Informally, it spends almost all its time in the loop of lines (2) through (4), as we might expect, simply from the fact that, for large n, the area of the matrix, n^2, is much larger than its diagonal, which consists of n cells. ◆

Example 3.9 is just an application of the rule that low order terms don't matter, since we threw away the terms 1 and n, which are lower-degree polynomials than n^2. However, the rule of sums allows us to do more than just throw away low-order terms. If we have any constant number of terms that are, to within big-oh, the same, such as a sequence of 10 assignment statements, each of which takes $O(1)$ time, then we can "add" ten $O(1)$'s to get $O(1)$. Less formally, the sum of 10 constants is still a constant. To see why, note that 1 is $O(1)$, so that any of the ten $O(1)$'s, can be "added" to any other to get $O(1)$ as a result. We keep combining terms until only one $O(1)$ is left.

However, we must be careful not to confuse "a constant number" of some term like $O(1)$ with a number of these terms that varies with the input size. For example, we might be tempted to observe that it takes $O(1)$ time to go once around the loop of lines (5) and (6) of Fig. 3.7. The number of times we go around the loop is n, so that the running time for lines (5) and (6) together is $O(1) + O(1) + O(1) + \cdots$ (n times). The rule for sums tells us that the sum of two $O(1)$'s is $O(1)$, and by induction we can show that the sum of any constant number of $O(1)$'s is $O(1)$. However, in this program, n is not a constant; it varies with the input size. Thus, no one sequence of applications of the sum rule tells us that n $O(1)$'s has any value in particular. Of course, if we think about the matter, we know that the sum of n c's, where c is some constant, is cn, a function that is $O(n)$, and that is the true running time of lines (5) and (6).

Incommensurate Functions

It would be nice if any two functions $f(n)$ and $g(n)$ could be compared by big-oh; that is, either $f(n)$ is $O(g(n))$, or $g(n)$ is $O(f(n))$ (or both, since as we observed, there are functions such as $2n^2$ and $n^2 + 3n$ that are each big-oh of the other). Unfortunately, there are pairs of *incommensurate* functions, neither of which is big-oh of the other.

✦ **Example 3.10.** Consider the function $f(n)$ that is n for odd n and n^2 for even n. That is, $f(1) = 1$, $f(2) = 4$, $f(3) = 3$, $f(4) = 16$, $f(5) = 5$, and so on. Similarly, let $g(n)$ be n^2 for odd n and let $g(n)$ be n for even n. Then $f(n)$ cannot be $O(g(n))$, because of the even n's. For as we observed in Section 3.4, n^2 is definitely not $O(n)$. Similarly, $g(n)$ cannot be $O(f(n))$, because of the odd n's, where the values of g outrace the corresponding values of f. ✦

EXERCISES

3.5.1: Prove the following:

a) n^a is $O(n^b)$ if $a \le b$.
b) n^a is not $O(n^b)$ if $a > b$.
c) a^n is $O(b^n)$ if $1 < a \le b$.
d) a^n is not $O(b^n)$ if $1 < b < a$.
e) n^a is $O(b^n)$ for any a, and for any $b > 1$.
f) a^n is not $O(n^b)$ for any b, and for any $a > 1$.
g) $(\log n)^a$ is $O(n^b)$ for any a, and for any $b > 0$.
h) n^a is not $O((\log n)^b)$ for any b, and for any $a > 0$.

3.5.2: Show that $f(n) + g(n)$ is $O\left(\max(f(n), g(n))\right)$.

3.5.3: Suppose that $T(n)$ is $O(f(n))$ and $g(n)$ is a function whose value is never negative. Prove that $g(n)T(n)$ is $O(g(n)f(n))$.

3.5.4: Suppose that $S(n)$ is $O(f(n))$ and $T(n)$ is $O(g(n))$. Assume that none of these functions is negative for any n. Prove that $S(n)T(n)$ is $O(f(n)g(n))$.

3.5.5: Suppose that $f(n)$ is $O(g(n))$. Show that $\max(f(n), g(n))$ is $O(g(n))$.

3.5.6*: Show that if $f_1(n)$ and $f_2(n)$ are both tight bounds on some function $T(n)$, then $f_1(n)$ and $f_2(n)$ are each big-oh of the other.

3.5.7*: Show that $\log_2 n$ is not $O\big(f(n)\big)$, where $f(n)$ is the function from Fig. 3.6.

3.5.8: In the program of Fig. 3.7, we created an identity matrix by first putting 0's everywhere and then putting 1's along the diagonal. It might seem that a faster way to do the job is to replace line (4) by a test that asks if $i = j$, putting 1 in `A[i][j]` if so and 0 if not. We can then eliminate lines (5) and (6).

a)   Write this program.

b)*   Consider the programs of Fig. 3.7 and your answer to (a). Making simplifying assumptions like those of Example 3.1, compute the number of time units taken by each of the programs. Which is faster? Run the two programs on various-sized arrays and plot their running times.

✧✦✧ 3.6   Analyzing the Running Time of a Program

Armed with the concept of big-oh and the rules from Sections 3.4 and 3.5 for manipulating big-oh expressions, we shall now learn how to derive big-oh upper bounds on the running times of typical programs. Whenever possible, we shall look for simple and tight big-oh bounds. In this section and the next, we shall consider only programs without function calls (other than library functions such as `printf`), leaving the matter of function calls to Sections 3.8 and beyond.

We do not expect to be able to analyze arbitrary programs, since questions about running time are as hard as any in mathematics. On the other hand, we can discover the running time of most programs encountered in practice, once we learn some simple rules.

The Running Time of Simple Statements

We ask the reader to accept the principle that certain simple operations on data can be done in $O(1)$ time, that is, in time that is independent of the size of the input. These primitive operations in C consist of

1.   Arithmetic operations (e.g. `+` or `%`).

2.   Logical operations (e.g., `&&`).

3.   Comparison operations (e.g., `<=`).

4.   Structure accessing operations (e.g. array-indexing like `A[i]`, or pointer following with the `->` operator).

5.   Simple assignment such as copying a value into a variable.

6.   Calls to library functions (e.g., `scanf`, `printf`).

The justification for this principle requires a detailed study of the machine instructions (primitive steps) of a typical computer. Let us simply observe that each of the described operations can be done with some small number of machine instructions; often only one or two instructions are needed.

As a consequence, several kinds of statements in C can be executed in $O(1)$ time, that is, in some constant amount of time independent of input. These *simple statements* include

Simple statement

1.   Assignment statements that do not involve function calls in their expressions.

2.   Read statements.

3.   Write statements that do not require function calls to evaluate arguments.

4.   The jump statements **break, continue, goto,** and **return** *expression*, where *expression* does not contain a function call.

In (1) through (3), the statements each consist of some finite number of primitive operations, each of which we take on faith to require $O(1)$ time. The summation rule then tells us that the entire statements take $O(1)$ time. Of course, the constants hidden in the big-oh are larger for statements than for single primitive operations, but as we already know, we cannot associate concrete constants with running time of C statements anyway.

✦   **Example 3.11.** We observed in Example 3.9 that the read statement of line (1) of Fig. 3.7 and the assignments of lines (4) and (6) each take $O(1)$ time. For another illustration, consider the fragment of the selection-sort program shown in Fig. 3.8. The assignments of lines (2), (5), (6), (7), and (8) each take $O(1)$ time. ✦

```
(1)            for (i = 0; i < n-1; i++) {
(2)                small = i;
(3)                for (j = i+1; j < n; j++)
(4)                    if (A[j] < A[small])
(5)                        small = j;
(6)                temp = A[small];
(7)                A[small] = A[i];
(8)                A[i] = temp;
               }
```

Fig. 3.8. Selection-sort fragment.

Blocks of simple statements

Frequently, we find a block of simple statements that are executed consecutively. If the running time of each of these statements is $O(1)$, then the entire block takes $O(1)$ time, by the summation rule. That is, any constant number of $O(1)$'s sums to $O(1)$.

✦ **Example 3.12.** Lines (6) through (8) of Fig. 3.8 form a block, since they are always executed consecutively. Since each takes $O(1)$ time, the block of lines (6) to (8) takes $O(1)$ time.

Note that we should not include line (5) in the block, since it is part of the if-statement on line (4). That is, sometimes lines (6) to (8) are executed without executing line (5). ✦

The Running Time of Simple For-Loops

In C, many for-loops are formed by initializing an index variable to some value and incrementing that variable by 1 each time around the loop. The for-loop ends when the index reaches some limit. For instance, the for-loop of line (1) of Fig. 3.8 uses index variable i. It increments i by 1 each time around the loop, and the iterations stop when i reaches $n - 1$.

There are more complex for-loops in C that behave more like while-statements; these loops iterate an unpredictable number of times. We shall take up this sort of loop later in the section. However, for the moment, focus on the simple form of for-loop, where the difference between the final and initial values, divided by the amount by which the index variable is incremented tells us how many times we go around the loop. That count is exact, unless there are ways to exit the loop via a jump statement; it is an upper bound on the number of iterations in any case. For instance, the for-loop of line (1) of Fig. 3.8 iterates $((n - 1) - 0)/1 = n - 1$ times, since 0 is the initial value of i, $n - 1$ is the highest value reached by i (i.e., when i reaches $n - 1$, the loop stops and no iteration occurs with $i = n - 1$), and 1 is added to i at each iteration of the loop.

To bound the running time of the for-loop, we must obtain an upper bound on the amount of time spent in one iteration of the loop body. Note that the time for an iteration includes the time to increment the loop index (e.g., the increment statement i++ in line (1) of Fig. 3.8), which is $O(1)$, and the time to compare the loop index with the upper limit (e.g., the test statement i<n-1 in line (1) of Fig. 3.8), which is also $O(1)$. In all but the exceptional case where the loop body is empty, these $O(1)$'s can be dropped by the summation rule.

In the simplest case, where the time spent in the loop body is the same for each iteration, we can multiply the big-oh upper bound for the body by the number of times around the loop. Strictly speaking, we must then add $O(1)$ time to initialize the loop index and $O(1)$ time for the first comparison of the loop index with the limit, because we test one more time than we go around the loop. However, unless it is possible to execute the loop zero times, the time to initialize the loop and test the limit once is a low-order term that can be dropped by the summation rule.

✦ **Example 3.13.** Consider the for-loop of lines (3) and (4) in Fig. 3.7, which is

```
(3)          for (j = 0; j < n; j++)
(4)              A[i][j] = 0;
```

We know that line (4) takes $O(1)$ time. Clearly, we go around the loop n times, as we can determine by subtracting the lower limit from the upper limit found on line (3) and then adding 1. Since the body, line (4), takes $O(1)$ time, we can neglect the time to increment j and the time to compare j with n, both of which are also $O(1)$. Thus, the running time of lines (3) and (4) is the product of n and $O(1)$, which is

$O(n)$.

Similarly, we can bound the running time of the outer loop consisting of lines (2) through (4), which is

```
(2)              for (i = 0; i < n; i++)
(3)                  for (j = 0; j < n; j++)
(4)                      A[i][j] = 0;
```

We have already established that the loop of lines (3) and (4) takes $O(n)$ time. Thus, we can neglect the $O(1)$ time to increment i and to test whether $i < n$ in each iteration, concluding that each iteration of the outer loop takes $O(n)$ time. The initialization i = 0 of the outer loop and the $(n+1)$st test of the condition $i < n$ likewise take $O(1)$ time and can be neglected. Finally, we observe that we go around the outer loop n times, taking $O(n)$ time for each iteration, giving a total $O(n^2)$ running time. ✦

✦   **Example 3.14.** Now, let us consider the for-loop of lines (3) to (5) of Fig. 3.8. Here, the body is an if-statement, a construct we shall learn how to analyze next. It is not hard to deduce that line (4) takes $O(1)$ time to perform the test and line (5), if we execute it, takes $O(1)$ time because it is an assignment with no function calls. Thus, we take $O(1)$ time to execute the body of the for-loop, regardless of whether line (5) is executed. The incrementation and test in the loop add $O(1)$ time, so that the total time for one iteration of the loop is just $O(1)$.

Now we must calculate the number of times we go around the loop. The number of iterations is not related to n, the size of the input. Rather, the formula "last value minus initial value divided by the increment" gives us $(n - (i+1))/1$, or $n - i - 1$, as the number of times around the loop. Strictly speaking, that formula holds only if $i < n$. Fortunately, we can observe from line (1) of Fig. 3.8 that we do not enter the loop body of lines (2) through (8) unless $i \leq n-2$. Thus, not only is $n-i-1$ the number of iterations, but we also know that this number cannot be 0. We conclude that the time spent in the loop is $(n - i - 1) \times O(1)$, or $O(n - i - 1)$.[5] We do not have to add in $O(1)$ for initializing j, since we have established that $n-i-1$ cannot be 0. If we had not observed that $n - i - 1$ was positive, then we would have to write the upper bound on the running time as $O\big(\max(1, n - i - 1)\big)$. ✦

The Running Time of Selection Statements

An if-else selection statement has the form

```
    if (<condition>)
        <if-part>
    else
        <else-part>
```

where

1.   The condition is an expression to be evaluated,

---

[5] Technically, we have not discussed a big-oh operator applied to a function of more than one variable. In this case, we can regard $O(n - i - 1)$ as saying "at most some constant times $n - i - 1$." That is, we can consider $n - i - 1$ as a surrogate for a single variable.

2. The if-part is a statement that is executed only if the condition is true (the value of the expression is not zero), and

3. The else-part is a statement that is executed if the condition is false (evaluates to 0). The **else** followed by the $<$**else-part**$>$ is optional.

A condition, no matter how complex, requires the computer to perform only a constant number of primitive operations, as long as there are no function calls within the condition. Thus, the evaluation of the condition will take $O(1)$ time.

Suppose that there are no function calls in the condition, and that the if- and else-parts have big-oh upper bounds $f(n)$ and $g(n)$, respectively. Let us also suppose that $f(n)$ and $g(n)$ are not both 0; that is, while the else-part may be missing, the if-part is something other than an empty block. We leave as an exercise the question of determining what happens if both parts are missing or are empty blocks.

If $f(n)$ is $O\big(g(n)\big)$, then we can take $O\big(g(n)\big)$ to be an upper bound on the running time of the selection statement. The reason is that

1. We can neglect the $O(1)$ for the condition,

2. If the else-part is executed, $g(n)$ is known to be a bound on the running time, and

3. If the if-part is executed instead of the else-part, the running time will be $O\big(g(n)\big)$ because $f(n)$ is $O\big(g(n)\big)$.

Similarly, if $g(n)$ is $O\big(f(n)\big)$, we can bound the running time of the selection statement by $O\big(f(n)\big)$. Note that when the else-part is missing, as it often is, $g(n)$ is 0, which is surely $O\big(f(n)\big)$.

The problem case is when neither f nor g is big-oh of the other. We know that either the if-part or the else-part, but not both, will be executed, and so a safe upper bound on the running time is the larger of $f(n)$ and $g(n)$. Which is larger can depend on n, as we saw in Example 3.10. Thus, we must write the running time of the selection statement as $O\Big(\max\big(f(n), g(n)\big)\Big)$.

✦ **Example 3.15.** As we observed in Example 3.12, the selection statement of lines (4) and (5) of Fig. 3.8 has an if-part, line (5), which takes $O(1)$ time, and a missing else-part, which takes 0 time. Thus, $f(n)$ is 1 and $g(n)$ is 0. As $g(n)$ is $O\big(f(n)\big)$, we get $O(1)$ as an upper bound on running time for lines (4) and (5). Note that the $O(1)$ time to perform the test A[j] $<$ A[small] at line (4) can be neglected. ✦

✦ **Example 3.16.** For a more complicated example, consider the fragment of code in Fig. 3.9, which performs the (relatively pointless) task of either zeroing the matrix A or setting its diagonal to 1's. As we learned in Example 3.13, the running time of lines (2) through (4) is $O(n^2)$, while the running time of lines (5) and (6) is $O(n)$. Thus, $f(n)$ is n^2 here, and $g(n)$ is n. Since n is $O(n^2)$, we can neglect the time of the else-part and take $O(n^2)$ as a bound on the running time of the entire fragment of Fig. 3.9. That is to say, we have no idea if or when the condition of line (1) will be true, but the only safe upper bound results from assuming the worst: that the condition is true and the if-part is executed. ✦

```
(1)          if (A[1][1] == 0)
(2)              for (i = 0; i < n; i++)
(3)                  for (j = 0; j < n; j++)
(4)                      A[i][j] = 0;
             else
(5)              for (i = 0; i < n; i++)
(6)                  A[i][i] = 1;
```

Fig. 3.9. Example of an if-else selection statement.

The Running Time of Blocks

**Compound
statement**

We already mentioned that a sequence of assignments, reads, and writes, each of which takes $O(1)$ time, together takes $O(1)$ time. More generally, we must be able to combine sequences of statements, some of which are *compound statements*, that is, selection statements or loops. Such a sequence of simple and compound statements is called a *block*. The running time of a block is calculated by taking the sum of the big-oh upper bounds for each of the (possibly compound) statements in the block. With luck, we can use the summation rule to eliminate all but one of the terms in the sum.

✦   **Example 3.17.** In the selection sort fragment of Fig. 3.8, we can view the body of the outer loop, that is, lines (2) through (8), as a block. This block consists of five statements:

1.   The assignment of line (2)
2.   The loop of lines (3), (4), and (5)
3.   The assignment of line (6)
4.   The assignment of line (7)
5.   The assignment of line (8)

Note that the selection statement of lines (4) and (5), and the assignment of line (5), are not visible at the level of this block; they are hidden within a larger statement, the for-loop of lines (3) to (5).

We know that the four assignment statements take $O(1)$ time each. In Example 3.14 we learned that the running time of the second statement of the block — that is, lines (3) through (5) — is $O(n - i - 1)$. Thus, the running time of the block is

$$O(1) + O(n - i - 1) + O(1) + O(1) + O(1)$$

Since 1 is $O(n - i - 1)$ (recall we also deduced that i never gets higher than $n - 2$), we can eliminate all the $O(1)$'s by the summation rule. Thus, the entire block takes $O(n - i - 1)$ time.

For another example, consider the program fragment of Fig. 3.7 again. It can be considered a single block consisting of three statements:

1.   The read statement of line (1)
2.   The loop of lines (2) through (4)
3.   The loop of lines (5) and (6)

We know that line (1) takes $O(1)$ time. From Example 3.13, lines (2) through (4) take $O(n^2)$ time; lines (5) and (6) take $O(n)$ time. The block itself takes

$$O(1) + O(n^2) + O(n)$$

time. By the summation rule, we can eliminate $O(1)$ and $O(n)$ in favor of $O(n^2)$. We conclude that the fragment of Fig. 3.7 takes $O(n^2)$ time. ✦

The Running Time of Complex Loops

In C, there are while-, do-while-, and some for-loops that do not offer an explicit count of the number of times we go around the loop. For these loops, part of the analysis is an argument that provides an upper bound on the number of iterations of the loop. These proofs typically follow the pattern we learned in Section 2.5. That is, we prove some statement by induction on the number of times around the loop, and the statement implies that the loop condition must become false after the number of iterations reaches a certain limit.

We must also establish a bound on the time to perform one iteration of the loop. Thus, we examine the body and obtain a bound on its execution. To that, we must add $O(1)$ time to test the condition after the execution of the loop body, but unless the loop body is missing, we can neglect this $O(1)$ term. We get a bound on the running time of the loop by multiplying an upper bound on the number of iterations by our upper bound on the time for one iteration. Technically, if the loop is a for- or while-loop rather than a do-while-loop, we must include the time needed to test the condition the first time, before entering the body. However, that $O(1)$ term can normally be neglected.

✦ **Example 3.18.** Consider the program fragment shown in Fig. 3.10. The program searches an array `A[0..n-1]` for the location of an element x that is believed to be in the array.

```
(1)          i = 0;
(2)          while(x != A[i])
(3)              i++;
```

Fig. 3.10. Program fragment for linear search.

The two assignment statements (1) and (3) in Fig. 3.10 have a running time of $O(1)$. The while-loop of lines (2) and (3) may be executed as many as n times, but no more, because we assume one of the array elements is x. Since the loop body, line (3), requires time $O(1)$, the running time of the while-loop is $O(n)$. From the summation rule, the running time of the entire program fragment is $O(n)$, because that is the maximum of the time for the assignment of line (1) and the time for the while-loop. In Chapter 6, we shall see how this $O(n)$ program can be replaced by an $O(\log n)$ program using binary search. ✦

EXERCISES

3.6.1: In a for-loop headed

```
for (i = a; i <= b; i++)
```

how many times do we go around the loop, as a function of a and b? What about a for-loop headed

```
for (i = a; i <= b; i--)
```

What about A for-loop headed

```
for(i = a; i <= b; i = i+c)
```

3.6.2: Give a big-oh upper bound on the running time of the trivial selection statement

```
if ( C ) { }
```

where C is a condition that does not involve any function calls.

3.6.3: Repeat Exercise 3.6.2 for the trivial while-loop

```
while ( C ) { }
```

3.6.4*: Give a rule for the running time of a C switch-statement.

3.6.5: Give a rule for the running time of a selection statement in which we can tell which branch is taken, such as

```
if (1==2)
    something O(f(n));
else
    something O(g(n));
```

3.6.6: Give a rule for the running time of a degenerate while-loop, in which the condition is known to be false right from the start, such as

```
while (1 != 1)
    something O(f(n));
```

❖❖ 3.7 A Recursive Rule for Bounding Running Time

In the previous section, we informally described a number of rules for defining the running time of certain program constructs in terms of the running times of their parts. For instance, we said that the time of a for-loop is essentially the time taken by the body multiplied by the number of iterations. Hidden among these rules was the notion that programs are built using inductive rules by which compound statements (loops, selections, and other statements that have substatements as constituent parts) are constructed from a basis consisting of simple statements such as assignment, read, write, and jump statements. The inductive rules covered loop formation, selection statements, and blocks, which are sequences of compound statements.

We shall state some syntactic rules for building statements of C as a recursive definition. These rules correspond to the grammatical rules for defining C that often appear in a text on C. We shall see in Chapter 11 that grammars can serve as a succinct recursive notation for specifying the syntax of programming languages.

More Defensive Programming

If you think that the array **A** in Example 3.18 will always have the element x just because we believe it does, there's a bridge we'd like to sell you. Notice that if x fails to appear in the array, the loop of Fig. 3.10 will eventually err by trying to access an element of the array that is beyond the array's upper limit.

Fortunately, there is a simple way to avoid this error without spending a lot of extra time in each iteration of the loop. We allow an extra $(n + 1)$st cell at the end of the array, and before starting the loop, we place x there. Then we really can be sure that x will appear somewhere in the array. When the loop ends, we test to see whether $i = n$. If so, then x wasn't really in the array, and we fell through the array to the copy of x we had placed as a *sentinel*. If $i < n$, then i does indicate a position where x appears. An example program with this protection feature is

Sentinel

```
A[n] = x;
i = 0;
while (x != A[i])
    i++;
if (i == n) /* do something appropriate to the case
                      that x is not in the array */
else /* do something appropriate to the case
                      that x is found at position i */
```

BASIS. The following are simple statements in C:

1. *Expressions*, including assignment statements and read and write statements; the latter are calls to functions such as **printf** and **scanf**.

2. *Jump statements*, including **goto**'s, **break**'s, **continue**'s, and **return**'s.

3. The *null statement*.

Note that in C, simple statements end in a semicolon, which we take to be part of the statement.

INDUCTION. The following rules let us construct statements from smaller statements:

1. *While-statement.* If S is a statement and C is a condition (an expression with an arithmetic value), then

    while (C) S

    is a statement. The body S is executed as long as C is true (has a nonzero value).

2. *Do-while-statement.* If S is a statement and C is a condition, then

    do S **while** (C) ;

    is a statement. The do-while is similar to the while-statement except that the body S is executed at least once.

3. *For-statement.* If S is a statement and E_1, E_2, and E_3 are expressions, then

    for (E_1 ; E_2 ; E_3) S

    is a statement. The first expression E_1 is evaluated once and specifies the initialization for the loop body S. The second expression E_2 is the test for loop termination, which is evaluated before each iteration. If its value is nonzero, the body is executed; otherwise, the for-loop is terminated. The third expression E_3 is evaluated after each iteration and specifies the reinitialization (incrementation) for the next iteration of the loop. For instance, a common for-loop is

    ```
    for (i = 0; i < n; i++) S
    ```

    where S is iterated n times with i having the values $0, 1, \ldots, n-1$. Here, `i = 0` is the initialization, `i < n` is the termination test, and `i++` is the reinitialization.

4. *Selection statement.* If S_1 and S_2 are statements and C is a condition, then

    if (C) S_1 **else** S_2

    is a statement, and

    if (C) S_1

    is also a statement. In the first case, if C is true (nonzero), then S_1 is executed; otherwise, S_2 is executed. In the second case, S_1 is executed only if C is true.

5. *Block.* If $S_1, S_2, \ldots, S_n$ are statements, then

    $\{S_1 \ S_2 \cdots S_n\}$

    is a statement.

We have omitted from this list the switch-statement, which has a complex form but can be thought of as nested selection statements for analysis of running time.

Using this recursive definition of statements, it is possible to parse a program by identifying its constituent parts. That is, we begin with the simple statements and group them into progressively larger compound statements.

✦   **Example 3.19.** Consider the selection-sort program fragment shown in Fig. 3.11. For the basis, each of the assignments, lines (2), (5), (6), (7), and (8), is a statement by itself. Then lines (4) and (5) are grouped into a selection statement. Next lines (3) through (5) are grouped into a for-statement. Then lines (2) through (8) are grouped into a block. Finally, the entire program fragment is a for-statement. ✦

A Tree Representation of a Program's Structure

We can represent the structure of programs by a tree such as that shown in Fig. 3.12. Leaves (the circles) are simple statements and other nodes represent compound statements.[6] Nodes are labeled by the kind of construct they represent and by the

---

[6] Trees are discussed in detail in Chapter 5.

```
(1)              for (i = 0; i < n-1; i++) {
(2)                  small = i;
(3)                  for (j = i+1; j < n; j++)
(4)                      if (A[j] < A[small])
(5)                          small = j;
(6)                  temp = A[small];
(7)                  A[small] = A[i];
(8)                  A[i] = temp;
                 }
```

Fig. 3.11. Selection sort fragment.

Structure tree

line or lines of the program that form the simple or compound statement represented by the node. From each node N that represents a compound statement we find lines downward to its "children" nodes. The children of node N represent the substatements forming the compound statement that N represents. Such a tree is called the *structure tree* for a program.

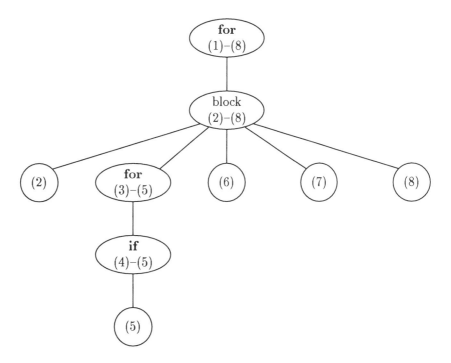

Fig. 3.12. Tree showing grouping of statements.

✦ **Example 3.20.** Figure 3.12 is the structure tree for the program fragment of Fig. 3.11. Each of the circles is a leaf representing one of the five assignment statements of Fig. 3.11. We have omitted from Fig. 3.12 an indication that these five statements are assignment statements.

At the top (the "root") of the tree is a node representing the entire fragment of lines (1) through (8); it is a for-statement. The body of the for-loop is a block consisting of lines (2) through (8).[7] This block is represented by a node just below the root. That block node has five children, representing the five statements of the block. Four of them are assignment statements, lines (2), (6), (7), and (8). The fifth is the for-loop of lines (3) through (5).

The node for this for-loop has a child representing its body, the if-statement of lines (4) and (5). The latter node has a child representing its constituent statement, the assignment of line (5). ✦

Climbing the Structure Tree to Determine Running Time

Just as program structures are built recursively, we can define big-oh upper bounds on the running time of programs, using an analogous recursive method. As in Section 3.6, we presume that there are no function calls within the expressions that form assignment statements, print statements, conditions in selections, conditions in while-, for-, or do-while- loops, or the initialization or reinitialization of a for-loop. The only exception is a call to a read- or write-function such as `printf`.

BASIS. The bound for a simple statement — that is, for an assignment, a read, a write, or a jump — is $O(1)$.

INDUCTION. For the five compound constructs we have discussed, the rules for computing their running time are as follows.

1. *While-statement.* Let $O(f(n))$ be the upper bound on the running time of the body of the while-statement; $f(n)$ was discovered by the recursive application of these rules. Let $g(n)$ be an upper bound on the number of times we may go around the loop. Then $O\Big(1 + \big(f(n) + 1\big)g(n)\Big)$ is an upper bound on the running time of the while-loop. That is, $O(f(n)+1)$ is an upper bound on the running time of the body plus the test after the body. The additional 1 at the beginning of the formula accounts for the first test, before entering the loop. In the common case where $f(n)$ and $g(n)$ are at least 1 (or we can define them to be 1 if their value would otherwise be 0), we can write the running time of the while-loop as $O(f(n)g(n))$. This common formula for running time is suggested by Fig. 3.13(a).

2. *Do-while-statement.* If $O(f(n))$ is an upper bound on the body of the loop and $g(n)$ is an upper bound on the number of times we can go around the loop, then $O\Big(\big(f(n)+1\big)g(n)\Big)$ is an upper bound on the running time of the do-while-loop. The "+1" represents the time to compute and test the condition at the end of each iteration of the loop. Note that for a do-while-loop, $g(n)$ is always at least 1. In the common case that $f(n) \geq 1$ for all n, the running time of the do-while-loop is $O(f(n)g(n))$. Figure 3.13(b) suggests the way that running time is computed for the common case of a do-while-loop.

---

[7] A more detailed structure tree would have children representing the expressions for the initialization, termination test, and reinitialization of the for-loop.

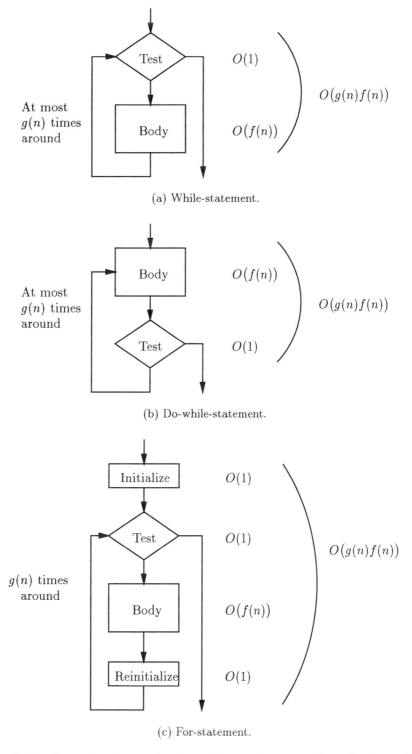

(a) While-statement.

(b) Do-while-statement.

(c) For-statement.

Fig. 3.13. Computing the running time of loop statements without function calls.

3. *For-statement.* If $O(f(n))$ is an upper bound on the running time of the body, and $g(n)$ is an upper bound on the number of times around the loop, then an upper bound on the time of a for-statement is $O\big(1 + (f(n) + 1)g(n)\big)$. The factor $f(n) + 1$ represents the cost of going around once, including the body, the test, and the reinitialization. The "1+" at the beginning represents the first initialization and the possibility that the first test is negative, resulting in zero iterations of the loop. In the common case that $f(n)$ and $g(n)$ are both at least 1, or can be redefined to be at least 1, then the running time of the for-statement is $O\big(f(n)g(n)\big)$, as is illustrated by Fig. 3.13(c).

4. *Selection statement.* If $O(f_1(n))$ and $O(f_2(n))$ are upper bounds on the running time of the if-part and the else-part, respectively ($f_2(n)$ is 0 if the else-part is missing), then an upper bound on the running time of the selection statement is $O\big(1 + \max(f_1(n), f_2(n))\big)$. The "1+" represents the test; in the common case, where at least one of $f_1(n)$ and $f_2(n)$ are positive for all n, the "1+" can be omitted. Further, if one of $f_1(n)$ and $f_2(n)$ is big-oh of the other, this expression may be simplified to whichever is the larger, as was stated in Exercise 3.5.5. Figure 3.14 suggests the computation of running time for an if-statement.

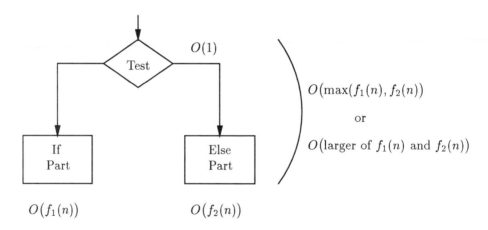

Fig. 3.14. Computing the running time of an if-statement without function calls.

5. *Block.* If $O(f_1(n)), O(f_2(n)), \ldots, O(f_k(n))$ are our upper bounds on the statements within the block, then $O\big(f_1(n) + f_2(n) + \cdots + f_k(n)\big)$ is an upper bound on the running time of the block. If possible, use the summation rule to simplify this expression. The rule is illustrated in Fig. 3.15.

We apply these rules traveling up the structure tree that represents the construction of compound statements from smaller statements. Alternatively, we can see the application of these rules as beginning with the simple statements covered by the basis and then proceeding to progressively larger compound statements, applying whichever of the five inductive rules is appropriate at each step. However we view the process of computing the upper bound on running time, we analyze

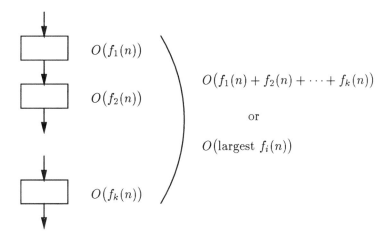

Fig. 3.15. Computing the running time of a block without function calls.

a compound statement only after we have analyzed all the statements that are its constituent parts.

✦   **Example 3.21.** Let us revisit our selection sort program of Fig. 3.11, whose structure tree is in Fig. 3.12. To begin, we know that each of the assignment statements at the leaves in Fig. 3.12 takes $O(1)$ time. Proceeding up the tree, we next come to the if-statement of lines (4) and (5). We recall from Example 3.15 that this compound statement takes $O(1)$ time.

Next as we travel up the tree (or proceed from smaller statements to their surrounding larger statements), we must analyze the for-loop of lines (3) to (5). We did so in Example 3.14, where we discovered that the time was $O(n - i - 1)$. Here, we have chosen to express the running time as a function of the two variables n and i. That choice presents us with some computational difficulties, and as we shall see, we could have chosen the looser upper bound of $O(n)$. Working with $O(n - i - 1)$ as our bound, we must now observe from line (1) of Fig. 3.11 that i can never get as large as $n - 1$. Thus, $n - i - 1$ is strictly greater than 0 and dominates $O(1)$. Consequently, we need not add to $O(n - i - 1)$ an $O(1)$ term for initializing the index j of the for-loop.

Now we come to the block of lines (2) through (8). As discussed in Example 3.17, the running time of this block is the sum of four $O(1)$'s corresponding to the four assignment statements, plus the term $O(n - i - 1)$ for the compound statement of lines (3) to (5). By the rule for sums, plus our observation that $i < n$, we drop the $O(1)$'s, leaving $O(n - i - 1)$ as the running time of the block.

Finally, we must consider the for-loop of lines (1) through (8). This loop was not analyzed in Section 3.6, but we can apply inductive rule (3). That rule needs an upper bound on the running time of the body, which is the block of lines (2) through (8). We just determined the bound $O(n - i - 1)$ for this block, presenting us with a situation we have not previously seen. While i is constant within the block, i is the index of the outer for-loop, and therefore varies within the loop. Thus, the bound $O(n - i - 1)$ makes no sense if we think of it as the running time of all iterations of the loop. Fortunately, we can see from line (1) that i is never below 0, and so $O(n-1)$ is an upper bound on $O(n-i-1)$. Moreover, by our rule that low-order terms don't matter, we can simplify $O(n-1)$ to $O(n)$.

Next, we need to determine the number of times we go around the loop. Since i ranges from 0 to $n-2$, evidently we go around $n-1$ times. When we multiply $n-1$ by $O(n)$, we get $O(n^2-n)$. Throwing away low-order terms again, we see that $O(n^2)$ is an upper bound on the running time of the whole selection sort program. That is to say, selection sort has a quadratic upper bound on its running time. The quadratic upper bound is the tightest possible, since we can show that if the elements are initially in reverse of sorted order, then selection sort does make $n(n-1)/2$ comparison steps. ✦

As we shall see, we can derive $n \log n$ upper and lower bounds for the running time of merge sort. In practice, merge sort is more efficient than selection sort for all but some small values of n. The reason merge sort is sometimes slower than selection sort is because the $O(n \log n)$ upper bound hides a larger constant than the $O(n^2)$ bound for selection sort. The true situation is a pair of crossing curves, as shown in Fig. 3.2 of Section 3.3.

More Precise Upper Bounds for Loop Running Times

We have suggested that to evaluate the running time of a loop we need to find a uniform bound that applies to each of the iterations of the loop. However, a more careful analysis of a loop would treat each iteration separately. We could instead sum the upper bounds for each iteration. Technically, we must include the time to increment the index (if the loop is a for-loop) and to test the loop condition in the rare situation when the time for these operations makes a difference. Generally, the more careful analysis doesn't change the answer, although there are some unusual loops in which most iterations take very little time, but one or a few take a lot of time. Then the sum of the times for each iteration might be significantly less than the product of the number of iterations times the maximum time taken by any iteration.

✦ **Example 3.22.** We shall perform this more precise analysis on the outer loop of selection sort. Despite this extra effort, we still get a quadratic upper bound. As Example 3.21 demonstrated, the running time of the iteration of the outer loop with the value i for the index variable i is $O(n-i-1)$. Thus an upper bound on the time taken by all iterations, as i ranges from its initial value 0 up to $n-2$, is $O\left(\sum_{i=0}^{n-2}(n-i-1)\right)$. The terms in this sum form an arithmetic progression, so we can use the formula "average of the first and last terms times the number of terms." That formula tells us that

$$\sum_{i=0}^{n-2}(n-i-1) = n(n-1)/2 = 0.5n^2 - 0.5n$$

Neglecting low-order terms and constant factors, we see that $O(0.5n^2 - 0.5n)$ is the same as $O(n^2)$. We again conclude that selection sort has a quadratic upper bound on its running time. ✦

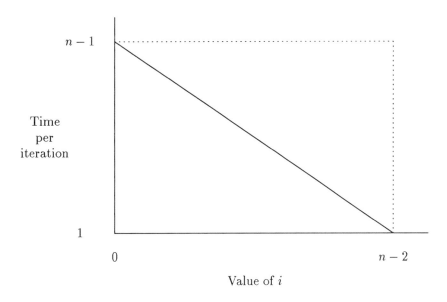

Fig. 3.16. Simple and precise estimates of loop running time.

The difference between the simple analysis in Example 3.21 and the more detailed analysis in Example 3.22 is illustrated by Fig. 3.16. In Example 3.21, we took the maximum time of any iteration as the time for each iteration, thus getting the area of the rectangle as our bound on the running time of the outer for-loop in Fig. 3.11. In Example 3.22, we bounded the running time of each iteration by the diagonal line, since the time for each iteration decreases linearly with i. Thus, we obtained the area of the triangle as our estimate of the running time. However, it is well known that the area of the triangle is half the area of the rectangle. Since the factor of 2 gets lost with the other constant factors that are hidden by the big-oh notation anyway, the two upper bounds on the running time are really the same.

EXERCISES

3.7.1: Figure 3.17 contains a C program to find the average of the elements of an array `A[0..n-1]` and to print the index of the element that is closest to average (a tie is broken in favor of the element appearing first). We assume that $n \geq 1$ and do not include the necessary check for an empty array. Build a structure tree showing how the statements are grouped into progressively more complex statements, and give a simple and tight big-oh upper bound on the running time for each of the statements in the tree. What is the running time of the entire program?

3.7.2: The fragment in Fig. 3.18 transforms an n by n matrix **A**. Show the structure tree for the fragment. Give a big-oh upper bound on the running time of each compound statement

a)   Making the bound for the two inner loops a function of n and i.
b)   Making the bound for all loops be a function of n only.

For the whole program, is there a big-oh difference between your answers to parts (a) and (b)?

```
        #include <stdio.h>
        #define MAX 100
        int A[MAX];

        main()
        {
            int closest, i, n;
            float avg, sum;

(1)         for (n = 0; n < MAX && scanf("%d", &A[n]) != EOF; n++)
(2)             ;
(3)         sum = 0;
(4)         for (i = 0; i < n; i++)
(5)             sum += A[i];
(6)         avg = sum/n;
(7)         closest = 0;
(8)         i = 1;
(9)         while (i < n) {
                /* squaring elements in the test below eliminates
                   the need to distinguish positive and negative
                   differences */
(10)            if ((A[i]-avg)*(A[i]-avg) <
                   (A[closest]-avg)*(A[closest]-avg))
(11)                    closest = i;
(12)            i++;
            }
(13)        printf("%d\n",closest);
        }
```

Fig. 3.17. Program for Exercise 3.7.1.

```
(1)    for (i = 0; i < n-1; i++)
(2)        for (j = i+1; j < n; j++)
(3)            for (k = i; k < n; k++)
(4)                A[j][k] = A[j][k] - A[i][k]*A[j][i]/A[i][i];
```

Fig. 3.18. Program for Exercise 3.7.2.

3.7.3*: Figure 3.19 contains a program fragment that applies the powers-of-2 operation discussed in Example 3.8 to the integers i from 1 to n. Show the structure tree for the fragment. Give a big-oh upper bound on the running time of each compound statement

a)   Making the bound for the while-loop a function of (the factors of) i.
b)   Making the bound for the while-loop a function of n only.

For the whole program, is there a big-oh difference between your answers to parts (a) and (b)?

```
(1)              for (i = 1; i <= n; i++) {
(2)                  m = 0;
(3)                  j = i;
(4)                  while (j%2 == 0) {
(5)                      j = j/2;
(6)                      m++;
                     }
             }
```

Fig. 3.19. Program for Exercise 3.7.3.

3.7.4: In Fig. 3.20 is a function that determines whether the argument n is a prime. Note that if n is not a prime, then it is divisible evenly by some integer i between 2 and $\sqrt{n}$. Show the structure tree for the function. Give a big-oh upper bound on the running time of each compound statement, as a function of n. What is the running time of the function as a whole?

```
             int prime(int n)
             {
                 int i;

(1)              i = 2;
(2)              while (i*i <= n)
(3)                  if (n%i == 0)
(4)                      return FALSE;
                     else
(5)                      i++;
(6)              return TRUE;
             }
```

Fig. 3.20. Program for Exercise 3.7.4.

❖❖ 3.8   Analyzing Programs with Function Calls

We now show how to analyze the running time of a program or program fragment that contains function calls. To begin, if all functions are nonrecursive, we can determine the running time of the functions making up the program one at a time, starting with those functions that do not call any other function. Then we evaluate the running times of the functions that call only functions whose running times we have already determined. We proceed in this fashion until we have evaluated the running time for all functions.

There are some complexities introduced by the fact that for different functions there may be different natural measures of the size of the input. In general, the input to a function is the list of the arguments of that function. If function F calls function G, we must relate the size measure for the arguments of G to the measure of size that is used for F. It is hard to give useful generalities, but some examples in this section and the next will help us see how the process of bounding the running time for functions works in simple cases.

Suppose we have determined that a good upper bound on the running time of a function F is $O(h(n))$, where n is a measure of the size of the arguments of F. Then when a call to F is made from within a simple statement (e.g., in an assignment), we add $O(h(n))$ to the cost of that statement.

```
        #include <stdio.h>
        int bar(int x, int n);
        int foo(int x, int n);

        main()
        {
            int a, n;

(1)         scanf("%d", &n);
(2)         a = foo(0,n);
(3)         printf("%d\n", bar(a,n));
        }

        int bar(int x, int n)
        {
            int i;

(4)         for (i = 1; i <= n; i++)
(5)             x += i;
(6)         return x;
        }

        int foo(int x, int n)
        {
            int i;

(7)         for (i = 1; i <= n; i++)
(8)             x += bar(i,n);
(9)         return x;
        }
```

Fig. 3.21. Program illustrating nonrecursive function calls.

When a function call with upper bound $O(h(n))$ appears in a condition of a while-, do-while-, or if-statement, or in the initialization, test, or reinitialization of a for-statement, the time of that function call is accounted for as follows:

1. If the function call is in the condition of a while- or do-while-loop, or in the condition or reinitialization of a for-loop, add $h(n)$ to the bound on the time for each iteration. Then proceed as in Section 3.7 to obtain the running time of the loop.

Program Analysis in a Nutshell

Here are the major points that you should take from Sections 3.7 and 3.8.

✦ The running time of a sequence of statements is the sum of the running times of the statements. Often, one of the statements dominates the others by having a running time that is at least as big as any. By the summation rule the big-oh running time of the sequence is just the running time of the dominant statement.

✦ The running time of a loop is computed by taking the running time of the body, plus any control steps (e.g., reinitializing the index of a for-loop and comparing it to the limit). Multiply this running time by an upper bound on the number of times the loop can be iterated. Then, add anything that is done just once, such as the initialization or the first test for termination, if the loop might be iterated zero times.

✦ The running time of a selection statement (if-else, e.g.) is the time to decide which branch to take plus the larger of the running times of the branches.

2. If the function call is in the initialization of a for-loop, add $O\big(h(n)\big)$ to the cost of the loop.

3. If the function call is in the condition of an if-statement, add $h(n)$ to the cost of the statement.

Calling graph

✦ **Example 3.23.** Let us analyze the (meaningless) program of Fig. 3.21. First, let us note that it is not a recursive program. The function `main` calls both functions `foo` and `bar`, and `foo` calls `bar`, but that is all. The diagram of Fig. 3.22, called a *calling graph*, indicates how functions call one another. Since there are no cycles, there is no recursion, and we can analyze the functions by starting with "group 0," those that do not call other functions (`bar` in this case), then working on "group 1," those that call only functions in group 0 (`foo` in this case), and then on "group 2," those that call only functions in groups 0 and 1 (`main` in this case). At this point, we are done, since all functions are in groups. In general, we would have to consider a larger number of groups, but as long as there are no cycles, we can eventually place each function in a group.

The order in which we analyze the running time of the functions is also the order in which we should examine them in order to gain an understanding of what the program does. Thus, let us first consider what the function `bar` does. The for-loop of lines (4) and (5) adds each of the integers 1 through n to x. As a result, $bar(x, n)$ is equal to $x + \sum_{i=1}^{n} i$. The summation $\sum_{i=1}^{n} i$ is another example of summing an arithmetic progression, which we can calculate by adding the first and last terms, multiplying by the number of terms, and dividing by 2. That is, $\sum_{i=1}^{n} i = (1 + n)n/2$. Thus, $bar(x, n) = x + n(n + 1)/2$.

Now, consider function `foo`, which adds to its argument `x` the sum

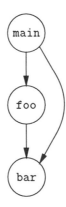

Fig. 3.22. Calling graph for Fig. 3.21.

Proofs and Program Understanding

The reader may notice that in our examination of the program in Fig. 3.21, we were able to understand what the program does, but we did not prove anything formally as we did in Chapter 2. However, there are many simple inductive proofs lurking just below the surface. For example, we need to prove by induction on the number of times around the loop of lines (4) and (5) that the value of x, just before we begin the iteration with value i for i, is the initial value of x plus $\sum_{j=1}^{i-1} j$. Note that if $i = 1$, then this sum consists of 0 terms and therefore has the value 0.

$$\sum_{i=1}^{n} bar(i, n)$$

From our understanding of bar we know that $bar(i, n) = i + n(n+1)/2$. Thus foo adds to x the quantity $\sum_{i=1}^{n}(i+n(n+1)/2)$. We have another arithmetic progression to sum, and this one requires more algebraic manipulation. However, the reader may check that the quantity foo adds to its argument x is $(n^3 + 2n^2 + n)/2$.

Finally, let us consider the function main. We read n at line (1). At line (2) we apply foo to 0 and n. By our understanding of foo, the value of foo(0,n) at line (2) will be 0 plus $(n^3 + 2n^2 + n)/2$. At line (3), we print the value of bar(foo(0,n),n), which, by our understanding of bar is the sum of $n(n+1)/2$ and the current value of foo(a,n). Thus, the value printed is $(n^3 + 3n^2 + 2n)/2$.

Now let us analyze the running time of the program in Fig. 3.21, working from bar to foo and then to main, as we did in Example 3.23. In this case, we shall take the value n to be the size of the input to all three functions. That is, even though we generally want to consider the "size" of all the arguments to a function, in this case the running time of the functions depends only on n.

To analyze bar, we note that line (5) takes $O(1)$ time. The for-loop of lines (4) and (5) iterates n times, and so the time for lines (4) and (5) is $O(n)$. Line (6) takes $O(1)$ time, and so the time for the block of lines (4) to (6) is $O(n)$.

Now we proceed to foo. The assignment in line (8) takes $O(1)$ plus the time of a call to bar(i,n). That call, we already know, takes $O(n)$ time, and so the time for line (8) is $O(n)$. The for-loop of lines (7) and (8) iterates n times, and so we multiply the $O(n)$ for the body by n to get $O(n^2)$ as the running time of a call to foo.

Finally, we may analyze main. Line (1) takes $O(1)$ time. The call to foo at line (2) takes $O(n^2)$ time, as we just deduced. The print-statement of line (3) takes $O(1)$ plus the time for a call to bar. The latter takes $O(n)$ time, and so line (3) as a whole takes $O(n^2) + O(n)$ time. The total time for the block of lines (1) through (3) is therefore $O(1) + O(1) + O(n^2) + O(n)$. By the rule for sums, we can eliminate all but the third term, concluding that the function main takes $O(n^2)$ time. That is, the call to foo at line (2) is the dominant cost. ✦

EXERCISES

3.8.1: Show the claim in Example 3.23, that

$$\sum_{i=1}^{n} (i + n(n+1)/2) = (n^3 + 2n^2 + n)/2$$

3.8.2: Suppose that $prime(n)$ is a function call that takes time $O(\sqrt{n})$. Consider a function whose body is

```
if ( prime(n) )
    A;
else
    B;
```

Give a simple and tight big-oh upper bound on the running time of this function, as a function of n, on the assumption that

a) A takes $O(n)$ time and B takes $O(1)$ time
b) A and B both take $O(1)$ time

3.8.3: Consider a function whose body is

```
sum = 0;
for (i = 1; i <= f(n); i++)
    sum += i;
```

where $f(n)$ is a function call. Give a simple and tight big-oh upper bound on the running time of this function, as a function of n, on the assumption that

a)   The running time of $f(n)$ is $O(n)$, and the value of $f(n)$ is $n!$
b)   The running time of $f(n)$ is $O(n)$, and the value of $f(n)$ is n
c)   The running time of $f(n)$ is $O(n^2)$, and the value of $f(n)$ is n
d)   The running time of $f(n)$ is $O(1)$, and the value of $f(n)$ is 0

3.8.4: Draw the calling graph for the functions in the merge sort program from Section 2.8. Is the program recursive?

3.8.5*: Suppose that line (7) in the function foo of Fig. 3.21 were replaced by

```
for (i = 1; i <= bar(n,n); i++)
```

What would the running time of main be then?

✦✦ 3.9   Analyzing Recursive Functions

Determining the running time of a function that calls itself recursively requires more work than analyzing nonrecursive functions. The analysis for a recursive function requires that we associate with each function F in a program an unknown running time $T_F(n)$. This unknown function represents F's running time as a function of n, the size of F's arguments. We then establish an inductive definition, called a *recurrence relation* for $T_F(n)$, that relates $T_F(n)$ to functions of the form $T_G(k)$ for the other functions G in the program and their associated argument sizes k. If F is directly recursive, then one or more of the G's will be the same as F.

Recurrence relation

The value of $T_F(n)$ is normally established by an induction on the argument size n. Thus, it is necessary to pick a notion of argument size that guarantees functions are called with progressively smaller arguments as the recursion proceeds. The requirement is the same as what we encountered in Section 2.9, when we tried to prove statements about recursive programs. That should be no surprise, because a statement about the running time of a program is just one example of something that we might try to prove about a program.

Once we have a suitable notion of argument size, we can consider two cases:

1. The argument size is sufficiently small that no recursive calls will be made by F. This case corresponds to the basis in an inductive definition of $T_F(n)$.

2. For larger argument sizes, one or more recursive calls may occur. Note that whatever recursive calls F makes, whether to itself or to some other function G, will be made with smaller arguments. This case corresponds to the inductive step in the definition of $T_F(n)$.

The recurrence relation defining $T_F(n)$ is derived by examining the code for function F and doing the following:

a) For each call to a function G or use of a function G in an expression (note that G may be F), use $T_G(k)$ as the running time of the call, where k is the appropriate measure of the size of the arguments in the call.

b) Evaluate the running time of the body of function F, using the same techniques as in previous sections, but leaving terms like $T_G(k)$ as unknown functions, rather than concrete functions such as n^2. These terms cannot generally be combined with concrete functions using simplification tricks such as the summation rule. We must analyze F twice — once on the assumption that F's argument size n is sufficiently small that no recursive function calls are made, and once assuming that n is not that small. As a result, we obtain two expressions for the running time of F — one (the *basis expression*) serving as the basis of the recurrence relation for $T_F(n)$, and the other (the *induction expression*) serving as the inductive part.

Basis and induction expressions

c) In the resulting basis and induction expressions for the running time of F, replace big-oh terms like $O(f(n))$ by a specific constant times the function involved — for example, $cf(n)$.

d) If a is a basis value for the input size, set $T_F(a)$ equal to the basis expression resulting from step (c) on the assumption that there are no recursive calls. Also, set $T_F(n)$ equal to the induction expression from (c) for the case where n is not a basis value.

```
            int fact(int n)
            {
(1)             if (n <= 1)
(2)                 return 1; /* basis */
            else
(3)                 return n*fact(n-1); /* induction */
            }
```

Fig. 3.23. Program to compute $n!$.

The running time of the entire function is determined by solving this recurrence relation. In Section 3.11, we shall give general techniques for solving recurrences of the kind that arise in the analysis of common recursive functions. For the moment, we solve these recurrences by ad hoc means.

✦   **Example 3.24.** Let us reconsider the recursive program from Section 2.7 to compute the factorial function; the code is shown in Fig. 3.23. Since there is only one function, **fact**, involved, we shall use $T(n)$ for the unknown running time of this function. We shall use n, the value of the argument, as the size of the argument. Clearly, recursive calls made by **fact** when the argument is n have a smaller argument, $n-1$ to be precise.

For the basis of the inductive definition of $T(n)$ we shall take $n = 1$, since no recursive call is made by **fact** when its argument is 1. With $n = 1$, the condition of line (1) is true, and so the call to **fact** executes lines (1) and (2). Each takes $O(1)$ time, and so the running time of **fact** in the basis case is $O(1)$. That is, $T(1)$ is $O(1)$.

Now, consider what happens when $n > 1$. The condition of line (1) is false, and so we execute only lines (1) and (3). Line (1) takes $O(1)$ time, and line (3) takes $O(1)$ for the multiplication and assignment, plus $T(n-1)$ for the recursive call to **fact**. That is, for $n > 1$, the running time of **fact** is $O(1) + T(n-1)$. We can thus define $T(n)$ by the following recurrence relation:

BASIS. $T(1) = O(1)$.

INDUCTION. $T(n) = O(1) + T(n-1)$, for $n > 1$.

We now invent constant symbols to stand for those constants hidden within the various big-oh expressions, as was suggested by rule (c) above. In this case, we can replace the $O(1)$ in the basis by some constant a, and the $O(1)$ in the induction by some constant b. These changes give us the following recurrence relation:

BASIS. $T(1) = a$.

INDUCTION. $T(n) = b + T(n-1)$, for $n > 1$.

Now we must solve this recurrence for $T(n)$. We can calculate the first few values easily. $T(1) = a$ by the basis. Thus, by the inductive rule, we have

$$T(2) = b + T(1) = a + b$$

Continuing to use the inductive rule, we get

$$T(3) = b + T(2) = b + (a + b) = a + 2b$$

Then

$$T(4) = b + T(3) = b + (a + 2b) = a + 3b$$

By this point, it should be no surprise if we guess that $T(n) = a + (n - 1)b$, for all $n \geq 1$. Indeed, computing some sample values, then guessing a solution, and finally proving our guess correct by an inductive proof is a common method of dealing with recurrences.

Repeated substitution

In this case, however, we can derive the solution directly by a method known as *repeated substitution*. First, let us make a substitution of variables, m for n, in the recursive equation, which now becomes

$$T(m) = b + T(m - 1), \text{ for } m > 1 \tag{3.3}$$

Now, we can substitute n, $n - 1$, $n - 2, \ldots, 2$ for m in equation (3.3) to get the sequence of equations

$$
\begin{array}{rlcl}
1) & T(n) & = & b + T(n - 1) \\
2) & T(n - 1) & = & b + T(n - 2) \\
3) & T(n - 2) & = & b + T(n - 3) \\
& & \cdots & \\
n - 1) & T(2) & = & b + T(1)
\end{array}
$$

Next, we can use line (2) above to substitute for $T(n-1)$ in (1), to get the equation

$$T(n) = b + \big(b + T(n - 2)\big) = 2b + T(n - 2)$$

Now, we use line (3) to substitute for $T(n - 2)$ in the above to get

$$T(n) = 2b + \big(b + T(n - 3)\big) = 3b + T(n - 3)$$

We proceed in this manner, each time replacing $T(n - i)$ by $b + T(n - i - 1)$, until we get down to $T(1)$. At that point, we have the equation

$$T(n) = (n - 1)b + T(1)$$

We can then use the basis to replace $T(1)$ by a, and conclude that $T(n) = a + (n-1)b$.

To make this analysis more formal, we need to prove by induction our intuitive observations about what happens when we repeatedly substitute for $T(n-i)$. Thus we shall prove the following by induction on i:

STATEMENT $S(i)$: If $1 \leq i < n$, then $T(n) = ib + T(n - i)$.

BASIS. The basis is $i = 1$. $S(1)$ says that $T(n) = b + T(n-1)$. This is the inductive part of the definition of $T(n)$ and therefore known to be true.

INDUCTION. If $i \geq n - 1$, there is nothing to prove. The reason is that statement $S(i + 1)$ begins, "If $1 \leq i + 1 < n \cdots$," and when the condition of an if-statement is false, the statement is true regardless of what follows the "then." In this case, where $i \geq n - 1$, the condition $i + 1 < n$ must be false, so $S(i + 1)$ is true.

The hard part is when $i \leq n-2$. In that case, $S(i)$ says that $T(n) = ib + T(n-i)$. Since $i \leq n - 2$, the argument of $T(n - i)$ is at least 2. Thus we can apply the inductive rule for T — that is, (3.3) with $n - i$ in place of m — to get the equation $T(n - i) = b + T(n - i - 1)$. When we substitute $b + T(n - i - 1)$ for $T(n - i)$ in the equation $T(n) = ib + T(n - i)$, we obtain $T(n) = ib + (b + T(n - i - 1))$, or regrouping terms,

$$T(n) = (i + 1)b + T(n - (i + 1))$$

This equation is the statement $S(i+1)$, and we have now proved the induction step.

We have now shown that $T(n) = a + (n - 1)b$. However, a and b are unknown constants. Thus, there is no point in presenting the solution this way. Rather, we can express $T(n)$ as a polynomial in n, namely, $bn + (a - b)$, and then replace terms by big-oh expressions, giving $O(n) + O(1)$. Using the summation rule, we can eliminate $O(1)$, which tells us that $T(n)$ is $O(n)$. That makes sense; it says that to compute $n!$, we make on the order of n calls to `fact` (the actual number is exactly n), each of which requires $O(1)$ time, excluding the time spent performing the recursive call to `fact`. ✦

EXERCISES

3.9.1: Set up a recurrence relation for the running time of the function `sum` mentioned in Exercise 2.9.2, as a function of the length of the list that is input to the program. Replace big-oh's by (unknown) constants, and try to solve your recurrence. What is the running time of `sum`?

3.9.2: Repeat Exercise 3.9.1 for the function `find0` from Exercise 2.9.3. What is a suitable size measure?

3.9.3*: Repeat Exercise 3.9.1 for the recursive selection sort program in Fig. 2.22 of Section 2.7. What is a suitable size measure?

Fibonacci
numbers

3.9.4**: Repeat Exercise 3.9.1 for the function of Fig. 3.24, which computes the Fibonacci numbers. (The first two are 1, and each succeeding number is the sum of the previous two. The first seven Fibonacci numbers are 1, 1, 2, 3, 5, 8, 13.) Note that the value of n is the appropriate size of an argument and that you need both 1 and 2 as basis cases.

```
int fibonacci(int n)
{
    if (n <= 2)
        return 1;
    else
        return fibonacci(n-1) + fibonacci(n-2);
}
```

Fig. 3.24. C function computing the Fibonacci numbers.

3.9.5*: Write a recursive program to compute $gcd(i, j)$, the greatest common divisor of two integers i and j, as outlined in Exercise 2.7.8. Show that the running time of the program is $O(\log i)$. *Hint*: Show that after two calls we invoke $gcd(m, n)$ where $m \leq i/2$.

❖❖ 3.10   Analysis of Merge Sort

We shall now analyze the merge sort algorithm that we presented in Section 2.8. First, we show that the **merge** and **split** functions each take $O(n)$ time on lists of length n, and then we use these bounds to show that the **MergeSort** function takes $O(n \log n)$ time on lists of length n.

Analysis of the Merge Function

We begin with the analysis of the recursive function **merge**, whose code we repeat as Fig. 3.25. The appropriate notion of size n for the argument of **merge** is the sum of the lengths of the lists *list*1 and *list*2. Thus, we let $T(n)$ be the time taken by **merge** when the sum of the lengths of its argument lists is n. We shall take $n = 1$ to be the basis case, and so we must analyze Fig. 3.25 on the assumption that one of **list1** and **list2** is empty and the other has only one element. There are two cases:

1. If the test of line (1) — that is, *list*1 equals **NULL** — succeeds, then we return **list2**, which takes $O(1)$ time. Lines (2) through (7) are not executed. Thus, the entire function call takes $O(1)$ time to test the selection of line (1) and $O(1)$ time to perform the assignment on line (1), a total of $O(1)$ time.

2. If the test of line (1) fails, then *list*1 is not empty. Since we assume that the sum of the lengths of the lists is only 1, *list*2 must therefore be empty. Thus, the test on line (2) — namely, *list*2 equals **NULL** — must succeed. We then take $O(1)$ time to perform the test of line (1), $O(1)$ to perform the test of line (2), and $O(1)$ to return **list1** on line (2). Lines (3) through (7) are not executed. Again, we take only $O(1)$ time.

We conclude that in the basis case **merge** takes $O(1)$ time.

Now let us consider the inductive case, where the sum of the list lengths is greater than 1. Of course, even if the sum of the lengths is 2 or more, one of the lists could still be empty. Thus, any of the four cases represented by the nested selection statements could be taken. The structure tree for the program of Fig. 3.25 is shown in Fig. 3.26. We can analyze the program by working from the bottom, up the structure tree.

The innermost selection begins with the "if" on line (3), where we test which list has the smaller first element and then either execute lines (4) and (5) or execute lines (6) and (7). The condition of line (3) takes $O(1)$ time to evaluate. Line (5) takes $O(1)$ time to evaluate, and line (4) takes $O(1)$ time plus $T(n - 1)$ time for the recursive call to **merge**. Note that $n - 1$ is the argument size for the recursive call, since we have eliminated exactly one element from one of the lists and left the other list as it was. Thus, the block of lines (4) and (5) takes $O(1) + T(n - 1)$ time.

The analysis for the else-part in lines (6) and (7) is exactly the same: line (7) takes $O(1)$ time and line (6) takes $O(1) + T(n - 1)$ time. Thus, when we take

```
            LIST merge(LIST list1, LIST list2)
            {
(1)             if (list1 == NULL) return list2;
(2)             else if (list2 == NULL) return list1;
(3)             else if (list1->element <= list2->element) {
(4)                 list1->next = merge(list1->next, list2);
(5)                 return list1;
            }
                else { /* list2 has smaller first element */
(6)                 list2->next = merge(list1, list2->next);
(7)                 return list2;
            }
            }
```

Fig. 3.25. The function merge.

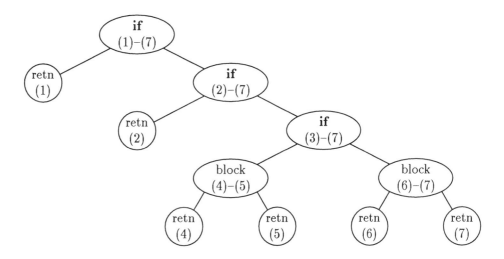

Fig. 3.26. Structure of merge.

the maximum of the running times of the if- and else-parts, we find these times to be the same. The $O(1)$ for the test of the condition can be neglected, and so we conclude that the running time of the innermost selection is $O(1) + T(n-1)$.

Now we proceed to the selection beginning on line (2), where we test whether *list2* equals NULL. The time for testing the condition is $O(1)$, and the time for the if-part, which is the return on line (2), is also $O(1)$. However, the else-part is the selection statement of lines (3) through (7), which we just determined takes $O(1) + T(n-1)$ time. Thus, the time for the selection of lines (2) through (7) is

$$O(1) + \max\big(O(1), O(1) + T(n-1)\big)$$

The second term of the maximum dominates the first and also dominates the $O(1)$ contributed by the test of the condition. Thus, the time for the if-statement beginning at line (2) is also $O(1) + T(n-1)$.

Finally, we perform the same analysis for the outermost if-statement. Essen-

A Common Form of Recursion

Many of the simplest recursive functions, such as **fact** and **merge**, perform some operation that takes $O(1)$ time and then make a recursive call to themselves on an argument one size smaller. Assuming the basis case takes $O(1)$ time, we see that such a function always leads to a recurrence relation $T(n) = O(1) + T(n-1)$. The solution for $T(n)$ is $O(n)$, or linear in the size of the argument. In Section 3.11 we shall see some generalizations of this principle.

tially, the dominant time is the else-part, which consists of lines (2) through (7). That is, the time for the cases in which there is a recursive call, lines (4) and (5) or lines (6) and (7), dominates the time for the cases in which there is no recursive call, represented by lines (1) and (2), and also dominates the time for all three tests on lines (1), (2), and (3). Thus, the time for the function **merge**, when $n > 1$, is bounded above by $O(1) + T(n-1)$. We therefore have the following recurrence relation for defining $T(n)$:

BASIS. $T(1) = O(1)$.

INDUCTION. $T(n) = O(1) + T(n-1)$, for $n > 1$.

These equations are exactly the same as those derived for the function **fact** in Example 3.24. Thus, the solution is the same and we can conclude that $T(n)$ is $O(n)$. That result makes intuitive sense, since **merge** works by eliminating an element from one of the lists, taking $O(1)$ time to do so, and then calling itself recursively on the remaining lists. It follows that the number of recursive calls will be no greater than the sum of the lengths of the lists. Since each call takes $O(1)$ time, exclusive of the time taken by its recursive call, we expect the time for **merge** to be $O(n)$.

```
        LIST split(LIST list)
        {
            LIST pSecondCell;

(1)         if (list == NULL) return NULL;
(2)         else if (list->next == NULL) return NULL;
            else { /* there are at least two cells */
(3)             pSecondCell = list->next;
(4)             list->next = pSecondCell->next;
(5)             pSecondCell->next = split(pSecondCell->next);
(6)             return pSecondCell;
            }
        }
```

Fig. 3.27. The function **split**.

Analysis of the Split Function

Now let us consider the `split` function, which we reproduce as Fig. 3.27. The analysis is quite similar to that for `merge`. We let the size n of the argument be the length of the list, and we here use $T(n)$ for the time taken by `split` on a list of length n.

For the basis, we take both $n = 0$ and $n = 1$. If $n = 0$ — that is, *list* is empty — the test of line (1) succeeds and we return NULL on line (1). Lines (2) through (6) are not executed, and we therefore take $O(1)$ time. If $n = 1$, that is, *list* is a single element, the test of line (1) fails, but the test of line (2) succeeds. We therefore return NULL on line (2) and do not execute lines (3) through (6). Again, only $O(1)$ time is needed for the two tests and one return statement.

For the induction, $n > 1$, there is a three-way selection branch, similar to the four-way branch we encountered in `merge`. To save time in analysis, we may observe — as we eventually concluded for `merge` — that we take $O(1)$ time to do one or both of the selection tests of lines (1) and (2). Also, in the cases in which one of these two tests is true, where we return on line (1) or (2), the additional time is only $O(1)$. The dominant time is the case in which both tests fail, that is, in which the list is of length at least 2; in this case we execute the statements of lines (3) through (6). All but the recursive call in line (5) contributes $O(1)$ time. The recursive call takes $T(n-2)$ time, since the argument list is the original value of `list`, missing its first two elements (to see why, refer to the material in Section 2.8, especially the diagram of Fig. 2.28). Thus, in the inductive case, $T(n)$ is $O(1) + T(n-2)$.

We may set up the following recurrence relation:

BASIS. $T(0) = O(1)$ and $T(1) = O(1)$.

INDUCTION. $T(n) = O(1) + T(n-2)$, for $n > 1$.

As in Example 3.24, we must next invent constants to represent the constants of proportionality hidden by the $O(1)$'s. We shall let a and b be the constants represented by $O(1)$ in the basis for the values of $T(0)$ and $T(1)$, respectively, and we shall use c for the constant represented by $O(1)$ in the inductive step. Thus, we may rewrite the recursive definition as

BASIS. $T(0) = a$ and $T(1) = b$.

INDUCTION. $T(n) = c + T(n-2)$ for $n \geq 2$.

Let us evaluate the first few values of $T(n)$. Evidently $T(0) = a$ and $T(1) = b$ by the basis. We may use the inductive step to deduce

$$
\begin{aligned}
T(2) &= c + T(0) &=& \ a + c \\
T(3) &= c + T(1) &=& \ b + c \\
T(4) &= c + T(2) &=& \ c + (a + c) &=& \ a + 2c \\
T(5) &= c + T(3) &=& \ c + (b + c) &=& \ b + 2c \\
T(6) &= c + T(4) &=& \ c + (a + 2c) &=& \ a + 3c
\end{aligned}
$$

The calculation of $T(n)$ is really two separate calculations, one for odd n and the other for even n. For even n, we get $T(n) = a + cn/2$. That makes sense, since with an even-length list, we eliminate two elements, taking time c to do so, and after $n/2$ recursive calls, we are left with an empty list, on which we make no more recursive calls and take a time.

On an odd-length list, we again eliminate two elements, taking time c to do so. After $(n-1)/2$ calls, we are down to a list of length 1, for which time b is required. Thus, the time for odd-length lists will be $b + c(n-1)/2$.

The inductive proofs of these observations closely parallel the proof in Example 3.24. That is, we prove the following:

STATEMENT $S(i)$: If $1 \le i \le n/2$, then $T(n) = ic + T(n - 2i)$.

In the proof, we use the inductive rule in the definition of $T(n)$, which we can rewrite with argument m as

$$T(m) = c + T(m - 2), \text{ for } m \ge 2 \tag{3.4}$$

We may then prove $S(i)$ by induction as follows:

BASIS. The basis, $i = 1$, is (3.4) with n in place of m.

INDUCTION. Because $S(i)$ has an if-then form, $S(i + 1)$ is always true if $i \ge n/2$. Thus, the inductive step — that $S(i)$ implies $S(i+1)$ — requires no proof if $i \ge n/2$.

The hard case occurs when $1 \le i < n/2$. In this situation, suppose that the inductive hypothesis $S(i)$ is true; $T(n) = ic + T(n - 2i)$. We substitute $n - 2i$ for m in (3.4), giving us

$$T(n - 2i) = c + T(n - 2i - 2)$$

If we substitute for $T(n - 2i)$ in $S(i)$, we get

$$T(n) = ic + \big(c + T(n - 2i - 2)\big)$$

If we then group terms, we get

$$T(n) = (i + 1)c + T\big(n - 2(i + 1)\big)$$

which is the statement $S(i + 1)$. We have thus proved the inductive step, and we conclude $T(n) = ic + T(n - 2i)$.

Now if n is even, let $i = n/2$. Then $S(n/2)$ says that $T(n) = cn/2 + T(0)$, which is $a + cn/2$. If n is odd, let $i = (n-1)/2$. $S((n-1)/2)$ tells us that $T(n)$ is

$$c(n - 1)/2 + T(1)$$

which equals $b + c(n - 1)/2$ since $T(1) = b$.

Finally, we must convert to big-oh notation the constants a, b, and c, which represent compiler- and machine-specific quantities. Both the polynomials $a + cn/2$ and $b + c(n - 1)/2$ have high-order terms proportional to n. Thus, the question whether n is odd or even is actually irrelevant; the running time of split is $O(n)$ in either case. Again, that is the intuitively correct answer, since on a list of length n, split makes about $n/2$ recursive calls, each taking $O(1)$ time.

```
        LIST MergeSort(LIST list)
        {
            LIST SecondList;

(1)         if (list == NULL) return NULL;
(2)         else if (list->next == NULL) return list;
            else {
                /* at least two elements on list */
(3)             SecondList = split(list);
(4)             return merge(MergeSort(list), MergeSort(SecondList));
            }
        }
```

Fig. 3.28. The merge sort algorithm.

The Function MergeSort

Finally, we come to the function MergeSort, which is reproduced in Fig. 3.28. The appropriate measure n of argument size is again the length of the list to be sorted. Here, we shall use $T(n)$ as the running time of MergeSort on a list of length n.

We take $n = 1$ as the basis case and $n > 1$ as the inductive case, where recursive calls are made. If we examine MergeSort, we observe that, unless we call MergeSort from another function with an argument that is an empty list, then there is no way to get a call with an empty list as argument. The reason is that we execute line (4) only when list has at least two elements, in which case the lists that result from a split will have at least one element each. Thus, we can ignore the case $n = 0$ and start our induction at $n = 1$.

BASIS. If list consists of a single element, then we execute lines (1) and (2), but none of the other code. Thus, in the basis case, $T(1)$ is $O(1)$.

INDUCTION. In the inductive case, the tests of lines (1) and (2) both fail, and so we execute the block of lines (3) and (4). To make things simpler, let us assume that n is a power of 2. The reason it helps to make this assumption is that when n is even, the split of the list is into two pieces of length exactly $n/2$. Moreover, if n is a power of 2, then $n/2$ is also a power of 2, and the divisions by 2 are all into equal-sized pieces until we get down to pieces of 1 element each, at which time the recursion ends. The time spent by MergeSort when $n > 1$ is the sum of the following terms:

1. $O(1)$ for the two tests

2. $O(1) + O(n)$ for the assignment and call to split on line (3)

3. $T(n/2)$ for the first recursive call to MergeSort on line (4)

4. $T(n/2)$ for the second recursive call to MergeSort on line (4)

5. $O(n)$ for the call to merge on line (4)

6. $O(1)$ for the return on line (4).

Inductions that Skip Some Values

The reader should not be concerned by the new kind of induction that is involved in the analysis of MergeSort, where we skip over all but the powers of 2 in our proof. In general, if $i_1, i_2, \ldots$ is a sequence of integers about which we want to prove a statement S, we can show $S(i_1)$ as a basis and then show for the induction that $S(i_j)$ implies $S(i_{j+1})$, for all j. That is an ordinary induction if we think of it as an induction on j. More precisely, define the statement S' by $S'(j) = S(i_j)$. Then we prove $S'(j)$ by induction on j. For the case at hand, $i_1 = 1$, $i_2 = 2$, $i_3 = 4$, and in general, $i_j = 2^{j-1}$.

Incidentally, note that $T(n)$, the running time of MergeSort, surely does not decrease as n increases. Thus, showing that $T(n)$ is $O(n \log n)$ for n equal to a power of 2 also shows that $T(n)$ is $O(n \log n)$ for all n.

If we add these terms, and drop the $O(1)$'s in favor of the larger $O(n)$'s that come from the calls to split and merge, we get the bound $2T(n/2) + O(n)$ for the time spent by MergeSort in the inductive case. We thus have the recurrence relation:

BASIS. $T(1) = O(1)$.

INDUCTION. $T(n) = 2T(n/2) + O(n)$, where n is a power of 2 and greater than 1.

Our next step is to replace the big-oh expressions by functions with concrete constants. We shall replace the $O(1)$ in the basis by constant a, and the $O(n)$ in the inductive step by bn, for some constant b. Our recurrence relation thus becomes

BASIS. $T(1) = a$.

INDUCTION. $T(n) = 2T(n/2) + bn$, where n is a power of 2 and greater than 1.

This recurrence is rather more complicated than the ones studied so far, but we can apply the same techniques. First, let us explore the values of $T(n)$ for some small n's. The basis tells us that $T(1) = a$. Then the inductive step says

$$
\begin{aligned}
T(2) &= 2T(1) + 2b && &&= 2a + 2b \\
T(4) &= 2T(2) + 4b &&= 2(2a + 2b) + 4b &&= 4a + 8b \\
T(8) &= 2T(4) + 8b &&= 2(4a + 8b) + 8b &&= 8a + 24b \\
T(16) &= 2T(8) + 16b &&= 2(8a + 24b) + 16b &&= 16a + 64b
\end{aligned}
$$

It may not be easy to see what is going on. Evidently, the coefficient of a keeps pace with the value of n; that is, $T(n)$ is n times a plus some number of b's. But the coefficient of b grows faster than any multiple of n. The relationship between n and the coefficient of b is summarized as follows:

Value of n	2	4	8	16
Coefficient of b	2	8	24	64
Ratio	1	2	3	4

The ratio is the coefficient of b divided by the value of n. Thus, it appears that the coefficient of b is n times another factor that grows by 1 each time n doubles. In particular, we can see that this ratio is $\log_2 n$, because $\log_2 2 = 1$, $\log_2 4 = 2$, $\log_2 8 = 3$, and $\log_2 16 = 4$. It is thus reasonable to conjecture that the solution to our recurrence relation is $T(n) = an + bn \log_2 n$, at least for n a power of 2. We shall see that this formula is correct.

To get a solution to the recurrence, let us follow the same strategy as for previous examples. We write the inductive rule with argument m, as

$$T(m) = 2T(m/2) + bm, \text{ for } m \text{ a power of 2 and } m > 1 \tag{3.5}$$

We then start with $T(n)$ and use (3.5) to replace $T(n)$ by an expression involving smaller values of the argument; in this case, the replacing expression involves $T(n/2)$. That is, we begin with

$$T(n) = 2T(n/2) + bn \tag{3.6}$$

Next, we use (3.5), with $n/2$ in place of m, to get a replacement for $T(n/2)$ in (3.6). That is, (3.5) says that $T(n/2) = 2T(n/4) + bn/2$, and we can replace (3.6) by

$$T(n) = 2\big(2T(n/4) + bn/2\big) + bn = 4T(n/4) + 2bn$$

Then, we can replace $T(n/4)$ by $2T(n/8) + bn/4$; the justification is (3.5) with $n/4$ in place of m. That gives us

$$T(n) = 4\big(2T(n/8) + bn/4\big) + 2bn = 8T(n/8) + 3bn$$

The statement that we shall prove by induction on i is

STATEMENT $S(i)$: If $1 \leq i \leq \log_2 n$, then $T(n) = 2^i T(n/2^i) + ibn$.

BASIS. For $i = 1$, the statement $S(1)$ says that $T(n) = 2T(n/2) + bn$. This equality is the inductive rule in the definition of $T(n)$, the running time of merge and sort, so we know that the basis holds.

INDUCTION. As in similar inductions where the inductive hypothesis is of the if-then form, the inductive step holds whenever i is outside the assumed range; here, $i \geq \log_2 n$ is the simple case, where $S(i + 1)$ is seen to hold.

For the hard part, suppose that $i < \log_2 n$. Also, assume the inductive hypothesis $S(i)$; that is, $T(n) = 2^i T(n/2^i) + ibn$. Substitute $n/2^i$ for m in (3.5) to get

$$T(n/2^i) = 2T(n/2^{i+1}) + bn/2^i \tag{3.7}$$

Substitute the right side of (3.7) for $T(n/2^i)$ in $S(i)$ to get

$$
\begin{aligned}
T(n) &= 2^i\big(2T(n/2^{i+1}) + bn/2^i\big) + ibn \\
&= 2^{i+1}T(n/2^{i+1}) + bn + ibn \\
&= 2^{i+1}T(n/2^{i+1}) + (i+1)bn
\end{aligned}
$$

The last equality is the statement $S(i + 1)$, and so we have proved the inductive step.

We conclude that the equality $S(i)$ — that is, $T(n) = 2^i T(n/2^i) + ibn$ — holds for any i between 1 and $\log_2 n$. Now consider the formula $S(\log_2 n)$, that is,

$$T(n) = 2^{\log_2 n} T(n/2^{\log_2 n}) + (\log_2 n)bn$$

We know that $2^{\log_2 n} = n$ (recall that the definition of $\log_2 n$ is the power to which we must raise 2 to equal n). Also, $n/2^{\log_2 n} = 1$. Thus, $S(\log_2 n)$ can be written

$$T(n) = nT(1) + bn \log_2 n$$

We also know that $T(1) = a$, by the basis of the definition of T. Thus,

$$T(n) = an + bn \log_2 n$$

After this analysis, we must replace the constants a and b by big-oh expressions. That is, $T(n)$ is $O(n) + O(n \log n)$.[8] Since n grows more slowly than $n \log n$, we may neglect the $O(n)$ term and say that $T(n)$ is $O(n \log n)$. That is, merge sort is an $O(n \log n)$-time algorithm. Remember that selection sort was shown to take $O(n^2)$ time. Although strictly speaking, $O(n^2)$ is only an upper bound, it is in fact the tightest simple bound for selection sort. Thus, we can be sure that, as n gets large, merge sort will always run faster than selection sort. In practice, merge sort is faster than selection sort for n's larger than a few dozen.

EXERCISES

3.10.1: Draw structure trees for the functions

a) `split`
b) `MergeSort`

Indicate the running time for each node of the trees.

3.10.2*: Define a function k-mergesort that splits a list into k pieces, sorts each piece, and then merges the result.

a)   What is the running time of k-mergesort as a function of k and n?
b)**What value of k gives the fastest algorithm (as a function of n)? This problem requires that you estimate the running times sufficiently precisely that you can distinguish constant factors. Since you cannot be that precise in practice, for the reasons we discussed at the beginning of the chapter, you really need to examine how the running time from (a) varies with k and get an approximate minimum.

❖❖ 3.11   Solving Recurrence Relations

There are many techniques for solving recurrence relations. In this section, we shall discuss two such approaches. The first, which we have already seen, is repeatedly substituting the inductive rule into itself until we get a relationship between $T(n)$ and $T(1)$ or — if 1 is not the basis — between $T(n)$ and $T(i)$ for some i that is covered by the basis. The second method we introduce is guessing a solution and checking its correctness by substituting into the basis and the inductive rules.

---

[8] Remember that inside a big-oh expression, we do not have to specify the base of a logarithm, because logarithms to all bases are the same, to within a constant factor.

In the previous two sections, we have solved exactly for $T(n)$. However, since $T(n)$ is really a big-oh upper bound on the exact running time, it is sufficient to find a tight upper bound on $T(n)$. Thus, especially for the "guess-and-check" approach, we require only that the solution be an upper bound on the true solution to the recurrence.

Solving Recurrences by Repeated Substitution

Probably the simplest form of recurrence that we encounter in practice is that of Example 3.24:

BASIS. $T(1) = a$.

INDUCTION. $T(n) = T(n-1) + b$, for $n > 1$.

We can generalize this form slightly if we allow the addition of some function $g(n)$ in place of the constant b in the induction. We can write this form as

BASIS. $T(1) = a$.

INDUCTION. $T(n) = T(n-1) + g(n)$, for $n > 1$.

This form arises whenever we have a recursive function that takes time $g(n)$ and then calls itself with an argument one smaller than the argument with which the current function call was made. Examples are the factorial function of Example 3.24, the function **merge** of Section 3.10, and the recursive selection sort of Section 2.7. In the first two of these functions, $g(n)$ is a constant, and in the third it is linear in n. The function **split** of Section 3.10 is almost of this form; it calls itself with an argument that is smaller by 2. We shall see that this difference is unimportant.

Let us solve this recurrence by repeated substitution. As in Example 3.24, we first write the inductive rule with the argument m, as

$$T(m) = T(m-1) + g(m)$$

and then proceed to substitute for T repeatedly in the right side of the original inductive rule. Doing this, we get the sequence of expressions

$$
\begin{aligned}
T(n) &= T(n-1) + g(n) \\
&= T(n-2) + g(n-1) + g(n) \\
&= T(n-3) + g(n-2) + g(n-1) + g(n) \\
&\quad \cdots \\
&= T(n-i) + g(n-i+1) + g(n-i+2) + \cdots + g(n-1) + g(n)
\end{aligned}
$$

Using the technique in Example 3.24, we can prove by induction on i, for $i = 1, 2, \ldots, n-1$, that

$$T(n) = T(n-i) + \sum_{j=0}^{i-1} g(n-j)$$

We want to pick a value for i so that $T(n-i)$ is covered by the basis; thus, we pick $i = n - 1$. Since $T(1) = a$, we have $T(n) = a + \sum_{j=0}^{n-2} g(n-j)$. Put another way, $T(n)$ is the constant a plus the sum of all the values of g from 2 to n, or $a + g(2) + g(3) + \cdots + g(n)$. Unless all the $g(j)$'s are 0, the a term will not matter when we convert this expression to a big-oh expression, and so we generally just need the sum of the $g(j)$'s.

✦ **Example 3.25.** Consider the recursive selection sort function of Fig. 2.22, the body of which we reproduce as Fig. 3.29. If we let $T(m)$ be the running time of the function `SelectionSort` when given an array of m elements to sort (that is, when the value of its argument i is $n - m$), we can develop a recurrence relation for $T(m)$ as follows. First, the basis case is $m = 1$. Here, only line (1) is executed, taking $O(1)$ time.

```
(1)        if (i < n-1) {
(2)                small = i;
(3)                for (j = i+1; j < n; j++)
(4)                    if (A[j] < A[small])
(5)                        small = j;
(6)                temp = A[small];
(7)                A[small] = A[i];
(8)                A[i] = temp;
(9)                recSS(A, i+1, n);
           }
      }
```

Fig. 3.29. Recursive selection sort.

For the inductive case, $m > 1$, we execute the test of line (1) and the assignments of lines (2), (6), (7), and (8), all of which take $O(1)$ time. The for-loop of lines (3) to (5) takes $O(n - i)$ time, or $O(m)$ time, as we discussed in connection with the iterative selection sort program in Example 3.17. To review why, note that the body, lines (4) and (5), takes $O(1)$ time, and we go $m - 1$ times around the loop. Thus, the time of the for-loop dominates lines (1) through (8), and we can write $T(m)$, the time of the entire function, as $T(m-1) + O(m)$. The second term, $O(m)$, covers lines (1) through (8), and the $T(m-1)$ term is the time for line (9), the recursive call. If we replace the hidden constant factors in the big-oh expressions by concrete constants, we get the recurrence relation

BASIS. $T(1) = a$.

INDUCTION. $T(m) = T(m-1) + bm$, for $m > 1$.

This recurrence is of the form we studied, with $g(m) = bm$. That is, the solution is

$$T(m) = a + \sum_{j=0}^{m-2} b(m-j)$$

$$= a + 2b + 3b + \cdots + mb$$

$$= a + b(m-1)(m+2)/2$$

Thus, $T(m)$ is $O(m^2)$. Since we are interested in the running time of function SelectionSort on the entire array of length n, that is, when called with $i = 1$, we need the expression for $T(n)$ and find that it is $O(n^2)$. Thus, the recursive version of selection sort is quadratic, just like the iterative version. ✦

Another common form of recurrence generalizes the recurrence we derived for MergeSort in the previous section:

BASIS. $T(1) = a$.

INDUCTION. $T(n) = 2T(n/2) + g(n)$, for n a power of 2 and greater than 1.

This is the recurrence for a recursive algorithm that solves a problem of size n by subdividing it into two subproblems, each of size $n/2$. Here $g(n)$ is the amount of time taken to create the subproblems and combine the solutions. For example, MergeSort divides a problem of size n into two problems of size $n/2$. The function $g(n)$ is bn for some constant b, since the time taken by MergeSort exclusive of recursive calls to itself is $O(n)$, principally for the split and merge algorithms.

To solve this recurrence, we substitute for T on the right side. Here we assume that $n = 2^k$ for some k. The recursive equation can be written with m as its argument: $T(m) = 2T(m/2) + g(m)$. If we substitute $n/2^i$ for m, we get

$$T(n/2^i) = 2T(n/2^{i+1}) + g(n/2^i) \tag{3.8}$$

If we start with the inductive rule and proceed to substitute for T using (3.8) with progressively greater values of i, we find

$$\begin{aligned}
T(n) &= 2T(n/2) + g(n) \\
&= 2\big(2T(n/2^2) + g(n/2)\big) + g(n) \\
&= 2^2 T(n/2^2) + 2g(n/2) + g(n) \\
&= 2^2\big(2T(n/2^3) + g(n/2^2)\big) + 2g(n/2) + g(n) \\
&= 2^3 T(n/2^3) + 2^2 g(n/2^2) + 2g(n/2) + g(n) \\
&\cdots \\
&= 2^i T(n/2^i) + \sum_{j=0}^{i-1} 2^j g(n/2^j)
\end{aligned}$$

If $n = 2^k$, we know that $T(n/2^k) = T(1) = a$. Thus, when $i = k$, that is, when $i = \log_2 n$, we obtain the solution

$$T(n) = an + \sum_{j=0}^{(\log_2 n)-1} 2^j g(n/2^j) \tag{3.9}$$

to our recurrence.

Intuitively, the first term of (3.9) represents the contribution of the basis value a. That is, there are n calls to the recursive function with an argument of size 1. The summation is the contribution of the recursion, and it represents the work performed by all the calls with argument size greater than 1.

Figure 3.30 suggests the accumulation of time during the execution of **Merge-Sort**. It represents the time to sort eight elements. The first row represents the work on the outermost call, involving all eight elements; the second row represents the work of the two calls with four elements each; and the third row is the four calls with two elements each. Finally, the bottom row represents the eight calls to **MergeSort** with a list of length one. In general, if there are n elements in the original unsorted list, there will be $\log_2 n$ levels at which bn work is done by calls to **MergeSort** that result in other calls. The accumulated time of all these calls is thus $bn \log_2 n$. There will be one level at which calls are made that do not result in further calls, and an is the total time spent by these calls. Note that the first $\log_2 n$ levels represent the terms of the summation in (3.9) and the lowest level represents the term an.

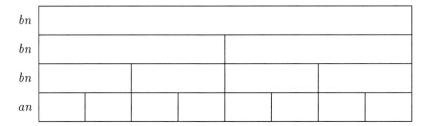

Fig. 3.30. Time spent by the calls to mergesort.

✦ **Example 3.26.** In the case of **MergeSort**, the function $g(n)$ is bn for some constant b. The solution (3.9) with these parameters is therefore

$$
\begin{aligned}
T(n) &= an + \sum_{j=0}^{(\log_2 n)-1} 2^j bn/2^j \\
&= an + bn \sum_{j=0}^{(\log_2 n)-1} 1 \\
&= an + bn \log n
\end{aligned}
$$

The last equality comes from the fact there are $\log_2 n$ terms in the sum and each term is 1. Thus, when $g(n)$ is linear, the solution to (3.9) is $O(n \log n)$. ✦

Solving Recurrences by Guessing a Solution

Another useful approach to solving recurrences is to guess a solution $f(n)$ and then use the recurrence to show that $T(n) \leq f(n)$. That may not give the exact value of $T(n)$, but if it gives a tight upper bound, we are satisfied. Often we guess only the functional form of $f(n)$, leaving some parameters unspecified; for example, we may guess that $f(n) = an^b$, for some a and b. The values of the parameters will be forced, as we try to prove $T(n) \le f(n)$ for all n.

Although we may consider it bizarre to imagine that we can guess solutions accurately, we can frequently deduce the high-order term by looking at the values of $T(n)$ for a few small values of n. We then throw in some lower-order terms as well, and see whether their coefficients turn out to be nonzero.[9]

✦   **Example 3.27.** Let us again examine the `MergeSort` recurrence relation from the previous section, which we wrote as

BASIS. $T(1) = a$.

INDUCTION. $T(n) = 2T(n/2) + bn$, for n a power of 2 and greater than 1.

We are going to guess that an upper bound to $T(n)$ is $f(n) = cn \log_2 n + d$ for some constants c and d. Recall that this form is not exactly right; in the previous example we derived the solution and saw that it had an $O(n \log n)$ term with an $O(n)$ term, rather than with a constant term. However, this guess turns out to be good enough to prove an $O(n \log n)$ upper bound on $T(n)$.

We shall use complete induction on n to prove the following, for some constants c and d:

STATEMENT $S(n)$: If n is a power of 2 and $n \ge 1$, then $T(n) \le f(n)$, where $f(n)$ is the function $cn \log_2 n + d$.

BASIS. When $n = 1$, $T(1) \le f(1)$ provided $a \le d$. The reason is that the $cn \log_2 n$ term of $f(n)$ is 0 when $n = 1$, so that $f(1) = d$, and it is given that $T(1) = a$.

INDUCTION. Let us assume $S(i)$ for all $i < n$, and prove $S(n)$ for some $n > 1$.[10] If n is not a power of 2, there is nothing to prove, since the if-portion of the if-then statement $S(n)$ is not true. Thus, consider the hard case, in which n is a power of 2. We may assume $S(n/2)$, that is,

$$T(n/2) \le (cn/2) \log_2(n/2) + d$$

because it is part of the inductive hypothesis. For the inductive step, we need to show that

$$T(n) \le f(n) = cn \log_2 n + d$$

When $n \ge 2$, the inductive part of the definition of $T(n)$ tells us that

$$T(n) \le 2T(n/2) + bn$$

---

[9]   If it is any comfort, the theory of differential equations, which in many ways resembles the theory of recurrence equations, also relies on known solutions to equations of a few common forms and then educated guessing to solve other equations.

[10]   In most complete inductions we assume $S(i)$ for i up to n and prove $S(n+1)$. In this case it is notationally simpler to prove $S(n)$ from $S(i)$, for $i < n$, which amounts to the same thing.

Manipulating Inequalities

In Example 3.27 we derive one inequality, $T(n) \leq cn \log_2 n + d$, from another,

$$T(n) \leq cn \log_2 n + (b - c)n + 2d$$

Our method was to find an "excess" and requiring it to be at most 0. The general principle is that if we have an inequality $A \leq B + E$, and if we want to show that $A \leq B$, then it is sufficient to show that $E \leq 0$. In Example 3.27, A is $T(n)$, B is $cn \log_2 n + d$, and E, the excess, is $(b - c)n + d$.

Using the inductive hypothesis to bound $T(n/2)$, we have

$$T(n) \leq 2[c(n/2) \log_2(n/2) + d] + bn$$

Since $\log_2(n/2) = \log_2 n - \log_2 2 = \log_2 n - 1$, we may simplify this expression to

$$T(n) \leq cn \log_2 n + (b - c)n + 2d \tag{3.10}$$

We now show that $T(n) \leq cn \log_2 n + d$, provided that the excess over $cn \log_2 n + d$ on the right side of (3.10) is at most 0; that is, $(b - c)n + d \leq 0$. Since $n > 1$, this inequality is true when $d \geq 0$ and $b - c \leq -d$.

We now have three constraints for $f(n) = cn \log n + d$ to be an upper bound on $T(n)$:

1.   The constraint $a \leq d$ comes from the basis.

2. $d \geq 0$ comes from the induction, but since we know that $a > 0$, this inequality is superseded by (1).

3. $b - c \leq -d$, or $c \geq b + d$, also comes from the induction.

These constraints are obviously satisfied if we let $d = a$ and $c = a + b$. We have now shown by induction on n that for all $n \geq 1$ and a power of 2,

$$T(n) \leq (a + b)n \log_2 n + a$$

This argument shows that $T(n)$ is $O(n \log n)$, that is, that $T(n)$ does not grow any faster than $n \log n$. However, the bound $(a + b)n \log_2 n + a$ that we obtained is slightly larger than the exact answer that we obtained in Example 3.26, which was $bn \log_2 n + an$. At least we were successful in obtaining a bound. Had we taken the simpler guess of $f(n) = cn \log_2 n$, we would have failed, because there is no value of c that can make $f(1) \geq a$. The reason is that $c \times 1 \times \log_2 1 = 0$, so that $f(1) = 0$. If $a > 0$, we evidently cannot make $f(1) \geq a$. ✦

✦ **Example 3.28.** Now let us consider a recurrence relation that we shall encounter later in the book:

BASIS. $G(1) = 3$.

INDUCTION. $G(n) = (2^{n/2} + 1)G(n/2)$, for $n > 1$.

Summary of Solutions

In the table below, we list the solutions to some of the most common recurrence relations, including some we have not covered in this section. In each case, we assume that the basis equation is $T(1) = a$ and that $k \geq 0$.

INDUCTIVE EQUATION	$T(n)$
$T(n) = T(n-1) + bn^k$	$O(n^{k+1})$
$T(n) = cT(n-1) + bn^k$, for $c > 1$	$O(c^n)$
$T(n) = cT(n/d) + bn^k$, for $c > d^k$	$O(n^{\log_d c})$
$T(n) = cT(n/d) + bn^k$, for $c < d^k$	$O(n^k)$
$T(n) = cT(n/d) + bn^k$, for $c = d^k$	$O(n^k \log n)$

All the above also hold if bn^k is replaced by any kth-degree polynomial.

This recurrence has actual numbers, like 3, instead of symbolic constants like a. In Chapter 13, we shall use recurrences such as this to count the number of gates in a circuit, and gates can be counted exactly, without needing the big-oh notation to hide unknowable constant factors.

If we think about a solution by repeated substitution, we might see that we are going to make $\log_2 n - 1$ substitutions before $G(n)$ is expressed in terms of $G(1)$. As we make the substitutions, we generate factors

$$(2^{n/2} + 1)(2^{n/4} + 1)(2^{n/8} + 1) \cdots (2^1 + 1)$$

If we neglect the "+1" term in each factor, we have approximately the product $2^{n/2}2^{n/4}2^{n/8} \cdots 2^1$, which is

$$2^{n/2 + n/4 + n/8 + \cdots + 1}$$

or 2^{n-1} if we sum the geometric series in the exponent. That is half of 2^n, and so we might guess that 2^n is a term in the solution $G(n)$. However, if we guess that $f(n) = c2^n$ is an upper bound on $G(n)$, we shall fail, as the reader may check. That is, we get two inequalities involving c that have no solution.

We shall thus guess the next simplest form, $f(n) = c2^n + d$, and here we shall be successful. That is, we can prove the following statement by complete induction on n for some constants c and d:

STATEMENT $S(n)$: If n is a power of 2 and $n \geq 1$, then $G(n) \leq c2^n + d$.

BASIS. If $n = 1$, then we must show that $G(1) \leq c2^1 + d$, that is, that $3 \leq 2c + d$. This inequality becomes one of the constraints on c and d.

INDUCTION. As in Example 3.27, the only hard part occurs when n is a power of 2 and we want to prove $S(n)$ from $S(n/2)$. The equation in this case is

$$G(n/2) \leq c2^{n/2} + d$$

We must prove $S(n)$, which is $G(n) \leq c2^n + d$. We start with the inductive definition of G,

$$G(n) = (2^{n/2} + 1)G(n/2)$$

and then substitute our upper bound for $G(n/2)$, converting this expression to

$$G(n) \leq (2^{n/2} + 1)(c2^{n/2} + d)$$

Simplifying, we get

$$G(n) \leq c2^n + (c + d)2^{n/2} + d$$

That will give the desired upper bound, $c2^n + d$, on $G(n)$, provided that the excess on the right, $(c + d)2^{n/2}$, is no more than 0. It is thus sufficient that $c + d \leq 0$.

We need to select c and d to satisfy the two inequalities

1. $2c + d \geq 3$, from the basis, and

2. $c + d \leq 0$, from the induction.

For example, these inequalities are satisfied if $c = 3$ and $d = -3$. Then we know that $G(n) \leq 3(2^n - 1)$. Thus, $G(n)$ grows exponentially with n. It happens that this function is the exact solution, that is, that $G(n) = 3(2^n - 1)$, as the reader may prove by induction on n. ✦

EXERCISES

3.11.1: Let $T(n)$ be defined by the recurrence

$$T(n) = T(n - 1) + g(n), \text{ for } n > 1$$

Prove by induction on i that if $1 \leq i < n$, then

$$T(n) = T(n - i) + \sum_{j=0}^{i-1} g(n - j)$$

3.11.2: Suppose we have a recurrence of the form

$$T(1) = a$$
$$T(n) = T(n - 1) + g(n), \text{ for } n > 1$$

Give tight big-oh upper bounds on the solution if $g(n)$ is

a) n^2
b) $n^2 + 3n$
c) $n^{3/2}$
d) $n \log n$
e) 2^n

3.11.3: Suppose we have a recurrence of the form

$$T(1) = a$$
$$T(n) = T(n/2) + g(n), \text{ for } n \text{ a power of 2 and } n > 1$$

Give tight big-oh upper bounds on the solution if $g(n)$ is

a) n^2
b) $2n$
c) 10
d) $n \log n$
e) 2^n

3.11.4*: Guess each of the following as the solution to the recurrence

$T(1) = a$
$T(n) = 2T(n/2) + bn$, for n a power of 2 and $n > 1$

a) $cn \log_2 n + dn + e$
b) $cn + d$
c) cn^2

What constraints on the unknown constants c, d, and e are implied? For which of these forms does there exist an upper bound on $T(n)$?

3.11.5: Show that if we guess $G(n) \leq c2^n$ for the recurrence of Example 3.28, we fail to find a solution.

3.11.6*: Show that if

$T(1) = a$
$T(n) = T(n-1) + n^k$, for $n > 1$

then $T(n)$ is $O(n^{k+1})$. You may assume $k \geq 0$. Also, show that this is the tightest simple big-oh upper bound, that is, that $T(n)$ is not $O(n^m)$ if $m < k + 1$. *Hint*: Expand $T(n)$ in terms of $T(n-i)$, for $i = 1, 2, \ldots$, to get the upper bound. For the lower bound, show that $T(n)$ is at least cn^{k+1} for some particular $c > 0$.

3.11.7**: Show that if

$T(1) = a$
$T(n) = cT(n-1) + p(n)$, for $n > 1$

where $p(n)$ is any polynomial in n and $c > 1$, then $T(n)$ is $O(c^n)$. Also, show that this is the tightest simple big-oh upper bound, that is, that $T(n)$ is not $O(d^n)$ if $d < c$.

3.11.8**: Consider the recurrence

$T(1) = a$
$T(n) = cT(n/d) + bn^k$, for n a power of d

Iteratively expand $T(n)$ in terms of $T(n/d^i)$ for $i = 1, 2, \ldots$. Show that

a) If $c > d^k$, then $T(n)$ is $O(n^{\log_d c})$
b) If $c = d^k$, then $T(n)$ is $O(n^k \log n)$
c) If $c < d^k$, then $T(n)$ is $O(n^k)$

3.11.9: Solve the following recurrences, each of which has $T(1) = a$:

a) $T(n) = 3T(n/2) + n^2$, for n a power of 2 and $n > 1$
b) $T(n) = 10T(n/3) + n^2$, for n a power of 3 and $n > 1$
c) $T(n) = 16T(n/4) + n^2$, for n a power of 4 and $n > 1$

You may use the solutions of Exercise 3.11.8.

3.11.10: Solve the recurrence

$$T(1) = 1$$
$$T(n) = 3^n T(n/2), \text{ for } n \text{ a power of 2 and } n > 1$$

3.11.11: The *Fibonacci recurrence* is $F(0) = F(1) = 1$, and

$$F(n) = F(n-1) + F(n-2), \text{ for } n > 1$$

Golden ratio

The values $F(0), F(1), F(2), \ldots$ form the sequence of Fibonacci numbers, in which each number after the first two is the sum of the two previous numbers. (See Exercise 3.9.4.) Let $r = (1 + \sqrt{5})/2$. This constant r is called the *golden ratio* and its value is about 1.62. Show that $F(n)$ is $O(r^n)$. *Hint*: For the induction, it helps to guess that $F(n) \le ar^n$ for some n, and attempt to prove that inequality by induction on n. The basis must incorporate the two values $n = 0$ and $n = 1$. In the inductive step, it helps to notice that r satisfies the equation $r^2 = r + 1$.

✦✦ 3.12   Summary of Chapter 3

Here are the important concepts covered in Chapter 3.

✦   Many factors go into the selection of an algorithm for a program, but simplicity, ease of implementation, and efficiency often dominate.

✦   Big-oh expressions provide a convenient notation for upper bounds on the running times of programs.

✦   There are recursive rules for evaluating the running time of the various compound statements of C, such as for-loops and conditions, in terms of the running times of their constituent parts.

✦   We can evaluate the running time of a function by drawing a structure tree that represents the nesting structure of statements and evaluating the running time of the various pieces in a bottom-up order.

✦   Recurrence relations are a natural way to model the running time of recursive programs.

✦   We can solve recurrence relations either by iterated substitution or by guessing a solution and checking our guess is correct.

Divide and conquer is an important algorithm-design technique in which a problem is partitioned into subproblems, the solutions to which can be combined to provide a solution to the whole problem. A few rules of thumb can be used to evaluate the running time of the resulting algorithm: A function that takes time $O(1)$ and then calls itself on a subproblem of size $n-1$ takes time $O(n)$. Examples are the factorial function and the merge function.

✦   More generally, a function that takes time $O(n^k)$ and then calls itself on a subproblem of size $n - 1$ takes time $O(n^{k+1})$.

♦ If a function calls itself twice but the recursion goes on for $\log_2 n$ levels (as in merge sort), then the total running time is $O(n \log n)$ times the work done at each call, plus $O(n)$ times the work done at the basis. In the case of merge sort, the work at each call, including basis calls, is $O(1)$, so the total running time is $O(n \log n) + O(n)$, or just $O(n \log n)$.

♦ If a function calls itself twice and the recursion goes on for n levels (as in the Fibonacci program of Exercise 3.9.4), then the running time is exponential in n.

✦✦✦ 3.13 Bibliographic Notes for Chapter 3

The study of the running time of programs and the computational complexity of problems was pioneered by Hartmanis and Stearns [1964]. Knuth [1968] was the book that established the study of the running time of algorithms as an essential ingredient in computer science.

Since that time, a rich theory for the difficulty of problems has been developed. Many of the key ideas are found in Aho, Hopcroft, and Ullman [1974, 1983].

In this chapter, we have concentrated on upper bounds for the running times of programs. Knuth [1976] describes analogous notations for lower bounds and exact bounds on running times.

For more discussion of divide and conquer as an algorithm-design technique, see Aho, Hopcroft, and Ullman [1974] or Borodin and Munro [1975]. Additional information on techniques for solving recurrence relations can be found in Graham, Knuth, and Patashnik [1989].

Aho, A. V., J. E. Hopcroft, and J. D. Ullman [1974]. *The Design and Analysis of Computer Algorithms*, Addison-Wesley, Reading, Mass.

Aho, A. V., J. E. Hopcroft, and J. D. Ullman [1983]. *Data Structures and Algorithms*, Addison-Wesley, Reading, Mass.

Borodin, A. B., and I. Munro [1975]. *The Computational Complexity of Algebraic and Numeric Problems*, American Elsevier, New York.

Graham, R. L., D. E. Knuth, and O. Patashnik [1989]. *Concrete Mathematics: a Foundation for Computer Science*, Addison-Wesley, Reading, Mass.

Knuth, D. E. [1968]. *The Art of Computer Programming* Vol. I: *Fundamental Algorithms*, Addison-Wesley, Reading, Mass.

Knuth, D. E. [1976]. "Big omicron, big omega, and big theta," *ACM SIGACT News* **8**:2, pp. 18–23.

CHAPTER 4

Combinatorics and Probability

❖❖

In computer science we frequently need to count things and measure the likelihood of events. The science of counting is captured by a branch of mathematics called *combinatorics*. The concepts that surround attempts to measure the likelihood of events are embodied in a field called *probability theory*. This chapter introduces the rudiments of these two fields. We shall learn how to answer questions such as how many execution paths are there in a program, or what is the likelihood of occurrence of a given path?

❖❖ 4.1 What This Chapter Is About

We shall study combinatorics, or "counting," by presenting a sequence of increasingly more complex situations, each of which is represented by a simple paradigm problem. For each problem, we derive a formula that lets us determine the number of possible outcomes. The problems we study are:

✦   Counting assignments (Section 4.2). The paradigm problem is how many ways can we paint a row of n houses, each in any of k colors.

✦   Counting permutations (Section 4.3). The paradigm problem here is to determine the number of different orderings for n distinct items.

✦   Counting ordered selections (Section 4.4), that is, the number of ways to pick k things out of n and arrange the k things in order. The paradigm problem is counting the number of ways different horses can win, place, and show in a horse race.

✦   Counting the combinations of m things out of n (Section 4.5), that is, the selection of m from n distinct objects, without regard to the order of the selected objects. The paradigm problem is counting the number of possible poker hands.

156

◆   Counting permutations with some identical items (Section 4.6). The paradigm problem is counting the number of anagrams of a word that may have some letters appearing more than once.

◆   Counting the number of ways objects, some of which may be identical, can be distributed among bins (Section 4.7). The paradigm problem is counting the number of ways of distributing fruits to children.

In the second half of this chapter we discuss probability theory, covering the following topics:

◆   Basic concepts: probability spaces, experiments, events, probabilities of events.

◆   Conditional probabilities and independence of events. These concepts help us think about how observation of the outcome of one experiment, e.g., the drawing of a card, influences the probability of future events.

◆   Probabilistic reasoning and ways that we can estimate probabilities of combinations of events from limited data about the probabilities and conditional probabilities of events.

We also discuss some applications of probability theory to computing, including systems for making likely inferences from data and a class of useful algorithms that work "with high probability" but are not guaranteed to work all the time.

❖❖ 4.2   Counting Assignments

One of the simplest but most important counting problems deals with a list of items, to each of which we must assign one of a fixed set of values. We need to determine how many different assignments of values to items are possible.

◆   **Example 4.1.** A typical example is suggested by Fig. 4.1, where we have four houses in a row, and we may paint each in one of three colors: red, green, or blue. Here, the houses are the "items" mentioned above, and the colors are the "values." Figure 4.1 shows one possible assignment of colors, in which the first house is painted red, the second and fourth blue, and the third green.

Red   Blue   Green   Blue

Fig. 4.1. One assignment of colors to houses.

To answer the question, "How many different assignments are there?" we first need to define what we mean by an "assignment." In this case, an assignment is a list of four values, in which each value is chosen from one of the three colors red, green, or blue. We shall represent these colors by the letters R, G, and B. Two such lists are *different* if and only if they differ in at least one position.

In the example of houses and colors, we can choose any of three colors for the first house. Whatever color we choose for the first house, there are three colors in which to paint the second house. There are thus nine different ways to paint the first two houses, corresponding to the nine different pairs of letters, each letter chosen from R, G, and B. Similarly, for each of the nine assignments of colors to the first two houses, we may select a color for the third house in three possible ways. Thus, there are $9 \times 3 = 27$ ways to paint the first three houses. Finally, each of these 27 assignments can be extended to the fourth house in 3 different ways, giving a total of $27 \times 3 = 81$ assignments of colors to the houses. ✦

The Rule for Counting Assignments

Assignment

We can extend the above example. In the general setting, we have a list of n "items," such as the houses in Example 4.1. There is also a set of k "values," such as the colors in Example 4.1, any one of which can be assigned to an item. An *assignment* is a list of n values $(v_1, v_2, \ldots, v_n)$. Each of $v_1, v_2, \ldots, v_n$ is chosen to be one of the k values. This assignment assigns the value v_i to the ith item, for $i = 1, 2, \ldots, n$.

There are k^n different assignments when there are n items and each item is to be assigned one of k values. For instance, in Example 4.1 we had $n = 4$ items, the houses, and $k = 3$ values, the colors. We calculated that there were 81 different assignments. Note that $3^4 = 81$. We can prove the general rule by an induction on n.

STATEMENT $S(n)$: The number of ways to assign any one of k values to each of n items is k^n.

BASIS. The basis is $n = 1$. If there is one item, we can choose any of the k values for it. Thus there are k different assignments. Since $k^1 = k$, the basis is proved.

INDUCTION. Suppose the statement $S(n)$ is true, and consider $S(n + 1)$, the statement that there are k^{n+1} ways to assign one of k values to each of $n+1$ items. We may break any such assignment into a choice of value for the first item and, for each choice of first value, an assignment of values to the remaining n items. There are k choices of value for the first item. For each such choice, by the inductive hypothesis there are k^n assignments of values to the remaining n items. The total number of assignments is thus $k \times k^n$, or k^{n+1}. We have thus proved $S(n + 1)$ and completed the induction.

Figure 4.2 suggests this selection of first value and the associated choices of assignment for the remaining items in the case that $n + 1 = 4$ and $k = 3$, using as a concrete example the four houses and three colors of Example 4.1. There, we assume by the inductive hypothesis that there are 27 assignments of three colors to three houses.

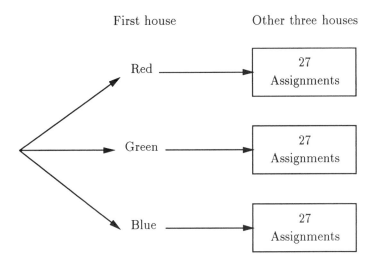

First house   Other three houses

Fig. 4.2. The number of ways to paint 4 houses using 3 colors.

Counting Bit Strings

Bit

In computer systems, we frequently encounter strings of 0's and 1's, and these strings often are used as the names of objects. For example, we may purchase a computer with "64 megabytes of main memory." Each of the bytes has a name, and that name is a sequence of 26 *bits*, each of which is either a 0 or 1. The string of 0's and 1's representing the name is called a *bit string*.

Why 26 bits for a 64-megabyte memory? The answer lies in an assignment-counting problem. When we count the number of bit strings of length n, we may think of the "items" as the positions of the string, each of which may hold a 0 or a 1. The "values" are thus 0 and 1. Since there are two values, we have $k = 2$, and the number of assignments of 2 values to each of n items is 2^n.

If $n = 26$ — that is, we consider bit strings of length 26 — there are 2^{26} possible strings. The exact value of 2^{26} is 67,108,864. In computer parlance, this number is thought of as "64 million," although obviously the true number is about 5% higher. The box about powers of 2 tells us a little about the subject and tries to explain the general rules involved in naming the powers of 2.

EXERCISES

4.2.1: In how many ways can we paint

a)   Three houses, each in any of four colors
b)   Five houses, each in any of five colors
c)   Two houses, each in any of ten colors

4.2.2: Suppose a computer password consists of eight to ten letters and/or digits. How many different possible passwords are there? Remember that an upper-case letter is different from a lower-case one.

4.2.3*: Consider the function f in Fig. 4.3. How many different values can f return?

```
int f(int x)
{
    int n;

    n = 1;
    if (x%2 == 0) n *= 2;
    if (x%3 == 0) n *= 3;
    if (x%5 == 0) n *= 5;
    if (x%7 == 0) n *= 7;
    if (x%11 == 0) n *= 11;
    if (x%13 == 0) n *= 13;
    if (x%17 == 0) n *= 17;
    if (x%19 == 0) n *= 19;
    return n;
}
```

Fig. 4.3. Function `f`.

4.2.4: In the game of "Hollywood squares," X's and O's may be placed in any of the nine squares of a tic-tac-toe board (a 3×3 matrix) in any combination (i.e., unlike ordinary tic-tac-toe, it is not necessary that X's and O's be placed alternately, so, for example, all the squares could wind up with X's). Squares may also be blank, i.e., not containing either an X or and O. How many different boards are there?

4.2.5: How many different strings of length n can be formed from the ten digits? A digit may appear any number of times in the string or not at all.

4.2.6: How many different strings of length n can be formed from the 26 lower-case letters? A letter may appear any number of times or not at all.

4.2.7: Convert the following into K's, M's, G's, T's, or P's, according to the rules of the box in Section 4.2: (a) 2^{13} (b) 2^{17} (c) 2^{24} (d) 2^{38} (e) 2^{45} (f) 2^{59}.

4.2.8*: Convert the following powers of 10 into approximate powers of 2: (a) 10^{12} (b) 10^{18} (c) 10^{99}.

❖ 4.3   Counting Permutations

In this section we shall address another fundamental counting problem: Given n distinct objects, in how many different ways can we order those objects in a line? Such an ordering is called a *permutation* of the objects. We shall let $\Pi(n)$ stand for the number of permutations of n objects.

As one example of where counting permutations is significant in computer science, suppose we are given n objects, $a_1, a_2, \ldots, a_n$, to sort. If we know nothing about the objects, it is possible that any order will be the correct sorted order, and thus the number of possible outcomes of the sort will be equal to $\Pi(n)$, the number of permutations of n objects. We shall soon see that this observation helps us argue that general-purpose sorting algorithms require time proportional to $n \log n$, and therefore that algorithms like merge sort, which we saw in Section 3.10 takes

---

K's and M's and Powers of 2

A useful trick for converting powers of 2 into decimal is to notice that 2^{10}, or 1024, is very close to one thousand. Thus 2^{30} is $(2^{10})^3$, or about 1000^3, that is, a billion. Then, $2^{32} = 4 \times 2^{30}$, or about four billion. In fact, computer scientists often accept the fiction that 2^{10} is *exactly* 1000 and speak of 2^{10} as "1K"; the K stands for "kilo." We convert 2^{15}, for example, into "32K," because

$$2^{15} = 2^5 \times 2^{10} = 32 \times \text{"1000"}$$

But 2^{20}, which is exactly 1,048,576, we call "1M," or "one million," rather than "1000K" or "1024K." For powers of 2 between 20 and 29, we factor out 2^{20}. Thus, 2^{26} is $2^6 \times 2^{20}$ or 64 "million." That is why 2^{26} bytes is referred to as 64 million bytes or 64 "megabytes."

Below is a table that gives the terms for various powers of 10 and their rough equivalents in powers of 2.

PREFIX	LETTER	VALUE
Kilo	K	10^3 or 2^{10}
Mega	M	10^6 or 2^{20}
Giga	G	10^9 or 2^{30}
Tera	T	10^{12} or 2^{40}
Peta	P	10^{15} or 2^{50}

This table suggests that for powers of 2 beyond 29 we factor out 2^{30}, 2^{40}, or 2 raised to whatever multiple-of-10 power we can. The remaining powers of 2 name the number of giga-, tera-, or peta- of whatever unit we are measuring. For example, 2^{43} bytes is 8 terabytes.

$O(n \log n)$ time, are to within a constant factor as fast as can be.

There are many other applications of the counting rule for permutations. For example, it figures heavily in more complex counting questions like combinations and probabilities, as we shall see in later sections.

♦ **Example 4.2.** To develop some intuition, let us enumerate the permutations of small numbers of objects. First, it should be clear that $\Pi(1) = 1$. That is, if there is only one object A, there is only one order: A.

Now suppose there are two objects, A and B. We may select one of the two objects to be first and then the remaining object is second. Thus there are two orders: AB and BA. Therefore, $\Pi(2) = 2 \times 1 = 2$.

Next, let there be three objects: A, B, and C. We may select any of the three to be first. Consider the case in which we select A to be first. Then the remaining two objects, B and C, can be arranged in either of the two orders for two objects to complete the permutation. We thus see that there are two orders that begin with A, namely ABC and ACB.

Similarly, if we start with B, there are two ways to complete the order, corresponding to the two ways in which we may order the remaining objects A and C. We thus have orders BAC and BCA. Finally, if we start with C first, we can order the remaining objects A and B in the two possible ways, giving us orders CAB and CBA. These six orders,

$$ABC, \ ACB, \ BAC, \ BCA, \ CAB, \ CBA$$

are all the possible orders of three elements. That is, $\Pi(3) = 3 \times 2 \times 1 = 6$.

Next, consider how many permutations there are for 4 objects: A, B, C, and D. If we pick A first, we may follow A by the objects B, C, and D in any of their 6 orders. Similarly, if we pick B first, we can order the remaining A, C, and D in any of their 6 ways. The general pattern should now be clear. We can pick any of the four elements first, and for each such selection, we can order the remaining three elements in any of the $\Pi(3) = 6$ possible ways. It is important to note that the number of permutations of the three objects does not depend on which three elements they are. We conclude that the number of permutations of 4 objects is 4 times the number of permutations of 3 objects. ✦

More generally,

$$\Pi(n + 1) = (n + 1)\Pi(n) \text{ for any } n \geq 1 \tag{4.1}$$

That is, to count the permutations of $n + 1$ objects we may pick any of the $n + 1$ objects to be first. We are then left with n remaining objects, and these can be permuted in $\Pi(n)$ ways, as suggested in Fig. 4.4. For our example where $n + 1 = 4$, we have $\Pi(4) = 4 \times \Pi(3) = 4 \times 6 = 24$.

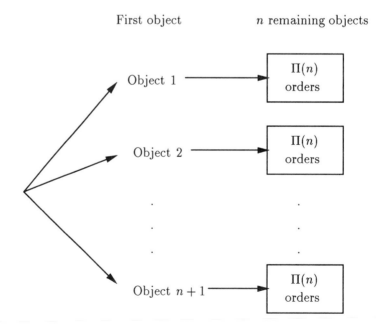

Fig. 4.4. The permutations of $n + 1$ objects.

The Formula for Permutations

Equation (4.1) is the inductive step in the definition of the factorial function introduced in Section 2.5. Thus it should not be a surprise that $\Pi(n)$ equals $n!$. We can prove this equivalence by a simple induction.

STATEMENT $S(n)$: $\Pi(n) = n!$ for all $n \geq 1$.

BASIS. For $n = 1$, $S(1)$ says that there is 1 permutation of 1 object. We observed this simple point in Example 4.2.

INDUCTION. Suppose $\Pi(n) = n!$. Then $S(n+1)$, which we must prove, says that $\Pi(n+1) = (n+1)!$. We start with Equation (4.1), which says that

$$\Pi(n+1) = (n+1) \times \Pi(n)$$

By the inductive hypothesis, $\Pi(n) = n!$. Thus, $\Pi(n+1) = (n+1)n!$. Since

$$n! = n \times (n-1) \times \cdots \times 1$$

it must be that $(n+1) \times n! = (n+1) \times n \times (n-1) \times \cdots \times 1$. But the latter product is $(n+1)!$, which proves $S(n+1)$.

✦ **Example 4.3.** As a result of the formula $\Pi(n) = n!$, we conclude that the number of permutations of 4 objects is $4! = 4 \times 3 \times 2 \times 1 = 24$, as we saw above. As another example, the number of permutations of 7 objects is $7! = 5040$. ✦

How Long Does it Take to Sort?

One of the interesting uses of the formula for counting permutations is in a proof that sorting algorithms must take at least time proportional to $n \log n$ to sort n elements, unless they make use of some special properties of the elements. For example, as we note in the box on special-case sorting algorithms, we can do better than proportional to $n \log n$ if we write a sorting algorithm that works only for small integers.

However, if a sorting algorithm works on any kind of data, as long as it can be compared by some "less than" notion, then the only way the algorithm can decide on the proper order is to consider the outcome of a test for whether one of two elements is less than the other. A sorting algorithm is called a *general-purpose sorting algorithm* if its only operation upon the elements to be sorted is a comparison between two of them to determine their relative order. For instance, selection sort and merge sort of Chapter 2 each make their decisions that way. Even though we wrote them for integer data, we could have written them more generally by replacing comparisons like

General purpose sorting algorithm

```
if (A[j] < A[small])
```

on line (4) of Fig. 2.2 by a test that calls a Boolean-valued function such as

```
if (lessThan(A[j], A[small]))
```

Suppose we are given n distinct elements to sort. The answer — that is, the correct sorted order — can be any of the $n!$ permutations of these elements. If our algorithm for sorting arbitrary types of elements is to work correctly, it must be able to distinguish all $n!$ different possible answers.

Consider the first comparison of elements that the algorithm makes, say

```
lessThan(X,Y)
```

For each of the $n!$ possible sorted orders, either X is less than Y or it is not. Thus, the $n!$ possible orders are divided into two groups, those for which the answer to the first test is "yes" and those for which it is "no."

One of these groups must have at least $n!/2$ members. For if both groups have fewer than $n!/2$ members, then the total number of orders is less than $n!/2 + n!/2$, or less than $n!$ orders. But this upper limit on orders contradicts the fact that we started with exactly $n!$ orders.

Now consider the second test, on the assumption that the outcome of the comparison between X and Y was such that the larger of the two groups of possible orders remains (take either outcome if the groups are the same size). That is, at least $n!/2$ orders remain, among which the algorithm must distinguish. The second comparison likewise has two possible outcomes, and at least half the remaining orders will be consistent with one of these outcomes. Thus, we can find a group of at least $n!/4$ orders consistent with the first two tests.

We can repeat this argument until the algorithm has determined the correct sorted order. At each step, by focusing on the outcome with the larger population of consistent possible orders, we are left with at least half as many possible orders as at the previous step. Thus, we can find a sequence of tests and outcomes such that after the ith test, there are at least $n!/2^i$ orders consistent with all these outcomes.

Since we cannot finish sorting until every sequence of tests and outcomes is consistent with at most one sorted order, the number of tests t made before we finish must satisfy the equation

$$n!/2^t \leq 1 \tag{4.2}$$

If we take logarithms base 2 of both sides of Equation (4.2) we have $\log_2 n! - t \leq 0$, or

$$t \geq \log_2(n!)$$

We shall see that $\log_2(n!)$ is about $n \log_2 n$. But first, let us consider an example of the process of splitting the possible orders.

♦ **Example 4.3.** Let us consider how the selection sort algorithm of Fig. 2.2 makes its decisions when given three elements (a, b, c) to sort. The first comparison is between a and b, as suggested at the top of Fig. 4.5, where we show in the box that all 6 possible orders are consistent before we make any tests. After the test, the orders abc, acb, and cab are consistent with the "yes" outcome (i.e., $a < b$), while the orders bac, bca, and cba are consistent with the opposite outcome, where $b > a$. We again show in a box the consistent orders in each case.

In the algorithm of Fig. 2.2, the index of the smaller becomes the value small. Thus, we next compare c with the smaller of a and b. Note that which test is made next depends on the outcome of previous tests.

After making the second decision, the smallest of the three is moved into the first position of the array, and a third comparison is made to determine which of the remaining elements is the larger. That comparison is the last comparison made by the algorithm when three elements are to be sorted. As we see at the bottom of Fig. 4.5, sometimes that decision is determined. For example, if we have already found $a < b$ and $c < a$, then c is the smallest and the last comparison of a and b must find a smaller.

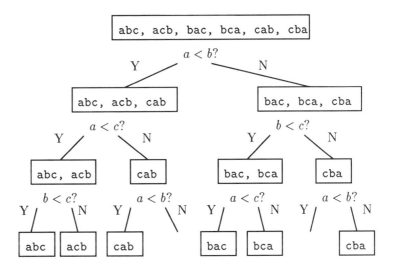

Fig. 4.5. Decision tree for selection sorting of 3 elements.

In this example, all paths involve 3 decisions, and at the end there is at most one consistent order, which is the correct sorted order. The two paths with no consistent order never occur. Equation (4.2) tells us that the number of tests t must be at least $\log_2 3!$, which is $\log_2 6$. Since 6 is between 2^2 and 2^3, we know that $\log_2 6$ will be between 2 and 3. Thus, at least some sequences of outcomes in any algorithm that sorts three elements must make 3 tests. Since selection sort makes only 3 tests for 3 elements, it is at least as good as any other sorting algorithm for 3 elements in the worst case. Of course, as the number of elements becomes large, we know that selection sort is not as good as can be done, since it is an $O(n^2)$ sorting algorithm and there are better algorithms such as merge sort. ✦

We must now estimate how large $\log_2 n!$ is. Since $n!$ is the product of all the integers from 1 to n, it is surely larger than the product of only the $\frac{n}{2} + 1$ integers from $n/2$ through n. This product is in turn at least as large as $n/2$ multiplied by itself $n/2$ times, or $(n/2)^{n/2}$. Thus, $\log_2 n!$ is at least $\log_2\big((n/2)^{n/2}\big)$. But the latter is $\frac{n}{2}(\log_2 n - \log_2 2)$, which is

$$\frac{n}{2}(\log_2 n - 1)$$

For large n, this formula is approximately $(n \log_2 n)/2$.

A more careful analysis will tell us that the factor of $1/2$ does not have to be there. That is, $\log_2 n!$ is very close to $n \log_2 n$ rather than to half that expression.

A Linear-Time Special-Purpose Sorting Algorithm

If we restrict the inputs on which a sorting algorithm will work, it can in one step divide the possible orders into more than 2 parts and thus work in less than time proportional to $n \log n$. Here is a simple example that works if the input is n distinct integers, each chosen in the range 0 to $2n - 1$.

```
(1)    for (i = 0; i < 2*n; i++)
(2)        count[i] = 0;
(3)    for (i = 0; i < n; i++)
(4)        count[a[i]]++;
(5)    for (i = 0; i < 2*n; i++)
(6)        if (count[i] > 0)
(7)            printf("%d\n", i);
```

We assume the input is in an array a of length n. In lines (1) and (2) we initialize an array count of length $2n$ to 0. Then in lines (3) and (4) we add 1 to the count for x if x is the value of a[i], the ith input element. Finally, in the last three lines we print each of the integers i such that count[i] is positive. Thus we print those elements appearing one or more times in the input and, on the assumption the inputs are distinct, it prints all the input elements, sorted smallest first.

We can analyze the running time of this algorithm easily. Lines (1) and (2) are a loop that iterates $2n$ times and has a body taking $O(1)$ time. Thus, it takes $O(n)$ time. The same applies to the loop of lines (3) and (4), but it iterates n times rather than $2n$ times; it too takes $O(n)$ time. Finally, the body of the loop of lines (5) through (7) takes $O(1)$ time and it is iterated $2n$ times. Thus, all three loops take $O(n)$ time, and the entire sorting algorithm likewise takes $O(n)$ time. Note that if given an input for which the algorithm is not tailored, such as integers in a range larger than 0 through $2n - 1$, the program above fails to sort correctly.

We have shown only that any general-purpose sorting algorithm must have some input for which it makes about $n \log_2 n$ comparisons or more. Thus any general-purpose sorting algorithm must take at least time proportional to $n \log n$ in the worst case. In fact, it can be shown that the same applies to the "average" input. That is, the average over all inputs of the time taken by a general-purpose sorting algorithm must be at least proportional to $n \log n$. Thus, merge sort is about as good as we can do, since it has this big-oh running time for all inputs.

EXERCISES

4.3.1: Suppose we have selected 9 players for a baseball team.

a)   How many possible batting orders are there?
b)   If the pitcher has to bat last, how many possible batting orders are there?

4.3.2: How many comparisons does the selection sort algorithm of Fig. 2.2 make if there are 4 elements? Is this number the best possible? Show the top 3 levels of the decision tree in the style of Fig. 4.5.

4.3.3: How many comparisons does the merge sort algorithm of Section 2.8 make if there are 4 elements? Is this number the best possible? Show the top 3 levels of the decision tree in the style of Fig. 4.5.

4.3.4*: Are there more assignments of n values to n items or permutations of $n + 1$ items? *Note*: The answer may not be the same for all n.

4.3.5*: Are there more assignments of $n/2$ values to n items than there are permutations of n items?

4.3.6**: Show how to sort n integers in the range 0 to $n^2 - 1$ in $O(n)$ time.

✦✦ 4.4   Ordered Selections

Sometimes we wish to select only some of the items in a set and give them an order. Let us generalize the function $\Pi(n)$ that counted permutations in the previous section to a two-argument function $\Pi(n, m)$, which we define to be the number of ways we can select m items from n in such a way that order matters for the selected items, but there is no order for the unselected items. Thus, $\Pi(n) = \Pi(n, n)$.

✦   **Example 4.5.** A horse race awards prizes to the first three finishers; the first horse is said to "win," the second to "place," and the third to "show." Suppose there are 10 horses in a race. How many different awards for win, place, and show are there?

Clearly, any of the 10 horses can be the winner. Given which horse is the winner, any of the 9 remaining horses can place. Thus, there are $10 \times 9 = 90$ choices for horses in first and second positions. For any of these 90 selections of win and place, there are 8 remaining horses. Any of these can finish third. Thus, there are $90 \times 8 = 720$ selections of win, place, and show. Figure 4.6 suggests all these possible selections, concentrating on the case where 3 is selected first and 1 is selected second. ✦

The General Rule for Selections Without Replacement

Let us now deduce the formula for $\Pi(n, m)$. Following Example 4.5, we know that there are n choices for the first selection. Whatever selection is first made, there will be $n - 1$ remaining items to choose from. Thus, the second choice can be made in $n - 1$ different ways, and the first two choices occur in $n(n - 1)$ ways. Similarly, for the third choice we are left with $n - 2$ unselected items, so the third choice can be made in $n - 2$ different ways. Hence the first three choices can occur in $n(n - 1)(n - 2)$ distinct ways.

We proceed in this way until m choices have been made. Each choice is made from one fewer item than the choice before. The conclusion is that we may select m items from n without replacement but with order significant in

$$\Pi(n, m) = n(n - 1)(n - 2) \cdots (n - m + 1) \tag{4.3}$$

different ways. That is, expression (4.3) is the product of the m integers starting and n and counting down.

Another way to write (4.3) is as $n!/(n - m)!$. That is,

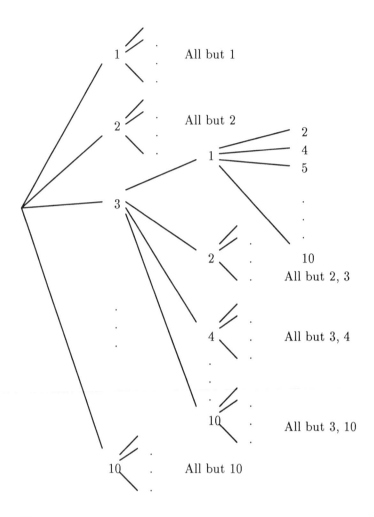

Fig. 4.6. Ordered selection of three things out of 10.

$$\frac{n!}{(n-m)!} = \frac{n(n-1)\cdots(n-m+1)(n-m)(n-m-1)\cdots(1)}{(n-m)(n-m-1)\cdots(1)}$$

The denominator is the product of the integers from 1 to $n-m$. The numerator is the product of the integers from 1 to n. Since the last $n-m$ factors in the numerator and denominator above are the same, $(n-m)(n-m-1)\cdots(1)$, they cancel and the result is that

$$\frac{n!}{(n-m)!} = n(n-1)\cdots(n-m+1)$$

This formula is the same as that in (4.3), which shows that $\Pi(n,m) = n!/(n-m)!$.

Example 4.6. Consider the case from Example 4.5, where $n = 10$ and $m = 3$. We observed that $\Pi(10,3) = 10 \times 9 \times 8 = 720$. The formula (4.3) says that $\Pi(10,3) = 10!/7!$, or

Selections With and Without Replacement

The problem considered in Example 4.5 differs only slightly from the assignment problem considered in Section 4.2. In terms of houses and colors, we could almost see the selection of the first three finishing horses as an assignment of one of ten horses (the "colors") to each of three finishing positions (the "houses"). The only difference is that, while we are free to paint several houses the same color, it makes no sense to say that one horse finished both first and third, for example. Thus, while the number of ways to color three houses in any of ten colors is 10^3 or $10 \times 10 \times 10$, the number of ways to select the first three finishers out of 10 is $10 \times 9 \times 8$.

Selection with replacement

We sometimes refer to the kind of selection we did in Section 4.2 as *selection with replacement*. That is, when we select a color, say red, for a house, we "replace" red into the pool of possible colors. We are then free to select red again for one or more additional houses.

Selection without replacement

On the other hand, the sort of selection we discussed in Example 4.5 is called *selection without replacement*. Here, if the horse Sea Biscuit is selected to be the winner, then Sea Biscuit is not replaced in the pool of horses that can place or show. Similarly, if Secretariat is selected for second place, he is not eligible to be the third-place horse also.

$$\frac{10 \times 9 \times 8 \times 7 \times 6 \times 5 \times 4 \times 3 \times 2 \times 1}{7 \times 6 \times 5 \times 4 \times 3 \times 2 \times 1}$$

The factors from 1 through 7 appear in both numerator and denominator and thus cancel. The result is the product of the integers from 8 through 10, or $10 \times 9 \times 8$, as we saw in Example 4.5. ✦

EXERCISES

4.4.1: How many ways are there to form a sequence of m letters out of the 26 letters, if no letter is allowed to appear more than once, for (a) $m = 3$ (b) $m = 5$.

4.4.2: In a class of 200 students, we wish to elect a President, Vice President, Secretary, and Treasurer. In how many ways can these four officers be selected?

4.4.3: Compute the following quotients of factorials: (a) 100!/97! (b) 200!/195!.

Mastermind

4.4.4: The game of Mastermind requires players to select a "code" consisting of a sequence of four pegs, each of which may be of any of six colors: red, green, blue, yellow, white, and black.

a)   How may different codes are there?

b*) How may different codes are there that have two or more pegs of the same color? *Hint*: This quantity is the difference between the answer to (a) and another easily computed quantity.

c)   How many codes are there that have no red peg?

d*) How many codes are there that have no red peg but have at least two pegs of the same color?

Quotients of Factorials

Note that in general, $a!/b!$ is the product of the integers between $b+1$ and a, as long as $b < a$. It is much easier to calculate the quotient of factorials as

$$a \times (a-1) \times \cdots \times (b+1)$$

than to compute each factorial and divide, especially if b is not much less than a.

4.4.5*: Prove by induction on n that for any m between 1 and n, $\Pi(n,m) = n!/(n-m)!$.

4.4.6*: Prove by induction on $a - b$ that $a!/b! = a(a-1)(a-2)\cdots(a-b+1)$.

✦✦ 4.5   Unordered Selections

There are many situations in which we wish to count the ways to select a set of items, but the order in which the selections are made does not matter. In terms of the horse race example of the previous section, we may wish to know which horses were the first three to finish, but we do not care about the order in which these three finished. Put another way, we wish to know how many ways we can select three horses out of n to be the top three finishers.

✦ **Example 4.7.** Let us again assume $n = 10$. We know from Example 4.5 that there are 720 ways to select three horses, say A, B, and C, to be the win, place, and show horses, respectively. However, now we do not care about the order of finish of these three horses, only that A, B, and C were the first three finishers in some order. Thus, we shall get the answer "A, B, and C are the three best horses" in six different ways, corresponding to the ways that these three horses can be ordered among the top three. We know there are exactly six ways, because the number of ways to order 3 items is $\Pi(3) = 3! = 6$. However, if there is any doubt, the six ways are seen in Fig. 4.7.

Win	Place	Show
A	B	C
A	C	B
B	A	C
B	C	A
C	A	B
C	B	A

Fig. 4.7. Six orders in which a set of three horses may finish.

What is true for the set of horses A, B, and C is true of any set of three horses. Each set of three horses will appear exactly 6 times, in all of their possible orders, when we count the ordered selections of three horses out of 10. Thus, if we wish to count only the sets of three horses that may be the three top finishers, we must divide $\Pi(10, 3)$ by 6. Thus, there are $720/6 = 120$ different sets of three horses out of 10. ✦

✦ **Example 4.8.** Let us count the number of poker hands. In poker, each player is dealt five cards from a 52-card deck. We do not care in what order the five cards are dealt, just what five cards we have. To count the number of sets of five cards we may be dealt, we could start by calculating $\Pi(52, 5)$, which is the number of ordered selections of five objects out of 52. This number is $52!/(52 - 5)!$, which is $52!/47!$, or $52 \times 51 \times 50 \times 49 \times 48 = 311{,}875{,}200$.

However, just as the three fastest horses in Example 4.7 appear in $3! = 6$ different orders, any set of five cards to appear in $\Pi(5) = 5! = 120$ different orders. Thus, to count the number of poker hands without regard to order of selection, we must take the number of ordered selections and divide by 120. The result is $311{,}875{,}200/120 = 2{,}598{,}960$ different hands. ✦

Counting Combinations

Let us now generalize Examples 4.7 and 4.8 to get a formula for the number of ways to select m items out of n without regard to order of selection. This function is usually written $\binom{n}{m}$ and spoken "n choose m" or "combinations of m things out of n." To compute $\binom{n}{m}$, we start with $\Pi(n, m) = n!/(n - m)!$, the number of ordered selections of m things out of n. We then group these ordered selections according to the set of m items selected. Since these m items can be ordered in $\Pi(m) = m!$ different ways, the groups will each have $m!$ members. We must divide the number of ordered selections by $m!$ to get the number of unordered selections. That is,

Combinations of m things out of n

$$\binom{n}{m} = \frac{\Pi(n, m)}{\Pi(m)} = \frac{n!}{(n - m)! \times m!} \tag{4.4}$$

✦ **Example 4.9.** Let us repeat Example 4.8, using formula (4.4) with $n = 52$ and $m = 5$. We have $\binom{52}{5} = 52!/(47! \times 5!)$. If we cancel the 47! with the last 47 factors of 52! and expand 5!, we can write

$$\binom{52}{5} = \frac{52 \times 51 \times 50 \times 49 \times 48}{5 \times 4 \times 3 \times 2 \times 1}$$

Simplifying, we get $\binom{52}{5} = 26 \times 17 \times 10 \times 49 \times 12 = 2{,}598{,}960$. ✦

A Recursive Definition of n Choose m

If we think recursively about the number of ways to select m items out of n, we can develop a recursive algorithm to compute $\binom{n}{m}$.

BASIS. $\binom{n}{0} = 1$ for any $n \geq 1$. That is, there is only one way to pick zero things out of n: pick nothing. Also, $\binom{n}{n} = 1$; that is, the only way to pick n things out of n is to pick them all.

INDUCTION. If $0 < m < n$, then $\binom{n}{m} = \binom{n-1}{m} + \binom{n-1}{m-1}$. That is, if we wish to pick m things out of n, we can either

i) Not pick the first element, and then pick m things from the remaining $n - 1$ elements. The term $\binom{n-1}{m}$ counts this number of possibilities.

or

ii) Pick the first element and then select $m - 1$ things from among the remaining $n - 1$ elements. The term $\binom{n-1}{m-1}$ counts these possibilities.

Incidently, while the idea of the induction should be clear — we proceed from the simplest cases of picking all or none to more complicated cases where we pick some but not all — we have to be careful to state what quantity the induction is "on." One way to look at this induction is that it is a complete induction on the product of n and the minimum of m and $n - m$. Then the basis case occurs when this product is 0 and the induction is for larger values of the product. We have to check for the induction that $n \times \min(m, n - m)$ is always greater than $(n - 1) \times \min(n, n - m - 1)$ and $(n - 1) \times \min(m - 1, n - m)$ when $0 < m < n$. This check is left as an exercise.

Pascal's triangle   This recursion is often displayed by *Pascal's triangle*, illustrated in Fig. 4.8, where the borders are all 1's (for the basis) and each interior entry is the sum of the two numbers above it to the northeast and northwest (for the induction). Then $\binom{n}{m}$ can be read from the $(m + 1)$st entry of the $(n + 1)$st row.

$$
\begin{array}{ccccccccc}
 & & & & 1 & & & & \\
 & & & 1 & & 1 & & & \\
 & & 1 & & 2 & & 1 & & \\
 & 1 & & 3 & & 3 & & 1 & \\
1 & & 4 & & 6 & & 4 & & 1
\end{array}
$$

Fig. 4.8. The first rows of Pascal's triangle.

✦   **Example 4.10.** Consider the case where $n = 4$ and $m = 2$. We find the value of $\binom{4}{2}$ in the 3rd entry of the 5th row of Fig. 4.8. This entry is 6, and it is easy to check that $\binom{4}{2} = 4!/(2! \times 2!) = 24/(2 \times 2) = 6$. ✦

The two ways we have to compute $\binom{n}{m}$ — by formula (4.4) or by the above recursion — each compute the same value, naturally. We can argue so by appeal to physical reasoning. Both methods compute the number of ways to select m items out of n in an unordered fashion, so they must produce the same value. However, we can also prove the equality of the two approaches by an induction on n. We leave this proof as an exercise.

Running Time of Algorithms to Compute $\binom{n}{m}$

As we saw in Example 4.9, when we use formula (4.4) to compute $\binom{n}{m}$ we can cancel $(n - m)!$ in the denominator against the last $n - m$ factors in $n!$ to express $\binom{n}{m}$ as

$$\binom{n}{m} = \frac{n \times (n - 1) \times \cdots \times (n - m + 1)}{m \times (m - 1) \times \cdots \times 1} \tag{4.5}$$

If m is small compared to n, we can evaluate the above formula much faster than we can evaluate (4.4). In principle, the fragment of C code in Fig. 4.9 does the job.

```
(1)        c = 1;
(2)        for (i = n; i > n-m; i--)
(3)            c *= i;
(4)        for (i = 2; i <= m; i++)
(5)            c /= i;
```

Fig. 4.9. Code to compute $\binom{n}{m}$.

Line (1) initializes c to 1; c will become the result, $\binom{n}{m}$. Lines (2) and (3) multiply c by each of the integers between $n - m + 1$ and n. Then, lines (4) and (5) divide c by each of the integers between 2 and m. Thus, Fig. 4.9 implements the formula of Equation (4.5).

For the running time of Fig. 4.9, we have only to observe that the two loops, lines (2) – (3) and lines (4) – (5), each iterate m times and have a body that takes $O(1)$ time. Thus, the running time is $O(m)$.

In the case that m is close to n but $n - m$ is small, we can interchange the role of m and $n - m$. That is, we can cancel factors of $n!$ and $m!$, getting $n(n - 1) \cdots (m + 1)$ and divide that by $(n - m)!$. This approach gives us an alternative to (4.5), which is

$$\binom{n}{m} = \frac{n \times (n - 1) \times \cdots \times (m + 1)}{(n - m) \times (n - m - 1) \times \cdots \times 1} \tag{4.6}$$

Likewise, there is a code fragment similar to Fig. 4.9 that implements formula (4.6) and takes time $O(n - m)$. Since both $n - m$ and m must be n or less for $\binom{n}{m}$ to be defined, we know that either way, $O(n)$ is a bound on the running time. Moreover, when m is either close to 0 or close to n, then the running time of the better of the two approaches is much less than $O(n)$.

However, Fig. 4.9 is flawed in an important way. It starts by computing the product of a number of integers and then divides by an equal number of integers. Since ordinary computer arithmetic can only deal with integers of a limited size (often, about two billion is as large as an integer can get), we run the risk of computing an intermediate result after line (3) of Fig. 4.9 that overflows the limit on integer size. That may be the case even though the value of $\binom{n}{m}$ is small enough to be represented in the computer.

A more desirable approach is to alternate multiplications and divisions. Start by multiplying by n, then divide by m. Multiply by $n - 1$; then divide by $m - 1$, and so on. The problem with this approach is that we have no reason to believe the result will be an integer at each stage. For instance, in Example 4.9 we would begin by multiplying by 52 and dividing by 5. The result is already not an integer.

Formulas for $\binom{n}{m}$ Must Yield Integers

It may not be obvious why the quotients of many factors in Equations (4.4), (4.5), or (4.6) must always turn out to be an integer. The only simple argument is to appeal to physical reasoning. The formulas all compute the number of ways to choose m things out of n, and this number must be some integer.

It is much harder to argue this fact from properties of integers, without appealing to the physical meaning of the formulas. It can in fact be shown by a careful analysis of the number of factors of each prime in numerator and denominator. As a sample, look at the expression in Example 4.9. There is a 5 in the denominator, and there are 5 factors in the numerator. Since these factors are consecutive, we know one of them must be divisible by 5; it happens to be the middle factor, 50. Thus, the 5 in the denominator surely cancels.

Thus, we need to convert to floating-point numbers before doing any calculation. We leave this modification as an exercise.

Now, let us consider the recursive algorithm to compute $\binom{n}{m}$. We can implement it by the simple recursive function of Fig. 4.10.

```
         /* compute n choose m for 0 <= m <= n */
         int choose(int n, int m)
         {
             int n, m;

(1)          if (m < 0 || m > n) {/* error conditions */
(2)              printf("invalid input\n");
(3)              return 0;
             }
(4)          else if (m == 0 || m == n) /* basis case */
(5)              return 1;
             else /* induction */
(6)              return (choose(n-1, m-1) + choose(n-1, m));
         }
```

Fig. 4.10. Recursive function to compute $\binom{n}{m}$.

The function of Fig. 4.10 is not efficient; it creates an exponential explosion in the number of calls to choose. The reason is that when called with n as its first argument, it usually makes two recursive calls at line (6) with first argument $n-1$. Thus, we might expect the number of calls made to double when n increases by 1. Unfortunately, the exact number of recursive calls made is harder to count. The reason is that the basis case on lines (4) and (5) can apply not only when $n = 1$, but for higher n, provided m has the value 0 or n.

We can prove a simple, but slightly pessimistic upper bound as follows. Let $T(n)$ be the running time of Fig. 4.10 with first argument n. We can prove that $T(n)$ is $O(2^n)$ simply. Let a be the total running time of lines (1) through (5), plus that part of line (6) that is involved in the calls and return, but not the time of the recursive calls themselves. Then we can prove by induction on n:

STATEMENT $S(n)$: If `choose` is called with first argument n and some second argument m between 0 and n, then the running time $T(n)$ of the call is at most $a(2^n - 1)$.

BASIS. $n = 1$. Then it must be that either $m = 0$ or $m = 1 = n$. Thus, the basis case on lines (4) and (5) applies and we make no recursive calls. The time for lines (1) through (5) is included in a. Since $S(1)$ says that $T(1)$ is at most $a(2^1 - 1) = a$, we have proved the basis.

INDUCTION. Assume $S(n)$; that is, $T(n) \le a(2^n - 1)$. To prove $S(n+1)$, suppose we call `choose` with first argument $n + 1$. Then Fig. 4.10 takes time a plus the time of the two recursive calls on line (6). By the inductive hypothesis, each call takes at most time $a(2^n - 1)$. Thus, the total time consumed is at most

$$a + 2a(2^n - 1) = a(1 + 2^{n+1} - 2) = a(2^{n+1} - 1)$$

This calculation proves $S(n+1)$ and proves the induction.

We have thus proved that $T(n) \le a(2^n - 1)$. Dropping the constant factor and the low-order terms, we see that $T(n)$ is $O(2^n)$.

Curiously, while in our analyses of Chapter 3 we easily proved a smooth and tight upper bound on running time, the $O(2^n)$ bound on $T(n)$ is smooth but not tight. The proper smooth, tight upper bound is slightly less: $O(2^n/\sqrt{n})$. A proof of this fact is quite difficult, but we leave as an exercise the easier fact that the running time of Fig. 4.10 is proportional to the value it returns: $\binom{n}{m}$. An important observation is that the recursive algorithm of Fig. 4.10 is much less efficient that the linear algorithm of Fig. 4.9. This example is one where recursion hurts considerably.

The Shape of the Function $\binom{n}{m}$

Bell curve

For a fixed value of n, the function of m that is $\binom{n}{m}$ has a number of interesting properties. For a large value of n, its form is the bell-shaped curve suggested in Fig. 4.11. We immediately notice that this function is symmetric around the midpoint $n/2$; this is easy to check using formula (4.4) that states $\binom{n}{m} = \binom{n}{n-m}$.

The maximum height at the center, that is, $\binom{n}{n/2}$, is approximately $2^n/\sqrt{\pi n/2}$. For example, if $n = 10$, this formula gives 258.37, while $\binom{10}{5} = 252$.

The "thick part" of the curve extends for approximately $\sqrt{n}$ on either side of the midpoint. For example, if $n = 10,000$, then for m between 4900 and 5100 the value of $\binom{10,000}{m}$ is close to the maximum. For m outside this range, the value of $\binom{10,000}{m}$ falls off very rapidly.

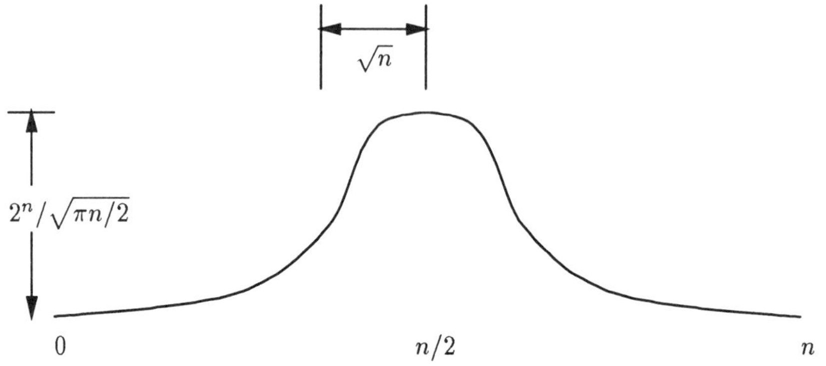

Fig. 4.11. The function $\binom{n}{m}$ for fixed n.

Binomial Coefficients

Binomial

The function $\binom{n}{m}$, in addition to its use in counting, gives us the *binomial coefficients*. These numbers are found when we expand a two-term polynomial (a *binomial*) raised to a power, such as $(x + y)^n$.

When we expand $(x + y)^n$, we get 2^n terms, each of which is $x^m y^{n-m}$ for some m between 0 and n. That is, from each of the factors $x + y$ we may choose either x or y to contribute as a factor in a particular term. The coefficient of $x^m y^{n-m}$ in the expansion is the number of terms that are composed of m choices of x and the remaining $n - m$ choices of y.

✦ **Example 4.11.** Consider the case $n = 4$, that is, the product

$$(x + y)(x + y)(x + y)(x + y)$$

There are 16 terms, of which only one is $x^4 y^0$ (or just x^4). This term is the one we get if we select x from each of the four factors. On the other hand, there are four terms $x^3 y$, corresponding to the fact that we can select y from any of the four factors and x from the remaining three factors. Symmetrically, we know that there is one term y^4 and four terms xy^3.

How many terms $x^2 y^2$ are there? We get such a term if we select x from two of the four factors and y from the remaining two. Thus, we must count the number of ways to select two of the factors out of four. Since the order in which we select the two doesn't matter, this count is $\binom{4}{2} = 4!/(2! \times 2!) = 24/4 = 6$. Thus, there are six terms $x^2 y^2$. The complete expansion is

$$(x + y)^4 = x^4 + 4x^3 y + 6x^2 y^2 + 4xy^3 + y^4$$

Notice that the coefficients of the terms on the right side of the equality, $(1, 4, 6, 4, 1)$, are exactly a row of Pascal's triangle in Fig. 4.8. That is no coincidence, as we shall see. ✦

We can generalize the idea that we used to calculate the coefficient of $x^2 y^2$ in Example 4.11. The coefficient of $x^m y^{n-m}$ in the expansion of $(x + y)^n$ is $\binom{n}{m}$. The reason is that we get a term $x^m y^{n-m}$ whenever we select m of the n factors to provide an x and the remainder of the factors to provide y. The number of ways to choose m factors out of n is $\binom{n}{m}$.

There is another interesting consequence of the relationship between binomial coefficients and the function $\binom{n}{m}$. We just observed that

$$(x + y)^n = \sum_{m=0}^{n} \binom{n}{m} x^m y^{n-m}$$

Let $x = y = 1$. Then $(x + y)^n = 2^n$. All powers of x and y are 1, so the above equation becomes

$$2^n = \sum_{m=0}^{n} \binom{n}{m}$$

Put another way, the sum of all the binomial coefficients for a fixed n is 2^n. In particular, each coefficient $\binom{n}{m}$ is less than 2^n. The implication of Fig. 4.11 is that for m around $n/2$, $\binom{n}{m}$ is quite close to 2^n. Since the area under the curve of Fig. 4.11 is 2^n, we see why only a few values near the middle can be large.

EXERCISES

4.5.1: Compute the following values: (a) $\binom{7}{3}$ (b) $\binom{8}{3}$ (c) $\binom{10}{7}$ (d) $\binom{12}{11}$.

4.5.2: In how many ways can we choose a set of 5 different letters out of the 26 possible lower-case letters?

4.5.3: What is the coefficient of

a) $x^3 y^4$ in the expansion $(x + y)^7$
b) $x^5 y^3$ in the expansion of $(x + y)^8$

4.5.4*: At Real Security, Inc., computer passwords are required to have four digits (of 10 possible) and six letters (of 52 possible). Letters and digits may repeat. How many different possible passwords are there? *Hint*: Start by counting the number of ways to select the four positions holding digits.

4.5.5*: How many sequences of 5 letters are there in which exactly two are vowels?

4.5.6: Rewrite the fragment of Fig. 4.9 to take advantage of the case when $n - m$ is small compared with n.

4.5.7: Rewrite the fragment of Fig. 4.9 to convert to floating-point numbers and alternately multiply and divide.

4.5.8: Prove that if $0 \leq m \leq n$, then $\binom{n}{m} = \binom{n}{n-m}$

a)   By appealing to the meaning of the function $\binom{n}{m}$
b)   By using Equation 4.4

4.5.9*: Prove by induction on n that the recursive definition of $\binom{n}{m}$ correctly defines $\binom{n}{m}$ to be equal to $n!/((n - m)! \times m!)$.

4.5.10**: Show by induction on n that the running time of the recursive function `choose(n,m)` of Fig. 4.10 is at most $c\binom{n}{m}$ for some constant c.

4.5.11*: Show that $n \times \min(m, n - m)$ is always greater than

$$(n-1) \times \min(n, n-m-1)$$

and $(n-1) \times \min(m-1, n-m)$ when $0 < m < n$.

✦✦ 4.6   Orderings With Identical Items

In this section, we shall examine a class of selection problems in which some of the items are indistinguishable from one another, but the order of appearance of the items matters when items can be distinguished. The next section will address a similar class of problems where we do not care about order, and some items are indistinguishable.

Anagrams   ✦   **Example 4.12.** *Anagram* puzzles give us a list of letters, which we are asked to rearrange to form a word. We can solve such problems mechanically if we have a dictionary of legal words and we can generate all the possible orderings of the letters. Chapter 10 considers efficient ways to check whether a given sequence of letters is in the dictionary. But now, considering combinatorial problems, we might start by asking how many different potential words we must check for presence in the dictionary.

For some anagrams, the count is easy. Suppose we are given the letters `abenst`. There are six letters, which may be ordered in $\Pi(6) = 6! = 720$ ways. One of these 720 ways is `absent`, the "solution" to the puzzle.

However, anagrams often contain duplicate letters. Consider the puzzle `eilltt`. There are not 720 different sequences of these letters. For example, interchanging the positions in which the two `t`'s appear does not make the word different.

Suppose we "tagged" the `t`'s and `l`'s so we could distinguish between them, say t_1, t_2, l_1, and l_2. Then we would have 720 orders of tagged letters. However, pair of orders that differ only in the position of the tagged `l`'s, such as $l_1it_2t_1l_2e$ and $l_2it_2t_1l_1e$, are not really different. Since all 720 orders group into pairs differing only in the subscript on the `l`'s, we can account for the fact that the `l`'s are really identical if we divide the number of strings of letters by 2. We conclude that the number of different anagrams in which the `t`'s are tagged but the `l`'s are not is 720/2=360.

Similarly, we may pair the strings with only `t`'s tagged if they differ only in the subscript of the `t`'s. For example, lit_1t_2le and lit_2t_1le are paired. Thus, if we divide by 2 again, we have the number of different anagram strings with the tags removed from both `t`'s and `l`'s. This number is $360/2 = 180$. We conclude that there are 180 different anagrams of `eilltt`. ✦

We may generalize the idea of Example 4.12 to a situation where there are n items, and these items are divided into k groups. Members of each group are indistinguishable, but members of different groups are distinguishable. We may let m_i be the number of items in the ith group, for $i = 1, 2, \ldots, k$.

✦   **Example 4.13.** Reconsider the anagram problem `eilltt` from Example 4.12. Here, there are six items, so $n = 6$. The number of groups k is 4, since there are

4 different letters. Two of the groups have one member (e and i), while the other two groups have two members. We may thus take $i_1 = i_2 = 1$ and $i_3 = i_4 = 2$. ✦

If we tag the items so members of a group are distinguishable, then there are $n!$ different orders. However, if there are i_1 members of the first group, these tagged items may appear in $i_1!$ different orders. Thus, when we remove the tags from the items in group 1, we cluster the orders into sets of size $i_1!$ that become identical. We must thus divide the number of orders by $i_1!$ to account for the removal of tags from group 1.

Similarly, removing the tags from each group in turn forces us to divide the number of distinguishable orders by $i_2!$, by $i_3!$, and so on. For those i_j's that are 1, this division is by $1! = 1$ and thus has no effect. However, we must divide by the factorial of the size of each group of more than one item. That is what happened in Example 4.12. There were two groups with more than one member, each of size 2, and we divided by $2!$ twice. We can state and prove the general rule by induction on k.

STATEMENT $S(k)$: If there are n items divided into k groups of sizes $i_1, i_2, \ldots, i_k$ respectively, items within a group are not distinguishable, but items in different groups are distinguishable, then the number of different distinguishable orders of the n items is

$$\frac{n!}{\prod_{j=1}^{k} i_j!} \tag{4.7}$$

BASIS. If $k = 1$, then there is one group of indistinguishable items, which gives us only one distinguishable order no matter how large n is. If $k = 1$ then i_1 must be n, and formula (4.7) reduces to $n!/n!$, or 1. Thus, $S(1)$ holds.

INDUCTION. Suppose $S(k)$ is true, and consider a situation with $k+1$ groups. Let the last group have $m = i_{k+1}$ members. These items will appear in m positions, and we can choose these positions in $\binom{n}{m}$ different ways. Once we have chosen the m positions, it does not matter which items in the last group we place in these positions, since they are indistinguishable.

Having chosen the positions for the last group, we have $n - m$ positions left to fill with the remaining k groups. The inductive hypothesis applies and tells us that each selection of positions for the last group can be coupled with $(n-m)!/\prod_{j=1}^{k} i_j!$ distinguishable orders in which to place the remaining groups in the remaining positions. This formula is just (4.7) with $n - m$ replacing n since there are only $n - m$ items remaining to be placed. The total number of ways to order the $k + 1$ groups is thus

$$\frac{\binom{n}{m}(n - m)!}{\prod_{j=1}^{k} i_j!} \tag{4.8}$$

Let us replace $\binom{n}{m}$ in (4.8) by its equivalent in factorials: $n!/\big((n-m)!m!\big)$. We then have

$$\frac{n!}{(n-m)!m!} \frac{(n-m)!}{\prod_{j=1}^{k} i_j!} \tag{4.9}$$

We may cancel $(n-m)!$ from numerator and denominator in (4.8). Also, remember that m is i_{k+1}, the number of members in the $(k+1)$st group. We thus discover that the number of orders is

$$\frac{n!}{\prod_{j=1}^{k+1} i_j!}$$

This formula is exactly what is given by $S(k+1)$.

✦ **Example 4.14.** An explorer has rations for two weeks, consisting of 4 cans of Tuna, 7 cans of Spam, and 3 cans of Beanie Weenies. If he opens one can each day, in how many orders can he consume the rations? Here, there are 14 items divided into groups of 4, 7, and 3 identical items. In terms of Equation (4.7), $n = 14$, $k = 3$, $i_1 = 4$, $i_2 = 7$, and $i_3 = 3$. The number of orders is thus

$$\frac{14!}{4!7!3!}$$

Let us begin by canceling the 7! in the denominator with the last 7 factors in 14! of the numerator. That gives us

$$\frac{14 \times 13 \times 12 \times 11 \times 10 \times 9 \times 8}{4 \times 3 \times 2 \times 1 \times 3 \times 2 \times 1}$$

Continuing to cancel factors in the numerator and denominator, we find the resulting product is 120,120. That is, there are over a hundred thousand ways in which to consume the rations. None sounds very appetizing. ✦

EXERCISES

4.6.1: Count the number of anagrams of the following words: (a) `error` (b) `street` (c) `allele` (d) `Mississippi`.

4.6.2: In how many ways can we arrange in a line

a)   Three apples, four pears, and five bananas
b)   Two apples, six pears, three bananas, and two plums

4.6.3*: In how many ways can we place a white king, a black king, two white knights, and a black rook on the chessboard?

4.6.4*: One hundred people participate in a lottery. One will win the grand prize of $1000, and five more will win consolation prizes of a $50 savings bond. How many different possible outcomes of the lottery are there?

4.6.5: Write a simple formula for the number of orders in which we may place $2n$ objects that occur in n pairs of two identical objects each.

❖❖ 4.7 Distribution of Objects to Bins

Our next class of counting problems involve the selection of a bin in which to place each of several objects. The objects may or may not be identical, but the bins are distinguishable. We must count the number of ways in which the bins can be filled.

✦ **Example 4.15.** Kathy, Peter, and Susan are three children. We have four apples to distribute among them, without cutting apples into parts. In how many different ways may the children receive apples?

There are sufficiently few ways that we can enumerate them. Kathy may receive anything from 0 to 4 apples, and whatever remains can be divided between Peter and Susan in only a few ways. If we let (i, j, k) represent the situation in which Kathy receives i apples, Peter receives j, and Susan receives k, the 15 possibilities are as shown in Fig. 4.12. Each row corresponds to the number of apples given to Kathy.

(0,0,4)	(0,1,3)	(0,2,2)	(0,3,1)	(0,4,0)
(1,0,3)	(1,1,2)	(1,2,1)	(1,3,0)	
(2,0,2)	(2,1,1)	(2,2,0)		
(3,0,1)	(3,1,0)			
(4,0,0)				

Fig. 4.12. Four apples can be distributed to three children in 15 ways.

There is a trick to counting the number of ways to distribute identical objects to bins. Suppose we have four letter **A**'s representing apples. Let us also use two *'s which will represent partitions between the apples belonging to different children. We order the **A**'s and *'s as we like and interpret all **A**'s before the first * as being apples belonging to Kathy. Those **A**'s between the two *'s belong to Peter, and the **A**'s after the second * are apples belonging to Susan. For instance, **AA*A*A** represents the distribution (2,1,1), where Kathy gets two apples and the other two children get one each. Sequence **AAA*A*** represents the situation (3,1,0), where Kathy gets three, Peter gets one, and Susan gets none.

Thus, each distribution of apples to bins is associated with a unique string of 4 **A**'s and 2 *'s. How many such strings are there? Think of the six positions forming such a string. Any four of those positions may be selected to hold the **A**'s; the other two will hold the *'s. The number of ways to select 4 items out of 6 is $\binom{6}{4}$, as we learned in Section 4.5. Since $\binom{6}{4} = 15$, we again conclude that there are 15 ways to distribute four apples to three children. ✦

The General Rule for Distribution to Bins

We can generalize the problem of Example 4.15 as follows. Suppose we are given n bins; these correspond to the three children in the example. Suppose also we are given m identical objects to place arbitrarily into the bins. How many distributions into bins are there.

We may again think of strings of **A**'s and *'s. The **A**'s now represent the objects, and the *'s represent boundaries between the bins. If there are n objects, we use n

A's, and if there are m bins, we need $m - 1$ *'s to serve as boundaries between the portions for the various bins. Thus, strings are of length $n + m - 1$.

We may choose any n of these positions to hold A's, and the rest will hold *'s. There are thus $\binom{n+m-1}{n}$ strings of A's and *'s, so there are this many distributions of objects to bins. In Example 4.15 we had $n = 4$ and $m = 3$, and we concluded that there were $\binom{n+m-1}{n} = \binom{6}{4}$ distributions.

Chuck-a-Luck ✦ **Example 4.16.** In the game of Chuck-a-Luck we throw three dice, each with six sides numbered 1 through 6. Players bet a dollar on a number. If the number does not come up, the dollar is lost. If the number comes up one or more times, the player wins as many dollars as there are occurrences of the number.

We would like to count the "outcomes," but there may initially be some question about what an "outcome" is. If we were to color the dice different colors so we could tell them apart, we could see this counting problem as that of Section 4.2, where we assign one of six numbers to each of three dice. We know there are $6^3 = 216$ ways to make this assignment.

However, the dice ordinarily aren't distinguishable, and the order in which the numbers come up doesn't matter; it is only the occurrences of each number that determines which players get paid and how much. For instance, we might observe that 1 comes up on two dice and 6 comes up on the third. The 6 might have appeared on the first, second, or third die, but it doesn't matter which.

Thus, we can see the problem as one of distribution of identical objects to bins. The "bins" are the numbers 1 through 6, and the "objects" are the three dice. A die is "distributed" to the bin corresponding to the number thrown on that die. Thus, there are $\binom{6+3-1}{3} = \binom{8}{3} = 56$ different outcomes in Chuck-a-Luck. ✦

Distributing Distinguishable Objects

We can extend the previous formula to allow for distribution into m bins of a collection of n objects that fall into k different classes. Objects within a class are indistinguishable from each other, but are distinguishable from those of other classes. Let us use symbol a_i to represent members of the ith class. We may thus form strings consisting of

1. For each class i, as many a_i's as there are members of that class.
2. $m - 1$ *'s to represent the boundaries between the m bins.

The length of these strings is thus $n + m - 1$. Note that the *'s form a $(k + 1)$st class, with m members.

We learned how to count the number of such strings in Section 4.6. There are

$$\frac{(n + m - 1)!}{(m - 1)! \prod_{j=1}^{k} i_j!}$$

strings, where i_j is the number of members of the jth class.

✦ **Example 4.17.** Suppose we have three apples, two pears, and a banana to distribute to Kathy, Peter, and Susan. Then $m = 3$, the number of "bins," which is the number of children. There are $k = 3$ groups, with $i_1 = 3$, $i_2 = 2$, and $i_3 = 1$. Since there are 6 objects in all, $n = 6$, and the strings in question are of length

Comparison of Counting Problems

In this and the previous five sections we have considered six different counting problems. Each can be thought of as assigning objects to certain positions. For example, the assignment problem of Section 4.2 may be thought of as one where we are given n positions (corresponding to the houses) and and infinite supply of objects of k different types (the colors). We can classify these problems along three axes:

1. Do they place all the given objects?
2. Is the order in which objects are assigned important?
3. Are all the objects distinct, or are some indistinguishable?

Here is a table indicating the differences between the problems mentioned in each of these sections.

SECTION	TYPICAL PROBLEM	MUST USE ALL?	ORDER IMPORTANT?	IDENTICAL OBJECTS?
4.2	Painting houses	N	Y	N
4.3	Sorting	Y	Y	N
4.4	Horse race	N	Y	N
4.5	Poker hands	N	N	Y
4.6	Anagrams	Y	Y	Y
4.7	Apples to children	Y	N	Y

The problems of Sections 4.2 and 4.4 are not differentiated in the table above. The distinction is one of replacement, as discussed in the box on "Selections With and Without Replacement" in Section 4.4. That is, in Section 4.2 we had an infinite supply of each "color" and could select a color many times. In Section 4.4, a "horse" selected is not available for later selections.

$n + m - 1 = 8$. The strings consist of three A's standing for apples, two P's standing for pears, one B standing for the banana, and two *'s, the boundaries between the shares of the children. The formula for the number of distributions is thus

$$\frac{(n + m - 1)!}{(m - 1)! i_1! i_2! i_3!} = \frac{8!}{2! 3! 2! 1!} = 1680$$

ways in which these fruits may be distributed to Kathy, Peter, and Susan. ✦

EXERCISES

4.7.1: In how many ways can we distribute

a) Six apples to four children
b) Four apples to six children
c) Six apples and three pears to five children
d) Two apples, five pears, and six bananas to three children

4.7.2: How many outcomes are there if we throw

(a) Four indistinguishable dice

b) Five indistinguishable dice

4.7.3*: How many ways can we distribute seven apples to three children so that each child gets at least one apple?

4.7.4*: Suppose we start at the lower-left corner of a chessboard and move to the upper-right corner, making moves that are each either one square up or one square right. In how many ways can we make the journey?

4.7.5*: Generalize Exercise 4.7.4. If we have a rectangle of n squares by m squares, and we move only one square up or one square right, in how many ways can we move from lower-left to upper-right?

✦✦ 4.8 Combining Counting Rules

The subject of combinatorics offers myriad challenges, and few are as simple as those discussed so far in this chapter. However, the rules learned so far are valuable building blocks that may be combined in various ways to count more complex structures. In this section, we shall learn three useful "tricks" for counting:

1. Express a count as a sequence of choices.

2. Express a count as a difference of counts.

3. Express a count as a sum of counts for subcases.

Breaking a Count Into a Sequence of Choices

One useful approach to be taken, when faced with the problem of counting some class of arrangements is to describe the things to be counted in terms of a series of choices, each of which refines the description of a particular member of the class. In this section we present a series of examples intended to suggest some of the possibilities.

✦ **Example 4.18.** Let us count the number of poker hands that are one-pair hands. A hand with one pair consists of two cards of one rank and three cards of ranks[1] that are different and also distinct from the rank of the pair. We can describe all one-pair hands by the following steps.

1. Select the rank of the pair.

2. Select the three ranks for the other three cards from the remaining 12 ranks.

3. Select the suits for the two cards of the pair.

4. Select the suits for each of the other three cards.

---

[1] The 13 ranks are Ace, King, Queen, Jack, and 10 through 2.

If we multiply all these numbers together, we shall have the number of one-pair hands. Note that the order in which the cards appear in the hand is not important, as we discussed in Example 4.8, and we have made no attempt to specify the order.

Now, let us take each of these factors in turn. We can select the rank of the pair in 13 different ways. Whichever rank we select for the pair, we have 12 ranks left. We must select 3 of these for the remaining cards of the hand. This is a selection in which order is unimportant, as discussed in Section 4.5. We may perform this selection in $\binom{12}{3} = 220$ ways.

Now, we must select the suits for the pair. There are four suits, and we must select two of them. Again we have an unordered selection, which we may do in $\binom{4}{2} = 6$ ways. Finally, we must select a suit for each of the three remaining cards. Each has 4 choices of suit, so we have an assignment like those of Section 4.2. We may make this assignment in $4^3 = 64$ ways.

The total number of one-pair hands is thus $13 \times 220 \times 6 \times 64 = 1,098,240$. This number is over 40% of the total number of 2,598,960 poker hands. ✦

Computing a Count as a Difference of Counts

Another useful technique is to express what we want to count as the difference between some more general class C of arrangements and those in C that do not meet the condition for the thing we want to count.

✦   **Example 4.19.** There are a number of other poker hands — two pairs, three of a kind, four of a kind, and full house — that can be counted in a manner similar to Example 4.18. However, there are other hands that require a different approach.

First, let us consider a straight-flush, which is five cards of consecutive rank (a straight) of the same suit (a flush). First, each straight begins with one of the nine ranks 2 through 10 as the lowest card. That is, the straights are 2-3-4-5-6, 3-4-5-6-7, and so on, up to 10-Jack-Queen-King-Ace. Once the ranks are determined, the straight-flush can be completely specified by giving the suit. Thus, we can count the straight-flushes by

1.   Select the lowest rank in the straight (9 choices).

2.   Select the suit (4 choices).

Thus, there are $9 \times 4 = 36$ straight-flushes.

Now, let us count the straights, that is, those hands whose ranks are consecutive but that are not straight-flushes. We shall first count all those hands with consecutive ranks, regardless of whether the suits are the same, and then subtract the 36 straight-flushes. To count hands with consecutive ranks, we can

1.   Select the low rank (9 choices).

2.   Assign a suit to each of the five ranks ($4^5 = 1024$ choices, as in Section 4.2).

The number of straights and straight-flushes is thus $9 \times 1024 = 9216$. When we subtract the straight-flushes, we are left with $9216 - 36 = 9180$ hands that are classified as straights.

Next, let us count the number of flushes. Again, we shall first include the straight-flushes and then subtract 36. We can define a flush by

1. Select the suit (4 choices).

2. Select the five ranks out of thirteen ranks in any of $\binom{13}{5} = 1287$ ways, as in Section 4.5.

We conclude that the number of flushes is $4 \times 1287 - 36 = 5112$. ✦

Expressing a Count as a Sum of Subcases

Our third "trick" is to be methodical when faced with a problem that is too hard to solve directly. We break the problem of counting a class C into two or more separate problems, where each member of class C is covered by exactly one of the subproblems.

✦   **Example 4.20.** Suppose we toss a sequence of 10 coins. In how many sequences will 8 or more of the coins be heads? If we wanted to know how many sequences had exactly 8 heads, we could answer the problem by the method of Section 4.5. That is, there are 10 coins, and we wish to select 8 of them to be heads. We can do so in $\binom{10}{8} = 45$ ways.

To solve the problem of counting sequences of 8 or more heads, we break it into the three subproblems of counting sequences with exactly 8 heads, exactly 9 heads, and exactly 10 heads. We already did the first. The number of sequences with 9 heads is $\binom{10}{9} = 10$, and there is $\binom{10}{10} = 1$ sequence with all 10 heads. Thus, the number of sequences with 8 or more heads is $45 + 10 + 1 = 56$. ✦

✦   **Example 4.21.** Let us reconsider the problem of counting the outcomes in Chuck-a-Luck, which we solved in Example 4.16. Another approach is to divide the problem into three subproblems, depending on whether the number of different numbers showing is 3, 2, or 1.

a) We can count the number of outcomes with three different numbers using the technique of Section 4.5. That is, we must select 3 out of the 6 possible numbers on a die, and we can do so in $\binom{6}{3} = 20$ different ways.

b) Next, we must count the number of outcomes with two of one number and one of another. There are 6 choices for the number that appears twice, and no matter which number we choose to appear twice, there are 5 choices for the number that appears once. There are thus $6 \times 5 = 30$ outcomes with two of one number and one of another.

c) One number on all three dice can occur in 6 different ways, one for each of the numbers on a die.

Thus, the number of possible outcomes is $20 + 30 + 6 = 56$, as we also deduced in Example 4.16. ✦

EXERCISES

4.8.1*: Count the number of poker hands of the following types:

a)   Two pairs
b)   Three of a kind
c)   Full house
d)   Four of a kind

Be careful when counting one type of hand not to include hands that are better. For example, in (a), make sure that the two pairs are different (so you don't really have four of a kind) and the fifth card is different from the pairs (so you don't have a full house).

Blackjack

4.8.2*: A *blackjack* consists of two cards, one of which is an Ace and the other of which is a 10-point card, either a 10, Jack, Queen, or King.

a)   How many different blackjacks are there in a 52-card deck?

b)   In the game blackjack, one card is dealt down and the other is dealt up. Thus, in a sense order of the two cards matters. In this case, how many different blackjacks are there?

Pinochle deck

c)   In a pinochle deck there are eight cards of each rank 9, 10, Jack, Queen, King, Ace (two indistinguishable cards of each suit) and no other cards. How many blackjacks are there, assuming order is unimportant?

4.8.3: How many poker hands are "nothing" (i.e., not one-pair or better)? You may use the results of Examples 4.18 and 4.19 as well as the answer to Exercise 4.8.1.

4.8.4: If we toss 12 coins in sequence, how many have

a)   At least 9 heads
b)   At most 4 heads
c)   Between 5 and 7 heads
d)   Fewer than 2 or more than 10 heads

4.8.5*: How many outcomes in Chuck-a-Luck have at least one 1?

4.8.6*: How many anagrams of the word `little` are there in which the two `t`'s are not adjacent?

Bridge

4.8.7**: A bridge hand consists of 13 of the 52 cards. We often classify hands by "distribution," that is, the way cards are grouped into suits. For example, a hand of 4-3-3-3 distribution has four of one suit and three of each of the other suits. A hand with 5-4-3-1 distribution has one suit of five cards, one of four, one of three, and one of one card. Count the number of hands with the following distributions: (a) 4-3-3-3 (b) 5-4-3-1 (c) 4-4-3-2 (d) 9-2-2-0.

✦✦ 4.9   Introduction to Probability Theory

Probability theory, along with its general importance, has many uses in computer science. One important application is the estimation of the running time of programs in the case of average or typical inputs. This evaluation is important for those algorithms whose worst-case running time is very much larger than the average running time. We shall see examples of such evaluations shortly.

Another use of probability is in designing algorithms for making decisions in the presence of uncertainty. For example, we can use probability theory to design algorithms for making the best possible medical diagnosis from available information or algorithms for allocating resources on the basis of expected future needs.

Probability Spaces

Experiment, outcome

When we speak of a *probability space*, we mean a finite set of points, each of which represents one possible *outcome* of an *experiment*. Each point x has associated with it a nonnegative real number called the *probability of x*, such that the sum of the probabilities of all the points is 1. One also speaks of probability spaces that have infinite numbers of points, although there is little application for these in computer science, and we shall not deal with them here.

Commonly, the points of a probability space have equal probability. Unless we state otherwise, you may assume that the probabilities of the various points in a probability space are equal. Thus, if there are n points in the probability space the probability of each point is $1/n$.

♦ **Example 4.22.** In Fig. 4.13 is a probability space with six points. The points are each identified with one of the numbers from 1 to 6, and we may think of this space as representing the outcomes of the "experiment" of throwing a single fair die. That is, one of the six numbers will appear on top of the die, and each number is equally likely to appear, that is, 1/6th of the time. ♦

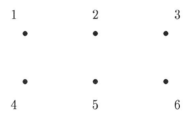

Fig. 4.13. A probability space with six points.

Event

Any subset of the points in a probability space is called an *event*. The *probability* of an event E, denoted PROB(E), is the sum of the probabilities of the points in E. If the points are all equally likely, then we can compute the probability of E by dividing the number of points in E by the number of points in the total probability space.

Probability Calculations

Often, the calculation of the probability of an event involves combinatorics. We must count the number of points in the event as well as the number of points in the entire probability space. When points are equally likely, the ratio of these two counts is the probability of the event. We shall give a series of examples to illustrate the calculation of probabilities in this fashion.

Infinite Probability Spaces

In certain circumstances, we can imagine that a probability space has an infinite number of points. The probability of any given point may be infinitesimal, and we can only associate finite probabilities with some collections of points. For a simple example, here is a probability space, the square, whose points are all the points of the plane within the square.

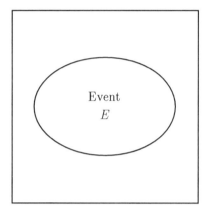

We may suppose that any point in the square is equally likely to be chosen. The "experiment" may be thought of as throwing a dart at the square in such a way that the dart is equally likely to wind up anywhere within the square, but not outside it. Although any point has only infinitesimal probability of being hit, the probability of a region of the square is the ratio of the area of the region to the area of the entire square. Thus, we can compute the probability of certain events.

For example, we show within the probability space an event E consisting of an ellipse contained within the square. Let us suppose the area of the ellipse is 29% of the area of the square. Then PROB(E) is 0.29. That is, if the dart is thrown at random at the square, 29% of the time the dart will land within the ellipse.

◆ **Example 4.23.** Figure 4.14 shows the probability space representing the throw of two dice. That is, the experiment is the tossing of two dice, in order, and observing the numbers on their upper faces. Assuming the dice are fair, there are 36 equally likely points, or outcomes of the experiment, so each point has probability 1/36. Each point corresponds to the assignment of one of six values to each die. For example, $(2, 3)$ represents the outcome where 2 appears on the first die and 3 on the second. Pair $(3, 2)$ represents 3 on the first die and 2 on the second.

The outlined region represents the event "craps," that is, a total 7 or 11 on the two dice. There are eight points in this event, six where the total is 7 and two where the total is 11. The probability of throwing craps is thus 8/36, or about 22%. ◆

◆ **Example 4.24.** Let us calculate the probability that a poker hand is a one-pair hand. We learned in Example 4.8 that there are 2,598,960 different poker hands. Consider the experiment of dealing a poker hand fairly, that is, with all hands equally likely. Thus, the probability space for this experiment has 2,598,960

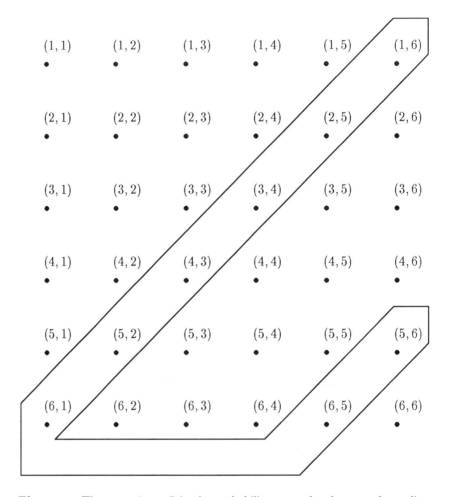

Fig. 4.14. The event "craps" in the probability space for the toss of two dice.

points. We also learned in Example 4.18 that 1,098,240 of these points represent hands classified as one pair. Assuming all hands are equally likely to be dealt, the probability of the event "one pair" is 1,098,240/2,598,960, or about 42%. ✦

Keno

✦ **Example 4.25.** In the game of Keno, twenty of the numbers from 1 to 80 are selected at random. Before the selection, players may guess some numbers; we shall concentrate on the "5-spot game," where players guess five numbers. A player who guesses correctly three, four, or five of the twenty selected numbers is rewarded; the amount of the payoff increases with the number of correct guesses. We shall calculate the probability that a player guesses exactly three numbers correctly in a 5-spot game. The probabilities of guessing four or five correctly are left as exercises.

To begin, the appropriate probability space has one point for each possible selection of twenty numbers from 1 to 80. The number of such selections is

$$\binom{80}{20} = \frac{80!}{20!60!}$$

When are Outcomes Random?

We have assumed in our examples that certain experiments have "random" outcomes; that is, all possible outcomes are equally likely. In some cases the justification for this assumptions comes from physics. For instance, when throwing fair (unweighted) dice, we assume that it is not physically possible to control the toss in such a way that one face is more likely than others to appear on top. That is a valid assumption in practice. Similarly, we assume that a fairly shuffled deck will not bias the outcome, and any card is equally likely to be found in any position in the deck.

In other cases, we find that what we imagine is random is actually not random at all, but is the result of a process that is predictable in principle but unpredictable in practice. For example, the numbers in a Keno game may be generated by a computer executing a particular algorithm, and yet without access to secret information used by the computer, it is impossible to predict the outcome.

Random number generator

All computer-generated "random" sequences of outcomes are the result of a special kind of algorithm called a *random number generator*. Designing one of these algorithms requires knowledge of some specialized mathematics and is beyond the scope of this book. However, we can offer an example of a random number generator that works fairly well in practice, called a *linear congruential generator*.

We specify constants $a \geq 2$, $b \geq 1$, $x_0 \geq 0$, and a modulus $m > \max(a, b, x_0)$. We can generate a sequence of numbers $x_0, x_1, x_2, \ldots$ using the formula

$$x_{n+1} = (ax_n + b) \bmod m$$

For suitable choices of a, b, m, and x_0, the resulting sequence of numbers will appear quite random, even though they are constructed from the "seed" x_0 by a specific algorithm.

Sequences generated by a random number generator have many uses. For instance, we can select numbers in a Keno game by taking numbers from the sequence described above, dividing each by 80, taking the remainder, and adding 1 to get a "random" number from 1 to 80. We keep doing so, throwing away repeated numbers, until twenty numbers are selected. The game will be perceived as fair, as long as no one knows the generation algorithm and the seed.

---

a number so huge that we are fortunate we do not have to write it down.

Now we must count the number of selections of twenty numbers out of eighty that include three of the five numbers chosen by the player and seventeen numbers from the seventy-five that the player has not chosen. We can choose three of the five in $\binom{5}{3} = 10$ ways, and we can choose seventeen from the remaining seventy-five in $\binom{75}{17} = \frac{75!}{17!58!}$ ways.

The ratio of the number of outcomes where the player picks three out of five to the total number of selections is thus

$$\frac{10 \frac{75!}{17!58!}}{\frac{80!}{20!60!}}$$

If we multiply top and bottom by $\frac{20!60!}{80!}$, the above becomes

$$10(\frac{75!}{17!58!})(\frac{20!60!}{80!})$$

Now, we find in the numerator and denominator pairs of factorials that are close and can almost be canceled. For instance, 75! in the numerator and 80! in the denominator can be replaced by the product of the five numbers from 80 down to 76 in the denominator. The resulting simplification is

$$\frac{10 \times 60 \times 59 \times 20 \times 19 \times 18}{80 \times 79 \times 78 \times 77 \times 76}$$

Now we have a computation that involves manageable numbers. The result is about 0.084. That is, about 8.4% of the time the player guesses three out of five correctly. ✦

Fundamental Relationships

Let us close this section by observing several important properties of probabilities. First, if p is the probability of any event, then

$$0 \leq p \leq 1$$

That is, any event consists of 0 or more points, so its probability cannot be negative. Also, no event can consist of more points than are in the entire probability space, so its probability cannot exceed 1.

Complement event

Second, let E be an event in a probability space P. Then the *complement event* $\bar{E}$ for E is the set of points of P that are not in event E. We may observe that

$$\text{PROB}(E) + \text{PROB}(\bar{E}) = 1$$

or put another way, $\text{PROB}(\bar{E}) = 1 - \text{PROB}(E)$. The reason is that every point in P is either in E or in $\bar{E}$, but not both.

EXERCISES

4.9.1: Using the probability space for the toss of two fair dice shown in Fig. 4.14, give the probabilities of the following events:

a)   A six is thrown (i.e., the sum of the dice is 6)
b)   A ten is thrown
c)   The sum of the dice is odd
d)   The sum of the dice is between 5 and 9

4.9.2*: Calculate the probabilities of the following events. The probability space is the deal of two cards in order from an ordinary 52-card deck.

a)   At least one card is an Ace
b)   The cards are of the same rank
c)   The cards are of the same suit
d)   The cards are of the same rank and suit
e)   The cards are the same either in rank or in suit
f)   The first card is of a higher rank than the second card

4.9.3*: A dart is thrown at a one foot square on the wall, with equal likelihood of entering the square at any point. What is the probability that the dart is thrown

a) Within three inches of the center?
b) Within three inches of the border?

Note that for this exercise, the probability space is an infinite one-foot square, with all points within it equally likely.

4.9.4: Calculate the probability of the player in a 5-spot game of Keno guessing

a) Four out of five
b) All five

4.9.5: Write a C program to implement a linear congruential random number generator. Plot a histogram of the frequencies of the least significant digits of the first 100 numbers generated. What property should this histogram have?

❖❖ 4.10 Conditional Probability

In this section we shall develop a number of formulas and strategies for thinking about relationships among the probabilities of several events. One important development is a notion of independent experiments, where the outcome of one experiment does not affect the outcome of others. We shall also use our techniques to calculate probabilities in some complicated situations.

These developments depend upon a notion of "conditional probability." Informally, if we conduct an experiment and we find that an event E has occurred, it may or may not be the case that the point representing the outcome is also in some other event F. Figure 4.15 suggests this situation. The conditional probability of F given E is the probability that F has also occurred.

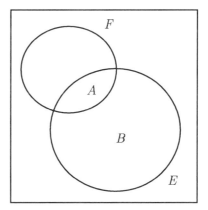

Fig. 4.15. The conditional probability of F given E is the probability that the outcome is in A divided by the probability that the outcome is in A or B.

Formally, if E and F are two events in a probability space, we say the *conditional probability of F given E*, denoted $\text{PROB}(F/E)$, is the sum of the probabilities of the points that are in both E and F divided by the sum of the probabilities of the points in E. In Fig. 4.15, region A is those points that are in both E and F, and B is those points that are in E but not F. If all points are equally likely, then

PROB(F/E) is the number of points in A divided by the sum of the numbers of points in A and B.

◆ **Example 4.26.** Let us consider the probability space of Fig. 4.14, which represents the toss of two dice. Let the event E be the six points in which the first die comes out 1, and let the event F be the six points in which the second die comes out 1. The situation is shown in Fig. 4.16. There is one point in both E and F, namely the point $(1,1)$. There are five points in E that are not in F. Thus, the conditional probability PROB(F/E) is $1/6$. That is, the chance that the second die is 1, given that the first die is 1, is $1/6$.

We may notice that this conditional probability is exactly the same as the probability of F itself. That is, since F has 6 out of the 36 points in the space, PROB(F) $= 6/36 = 1/6$. Intuitively, the probability of throwing 1 on the second die is not affected by the fact that 1 has been thrown on the first die. We shall soon define the notion of "independent experiments," such as the throwing of dice in sequence, where the outcome of one experiment does not influence the outcome of the others. In these cases, if E and F are events representing outcomes of the two experiments, we expect that PROB(F/E) = PROB(F). We have just seen an example of this phenomenon. ◆

◆ **Example 4.27.** Suppose our experiment is the deal of two cards, in order, from the usual 52-card deck. The number of points in this experiment of selection without replacement (as in Section 4.4) is $52 \times 51 = 2652$. We shall assume that the deal is fair, so each point has the same probability.

Let the event E be that the first card is an Ace, and let event F be that the second card is an Ace. Then the number of points in E is $4 \times 51 = 204$. That is, the first card must be one of the four Aces, and the second card can be any of 51 cards, excluding the Ace that was chosen first. Thus, PROB(E) $= 204/2652 = 1/13$. That result matches our intuition. All 13 ranks being equally likely, we expect that one time in 13 an Ace will appear first.

Similarly, the number of points in event F is $51 \times 4 = 204$. We can choose any of the 4 Aces for the second card and any of the remaining 51 cards for the first card. The fact that the first card is theoretically dealt first is irrelevant. There are thus 204 outcomes in which an Ace appears in the second position. Therefore, PROB(F) $= 1/13$ just as for E. Again, this result meets our intuition that one time in 13 an Ace will be dealt as the second card.

Now, let us compute PROB(F/E). Of the 204 points in E, there are 12 that have an Ace in the second position and therefore are also in F. That is, all points in E have an Ace in the first position. We may select this Ace in 4 different ways, corresponding to the 4 suits. For each selection, we have 3 different choices of Ace for the second position. Thus, the number of choices of two Aces with order considered is 4×3 according to the technique of Section 4.4.

Therefore, the conditional probability PROB(F/E) is $12/204$, or $1/17$. We notice that the conditional probability of F given E is not the same as the probability of F in this example. That also makes intuitive sense. The probability of getting an Ace in the second position goes down when we know there is an Ace in the first position. For then, there are only 3 Aces remaining out of 51 cards, and $3/51 = 1/17$.

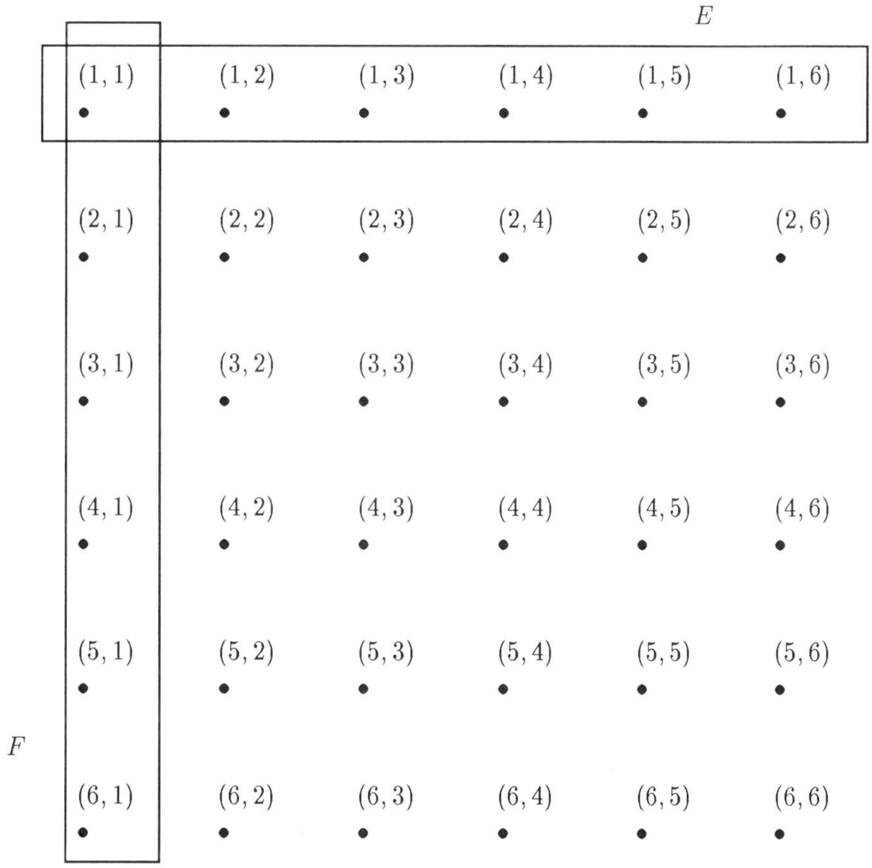

E

(1,1) •	(1,2) •	(1,3) •	(1,4) •	(1,5) •	(1,6) •
(2,1) •	(2,2) •	(2,3) •	(2,4) •	(2,5) •	(2,6) •
(3,1) •	(3,2) •	(3,3) •	(3,4) •	(3,5) •	(3,6) •
(4,1) •	(4,2) •	(4,3) •	(4,4) •	(4,5) •	(4,6) •
(5,1) •	(5,2) •	(5,3) •	(5,4) •	(5,5) •	(5,6) •
(6,1) •	(6,2) •	(6,3) •	(6,4) •	(6,5) •	(6,6) •

F

Fig. 4.16. Events representing 1 on the first or second dice.

In comparison, if we know nothing about the first card, there are 4 Aces out of 52 that we may receive as the second card. ✦

Independent Experiments

Joint
probability
space

As we suggested in Examples 4.23, 4.26, and 4.27, we sometimes form a probability space representing the outcomes of two or more experiments. In the simplest cases, the points in this joint probability space are lists of outcomes, one for each of the experiments. Figure 4.16 is an example of a probability space that is joint between two experiments. In other situations, where there is a connection between the outcomes of the experiments, the joint space may have some points missing. Example 4.27 discussed such a case, where the joint space represented the deal of two cards and the pairs of outcomes in which the two cards are identical are not possible.

There is an intuitive notion of the outcome of one experiment X being "independent" of previous experiments in the sequence, meaning that the probabilities of the various outcomes of X do not depend on the outcomes of the previous experiments. Thus, in Example 4.26 we argued that the roll of the second die is independent of the roll of the first die, while in Example 4.27 we saw that the second card dealt was not independent of the first, since the first card was then unavailable.

In defining independence, we shall focus on two experiments. However, since either experiment may itself be the sequence of several experiments, we effectively cover the case of many experiments. We must begin with a probability space that represents the outcome of two successive experiments, X_1 and X_2.

✦ **Example 4.28.** Figure 4.14 illustrates a joint probability space in which experiment X_1 is the throw of the first die and X_2 is the throw of the second die. Here, every pair of outcomes is represented by one point, and the points have equal probability, $1/36$.

In Example 4.27 we discussed a space of 2652 points representing the selection of two cards in order. This space consists of all pairs (C, D) in which C and D are cards, and $C \neq D$. Again, each of these points has the same probability, $1/2652$. ✦

In the probability space representing the outcomes of X_1 followed by X_2, there are events that represent the outcome of one of the experiments. That is, if a is a possible outcome of experiment X_1, then there is an event consisting of all those points in which the outcome of the first experiment is a. Let us call this event E_a. Similarly, if b is a possible outcome of X_2, then there is an event F_b consisting of all those points in which the outcome of the second experiment is b.

✦ **Example 4.29.** In Fig. 4.16, E is E_1, the event of all points for which the outcome of the first experiment is 1. Likewise, F is the event F_1, whose points are those where the outcome of the second experiment is 1. More generally, each row corresponds to one of the six possible outcomes of the first experiment, and each column corresponds to one of the six possible outcomes of the second experiment. ✦

Independence   Formally, we say that experiment X_2 is *independent of* experiment X_1 if for all outcomes a for X_1 and all outcomes b for X_2, $\text{PROB}(F_b/E_a) = \text{PROB}(F_b)$. That is, no matter what the outcome of experiment X_1, the conditional probability of each outcome of X_2 is the same as it is in the whole probability space.

✦ **Example 4.30.** Returning to the probability space of Fig. 4.16 representing the toss of two dice, let a and b each be any of the numbers from 1 to 6. Let E_a be the event that the first die is a and F_b be the event that the second die is b. We note that the probability of each of these events is $1/6$; they are each one row or column. For any a and b, $\text{PROB}(F_b/E_a)$ is also $1/6$. We argued this fact for the case $a = b = 1$ in Example 4.26, but the same argument applies to any two outcomes a and b, because their events have exactly one point in common. Thus, the tosses of the two dice are independent.

On the other hand, in the card-based Example 4.27, we do not get independence. Here, the experiment X_1 is the selection of the first card, and the experiment X_2 is the selection of the second card from the remaining deck. Consider an event like $F_{A\spadesuit}$ — that is, the second card is the Ace of Spades. It is easy to count that the probability of this event, $\text{PROB}(F_{A\spadesuit})$, is 1/52.

Now, consider an event like $E_{3\clubsuit}$, the first card is the Three of Clubs. The number of points in both $E_{3\clubsuit}$ and $F_{A\spadesuit}$ is 1, namely the point $(3\clubsuit, A\spadesuit)$. The total number of points in $E_{3\clubsuit}$ is 51, namely those points of the form $(3\clubsuit, C)$ where C is any card but the Three of Clubs. Thus, the conditional probability $\text{PROB}(F_{A\spadesuit}/E_{3\clubsuit})$ is 1/51, not 1/52 as it would have to be if the two experiments were independent.

For a more extreme example, consider the event $E_{A\spadesuit}$ in which the first card is the Ace of Spades. Since $E_{A\spadesuit}$ and $F_{A\spadesuit}$ have no point in common, $\text{PROB}(F_{A\spadesuit}/E_{A\spadesuit})$ is 0 instead of 1/52. ✦

A Distributive Law for Probabilities

Region

Sometimes it is easier to calculate the probability of an event if we first divide the probability space into regions[2] that partition the space. That is, every point is in exactly one region. Typically, the probability space represents the outcome of a sequence of experiments, and the regions, which are themselves events, correspond to the possible outcomes of one of these experiments.

Suppose we wish to calculate the probability of event E in a space of n points that is divided into k regions, $R_1, R_2, \ldots, R_k$. For simplicity, we shall assume that all points have equal probability, although the conclusion we draw holds as well if the points have differing probabilities. Let event E consist of m points. Let region R_i have r_i points, for $i = 1, 2, \ldots, k$. Finally, let the number of points of E that lie in region R_i be e_i. Note that $\sum_{i=1}^{k} r_i = n$, and $\sum_{i=1}^{k} e_i = m$. The reason in each case is that points are each in one and only one region.

We know $\text{PROB}(E) = m/n$, because m/n is the fraction of points in E. If we replace m by the sum of the e_i's we get

$$\text{PROB}(E) = \sum_{i=1}^{k} \frac{e_i}{n}$$

Next, introduce factor r_i in both the numerator and denominator in each term of the sum above. The result is

$$\text{PROB}(E) = \sum_{i=1}^{k} \left(\frac{e_i}{r_i}\right)\left(\frac{r_i}{n}\right)$$

Now, notice that $r_i/n = \text{PROB}(R_i)$; that is, r_i/n is the fraction of the entire space in region R_i. Also, e_i/r_i is $\text{PROB}(E/R_i)$, the conditional probability of event E given event R_i. Put another way, e_i/r_i is the fraction of the points in region R_i that are in E. The result is the following formula for the probability of an event E.

$$\text{PROB}(E) = \sum_{i=1}^{k} \text{PROB}(E/R_i)\text{PROB}(R_i) \tag{4.10}$$

Informally, the probability of E is the sum over all regions of the probability of being in that region times the probability of E within that region.

---

[2] A "region" is synonymous with an "event," that is, a subset of a probability space. However, we shall use the term region to emphasize the fact that the space is being partitioned into events that completely cover the space and do not overlap.

✦ **Example 4.31.** The diagram in Fig. 4.17 suggests how Equation (4.10) is to be applied. There we see a probability space that has been divided vertically into three regions, R_1, R_2, and R_3. There is an event E, which we doubly outline. We let a through f be the numbers of points in the six sets shown.

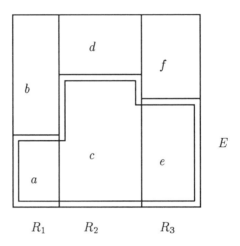

Fig. 4.17. A probability space divided into regions.

Let $n = a + b + c + d + e + f$. Then $\text{PROB}(R_1) = (a + b)/n$, $\text{PROB}(R_2) = (c + d)/n$, and $\text{PROB}(R_3) = (e + f)/n$. Next, the conditional probabilities of E in the three regions are $\text{PROB}(E/R_1) = a/(a + b)$, $\text{PROB}(E/R_2) = c/(c + d)$, and $\text{PROB}(E/R_3) = e/(e + f)$. Now, to evaluate formula (4.10), we have

$$\text{PROB}(E) = \text{PROB}(E/R_1)\text{PROB}(R_1) + \text{PROB}(E/R_2)\text{PROB}(R_2) +$$
$$\text{PROB}(E/R_3)\text{PROB}(R_3)$$

This formula, in terms of the parameters a through f, is

$$\text{PROB}(E) = (\frac{a}{a + b})(\frac{a + b}{n}) + (\frac{c}{c + d})(\frac{c + d}{n}) + (\frac{e}{e + f})(\frac{e + f}{n})$$
$$= \frac{a}{n} + \frac{c}{n} + \frac{e}{n}$$

Notice that the same result can be obtained by simply comparing the numbers of points in the three areas labeled a, c, and e with the size of the entire space. This fraction, $(a + c + e)/n$, is exactly what the formula above gives for the probability of E. That observation illustrates Equation (4.10). ✦

✦ **Example 4.32.** Let us use Equation (4.10) to compute the probability of the event E that two cards dealt in order are both Aces. The probability space is the 2652 points discussed in Example 4.27. We shall divide this space into two regions:

R_1: Those points in which the first card is an Ace. There are $4 \times 51 = 204$ such points, since we may pick the first card to be an Ace in 4 ways, and there are then 51 choices of second card.

R_2: The remaining 2448 points.

Equation (4.10) in this case becomes

$$\text{PROB}(E) = \text{PROB}(E/R_1)\text{PROB}(R_1) + \text{PROB}(E/R_2)\text{PROB}(R_2)$$

Clearly $\text{PROB}(E/R_2)$, the conditional probability of E given R_2, is 0. There is no way to get two Aces if the first card is not an Ace. We must thus compute $\text{PROB}(E/R_1)\text{PROB}(R_1)$, and this value is $\text{PROB}(E)$. Now $\text{PROB}(R_1) = 204/2652 = 1/13$. In other words, the chance of getting an Ace as the first card is $1/13$. Since there are thirteen ranks, that probability makes sense.

Now, we need to compute $\text{PROB}(E/R_1)$. If the first card is an Ace, then there remain 3 Aces out of 51 cards. Thus, $\text{PROB}(E/R_1) = 3/51 = 1/17$. We conclude that $\text{PROB}(E) = (1/17)(1/13) = 1/221$. ✦

✦ **Example 4.33.** Let us apply Equation (4.10) to the problem of computing the probability of the event E that at least one 1 appears in the toss of three dice, as in the game Chuck-a-Luck described in Example 4.16. First, we must understand that the notion of an "outcome" described in that example does not match the notion of a point in a probability space. In Example 4.16 we established that there were 56 different "outcomes," which were defined to be the numbers of occurrences of 1 through 6 on the faces of the dice. For instance, "a 4, a 5, and a 6" is one possible outcome; "two 3's and a 4" is another. However, not all outcomes in this sense have the same probability. In particular, outcomes with three different numbers showing have twice the probability of outcomes with two of one number and six times the probability of an outcome where all three dice show the same number.

While we could use the probability space whose points are "outcomes " in the sense of Example 4.16, it is more more natural to consider the order in which the dice are rolled and thus develop a probability space whose points have equal probability. There are $6^3 = 216$ different outcomes corresponding to the roll of three dice, in order, and each of these outcomes has probability $1/216$.

We could calculate the probability of at least one 1 in a direct manner, without using Equation (4.10). First, calculate the number of rolls in which no 1 appears. We can assign to each of the three dice any of the numbers from 2 to 6. There are thus $5^3 = 125$ points in the space that have no 1, and $216 - 125 = 91$ points that do have a 1. Therefore, $\text{PROB}(E) = 91/216$, or about 42%.

The approach above is short but requires that we use several "tricks." Another way to calculate the probability "by force" is to divide the space into three regions, corresponding to the cases in which there are one, two, or three different numbers showing. Let R_i be the region of points with i different numbers. We can calculate the probabilities of the various regions as follows. For R_3 there are only six points, one for each of the numbers 1 through 6 that may appear on all three dice. For R_1 there are $6 \times 5 \times 4 = 120$ ways to select three different numbers out of six, according to the rule of Section 4.4. Thus, R_2 must have the remaining $216 - 6 - 120 = 90$ points.[3] The probabilities of the regions are $\text{PROB}(R_1) = 6/216 = 1/36$, $\text{PROB}(R_2) = 90/216 = 5/12$, and $\text{PROB}(R_3) = 120/216 = 5/9$.

Next, we can calculate the conditional probabilities. If there are three numbers out of the possible six showing, the probability is $1/2$ that one of them is 1. If two

---

[3] We can compute this number directly by multiplying 6 ways that we can choose the number to appear twice, times 5 ways we can pick the number on the remaining dice, times $\binom{3}{1} = 3$ ways we can pick the die that has the unique number. Note that $6 \times 5 \times 3 = 90$.

numbers are showing, the probability is 1/3 that 1 appears at least once. If only one number shows, there is a 1/6 chance that it is 1. Thus, $\text{PROB}(E/R_1) = 1/6$, $\text{PROB}(E/R_2) = 1/3$, and $\text{PROB}(E/R_3) = 1/2$. We can put all these probabilities together to evaluate (4.10). The result is

$$\begin{aligned} \text{PROB}(E) &= (1/6)(1/36) + (1/3)(5/12) + (1/2)(5/9) \\ &= 1/216 + 5/36 + 5/18 = 91/216 \end{aligned}$$

This fraction agrees with the direct calculation, of course. If we see the "trick" of the direct calculation, that approach is considerably easier. However, breaking the problem into regions is frequently a more reliable way to guarantee success. ✦

A Product Rule for Independent Experiments

A common type of probability problem asks for the probability of a sequence of outcomes to a sequence of independent experiments. In that case, Equation (4.10) has an especially simple form, and it tells us that the probability of a sequence of outcomes is the product of the probabilities of each outcome by itself.

First, whenever we divide the probability space into k regions of equal size, we know that $\text{PROB}(R_i) = 1/k$ for all i. Thus (4.10) reduces to

$$\text{PROB}(E) = \sum_{i=1}^{k} \frac{1}{k} \text{PROB}(E/R_i) \tag{4.11}$$

A useful way to look at (4.11) is that the probability of E is the average over all regions of the probability of E given we are in that region.

Now, consider a probability space that represents the outcomes of two independent experiments X_1 and X_2. We may divide this space into k regions, each the set of points for which the outcome of X_1 has a particular value. Then each of the regions has the same probability, $1/k$.

Suppose we want to calculate the probability of the event E in which X_1 has the outcome a and X_2 has the outcome b. We may use formula (4.11). If R_i is not the region corresponding to outcome a for X_1, then $\text{PROB}(E/R_i) = 0$. Thus, all but the term for the region of a drops out of (4.11). If R_a is that region, we get

$$\text{PROB}(E) = \frac{1}{k} \text{PROB}(E/R_a) \tag{4.12}$$

What is $\text{PROB}(E/R_a)$? It is the probability that X_1 has outcome a and X_2 has outcome b, given that X_1 has outcome a. Since we are given that X_1 has outcome a, $\text{PROB}(E/R_a)$ is just the probability that X_2 has outcome b given that X_1 has outcome a. Since X_1 and X_2 are independent, $\text{PROB}(E/R_a)$ is just the probability that X_2 has outcome b. If there are m possible outcomes for X_2, then $\text{PROB}(E/R_a)$ is $1/m$. Then (4.12) becomes

$$\text{PROB}(E) = (\frac{1}{k})(\frac{1}{m})$$

We may generalize the above reasoning to any number of experiments. To do so, we let experiment X_1 be a sequence of experiments and show by induction on the total number of independent experiments that the probability of all having a particular sequence of outcomes is the product of the probabilities of each outcome.

Using Independence to Simplify Calculations

There are many opportunities to simplify probability calculations if we know that experiments are independent. The product rule is one such example. Another is that whenever event E is the set of points with a particular outcome from experiment X_1, and F is the set of points with a particular outcome of another, independent experiment X_2, then $\text{PROB}(E/F) = \text{PROB}(E)$.

In principle, telling whether two experiments are independent is a complex task involving examination of the probability space representing pairs of outcomes of each experiment. However, often we can appeal to the physics of the situation to conclude that experiments are independent without doing this calculation. For example, when we throw dice in sequence, there is no physical reason why the outcome of one would influence the other, so they must be independent experiments. Contrast the situation of dice with the deal of several cards from a deck. Since cards dealt are unavailable to be dealt at a future step, we do not expect successive cards to be independent of each other. We in fact observed this lack of independence in Example 4.29.

♦ **Example 4.34.** The probability that the last four digits of a phone number are 1234 is 0.0001. The selection of each digit is an experiment with ten possible outcomes: 0 through 9. Moreover, each selection is independent of the other selections, since we are performing a "selection with replacement" as in Section 4.2. The probability that the first digit is 1 is 1/10. Similarly, the probability that the second digit is 2 is 1/10, and likewise for the other two digits. The probability of the event that the four digits are 1234 in order is $(1/10)^4 = 0.0001$. ♦

EXERCISES

4.10.1: Using the space of Fig. 4.14, give the conditional probabilities of the following pairs of events.

a) The second die is even, given that the first die is odd
b) The first die is even, given that the second die is at least 3
c) The sum of the dice is at least 7, given that the first die is 4
d) The second die is 3, given that the sum of the dice is 8

4.10.2: Divide the Chuck-a-Luck (see Example 4.16) probability space into three regions, as in Example 4.33. Use this division and Equation 4.10 to compute the probability that

a) There are at least two 1's showing
b) All three dice are 1
c) There is exactly one 1 showing

4.10.3: Show that in Chuck-a-Luck, the probability of any event in which all three dice have different values is twice the probability of any event where one number appears exactly twice and six times the probability of any event in which all three dice show the same number.

4.10.4*: Show by induction on n that if there are n experiments, each of which is independent of those that go before, then the probability of any sequence of outcomes is the product of the probabilities of each outcome in its own experiment.

4.10.5*: Show that if $\text{PROB}(F/E) = \text{PROB}(F)$, then $\text{PROB}(E/F) = \text{PROB}(E)$. Thus, show that if experiment X_1 is independent of experiment X_2, then X_2 is independent of X_1.

4.10.6*: Consider the set of sequences of seven letters chosen from W and L. We may think of these sequences as representing the outcomes of a match of seven games, where W means the first team wins the game and L means the second team wins the game. The match is won by the first team to win four games (thus, some games may never get played, but we need to include their hypothetical outcomes in the points in order that we have a probability space of equally likely points).

a) What is the probability that a team will win the match, given that it has won the first game?

b) What is the probability that a team will win the match, given that it has won the first two games?

c) What is the probability that a team will win the match, given that it has won two out of the first three games?

4.10.7**: There are three prisoners, A, B, and C. They are told one and only one is to be shot and that the guard knows who. A asks the guard to tell him the name of one of the other prisoners who will *not* be shot. The guard answers that B will not be shot.

A reasons that either he or C will be shot, so the probability that A will be shot is 1/2. On the other hand, reasons A, no matter who is to be shot, the guard knows somebody besides A who will not be shot, so he always has an answer to A's question. Therefore, the asking and answering of the question provides no information about whether or not A is to be shot, so the probability that A will be shot is still 1/3, as it was before the question was asked.

What is the true probability that A will be shot after the sequence of events described above? *Hint*: You need to construct an appropriate probability space, one that represents not only the experiment in which a prisoner is chosen to be shot but also the possibility that the guard has a choice of whether to answer "B" or "C," and the experiment in which he chooses one if so.

4.10.8*: Suppose that E is an event in a space that is partitioned into k regions $R_1, R_2, \ldots, R_k$. Show that

$$\text{PROB}(R_j/E) = \frac{\text{PROB}(R_j)\text{PROB}(E/R_j)}{\sum_{i=1}^{k} \text{PROB}(R_i)\text{PROB}(E/R_i)}$$

Bayes' Rule

This formula is called *Bayes' Rule*. It gives a value for the probability of R_j given that E has been observed. For Example 4.31, calculate $\text{PROB}(R_1/E)$, $\text{PROB}(R_2/E)$, and $\text{PROB}(R_3/E)$ using Bayes' rule.

❖❖ 4.11 Probabilistic Reasoning

An important application of probability in computing is in the design of systems that predict events. An example is a medical diagnosis system. Ideally, the process of diagnosis consists of performing tests or observing symptoms until the outcome of the tests and presence or absence of certain symptoms is sufficient for the physician to determine what disease the patient has. In practice, however, diagnoses are rarely certain. Rather, a diagnosis is the most likely disease, or a disease whose conditional probability, given the outcomes of the experiments that are the tests and observations of symptoms, is highest.

Let us consider an overly simple example that has the flavor of diagnosis using probability. Suppose it is known that when a patient has a headache, the probability that he has the flu is 50%. That is,

$$\text{PROB}(\text{Flu}/\text{Headache}) = 0.5$$

In the above, we interpret Flu as the name of an event that can be interpreted as "the patient has the flu." Similarly, Headache is the name of the event that the patient complains of a headache.

Suppose we also know that when the patient's temperature is measured at 102 (Fahrenheit) or above, the probability is 60% that he has the flu. If we allow Fever to be the name of the event that the patient's temperature is at least 102, then we can write this observation as

$$\text{PROB}(\text{Flu}/\text{Fever}) = 0.6$$

Now, consider the following diagnosis situation. A patient comes to the doctor complaining of a headache. The doctor takes his temperature and finds it is 102. What is the probability that the patient has the flu?

The situation is suggested by Fig. 4.18. There we see the three events Flu, Headache, and Fever, which together divide the space into 8 regions, which we indicate by letters a through h. For example, c is the event that the patient has a headache and flu, but not a fever.

The given information about probabilities puts some constraints on the sizes of the events in Fig. 4.18. Let us use the letters a through h as standing not only for the regions indicated in Fig. 4.18 but as the probabilities of those events. Then the condition that $\text{PROB}(\text{Flu}/\text{Headache}) = 0.5$ says that the sum of regions $c + f$ is half the total size of the headache event, or put another way:

$$c + f = d + g \tag{4.13}$$

Similarly, the fact that $\text{PROB}(\text{Flu}/\text{Fever}) = 0.6$ says that $e + f$ is 3/5 of the total size of the Fever event, or:

$$e + f = \tfrac{3}{2}(g + h) \tag{4.14}$$

Now, let us interpret the question: what is the probability of flu, given both a fever and a headache? The fact that there is both fever and headache says that we are either in region f or region g. In region f the diagnosis of flu is correct, and in g it is not. Thus, the probability of flu is $f/(f + g)$.

What is the value of $f/(f + g)$? The answer may be surprising. We have absolutely no information about the probability of flu; it could be 0 or 1 or anything in between. Here are two examples of how the points of the probability space of Fig. 4.18 could actually be distributed.

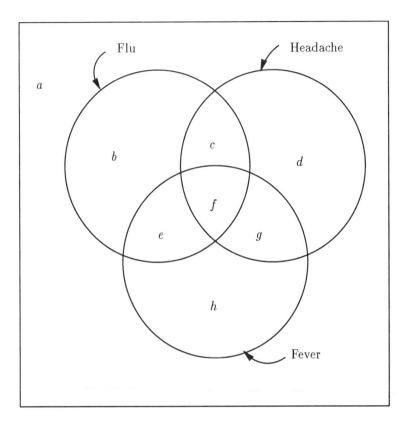

Fig. 4.18. The events Flu, Headache, and Fever.

✦ **Example 4.35.** Suppose that in Fig. 4.18 the probabilities associated with the various events are: $d = f = 0.3$, $a = h = 0.2$, and the four other regions have probability 0. Note that these values satisfy the constraining equations (4.13) and (4.14). In this example, $f/(f+g) = 1$; that is, a patient with both a headache and fever is certain to have the flu. Then the probability space of Fig. 4.18 actually looks like that of Fig. 4.19. There we see that whenever a patient has both a fever and headache, he has the flu, and conversely, whenever he has the flu, he has both fever and headache.[4] ✦

✦ **Example 4.36.** Another example is given by the probabilities $c = g = 0.2$, $a = e = 0.3$, with other probabilities 0. Again, Equations (4.13) and (4.14) are satisfied. Now, however, $f/(f+g) = 0$. That is, if you have both a fever and headache, then you are certain *not* to have the flu, a rather doubtful statement, but one that is not ruled out by Equations (4.13) and (4.14). The situation is shown in Fig. 4.20. ✦

---

[4] Although there are other examples where $b \neq 0$ — that is, one can have the flu and yet have neither fever nor headache — yet $f/(f+g) = 1$.

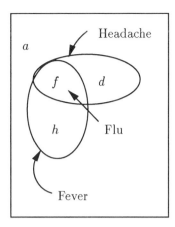

Fig. 4.19. Example of space where Fever and Headache guarantee Flu.

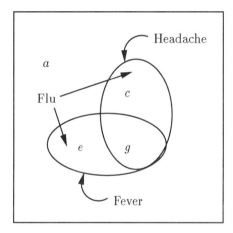

Fig. 4.20. Example of space where Fever and Headache guarantee no Flu.

Probability of the OR of Two Events

If we cannot tell anything about what happens when a patient has both fever and headache in the previous scenario, we might wonder whether there is anything we *can* say. In simpler situations there is indeed some limit to how probabilities behave when events are combined. Perhaps the most straightforward situation occurs when **Disjunction** we combine two events with *disjunction* or logical-OR.

◆ **Example 4.37.** Referring again to the situation of Fig. 4.18, suppose we are told that at any time, 2% of the population has a fever and 3% of the population has a headache. That is, the size of the event Fever is 0.02, and the size of the event Headache is 0.03. What fraction of the population has either a fever or a headache, or both?

The answer is that between 3% and 5% of the population has at least one. To see why, let us do some calculation in terms of the eight regions defined in Fig. 4.18.

If Fever has probability 0.02, that says

$$e + h + f + g = 0.02 \tag{4.15}$$

If Headache has probability 0.03, then

$$c + d + f + g = 0.03 \tag{4.16}$$

We are asked what is the size of the regions that are in either Fever or Headache or both; that is, how large is $e + h + f + g + c + d$?

If we add (4.15) and (4.16), we get $e + h + 2(f + g) + c + d = 0.05$, or put another way,

$$e + h + f + g + c + d = 0.05 - (f + g) \tag{4.17}$$

Since the probability of Fever-or-Headache is the left side of (4.17), it is also the right side, or $0.05 - (f + g)$.

At the minimum, $f + g$ is 0, so the probability of Fever-or-Headache can be as high as 0.05, but no higher. That is, it is possible that fever and headache never occur together. Then the regions f and g are empty, $e + h = 0.02$, and $c + d = 0.03$. In this case, the probability of Fever-or-Headache is the sum of the probability of Fever and the Probability of Headache.

What is the maximum value $f + g$ could have? Surely $f + g$ is no bigger than the entire Fever event and no bigger than the entire Headache event. Since Fever is smaller, we see that $f + g \leq 0.02$. Thus, the smallest the probability of Fever-or-Headache could be is $0 - 05 - 0.02$, or 0.03. This result happens to be the probability of Headache, the larger of the two events. That is no coincidence. Another way to look at it is that the smallest size Fever-or-Headache could have occurs when the smaller of the two events is wholly contained within the larger. In this example, that occurs when $e + h = 0$, and Fever is contained within Headache. In that case, you cannot have a fever unless you also have a headache, so the probability of Fever-or-Headache is the same as the probability of Headache alone, or 0.03. ✦

Rule for sums

We can generalize our explorations of Example 4.37 to any two events. The *rule for sums* is as follows. If E and F are any two events, and G is the event that either E or F or both occurs, then

$$\max\big(\text{PROB}(E), \text{PROB}(F)\big) \leq \text{PROB}(G) \leq \text{PROB}(E) + \text{PROB}(F) \tag{4.18}$$

That is, the probability of E-or-F is between the larger of the probabilities of E and F and the sum of those probabilities.

The same idea holds within any other event H. That is, all the probabilities in (4.18) may be made conditional on event H, giving us the more general rule

$$\max\big(\text{PROB}(E/H), \text{PROB}(F/H)\big) \leq \text{PROB}(G/H)$$
$$\leq \text{PROB}(E/H) + \text{PROB}(F/H) \tag{4.19}$$

✦ **Example 4.38.** Suppose, in the scenario of Fig. 4.18 we are told that 70% of all people with the flu have a fever, and 80% of all people with the flu have a headache. Then in (4.19), Flu is the event H, E is the event Fever, F is Headache, and G is Headache-or-Fever. We are told that $\text{PROB}(E/H) = \text{PROB}(\text{Fever/Flu}) = 0.7$, and $\text{PROB}(F/H) = \text{PROB}(\text{Headache/Flu}) = 0.8$.

Rule (4.19) says that $\text{PROB}(G/H)$ is at least the larger of 0.7 and 0.8. That is, if you have the flu, then the probability that you have a fever or headache or both is at least 0.8. Rule (4.19) also says that $\text{PROB}(G/H)$ is at most

$$\text{PROB}(E/H) + \text{PROB}(F/H)$$

or $0.7 + 0.8 = 1.5$. However, that upper bound is not useful. We know that no event can have probability greater than 1, so 1 is a better upper bound on $\text{PROB}(G/H)$. ✦

Probability of the AND of Events

Suppose we are again told that the probability of Fever is 0.02 and the probability of Headache is 0.03. What is the probability of Fever-and-Headache, that is, the probability that a person has both fever and headache? As for the OR of two events, we cannot tell exactly, but sometimes we can put some limits on the probability of **Conjunction** the *conjunction* (logical AND) of two events.

In terms of Fig. 4.18, we are asking how big $f + g$ can be. We already observed in connection with the OR of events that $f + g$ is largest when the smaller of the two events, Fever in this case, is wholly contained within the other. Then, all the probability of Fever is concentrated in $f + g$, and we have $f + g = 0.02$. That is, the probability of Fever-and-Headache is at most 0.02, the probability of Fever alone. In general, the probability of the AND of two events cannot exceed the probability of the smaller.

How small can $f + g$ be? Evidently there is nothing that prevents Fever and Headache from being disjoint, so $f + g$ could be 0. That is, there may be no one who has both a fever and headache.

Yet the above idea does not generalize completely. Suppose that instead of the tiny probabilities 0.02 and 0.03 for the events Fever and Headache, we found that 60% had a fever and 70% had a headache. Is it possible that no one has both a fever and a headache? If $f + g = 0$ in this situation, then $e + h = 0.6$, and $c + d = 0.7$. Then $e + h + c + d = 1.3$, which is impossible. That is, we would have in Fig. 4.18 an event, $e + h + c + d$, with a probability greater than 1.

Evidently, the size of the AND of two events cannot be smaller than the sum of the probabilities of the events minus 1. If not, then the OR of the same two events has a probability greater than 1. This observation is summarized in the *rule for* **Rule for** *products*. If E and F are two events, and G is the event that both of E and F **products** occur, then

$$\text{PROB}(E) + \text{PROB}(F) - 1 \leq \text{PROB}(G) \leq \min(\text{PROB}(E), \text{PROB}(F))$$

As with the rule for sums, the same idea applies to probabilities that are conditional upon some other event H. That is,

$$\text{PROB}(E/H) + \text{PROB}(F/H) - 1 \leq \text{PROB}(G/H)$$
$$\leq \min(\text{PROB}(E/H), \text{PROB}(F/H)) \tag{4.20}$$

✦ **Example 4.38.** Again referring to Fig. 4.18, suppose that 70% of those with the flu have a fever and 80% have a headache. How many have both a fever and a headache? According to (4.20) with H the event Flu, the probability of both a fever and headache, given that the person has the flu, is at least $0.7 + 0.8 - 1 = 0.5$ and at most $\min(0.7, 0.8) = 0.7$. ✦

Summary of Rules Involving Several Events

The following summarizes rules of this section and rules about independent events from the last section. Suppose E and F are events with probabilities p and q, respectively. Then

✦ The probability of event E-or-F (i.e., at least one of E and F) is at least $\max(p, q)$ and at most $p + q$ (or 1 if $p + q > 1$).

✦ The probability of event E-and-F (i.e., both E and F) is at most $\min(p, q)$ and at least $p + q - 1$ (or 0 if $p + q < 1$).

✦ If E and F are independent events, then the probability of E-and-F is pq.

✦ If E and F are independent events, then the probability of E-or-F is $p + q - pq$.

The latter rule requires some thought. The probability of E-or-F is $p + q$ minus the fraction of the space that is in both events, since the latter space is counted twice when we add the probabilities of E and F. The points in both E and F are exactly the event E-and-F, whose probability is pq. Thus,

$$\text{PROB}(E\text{-or-}F) = \text{PROB}(E) + \text{PROB}(F) - \text{PROB}(E\text{-and-}F) = p + q - pq$$

The diagram below illustrates the relationships between these various events.

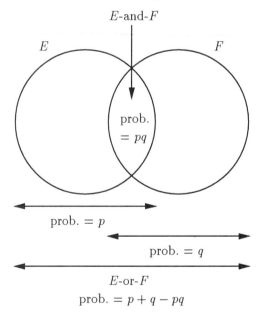

Some Ways to Deal With Relationships Among Events

Compound event

In applications that require us to compute the probability of *compound* events (events that are the **AND** or **OR** of several other events), often we do not need to know exact probabilities. Rather, we need to determine what is the most likely situation or a situation that has high probability (i.e., probability close to 1). Thus, the range of probabilities that a compound event may not present a great problem, as long as we can deduce that the probability of the event is "high."

For instance, in the medical diagnosis problem introduced in Example 4.35, we may never be able to deduce with probability 1 that the patient has the flu. But as long as the combination of observed symptoms and symptoms not present in the patient together allow us to conclude that the probability he has the flu is very high, then it may make good sense to treat the patient for flu.

However, we observed in Example 4.35 that we could say essentially nothing about the probability that a patient with both a headache and fever has the flu, even though we know that each symptom by itself strongly suggests the flu. A real reasoning system needs more information or more rules from which it can estimate probabilities. As a simple example, we might be given explicitly the probability PROB(Flu/Headache-and-Fever). That would settle the question immediately.

However, if there are n events $E_1, E_2, \ldots, E_n$ that in some combination might let us conclude another event F, then we need to give explicitly $2^n - 1$ different probabilities. These are the conditional probabilities of F given each set of one or more of $E_1, E_2, \ldots, E_n$.

✦ **Example 4.40.** For the case $n = 2$, such as Example 4.35, we need only give three conditional probabilities. Thus we might assert, as we did previously, that PROB(Flu/Fever) = 0.6 and PROB(Flu/Headache) = 0.5. Then, we might add information such as PROB(Flu/Fever-and-Headache) = 0.9. ✦

Implication of events

To avoid having to specify an exponential number of conditional probabilities, there are many types of restrictions that have been used to help us deduce or estimate probabilities. A simple one is a statement that one event *implies* another; that is, the first event is a subset of the second event. Often, such information tells us something useful.

✦ **Example 4.41.** Suppose we state that whenever one has the flu, one is sure to have a headache. In terms of Fig. 4.18, we are saying that regions b and e are empty. Suppose also that whenever one has the flu, one also has a fever. Then region c of Fig. 4.18 is also empty. Figure 4.22 suggests the simplification to Fig. 4.18 that results from these two assumptions.

Under the conditions that b, c, and e are all 0, and again assuming that PROB(Flu/Headache) = 0.5 and PROB(Flu/Fever) = 0.6, we can rewrite Equations (4.13) and (4.14) as

$$f = d + g$$
$$f = \tfrac{3}{2}(g + h)$$

Since d and h are both at least 0, the first equation says $f \geq g$ and the second says $f \geq 3g/2$.

Now, let us see what we know about the probability of flu, given both fever and headache, that is, PROB(Flu/Fever-and-Headache). This conditional probability in either Fig. 4.18 or Fig. 4.22 is $f/(f + g)$. Since $f \geq 3g/2$, we conclude that $f/(f+g) \geq 0.6$. That is, the probability is at least 0.6 that a patient with headache and fever has the flu. ✦

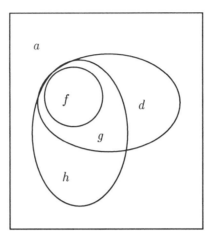

Fig. 4.22. Here, Flu implies both Headache and Fever.

We can generalize Example 4.41 to apply to any three events, two of which are implied by the third. Suppose E, F, and G are events, and

$$\text{PROB}(E/G) = \text{PROB}(F/G) = 1$$

That is, whenever G occurs, E and F are certain to occur as well. Suppose further that $\text{PROB}(G/E) = p$ and $\text{PROB}(G/F) = q$. Then

$$\text{PROB}(G/E\text{-and-}F) \geq \max(p, q) \tag{4.21}$$

The reason Equation (4.21) holds can be seen from Fig. 4.22, if we interpret Flu as G, Fever as E, and Headache as F. Then $p = f/(f+g+h)$ and $q = f/(f+g+d)$. Since d and h are at least 0, it follows that $p \leq f/(f+g)$ and $q \leq f/(f+g)$. But $f/(f+g)$ is $\text{PROB}(G/E\text{-and-}F)$. Thus, this conditional probability is equal to or greater than the larger of p and q.

EXERCISES

4.11.1: Generalize the rule of sums and the rule of products to more than two events. That is, if $E_1, E_2, \ldots, E_n$ are events with probabilities $p_1, p_2, \ldots, p_n$, respectively,

a)   What can we say about the probability that at least one of the n events occur?

b)   What can we say about the probability that all n events occur?

4.11.2*: If $\text{PROB}(F/E) = p$, what, if anything, can we say about

a) $\text{PROB}(F/\bar{E})$

b) $\text{PROB}(\bar{F}/E)$

c) $\text{PROB}(\bar{F}/\bar{E})$

Recall that $\bar{E}$ is the complement event for E and $\bar{F}$ is the complement event for F.

Other Applications of Probabilistic Reasoning

We have seen in this section a tiny illustration of an important application of probabilistic reasoning: medical diagnosis. Here are some of the other areas in which similar ideas appear in computer solutions.

✦ *Systems diagnosis.* A device fails, exhibiting some incorrect behavior. For example, a computer's screen is blank but the disk is running. What has caused the problem?

✦ *Corporate planning.* Given probabilities of economic conditions, such as a rise in inflation, a decrease in supply of a certain commodity, and so on, what strategies have the greatest probability of success?

Fuzzy logic

✦ *Intelligent appliances.* State-of-the-art appliances of many sorts use probabilistic reasoning (often referred to as "fuzzy logic") to make decisions for the user. For example, a washing machine can spin and weigh its load and predict the most likely kind of fabric (e.g., wash-and-wear or woolens), adjusting the cycle accordingly.

4.11.3: An intelligent building control tries to predict whether it will be a "cold" night, which we shall take to mean that the nighttime low is at least 20 degrees colder than the daytime high. It knows that when the sunlight falling on its sensor is high just before sunset, there is a 60% probability of a cold night (because there is apparently no cloud cover, allowing heat to radiate more easily from the earth). It also knows that if the change in temperature the hour after sunset is at least 5 degrees, then the probability is 70% of a cold night. Refer to these three events as Cold, High, and Dropping, respectively. Let us suppose also that PROB(High) = 0.4 and PROB(Dropping) = 0.3.

a) Give upper and lower limits on PROB(High-and-Dropping).

b) Give upper and lower limits on PROB(High-or-Dropping).

c) Suppose we are also told that whenever it is going to be cold at night, the sunlight sensor reads high, and the temperature drops at least 4 degrees after sunset, i.e., PROB(High/Cold) and PROB(Dropping/Cold) are both 1. Give upper and lower limits on PROB(Cold/High-and-Dropping).

d**)Under the same assumption as part (c), give upper and lower limits on

PROB(Cold/High-or-Dropping)

Note that this problem requires reasoning not covered in the section.

4.11.4*: In many situations, such as Example 4.35, two or more events mutually reinforce a conclusion. That is, we expect intuitively that whatever

PROB(Flu/Headache)

Reinforcing events

may be, being told that the patient has a fever as well as a headache increases the probability of flu. Say that event E *reinforces* event F in the conclusion G if PROB(G/E-and-F) ≥ PROB(G/F). Show that if events E and F each reinforce the other in the conclusion G, then Equation (4.21) holds. That is, the conditional probability of G given E and F is at least the larger of the conditional probability of G given E and the conditional probability of G given F.

❖❖ 4.12   Expected Value Calculations

Commonly, the possible outcomes of an experiment have associated values. In this section, we shall use simple gambling games as examples, where money is won or lost depending on the outcome of the experiment. In the next section, we shall discuss more complex examples from computer science, where we compute the expected running time of certain algorithms.

Payoff function

Suppose we have a probability space and a *payoff function* f on the points of that space. The *expected value* of f is the sum over all points x of $f(x)\text{PROB}(x)$. We denote this value by $\text{EV}(f)$. When all points are equally likely, we can compute the expected value $\text{EV}(f)$ by

1. Summing $f(x)$ for all x in the space and then
2. Dividing by the number of points in the space.

Mean value

The expected value is sometimes called the *mean* value and it can be thought of as a "center of gravity."

❖ **Example 4.42.** Suppose the space is the six points representing the outcomes of the throw of a fair die. These points are naturally thought of as integers 1 through 6. Let the payoff function be the identity function; that is, $f(i) = i$ for $i = 1, 2, \ldots, 6$. Then the expected value of f is

$$\text{EV}(f) = \big(f(1) + f(2) + f(3) + f(4) + f(5) + f(6)\big)/6$$
$$= (1 + 2 + 3 + 4 + 5 + 6)/6 = 21/6 = 3.5$$

That is, the expected value of the number on a die is 3.5.

As another example, let g be the payoff function $g(i) = i^2$. Then, for the same experiment — the throw of one die — the expected value of g is

$$\text{EV}(g) = (1^2 + 2^2 + 3^2 + 4^2 + 5^2 + 6^2)/6$$
$$= (1 + 4 + 9 + 16 + 25 + 36)/6 = 91/6 = 15.17$$

Informally, the expected value for the square of the number thrown on a die is 15.17 ❖

❖ **Example 4.43.** Let us reconsider the game of Chuck-a-Luck, first introduced in Example 4.16. The payoff rules for this game are as follows. A player bets one dollar on a number. If that number comes up one or more times, then the player receives as many dollars as his number appears. If the number does not come up at all, then the player loses his dollar.

The probability space for Chuck-a-Luck is the 216 points consisting of the triples of numbers between 1 and 6. These points represent the outcome of the toss of three dice. Let us suppose that the player bets on number 1. It should be clear that the expected value of the player's winnings or losings does not depend on the number bet on, as long as the dice are fair.

The payoff function f for this game is:

0. $g(i, j, k) = -1$ if none of i, j, or k is 1. That is, the player loses a dollar if there are no 1's.

1. $g(i, j, k) = 1$ if exactly one of i, j, or k is 1.

2. $g(i, j, k) = 2$ if exactly two of i, j, or k are 1.

3. $g(i, j, k) = 3$ if all three of i, j, or k are 1.

Our problem then is to average g over the 216 points. Since enumeration of all these points is tedious, we are better off trying to count the number of points with each of the four different outcomes.

First, let us count the number of triples with no 1's. There are five numbers to chose from in each position, so we have an assignment problem as in Section 4.2. There are thus $5^3 = 125$ points with no 1's. These 125 points contribute -125 to the sum of the payoffs, by rule (0) above.

Next, let us count the number of triples with exactly one 1. The 1 can appear in any of the three places. For each place that holds the 1, there are choices of five numbers for each of the other two places. Thus, the number of points with exactly one 1 is $3 \times 5 \times 5 = 75$. These points contribute $+75$ to the payoff by rule (1).

The number of points with all three 1's is clearly one, so this possibility contributes $+3$ to the payoff. The remaining $216 - 125 - 75 - 1 = 15$ points must have two 1's, so these 15 points contribute $+30$ to the payoff by rule (2).

Finally, we can compute the expected value of the game by adding the payoffs from each of the four types of points and dividing by the total number of points. Thus calculation is

$$\mathrm{EV}(f) = (-125 + 75 + 30 + 3)/216 = -17/216 = -0.079$$

That is, on the average, the player loses almost 8 cents for every dollar wagered. This result may be surprising, since the game superficially looks like an even bet. This point is discussed in the exercises. ✦

As Example 4.43 suggests, it is sometimes easier to group the points according to the value of their payoff function. In general, suppose we have a probability space with a payoff function f, and f has a finite number of different values that it produces. For instance, in Example 4.43 f produced only the values -1, 1, 2, and 3. For each value v produced by f, let E_v be the event consisting of the points x such that $f(x) = v$. That is, E_v is the set of points on which f produces value v. Then

$$\mathrm{EV}(f) = \sum_v v \, \mathrm{PROB}(E_v) \tag{4.22}$$

In the common case where the points have equal probability, let n_v be the number of points in event E_v and let n be the total number of points in the space. Then $\mathrm{PROB}(E_v)$ is n_v/n, and we may write

$$\mathrm{EV}(f) = \left(\sum_v v n_v\right)/n$$

✦ **Example 4.44.** In Example 4.25, we introduced the game of Keno, and computed the probability of guessing three out of 5 correct. Now let us compute the expected value of the payoff in the 5-spot game of Keno. Recall that in the 5-spot game, the player guesses five numbers from 1 to 80. When the game is played, twenty numbers from 1 to 80 are selected. The player wins if three or more of those twenty numbers are among the five he selected.

However, the payoff depends on how many of the player's five numbers are correct. Typically, for a $1 bet, the player receives $2 if he guesses three out of five (i.e., the player has a net gain of $1). If he guesses four out of five, he receives $15, and for guessing all five, he is rewarded with $300. If he guesses fewer than three correctly, the player receives nothing, and loses his $1.

In Example 4.25, we calculated the probability of guessing three out of five to be 0.08394 (to four significant places). We can similarly calculate that the probability of guessing four out of five is 0.01209, and the probability of guessing all five is 0.0006449. Then, the probability of guessing fewer than three is 1 minus these three fractions, or 0.90333. The payoffs for fewer than three, for three, four, and five are −1, +1, +14, and +299, respectively. Thus, we may apply formula (4.22) to get the expected payoff of the 5-spot game of Keno. It is

$$0.90333 \times -1 + 0.08394 \times 1 + 0.01209 \times 14 + 0.0006449 \times 299 = -0.4573$$

Thus, the player loses almost 46 cents of every dollar he bets in this game. ✦

EXERCISES

4.12.1: Show that if we throw three dice, the expected number of 1's that will appear is 1/2.

4.12.2*: Since we win when there is a 1 and lose when there is not, why does not the fact in Exercise 4.12.1 imply that Chuck-a-Luck is an even game (i.e., the expected payoff by betting on 1, or any other number, is 0)?

4.12.3: Suppose that in a 4-spot game of Keno, where the player guesses four numbers, the payout is as follows: for guessing two, $1 (i.e., the player gets his dollar back); for guessing three, $4; for guessing all four, $50. What is the expected value of the payout?

4.12.4: Suppose in a 6-spot game of Keno, the payouts are as follows: for guessing three, $1; for four, $4; for five, $25; for guessing all six, $1000. What is the expected value of the payout?

4.12.5: Suppose we play a Chuck-a-Luck type of game with six dice. The player pays $1 to play, bets on a number, and throws the dice. He is rewarded with $1 for every time his selected number appears. For instance, if it appears once, the net payout is 0; if it appears twice, the net payout is +1, and so on. Is this a *fair game* (i.e., is the expected value of the payout 0)?

Fair game

4.12.6*: Based on the style of payout suggested by Exercise 4.12.5, we could modify the payout of the standard 3-dice form of Chuck-a-Luck so that the player pays some amount to play. He is then rewarded with $1 for every time his number appears. What is the proper amount the player should pay in order that this be a fair game?

❖❖ 4.13 Some Programming Applications of Probability

In this section, we shall consider two types of uses for probability calculations in computer science. The first is an analysis of the expected running time of an algorithm. The second is a new type of algorithm, often called a "Monte Carlo" algorithm, because it takes a risk of being incorrect. As we shall see, by adjusting parameters, it is possible to make Monte-Carlo algorithms correct with as high a probability as we like, except that we cannot reach probability 1, or absolute certainty.

A Probabilistic Analysis

Let us consider the following simple problem. Suppose we have an array of n integers, and we ask whether an integer x is an entry of the array A[0..n-1]. The algorithm in Fig.4.23 does as well as any. Note that it returns a type which we called BOOLEAN, defined to be a synonym for int in Section 1.6. Also in that section were defined the constants TRUE and FALSE, which stand for 1 and 0, respectively.

```
       BOOLEAN find(int x, int A[], int n)
       {
           int i;

(1)        for(i = 0; i < n; i++)
(2)            if(A[i] == x)
(3)                return TRUE;
(4)        return FALSE;
       }
```

Fig. 4.23. Finding an element x in an array A of size n.

The loop of lines (1) – (3) examines each entry of the array, and if x is found there, immediately terminates the loop with TRUE as our answer. If x is never found, we reach line (4) and return FALSE. Let the time taken by the body of the loop and the loop incrementation and test be c. Let d be the time of line (4) and the initialization of the loop. Then if x is not found, the running time of the function of Fig. 4.23 is $cn + d$, which is $O(n)$.

However, suppose x is found; what is the running time of Fig. 4.23 then? Clearly, the earlier x is found, the less time it takes. If x were somehow guaranteed to be in A[0], the time would be $O(1)$, since the loop would iterate only once. But if x were always at or near the end, the time would be $O(n)$.

Surely the worst case is when we find x at the last step, so $O(n)$ is a smooth and tight upper bound on the worst case. However, is it possible that the average case is much better than $O(n)$? In order to address this question, we need to define a probability space whose points represent the possible places in which x can be found. The simplest assumption is that x is equally likely to be placed in any of the n entries of array A. If so, then our space has n points, one representing each of the integers from 0 to $n - 1$, which are the bounds of the index of array A.

Our question then becomes: in this probability space, what is the expected value of the running time of the function of Fig. 4.23? Consider a point i in the space; i can be anything from 0 to $n - 1$. If x is in $\texttt{A[i]}$, then the loop will iterate $i + 1$ times. An upper bound on the running time is thus $ci + d$. This bound is off slightly in the constant d, since line (4) is never executed. However, the difference does not matter, since d will disappear when we translate to a big-oh expression anyway.

We must thus find the expected value of the function $f(i) = ci + d$ on this probability space. We sum $ci + d$ where i ranges from 0 to $n - 1$, and then divide by n, the number of points. That is,

$$\text{EV}(f) = \Big(\sum_{i=0}^{n-1} ci + d\Big)/n = \big(cn(n-1)/2 + dn\big)/n = c(n-1)/2 + d$$

For large n, this expression is about $cn/2$. Thus, $O(n)$ is the smooth and tight upper bound on this expected value. That is, the expected value is, to within a constant factor of about 2, the same as the worst case. This result makes intuitive sense. If x is equally likely to be anywhere in the array, it will "typically" be half way down the array, and we therefore do about half the work that would be done if x were not in the array at all, or if it were at the last element.

Algorithms That Use Probability

Deterministic algorithm

The algorithm of Fig. 4.23 was deterministic, in the sense that it always does the same thing on the same data. Only the analysis of the expected running time uses probability calculations. Almost every algorithm we meet is deterministic. However, there are some problems that are better solved with an algorithm that is not deterministic, but uses a selection from a probability space in some essential way. Making such a selection from an imagined probability space is not hard; we use a random number generator as discussed in the box in Section 4.9.

Monte-Carlo algorithm

One common type of probabilistic algorithm, called a *Monte-Carlo algorithm*, makes a random selection at each iteration. Based on this selection, it will either say "true," in which case that is guaranteed to be the correct answer, or it will say "I don't know," in which case the correct answer could be either "true" or "false." The possibilities are suggested by the probability space in Fig.4.24.

The probability that the algorithm will say "true" given that the answer is true is $a/(a + b)$. That is, this probability is the conditional probability of event a in Fig. 4.24 given a or b. As long as this probability p is greater than 0, we can iterate as many times as we like, and get rapidly decreasing probability of a failure. By "failure," we mean that the correct answer is "true," but on no iteration does the algorithm tell us so.

Since each iteration is an independent experiment, if the correct answer is "true" and we iterate n times, the probability that the algorithm will never say true is $(1 - p)^n$. As long as $1 - p$ is strictly less than 1, we know that $(1 - p)^n$ will decrease rapidly as n increases. For example, if $p = 1/2$, then $1 - p$ is also $1/2$. The quantity $(0.5)^n$ is about $1/1000$ for $n = 10$ (see the box in Section 4.2); it is $1/1000000$ for $n = 20$, and so on, decreasing by a factor of about 1000 every time n increases by 10.

The Monte-Carlo algorithm, then, is to run the experiment n times. If the answer to any experiment is "true," then the algorithm answers "true." If all answers are "false," then the algorithm answers "false." Thus,

1. If the correct answer is "false," the algorithm will surely answer "false."

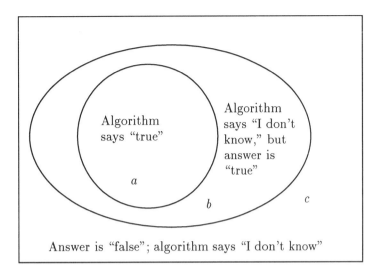

Fig. 4.24. Possible outcomes of one iteration of a Monte-Carlo algorithm.

2. If the correct answer is "true," then the algorithm answers "false" with proba-
    bility $(1-p)^n$, which we assume is very small because n is chosen large enough
    to make it small. The algorithm answers "true" with probability $1 - (1-p)^n$,
    which is presumably very close to 1.

Thus, there are no failures when the correct answer is "false" and very few failures
when the correct answer is "true."

✦ **Example 4.45.** Here is an example of a problem that can be solved more
efficiently using a Monte-Carlo algorithm. The XYZ computer company orders
boxes of chips that are supposed to be tested at the factory to make sure they are
all good. However, XYZ believes that some boxes have been leaving the factory
untested, in which case the probability that any given chip is bad is 1/10. A simple
approach solution would be for XYZ itself to test all the chips it receives, but this
process is expensive and time-consuming. If there are n chips in a box, the test of
a box takes $O(n)$ time.

A better approach is to use a Monte-Carlo algorithm. Select from each box k
chips at random to be tested. If a chip is bad, answer "true" — the box had not
been tested at the factory or else the bad chip would have been discovered. If the
chip is good, answer "I don't know," and go on to the next chip. If all k chips that
we test are good, declare the entire box to be good.

In terms of Fig. 4.24, region c represents the case that the chips are chosen
from a good box; region b is the case that the box is untested, but the chip happens
to be good; region a is the case that the box is untested, and the chip is bad. Our
assumption that 1/10 of the chips are bad if the box is untested says that the area
of the circle, a, is one-tenth of the area of the ellipse enclosing regions a and b.

Let us compute the probability of failure — all k chips are good, but the box
is untested. The probability of saying "I don't know" after testing one chip is
$1 - \frac{1}{10} = 0.9$. Since the events of testing each chip are independent, the probability
that we shall say "I don't know" to each of k chips is $(0.9)^k$. Suppose we pick

$k = 131$. Then the probability of failure, $(0.9)^{131}$, is almost exactly 0.000001, or one in a million. That is, if the box is good, we shall never find a bad chip in it, so we surely say the box is good. If the box is untested, then with probability 0.999999 we find a bad chip among the 131 we test and say the box needs full testing. With probability 0.000001, the box is untested, but we say it is a good box and do not test the remaining chips in the box.

The running time of this algorithm is $O(1)$. That is, the time to test at most 131 chips is a constant, independent of n, the number of chips in the box. Thus, compared with the more obvious algorithm of testing all the chips, the cost has gone down from $O(n)$ to $O(1)$ per box, at the cost of making an error once in every million untested boxes.

Moreover, we can make the probability of error as small as we like, by changing the number of chips we test before concluding we have a good box. For example, if we double the number of tested chips, to 262, then we square the probability of failure, which then becomes one in a trillion, or 10^{-12}. Also, we could save a constant factor in time at the cost of a higher failure rate. For instance, if we halved the number of chips tested, to 66 per box, we would have a failure rate of about one in a thousand untested boxes. ✦

EXERCISES

4.13.1: Which of 377, 383, 391 is prime?

4.13.2: Suppose that we used the function of Fig. 4.23 to search for element x, but the probability of finding x in entry i is proportional to $n - i$. That is, we can imagine a probability space with $n(n + 1)/2$ points, n of which represent situations where x is in A[0], $n - 1$ points represent situations where x is in A[1], and so on, down to one point that represents the possibility that x is in A[n-1]. What is the expected running time of the algorithm for this probability space?

4.13.3: In 1993, the National Basketball Association held a lottery in which the 11 teams that did not make the playoffs participated. At stake was the first choice in the player draft. The team with the worst record was given 11 tickets in the lottery, the next-worst team got 10, and so on, until the 11th-worst team was given one ticket. A ticket was picked at random and the first-place draft was awarded to the holder of that ticket. What is the expected value of the function $f(t)$ that is the finishing place (from the bottom) of the holder of the selected ticket t?

4.13.4**: The lottery described in Exercise 4.13.3 continued. The winning team had all their tickets removed, and another ticket was picked for second place in the draft. That winner's remaining tickets were removed, and a third ticket was selected for third place in the draft. What are the expected values of the finishing positions of the teams that got second and third places in the draft?

4.13.5*: Suppose that we are given an array of size n, either sorted or filled at random with integers. We wish to construct a Monte-Carlo algorithm that will either say "true" if it finds the array unsorted or will say "I don't know." By repeating the test k times, we'd like to know there is no more than a 2^{-k} probability of failure. Suggest such an algorithm. *Hint*: Make sure that your tests are independent. As an example of tests that are *not* independent, we might test whether A[0]<A[1] and that A[1]<A[2]. These tests are independent. However, if we then tested that

Testing Whether an Integer is a Prime

While Example 4.45 is not really a program, it still exhibits a useful algorithmic principle, and is in fact a realistic portrayal of a technique for measuring the reliability of manufactured goods. There are some interesting computer algorithms that use the Monte-Carlo idea as well.

Perhaps first among these is the problem of testing whether a number is a prime. That question is not an idle one of number theory. It turns out that many of the central ideas of computer security involve knowing that a very large number **Cryptography** is a prime. Roughly, when we encrypt information using n-digit primes, decrypting without knowing the secret key appears to involve guessing from among almost all of the 10^n possibilities. By making n sufficiently large, we can ensure that "breaking" the code requires either tremendous luck or more computer time than is available.

Thus, we would like a way to test whether a very large number is a prime, and to do so in time that is much less than the value of that prime; ideally we'd like it to take time proportional to the number of digits (i.e., proportional to the logarithm of the number). It seems that the problem of detecting composite numbers (nonprimes) is not hard. For example, every even number except 2 is composite, so it looks like half the problem is solved already. Similarly, those divisible by 3 have a sum of digits that is divisible by 3, so we can write a recursive algorithm to test for divisibility by 3 that is only a tiny bit slower than linear in the number of digits. However, the problem is still tricky for many numbers. For example, one of 377, 383, and 391 is prime. Which?

There is a Monte-Carlo algorithm that tests for composite numbers. On each iteration, it has at least probability $1/2$ of saying "true" if the number is composite, and never says "true" if the number is prime. The following is not the exact algorithm, but it works except for a small fraction of the composite numbers. The complete algorithm is beyond the scope of this book.

Fermat's theorem The algorithm is based on *Fermat's theorem*, which states that if p is a prime, and a is any integer between 1 and $p - 1$, then a^{p-1} leaves a remainder of 1 when divided by p. Moreover, it happens, except for that small number of "bad" composite numbers, that if a is chosen at random between 1 and $p - 1$, then the probability is at least $1/2$ that a^{p-1} will have a remainder other than 1 when divided by p. For example, let $p = 7$. Then $1^6, 2^6, \ldots, 6^6$ are respectively 1, 64, 729, 4096, 15625, and 46656. Their remainders when divided by 7 are all 1. However, if $p = 6$, a composite number, we have $1^5, 2^5, \ldots, 5^5$ equal to 1, 32, 243, 1024, and 3125, respectively, whose remainders when divided by 6 are 1, 2, 3, 4, and 5. Only 20% are 1.

Thus, the "algorithm" for testing whether a number p is a prime is to select k integers from 1 to $p - 1$, independently and at random. If for any selected a we find the remainder of a^{p-1}/p to be other than 1, we say p is composite; otherwise, we say it is prime. If it weren't for the "bad" composites, we could say that the probability of failure is at most 2^{-k}, since composites meet the test for a given a with probability at least $1/2$. If we make k something like 40, we have only a one in a trillion chance of accepting a composite as prime. To handle the "bad" composites, a more complex test is needed, however. This test is still polynomial in the number of digits in p, as is the simple test given above.

`A[0]<A[2]`, the test would not be independent, since knowing the first two hold we can be sure the third holds.

4.13.6**: Suppose we are given an array of size n filled with integers in the range 1 to n. These integers were either selected to be different, or they were selected at random and independently, so we can expect some equalities among entries in the array. Give a Monte-Carlo algorithm that has running time $O(\sqrt{n})$ and has at most a probability of 10^{-6} of saying the array was filled with distinct integers when in fact it was filled at random.

✦✦✦ 4.14   Summary of Chapter 4

The reader should remember the following formulas and paradigm problems for counting.

✦   The number of assignments of k values to n objects is k^n. The paradigm problem is painting n houses, each in any of k colors.

✦   We can arrange n distinct items in $n!$ different ways.

✦   We can select k items out of n and arrange the k selected items in any order in $n!/(n-k)!$ different ways. The paradigm problem is choosing the win, place, and show horses ($k = 3$) in a race with n horses.

✦   The number of ways to select m objects out of n, without order, is $\binom{n}{m}$, or $n!/\big(m!(n-m)!\big)$. The paradigm problem is dealing poker hands, where $n = 52$ and $m = 5$.

✦   If we want to order n items, some of which are identical, the number of ways to do so is computed as follows. Start with $n!$. Then, if one value appears $k > 1$ times among the n items, divide by $k!$. Perform this division for each value that appears more than once. The paradigm problem is counting anagrams of a word of length n, where we must divide $n!$ by $k!$ for each letter that appears k times in the word and $k > 1$.

✦   If we want to distribute n identical objects into m bins, we can do so in $\binom{n+m-1}{n}$ ways. The paradigm problem is distributing apples to children.

✦   If as above, some of the objects are not identical, we count the number of ways to distribute them to bins as follows. Start with $(n+m-1)!/(m-1)!$. Then, if there is a group of k identical objects, and $k > 1$, divide by $k!$. Perform the division for each value that appears more than once. The paradigm problem is distributing fruits of various kinds to children.

In addition, the reader should remember the following points about probability.

✦   A probability space consists of points, each of which is the outcome of an experiment. Each point x has associated with it a nonnegative number called the *probability of* x. The sum of the probabilities of the points in a probability space is 1.

♦   An event is a subset of the points in a probability space. The probability of an event is the sum of the probabilities of the points in the event. The probability of any event lies between 0 and 1.

♦   If all points are equally likely, the conditional probability of event F given event E is the fraction of the points in event E that are also in event F.

♦   Event E is independent of event F if the conditional probability of E given F is the same as the probability of E. If E is independent of F, then F is independent of E.

♦   The rule of sums says that the probability that one of two events E and F occurs is at least the larger of their probabilities and no greater than the sum of their probabilities (or no greater than 1 if the sum is above 1).

♦   The rule of products says that the probability that the outcome of an experiment is both in event E and in event F is no greater than the smaller of their probabilities and at least the sum of their probabilities minus 1 (or at least 0 if the latter is negative).

Finally, there are a number of applications to computer science of principles we learned in this chapter.

♦   Any sorting algorithm that works on arbitrary types of data that can be compared by "less than" requires time at least proportional to $n \log n$ to sort n items.

♦   The number of bit strings of length n is 2^n.

♦   Random number generators are programs that produce sequences of numbers that appear to be the result of independent experiments, although of course they are completely determined by the program.

♦   Systems for probabilistic reasoning need a way to express the probabilities of compound events that are formed from the occurrence of several events. The rules of sums and products sometimes help. We also learned some other simplifying assumptions that let us put bounds on the probability of compound events.

♦   Monte-Carlo algorithms use random numbers to produce either a desired result ("true") or no result at all. By repeating the algorithm a constant number of times, we can solve the problem at hand by concluding the answer is ("false") if none of the repetitions produces the answer "true." By selecting the number of repetitions, we can adjust the probability of incorrectly concluding "false" to be as low as we like, but not 0.

✦✦ 4.15   Bibliographic Notes for Chapter 4

A venerable and excellent introduction to combinatorics is Liu [1968]. Graham, Knuth, and Patashnik [1989] is a deeper discussion of the subject. Feller [1968] is the classic book on probability theory and its applications.

The Monte-Carlo algorithm for testing whether a number is a prime is from Rabin [1976]. A discussion of this algorithm and other interesting issues involving computer security and algorithms that use randomness in an important way can be found in Dewdeney [1993]. A more advanced discussion of these topics is presented in Papadimitriou [1994].

Dewdeney, A. K. [1993]. *The Turing Omnibus*, Computer Science Press, New York.

Feller, W. [1968]. *An Introduction to Probability Theory and Its Applications*, Third Edition, Wiley, New York.

Graham, R. L., D. E. Knuth, and O. Patashnik [1989]. *Concrete Mathematics: A Foundation for Computer Science*, Addison-Wesley, Reading, Mass.

Liu, C.-L. [1968]. *An Introduction to Combinatorial Mathematics*, McGraw-Hill, New York.

Papadimitriou, C. H. [1994]. *Computational Complexity*, Addison-Wesley, Reading, Mass.

Rabin, M. O. [1976]. "Probabilistic algorithms," in *Algorithms and Complexity: New Directions and Recent Trends* (J. F. Traub, ed.), pp. 21–39, Academic Press, New York.

CHAPTER

5

❖❖

The Tree
Data Model

There are many situations in which information has a hierarchical or nested structure like that found in family trees or organization charts. The abstraction that models hierarchical structure is called a *tree* and this data model is among the most fundamental in computer science. It is the model that underlies several programming languages, including Lisp.

Trees of various types appear in many of the chapters of this book. For instance, in Section 1.3 we saw how directories and files in some computer systems are organized into a tree structure. In Section 2.8 we used trees to show how lists are split recursively and then recombined in the merge sort algorithm. In Section 3.7 we used trees to illustrate how simple statements in a program can be combined to form progressively more complex statements.

❖❖ 5.1 What This Chapter Is About

The following themes form the major topics of this chapter:

✦ The terms and concepts related to trees (Section 5.2).

✦ The basic data structures used to represent trees in programs (Section 5.3).

✦ Recursive algorithms that operate on the nodes of a tree (Section 5.4).

✦ A method for making inductive proofs about trees, called structural induction, where we proceed from small trees to progressively larger ones (Section 5.5).

✦ The binary tree, which is a variant of a tree in which nodes have two "slots" for children (Section 5.6).

✦ The binary search tree, a data structure for maintaining a set of elements from which insertions and deletions are made (Sections 5.7 and 5.8).

♦ The priority queue, which is a set to which elements can be added, but from which only the maximum element can be deleted at any one time. An efficient data structure, called a partially ordered tree, is introduced for implementing priority queues, and an $O(n \log n)$ algorithm, called heapsort, for sorting n elements is derived using a balanced partially ordered tree data structure, called a heap (Sections 5.9 and 5.10).

✦✦ 5.2 Basic Terminology

Nodes and edges

Trees are sets of points, called *nodes*, and lines, called *edges*. An edge connects two distinct nodes. To be a tree, a collection of nodes and edges must satisfy certain properties; Fig. 5.1 is an example of a tree.

Root

1. In a tree, one node is distinguished and called the *root*. The root of a tree is generally drawn at the top. In Fig. 5.1, the root is n_1.

Parent and child

2. Every node c other than the root is connected by an edge to some one other node p called the *parent* of c. We also call c a *child* of p. We draw the parent of a node above that node. For example, in Fig. 5.1, n_1 is the parent of n_2, n_3, and n_4, while n_2 is the parent of n_5 and n_6. Said another way, n_2, n_3, and n_4 are children of n_1, while n_5 and n_6 are children of n_2.

All nodes are connected to the root

3. A tree is *connected* in the sense that if we start at any node n other than the root, move to the parent of n, to the parent of the parent of n, and so on, we eventually reach the root of the tree. For instance, starting at n_7, we move to its parent, n_4, and from there to n_4's parent, which is the root, n_1.

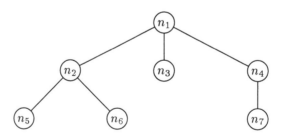

Fig. 5.1. Tree with seven nodes.

An Equivalent Recursive Definition of Trees

It is also possible to define trees recursively with an inductive definition that constructs larger trees out of smaller ones.

BASIS. A single node n is a tree. We say that n is the root of this one-node tree.

INDUCTION. Let r be a new node and let $T_1, T_2, \ldots, T_k$ be one or more trees with roots $c_1, c_2, \ldots, c_k$, respectively. We require that no node appear more than once in the T_i's; and of course r, being a "new" node, cannot appear in any of these trees. We form a new tree T from r and $T_1, T_2, \ldots, T_k$ as follows:

a)   Make r the root of tree T.

b)   Add an edge from r to each of $c_1, c_2, \ldots, c_k$, thereby making each of these nodes a child of the root r. Another way to view this step is that we have made r the parent of each of the roots of the trees $T_1, T_2, \ldots, T_k$.

✦ **Example 5.1.** We can use this recursive definition to construct the tree in Fig. 5.1. This construction also verifies that the structure in Fig. 5.1 is a tree. The nodes n_5 and n_6 are each trees themselves by the basis rule, which says that a single node can be considered a tree. Then we can apply the inductive rule to create a new tree with n_2 as the root r, and the tree T_1, consisting of n_5 alone, and the tree T_2, consisting of n_6 alone, as children of this new root. The nodes c_1 and c_2 are n_5 and n_6, respectively, since these are the roots of the trees T_1 and T_2. As a result, we can conclude that the structure

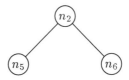

is a tree; its root is n_2.

Similarly, n_7 alone is a tree by the basis, and by the inductive rule, the structure

is a tree; its root is n_4.

Node n_3 by itself is a tree. Finally, if we take the node n_1 as r, and n_2, n_3, and n_4 as the roots of the three trees just mentioned, we create the structure in Fig. 5.1, verifying that it indeed is a tree. ✦

Paths, Ancestors, and Descendants

The parent-child relationship can be extended naturally to ancestors and descendants. Informally, the ancestors of a node are found by following the unique path from the node to its parent, to its parent's parent, and so on. Strictly speaking, a node is also its own ancestor. The descendant relationship is the inverse of the ancestor relationship, just as the parent and child relationships are inverses of each other. That is, node d is a descendant of node a if and only if a is an ancestor of d.

More formally, suppose $m_1, m_2, \ldots, m_k$ is a sequence of nodes in a tree such that m_1 is the parent of m_2, which is the parent of m_3, and so on, down to m_{k-1}, which is the parent of m_k. Then $m_1, m_2, \ldots, m_k$ is called a *path* from m_1 to m_k in the tree. The *length* of the path is $k - 1$, one less than the number of nodes on the path. Note that a path may consist of a single node (if $k = 1$), in which case the length of the path is 0.

Path length

✦ **Example 5.2.** In Fig. 5.1, n_1, n_2, n_6 is a path of length 2 from the root n_1 to the node n_6; n_1 is a path of length zero from n_1 to itself. ✦

Proper ancestor and descendant

If $m_1, m_2, \ldots, m_k$ is a path in a tree, node m_1 is called an *ancestor* of m_k and node m_k a *descendant* of m_1. If the path is of length 1 or more, then m_1 is called a *proper* ancestor of m_k and m_k a *proper* descendant of m_1. Again, remember that the case of a path of length 0 is possible, in which case the path lets us conclude that m_1 is an ancestor of itself and a descendant of itself, although not a proper ancestor or descendant. The root is an ancestor of every node in a tree and every node is a descendant of the root.

✦ **Example 5.3.** In Fig. 5.1, all seven nodes are descendants of n_1, and n_1 is an ancestor of all nodes. Also, all nodes but n_1 itself are proper descendants of n_1, and n_1 is a proper ancestor of all nodes in the tree but itself. The ancestors of n_5 are n_5, n_2, and n_1. The descendants of n_4 are n_4 and n_7. ✦

Sibling

Nodes that have the same parent are sometimes called *siblings*. For example, in Fig. 5.1, nodes n_2, n_3, and n_4 are siblings, and n_5 and n_6 are siblings.

Subtrees

In a tree T, a node n, together with all of its proper descendants, if any, is called a *subtree* of T. Node n is the root of this subtree. Notice that a subtree satisfies the three conditions for being a tree: it has a root, all other nodes in the subtree have a unique parent in the subtree, and by following parents from any node in the subtree, we eventually reach the root of the subtree.

✦ **Example 5.4.** Referring again to Fig. 5.1, node n_3 by itself is a subtree, since n_3 has no descendants other than itself. As another example, nodes n_2, n_5, and n_6 form a subtree, with root n_2, since these nodes are exactly the descendants of n_2. However, the two nodes n_2 and n_6 by themselves do not form a subtree without node n_5. Finally, the entire tree of Fig. 5.1 is a subtree of itself, with root n_1. ✦

Leaves and Interior Nodes

A *leaf* is a node of a tree that has no children. An *interior node* is a node that has one or more children. Thus, every node of a tree is either a leaf or an interior node, but not both. The root of a tree is normally an interior node, but if the tree consists of only one node, then that node is both the root and a leaf.

✦ **Example 5.5.** In Fig. 5.1, the leaves are n_5, n_6, n_3, and n_7. The nodes n_1, n_2, and n_4 are interior. ✦

Height and Depth

Level

In a tree, the *height* of a node n is the length of a longest path from n to a leaf. The *height of the tree* is the height of the root. The *depth*, or *level*, of a node n is the length of the path from the root to n.

✦ **Example 5.6.** In Fig. 5.1, node n_1 has height 2, n_2 has height 1, and leaf n_3 has height 0. In fact, any leaf has height 0. The tree in Fig. 5.1 has height 2. The depth of n_1 is 0, the depth of n_2 is 1, and the depth of n_5 is 2. ✦

Ordered Trees

Optionally, we can assign a left-to-right order to the children of any node. For example, the order of the children of n_1 in Fig. 5.1 is n_2 leftmost, then n_3, then n_4. This left-to-right ordering can be extended to order all the nodes in a tree. If m and n are siblings and m is to the left of n, then all of m's descendants are to the left of all of n's descendants.

✦ **Example 5.7.** In Fig. 5.1, the nodes of the subtree rooted at n_2 — that is, n_2, n_5, and n_6 — are all to the left of the nodes of the subtrees rooted at n_3 and n_4. Thus, n_2, n_5, and n_6 are all to the left of n_3, n_4, and n_7. ✦

In a tree, take any two nodes x and y neither of which is an ancestor of the other. As a consequence of the definition of "to the left," one of x and y will be to the left of the other. To tell which, follow the paths from x and y toward the root. At some point, perhaps at the root, perhaps lower, the paths will meet at some node z as suggested by Fig. 5.2. The paths from x and y reach z from two different nodes m and n, respectively; it is possible that $m = x$ and/or $n = y$, but it must be that $m \neq n$, or else the paths would have converged somewhere below z.

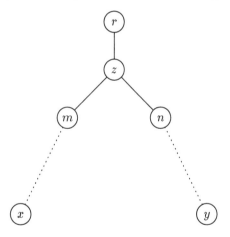

Fig. 5.2. Node x is to the left of node y.

Suppose m is to the left of n. Then since x is in the subtree rooted at m and y is in the subtree rooted at n, it follows that x is to the left of y. Similarly, if m were to the right of n, then x would be to the right of y.

✦ **Example 5.8.** Since no leaf can be an ancestor of another leaf, it follows that all leaves can be ordered "from the left." For instance, the order of the leaves in Fig. 5.1 is n_5, n_6, n_3, n_7. ✦

Labeled Trees

A *labeled* tree is a tree in which a label or value is associated with each node of the tree. We can think of the label as the information associated with a given node. The label can be something as simple, such as a single integer, or complex, such as the text of an entire document. We can change the label of a node, but we cannot change the name of a node.

If the name of a node is not important, we can represent a node by its label. However, the label does not always provide a unique name for a node, since several nodes may have the same label. Thus, many times we shall draw a node with both its label and its name. The following paragraphs illustrate the concept of a labeled tree and offer some samples.

Expression Trees — An Important Class of Trees

Arithmetic expressions are representable by labeled trees, and it is often quite helpful to visualize expressions as trees. In fact, *expression trees*, as they are sometimes called, specify the association of an expression's operands and its operators in a uniform way, regardless of whether the association is required by the placement of parentheses in the expression or by the precedence and associativity rules for the operators involved.

Let us recall the discussion of expressions in Section 2.6, especially Example 2.17, where we gave a recursive definition of expressions involving the usual arithmetic operators. By analogy with the recursive definition of expressions, we can recursively define the corresponding labeled tree. The general idea is that each time we form a larger expression by applying an operator to smaller expressions, we create a new node, labeled by that operator. The new node becomes the root of the tree for the large expression, and its children are the roots of the trees for the smaller expressions.

For instance, we can define the labeled trees for arithmetic expressions with the binary operators $+$, $-$, $\times$, and $/$, and the unary operator $-$, as follows.

BASIS. A single atomic operand (e.g., a variable, an integer, or a real, as in Section 2.6) is an expression, and its tree is a single node, labeled by that operand.

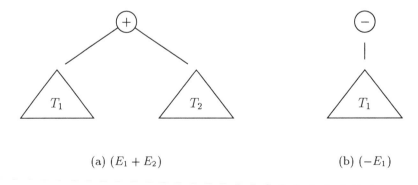

(a) $(E_1 + E_2)$ (b) $(-E_1)$

Fig. 5.3. Expression trees for $(E_1 + E_2)$ and $(-E_1)$.

INDUCTION. If E_1 and E_2 are expressions represented by trees T_1 and T_2, respectively, then the expression $(E_1 + E_2)$ is represented by the tree of Fig. 5.3(a), whose root is labeled $+$. This root has two children, which are the roots of T_1 and T_2, respectively, in that order. Similarly, the expressions $(E_1 - E_2)$, $(E_1 \times E_2)$, and (E_1/E_2) have expression trees with roots labeled $-$, $\times$, and $/$, respectively, and subtrees T_1 and T_2. Finally, we may apply the unary minus operator to one expression, E_1. We introduce a root labeled $-$, and its one child is the root of T_1; the tree for $(-E_1)$ is shown in Fig. 5.3(b).

✦ **Example 5.9.** In Example 2.17 we discussed the recursive construction of a sequence of six expressions from the basis and inductive rules. These expressions, listed in Fig. 2.16, were

i)	x	iv)	$(-(x + 10))$
ii)	10	v)	y
iii)	$(x + 10)$	vi)	$\left(y \times (-(x + 10))\right)$

Expressions (i), (ii), and (v) are single operands, and so the basis rule tells us that the trees of Fig. 5.4(a), (b), and (e), respectively, represent these expressions. Note that each of these trees consists of a single node to which we have given a name — n_1, n_2, and n_5, respectively — and a label, which is the operand in the circle.

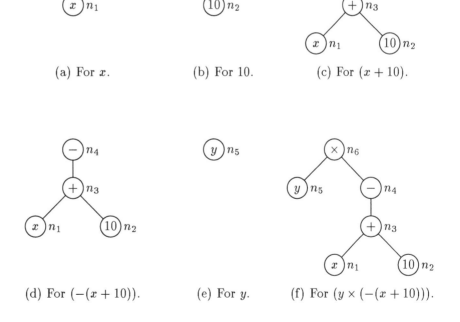

(a) For x.   (b) For 10.   (c) For $(x + 10)$.

(d) For $(-(x + 10))$.   (e) For y.   (f) For $(y \times (-(x + 10)))$.

Fig. 5.4. Construction of expression trees.

Expression (iii) is formed by applying the operator $+$ to the operands x and 10, and so we see in Fig. 5.4(c) the tree for this expression, with root labeled $+$, and the roots of the trees in Fig. 5.4(a) and (b) as its children. Expression (iv) is formed by applying unary − to expression *(iii)*, so that the tree for $\left(-(x + 10)\right)$, shown in Fig. 5.4(d), has root labeled − above the tree for $(x + 10)$. Finally, the tree for the expression $\left(y \times \left(-(x + 10)\right)\right)$, shown in Fig. 5.4(f), has a root labeled ×, whose children are the roots of the trees of Fig. 5.4(e) and (d), in that order. ◆

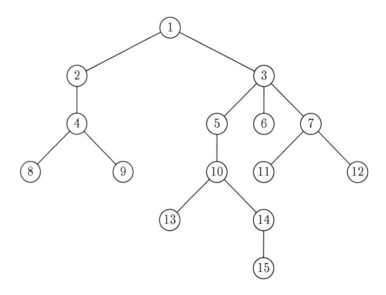

Fig. 5.5. Tree for Exercise 5.2.1.

EXERCISES

5.2.1: In Fig. 5.5 we see a tree. Tell what is described by each of the following phrases:

a)   The root of the tree
b)   The leaves of the tree
c)   The interior nodes of the tree
d)   The siblings of node 6
e)   The subtree with root 5
f)   The ancestors of node 10
g)   The descendants of node 10
h)   The nodes to the left of node 10
i)   The nodes to the right of node 10
j)   The longest path in the tree
k)   The height of node 3
l)   The depth of node 13
m) The height of the tree

5.2.2: Can a leaf in a tree ever have any (a) descendants? (b) proper descendants?

5.2.3: Prove that in a tree no leaf can be an ancestor of another leaf.

5.2.4*: Prove that the two definitions of trees in this section are equivalent. *Hint*: To show that a tree according the nonrecursive definition is a tree according the recursive definition, use induction on the number of nodes in the tree. In the opposite direction, use induction on the number of rounds used in the recursive definition.

5.2.5: Suppose we have a graph consisting of four nodes, r, a, b, and c. Node r is an isolated node and has no edges connecting it. The remaining three nodes form a cycle; that is, we have an edge connecting a and b, an edge connecting b and c, and an edge connecting c and a. Why is this graph not a tree?

5.2.6: In many kinds of trees, there is a significant distinction between the interior nodes and the leaves (or rather the labels of these two kinds of nodes). For example, in an expression tree, the interior nodes represent operators, and the leaves represent atomic operands. Give the distinction between interior nodes and leaves for each of the following kinds of trees:

a)   Trees representing directory structures, as in Section 1.3
b)   Trees representing the splitting and merging of lists for merge sort, as in Section 2.8
c)   Trees representing the structure of a function, as in Section 3.7

5.2.7: Give expression trees for the following expressions. Note that, as is customary with expressions, we have omitted redundant parentheses. You must first restore the proper pairs of parentheses, using the customary rules for precedence and associativity of operators.

a) $(x + 1) \times (x - y + 4)$
b) $1 + 2 + 3 + 4 + 5 + 6$
c) $9 \times 8 + 7 \times 6 + 5$

5.2.8: Show that if x and y are two distinct nodes in an ordered tree, then exactly one of the following conditions must hold:

a) x is a proper ancestor of y
b) x is a proper descendant of y
c) x is to the left of y
d) x is to the right of y

✧✧ 5.3   Data Structures for Trees

Many data structures can be used to represent trees. Which one we should use depends on the particular operations we want to perform. As a simple example, if all we ever want to do is to locate the parents of nodes, then we can represent each node by a structure consisting of a label plus a pointer to the structure representing the parent of that node.

As a general rule, the nodes of a tree can be represented by structures in which the fields link the nodes together in a manner similar to the way in which the nodes are connected in the abstract tree; the tree itself can be represented by a pointer to the root's structure. Thus, when we talk about representing trees, we are primarily interested in how the nodes are represented.

One distinction in representations concerns where the structures for the nodes "live" in the memory of the computer. In C, we can create the space for structures for nodes by using the function `malloc` from the standard library `stdlib.h`, in which case nodes "float" in memory and are accessible only through pointers. Alternatively, we can create an array of structures and use elements of the array to represent nodes. Again nodes can be linked according to their position in the tree, but it is also possible to visit nodes by walking down the array. We can thus access nodes without following a path through the tree. The disadvantage of an array-based representation is that we cannot create more nodes than there are elements in the array. In what follows, we shall assume that nodes are created by `malloc`, although in situations where there is a limit on how large trees can grow, an array of structures of the same type is a viable, and possibly preferred, alternative.

Array-of-Pointers Representation of Trees

One of the simplest ways of representing a tree is to use for each node a structure consisting of a field or fields for the label of the node, followed by an array of pointers to the children of that node. Such a structure is suggested by Fig. 5.6. The constant *bf* is the size of the array of pointers. It represents the maximum number of children a node can have, a quantity known as the *branching factor*. The ith component of the array at a node contains a pointer to the ith child of that node. A missing child can be represented by a NULL pointer.

Branching factor

info			
p_0	p_1	$\cdots$	p_{bf-1}

Fig. 5.6. Node represented by an array of pointers.

In C this data structure can be represented by the type declaration

```
typedef struct NODE *pNODE;
struct NODE {
    int info;
    pNODE children[BF];
};
```

Here, the field `info` represents the information that constitutes the label of a node and `BF` is the constant defined to be the branching factor. We shall see many variants of this declaration throughout this chapter.

In this and most other data structures for trees, we represent a tree by a pointer to the root node. Thus, `pNODE` also serves as the type of a tree. We could, in fact, use the type `TREE` in place of `pNODE`, and we shall adopt that convention when we talk about binary trees starting in Section 5.6. However, for the moment, we shall use the name `pNODE` for the type "pointer to node," since in some data structures, pointers to nodes are used for other purposes besides representing trees.

The array-of-pointers representation allows us to access the ith child of any node in $O(1)$ time. This representation, however, is very wasteful of space when only a few nodes in the tree have many children. In this case, most of the pointers in the arrays will be NULL.

Try to Remember Trie

The term "trie" comes from the middle of the word "retrieval." It was originally intended to be pronounced "tree." Fortunately, common parlance has switched to the distinguishing pronunciation "try."

◆ **Example 5.10.** A tree can be used to represent a collection of words in a way that makes it quite efficient to check whether a given sequence of characters is a valid word. In this type of tree, called a *trie,* each node except the root has an associated letter. The string of characters represented by a node n is the sequence of letters along the path from the root to n. Given a set of words, the trie consists of nodes for exactly those strings of characters that are prefixes of some word in the set. The label of a node consists of the letter represented by the node and also a Boolean telling whether or not the string from the root to that node forms a complete word; we shall use for the Boolean the integer 1 if so and 0 if not.[1]

Trie

For instance, suppose our "dictionary" consists of the four words **he**, **hers**, **his**, **she**. A trie for these words is shown in Fig. 5.7. To determine whether the word **he** is in the set, we start at the root n_1, move to the child n_2 labeled **h**, and then from that node move to its child n_4 labeled **e**. Since these nodes all exist in the tree, and n_4 has 1 as part of its label, we conclude that **he** is in the set.

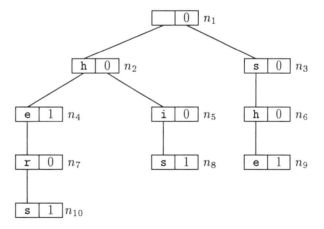

Fig. 5.7. Trie for words **he**, **hers**, **his**, and **she**.

As another example, suppose we want to determine whether **him** is in the set. We follow the path from the root to n_2 to n_5, which represents the prefix **hi**; but at n_5 we find no child corresponding to the letter **m**. We conclude that **him** is not in the set. Finally, if we search for the word **her**, we find our way from the root to node n_7. That node exists but does not have a 1. We therefore conclude that **her** is not in the set, although it is a proper prefix of a word, **hers**, in the set.

---

[1] In the previous section we acted as if the label was a single value. However, values can be of any type, and labels can be structures consisting of two or more fields. In this case, the label has one field that is a letter and a second that is an integer that is either 0 or 1.

Nodes in a trie have a branching factor equal to the number of different characters in the alphabet from which the words are formed. For example, if we do not distinguish between upper- and lower-case, and words contain no special characters such as apostrophes, then we can take the branching factor to be 26. The type of a node, including the two label fields, can be defined as in Fig. 5.8. In the array `children`, we assume that the letter `a` is represented by index 0, the letter `b` by index 1, and so on.

```
typedef struct NODE *pNODE;
struct NODE {
    char letter;
    int isWord;
    pNODE children[BF];
};
```

Fig. 5.8. Definition of an alphabetic trie.

The abstract trie of Fig. 5.7 can be represented by the data structure of Fig. 5.9. We represent nodes by showing the first two fields, `letter` and `isWord`, along with those elements of the array `children` that have non-`NULL` pointers. In the `children` array, for each non-`NULL` element, the letter indexing the array is shown in the entry above the pointer to the child, but that letter is not actually present in the structure. Note that the `letter` field of the root is irrelevant. ◆

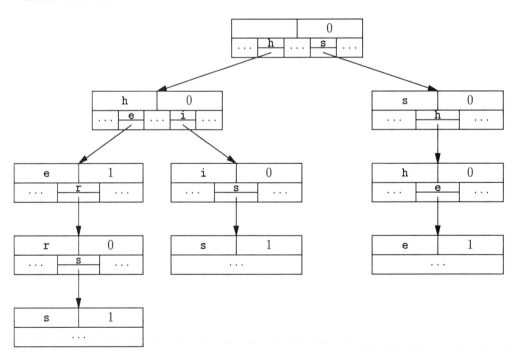

Fig. 5.9. Data structure for the trie of Fig. 5.7.

Leftmost-Child–Right-Sibling Representation of Trees

Using arrays of pointers for nodes is not necessarily space-efficient, because in typical cases, the great majority of pointers will be **NULL**. That is certainly the case in Fig. 5.9, where no node has more than two non-**NULL** pointers. In fact, if we think about it, we see that the number of pointers in any trie based on a 26-letter alphabet will have 26 times as many spaces for pointers as there are nodes. Since no node can have two parents and the root has no parent at all, it follows that among N nodes there are only $N - 1$ non-**NULL** pointers; that is, less than one out of 26 pointers is useful.

One way to overcome the space inefficiency of the array-of-pointers representation of a tree is to use linked lists to represent the children of nodes. The space occupied by a linked list for a node is proportional to the number of children of that node. There is, however, a time penalty with this representation; accessing the ith child takes $O(i)$ time, because we must traverse a list of length $i - 1$ to get to the ith node. In comparison, we can get to the ith child in $O(1)$ time, independent of i, using an array of pointers to the children.

In the representation of trees called *leftmost-child–right-sibling*, we put into each node a pointer only to its leftmost child; a node does not have pointers to any of its other children. To find the second and subsequent children of a node n, we create a linked list of those children, with each child c pointing to the child of n **Right sibling** immediately to the right of c. That node is called the *right sibling* of c.

◆ **Example 5.11.** In Fig. 5.1, n_3 is the right sibling of n_2, n_4 is the right sibling of n_3, and n_4 has no right sibling. We would find the children of n_1 by following its leftmost-child pointer to n_2, then the right-sibling pointer to n_3, and then the right-sibling pointer of n_3 to n_4. There, we would find a **NULL** right-sibling pointer and know that n_1 has no more children.

Figure 5.10 contains a sketch of the leftmost-child–right-sibling representation for the tree in Fig. 5.1. The downward arrows are the leftmost-child links; the sideways arrows are the right-sibling links. ◆

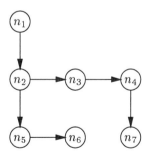

Fig. 5.10. Leftmost-child–right-sibling representation for the tree in Fig. 5.1.

In a leftmost-child–right-sibling representation of a tree, nodes can be defined as follows:

```
typedef struct NODE *pNODE;
struct NODE {
    int info;
    pNODE leftmostChild, rightSibling;
};
```

The field `info` holds the label associated with the node and it can have any type. The fields `leftmostChild` and `rightSibling` point to the leftmost child and right sibling of the node in question. Note that while `leftmostChild` gives information about the node itself, the field `rightSibling` at a node is really part of the linked list of children of that node's parent.

◆ **Example 5.12.** Let us represent the trie of Fig. 5.7 in the leftmost-child–right-sibling form. First, the type of nodes is

```
typedef struct NODE *pNODE;
struct NODE {
    char letter;
    int isWord;
    pNODE leftmostChild, rightSibling;
};
```

The first two fields represent information, according to the scheme described in Example 5.10. The trie of Fig. 5.7 is represented by the data structure shown in Fig. 5.11. Notice that each leaf has a `NULL` leftmost-child pointer, and each rightmost child has a `NULL` right-sibling pointer.

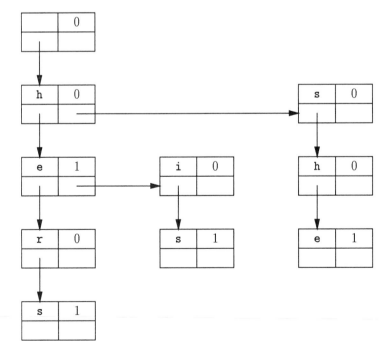

Fig. 5.11. Leftmost-child–right-sibling representation for the trie of Fig. 5.7.

As an example of how one uses the leftmost-child–right-sibling representation, we see in Fig. 5.12 a function **seek(let, n)** that takes a letter *let* and a pointer to a node *n* as arguments. It returns a pointer to the child of *n* that has *let* in its **letter** field, and it returns NULL if there is no such node. In the while loop of Fig. 5.12, each child of *n* is examined in turn. We reach line (6) if either *let* is found or we have examined all the children and thus have fallen out of the loop. In either case, **c** holds the correct value, a pointer to the child holding *let* if there is one, and NULL if not.

Notice that **seek** takes time proportional to the number of children that must be examined until we find the child we are looking for, and if we never find it, then the time is proportional to the number of children of node *n*. In comparison, using the array-of-pointers representation of trees, **seek** could simply return the value of the array element for letter *let*, taking $O(1)$ time. ✦

```
       pNODE seek(char let, pNODE n)
       {
(1)        c = n->leftmostChild;
(2)        while (c != NULL)
(3)            if (c->letter == let)
(4)                break;
           else
(5)                c = c->rightSibling;
(6)        return c;
       }
```

Fig. 5.12. Finding the child for a desired letter.

Parent Pointers

Sometimes, it is useful to include in the structure for each node a pointer to the parent. The root has a NULL parent pointer. For example, the structure of Example 5.12 could become

```
       typedef struct NODE *pNODE;
       struct NODE {
           char letter;
           int isWord;
           pNODE leftmostChild, rightSibling, parent;
       };
```

With this structure, it becomes possible to determine what word a given node represents. We repeatedly follow parent pointers until we come to the root, which we can identify because it alone has the value of **parent** equal to NULL. The **letter** fields encountered along the way spell the word, backward.

EXERCISES

5.3.1: For each node in the tree of Fig. 5.5, indicate the leftmost child and right sibling.

Comparison of Tree Representations

We summarize the relative merits of the array-of-pointers (trie) and the leftmost-child–right-sibling representations for trees:

✦   The array-of-pointers representation offers faster access to children, requiring $O(1)$ time to reach any child, no matter how many children there are.

✦   The leftmost-child–right-sibling representation uses less space. For instance, in our running example of the trie of Fig. 5.7, each node contains 26 pointers in the array representation and two pointers in the leftmost-child–right-sibling representation.

✦   The leftmost-child–right-sibling representation does not require that there be a limit on the branching factor of nodes. We can represent trees with any branching factor, without changing the data structure. However, if we use the array-of-pointers representation, once we choose the size of the array, we cannot represent a tree with a larger branching factor.

5.3.2: Represent the tree of Fig. 5.5

a)   As a trie with branching factor 3

b)   By leftmost-child and right-sibling pointers

How many bytes of memory are required by each representation?

5.3.3: Consider the following set of singular personal pronouns in English: I, my, mine, me, you, your, yours, he, his, him, she, her, hers. Augment the trie of Fig. 5.7 to include all thirteen of these words.

5.3.4: Suppose that a complete dictionary of English contains 2,000,000 words and that the number of prefixes of words — that is, strings of letters that can be extended at the end by zero or more additional letters to form a word — is 10,000,000.

a)   How many nodes would a trie for this dictionary have?

b)   Suppose that we use the structure in Example 5.10 to represent nodes. Let pointers require four bytes, and suppose that the information fields `letter` and `isWord` each take one byte. How many bytes would the trie require?

c)   Of the space calculated in part (b), how much is taken up by `NULL` pointers?

5.3.5: Suppose we represent the dictionary described in Exercise 5.3.4 by using the structure of Example 5.12 (a leftmost-child–right-sibling representation). Under the same assumptions about space required by pointers and information fields as in Exercise 5.3.4(b), how much space does the tree for the dictionary require? What portion of that space is `NULL` pointers?

Lowest common ancestor

5.3.6: In a tree, a node c is the *lowest common ancestor* of nodes x and y if c is an ancestor of both x and y, and no proper descendant of c is an ancestor of x and y. Write a program that will find the lowest common ancestor of any pair of nodes in a given tree. What is a good data structure for trees in such a program?

❖❖ 5.4   Recursions on Trees

The usefulness of trees is highlighted by the number of recursive operations on trees that can be written naturally and cleanly. Figure 5.13 suggests the general form of a recursive function $F(n)$ that takes a node n of a tree as argument. F first performs some steps (perhaps none), which we represent by action A_0. Then F calls itself on the first child, c_1, of n. During this recursive call, F will "explore" the subtree rooted at c_1, doing whatever it is F does to a tree. When that call returns to the call at node n, some other action — say A_1 — is performed. Then F is called on the second child of n, resulting in exploration of the second subtree, and so on, with actions at n alternating with calls to F on the children of n.

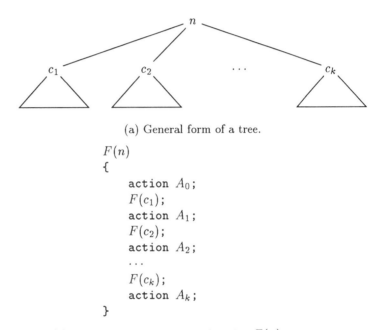

(a) General form of a tree.

```
F(n)
{
        action A_0;
        F(c_1);
        action A_1;
        F(c_2);
        action A_2;
        ...
        F(c_k);
        action A_k;
}
```

(b) General form of recursive function $F(n)$ on a tree.

Fig. 5.13.   A recursive function on a tree.

Preorder   ✦   **Example 5.13.** A simple recursion on a tree produces what is known as the *preorder listing* of the node labels of the tree. Here, action A_0 prints the label of the node, and the other actions do nothing other than some "bookkeeping" operations that enable us to visit each child of a given node. The effect is to print the labels as we would first meet them if we started at the root and circumnavigated the tree, visiting all the nodes in a counterclockwise tour. Note that we print the label of a node only the first time we visit that node. The circumnavigation is suggested by the arrow in Fig. 5.14, and the order in which the nodes are visited is $+a+*-b-c-*d*+$. The preorder listing is the sequence of node labels $+a*-bcd$.

Let us suppose that we use a leftmost-child–right-sibling representation of nodes in an expression tree, with labels consisting of a single character. The label of an

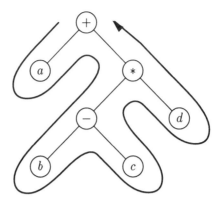

Fig. 5.14. An expression tree and its circumnavigation.

interior node is the arithmetic operator at that node, and the label of a leaf is a letter standing for an operand. Nodes and pointers to nodes can be defined as follows:

```
typedef struct NODE *pNODE;
struct NODE {
    char nodeLabel;
    pNODE leftmostChild, rightSibling;
};
```

The function **preorder** is shown in Fig. 5.15. In the explanation that follows, it is convenient to think of pointers to nodes as if they were the nodes themselves.

```
        void preorder(pNODE n)
        {
            pNODE c; /* a child of node n */
(1)         printf("%c\n", n->nodeLabel);
(2)         c = n->leftmostChild;
(3)         while (c != NULL) {
(4)             preorder(c);
(5)             c = c->rightSibling;
            }
        }
```

Fig. 5.15. Preorder traversal function.

Action "A_0" consists of the following parts of the program in Fig. 5.15:

1. Printing the label of node n, at line (1),

2. Initializing c to be the leftmost child of n, at line (2), and

3. Performing the first test for c != NULL, at line (3).

Line (2) initializes a loop in which c becomes each child of n, in turn. Note that if n is a leaf, then c is assigned the value **NULL** at line (2).

We go around the while-loop of lines (3) to (5) until we run out of children of n. For each child, we call the function **preorder** recursively on that child, at line (4), and then advance to the next child, at line (5). Each of the actions A_i, for $i \geq 1$, consists of line (5), which moves c through the children of n, and the test at line (3) to see whether we have exhausted the children. These actions are for bookkeeping only; in comparison, line (1) in action A_0 does the significant step, printing the label.

The sequence of events for calling **preorder** on the root of the tree in Fig. 5.14 is summarized in Fig. 5.16. The character at the left of each line is the label of the node n at which the call of **preorder(n)** is currently being executed. Because no two nodes have the same label, it is convenient here to use the label of a node as its name. Notice that the characters printed are $+a * -bcd$, in that order, which is the same as the order of circumnavigation. ✦

```
          call preorder(+)
(+)           print +
(+)           call preorder(a)
(a)               print a
(+)           call preorder(*)
(*)               print *
(*)               call preorder(-)
(-)                   print -
(-)                   call preorder(b)
(b)                       print b
(-)                   call preorder(c)
(c)                       print c
(*)               call preorder(d)
(d)                   print d
```

Fig. 5.16. Action of recursive function **preorder** on tree of Fig. 5.14.

Postorder

✦ **Example 5.14.** Another common way to order the nodes of the tree, called *postorder*, corresponds to circumnavigating the tree as in Fig. 5.14 but listing a node the last time it is visited, rather than the first. For instance, in Fig. 5.14, the postorder listing is $abc - d * +$.

To produce a postorder listing of the nodes, the last action does the printing, and so a node's label is printed after the postorder listing function is called on all of its children, in order from the left. The other actions initialize the loop through the children or move to the next child. Note that if a node is a leaf, all we do is list the label; there are no recursive calls.

If we use the representation of Example 5.13 for nodes, we can create postorder listings by the recursive function **postorder** of Fig. 5.17. The action of this function when called on the root of the tree in Fig. 5.14 is shown in Fig. 5.18. The same convention regarding node names is used here as in Fig. 5.16. ✦

```
        void postorder(pNODE n)
        {
            pNODE c; /* a child of node n */
(1)         c = n->leftmostChild;
(2)         while (c != NULL) {
(3)             postorder(c);
(4)             c = c->rightSibling;
            }
(5)         printf("%c\n", n->nodeLabel);
        }
```

Fig. 5.17. Recursive postorder function.

```
        call postorder(+)
(+)         call postorder(a)
(a)             print a
(+)         call postorder(*)
(*)             call postorder(-)
(-)                 call postorder(b)
(b)                     print b
(-)                 call postorder(c)
(c)                     print c
(-)                 print -
(*)             call postorder(d)
(d)                 print d
(*)             print *
(+)         print +
```

Fig. 5.18. Action of recursive function **postorder** on tree of Fig. 5.14.

✦ **Example 5.15.** Our next example requires us to perform significant actions among all of the recursive calls on subtrees. Suppose we are given an expression tree with integers as operands, and with binary operators, and we wish to produce the numerical value of the expression represented by the tree. We can do so by executing the following recursive algorithm on the expression tree.

Evaluating an expression tree

BASIS. For a leaf we produce the integer value of the node as the value of the tree.

INDUCTION. Suppose we wish to compute the value of the expression formed by the subtree rooted at some node n. We evaluate the subexpressions for the two subtrees rooted at the children of n; these are the values of the operands for the operator at n. We then apply the operator labeling n to the values of these two subtrees, and we have the value of the entire subtree rooted at n.

We define a pointer to a node and a node as follows:

Prefix and Postfix Expressions

When we list the labels of an expression tree in preorder, we get the *prefix expression* equivalent to the given expression. Similarly, the list of the labels of an expression tree in postorder yields the equivalent *postfix expression*. Expressions in the ordinary notation, where binary operators appear between their operands, are called *infix expressions*. For instance, the expression tree of Fig. 5.14 has the infix expression $a + (b - c) * d$. As we saw in Examples 5.13 and 5.14, the equivalent prefix expression is $+a * -bcd$, and the equivalent postfix expression is $abc - d * +$.

Infix expression

An interesting fact about prefix and postfix notations is that, as long as each operator has a unique number of arguments (e.g., we cannot use the same symbol for binary and unary minus), then no parentheses are ever needed, yet we can still unambiguously group operators with their operands.

We can construct an infix expression from a prefix expression as follows. In the prefix expression, we find an operator that is followed by the required number of operands, with no embedded operators. In the prefix expression $+a * -bcd$, for example, the subexpression $-bc$ is such a string, since the minus sign, like all operators in our running example, takes two operands. We replace this subexpression by a new symbol, say $x = -bc$, and repeat the process of identifying an operator followed by its operands. In our example, we now work with $+a * xd$. At this point we identify the subexpression $y = *xd$ and reduce the remaining string to $+ay$. Now the remaining string is just an instance of an operator and its operands, and so we convert it to the infix expression $a + y$.

We may now reconstruct the remainder of the infix expression by retracing these steps. We observe that the subexpression $y = *xd$ in infix is $x * d$, and so we may substitute for y in $a + y$ to get $a + (x * d)$. Note that in general, parentheses are needed in infix expressions, although in this case, we can omit them because of the convention that $*$ takes precedence over $+$ when grouping operands. Then we substitute for $x = -bc$ the infix expression $b - c$, and so our final expression is $a + \big((b - c) * d\big)$, which is the same as that represented by the tree of Fig. 5.14.

For a postfix expression, we can use a similar algorithm. The only difference is that we look for an operator preceded by the requisite number of operands in order to decompose a postfix expression.

```
typedef struct NODE *pNODE;
struct NODE {
    char op;
    int value;
    pNODE leftmostChild, rightSibling;
};
```

The field **op** will hold either the character for an arithmetic operator, or the character **i**, which stands for "integer" and identifies a node as a leaf. If the node is a leaf, then the **value** field holds the integer represented; **value** is not used at interior nodes.

This notation allows operators with any number of arguments, although we shall write code on the simplifying assumption that all operators are binary. The code appears in Fig. 5.19.

```
         int eval(pNODE n)
         {
             int val1, val2; /* values of first and second subtrees */
(1)          if (n->op) == 'i') /* n points to a leaf */
(2)              return n->value;
             else {/* n points to an interior node */
(3)              val1 = eval(n->leftmostChild);
(4)              val2 = eval(n->leftmostChild->rightSibling);
(5)              switch (n->op) {
(6)                  case '+': return val1 + val2;
(7)                  case '-': return val1 - val2;
(8)                  case '*': return val1 * val2;
(9)                  case '/': return val1 / val2;
             }
         }
         }
```

Fig. 5.19. Evaluating an arithmetic expression.

If the node n is a leaf, then the test of line (1) succeeds and we return the integer label of that leaf at line (2). If the node is not a leaf, then we evaluate its left operand at line (3) and its right operand at line (4), storing the results in **val1** and **val2**, respectively. Note in connection with line (4) that the second child of a node n is the right sibling of the leftmost child of the node n. Lines (5) through (9) form a switch statement, in which we decide what the operator at n is and apply the appropriate operation to the values of the left and right operands.

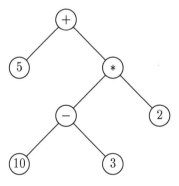

Fig. 5.20. An expression tree with integer operands.

For instance, consider the expression tree of Fig. 5.20. We see in Fig. 5.21 the sequence of calls and returns that are made at each node during the evaluation of this expression. As before, we have taken advantage of the fact that labels are unique and have named nodes by their labels. ◆

◆ **Example 5.16.** Sometimes we need to determine the height of each node in a

```
        call eval(+)
(+)         call eval(5)
(5)             return 5
(+)         call eval(*)
(*)             call eval(−)
(−)                 call eval(10)
(10)                    return 10
(−)                 call eval(3)
(3)                     return 3
(−)                 return 7
(*)             call eval(2)
(2)                 return 2
(*)             return 14
(+)         return 19
```

Fig. 5.21. Actions of function eval at each node on tree of Fig. 5.20.

tree. The height of a node can be defined recursively by the following function:

Computing the height of a tree

BASIS. The height of a leaf is 0.

INDUCTION. The height of an interior node is 1 greater than the largest of the heights of its children.

We can translate this definition into a recursive program that computes the height of each node into a field **height**:

BASIS. At a leaf, set the height to 0.

INDUCTION. At an interior node, recursively compute the heights of the children, find the maximum, add 1, and store the result into the **height** field.

This program is shown in Fig. 5.22. We assume that nodes are structures of the form

```
typedef struct NODE *pNODE;
struct NODE {
    int height;
    pNODE leftmostChild, rightSibling;
};
```

The function **computeHt** takes a pointer to a node as argument and computes the height of that node in the field **height**. If we call this function on the root of a tree, it will compute the heights of all the nodes of that tree.

At line (1) we initialize the height of n to 0. If n is a leaf, we are done, because the test of line (3) will fail immediately, and so the height of any leaf is computed to be 0. Line (2) sets c to be (a pointer to) the leftmost child of n. As we go around the loop of lines (3) through (7), c becomes each child of n in turn. We recursively compute the height of c at line (4). As we proceed, the value in n->height will

Still More Defensive Programming

Several aspects of the program in Fig. 5.19 exhibit a careless programming style that we would avoid were it not our aim to illustrate some points concisely. Specifically, we are following pointers without checking first whether they are NULL. Thus, in line (1), n could be NULL. We really should begin the program by saying

```
if (n != NULL) /* then do lines (1) to (9) */
else /* print an error message */
```

Even if n is not NULL, in line (3) we might find that its leftmostChild field is NULL, and so we should check whether n->leftmostChild is NULL, and if so, print an error message and not call eval. Similarly, even if the leftmost child of n exists, that node might not have a right sibling, and so before line (4) we need to check that

```
n->leftmostChild->rightSibling != NULL
```

It is also tempting to rely on the assumption that the information contained in the nodes of the tree is correct. For example, if a node is an interior node, it is labeled by a binary operator, and we have assumed it has two children and the pointers followed in lines (3) and (4) cannot possibly be NULL. However, it may be possible that the operator label is incorrect. To handle this situation properly, we should add a default case to the switch statement to detect unanticipated operator labels.

As a general rule, relying on the assumption that inputs to programs will always be correct is simplistic at best; in reality, "whatever can go wrong, will go wrong." A program, if it is used more than once, is bound to see data that is not of the form the programmer envisioned. One cannot be too careful in practice – blindly following NULL pointers or assuming that input data is always correct are common programming errors.

```
          void computeHt(pNODE n)
          {
              pNODE c;
(1)           n->height = 0;
(2)           c = n->leftmostChild;
(3)           while (c != NULL) {
(4)               computeHt(c);
(5)               if (c->height >= n->height)
(6)                   n->height = 1+c->height;
(7)               c = c->rightSibling;
              }
          }
```

Fig. 5.22. Procedure to compute the height of all the nodes of a tree.

be 1 greater than the height of the highest child seen so far, but 0 if we have not seen any children. Thus, lines (5) and (6) allow us to increase the height of n if we find a new child that is higher than any previous child. Also, for the first child, the test of line (5) will surely be satisfied, and we set n->height to 1 more than the height of the first child. When we fall out of the loop because we have seen all the children, n->height has been set to 1 more than the maximum height of any of n's children. ◆

EXERCISES

5.4.1: Write a recursive program to count the number of nodes in a tree that is represented by leftmost-child and right-sibling pointers.

5.4.2: Write a recursive program to find the maximum label of the nodes of a tree. Assume that the tree has integer labels, and that it is represented by leftmost-child and right-sibling pointers.

5.4.3: Modify the program in Fig. 5.19 to handle trees containing unary minus nodes.

5.4.4*: Write a recursive program that computes for a tree, represented by leftmost-child and right-sibling pointers, the number of *left-right pairs,* that is, pairs of nodes n and m such that n is to the left of node m. For example, in Fig. 5.20, node 5 is to the left of the nodes labeled $*$, $-$, 10, 3, and 2; node 10 is to the left of nodes 3 and 2; and node $-$ is to the left of node 2. Thus, the answer for this tree is eight pairs. *Hint*: Let your recursive function return two pieces of information when called on a node n: the number of left-right pairs in the subtree rooted at n, and also the number of nodes in the subtree rooted at n.

5.4.5: List the nodes of the tree in Fig. 5.5 (see the Exercises for Section 5.2) in (a) preorder and (b) postorder.

5.4.6: For each of the expressions

$i)$ $(x + y) * (x + z)$

$ii)$ $((x - y) * z + (y - w)) * x$

$iii)$ $\left(\left(((a * x + b) * x + c) * x + d \right) * x + e \right) * x + f$

do the following:

a)   Construct the expression tree.
b)   Find the equivalent prefix expression.
c)   Find the equivalent postfix expression.

5.4.7: Convert the expression $ab + c * de - /f+$ from postfix to (a) infix and (b) prefix.

5.4.8: Write a function that "circumnavigates" a tree, printing the name of a node each time it is passed.

5.4.9: What are the actions A_0, A_1, and so forth, for the postorder function in Fig. 5.17? ("Actions" are as indicated in Fig. 5.13.)

❖❖ 5.5 Structural Induction

In Chapters 2 and 3 we saw a number of inductive proofs of properties of integers. We would assume that some statement is true about n, or about all integers less than or equal to n, and use this inductive hypothesis to prove the same statement is true about $n + 1$. A similar but not identical form of proof, called "structural induction," is useful for proving properties about trees. Structural induction is analogous to recursive algorithms on trees, and this form of induction is generally the easiest to use when we wish to prove something about trees.

Suppose we want to prove that a statement $S(T)$ is true for all trees T. For a basis, we show that $S(T)$ is true when T consists of a single node. For the induction, we suppose that T is a tree with root r and children $c_1, c_2, \ldots, c_k$, for some $k \geq 1$. Let $T_1, T_2, \ldots, T_k$ be the subtrees of T whose roots are $c_1, c_2, \ldots, c_k$, respectively, as suggested by Fig. 5.23. Then the inductive step is to assume that $S(T_1), S(T_2), \ldots, S(T_k)$ are all true and prove $S(T)$. If we do so, then we can conclude that $S(T)$ is true for all trees T. This form of argument is called *structural induction*. Notice that a structural induction does not make reference to the exact number of nodes in a tree, except to distinguish the basis (one node) from the inductive step (more than one node).

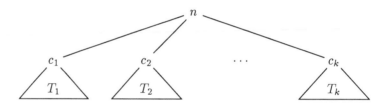

Fig. 5.23. A tree and its subtrees.

```
(1)        if (n->op) == 'i') /* n points to a leaf */
(2)            return n->value;
           else {/* n points to an interior node */
(3)            val1 = eval(n->leftmostChild);
(4)            val2 = eval(n->leftmostChild->rightSibling);
(5)            switch (n->op) {
(6)                case '+': return val1 + val2;
(7)                case '-': return val1 - val2;
(8)                case '*': return val1 * val2;
(9)                case '/': return val1 / val2;
               }
           }
```

Fig. 5.24. The body of the function `eval(n)` from Fig. 5.19.

✦ **Example 5.17.** A structural induction is generally needed to prove the correctness of a recursive program that acts on trees. As an example, let us reconsider the function **eval** of Fig. 5.19, the body of which we reproduce as Fig. 5.24. This function is applied to a tree T by being given a pointer to the root of T as the value of its argument n. It then computes the value of the expression represented by T. We shall prove by structural induction the following statement:

STATEMENT $S(T)$: The value returned by **eval** when called on the root of T equals the value of the arithmetic expression represented by T.

BASIS. For the basis, T consists of a single node. That is, the argument n is a (pointer to a) leaf. Since the **op** field has the value `'i'` when the node represents an operand, the test of line (1) in Fig. 5.24 succeeds, and the value of that operand is returned at line (2).

INDUCTION. Suppose the node n is not a (pointer to a) leaf. The inductive hypothesis is that $S(T')$ is true for each tree T' rooted at one of the children of n. We must use this reasoning to prove $S(T)$ for the tree T rooted at n.

Since our operators are assumed to be binary, n has two subtrees. By the inductive hypothesis, the values of **val1** and **val2** computed at lines (3) and (4) respectively, are the values of the left and right subtrees. Figure 5.25 suggests these two subtrees; **val1** holds the value of T_1 and **val2** holds the value of T_2.

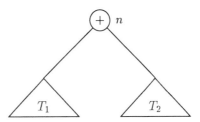

Fig. 5.25. The call $eval(n)$ returns the sum of the values of T_1 and T_2.

If we examine the switch statement of lines (5) through (9), we see that whatever operator appears at the root n is applied to the two values $val1$ and $val2$. For example, if the root holds +, as in Fig. 5.25, then at line (5) the value returned is $val1 + val2$, as it should be for an expression that is the sum of the expressions of trees T_1 and T_2. We have now completed the inductive step.

We conclude that $S(T)$ holds for all expression trees T, and, therefore, the function **eval** correctly evaluates trees that represent expressions. ✦

✦ **Example 5.18.** Now let us consider the function **computeHt** of Fig. 5.22, the body of which we reproduce as Fig. 5.26. This function takes as argument a (pointer to a) node n and computes the height of n. We shall prove the following statement by structural induction:

```
(1)                 n->height = 0;
(2)                 c = n->leftmostChild;
(3)                 while (c != NULL) {
(4)                     computeHt(c);
(5)                     if (c->height >= n->height)
(6)                         n->height = 1+c->height;
(7)                     c = c->rightSibling;
                    }
```

Fig. 5.26. The body of the function computeHt(n) from Fig. 5.22.

STATEMENT $S(T)$: When computeHt is called on a pointer to the root of tree T, the correct height of each node in T is stored in the height field of that node.

BASIS. If the tree T is a single node n, then at line (2) of Fig. 5.26, c will be given the value NULL, since n has no children. Thus, the test of line (3) fails immediately, and the body of the while-loop is never executed. Since line (1) sets n->height to 0, which is the correct value for a leaf, we conclude that $S(T)$ holds when T has a single node.

INDUCTION. Now suppose n is the root of a tree T that is not a single node. Then n has at least one child. We may assume by the inductive hypothesis that when computeHt(c) is called at line (4), the correct height is installed in the height field of each node in the subtree rooted at c, including c itself. We need to show that the while-loop of lines (3) through (7) correctly sets n->height to 1 more than the maximum of the heights of the children of n. To do so, we need to perform another induction, which is nested "inside" the structural induction, just as one loop might be nested within another loop in a program. This induction is an "ordinary" induction, not a structural induction, and its statement is

STATEMENT $S'(i)$: After the loop of lines (3) to (7) has been executed i times, the value of n->height is 1 more than the largest of the heights of the first i children of n.

BASIS. The basis is $i = 1$. Since n->height is set to 0 outside the loop — at line (1) — and surely no height can be less than 0, the test of line (5) will be satisfied. Line (6) sets n->height to 1 more than the height of its first child.

INDUCTION. Assume that $S'(i)$ is true. That is, after i iterations of the loop, n->height is 1 larger than the largest height among the first i children. If there is an $(i+1)$st child, then the test of line (3) will succeed and we execute the body an $(i+1)$st time. The test of line (5) compares the new height with the largest of the previous heights. If the new height, c->height, is less than 1 plus the largest of the first i heights, no change to n->height will be made. That is correct, since the maximum height of the first $i+1$ children is the same as the maximum height of the first i children. However, if the new height is greater than the previous maximum,

A Template for Structural Induction

The following is an outline for building correct structural inductions.

1. Specify the statement $S(T)$ to be proved, where T is a tree.

2. Prove the basis, that $S(T)$ is true whenever T is a tree with a single node.

3. Set up the inductive step by letting T be a tree with root r and $k \geq 1$ subtrees, $T_1, T_2, \ldots, T_k$. State that you assume the inductive hypothesis: that $S(T_i)$ is true for each of the subtrees T_i, $i = 1, 2, \ldots, k$.

4. Prove that $S(T)$ is true under the assumptions mentioned in (3).

---

then the test of line (5) will succeed, and `n->height` is set to 1 more than the height of the $(i+1)$st child, which is correct.

We can now return to the structural induction. When the test of line (3) fails, we have considered all the children of n. The inner induction, $S'(i)$, tells us that when i is the total number of children, `n->height` is 1 more than the largest height of any child of n. That is the correct height for n. The inductive hypothesis S applied to each of the children of n tells us that the correct height has been stored in each of their `height` fields. Since we just saw that n's height has also been correctly computed, we conclude that all the nodes in T have been assigned their correct height.

We have now completed the inductive step of the structural induction, and we conclude that `computeHt` correctly computes the height of each node of every tree on which it is called. ◆

Why Structural Induction Works

The explanation for why structural induction is a valid proof method is similar to the reason ordinary inductions work: if the conclusion were false, there would be a smallest counterexample, and that counterexample would violate either the basis or the induction. That is, suppose there is a statement $S(T)$ for which we have proved the basis and the structural induction step, yet there are one or more trees for which S is false. Let T_0 be a tree such that $S(T_0)$ is false, but let T_0 have as few nodes as any tree for which S is false.

There are two cases. First, suppose that T_0 consists of a single node. Then $S(T_0)$ is true by the basis, and so this case cannot occur.

The only other possibility is that T_0 has more than one node — say, m nodes — and therefore T_0 consists of a root r with one or more children. Let the trees rooted at these children be $T_1, T_2, \ldots, T_k$. We claim that none of $T_1, T_2, \ldots, T_k$ can have more than $m-1$ nodes. For if one — say T_i — did have m or more nodes, then T_0, which consists of T_i and the root node r, possibly along with other subtrees, would have at least $m+1$ nodes. That contradicts our assumption that T_0 has exactly m nodes.

Now since each of the subtrees $T_1, T_2, \ldots, T_k$ has $m-1$ or fewer nodes, we know that these trees cannot violate S, because we chose T_0 to be as small as any

A Relationship between Structural and Ordinary Induction

There is a sense in which structural induction really offers nothing new. Suppose we have a statement $S(T)$ about trees that we want to prove by structural induction. We could instead prove

STATEMENT $S'(i)$: For all trees T of i nodes, $S(T)$ is true.

$S'(i)$ has the form of an ordinary induction on the integer i, with basis $i = 1$. It can be proved by complete induction, where we assume $S'(j)$ for all $j \leq i$, and prove $S'(i + 1)$. This proof, however, would look exactly like the proof of $S(T)$, if we let T stand for an arbitrary tree of $i + 1$ nodes.

---

tree making S false. Thus, we know that $S(T_1), S(T_2), \ldots, S(T_k)$ are all true. The inductive step, which we assume proved, tells us that $S(T_0)$ is also true. Again we contradict the assumption that T_0 violates S.

We have considered the two possible cases, a tree of one node or a tree with more than one node, and have found that in either case, T_0 cannot be a violation of S. Therefore, S has no violations, and $S(T)$ must be true for all trees T.

EXERCISES

5.5.1: Prove by structural induction that

a)   The preorder traversal function of Fig. 5.15 prints the labels of the tree in preorder.
b)   The postorder function in Fig. 5.17 lists the labels in postorder.

5.5.2*: Suppose that a trie with branching factor b is represented by nodes in the format of Fig. 5.6. Prove by structural induction that if a tree T has n nodes, then there are $1 + (b - 1)n$ NULL pointers among its nodes. How many non-NULL pointers are there?

Degree of a node

5.5.3*: The *degree* of a node is the number of children that node has.[2] Prove by structural induction that in any tree T, the number of nodes is 1 more than the sum of the degrees of the nodes.

5.5.4*: Prove by structural induction that in any tree T, the number of leaves is 1 more than the number of nodes that have right siblings.

5.5.5*: Prove by structural induction that in any tree T represented by the leftmost-child–right-sibling data structure, the number of NULL pointers is 1 more than the number of nodes.

5.5.6*: At the beginning of Section 5.2 we gave recursive and nonrecursive definitions of trees. Use a structural induction to show that every tree in the recursive sense is a tree in the nonrecursive sense.

---

[2]   The branching factor and the degree are related concepts, but not the same. The branching factor is the maximum degree of any node in the tree.

A Fallacious Form of Tree Induction

It often is tempting to perform inductions on the number of nodes of the tree, where we assume a statement for n-node trees and prove it for $(n+1)$-node trees. This proof will be fallacious if we are not very careful.

When doing inductions on integers in Chapter 2, we suggested the proper methodology, in which we try to prove statement $S(n+1)$ by using $S(n)$; call this approach "leaning back." Sometimes one might be tempted to view this process as starting with $S(n)$ and proving $S(n+1)$; call this approach "pushing out." In the integer case, these are essentially the same idea. However, with trees, we cannot start by assuming the statement for an n-node tree, add a node somewhere, and claim that the result is proved for all $(n+1)$-node trees.

Danger: erroneous argument

For example, consider the claim $S(n)$: "all n-node trees have a path of length $n-1$." It is surely true for the basis, $n = 1$. In a false "induction," we might argue: "Assume an n-node tree T has a path of length $n-1$, say to node v. Add a child u to v. We now have an $(n+1)$-node tree with a path of length n, proving the inductive step."

This argument is, of course, fallacious because it does not prove the result for all $(n+1)$-node trees, just some selected trees. A correct proof does not "push out" from n to $n+1$ nodes, because we do not thus reach all possible trees. Rather, we must "lean back" by starting with an arbitrary $(n+1)$-node tree and carefully selecting a node to remove to get an n-node tree.

5.5.7**: Show the converse of Exercise 5.5.6: every tree in the nonrecursive sense is a tree in the recursive sense.

✥✥ 5.6 Binary Trees

This section presents another kind of tree, called a *binary tree*, which is different from the "ordinary" tree introduced in Section 5.2. In a binary tree, a node can have at most two children, and rather than counting children from the left, there are two "slots," one for a *left child* and the other for a *right child.* Either or both slots may be empty.

Left and right children

Fig. 5.27. The two binary trees with two nodes.

✦ **Example 5.19.** Figure 5.27 shows two binary trees. Each has node n_1 as root. The first has n_2 as the left child of the root and no right child. The second has no left child, and has n_2 as the right child of the root. In both trees, n_2 has neither a left nor a right child. These are the only binary trees with two nodes. ✦

We shall define binary trees recursively, as follows.

BASIS. The empty tree is a binary tree.

INDUCTION. If r is a node, and T_1 and T_2 are binary trees, then there is a binary tree with root r, left subtree T_1, and right subtree T_2, as suggested in Fig. 5.28. That is, the root of T_1 is the left child of r, unless T_1 is the empty tree, in which case r has no left child. Similarly, the root of T_2 is the right child of r, unless T_2 is empty, in which case r has no right child.

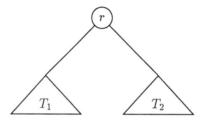

Fig. 5.28. Recursive construction of a binary tree.

Binary Tree Terminology

The notions of paths, ancestors, and descendants introduced in Section 5.2 also apply to binary trees. That is, left and right children are both regarded as "children." A path is still a sequence of nodes $m_1, m_2, \ldots, m_k$ such that m_{i+1} is a (left or right) child of m_i, for $i = 1, 2, \ldots, k-1$. This path is said to be from m_1 to m_k. The case $k = 1$ is permitted, where the path is just a single node.

The two children of a node, if they exist, are siblings. A leaf is a node with neither a left nor a right child; equivalently, a leaf is a node whose left and right subtrees are both empty. An interior node is a node that is not a leaf.

Path length, height, and depth are defined exactly as for ordinary trees. The length of a path in a binary tree is 1 less than the number of nodes; that is, the length is the number of parent-child steps along the path. The height of a node n is the length of the longest path from n to a descendant leaf. The height of a binary tree is the height of its root. The depth of a node n is the length of the path from the root to n.

✦ **Example 5.20.** Figure 5.29 shows the five shapes that a binary tree of three nodes can have. In each binary tree in Fig. 5.29, n_3 is a descendant of n_1, and there is a path from n_1 to n_3. Node n_3 is a leaf in each tree, while n_2 is a leaf in the middle tree and an interior node in the other four trees.

The height of n_3 is 0 in each tree, while the height of n_1 is 2 in all but the middle tree, where the height of n_1 is 1. The height of each tree is the same as the height of n_1 in that tree. Node n_3 is of depth 2 in all but the middle tree, where it is of depth 1. ✦

The Difference Between (Ordinary) Trees and Binary Trees

It is important to understand that while binary trees require us to distinguish whether a child is either a left child or a right child, ordinary trees require no such distinction. That is, binary trees are not just trees all of whose nodes have two or fewer children. Not only are the two trees in Fig. 5.27 different from each other, but they have no relation to the ordinary tree consisting of a root and a single child of the root:

Empty tree

There is another technical difference. While trees are defined to have at least one node, it is convenient to include the *empty tree*, the tree with no nodes, among the binary trees.

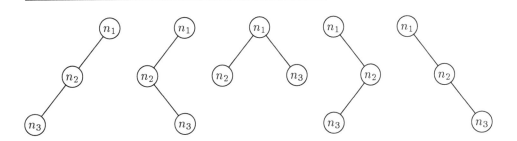

Fig. 5.29. The five binary trees with three nodes.

Data Structures for Binary Trees

There is one natural way to represent binary trees. Nodes are represented by records with two fields, `leftChild` and `rightChild`, pointing to the left and right children of the node, respectively. A NULL pointer in either of these fields indicates that the corresponding left or right subtree is missing — that is, that there is no left or right child, respectively.

A binary tree can be represented by a pointer to its root. The empty binary tree is represented naturally by NULL. Thus, the following type declarations represent binary trees:

```
typedef struct NODE *TREE;
struct NODE {
    TREE leftChild, rightChild;
};
```

Here, we call the type "pointer to node" by the name TREE, since the most common use for this type will be to represent trees and subtrees. We can interpret the `leftChild` and `rightChild` fields either as pointers to the children or as the left and right subtrees themselves.

Optionally, we can add to the structure for **NODE** a label field or fields, and/or we can add a pointer to the parent. Note that the type of the parent pointer is *NODE, or equivalently **TREE**.

Recursions on Binary Trees

There are many natural algorithms on binary trees that can be described recursively. The scheme for recursions is more limited than was the scheme of Fig. 5.13 for ordinary trees, since actions can only occur either before the left subtree is explored, between the exploration of the subtrees, or after both have been explored. The scheme for recursions on binary trees is suggested by Fig. 5.30.

```
{
    action A₀;
    recursive call on left subtree;
    action A₁;
    recursive call on right subtree;
    action A₂;
}
```

Fig. 5.30. Template of a recursive algorithm on a binary tree.

✦ **Example 5.21.** Expression trees with binary operators can be represented by binary trees. These binary trees are special, because nodes have either two children or none. (Binary trees in general can have nodes with one child.) For instance, the expression tree of Fig. 5.14, reproduced here as Fig. 5.31, can be thought of as a binary tree.

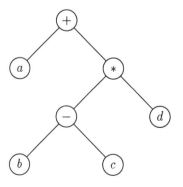

Fig. 5.31. The expression $a + (b - c) * d$ represented by a binary tree.

Suppose we use the type

```
typedef struct NODE *TREE;
struct NODE {
    char nodeLabel;
    TREE leftChild, rightChild;
};
```

for nodes and trees. Then Fig. 5.32 shows a recursive function that lists the labels of the nodes of a binary tree T in preorder.

```
      void preorder(TREE t)
      {
(1)       if (t != NULL) {
(2)           printf("%c\n", t->nodeLabel);
(3)           preorder(t->leftChild);
(4)           preorder(t->rightChild);
          }
      }
```

Fig. 5.32. Preorder listing of binary trees.

The behavior of this function is similar to that of the function of the same name in Fig. 5.15 that was designed to work on ordinary trees. The significant difference is that when the function of Fig. 5.32 comes to a leaf, it calls itself on the (missing) left and right children. These calls return immediately, because when t is **NULL**, none of the body of the function except the test of line (1) is executed. We could save the extra calls if we replaced lines (3) and (4) of Fig. 5.32 by

```
(3)   if (t->leftChild != NULL) preorder(t->leftChild);
(4)   if (t->rightChild != NULL) preorder(t->rightChild);
```

However, that would not protect us against a call to **preorder** from another function, with **NULL** as the argument. Thus, we would have to leave the test of line (1) in place for safety. ✦

EXERCISES

5.6.1: Write a function that prints an inorder listing of the (labels of the) nodes of a binary tree. Assume that the nodes are represented by records with left-child and right-child pointers, as described in this section.

5.6.2: Write a function that takes a binary expression tree and prints a fully parenthesized version of the represented expression. Assume the same data structure as in Exercise 5.6.1.

5.6.3*: Repeat Exercise 5.6.2 but print only the needed parentheses, assuming the usual precedence and associativity of arithmetic operators.

5.6.4: Write a function that produces the height of a binary tree.

Full binary tree

5.6.5: Define a node of a binary tree to be a *full* if it has both a left and a right child. Prove by structural induction that the number of full nodes in a binary tree is 1 fewer than the number of leaves.

Inorder Traversals

In addition to preorder and postorder listings of binary trees, there is another ordering of nodes that makes sense for binary trees only. An *inorder* listing of the nodes of a binary tree is formed by listing each node after exploring the left subtree, but before exploring the right subtree (i.e., in the position for action A_1 of Fig. 5.30). For example, on the tree of Fig. 5.31, the inorder listing would be $a + b - c * d$.

A preorder traversal of a binary tree that represents an expression produces the prefix form of that expression, and a postorder traversal of the same tree produces the postfix form of the expression. The inorder traversal almost produces the ordinary, or infix, form of an expression, but the parentheses are missing. That is, the tree of Fig. 5.31 represents the expression $a + (b - c) * d$, which is not the same as the inorder listing, $a + b - c * d$, but only because the necessary parentheses are missing from the latter.

To be sure that needed parentheses are present, we could parenthesize all operators. In this modified inorder traversal, action A_0, the step performed before exploring the left subtree, checks whether the label of the node is an operator and, if so, prints ' (', a left parenthesis. Similarly, action A_2, performed after exploring both subtrees, prints a right parenthesis, ') ', if the label is an operator. The result, applied to the binary tree of Fig. 5.31, would be $\left(a + \left((b - c) * d\right)\right)$, which has the needed pair of parentheses around $b - c$, along with two pairs of parentheses that are redundant.

5.6.6: Suppose we represent a binary tree by the left-child, right-child record type. Prove by structural induction that the number of **NULL** pointers is 1 greater than the number of nodes.

5.6.7**: Trees can be used to represent recursive calls. Each node represents a recursive call of some function F, and its children represent the calls made by F. In this exercise, we shall consider the recursion for $\binom{n}{m}$ given in Section 4.5, based on the recursion $\binom{n}{m} = \binom{n-1}{m} + \binom{n-1}{m-1}$. Each call can be represented by a binary tree. If a node corresponds to the computation of $\binom{n}{m}$, and the basis cases ($m = 0$ and $m = n$) do not apply, then the left child represents $\binom{n-1}{m}$ and the left child represents $\binom{n-1}{m-1}$. If the node represents a basis case, then it has neither left nor right child.

a) Prove by structural induction that a binary tree with root corresponding to $\binom{n}{m}$ has exactly $2\binom{n}{m} - 1$ nodes.

b) Use (a) to show that the running time of the recursive algorithm for $\binom{n}{m}$ is $O\left(\binom{n}{m}\right)$. Note that this running time is therefore also $O(2^n)$, but the latter is a smooth-but-not-tight bound.

✦✦ 5.7 Binary Search Trees

A common activity found in a variety of computer programs is the maintenance of

Structural Inductions on Binary Trees

A structural induction can be applied to a binary tree as well as to an ordinary tree. There is, in fact, a somewhat simpler scheme to use, in which the basis is an empty tree. Here is a summary of the technique.

1. Specify the statement $S(T)$ to be proved, where T is a binary tree.

2. Prove the basis, that $S(T)$ is true if T is the empty tree.

3. Set up the inductive step by letting T be a tree with root r and subtrees T_L and T_R. State that you assume the inductive hypothesis: that $S(T_L)$ and $S(T_R)$ are true.

4. Prove that $S(T)$ is true under the assumptions mentioned in (3).

a set of values from which we wish to

1. Insert elements into the set,
2. Delete elements from the set, and
3. Look up an element to see whether it is currently in the set.

One example is a dictionary of English words, where from time to time we insert a new word, such as `fax`, delete a word that has fallen into disuse, such as `aegilops`, or look up a string of letters to see whether it is a word (as part of a spelling-checker program, for instance).

Dictionary   Because this example is so familiar, a set upon which we can execute the operations *insert*, *delete*, and *lookup*, as defined above, is called a *dictionary*, no matter what the set is used for. As another example of a dictionary, a professor might keep a roll of the students in a class. Occasionally, a student will be added to the class (an insert), or will drop the class (a delete), or it will be necessary to tell whether a certain student is registered for the class (a lookup).

One good way to implement a dictionary is with a binary search tree, which is a kind of labeled binary tree. We assume that the labels of nodes are chosen from a set with a "less than" order, which we shall write as $<$. Examples include the reals or integers with the usual less than order; or character strings, with the lexicographic or alphabetic order represented by $<$.

Binary search   A *binary search tree (BST)* is a labeled binary tree in which the following
tree property   property holds at every node x in the tree: all nodes in the left subtree of x have labels less than the label of x, and all nodes in the right subtree have labels greater than the label of x. This property is called the *binary search tree property*.

✦   **Example 5.22.** Figure 5.33 shows a binary search tree for the set

{Hairy, Bashful, Grumpy, Sleepy, Sleazy, Happy}

where the $<$ order is lexicographic. Note that the names in the left subtree of the root are all lexicographically less than **Hairy**, while those in the right subtree are all lexicographically greater. This property holds at every node of the tree. ✦

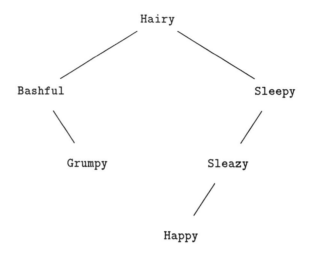

Fig. 5.33. Binary search tree with six nodes labeled by strings.

Implementation of a Dictionary as a Binary Search Tree

We can represent a binary search tree as any labeled binary tree. For example, we might define the type NODE by

```
typedef struct NODE *TREE;
struct NODE {
    ETYPE element;
    TREE leftChild, rightChild;
};
```

A binary search tree is represented by a pointer to the root node of the binary search tree. The type of an element, ETYPE, should be set appropriately. Throughout the programs of this section, we shall assume ETYPE is int so that comparisons between elements can be done simply using the arithmetic comparison operators <, == and >. In the examples involving lexicographic comparisons, we assume the comparisons in the programs will be done by the appropriate comparison functions lt, eq, and gt as discussed in Section 2.2.

Looking Up an Element in a Binary Search Tree

Suppose we want to look for an element x that may be in a dictionary represented by a binary search tree T. If we compare x with the element at the root of T, we can take advantage of the BST property to locate x quickly or determine that x is not present. If x is at the root, we are done. Otherwise, if x is less than the element at the root, x could be found only in the left subtree (by the BST property); and if x is greater, then it could be only in the right subtree (again, because of the BST property). That is, we can express the *lookup* operation by the following recursive algorithm.

BASIS. If the tree T is empty, then x is not present. If T is not empty, and x appears at the root, then x is present.

Abstract Data Types

A collection of operations, such as *insert*, *delete*, and *lookup*, that may be performed on a set of objects or a certain kind is sometimes called an *abstract data type* or ADT. The concept is also variously called a *class,* or a *module.* We shall study several abstract data types in Chapter 7, and in this chapter, we shall see one more, the priority queue.

An ADT can have more than one abstract implementation. For example, we shall see in this section that the binary search tree is a good way to implement the dictionary ADT. Lists are another plausible, though usually less efficient, way to implement the dictionary ADT. Section 7.6 covers hashing, another good implementation of the dictionary.

Each abstract implementation can, in turn, be implemented concretely by several different data structures. As an example, we shall use the left-child–right-child implementation of binary trees as a data structure implementing a binary search tree. This data structure, along with the appropriate functions for *insert*, *delete*, and *lookup*, becomes an implementation of the dictionary ADT.

An important reason for using ADT's in programs is that the data underlying the ADT is accessible only through the operations of the ADT, such as *insert*. This restriction is a form of defensive programming, protecting against accidental alteration of data by functions that manipulate the data in unexpected ways. A second important reason for using ADT's is that they allow us to redesign the data structures and functions implementing their operations, perhaps to improve the efficiency of operations, without having to worry about introducing errors into the rest of the program. There can be no new errors if the only interface to the ADT is through correctly rewritten functions for its operations.

INDUCTION. If T is not empty but x is not at the root, let y be the element at the root of T. If $x < y$ look up x only in the left subtree of the root, and if $x > y$ look up x only in the right subtree of y. The BST property guarantees that x cannot be in the subtree we do not search.

♦ **Example 5.23.** Suppose we want to look up `Grumpy` in the binary search tree of Fig. 5.33. We compare `Grumpy` with `Hairy` at the root and find that `Grumpy` precedes `Hairy` in lexicographic order. We thus call `lookup` on the left subtree.

The root of the left subtree is `Bashful`, and we compare this label with `Grumpy`, finding that the former precedes the latter. We thus call `lookup` recursively on the right subtree of `Bashful`. Now we find `Grumpy` at the root of this subtree and return `TRUE`. These steps would be carried out by a function modeled after Fig. 5.34 that dealt with lexicographic comparisons. ♦

More concretely, the recursive function `lookup(x,T)` in Fig. 5.34 implements this algorithm, using the left-child–right-child data structure. Note that `lookup` returns a value of type `BOOLEAN`, which is a defined type synonymous with `int`, but with the intent that only defined values `TRUE` and `FALSE`, defined to be 1 and 0, respectively, will be used. Type `BOOLEAN` was introduced in Section 1.6. Also, note that `lookup` is written only for types that can be compared by =, <, and so on. It would require rewriting for data like the character strings used in Example 5.23.

At line (1), `lookup` determines whether T is empty. If not, then at line (3) `lookup` determines whether x is stored at the current node. If x is not there, then `lookup` recursively searches the left subtree or right subtree depending on whether x is less than or greater than the element stored at the current node.

```
        BOOLEAN lookup(ETYPE x, TREE T)
        {
(1)         if (T == NULL)
(2)             return FALSE;
(3)         else if (x == T->element)
(4)             return TRUE;
(5)         else if (x < T->element)
(6)             return lookup(x, T->leftChild);
            else /* x must be > T->element */
(7)             return lookup(x, T->rightChild);
        }
```

Fig. 5.34. Function `lookup(x,T)` returns `TRUE` if x is in T, `FALSE` otherwise.

Inserting an Element into a Binary Search Tree

Adding a new element x to a binary search tree T is straightforward. The following recursive algorithm sketches the idea:

BASIS. If T is an empty tree, replace T by a tree consisting of a single node and place x at that node. If T is not empty and its root has element x, then x is already in the dictionary, and we do nothing.

INDUCTION. If T is not empty and does not have x at its root, then insert x into the left subtree if x is less than the element at the root, or insert x into the right subtree if x is greater than the element at the root.

The function `insert(x,T)` shown in Fig. 5.35 implements this algorithm for the left-child–right-child data structure. When we find that the value of T is **NULL** at line (1), we create a new node, which becomes the tree T. This tree is created by lines (2) through (5) and returned at line (10).

If x is not found at the root of T, then, at lines (6) through (9), `insert` is called on the left or right subtree, whichever is appropriate. The subtree, modified by the insertion, becomes the new value of the left or right subtree of the root of T at lines (7) or (9), respectively. Line (10) returns the augmented tree.

Notice that if x is at the root of T, then none of the tests of lines (1), (6), and (8) succeed. In this case, `insert` returns T without doing anything, which is correct, since x is already in the tree.

✦   **Example 5.24.** Let us continue with Example 5.23, understanding that technically, the comparison of character strings requires slightly different code from that of Fig. 5.35, in which arithmetic comparisons like < are replaced by calls to suitably defined functions like lt. Figure 5.36 shows the binary search tree of Fig. 5.33

```
      TREE insert(ETYPE x, TREE T)
      {
(1)       if (T == NULL) {
(2)           T = (TREE) malloc(sizeof(struct NODE));
(3)           T->element = x;
(4)           T->leftChild == NULL;
(5)           T->rightChild == NULL;
          }
(6)       else if (x < T->element)
(7)           T->leftChild = insert(x, T->leftChild);
(8)       else if (x > T->element)
(9)           T->rightChild = insert(x, T->rightChild);
(10)      return T;
      }
```

Fig. 5.35. Function insert(x,T) adds x to T.

after we insert **Filthy**. We begin by calling **insert** at the root, and we find that **Filthy** < **Hairy**. Thus, we call **insert** on the left child, at line (7) of Fig. 5.35. The result is that we find **Filthy** > **Bashful**, and so we call **insert** on the right child, at line (9). That takes us to **Grumpy**, which follows **Filthy** in lexicographic order, and we call **insert** on the left child of **Grumpy**.

The pointer to the left child of **Grumpy** is **NULL**, so at line (1) we discover that we must create a new node. This one-node tree is returned to the call of **insert** at the node for **Grumpy**, and the tree is installed as the value of the left child of **Grumpy** at line (7). The modified tree with **Grumpy** and **Filthy** is returned to the call of **insert** at the node labeled **Bashful**, and this modified tree becomes the right child of **Bashful**. Then, continuing up the tree, the new tree rooted at **Bashful** becomes the left child of the root of the entire tree. The final tree is shown in Fig. 5.36. ◆

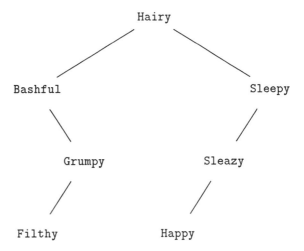

Fig. 5.36. Binary search tree after inserting **Filthy**.

Deleting an Element from a Binary Search Tree

Deleting an element x from a binary search tree is a little more complicated than *lookup* or *insert*. To begin, we may locate the node containing x; if there is no such node, we are done, since x is not in the tree to begin with. If x is at a leaf, we can simply delete the leaf. If x is at an interior node n, however, we cannot delete that node, because to do so would disconnect the tree.

We must rearrange the tree in some way so that the BST property is maintained and yet x is no longer present. There are two cases. First, if n has only one child, we can replace n by that child, and the BST property will be maintained.

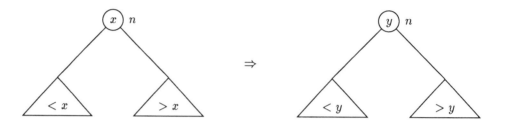

Fig. 5.37. To delete x, remove the node containing y, the smallest element in the right subtree, and then replace the label x by y at node n.

Second, suppose n has both children present. One strategy is to find the node m with label y, the smallest element in the right subtree of n, and replace x by y in node n, as suggested by Fig. 5.37. We can then remove node m from the right subtree.

The BST property continues to hold. The reason is that x is greater than everything in the left subtree of n, and so y, being greater than x (because y is in the right subtree of n), is also greater than everything in the left subtree of n. Thus, as far as the left subtree of n is concerned, y is a suitable element at n. As far as the right subtree of n is concerned, y is also suitable as the root, because y was chosen to be the smallest element in the right subtree.

```
        ETYPE deletemin(TREE *pT)
        {
            ETYPE min;

(1)         if ((*pT)->leftChild == NULL) {
(2)             min = (*pT)->element;
(3)             (*pT) = (*pT)->rightChild;
(4)             return min;
            }
            else
(5)             return deletemin(&((*pT)->leftChild));
        }
```

Fig. 5.38. Function `deletemin(pT)` removes and returns the smallest element from T.

It is convenient to define a function `deletemin(pT)`, shown in Fig. 5.38, to remove the node containing the smallest element from a nonempty binary search tree and to return the value of that smallest element. We pass to the function an argument that is the address of the pointer to the tree `T`. All references to `T` in the function are done indirectly through this pointer.

Call by reference

This style of tree manipulation, where we pass the function an argument that is a pointer to a place where a pointer to a node (i.e., a tree) is found, is called *call by reference*. It is essential in Fig. 5.38 because at line (3), where we have found a pointer to a node m whose left child is `NULL`, we wish to replace this pointer by another pointer — the pointer in the `rightChild` field of m. If the argument of *deletemin* were a pointer to a node, then the change would take place locally to the call to deletemin, and there would not actually be a change to the pointers in the tree itself. Incidentally, we could use the call-by-reference style to implement *insert* as well. In that case, we could modify the tree directly and not have to return a revised tree as we did in Fig. 5.35. We leave such a revised *insert* function as an exercise.

Now, let us see how Fig. 5.38 works. We locate the smallest element by following left children until we find a node whose left child is `NULL` at line (1) of Fig. 5.38. The element y at this node m must be the smallest in the subtree. To see why, first observe that y is smaller than the element at any ancestor of m in the subtree, because we have followed only left children. The only other nodes in the subtree are either in the right subtree of m, in which case their elements are surely larger than y by the BST property, or in the right subtree of one of m's ancestors. But elements in the right subtrees are greater than the element at some ancestor of m, and therefore greater than y, as suggested by Fig. 5.39.

Having found the smallest element in the subtree, we record this value at line (2), and at line (3) we replace the node of the smallest element by its right subtree. Note that when we delete the smallest element from the subtree, we always have the easy case of deletion, because there is no left subtree.

The only remaining point regarding `deletemin` is that when the test of line (1) fails, meaning that we are not yet at the smallest element, we proceed to the left child. That step is accomplished by the recursive call at line (5).

The function `delete(x,pT)` is shown in Fig. 5.40. If `pT` points to an empty tree T, there is nothing to do, and the test of line (1) makes sure that nothing is done. Otherwise, the tests of lines (2) and (4) handle the cases where x is not at the root, and we are directed to the left or right subtree, as appropriate. If we reach line (6), then x must be at the root of T, and we must replace the root node. Line (6) tests for the possibility that the left child is `NULL`, in which case we simply replace T by its right subtree at line (7). Similarly, if at line (8) we find that the right child is `NULL` then at line (9) we replace T by its left subtree. Note that if both children of the root are `NULL`, then we replace T by `NULL` at line (7).

The remaining case, where neither child is `NULL`, is handled at line (10). We call `deletemin`, which returns the smallest element, y, of the right subtree and also deletes y from that subtree. The assignment of line (10) replaces x by y at the root of T.

♦   **Example 5.25.** Figure 5.41 shows what would happen if we used a function similar to `delete` (but able to compare character strings) to remove `Hairy` from the

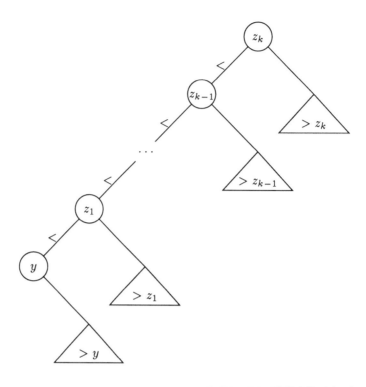

Fig. 5.39. All the other elements in the right subtree are greater than y.

```
      void delete(ETYPE x, TREE *pT)
      {
(1)       if ((*pT) != NULL)
(2)           if (x < (*pT)->element)
(3)               delete(x, &((*pT)->leftChild));
(4)           else if (x > (*pT)->element)
(5)               delete(x, &((*pT)->rightChild));
          else /* here, x is at the root of (*pT) */
(6)           if ((*pT)->leftChild == NULL)
(7)               (*pT) = (*pT)->rightChild;
(8)           else if ((*pT)->rightChild == NULL)
(9)               (*pT) = (*pT)->leftChild;
          else /* here, neither child is NULL */
(10)          (*pT)->element =
                      deletemin(&((*pT)->rightChild));
      }
```

Fig. 5.40. Function `delete(x,pT)` removes the element x from T.

binary search tree of Fig. 5.36. Since **Hairy** is at a node with two children, **delete** calls the function **deletemin**, which removes and returns the smallest element, **Happy**, from the right subtree of the root. **Happy** then becomes the label of the root of the tree, the node at which **Hairy** was stored. ◆

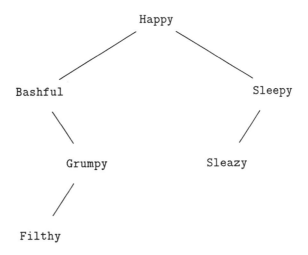

Fig. 5.41. Binary search tree after deleting Hairy.

EXERCISES

5.7.1: Suppose that we use a leftmost-child–right-sibling implementation for binary search trees. Rewrite the functions that implement the dictionary operations *insert*, *delete*, and *lookup* to work for this data structure.

5.7.2: Show what happens to the binary search tree of Fig. 5.33 if we insert the following dwarfs in order: **Doc**, **Dopey**, **Inky**, **Blinky**, **Pinky**, and **Sue**. Then show what happens when we delete in order: **Doc**, **Sleazy**, and **Hairy**.

5.7.3: Rewrite the functions **lookup**, **insert**, and **delete** to use lexicographic comparisons on strings instead of arithmetic comparisons on integers.

5.7.4*: Rewrite the function **insert** so that the tree argument is passed by reference.

5.7.5*: We wrote **delete** in the "call by reference" style. However, it is also possible to write it in a style like that of our **insert** function, where it takes a tree as argument (rather than a pointer to a tree) and returns the tree missing the deleted element. Write this version of the dictionary operation *delete*. *Note*: It is not really possible to have *deletemin* return a revised tree, since it must also return the minimum element. We could rewrite *deletemin* to return a structure with both the new tree and the minimum element, but that approach is not recommended.

5.7.6: Instead of handling the deletion of a node with two children by finding the least element in the right subtree, we could also find the greatest element in the left subtree and use that to replace the deleted element. Rewrite the functions **delete** and **deletemin** from Figs. 5.38 and 5.40 to incorporate this modification.

5.7.7*: Another way to handle *delete* when we need to remove the element at a node n that has parent p, (nonempty) left child l, and (nonempty) right child r is to find the node m holding the least element in the right subtree of n. Then, make r a left or right child of p, whichever n was, and make l the left child of m (note that

m cannot previously have had a left child). Show why this set of changes preserves the BST property. Would you prefer this strategy to the one described in Section 5.7? *Hint*: For both methods, consider their effect on the lengths of paths. As we shall see in the next section, short paths make the operations run fast.

5.7.8*: In this exercise, refer to the binary search tree represented in Fig. 5.39. Show by induction on i that if $1 \leq i \leq k$, then $y < z_i$. Then, show that y is the least element in the tree rooted at z_k.

5.7.9: Write a complete C program to implement a dictionary that stores integers. Accept commands of the form **x** i, where **x** is one of the letters **i** (insert), **d** (delete), and **l** (lookup). Integer i is the argument of the command, the integer to be inserted, deleted, or searched for.

❖❖ 5.8 Efficiency of Binary Search Tree Operations

The binary search tree provides a reasonably fast implementation of a dictionary. First, notice that each of the operations *insert*, *delete*, and *lookup* makes a number of recursive calls equal to the length of the path followed (but this path must include the route to the smallest element of the right subtree, in case **deletemin** is called). Also, a simple analysis of the functions **lookup**, **insert**, **delete**, and **deletemin** tells us that each operation takes $O(1)$ time, plus the time for one recursive call. Moreover, since this recursive call is always made at a child of the current node, the height of the node in each successive call decreases by at least 1.

Thus, if $T(h)$ is the time taken by any of these functions when called with a pointer to a node of height h, we have the following recurrence relation upper-bounding $T(h)$:

BASIS. $T(0) = O(1)$. That is, when called on a leaf, the call either terminates without further calls or makes a recursive call with a **NULL** argument and then returns without further calls. All of this work takes $O(1)$ time.

INDUCTION. $T(h) \leq T(h-1) + O(1)$ for $h \geq 1$. That is, the time taken by a call on any interior node is $O(1)$ plus the time for a recursive call, which is on a node of height at most $h-1$. If we make the reasonable assumption that $T(h)$ increases with increasing h, then the time for the recursive call is no greater than $T(h-1)$.

The solution to the recurrence for $T(h)$ is $O(h)$, as discussed in Section 3.9. Thus, the running time of each dictionary operation on a binary search tree of n nodes is at most proportional to the height of the tree. But what is the height of a typical binary search tree of n nodes?

The Worst Case

In the worst case, all the nodes in the binary tree will be arranged in a single path, like the tree of Fig. 5.42. That tree would result, for example, from taking a list of k elements in sorted order and inserting them one at a time into an initially empty tree. There are also trees in which the single path does not consist of right children

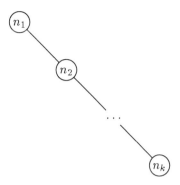

Fig. 5.42. A degenerate binary tree.

only but is a mixture of right and left children, with the path taking a turn either left or right at each interior node.

The height of a k-node tree like Fig. 5.42 is clearly $k - 1$. We thus expect that *lookup*, *insert*, and *delete* will take $O(k)$ time on a dictionary of k elements, if the representation of that dictionary happens to be one of these unfortunate trees. Intuitively, if we need to look for element x, on the average we shall find it halfway down the path, requiring us to look at $k/2$ nodes. If we fail to find x, we shall likewise have to search down the tree until we come to the place where x would be found, which will also be halfway down, on the average. Since each of the operations *lookup*, *insert*, and *delete* requires searching for the element involved, we know that these operations each take $O(k)$ time on the average, given one of the bad trees of the form of Fig. 5.42.

The Best Case

Complete tree

However, a binary tree need not grow long and thin like Fig. 5.42; it could be short and bushy like Fig. 5.43. A tree like the latter, where every interior node down to some level has both children present and the next level has all the leaves, is called a *full* or *complete* tree.

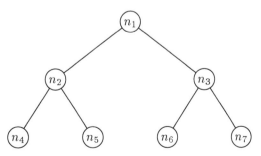

Fig. 5.43. Full binary tree with seven nodes.

A complete binary tree of height h has $2^{h+1} - 1$ nodes. We can prove this claim by induction on the height h.

BASIS. If $h = 0$, the tree consists of a single node. Since $2^{0+1} - 1 = 1$, the basis case holds.

INDUCTION. Suppose that a complete binary tree of height h has $2^{h+1} - 1$ nodes, and consider a complete binary tree of height $h + 1$. This tree consists of one node at the root and left and right subtrees that are complete binary trees of height h. For example, the height-2 complete binary tree of Fig. 5.43 consists of the root, n_1; a left subtree containing n_2, n_4, and n_5, which is a complete binary tree of height 1; and a right subtree consisting of the remaining three nodes, which is another complete binary tree of height 1. Now the number of nodes in two complete binary trees of height h is $2(2^h - 1)$, by the inductive hypothesis. When we add the root node, we find that a complete binary tree of height $h+1$ has $2(2^h - 1) + 1 = 2^{h+1} - 1$ nodes, which proves the inductive step.

Now we can invert this relationship and say that a complete binary tree of $k = 2^{h+1} - 1$ nodes has height h. Equivalently, $k + 1 = 2^{h+1}$. If we take logarithms, then $\log_2(k+1) = h+1$, or approximately, h is $O(\log k)$. Since the running time of *lookup*, *insert*, and *delete* is proportional to the height of the tree, we can conclude that on a complete binary tree, these operations take time that is logarithmic in the number of nodes. That performance is much better than the linear time taken for pessimal trees like Fig. 5.42. As the dictionary size becomes large, the running time of the dictionary operations grows much more slowly than the number of elements in the set.

The Typical Case

Is Fig. 5.42 or Fig. 5.43 the more common case? Actually, neither is common in practice, but the complete tree of Fig. 5.43 offers efficiency of the dictionary operations that is closer to what the typical case provides. That is, *lookup*, *insert*, and *delete* take logarithmic time, on the average.

A proof that the typical binary tree offers logarithmic time for the dictionary operations is difficult. The essential point of the proof is that the expected value of the length of a path from the root of such a tree to a random node is $O(\log n)$. A recurrence equation for this expected value is given in the exercises.

However, we can see intuitively why that should be the correct running time, as follows. The root of a binary tree divides the nodes, other than itself, into two subtrees. In the most even division, a k-node tree will have two subtrees of about $k/2$ nodes each. That case occurs if the root element happens to be exactly in the middle of the sorted list of elements. In the worst division, the root element is first or last among the elements of the dictionary and the division is into one subtree that is empty and another subtree of $k - 1$ nodes.

On the average, we could expect the root element to be halfway between the middle and the extremes in the sorted list; and we might expect that, on the average, about $k/4$ nodes go into the smaller subtree and $3k/4$ nodes into the larger. Let us assume that as we move down the tree we always move to the root of the larger subtree at each recursive call and that similar assumptions apply to the distribution of elements at each level. At the first level, the larger subtree will be divided in the 1:3 ratio, leaving a largest subtree of $(3/4)(3k/4)$, or $9k/16$, nodes at the second level. Thus, at the dth-level, we would expect the largest subtree to have about $(3/4)^d k$ nodes.

When d becomes sufficiently large, the quantity $(3/4)^d k$ will be close to 1, and we can expect that, at this level, the largest subtree will consist of a single leaf.

Thus, we ask, For what value of d is $(3/4)^d k \leq 1$? If we take logarithms to the base 2, we get

$$d \log_2(3/4) + \log_2 k \leq \log_2 1 \tag{5.1}$$

Now $\log_2 1 = 0$, and the quantity $\log_2(3/4)$ is a negative constant, about -0.4. Thus we can rewrite (5.1) as $\log_2 k \leq 0.4d$, or $d \geq (\log_2 k)/0.4 = 2.5 \log_2 k$.

Put another way, at a depth of about two and a half times the logarithm to the base 2 of the number of nodes, we expect to find only leaves (or to have found the leaves at higher levels). This argument justifies, but does not prove, the statement that the typical binary search tree will have a height that is proportional to the logarithm of the number of nodes in the tree.

EXERCISES

5.8.1: If tree T has height h and branching factor b, what are the largest and smallest numbers of nodes that T can have?

5.8.2**: Perform an experiment in which we choose one of the $n!$ orders for n different values and insert the values in this order into an initially empty binary search tree. Let $P(n)$ be the expected value of the depth of the node at which a particular value v among the n values is found after this experiment.

a)   Show that, for $n \geq 2$,

$$P(n) = 1 + \frac{2}{n^2} \sum_{k=1}^{n-1} k P(k)$$

b)   Prove that $P(n)$ is $O(\log n)$.

✦✦ 5.9   Priority Queues and Partially Ordered Trees

So far, we have seen only one abstract data type, the dictionary, and one implementation for it, the binary search tree. In this section we shall study another abstract data type and one of its most efficient implementations. This ADT, called a *priority queue*, is a set of elements each of which has an associated *priority*. For example, the elements could be records and the priority could be the value of one field of the record. The two operations associated with the priority queue ADT are the following:

1.   Inserting an element into the set (*insert*).

2.   Finding and deleting from the set an element of highest priority (this combined operation is called *deletemax*). The deleted element is returned by this function.

✦   **Example 5.26.** A time-shared operating system accepts requests for service from various sources, and these jobs may not all have the same priority. For example, at highest priority may be the system processes; these would include the "daemons" that watch for incoming data, such as the signal generated by a keystroke at a terminal or the arrival of a packet of bits over a local area network. Then may come user processes, the commands issued by ordinary users. Below these we may have certain background jobs such as backup of data to tape or long calculations that the user has designated to run with a low priority.

Jobs can be represented by records consisting of an integer ID for the job and an integer for the job's priority. That is, we might use the structure

```
struct ETYPE {
    int jobID;
    int priority;
};
```

for elements of a priority queue. When a new job is initiated, it gets an ID and a priority. We then execute the *insert* operation for this element on the priority queue of jobs waiting for service. When a processor becomes available, the system goes to the priority queue and executes the *deletemax* operation. The element returned by this operation is a waiting job of highest priority, and that is the one executed next. ✦

✦ **Example 5.27.** We can implement a sorting algorithm using the priority queue ADT. Suppose we are given the sequence of integers $a_1, a_2, \ldots, a_n$ to sort. We insert each into a priority queue, using the element's value as its priority. If we then execute *deletemax* n times, the integers will be selected highest first, or in the reverse of their sorted (lowest-first) order. We shall discuss this algorithm in more detail in the next section; it is known as heapsort. ✦

Partially Ordered Trees

An efficient way to implement a priority queue is by a *partially ordered tree* (*POT*), which is a labeled binary tree with the following properties:

1.   The labels of the nodes are elements with a "priority"; that priority may be the value of an element or the value of some component of an element.

2.   The element stored at a node has at least as large a priority as the elements stored at the children of that node.

POT property

Property 2 implies that the element at the root of any subtree is always a largest element of that subtree. We call property 2 the *partially ordered tree property,* or *POT property.*

✦ **Example 5.28.** Figure 5.44 shows a partially ordered tree with 10 elements. Here, as elsewhere in this section, we shall represent elements by their priorities, as if the element and the priority were the same thing. Note that equal elements can appear on different levels in the tree. To see that the POT property is satisfied at the root, note that 18, the element there, is no less than the elements 18 and 16 found at its children. Similarly, we can check that the POT property holds at every interior node. Thus, Fig. 5.44 is a partially ordered tree. ✦

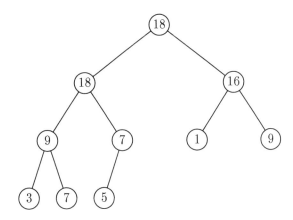

Fig. 5.44. Partially ordered tree with 10 nodes.

Partially ordered trees provide a useful abstract implementation for priority queues. Briefly, to execute *deletemax* we find the node at the root, which must be the maximum, and replace it by the rightmost node on the bottom level. However, when we do so, the POT property may be violated, and so we must restore that property by "bubbling down" the element newly placed at the root until it finds a suitable level where it is smaller than its parent but at least as large as any of its children. To execute *insert*, we can add a new leaf at the bottom level, as far left as possible, or at the left end of a new level if the bottom level is full. Again there may be a violation of the POT property, and if so, we "bubble up" the new element until it finds its rightful place.

Balanced POTs and Heaps

We say that a partially ordered tree is *balanced* if all possible nodes exist at all levels except the bottommost, and the leaves at the bottommost level are as far to the left as possible. This condition implies that if the tree has n nodes, then no path to a node from the root is longer than $\log_2 n$. The tree in Fig. 5.44 is a balanced POT.

Balanced POTs can be implemented using an array data structure called a *heap*, which provides a fast, compact implementation of the priority queue ADT. A heap is simply an array A with a special interpretation for the element indices. We start with the root in $A[1]$; $A[0]$ is not used. Following the root, the levels appear in order. Within a level, the nodes are ordered from left to right.

Thus, the left child of the root is in $A[2]$, and the right child of the root is in $A[3]$. In general, the left child of the node in $A[i]$ is in $A[2i]$ and the right child is in $A[2i + 1]$, if these children exist in the partially ordered tree. The balanced nature of the tree allows this representation. The POT property of the elements implies that if $A[i]$ has two children, then $A[i]$ is at least as large as $A[2i]$ and $A[2i + 1]$, and if $A[i]$ has one child, then $A[i]$ is at least as large as $A[2i]$.

◆ **Example 5.29.** The heap for the balanced partially ordered tree in Fig. 5.44 is shown in Fig. 5.45. For instance, $A[4]$ holds the value 9; this array element represents the left child of the left child of the root in Fig. 5.44. The children of this node are found in $A[8]$ and $A[9]$. Their elements, 3 and 7, are each no greater

1	2	3	4	5	6	7	8	9	10
18	18	16	9	7	1	9	3	7	5

Fig. 5.45. Heap for Fig. 5.44.

Layers of Implementation

It is useful to compare our two ADT's, the dictionary and the priority queue, and to notice that, in each case, we have given one abstract implementation and one data structure for that implementation. There are other abstract implementations for each, and other data structures for each abstract implementation. We promised to discuss other abstract implementations for the dictionary, such as the hash table, and in the exercises of Section 5.9 we suggest that the binary search tree may be a suitable abstract implementation for the priority queue. The table below summarizes what we already know about abstract implementations and data structures for the dictionary and the priority queue.

ADT	ABSTRACT IMPLEMENTATION	DATA STRUCTURE
dictionary	binary search tree	left-child–right-child structure
priority queue	balanced partially ordered tree	heap

than 9, as is required by the POT property. Array element $A[5]$, which corresponds to the right child of the left child of the root, has a left child in $A[10]$. It would have a right child in $A[11]$, but the partially ordered tree has only 10 elements at the moment, and so $A[11]$ is not part of the heap. ✦

While we have shown tree nodes and array elements as if they were the priorities themselves, in principle an entire record appears at the node or in the array. As we shall see, we shall have to do much swapping of elements between children and parents in a partially ordered tree or its heap representation. Thus, it is considerably more efficient if the array elements themselves are pointers to the records representing the objects in the priority queue and these records are stored in another array "outside" the heap. Then we can simply swap pointers, leaving the records in place.

Performing Priority Queue Operations on a Heap

Throughout this section and the next, we shall represent a heap by a global array `A[1..MAX]` of integers. We assume that elements are integers and are equal to their priorities. When elements are records, we can store pointers to the records in the array and determine the priority of an element from a field in its record.

Suppose that we have a heap of $n-1$ elements satisfying the POT property, and we add an nth element in $A[n]$. The POT property continues to hold everywhere, except perhaps between $A[n]$ and its parent. Thus, if $A[n]$ is larger than $A[n/2]$, the element at the parent, we must swap these elements. Now there may be a violation of the POT property between $A[n/2]$ and its parent. If so, we recursively "bubble up" the new element until it either reaches a position where the parent has a larger element or reaches the root.

Bubbling up   The C function `bubbleUp` to perform this operation is shown in Fig. 5.46. It makes use of a function `swap(A,i,j)` that exchanges the elements in $A[i]$ and $A[j]$; this function is also defined in Fig. 5.46. The operation of `bubbleUp` is simple. Given argument i indicating the node that, with its parent, possibly violates the POT property, we test whether $i = 1$ (that is, whether we are already at the root, so that no POT violation can occur), and if not, whether the element $A[i]$ is greater than the element at its parent. If so, we swap $A[i]$ with its parent and recursively call `bubbleUp` at the parent.

```c
void swap(int A[], int i, int j)
{
    int temp;

    temp = A[i];
    A[i] = A[j];
    A[j] = temp;
}

void bubbleUp(int A[], int i)
{
    if (i > 1 && A[i] > A[i/2]) {
        swap(A, i, i/2);
        bubbleUp(A, i/2);
    }
}
```

Fig. 5.46. The function `swap` exchanges array elements, and the function `bubbleUp` pushes a new element of a heap into its rightful place.

✦ **Example 5.30.** Suppose we start with the heap of Fig. 5.45 and we add an eleventh element, with priority 13. This element goes in $A[11]$, giving us the array

1	2	3	4	5	6	7	8	9	10	11
18	18	16	9	7	1	9	3	7	5	13

We now call `bubbleUp(A,11)`, which compares $A[11]$ with $A[5]$ and finds that we must swap these elements because $A[11]$ is larger. That is, $A[5]$ and $A[11]$ violate the POT property. Thus, the array becomes

1	2	3	4	5	6	7	8	9	10	11
18	18	16	9	13	1	9	3	7	5	7

Now we call `bubbleUp(A,5)`. This results in comparison of $A[2]$ and $A[5]$. Since $A[2]$ is larger, there is no POT violation, and `bubbleUp(A,5)` does nothing. We have now restored the POT property to the array. ✦

Implementation of insert

We now show how to implement the priority queue operation *insert*. Let n be the current number of elements in the priority queue, and assume `A[1..n]` already satisfies the POT property. We increment n and then store the element to be inserted into the new `A[n]`. Finally, we call `bubbleUp(A,n)`. The code for *insert* is shown in Fig. 5.47. The argument x is the element to be inserted, and the argument pn is a pointer to the current size of the priority queue. Note that n must be passed by reference — that is, by a pointer to n — so that when n is incremented the change has an affect that is not local only to *insert*. A check that $n < MAX$ is omitted.

```
void insert(int A[], int x, int *pn)
{
    (*pn)++;
    A[*pn] = x;
    bubbleUp(A, *pn);
}
```

Fig. 5.47. Priority queue operation *insert* implemented on a heap.

To implement the priority queue operation *deletemax*, we need another operation on heaps or partially ordered trees, this time to bubble down an element at the root that may violate the POT property. Suppose that $A[i]$ is a potential violator of the POT property, in that it may be smaller than one or both of its children, $A[2i]$ and $A[2i + 1]$. We can swap $A[i]$ with one of its children, but we must be careful which one. If we swap with the larger of the children, then we are sure not to introduce a POT violation between the two former children of $A[i]$, one of which has now become the parent of the other.

Bubbling down

The function `bubbleDown` of Fig. 5.48 implements this operation. After selecting a child with which to swap $A[i]$, it calls itself recursively to eliminate a possible POT violation between the element $A[i]$ in its new position — which is now `A[2i]` or `A[2i+1]` — and one of its new children. The argument n is the number of elements in the heap, or, equivalently, the index of the last element.

This function is a bit tricky. We have to decide which child of $A[i]$ to swap with, if any, and the first thing we do is assume that the larger child is $A[2i]$, at line (1) of Fig. 5.48. If the right child exists (i.e., *child* $< n$) and the right child is the larger, then the tests of line (2) are met and at line (3) we make *child* be the right child of $A[i]$.

Now at line (4) we test for two things. First, it is possible that $A[i]$ really has no children in the heap. We therefore check whether $A[i]$ is an interior node by asking whether *child* $\leq n$. The second test of line (4) is whether $A[i]$ is less than $A[child]$. If both these conditions are met, then at line (5) we swap $A[i]$ with its larger child, and at line (6) we recursively call `bubbleDown`, to push the offending element further down, if necessary.

Implementation of deletemax

We can use `bubbleDown` to implement the priority queue operation *deletemax* as shown in Fig. 5.49. The function `deletemax` takes as arguments an array A and

```
        void bubbleDown(int A[], int i, int n)
        {
            int child;

(1)         child = 2*i;
(2)         if (child < n && A[child+1] > A[child])
(3)             ++child;
(4)         if (child <= n && A[i] < A[child]) {
(5)             swap(A, i, child);
(6)             bubbleDown(A, child, n);
            }
        }
```

Fig. 5.48. bubbleDown pushes a POT violator down to its proper position.

a pointer pn to the number n that is the number of elements currently in the heap. We omit a test that $n > 0$.

In line (1), we swap the element at the root, which is to be deleted, with the last element, in A[n]. Technically, we should return the deleted element, but, as we shall see, it is convenient to put it in A[n], which will no longer be part of the heap.

At line (2), we decrement n by 1, effectively deleting the largest element, now residing in the old A[n]. Since the root may now violate the POT property, we call bubbleDown(A,1,n) at line (3), which will recursively push the offending element down until it either reaches a point where it is no less than either of its children, or becomes a leaf; either way, there is no violation of the POT property.

```
        void deletemax(int A[], int *pn)
        {
(1)         swap(A, 1, *pn);
(2)         --(*pn);
(3)         bubbleDown(A, 1, *pn);
        }
```

Fig. 5.49. Priority queue operation *deletemax* implemented by a heap.

◆ **Example 5.31.** Suppose we start with the heap of Fig. 5.45 and execute *deletemax*. After swapping $A[1]$ and $A[10]$, we set n to 9. The heap then becomes

1	2	3	4	5	6	7	8	9
5	18	16	9	7	1	9	3	7

When we execute bubbleDown(A,1,9), we set *child* to 2. Since $A[2] \geq A[3]$, we do not increment *child* at line (3) of Fig. 5.48. Then since *child* $\leq n$ and $A[1] < A[2]$, we swap these elements, to obtain the array

1	2	3	4	5	6	7	8	9
18	5	16	9	7	1	9	3	7

We then call bubbleDown(A,2,9). That requires us to compare $A[4]$ with $A[5]$ at line (2), and we find that the former is larger. Thus, $child = 4$ at line (4) of Fig. 5.48. When we find that $A[2] < A[4]$, we swap these elements and call bubbleDown(A,4,9) on the array

1	2	3	4	5	6	7	8	9
18	9	16	5	7	1	9	3	7

Next, we compare $A[8]$ and $A[9]$, finding that the latter is larger, so that $child = 9$ at line (4) of bubbleDown(A,4,9). We again perform the swap, since $A[4] < A[9]$, resulting in the array

1	2	3	4	5	6	7	8	9
18	9	16	7	7	1	9	3	5

Next, we call bubbleDown(A,9,9). We set $child$ to 18 at line (1), and the first test of line (2) fails, because $child < n$ is false. Similarly, the test of line (4) fails, and we make no swap or recursive call. The array is now a heap with the POT property restored. ✦

Running Time of Priority Queue Operations

The heap implementation of priority queues offers $O(\log n)$ running time per *insert* or *deletemax* operation. To see why, let us first consider the *insert* program of Fig. 5.47. This program evidently takes $O(1)$ time for the first two steps, plus whatever the call to bubbleUp takes. Thus, we need to determine the running time of bubbleUp.

Informally, we notice that each time bubbleUp calls itself recursively, we are at a node one position closer to the root. Since a balanced partially ordered tree has height approximately $\log_2 n$, the number of recursive calls is $O(\log_2 n)$. Since each call to bubbleUp takes time $O(1)$ plus the time of the recursive call, if any, the total time should be $O(\log n)$.

More formally, let $T(i)$ be the running time of bubbleUp(A,i). Then we can create a recurrence relation for $T(i)$ as follows.

BASIS. If $i = 1$, then $T(i)$ is $O(1)$, since it is easy to check that the bubbleUp program of Fig. 5.46 does not make any recursive calls and only the test of the if-statement is executed.

INDUCTION. If $i > 1$, then the if-statement test may fail anyway, because $A[i]$ does not need to rise further. If the test succeeds, then we execute *swap*, which takes $O(1)$ time, plus a recursive call to bubbleUp with an argument $i/2$ (or slightly less if i is odd). Thus $T(i) \leq T(i/2) + O(1)$.

We thus have, for some constants a and b, the recurrence

$$T(1) = a$$
$$T(i) = T(i/2) + b \text{ for } i > 1$$

as an upper bound on the running time of `bubbleUp`. If we expand $T(i/2)$ we get

$$T(i) = T(i/2^j) + bj \tag{5.2}$$

for each j. As in Section 3.10, we choose the value of j that makes $T(i/2^j)$ simplest. In this case, we make j equal to $\log_2 i$, so that $i/2^j = 1$. Thus, (5.2) becomes $T(i) = a + b\log_2 i$; that is, $T(i)$ is $O(\log i)$. Since `bubbleUp` is $O(\log i)$, so is *insert*.

Now consider *deletemax*. We can see from Fig. 5.49 that the running time of *deletemax* is $O(1)$ plus the running time of `bubbleDown`. The analysis of `bubbleDown`, in Fig. 5.48, is essentially the same as that of `bubbleUp`. We omit it and conclude that `bubbleDown` and *deletemax* also take $O(\log n)$ time.

EXERCISES

5.9.1: Starting with the heap of Fig. 5.45, show what happens when we

a)   Insert 3
b)   Insert 20
c)   Delete the maximum element
d)   Again delete the maximum element

5.9.2: Prove Equation (5.2) by induction on i.

5.9.3: Prove by induction on the depth of the POT-property violation that the function `bubbleUp` of Fig. 5.46 correctly restores a tree with one violation to a tree that has the POT property.

5.9.4: Prove that the function `insert(A,x,n)` makes `A` into a heap of size n, if `A` was previously a heap of size $n - 1$. You may use Exercise 5.9.3. What happens if `A` was not previously a heap?

5.9.5: Prove by induction on the height of the POT-property violation that the function `bubbleDown` of Fig. 5.48 correctly restores a tree with one violation to a tree that has the POT property.

5.9.6: Prove that `deletemax(A,n)` makes a heap of size n into one of size $n - 1$. What happens if `A` was not previously a heap?

5.9.7: Prove that `bubbleDown(A,1,n)` takes $O(\log n)$ time on a heap of length n.

5.9.8**: What is the probability that an n-element heap, with distinct element priorities chosen at random, is a partially ordered tree? If you cannot derive the general rule, write a recursive function to compute the probability as a function of n.

5.9.9: We do not need to use a heap to implement a partially ordered tree. Suppose we use the conventional left-child–right-child data structure for binary trees. Show how to implement the functions `bubbleDown`, `insert`, and `deletemax` using this structure instead of the heap structure.

5.9.10*: A binary search tree can be used as an abstract implementation of a priority queue. Show how the operations *insert* and *deletemax* can be implemented using a binary search tree with the left-child–right-child data structure. What is the running time of these operations (a) in the worst case and (b) on the average?

❖❖ 5.10 Heapsort: Sorting with Balanced POTs

We shall now describe the algorithm known as *heapsort*. It sorts an array A[1..n] in two phases. In the first phase, heapsort gives A the POT property. The second phase of heapsort repeatedly selects the largest remaining element from the heap until the heap consists of only the smallest element, whereupon the array A is sorted.

heap	large elements, sorted

↑   ↑   ↑
1   i n

Fig. 5.50. Condition of array A during heapsort.

Figure 5.50 shows the array A during the second phase. The initial part of the array has the POT property, and the remaining part has its elements sorted in nondecreasing order. Furthermore, the elements in the sorted part are the largest $n - i$ elements in the array. During the second phase, i is allowed to run from n down to 1, so that the heap, initially the entire array A, eventually shrinks until it is only the smallest element, located in A[1]. In more detail, the second phase consists of the following steps.

1. $A[1]$, the largest element in A[1..i], is exchanged with $A[i]$. Since all elements in A[i+1..n] are as large as or larger than any of A[1..i], and since we just moved the largest of the latter group of elements to position i, we know that A[i..n] are the largest $n - i + 1$ elements and are in sorted order.

2. The value i is decremented, reducing the size of the heap by 1.

3. The POT property is restored to the initial part of the array by bubbling down the element at the root, which we just moved to $A[1]$.

❖   **Example 5.32.** Consider the array in Fig. 5.45, which has the POT property. Let us go through the first iteration of the second phase. In the first step, we exchange $A[1]$ and $A[10]$ to get:

1	2	3	4	5	6	7	8	9	10
5	18	16	9	7	1	9	3	7	18

The second step reduces the heap size to 9, and the third step restores the POT property to the first nine elements by calling bubbleDown(1). In this call, $A[1]$ and $A[2]$ are exchanged:

1	2	3	4	5	6	7	8	9	10
18	5	16	9	7	1	9	3	7	18

Then, $A[2]$ and $A[4]$ are exchanged:

1	2	3	4	5	6	7	8	9	10
18	9	16	5	7	1	9	3	7	18

Finally, $A[4]$ and $A[9]$ are exchanged:

1	2	3	4	5	6	7	8	9	10
18	9	16	7	7	1	9	3	5	18

At this point, `A[1..9]` has the POT property.

The second iteration of phase 2 begins by swapping the element 18 in `A[1]` with the element 5 in `A[9]`. After bubbling 5 down, the array becomes

1	2	3	4	5	6	7	8	9	10
16	9	9	7	7	1	5	3	18	18

At this stage, the last two elements of the array are the two largest elements, in sorted order.

Phase 2 continues until the array is completely sorted:

1	2	3	4	5	6	7	8	9	10
1	3	5	7	7	9	9	16	18	18

✦

Heapifying an Array

We could describe heapsort informally as follows:

```
for (i = 1; i <= n; i++)
    insert(aᵢ);
for (i = 1; i <= n; i++)
    deletemax
```

To implement this algorithm, we insert the n elements $a_1, a_2, \ldots, a_n$ to be sorted into a heap that is initially empty. We then perform *deletemax* n times, getting the elements in largest-first order. The arrangement of Fig. 5.50 allows us to store the deleted elements in the tail of the array, as we shrink the heap portion of that array.

Since we just argued in the last section that *insert* and *deletemax* take $O(\log n)$ time each, and since we evidently execute each operation n times, we have an $O(n \log n)$ sorting algorithm, which is comparable to merge sort. In fact, heapsort can be superior to merge sort in a situation in which we only need a few of the largest elements, rather than the entire sorted list. The reason is that we can make the array be a heap in $O(n)$ time, rather than $O(n \log n)$ time, if we use the function `heapify` of Fig. 5.51.

```
void heapify(int A[], int n)
{
    int i;

    for (i = n/2; i >= 1; i--)
        bubbleDown(A, i, n);
}
```

Fig. 5.51. Heapifying an array.

Running Time of Heapify

At first, it might appear that the $n/2$ calls to bubbleDown in Fig. 5.51 should take $O(n \log n)$ time in total, because $\log n$ is the only upper bound we know on the running time of bubbleDown. However, we can get a tighter bound, $O(n)$, if we exploit the fact that most of the sequences that bubble down elements are very short.

To begin, we did not even have to call bubbleDown on the second half of the array, because all the elements there are leaves. On the second quarter of the array, that is,

```
A[(n/4)+1..n/2]
```

we may call bubbleDown once, if the element is smaller than either of its children; but those children are in the second half, and therefore are leaves. Thus, in the second quarter of A, we call bubbleDown at most once. Similarly, in the second eighth of the array, we call bubbleDown at most twice, and so on. The number of calls to bubbleDown in the various regions of the array is indicated in Fig. 5.52.

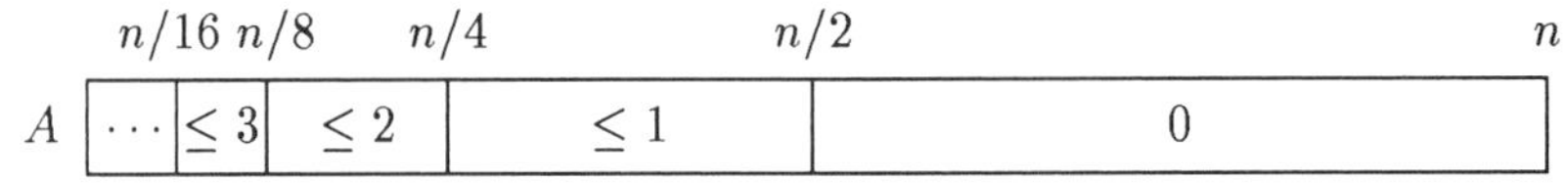

Fig. 5.52. The number of calls to bubbleDown decreases rapidly as we go through the array from low to high indices.

Let us count the number of calls to bubbleDown made by heapify, including recursive calls. From Fig. 5.52 we see that it is possible to divide A into *zones*, where the ith zone consists of A[j] for j greater than $n/2^{i+1}$ but no greater than $n/2^i$. The number of elements in zone i is thus $n/2^{i+1}$, and there are at most i calls to bubbleDown for each element in zone i. Further, the zones $i > \log_2 n$ are empty, since they contain at most $n/2^{1+\log_2 n} = 1/2$ element. The element A[1] is the sole occupant of zone $\log_2 n$. We thus need to compute the sum

$$\sum_{i=1}^{\log_2 n} in/2^{i+1} \tag{5.3}$$

We can provide an upper bound on the finite sum (5.3) by extending it to an infinite sum and then pulling out the factor $n/2$:

$$\frac{n}{2} \sum_{i=1}^{\infty} i/2^i \tag{5.4}$$

We must now get an upper bound on the sum in (5.4). This sum, $\sum_{i=1}^{\infty} i/2^i$, can be written as

$$(1/2) + (1/4 + 1/4) + (1/8 + 1/8 + 1/8) + (1/16 + 1/16 + 1/16 + 1/16) + \cdots$$

We can write these inverse powers of 2 as the triangle shown in Fig. 5.53. Each row is an infinite geometric series with ratio $1/2$, which sums to twice the first term in the series, as indicated at the right edge of Fig. 5.53. The row sums form another geometric series, which sums to 2.

$$
\begin{array}{ccccccccccc}
1/2 & + & 1/4 & + & 1/8 & + & 1/16 & + & \cdots & = & 1 \\
 & & 1/4 & + & 1/8 & + & 1/16 & + & \cdots & = & 1/2 \\
 & & & & 1/8 & + & 1/16 & + & \cdots & = & 1/4 \\
 & & & & & & 1/16 & + & \cdots & = & 1/8 \\
 & & & & & & & & \cdots & = & \cdots
\end{array}
$$

Fig. 5.53. Arranging $\sum_{i=1}^{\infty} i/2^i$ as a triangular sum.

It follows that (5.4) is upper-bounded by $(n/2) \times 2 = n$. That is, the number of calls to `bubbleDown` in the function `heapify` is no greater than n. Since we have already established that each call takes $O(1)$ time, exclusive of any recursive calls, we conclude that the total time taken by `heapify` is $O(n)$.

The Complete Heapsort Algorithm

The C program for heapsort is shown in Fig. 5.54. It uses an array of integers `A[1..MAX]` for the heap. The elements to be sorted are inserted in `A[1..n]`. The definitions of the function declarations in Fig. 5.54 are contained in Sections 5.9 and 5.10.

Line (1) calls `heapify`, which turns the n elements to be sorted into a heap; and line (2) initializes `i`, which marks the end of the heap, to n. The loop of lines (3) and (4) applies `deletemax` $n-1$ times. We should examine the code of Fig. 5.49 again to observe that `deletemax(A,i)` swaps the maximum element of the remaining heap — which is always in `A[1]` — with $A[i]$. As a side effect, i is decremented by 1, so that the size of the heap shrinks by 1. The element "deleted" by `deletemax` at line (4) is now part of the sorted tail of the array. It is less than or equal to any element in the previous tail, `A[i+1..n]`, but greater than or equal to any element still in the heap. Thus, the claimed property is maintained; all the heap elements precede all the elements of the tail.

Running Time of Heapsort

We have just established that `heapify` in line (1) takes time proportional to n. Line (2) clearly takes $O(1)$ time. Since i decreases by 1 each time around the loop of lines (3) and (4), the number of times around the loop is $n-1$. The call to `deletemax` at line (4) takes $O(\log n)$ time. Thus, the total time for the loop is $O(n \log n)$. That time dominates lines (1) and (2), and so the running time of `heapsort` is $O(n \log n)$ on n elements.

```
#include <stdio.h>

#define MAX 100

int A[MAX+1];

void bubbleDown(int A[], int i, int n);
void deletemax(int A[], int *pn);
void heapify(int A[], int n);
void heapsort(int A[], int n);
void swap(int A[], int i, int j);

main()
{
    int i, n, x;

    n = 0;
    while (n < MAX && scanf("%d", &x) != EOF)
        A[++n] = x;
    heapsort(A, n);
    for (i = 1; i <= n; i++)
        printf("%d\n", A[i]);
}

void heapsort(int A[], int n)
{
    int i;

(1)     heapify(A, n);
(2)     i = n;
(3)     while (i > 1)
(4)         deletemax(A, &i);
}
```

Fig. 5.54. Heapsorting an array.

EXERCISES

5.10.1: Apply heapsort to the list of elements 3, 1, 4, 1, 5, 9, 2, 6, 5.

5.10.2*: Give an $O(n)$ running time algorithm that finds the $\sqrt{n}$ largest elements in a list of n elements.

❖❖ 5.11   Summary of Chapter 5

The reader should take away the following points from Chapter 5:

✦   Trees are an important data model for representing hierarchical information.

✦ Many data structures involving combinations of arrays and pointers can be used to implement trees, and the data structure of choice depends on the operations performed on the tree.

✦ Two of the most important representations for tree nodes are the leftmost-child–right-sibling representation and the trie (array of pointers to children).

✦ Recursive algorithms and proofs are well suited for trees. A variant of our basic induction scheme, called structural induction, is effectively a complete induction on the number of nodes in a tree.

✦ The binary tree is a variant of the tree model in which each node has (optional) left and right children.

✦ A binary search tree is a labeled binary tree with the "binary search tree property" that all the labels in the left subtree precede the label at a node, and all labels in the right subtree follow the label at the node.

✦ The dictionary abstract data type is a set upon which we can perform the operations *insert*, *delete*, and *lookup*. The binary search tree efficiently implements dictionaries.

✦ A priority queue is another abstract data type, a set upon which we can perform the operations *insert* and *deletemax*.

✦ A partially ordered tree is a labeled binary tree with the property that the label at any node is at least as great as the label at its children.

✦ Balanced partially ordered trees, where the nodes fully occupy levels from the root to the lowest level, where only the leftmost positions are occupied, can be implemented by an array structure called a heap. This structure provides an $O(\log n)$ implementation of a priority queue and leads to an $O(n \log n)$ sorting algorithm called heapsort.

✦✦ 5.12   Bibliographic Notes for Chapter 5

The trie representation of trees is from Fredkin [1960]. The binary search tree was invented independently by a number of people, and the reader is referred to Knuth [1973] for a history as well as a great deal more information on various kinds of search trees. For more advanced applications of trees, see Tarjan [1983].

Williams [1964] devised the heap implementation of balanced partially ordered trees. Floyd [1964] describes an efficient version of heapsort.

Floyd, R. W. [1964]. "Algorithm 245: Treesort 3," *Comm. ACM* **7**:12, pp. 701.

Fredkin, E. [1960]. "Trie memory," *Comm. ACM* **3**:4, pp. 490–500.

Knuth, D. E. [1973]. *The Art of Computer Programming*, Vol. III, *Sorting and Searching*, 2nd ed., Addison-Wesley, Reading, Mass.

Tarjan, R. E. [1983]. *Data Structures and Network Algorithms*, SIAM Press, Philadelphia.

Williams, J. W. J. [1964]. "Algorithm 232: Heapsort," *Comm. ACM* **7**:6, pp. 347–348.

CHAPTER | 6

❖

The List
Data Model

Like trees, lists are among the most basic of data models used in computer programs. Lists are, in a sense, simple forms of trees, because one can think of a list as a binary tree in which every left child is a leaf. However, lists also present some aspects that are not special cases of what we have learned about trees. For instance, we shall talk about operations on lists, such as pushing and popping, that have no common analog for trees, and we shall talk of character strings, which are special and important kinds of lists requiring their own data structures.

❖❖ 6.1 What This Chapter Is About

We introduce list terminology in Section 6.2. Then in the remainder of the chapter we present the following topics:

✦ The basic operations on lists (Section 6.3).

✦ Implementations of abstract lists by data structures, especially the linked-list data structure (Section 6.4) and an array data structure (Section 6.5).

✦ The stack, a list upon which we insert and delete at only one end (Section 6.6).

✦ The queue, a list upon which we insert at one end and delete at the other (Section 6.8).

✦ Character strings and the special data structures we use to represent them (Section 6.10).

Further, we shall study in detail two applications of lists:

✦ The run-time stack and the way C and many other languages implement recursive functions (Section 6.7).

♦ The problem of finding longest common subsequences of two strings, and its solution by a "dynamic programming," or table-filling, algorithm (Section 6.9).

✦✦ 6.2 Basic Terminology

List

A *list* is a finite sequence of zero or more elements. If the elements are all of type T, then we say that the type of the list is "list of T." Thus we can have lists of integers, lists of real numbers, lists of structures, lists of lists of integers, and so on. We generally expect the elements of a list to be of some one type. However, since a type can be the union of several types, the restriction to a single "type" can be circumvented.

A list is often written with its elements separated by commas and enclosed in parentheses:

$$(a_1, a_2, \ldots, a_n)$$

where the a_i's are the elements of the list.

Character string

In some situations we shall not show commas or parentheses explicitly. In particular, we shall study *character strings*, which are lists of characters. Character strings are generally written with no comma or other separating marks and with no surrounding parentheses. Elements of character strings will normally be written in typewriter font. Thus `foo` is the list of three characters of which the first is `f` and the second and third are `o`.

♦ **Example 6.1.** Here are some examples of lists.

1. The list of prime numbers less than 20, in order of size:

   (2, 3, 5, 7, 11, 13, 17, 19)

2. The list of noble gasses, in order of atomic weight:

   (helium, neon, argon, krypton, xenon, radon)

3. The list of the numbers of days in the months of a non-leap year:

   (31, 28, 31, 30, 31, 30, 31, 31, 30, 31, 30, 31)

As this example reminds us, the same element can appear more than once on a list. ♦

♦ **Example 6.2.** A line of text is another example of a list. The individual characters making up the line are the elements of this list, so the list is a character string. This character string usually includes several occurrences of the blank character, and normally the last character in a line of text is the "newline" character.

As another example, a document can be viewed as a list. Here the elements of the list are the lines of text. Thus a document is a list whose elements that are themselves lists, character strings in particular. ♦

✦ **Example 6.3.** A point in n-dimensional space can be represented by a list of n real numbers. For example, the vertices of the unit cube can be represented by the triples shown in Fig. 6.1. The three elements on each list represent the coordinates of a point that is one of the eight corners (or "vertices") of the cube. The first component represents the x-coordinate (horizontal), the second represents the y-coordinate (into the page), and the third represents the z-coordinate (vertical). ✦

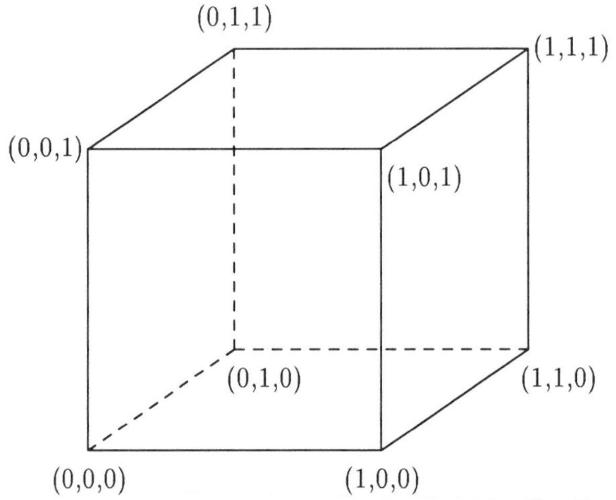

Fig. 6.1. The vertices of the unit cube represented as triples.

The Length of a List

Empty list

The *length* of a list is the number of occurrences of elements on the list. If the number of elements is zero, then the list is said to be *empty*. We use the Greek letter ϵ (epsilon) to represent the empty list. We can also represent the empty list by a pair of parentheses surrounding nothing: (). It is important to remember that length counts positions, not distinct symbols, and so a symbol appearing k times on a list adds k to the length of the list.

✦ **Example 6.4.** The length of list (1) in Example 6.1 is 8, and the length of list (2) is 6. The length of list (3) is 12, since there is one position for each month. The fact that there are only three different numbers on the list is irrelevant as far as the length of the list is concerned. ✦

Parts of a List

Head and tail of a list

If a list is not empty, then it consists of a first element, called the *head* and the remainder of the list, called the *tail*. For instance, the head of list (2) in Example 6.1 is helium, while the tail is the list consisting of the remaining five elements,

(neon, argon, krypton, xenon, radon)

Elements and Lists of Length 1

It is important to remember that the head of a list is an element, while the tail of a list is a list. Moreover, we should not confuse the head of a list — say a — with the list of length 1 containing only the element a, which would normally be written with parentheses as (a). If the element a is of type T, then the list (a) is of type "list of T."

Failure to recognize the difference leads to programming errors when we implement lists by data structures. For example, we may represent lists by linked cells, which are typically structures with an **element** field of some type T, holding an element, and a **next** field holding a pointer to the next cell. Then element a is of type T, while the list (a) is a cell with **element** field holding a and **next** field holding **NULL**.

Sublist

If $L = (a_1, a_2, \ldots, a_n)$ is a list, then for any i and j such that $1 \leq i \leq j \leq n$, $(a_i, a_{i+1}, \ldots, a_j)$ is said to be a *sublist* of L. That is, a sublist is formed by starting at some position i, and taking all the elements up to some position j. We also say that ϵ, the empty list, is a sublist of any list.

Subsequence

A *subsequence* of the list $L = (a_1, a_2, \ldots, a_n)$ is a list formed by striking out zero or more elements of L. The remaining elements, which form the subsequence, must appear in the same order in which they appear in L, but the elements of the subsequence need not be consecutive in L. Note that ϵ and the list L itself are always subsequences, as well as sublists, of L.

✦ **Example 6.5.** Let L be the character string abc. The sublists of L are

ϵ, a, b, c, ab, bc, abc

These are all subsequences of L as well, and in addition, ac is a subsequence, but not a sublist.

For another example, let L be the character string abab. Then the sublists are

ϵ, a, b, ab, ba, aba, bab, abab

These are also subsequences of L, and in addition, L has the subsequences aa, bb, aab, and abb. Notice that a character string like bba is not a subsequence of L. Even though L has two b's and an a, they do not appear in such an order in L that we can form bba by striking out elements of L. That is, there is no a after the second b in L. ✦

Prefix and suffix

A *prefix* of a list is any sublist that starts at the beginning of the list. A *suffix* is a sublist that terminates at the end of the list. As special cases, we regard ϵ as both a prefix and a suffix of any list.

✦ **Example 6.6.** The prefixes of the list abc are ϵ, a, ab, and abc. Its suffixes are ϵ, c, bc, and abc. ✦

Car and Cdr

In the programming language Lisp, the head is called the *car* and the tail is called the *cdr* (pronounced "cudder"). The terms "*car*" and "*cdr*" arose from the names given to two fields of a machine instruction on an IBM 709, the computer on which Lisp was first implemented. Car stands for "contents of the address register," and cdr stands for "contents of the decrement register." In a sense, memory words were seen as cells with **element** and **next** fields, corresponding to the car and cdr, respectively.

The Position of an Element on a List

Each element on a list is associated with a *position*. If $(a_1, a_2, \ldots, a_n)$ is a list and $n \geq 1$, then a_1 is said to be *first* element, a_2 the second, and so on, with a_n the *last* element. We also say that element a_i occurs at *position i*. In addition, a_i is said to *follow* a_{i-1} and to *precede* a_{i+1}. A position holding element a is said to be an *occurrence* of a.

Occurrence of an element

The number of positions on a list equals the length of the list. It is possible for the same element to appear at two or more positions. Thus it is important not to confuse a position with the element at that position. For instance, list (3) in Example 6.1 has twelve positions, seven of which hold 31 — namely, positions 1, 3, 5, 7, 8, 10, and 12.

EXERCISES

6.2.1: Answer the following questions about the list $(2, 7, 1, 8, 2)$.

a) What is the length?
b) What are all the prefixes?
c) What are all the suffixes?
d) What are all the sublists?
e) How many subsequences are there?
f) What is the head?
g) What is the tail?
h) How many positions are there?

6.2.2: Repeat Exercise 6.2.1 for the character string **banana**.

6.2.3**: In a list of length $n \geq 0$, what are the largest and smallest possible numbers of (a) prefixes (b) sublists (c) subsequences?

6.2.4: If the tail of the tail of the list L is the empty list, what is the length of L?

6.2.5*: Bea Fuddled wrote a list whose elements are lists of integers, but omitted the parentheses: 1,2,3. There are many lists of lists that could have been represented, such as $\big((1), (2, 3)\big)$. What are all the possible lists that do not have the empty list as an element?

✦✦ 6.3 Operations on Lists

A great variety of operations can be performed on lists. In Chapter 2, when we discussed merge sort, the basic problem was to sort a list, but we also needed to split a list into two, and to merge two sorted lists. Formally, the operation of *sorting* a list $(a_1, a_2, \ldots, a_n)$ amounts to replacing the list with a list consisting of a permutation of its elements, $(b_1, b_2, \ldots, b_n)$, such that $b_1 \leq b_2 \leq \cdots \leq b_n$. Here, as before, $\leq$ represents an ordering of the elements, such as "less than or equal to" on integers or reals, or lexicographic order on strings. The operation of *merging* two sorted lists consists of constructing from them a sorted list containing the same elements as the two given lists. Multiplicity must be preserved; that is, if there are k occurrences of element a among the two given lists, then the resulting list has k occurrences of a. Review Section 2.8 for examples of these two operations on lists.

Sorting and merging

Insertion, Deletion, and Lookup

Recall from Section 5.7 that a "dictionary" is a set of elements on which we perform the operations *insert*, *delete*, and *lookup*. There is an important difference between sets and lists. An element can never appear more than once in a set, although, as we have seen, an element can appear more than once on a list; this and other issues regarding sets are discussed in Chapter 7. However, lists can implement sets, in the sense that the elements in a set $\{a_1, a_2, \ldots, a_n\}$ can be placed in a list in any order, for example, the order $(a_1, a_2, \ldots, a_n)$, or the order $(a_n, a_{n-1}, \ldots, a_1)$. Thus it should be no surprise that there are operations on lists analogous to the dictionary operations on sets.

1. We can *insert* an element x onto a list L. In principle, x could appear anywhere on the list, and it does not matter if x already appears in L one or more times. We insert by adding one more occurrence of x. As a special case, if we make x the head of the new list (and therefore make L the tail), we say that we *push* x onto the list L. If $L = (a_1, \ldots, a_n)$, the resulting list is $(x, a_1, \ldots, a_n)$.

2. We can *delete* an element x from a list L. Here, we delete an occurrence of x from L. If there is more than one occurrence, we could specify which occurrence to delete; for example, we could always delete the first occurrence. If we want to delete all occurrences of x, we repeat the deletion until no more x's remain. If x is not present on list L, the deletion has no effect. As a special case, if we delete the head element of the list, so that the list $(x, a_1, \ldots, a_n)$ becomes $(a_1, \ldots, a_n)$, we are said to *pop* the list.

3. We can *lookup* an element x on a list L. This operation returns TRUE or FALSE, depending on whether x is or is not an element on the list.

✦ **Example 6.7.** Let L be the list $(1, 2, 3, 2)$. The result of *insert*$(1, L)$ could be the list $(1, 1, 2, 3, 2)$, if we chose to push 1, that is, to insert 1 at the beginning. We could also insert the new 1 at the end, yielding $(1, 2, 3, 2, 1)$. Alternatively, the new 1 could be placed in any of three positions interior to the list L.

The result of *delete*$(2, L)$ is the list $(1, 3, 2)$ if we delete the first occurrence of 2. If we ask *lookup*(x, L), the answer is TRUE if x is 1, 2, or 3, but FALSE if x is any other value. ✦

Concatenation

We *concatenate* two lists L and M by forming the list that begins with the elements of L and then continues with the elements of M. That is, if $L = (a_1, a_2, \ldots, a_n)$ and $M = (b_1, b_2, \ldots, b_k)$, then LM, the concatenation of L and M, is the list

$$(a_1, a_2, \ldots, a_n, b_1, b_2, \ldots, b_k)$$

Identity for concatenation

Note that the empty list is the identity for concatenation. That is, for any list L, we have $\epsilon L = L \epsilon = L$.

✦ **Example 6.8.** If L is the list $(1, 2, 3)$ and M is the list $(3, 1)$, then LM is the list $(1, 2, 3, 3, 1)$. If L is the character string **dog** and M is the character string **house**, then LM is the character string **doghouse**. ✦

Other List Operations

Another family of operations on lists refers to particular positions of the list. For example,

First and last of lists

a)   The operation $first(L)$ returns the first element (head) of list L, and $last(L)$ returns the last element of L. Both cause an error if L is an empty list.

Retrieve

b)   The operation $retrieve(i, L)$ returns the element at the ith position of list L. It is an error if L has length less than i.

There are additional operations that involve the length of a list. Some common operations are:

c) $length(L)$, which returns the length of list L.

isEmpty

d) $isEmpty(L)$, which returns **TRUE** if L is an empty list and returns **FALSE** if not. Similarly, $isNotEmpty(L)$ would return the opposite.

EXERCISES

6.3.1: Let L be the list $(3, 1, 4, 1, 5, 9)$.

a)   What is the value of $delete(5, L)$?
b)   What is the value of $delete(1, L)$?
c)   What is the result of popping L?
d)   What is the result of pushing 2 onto list L?
e)   What is returned if we perform $lookup$ with the element 6 and list L?
f)   If M is the list $(6, 7, 8)$, what is the value of LM (the concatenation of L and M)? What is ML?
g)   What is $first(L)$? What is $last(L)$?
h)   What is the result of $retrieve(3, L)$?
i)   What is the value of $length(L)$?
j)   What is the value of $isEmpty(L)$?

6.3.2**: If L and M are lists, under what conditions is $LM = ML$?

6.3.3**: Let x be an element and L a list. Under what conditions are the following equations true?

a) $delete\bigl(x,\ insert(x,L)\bigr) = L$
b) $insert\bigl(x,\ delete(x,L)\bigr) = L$
c) $first(L) = retrieve(1,L)$
d) $last(L) = retrieve\bigl(length(L),\ L\bigr)$

✧✧ 6.4 The Linked-List Data Structure

The easiest way to implement a list is to use a linked list of cells. Each cell consists of two fields, one containing an element of the list, the other a pointer to the next cell on the linked list. In this chapter we shall make the simplifying assumption that elements are integers. Not only may we use the specific type **int** for the type of elements, but we can compare elements by the standard comparison operators ==, <, and so on. The exercises invite the reader to develop variants of our functions that work for arbitrary types, where comparisons are made by user-defined functions such as *eq* to test equality, $lt(x,y)$ to test if x precedes y in some ordering, and so on.

In what follows, we shall use our macro from Section 1.6:

```
DefCell(int, CELL, LIST);
```

which expands into our standard structure for cells and lists:

```
typedef struct CELL *LIST;
struct CELL {
    int element;
    LIST next;
};
```

Note that **LIST** is the type of a pointer to a cell. In effect, the **next** field of each cell points both to the next cell and to the entire remainder of the list.

Figure 6.2 shows a linked list that represents the abstract list

$$L = (a_1, a_2, \ldots, a_n)$$

There is one cell for each element; the element a_i appears in the **element** field of the ith cell. The pointer in the ith cell points to the $(i+1)$st cell, for $i = 1, 2, \ldots, n-1$, and the pointer in the last cell is **NULL**, indicating the end of the list. Outside the list is a pointer, named **L**, that points to the first cell of the list; **L** is of type **LIST**. If the list L were empty, then the value of **L** would be **NULL**.

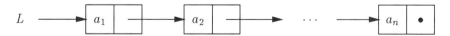

Fig. 6.2. A linked list representing the list $L = (a_1, a_2, \ldots, a_n)$.

Implementation of Dictionary Operations by Linked Lists

Let us consider how we can implement the dictionary operations if we represent the dictionary by a linked list. The following operations on dictionaries were defined in Section 5.7.

Lists and Linked Lists

Remember that a list is an abstract, or mathematical model. The linked list is a simple data structure, which was mentioned in Chapter 1. A linked list is one way to implement the list data model, although, as we shall see, it is not the only way. At any rate, this is a good time to remember once more the distinction between models and the data structures that implement them.

1. $insert(x, D)$, to insert element x into dictionary D,

2. $delete(x, D)$, to delete element x from dictionary D, and

3. $lookup(x, D)$, to determine whether element x is in dictionary D,

We shall see that the linked list is a simpler data structure for implementing dictionaries than the binary search tree that we discussed in the previous chapter. However, the running time of the dictionary operations when using the linked-list representation is not as good as when using the binary search tree. In Chapter 7 we shall see an even better implementation for dictionaries — the hash table — which makes use, as subroutines, of the dictionary operations on lists.

We shall assume that our dictionary contains integers, and cells are defined as they were at the beginning of this section. Then the type of a dictionary is **LIST**, also as defined at the beginning of this section. The dictionary containing the set of elements $\{a_1, a_2, \ldots, a_n\}$ could be represented by the linked list of Fig. 6.2. There are many other lists that could represent the same set, since order of elements is not important in sets.

Lookup

To perform $lookup(x, D)$, we examine each cell of the list representing D to see whether it holds the desired element x. If so, we return **TRUE**. If we reach the end of the list without finding x, we return **FALSE**. As before, the defined constants **TRUE** and **FALSE** stand for the constants 1 and 0, and **BOOLEAN** for the defined type **int**. A recursive function **lookup(x,D)** is shown in Fig. 6.3.

```
BOOLEAN lookup(int x, LIST L)
{
    if (L == NULL)
        return FALSE;
    else if (x == L->element)
        return TRUE;
    else
        return lookup(x, L->next);
}
```

Fig. 6.3. Lookup on a linked list.

If the list has length n, we claim that the function of Fig. 6.3 takes $O(n)$ time. Except for the recursive call at the end, **lookup** takes $O(1)$ time. When the call is made, the length of the remaining list is 1 less than the length of the list L. Thus it should surprise no one that lookup on a list of length n takes $O(n)$ time. More formally, the following recurrence relation gives the running time $T(n)$ of lookup when the list L pointed to by the second argument has length n.

BASIS. $T(0)$ is $O(1)$, because there is no recursive call when L is NULL.

INDUCTION. $T(n) = T(n-1) + O(1)$.

The solution to this recurrence is $T(n) = O(n)$, as we saw several times in Chapter 3. Since a dictionary of n elements is represented by a list of length n, *lookup* takes $O(n)$ time on a dictionary of size n.

Unfortunately, the average time for a successful lookup is also proportional to n. For if we are looking for an element x known to be in D, the expected value of the position of x in the list is $(n+1)/2$. That is, x could be anywhere from the first to the nth element, with equal probability. Thus, the expected number of recursive calls to lookup is $(n + 1)/2$. Since each takes $O(1)$ time, the average successful lookup takes $O(n)$ time. Of course, if the lookup is unsuccessful, we make all n calls before reaching the end of the list and returning FALSE.

Deletion

A function to delete an element x from a linked list is shown in Fig. 6.4. The second parameter pL is a pointer to the list L (rather than the list L itself). We use the "call by reference" style here because we want delete to remove the cell containing x from the list. As we move down the list, pL holds a pointer to a pointer to the "current" cell. If we find x in the current cell C, at line (2), then we change the pointer to cell C at line (3), so that it points to the cell following C on the list. If C happens to be last on the list, the former pointer to C becomes NULL. If x is not the current element, then at line (4) we recursively delete x from the tail of the list.

Note that the test at line (1) causes the function to return with no action if the list is empty. That is because x is not present on an empty list, and we need not do anything to remove x from the dictionary. If D is a linked list representing a dictionary, then a call to delete(x, &D) initiates the deletion of x from the dictionary D.

```
        void delete(int x, LIST *pL)
        {
(1)         if ((*pL) != NULL)
(2)             if (x == (*pL)->element)
(3)                 (*pL) = (*pL)->next;
                else
(4)                 delete(x, &((*pL)->next));
        }
```

Fig. 6.4. Deleting an element.

If the element x is not on the list for the dictionary D, then we run down to the end of the list, taking $O(1)$ time for each element. The analysis is similar to that for the **lookup** function of Fig. 6.3, and we leave the details for the reader. Thus the time to delete an element not in D is $O(n)$ if D has n elements. If x is in the dictionary D, then, on the average, we shall encounter x halfway down the list. Therefore we search $(n + 1)/2$ cells on the average, and the running time of a successful deletion is also $O(n)$.

Insertion

A function to insert an element x into a linked list is shown in Fig. 6.5. To insert x, we need to check that x is not already on the list (if it is, we do nothing). If x is not already present, we must add it to the list. It does not matter where in the list we add x, but the function in Fig. 6.5 adds x to the end of the list. When at line (1) we detect the **NULL** at the end, we are therefore sure that x is not already on the list. Then, lines (2) through (4) append x to the end of the list.

If the list is not **NULL**, line (5) checks for x at the current cell. If x is not there, line (6) makes a recursive call on the tail. If x is found at line (5), then function **insert** terminates with no recursive call and with no change to the list L. A call to **insert(x, &D)** initiates the insertion of x into dictionary D.

```
        void insert(int x, LIST *pL)
        {
(1)         if ((*pL) == NULL) {
(2)             (*pL) = (LIST) malloc(sizeof(struct CELL));
(3)             (*pL)->element = x;
(4)             (*pL)->next = NULL;
            }
(5)         else if (x != (*pL)->element)
(6)             insert(x, &((*pL)->next));
        }
```

Fig. 6.5. Inserting an element.

As in the case of lookup and deletion, if we do not find x on the list, we travel to the end, taking $O(n)$ time. If we do find x, then on the average we travel halfway[1] down the list, and we still take $O(n)$ time on the average.

A Variant Approach with Duplicates

We can make insertion run faster if we do not check for the presence of x on the list before inserting it. However, as a consequence, there may be several copies of an element on the list representing a dictionary.

To execute the dictionary operation $insert(x, D)$ we simply create a new cell, put x in it, and push that cell onto the front of the list for D. This operation takes $O(1)$ time.

The lookup operation is exactly the same as in Fig. 6.3. The only nuance is that we may have to search a longer list, because the length of the list representing dictionary D may be greater than the number of members of D.

---

[1] In the following analyses, we shall use terms like "halfway" or "$n/2$" when we mean the middle of a list of length n. Strictly speaking, $(n + 1)/2$ is more accurate.

Abstraction Versus Implementation Again

It may be surprising to see us using duplicates in lists that represent dictionaries, since the abstract data type DICTIONARY is defined as a set, and sets do not have duplicates. However, it is not the dictionary that has duplicates. Rather the data structure implementing the dictionary is allowed to have duplicates. But even when x appears several times on a linked list, it is only present once in the dictionary that the linked list represents.

Deletion is slightly different. We cannot stop our search for x when we encounter a cell with element x, because there could be other copies of x. Thus we must delete x from the tail of a list L, even when the head of L contains x. As a result, not only do we have longer lists to contend with, but to achieve a successful deletion we must search every cell rather than an average of half the list, as we could for the case in which no duplicates were allowed on the list. The details of these versions of the dictionary operations are left as an exercise.

In summary, by allowing duplicates, we make insertion faster, $O(1)$ instead of $O(n)$. However, successful deletions require search of the entire list, rather than an average of half the list, and for both lookup and deletion, we must contend with lists that are longer than when duplicates are not allowed, although how much longer depends on how often we insert an element that is already present in the dictionary.

Which method to choose is a bit subtle. Clearly, if insertions predominate, we should allow duplicates. In the extreme case, where we do only insertions but never lookup or deletion, we get performance of $O(1)$ per operation, instead of $O(n)$.[2] If we can be sure, for some reason, that we shall never insert an element already in the dictionary, then we can use both the fast insertion and the fast deletion, where we stop when we find one occurrence of the element to be deleted. On the other hand, if we may insert duplicate elements, and lookups or deletions predominate, then we are best off checking for the presence of x before inserting it, as in the *insert* function of Fig. 6.5.

Sorted Lists to Represent Dictionaries

Another alternative is to keep elements sorted in increasing order on the list representing a dictionary D. Then, if we wish to lookup element x, we have only to go as far as the position in which x would appear; on the average, that is halfway down the list. If we meet an element greater than x, then there is no hope of finding x later in the list. We thus avoid going all the way down the list on unsuccessful searches. That saves us about a factor of 2, although the exact factor is somewhat clouded because we have to ask whether x follows in sorted order each of the elements we meet on the list, which is an additional step at each cell. However, the same factor in savings is gained on unsuccessful searches during insertion and deletion.

A lookup function for sorted lists is shown in Fig. 6.6. We leave to the reader the exercise of modifying the functions of Figs. 6.4 and 6.5 to work on sorted lists.

---

[2] But why bother inserting into a dictionary if we never look to see what is there?

```
BOOLEAN lookup(int x, LIST L)
{
    if (L == NULL)
        return FALSE;
    else if (x > L->element)
        return lookup(x, L->next);
    else if (x == L->element)
        return TRUE;
    else /* here x < L->element, and so x could not be
            on the sorted list L */
        return FALSE;
}
```

Fig. 6.6. Lookup on a sorted list.

Comparison of Methods

The table in Fig. 6.7 indicates the number of cells we must search for each of the three dictionary operations, for each of the three list-based representations of dictionaries we have discussed. We take n to be the number of elements in the dictionary, which is also the length of the list if no duplicates are allowed. We use m for the length of the list when duplicates are allowed. We know that $m \geq n$, but we do not know how much greater m is than n. Where we use $n/2 \to n$ we mean that the number of cells is an average of $n/2$ when the search is successful, and n when unsuccessful. The entry $n/2 \to m$ indicates that on a successful lookup we shall see $n/2$ elements of the dictionary, on the average, before seeing the one we want,[3] but on an unsuccessful search, we must go all the way to the end of a list of length m.

	INSERT	DELETE	LOOKUP
No duplicates	$n/2 \to n$	$n/2 \to n$	$n/2 \to n$
Duplicates	0	m	$n/2 \to m$
Sorted	$n/2$	$n/2$	$n/2$

Fig. 6.7. Number of cells searched by three methods of
representing dictionaries by linked lists.

Notice that all of these running times, except for insertion with duplicates, are worse than the average running times for dictionary operations when the data structure is a binary search tree. As we saw in Section 5.8, dictionary operations take only $O(\log n)$ time on the average when a binary search tree is used.

---

[3] In fact, since there may be duplicates, we may have to examine somewhat more than $n/2$ cells before we can expect to see $n/2$ different elements.

Judicious Ordering of Tests

Notice the order in which the three tests of Fig. 6.6 are made. We have no choice but to test that L is not **NULL** first, since if L is **NULL** the other two tests will cause an error. Let y be the value of **L->element**. Then in all but the last cell we visit, we shall have $x < y$. The reason is that if we have $x = y$, we terminate the lookup successfully, and if we have $x > y$, we terminate with failure to find x. Thus we make the test $x < y$ first, and only if that fails do we need to separate the other two cases. That ordering of tests follows a general principle: we want to test for the most common cases first, and thus save in the total number of tests we perform, on the average.

If we visit k cells, then we test k times whether L is **NULL** and we test k times whether x is less than y. Once, we shall test whether $x = y$, making a total of $2k + 1$ tests. That is only one more test than we make in the **lookup** function of Fig. 6.3 — which uses unsorted lists — in the case that the element x is found. If the element is not found, we shall expect to use many fewer tests in Fig. 6.6 than in Fig. 6.3, because we can, on the average, stop after examining only half the cells with Fig. 6.6. Thus although the big-oh running times of the dictionary operations using either sorted or unsorted lists is $O(n)$, there is usually a slight advantage in the constant factor if we use sorted lists.

Doubly Linked Lists

In a linked list it is not easy to move from a cell toward the beginning of the list. The doubly linked list is a data structure that facilitates movement both forward and backward in a list. The cells of a doubly linked list of integers contain three fields:

```
typedef struct CELL *LIST;
struct CELL {
    LIST previous;
    int element;
    LIST next;
};
```

The additional field contains a pointer to the previous cell on the list. Figure 6.8 shows a doubly linked list data structure that represents the list $L = (a_1, a_2, \ldots, a_n)$.

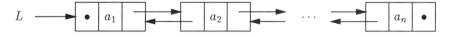

Fig. 6.8. A doubly linked list representing the list $L = (a_1, a_2, \ldots, a_n)$.

Dictionary operations on a doubly linked list structure are essentially the same as those on a singly linked list. To see the advantage of doubly linked lists, consider the operation of deleting an element a_i, given only a pointer to the cell containing that element. With a singly linked list, we would have to find the previous cell by searching the list from the beginning. With a doubly linked list, we can do the task in $O(1)$ time by a sequence of pointer manipulations, as shown in Fig. 6.9.

```
        void delete(LIST p, LIST *pL)
        {
            /* p is a pointer to the cell to be deleted,
               and pL points to the list */
(1)         if (p->next != NULL)
(2)             p->next->previous = p->previous;
(3)         if (p->previous == NULL) /* p points to first cell */
(4)             (*pL) = p->next;
            else
(5)             p->previous->next = p->next;
        }
```

Fig. 6.9. Deleting a cell from a doubly linked list.

The function delete(p,pL) shown in Fig. 6.9 takes as arguments a pointer p to the cell to be deleted, and pL, which is a pointer to the list L itself. That is, pL is the address of a pointer to the first cell on the list. In line (1) of Fig. 6.9 we check that p does not point to the last cell. If it does not, then at line (2) we make the backward pointer of the following cell point to the cell before p (or we make it equal to NULL if p happens to point to the first cell).

Line (3) tests whether p is the first cell. If so, then at line (4) we make L point to the second cell. Note that in this case, line (2) has made the **previous** field of the second cell NULL. If p does not point to the first cell, then at line (5) we make the forward pointer of the previous cell point to the cell following p. That way, the cell pointed to by p has effectively been spliced out of the list; the previous and next cells point to each other.

EXERCISES

6.4.1: Set up the recurrence relations for the running times of (a) delete in Fig. 6.4 (b) insert in Fig. 6.5. What are their solutions?

6.4.2: Write C functions for dictionary operations *insert*, *lookup* and *delete* using linked lists with duplicates.

6.4.3: Write C functions for *insert* and *delete*, using sorted lists as in Fig. 6.6.

6.4.4: Write a C function that inserts an element x into a new cell that follows the cell pointed to by p on a doubly linked list. Figure 6.9 is a similar function for deletion, but for insertion, we don't need to know the list header L.

6.4.5: If we use the doubly linked data structure for lists, an option is to represent a list not by a pointer to a cell, but by a cell with the element field unused. Note that this "header" cell is not itself a part of the list. The **next** field of the header points to the first true cell of the list, and the **previous** field of the first cell points to the header cell. We can then delete the cell (not the header) pointed to by pointer p without knowing the header L, as we needed to know in Fig. 6.9. Write a C function to delete from a doubly linked list using the format described here.

6.4.6: Write recursive functions for (a) *retrieve(i, L)* (b) *length(L)* (c) *last(L)* using the linked-list data structure.

6.4.7: Extend each of the following functions to cells with an arbitrary type `ETYPE` for elements, using functions $eq(x, y)$ to test if x and y are equal and $lt(x, y)$ to tell if x precedes y in an ordering of the elements of `ETYPE`.

a)   *lookup* as in Fig. 6.3.
b)   *delete* as in Fig. 6.4.
c)   *insert* as in Fig. 6.5.
d)   *insert*, *delete*, and *lookup* using lists with duplicates.
e)   *insert*, *delete*, and *lookup* using sorted lists.

❖❖ 6.5   Array-Based Implementation of Lists

Another common way to implement a list is to create a structure consisting of

1.   An array to hold the elements and

2.   A variable `length` to keep track of the count of the number of elements currently in the list.

Figure 6.10 shows how we might represent the list $(a_0, a_1, \ldots, a_{n-1})$ using an array `A[0..MAX-1]`. Elements $a_0, a_1, \ldots, a_{n-1}$ are stored in `A[0..n-1]`, and $length = n$.

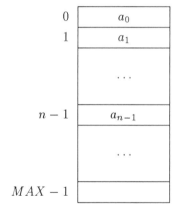

Fig. 6.10. The array `A` holding the list $(a_0, a_1, \ldots, a_{n-1})$.

As in the previous section, we assume that list elements are integers and invite the reader to generalize the functions to arbitrary types. The structure declaration for this array-based implementation of lists is:

```
typedef struct {
    int A[MAX];
    int length;
} LIST;
```

Here, **LIST** is a structure of two fields; the first is an array **A** that stores the elements, the second an integer **length** that contains the number of elements currently on the list. The quantity **MAX** is a user-defined constant that bounds the number of elements that will ever be stored on the list.

The array-based representation of lists is in many ways more convenient than the linked-list representation. It does suffer, however, from the limitation that lists cannot grow longer than the array, which can cause an insertion to fail. In the linked-list representation, we can grow lists as long as we have available computer memory.

We can perform the dictionary operations on array-based lists in roughly the same time as on lists in the linked-list representation. To insert x, we look for x, and if we do not find it, we check whether $length < MAX$. If not, there is an error condition, as we cannot fit the new element into the array. Otherwise, we store x in **A[length]** and then increase $length$ by 1. To delete x, we again lookup x, and if found, we shift all following elements of **A** down by one position; then, we decrement $length$ by 1. The details of functions to implement *insert* and *delete* are left as exercises. We shall concentrate on the details of *lookup* below.

Lookup with Linear Search

Figure 6.11 is a function that implements the operation *lookup*. Because the array **A** may be large, we choose to pass a pointer **pL** to the structure of type **LIST** as a formal parameter to *lookup*. Within the function, the two fields of the structure can then be referred to as **pL->A[i]** and **pL->length**.

Starting with $i = 0$, the for-loop of lines (1) to (3) examines each location of the array in turn, until it either reaches the last occupied location or finds x. If it finds x, it returns **TRUE**. If it has examined each element in the list without finding x, it returns **FALSE** at line (4). This method of lookup is called *linear* or *sequential* search.

```
        BOOLEAN lookup(int x, LIST *pL)
        {
            int i;

(1)         for (i = 0; i < pL->length; i++)
(2)             if (x == pL->A[i])
(3)                 return TRUE;
(4)         return FALSE;
        }
```

Fig. 6.11. Function that does lookup by linear search.

It is easy to see that, on the average, we search half the array **A[0..length-1]** before finding x if it is present. Thus letting n be the value of **length**, we take $O(n)$ time to perform a lookup. If x is not present, we search the whole array **A[0..length-1]**, again requiring $O(n)$ time. This performance is the same as for a linked-list representation of a list.

The Importance of Constant Factors in Practice

Throughout Chapter 3, we emphasized the importance of big-oh measures of running time, and we may have given the impression that big-oh is all that matters or that any $O(n)$ algorithm is as good as any other $O(n)$ algorithm for the same job. Yet here, in our discussion of sentinels, and in other sections, we have examined rather carefully the constant factor hidden by the $O(n)$. The reason is simple. While it is true that big-oh measures of running time dominate constant factors, it is also true that everybody studying the subject learns that fairly quickly. We learn, for example, to use an $O(n \log n)$ running time sort whenever n is large enough to matter. A competitive edge in the performance of software frequently comes from improving the constant factor in an algorithm that already has the right "big-oh" running time, and this edge frequently translates into the success or failure of a commercial software product.

Lookup with Sentinels

We can simplify the code in the for-loop of Fig 6.11 and speed up the program by temporarily inserting x at the end of the list. This x at the end of the list is called a *sentinel*. The technique was first mentioned in a box on "More Defensive Programming" in Section 3.6, and it has an important application here. Assuming that there always is an extra slot at the end of the list, we can use the program in Fig. 6.12 to search for x. The running time of the program is still $O(n)$, but the constant of proportionality is smaller because the number of machine instructions required by the body and test of the loop will typically be smaller for Fig. 6.12 than for Fig. 6.11.

```
        BOOLEAN lookup(int x, LIST *pL)
        {
            int i;

(1)         pL->A[pL->length] = x;
(2)         i = 0;
(3)         while (x != pL->A[i])
(4)             i++;
(5)         return (i < pL->length);
        }
```

Fig. 6.12. Function that does lookup with a sentinel.

The sentinel is placed just beyond the list by line (1). Note that since *length* does not change, this x is not really part of the list. The loop of lines (3) and (4) increases i until we find x. Note that we are guaranteed to find x even if the list is empty, because of the sentinel. After finding x, we test at line (5) whether we have found a real occurrence of x (that is, $i < length$), or whether we have found the sentinel (that is, $i = length$). Note that if we are using a sentinel, it is essential that *length* be kept strictly less than MAX, or else there will be no place to put the sentinel.

Lookup on Sorted Lists with Binary Search

Suppose L is a list in which the elements $a_0, a_1, \ldots, a_{n-1}$ have been sorted in non-decreasing order. If the sorted list is stored in an array `A[0..n-1]`, we can speed lookups considerably by using a technique known as *binary search*. We must first find the index m of the middle element; that is, $m = \lfloor (n-1)/2 \rfloor$.[4] Then we compare element x with $A[m]$. If they are equal, we have found x. If $x < A[m]$, we recursively repeat the search on the sublist `A[0..m-1]`. If $x > A[m]$, we recursively repeat the search on the sublist `A[m+1..n-1]`. If at any time we try to search an empty list, we report failure. Figure 6.13 illustrates the division process.

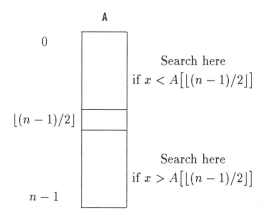

Fig. 6.13. Binary search divides a range in two.

The code for a function *binsearch* to locate x in a sorted array A is shown in Fig. 6.14. The function uses the variables `low` and `high` for the lower and upper bounds of the range in which x might lie. If the lower range exceeds the upper, we have failed to find x; the function terminates and returns `FALSE`.

Otherwise, *binsearch* computes the midpoint of the range, by

$$mid = \lfloor (low + high)/2 \rfloor$$

Then the function examines $A[mid]$, the element at the middle of the range, to determine whether x is there. If not, it continues the search in the lower or upper half of the range, depending on whether x is less than or greater than $A[mid]$. This idea generalizes the division suggested in Fig. 6.13, where *low* was 0 and *high* was $n - 1$.

The function `binsearch` can be proved correct using the inductive assertion that if x is in the array, then it must lie within the range `A[low..high]`. The proof is by induction on the difference $high - low$ and is left as an exercise.

At each iteration, *binsearch* either

1.   Finds the element x when it reaches line (8) or

---

[4] The notation $\lfloor a \rfloor$, the *floor* of a, is the integer part of a. Thus $\lfloor 6.5 \rfloor = 6$ and $\lfloor 6 \rfloor = 6$. Also, $\lceil a \rceil$, the *ceiling* of a, is the smallest integer greater than or equal to a. For instance, $\lceil 6.5 \rceil = 7$ and $\lceil 6 \rceil = 6$.

```
        BOOLEAN binsearch(int x, int A[], int low, int high)
        {
            int mid;

(1)         if (low > high)
(2)             return FALSE;
            else {
(3)             mid = (low + high)/2;
(4)             if (x < A[mid])
(5)                 return binsearch(x, A, low, mid-1);
(6)             else if (x > A[mid])
(7)                 return binsearch(x, A, mid+1, high);
                else /* x == A[mid] */
(8)                 return TRUE;
            }
        }
```

Fig. 6.14. Function that does lookup using binary search.

2. Calls itself recursively at line (5) or line (7) on a sublist that is at most half as long as the array `A[low..high]` that it was given to search.

Starting with an array of length n, we cannot divide the length of the array to be searched in half more than $\log_2 n$ times before it has length 1, whereupon we either find x at `A[mid]`, or we fail to find x at all after a call on the empty list.

To look for x in an array `A` with n elements, we call `binsearch(x,A,0,n-1)`. We see that `binsearch` calls itself $O(\log n)$ times at most. At each call, we spend $O(1)$ time, plus the time of the recursive call. The running time of binary search is therefore $O(\log n)$. That compares favorably with the linear search, which takes $O(n)$ time on the average, as we have seen.

EXERCISES

6.5.1: Write functions to (a) insert x and (b) delete x from a list L, using linear search of an array.

6.5.2: Repeat Exercise 6.5.1 for an array with sentinels.

6.5.3: Repeat Exercise 6.5.1 for a sorted array.

6.5.4: Write the following functions assuming that list elements are of some arbitrary type **ETYPE**, for which we have functions $eq(x, y)$ that tells whether x and y are equal and $lt(x, y)$ telling whether x precedes y in the order of elements of type **ETYPE**.

a) Function *lookup* of Fig. 6.11.
b) Function *lookup* of Fig. 6.12.
c) Function *binsearch* of Fig. 6.14.

Probes in binary search

6.5.5**: Let $P(k)$ be the length $(high - low + 1)$ of the longest array such that the binary search algorithm of Fig. 6.14 never makes more than k *probes* [evaluations of mid at line (3)]. For example, $P(1) = 1$, and $P(2) = 3$. Write a recurrence relation for $P(k)$. What is the solution to your recurrence relation? Does it demonstrate that binary search makes $O(\log n)$ probes?

6.5.6*: Prove by induction on the difference between *low* and *high* that if x is in the range A[low..high], then the binary search algorithm of Fig. 6.14 will find x.

6.5.7: Suppose we allowed arrays to have duplicates, so insertion could be done in $O(1)$ time. Write *insert*, *delete*, and *lookup* functions for this data structure.

6.5.8: Rewrite the binary search program to use iteration rather than recursion.

6.5.9**: Set up and solve a recurrence relation for the running time of binary search on an array of n elements. *Hint*: To simplify, it helps to take $T(n)$ as an upper bound on the running time of binary search on any array of n or fewer elements (rather than on exactly n elements, as would be our usual approach).

Ternary search

6.5.10: In *ternary search*, given a range *low* to *high*, we compute the approximate 1/3 point of the range,

$$first = \lfloor (2 \times low + high)/3 \rfloor$$

and compare the lookup element x with $A[first]$. If $x > A[first]$, we compute the approximate 2/3 point,

$$second = \lceil (low + 2 \times high)/3 \rceil$$

and compare x with $A[second]$. Thus we isolate x to within one of three ranges, each no more than one third the range *low* to *high*. Write a function to perform ternary search.

6.5.11**: Repeat Exercise 6.5.5 for ternary search. That is, find and solve a recurrence relation for the largest array that requires no more than k probes during ternary search. How do the number of probes required for binary and ternary search compare? That is, for a given k, can we handle larger arrays by binary search or by ternary search?

✦✦ 6.6 Stacks

Top of stack

A *stack* is an abstract data type based on the list data model in which all operations are performed at one end of the list, which is called the *top* of the stack. The term "LIFO (for last-in first-out) list" is a synonym for stack.

The abstract model of a stack is the same as that of a list — that is, a sequence of elements $a_1, a_2, \ldots, a_n$ of some one type. What distinguishes stacks from general lists is the particular set of operations permitted. We shall give a more complete set of operations later, but for the moment, we note that the quintessential stack oper-

Push and pop

ations are *push* and *pop*, where $push(x)$ puts the element x on top of the stack and *pop* removes the topmost element from the stack. If we write stacks with the top at the right end, the operation $push(x)$ applied to the list $(a_1, a_2, \ldots, a_n)$ yields the list $(a_1, a_2, \ldots, a_n, x)$. Popping the list $(a_1, a_2, \ldots, a_n)$ yields the list $(a_1, a_2, \ldots, a_{n-1})$; popping the empty list, ϵ, is impossible and causes an error condition,

✦ **Example 6.9.** Many compilers begin by turning the infix expressions that appear in programs into equivalent postfix expressions. For example, the expression $(3+4) \times 2$ is $3\ 4 + 2 \times$ in postfix notation. A stack can be used to evaluate postfix expressions. Starting with an empty stack, we scan the postfix expression from left to right. Each time we encounter an argument, we push it onto the stack. When we encounter an operator, we pop the stack twice, remembering the operands popped. We then apply the operator to the two popped values (with the second as the left operand) and push the result onto the stack. Figure 6.15 shows the stack after each step in the processing of the postfix expression $3\ 4 + 2 \times$. The result, 14, remains on the stack after processing. ✦

Symbol Processed	Stack	Actions
initial	ϵ	
3	3	*push* 3
4	3, 4	*push* 4
+	ϵ	*pop* 4; *pop* 3
		compute $7 = 3 + 4$
	7	*push* 7
2	7, 2	*push* 2
×	ϵ	*pop* 2; *pop* 7
		compute $14 = 7 \times 2$
	14	*push* 14

Fig. 6.15. Evaluating a postfix expression using a stack.

Operations on a Stack

The two previous ADT's we discussed, the dictionary and the priority queue, each had a definite set of associated operations. The stack is really a family of similar ADT's with the same underlying model, but with some variation in the set of allowable operations. In this section, we shall discuss the common operations on stacks and show two data structures that can serve as implementations for the stack, one based on linked lists and the other on arrays.

In any collection of stack operations we expect to see *push* and *pop*, as we mentioned. There is another common thread to the operations chosen for the stack ADT(s): they can all be implemented simply in $O(1)$ time, independent of the number of elements on the stack. You can check as an exercise that for the two data structures suggested, all operations require only constant time.

In addition to *push* and *pop*, we generally need an operation *clear* that initializes the stack to be empty. In Example 6.9, we tacitly assumed that the stack started out empty, without explaining how it got that way. Another possible operation is a test to determine whether the stack is currently empty.

The last of the operations we shall consider is a test whether the stack is "full." Now in our abstract model of a stack, there is no notion of a full stack, since a stack is a list and lists can grow as long as we like, in principle. However, in any implementation of a stack, there will be some length beyond which it cannot grow. The most common example is when we represent a list or stack by an array. As

The ADT stack

Clear stack

Full and empty stacks

seen in the previous section, we had to assume the list would not grow beyond the constant **MAX**, or our implementation of *insert* would not work.

The formal definitions of the operations we shall use in our implementation of stacks are the following. Let S be a stack of type **ETYPE** and x an element of type **ETYPE**.

1. *clear*(S). Make the stack S empty.

2. *isEmpty*(S). Return **TRUE** if S is empty, **FALSE** otherwise.

3. *isFull*(S). Return **TRUE** if S is full, **FALSE** otherwise.

4. *pop*(S, x). If S is empty, return **FALSE**; otherwise, set x to the value of the top element on stack S, remove this element from S, and return **TRUE**.

5. *push*(x, S). If S is full, return **FALSE**; otherwise, add the element x to the top of S and return **TRUE**.

There is a common variation of *pop* that assumes S is nonempty. It takes only S as an argument and returns the element x that is popped. Yet another alternative version of *pop* does not return a value at all; it just removes the element at the top of the stack. Similarly, we may write *push* with the assumption that S is not "full." In that case, *push* does not return any value.

Array Implementation of Stacks

The implementations we used for lists can also be used for stacks. We shall discuss an array-based implementation first, followed by a linked-list representation. In each case, we take the type of elements to be **int**. Generalizations are left as exercises.

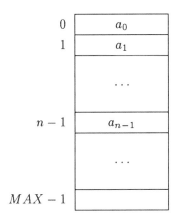

Fig. 6.16. An array representing a stack.

The declaration for an array-based stack of integers is

```
typedef struct {
    int A[MAX];
    int top;
} STACK;
```

```
void clear(STACK *pS)
{
    pS->top = -1;
}

BOOLEAN isEmpty(STACK *pS)
{
    return (pS->top < 0);
}

BOOLEAN isFull(STACK *pS)
{
    return (pS->top >= MAX-1);
}

BOOLEAN pop(STACK *pS, int *px)
{
    if (isEmpty(pS))
        return FALSE;
    else {
        (*px) = pS->A[(pS->top)--];
        return TRUE;
    }
}

BOOLEAN push(int x, STACK *pS)
{
    if (isFull(pS))
        return FALSE;
    else {
        pS->A[++(pS->top)] = x;
        return TRUE;
    }
}
```

Fig. 6.17. Functions to implement stack operations on arrays.

With an array-based implementation, the stack can grow either upward (from lower locations to higher) or downward (from higher locations to lower). We choose to have the stack grow upward;[5] that is, the oldest element a_0 in the stack is in location 0, the next-to-oldest element a_1 is in location 1, and the most recently inserted element a_{n-1} is in the location $n - 1$.

The field **top** in the array structure indicates the position of the top of stack. Thus, in Fig. 6.16, **top** has the value $n-1$. An empty stack is represented by having $top = -1$. In that case, the content of array **A** is irrelevant, there being no elements on the stack.

The programs for the five stack operations defined earlier in this section are

---

[5] Thus the "top" of the stack is physically shown at the bottom of the page, an unfortunate but quite standard convention.

```
void clear(STACK *pS)
{
    (*pS) = NULL;
}

BOOLEAN isEmpty(STACK *pS)
{
    return ((*pS) == NULL);
}

BOOLEAN isFull(STACK *pS)
{
    return FALSE;
}

BOOLEAN pop(STACK *pS, int *px)
{
    if ((*pS) == NULL)
        return FALSE;
    else {
        (*px) = (*pS)->element;
        (*pS) = (*pS)->next;
        return TRUE;
    }
}

BOOLEAN push(int x, STACK *pS)
{
    STACK newCell;

    newCell = (STACK) malloc(sizeof(struct CELL));
    newCell->element = x;
    newCell->next = (*pS);
    (*pS) = newCell;
    return TRUE;
}
```

Fig. 6.18. Functions to implement stacks by linked lists.

shown in Fig. 6.17. We pass stacks by reference to avoid having to copy large arrays that are arguments of the functions.

Linked-List Implementation of a Stack

We can represent a stack by a linked-list data structure, like any list. However, it is convenient if the top of the stack is the front of the list. That way, we can push and pop at the head of the list, which takes only $O(1)$ time. If we had to find the end of the list to push or pop, it would take $O(n)$ time to do these operations on a stack of length n. However, as a consequence, the stack $S = (a_1, a_2, \ldots, a_n)$ must be represented "backward" by the linked list, as:

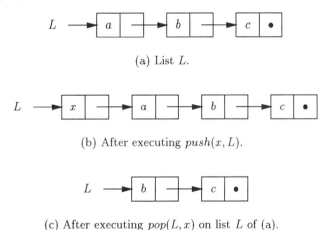

The type definition macro we have used for list cells can as well be used for stacks. The macro

        DefCell(int, CELL, STACK);

defines stacks of integers, expanding into

        typdef struct CELL *STACK;
        struct CELL {
            int element;
            STACK next;
        };

With this representation, the five operations can be implemented by the functions in Fig. 6.18. We assume that `malloc` never runs out of space, which means that the *isFull* operation always returns **FALSE**, and the *push* operation never fails.

The effects of *push* and *pop* on a stack implemented as a linked list are illustrated in Fig. 6.19.

(a) List L.

(b) After executing $push(x, L)$.

(c) After executing $pop(L, x)$ on list L of (a).

Fig. 6.19. Push and pop operations on a stack implemented as a linked list.

EXERCISES

6.6.1: Show the stack that remains after executing the following sequence of operations, starting with an empty stack: $push(a)$, $push(b)$, pop, $push(c)$, $push(d)$, pop, $push(e)$, pop, pop.

6.6.2: Using only the five operations on stacks discussed in this section to manipulate the stack, write a C program to evaluate postfix expressions with integer operands and the four usual arithmetic operators, following the algorithm suggested in Example 6.9. Show that you can use either the array or the linked-list implementation with your program by defining the data type **STACK** appropriately and including with your program first the functions of Fig. 6.17, and then the functions of Fig. 6.18.

6.6.3*: How would you use a stack to evaluate prefix expressions?

6.6.4: Compute the running time of each of the functions in Figs. 6.17 and 6.18. Are they all $O(1)$?

6.6.5: Sometimes, a stack ADT uses an operation top, where $top(S)$ returns the top element of stack S, which must be assumed nonempty. Write functions for top that can be used with

a) The array data structure
b) The linked-list data structure

that we defined for stacks in this section. Do your implementations of top all take $O(1)$ time?

6.6.6: Simulate a stack evaluating the following postfix expressions.

a) $ab + cd \times +e\times$
b) $abcde + + + +$
c) $ab + c + d + e+$

6.6.7*: Suppose we start with an empty stack and perform some push and pop operations. If the stack after these operations is $(a_1, a_2, \ldots, a_n)$ (top at the right), prove that a_i was pushed before a_{i+1} was pushed, for $i = 1, 2, \ldots, n - 1$.

❖❖ 6.7 Implementing Function Calls Using a Stack

An important application of stacks is normally hidden from view: a stack is used to allocate space in the computer's memory to the variables belonging to the various functions of a program. We shall discuss the mechanism used in C, although a similar mechanism is used in almost every other programming language as well.

```
            int fact(int n)
            {
(1)             if (n <= 1)
(2)                 return 1; /* basis */
                else
(3)                 return n*fact(n-1); /* induction */
            }
```

Fig. 6.20. Recursive function to compute $n!$.

To see what the problem is, consider the simple, recursive factorial function **fact** from Section 2.7, which we reproduce here as Fig. 6.20. The function has a parameter **n** and a return value. As **fact** calls itself recursively, different calls are active at the same time. These calls have different values of the parameter **n** and produce different return values. Where are these different objects with the same names kept?

Run-time organization

To answer the question, we must learn a little about the *run-time organization* associated with a programming language. The run-time organization is the plan used to subdivide the computer's memory into regions to hold the various data items

**Activation
record**

used by a program. When a program is run, each execution of a function is called an *activation*. The data objects associated with each activation are stored in the memory of the computer in a block called an *activation record* for that activation. The data objects include parameters, the return value, the return address, and any variables local to the function.

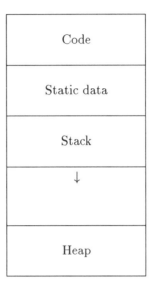

Fig. 6.21. Typical run-time memory organization.

**Static data
Run-time stack**

Figure 6.21 shows a typical subdivision of run-time memory. The first area contains the object code for the program being executed. The next area contains the static data for the program, such as the values of certain constants and external variables used by the program. The third area is the *run-time stack,* which grows downward toward the higher addresses in memory. At the highest-numbered memory locations is the *heap,* an area set aside for the objects that are dynamically allocated using `malloc`.[6]

The run-time stack holds the activation records for all the currently live activations. A stack is the appropriate structure, because when we call a function, we can push an activation record onto the stack. At all times, the currently executing activation A_1 has its activation record at the top of the stack. Just below the top of the stack is the activation record for the activation A_2 that called A_1. Below A_2's activation record is the record for the activation that called A_2, and so on. When a function returns, we pop its activation record off the top of stack, exposing the activation record of the function that called it. That is exactly the right thing to do, because when a function returns, control passes to the calling function.

✦ **Example 6.10.** Consider the skeletal program shown in Fig. 6.22. This program is nonrecursive, and there is never more than one activation for any one function.

---

[6] Do not confuse this use of the term "heap" with the heap data structure discussed in Section 5.9.

```
        void P();
        void Q();

        main() {
            int x, y, z;

            P(); /* Here */
        }

        void P();
        {
            int p1, p2;

            Q();
        }

        void Q()
        {
            int q1, q2, q3;
                . . .
        }
```

Fig. 6.22. Skeletal program.

When the main function starts to execute, its activation record containing the space for the variables x, y, and z is pushed onto the stack. When function P is called, at the place marked **Here**, its activation record, which contains the space for the variables p1 and p2, is pushed onto the stack.[7] When P calls Q, Q's activation record is pushed onto the stack. At this point, the stack is as shown in Fig. 6.23.

When Q finishes executing, its activation record is popped off the stack. At that time, P is also finished, and so its activation record is popped. Finally, **main** too is finished and has its activation record popped off the stack. Now the stack is empty, and the program is finished. ✦

✦ **Example 6.11.** Consider the recursive function **fact** from Fig. 6.20. There may be many activations of **fact** live at any one time, but each one will have an activation record of the same form, namely

consisting of a word for the parameter n, which is filled initially, and a word for the return value, which we have denoted **fact**. The return value is not filled until the last step of the activation, just before the return.

---

[7] Notice that the activation record for P has two data objects, and so is of a "type" different from that of the activation record for the main program. However, we may regard all activation record forms for a program as variants of a single record type, thus preserving the viewpoint that a stack has all its elements of the same type.

x
y
z
p1
p2
q1
q2
q3

Fig. 6.23. Run-time stack when function Q is executing.

Suppose we call `fact(4)`. Then we create one activation record, of the form

n	4
fact	–

As `fact(4)` calls `fact(3)`, we next push an activation record for that activation onto the run-time stack, which now appears as

n	4
fact	–
n	3
fact	–

Note that there are two locations named **n** and two named `fact`. There is no confusion, since they belong to different activations and only one activation record can be at the top of the stack at any one time: the activation record belonging to the currently executing activation.

n	4
fact	–
n	3
fact	–
n	2
fact	–
n	1
fact	–

Fig. 6.24. Activation records during execution of `fact`.

Then `fact(3)` calls `fact(2)`, which calls `fact(1)`. At that point, the run-time stack is as in Fig. 6.24. Now `fact(1)` makes no recursive call, but assigns $fact = 1$. The value 1 is thus placed in the slot of the top activation record reserved for `fact`.

n	4
fact	–
n	3
fact	–
n	2
fact	–
n	1
fact	1

Fig. 6.25. After `fact(1)` computes its value.

The other slots labeled `fact` are unaffected, as shown in Fig. 6.25.

Then, `fact(1)` returns, exposing the activation record for `fact(2)` and returning control to the activation `fact(2)` at the point where `fact(1)` was called. The return value, 1, from `fact(1)` is multiplied by the value of n in the activation record for `fact(2)`, and the product is placed in the slot for `fact` of that activation record, as required by line (3) in Fig. 6.20. The resulting stack is shown in Fig. 6.26.

n	4
fact	–
n	3
fact	–
n	2
fact	2

Fig. 6.26. After `fact(2)` computes its value.

Similarly, `fact(2)` then returns control to `fact(3)`, and the activation record for `fact(2)` is popped off the stack. The return value, 2, multiplies n of `fact(3)`, producing the return value 6. Then, `fact(3)` returns, and its return value multiplies `n` in `fact(4)`, producing the return value 24. The stack is now

n	4
fact	24

At this point, `fact(4)` returns to some hypothetical calling function whose activation record (not shown) is below that of `fact(4)` on the stack. However, it would receive the return value 24 as the value of `fact(4)`, and would proceed with its own execution. ◆

EXERCISES

6.7.1: Consider the C program of Fig. 6.27. The activation record for **main** has a slot for the integer **i**. The important data in the activation record for **sum** is

```
      #define MAX 4
      int A[MAX];
      int sum(int i);

      main()
      {
          int i;

(1)       for (i = 0; i < MAX; i++)
(2)           scanf("%d", &A[i]);
(3)       printf("\n", sum(0));
      }

      int sum(int i)
      {
(4)       if (i > MAX)
(5)           return 0;
          else
(6)           return A[i] + sum(i+1);
      }
```

Fig. 6.27. Program for Exercise 6.7.1.

1. The parameter i.
2. The return value.
3. An unnamed temporary location, which we shall call temp, to store the value of sum(i+1). The latter is computed in line (6) and then added to $A[i]$ to form the return value.

Show the stack of activation records immediately before and immediately after each call to sum, on the assumption that the value of $A[i]$ is $10i$. That is, show the stack immediately after we have pushed an activation record for sum, and just before we pop an activation record off the stack. You need not show the contents of the bottom activation record (for main) each time.

```
      void delete(int x, LIST *pL)
      {
          if ((*pL) != NULL)
              if (x == (*pL)->element)
                  (*pL) = (*pL)->next;
              else
                  delete(x, &((*pL)->next));
      end
```

Fig. 6.28. Function for Exercise 6.7.2.

6.7.2*: The function **delete** of Fig. 6.28 removes the first occurrence of integer x from a linked list composed of the usual cells defined by

```
DefCell(int, CELL, LIST);
```

The activation record for **delete** consists of the parameters **x** and **pL**. However, since **pL** is a pointer to a list, the value of the second parameter in the activation record is not a pointer to the first cell on the list, but rather a pointer to a pointer to the first cell. Typically, an activation record will hold a pointer to the **next** field of some cell. Show the sequence of stacks when **delete(3,&L)** is called (from some other function) and L is a pointer to the first cell of a linked list containing elements 1, 2, 3, and 4, in that order.

✦✦ 6.8 Queues

Another important ADT based on the list data model is the *queue*, a restricted form of list in which elements are inserted at one end, the *rear*, and removed from the other end, the *front*. The term "FIFO (first-in first-out) list" is a synonym for queue.

Front and rear of queue

The intuitive idea behind a queue is a line at a cashier's window. People enter the line at the rear and receive service once they reach the front. Unlike a stack, there is fairness to a queue; people are served in the order in which they enter the line. Thus the person who has waited the longest is the one who is served next.

Operations on a Queue

The abstract model of a queue is the same as that of a list (or a stack), but the operations applied are special. The two operations that are characteristic of a queue are *enqueue* and *dequeue*; *enqueue(x)* adds x to the rear of a queue, *dequeue* removes the element from the front of the queue. As is true of stacks, there are certain other useful operations that we may want to apply to queues.

Enqueue and dequeue

Let Q be a queue whose elements are of type **ETYPE**, and let x be an element of type **ETYPE**. We shall consider the following operations on queues:

1. *clear(Q)*. Make the queue Q empty.

2. *dequeue(Q, x)*. If Q is empty, return **FALSE**; otherwise, set x to the value of the element at the front of Q, remove this element from Q, and return **TRUE**.

3. *enqueue(x, Q)*. If Q is full, return **FALSE**; otherwise, add the element x to the rear of Q and return **TRUE**.

4. *isEmpty(Q)*. Return **TRUE** if Q is empty and **FALSE** otherwise.

5. *isFull(Q)*. Return **TRUE** if Q is full and **FALSE** otherwise.

As with stacks, we can have more "trusting" versions of *enqueue* and *dequeue* that do not check for a full or empty queue, respectively. Then *enqueue* does not return a value, and *dequeue* takes only Q as an argument and returns the value dequeued.

A Linked-List Implementation of Queues

A useful data structure for queues is based on linked lists. We start with the usual definition of cells given by the macro

```
void clear(QUEUE *pQ)
{
    pQ->front = NULL;
}

BOOLEAN isEmpty(QUEUE *pQ)
{
    return (pQ->front == NULL);
}

BOOLEAN isFull(QUEUE *pQ)
{
    return FALSE;
}

BOOLEAN dequeue(QUEUE *pQ, int *px)
{
    if (isEmpty(pQ))
        return FALSE;
    else {
        (*px) = pQ->front->element;
        pQ->front = pQ->front->next;
        return TRUE;
    }
}

BOOLEAN enqueue(int x, QUEUE *pQ)
{
    if (isEmpty(pQ)) {
        pQ->front = (LIST) malloc(sizeof(struct CELL));
        pQ->rear = pQ->front;
    }
    else {
        pQ->rear->next = (LIST) malloc(sizeof(struct CELL));
        pQ->rear = pQ->rear->next;
    }
    pQ->rear->element = x;
    pQ->rear->next = NULL;
    return TRUE;
}
```

Fig. 6.29. Procedures to implement linked-list queue operations.

```
DefCell(int, CELL, LIST);
```

As previously in this chapter, we assume that elements of our queues are integers and invite the reader to generalize our functions to arbitrary element types.

The elements of a queue will be stored on a linked list of cells. A queue itself is a structure with two pointers — one to the front cell (the first on the linked list) and another to the rear cell (the last on the linked list). That is, we define

More Abstract Data Types

We can add the stack and queue to the table of ADT's that we started in Section 5.9. We covered two data structures for the stack in Section 6.6, and one data structure for the queue in Section 6.8. Exercise 6.8.3 covers another data structure, the "circular array," for the queue.

ADT	Stack	Queue
Abstract Implementation	List	List
Data Structures	1) Linked List 2) Array	1) Linked List 2) Circular Array

```
typedef struct {
    LIST front, rear;
} QUEUE;
```

If the queue is empty, **front** will be **NULL**, and the value of **rear** is then irrelevant.

Figure 6.29 gives programs for the queue operations mentioned in this section. Note that when a linked list is used there is no notion of a "full" queue, and so *isFull* returns **FALSE** always. However, if we used some sort of array-based implementation of a queue, there would be the possibility of a full queue.

EXERCISES

6.8.1: Show the queue that remains after executing the following sequence of operations, starting with an empty queue: *enqueue(a)*, *enqueue(b)*, *dequeue*, *enqueue(c)*, *enqueue(d)*, *dequeue*, *enqueue(e)*, *dequeue*, *dequeue*.

6.8.2: Show that each of the functions in Fig. 6.29 can be executed in $O(1)$ time, regardless of the length of the queue.

6.8.3*: We can represent a queue by an array, provided that the queue does not grow too long. In order to make the operations take $O(1)$ time, we must think of the array as *circular*. That is, the array A[0..n-1] can be thought of as having A[1] follow A[0], A[2] follow A[1], and so on, up to A[n-1] following A[n-2], but also A[0] follows A[n-1]. The queue is represented by a pair of integers **front** and **rear** that indicate the positions of the front and rear elements of the queue. An empty queue is represented by having *front* be the position that follows *rear* in the circular sense; for example, *front* = 23 and *rear* = 22, or *front* = 0 and *rear* = $n - 1$. Note that therefore, the queue cannot have n elements, or that condition too would be represented by *front* immediately following *rear*. Thus the queue is full when it has $n - 1$ elements, not when it has n elements. Write functions for the queue operations assuming the circular array data structure. Do not forget to check for full and empty queues.

Circular array

6.8.4*: Show that if $(a_1, a_2, \ldots, a_n)$ is a queue with a_1 at the front, then a_i was enqueued before a_{i+1}, for $i = 1, 2, \ldots, n-1$.

✦✦ 6.9 Longest Common Subsequences

This section is devoted to an interesting problem about lists. Suppose we have two lists and we want to know what differences there are between them. This problem appears in many different guises; perhaps the most common occurs when the two lists represent two different versions of a text file and we want to determine which lines are common to the two versions. For notational convenience, throughout this section we shall assume that lists are character strings.

A useful way to think about this problem is to treat the two files as sequences of symbols, $x = a_1 \cdots a_m$ and $y = b_1 \cdots b_n$, where a_i represents the ith line of the first file and b_j represents the jth line of the second file. Thus an abstract symbol like a_i may really be a "big" object, perhaps a full sentence.

Diff command
There is a UNIX command `diff` that compares two text files for their differences. One file, x, might be the current version of a program and the other, y, might be the version of the program before a small change was made. We could use `diff` to remind ourselves of the changes that were made turning y into x. The typical changes that are made to a text file are

1. Inserting a line.

2. Deleting a line.

A modification of a line can be treated as a deletion followed by an insertion.

Usually, if we examine two text files in which a small number of such changes have been made when transforming one into the other, it is easy to see which lines correspond to which, and which lines have been deleted and which inserted. The `diff` command makes the assumption that one can identify what the changes are by
LCS
first finding a *longest common subsequence*, or *LCS*, of the two lists whose elements are the lines of the two text files involved. An LCS represents those lines that have not been changed.

Recall that a subsequence is formed from a list by deleting zero or more ele-
Common subsequence
ments, keeping the remaining elements in order. A *common subsequence* of two lists is a list that is a subsequence of both. A longest common subsequence of two lists is a common subsequence that is as long as any common subsequence of the two lists.

✦ **Example 6.12.** In what follows, we can think of characters like a, b, or c, as standing for lines of a text file, or as any other type of elements if we wish. As an example, baba and cbba are both longest common subsequences of abcabba and cbabac. We see that baba is a subsequence of abcabba, because we may take positions 2, 4, 5, and 7 of the latter string to form baba. String baba is also a subsequence of cbabac, because we may take positions 2, 3, 4, and 5. Similarly, cbba is formed from positions 3, 5, 6, and 7 of abcabba and from positions 1, 2, 4, and 5 of cbabac. Thus cbba too is a common subsequence of these strings. We must convince ourselves that these are longest common subsequences; that is, there are no common subsequences of length five or more. That fact will follow from the algorithm we describe next. ✦

A Recursion That Computes the LCS

We offer a recursive definition of the length of the LCS of two lists. This definition will let us calculate the length easily, and by examining the table it constructs, we can then discover one of the possible LCS's itself, rather than just its length. From the LCS, we can deduce what changes were made to the text files in question; essentially, everything that is not part of the LCS is a change.

To find the length of an LCS of lists x and y, we need to find the lengths of the LCS's of all pairs of prefixes, one from x and the other from y. Recall that a prefix is an initial sublist of a list, so that, for instance, the prefixes of cbabac are ϵ, c, cb, cba, and so on. Suppose that $x = (a_1, a_2, \ldots, a_m)$ and $y = (b_1, b_2, \ldots, b_n)$. For each i and j, where i is between 0 and m and j is between 0 and n, we can ask for an LCS of the prefix $(a_1, \ldots, a_i)$ from x and the prefix $(b_1, \ldots, b_j)$ from y.

If either i or j is 0, then one of the prefixes is ϵ, and the only possible common subsequence of the two prefixes is ϵ. Thus when either i or j is 0, the length of the LCS is 0. This observation is formalized in both the basis and rule (1) of the induction that follows our informal discussion of how the LCS is computed.

Now consider the case where both i and j are greater than 0. It helps to think of an LCS as a matching between certain positions of the two strings involved. That is, for each element of the LCS, we match the two positions of the two strings from which that element comes. Matched positions must have the same symbols, and the lines between matched positions must not cross.

✦ **Example 6.13.** Figure 6.30(a) shows one of two possible matchings between strings abcabba and cbabac corresponding to the common subsequence baba and Fig. 6.30(b) shows a matching corresponding to cbba. ✦

(a) For baba.   (b) For cbba.

Fig. 6.30. LCS's as matchings between positions.

Thus let us consider any matching between prefixes $(a_1, \ldots, a_i)$ and $(b_1, \ldots, b_j)$. There are two cases, depending on whether or not the last symbols of the two lists are equal.

a)   If $a_i \neq b_j$, then the matching cannot include both a_i and b_j. Thus an LCS of $(a_1, \ldots, a_i)$ and $(b_1, \ldots, b_j)$ must be either

    i)   An LCS of $(a_1, \ldots, a_{i-1})$ and $(b_1, \ldots, b_j)$, or

    ii)   An LCS of $(a_1, \ldots, a_i)$ and $(b_1, \ldots, b_{j-1})$.

If we have already found the lengths of the LCS's of these two pairs of prefixes, then we can take the larger to be the length of the LCS of $(a_1, \ldots, a_i)$ and $(b_1, \ldots, b_j)$. This situation is formalized in rule (2) of the induction that follows.

b)   If $a_i = b_j$, we can match a_i and b_j, and the matching will not interfere with any other potential matches. Thus the length of the LCS of $(a_1, \ldots, a_i)$ and $(b_1, \ldots, b_j)$ is 1 greater than the length of the LCS of $(a_1, \ldots, a_{i-1})$ and $(b_1, \ldots, b_{j-1})$. This situation is formalized in rule (3) of the following induction.

These observations let us give a recursive definition for $L(i, j)$, the length of the LCS of $(a_1, \ldots, a_i)$ and $(b_1, \ldots, b_j)$. We use complete induction on the sum $i + j$.

BASIS. If $i + j = 0$, then both i and j are 0, and so the LCS is ϵ. Thus $L(0, 0) = 0$.

INDUCTION. Consider i and j, and suppose we have already computed $L(g, h)$ for any g and h such that $g + h < i + j$. There are three cases to consider.

1.   If either i or j is 0, then $L(i, j) = 0$.

2.   If $i > 0$ and $j > 0$, and $a_i \neq b_j$, then $L(i, j) = \max\bigl(L(i, j-1), L(i-1, j)\bigr)$.

3.   If $i > 0$ and $j > 0$, and $a_i = b_j$, then $L(i, j) = 1 + L(i-1, j-1)$.

A Dynamic Programming Algorithm for the LCS

Ultimately what we want is $L(m, n)$, the length of an LCS for the two lists x and y. If we write a recursive program based on the preceding induction, it will take time that is exponential in the smaller of m and n. That is far too much time to make the simple recursive algorithm practical for, say, $n = m = 100$. The reason this recursion does so badly is a bit subtle. To begin, suppose there are no matches at all between characters in the lists x and y, and we call $L(3, 3)$. That results in calls to $L(2, 3)$ and $L(3, 2)$. But each of these calls results in a call to $L(2, 2)$. We thus do the work of $L(2, 2)$ twice. The number of times $L(i, j)$ is called increases rapidly as the arguments of L become smaller. If we continue the trace of calls, we find that $L(1, 1)$ is called 6 times, $L(0, 1)$ and $L(1, 0)$ are called 10 times each, and $L(0, 0)$ is called 20 times.

We can do much better if we build a two-dimensional table, or array, to store $L(i, j)$ for the various values of i and j. If we compute the values in order of the induction — that is, smallest values of $i + j$ first — then the needed values of L are always in the table when we compute $L(i, j)$. In fact, it is easier to compute L by rows, that is, for $i = 0, 1, 2$, and so on; within a row, compute by columns, for $j = 0, 1, 2$, and so on. Again, we can be sure of finding the needed values in the table when we compute $L(i, j)$, and no recursive calls are necessary. As a result, it takes only $O(1)$ time to compute each entry of the table, and a table for the LCS of lists of length m and n can be constructed in $O(mn)$ time.

In Fig. 6.31 we see C code that fills this table, working by row rather than by the sum $i + j$. We assume that the list x is stored in an array `a[1..m]` and y is stored in `b[1..n]`. Note that the 0th elements of these are unused; doing so simplifies the notation in Fig. 6.31. We leave it as an exercise to show that the running time of this program is $O(mn)$ on lists of length m and n.[8]

---

[8]   Strictly speaking, we discussed only big-oh expressions that are a function of one variable. However, the meaning here should be clear. If $T(m, n)$ is the running time of the program

```
for (j = 0; j <= n; j++)
    L[0][j] = 0;
for (i = 1; i <= m; i++) {
    L[i][0] = 0;
    for (j = 1; j <= n; j++)
        if (a[i] != b[j])
            if (L[i-1][j] >= L[i][j-1])
                L[i][j] = L[i-1][j];
            else
                L[i][j] = L[i][j-1];
        else /* a[i] == b[j] */
            L[i][j] = 1 + L[i-1][j-1];
}
```

Fig. 6.31. C fragment to fill the LCS table.

Dynamic Programming

The term "dynamic programming" comes from a general theory developed by R. E. Bellman in the 1950's for solving problems in control systems. People who work in the field of artificial intelligence often speak of the technique under the name *memoing* or *tabulation*.

Memoing

A table-filling technique like this example is often called a *dynamic programming algorithm*. As in this case, it can be much more efficient than a straightforward implementation of a recursion that solves the same subproblem repeatedly.

Dynamic
programming
algorithm

♦ **Example 6.14.** Let x be the list cbabac and y the list abcabba. Figure 6.32 shows the table constructed for these two lists. For instance, $L(6,7)$ is a case where $a_6 \neq b_7$. Thus $L(6,7)$ is the larger of the entries just below and just to the left. Since these are 4 and 3, respectively, we set $L(6,7)$, the entry in the upper right corner, to 4. Now consider $L(4,5)$. Since both a_4 and b_5 are the symbol b, we add 1 to the entry $L(3,4)$ that we find to the lower left. Since that entry is 2, we set $L(4,5)$ to 3. ♦

Recovery of an LCS

We now have a table giving us the length of the LCS, not only for the lists in question, but for each pair of their prefixes. From this information we must deduce one of the possible LCS's for the two lists in question. To do so, we shall find the matching pairs of elements that form one of the LCS's. We shall find a path through the table, beginning at the upper right corner; this path will identify an LCS.

Suppose that our path, starting at the upper right corner, has taken us to row i and column j, the point in the table that corresponds to the pair of elements a_i

---

on lists of length m and n, then there are constants m_0, n_0, and c such that for all $m \geq m_0$ and $n \geq n_0$, $T(m,n) \leq cmn$.

c	6	0	1	2	3	3	3	3	4
a	5	0	1	2	2	3	3	3	4
b	4	0	1	2	2	2	3	3	3
a	3	0	1	1	1	2	2	2	3
b	2	0	0	1	1	1	2	2	2
c	1	0	0	0	1	1	1	1	1
	0	0	0	0	0	0	0	0	0
		0	1	2	3	4	5	6	7
			a	b	c	a	b	b	a

Fig. 6.32. Table of longest common subsequences for cbabac and abcabba.

and b_j. If $a_i = b_j$, then $L(i, j)$ was chosen to be $1 + L(i-1, j-1)$. We thus treat a_i and b_j as a matched pair of elements, and we shall include the symbol that is a_i (and also b_j) in the LCS, ahead of all the elements of the LCS found so far. We then move our path down and to the left, that is, to row $i-1$ and column $j-1$.

However, it is also possible that $a_i \neq b_j$. If so, then $L(i, j)$ must equal at least one of $L(i-1, j)$ and $L(i, j-1)$. If $L(i, j) = L(i-1, j)$, we shall move our path one row down, and if not, we know that $L(i, j) = L(i, j-1)$, and we shall move our path one column left.

When we follow this rule, we eventually arrive at the lower left corner. At that point, we have selected a certain sequence of elements for our LCS, and the LCS itself is the list of these elements, in the reverse of the order in which they were selected.

c	6	0	1	2	3	3	3	3	**4**
a	5	0	1	2	2	3	3	3	**4**
b	4	0	1	2	2	2	3	**3**	3
a	3	0	1	1	1	2	**2**	2	3
b	2	0	0	1	1	1	**2**	2	2
c	1	0	0	0	**1**	**1**	1	1	1
	0	**0**	**0**	**0**	0	0	0	0	0
		0	1	2	3	4	5	6	7
			a	b	c	a	b	b	a

Fig. 6.33. A path that finds the LCS caba.

✦ **Example 6.15.** The table of Fig. 6.32 is shown again in Fig. 6.33, with a path shown in bold. We start with $L(6, 7)$, which is 4. Since $a_6 \neq b_7$, we look immediately to the left and down to find the value 4, which must appear in at least one of these places. In this case, 4 appears only below, and so we go to $L(5, 7)$. Now $a_5 = b_7$; both are a. Thus a is the last symbol of the LCS, and we move southwest, to $L(4, 6)$.

Since a_4 and b_6 are both b, we include b, ahead of a, in the LCS being formed, and we again move southwest, to $L(3, 5)$. Here, we find $a_3 \neq b_5$, but $L(3, 5)$, which is 2, equals both the entry below and the entry to the left. We have elected in this situation to move down, so we next move to $L(2, 5)$. There we find $a_2 = b_5 = $ b, and so we put a b ahead of the LCS being formed and move southwest to $L(1, 4)$.

Since $a_1 \neq b_4$ and only the entry to the left has the same value (1) as $L(1, 4)$, we move to $L(1, 3)$. Now we have $a_1 = b_3 = $ c, and so we add c to the beginning of the LCS and move to $L(0, 2)$. At this point, we have no choice but to move left to $L(0, 1)$ and then $L(0, 0)$, and we are done. The resulting LCS consists of the four characters we discovered, in the reverse order, or cbba. That happens to be one of the two LCS's we mentioned in Example 6.12. We can obtain other LCS's by choosing to go left instead of down when $L(i, j)$ equals both $L(i, j - 1)$ and $L(i - 1, j)$, and by choosing to go left or down when one of these equals $L(i, j)$, even in the situation when $a_i = b_j$ (i.e., by skipping certain matches in favor of matches farther to the left). ✦

We can prove that this path finding algorithm always finds an LCS. The statement that we prove by complete induction on the sum of the lengths of the lists is:

STATEMENT $S(k)$: If we find ourselves at row i and column j, where $i + j = k$, and if $L(i, j) = v$, then we subsequently discover v elements for our LCS.

BASIS. The basis is $k = 0$. If $i + j = 0$, then both i and j are 0. We have finished our path and find no more elements for the LCS. As we know $L(0, 0) = 0$, the inductive hypothesis holds for $i + j = 0$.

INDUCTION. Assume the inductive hypothesis for sums k or less, and let $i + j = k + 1$. Suppose we are at $L(i, j)$, which has value v. If $a_i = b_j$, then we find one match and move to $L(i - 1, j - 1)$. Since the sum $(i - 1) + (j - 1)$ is less than $i + j$, the inductive hypothesis applies. Since $L(i - 1, j - 1)$ must be $v - 1$, we know that we shall find $v - 1$ more elements for our LCS, which, with the one element just found, will give us v elements. That observation proves the inductive hypothesis in this case.

The only other case is when $a_i \neq b_j$. Then, either $L(i - 1, j)$ or $L(i, j - 1)$, or both, must have the value v, and we move to one of these positions that does have the value v. Since the sum of the row and column is $i + j - 1$ in either case, the inductive hypothesis applies, and we conclude that we find v elements for the LCS. Again we can conclude that $S(k + 1)$ is true. Since we have considered all cases, we are done and conclude that if we are at an entry $L(i, j)$, we always find $L(i, j)$ elements for our LCS.

EXERCISES

6.9.1: What is the length of the LCS of the lists

a)   banana and cabana
b)   abaacbacab and bacabbcaba

6.9.2*: Find all the LCS's of the pairs of lists from Exercise 6.9.1. *Hint*: After building the table from Exercise 6.9.1, trace backward from the upper right corner, following each choice in turn when you come to a point that could be explained in two or three different ways.

6.9.3**: Suppose we use the recursive algorithm for computing the LCS that we described first (instead of the table-filling program that we recommend). If we call $L(4, 4)$ with two lists having no symbols in common, how many calls to $L(1, 1)$ are made? *Hint*: Use a table-filling (dynamic programming) algorithm to compute a table giving the value of $L(i, j)$ for all i and j. Compare your result with Pascal's triangle from Section 4.5. What does this relationship suggest about a formula for the number of calls?

6.9.4**: Suppose we have two lists x and y, each of length n. For n below a certain size, there can be at most one string that is an LCS of x and y (although that string may occur in different positions of x and/or y). For example, if $n = 1$, then the LCS can only be ϵ, unless x and y are both the same symbol a, in which case a is the only LCS. What is the smallest value of n for which x and y can have two different LCS's?

6.9.5: Show that the program of Fig. 6.31 has running time $O(mn)$.

6.9.6: Write a C program to take a table, such as that computed by the program of Fig. 6.31, and find the positions, in each string, of one LCS. What is the running time of your program, if the table is m by n?

6.9.7: In the beginning of this section, we suggested that the length of an LCS and the size of the largest matching between positions of two strings were related.

a*) Prove by induction on k that if two strings have a common subsequence of length k, then they have a matching of length k.

b) Prove that if two strings have a matching of length k, then they have a common subsequence of length k.

c) Conclude from (a) and (b) that the lengths of the LCS and the greatest size of a matching are the same.

❖❖ 6.10 Representing Character Strings

Character strings are probably the most common form of list encountered in practice. There are a great many ways to represent strings, and some of these techniques are rarely appropriate for other kinds of lists. Therefore, we shall devote this section to the special issues regarding character strings.

First, we should realize that storing a single character string is rarely the whole problem. Often, we have a large number of character strings, each rather short. They may form a dictionary, meaning that we insert and delete strings from the population as time goes on, or they may be a *static* set of strings, unchanging over time. The following are two typical examples.

Concordance   1.   A useful tool for studying texts is a *concordance,* a list of all the words used in the document and the places in which they occur. There will typically be tens of thousands of different words used in a large document, and each occurrence must be stored once. The set of words used is static; that is, once formed it does not change, except perhaps if there were errors in the original concordance.

2.   The compiler that turns a C program into machine code must keep track of all the character strings that represent variables of the program. A large program may have hundreds or thousands of variable names, especially when we remember that two local variables named i that are declared in two functions are really two distinct variables. As the compiler scans the program, it finds new variable names and inserts them into the set of names. Once the compiler has finished compiling a function, the variables of that function are not available to subsequent functions, and so may be deleted.

In both of these examples, there will be many short character strings. Short words abound in English, and programmers like to use single letters such as i or x for variables. On the other hand, there is no limit on the length of words, either in English texts or in programs.

Character Strings in C

Null character   Character-string constants, as might appear in a C program, are stored as arrays of characters, followed by the special character '\0', called the *null character,* whose value is 0. However, in applications such as the ones mentioned above, we need the facility to create and store new strings as a program runs. Thus, we need a data structure in which we can store arbitrary character strings. Some of the possibilities are:

1.   Use a fixed-length array to hold character strings. Strings shorter than the array are followed by a null character. Strings longer than the array cannot be **Truncation**   stored in their entirety. They must be *truncated* by storing only their prefix of length equal to the length of the array.

2.   A scheme similar to (1), but assume that every string, or prefix of a truncated string, is followed by the null character. This approach simplifies the reading of strings, but it reduces by one the number of string characters that can be stored.

3.   A scheme similar to (1), but instead of following strings by a null character, use another integer *length* to indicate how long the string really is.

4.   To avoid the restriction of a maximum string length, we can store the characters of the string as the elements of a linked list. Possibly, several characters can be stored in one cell.

5.   We may create a large array of characters in which individual character strings are placed. A string is then represented by a pointer to a place in the array where the string begins. Strings may be terminated by a null character or they may have an associated length.

Fixed-Length Array Representations

Let us consider a structure of type (1) above, where strings are represented by fixed-length arrays. In the following example, we create structures that have a fixed-length array as one of their fields.

✦ **Example 6.16.** Consider the data structure we might use to hold one entry in a concordance, that is, a single word and its associated information. We need to hold

1. The word itself.
2. The number of times the word appears.
3. A list of the lines of the document in which there are one or more occurrences of the word.

Thus we might use the following structure:

```
typedef struct {
    char word[MAX];
    int occurrences;
    LIST lines;
} WORDCELL;
```

Here, MAX is the maximum length of a word. All WORDCELL structures have an array called **word** of MAX bytes, no matter how short the word happens to be.

The field **occurrences** is a count of the number of times the word appears, and **lines** is a pointer to the beginning of a linked list of cells. These cells are of the conventional type defined by the macro

```
DefCell(int, CELL, LIST);
```

Each cell holds one integer, representing a line on which there are one or more occurrences of the word in question. Note that **occurrences** could be larger than the length of the list, if the word appeared several times on one line.

In Fig. 6.34 we see the structure for the word **earth** in the first chapter of Genesis. We assume MAX is at least 6. The complete list of line (verse) numbers is (1, 2, 10, 11, 12, 15, 17, 20, 22, 24, 25, 26, 28, 29, 30).

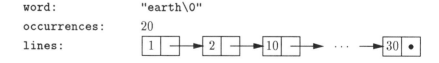

Fig. 6.34. Concordance entry for the word **earth** in the first chapter of Genesis.

The entire concordance might consist of a collection of structures of type WORD-CELL. These might, for example, be organized in a binary search tree, with the < ordering of structures based on the alphabetic order of words. That structure would allow relatively fast access to words as we use the concordance. It would also allow us to create the concordance efficiently as we scan the text to locate and list the occurrences of the various words. To use the binary tree structure we would require left- and right-child fields in the type WORDCELL. We could also arrange these structures in a linked list, by adding a "next" field to the type WORDCELL instead. That would be a simpler structure, but it would be less efficient if the number of words is large. We shall see, in the next chapter, how to arrange these structures in a hash table, which probably offers the best performance of all data structures for this problem. ✦

Linked Lists for Character Strings

The limitation on the length of character strings, and the need to allocate a fixed amount of space no matter how short the string, are two disadvantages of the previous implementation of character strings. However, C and other languages allow us to build other, more flexible data structures to represent strings. For example, if we are concerned that there be no upper limit on the length of a character string, we can use conventional linked lists of characters to hold character strings. That is, we can declare a type

```
typedef struct CHARCELL *CHARSTRING;
struct CHARCELL {
    char character;
    CHARSTRING next;
};
```

In the type WORDCELL, CHARSTRING becomes the type of the field word, as

```
typedef {
    CHARSTRING word;
    int occurrences;
    LIST lines;
} WORDCELL;
```

For example, the word earth would be represented by

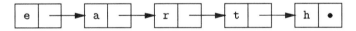

This scheme removes any upper limit on the length of words, but it is, in practice, not very economical of space. The reason is that each structure of type **CHARCELL** takes at least five bytes, assuming one for the character and a typical four for a pointer to the next cell on the list. Thus, the great majority of the space is used for the "overhead" of pointers rather than the "payload" of characters.

Packing
characters into
cells

We can be a bit more clever, however, if we pack several bytes into the data field of each cell. For example, if we put four characters into each cell, and pointers consume four bytes, then half our space will be used for "payload," compared with 20% payload in the one-character-per-cell scheme. The only caution is that we must have some character, such as the null character, that can serve as a string-terminating character, as is the case for character strings stored in arrays. In general, if CPC (characters per cell) is the number of characters that we are willing to place in one cell, we can declare cells by

```
typedef struct CHARCELL *CHARSTRING;
struct CHARCELL {
    char characters[CPC];
    CHARSTRING next;
};
```

For example, if CPC = 4, then we could store the word **earth** in two cells, as

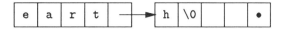

We could also increase CPC above 4. As we do so, the fraction of space taken for pointers decreases, which is good; it means that the overhead of using linked lists rather than arrays is dropping. On the other hand, if we used a very large value for CPC, we would find that almost all words used only one cell, but that cell would have many unused locations in it, just as an array of length CPC would.

✦ **Example 6.17.** Let us suppose that in our population of character strings, 30% are between 1 and 4 characters long, 40% between 5 and 8 characters, 20% in the range 9–12, and 10% in the range 13–16. Then the table in Fig. 6.35 gives the number of bytes devoted to linked lists representing words in the four ranges, for four values of CPC, namely, 4, 8, 12, and 16. For our assumption about word-length frequencies, CPC = 8 comes out best, with an average usage of 15.6 bytes That is, we are best off using cells with room for 8 bytes, using a total of 12 bytes per cell, including the 4 bytes for the **next** pointer. Note that the total space cost, which is 19.6 bytes when we include a pointer to the front of the list, is not as good as using 16 bytes for a character array. However, the linked-list scheme can accommodate strings longer than 16 characters, even though our assumptions put a 0% probability on finding such strings. ✦

		CHARACTERS PER CELL			
RANGE	PROBABILITY	4	8	12	16
1-4	.3	8	12	16	20
5-8	.4	16	12	16	20
9-12	.2	24	24	16	20
13-16	.1	32	24	32	20
Avg.		16.8	15.6	17.6	20.0

Fig. 6.35. Numbers of bytes used for strings in various length ranges by different values of CPC.

Mass Storage of Character Strings

Endmarker

There is another approach to the storage of large numbers of character strings that combines the advantage of array storage (little overhead) with the advantages of linked-list storage (no wasted space due to padding, and no limit on string length). We create one very long array of characters, into which we shall store each character string. To tell where one string ends and the next begins, we need a special character called the *endmarker.* The endmarker character cannot appear as part of a legitimate character string. In what follows, we shall use * as the endmarker, for visibility, although it is more usual to choose a nonprinting character, such as the null character.

✦   **Example 6.18.** Suppose we declare an array **space** by

```
char space[MAX];
```

We can then store a word by giving a pointer to the first position of **space** devoted to that word. The **WORDCELL** structure, analogous to that of Example 6.16, would then be

```
typedef struct {
    char *word;
    int occurrences;
    LIST lines;
} WORDCELL;
```

In Fig. 6.36 we see the **WORDCELL** structure for the word **the** in a concordance based on the book of Genesis. The pointer **word** refers us to **space[3]**, where we see the beginning of the word **the**.

Note that the lowest elements of the array **space** might appear to contain the text itself. However, that would not continue to be the case for long. Even if the next elements contain the words **beginning**, **God**, and **created**, the second **the** would not appear again in the array **space**. Rather, that word would be accounted for by adding to the number of occurrences in the **WORDCELL** structure for **the**. As we proceeded through the book and found more repetitions of words, the entries in **space** would stop resembling the biblical text itself. ✦

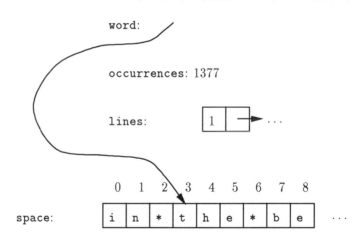

Fig. 6.36. Representing words by indices into string space.

As in Example 6.16, the structures of Example 6.18 can be formed into data structures such as binary search trees or linked lists by adding the appropriate pointer fields to the **WORDCELL** structure. The function $lt(W_1, W_2)$ that compares two **WORDCELL**'s W_1 and W_2 follows the **word** fields of these structures and compares them lexicographically.

To build a concordance using such a binary search tree, we maintain a pointer **available** to the first unoccupied position in the array **space**. Initially, **available** points to **space[0]**. Suppose we are scanning the text for which the concordance

What Happens When We Run Out of Space?

We have assumed that `space` is so large that there is always room to add a new word. Actually, each time we add a character we must be careful that the current position into which we write is less than `MAX`.

If we want to enter new words after running out of space, we need to be prepared to obtain new blocks of space when the old one runs out. Instead of creating just one array `space`, we can define a character-array type

```
typedef char SPACE[MAX];
```

We can then create a new array, the first character of which is pointed to by `available`, by

```
available = (char *) malloc(sizeof(SPACE));
```

It is useful to remember the end of this array by immediately assigning

```
last = available + MAX;
```

We then insert words into the array pointed to by `available`. If we can no longer fit words into this array, we call `malloc` to create another character array. Of course we must be careful not to write past the end of the array, and if we are presented with a string of length greater than MAX, there is no way we can store the word in this scheme.

---

is being built and we find the next word — say, `the`. We do not know whether or not `the` is already in the binary search tree. We thus temporarily add `the*` to the position indicated by `available` and the three following positions. We remember that the newly added word takes up 4 bytes.

Now we can search for the word `the` in the binary search tree. If found, we add 1 to its count of occurrences and insert the current line into the list of lines. If not found, we create a new node — which includes the fields of the `WORDCELL` structure, plus left- and right-child pointers (both `NULL`) — and insert it into the tree at the proper place. We set the `word` field in the new node to *available*, so that it refers to our copy of the word `the`. We set `occurrences` to 1 and create a list for the field `lines` consisting of only the current line of text. Finally, we must add 4 to `available`, since the word `the` has now been added permanently to the `space` array.

EXERCISES

6.10.1: For the structure type `WORDCELL` discussed in Example 6.16, write the following programs:

a)   A function `create` that returns a pointer to a structure of type `WORDCELL`.

b)   A function `insert(WORDCELL *pWC, int line)` that takes a pointer to the structure `WORDCELL` and a line number, adds 1 to the number of occurrences for that word, and adds that line to the list of lines if it is not already there.

6.10.2: Redo Example 6.17 under the assumption that any word length from 1 to 40 is equally likely; that is, 10% of the words are of length 1–4, 10% are of length 5–8, and so on, up to 10% in the range 37–40. What is the average number of bytes required if CPC is 4, 8, ..., 40?

6.10.3*: If, in the model of Example 6.17, all word lengths from 1 to n are equally likely, what value of CPC, as a function of n, minimizes the number of bytes used? If you cannot get the exact answer, a big-oh approximation is useful.

6.10.4*: One advantage of using the structure of Example 6.18 is that one can share parts of the space array among two or more words. For example, the structure for the word he could have word field equal to 5 in the array of Fig. 6.36. Compress the words all, call, man, mania, maniac, recall, two, woman into as few elements of the space array as you can. How much space do you save by compression?

6.10.5*: Another approach to storing words is to eliminate the endmarker character from the space array. Instead, we add a length field to the WORDCELL structures of Example 6.18, to tell us how many characters from the first character, as indicated by the word field, are included in the word. Assuming that integers take four bytes, does this scheme save or cost space, compared with the scheme described in Example 6.18? What if integers could be stored in one byte?

6.10.6**: The scheme described in Exercise 6.10.5 also gives us opportunities to compress the space array. Now words can overlap even if neither is a suffix of the other. How many elements of the space array do you need to store the words in the list of Exercise 6.10.4, using the scheme of Exercise 6.10.5?

6.10.7: Write a program to take two WORDCELL's as discussed in Example 6.18 and determine which one's word precedes the other in lexicographic order. Recall that words are terminated by * in this example.

✦✦ 6.11   Summary of Chapter 6

The following points were covered in Chapter 6.

✦   Lists are an important data model representing sequences of elements.

✦   Linked lists and arrays are two data structures that can be used to implement lists.

✦   Lists are a simple implementation of dictionaries, but their efficiency does not compare with that of the binary search tree of Chapter 5 or the hash table to be covered in Chapter 7.

✦   Placing a "sentinel" at the end of an array to make sure we find the element we are seeking is a useful efficiency improver.

✦   Stacks and queues are important special kinds of lists.

✦   The stack is used "behind the scenes" to implement recursive functions.

♦ A character string is an important special case of a list, and we have a number of special data structures for representing character strings efficiently. These include linked lists that hold several characters per cell and large arrays shared by many character strings.

♦ The problem of finding longest common subsequences can be solved efficiently by a technique known as "dynamic programming," in which we fill a table of information in the proper order.

✦✧ 6.12 Bibliographic Notes for Chapter 6

Knuth [1968] is still the fundamental source on list data structures. While it is hard to trace the origins of very basic notions such as "list" or "stack," the first programming language to use lists as a part of its data model was IPL-V (Newell et al. [1961]), although among the early list-processing languages, only Lisp (McCarthy et al. [1962]) survives among the currently important languages. Lisp, by the way, stands for "LISt Processing."

The use of stacks in run-time implementation of recursive programs is discussed in more detail in Aho, Sethi, and Ullman [1986].

The longest-common-subsequence algorithm described in Section 6.9 is by Wagner and Fischer [1975]. The algorithm actually used in the UNIX `diff` command is described in Hunt and Szymanski [1977]. Aho [1990] surveys a number of algorithms involving the matching of character strings.

Dynamic programming as an abstract technique was described by Bellman [1957]. Aho, Hopcroft, and Ullman [1983] give a number of examples of algorithms using dynamic programming.

Aho, A. V. [1990]. "Algorithms for finding patterns in strings," in *Handbook of Theoretical Computer Science* Vol. A: *Algorithms and Complexity* (J. Van Leeuwen, ed.), MIT Press, Cambridge, Mass.

Aho, A. V., J. E. Hopcroft, and J. D. Ullman [1983]. *Data Structures and Algorithms*, Addison-Wesley, Reading, Mass.

Aho, A. V., R. Sethi, and J. D. Ullman [1986]. *Compilers: Principles, Techniques, and Tools*, Addison-Wesley, Reading, Mass.

Bellman, R. E. [1957]. *Dynamic Programming*, Princeton University Press, Princeton, NJ.

Hunt, J. W. and T. G. Szymanski [1977]. "A fast algorithm for computing longest common subsequences," *Comm. ACM* **20**:5, pp. 350–353.

Knuth, D. E. [1968]. *The Art of Computer Programming*, Vol. I, *Fundamental Algorithms*, Addison-Wesley, Reading, Mass.

McCarthy, J. et al. [1962]. *LISP 1.5 Programmer's Manual*, MIT Computation Center and Research Laboratory of Electronics, Cambridge, Mass.

Newell, A., F. M. Tonge, E. A. Feigenbaum, B. F. Green, and G. H. Mealy [1961]. *Information Processing Language-V Manual*, Prentice-Hall, Englewood Cliffs, New Jersey.

Wagner, R. A. and M. J. Fischer [1975]. "The string to string correction problem," *J. ACM* **21**:1, pp. 168–173.

CHAPTER 7

❖

The Set Data Model

The set is the most fundamental data model of mathematics. Every concept in mathematics, from trees to real numbers, is expressible as a special kind of set. In this book, we have seen sets in the guise of events in a probability space. The dictionary abstract data type is a kind of set, on which particular operations — *insert*, *delete*, and *lookup* — are performed. Thus, it should not be surprising that sets are also a fundamental model of computer science. In this chapter, we learn the basic definitions concerning sets and then consider algorithms for efficiently implementing set operations.

❖ 7.1 What This Chapter Is About

This chapter covers the following topics:

❖ The basic definitions of set theory and the principal operations on sets (Sections 7.2–7.3).

❖ The three most common data structures used to implement sets: linked lists, characteristic vectors, and hash tables. We compare these data structures with respect to their relative efficiency in supporting various operations on sets (Sections 7.4–7.6).

❖ Relations and functions as sets of pairs (Section 7.7).

❖ Data structures for representing relations and functions (Sections 7.8–7.9).

❖ Special kinds of binary relations, such as partial orders and equivalence relations (Section 7.10).

❖ Infinite sets (Section 7.11).

✦✦ 7.2 Basic Definitions

In mathematics, the term "set" is not defined explicitly. Rather, like terms such as "point" and "line" in geometry, the term set is defined by its properties. Specifically, there is a notion of *membership* that makes sense only for sets. When S is a set and x is anything, we can ask the question, "Is x a member of set S?" The set S then consists of all those elements x for which x is a member of S. The following points summarize some important notations for talking about sets.

1. The expression $x \in S$ means that the element x is a member of the set S.

2. If $x_1, x_2, \ldots, x_n$ are all the members of set S, then we can write

    $$S = \{x_1, x_2, \ldots, x_n\}$$

    Here, each of the x's must be distinct; we cannot repeat an element twice in a set. However, the order in which the members of a set are listed is arbitrary.

Empty set

3. The empty set, denoted $\emptyset$, is the set that has no members. That is, $x \in \emptyset$ is false, no matter what x is.

✦ **Example 7.1.** Let $S = \{1, 3, 6\}$; that is, let S be the set that has the integers 1, 3, and 6, and nothing else, as members. We can say $1 \in S$, $3 \in S$, and $6 \in S$. However, the statement $2 \in S$ is false, as is the statement that any other thing is a member of S.

Sets can also have other sets as members. For example, let $T = \{\{1, 2\}, 3, \emptyset\}$. Then T has three members. First is the set $\{1, 2\}$, that is, the set with 1 and 2 as is sole members. Second is the integer 3. Third is the empty set. The following are true statements: $\{1, 2\} \in T$, $3 \in T$, and $\emptyset \in T$. However, $1 \in T$ is false. That is, the fact that 1 is a member of a member of T does not mean that 1 is a member of T itself. ✦

Atoms

In formal set theory, there really is nothing but sets. However, in our informal set theory, and in data structures and algorithms based on sets, it is convenient to assume the existence of certain *atoms,* which are elements that are not sets. An atom can be a member of a set, but nothing can be a member of an atom. It is important to remember that the empty set, like the atoms, has no members. However, the empty set is a set rather than an atom.

We shall generally assume that integers and lowercase letters denote atoms. When talking about data structures, it is often convenient to use complex data types as the types of atoms. Thus, atoms may be structures or arrays, and not be very "atomic" at all.

Definition of Sets by Abstraction

Enumeration of the members of a set is not the only way we may define sets. Often, it is more convenient to start with some set S and some property of elements P, and define the set of those elements in S that have property P. The notation for this operation, which is called *abstraction,* is

Sets and Lists

Although our notation for a list, such as $(x_1, x_2, \ldots, x_n)$, and our notation for a set, $\{x_1, x_2, \ldots, x_n\}$, look very much alike, there are important differences. First, the order of elements in a set is irrelevant. The set we write as $\{1, 2\}$ could just as well be written $\{2, 1\}$. In contrast, the list $(1, 2)$ is not the same as the list $(2, 1)$.

Second, a list may have repetitions. For example, the list $(1, 2, 2)$ has three elements; the first is 1, the second is 2, and the third is also 2. However, the set notation $\{1, 2, 2\}$ makes no sense. We cannot have an element, such as 2, occur as a member of a set more than once. If this notation means anything, it is the same as $\{1, 2\}$ or $\{2, 1\}$ — that is, the set with 1 and 2 as members, and no other members.

Multiset or bag   Sometimes we speak of a *multiset* or *bag,* which is a set whose elements are allowed to have a multiplicity greater than 1. For example, we could speak of the multiset that contains 1 once and 2 twice. Multisets are not the same as lists, because they still have no order associated with their elements.

$$\{x \mid x \in S \text{ and } P(x)\}$$

or "the set of elements x in S such that x has property P."

Set former   The preceding expression is called a *set former.* The variable x in the set former is local to the expression, and we could just as well have written

$$\{y \mid y \in S \text{ and } P(y)\}$$

to describe the same set.

◆ **Example 7.2.** Let S be the set $\{1, 3, 6\}$ from Example 7.1. Let $P(x)$ be the property "x is odd." Then

$$\{x \mid x \in S \text{ and } x \text{ is odd }\}$$

is another way of defining the set $\{1, 3\}$. That is, we accept the elements 1 and 3 from S because they are odd, but we reject 6 because it is not odd.

As another example, consider the set $T = \{\{1, 2\}, 3, \emptyset\}$ from Example 7.1. Then

$$\{A \mid A \in T \text{ and } A \text{ is a set }\}$$

denotes the set $\{\{1, 2\}, \emptyset\}$. ◆

Equality of Sets

We must not confuse what a set *is* with how it is represented. Two sets are *equal,* that is, they are really the same set, if they have exactly the same members. Thus, most sets have many different representations, including those that explicitly enumerate their elements in some order and representations that use abstraction.

◆ **Example 7.3.** The set $\{1, 2\}$ is the set that has exactly the elements 1 and 2 as members. We can present these elements in either order, so $\{1, 2\} = \{2, 1\}$. There are also many ways to express this set by abstraction. For example,

$$\{x \mid x \in \{1, 2, 3\} \text{ and } x < 3\}$$

is equal to the set $\{1, 2\}$. ✦

Infinite Sets

It is comforting to assume that sets are *finite* — that is, that there is some particular integer n such that the set at hand has exactly n members. For example, the set $\{1, 3, 6\}$ has three members. However, some sets are *infinite,* meaning there is no integer that is the number of elements in the set. We are familiar with infinite sets such as

1.   **N**, the set of nonnegative integers
2.   **Z**, the set of nonnegative and negative integers
3.   **R**, the set of real numbers
4.   **C**, the set of complex numbers

From these sets, we can create other infinite sets by abstraction.

✦   **Example 7.4.** The set former

$$\{x \mid x \in \mathbf{Z} \text{ and } x < 3\}$$

stands for the set of all the negative integers, plus 0, 1, and 2. The set former

$$\{x \mid x \in \mathbf{Z} \text{ and } \sqrt{x} \in \mathbf{Z}\}$$

represents the set of integers that are perfect squares, that is, $\{0, 1, 4, 9, 16, \dots\}$.

For a third example, let $P(x)$ be the property that x is prime (i.e., $x > 1$ and x has no divisors except 1 and x itself). Then the set of primes is denoted

$$\{x \mid x \in \mathbf{N} \text{ and } P(x)\}$$

This expression denotes the infinite set $\{2, 3, 5, 7, 11, \dots\}$. ✦

There are some subtle and interesting properties of infinite sets. We shall take up the matter again in Section 7.11.

EXERCISES

7.2.1: What are the members of the set $\{\{a, b\}, \{a\}, \{b, c\}\}$?

7.2.2: Write set-former expressions for the following:

a)   The set of integers greater than 1000.
b)   The set of even integers.

7.2.3: Find two different representations for the following sets, one using abstraction, the other not.

a) $\{a, b, c\}$.
b) $\{0, 1, 5\}$.

Russell's Paradox

One might wonder why the operation of abstraction requires that we designate some other set from which the elements of the new set must come. Why can't we just use an expression like $\{x \mid P(x)\}$, for example,

$$\{x \mid x \text{ is blue }\}$$

to define the set of all blue things? The reason is that allowing such a general way to define sets gets us into a logical inconsistency discovered by Bertrand Russell and called *Russell's paradox*. We may have met this paradox informally when we heard about the town where the barber shaves everyone who doesn't shave himself, and then were asked whether the barber shaves himself. If he does, then he doesn't, and if he doesn't, he does. The way out of this anomaly is to realize that the statement "shaves everyone who doesn't shave himself," while it looks reasonable, actually makes no formal sense.

To understand Russell's paradox concerning sets, suppose we could define sets of the form $\{x \mid P(x)\}$ for any property P. Then let $P(x)$ be the property "x is not a member of x." That is, let P be true of a set x if x is not a member of itself. Let S be the set

$$S = \{x \mid x \text{ is not a member of } x\}$$

Now we can ask, "Is set S a member of itself?"

Case 1: Suppose that S is not a member of S. Then $P(S)$ is true, and so S is a member of the set $\{x \mid x \text{ is not a member of } x\}$. But that set is S, and so by assuming that S is not a member of itself, we prove that S is indeed a member of itself. Thus, it cannot be that S is not a member of itself.

Case 2: Suppose that S is a member of itself. Then S is not a member of

$$\{x \mid x \text{ is not a member of } x\}$$

But again, that set is S, and so we conclude that S is not a member of itself.

Thus, when we start by assuming that $P(S)$ is false, we prove that it is true, and when we start by assuming that $P(S)$ is true, we wind up proving that it is false. Since we arrive at a contradiction either way, we are forced to blame the notation. That is, the real problem is that it makes no sense to define the set S as we did.

Another interesting consequence of Russell's paradox is that it makes no sense to suppose there is a "set of all elements." If there were such a "universal set" — say U — then we could speak of

Universal set

$$\{x \mid x \in U \text{ and } x \text{ is not a member of } x\}$$

and we would again have Russell's paradox. We would then be forced to give up abstraction altogether, and that operation is far too useful to drop.

✦✪✦ 7.3 Operations on Sets

There are special operations that are commonly performed on sets, such as union and intersection. You are probably familiar with many of them, but we shall review the most important operations here. In the next sections we discuss some implementations of these operations.

Union, Intersection, and Difference

Perhaps the most common ways to combine sets are with the following three operations:

1. The *union* of two sets S and T, denoted $S \cup T$, is the set containing the elements that are in S or T, or both.

2. The *intersection* of sets S and T, written $S \cap T$, is the set containing the elements that are in both S and T.

3. The *difference* of sets S and T, denoted $S - T$, is the set containing those elements that are in S but not in T.

✦ **Example 7.5.** Let S be the set $\{1, 2, 3\}$ and T the set $\{3, 4, 5\}$. Then

$$S \cup T = \{1, 2, 3, 4, 5\}, S \cap T = \{3\}, \text{ and } S - T = \{1, 2\}$$

That is, $S \cup T$ contains all the elements appearing in either S or T. Although 3 appears in both S and T, there is, of course, only one occurrence of 3 in $S \cup T$, because elements cannot appear more than once in a set. $S \cap T$ contains only 3, because no other element appears in both S and T. Finally, $S - T$ contains 1 and 2, because these appear in S and do not appear in T. The element 3 is not present in $S - T$, because although it appears in S, it also appears in T. ✦

When the sets S and T are events in a probability space, the union, intersection, and difference have a natural meaning. $S \cup T$ is the event that either S or T (or both) occurs. $S \cap T$ is the event that both S and T occur. $S - T$ is the event that S, but not T occurs. However, if S is the set that is the entire probability space, then $S - T$ is the event "T does not occur," that is, the complement of T.

Venn Diagrams

It is often helpful to see operations involving sets as pictures called *Venn diagrams*. Figure 7.1 is a Venn diagram showing two sets, S and T, each of which is represented by an ellipse. The two ellipses divide the plane into four regions, which we have numbered 1 to 4.

1. Region 1 represents those elements that are in neither S nor T.
2. Region 2 represents $S - T$, those elements that are in S but not in T.
3. Region 3 represents $S \cap T$, those elements that are in both S and T.
4. Region 4 represents $T - S$, those elements that are in T but not in S.
5. Regions 2, 3, and 4 combined represent $S \cup T$, those elements that are in S or T, or both.

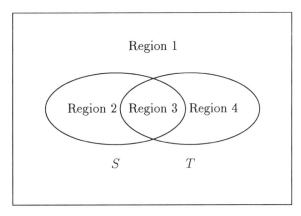

Fig. 7.1. Regions representing Venn diagrams for the basic set operations.

What Is an Algebra?

We may think that the term "algebra" refers to solving word problems, finding roots of polynomials, and other matters covered in a high school algebra course. To a mathematician, however, the term algebra refers to any sort of system in which there are operands and operators from which one builds expressions. For an algebra to be interesting and useful, it usually has special constants and *laws* that allow us to transform one expression into another "equivalent" expression.

The most familiar algebra is that in which operands are integers, reals, or perhaps complex numbers — or variables representing values from one of these classes — and the operators are the ordinary arithmetic operators: addition, multiplication, subtraction, and division. The constants 0 and 1 are special and satisfy laws like $x + 0 = x$. In manipulating arithmetic expressions, we use laws such as the distributive law, which lets us replace any expression of the form $a \times b + a \times c$ by an equivalent expression $a \times (b + c)$. Notice that by making this transformation, we reduce the number of arithmetic operations by 1. Often the purpose of algebraic manipulation of expressions, such as this one, is to find an equivalent expression whose evaluation takes less time than the evaluation of the original.

Throughout this book, we shall meet various kinds of algebras. Section 8.7 introduces relational algebra, a generalization of the algebra of sets that we discuss here. Section 10.5 talks about the algebra of *regular expressions* for describing patterns of character strings. Section 12.8 introduces the reader to the *Boolean* algebra of logic.

While we have suggested that Region 1 in Fig. 7.1 has finite extent, we should remember that this region represents everything outside S and T. Thus, this region is *not* a set. If it were, we could take its union with S and T to get the "universal set," which we know by Russell's paradox does not exist. Nevertheless, it is often convenient to draw as a region the elements that are not in any of the sets represented explicitly in the Venn diagram, as we did in Fig. 7.1.

Algebraic Laws For Union, Intersection, and Difference

Mirroring the algebra of arithmetic operations such as + and *, one can define an algebra of sets in which the operators are union, intersection, and difference and the operands are sets or variables denoting sets. Once we allow ourselves to build up complicated expressions like $R \cup ((S \cap T) - U)$, we can ask whether two expressions are *equivalent,* that is, whether they always denote the same set regardless of what sets we substitute for the operands that are variables. By substituting one expression for an equivalent expression, sometimes we can simplify expressions involving sets so that they may be evaluated more efficiently.

Equivalent expressions

In what follows, we shall list the most important *algebraic laws* — that is, statements asserting that one expression is equivalent to another — for union, intersection, and difference of sets. The symbol $\equiv$ is used to denote equivalence of expressions.

In many of these algebraic laws, there is an analogy between union, intersection, and difference of sets, on one hand, and addition, multiplication, and subtraction of integers on the other hand. We shall, however, point out those laws that do not have analogs for ordinary arithmetic.

a) *The commutative law of union:* $(S \cup T) \equiv (T \cup S)$. That is, it does not matter which of two sets appears first in a union. The reason this law holds is simple. The element x is in $S \cup T$ if x is in S or if x is in T, or both. That is exactly the condition under which x is in $T \cup S$.

b) *The associative law of union:* $(S \cup (T \cup R)) \equiv ((S \cup T) \cup R)$. That is, the union of three sets can be written either by first taking the union of the first two or the last two; in either case, the result will be the same. We can justify this law as we did the commutative law, by arguing that an element is in the set on the left if and only if it is in the set on the right. The intuitive reason is that both sets contain exactly those elements that are in either S, T, or R, or any two or three of them.

The commutative and associative laws of union together tell us that we can take the union of a collection of sets in any order. The result will always be the same set of elements, namely those elements that are in one or more of the sets. The argument is like the one we presented for addition, which is another commutative and associative operation, in Section 2.4. There, we showed that all ways to group a sum led to the same result.

c) *The commutative law of intersection:* $(S \cap T) \equiv (T \cap S)$. Intuitively, an element x is in the sets $S \cap T$ and $T \cap S$ under exactly the same circumstances: when x is in S and x is in T.

d) *The associative law of intersection:* $(S \cap (T \cap R)) \equiv ((S \cap T) \cap R)$. Intuitively, x is in either of these sets exactly when x is in all three of S, T, and R. Like addition or union, the intersection of any collection of sets may be grouped as we choose, and the result will be the same; in particular, it will be the set of elements in all the sets.

e) *Distributive law of intersection over union:* Just as we know that multiplication distributes over addition — that is, $a \times (b + c) = a \times b + a \times c$ — the law

$$(S \cap (T \cup R)) \equiv ((S \cap T) \cup (S \cap R))$$

holds for sets. Intuitively, an element x is in each of these sets exactly when x is in S and also in at least one of T and R. Similarly, by the commutativity of union and intersection, we can distribute intersections from the right, as

$$((T \cup R) \cap S) \equiv ((T \cap S) \cup (R \cap S))$$

f)   *Distributive law of union over intersection*: Similarly,

$$\big(S \cup (T \cap R)\big) \equiv \big((S \cup T) \cap (S \cup R)\big)$$

holds. Both the left and right sides are sets that contain an element x exactly when x is either in S, or is in both T and R. Notice that the analogous law of arithmetic, where union is replaced by addition and intersection by multiplication, is false. That is, $a + b \times c$ is generally not equal to $(a + b) \times (a + c)$. Here is one of several places where the analogy between set operations and arithmetic operations breaks down. However, as in (e), we can use the commutativity of union to get the equivalent law

$$((T \cap R) \cup S) \equiv ((T \cup S) \cap (R \cup S))$$

✦   **Example 7.6.** Let $S = \{1, 2, 3\}$, $T = \{3, 4, 5\}$, and $R = \{1, 4, 6\}$. Then

$$
\begin{aligned}
S \cup (T \cap R) &= \{1, 2, 3\} \cup (\{3, 4, 5\} \cap \{1, 4, 6\}) \\
&= \{1, 2, 3\} \cup \{4\} \\
&= \{1, 2, 3, 4\}
\end{aligned}
$$

On the other hand,

$$
\begin{aligned}
(S \cup T) \cap (S \cup R) &= (\{1, 2, 3\} \cup \{3, 4, 5\}) \cap (\{1, 2, 3\} \cup \{1, 4, 6\}) \\
&= \{1, 2, 3, 4, 5\} \cap \{1, 2, 3, 4, 6\} \\
&= \{1, 2, 3, 4\}
\end{aligned}
$$

Thus, the distributive law of union over intersection holds in this case. That doesn't prove that the law holds in general, of course, but the intuitive argument we gave with rule (f) should be convincing. ✦

g)   *Associative law of union and difference*: $\big(S - (T \cup R)\big) \equiv \big((S - T) - R\big)$. Both sides contain an element x exactly when x is in S but in neither T nor R. Notice that this law is analogous to the arithmetic law $a - (b + c) = (a - b) - c$.

h)   *Distributive law of difference over union*: $\big((S \cup T) - R\big) \equiv \big((S - R) \cup (T - R)\big)$. In justification, an element x is in either set when it is not in R, but is in either S or T, or both. Here is another point at which the analogy with addition and subtraction breaks down; it is not true that $(a + b) - c = (a - c) + (b - c)$, unless $c = 0$.

i)   *The empty set is the identity for union*. That is, $(S \cup \emptyset) \equiv S$, and by commutativity of union, $(\emptyset \cup S) \equiv S$. Informally, an element x can be in $S \cup \emptyset$ only when x is in S, since x cannot be in $\emptyset$.

Note that there is no identity for intersection. We might imagine that the set of "all elements" could serve as the identity for intersection, since the intersection of a set S with this "set" would surely be S. However, as mentioned in connection with Russell's paradox, there cannot be a "set of all elements."

Idempotence

j)   *Idempotence of union.* An operator is said to be *idempotent* if, when applied to two copies of the same value, the result is that value. We see that $(S \cup S) \equiv S$. That is, an element x is in $S \cup S$ exactly when it is in S. Again the analogy with arithmetic fails, since $a + a$ is generally not equal to a.

k)   *Idempotence of intersection.* Similarly, we have $(S \cap S) \equiv S$.

There are a number of laws relating the empty set to operations besides union. We list them here.

l) $(S - S) \equiv \emptyset$.

m) $(\emptyset - S) \equiv \emptyset$.

n) $(\emptyset \cap S) \equiv \emptyset$, and by commutativity of intersection, $(S \cap \emptyset) \equiv \emptyset$.

Proving Equivalences by Venn Diagrams

Figure 7.2 illustrates the distributive law for intersection over union by a Venn diagram. This diagram shows three sets, S, T, and R, which divide the plane into eight regions, numbered 1 through 8. These regions correspond to the eight possible relationships (in or out) that an element can have with the three sets.

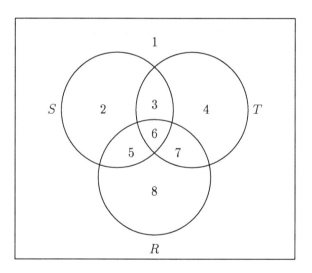

Fig. 7.2. Venn diagram showing the distributive law of intersection over union: $S \cap (T \cup R)$ consists of regions 3, 5, and 6, as does $(S \cap T) \cup (S \cap R)$.

We can use the diagram to help us keep track of the values of various subexpressions. For instance, $T \cup R$ is regions 3, 4, 5, 6, 7, and 8. Since S is regions 2, 3, 5, and 6, it follows that $S \cap (T \cup R)$ is regions 3, 5, and 6. Similarly, $S \cap T$ is regions 3 and 6, while $S \cap R$ is regions 5 and 6. It follows that $(S \cap T) \cup (S \cap R)$ is the same regions 3, 5, and 6, proving that

$$(S \cap (T \cup R)) \equiv ((S \cap T) \cup (S \cap R))$$

In general, we can prove an equivalence by considering one representative element from each region and checking that it is either in the set described by both sides of the equivalence or in neither of those sets. This method is very close to the truth-table method by which we prove algebraic laws for propositional logic in Chapter 12.

Proving Equivalences by Applying Transformations

Another way to prove two expressions equivalent is by turning one into the other using one or more of the algebraic laws we have already seen. We shall give a more formal treatment of how expressions are manipulated in Chapter 12, but for the present, let us observe that we can

1.   Substitute any expression for any variable in an equivalence, provided that we substitute for all occurrences of that variable. The equivalence remains true.

2.   Substitute, for a subexpression E in some equivalence, an expression F that is known to be equivalent to E. The equivalence remains true.

In addition, we can write any of the equivalences that were stated as laws and assume that equivalence is true.

◆ **Example 7.7.** We shall prove the equivalence $\big(S - (S \cup R)\big) \equiv \emptyset$. Let us start with law (g), the associative law for union and difference, which is

$$\big(S - (T \cup R)\big) \equiv \big((S - T) - R\big)$$

We substitute S for each of the two occurrences of T to get a new equivalence:

$$\big(S - (S \cup R)\big) \equiv \big((S - S) - R\big)$$

By law (l), $(S - S) \equiv \emptyset$. Thus, we may substitute $\emptyset$ for $(S - S)$ above to get:

$$\big(S - (S \cup R)\big) \equiv (\emptyset - R)$$

Law (m), with R substituted for S says that $\emptyset - R \equiv \emptyset$. We may thus substitute $\emptyset$ for $\emptyset - R$ and conclude that $\big(S - (S \cup R)\big) \equiv \emptyset$. ◆

The Subset Relationship

There is a family of comparison operators among sets that is analogous to the comparisons among numbers. If S and T are sets, we say that $S \subseteq T$ if every member of S is also a member of T. We can express this in words several ways: "S is a subset of T," "T is a superset of S," "S is contained in T," or "T contains S."

Containment of sets

We say that $S \subset T$, if $S \subseteq T$, and there is at least one element of T that is not also a member of S. The $S \subset T$ relationship can be read "S is a proper subset of T," "T is a proper superset of S," "S is properly contained in T," or "T properly contains S."

Proper subset

As with "less than," we can reverse the direction of the comparison; $S \supset T$ is synonymous with $T \subset S$, and $S \supseteq T$ is synonymous with $T \subseteq S$.

◆ **Example 7.8.** The following comparisons are all true:

1. $\{1, 2\} \subseteq \{1, 2, 3\}$

2. $\{1, 2\} \subset \{1, 2, 3\}$

3. $\{1, 2\} \subseteq \{1, 2\}$

Note that a set is always a subset of itself but a set is never a proper subset of itself, so that $\{1, 2\} \subset \{1, 2\}$ is false. ✦

There are a number of algebraic laws involving the subset operator and the other operators that we have already seen. We list some of them here.

o) $\emptyset \subseteq S$ for any set S.

p) If $S \subseteq T$, then

   i) $(S \cup T) \equiv T$,

   ii) $(S \cap T) \equiv S$, and

   iii) $(S - T) \equiv \emptyset$.

Proving Equivalences by Showing Containments

Two sets S and T are equal if and only if $S \subseteq T$ and $T \subseteq S$; that is, each is a subset of the other. For if every element in S is an element of T and vice versa, then S and T have exactly the same members and thus are equal. Conversely, if S and T have exactly the same members, then surely $S \subseteq T$ and $T \subseteq S$ are true. This rule is analogous to the arithmetic rule that $a = b$ if and only if both $a \leq b$ and $b \leq a$ are true.

We can show the equivalence of two expressions E and F by showing that the set denoted by each is contained in the set denoted by the other. That is, we

1. Consider an arbitrary element x in E and prove that it is also in F, and then

2. Consider an arbitrary element x in F and prove that it is also in E.

Note that both proofs are necessary in order to prove that $E \equiv F$.

	STEP	REASON
1)	x is in $S - (T \cup R)$	Given
2)	x is in S	Definition of $-$ and (1)
3)	x is not in $T \cup R$	Definition of $-$ and (1)
4)	x is not in T	Definition of $\cup$ and (3)
5)	x is not in R	Definition of $\cup$ and (3)
6)	x is in $S - T$	Definition of $-$ with (2) and (4)
7)	x is in $(S - T) - R$	Definition of $-$ with (6) and (5)

Fig. 7.3. Proof of one half of the associative law for union and difference.

✦ **Example 7.9.** Let us prove the associative law for union and difference,

$$\left(S - (T \cup R)\right) \equiv \left((S - T) - R\right)$$

We start by assuming that x is in the expression on the left. The sequence of steps is shown in Fig. 7.3. Note that in steps (4) and (5), we use the definition of union backwards. That is, (3) tells us that x is not in $T \cup R$. If x were in T, (3) would be wrong, and so we can conclude that x is not in T. Similarly, x is not in R.

	STEP	REASON
1)	x is in $(S - T) - R$	Given
2)	x is in $S - T$	Definition of $-$ and (1)
3)	x is not in R	Definition of $-$ and (1)
4)	x is in S	Definition of $-$ and (2)
5)	x is not in T	Definition of $-$ and (2)
6)	x is not in $T \cup R$	Definition of $\cup$ with (3) and (5)
7)	x is in $S - (T \cup R)$	Definition of $-$ with (4) and (6)

Fig. 7.4. Second half of the proof of the associative law for union and difference.

We are not done; we must now start by assuming that x is in $(S - T) - R$ and show that it is in $S - (T \cup R)$. The steps are shown in Fig. 7.4. ✦

✦ **Example 7.10.** As another example, let us prove part of (p), the rule that if $S \subseteq T$, then $S \cup T \equiv T$. We begin by assuming that x is in $S \cup T$. We know by the definition of union that either

1. x is in S or

2. x is in T.

In case (1), since $S \subseteq T$ is assumed, we know that x is in T. In case (2), we immediately see that x is in T. Thus, in either case x is in T, and we have completed the first half of the proof, the statement that $(S \cup T) \subseteq T$.

Now let us assume that x is in T. Then x is in $S \cup T$ by the definition of union. Thus, $T \subseteq (S \cup T)$, which is the second half of the proof. We conclude that if $S \subseteq T$ then $(S \cup T) \equiv T$. ✦

The Power Set of a Set

If S is any set, the *power set* of S is the set of subsets of S. We shall use $\mathbf{P}(S)$ to denote the power set of S, although the notation 2^S is also used.

✦ **Example 7.11.** Let $S = \{1, 2, 3\}$. Then

$$\mathbf{P}(S) = \{\emptyset, \{1\}, \{2\}, \{3\}, \{1, 2\}, \{1, 3\}, \{2, 3\}, \{1, 2, 3\}\}$$

Singleton set

That is, $\mathbf{P}(S)$ is a set with eight members; each member is itself a set. The empty set is in $\mathbf{P}(S)$, since surely $\emptyset \subseteq S$. The *singletons* — sets with one member of S, namely, $\{1\}$, $\{2\}$, and $\{3\}$ — are in $\mathbf{P}(S)$. Likewise, the three sets with two of the three members of S are in $\mathbf{P}(S)$, and S itself is a member of $\mathbf{P}(S)$.

As another example, $\mathbf{P}(\emptyset) = \{\emptyset\}$ since $\emptyset \subseteq S$, but for no set S besides the empty set is $S \subseteq \emptyset$. Note that $\{\emptyset\}$, the set containing the empty set, is not the same as the empty set. In particular, the former has a member, namely $\emptyset$, while the empty set has no members. ✦

The Size of Power Sets

If S has n members, then $\mathbf{P}(S)$ has 2^n members. In Example 7.11 we saw that a set of three members has a power set of $2^3 = 8$ members. Also, $2^0 = 1$, and we saw that the empty set, which contains zero elements, has a power set of one element.

Let $S = \{a_1, a_2, \ldots, a_n\}$, where $a_1, a_2, \ldots, a_n$ are any n elements. We shall now prove by induction on n that $\mathbf{P}(S)$ has 2^n members.

BASIS. If $n = 0$, then S is $\emptyset$. We have already observed that $\mathbf{P}(\emptyset)$ has one member. Since $2^0 = 1$, we have proved the basis.

INDUCTION. Suppose that when $S = \{a_1, a_2, \ldots, a_n\}$, $\mathbf{P}(S)$ has 2^n members. Let a_{n+1} be a new element, and let $T = S \cup \{a_{n+1}\}$, a set of $n + 1$ members. Now a subset of T either does not have or does have a_{n+1} as a member. Let us consider these two cases in turn.

1. The subsets of T that do not include a_{n+1} are also subsets of S, and therefore in $\mathbf{P}(S)$. By the inductive hypothesis, there are exactly 2^n such sets.

2. If R is a subset of T that includes a_{n+1}, let $Q = R - \{a_{n+1}\}$; that is, Q is R with a_{n+1} removed. Then Q is a subset of S. By the inductive hypothesis, there are exactly 2^n possible sets Q, and each one corresponds to a unique set R, which is $Q \cup \{a_{n+1}\}$.

We conclude that there are exactly 2×2^n, or 2^{n+1}, subsets of T, half that are subsets of S, and half that are formed from a subset of S by including a_{n+1}. Thus, the inductive step is proved; given that any set S of n elements has 2^n subsets, we have shown that any set T of $n + 1$ elements has 2^{n+1} subsets.

EXERCISES

7.3.1: In Fig. 7.2, we showed two expressions for the set of regions $\{3, 5, 6\}$. However, each of the regions can be represented by expressions involving S, T, and R and the operators union, intersection, and difference. Write two different expressions for each of the following:

a)   Region 6 alone
b)   Regions 2 and 4 together
c)   Regions 2, 4, and 8 together

7.3.2: Use Venn diagrams to show the following algebraic laws. For each subexpression involved in the equivalence, indicate the set of regions it represents.

a) $(S \cup (T \cap R)) \equiv ((S \cup T) \cap (S \cup R))$
b) $((S \cup T) - R) \equiv ((S - R) \cup (T - R))$
c) $(S - (T \cup R)) \equiv ((S - T) - R)$

7.3.3: Show each of the equivalences from Exercise 7.3.2 by showing containment of each side in the other.

7.3.4: Assuming $S \subseteq T$, prove the following by showing that each side of the equivalence is a subset of the other:

a) $(S \cap T) \equiv S$
b) $(S - T) \equiv \emptyset$

7.3.5*: Into how many regions does a Venn diagram with n sets divide the plane, assuming that no set is a subset of any other? Suppose that of the n sets there is one that is a subset of one other, but there are no other containments. Then some regions would be empty. For example, in Fig. 7.1, if $S \subseteq T$, then region 2 would be empty, because there is no element that is in S but not in T. In general, how many nonempty regions would there be?

7.3.6: Prove that if $S \subseteq T$, then $\mathbf{P}(S) \subseteq \mathbf{P}(T)$.

7.3.7*: In C we can represent a set S whose members are sets by a linked list whose elements are the headers for lists; each such list represents a set that is one of the members of S. Write a C program that takes a list of elements representing a set (i.e., a list in which all the elements are distinct) and returns the power set of the given set. What is the running time of your program? *Hint*: Use the inductive proof that there are 2^n members in the power set of a set of n elements to devise a recursive algorithm that creates the power set. If you are clever, you can use the same list as part of several sets, to avoid copying the lists that represent members of the power set, thus saving both time and space.

7.3.8: Show that

a) $\mathbf{P}(S) \cup \mathbf{P}(T) \subseteq \mathbf{P}(S \cup T)$
b) $\mathbf{P}(S \cap T) \subseteq \mathbf{P}(S) \cap \mathbf{P}(T)$

Are either (a) or (b) true if containment is replaced by equivalence?

7.3.9: What is $\mathbf{P}(\mathbf{P}(\mathbf{P}(\emptyset)))$?

7.3.10*: If we apply the power-set operator n times, starting with $\emptyset$, how many members does the resulting set have? For an example, Exercise 7.3.9 is the case $n = 3$.

❖ 7.4   List Implementation of Sets

We have already seen, in Section 6.4, how to implement the dictionary operations *insert*, *delete*, and *lookup* using a linked-list data structure. We also observed there that the expected running time of these operations is $O(n)$ if the set has n elements. This running time is not as good as the $O(\log n)$ average time taken for the dictionary operations using a balanced binary search tree data structure, as in Section 5.8. On the other hand, as we shall see in Section 7.6, a linked-list representation of dictionaries plays an essential role in the hash-table data structure for dictionaries, which is generally faster than the binary search tree.

Union, Intersection, and Difference

The basic set operations such as union can profit from the use of linked lists as a data structure, although the proper techniques are somewhat different from what we use for the dictionary operations. In particular, sorting the lists significantly improvess the running time for union, intersection, and difference. As we saw in Section 6.4, sorting makes only a small improvement in the running time of dictionary operations.

To begin, let us see what problems arise when we represent sets by unsorted lists. In this case, we must compare each element of each set with each element of the other. Thus, to take the union, intersection, or difference of sets of size n and m requires $O(mn)$ time. For example, to create a list U that represents the union of two sets S and T, we may start by copying the list for S onto the initially empty list U. Then we examine each element of T and see whether it is in S. If not, we add the element to U. The idea is sketched in Fig. 7.5.

```
(1)    copy S to U;
(2)    for (each x in T)
(3)        if (!lookup(x, S))
(4)            insert(x, U);
```

Fig. 7.5. Pseudocode sketch of the algorithm for taking the union of sets represented by unsorted lists.

Suppose S has n members and T has m members. The operation in line (1), copying S to U, can easily be accomplished in $O(n)$ time. The lookup of line (3) takes $O(n)$ time. We only execute the insertion of line (4) if we know from line (3) that x is not in S. Since x can only appear once on the list for T, we know that x is not yet in U. Therefore, it is safe to place x at the front of U's list, and line (4) can be accomplished in $O(1)$ time. The for-loop of lines (2) through (4) is iterated m times, and its body takes time $O(n)$. Thus, the time for lines (2) to (4) is $O(mn)$, which dominates the $O(n)$ for line (1).

There are similar algorithms for intersection and difference, each taking $O(mn)$ time. We leave these algorithms for the reader to design.

Union, Intersection, and Difference Using Sorted Lists

We can perform unions, intersections, and set differences much faster when the lists representing the sets are sorted. In fact, we shall see that it pays to sort the lists before performing these operations, even if the lists are not initially sorted. For example, consider the computation of $S \cup T$, where S and T are represented by sorted lists. The process is similar to the merge algorithm of Section 2.8. One difference is that when there is a tie for smallest between the elements currently at the fronts of the two lists, we make only one copy of the element, rather than two copies as we must for merge. The other difference is that we cannot simply remove elements from the lists for S and T for the union, since we should not destroy S or

T while creating their union. Instead, we must make copies of all elements to form the union.

We assume that the types LIST and CELL are defined as before, by the macro

    DefCell(int, CELL, LIST);

The function setUnion is shown in Fig. 7.6. It makes use of an auxiliary function $assemble(x, L, M)$ that creates a new cell at line (1), places element x in that cell at line (2), and calls setUnion at line (3) to take the union of the lists L and M. Then assemble returns a cell for x followed by the list that results from applying setUnion to L and M. Note that the functions assemble and setUnion are mutually recursive; each calls the other.

Function setUnion selects the least element from its two given sorted lists and passes to assemble the chosen element and the remainders of the two lists. There are six cases for setUnion, depending on whether or not one of its lists is NULL, and if not, which of the two elements at the heads of the lists precedes the other.

1. If both lists are NULL, setUnion simply returns NULL, ending the recursion. This case is lines (5) and (6) of Fig. 7.6.

2. If L is NULL and M is not, then at lines (7) and (8) we assemble the union by taking the first element from M, followed by the "union" of the NULL list with the tail of M. Note that, in this case, successive calls to setUnion result in M being copied.

3. If M is NULL but L is not, then at lines (9) and (10) we do the opposite, assembling the answer from the first element of L and the tail of L.

4. If the first elements of L and M are the same, then at lines (11) and (12) we assemble the answer from one copy of this element, referred to as L->element, and the tails of L and M.

5. If the first element of L precedes that of M, then at lines (13) and (14) we assemble the answer from this smallest element, the tail of L, and the entire list M.

6. Symmetrically, at lines (15) and (16), if M has the smallest element, then we assemble the answer from that element, the entire list L, and the tail of M.

◆ **Example 7.12.** Suppose S is $\{1, 3, 6\}$ and T is $\{5, 3\}$. The sorted lists representing these sets are $L = (1, 3, 6)$ and $M = (3, 5)$. We call $setUnion(L, M)$ to take the union. Since the first element of L, which is 1, precedes the first element of M, which is 3, case (5) applies, and we assemble the answer from 1, the tail of L, which we shall call $L_1 = (3, 6)$, and M. Function $assemble(1, L_1, M)$ calls $setUnion(L_1, M)$ at line (3), and the result is the list with first element 1 and tail equal to whatever the union is.

This call to setUnion is case (4), where the two leading elements are equal; both are 3 here. Thus, we assemble the union from one copy of element 3 and the tails of the lists L_1 and M. These tails are L_2, consisting of only the element 6, and M_1, consisting of only the element 5. The next call is $setUnion(L_2, M_1)$, which is an instance of case (6). We thus add 5 to the union and call $setUnion(L_2, \text{NULL})$. That is case (3), generating 6 for the union and calling $setUnion(\text{NULL}, \text{NULL})$. Here, we

```
        LIST setUnion(LIST L, LIST M);
        LIST assemble(int x, LIST L, LIST M);

        /* assemble produces a list whose head element is x and
           whose tail is the union of lists L and M */

        LIST assemble(int x, LIST L, LIST M)
        {
            LIST first;

(1)         first = (LIST) malloc(sizeof(struct CELL));
(2)         first->element = x;
(3)         first->next = setUnion(L, M);
(4)         return first;
        }


        /* setUnion returns a list that is the union of L and M */

        LIST setUnion(LIST L, LIST M)
        {
(5)         if (L == NULL && M == NULL)
(6)             return NULL;
(7)         else if (L == NULL) /* M cannot be NULL here */
(8)             return assemble(M->element, NULL, M->next);
(9)         else if (M == NULL) /* L cannot be NULL here */
(10)            return assemble(L->element, L->next, NULL);
            /* if we reach here, neither L nor M can be NULL */
(11)        else if (L->element == M->element)
(12)            return assemble(L->element, L->next, M->next);
(13)        else if (L->element < M->element)
(14)            return assemble(L->element, L->next, M);
(15)        else /* here, M->element < L->element */
(16)            return assemble(M->element, L, M->next);
        }
```

Fig. 7.6. Computing the union of sets represented by sorted lists.

have case (1), and the recursion ends. The result of the initial call to setUnion is the list $(1, 3, 5, 6)$. Figure 7.7 shows in detail the sequence of calls and returns made on this example data. ✦

Notice that the list generated by setUnion always comes out in sorted order. We can see why the algorithm works, by observing that whichever case applies, each element in lists L or M is either copied to the output, by becoming the first parameter in a call to assemble, or remains on the lists that are passed as parameters in the recursive call to setUnion.

Running Time of Union

If we call setUnion on sets with n and m elements, respectively, then the time taken

call $setUnion\big((1,3,6),(3,5)\big)$
    call $assemble\big(1,(3,6),(3,5)\big)$
        call $setUnion\big((3,6),(3,5)\big)$
            call $assemble\big(3,(6),(5)\big)$
                call $setUnion\big((6),(5)\big)$
                    call $assemble\big(5,(6),\text{NULL}\big)$
                        call $setUnion\big((6),\text{NULL}\big)$
                            call $assemble\big(6,\text{NULL},\text{NULL}\big)$
                                call $setUnion(\text{NULL},\text{NULL})$
                              return NULL
                          return (6)
                      return (6)
                  return (5,6)
              return (5,6)
            return (3,5,6)
        return (3,5,6)
    return (1,3,5,6)
return (1,3,5,6)

Fig. 7.7. Sequence of calls and returns for Example 7.12.

Big-Oh for Functions of More Than One Variable

As we pointed out in Section 6.9, the notion of big-oh, which we defined only for functions of one variable, can be applied naturally to functions of more than one variable. We say that $f(x_1,\ldots,x_k)$ is $O\big(g(x_1,\ldots,x_k)\big)$ if there are constants c and $a_1,\ldots,a_k$ such that whenever $x_i \geq a_i$ for all $i = 1,\ldots,k$, it is the case that $f(x_1,\ldots,x_k) \leq cg(x_1,\ldots,x_k)$. In particular, note that even though $m+n$ is greater than mn when one of m and n is 0 and the other is greater than 0, we can still say that $m + n$ is $O(mn)$, by choosing constants c, a_1, and a_2 all equal to 1.

by setUnion is $O(m+n)$. To see why, note that calls to assemble spend $O(1)$ time creating a cell for the output list and then calling setUnion on the remaining lists. Thus, the calls to assemble in Fig. 7.6 can be thought of as costing $O(1)$ time plus the time for a call to setUnion on lists the sum of whose lengths is either one less than that of L and M, or in case (4), two less. Further, all the work in setUnion, exclusive of the call to assemble, takes $O(1)$ time.

It follows that when setUnion is called on lists of total length $m+n$, it will result in at most $m + n$ recursive calls to setUnion and an equal number to assemble. Each takes $O(1)$ time, exclusive of the time taken by the recursive call. Thus, the time to take the union is $O(m + n)$, that is, proportional to the sum of the sizes of the sets.

This time is less than that of the $O(mn)$ time needed to take the union of sets represented by unsorted lists. In fact, if the lists for our sets are not sorted, we can sort them in $O(n \log n + m \log m)$ time, and then take the union of the sorted lists. Since $n \log n$ dominates n and $m \log m$ dominates m, we can express the total cost of sorting and taking the union as $O(n \log n + m \log m)$. That expression can be greater than $O(mn)$, but is less whenever n and m are close in value — that is, whenever the sets are approximately the same size. Thus, it usually makes sense to sort before taking the union.

Intersection and Difference

The idea in the algorithm for union outlined in Fig. 7.6 works for intersections and differences of sets as well: when the sets are represented by sorted lists, intersection and difference are also performed in linear time. For intersection, we want to copy an element to the output only if it appears on both lists, as in case (4). If either list is NULL, we cannot have any elements in the intersection, and so cases (1), (2), and (3) can be replaced by a step that returns NULL. In case (4), we copy the element at the heads of the lists to the intersection. In cases (5) and (6), where the heads of the lists are different, the smaller cannot appear on both lists, and so we do not add anything to the intersection but pop the smaller off its list and take the intersection of the remainders.

To see why that makes sense, suppose, for example, that a is at the head of list L, that b is at the head of list M, and that $a < b$. Then a cannot appear on the sorted list M, and so we can rule out the possibility that a is on both lists. However, b can appear on list L somewhere after a, so that we may still be able to use b from M. Thus, we need to take the intersection of the tail of L with the entire list M. Conversely, if b were less than a, we would take the intersection of L with the tail of M. C code to compute the intersection is shown in Fig. 7.8. It is also necessary to modify assemble to call intersection instead of setUnion. We leave this change as well as a program to compute the difference of sorted lists as exercises.

```
LIST intersection(LIST L, LIST M)
{
    if (L == NULL || M == NULL)
        return NULL;
    else if (L->element == M->element)
        return assemble(L->element, L->next, M->next);
    else if (L->element < M->element)
        return intersection(L->next, M);
    else /* here, M->element < L->element */
        return intersection(L, M->next);
}
```

Fig. 7.8. Computing the intersection of sets represented by sorted lists.
A new version of assemble is required.

EXERCISES

7.4.1: Write C programs for taking the (a) union, (b) intersection, and (c) difference of sets represented by unsorted lists.

7.4.2: Modify the program of Fig. 7.6 so that it takes the (a) intersection and (b) difference of sets represented by sorted lists.

7.4.3: The functions `assemble` and `setUnion` from Fig. 7.6 leave the lists whose union they take intact; that is, they make copies of elements rather than use the cells of the given lists themselves. Can you simplify the program by allowing it to destroy the given lists as it takes their union?

7.4.4*: Prove by induction on the sum of the lengths of the lists given as parameters that `setUnion` from Fig. 7.6 returns the union of the given lists.

Symmetric difference

7.4.5*: The *symmetric difference* of two sets S and T is $(S - T) \cup (T - S)$, that is, the elements that are in exactly one of S and T. Write a program to take the symmetric difference of two sets that are represented by sorted lists. Your program should make one pass through the lists, like Fig. 7.6, rather than call routines for union and difference.

7.4.6*: We analyzed the program of Fig. 7.6 informally by arguing that if the total of the lengths of the lists was n, there were $O(n)$ calls to `setUnion` and `assemble` and each call took $O(1)$ time plus whatever time the recursive call took. We can formalize this argument by letting $T_U(n)$ be the running time for `setUnion` and $T_A(n)$ be the running time of `assemble` on lists of total length n. Write recursive rules defining T_U and T_A in terms of each other. Substitute to eliminate T_A, and set up a conventional recurrence for T_U. Solve that recurrence. Does it show that `setUnion` takes $O(n)$ time?

✦✥ 7.5 Characteristic-Vector Implementation of Sets

Frequently, the sets we encounter are each subsets of some small set U, which we shall refer to as the "universal set."[1] For example, a hand of cards is a subset of the set of all 52 cards. When the sets with which we are concerned are each subsets of some small set U, there is a representation of sets that is much more efficient than the list representation discussed in the previous section. We order the elements of U in some way so that each element of U can be associated with a unique "position," which is an integer from 0 up to $n - 1$, where n is the number of elements in U.

Then, given a set S that is contained in U, we can represent S by a *characteristic vector* of 0's and 1's, such that for each element x of U, if x is in S, the position corresponding to x has a 1, and if x is not in S, then that position has a 0.

✦ **Example 7.13.** Let U be the set of cards. We may order the cards any way we choose, but one reasonable scheme is to order them by suits: clubs, then diamonds, then hearts, then spades. Then, within a suit, we order the cards ace, 2, 3, ..., 10, jack, queen, king. For instance, the position of the ace of clubs is 0, the king of clubs is 12, the ace of diamonds is 13, and the jack of spades is 49. A royal flush in hearts is represented by the characteristic vector

0000000000000000000000000010000000011110000000000000

---

[1] Of course U cannot be a true universal set, or set of all sets, which we argued does not exist because of Russell's paradox.

The first 1, in position 26, represents the ace of hearts; and the other four 1's, in positions 35 through 38, represent the 10, jack, queen, and king of hearts.

The set of all clubs is represented by

1111111111111100000000000000000000000000000000000000

and the set of all picture cards is represented by

0000000000011100000000001110000000000111000000000111

◆

Array Implementation of Sets

We can represent characteristic vectors for subsets of a universal set of n elements using Boolean arrays of the following type:

```
typedef BOOLEAN USET[n];
```

The type **BOOLEAN** is as described in Section 1.6. To insert the element corresponding to position i into a set S declared to be of type **USET**, we have only to execute

```
S[i] = TRUE;
```

Similarly, to delete the element corresponding to position i from S, we do

```
S[i] = FALSE;
```

If we want to look up this element, we have only to return the value $S[i]$, which tells us whether the ith element is present in S or not.

Note that each of the dictionary operations *insert*, *delete*, and *lookup* thus takes $O(1)$ time, when sets are represented by characteristic vectors. The only disadvantage to this technique is that all sets must be subsets of some universal set U. Moreover, the universal set must be small; otherwise, the length of the arrays becomes so large that we cannot store them conveniently. In fact, since we shall normally have to initialize all elements of the array for a set S to **TRUE** or **FALSE**, the initialization of any subset of U (even $\emptyset$) must take time proportional to the size of U. If U had a large number of elements, the time to initialize a set could dominate the cost of all other operations.

To form the union of two sets that are subsets of a common universal set of n elements, and that are represented by characteristic vectors S and T, we define another characteristic vector R to be the bitwise **OR** of the characteristic vectors S and T:

```
R[i] = S[i] || T[i], for 0 ≤ i < n
```

Similarly, we can make R represent the intersection of S and T by taking the bitwise **AND** of S and T:

```
R[i] = S[i] && T[i], for 0 ≤ i < n
```

Finally, we can make R represent the set difference $S - T$ as follows:

```
R[i] = S[i] && !T[i], for 0 ≤ i < n
```

The arrays representing characteristic vectors and the Boolean operations on them can be implemented using the bitwise operators of C if we define the type **BOOLEAN** appropriately. However, the code is machine specific, and so we shall not present any details here. A portable (but more space consuming) implementation of characteristic vectors can be accomplished with arrays of **int**'s of the appropriate size, and this is the definition of **BOOLEAN** that we have assumed.

✦ **Example 7.14.** Let us consider sets of apple varieties. Our universal set will consist of the six varieties listed in Fig. 7.9; the order of their listing indicates their position in characteristic vectors.

	VARIETY	COLOR	RIPENS
0)	Delicious	red	late
1)	Granny Smith	green	early
2)	Gravenstein	red	early
3)	Jonathan	red	early
4)	McIntosh	red	late
5)	Pippin	green	late

Fig. 7.9. Characteristics of some apple varieties.

The set of red apples is represented by the characteristic vector

$$Red = 101110$$

and the set of early apples is represented by

$$Early = 011100$$

Thus, the set of apples that are either red or early, that is, $Red \cup Early$, is represented by the characteristic vector 111110. Note that this vector has a 1 in those positions where either the vector for Red, that is, 101110, or the vector for $Early$, that is, 011100, or both, have a 1.

We can find the characteristic vector for $Red \cap Early$, the set of apples that are both red and early, by placing a 1 in those positions where both 101110 and 011100 have 1. The resulting vector is 001100, representing the set of apples {Gravenstein, Jonathan}. The set of apples that are red but not early, that is,

$$Red - Early$$

is represented by the vector 100010. The set is {Delicious, McIntosh}. ✦

Notice that the time to perform union, intersection, and difference using characteristic vectors is proportional to the length of the vectors. That length is not directly related to the size of the sets, but is equal to the size of the universal set. If the sets have a reasonable fraction of the elements in the universal set, then the time for union, intersection, and difference is proportional to the sizes of the sets involved. That is better than the $O(n \log n)$ time for sorted lists, and much better than the $O(n^2)$ time for unsorted lists. However, the drawback of characteristic vectors is that, should the sets be much smaller than the universal set, the running time of these operations can be far greater than the sizes of the sets involved.

EXERCISES

7.5.1: Give the characteristic vectors of the following sets of cards. For convenience, you can use 0^k to represent k consecutive 0's and 1^k for k consecutive 1's.

a)   The cards found in a pinochle deck

b)   The red cards

c)   The one-eyed jacks and the suicide king

7.5.2: Using bitwise operators, write C programs to compute the (a) union and (b) difference of two sets of cards, the first represented by words $a1$ and $a2$, the second represented by $b1$ and $b2$.

7.5.3*: Suppose we wanted to represent a bag (multiset) whose elements were contained in some small universal set U. How could we generalize the characteristic-vector method of representation to bags? Show how to perform (a) *insert*, (b) *delete*, and (c) *lookup* on bags represented this way. Note that bag *lookup*(x) returns the number of times x appears in the bag.

✦✦ 7.6   Hashing

The characteristic-vector representation of dictionaries, when it can be used, allows us to access directly the place where an element is represented, that is, to access the position in the array that is indexed by the value of the element. However, as we mentioned, we cannot allow our universal set to be too large, or the array will be too long to fit in the available memory of the computer. Even if it did fit, the time to initialize the array would be prohibitive. For example, suppose we wanted to store a real dictionary of words in the English language, and also suppose we were willing to ignore words longer than 10 letters. We would still have $26^{10} + 26^9 + \cdots + 26$ possible words, or over 10^{14} words. Each of these possible words would require a position in the array.

At any time, however, there are only about a million words in the English language, so that only one out of 100 million of the array entries would be TRUE. Perhaps we could collapse the array, so that many possible words could share an entry. For example, suppose we assigned the first 100 million possible words to the first cell of the array, the next 100 million possibilities to the second cell, and so on, up to the millionth cell. There are two problems with this arrangement:

1.   It is no longer enough just to put TRUE in a cell, because we won't know which of the 100 million possible words are actually present in the dictionary, or if in fact more than one word in any one group is present.

2. If, for example, the first 100 million possible words include all the short words, then we would expect many more than the average number of words from the dictionary to fall into this group of possible words. Note that our arrangement has as many cells of the array as there are words in the dictionary, and so we expect the average cell to represent one word; but surely there are in English many thousands of words in the first group, which would include all the words of up to five letters, and some of the six-letter words.

To solve problem (1), we need to list, in each cell of the array, all the words in its group that are present in the dictionary. That is, the array cell becomes the header of a linked list with these words. To solve problem (2), we need to be careful how we assign potential words to groups. We must distribute elements among groups so that it is unlikely (although never impossible) that there will be many elements in a single group. Note that if there are a large number of elements in a group, and we represent groups by linked lists, then lookup will be very slow for members of a large group.

The Hash Table Data Structure

We have now evolved from the characteristic vector — a valuable data structure that is of limited use — to a structure called a *hash table* that is useful for any dictionary whatsoever, and for many other purposes as well.[2] The speed of the hash table for the dictionary operations can be made $O(1)$ on the average, independent of the size of the dictionary, and independent of the size of the universal set from which the dictionary is drawn. A picture of a hash table appears in Fig. 7.10. However, we show the list for only one group, that to which x belongs.

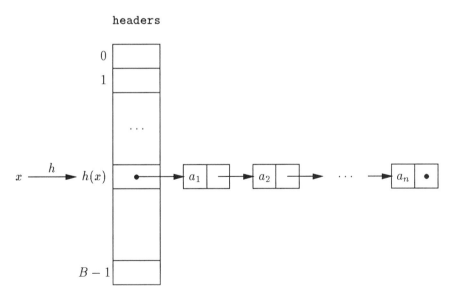

Fig. 7.10. A hash table.

---

[2] Although in situations where a characteristic vector is feasible, we would normally prefer that representation over any other.

Bucket

There is a *hash function* that takes an element x as argument and produces an integer value between 0 and $B - 1$, where B is the number of *buckets* in the hash table. The value $h(x)$ is the bucket in which we place the element x. Thus, the buckets correspond to the "groups" of words that we talked about in the preceding informal discussion, and the hash function is used to decide to which bucket a given element belongs.

Hash function

The appropriate hash function to use depends on the type of the elements. For example,

1. If elements are integers, we could let $h(x)$ be x % B, that is, the remainder when x is divided by B. That number is always in the required range, 0 to $B - 1$.

2. If the elements are character strings, we can take an element $x = a_1 a_2 \cdots a_k$, where each a_i is a character, and compute $y = a_1 + a_2 + \cdots + a_k$, since a **char** in C is a small integer. We then have an integer y that is the sum of the integer equivalents of all the characters in the string x. If we divide y by B and take the remainder, we have a bucket number in the range 0 to $B - 1$.

What is important is that the hash function "hashes" the element. That is, h wildly mixes up the buckets into which elements fall, so they tend to fall in approximately equal numbers into all the buckets. This equitable distribution must occur even for a fairly regular pattern of elements, such as consecutive integers or character strings that differ in only one position.

Each bucket consists of a linked list wherein are stored all the elements of the set that are sent by the hash function to that bucket. To find an element x, we compute $h(x)$, which gives us a bucket number. If x is anywhere, it is in that bucket, so that we may search for x by running down the list for that bucket. In effect, the hash table allows us to use the (slow) list representation for sets, but, by dividing the set into B buckets, allows us to search lists that are only $1/B$ as long as the size of the set, on the average. If we make B roughly as large as the set, then buckets will average only one element, and we can find elements in an average of $O(1)$ time, just as for the characteristic-vector representation of sets.

✦ **Example 7.15.** Suppose we wish to store a set of character strings of up to 32 characters, where each string is terminated by the null character. We shall use the hash function outlined in (2) above, with $B = 5$, that is, a five-bucket hash table. To compute the hash value of each element, we sum the integer values of the characters in each string, up to but not including the null character. The following declarations give us the desired types.

```
(1)      #define B 5
(2)      typedef char ETYPE[32];
(3)      DefCell(ETYPE, CELL, LIST);
(4)      typedef LIST HASHTABLE[B];
```

Line (1) defines the constant B to be the number of buckets, 5. Line (2) defines the type **ETYPE** to be arrays of 32 characters. Line (3) is our usual definition of cells and linked lists, but here the element type is **ETYPE**, that is, 32-character arrays. Line (4) defines a hashtable to be an array of B lists. If we then declare

```
HASHTABLE headers;
```

the array **headers** is of the appropriate type to contain the bucket headers for our hash table.

```
int h(ETYPE x)
{
    int i, sum;

    sum = 0;
    for (i = 0; x[i] != '\0'; i++)
        sum += x[i];
    return sum % B;
}
```

Fig. 7.11. A hash function that sums the integer equivalents of characters, assuming **ETYPE** is an array of characters.

Now, we must define the hash function h. The code for this function is shown in Fig. 7.11. The integer equivalent of each of the characters of the string x is summed in the variable **sum**. The last step computes and returns as the value of the hash function h the remainder of this sum when it is divided by the number of buckets B.

Let us consider some examples of words and the buckets into which the function h puts them. We shall enter into the hash table the seven words[3]

> **anyone lived in a pretty how town**

In order to compute $h($**anyone**$)$, we need to understand the integer values of characters. In the usual ASCII code for characters, the lower-case letters have integer values starting at 97 for **a** (that's 1100001 in binary), 98 for **b**, and so on, up to 122 for **z**. The upper-case letters correspond to integers that are 32 less than their lower-case equivalents — that is, from 65 for **A** (1000001 in binary) to 90 for **Z**.

Thus, the integer equivalents for the characters in **anyone** are 97, 110, 121, 111, 110, 101. The sum of these is 650. When we divide by B, which is 5, we get the remainder 0. Thus, **anyone** belongs in bucket 0. The seven words of our example are assigned, by the hash function of Fig. 7.11, to the buckets indicated in Fig. 7.12.

We see that three of the seven words have been assigned to one bucket, number 0. Two words are assigned to bucket 2, and one each to buckets 1 and 4. That is somewhat less even a distribution than would be typical, but with a small number of words and buckets, we should expect anomalies. As the number of words becomes large, they will tend to distribute themselves among the five buckets approximately evenly. The hash table, after insertion of these seven words, is shown in Fig. 7.13. ✦

Implementing the Dictionary Operations by a Hash Table

To insert, delete, or look up an element x in a dictionary that is represented by a hash table, there is a simple three-step process:

---

[3] The words are from a poem of the same name by e. e. cummings. The poem doesn't get any easier to decode. The next line is "with up so floating many bells down."

WORD	SUM	BUCKET
anyone	650	0
lived	532	2
in	215	0
a	97	2
pretty	680	0
how	334	4
town	456	1

Fig. 7.12. Words, their values, and their buckets.

headers

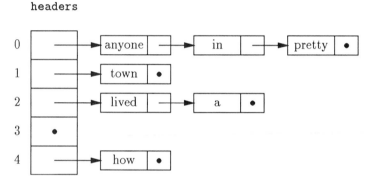

Fig. 7.13. Hash table holding seven elements.

1.   Compute the proper bucket, which is $h(x)$.

2.   Use the array of header pointers to find the list of elements for the bucket numbered $h(x)$.

3.   Perform the operation on this list, just as if the list represented the entire set.

The algorithms in Section 6.4 can be used for the list operations after suitable modifications for the fact that elements here are character strings while in Section 6.4 elements were integers. As an example, we show the complete function for inserting an element into a hash table in Fig. 7.14. You can develop similar functions for **delete** and **lookup** as an exercise.

To understand Fig. 7.14, it helps to notice that the function **bucketInsert** is similar to the function **insert** from Fig. 6.5. At line (1) we test to see whether we have reached the end of the list. If we have, then we create a new cell at line (2). However, at line (3), instead of storing an integer into the newly created cell, we use the function **strcpy** from the standard header file **string.h** to copy the string x into the element field of the cell.

Also, at line (5), to test if x has not yet been found on the list, we use function **strcmp** from **string.h**. That function returns 0 if and only if x and the element in the current cell are equal. Thus, we continue down the list as long as the value of the comparison is nonzero, that is, as long as the current element is not x.

The function **insert** here consists of a single line, in which we call **buck-**

```
         #include <string.h>

         void bucketInsert(ETYPE x, LIST *pL)
         {
(1)          if ((*pL) == NULL) {
(2)              (*pL) = (LIST) malloc(sizeof(struct CELL));
(3)              strcpy((*pL)->element, x);
(4)              (*pL)->next = NULL;
             }
(5)          else if (strcmp((*pL)->element, x)) /* x and element
                         are different */
(6)              bucketInsert(x, &((*pL)->next));
         }

         void insert(ETYPE x, HASHTABLE H)
         {
(7)          bucketInsert(x, &(H[h(x)]));
         }
```

Fig. 7.14. Inserting an element into a hash table.

etInsert after first finding the element of the array that is the header for the appropriate bucket, $h(x)$. We assume that the hash function h is defined elsewhere. Also recall that the type HASHTABLE means that H is an array of pointers to cells (i.e., an array of lists).

◆ **Example 7.16.** Suppose we wish to delete the element in from the hash table of Fig. 7.13, assuming the hash function described in Example 7.15. The delete operation is carried out essentially like the function insert of Fig. 7.14. We compute $h(\text{in})$, which is 0. We thus go to the header for bucket number 0. The second cell on the list for this bucket holds in, and we delete that cell. The detailed C program is left as an exercise. ◆

Running Time of Hash Table Operations

As we can see by examining Fig. 7.14, the time taken by the function *insert* to find the header of the appropriate bucket is $O(1)$, assuming that the time to compute $h(x)$ is a constant independent of the number of elements stored in the hash table.[4] To this constant we must add on the average an additional $O(n/B)$ time, if n is the number of elements in the hash table and B is the number of buckets. The reason is that *bucketInsert* will take time proportional to the length of the list, and that length, on the average, must be the total number of elements divided by the number of buckets, or n/B.

An interesting consequence is that if we make B approximately equal to the number of elements in the set — that is, n and B are close — then n/B is about 1

---

[4] That would be the case for the hash function of Fig. 7.11, or most other hash functions encountered in practice. The time for computing the bucket number may depend on the type of the element — longer strings may require the summation of more integers, for example — but the time is not dependent on the number of elements stored.

and the dictionary operations on a hash table take $O(1)$ time each, on the average, just as when we use a characteristic-vector representation. If we try to do better by making B much larger than n, so that most buckets are empty, it still takes us $O(1)$ time to find the bucket header, and so the running time does not improve significantly once B becomes larger than n.

Restructuring hash tables

We must also consider that in some circumstances it may not be possible to keep B close to n all the time. If the set is growing rapidly, then n increases while B remains fixed, so that ultimately n/B becomes large. It is possible to restructure the hash table by picking a larger value for B and then inserting each of the elements into the new table. It takes $O(n)$ time to do so, but that time is no greater than the $O(n)$ time that must be spent inserting the n elements into the hash table in the first place. (Note that n insertions, at $O(1)$ average time per insertion, require $O(n)$ time in all.)

EXERCISES

7.6.1: Continue filling the hash table of Fig. 7.13 with the words `with up so floating many bells down`.

7.6.2*: Comment on how effective the following hash functions would be at dividing typical sets of English words into buckets of roughly equal size:

a) Use $B = 10$, and let $h(x)$ be the remainder when the length of the word x is divided by 10.

b) Use $B = 128$, and let $h(x)$ be the integer value of the last character of x.

c) Use $B = 10$. Take the sum of the values of the characters in x. Square the result, and take the remainder when divided by 10.

7.6.3: Write C programs for performing (a) *delete* and (b) *lookup* in a hash table, using the same assumptions as for the code in Fig. 7.14.

❖❖ 7.7 Relations and Functions

While we have generally assumed that elements of sets are atomic, in practice it is often useful to give elements some structure. For example, in the previous section we talked about elements that were character strings of length 32. Another important structure for elements is fixed-length lists, which are similar to C structures. Lists used as set elements will be called *tuples*, and each list element is called a *component* of the tuple.

Tuple, component

The number of components a tuple has is called its *arity*. For example, (a, b) is a tuple of arity 2; its first component is a and its second component is b. A tuple of arity k is also called a *k-tuple*.

Arity: unary, binary

A set of elements, each of which is a tuple of the same arity, — say, k — is called a *relation*. The arity of this relation is k. A tuple or relation of arity 1 is *unary*. If the arity is 2, it is *binary*, and in general, if the arity is k, then the tuple or relation is *k-ary*.

✦ **Example 7.17.** The relation $R = \{(1, 2),\ (1, 3),\ (2, 2)\}$ is a relation of arity 2, or a binary relation. Its members are $(1, 2)$, $(1, 3)$, and $(2, 2)$, each of which is a tuple of arity 2. ✦

In this section, we shall consider primarily binary relations. There are also many important applications of nonbinary relations, especially in representing and manipulating tabular data (as in relational databases). We shall discuss this topic extensively in Chapter 8.

Cartesian Products

Before studying binary relations formally, we need to define another operator on sets. Let A and B be two sets. Then the *product* of A and B, denoted $A \times B$, is defined as the set of pairs in which the first component is chosen from A and the second component from B. That is,

$$A \times B = \{(a, b) \mid a \in A \text{ and } b \in B\}$$

The product is sometimes called the *Cartesian* product, after the French mathematician René Descartes.

✦ **Example 7.18.** Recall that $\mathbf{Z}$ is the conventional symbol for the set of all integers. Thus, $\mathbf{Z} \times \mathbf{Z}$ stands for the set of pairs of integers.

As another example, if A is the two-element set $\{1, 2\}$ and B is the three-element set $\{a, b, c\}$, then $A \times B$ is the six-element set

$$\{(1, a),\ (1, b),\ (1, c),\ (2, a),\ (2, b),\ (2, c)\}$$

Note that the product of sets is aptly named, because if A and B are finite sets, then the number of elements in $A \times B$ is the product of the number of elements in A and the number of elements in B. ✦

Cartesian Product of More Than Two Sets

Unlike the arithmetic product, the Cartesian product does not have the common properties of commutativity or associativity. It is easy to find examples where

$$A \times B \neq B \times A$$

disproving commutativity. The associative law does not even make sense, because $(A \times B) \times C$ would have as members pairs like $\big((a, b), c\big)$, while members of $A \times (B \times C)$ would be pairs of the form $\big(a, (b, c)\big)$.

k-way product
of sets

Since we shall need on several occasions to talk about sets of tuples with more than two components, we need to extend the product notation to a k-way product. We let $A_1 \times A_2 \times \cdots \times A_k$ stand for the *product* of sets $A_1, A_2, \ldots, A_k$, that is, the set of k-tuples $(a_1, a_2, \ldots, a_k)$ such that $a_1 \in A_1$, $a_2 \in A_2, \ldots$, and $a_k \in A_k$.

✦ **Example 7.19.** $\mathbf{Z} \times \mathbf{Z} \times \mathbf{Z}$ represents the set of triples of integers (i, j, k) — it contains, for example, the triple $(1, 2, 3)$. This three-way product should not be confused with $(\mathbf{Z} \times \mathbf{Z}) \times \mathbf{Z}$, which represents pairs like $((1, 2), 3)$, or $\mathbf{Z} \times (\mathbf{Z} \times \mathbf{Z})$, which represents pairs like $(1, (2, 3))$.

On the other hand, note that all three product expressions can be represented by structures consisting of three integer fields. The distinction is in how one interprets the structures of this type. Thus, we often feel free to "confuse" parenthesized and unparenthesized product expressions. Similarly, the three C type declarations

```
struct {int f1; int f2; int f3;};
struct {struct {int f1; int f2;}; int f3;};
struct {int f1; struct {int f2; int f3;};};
```

would all be stored in a similar way — only the notation for accessing fields would differ. ✦

Binary Relations

A binary relation R is a set of pairs that is a subset of the product of two sets A and B. If a relation R is a subset of $A \times B$, we say that R is *from A to B*. We call *Domain, range* A the *domain* and B the *range* of the relation. If B is the same as A, we say that R is a relation *on* A or "on the domain" A.

✦ **Example 7.20.** The arithmetic relation $<$ on integers is a subset of $\mathbf{Z} \times \mathbf{Z}$, consisting of those pairs (a, b) such that a is less than b. Thus, the symbol $<$ may be regarded as the name of the set

$$\{(a, b) \mid (a, b) \in \mathbf{Z} \times \mathbf{Z}, \text{ and } a \text{ is less than } b\}$$

We then use $a < b$ as a shorthand for "$(a, b) \in <$," or "(a, b) is a member of the relation $<$." The other arithmetic relations on integers, such as $>$ or $\leq$, can be defined similarly, as can the arithmetic comparisons on real numbers.

For another example, consider the relation R from Example 7.17. Its domain and range are uncertain. We know that 1 and 2 must be in the domain, because these integers appear as first components of tuples in R. Similarly, we know that the range of R must include 2 and 3. However, we could regard R as a relation from $\{1, 2\}$ to $\{2, 3\}$, or as a relation from $\mathbf{Z}$ to $\mathbf{Z}$, as two examples among an infinity of choices. ✦

Infix Notation for Relations

As we suggested in Example 7.20, it is common to use an infix notation for binary relations, so that a relation like $<$, which is really a set of pairs, can be written between the components of pairs in the relation. That is why we commonly find expressions like $1 < 2$ and $4 \geq 4$, rather than the more pedantic "$(1, 2) \in <$" or "$(4, 4) \in \geq$."

✦ **Example 7.21.** The same notation can be used for arbitrary binary relations. For instance, the relation R from Example 7.17 can be written as the three "facts" $1R2$, $1R3$, and $2R2$. ✦

Declared and Current Domains and Ranges

The second part of Example 7.20 underscores the point that we cannot tell the domain or range of a relation just by looking at it. Surely the set of elements appearing in first components must be a subset of the domain, and the set of elements that occur in second components must be a subset of the range. However, there could be other elements in the domain or range.

The difference is not important when a relation does not change. However, we shall see in Sections 7.8 and 7.9, and also in Chapter 8, that relations whose values change are very important. For example, we might speak of a relation whose domain is the students in a class, and whose range is integers, representing total scores on homework. Before the class starts, there are no pairs in this relation. After the first assignment is graded, there is one pair for each student. As time goes on, students drop the class or are added to the class, and scores increase.

Current domain, range

Declared domain, range

We could define the domain of this relation to be the set of all students registered at the university and the range to be the set of integers. Surely, at any time, the value of the relation is a subset of the Cartesian product of these two sets. On the other hand, at any time, the relation has a *current domain* and a *current range*, which are the sets of elements appearing in first and second components, respectively, of the pairs in the relation. When we need to make a distinction, we can call the domain and range the *declared* domain and range. The current domain and range will always be a subset of the declared domain and range, respectively.

Graphs for Binary Relations

We can represent a relation R whose domain is A and whose range is B by a graph. We draw a node for each element that is in A and/or B. If aRb, then we draw an arrow ("arc") from a to b. (General graphs are discussed in more detail in Chapter 9.)

✦ **Example 7.22.** The graph for the relation R from Example 7.17 is shown in Fig. 7.15. It has nodes for the elements 1, 2, and 3. Since $1R2$, there is an arc from node 1 to node 2. Since $1R3$, there is an arc from 1 to 3, and since $2R2$, there is an arc from node 2 to itself. There are no other arcs, because there are no other pairs in R. ✦

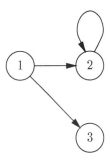

Fig. 7.15. Graph for the relation $\{(1,2),\ (1,3),\ (2,2)\}$.

Functions

Suppose a relation R, from domain A to range B, has the property that for every member a of A there is at most one element b in B such that aRb. Then R is said **Partial function** to be a *partial function from domain A to range B*.

Total function If for every member a of A there is exactly one element b in B such that aRb, then R is said to be a *total function* from A to B. The difference between a partial function and a total function is that a partial function can be undefined on some elements of its domain; for example, for some a in A, there may be no b in B such that aRb. We shall use the term "function" to refer to the more general notion of a partial function, but whenever the distinction between a partial function and a total function is important, we shall use the word "partial."

There a common notation used to describe functions. We often write $R(a) = b$ if b is the unique element such that aRb.

◆ **Example 7.23.** Let S be the total function from $\mathbf{Z}$ to $\mathbf{Z}$ given by

$$\{(a, b) \mid b = a^2\}$$

that is, the set of pairs of integers whose second component is the square of the first component. Then S has such members as $(3, 9)$, $(-4, 16)$, and $(0, 0)$. We can express the fact that S is the squaring function by writing $S(3) = 9$, $S(-4) = 16$, and $S(0) = 0$. ◆

Notice that the set-theoretic notion of a function is not much different from the notion of a function that we encountered in C. That is, suppose **s** is a C function declared as

```
int s(int a)
{
    return a*a;
}
```

that takes an integer and returns its square. We usually think of **s(a)** as being the same function as $S(a)$, although the former is a way to compute squares and the latter only defines the operation of squaring abstractly. Also note that in practice **s(a)** is always a partial function, since there are many values of **a** for which **s(a)** will not return an integer because of the finiteness of computer arithmetic.

C has functions that take more than one parameter. A C function **f** that takes two integer parameters **a** and **b**, returning an integer, is a function from $\mathbf{Z} \times \mathbf{Z}$ to $\mathbf{Z}$. Similarly, if the two parameters are of types that make them belong to sets A and B, respectively, and **f** returns a member of type C, then **f** is a function from $A \times B$ to C. More generally, if **f** takes k parameters — say, from sets $A_1, A_2, \ldots, A_k$, respectively — and returns a member of set B, then we say that **f** is a function from $A_1 \times A_2 \times \cdots \times A_k$ to B.

For example, we can regard the function **lookup(x,L)** from Section 6.4 as a function from $\mathbf{Z} \times L$ to $\{\text{TRUE}, \text{FALSE}\}$. Here, L is the set of linked lists of integers.

Formally, a function from domain $A_1 \times \cdots \times A_k$ to range B is a set of pairs of the form $\big((a_1, \ldots, a_k), b\big)$, where each a_i is in set A_i and b is in B. Notice that the first element of the pair is itself a k-tuple. For example, the function **lookup(x,L)** discussed above can be thought of as the set of pairs $\big((x, L), t\big)$, where x is an

The Many Notations for Functions

A function F from, say, $A \times B$ to C is technically a subset of $(A \times B) \times C$. A typical pair in the function F would thus have the form $((a, b), c)$, where a, b, and c are members of A, B, and C, respectively. Using the special notation for functions, we can write $F(a, b) = c$.

We can also view F as a relation from $A \times B$ to C, since every function is a relation. Using the infix notation for relations, the fact that $((a, b), c)$ is in F could also be written $(a, b)Fc$.

When we extend the Cartesian product to more than two sets, we may wish to remove parentheses from product expressions. Thus, we might identify $(A \times B) \times C$ with the technically inequivalent expression $A \times B \times C$. In that case, a typical member of F could be written (a, b, c). If we stored F as a set of such triples, we would have to remember that the first two components together make up the domain element and the third component is the range element.

---

integer, L is a list of integers, and t is either **TRUE** or **FALSE**, depending on whether x is or is not on the list L. We can think of a function, whether written in C or as formally defined in set theory, as a box that takes a value from the domain set and produces a value from the range set, as suggested in Fig. 7.16 for the function **lookup**.

Fig. 7.16. A function associates elements from the domain
with unique elements from the range.

One-to-One Correspondences

Let F be a partial function from domain A to range B with the following properties:

1. For every element a in A, there is an element b in B such that $F(a) = b$.

2. For every b in B, there is some a in A such that $F(a) = b$.

3. For no b in B are there two elements a_1 and a_2 in A such that $F(a_1)$ and $F(a_2)$ are both b.

Then F is said to be a *one-to-one correspondence* from A to B. The term *bijection* is also used for a one-to-one correspondence.

Property (1) says that F is a total function from A to B. Property (2) is the condition of being *onto*: F is a total function from A onto B. Some mathematicians **Surjection** use the term *surjection* for a total function that is onto.

Properties (2) and (3) together say that F behaves like a total function from **Injection** B to A. A total function with property (3) is sometimes called an *injection*.

A one-to-one correspondence is basically a total function in both directions, but it is important to observe that whether F is a one-to-one correspondence depends not only on the pairs in F, but on the declared domain and range. For example, we could take any one-to-one correspondence from A to B and change the domain by adding to A some new element e not mentioned in F. F would not be a one-to-one correspondence from $A \cup \{e\}$ to B.

Example 7.24. The squaring function S from $\mathbf{Z}$ to $\mathbf{Z}$ of Example 7.23 is not a one-to-one correspondence. It does satisfy property (1), since for every integer i there is some integer, namely, i^2, such that $S(i) = i^2$. However, it fails to satisfy (2), since there are some b's in $\mathbf{Z}$ — in particular all the negative integers — that are not $S(a)$ for any a. S also fails to satisfy (3), since there are many examples of two distinct a's for which $S(a)$ equals the same b. For instance, $S(3) = 9$ and $S(-3) = 9$.

For an example of a one-to-one correspondence, consider the total function P from $\mathbf{Z}$ to $\mathbf{Z}$ defined by $P(a) = a+1$. That is, P adds 1 to any integer. For instance, $P(5) = 6$, and $P(-5) = -4$. An alternative way to look at the situation is that P consists of the tuples

$$\{ \ldots, \ (-2,-1), \ (-1,0), \ (0,1), \ (1,2), \ldots \}$$

or that it has the graph of Fig. 7.17.

We claim that P is a one-to-one correspondence from integers to integers. First, it is a partial function, since when we add 1 to an integer a we get the unique integer $a+1$. It satisfies property (1), since for every integer a, there is some integer $a+1$, which is $P(a)$. Property (2) is also satisfied, since for every integer b there is some integer, namely, $b-1$, such that $P(b-1) = b$. Finally, property (3) is satisfied, because for an integer b there cannot be two distinct integers such that when you add 1 to either, the result is b. ◆

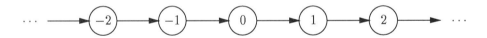

Fig. 7.17. Graph for the relation that is the function $P(a) = a + 1$.

A one-to-one correspondence from A to B is a way of establishing a unique association between the elements of A and B. For example, if we clap our hands together, the left and right thumbs touch, the left and right index fingers touch, and so on. We can think of this association between the set of fingers on the left hand and the fingers on the right hand as a one-to-one correspondence F, defined by $F(\text{"left thumb"}) = \text{"right thumb"}$, $F(\text{"left index finger"}) = \text{"right index finger"}$, and so on. We could similarly think of the association as the inverse function, from the right hand to the left. In general, a one-to-one correspondence from A to B can be inverted by switching the order of components in its pairs, to become a one-to-one correspondence from B to A.

A consequence of the existence of this one-to-one correspondence between hands is that the number of fingers on each hand is the same. That seems a natural and intuitive notion; two sets have the same number of elements exactly when there is a one-to-one correspondence from one set to the other. However, we shall see in Section 7.11 that when sets are infinite, there are some surprising conclusions we are forced to draw from this definition of "same number of elements."

EXERCISES

7.7.1: Give an example of sets A and B for which $A \times B$ is not the same as $B \times A$.

7.7.2: Let R be the relation defined by aRb, bRc, cRd, aRc, and bRd.

a) Draw the graph of R.
b) Is R a function?
c) Name two possible domains for R; name two possible ranges.
d) What is the smallest set S such that R is a relation on S (i.e., the domain and the range can both be S)?

7.7.3: Let T be a tree and let S be the set of nodes of T. Let R be the "child-parent" relation; that is, cRp if and only if c is a child of p. Answer the following, and justify your answers:

a) Is R a partial function, no matter what tree T is?
b) Is R a total function from S to S no matter what T is?
c) Can R ever be a one-to-one correspondence (i.e., for some tree T)?
d) What does the graph for R look like?

7.7.4: Let R be the relation on the set of integers $\{1, 2, \ldots, 10\}$ defined by aRb if a and b are distinct and have a common divisor other than 1. For example, $2R4$ and $6R9$, but not $2R3$.

a) Draw the graph for R.
b) Is R a function? Why or why not?

7.7.5*: Although we observed that $S = (A \times B) \times C$ and $T = A \times (B \times C)$ are not the same set, we can show that they are "essentially the same" by exhibiting a natural one-to-one correspondence between them. For each $((a, b), c)$ in S, let

$$F\Big(\big((a, b), c\big)\Big) = \big(a, (b, c)\big)$$

Show that F is a one-to-one correspondence from S to T.

7.7.6: What do the three statements $F(10) = 20$, $10F20$, and $(10, 20) \in F$ have in common?

Inverse relation **7.7.7***: The *inverse* of a relation R is the set of pairs (b, a) such that (a, b) is in R.

a) Explain how to get the graph of the inverse of R from the graph for R.
b) If R is a total function, is the inverse of R necessarily a function? What if R is a one-to-one correspondence?

7.7.8: Show that a relation is a one-to-one correspondence if and only if it is a total function and its inverse is also a total function.

✦✧ 7.8 Implementing Functions as Data

In a programming language, functions are usually implemented by code, but when their domain is small, they can be implemented using techniques quite similar to the ones we used for sets. In this section we shall discuss the use of linked lists, characteristic vectors, and hash tables to implement finite functions.

Functions as Programs and Functions as Data

While we drew a strong analogy in Section 7.7 between the abstract notion of a function and a function as implemented in C, we should also be aware of an important difference. If F is a C function and x a member of its domain set, then F tells us how to compute the value $F(x)$. The same program works for any value x.

However, when we represent functions as data, we require, first of all, that the function consists of a finite set of pairs. Second, it is normal that the pairs are essentially unpredictable. That is, there is no convenient way to compute, given x, the value $F(x)$. The best we can do is create a table giving each of the pairs

$$(a_1, b_1), \ (a_2, b_2), \ldots, (a_n, b_n)$$

such that $F(a_i) = b_i$. Such a function is effectively data, rather than a program, even though we could, in principle, create a program that could store the table as part of itself and from the internal table look up $F(x)$, given x. However, a more productive approach is to store the table separately as data and look up values by a general-purpose algorithm that will work for any such function.

Operations on Functions

The operations we most commonly perform on functions are similar to those for dictionaries. Suppose F is a function from domain set A to range set B. Then we may

1. *Insert* a new pair (a, b), such that $F(a) = b$. The only nuance is that, since F must be a function, should there already be a pair (a, c) for any c, this pair must be replaced by (a, b).

2. *Delete* the value associated with $F(a)$. Here, we need to give only the domain value a. If there is any b such that $F(a) = b$, the pair (a, b) is removed from the set. If there is no such pair, then no change is made.

3. *Lookup* the value associated with $F(a)$; that is, given domain value a, we return the value b such that $F(a) = b$. If there is no such pair (a, b) in the set, then we return some special value warning that $F(a)$ is undefined.

✦ **Example 7.25.** Suppose F consists of the pairs $\{(3, 9), \ (-4, 16), \ (0, 0)\}$; that is, $F(3) = 9$; $F(-4) = 16$, and $F(0) = 0$. Then *lookup*(3) returns 9, and *lookup*(2) returns a value indicating that no value is defined for $F(2)$. If F is the "squaring" function, the value -1 might be used to indicate a missing value, since -1 is not the true square of any integer.

The operation *delete*(3) removes the pair $(3, 9)$, while *delete*(2) has no effect. If we execute *insert*(5, 25), the pair $(5, 25)$ is added to the set F, or equivalently, we now have $F(5) = 25$. If we execute *insert*(3, 10), the old pair $(3, 9)$ is removed from F, and the new pair $(3, 10)$ is added to F, so that now $F(3) = 10$. ✦

Linked-List Representation of Functions

A function, being a set of pairs, can be stored in a linked list just like any other set. It is useful to define cells with three fields, one for the domain value, one for the range value, and one for a next-cell pointer. For example, we could define cells as

```
typedef struct CELL *LIST;
struct CELL {
    DTYPE domain;
    RTYPE range;
    LIST next;
};
```

where DTYPE is the type for domain elements and RTYPE is the type for range elements. Then a function is represented by a pointer to (the first cell of) a linked list.

The function in Fig. 7.18 performs the operation $insert(a, b, L)$, assuming that DTYPE and RTYPE are both arrays of 32 characters. We search for a cell containing a in the domain field. If found, we set its range field to b. If we reach the end of the list, we create a new cell and store (a, b) therein. Otherwise, we test whether the cell has domain element a. If so, we change the range value to b, and we are done. If the domain has a value other than a, then we recursively insert into the tail of the list.

```
typedef char DTYPE[32], RTYPE[32];

void insert(DTYPE a, RTYPE b, LIST *pL)
{
    if ((*pL) == NULL) {/* at end of list */
        (*pL) = (LIST) malloc(sizeof(struct CELL));
        strcpy((*pL)->domain, a);
        strcpy((*pL)->range, b);
        (*pL)->next = NULL;
    }
    else if (!strcmp(a, (*pL)->domain)) /* a = domain element;
            change F(a) */
        strcpy((*pL)->range, b);
    else /* domain element is not a */
        insert(a, b, &((*pL)->next));
};
```

Fig. 7.18. Inserting a new fact into a function represented as a linked list.

If the function F has n pairs, then *insert* takes $O(n)$ time on the average. Likewise, the analogous *delete* and *lookup* functions for a function represented as a linked list require $O(n)$ time on the average.

Vector Representation of Functions

Suppose the declared domain is the integers 0 through $DNUM - 1$, or it can be regarded as such, perhaps by being an enumeration type. Then we can use a generalization of a characteristic vector to represent functions. Define a type FUNCT for the characteristic vector as

```
typedef RTYPE FUNCT[DNUM];
```

Here it is essential that either the function be total or that RTYPE contain a value that we can interpret as "no value."

✦ **Example 7.26.** Suppose we want to store information about apples, like the harvest information of Fig. 7.9, but we now want to give the actual month of harvest, rather than the binary choice early/late. We can associate an integer constant with each element in the domain and range by defining the enumeration types

```
enum APPLES {Delicious, GrannySmith, Jonathan, McIntosh,
            Gravenstein, Pippin};
enum MONTHS {Unknown, Jan, Feb, Mar, Apr, May, Jun, Jul, Aug,
            Sep, Oct, Nov, Dec};
```

This declaration associates 0 with the identifier Delicious, 1 with GrannySmith, and so on. It also associates 0 with Unknown, 1 with Jan, and so on. The identifier Unknown indicates that the harvest month is not known. We can now declare an array

```
int Harvest[6];
```

with the intention that the array Harvest represents the set of pairs in Fig. 7.19. Then the array Harvest appears as in Fig. 7.20, where, for example, the entry Harvest[Delicious] = Oct means Harvest[0] = 10. ✦

APPLE	HARVEST MONTH
Delicious	Oct
Granny Smith	Aug
Jonathan	Sep
McIntosh	Oct
Gravenstein	Sep
Pippin	Nov

Fig. 7.19. Harvest months of apples.

Hash-Table Representation of Functions

We can store the pairs belonging to a function in a hash table. The crucial point is that we apply the hash function only to the domain element to determine the bucket of the pair. The cells in the linked lists forming the buckets have one field for the domain element, another for the corresponding range element, and a third to link one cell to the next on the list. An example should make the technique clear.

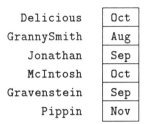

Delicious	Oct
GrannySmith	Aug
Jonathan	Sep
McIntosh	Oct
Gravenstein	Sep
Pippin	Nov

Fig. 7.20. The array Harvest.

◆   **Example 7.27.** Let us use the same data about apples that appeared in Example 7.26, except now we shall use the actual names rather than integers to represent the domain. To represent the function Harvest, we shall use a hash table with five buckets. We shall define APPLES to be 32-character arrays, while MONTHS is an enumeration as in Example 7.26. The buckets are linked lists with field **variety** for a domain element of type APPLES, field **harvested** for a range element of type **int** (a month), and a link field **next** to the next element of the list.

We shall use a hash function h similar to that shown in Fig. 7.11 of Section 7.6. Of course, h is applied to domain elements only — that is, to character strings of length 32, consisting of the name of an apple variety.

Now, we can define the type HASHTABLE as an array of B LIST's. B is the number of buckets, which we have taken to be 5. All these declarations appear in the beginning of Fig. 7.22. We may then declare a hash table **Harvest** to represent the desired function.

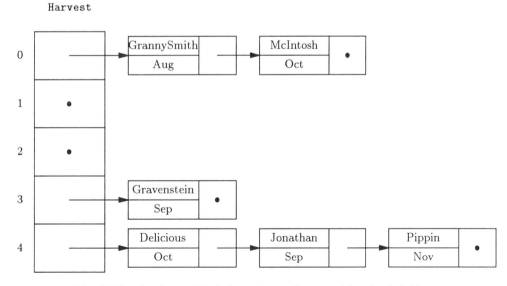

Fig. 7.21. Apples and their harvest months stored in a hash table.

After inserting the six apple varieties listed in Fig. 7.19, the arrangement of cells within buckets is shown in Fig. 7.21. For example, the word **Delicious** yields the sum 929 if we add up the integer values of the nine characters. Since the remainder when 929 is divided by 5 is 4, the Delicious apple belongs in bucket 4. The cell for Delicious has that string in the **variety** field, the month **Oct** in the **harvested** field, and a pointer to the next cell of the bucket. ✦

```
#include <string.h>
#define B 5

typedef char APPLES[32];
enum MONTHS {Unknown, Jan, Feb, Mar, Apr, May, Jun, Jul, Aug,
            Sep, Oct, Nov, Dec};
typedef struct CELL *LIST;
struct CELL {
    APPLES variety;
    int harvested;
    LIST next;
};
typedef LIST HASHTABLE[B];

int lookupBucket(APPLES a, LIST L)
{
    if (L == NULL)
        return Unknown;
    if (!strcmp(a, L->variety)) /* found */
        return L->harvested;
    else /* a not found; examine tail */
        return lookupBucket(a, L->next);
}

int lookup(APPLES a, HASHTABLE H)
{
    return lookupBucket(a, H[h(a)]);
}
```

Fig. 7.22. Lookup for a function represented by a hash table.

Operations on Functions Represented by a Hash Table

Each of the operations *insert*, *delete*, and *lookup* start with a domain value that we hash to find a bucket. To insert the pair (a, b), we find the bucket $h(a)$ and search its list. The action is then the same as the function to insert a function pair into a list, given in Fig. 7.18.

To execute *delete(a)*, we find bucket $h(a)$, search for a cell with domain value a, and delete that cell from the list, when and if it is found. The *lookup(a)* operation is executed by again hashing a and searching the bucket $h(a)$ for a cell with domain value a. If such a cell is found, the associated range value is returned.

For example, the function **lookup(a, H)** is shown in Fig. 7.22. The function **lookupBucket(a, L)** runs down the list L for a bucket and returns the value

$$harvested(a)$$

Vectors versus Hash Tables

There is a fundamental difference in the way we viewed the information about apples in Examples 7.26 and 7.27. In the characteristic-vector approach, apple varieties were a fixed set, which became an enumerated type. There is no way, while a C program is running, to change the set of apple names, and it is meaningless to perform a lookup with a name that is not part of our enumerated set.

On the other hand, when we set the same function up as a hash table, we treated the apple names as character strings, rather than members of an enumerated type. As a consequence, it is possible to modify the set of names while the program is running — say, in response to some input data about new apple varieties. It makes sense for a lookup to be performed for a variety not in the hash table, and we had to make provisions, by the addition of a "month" Unknown, for the possibility that we would look up a variety that was not mentioned in our table. Thus, the hash table offers increased flexibility over the characteristic vector, at some cost in speed.

that is, the month in which apple variety a is harvested. If the month is undefined, it returns the value Unknown.

Efficiency of Operations on Functions

The times required for the operations on functions for the three representations we have discussed here are the same as for the operations of the same names on dictionaries. That is, if the function consists of n pairs, then the linked-list representation requires $O(n)$ time per operation on the average. The characteristic-vector approach requires only $O(1)$ time per operation, but, as for dictionaries, it can be used only if the domain type is of limited size. The hash table with B buckets offers average time per operation of $O(n/B)$. If it is possible to make B close to n, then $O(1)$ time per operation, on the average, can be achieved.

EXERCISES

7.8.1: Write functions that perform (a) *delete* and (b) *lookup* on functions represented by linked lists, analogous to the *insert* function of Fig. 7.18.

7.8.2: Write functions that perform (a) *insert*, (b) *delete*, and (c) *lookup* on a function represented by a vector, that is, an array of RTYPE's indexed by integers representing DTYPE's.

7.8.3: Write functions that perform (a) *insert* and (b) *delete* on functions represented by hash tables, analogous to the *lookup* function of Fig. 7.22.

7.8.4: A binary search tree can also be used to represent functions as data. Define appropriate data structures for a binary search tree to hold the apple information in Fig. 7.19, and implement (a) *insert*, (b) *delete*, and (c) *lookup* using these structures.

7.8.5: Design an information retrieval system to keep track of information about at bats and hits for baseball players. Your system should accept triples of the form

Ruth 5 2

to indicate that Ruth in 5 at bats got 2 hits. The entry for Ruth should be updated appropriately. You should also be able to query the number of at bats and hits for any player. Implement your system so that the functions *insert* and *lookup* will work on any data structure as long as they use the proper subroutines and types.

✦✦ 7.9 Implementing Binary Relations

The implementation of binary relations differs in some details from the implementation of functions. Recall that both binary relations and functions are sets of pairs, but a function has for each domain element a at most one pair of the form (a, b) for any b. In contrast, a binary relation can have any number of range elements associated with a given domain element a.

In this section, we shall first consider the meaning of insertion, deletion, and lookup for binary relations. Then we see how the three implementations we have been using — linked lists, characteristic vectors, and hash tables — generalize to binary relations. In Chapter 8, we shall discuss implementation of relations with more than two components. Frequently, data structures for such relations are built from the structures for functions and binary relations.

Operations on Binary Relations

When we insert a pair (a, b) into a binary relation R, we do not have to concern ourselves with whether or not there already is a pair (a, c) in R, for some $c \neq b$, as we do when we insert (a, b) into a function. The reason, of course, is that there is no limit on the number of pairs in R that can have the domain value a. Thus, we shall simply insert the pair (a, b) into R as we would insert an element into any set.

Likewise, deletion of a pair (a, b) from a relation is similar to deletion of an element from a set: we look for the pair and remove it if it is present.

The *lookup* operation can be defined in several ways. For example, we could take a pair (a, b) and ask whether this pair is in R. However, if we interpret *lookup* thus, along with the *insert* and *delete* operations we just defined, a relation behaves like any dictionary. The fact that the elements being operated upon are pairs, rather than atomic, is a minor detail; it just affects the type of elements in the dictionary.

However, it is often useful to define *lookup* to take a domain element a and return all the range elements b such that (a, b) is in the binary relation R. This interpretation of *lookup* gives us an abstract data type that is somewhat different from the dictionary, and it has certain uses that are distinct from those of the dictionary ADT.

✦ **Example 7.28.** Most varieties of plums require one of several other specific varieties for pollination; without the appropriate "pollinizer," the tree cannot bear fruit. A few varieties are "self-fertile": they can serve as their own pollinizer. Figure 7.23 shows a binary relation on the set of plum varieties. A pair (a, b) in this relation means that variety b is a pollinizer for variety a.

Inserting a pair into this table corresponds to asserting that one variety is a pollinizer for another. For example, if a new variety is developed, we might enter into the relation facts about which varieties pollinize the new variety, and which it

VARIETY	POLLINIZER
Beauty	Santa Rosa
Santa Rosa	Santa Rosa
Burbank	Beauty
Burbank	Santa Rosa
Eldorado	Santa Rosa
Eldorado	Wickson
Wickson	Santa Rosa
Wickson	Beauty

Fig. 7.23. Pollinizers for certain plum varieties.

More General Operations on Relations

We may want more information than the three operations *insert*, *delete*, and *lookup* can provide when applied to the plum varieties of Example 7.28. For example, we may want to ask "What varieties does Santa Rosa pollinate?" or "Does Eldorado pollinate Beauty?" Some data structures, such as a linked list, allow us to answer questions like these as fast as we can perform the three basic dictionary operations, if for no other reason than that linked lists are not very efficient for any of these operations.

A hash table based on domain elements does not help answer questions in which we are given a range element and must find all the associated domain elements — for instance, "What varieties does Santa Rosa pollinate?" We could, of course, base the hash function on range elements, but then we could not answer easily questions like "What pollinates Burbank?" We could base the hash function on a combination of the domain and range values, but then we couldn't answer either type of query efficiently; we could only answer easily questions like "Does Eldorado pollinate Beauty?"

There are ways to get questions of all these types answered efficiently. We shall have to wait, however, until the next chapter, on the relational model, to learn the techniques.

can pollinize. Deletion of a pair corresponds to a retraction of the assertion that one variety can pollinize another.

The lookup operation we defined takes a variety a as argument, looks in the first column for all pairs having the value a, and returns the set of associated range values. That is, we ask, "What varieties can pollinize variety a?" This question seems to be the one we are most likely to ask about the information in this table, because when we plant a plum tree, we must make sure that, if it is not self-fertile, then there is a pollinizer nearby. For instance, if we invoke *lookup*(Burbank), we expect the answer {Beauty, Santa Rosa}. ◆

Linked-List Implementation of Binary Relations

We can link the pairs of a relation in a list if we like. The cells of this list consist of a domain element, a range element, and a pointer to the next cell, just like the cells for functions. Insertion and deletion are carried out as for ordinary sets, as discussed in Section 6.4. The only nuance is that equality of set members is determined by comparing both the field holding the domain element and the field holding the range element.

Lookup is a somewhat different operation from the operations of the same name we have encountered previously. We must go down the list, looking for cells with a particular domain value a, and we must assemble a list of the associated range values. An example will show the mechanics of the *lookup* operation on linked lists.

✦ **Example 7.29.** Suppose we want to implement the plum relation of Example 7.28 as a linked list. We could define the type **PVARIETY** as a character string of length 32; and cells, whose type we shall call **RCELL** (relation cell), can be defined by a structure:

```
typedef char PVARIETY[32];
typedef struct RCELL *RLIST;
struct RCELL {
    PVARIETY variety;
    PVARIETY pollinizer;
    RLIST next;
};
```

We also need a cell containing one plum variety and a pointer to the next cell, in order to build a list of the pollinizers of a given variety, and thus to answer a *lookup* query. This type we shall call **PCELL**, and we define

```
typedef struct PCELL *PLIST;
struct PCELL {
    PVARIETY pollinizer;
    PLIST next;
};
```

We can then define *lookup* by the function in Fig. 7.24.

The function *lookup* takes a domain element a and a pointer to the first cell of a linked list of pairs as arguments. We perform the *lookup*(a) operation on a relation R by calling **lookup(a,L)**, where L is a pointer to the first cell on the linked list representing relation R. Lines (1) and (2) are simple. If the list is empty, we return **NULL**, since surely there are no pairs with first component a in an empty list.

The hard case occurs when a is found in the domain field, called **variety**, in the first cell of the list. This case is detected at line (3) and handled by lines (4) through (7). We create at line (4) a new cell of type **PCELL**, which becomes the first cell on the list of **PCELL**'s that we shall return. Line (5) copies the associated range value into this new cell. Then at line (6) we call **lookup** recursively on the tail of the list L. The return value from this call, which is a pointer to the first cell on the resulting list (**NULL** if the list is empty), becomes the **next** field of the cell we created at line (4). Then at line (7) we return a pointer to the newly created cell, which holds one range value and is linked to cells holding other range values for domain value a, if any exist.

The last case occurs when the desired domain value a is not found in the first cell of the list L. Then we just call *lookup* on the tail of the list, at line (8), and

```
        PLIST lookup(PVARIETY a, RLIST L)
        {
            PLIST P;

(1)         if (L == NULL)
(2)             return NULL;
(3)         else if (!strcmp(L->variety, a)) /* L->variety == a */ {
(4)             P = (PLIST) malloc(sizeof(struct PCELL));
(5)             strcpy(P->pollinizer, L->pollinizer);
(6)             P->next = lookup(a, L->next);
(7)             return P;
            }
            else /* a not the domain value of current pair */
(8)             return lookup(a, L->next);
        }
```

Fig. 7.24. Lookup in a binary relation represented by a linked list.

return whatever that call returns. ✦

A Characteristic-Vector Approach

For sets and for functions, we saw that we could create an array indexed by elements of a "universal" set and place appropriate values in the array. For sets, the appropriate array values are **TRUE** and **FALSE**, and for functions they are those values that can appear in the range, plus (usually) a special value that means "none."

For binary relations, we can index an array by members of a small declared domain, just as we did for functions. However, we cannot use a single value as an array element, because a relation can have any number of range values for a given domain value. The best we can do is to use as an array element the header of a linked list that contains all the range values associated with a given domain value.

✦ **Example 7.30.** Let us redo the plum example using this organization. As was pointed out in the last section, when we use a characteristic-vector style, we must fix the set of values, in the domain at least; there is no such constraint for linked-list or hash-table representations. Thus, we must redeclare the **PVARIETY** type to be an enumerated type:

```
        enum PVARIETY {Beauty, SantaRosa, Burbank, Eldorado, Wickson};
```

We can continue to use the **PCELL** type for lists of varieties, as defined in Example 7.29. Then we may define the array

```
        PLIST Pollinizers[5];
```

That is, the array representing the relation of Fig. 7.23 is indexed by the varieties mentioned in that figure, and the value associated with each variety is a pointer to the first cell on its list of pollinizers. Figure 7.25 shows the pairs of Fig. 7.23 represented in this way. ✦

Pollinizers

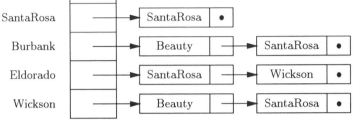

Fig. 7.25. Characteristic-vector representation of the pollinizers relation.

Insertion and deletion of pairs is performed by going to the appropriate array element and thence to the linked list. At that point, insertion in or deletion from the list is performed normally. For example, if we determined that Wickson cannot adequately pollinate Eldorado, we could execute the operation

delete(Eldorado, Wickson)

The header of the list for Eldorado is found in `Pollinizers[Eldorado]`, and from there we go down the list until we find a cell holding Wickson and delete it.

Lookup is trivial; we have only to return the pointer found in the appropriate array entry. For example, to answer the query `lookup(Burbank, Pollinizers)`, we simply return the list `Pollinizers[Burbank]`.

Hash-Table Implementation of Binary Relations

We may store a given binary relation R in a hash table, using a hash function that depends only on the first component of a pair. That is, the pair (a, b) will be placed in bucket $h(a)$, where h is the hash function. Note that this arrangement is exactly the same as that for a function; the only difference is that for a binary relation a bucket may contain more than one pair with a given value a as the first component, whereas for a function, it could never contain more than one such pair.

To insert the pair (a, b), we compute $h(a)$ and examine the bucket with that number to be sure that (a, b) is not already there. If it is not, we append (a, b) to the end of the list for that bucket. To delete (a, b), we go to the bucket $h(a)$, search for this pair, and remove it from the list if it is there.

To execute $lookup(a)$, we again find the bucket $h(a)$ and go down the list for this bucket, collecting all the b's that appear in cells with first component a. The *lookup* function of Fig. 7.24, which we wrote for a linked list, applies equally well to the list that forms one bucket of a hash table.

Running Time of Operations on a Binary Relation

The performance of the three representations for binary relations is not much different from the performance of the same structures on functions or dictionaries. Consider first the list representation. While we have not written the functions for *insert* and *delete*, we should be able to visualize that these functions will run down the entire list, searching for the target pair, and stop upon finding it. On a list of length n, this search takes $O(n)$ average time, since we must scan the entire list if the pair is not found and, on the average, half the list if it is found.

For *lookup*, an examination of Fig. 7.24 should convince us that this function takes $O(1)$ time plus a recursive call on the tail of a list. We thus make n calls if the list is of length n, for a total time of $O(n)$.

Now consider the generalized characteristic vector. The operation *lookup(a)* is easiest. We go to the array element indexed by a, and there we find our answer, a list of all the b's such that (a, b) is in the relation. We don't even have to examine the elements or copy them. Thus, *lookup* takes $O(1)$ time when characteristic vectors are used.

On the other hand, *insert* and *delete* are less simple. To insert (a, b), we can go to the array element indexed by a easily enough, but we must search the entire list to make sure that (a, b) is not already there.[5] That requires an amount of time proportional to the average length of a list, that is, to the average number of range values associated with a given domain value. We shall call this parameter m. Another way to look at m is that it is n, the total number of pairs in the relation, divided by the number of different domain values. If we assume that any list is as likely to be searched as any other, then we require $O(m)$ time on the average to perform an *insert* or a *delete*.

Finally, let us consider the hash table. If there are n pairs in our relation and B buckets, we expect there to be an average of n/B pairs per bucket. However, the parameter m must be figured in as well. If there are n/m different domain values, then at most n/m buckets can be nonempty, since the bucket for a pair is determined only by the domain value. Thus, m is a lower bound on the average size of a bucket, regardless of B. Since n/B is also a lower bound, the time to perform one of the three operations is $O(\max(m, n/B))$.

✦ **Example 7.31.** Suppose there is a relation of 1000 pairs, distributed among 100 domain values. Then the typical domain value has 10 associated range values; that is, $m = 10$. If we use 1000 buckets — that is, $B = 1000$ — then m is greater than n/B, which is 1, and we expect the average bucket that we might actually search (because its number is $h(a)$ for some domain value a that appears in the relation) to have about 10 pairs. In fact, it will have on the average slightly more, because by coincidence, the same bucket could be $h(a_1)$ and $h(a_2)$ for different domain values a_1 and a_2. If we choose $B = 100$, then $m = n/B = 10$, and we would again expect each bucket we might search to have about 10 elements. As just mentioned, the actual number is slightly more because of coincidences, where two or more domain values hash to the same bucket. ✦

EXERCISES

7.9.1: Using the data types from Example 7.29, write a function that takes a pollinizer value b and a list of variety-pollinizer pairs, and returns a list of the varieties that are pollinated by b.

---

[5] We could insert the pair without regard for whether it is already present, but that would have both the advantages and disadvantages of the list representation discussed in Section 6.4, where we allowed duplicates.

"Dictionary Operations" on Functions and Relations

A set of pairs might be thought of as a set, as a function, or as a relation. For each of these cases, we have defined operations *insert*, *delete*, and *lookup* suitably. These operations differ in form. Most of the time, the operation takes both the domain and range element of the pair. However, sometimes only the domain element is used as an argument. The table below summarizes the differences in the use of these three operations.

	Set of Pairs	Function	Relation
Insert	Domain and Range	Domain and Range	Domain and Range
Delete	Domain and Range	Domain only	Domain and Range
Lookup	Domain and Range	Domain only	Domain only

7.9.2: Write (a) *insert* and (b) *delete* routines for variety-pollinizer pairs using the assumptions of Example 7.29.

7.9.3: Write (a) *insert*, (b) *delete*, and (c) *lookup* functions for a relation represented by the vector data structure of Example 7.30. When inserting, do not forget to check for an identical pair already in the relation.

7.9.4: Design a hash-table data structure to represent the pollinizer relation that forms the primary example of this section. Write functions for the operations *insert*, *delete*, and *lookup*.

7.9.5*: Prove that the function `lookup` of Fig. 7.24 works correctly, by showing by induction on the length of list L that `lookup` returns a list of all the elements b such that the pair (a, b) is on the list L.

7.9.6*: Design a data structure that allows $O(1)$ average time to perform each of the operations *insert*, *delete*, *lookup*, and *inverseLookup*. The latter operation takes a range element and finds the associated domain elements.

7.9.7: In this section and the previous, we defined some new abstract data types that had operations we called *insert*, *delete*, and *lookup*. However, these operations were defined slightly differently from the operations of the same name on dictionaries. Make a table for the ADT's DICTIONARY, FUNCTION (as discussed in Section 7.8), and RELATION (as discussed in this section) and indicate the possible abstract implementations and the data structures that support them. For each, indicate the running time of each operation.

❖❖ 7.10 Some Special Properties of Binary Relations

In this section we shall consider some of the special properties that certain useful binary relations have. We begin by defining some basic properties: transitivity, reflexivity, symmetry, and antisymmetry. These are combined to form common types of binary relations: partial orders, total orders, and equivalence relations.

Transitivity

Let R be a binary relation on the domain D. We say that the relation R is *transitive* if whenever aRb and bRc are true, aRc is also true. Figure 7.26 illustrates the transitivity property as it appears in the graph of a relation. Whenever the dotted arrows from a to b and from b to c appear in the diagram, for some particular a, b, and c, then the solid arrow from a to c must also be in the diagram. It is important to remember that transitivity, like the other properties to be defined in this section, pertains to the relation as a whole. It is not enough that the property be satisfied for three particular domain elements; it must be satisfied for all triples a, b, and c in the declared domain D.

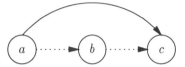

Fig. 7.26. Transitivity condition requires that if both the arcs aRb and bRc are present in the graph of a relation, then so is the arc aRc.

✦   **Example 7.32.** Consider the relation $<$ on $\mathbf{Z}$, the set of integers. That is, $<$ is the set of pairs of integers (a, b) such that a is less than b. The relation $<$ is transitive, because if $a < b$ and $b < c$, we know that $a < c$. Similarly, the relations $\leq$, $>$, and $\geq$ on integers are transitive. These four comparison relations are likewise transitive on the set of real numbers.

However, consider the relation $\neq$ on the integers (or the reals for that matter). This relation is not transitive. For instance, let a and c both be 3, and let b be 5. Then $a \neq b$ and $b \neq c$ are both true. If the relation were transitive, we would have $a \neq c$. But that says $3 \neq 3$, which is wrong. We conclude that $\neq$ is not transitive.

Transitivity of subset
For another example of a transitive relation, consider $\subseteq$, the subset relation. We might like to consider the relation as being the set of all pairs of sets (S, T) such that $S \subseteq T$, but to imagine that there is such a set would lead us to Russell's paradox again. However, suppose we have a "universal" set U. We can let $\subseteq_U$ be the set of pairs of sets

$$\{(S, T) \mid S \subseteq T \text{ and } T \subseteq U\}$$

Then $\subseteq_U$ is a relation on $\mathbf{P}(U)$, the power set of U, and we can think of $\subseteq_U$ as the subset relation.

For instance, let $U = \{1, 2\}$. Then $\subseteq_{\{1,2\}}$ consists of the nine (S, T)-pairs shown in Fig. 7.27. Thus, $\subseteq_U$ contains exactly those pairs such that the first component is a subset (not necessarily proper) of the second component and both are subsets of $\{1, 2\}$.

It is easy to check that $\subseteq_U$ is transitive, no matter what the universal set U is. If $A \subseteq B$ and $B \subseteq C$, then it must be that $A \subseteq C$. The reason is that for every x in A, we know that x is in B, because $A \subseteq B$. Since x is in B, we know that x is in C, because $B \subseteq C$. Thus, every element of A is an element of C. Therefore, $A \subseteq C$. ✦

S	T
$\emptyset$	$\emptyset$
$\emptyset$	$\{1\}$
$\emptyset$	$\{2\}$
$\emptyset$	$\{1,2\}$
$\{1\}$	$\{1\}$
$\{1\}$	$\{1,2\}$
$\{2\}$	$\{2\}$
$\{2\}$	$\{1,2\}$
$\{1,2\}$	$\{1,2\}$

Fig. 7.27. The pairs in the relation $\subseteq_{\{1,2\}}$.

Reflexivity

Some binary relations R have the property that for every element a in the declared domain, R has the pair (a, a); that is, aRa. If so, we say that R is *reflexive.* Figure 7.28 suggests that the graph of a reflexive relation has a loop on every element of its declared domain. The graph may have other arrows in addition to the loops. However, it is not sufficient that there be loops for the elements of the current domain; there must be one for each element of the declared domain.

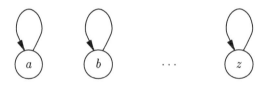

Fig. 7.28. A reflexive relation R has xRx for every x in its declared domain.

◆ **Example 7.33.** The relation $\geq$ on the reals is reflexive. For each real number a, we have $a \geq a$. Similarly, $\leq$ is reflexive, and both these relations are also reflexive on the integers. However, $<$ and $>$ are not reflexive, since $a < a$ and $a > a$ are each false for at least one value of a; in fact, they are both false for all a.

The subset relations $\subseteq_U$ defined in Example 7.32 are also reflexive, since $A \subseteq A$ for any set A. However, the similarly defined relations $\subset_U$ that contain the pair (S, T) if $T \subseteq U$ and $S \subset T$ — that is, S is a proper subset of T — are not reflexive. The reason is that $A \subset A$ is false for some A (in fact, for all A). ◆

Symmetry and Antisymmetry

Inverse relation

Let R be a binary relation. As defined in Exercise 7.7.7, the *inverse* of R is the set of pairs of R with the components reversed. That is, the inverse of R, denoted R^{-1}, is

$$\{(b, a) \mid (a, b) \in R\}$$

For example, $>$ is the inverse of $<$, since $a > b$ exactly when $b < a$. Likewise, $\geq$ is the inverse of $\leq$.

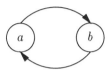

Fig. 7.29. Symmetry requires that if aRb, then bRa as well.

We say that R is *symmetric* if it is its own inverse. That is, R is symmetric if, whenever aRb, we also have bRa. Figure 7.29 suggests what symmetry looks like in the graph of a relation. Whenever the forward arc is present, the backward arc must also be present.

We say that R is *antisymmetric* if aRb and bRa are both true only when $a = b$. Note that it is not necessary that aRa be true for any particular a in an antisymmetric relation. However, an antisymmetric relation can be reflexive. Figure 7.30 shows how the antisymmetry condition relates to graphs of relations.

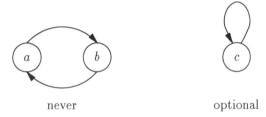

never   optional

Fig. 7.30. An antisymmetric relation cannot have a cycle involving two elements, but loops on a single element are permitted.

✦   **Example 7.34.** The relation $\leq$ on integers or reals is antisymmetric, because if $a \leq b$ and $b \leq a$, it must be that $a = b$. The relation $<$ is also antisymmetric, because under no circumstances are $a < b$ and $b < a$ both true. Similarly, $\geq$ and $>$ are antisymmetric, as are the subset relations $\subseteq_U$ that we discussed in Example 7.32.

However, note that $\leq$ is not symmetric. For example, $3 \leq 5$, but $5 \leq 3$ is false. Likewise, none of the other relations mentioned in the previous paragraph is symmetric.

An example of a symmetric relation is $\neq$ on the integers. That is, if $a \neq b$, then surely $b \neq a$. ✦

Pitfalls in Property Definitions

As we have pointed out, the definition of a property is a general condition, one that applies to all elements of the domain. For example, in order for a relation R on declared domain D to be reflexive, we need to have aRa for every $a \in D$. It is not sufficient for aRa to be true for one a, nor does it make sense to say that a relation is reflexive for some elements and not others. If there is even one a in D for which aRa is false, then R is not reflexive. (Thus, reflexivity may depend on the domain, as well as on the relation R.)

Also, a condition like transitivity — "if aRb and bRc then aRc" — is of the form "if A then B." Remember that we can satisfy such a statement either by making B true or by making A false. Thus, for a given triple a, b, and c, the transitivity condition is satisfied whenever aRb is false, or whenever bRc is false, or whenever aRc is true. As an extreme example, the empty relation is transitive, symmetric, and antisymmetric, because the "if" condition is never satisfied. However, the empty relation is not reflexive, unless the declared domain is $\emptyset$.

Partial Orders and Total Orders

Comparable elements

A *partial order* is a transitive and antisymmetric binary relation. A relation is said to be a *total order* if in addition to being transitive and antisymmetric, it makes every pair of elements in the domain *comparable*. That is to say, if R is a total order, and if a and b are any two elements in its domain, then either aRb or bRa is true. Note that every total order is reflexive, because we may let a and b be the same element, whereupon the comparability requirement tells us that aRa.

✦ **Example 7.35.** The arithmetic comparisons $\leq$ and $\geq$ on integers or reals are total orders and therefore are also partial orders. Notice that for any a and b, either $a \leq b$ or $b \leq a$, but both are true exactly when $a = b$.

The comparisons $<$ and $>$ are partial orders but not total orders. While they are antisymmetric, they are not reflexive; that is, neither $a < a$ nor $a > a$ is true.

The subset relations $\subseteq_U$ and $\subset_U$ on 2^U for some universal set U are partial orders. We already observed that they are transitive and antisymmetric. These relations are not total orders, however, as long as U has at least two members, since then there are incomparable elements. For example, let $U = \{1, 2\}$. Then $\{1\}$ and $\{2\}$ are subsets of U, but neither is a subset of the other. ✦

One can view a total order R as a linear sequence of elements, as suggested in Fig. 7.31, where whenever aRb for distinct elements a and b, a appears to the left of b along the line. For example, if R is $\leq$ on the integers, then the elements along the line would be $\ldots, -2, -1, 0, 1, 2, \ldots$. If R is $\leq$ on the reals, then the points correspond to the points along the real line, as if the line were an infinite ruler; the real number x is found x units to the right of the 0 mark if x is nonnegative, and $-x$ units to the left of the zero mark if x is negative.

If R is a partial order but not a total order, we can also draw the elements of the domain in such a way that if aRb, then a is to the left of b. However, because there may be some incomparable elements, we cannot necessarily draw the elements

Fig. 7.31. Picture of a total order on $a_1, a_2, a_3, \ldots, a_n$.

in one line so that the relation R means "to the left."

◆

Reduced graph

Example 7.36. Figure 7.32 represents the partial order $\subseteq_{\{1,2,3\}}$. We have drawn the relation as a *reduced graph*, in which we have omitted arcs that can be inferred by transitivity. That is, $S \subseteq_{\{1,2,3\}} T$ if either

1. $S = T$,
2.   There is an arc from S to T, or
3.   There is a path of two or more arcs leading from S to T.

For example, we know that $\emptyset \subseteq_{\{1,2,3\}} \{1,3\}$, because of the path from $\emptyset$ to $\{1\}$ to $\{1,3\}$. ◆

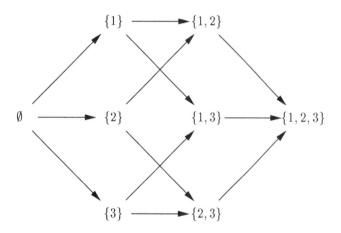

Fig. 7.32. Reduced graph for the partial order $\subseteq_{\{1,2,3\}}$.

Equivalence Relations

An *equivalence relation* is a binary relation that is reflexive, symmetric, and transitive. This kind of relation is quite different from the partial orders and total orders we have met in our previous examples. In fact, a partial order can never be an equivalence relation, except in the trivial cases that the declared domain is empty, or there is only one element a in the declared domain and the relation is $\{(a, a)\}$.

◆

Example 7.37. A relation like $\leq$ on integers is not an equivalence relation. Although it is transitive and reflexive, it is not symmetric. If $a \leq b$, we do not have $b \leq a$, except if $a = b$.

For an example that is an equivalence relation, let R consist of those pairs of integers (a, b) such that $a - b$ is an integer multiple of 3. For example $3R9$, since

$3 - 9 = -6 = 3 \times (-2)$. Also, $5R(-4)$, since $5 - (-4) = 9 = 3 \times 3$. However, $(1, 2)$ is not in R (or we can say "$1R2$ is false"), since $1 - 2 = -1$, which is not an integer multiple of 3. We can demonstrate that R is an equivalence relation, as follows:

1. R is reflexive, since aRa for any integer a, because $a - a$ is zero, which is a multiple of 3.

2. R is symmetric. If $a - b$ is a multiple of 3 — say, $3c$ for some integer c — then $b - a$ is $-3c$ and is therefore also an integer multiple of 3.

3. R is transitive. Suppose aRb and bRc. That is, $a - b$ is a multiple of 3, say, $3d$; and $b - c$ is a multiple of 3, say, $3e$. Then

$$a - c = (a - b) + (b - c) = 3d + 3e = 3(d + e)$$

and so $a - c$ is also a multiple of 3. Thus, aRb and bRc imply aRc, which means that R is transitive.

For another example, let S be the set of cities of the world, and let T be the relation defined by aTb if a and b are connected by roads, that is, if it is possible to drive by car from a to b. Thus, the pair (Toronto, New York) is in T, but

(Honolulu, Anchorage)

is not. We claim that T is an equivalence relation.

T is reflexive, since trivially every city is connected to itself. T is symmetric because if a is connected to b, then b is connected to a. T is transitive because if a is connected to b and b is connected to c, then a is connected to c; we can travel from a to c via b, if no shorter route exists. ✦

Equivalence Classes

Another way to view an equivalence relation is that it partitions its domain into *equivalence classes*. If R is an equivalence relation on a domain D, then we can divide D into equivalence classes so that

1. Each domain element is in exactly one equivalence class.

2. If aRb, then a and b are in the same equivalence class.

3. If aRb is false, then a and b are in different equivalence classes.

✦ **Example 7.38.** Consider the relation R of Example 7.37, where aRb when $a - b$ is a multiple of 3. One equivalence class is the set of integers that are exactly divisible by 3, that is, those that leave a remainder of 0 when divided by 3. This class is $\{\ldots, -3, 0, 3, 6, \ldots\}$. A second is the set of integers that leave a remainder of 1 when divided by 3, that is, $\{\ldots, -2, 1, 4, 7, \ldots\}$. The last class is the set of integers that leave a remainder of 2 when divided by 3. This class is $\{\ldots, -1, 2, 5, 8, \ldots\}$. The classes partition the set of integers into three disjoint sets, as suggested by Fig. 7.33.

Notice that when two integers leave the same remainder when divided by 3, then their difference is evenly divided by 3. For instance, $14 = 3 \times 4 + 2$ and $5 = 3 \times 1 + 2$. Thus, $14 - 5 = 3 \times 4 - 3 \times 1 + 2 - 2 = 3 \times 3$. We therefore know that $14R5$. On the other hand, if two integers leave different remainders when divided by

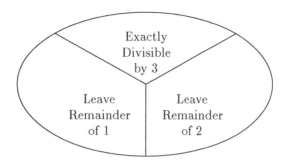

Fig. 7.33. Equivalence classes for the relation on the integers:
"Difference is divisible by 3."

3, their difference surely is not evenly divisible by 3. Thus, integers from different
classes, like 5 and 7, are not related by R. ✦

To construct the equivalence classes for an equivalence relation R, let $class(a)$
be the set of elements b such that aRb. For example, if our equivalence relation is
the one we called R in Example 7.37, then $class(4)$ is the set of integers that leave
a remainder of 1 when divided by 3; that is $class(4) = \{\ldots, -2, 1, 4, 7, \ldots\}$.

Notice that if we let a vary over each of the elements of the domain, we typically
get the same class many times. In fact, when aRb, then $class(a) = class(b)$. To
see why, suppose that c is in $class(a)$. Then aRc, by definition of $class$. Since we
are given that aRb, by symmetry it follows that bRa. By transitivity, bRa and aRc
imply bRc. But bRc says that c is in $class(b)$. Thus, every element in $class(a)$ is in
$class(b)$. Since the same argument tells us that, as long as aRb, every element in
$class(b)$ is also in $class(a)$, we conclude that $class(a)$ and $class(b)$ are identical.

However, if $class(a)$ is not the same as $class(b)$, then these classes can have
no element in common. Suppose otherwise. Then there must be some c in both
$class(a)$ and $class(b)$. By our previous assumption, we know that aRc and bRc.
By symmetry, cRb. By transitivity, aRc and cRb imply aRb. But we just showed
that whenever aRb is true, $class(a)$ and $class(b)$ are the same. Since we assumed
these classes were not the same, we have a contradiction. Therefore, the assumed c
in the intersection of $class(a)$ and $class(b)$ cannot exist.

There is one more observation we need to make: every domain element is in
some equivalence class. In particular, a is always in $class(a)$, because reflexivity
tells us aRa.

We can now conclude that an equivalence relation divides its domain into equivalence classes that are disjoint and that place each element into exactly one class.
Example 7.38 illustrated this phenomenon.

Closures of Relations

A common operation on relations is to take a relation that does not have some
property and add as few pairs as possible to create a relation that does have that
property. The resulting relation is called the *closure* (for that property) of the
original relation.

Transitive
closure

✦ **Example 7.39.** We discussed reduced graphs in connection with Fig. 7.32. Although we were representing a transitive relation, $\subseteq_{\{1,2,3\}}$, we drew arcs corresponding to only a subset of the pairs in the relation. We can reconstruct the entire relation by applying the transitive law to infer new pairs, until no new pairs can be inferred. For example, we see that there are arcs corresponding to the pairs $(\{1\}, \{1, 3\})$ and $(\{1, 3\}, \{1, 2, 3\})$, and so the transitive law tells us that the pair $(\{1\}, \{1, 2, 3\})$ must also be in the relation. Then this pair, together with the pair $(\emptyset, \{1\})$ tells us that $(\emptyset, \{1, 2, 3\})$ is in the relation. To these we must add the "reflexive" pairs (S, S), for each set S that is a subset of $\{1, 2, 3\}$. In this manner, we can reconstruct all the pairs in the relation $\subseteq_{\{1,2,3\}}$. ✦

Topological
sorting

Another useful closure operation is *topological sorting,* where we take a partial order and add tuples until it becomes a total order. While the transitive closure of a binary relation is unique, there are frequently several total orders that contain a given partial order. We shall learn in Chapter 9 of a surprisingly efficient algorithm for topological sorting. For the moment, let us consider an example where topological sorting is useful.

✦ **Example 7.40.** It is common to represent a sequence of tasks that must be performed in a manufacturing process by a set of "precedences" that must be obeyed. For a simple example, you must put on your left sock before your left shoe, and your right sock before your right shoe. However, there are no other precedences that must be obeyed. We can represent these precedences by a set consisting of the two pairs $(leftsock, leftshoe)$ and $(rightsock, rightshoe)$. This set is a partial order.

We can extend this relation to six different total orders. One is the total order in which we dress the left foot first; this relation is a set that contains the ten pairs

$(leftsock, leftsock)$ $(leftsock, leftshoe)$ $(leftsock, rightsock)$ $(leftsock, rightshoe)$
$(leftshoe, leftshoe)$ $(leftshoe, rightsock)$ $(leftshoe, rightshoe)$
$(rightsock, rightsock)$ $(rightsock, rightshoe)$
$(rightshoe, rightshoe)$

We can think of this total order as the linear arrangement

$$leftsock \rightarrow leftshoe \rightarrow rightsock \rightarrow rightshoe$$

There is the analogous procedure where we dress the right foot first.

There are four other possible total orders consistent with the original partial order, where we first put on the socks and then the shoes. These are represented by the linear arrangements

$$leftsock \rightarrow rightsock \rightarrow leftshoe \rightarrow rightshoe$$
$$leftsock \rightarrow rightsock \rightarrow rightshoe \rightarrow leftshoe$$
$$rightsock \rightarrow leftsock \rightarrow leftshoe \rightarrow rightshoe$$
$$rightsock \rightarrow leftsock \rightarrow rightshoe \rightarrow leftshoe$$

✦

A third form of closure is to find the smallest equivalence relation containing a given relation. For example, a road map represents a relation consisting of pairs of cities connected by road segments having no intermediate cities. To determine the

Connected components

road-connected cities, we can apply reflexivity, transitivity, and symmetry to infer those pairs of cities that are connected by some sequence of these elementary roads. This form of closure is called finding the "connected components" in a graph, and an efficient algorithm for the problem will be discussed in Chapter 9.

EXERCISES

7.10.1: Give an example of a relation that is reflexive for one declared domain but not reflexive for another declared domain. Remember that for D to be a possible domain for a relation R, D must include every element that appears in a pair of R but it may also include more elements.

7.10.2**: How many pairs are there in the relation $\subseteq_{\{1,2,3\}}$? In general, how many pairs are there in $\subseteq_U$, if U has n elements? *Hint*: Try to guess the function from a few cases like the two-element case (Fig. 7.27) where there are 9 pairs. Then prove your guess correct by induction.

7.10.3: Consider the binary relation R on the domain of four-letter strings defined by sRt if t is formed from the string s by cycling its characters one position left. That is, $abcdRbcda$, where a, b, c, and d are individual letters. Determine whether R is (a) reflexive, (b) symmetric, (c) transitive, (d) a partial order, and/or (e) an equivalence relation. Give a brief argument why, or a counterexample, in each case.

7.10.4: Consider the domain of four-letter strings in Exercise 7.10.3. Let S be the binary relation consisting of R applied 0 or more times. Thus, $abcdSabcd$, $abcdSbcda$, $abcdScdab$, and $abcdSdabc$. Put another way, a string is related by S to any of its rotations. Answer the five questions from Exercise 7.10.3 for the relation S. Again, give justification in each case.

7.10.5*: What is wrong with the following "proof"?

(Non)Theorem: If binary relation R is symmetric and transitive, then R is reflexive.

(Non)Proof: Let x be some member of the domain of R. Pick y such that xRy. By symmetry, yRx. By transitivity, xRy and yRx imply xRx. Since x is an arbitrary member of R's domain, we have shown that xRx for every element in the domain of R, which "proves" that R is reflexive.

7.10.6: Give examples of relations with declared domain $\{1, 2, 3\}$ that are

a)   Reflexive and transitive, but not symmetric
b)   Reflexive and symmetric, but not transitive
c)   Symmetric and transitive, but not reflexive
d)   Symmetric and antisymmetric
e)   Reflexive, transitive, and a total function
f)   Antisymmetric and a one-to-one correspondence

7.10.7*: How many arcs are saved if we use the reduced graph for the relation $\subseteq_U$, where U has n elements, rather than the full graph?

7.10.8: Are (a) $\subseteq_U$ and (b) $\subset_U$ either partial orders or total orders when U has one element? What if U has zero elements?

7.10.9*: Show by induction on n, starting at $n = 1$, that if there is a sequence of n pairs $a_0 R a_1, a_1 R a_2, \ldots, a_{n-1} R a_n$, and if R is a transitive relation, then $a_0 R a_n$. That is, show that if there is any path in the graph of a transitive relation, then there is an arc from the beginning of the path to the end.

7.10.10: Find the smallest equivalence relation containing the pairs (a, b), (a, c), (d, e), and (b, f).

7.10.11: Let R be the relation on the set of integers such that $a R b$ if a and b are distinct and have a common divisor other than 1. Determine whether R is (a) reflexive, (b) symmetric, (c) transitive, (d) a partial order, and/or (e) an equivalence relation.

7.10.12: Repeat Exercise 7.10.11 for the relation R_T on the nodes of a particular tree T defined by $a R_T b$ if and only if a is an ancestor of b in tree T. However, unlike Exercise 7.10.11, your possible answers are "yes," "no," or "it depends on what tree T is."

7.10.13: Repeat Exercise 7.10.12 for relation S_T on the nodes of a particular tree T defined by $a S_T b$ if and only if a is to the left of b in tree T.

❖❖ 7.11   Infinite Sets

All of the sets that one would implement in a computer program are finite, or limited, in extent; one could not store them in a computer's memory if they were not. Many sets in mathematics, such as the integers or reals, are infinite in extent. These remarks seem intuitively clear, but what distinguishes a finite set from an infinite one?

The distinction between finite and infinite is rather surprising. A finite set is one that does not have the same number of elements as any of its proper subsets. Recall from Section 7.7 that we said we could use the existence of a one-to-one correspondence between two sets to establish that that they are *equipotent*, that is,

Equipotent sets

they have the same number of members.

If we take a finite set such as $S = \{1, 2, 3, 4\}$ and any proper subset of it, such as $T = \{1, 2, 3\}$, there is no way to find a one-to-one correspondence between the two sets. For example, we could map 4 of S to 3 of T, 3 of S to 2 of T, and 2 of S to 1 of T, but then we would have no member of T to associate with 1 of S. Any other attempt to build a one-to-one correspondence from S to T must likewise fail.

Your intuition might suggest that the same should hold for any set whatsoever: how could a set have the same number of elements as a set formed by throwing away one or more of its elements? Consider the natural numbers (nonnegative integers) $\mathbf{N}$ and the proper subset of $\mathbf{N}$ formed by throwing away 0; call it $\mathbf{N} - \{0\}$, or $\{1, 2, 3, \ldots\}$. Then consider the one-to-one correspondence F from $\mathbf{N}$ to $\mathbf{N} - \{0\}$ defined by $F(0) = 1$, $F(1) = 2$, and, in general, $F(i) = i + 1$.

Surprisingly, F is a one-to-one correspondence from $\mathbf{N}$ to $\mathbf{N} - \{0\}$. For each i in $\mathbf{N}$, there is at most one j such that $F(i) = j$, so F is a function. In fact, there is exactly one such j, namely $i + 1$, so that condition (1) in the definition of one-to-one correspondence (see Section 7.7) is satisfied. For every j in $\mathbf{N} - \{0\}$ there is some i such that $F(i) = j$, namely, $i = j - 1$. Thus condition (2) in the definition of one-to-one correspondence is satisfied. Finally, there cannot be two

Infinite Hotels

To help you appreciate that there are as many numbers from 0 up as from 1 up, imagine a hotel with an infinite number of rooms, numbered 0, 1, 2, and so on; for any integer, there is a room with that integer as room number. At a certain time, there is a guest in each room. A kangaroo comes to the front desk and asks for a room. The desk clerk says, "We don't see many kangaroos around here." Wait — that's another story. Actually, the desk clerk makes room for the kangaroo as follows. He moves the guest in room 0 to room 1, the guest in room 1 to room 2, and so on. All the old guests still have a room, and now room 0 is vacant, and the kangaroo goes there. The reason this "trick" works is that there are truly the same number of rooms numbered from 1 up as are numbered from 0 up.

---

distinct numbers i_1 and i_2 in $\mathbf{N}$ such that $F(i_1)$ and $F(i_2)$ are both j, because then $i_1 + 1$ and $i_2 + 1$ would both be j, from which we would conclude that $i_1 = i_2$. We are forced to conclude that F is a one-to-one correspondence between $\mathbf{N}$ and its proper subset $\mathbf{N} - \{0\}$.

Formal Definition of Infinite Sets

The definition accepted by mathematicians of an *infinite set* is one that has a one-to-one correspondence between itself and at least one of its proper subsets. There are more extreme examples of how an infinite set and a proper subset can have a one-to-one correspondence between them.

◆ **Example 7.41.** The set of natural numbers and the set of even natural numbers are equipotent. Let $F(i) = 2i$. Then F is a one-to-one correspondence that maps 0 to 0, 1 to 2, 2 to 4, 3 to 6, and in general, every natural number to a unique natural number, its double.

Similarly, $\mathbf{Z}$ and $\mathbf{N}$ are the same size; that is, there are as many nonnegative and negative integers as nonnegative integers. Let $F(i) = 2i$ for all $i \geq 0$, and let $F(i) = -2i - 1$ for $i < 0$. Then 0 goes to 0, 1 to 2, -1 to 1, 2 to 4, -2 to 3, and so on. Every integer is sent to a unique nonnegative integer, with the negative integers going to odd numbers and the nonnegative integers to even numbers.

Even more surprising, the set of pairs of natural numbers is equinumerous with $\mathbf{N}$ itself. To see how the one-to-one correspondence is constructed, consider Fig. 7.34, which shows the pairs in $\mathbf{N} \times \mathbf{N}$ arranged in an infinite square. We order the pairs according to their sum, and among pairs of equal sum, by order of their first components. This order begins $(0,0)$, $(0,1)$, $(1,0)$, $(0,2)$, $(1,1)$, $(2,0)$, $(0,3)$, $(1,2)$, and so on, as suggested by Fig. 7.34.

Now, every pair has a place in the order. The reason is that for any pair (i, j), there are only a finite number of pairs with a smaller sum, and a finite number with the same sum and a smaller value of i. In fact, we can calculate the position of the pair (i, j) in the order; it is $(i + j)(i + j + 1)/2 + i$. That is, our one-to-one correspondence associates the pair (i, j) with the unique natural number $(i + j)(i + j + 1)/2 + i$.

Notice that we have to be careful how we order pairs. Had we ordered them by rows in Fig. 7.34, we would never get to the pairs on the second or higher rows,

$$
\begin{array}{r|lllll}
5 & 15 \\
\uparrow \quad 4 & 10 & 16 \\
j \quad 3 & 6 & 11 \\
2 & 3 & 7 & 12 \\
1 & 1 & 4 & 8 & 13 \\
0 & 0 & 2 & 5 & 9 & 14 \\
\hline
 & 0 & 1 & 2 & 3 & 4 & 5 \\
 & & & i & \rightarrow
\end{array}
$$

Fig. 7.34. Ordering pairs of natural numbers.

Every Set Is Either Finite or Infinite

At first glance, it might appear that there are things that are not quite finite and not quite infinite. For example, when we talked about linked lists, we put no limit on the length of a linked list. Yet whenever a linked list is created during the execution of a program, it has a finite length. Thus, we can make the following distinctions:

1. Every linked list is finite in length; that is, it has a finite number of cells.

2. The length of a linked list may be any nonnegative integer, and the set of possible lengths of linked lists is infinite.

because there are an infinite number of pairs on each row. Similarly, ordering by columns would not work. ◆

The formal definition of infinite sets is interesting, but that definition may not meet our intuition of what infinite sets are. For example, one might expect that an infinite set was one that, for every integer n, contained at least n elements. Fortunately, this property can be proved for every set that the formal definition tells us is infinite. The proof is an example of induction.

STATEMENT $S(n)$: If I is an infinite set, then I has a subset with n elements.

BASIS. Let $n = 0$. Surely $\emptyset \subseteq I$.

INDUCTION. Assume $S(n)$ for some $n \geq 0$. We shall prove that I has a subset with $n+1$ elements. By the inductive hypothesis, I has a subset T with n elements. By the formal definition of an infinite set, there is a proper subset $J \subset I$ and a 1-1 correspondence f from I to J. Let a be an element in $I - J$; surely a exists because J is a proper subset.

Consider R, the *image* of T under f, that is, if $T = \{b_1, \ldots, b_n\}$, then $R = \{f(b_1), \ldots, f(b_n)\}$. Since f is 1-1, each of $f(b_1), \ldots, f(b_n)$ are different, so R is of size n. Since f is from I to J, each of the $f(b_k)$'s is in J; that is, $R \subseteq J$. Thus, a

Cardinality of Sets

We defined two sets S and T to be equipotent (equal in size) if there is a one-to-one correspondence from S to T. Equipotence is an equivalence relation on any set of sets, and we leave this point as an exercise. The equivalence class to which a set S belongs is said to be the *cardinality* of S. For example, the empty set belongs to an equivalence class by itself; we can identify this class with cardinality 0. The class containing the set $\{a\}$, where a is any element, is cardinality 1, the class containing the set $\{a, b\}$ is cardinality 2, and so on.

Countable set, aleph-zero

The class containing $\mathbf{N}$ is "the cardinality of the integers," usually given the name *aleph-zero,* and a set in this class is said to be *countable.* The set of real numbers belongs to another equivalence class, often called *the continuum.* There are, in fact, an infinite number of different infinite cardinalities.

cannot be in R. It follows that $R \cup \{a\}$ is a subset of I with $n + 1$ elements, proving $S(n + 1)$.

Countable and Uncountable Sets

From Example 7.41, we might think that all infinite sets are equipotent. We've seen that $\mathbf{Z}$, the set of integers, and $\mathbf{N}$, the set of nonnegative integers, are the same size, as are some infinite subsets of these that intuitively "seem" smaller than $\mathbf{N}$. Since we saw in Example 7.41 that the pairs of natural numbers are equinumerous with $\mathbf{N}$, it follows that the nonnegative rational numbers are equinumerous with the natural numbers, since a rational is just a pair of natural numbers, its numerator and denominator. Likewise, the (nonnegative and negative) rationals can be shown to be just as numerous as the integers, and therefore as the natural numbers.

Any set S for which there is a one-to-one correspondence from S to $\mathbf{N}$ is said to be *countable.* The use of the term "countable" makes sense, because S must have an element corresponding to 0, an element corresponding to 1, and so on, so that we can "count" the members of S. From what we just said, the integers, the rationals, the even numbers, and the set of pairs of natural numbers are all countable sets. There are many other countable sets, and we leave the discovery of the appropriate one-to-one correspondences as exercises.

However, there are infinite sets that are not countable. In particular, the real numbers are not countable. In fact, we shall show that there are more real numbers between 0 and 1 than there are natural numbers. The crux of the argument is that the real numbers between 0 and 1 can each be represented by a decimal fraction of infinite length. We shall number the positions to the right of the decimal point 0, 1, and so on. If the reals between 0 and 1 are countable, then we can number them, r_0, r_1, and so on. We can then arrange the reals in an infinite square table, as suggested by Fig. 7.35. In our hypothetical listing of the real numbers between 0 and 1, $\pi/10$ is assigned to row zero, 5/9 is assigned to row one, 5/8 is assigned to row two, 4/33 is assigned to row three, and so on.

Diagonalization

However, we can prove that Fig. 7.35 does not really represent a listing of all the reals in the range 0 to 1. Our proof is of a type known as a *diagonalization,* where we use the diagonal of the table to create a value that cannot be in the list of reals. We create a new real number r with decimal representation $.a_0 a_1 a_2 \cdots$.

		POSITIONS							
		0	1	2	3	4	5	6	$\cdots$
	0	3	1	4	1	5	9	2	$\cdots$
REAL	1	5	5	5	5	5	5	5	$\cdots$
NUMBERS	2	6	2	5	0	0	0	0	$\cdots$
$\downarrow$	3	1	2	1	2	1	2	1	$\cdots$
	4								

Fig. 7.35. Hypothetical table of real numbers, assuming that the reals are countable.

The value of the ith digit, a_i, depends on that of the ith diagonal digit, that is, on the value found at the ith position of the ith real. If this value is 0 through 4, we let $a_i = 8$. If the value at the ith diagonal position is 5 through 9, then $a_i = 1$.

◆ **Example 7.42.** Given the part of the table suggested by Fig. 7.35, our real number r begins .8118$\cdots$. To see why, note that the value at position 0 of real 0 is 3, and so $a_0 = 8$. The value at position 1 of real 1 is 5, and so $a_1 = 1$. Continuing, the value at position 2 of real 2 is 5 and the value at position 3 of real 3 is 2, and so the next two digits are 18. ◆

We claim that r does not appear anywhere in the hypothetical list of reals, even though we supposed that all real numbers from 0 to 1 were in the list. Suppose r were r_j, the real number associated with row j. Consider the difference d between r and r_j. We know that a_j, the digit in position j of the decimal expansion of r, was specifically chosen to differ by at least 4 and at most 8 from the digit in the jth position of r_j. Thus, the contribution to d from the jth position is between $4/10^{j+1}$ and $8/10^{j+1}$.

The contribution to d from all positions after the jth is no more than $1/10^{j+1}$, since that would be the difference if one of r and r_j had all 0's there and the other had all 9's. Hence, the contribution to d from all positions j and greater is between $3/10^{j+1}$ and $9/10^{j+1}$.

Finally, in positions before the jth, r and r_j are either the same, in which case the contribution to d from the first $j-1$ positions is 0, or r and r_j differ by at least $1/10^j$. In either case, we see that d cannot be 0. Thus, r and r_j cannot be the same real number.

We conclude that r does not appear in the list of real numbers. Thus, our hypothetical one-to-one correspondence from the nonnegative integers to the reals between 0 and 1 is not one to one. We have shown there is at least one real number in that range, namely r, that is not associated with any integer.

EXERCISES

7.11.1: Show that equipotence is an equivalence relation. *Hint*: The hard part is transitivity, showing that if there is a one-to-one correspondence f from S to T, and a one-to-one correspondence g from T to R, then there is a one-to-one correspondence from S to R. This function is the *composition* of f and g, that is, the function that sends each element x in S to $g\big(f(x)\big)$ in R.

Composition of
functions

7.11.2: In the ordering of pairs in Fig. 7.34, what pair is assigned number 100?

7.11.3*: Show that the following sets are countable (have a one-to-one correspondence between them and the natural numbers):

a)   The set of perfect squares
b)   The set of triples (i, j, k) of natural numbers
c)   The set of powers of 2
d)   The set of finite sets of natural numbers

7.11.4**: Show that $\mathbf{P(N)}$, the power set of the natural numbers, has the same cardinality as the reals — that is, there is a one-to-one correspondence from $\mathbf{P(N)}$ to the reals between 0 and 1. Note that this conclusion does not contradict Exercise 7.11.3(d), because here we are talking about finite and infinite sets of integers, while there we counted only finite sets. *Hint*: The following construction almost works, but needs to be fixed. Consider the characteristic vector for any set of natural numbers. This vector is an infinite sequence of 0's and 1's. For example, $\{0, 1\}$ has the characteristic vector $1100\cdots$, and the set of odd numbers has the characteristic vector $010101\cdots$. If we put a decimal point in front of a characteristic vector, we have a binary fraction between 0 and 1, which represents a real number. Thus, every set is sent to a real in the range 0 to 1, and every real number in that range can be associated with a set, by turning its binary representation into a characteristic vector. The reason this association is not a one-to-one correspondence is that certain reals have two binary representations. For example, $.11000\cdots$ and $.10111\cdots$ both represent the real number $3/4$. However, these sequences as characteristic vectors represent different sets; the first is $\{0, 1\}$ and the second is the set of all integers except 1. You can modify this construction to define a one-to-one correspondence.

7.11.5**: Show that there is a one-to-one correspondence from pairs of reals in the range 0 to 1 to reals in that range. *Hint*: It is not possible to imitate the table of Fig. 7.34 directly. However, we may take a pair of reals, say, (r, s), and combine the infinite decimal fractions for r and s to make a unique new real number t. This number will not be related to r and s by any simple arithmetic expression, but from t, we can recover r and s uniquely. The reader must discover a way to construct the decimal expansion of t from the expansions of r and s.

7.11.6**: Show that whenever a set S contains subsets of all integer sizes $0, 1, \ldots,$ then it is an infinite set according to the formal definition of "infinite"; that is, S has a one-to-one correspondence with one of its proper subsets.

✦✦ 7.12   Summary of Chapter 7

You should take away the following points from Chapter 7:

✦   The concept of a set is fundamental to both mathematics and computer science.

✦   The common operations on sets such as union, intersection, and difference can be visualized in terms of Venn diagrams.

✦   Algebraic laws can be used to manipulate and simplify expressions involving sets and operations on sets.

✦ Linked lists, characteristic vectors, and hash tables provide three basic ways to represent sets. Linked lists offer the greatest flexibility for most set operations but are not always the most efficient. Characteristic vectors provide the greatest speed for certain set operations but can be used only when the universal set is small. Hash tables are often the method of choice, providing both economy of representation and speed of access.

✦ (Binary) relations are sets of pairs. A function is a relation in which there is at most one tuple with a given first component.

✦ A one-to-one correspondence between two sets is a function that associates a unique element of the second set with each element of the first, and vice versa.

✦ There are a number of significant properties of binary relations: reflexivity, transitivity, symmetry, and asymmetry are among the most important.

✦ Partial orders, total orders, and equivalence relations are important special cases of binary relations.

✦ Infinite sets are those sets that have a one-to-one correspondence with one of their proper subsets.

✦ Some infinite sets are "countable," that is, they have a one-to-one correspondence with the integers. Other infinite sets, such as the reals, are not countable.

✦ The data structures and operations defined on sets and relations in this chapter will be used in many different ways in the remainder of this book.

✦✦ 7.13 Bibliographic Notes for Chapter 7

Halmos [1974] provides a good introduction to set theory. Hashing techniques were first developed in the 1950's, and Peterson [1957] covers the early techniques. Knuth [1973] and Morris [1968] contain additional material on hashing techniques. Reingold [1972] discusses the computational complexity of basic set operations. The theory of infinite sets was developed by Cantor [1915].

Cantor, G. [1915]. "Contributions to the founding of the theory of transfinite numbers," reprinted by Dover Press, New York.

Halmos, P. R. [1974]. *Naive Set Theory*, Springer-Verlag, New York.

Knuth, D. E. [1973]. *The Art of Computer Programming*, Vol. III, *Sorting and Searching*, Addison-Wesley, Reading, Mass.

Morris, R. [1968]. "Scatter storage techniques," *Comm. ACM* **11**:1, pp. 35–44.

Peterson, W. W. [1957]. "Addressing for random access storage," *IBM J. Research and Development* **1**:7, pp. 130–146.

Reingold, E. M. [1972]. "On the optimality of some set algorithms," *J. ACM* **19**:4, pp. 649–659.

CHAPTER | 8

❖❖

The Relational
Data Model

One of the most important applications for computers is storing and managing information. The manner in which information is organized can have a profound effect on how easy it is to access and manage. Perhaps the simplest but most versatile way to organize information is to store it in tables.

The relational model is centered on this idea: the organization of data into collections of two-dimensional tables called "relations." We can also think of the relational model as a generalization of the set data model that we discussed in Chapter 7, extending binary relations to relations of arbitrary arity.

Database

Originally, the relational data model was developed for *databases* — that is, information stored over a long period of time in a computer system — and for *database management systems*, the software that allows people to store, access, and modify this information. Databases still provide us with important motivation for understanding the relational data model. They are found today not only in their original, large-scale applications such as airline reservation systems or banking systems, but in desktop computers handling individual activities such as maintaining expense records, homework grades, and many other uses.

Other kinds of software besides database systems can make good use of tables of information as well, and the relational data model helps us design these tables and develop the data structures that we need to access them efficiently. For example, such tables are used by compilers to store information about the variables used in the program, keeping track of their data type and of the functions for which they are defined.

❖❖ 8.1 What This Chapter Is About

There are three intertwined themes in this chapter. First, we introduce you to the design of information structures using the relational model. We shall see that

❖ Tables of information, called "relations," are a powerful and flexible way to represent information (Section 8.2).

✦ An important part of the design process is selecting "attributes," or properties of the described objects, that can be kept together in a table, without introducing "redundancy," a situation where a fact is repeated several times (Section 8.2).

✦ The columns of a table are named by attributes. The "key" for a table (or relation) is a set of attributes whose values uniquely determine the values of a whole row of the table. Knowing the key for a table helps us design data structures for the table (Section 8.3).

✦ Indexes are data structures that help us retrieve or change information in tables quickly. Judicious selection of indexes is essential if we want to operate on our tables efficiently (Sections 8.4, 8.5, and 8.6).

The second theme is the way data structures can speed access to information. We shall learn that

✦ Primary index structures, such as hash tables, arrange the various rows of a table in the memory of a computer. The right structure can enhance efficiency for many operations (Section 8.4).

✦ Secondary indexes provide additional structure and help perform other operations efficiently (Sections 8.5 and 8.6).

Our third theme is a very high-level way of expressing "queries," that is, questions about the information in a collection of tables. The following points are made:

✦ Relational algebra is a powerful notation for expressing queries without giving details about how the operations are to be carried out (Section 8.7).

✦ The operators of relational algebra can be implemented using the data structures discussed in this chapter (Section 8.8).

✦ In order that we may get answers quickly to queries expressed in relational algebra, it is often necessary to "optimize" them, that is, to use algebraic laws to convert an expression into an equivalent expression with a faster evaluation strategy. We learn some of the techniques in Section 8.9.

✦✦✦ 8.2 Relations

Section 7.7 introduced the notion of a "relation" as a set of tuples. Each tuple of a relation is a list of components, and each relation has a fixed arity, which is the number of components each of its tuples has. While we studied primarily binary relations, that is, relations of arity 2, we indicated that relations of other arities were possible, and indeed can be quite useful.

The relational model uses a notion of "relation" that is closely related to this set-theoretic definition, but differs in some details. In the relational model, information is stored in tables such as the one shown in Fig. 8.1. This particular table represents data that might be stored in a registrar's computer about courses, students who have taken them, and the grades they obtained.

Attribute   The columns of the table are given names, called *attributes*. In Fig. 8.1, the attributes are Course, StudentId, and Grade.

Course	StudentId	Grade
CS101	12345	A
CS101	67890	B
EE200	12345	C
EE200	22222	B+
CS101	33333	A−
PH100	67890	C+

Fig. 8.1. A table of information.

Relations as Sets Versus Relations as Tables

In the relational model, as in our discussion of set-theoretic relations in Section 7.7, a relation is a set of tuples. Thus the order in which the rows of a table are listed has no significance, and we can rearrange the rows in any way without changing the value of the table, just as we can we rearrange the order of elements in a set without changing the value of the set.

The order of the components in each row of a table is significant, since different columns are named differently, and each component must represent an item of the kind indicated by the header of its column. In the relational model, however, we may permute the order of the columns along with the names of their headers and keep the relation the same. This aspect of database relations is different from set-theoretic relations, but rarely shall we reorder the columns of a table, and so we can keep the same terminology. In cases of doubt, the term "relation" in this chapter will always have the database meaning.

Tuple

Each row in the table is called a *tuple* and represents a basic fact. The first row, (CS101, 12345, A), represents the fact that the student with ID number 12345 got an A in the course CS101.

A table has two aspects:

1.   The set of column names, and

2.   The rows containing the information.

The term "relation" refers to the latter, that is, the set of rows. Each row represents a tuple of the relation, and the order in which the rows appear in the table is immaterial. No two rows of the same table may have identical values in all columns.

Relation scheme

Item (1), the set of column names (attributes) is called the *scheme* of the relation. The order in which the attributes appear in the scheme is immaterial, but we need to know the correspondence between the attributes and the columns of the table in order to write the tuples properly. Frequently, we shall use the scheme as the name of the relation. Thus the table in Fig. 8.1 will often be called the Course-StudentId-Grade relation. Alternatively, we could give the relation a name, like *CSG*.

Representing Relations

As sets, there are a variety of ways to represent relations by data structures. A table looks as though its rows should be structures, with fields corresponding to the column names. For example, the tuples in the relation of Fig. 8.1 could be represented by structures of the type

```
struct CSG {
    char Course[5];
    int StudentId;
    char Grade[2];
};
```

The table itself could be represented in any of a number of ways, such as

1. An array of structures of this type.

2. A linked list of structures of this type, with the addition of a **next** field to link the cells of the list.

Additionally, we can identify one or more attributes as the "domain" of the relation and regard the remainder of the attributes as the "range." For instance, the relation of Fig. 8.1 could be viewed as a relation from domain Course to a range consisting of StudentId-Grade pairs. We could then store the relation in a hash table according to the scheme for binary relations that we discussed in Section 7.9. That is, we hash Course values, and the elements in buckets are Course-StudentId-Grade triples. We shall take up this issue of data structures for relations in more detail, starting in Section 8.4.

Databases

A collection of relations is called a *database*. The first thing we need to do when designing a database for some application is to decide on how the information to be stored should be arranged into tables. Design of a database, like all design problems, is a matter of business needs and judgment. In an example to follow, we shall expand our application of a registrar's database involving courses, and thereby expose some of the principles of good database design.

Some of the most powerful operations on a database involve the use of several relations to represent coordinated types of data. By setting up appropriate data structures, we can jump from one relation to another efficiently, and thus obtain information from the database that we could not uncover from a single relation. The data structures and algorithms involved in "navigating" among relations will be discussed in Sections 8.6 and 8.8.

Database scheme

The set of schemes for the various relations in a database is called the *scheme* of the database. Notice the difference between the scheme for the database, which tells us something about how information is organized in the database, and the set of tuples in each relation, which is the actual information stored in the database.

◆   **Example 8.1.** Let us supplement the relation of Fig. 8.1, which has scheme

{Course, StudentId, Grade}

with four other relations. Their schemes and intuitive meanings are:

1.   {StudentId, Name, Address, Phone}. The student whose ID appears in the first component of a tuple has name, address, and phone number equal to the values appearing in the second, third, and fourth components, respectively.

2.   {Course, Prerequisite}. The course named in the second component of a tuple is a prerequisite for the course named in the first component of that tuple.

3.   {Course, Day, Hour}. The course named in the first component meets on the day specified by the second component, at the hour named in the third component.

4.   {Course, Room}. The course named in the first component meets in the room indicated by the second component.

These four schemes, plus the scheme {Course, StudentId, Grade} mentioned earlier, form the database scheme for a running example in this chapter. We also need to offer an example of a possible "current value" for the database. Figure 8.1 gave an example for the Course-StudentId-Grade relation, and example relations for the other four schemes are shown in Fig. 8.2. Keep in mind that these relations are all much shorter than we would find in reality; we are just offering some sample tuples for each. ✦

Queries on a Database

We saw in Chapter 7 some of the most important operations performed on relations and functions; they were called *insert*, *delete*, and *lookup*, although their appropriate meanings differed, depending on whether we were dealing with a dictionary, a function, or a binary relation. There is a great variety of operations one can perform on database relations, especially on combinations of two or more relations, and we shall give a feel for this spectrum of operations in Section 8.7. For the moment, let us focus on the basic operations that we might perform on a single relation. These are a natural generalization of the operations discussed in the previous chapter.

1.   *insert*(t, R). We add the tuple t to the relation R, if it is not already there. This operation is in the same spirit as *insert* for dictionaries or binary relations.

2.   *delete*(X, R). Here, X is intended to be a specification of some tuples. It consists of components for each of the attributes of R, and each component can be either

  a)   A value, or
  b)   The symbol *, which means that any value is acceptable.

The effect of this operation is to delete all tuples that match the specification X. For example, if we cancel CS101, we want to delete all tuples of the

       Course-Day-Hour

relation that have Course = "CS101." We could express this condition by

       delete$(($"CS101"$, *, *),$ Course-Day-Hour$)$

That operation would delete the first three tuples of the relation in Fig. 8.2(c), because their first components each are the same value as the first component of the specification, and their second and third components all match *, as any values do.

StudentId	Name	Address	Phone
12345	C. Brown	12 Apple St.	555-1234
67890	L. Van Pelt	34 Pear Ave.	555-5678
22222	P. Patty	56 Grape Blvd.	555-9999

(a) StudentId-Name-Address-Phone

Course	Prerequisite
CS101	CS100
EE200	EE005
EE200	CS100
CS120	CS101
CS121	CS120
CS205	CS101
CS206	CS121
CS206	CS205

(b) Course-Prerequisite

Course	Day	Hour
CS101	M	9AM
CS101	W	9AM
CS101	F	9AM
EE200	Tu	10AM
EE200	W	1PM
EE200	Th	10AM

(c) Course-Day-Hour

Course	Room
CS101	Turing Aud.
EE200	25 Ohm Hall
PH100	Newton Lab.

(d) Course-Room

Fig. 8.2. Sample relations.

3. *lookup*(X, R). The result of this operation is the set of tuples in R that match the specification X; the latter is a symbolic tuple as described in the preceding item (2). For example, if we wanted to know for what courses CS101 is a prerequisite, we could ask

$$lookup((*, \text{``CS101''}), \text{Course-Prerequisite})$$

The result would be the set of two matching tuples

(CS120, CS101)
(CS205, CS101)

✦ **Example 8.2.** Here are some more examples of operations on our registrar's database:

a) *lookup*(("CS101", 12345, ∗), Course-StudentId-Grade) finds the grade of the student with ID 12345 in CS101. Formally, the result is the one matching tuple, namely the first tuple in Fig. 8.1.

b) *lookup*(("CS205", "CS120"), Course-Prerequisite) asks whether CS120 is a prerequisite of CS205. Formally, it produces as an answer either the single tuple ("CS205", "CS120") if that tuple is in the relation, or the empty set if not. For the particular relation of Fig. 8.2(b), the empty set is the answer.

c) *delete*(("CS101", ∗), Course-Room) drops the first tuple from the relation of Fig. 8.2(d).

d) *insert*(("CS205", "CS120"), Course-Prerequisite) makes CS120 a prerequisite of CS205.

e) *insert*(("CS205", "CS101"), Course-Prerequisite) has no effect on the relation of Fig. 8.2(b), because the inserted tuple is already there. ✦

The Design of Data Structures for Relations

In much of the rest of this chapter, we are going to discuss the issue of how one selects a data structure for a relation. We have already seen some of the problem when we discussed the implementation of binary relations in Section 7.9. The relation Variety-Pollinizer was given a hash table on Variety as its data structure, and we observed that the structure was very useful for answering queries like

$$lookup\big((\text{``Wickson''}, ∗), \text{Variety-Pollinizer}\big)$$

because the value "Wickson" lets us find a specific bucket in which to search. But that structure was of no help answering queries like

$$lookup\big((∗, \text{``Wickson''}), \text{Variety-Pollinizer}\big)$$

because we would have to look in all buckets.

Whether a hash table on Variety is an adequate data structure depends on the expected mix of queries. If we expect the variety always to be specified, then a hash table is adequate, and if we expect the variety sometimes not to be specified, as in the preceding query, then we need to design a more powerful data structure.

The selection of a data structure is one of the essential design issues we tackle in this chapter. In the next section, we shall generalize the basic data structures for functions and relations from Sections 7.8 and 7.9, to allow for several attributes in either the domain or the range. These structures will be called "primary index structures." Then, in Section 8.5 we introduce "secondary index structures," which are additional structures that allow us to answer a greater variety of queries efficiently. At that point, we shall see how both the above queries, and others we might ask about the Variety-Pollinizer relation, can be answered efficiently, that is, in about as much time as it takes to list all the answers.

Design I: Selecting a Database Scheme

An important issue when we use the relational data model is how we select an appropriate database scheme. For instance, why did we separate information about courses into five relations, rather than have one table with scheme

{Course, StudentId, Grade, Prerequisite, Day, Hour, Room}

The intuitive reason is that

✦   If we combine into one relation scheme information of two independent types, we may be forced to repeat the same fact many times.

For example, prerequisite information about a course is independent of day and hour information. If we were to combine prerequisite and day-hour information, we would have to list the prerequisites for a course in conjunction with every meeting of the course, and vice versa. Then the data about EE200 found in Fig. 8.2(b) and (c), if put into a single relation with scheme

{Course, Prerequisite, Day, Hour}

would look like

Course	Prerequisite	Day	Hour
EE200	EE005	Tu	10AM
EE200	EE005	W	1PM
EE200	EE005	Th	10AM
EE200	CS100	Tu	10AM
EE200	CS100	W	1PM
EE200	CS100	Th	10AM

Notice that we take six tuples, with four components each, to do the work previously done by five tuples, with two or three components each.

✦   Conversely, do not separate attributes when they represent connected information.

For example, we cannot replace the Course-Day-Hour relation by two relations, one with scheme Course-Day and the other with scheme Course-Hour. For then, we could only tell that EE200 meets Tuesday, Wednesday, and Thursday, and that it has meetings at 10AM and 1PM, but we could not tell when it met on each of its three days.

EXERCISES

8.2.1: Give appropriate structure declarations for the tuples of the relations of Fig. 8.2(a) through (d).

8.2.2*: What is an appropriate database scheme for

a)   A telephone directory, including all the information normally found in a directory, such as area codes.

b) A dictionary of the English language, including all the information normally found in the dictionary, such as word origins and parts of speech.

c) A calendar, including information normally found on a calendar such as holidays, good for the years 1 through 4000.

✦✦ 8.3   Keys

Many database relations can be considered functions from one set of attributes to the remaining attributes. For example, we might choose to view the

Course-StudentId-Grade

relation as a function whose domain is Course-StudentId pairs and whose range is Grade. Because functions have somewhat simpler data structures than general relations, it helps if we know a set of attributes that can serve as the domain of a function. Such a set of attributes is called a "key."

More formally, a *key* for a relation is a set of one or more attributes such that under no circumstances will the relation have two tuples whose values agree in each column headed by a key attribute. Frequently, there are several different sets of attributes that could serve as a key for a relation, but we normally pick one and refer to it as "the key."

Finding Keys

Because keys can be used as the domain of a function, they play an important role in the next section when we discuss primary index structures. In general, we cannot deduce or prove that a set of attributes forms a key; rather, we need to examine carefully our assumptions about the application being modeled and how they are reflected in the database scheme we are designing. Only then can we know whether it is appropriate to use a given set of attributes as a key. There follows a sequence of examples that illustrate some of the issues.

✦   **Example 8.3.** Consider the relation StudentId-Name-Address-Phone of Fig. 8.2(a). Evidently, the intent is that each tuple gives information about a different student. We do not expect to find two tuples with the same ID number, because the whole purpose of such a number is to give each student a unique identifier.

If we have two tuples with identical student ID numbers in the same relation, then one of two things has gone wrong.

1. If the two tuples are identical in all components, then we have violated our assumption that a relation is a set, because no element can appear more than once in a set.

2. If the two tuples have identical ID numbers but disagree in at least one of the Name, Address, or Phone columns, then there is something wrong with the data. Either we have two different students with the same ID (if the tuples differ in Name), or we have mistakenly recorded two different addresses and/or phone numbers for the same student.

Thus it is reasonable to take the StudentId attribute by itself as a key for the StudentId-Name-Address-Phone relation.

However, in declaring StudentId a key, we have made a critical assumption, enunciated in item (2) preceding, that we never want to store two names, addresses, or phone numbers for one student. But we could just as well have decided otherwise, for example, that we want to store for each student both a home address and a campus address. If so, we would probably be better off designing the relation to have five attributes, with Address replaced by HomeAddress and LocalAddress, rather than have two tuples for each student, with all but the Address component the same. If we did use two tuples — differing in their Address components only — then StudentId would no longer be a key but {StudentId, Address} would be a key. ✦

✦ **Example 8.4.** Examining the Course-StudentId-Grade relation of Fig. 8.1, we might imagine that Grade was a key, since we see no two tuples with the same grade. However, this reasoning is fallacious. In this little example of six tuples, no two tuples hold the same grade; but in a typical Course-StudentId-Grade relation, which would have thousands or tens of thousands of tuples, surely there would be many grades appearing more than once.

Most probably, the intent of the designers of the database is that Course and StudentId together form a key. That is, assuming students cannot take the same course twice, we could not have two different grades assigned to the same student in the same course; hence, there could not be two different tuples that agreed in both Course and StudentId. Since we would expect to find many tuples with the same Course component and many tuples with the same StudentId component, neither Course nor StudentId by itself would be a key.

However, our assumption that students can get only one grade in any course is another design decision that could be questioned, depending on the policy of the school. Perhaps when course content changes sufficiently, a student may reregister for the course. If that were the case, we would not declare {Course, StudentId} to be a key for the Course-StudentId-Grade relation; rather, the set of all three attributes would be the only key. (Note that the set of all attributes for a relation can always be used as a key, since two identical tuples cannot appear in a relation.) In fact, it would be better to add a fourth attribute, Date, to indicate when a course was taken. Then we could handle the situation where a student took the same course twice and got the same grade each time. ✦

✦ **Example 8.5.** In the Course-Prerequisite relation of Fig. 8.2(b), neither attribute by itself is a key, but the two attributes together form a key. ✦

✦ **Example 8.6.** In the Course-Day-Hour relation of Fig. 8.2(c), all three attributes form the only reasonable key. Perhaps Course and Day alone could be declared a key, but then it would be impossible to store the fact that a course met twice in one day (e.g., for a lecture and a lab). ✦

Design II: Selecting a Key

Determining a key for a relation is an important aspect of database design; it is used when we select a primary index structure in Section 8.4.

✦ You can't tell the key by looking at an example value for the relation.

That is, appearances can be deceptive, as in the matter of Grade for the Course-StudentId-Grade relation of Fig. 8.1, which we discuss in Example 8.4.

✦ There is no one "right" key selection; what is a key depends on assumptions made about the types of data the relations will hold.

✦ **Example 8.7.** Finally, consider the Course-Room relation of Fig. 8.2(d). We believe that Course is a key; that is, no course meets in two or more different rooms. If that were not the case, then we should have combined the Course-Room relation with the Course-Day-Hour relation, so we could tell which meetings of a course were held in which rooms. ✦

EXERCISES

8.3.1*: Suppose we want to store home and local addresses and also home and local phones for students in the StudentId-Name-Address-Phone relation.

a) What would then be the most suitable key for the relation?

b) This change causes redundancy; for example, the name of a student could be repeated four times as his or her two addresses and two phones are combined in all possible ways in different tuples. We suggested in Example 8.3 that one solution is to use separate attributes for the different addresses and different phones. What would the relation scheme be then? What would be the most suitable key for this relation?

c) Another approach to handling redundancy, which we suggested in Section 8.2, is to split the relation into two relations, with different schemes, that together hold all the information of the original. Into what relations should we split StudentId-Name-Address-Phone, if we are going to allow multiple addresses and phones for one student? What would be the most suitable keys for these relations? *Hint*: A critical issue is whether addresses and phones are independent. That is, would you expect a phone number to ring in all addresses belonging to one student (in which case address and phone are independent), or are phones associated with single addresses?

8.3.2*: The Department of Motor Vehicles keeps a database with the following kinds of information.

1. The name of a driver (Name).
2. The address of a driver (Addr).
3. The license number of a driver (LicenseNo).
4. The serial number of an automobile (SerialNo).
5. The manufacturer of an automobile (Manf).
6. The model name of an automobile (Model).

7.   The registration (license plate) number of an automobile (RegNo).

The DMV wants to associate with each driver the relevant information: address, driver's license, and autos owned. It wants to associate with each auto the relevant information: owner(s), serial number, manufacturer, model, and registration. We assume that you are familiar with the basics of operation of the DMV; for example, it strives not to issue the same license plate to two cars. You may not know (but it is a fact) that no two autos, even with different manufacturers, will be given the same serial number.

a)   Select a database scheme — that is, a collection of relation schemes — each consisting of a set of the attributes 1 through 7 listed above. You must allow any of the desired connections to be found from the data stored in these relations, and you must avoid redundancy; that is, your scheme should not require you to store the same fact repeatedly.

b)   Suggest what attributes, if any, could serve as keys for your relations from part (a).

✦✦ 8.4   Primary Storage Structures for Relations

In Sections 7.8 and 7.9 we saw how certain operations on functions and binary relations were speeded up by storing pairs according to their domain value. In terms of the general *insert*, *delete*, and *lookup* operations that we defined in Section 8.2, the operations that are helped are those where the domain value is specified. Recalling the Variety-Pollinizer relation from Section 7.9 again, if we regard Variety as the domain of the relation, then we favor operations that specify a variety but we do not care whether a pollinizer is specified.

Here are some structures we might use to represent a relation.

1.   A binary search tree, with a "less than" relation on domain values to guide the placement of tuples, can serve to facilitate operations in which a domain value is specified.

2.   An array used as a characteristic vector, with domain values as the array index, can sometimes serve.

3.   A hash table in which we hash domain values to find buckets will serve.

4.   In principle, a linked list of tuples is a candidate structure. We shall ignore this possibility, since it does not facilitate operations of any sort.

Domain and range attributes

The same structures work when the relation is not binary. In place of a single attribute for the domain, we may have a combination of k attributes, which we call the *domain attributes* or just the "domain" when it is clear we are referring to a set of attributes. Then, domain values are k-tuples, with one component for each attribute of the domain. The *range attributes* are all those attributes other than the domain attributes. The range values may also have several components, one for each attribute of the range.

In general, we have to pick which attributes we want for the domain. The easiest case occurs when there is one or a small number of attributes that serve as a key for the relation. Then it is common to choose the key attribute(s) as the domain and the rest as the range. In cases where there is no key (except the set of all attributes, which is not a useful key), we may pick any set of attributes as the domain. For example, we might consider typical operations that we expect to perform on the relation and pick for the domain an attribute we expect will be specified frequently. We shall see some concrete examples shortly.

Once we have selected a domain, we can select any of the four data structures just named to represent the relation, or indeed we could select another structure. However, it is common to choose a hash table based on domain values as the index, and we shall generally do so here.

Primary index   The chosen structure is said to be the *primary index structure* for the relation. The adjective "primary" refers to the fact that the location of tuples is determined by this structure. An *index* is a data structure that helps find tuples, given a value for one or more components of the desired tuples. In the next section, we shall discuss "secondary" indexes, which help answer queries but do not affect the location of the data.

```
typedef struct TUPLE *TUPLELIST;
struct TUPLE {
    int StudentId;
    char Name[30];
    char Address[50];
    char Phone[8];
    TUPLELIST next;
};
typedef TUPLELIST HASHTABLE[1009];
```

Fig. 8.3. Types for a hash table as primary index structure.

♦   **Example 8.8.** Let us consider the StudentId-Name-Address-Phone relation, which has key StudentId. This attribute will serve as our domain, and the other three attributes will form the range. We may thus see the relation as a function from StudentId to Name-Address-Phone triples.

As with all functions, we select a hash function that takes a domain value as argument and produces a bucket number as result. In this case, the hash function takes student ID numbers, which are integers, as arguments. We shall choose the number of buckets, B, to be 1009,[1] and the hash function to be

$$h(x) = x \ \% \ 1009$$

This hash function maps ID's to integers in the range 0 to 1008.

An array of 1009 bucket headers takes us to a list of structures. The structures on the list for bucket i each represent a tuple whose StudentId component is an integer whose remainder, when divided by 1009, is i. For the StudentId-Name-Address-Phone relation, the declarations in Fig. 8.3 are suitable for the structures

---

[1] 1009 is a convenient prime around 1000. We might choose about 1000 buckets if there were several thousand students in our database, so that the average number of tuples in a bucket would be small.

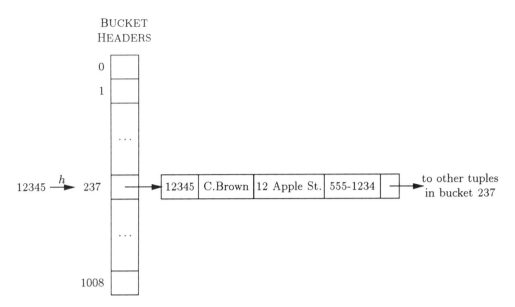

Fig. 8.4. Hash table representing StudentId-Name-Address-Phone relation.

in the linked lists of the buckets and for the bucket header array. Figure 8.4 suggests what the hash table would look like. ✦

✦ **Example 8.9.** For a more complicated example, consider the Course-StudentId-Grade relation. We could use as a primary structure a hash table whose hash function took as argument both the course and the student (i.e., both attributes of the key for this relation). Such a hash function might take the characters of the course name, treat them as integers, add those integers to the student ID number, and divide by 1009, taking the remainder.

That data structure would be useful if all we ever did was look up grades, given a course and a student ID — that is, we performed operations like

$$lookup((\text{``CS101''}, 12345, *), \text{Course-StudentId-Grade})$$

However, it is not useful for operations such as

1. Finding all the students taking CS101, or

2. Finding all the courses being taken by the student whose ID is 12345.

In either case, we would not be able to compute a value for the hash function. For example, given only the course, we do not have a student ID to add to the sum of the characters converted to integers, and thus have no value to divide by 1009 to get the bucket number.

However, suppose it is quite common to ask queries like, "Who is taking CS101?," that is,

$$lookup((\text{``CS101''}, *, *), \text{Course-StudentId-Grade})$$

Design III: Choosing a Primary Index

✦   It is often useful to make the key for a relation scheme be the domain of a function and the remaining attributes be the range.

Then, the relation can be implemented as if it were a function, using a primary index such as a hash table, with the hash function based on the key attributes.

✦   However, if the most common type of query specifies values for an attribute or a set of attributes that do not form a key, we may prefer to use this set of attributes as the domain, with the other attributes as the range.

We may then implement this relation as a binary relation (e.g., by a hash table). The only problem is that the division of the tuples into buckets may not be as even as we would expect were the domain a key.

✦   The choice of domain for the primary index structure probably has the greatest influence over the speed with which we can execute "typical" queries.

We might find it more efficient to use a primary structure based only on the value of the Course component. That is, we may regard our relation as a binary relation in the set-theoretic sense, with domain equal to Course and range the StudentId-Grade pairs.

For instance, suppose we convert the characters of the course name to integers, sum them, divide by 197, and take the remainder. Then the tuples of the

> Course-StudentId-Grade

relation would be divided by this hash function into 197 buckets, numbered 0 through 196. However, if CS101 has 100 students, then there would be at least 100 structures in its bucket, regardless of how many buckets we chose for our hash table; that is the disadvantage of using something other than a key on which to base our primary index structure. There could even be more than 100 structures, if some other course were hashed to the same bucket as CS101.

On the other hand, we still get help when we want to find the students in a given course. If the number of courses is significantly more than 197, then on the average, we shall have to search something like 1/197 of the entire

> Course-StudentId-Grade

relation, which is a great saving. Moreover, we get some help when performing operations like looking up a particular student's grade in a particular course, or inserting or deleting a Course-StudentId-Grade tuple. In each case, we can use the Course value to restrict our search to one of the 197 buckets of the hash table. The only sort of operation for which no help is provided is one in which no course is specified. For example, to find the courses taken by student 12345, we must search all the buckets. Such a query can be made more efficient only if we use a secondary index structure, as discussed in the next section. ✦

Insert, Delete, and Lookup Operations

The way in which we use a primary index structure to perform the operations *insert*, *delete*, and *lookup* should be obvious, given our discussion of the same subject for binary relations in Chapter 7. To review the ideas, let us focus on a hash table as the primary index structure. If the operation specifies a value for the domain, then we hash this value to find a bucket.

1. To insert a tuple t, we examine the bucket to check that t is not already there, and we create a new cell on the bucket's list for t if it is not.

2. To delete tuples that match a specification X, we find the domain value from X, hash to find the proper bucket, and run down the list for this bucket, deleting each tuple that matches the specification X.

3. To lookup tuples according to a specification X, we again find the domain value from X and hash that value to find the proper bucket. We run down the list for that bucket, producing as an answer each tuple on the list that matches the specification X.

If the operation does not specify the domain value, we are not so fortunate. An *insert* operation always specifies the inserted tuple completely, but a *delete* or *lookup* might not. In those cases, we must search all the bucket lists for matching tuples and delete or list them, respectively.

EXERCISES

8.4.1: The DMV database of Exercise 8.3.2 should be designed to handle the following sorts of queries, all of which may be assumed to occur with significant frequency.

1. What is the address of a given driver?
2. What is the license number of a given driver?
3. What is the name of the driver with a given license number?
4. What is the name of the driver who owns a given automobile, identified by its registration number?
5. What are the serial number, manufacturer, and model of the automobile with a given registration number?
6. Who owns the automobile with a given registration number?

Suggest appropriate primary index structures for the relations you designed in Exercise 8.3.2, using a hash table in each case. State your assumptions about how many drivers and automobiles there are. Tell how many buckets you suggest, as well as what the domain attribute(s) are. How many of these types of queries can you answer efficiently, that is, in average time $O(1)$ independent of the size of the relations?

8.4.2: The primary structure for the Course-Day-Hour relation of Fig. 8.2(c) might depend on the typical operations we intended to perform. Suggest an appropriate hash table, including both the attributes in the domain and the number of buckets if the typical queries are of each of the following forms. You may make reasonable assumptions about how many courses and different class periods there are. In each case, a specified value like "CS101" is intended to represent a "typical" value; in this case, we would mean that Course is specified to be some particular course.

a) *lookup*(("CS101", "M", ∗), Course-Day-Hour).

b) *lookup*((∗, "M", "9AM"), Course-Day-Hour).

c) *delete*(("CS101", ∗, ∗), Course-Day-Hour).

d) Half of type (a) and half of type (b).

e) Half of type (a) and half of type (c).

f) Half of type (b) and half of type (c).

✦✦ 8.5 Secondary Index Structures

Suppose we store the StudentId-Name-Address-Phone relation in a hash table, where the hash function is based on the key StudentId, as in Fig. 8.4. This primary index structure helps us answer queries in which the student ID number is specified. However, perhaps we wish to ask questions in terms of students' names, rather than impersonal — and probably unknown — ID's. For example, we might ask, "What is the phone number of the student named C. Brown?" Now, our primary index structure gives no help. We must go to each bucket and examine the lists of records until we find one whose Name field has value "C. Brown."

To answer such a query rapidly, we need an additional data structure that takes us from a name to the tuple or tuples with that name in the Name component of the tuple.[2] A data structure that helps us find tuples — given a value for a certain attribute or attributes — but is not used to position the tuples within the overall structure, is called a *secondary index*.

What we want for our secondary index is a binary relation whose

1. Domain is Name.

2. Range is the set of pointers to tuples of the StudentId-Name-Address-Phone relation.

In general, a secondary index on attribute A of relation R is a set of pairs (v, p), where

a) v is a value for attribute A, and

b) p is a pointer to one of the tuples, in the primary index structure for relation R, whose A-component has the value v.

The secondary index has one such pair for each tuple with the value v in attribute A.

We may use any of the data structures for binary relations for storing secondary indexes. Usually, we would expect to use a hash table on the value of the attribute A. As long as the number of buckets is no greater than the number of different values of attribute A, we can normally expect good performance — that is, $O(n/B)$ time, on the average — to find one pair (v, p) in the hash table, given a desired value of v. (Here, n is the number of pairs and B is the number of buckets.) To show that other structures are possible for secondary (or primary) indexes, in the next example we shall use a binary search tree as a secondary index.

---

[2] Remember that Name is not a key for the StudentId-Name-Address-Phone relation, despite the fact that in the sample relation of Fig. 8.2(a), there are no tuples that have the same Name value. For example, if Linus goes to the same college as Lucy, we could find two tuples with Name equal to "L. Van Pelt," but with different student ID's.

◆   **Example 8.10.** Let us develop a data structure for the

StudentId-Name-Address-Phone

relation of Fig. 8.2(a) that uses a hash table on StudentId as a primary index and a binary search tree as a secondary index for attribute Name. To simplify the presentation, we shall use a hash table with only two buckets for the primary structure, and the hash function we use is the remainder when the student ID is divided by 2. That is, the even ID's go into bucket 0 and the odd ID's into bucket 1.

```
typedef struct TUPLE *TUPLELIST;
struct TUPLE {
    int StudentId;
    char Name[30];
    char Address[50];
    char Phone[8];
    TUPLELIST next;
};

typedef TUPLELIST HASHTABLE[2];

typedef struct NODE *TREE;
struct NODE {
    char Name[30];
    TUPLELIST toTuple; /* really a pointer to a tuple */
    TREE lc;
    TREE rc;
};
```

Fig. 8.5. Types for a primary and a secondary index.

For the secondary index, we shall use a binary search tree, whose nodes store elements that are pairs consisting of the name of a student and a pointer to a tuple. The tuples themselves are stored as records, which are linked in a list to form one of the buckets of the hash table, and so the pointers to tuples are really pointers to records. Thus we need the structures of Fig. 8.5. The types **TUPLE** and **HASHTABLE** are the same as in Fig. 8.3, except that we are now using two buckets rather than 1009 buckets.

The type **NODE** is a binary tree node with two fields, **Name** and **toTuple**, representing the element at the node — that is, a student's name — and a pointer to a record where the tuple for that student is kept. The remaining two fields, **lc** and **rc**, are intended to be pointers to the left and right children of the node. We shall use alphabetic order on the last names of students as the "less than" order with which we compare elements at the nodes of the tree. The secondary index itself is a variable of type **TREE** — that is, a pointer to a node — and it takes us to the root of the binary search tree.

An example of the entire structure is shown in Fig. 8.6. To save space, the Address and Phone components of tuples are not shown. The Li's indicate the memory locations at which the records of the primary index structure are stored.

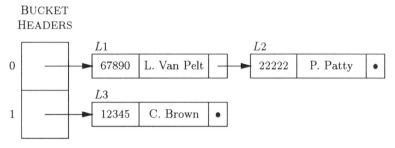

(a) Primary index structure

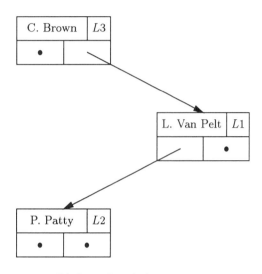

(b) Secondary index structure

Fig. 8.6. Example of primary and secondary index structures.

Now, if we want to answer a query like "What is P. Patty's phone number," we go to the root of the secondary index, look up the node with **Name** field "P. Patty," and follow the pointer in the **toTuple** field (shown as *L2* in Fig. 8.6). That gets us to the record for P. Patty, and from that record we can consult the **Phone** field and produce the answer to the query. ✦

Secondary Indexes on a Nonkey Field

It appeared that the attribute Name on which we built a secondary index in Example 8.10 was a key, because no name occurs more than once. As we know, however, it is possible that two students will have the same name, and so Name really is not a key. Nonkeyness, as we discussed in Section 7.9, does not affect the hash table data structure, although it may cause tuples to be distributed less evenly among buckets than we might expect.

A binary search tree is another matter, because that data structure does not handle two elements, neither of which is "less than" the other, as would be the case if we had two pairs with the same name and different pointers. A simple fix to the

---

Design IV: When Should We Create a Secondary Index?

The existence of secondary indexes generally makes it easier to look up a tuple, given the values of one or more of its components. However,

✦   Each secondary index we create costs time when we insert or delete information in the relation.

✦   Thus it makes sense to build a secondary index on only those attributes that we are likely to need for looking up data.

For example, if we never intend to find a student given the phone number alone, then it is wasteful to create a secondary index on the Phone attribute of the

StudentId-Name-Address-Phone

relation.

---

structure of Fig. 8.5 is to use the field `toTuple` as the header of a linked list of pointers to tuples, one pointer for each tuple with a given value in the `Name` field. For instance, if there were several P. Patty's, the bottom node in Fig. 8.6(b) would have, in place of $L2$, the header of a linked list. The elements of that list would be the pointers to the various tuples that had Name attribute equal to "P. Patty."

Updating Secondary Index Structures

When there are one or more secondary indexes for a relation, the insertion and deletion of tuples becomes more difficult. In addition to updating the primary index structure as outlined in Section 8.4, we may need to update each of the secondary index structures as well. The following methods can be used to update a secondary index structure for A when a tuple involving attribute A is inserted or deleted.

1.   *Insertion.* If we insert a new tuple with value v in the component for attribute A, we must create a pair (v, p), where p points to the new record in the primary structure. Then, we insert the pair (v, p) into the secondary index.

2.   *Deletion.* When we delete a tuple that has value v in the component for A, we must first remember a pointer — call it p — to the tuple we have just deleted. Then, we go into the secondary index structure and examine all the pairs with first component v, until we find the one with second component p. That pair is then deleted from the secondary index structure.

EXERCISES

8.5.1: Show how to modify the binary search tree structure of Fig. 8.5 to allow for the possibility that there are several tuples in the StudentId-Name-Address-Phone relation that have the same student name. Write a C function that takes a name and lists all the tuples of the relation that have that name for the Name attribute.

8.5.2**: Suppose that we have decided to store the

StudentId-Name-Address-Phone

relation with a primary index on StudentId. We may also decide to create some secondary indexes. Suppose that all lookups will specify only one attribute, either Name, Address, or Phone. Assume that 75% of all lookups specify Name, 20% specify Address, and 5% specify Phone. Suppose that the cost of an insertion or a deletion is 1 time unit, plus 1/2 time unit for each secondary index we choose to build (e.g., the cost is 2.5 time units if we build all three secondary indexes). Let the cost of a lookup be 1 unit if we specify an attribute for which there is a secondary index, and 10 units if there is no secondary index on the specified attribute. Let a be the fraction of operations that are insertions or deletions of tuples with all attributes specified; the remaining fraction $1 - a$ of the operations are lookups specifying one of the attributes, according to the probabilities we assumed [e.g., $.75(1 - a)$ of all operations are lookups given a Name value]. If our goal is to minimize the average time of an operation, which secondary indexes should we create if the value of parameter a is (a) .01 (b) .1 (c) .5 (d) .9 (e) .99?

8.5.3: Suppose that the DMV wants to be able to answer the following types of queries efficiently, that is, much faster than by searching entire relations.

i)   Given a driver's name, find the driver's license(s) issued to people with that name.
ii)   Given a driver's license number, find the name of the driver.
iii)   Given a driver's license number, find the registration numbers of the auto(s) owned by this driver.
iv)   Given an address, find all the drivers' names at that address.
v)   Given a registration number (i.e., a license plate), find the driver's license(s) of the owner(s) of the auto.

Suggest a suitable data structure for your relations from Exercise 8.3.2 that will allow all these queries to be answered efficiently. It is sufficient to suppose that each index will be built from a hash table and tell what the primary and secondary indexes are for each relation. Explain how you would then answer each type of query.

8.5.4*: Suppose that it is desired to find efficiently the pointers in a given secondary index that point to a particular tuple t in the primary index structure. Suggest a data structure that allows us to find these pointers in time proportional to the number of pointers found. What operations are made more time-consuming because of this additional structure?

✦✦ 8.6   Navigation among Relations

Until now, we have considered only operations involving a single relation, such as finding a tuple given values for one or more of its components. The power of the relational model can be seen best when we consider operations that require us to "navigate," or jump from one relation to another. For example, we could answer the query "What grade did the student with ID 12345 get in CS101?" by working entirely within the Course-StudentId-Grade relation. But it would be more natural to ask, "What grade did C. Brown get in CS101?" That query cannot be answered within the Course-StudentId-Grade relation alone, because that relation uses student ID's, rather than names.

To answer the query, we must first consult the StudentId-Name-Address-Phone relation and translate the name "C. Brown" into a student ID (or ID's, since it is possible that there are two or more students with the same name and different ID's). Then, for each such ID, we search the Course-StudentId-Grade relation for tuples with this ID and with course component equal to "CS101." From each such tuple we can read the grade of some student named C. Brown in course CS101. Figure 8.7 suggests how this query connects given values to the relations and to the desired answers.

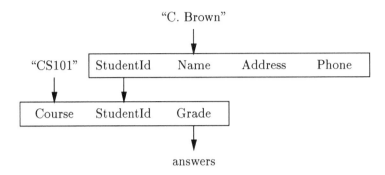

Fig. 8.7. Diagram of the query "What grade did C. Brown get in CS101?"

If there are no indexes we can use, then answering this query can be quite time-consuming. Suppose that there are n tuples in the

StudentId-Name-Address-Phone

relation and m tuples in the Course-StudentId-Grade relation. Also assume that there are k students with the name "C. Brown." A sketch of the algorithm for finding the grades of this student or students in CS101, assuming there are no indexes we can use, is shown in Fig. 8.8.

```
(1)    for each tuple t in StudentId-Name-Address-Phone do
(2)        if t has "C. Brown" in its Name component then begin
(3)            let i be the StudentId component of tuple t;
(4)            for each tuple s in Course-StudentId-Grade do
(5)                if s has Course component "CS101" and
                        StudentId component i then
(6)                    print the Grade component of tuple s;
           end
```

Fig. 8.8. Finding the grade of C. Brown in CS101.

Let us determine the running time of the program in Fig. 8.8. Starting from the inside out, the print statement of line (6) takes $O(1)$ time. The conditional statement of lines (5) and (6) also takes $O(1)$ time, since the test of line (5) is an $O(1)$-time test. Since we assume that there are m tuples in the relation

Course-StudentId-Grade

the loop of lines (4) through (6) is iterated m times and thus takes $O(m)$ time in total. Since line (3) takes $O(1)$ time, the block of lines (3) to (6) takes $O(m)$ time.

Now consider the if-statement of lines (2) to (6). Since the test of line (2) takes $O(1)$ time, the entire if-statement takes $O(1)$ time if the condition is false and $O(m)$ time if it is true. However, we have assumed that the condition is true for k tuples and false for the rest; that is, there are k tuples t for which the name component is "C. Brown." Since there is so much difference between the times taken when the condition is true and when it is false, we should be careful how we analyze the for-loop of lines (1) to (6). That is, instead of counting the number of times around the loop and multiplying by the greatest time the body can take, we shall consider separately the two outcomes of the test at line (2).

First, we go around the loop n times, because that is the number of different values of t. For the k tuples t on which the test at line (2) is true, we take $O(m)$ time each, or a total of $O(km)$ time. For the remaining $n - k$ tuples for which the test is false, we take $O(1)$ time per tuple, or $O(n - k)$ total. Since k is presumably much less than n, we can take $O(n)$ as a simpler but tight upper bound instead of $O(n - k)$. Thus the cost of the entire program is $O(n + km)$. In the likely case where $k = 1$, when there is only one student with the given name, the time required, $O(n + m)$, is proportional to the sum of the sizes of the two relations involved. If k is greater than 1, the time is greater still.

Speeding Navigation by Using Indexes

With the right indexes, we can answer the same query in $O(k)$ average time — that is, $O(1)$ time if k, the number of students with the name C. Brown, is 1. That makes sense, since all we must do is examine $2k$ tuples, k from each of the two relations. The indexes allow us to focus on the needed tuples in $O(1)$ average time for each tuple, if a hash table with the right number of buckets is used. If we have an index on Name for the StudentId-Name-Address-Phone relation, and an index on the combination of Course and StudentId for the Course-StudentId-Grade relation, then the algorithm for finding the grade of C. Brown in CS101 is as sketched in Fig. 8.9.

(1) using the index on Name, find each tuple in the
  StudentId-Name-Address-Grade relation that has Name
  component "C. Brown";
(2) **for** each tuple t found in (1) **do begin**
(3) let i be the StudentId component of tuple t;
(4) using the index on Course and StudentId in the
   Course-StudentId-Grade relation, find the tuple
   s with Course component "CS101" and StudentId
   component i;
(5) **print** the Grade component of tuple s;
  end

Fig. 8.9. Finding the grade of C. Brown in CS101 using indexes.

Let us assume that the index on Name is a hash table with about n buckets, used as a secondary index. Since n is the number of tuples in the

StudentId-Name-Address-Grade

relation, the buckets have $O(1)$ tuples each, on the average. Finding the bucket for Name value "C. Brown" takes $O(1)$ time. If there are k tuples with this name, it will take $O(k)$ time to find these tuples in the bucket and $O(1)$ time to skip over possible other tuples in the bucket. Thus line (1) of Fig. 8.9 takes $O(k)$ time on the average.

The loop of lines (2) through (5) is executed k times. Let us suppose we store the k tuples t that were found at line (1) in a linked list. Then the cost of going around the loop by finding the next tuple t or discovering that there are no more tuples is $O(1)$, as are the costs of lines (3) and (5). We claim that line (4) can also be executed in $O(1)$ time, and therefore the loop of lines (2) to (5) takes $O(k)$ time.

We analyze line (4) as follows. Line (4) requires the lookup of a single tuple, given its key value. Let us suppose that the Course-StudentId-Grade relation has a primary index on its key, {Course, StudentId}, and that this index is a hash table with about m buckets. Then the average number of tuples per bucket is $O(1)$, and therefore line (4) of Fig. 8.9 takes $O(1)$ time. We conclude that the body of the loop of lines (2) through (5) takes $O(1)$ average time, and thus the entire program of Fig. 8.9 takes $O(k)$ average time. That is, the cost is proportional to the number of students with the particular name we query about, regardless of the size of the relations involved.

Navigating over Many Relations

The same techniques that let us navigate efficiently from one relation to another also allow navigation involving many relations. For example, suppose we wanted to know, "Where is C. Brown 9AM Monday mornings?" Assuming that he is in some class, we can find the answer to this query by finding the courses C. Brown is taking, seeing whether any of them meet 9AM Mondays, and, if so, finding the room in which the course meets. Figure 8.10 suggests the navigation through relations from the given value "C. Brown" to the answer.

The following plan assumes that there is a unique student named C. Brown; if there is more than one, then we can get the rooms in which one or more of them are found at 9AM Mondays. It also assumes that this student has not registered for conflicting courses; that is, he is taking at most one course that meets at 9AM on Mondays.

1. Find the student ID for C. Brown, using the StudentId-Name-Address-Phone relation for C. Brown. Let this ID number be i.

2. Look up in the Course-StudentId-Grade relation all tuples with StudentId component i. Let $\{c_1, \ldots, c_k\}$ be the set of Course values in these tuples.

3. In the Course-Day-Hour relation, look for tuples with Course component c_i, that is, one of the courses found in step (2). There should be at most one that has both "M" in the Day component and "9AM" in the Hour component.

4. If a course c is found in step (3), then look up in the Course-Room relation the room in which course c meets. That is where C. Brown will be found on Mondays at 9AM, assuming that he hasn't decided to take a long weekend.

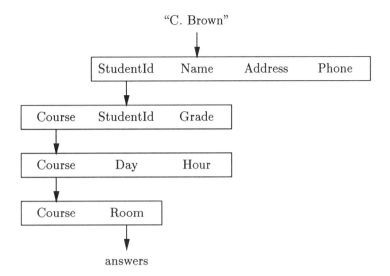

Fig. 8.10. Diagram of the query "Where is C. Brown
at 9AM on Mondays?"

If we do not have indexes, then the best we can hope for is that we can execute this plan in time proportional to the sum of the sizes of the four relations involved. However, there are a number of indexes we can take advantage of.

a) In step (1), we can use an index on the Name component of the

> StudentId-Name-Address-Phone

relation to get the student ID of C. Brown in $O(1)$ average time.

b) In step (2), we can take advantage of an index on the StudentId component of Course-StudentId-Grade to get in $O(k)$ time all the courses C. Brown is taking, if he is taking k courses.

c) In step (3), we can take advantage of an index on Course in the

> Course-Day-Hour

relation to find all the meetings of the k courses from step (2) in average time proportional to the sum of the numbers of meetings of these courses. If we assume that no course meets more than five times a week, then there are at most $5k$ tuples, and we can find them in $O(k)$ average time. If there is no index on Course for this relation, but there is an index on Day and/or Hour, we can take some advantage of such an index, although we may look at far more than $O(k)$ tuples, depending on how many courses there are that meet on Monday or that meet at 9AM on some day.

d) In step (4), we can take advantage of an index on Course for the Course-Room relation. In that case, we can retrieve the desired room in $O(1)$ average time.

We conclude that, with all the right indexes, we can answer this very complicated query in $O(k)$ average time. Since k, the number of courses taken by C. Brown, can be assumed small — say, 5 or so — this amount of time is normally quite small,

---

Summary: Fast Access to Relations

It is useful to review how our capability to get answers from relations has grown. We began in Section 7.8 by using a hash table, or another structure such as a binary search tree or a (generalized) characteristic vector, to implement functions, which in the context of this chapter are binary relations whose domain is a key. Then, in Section 7.9, we saw that these ideas worked even when the domain was not a key, as long as the relation was binary.

In Section 8.4, we saw that there was no requirement that the relation be binary; we could regard all attributes that are part of the key as a single "domain" set, and all the other attributes as a single "range" set. Further, we saw in Section 8.4 that the domain did not have to be a key.

In Section 8.5 we learned that we could use more than one index structure on a relation to allow fast access based on attributes that are not part of the domain, and in Section 8.6 we saw that it is possible to use a combination of indexes on several relations to perform complex retrievals of information in time proportional to the number of tuples we actually visit.

---

and in particular is independent of the sizes of any of the relations involved.

EXERCISES

8.6.1: Suppose that the Course-StudentId-Grade relation in Fig. 8.9 did not have an index on Course-StudentId pairs, but rather had an index on Course alone. How would that affect the running time of Fig. 8.9? What if the index were only on StudentId?

8.6.2: Discuss how the following queries can be answered efficiently. In each case, state what assumptions you make about the number of elements in intermediate sets (e.g., the number of courses taken by C. Brown), and also state what indexes you assume exist.

a) Find all the prerequisites of the courses taken by C. Brown.
b) Find the phone numbers of all the students taking a course that meets in Turing Aud.
c) Find the prerequisites of the prerequisites of CS206.

8.6.3: Assuming no indexes, how much time would each of the queries in Exercise 8.6.2 take, as a function of the sizes of the relations involved, assuming straightforward iterations over all tuples, as in the examples of this section?

❖❖ 8.7   An Algebra of Relations

In Section 8.6 we saw that a query involving several relations can be quite complicated. It is useful to express such queries in language that is much "higher-level" than C, in the sense that the query expresses what we want (e.g., all tuples with Course component equal to "CS101") without having to deal with issues such as lookup in indexes, as a C program would. For this purpose, a language called *relational algebra* has been developed.

Like any algebra, relational algebra allows us to rephrase queries by applying algebraic laws. Since complicated queries often have many different sequences of steps whereby their answer can be obtained from the stored data, and since different algebraic expressions represent different sequences of steps, relational algebra provides an excellent example of algebra as a design theory. In fact, the improvement in efficiency made possible by transforming expressions of relational algebra is arguably the most striking example of the power of algebra that we find in computer science. The ability to "optimize" queries by algebraic transformation is the subject of Section 8.9.

Operands of Relational Algebra

Constant arguments

In relational algebra, the operands are relations. As in other algebras, operands can be either constants — specific relations in this case — or variables representing unknown relations. However, whether a variable or a constant, each operand has a specific scheme (list of attributes naming its columns). Thus a constant argument might be shown as

A	B	C
0	1	2
0	3	4
5	2	3

This relation has scheme $\{A, B, C\}$, and it has three tuples, $(0, 1, 2)$, $(0, 3, 4)$, and $(5, 2, 3)$.

Variable arguments

A variable argument might be represented by $R(A, B, C)$, which denotes a relation called R, whose columns are named A, B, and C but whose set of tuples is unknown. If the scheme $\{A, B, C\}$ for R is understood or irrelevant, we can just use R as the operand.

Set Operators of Relational Algebra

Union, intersection, and difference

The first three operators we shall use are common set operations: union, intersection, and set difference, which were discussed in Section 7.3. We place one requirement on the operands of these operators: the schemes of the two operands must be the same. The scheme of the result is then naturally taken to be the scheme of either argument.

◆ **Example 8.11.** Let R and S be the relations of Fig. 8.11(a) and (b), respectively. Note that both relations have the scheme $\{A, B\}$. The union operator produces a relation with each tuple that appears in either R or S, or both. Note that since relations are sets, they can never have two or more copies of the same tuple, even though a tuple appears in both R and S, as does the tuple $(0, 1)$ in this example. The relation $R \cup S$ is shown in Fig. 8.11(c).

The intersection operator produces the relation that has those tuples appearing in both operands. Thus the relation $R \cap S$ has only the tuple $(0, 1)$, as shown in Fig. 8.11(d). The set difference produces a relation with those tuples in the first relation that are not also in the second. The relation $R - S$, shown in Fig. 8.11(e),

A	B
0	1
2	3

(a) R

A	B
0	1
4	5

(b) S

A	B
0	1
2	3
4	5

(c) $R \cup S$

A	B
0	1

(d) $R \cap S$

A	B
2	3

(e) $R - S$

Fig. 8.11. Examples of operations of relational algebra.

has the tuple $(2, 3)$ of R, because that tuple is not in S, but does not have the tuple $(0, 1)$ of R, because that tuple is also in S. ✦

The Selection Operator

The other operators of relational algebra are designed to perform the kinds of actions we have studied in this chapter. For example, we have frequently wanted to extract from a relation tuples meeting certain conditions, such as all tuples from the

Course-StudentId-Grade

relation that have Course component "CS101." For this purpose, we use the *selection* operator. This operator takes a single relation as operand, but also has a conditional expression as a "parameter." We write the selection operator $\sigma_C(R)$, where σ (Greek lower-case sigma) is the symbol for selection, C is the condition, and R is the relation operand. The condition C is allowed to have operands that are attributes from the scheme of R, as well as constants. The operators allowed in C are the usual ones for C conditional expressions, that is, arithmetic comparisons and the logical connectives.

The result of this operation is a relation whose scheme is the same as that of R. Into this relation we put every tuple t of R such that condition C becomes true when we substitute for each attribute A the component of tuple t in the column for A.

✦ **Example 8.12.** Let CSG stand for the Course-StudentId-Grade relation of Fig. 8.1. If we want those tuples that have Course component "CS101," we can write the expression

$$\sigma_{\text{Course}=\text{"CS101"}}(CSG)$$

The result of this expression is a relation with the same scheme as CSG, that is, {Course, StudentId, Grade}, and the set of tuples shown in Fig. 8.12. That is, the condition becomes true only for those tuples where the Course component is "CS101." For then, when we substitute "CS101" for Course, the condition becomes "CS101" = "CS101." If the tuple has any other value, such as "EE200", in the Course component, we get an expression like "EE200" = "CS101," which is false. ✦

Course	StudentId	Grade
CS101	12345	A
CS101	67890	B
CS101	33333	A−

Fig. 8.12. Result of expression $\sigma_{\text{Course}=\text{``CS101''}}(CSG)$.

The Projection Operator

Whereas the selection operator makes a copy of the relation with some rows deleted, we often want to make a copy in which some columns are eliminated. For that purpose we have the *projection operator,* represented by the symbol π. Like selection, the projection operator takes a single relation as argument, and it also takes a parameter, which is a list of attributes, chosen from the scheme of the relation that is the argument.

If R is a relation with set of attributes $\{A_1, \ldots, A_k\}$, and $(B_1, \ldots, B_n)$ is a list of some of the A's, then $\pi_{B_1,\ldots,B_n}(R)$, the *projection of R onto attributes $B_1, \ldots, B_n$,* is the set of tuples formed as follows. Take each tuple t in R, and extract its components in attributes $B_1, \ldots, B_n$; say these components are $b_1, \ldots, b_n$, respectively. Then add the tuple $(b_1, \ldots, b_n)$ to the relation $\pi_{B_1,\ldots,B_n}(R)$. Note that two or more tuples of R may have the same components in all of $B_1, \ldots, B_n$. If so, only one copy of the projection of those tuples goes into $\pi_{B_1,\ldots,B_n}(R)$, since that relation, like all relations, cannot have more than one copy of any tuple.

✦ **Example 8.13.** Suppose we wanted to see only the student ID's for the students who are taking CS101. We could apply the same selection as in Example 8.12, which gives us all the tuples for CS101 in the CSG relation, but we then must project out the course and grade; that is, we project onto StudentId alone. The expression that performs both operations is

$$\pi_{\text{StudentId}}\left(\sigma_{\text{Course}=\text{``CS101''}}(CSG)\right)$$

The result of this expression is the relation of Fig. 8.12 projected onto its StudentId component — that is, the unary relation of Fig. 8.13. ✦

StudentId
12345
67890
33333

Fig. 8.13. Students taking CS101.

Joining Relations

Finally, we need a way to express the idea that two relations are connected, so that we can navigate from one to the other. For this purpose, we use the *join* operator, which we denote $\bowtie$.[3] Suppose we have two relations R and S, with sets of attributes (schemes) $\{A_1, \ldots, A_n\}$ and $\{B_1, \ldots, B_m\}$, respectively. We pick one attribute from each set — say, A_i and B_j — and these attributes become parameters of the join operation with arguments R and S.

The join of R and S, written $R \underset{A_i = B_j}{\bowtie} S$, is formed by taking each tuple r from R and each tuple s from S and comparing them. If the component of r for A_i equals the component of s for B_j, then we form one tuple from r and s; otherwise, no tuple is created from the pairing of r and s. We form a tuple from r and s by taking the components of r and following them by all the components of s, but omitting the component for B_j, which is the same as the A_i component of r anyway.

The relation $R \underset{A_i = B_j}{\bowtie} S$ is the set of tuples formed in this manner. Note that there could be no tuples in this relation, if no value appearing in the A_i column of R also appeared in the B_j column of S. At the other extreme, every tuple of R could have the same value in the A_i component, and this component could also appear in the B_j component of every tuple in S. Then, the number of tuples in the join would be the product of the number of tuples in R and the number in S, since every pair of tuples would match. Generally, the truth lies somewhere between these extremes; each tuple of R pairs with some but not all of the tuples of S.

The scheme of the joined relation is

$$\{A_1, \ldots, A_n, B_1, \ldots, B_{j-1}, B_{j+1}, \ldots, B_m\}$$

that is, the set of all attributes of R and S except for B_j. However, there could be two occurrences of the same name on this list, if one of the A's was the same as one of the B's (other than B_j, which is not an attribute of the join). If that is the case, we shall insist that one of the pair of identical attributes be renamed.

✦ **Example 8.14.** Suppose we want to perform some operation connecting the

   Course-Day-Hour

relation (which we abbreviate to CDH), and the Course-Room relation (CR). For instance, we might want to know at what times each room is occupied by some course. To answer that query, we must pair each tuple from CR with each tuple from CDH, provided that the Course components of the two tuples are the same —

---

[3] The "join" that we describe here is less general than that normally found in relational algebra but will serve to get the flavor of the operator without going into all the complexities of the subject.

that is, if the tuples are talking about the same course. Thus if we join CR with CDH, requiring equality of the two Course attributes, we shall get a relation with scheme

{Course, Room, Day, Hour}

that contains each tuple (c, r, d, h) such that (c, r) is a tuple of CR and (c, d, h) is a tuple of CDH. The expression defining this relation is

$$CR \underset{\text{Course=Course}}{\bowtie} CDH$$

and the value of the relation produced by this expression, assuming that the relations have the tuples found in Fig. 8.2, is as shown in Fig. 8.14.

Course	Room	Day	Hour
CS101	Turing Aud.	M	9AM
CS101	Turing Aud.	W	9AM
CS101	Turing Aud.	F	9AM
EE200	25 Ohm Hall	Tu	10AM
EE200	25 Ohm Hall	W	1PM
EE200	25 Ohm Hall	Th	10AM

Fig. 8.14. Join of CR and CDH on Course = Course.

To see how the relation of Fig. 8.14 is constructed, consider the first tuple of CR, which is (CS101, Turing Aud.). We examine the tuples of CDH for those that have the same Course value, that is, "CS101." In Fig. 8.2(c), we find that the first three tuples match, and from each of them, we construct one of the first three tuples of Fig. 8.14. For example, the first tuple of CDH, which is (CS101, M, 9AM), joins with tuple (CS101, Turing Aud.) to create the first tuple of Fig. 8.14. Notice how that tuple agrees with each of the two tuples from which it is constructed.

Similarly, the second tuple of CR, (EE200, 25 Ohm Hall), shares a common Course component with each of the last three tuples of CDH. These three pairings give rise to the last three tuples of Fig. 8.14. The last tuple of CR,

(PH100, Newton Lab.)

does not have the same Course component as any tuple of CDH. Thus that tuple does not contribute anything at all to the join. ✦

Natural Join

When we join two relations R and S, it is common that the attributes we equate have the same name. If, in addition, R and S have no other attribute names in common, then we can omit the parameter of the join and simply write $R \bowtie S$. Such a join is called a *natural join.*

For instance, the join in Example 8.14 is a natural join. The equated attributes are both called Course, and the remaining attributes of CR and CDH all have distinct names. Thus we could have written this join simply as $CR \bowtie CDH$.

Expression Trees for Relational Algebra Expressions

Just as we draw expression trees for arithmetic expressions, we can represent a relational algebra expression as a tree. The leaves are labeled by operands, that is, by specific relations or variables representing relations. Each interior node is labeled by an operator, including the parameter of the operator if it is a selection, projection, or join (except a natural join, which needs no parameter). The children of each interior node N are the node or nodes representing the operands to which the operator at node N is applied.

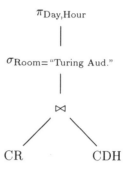

Fig. 8.15. Expression tree in relational algebra.

✦ **Example 8.15.** Building on Example 8.14, suppose we wanted to see not the entire relation $CR \bowtie CDH$, but just the Day-Hour pairs during which Turing Aud. is occupied by some course. Then we need to take the relation of Fig. 8.14 and

1. Select for those tuples having Room component "Turing Aud.," and
2. Project onto attributes Day and Hour.

The expression that performs the join, selection, and projection, in that order, is

$$\pi_{\text{Day,Hour}}\big(\sigma_{\text{Room}=\text{``Turing Aud.''}}\,(CR \bowtie CDH)\big)$$

Alternatively, we could display this expression as the tree shown in Fig. 8.15. The relation computed at the join node appeared in Fig. 8.14. The relation for the selection node is the first three tuples in Fig. 8.14, because these have "Turing Aud." in their Room component. The relation for the root of the expression is shown in Fig. 8.16, that is, the Day and Hour components of the latter three tuples. ✦

Day	Hour
M	9AM
W	9AM
F	9AM

Fig. 8.16. Result of expression in Fig. 8.15.

SQL, a Language Based on Relational Algebra

Many modern database systems use a language called SQL (Structured Query Language) for expressing queries. While a complete guide to that language is beyond the scope of this book, we can give the reader a feel for SQL with a few examples.

```
SELECT StudentId
FROM CSG
WHERE Course = "CS101"
```

is SQL's way of expressing the query of Example 8.13, that is,

$$\pi_{\text{StudentId}}\left(\sigma_{\text{Course}=\text{"CS101"}}(CSG)\right)$$

The FROM-clause indicates the relation to which the query is applied. The WHERE-clause gives the condition of the selection, and the SELECT-clause gives the list of attributes onto which the answer is projected. (It is unfortunate that the keyword SELECT in SQL corresponds not to the relational algebra operator called "selection" but to the operator called "projection.")

For a more complicated example, we can express the query of Example 8.15, which is $\pi_{\text{Day,Hour}}\left(\sigma_{\text{Room}=\text{"Turing Aud."}}(CR \bowtie CDH)\right)$, by the SQL program

```
SELECT Day, Hour
FROM CR, CDH
WHERE CR.Course = CDH.Course AND Room = "Turing Aud."
```

Here, the FROM-clause tells us we are going to join the two relations CR and CDH. The first part of the WHERE-clause is the join condition; it says that the Course attribute of CR must equal the Course attribute in CDH. The second part of the WHERE-clause is the selection condition. The SELECT-clause gives us the attributes in the projection.

EXERCISES

8.7.1: Express the queries of Exercise 8.4.2(a, b, c) in relational algebra. Assume that what is wanted as an answer is the complete tuple(s).

8.7.2: Repeat Exercise 8.7.1, assuming that what is wanted is only the components that have a ∗ in the specification.

8.7.3: Express the queries of Exercise 8.6.2(a, b, c) in relational algebra. Note that in part (c), you will have to rename some attributes in order to take the join of a relation with itself.

8.7.4: Express the query "Where is C. Brown at 9AM on Monday?" in relational algebra. The discussion at the end of Section 8.6 should indicate the joins necessary to answer this query.

8.7.5: Draw expression trees for the queries of Exercise 8.7.2(a) through (c), Exercise 8.7.3(a) through (c), and Exercise 8.7.4.

❖❖ 8.8   Implementing Relational Algebra Operations

Using the right data structures and algorithms for relational algebra operations can speed up database queries. In this section, we shall consider some of the simpler and more common strategies for implementing relational algebra operations.

Implementing Union, Intersection, and Difference

The three basic set operations can be implemented in the same way for relations as for sets. We can take the union of two sets or relations by sorting both sets and merging, as discussed in Section 7.4. The intersection and difference can be taken by a similar technique. If the relations have n tuples each, it takes $O(n \log n)$ time to sort them and $O(n)$ time to do the merging, or $O(n \log n)$ total.

However, there are several other ways we could take the union of relations R and S, and these are sometimes more efficient. First, we might not worry about eliminating the duplicate copy of a tuple that appears in both R and S. We could construct $R \cup S$ by making a copy of R, say, as a linked list, and then appending all the tuples of S, without checking whether a tuple of S is also in R. This operation can be done in time proportional to the sum of the sizes of R and S. The drawback is that the result is not, strictly speaking, the union, since it can have duplicate tuples. However, perhaps the presence of duplicates does not matter, because they are expected to be rare. Or, we might find it more convenient to eliminate the duplicates at a later stage, such as by sorting after taking the union of several more relations.

Another option is to use an index. For example, suppose that S has an index on attribute A, and that this attribute is a key for S. Then we can take the union $R \cup S$ by starting with the tuples of S, and examining each tuple t of R, in its turn. We find the value of t in its component A — let us call it a — and use the index to look up the tuple of S that has the value a in its A-component. If this tuple in S is identical to t, then we do not add t to the union a second time; but if there is no tuple with key value a in S, or if the tuple with this key value differs from t, then we add t to the union.

If the index gives us $O(1)$ average time to look up a tuple, given its key value, then this method takes average time proportional to the sum of the sizes of R and S. Moreover, the resulting relation will have no duplicates, as long as neither R nor S has duplicates.

Implementing Projection

In principle, when we perform a projection, we have no choice but to run through every tuple and make a copy that omits the components corresponding to attributes not on the projection list. Indexes do not help us at all. Moreover, after we compute the projection of each tuple, we may find that we are left with many duplicates.

For example, suppose we have a relation R with scheme (A, B, C) and we compute $\pi_{A,B}(R)$. Even though R cannot have tuples that agree on all of A, B, and C, it may have many tuples with the same values for attributes A and B but different values for C. Then all these tuples will yield the same tuple in the projection.

Thus, after we compute a projection such as $S = \pi_L(R)$, for some relation R and list of attributes L, we must eliminate duplicates. For example, we could sort S and then run through the tuples in the sorted order. Any tuple that is the same as the previous tuple in the order will be eliminated. Another way to eliminate duplicates is to treat the relation S as an ordinary set. Each time we generate a tuple by projecting a tuple of R onto the attributes in the list L, we insert it into the set. As with all insertions into a set, if the element inserted is already there, we do nothing. A structure such as a hash table will serve adequately to represent the set S of tuples generated by the projection.

To sort the relation S before eliminating duplicates requires $O(n \log n)$ time if there are n tuples in the relation R. If we instead hash tuples of S as we generate them and we use a number of buckets proportional to n, then the entire projection will take $O(n)$ time, on the average. Thus hashing is normally slightly better than sorting.

Implementing Selection

When we perform a selection $S = \sigma_C(R)$ and there are no indexes on R, then we have no choice but to run through all the tuples of R to apply the condition C. Regardless of how we perform the selection, we know that there can be no duplicates in the result S, as long as R has no duplicates.

However, if there are indexes on R, then we can often take advantage of one of them to home in on the tuples that meet the condition C, and we can thus avoid looking at most or all of the tuples that do not meet condition C. The simplest situation occurs when condition C is of the form $A = b$, where A is an attribute of R and b is a constant. If R has an index on A, then we can retrieve all the tuples that meet this condition by looking up b in the index.

If condition C is the logical **AND** of several conditions, then we can use any one of them to look up tuples using an index, and then check the retrieved tuples to see which ones meet the remaining conditions. For example, suppose condition C is

$$(A = a) \text{ AND } (B = b)$$

Then we have the choice of using an index on A or an index on B, if either or both exists. Suppose that there is an index on B, and either there is no index on A or we prefer to use the index on B. Then we get all the tuples of R that have the value b in their B component. Each of these tuples that has a in the A component belongs in the relation S, the result of the selection; other retrieved tuples do not. The time taken for the selection is proportional to the number of tuples with B value b, which generally lies somewhere between the number of tuples in R and the number of tuples in the answer, S.

Implementing Join

Suppose we want to take the natural join of relation R with scheme $\{A, B\}$ and relation S with scheme $\{B, C\}$. Suppose also that the join is the natural join, with equality between the B attributes of the two relations.[4] How we perform this join depends on what indexes on attribute B we can find. The issues are similar to those discussed in Section 8.6, when we considered how to navigate among relations, because the join is the essence of navigation.

Nested-loop join   There is an obvious and slow way to compute the join, called *nested-loop join*. We compare every tuple of one relation with every tuple of the other relation, as

---

[4] We show for each relation only one attribute (A and C, respectively) that is not involved in the join, but the ideas mentioned here clearly carry over to relations with many attributes.

Index-join

Sort-join

for each tuple r in R **do**
    for each tuple s in S **do**
        if r and s agree on their B attributes **then**
            print the tuple agreeing with r and s
            on attributes A, B, and C;

However, there are several more efficient ways to take a join. One is an *index-join*. Suppose S has an index on B. Then we can visit every tuple t of R and find its B component — say, b. We look up b in the index for S, and thus obtain all the tuples that match t in B-values.

Similarly, if R has an index on B, we can run through the tuples of S. For each such tuple, we look up the corresponding tuples of R by using the B index of R. If both R and S have indexes on B, we can choose either one to use. As we shall see, it makes a difference in the amount of time the join takes.

If there are no indexes on B, we can still do better than a nested-loop join by a technique called *sort-join*. We begin by merging the tuples of R and S, but reorganizing them so that the B components are first in all tuples, and tuples have an extra component that is either R (when the tuple comes from relation R) or S (when the tuple comes from S). That is, a tuple (a, b) from R becomes (b, a, R), while tuple (b, c) from S becomes (b, c, S).

We sort the merged list of tuples on the first, or b, component. Now, all the tuples of both relations that join because of a common B value are consecutive in the ordering, although tuples from the two relations may be mixed.[5] We visit the tuples with each given B value in turn, by going down the sorted list. When we come to the tuples with B value b, we can pair all the tuples from R with those from S. Since these tuples all have the same B value, they all join, and the time taken to produce the tuples of the joined relation is proportional to the number of tuples produced, except in the case that there are no tuples from R or no tuples from S. In the latter case, we must still take time proportional to the number of tuples with B value b, just to examine each once and skip over them on the sorted list.

✦ **Example 8.16.** Suppose we want to join the relation CDH from Fig. 8.2(c) with the relation CR from Fig. 8.2(d). Here, Course plays the role of attribute B, Day and Hour together play the role of A, and Room is C. The six tuples from CDH and the three from CR are first padded with the name of the relation. No reordering of components is necessary, because Course is first in both relations. When we compare tuples, we first compare the Course components, using lexicographic order to determine which course name comes first in the order. If there is a tie, that is, if the course names are the same, we compare the last components, where we take CDH to precede CR. If there is still a tie, we can allow either tuple to precede the other.

Then one sorted order of the tuples will be as shown in Fig. 8.17. Note that this list is not a relation, because it has tuples of varying lengths. However, it does group the tuples for CS101 and the tuples for EE200, so that we can easily take the

---

[5] We could arrange while sorting that the last component — that is, the relation name — be taken into account, so that a tuple with a given B value from relation R is deemed to precede a tuple with the same B value from S. Then, the tuples with a common B value would appear with the tuples from R first, and then the tuples from S.

CS101	M	9AM	CDH
CS101	W	9AM	CDH
CS101	F	9AM	CDH
CS101	Turing Aud.	CR	
EE200	Tu	10AM	CDH
EE200	W	1PM	CDH
EE200	F	10AM	CDH
EE200	25 Ohm Hall	CR	
PH100	Newton Lab.	CR	

Fig. 8.17. Sorted list of tuples from CDH and CR.

join of these groups of tuples. ✦

Comparison of Join Methods

Suppose we join the relation R, with scheme $\{A, B\}$, and the relation S, with scheme $\{B, C\}$, and let R and S have r tuples and s tuples, respectively. Also, let the number of tuples in the join be m. Remember that m could be as large as rs, if each tuple of R joins with each tuple of S (because they all have the same B value), but m could also be as small as 0, if no tuple of R has a B value in common with any tuple of S. Finally, let us assume that we can look up any value in any index in $O(1)$ time, on the average, as we could if the index were a hash table with a sufficiently large number of buckets.

Every method for joining will take at least $O(m)$ time, just to produce the output. However, some methods will take more. If we use nested-loop join, it takes time rs to perform the comparisons. Since $m \leq rs$, we can neglect the time to produce the output and say that the cost of pairing all tuples is $O(rs)$.

On the other hand, we could sort the relations. If we use an algorithm like merge sort to sort the combined list of $r + s$ tuples, the time required is

$$O\big((r + s) \log(r + s)\big)$$

Building the output tuples from adjacent tuples in the sorted list will take $O(r + s)$ time to examine the list, plus $O(m)$ time to produce the output. The time to sort dominates the $O(r + s)$ term, but the $O(m)$ cost to produce the output can be greater or less than the sorting time. Thus we must include both terms in the running time of the algorithm that joins by sorting; this running time is thus

$$O\big(m + (r + s) \log(r + s)\big)$$

Since m is never greater than rs, and $(r + s) \log(r + s)$ is greater than rs only in some unusual cases (for example, when r or s is 0), we conclude that sort-join is generally faster than nested-loop join.

Now suppose we have an index on B in the relation S. It takes $O(r)$ time to look at each tuple of R and look up its B value in the index. To this time we must add the $O(m)$ cost of retrieving the matching tuples for the various B values and of producing the output tuples. Since m can be greater than or less than r, the expression for the cost of this index-join is $O(m + r)$. Similarly, if there is an index on B for relation R, we can perform the index-join in $O(m + s)$ time. Since both r and s are smaller than $(r + s) \log(r + s)$, except in some unusual situations such as $r + s \leq 1$, the running time of index-join is smaller than that of sort-join. Of course, we need an index on one of the attributes involved in the join, if we are to do an index-join, while a sort-join can be done on any relations.

EXERCISES

8.8.1: Suppose that the StudentId-Name-Address-Phone relation ($SNAP$) of Fig. 8.2(a) is stored with a primary index on StudentId (the key) and a secondary index on Phone. How would you compute most efficiently the answer to the query $\sigma_C(SNAP)$ if C were

a) StudentId = 12345 **AND** Address $\neq$ "45 Kumquat Blvd"?
b) Name = "C. Brown" **AND** Phone = 555-1357?
c) Name = "C. Brown" **OR** Phone = 555-1357?

8.8.2: Show how to sort-join the relations CSG from Fig. 8.1 and $SNAP$ from Fig. 8.2(a) by sorting the merged list of tuples as in Example 8.16. Assume the natural join, or equality on the StudentId components, is wanted. Show the result of the sort, analogous to Fig. 8.17, and give the tuples in the result of the join.

8.8.3*: Suppose that we join relations R and S, each with n tuples, and the result has $O(n^{3/2})$ tuples. Write formulas for the big-oh running time, as a function of n, for the following techniques for taking the join:

a) Nested-loop join
b) Sort-join
c) Index-join, using an index on the join attribute of R
d) Index-join, using an index on the join attribute of S

8.8.4*: We proposed taking the union of two relations by using an index on an attribute A that was a key for one of the relations. Is the method a reasonable way to take a union if the attribute A that has an index is not a key?

8.8.5*: Suppose we want to compute (a) $R \cap S$ (b) $R - S$ using an index on attribute A for one of R and S. Can we obtain running time close to the sum of the sizes of the two relations?

8.8.6: If we project a relation R onto a set of attributes that contains a key for R, do we need to eliminate duplicates? Why?

✦✦ 8.9   Algebraic Laws for Relations

As with other algebras, by transforming expressions we often have the opportunity to "optimize" expressions. That is, we can take an expression that is expensive to evaluate and turn it into an equivalent expression whose evaluation has a lower cost. While transformations to arithmetic or logical expressions sometimes save a few operations, the right transformations applied to expressions of relational algebra can save orders of magnitude in the time it takes to evaluate the expression. Because of the tremendous difference between the running times of optimized and unoptimized relational algebra expressions, our ability to optimize such expressions is essential if programmers are going to program in very high-level languages, like the language SQL that we mentioned in Section 8.7.

Laws Involving Union, Intersection, and Difference

Section 7.3 covered the principal algebraic laws for union, intersection, and difference of sets. They apply to relations as a special case, although the reader should bear in mind the requirement of the relational model that the schemes of the relations involved in these operations be the same.

Laws Involving Join

Commutativity of join

In one sense, the join operator is commutative, and in another sense it is not. Suppose we take the natural join $R \bowtie S$, where R has attributes A and B while S has attributes B and C. Then the columns of the scheme for $R \bowtie S$ are A, B, and C, in that order. If we take $S \bowtie R$ instead, we get essentially the same tuples, but the order of the columns is B, C, and then A. Thus if we insist that order of columns matters, join is not commutative. However, if we accept that a relation, with its columns permuted along with their column names, is really the same relation, then we can consider the join commutative; that point of view will be adopted here.

Nonassociativity of join

The join operator does not always obey the associative law. For example, suppose relations R, S, and T have schemes $\{A, B\}$, $\{B, C\}$, and $\{A, D\}$, respectively. Suppose we take the natural join $(R \bowtie S) \bowtie T$, where we first equate the B components of R and S and then equate the A component of the result with the A component of relation T. If we associate from the right instead of the left, we get $R \bowtie (S \bowtie T)$. Relations S and T have schemes $\{B, C\}$ and $\{A, D\}$, respectively. There is no pair of attributes we can choose to equate that will achieve the same effect as the natural join.

However, there are some conditions under which the associative law holds for $\bowtie$. We leave it as an exercise for the reader to show that

$$\left(\left(R \underset{A=B}{\bowtie} S \right) \underset{C=D}{\bowtie} T \right) \equiv \left(R \underset{A=B}{\bowtie} \left(S \underset{C=D}{\bowtie} T \right) \right)$$

whenever A is an attribute of R, B and C are different attributes of S, and D is an attribute of T.

Laws Involving Selection

The most useful laws of relational algebra involve the selection operator. If the selection condition requires that a specified component have a certain value, as is often the case in practice, then the relation that is the result of the selection will tend to have many fewer tuples than the relation to which the selection is applied. Since operations in general take less time if they are applied to smaller relations, it is extremely advantageous to apply a selection as soon as we can. In algebraic terms, we apply selections early by using a law that lets a selection pass down the expression tree, below other operators.

An example of such a law is

$$\left(\sigma_C (R \bowtie S) \right) \equiv \left(\sigma_C (R) \bowtie S \right)$$

which holds provided that all attributes mentioned in condition C are attributes of relation R. Similarly, if all attributes mentioned by C are attributes of S, we can push the selection down to S, using the law

$$\left(\sigma_C (R \bowtie S) \right) \equiv \left(R \bowtie \sigma_C (S) \right)$$

Pushing selections

Either law is referred to as *selection pushing.*

When we have a complex condition in a selection, sometimes we can push part of it one way and part of it the other way, through a join. In order to split a selection into two or more parts, we need the law

$$\sigma_{C \text{ AND } D}(R) \equiv \sigma_C\big(\sigma_D(R)\big)$$

Selection splitting

Notice that we can only split a condition into two parts — C and D here — if the parts are connected by **AND**. Intuitively, when we select for the **AND** of two conditions C and D, we can either examine each tuple of the relation R and see whether the tuple satisfies both C and D, or we can examine all the tuples of R, selecting those that satisfy D, and then examine the tuples that satisfy D to see which of them satisfy C. We call this law *selection splitting.*

Another necessary law is the commutativity of selections. If we apply two selections to a relation, it does not matter in what order we apply the selections; the selected tuples will still be the same. Formally, we may write

Commutativity of selection

$$\sigma_C\big(\sigma_D(R)\big) \equiv \sigma_D\big(\sigma_C(R)\big)$$

for any conditions C and D.

✦ **Example 8.17.** Let us take up the complex query that we first considered in Section 8.6: "Where is C. Brown 9 AM on Mondays?" This query involves navigating over the four relations

1. *CSG* (Course-StudentId-Grade),

2. *SNAP* (StudentId-Name-Address-Phone),

3. *CDH* (Course-Day-Hour), and

4. *CR* (Course-Room).

To get an algebraic expression for the query, we can start by taking the natural join of all four relations. That is, we connect *CSG* and *SNAP* by equating the StudentId components. Think of this operation as extending each

      Course-StudentId-Grade

tuple by adding components for the name, address, and phone of the student mentioned in the tuple. Of course, we wouldn't want to store data this way, because it forces us to repeat the information about each student once for each course the student takes. However, we are not storing this data, but just designing an expression to compute it.

To the result of $CSG \bowtie SNAP$ we join CDH, by equating on the Course components. That join has the effect of taking each *CSG* tuple (already extended by the student information), making one copy for each meeting of the course, and extending each tuple by one of the possible Day and Hour values. Finally, we join the result of $(CSG \bowtie SNAP) \bowtie CDH$ with the *CR* relation, equating Course components, which has the effect of extending each tuple by adding a component with the room in which the course meets. The resulting relation has scheme

      {Course, StudentId, Grade, Name, Address, Phone, Day, Hour, Room}

and the meaning of a tuple $(c, s, g, n, a, p, d, h, r)$ is that

1. Student s took course c and got grade g.

2. The name of the student with ID number s is n, his or her address is a, and phone is p.

3. The course c meets in room r, and one meeting of the course is on day d at hour h.

To this set of tuples, we must apply the selection that restricts our consideration to the relevant tuples, namely, those in which the Name component is "C. Brown," the Day component is "M," and the Hour component is "9AM." There will be at most one such tuple, on the assumption that C. Brown is taking at most one course meeting at 9AM on Mondays. Since the answer we want is the Room component of this tuple, we finish our expression by projecting onto Room. The expression tree for our query is shown in Fig. 8.18. It consists of the four-way join, followed by the selection, and then the projection.

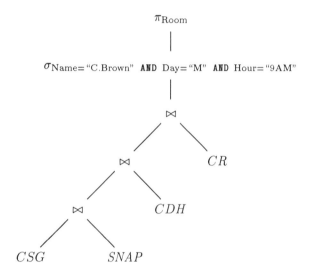

Fig. 8.18. Initial expression to determine where C. Brown is at 9AM, Mondays.

If we were to evaluate the expression of Fig. 8.18 as written, we would construct an enormous relation by joining CSG, $SNAP$, CDH, and CR, and then restrict it to a single tuple and project that tuple to a single component. Remember from Section 8.6 that it is not necessary to build such a big relation; we can "push the selection down the tree" to restrict the relations involved in the join, thus limiting greatly the sizes of the relations we do construct.

Our first step is shown in Fig. 8.19(a). Notice that the selection involves only attributes Name, Day, and Hour. None of these come from the right operand of the top join in Fig. 8.18; they all come from the left side, which is the join of CSG, $SNAP$, and CDH. Thus we may push the selection below the top join and have it apply to the left operand only, as we see in Fig. 8.19(a).

Now we cannot push the selection further, because one of the attributes involved, Name, comes from the left operand of the middle join in Fig. 8.19(a), while the other attributes, Day and Hour, come from the right operand, the relation

CDH. Thus we must split the condition in the selection, which is the **AND** of three conditions. We could split into three selections, but in this example it suffices to split the condition Name = "C. Brown" off from the other two. The result of the split is shown in Fig. 8.19(b).

Now, the selection involving Day and Hour can be pushed down to the right operand of the middle join, since the right operand, the relation CDH, has both attributes Day and Hour. Then the other selection, involving Name, can be pushed to the left operand of the middle join, since that operand, $CSG \bowtie SNAP$, has Name as an attribute. These two changes yield the expression tree shown in Fig. 8.19(c).

Finally, the selection on Name involves an attribute of $SNAP$, and so we can push this selection to the right operand of the bottom join. This change is shown in Fig. 8.19(d).

Now we have an expression that gives us almost the same plan as we developed in Section 8.6 for this query. We begin at the bottom of the expression in Fig. 8.19(d) by finding the student ID(s) for the student(s) named "C. Brown." By joining the tuples of $SNAP$ that have Name = "C. Brown" with the CSG relation, we get the courses taken by C. Brown. When we apply the second selection to relation CDH, we get the courses that meet at 9AM on Mondays. The middle join in Fig. 8.19(d) thus gives us tuples with a course that both is taken by C. Brown and meets at 9AM Mondays. The top join gets the rooms in which those courses meet, and the projection gives us these rooms as answer.

The major difference between this plan and the plan of Section 8.6 is that the latter projects away useless components of tuples, while the plan here carries them along until the end. Thus to complete our optimization of expressions of relational algebra, we need laws that push projections down the tree. These laws are not all the same as the laws for selection, as we shall see in the next subsection. ✦

Laws Involving Projection

First, whereas selections can be pushed below a union, an intersection, or a set difference (provided that we push the selection to *both* operands), projections push below unions only. That is, the law

$$\big(\pi_L(R \cup S)\big) \equiv \big(\pi_L(R) \cup \pi_L(S)\big)$$

holds. However, it is not true that $\pi_L(R \cap S)$ is necessarily the same as

$$\pi_L(R) \cap \pi_L(S)$$

For example, suppose that R and S are relations with scheme $\{A, B\}$, R contains only the tuple (a, b), and S contains only the tuple (a, c). Then $\pi_A(R) \cap \pi_A(S)$ contains the (one-component) tuple (a), while $\pi_A(R \cap S)$ does not (because $R \cap S$ is empty). Thus we have a situation in which

$$\big(\pi_A(R \cap S)\big) \neq \big(\pi_A(R) \cap \pi_A(S)\big)$$

Projection pushing

It is possible to push a projection below a join. In general, we need a projection operator for each operand of the join. If we have an expression $\pi_L(R \underset{A=B}{\bowtie} S)$, then the attributes of R that we need are those appearing in the list of attributes L, and the attribute A, which is the attribute from R upon which the join is based. Similarly, from S we need those attributes that are on the list L, and we also need the join attribute B, regardless of whether it is or is not on L. Formally, the law for pushing projections below joins is

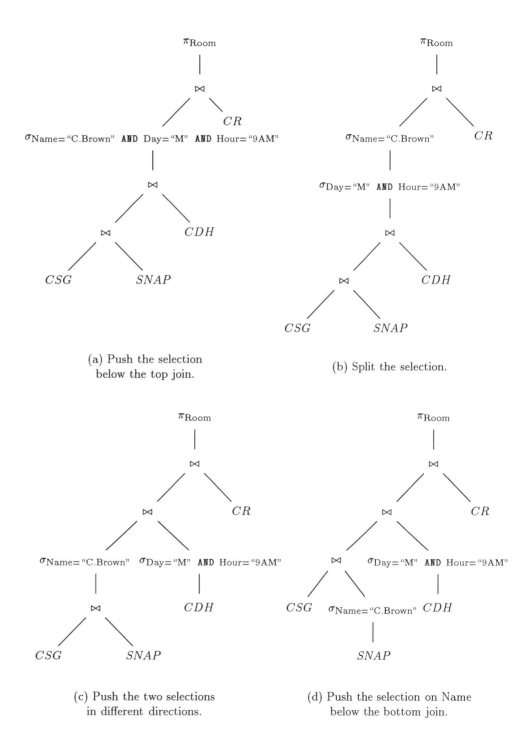

(a) Push the selection
below the top join.

(b) Split the selection.

(c) Push the two selections
in different directions.

(d) Push the selection on Name
below the bottom join.

Fig. 8.19. Pushing the selection down.

$$\left(\pi_L(R \underset{A=B}{\bowtie} S)\right) \equiv \left(\pi_L\left(\pi_M(R) \underset{A=B}{\bowtie} \pi_N(S)\right)\right)$$

where

1. List M consists of those attributes of L that are in the scheme for R, followed by attribute A if it is not on L, and

2. List N is the attributes of L that are in the scheme of S, followed by B if that attribute is not on list L.

Note that the useful way in which to apply this *projection pushing* law is from left to right, even though we thereby introduce two additional projections and do not get rid of any. The reason is that it is usually beneficial to project out what attributes we can as early as possible, that is, as far down the tree as we can. We still may have to do the projection onto the list L after the join, in the situation where the join attribute A is not on the list L (recall that the other join attribute, B from S, will not appear in the join anyway).

Sometimes, the lists M and/or N consist of all attributes of R or S, respectively. If so, there is no point in performing the projection, since it has no effect, except perhaps a pointless permutation of the columns of the relation. Thus we shall use the following law.

$$\pi_L(R) \equiv R$$

provided that list L consists of all the attributes in the scheme for R. Note that this law takes the point of view that relations are not changed by permutations of their columns.

There is also a situation in which we do not want to bother projecting. Suppose we have a subexpression $\pi_L(R)$ that is part of a larger expression, and let R be a single relation (rather than an expression involving one or more occurrences of operators). Suppose also that above this subexpression in the expression tree is another projection. To perform the projection on R now requires us to examine the entire relation, regardless of the existence of indexes. If we instead carry along the attributes of R not on the list L, until the next opportunity to project out those attributes, we are frequently able to save a significant amount of time.

For instance, we shall, in the next example, discuss a subexpression

$$\pi_{\text{Course,StudentId}}(CSG)$$

which has the effect of getting rid of grades. Since our entire expression, which is for the query of Example 8.17, eventually focuses on a few tuples of the CSG relation, we are much better off projecting out grades later; by so doing, we avoid ever examining the entire CSG relation.

✦ **Example 8.18.** Let us proceed from Fig. 8.19(d) to push projections down. The projection at the root is first pushed below the top join. The projection list consists of only Room, and the join attribute on both sides of the join is Course. Thus on the left we project onto Course alone, since Room is not an attribute of the expression on the left. The right operand of the join is projected onto both Course and Room. Since these are all the attributes of the operand CR, we can omit the projection. The resulting expression is shown in Fig. 8.20(a).

Now, we can push the projection onto Course below the middle join. Since

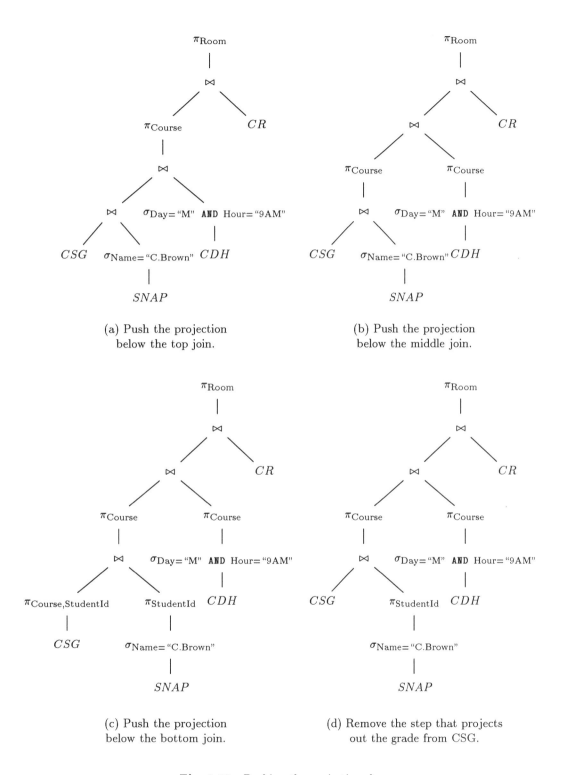

(a) Push the projection
below the top join.

(b) Push the projection
below the middle join.

(c) Push the projection
below the bottom join.

(d) Remove the step that projects
out the grade from CSG.

Fig. 8.20. Pushing the projection down.

Course is also the join attribute on both sides, we introduce two operators π_{Course} below the middle join. Since the result of the middle join then has only attribute Course, we no longer need the projection above that join; the new expression is shown in Fig. 8.20(b). Note that this join, involving two relations whose tuples have only the one component Course, is effectively an intersection of sets. That makes sense — it intersects the set of courses C. Brown is taking with the set of courses that meet at 9AM Mondays.

At this point, we need to push π_{Course} below the bottom join. The join attribute is StudentId on both sides, and so the projection list on the left is (Course, StudentId) and the list on the right is just StudentId (because Course is not an attribute of the expression on the right). The expression that results is shown in Fig. 8.20(c).

Finally, as we mentioned just before the example, it is advantageous here not to project Grade out of the CSG relation immediately. Above that projection we meet the operator π_{Course}, which will get rid of the grades anyway. If we instead use the expression of Fig. 8.20(d), we have essentially the plan of Section 8.6 for this query. That is, the expression $\pi_{\text{StudentId}}\big(\sigma_{\text{Name}=\text{"C.Brown"}}(SNAP)\big)$ gives us the student ID(s) for students named "C. Brown," and the first join followed by projection π_{Course} gives us the courses taken by those students. If there is an index on Name for relation $SNAP$ and there is an index on StudentId for relation CSG, then these operations are performed quickly.

The subexpression $\pi_{\text{Course}}\big(\sigma_{\text{Day}=\text{"M"} \text{ AND } \text{Hour}=\text{"9AM"}}(CDH)\big)$ has as its value the courses that meet at 9AM Mondays, and the middle join intersects these sets to give us the courses taken by a student named "C. Brown" that meet at 9AM Mondays. Finally, the top join followed by projection looks up these courses in the CR relation (a fast operation if there is an index on Course), and produces the associated rooms as answer. ✦

EXERCISES

8.9.1*: Prove that

$$\big((R \underset{A=B}{\bowtie} S) \underset{C=D}{\bowtie} T\big) \equiv \big(R \underset{A=B}{\bowtie} (S \underset{C=D}{\bowtie} T)\big)$$

whenever A is an attribute of R, B and C are different attributes of S, and D is an attribute of T. Why is it important that $B \neq C$? *Hint*: Remember that certain attributes disappear when a join is taken.

8.9.2*: Prove that

$$\big((R \underset{A=B}{\bowtie} S) \underset{A=C}{\bowtie} T\big) \equiv \big(R \underset{A=B}{\bowtie} (S \underset{B=C}{\bowtie} T)\big)$$

whenever A is an attribute of R, B is an attribute of S, and C is an attribute of T.

8.9.3: Take each of your relational algebra queries from Exercise 8.7.3 and push selections and projections down as far as you can.

8.9.4: Let us make the following gross simplifications regarding the number of tuples that appear in relations that are the result of the operations of relational algebra.

i) Each operand relation has 1000 tuples.

ii) When we join relations with n and m tuples, respectively, the resulting relation has $mn/100$ tuples.

iii) When we perform a selection whose condition is the **AND** of k conditions, each of which equates an attribute to a constant value, we divide the size of the relation by 10^k.

iv) When we perform a projection, the size of the relation does not change.

Further, let us estimate the cost of evaluating an expression by the sum of the sizes of the relations computed for each interior node. Give the costs of each of the expressions in Figs. 8.18, 8.19(a) through (d), and 8.20(a) through (d).

8.9.5*: Prove the selection-pushing law

$$\big(\sigma_C(R \bowtie S)\big) \equiv \big((\sigma_C(R)) \bowtie S\big)$$

Hint: To prove the equality of two sets, it is often easiest to show that each is a subset of the other, as discussed in Section 7.3.

8.9.6*: Prove the laws

a) $\big(\sigma_C(R \cap S)\big) \equiv \big(\sigma_C(R) \cap \sigma_C(S)\big)$

b) $\big(\sigma_C(R \cup S)\big) \equiv \big(\sigma_C(R) \cup \sigma_C(S)\big)$

c) $\big(\sigma_C(R - S)\big) \equiv \big(\sigma_C(R) - \sigma_C(S)\big)$

8.9.7*: Give an example to show that the law

$$\big(\pi_L(R - S)\big) \equiv \big(\pi_L(R) - \pi_L(S)\big)$$

does not hold.

8.9.8**: It is sometimes possible to push a selection down both ways through a join, using the "equivalence"

$$\sigma_C(R \bowtie S) \equiv \big(\sigma_C(R) \bowtie \sigma_C(S)\big) \tag{8.1}$$

a) Under what circumstances is Equation (8.1) truly an equivalence?

b) If (8.1) is valid, when would it be better to use this law, rather than push the selection down only to R or only to S?

❖❖ 8.10 Summary of Chapter 8

You should remember the following points from this chapter.

✦ Two-dimensional tables, called relations, are a versatile way to store information.

✦ Rows of a relation are called "tuples," and the columns are named by "attributes."

✦ A "primary index" represents the tuples of a relation as data structures and distributes them in such a way that operations using values in certain attributes — the "domain" for the index — are facilitated.

✦ A "key" for a relation is a set of attributes that uniquely determine values for the other attributes of the relation. Often, a primary index uses a key for its domain.

✦ "Secondary indexes" are data structures that facilitate operations that specify a particular attribute, usually one not part of the domain for the primary index.

✦ Relational algebra is a high-level notation for specifying queries about one or more relations. Its principal operations are union, intersection, difference, selection, projection, and join.

✦ There are a number of ways to implement joins more efficiently than the obvious "nested-loop join," which pairs each tuple of one relation with each tuple of the other. Index-join and sort-join run in time that is close to what it takes to look at the two relations involved and produce the result of the join.

✦ Optimization of expressions in relational algebra can make significant improvements in the running time for evaluation of expressions and is therefore essential if languages based on relational algebra are to be used in practice to express queries.

✦ A number of ways to improve the running time of a given expression are known. Pushing down selections is often the most profitable.

❖❖ 8.11   Bibliographic Notes for Chapter 8

Further study of database systems, especially those based on the relational model, can be found in Ullman [1988].

The paper by Codd [1970] is generally regarded as the origin of the relational data model, although there were a number of earlier works that contained some of the ideas. The first implementations of systems using this model were INGRES (Stonebraker et al. [1976]) at Berkeley and System R (Astrahan et al. [1976]) at IBM. The latter is the origin of the language SQL sampled in Section 8.7 and found in many database management systems today; see Chamberlin et al. [1976]. The relational model is also found in the UNIX command awk (Aho, Kernighan, and Weinberger [1988]).

Aho, A. V., B. W. Kernighan, and P. J. Weinberger [1988]. *The AWK programming Language*, Addison-Wesley, Reading, Mass.

Astrahan, M. M., et al. [1976]. "System R: a relational approach to data management," *ACM Trans. on Database Systems* **1**:2, pp. 97–137.

Chamberlin, D. D., et al. [1976]. "SEQUEL 2: a unified approach to data definition, manipulation, and control," *IBM J. Research and Development* **20**:6, pp. 560–575.

Codd, E. F. [1970]. "A relational model for large shared data banks," *Comm. ACM* **13**:6, pp. 377–387.

Stonebraker, M., E. Wong, P. Kreps, and G. Held [1976]. "The design and implementation of INGRES," *ACM Trans. on Database Systems* **1**:3, pp. 189–222.

Ullman, J. D. [1988]. *Principles of Database and Knowledge-Base Systems* (two volumes) Computer Science Press, New York.

CHAPTER 9

❖

The Graph
Data Model

A graph is, in a sense, nothing more than a binary relation. However, it has a powerful visualization as a set of points (called nodes) connected by lines (called edges) or by arrows (called arcs). In this regard, the graph is a generalization of the tree data model that we studied in Chapter 5. Like trees, graphs come in several forms: directed/undirected, and labeled/unlabeled.

Also like trees, graphs are useful in a wide spectrum of problems such as computing distances, finding circularities in relationships, and determining connectivities. We have already seen graphs used to represent the structure of programs in Chapter 2. Graphs were used in Chapter 7 to represent binary relations and to illustrate certain properties of relations, like commutativity. We shall see graphs used to represent automata in Chapter 10 and to represent electronic circuits in Chapter 13. Several other important applications of graphs are discussed in this chapter.

❖❖ 9.1 What This Chapter Is About

The main topics of this chapter are

❖ The definitions concerning directed and undirected graphs (Sections 9.2 and 9.10).

❖ The two principal data structures for representing graphs: adjacency lists and adjacency matrices (Section 9.3).

❖ An algorithm and data structure for finding the connected components of an undirected graph (Section 9.4).

❖ A technique for finding minimal spanning trees (Section 9.5).

❖ A useful technique for exploring graphs, called "depth-first search" (Section 9.6).

◆ Applications of depth-first search to test whether a directed graph has a cycle, to find a topological order for acyclic graphs, and to determine whether there is a path from one node to another (Section 9.7).

◆ Dijkstra's algorithm for finding shortest paths (Section 9.8). This algorithm finds the minimum distance from one "source" node to every node.

◆ Floyd's algorithm for finding the minimum distance between any two nodes (Section 9.9).

Many of the algorithms in this chapter are examples of useful techniques that are much more efficient than the obvious way of solving the given problem.

✦✦ 9.2 Basic Concepts

Directed graph

A *directed graph,* consists of

1. A set N of *nodes* and

Nodes and arcs

2. A binary relation A on N. We call A the set of *arcs* of the directed graph. Arcs are thus pairs of nodes.

Graphs are drawn as suggested in Fig. 9.1. Each node is represented by a circle, with the name of the node inside. We shall usually name the nodes by integers starting at 0, or we shall use an equivalent enumeration. In Fig. 9.1, the set of nodes is $N = \{0, 1, 2, 3, 4\}$.

Each arc (u, v) in A is represented by an arrow from u to v. In Fig. 9.1, the set of arcs is

$$A = \{(0,0),\ (0,1),\ (0,2),\ (1,3),\ (2,0),\ (2,1),\ (2,4),\ (3,2),\ (3,4),\ (4,1)\}$$

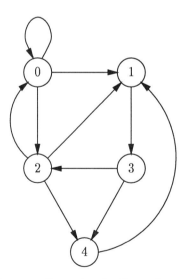

Fig. 9.1. Example of a directed graph.

Head and tail

In text, it is customary to represent an arc (u, v) as $u \rightarrow v$. We call v the *head* of the arc and u the *tail* to conform with the notion that v is at the head of the

Loop

arrow and u is at its tail. For example, $0 \to 1$ is an arc of Fig. 9.1; its head is node 1 and its tail is node 0. Another arc is $0 \to 0$; such an arc from a node to itself is called a *loop*. For this arc, both the head and the tail are node 0.

Predecessors and Successors

When $u \to v$ is an arc, we can also say that u is a *predecessor* of v, and that v is a *successor* of u. Thus, the arc $0 \to 1$ tells us that 0 is a predecessor of 1 and that 1 is a successor of 0. The arc $0 \to 0$ tells us that node 0 is both a predecessor and a successor of itself.

Labels

As for trees, it is permissible to attach a *label* to each node. Labels will be drawn near their node. Similarly, we can label arcs by placing the label near the middle of the arc. Any type can be used as a node label or an arc label. For instance, Fig. 9.2 shows a node named 1, with a label "dog," a node named 2, labeled "cat," and an arc $1 \to 2$ labeled "bites."

Fig. 9.2. A labeled graph with two nodes.

Again as with trees, we should not confuse the name of a node with its label. Node names must be unique in a graph, but two or more nodes can have the same label.

Paths

Length of a path

A *path* in a directed graph is a list of nodes $(v_1, v_2, \ldots, v_k)$ such that there is an arc from each node to the next, that is, $v_i \to v_{i+1}$ for $i = 1, 2, \ldots, k-1$. The *length* of the path is $k - 1$, the number of arcs along the path. For example, $(0, 1, 3)$ is a path of length two in Fig. 9.1.

The trivial case $k = 1$ is permitted. That is, any node v by itself is a path of length zero from v to v. This path has no arcs.

Cyclic and Acyclic Graphs

Length of a cycle

A *cycle* in a directed graph is a path of length 1 or more that begins and ends at the same node. The *length of the cycle* is the length of the path. Note that a trivial path of length 0 is not a cycle, even though it "begins and ends at the same node." However, a path consisting of a single arc $v \to v$ is a cycle of length 1.

✦ **Example 9.1.** Consider the graph of Fig. 9.1. There is a cycle $(0, 0)$ of length 1 because of the loop $0 \to 0$. There is a cycle $(0, 2, 0)$ of length 2 because of the arcs $0 \to 2$ and $2 \to 0$. Similarly, $(1, 3, 2, 1)$ is a cycle of length 3, and $(1, 3, 2, 4, 1)$ is a cycle of length 4. ✦

Equivalent cycles

Note that a cycle can be written to start and end at any of its nodes. That is, the cycle $(v_1, v_2, \ldots, v_k, v_1)$ could also be written as $(v_2, \ldots, v_k, v_1, v_2)$ or as $(v_3, \ldots, v_k, v_1, v_2, v_3)$, and so on. For example, the cycle $(1, 3, 2, 4, 1)$ could also have been written as $(2, 4, 1, 3, 2)$.

Simple cycle

On every cycle, the first and last nodes are the same. We say that a cycle $(v_1, v_2, \ldots, v_k, v_1)$ is *simple* if no node appears more than once among $v_1, \ldots, v_k$; that is, the only repetition in a simple cycle occurs at the final node.

✦ **Example 9.2.** All the cycles in Example 9.1 are simple. In Fig. 9.1 the cycle $(0, 2, 0)$ is simple. However, there are cycles that are not simple, such as $(0, 2, 1, 3, 2, 0)$ in which node 2 appears twice. ✦

Given a nonsimple cycle containing node v, we can find a simple cycle containing v. To see why, write the cycle to begin and end at v, as in $(v, v_1, v_2, \ldots, v_k, v)$. If the cycle is not simple, then either

1. v appears three or more times, or
2. There is some node u other than v that appears twice; that is, the cycle must look like $(v, \ldots, u, \ldots, u, \ldots, v)$.

In case (1), we can remove everything up to, but not including, the next-to-last occurrence of v. The result is a shorter cycle from v to v. In case (2), we can remove the section from u to u, replacing it by a single occurrence of u, to get the cycle $(v, \ldots, u, \ldots, v)$. The result must still be a cycle in either case, because each arc of the result is present in the original cycle, and therefore is present in the graph.

It may be necessary to repeat this transformation several times before the cycle becomes simple. Since the cycle always gets shorter with each iteration, eventually we must arrive at a simple cycle. What we have just shown is that if there is a cycle in a graph, then there must be at least one simple cycle.

✦ **Example 9.3.** Given the cycle $(0, 2, 1, 3, 2, 0)$, we can remove the first 2 and the following $1, 3$ to get the simple cycle $(0, 2, 0)$. In physical terms, we started with the cycle that begins at 0, goes to 2, then 1, then 3, back to 2, and finally back to 0. The first time we are at 2, we can pretend it is the second time, skip going to 1 and 3, and proceed right back to 0.

For another example, consider the nonsimple cycle $(0, 0, 0)$. As 0 appears three times, we remove the first 0, that is, everything up to but not including the next-to-last 0. Physically, we have replaced the path in which we went around the loop $0 \to 0$ twice by the path in which we go around once. ✦

Cyclic graph

If a graph has one or more cycles, we say the graph is *cyclic*. If there are no cycles, the graph is said to be *acyclic*. By what we just argued about simple cycles, a graph is cyclic if and only if it has a simple cycle, because if it has any cycles at all, it will have a simple cycle.

✦ **Example 9.4.** We mentioned in Section 3.8 that we could represent the calls

Calling graph

made by a collection of functions with a directed graph called the "calling graph." The nodes are the functions, and there is an arc $P \to Q$ if function P calls function Q. For instance, Fig. 9.3 shows the calling graph associated with the merge sort algorithm of Section 2.9.

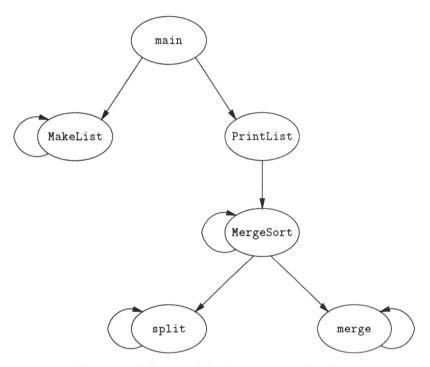

Fig. 9.3. Calling graph for the mergesort algorithm.

The existence of a cycle in the calling graph implies a recursion in the algorithm. In Fig. 9.3 there are four simple cycles, one around each of the nodes **MakeList**, **MergeSort**, **split**, and **merge**. Each cycle is a trivial loop. Recall that all these functions call themselves, and thus are recursive. Recursions in which a function calls itself are by far the most common kind, and each of these appears as a loop in the calling graph. We call these recursions *direct*. However, one occasionally sees an *indirect* recursion, in which there is a cycle of length greater than 1. For instance, the graph

Direct and indirect recursion

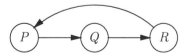

represents a function P that calls function Q, which calls function R, which calls function P. ✦

Acyclic Paths

A path is said to be *acyclic* if no node appears more than once on the path. Clearly, no cycle is acyclic. The argument that we just gave to show that for every cycle there is a simple cycle also demonstrates the following principle. If there is any path at all from u to v, then there is an acyclic path from u to v. To see why, start with any path from u to v. If there is a repetition of some node w, which could be u or v, replace the two occurrences of w and everything in between by one occurrence of w. As for the case of cycles, we may have to repeat this process several times, but eventually we reduce the path to an acyclic path.

✦ **Example 9.5.** Consider the graph of Fig 9.1 again. The path $(0, 1, 3, 2, 1, 3, 4)$ is a path from 0 to 4 that contains a cycle. We can focus on the two occurrences of node 1, and replace them, and the 3, 2 between them, by 1, leaving $(0, 1, 3, 4)$, which is an acyclic path because no node appears twice. We could also have obtained the same result by focusing on the two occurrences of node 3. ✦

Undirected Graphs

Edge

Neighbors

Sometimes it makes sense to connect nodes by lines that have no direction, called *edges*. Formally, an edge is a set of two nodes. The edge $\{u, v\}$ says that nodes u and v are connected in both directions.[1] If $\{u, v\}$ is an edge, then nodes u and v are said to be *adjacent* or to be *neighbors*. A graph with edges, that is, a graph with a symmetric arc relation, is called an *undirected graph*.

✦ **Example 9.6.** Figure 9.4 represents a partial road map of the Hawaiian Islands, indicating some of the principal cities. Cities with a road between them are indicated by an edge, and the edge is labeled by the driving distance. It is natural to represent roads by edges, rather than arcs, because roads are normally two-way. ✦

Paths and Cycles in Undirected Graphs

A *path* in an undirected graph is a list of nodes $(v_1, v_2, \ldots, v_k)$ such that each node and the next are connected by an edge. That is, $\{v_i, v_{i+1}\}$ is an edge for $i = 1, 2, \ldots, k - 1$. Note that edges, being sets, do not have their elements in any particular order. Thus, the edge $\{v_i, v_{i+1}\}$ could just as well appear as $\{v_{i+1}, v_i\}$.

The *length* of the path $(v_1, v_2, \ldots, v_k)$ is $k - 1$. As with directed graphs, a node by itself is a path of length 0.

Defining cycles in undirected graphs is a little tricky. The problem is that we do not want to consider a path such as (u, v, u), which exists whenever there is an edge $\{u, v\}$, to be a cycle. Similarly, if $(v_1, v_2, \ldots, v_k)$ is a path, we can traverse it forward and backward, but we do not want to call the path

$$(v_1, v_2, \ldots, v_{k-1}, v_k, v_{k-1}, \ldots, v_2, v_1)$$

---

[1] Note that the edge is required to have exactly two nodes. A singleton set consisting of one node is not an edge. Thus, although an arc from a node to itself is permitted, we do not permit a looping edge from a node to itself. Some definitions of "undirected graph" do permit such loops.

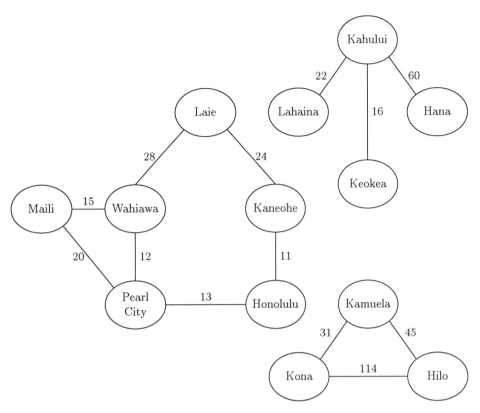

Fig. 9.4. An undirected graph representing roads in three Hawaiian Islands Oahu, Maui, and Hawaii (clockwise from the left).

a cycle.

Simple cycle

Perhaps the easiest approach is to define a *simple cycle* in an undirected graph to be a path of length three or more that begins and ends at the same node, and with the exception of the last node does not repeat any node. The notion of a nonsimple cycle in an undirected graph is not generally useful, and we shall not pursue this concept.

Equivalent cycles

As with directed cycles, we regard two undirected cycles as the same if they consist of the same nodes in the same order, with a different starting point. Undirected cycles are also the same if they consist of the same nodes in reverse order. Formally, the simple cycle $(v_1, v_2, \ldots, v_k)$ is equivalent, for each i between 1 and k, to the cycle $(v_i, v_{i+1}, \ldots, v_k, v_1, v_2, \ldots, v_{i-1})$ and to the cycle

$$(v_i, v_{i-1}, \ldots, v_1, v_k, v_{k-1}, \ldots, v_{i+1})$$

✦ **Example 9.7.** In Fig. 9.4,

(Wahiawa, Pearl City, Maili, Wahiawa)

is a simple cycle of length three. It could have been written equivalently as

(Maili, Wahiawa, Pearl City, Maili)

by starting at Maili and proceeding in the same order around the circle. Likewise, it could have been written to start at Pearl City and proceed around the circle in reverse order:

(Pearl City, Maili, Wahiawa, Pearl City)

For another example,

(Laie, Wahiawa, Pearl City, Honolulu, Kaneohe, Laie)

is a simple cycle of length five. ✦

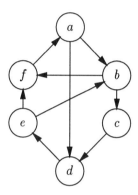

Fig. 9.5. Directed graph for Exercises 9.2.1 and 9.2.2.

EXERCISES

9.2.1: Consider the graph of Fig. 9.5.

a) How many arcs are there?
b) How many acyclic paths are there from node a to node d? What are they?
c) What are the predecessors of node b?
d) What are the successors of node b?
e) How many simple cycles are there? List them. Do not repeat paths that differ only in the starting point (see Exercise 9.2.8).
f) List all the nonsimple cycles of length up to 7.

9.2.2: Consider the graph of Fig. 9.5 to be an undirected graph, by replacing each arc $u \rightarrow v$ by an edge $\{u, v\}$.

a) Find all the paths from a to d that do not repeat any node.
b) How many simple cycles are there that include all six nodes? List these cycles.
c) What are the neighbors of node a?

9.2.3*: If a graph has 10 nodes, what is the largest number of arcs it can have? What is the smallest possible number of arcs? In general, if a graph has n nodes, what are the minimum and maximum number of arcs?

9.2.4*: Repeat Exercise 9.2.3 for the edges of an undirected graph.

9.2.5**: If a directed graph is acyclic and has n nodes, what is the largest possible number of arcs?

9.2.6: Find an example of indirect recursion among the functions so far in this book.

9.2.7: Write the cycle $(0, 1, 2, 0)$ in all possible ways.

9.2.8*: Let G be a directed graph and let R be the relation on the cycles of G defined by $(u_1, \ldots, u_k, u_1)R(v_1, \ldots, v_k, v_1)$ if and only if $(u_1, \ldots, u_k, u_1)$ and $(v_1, \ldots, v_k, v_1)$ represent the same cycle. Show that R is an equivalence relation on the cycles of G.

9.2.9*: Show that the relation S defined on the nodes of a graph by uSv if and only if $u = v$ or there is some cycle that includes both nodes u and v, is an equivalence relation.

9.2.10*: When we discussed simple cycles in undirected graphs, we mentioned that two cycles were really the same if they were the same nodes, either in order, or in reverse order, but with a different starting point. Show that the relation R consisting of pairs of representations for the same simple cycle is an equivalence relation.

✦✦ 9.3 Implementation of Graphs

There are two standard ways to represent a graph. One, called *adjacency lists*, is familiar from the implementation of binary relations in general. The second, called *adjacency matrices*, is a new way to represent binary relations, and is more suitable for relations where the number of pairs is a sizable fraction of the total number of pairs that could possibly exist over a given domain. We shall consider these representations, first for directed graphs, then for undirected graphs.

Adjacency Lists

Let nodes be named either by the integers $0, 1, \ldots, MAX - 1$ or by an equivalent enumerated type. In general, we shall use `NODE` as the type of nodes, but we may suppose that `NODE` is a synonym for `int`. Then we can use the generalized characteristic-vector approach, introduced in Section 7.9, to represent the set of arcs. This representation is called *adjacency lists*. We define linked lists of nodes by

```
typedef struct CELL *LIST;
struct CELL {
    NODE nodeName;
    LIST next;
};
```

and then create an array

```
LIST successors[MAX];
```

That is, the entry `successors[u]` contains a pointer to a linked list of all the successors of node u.

successors

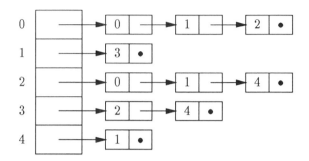

Fig. 9.6. Adjacency-list representation of the graph shown in Fig. 9.1.

♦ **Example 9.8.** The graph of Fig. 9.1 can be represented by the adjacency lists shown in Fig. 9.6. We have sorted the adjacency lists by node number, but the successors of a node can appear in any order on its adjacency list. ♦

Adjacency Matrices

Another common way to represent directed graphs is as *adjacency matrices.* We can create a two-dimensional array

```
BOOLEAN arcs[MAX][MAX];
```

in which the value of `arcs[u][v]` is TRUE if there is an arc $u \to v$, and FALSE if not.

♦ **Example 9.9.** The adjacency matrix for the graph of Fig. 9.1 is shown in Fig. 9.7. We use 1 for TRUE and 0 for FALSE. ♦

	0	1	2	3	4
0	1	1	1	0	0
1	0	0	0	1	0
2	1	1	0	0	1
3	0	0	1	0	1
4	0	1	0	0	0

Fig. 9.7. Adjacency matrix representing the graph of Fig. 9.1.

Operations on Graphs

We can see some of the distinctions between the two graph representations if we consider some simple operations on graphs. Perhaps the most basic operation is to determine whether there is an arc $u \to v$ from a node u to a node v. In the adjacency matrix, it takes $O(1)$ time to look up `arcs[u][v]` to see whether the entry there is TRUE or not.

Comparison of Adjacency Matrices and Adjacency Lists

Dense and sparse graphs

We tend to prefer adjacency matrices when the graphs are *dense,* that is, when the number of arcs is near the maximum possible number, which is n^2 for a graph of n nodes. However, if the graph is *sparse,* that is, if most of the possible arcs are not present, then the adjacency-list representation may save space. To see why, note that an adjacency matrix for an n-node graph has n^2 bits (provided we represent **TRUE** and **FALSE** by single bits rather than integers as we have done in this section).

In a typical computer, a structure consisting of an integer and a pointer, like our adjacency list cells, will use 32 bits to represent the integer and 32 bits to represent the pointer, or 64 bits total. Thus, if the number of arcs is a, we need about $64a$ bits for the lists, and $32n$ bits for the array of n headers. The adjacency list will use less space than the adjacency matrix if $32n + 64a < n^2$, that is, if $a < n^2/64 - n/2$. If n is large, we can neglect the $n/2$ term and approximate the previous inequality by $a < n^2/64$, that is, if fewer than 1/64th of the possible arcs are actually present. More detailed arguments favoring one or the other representation are presented when we discuss operations on graphs. The following table summarizes the preferred representations for various operations.

OPERATION	DENSE GRAPH	SPARSE GRAPH
Look up an arc	Adjacency matrix	Either
Find successors	Either	Adjacency lists
Find predecessors	Adjacency matrix	Either

With adjacency lists, it takes $O(1)$ time to find the header of the adjacency list for u. We must then traverse this list to the end if v is not there, or half the way down the list on the average if v is present. If there are a arcs and n nodes in the graph, then we take time $O(1 + a/n)$ on the average to do the lookup. If a is no more than a constant factor times n, this quantity is $O(1)$. However, the larger a is when compared with n, the longer it takes to tell whether an arc is present using the adjacency list representation. In the extreme case where a is around n^2, its maximum possible value, there are around n nodes on each adjacency list. In this case, it takes $O(n)$ time on the average to find a given arc. Put another way, the denser a graph is, the more we prefer the adjacency matrix to adjacency lists, when we need to look up a given arc.

On the other hand, we often need to find all the successors of a given node u. Using adjacency lists, we go to `successors[u]` and traverse the list, in average time $O(a/n)$, to find all the successors. If a is comparable to n, then we find all the successors of u in $O(1)$ time. But with adjacency matrices, we must examine the entire row for node u, taking $O(n)$ time no matter what a is. Thus, for graphs with a small number of edges per node, adjacency lists are much faster than adjacency matrices when we need to examine all the successors of a given node.

However, suppose we want to find all the predecessors of a given node v. With an adjacency matrix, we can examine the column for v; a 1 in the row for u means that u is a predecessor of v. This examination takes $O(n)$ time. The adjacency-list representation gives us no help finding predecessors. We must examine the adjacency list for every node u, to see if that list includes v. Thus, we may examine

A Matter of Degree

The number of arcs out of a node v is called the *out-degree* of v. Thus, the out-degree of a node equals the length of its adjacency list; it also equals the number of 1's in the row for v in the adjacency matrix. The number of arcs into node v is the *in-degree* of v. The in-degree measures the number of times v appears on the adjacency list of some node, and it is the number of 1's found in the column for v in the adjacency matrix.

In an undirected graph, we do not distinguish between edges coming in or going out of a node. For an undirected graph, the *degree* of node v is the number of neighbors of v, that is, the number of edges $\{u, v\}$ containing v for some node u. Remember that in a set, order of members is unimportant, so $\{u, v\}$ and $\{v, u\}$ are the same edge, and are counted only once. The *degree of an undirected graph* is the maximum degree of any node in the graph. For example, if we regard a binary tree as an undirected graph, its degree is 3, since a node can only have edges to its parent, its left child, and its right child. For a directed graph, we can say that the *in-degree of a graph* is the maximum of the in-degrees of its nodes, and likewise, the *out-degree of a graph* is the maximum of the out-degrees of its nodes.

(Margin notes: **In- and Out-degree**, **Degree of a graph**)

all the cells of all the adjacency lists, and we shall probably examine most of them. Since the number of cells in the entire adjacency list structure is equal to a, the number of arcs of the graph, the time to find predecessors using adjacency lists is thus $O(a)$ on a graph of a arcs. Here, the advantage goes to the adjacency matrix; and the denser the graph, the greater the advantage.

Implementing Undirected Graphs

If a graph is undirected, we can pretend that each edge is replaced by arcs in both directions, and represent the resulting directed graph by either adjacency lists or an adjacency matrix. If we use an adjacency matrix, the matrix is *symmetric*. That is, if we call the matrix **edges**, then $edges[u][v] = edges[v][u]$. If we use an adjacency-list representation, then the edge $\{u, v\}$ is represented twice. We find v on the adjacency list for u and we find u on the list for v. That arrangement is often useful, since we cannot tell in advance whether we are more likely to follow the edge $\{u, v\}$ from u to v or from v to u.

(Margin note: **Symmetric adjacency matrix**)

	Laie	Kaneohe	Honolulu	PearlCity	Maili	Wahiawa
Laie	0	1	0	0	0	1
Kaneohe	1	0	1	0	0	0
Honolulu	0	1	0	1	0	0
PearlCity	0	0	1	0	1	1
Maili	0	0	0	1	0	1
Wahiawa	1	0	0	1	1	0

Fig. 9.8. Adjacency-matrix representation of an undirected graph from Fig. 9.4.

✦ **Example 9.10.** Consider how to represent the largest component of the undirected graph of Fig. 9.4 (which represents six cities on the island of Oahu). For the moment, we shall ignore the labels on the edges. The adjacency matrix representation is shown in Fig. 9.8. Notice that the matrix is symmetric.

Figure 9.9 shows the representation by adjacency lists. In both cases, we are using an enumeration type

```
enum CITYTYPE {Laie, Kaneohe, Honolulu,
        PearlCity, Maili, Wahiawa};
```

to index arrays. That arrangement is somewhat rigid, since it does not allow any changes in the set of nodes of the graph. We shall give a similar example shortly where we name nodes explicitly by integers, and use city names as node labels, for more flexibility in changing the set of nodes. ✦

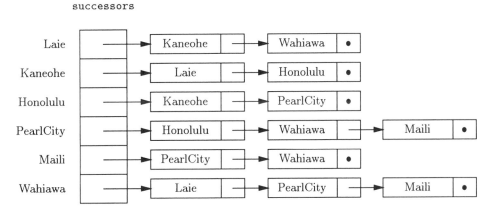

Fig. 9.9. Adjacency-list representation of an undirected graph from Fig. 9.4.

Representing Labeled Graphs

Suppose a graph has labels on its arcs (or edges if it is undirected). Using an adjacency matrix, we can replace the 1 that represents the presence of arc $u \to v$ in the graph by the label of this arc. It is necessary that we have some value that is permissible as a matrix entry but cannot be mistaken for a label; we use this value to represent the absence of an arc.

If we represent the graph by adjacency lists, we add to the cells forming the lists an additional field `nodeLabel`. If there is an arc $u \to v$ with label L, then on the adjacency list for node u we shall find a cell with v in its `nodeName` field and L in its `nodeLabel` field. That value represents the label of the arc.

We represent labels on nodes in a different way. For an adjacency matrix, we simply create another array, say `NodeLabels`, and let `NodeLabels[u]` be the label of node `u`. When we use adjacency lists, we already have an array of headers indexed by nodes. We change this array so that it has elements that are structures, one field for the node label and one field pointing to the beginning of the adjacency list.

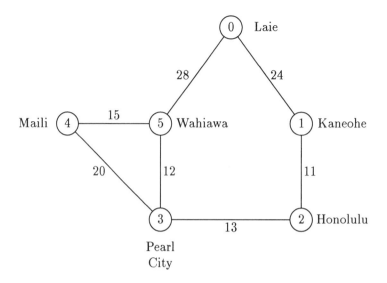

Fig. 9.10. Map of Oahu with nodes named by integers and labeled by cities.

cities

0	Laie
1	Kaneohe
2	Honolulu
3	PearlCity
4	Maili
5	Wahiawa

distances

	0	1	2	3	4	5
0	−1	24	−1	−1	−1	28
1	24	−1	11	−1	−1	−1
2	−1	11	−1	13	−1	−1
3	−1	−1	13	−1	20	12
4	−1	−1	−1	20	−1	15
5	28	−1	−1	12	15	−1

Fig. 9.11. Adjacency-matrix representation of a directed graph.

✦ **Example 9.11.** Let us again represent the large component of the graph of Fig. 9.4, but this time, we shall incorporate the edge labels, which are distances. Furthermore, we shall give the nodes integer names, starting with 0 for Laie, and proceeding clockwise. The city names themselves are indicated by node labels. We shall take the type of node labels to be character arrays of length 32. This representation is more flexible than that of Example 9.10, since if we allocate extra places in the array, we can add cities should we wish. The resulting graph is redrawn in Fig. 9.10, and the adjacency matrix representation is in Fig. 9.11.

Notice that there are really two parts to this representation: the array `cities`, indicating the city that each of the integers 0 through 5 stands for, and the matrix `distances`, indicating the presence or absence of edges and the labels of present edges. We use -1 as a value that cannot be mistaken for a label, since in this example, labels, representing distances, must be positive.

We could declare this structure as follows:

```
typedef char CITYTYPE[32];
typedef CITYTYPE cities[MAX];
int distances[MAX][MAX];
```

Here, MAX is some number at least 6; it limits the number of nodes that can ever appear in our graph. `CITYTYPE` is defined to be 32-character arrays, and the array `cities` gives the labels of the various nodes. For example, we expect $cities[0]$ to be `"Laie"`.

An alternative representation of the graph of Fig. 9.10 is by adjacency lists. Suppose the constant MAX and the type `CITYTYPE` are as above. We define the types `CELL` and `LIST` by

```
typedef struct CELL *LIST;
struct CELL {
    NODE nodeName;
    int distance;
    LIST next;
};
```

Next, we declare the array `cities` by

```
struct {
    CITYTYPE city;
    LIST adjacent;
} cities[MAX];
```

Figure 9.12 shows the graph of Fig. 9.10 represented in this manner. ✦

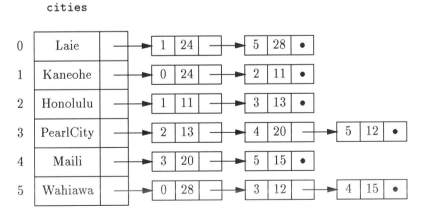

Fig. 9.12. Adjacency-list representation of graph with node and edge labels.

EXERCISES

9.3.1: Represent the graph of Fig. 9.5 (see the exercises of Section 9.2) by

a)   Adjacency lists

b)   An adjacency matrix

Give the appropriate type definitions in each case.

9.3.2: Suppose the arcs of Fig. 9.5 were instead edges (i.e., the graph were undirected). Repeat Exercise 9.3.1 for the undirected graph.

9.3.3: Let us label each of the arcs of the directed graph of Fig. 9.5 by the character string of length 2 consisting of the tail followed by the head. For example, the arc $a \rightarrow b$ is labeled by the character string **ab**. Also, suppose each node is labeled by the capital letter corresponding to its name. For instance, the node named a is labeled **A**. Repeat Exercise 9.3.1 for this labeled, directed graph.

9.3.4*: What is the relationship between the adjacency-matrix representation of an unlabeled graph and the characteristic-vector representation of a set of arcs?

9.3.5*: Prove by induction on n that in an undirected graph of n nodes, the sum of the degrees of the nodes is twice the number of edges. *Note.* A proof without using induction is also possible, but here an inductive proof is required.

9.3.6: Design algorithms to insert and delete arcs from an (a) adjacency-matrix (b) adjacency-list representation of a directed graph.

9.3.7: Repeat Exercise 9.3.6 for an undirected graph.

9.3.8: We can add a "predecessor list" to the adjacency-list representation of a directed or undirected graph. When is this representation preferred for the operations of

a)   Looking up an arc?

b)   Finding all successors?

c)   Finding all predecessors?

Consider both dense and sparse graphs in your analysis.

❖❖ 9.4 Connected Components of an Undirected Graph

We can divide any undirected graph into one or more *connected components.* Each connected component is a set of nodes with paths from any member of the component to any other. Moreover, the connected components are maximal, that is, for no node in the component is there a path to any node outside the component. If a graph consists of a single connected component, then we say the graph is *connected.*

Connected
graph

Physical Interpretation of Connected Components

If we are given a drawing of an undirected graph, it is easy to see the connected components. Imagine that the edges are strings. If we pick up any node, the connected component of which it is a member will come up with it, and members of all other connected components will stay where they are. Of course, what is easy to do by "eyeball" is not necessarily easy to do by computer. An algorithm to find the connected components of a graph is the principal subject of this section.

✦ **Example 9.12.** Consider again the graph of the Hawaiian Islands in Fig. 9.4. There are three connected components, corresponding to three islands. The largest component consists of Laie, Kaneohe, Honolulu, Pearl City, Maili, and Wahiawa. These are cities on the island of Oahu, and they are clearly mutually connected by roads, that is, by paths of edges. Also, clearly, there are no roads leading from Oahu to any other island. In graph-theoretic terms, there are no paths from any of the six cities mentioned above to any of the other cities in Fig. 9.4.

A second component consists of the cities of Lahaina, Kahului, Hana, and Keokea; these are cities on the island of Maui. The third component is the cities of Hilo, Kona, and Kamuela, on the "big island" of Hawaii. ✦

Connected Components as Equivalence Classes

Another useful way to look at connected components is that they are the equivalence classes of the equivalence relation P defined on the nodes of the undirected graph by: uPv if and only if there is a path from u to v. It is easy to check that P is an equivalence relation.

1. P is reflexive, that is, uPu for any node u, since there is a path of length 0 from any node to itself.

2. P is symmetric. If uPv, then there is a path from u to v. Since the graph is undirected, the reverse sequence of nodes is also a path. Thus vPu.

3. P is transitive. Suppose uPw and wPv are true. Then there is a path, say

$$(x_1, x_2, \ldots, x_j)$$

from u to w. Here, $u = x_1$ and $w = x_j$. Also, there is a path $(y_1, y_2, \ldots, y_k)$ from w to v where $w = y_1$ and $v = y_k$. If we put these paths together, we get a path from u to v, namely

$$(u = x_1, x_2, \cdots, x_j = w = y_1, y_2, \cdots, y_k = v)$$

✦ **Example 9.13.** Consider the path

(Honolulu, PearlCity, Wahiawa, Maili)

from Honolulu to Maili in Fig. 9.10. Also consider the path

(Maili, PearlCity, Wahiawa, Laie)

from Maili to Laie in the same graph. If we put these paths together, we get a path from Honolulu to Laie:

(Honolulu, PearlCity, Wahiawa, Maili, PearlCity, Wahiawa, Laie)

It happens that this path is cyclic. As mentioned in Section 9.2, we can always remove cycles to get an acyclic path. In this case, one way to do so is to replace the two occurrences of Wahiawa and the nodes in between by one occurrence of Wahiawa to get

(Honolulu, PearlCity, Wahiawa, Laie)

which is an acyclic path from Honolulu to Laie. ✦

Since P is an equivalence relation, it partitions the set of nodes of the undirected graph in question into equivalence classes. The class containing node v is the set of nodes u such that vPu, that is, the set of nodes connected to v by a path. Moreover, another property of equivalence classes is that if nodes u and v are in different classes, then it is not possible that uPv; that is, there is never a path from a node in one equivalence class to a node in another. Thus, the equivalence classes defined by the "path" relation P are exactly the connected components of the graph.

An Algorithm for Computing the Connected Components

Suppose we want to construct the connected components of a graph G. One approach is to begin with a graph G_0 consisting of the nodes of G with none of the edges. We then consider the edges of G, one at a time, to construct a sequence of graphs $G_0, G_1, \ldots$, where G_i consists of the nodes of G and the first i edges of G.

BASIS. G_0 consists of only the nodes of G with none of the edges. Every node is in a component by itself.

INDUCTION. Suppose we have the connected components for the graph G_i after considering the first i edges, and we now consider the $(i + 1)$st edge, $\{u, v\}$.

1. If u and v are in the same component of G_i, then G_{i+1} has the same set of connected components as G_i, because the new edge does not connect any nodes that were not already connected.

2. If u and v are in different components, we merge the components containing u and v to get the connected components for G_{i+1}. Figure 9.13 suggests why there is a path from any node x in the component of u, to any node y in the component of v. We follow the path in the first component from x to u, then the edge $\{u, v\}$, and finally the path from v to y that we know exists in the second component.

When we have considered all edges in this manner, we have the connected components of the full graph.

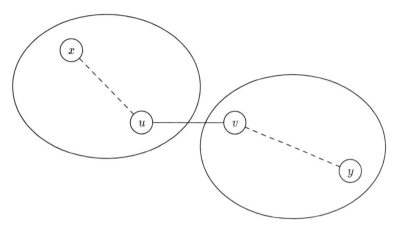

Fig. 9.13. Adding edge $\{u, v\}$ connects the components containing u and v.

♦ **Example 9.14.** Let us consider the graph of Fig. 9.4. We can consider edges in any order, but for reasons having to do with an algorithm in the next section, let us list the edges in order of the edge labels, smallest first. This list of edges is shown in Fig. 9.14.

Initially, all thirteen nodes are in components of their own. When we consider edge 1, {Kaneohe, Honolulu}, we merge these two nodes into a single component. The second edge, {Wahiawa, PearlCity}, merges those two cities. The third edge is {PearlCity, Honolulu}. That edge merges the components containing these two cities. Presently, each of these components contains two cities, so we now have one component with four cities, namely

{Wahiawa, PearlCity, Honolulu, Kaneohe}

All other cities are still in components by themselves.

EDGE	CITY 1	CITY 2	DISTANCE
1	Kaneohe	Honolulu	11
2	Wahiawa	PearlCity	12
3	PearlCity	Honolulu	13
4	Wahiawa	Maili	15
5	Kahului	Keokea	16
6	Maili	PearlCity	20
7	Lahaina	Kahului	22
8	Laie	Kaneohe	24
9	Laie	Wahiawa	28
10	Kona	Kamuela	31
11	Kamuela	Hilo	45
12	Kahului	Hana	60
13	Kona	Hilo	114

Fig. 9.14. Edges of Fig. 9.4 in order of labels.

Edge 4 is {Maili, Wahiawa} and adds Maili to the large component. The fifth edge is {Kahului, Keokea}, which merges these two cities into a component. When we consider edge 6, {Maili, PearlCity}, we see a new phenomenon: both ends of the edge are already in the same component. We therefore do no merging with edge 6.

Edge 7 is {Lahaina, Kahului}, and it adds the node Lahaina to the component {Kahului, Keokea}, forming the component {Lahaina, Kahului, Keokea}. Edge 8 adds Laie to the largest component, which is now

{Laie, Kaneohe, Honolulu, PearlCity, Wahiawa, Maili}

The ninth edge, {Laie, Wahiawa}, connects two cities in this component and is thus ignored.

Edge 10 groups Kamuela and Kona into a component, and edge 11 adds Hilo to this component. Edge 12 adds Hana to the component of

{Lahaina, Kahului, Keokea}

Finally, edge 13, {Hilo, Kona}, connects two cities already in the same component. Thus,

{Laie, Kaneohe, Honolulu, PearlCity, Wahiawa, Maili}
{Lahaina, Kahului, Keokea, Hana}
{Kamuela, Hilo, Kona}

is the final set of connected components. ✦

A Data Structure for Forming Components

If we consider the algorithm described informally above, we need to be able to do two things quickly:

1. Given a node, find its current component.

2. Merge two components into one.

There are a number of data structures that can support these operations. We shall study one simple idea that gives surprisingly good performance. The key is to put the nodes of each component into a tree.[2] The component is represented by the root of the tree. The two operations above can now be implemented as follows:

1. To find the component of a node in the graph, we go to the representative of that node in the tree and follow the path in that tree to the root, which represents the component.

2. To merge two different components, we make the root of one component a child of the root of the other.

---

[2] It is important to understand that, in what follows, the "tree" and the "graph" are distinct structures. There is a one-to-one correspondence between the nodes of the graph and the nodes of the tree; that is, each tree node represents a graph node. However, the parent-child edges of the tree are not necessarily edges in the graph.

✦ **Example 9.15.** Let us follow the steps of Example 9.14, showing the trees created at certain steps. Initially, every node is in a one-node tree by itself. The first edge, {Kaneohe, Honolulu}, causes us to merge two one-node trees, {Kaneohe} and {Honolulu}, into one two-node tree, {Kaneohe, Honolulu}. Either node could be made a child of the other. Let us suppose that Honolulu is made the child of the root Kaneohe.

Similarly, the second edge, {Wahiawa, PearlCity}, merges two trees, and we may suppose that PearlCity is made the child of the root Wahiawa. At this point, the current collection of components is represented by the two trees in Fig. 9.15 and nine one-node trees.

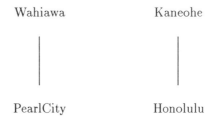

Fig. 9.15. The first two nontrivial trees as we merge components.

The third edge, {PearlCity, Honolulu}, merges these two components. Let us suppose that Wahiawa is made a child of the other root, Kaneohe. Then the resulting component is represented by the tree of Fig. 9.16.

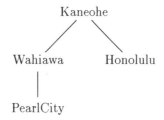

Fig. 9.16. Tree representing component of four nodes.

When we consider the fourth edge, {Wahiawa, Maili}, we merge Maili into the component represented by the tree of Fig. 9.16. We could either make Maili a child of Kaneohe, or make Kaneohe a child of Maili. We prefer the former, since that keeps the height of the tree small, while making the root of the large component a child of the root of the small component tends to make paths in the tree larger. Large paths, in turn, cause us to take more time following a path to the root, which we need to do to determine the component of a node. By following that policy and making arbitrary decisions when components have the same height, we might wind up with the three trees in Fig. 9.17 that represent the three final connected components. ✦

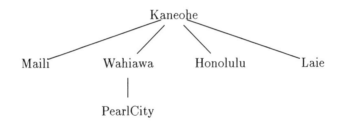

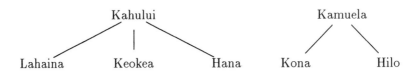

Fig. 9.17. Trees representing final connected components using tree-merging algorithm.

Following the lesson of Example 9.15, we formulate a policy that whenever we merge two trees, the root of lesser height becomes a child of the root with greater height. Ties can be broken arbitrarily. The important gain from this policy is that heights of trees can only grow logarithmically with the number of nodes in the trees, and in practice, the height is often smaller. Therefore, when we follow a path from a tree node to its root, we take at most time proportional to the logarithm of the number of nodes in the tree. We can derive the logarithmic bound by proving the following statement by induction on the height h.

STATEMENT $S(h)$: A tree of height h, formed by the policy of merging lower into higher, has at least 2^h nodes.

BASIS. The basis is $h = 0$. Such a tree must be a single node, and since $2^0 = 1$, the statement $S(0)$ is true.

INDUCTION. Suppose $S(h)$ is true for some $h \geq 0$, and consider a tree T of height $h + 1$. At some time during the formation of T by mergers, the height first reached $h + 1$. The only way to get a tree of height $h + 1$ is to make the root of some tree T_1, of height h, a child of the root of some tree T_2. T is T_1 plus T_2, plus perhaps other nodes that were added later, as suggested by Fig. 9.18.

Now T_1, by the inductive hypothesis, has at least 2^h nodes. Since its root was made a child of the root of T_2, the height of T_2 is also at least h. Thus, T_2 also has at least 2^h nodes. T consists of T_1, T_2, and perhaps more, so T has at least $2^h + 2^h = 2^{h+1}$ nodes. That statement is $S(h+1)$, and we have proved the inductive step.

We now know that if a tree has n nodes and height h, it must be that $n \geq 2^h$. Taking logarithms of both sides, we have $\log_2 n \geq h$; that is, the height of the tree

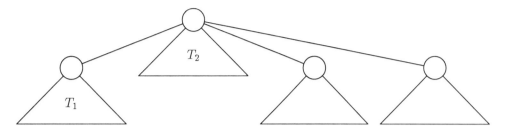

Fig. 9.18. Forming a tree of height $h + 1$.

cannot be greater than the logarithm of the number of nodes. Consequently, when we follow any path from a node to its root, we take $O(\log n)$ time.

We shall now describe in more detail the data structure that implements these ideas. First, suppose that there is a type **NODE** representing nodes. As before, we assume the type **NODE** is **int** and **MAX** is at least the number of nodes in the graph. For our example of Fig. 9.4, we shall let **MAX** be 13.

We shall also assume that there is a list **edges** consisting of cells of type **EDGE**. These cells are defined by

```
typedef struct EDGE *EDGELIST;
struct EDGE {
    NODE node1, node2;
    EDGELIST next;
};
```

Finally, for each node of the graph, we need a corresponding tree node. Tree nodes will be structures of type **TREENODE**, consisting of

1. A parent pointer, so that we can build a tree on the graph's nodes, and follow the tree to its root. A root node will be identified by having **NULL** as its parent.

2. The height of the tree of which a given node is the root. The height will only be used if the node is presently a root.

We may thus define type **TREENODE** by

```
typedef struct TREENODE *TREE;
struct TREENODE {
    int height;
    TREE parent;
}:
```

We shall define an array

```
TREE nodes[MAX];
```

to associate with each graph node a node in some tree. It is important to realize that each entry in the array **nodes** is a pointer to a node in the tree, yet this entry is the sole representative of the node in the graph.

Two important auxiliary functions are shown in Fig. 9.19. The first, **find**, takes a node a, gets a pointer to the corresponding tree node, x, and follows the parent pointers in x and its ancestors, until it comes to the root. This search for the root is performed by lines (2) and (3). If the root is found, a pointer to the root is returned at line (4). Note that at line (1), the type **NODE** must be **int** so it may

```
      /* return the root of the tree containing the tree node x
          corresponding to graph node a */
      TREE find(NODE a, TREE nodes[]);
      {
          TREE x;

(1)       x = nodes[a];
(2)       while (x->parent != NULL)
(3)           x = x->parent;
(4)       return x;
      }



      /* merge the trees with roots x and y into one tree,
          by making the root of the lower a child of
          the root of the higher */
      void merge(TREE x, TREE y)
      {
          TREE higher, lower;

(5)       if (x->height > y->height) {
(6)           higher = x;
(7)           lower = y;
          }
          else {
(8)           higher = y;
(9)           lower = x;
          }
(10)      lower->parent = higher;
(11)      if (lower->height == higher->height)
(12)          ++(higher->height);
      }
```

Fig. 9.19. Auxiliary functions find and merge.

be used to index the array **nodes**.

The second function, **merge**,[3] takes pointers to two tree nodes, x and y, which must be the roots of distinct trees for the merger to work properly. The test of line (5) determines which of the roots has the greater height; ties are broken in favor of y. The higher is assigned to the local variable **higher** and the lower to the local variable **lower** at lines (6–7) or lines (8–9), whichever is appropriate. Then at line (10) the lower is made a child of the higher and at lines (11) and (12) the height of the higher, which is now the root of the combined tree, is incremented by one if the heights of T_1 and T_2 are equal. The height of the lower remains as it was, but it is now meaningless, because the lower is no longer a root.

The heart of the algorithm to find connected components is shown in Fig. 9.20.

---

[3] Do not confuse this function with a function of the same name used for merge sorting in Chapters 2 and 3.

```
#include <stdio.h>
#include <stdlib.h>

#define MAX 13
typedef int NODE;
typedef struct EDGE *EDGELIST;
struct EDGE {
    NODE node1, node2;
    EDGELIST next;
};

typedef struct TREENODE *TREE;
struct TREENODE {
    int height;
    TREE parent;
};

TREE find(NODE a, TREE nodes[]);
void merge(TREE x, TREE y);
EDGELIST makeEdges();

main()
{
    NODE u;
    TREE a, b;
    EDGELIST e;
    TREE nodes[MAX];

    /* initialize nodes so each node is in a tree by itself */
(1)  for (u = 0; u < MAX; u++) {
(2)      nodes[u] = (TREE) malloc(sizeof(struct TREENODE));
(3)      nodes[u]->parent = NULL;
(4)      nodes[u]->height = 0;
     }

     /* initialize e as the list of edges of the graph */
(5)  e = makeEdges();

     /* examine each edge, and if its ends are in different
        components, then merge them */
(6)  while (e != NULL) {
(7)      a = find(e->node1, nodes);
(8)      b = find(e->node2, nodes);
(9)      if (a != b)
(10)         merge(a, b);
(11)     e = e->next;
     }
}
```

Fig. 9.20. C program to find connected components.

Better Algorithms for Connected Components

We shall see, when we learn about depth-first search in Section 9.6, that there is actually a better way to compute connected components, one that takes only $O(m)$ time, instead of $O(m \log n)$ time. However, the data structure given in Section 9.4 is useful in its own right, and we shall see in Section 9.5 another program that uses this data structure.

We assume that the function **makeEdges()** turns the graph at hand into a list of edges. The code for this function is not shown.

Lines (1) through (4) of Fig. 9.20 go down the array **nodes**, and for each node, a tree node is created at line (2). Its **parent** field is set to **NULL** at line (3), making it the root of its own tree, and its **height** field is set to 0 at line (4), reflecting the fact that the node is alone in its tree.

Line (5) then initializes **e** to point to the first edge on the list of edges, and the loop of lines (6) through (11) examines each edge in turn. At lines (7) and (8) we find the roots of the two ends of the current edge. Then at line (9) we test to see if these roots are different tree nodes. If so, the ends of the current edge are in different components, and we merge these components at line (10). If the two ends of the edge are in the same component, we skip line (10), so no change to the collection of trees is made. Finally, line (11) advances us along the list of edges.

Running Time of the Connected Components Algorithm

Let us determine how long the algorithm of Fig. 9.20 takes to process a graph. Suppose the graph has n nodes, and let m be the larger of the number of nodes and the number of edges.[4] First, let us examine the auxiliary functions. We argued that the policy of merging lower trees into higher ones guarantees that the path from any tree node to its root cannot be longer than $\log n$. Thus, **find** takes $O(\log n)$ time.

Next, let us examine the function **merge** from Fig. 9.19. Each of its statements takes $O(1)$ time. Since there are no loops or function calls, the entire function takes $O(1)$ time.

Finally, let us examine the main program of Fig. 9.20. The body of the for-loop of lines (1) to (4) takes $O(1)$ time, and the loop is iterated n times. Thus, the time for lines (1) through (4) is $O(n)$. Let us assume line (5) takes $O(m)$ time. Finally, consider the while-loop of lines (6) to (11). In the body, lines (7) and (8) each take $O(\log n)$ time, since they are calls to a function, **find**, that we just determined takes $O(\log n)$ time. Lines (9) and (11) clearly take $O(1)$ time. Line (10) likewise takes $O(1)$ time, because we just determined that function **merge** takes $O(1)$ time. Thus, the entire body takes $O(\log n)$ time. The while-loop iterates m times, where m is the number of edges. Thus, the time for this loop is $O(m \log n)$, that is, the number of iterations times the bound on the time for the body.

In general, then, the running time of the entire program can be expressed as $O(n + m + m \log n)$. However, m is at least n, and so the $m \log n$ term dominates the other terms. Thus, the running time of the program in Fig. 9.20 is $O(m \log n)$.

---

[4] It is normal to think of m as the number of edges, but in some graphs, there are more nodes than edges.

CITY 1	CITY 2	DISTANCE
Marquette	Sault Ste. Marie	153
Saginaw	Flint	31
Grand Rapids	Lansing	60
Detroit	Lansing	78
Escanba	Sault Ste. Marie	175
Ann Arbor	Detroit	28
Ann Arbor	Battle Creek	89
Battle Creek	Kalamazoo	21
Menominee	Escanba	56
Kalamazoo	Grand Rapids	45
Escanba	Marquette	78
Battle Creek	Lansing	40
Flint	Detroit	58

Fig. 9.21. Some distances within the state of Michigan.

EXERCISES

9.4.1: Figure 9.21 lists some cities in the state of Michigan and the road mileage between them. For the purposes of this exercise, ignore the mileage. Construct the connected components of the graph by examining each edge in the manner described in this section.

9.4.2*: Prove, by induction on k, that a connected component of k nodes has at least $k - 1$ edges.

9.4.3*: There is a simpler way to implement "merge" and "find," in which we keep an array indexed by nodes, giving the component of each node. Initially, each node is in a component by itself, and we name the component by the node. To find the component of a node, we simply look up the corresponding array entry. To merge components, we run down the array, changing each occurrence of the first component to the second.

a)   Write a C program to implement this algorithm.

b)   As a function of n, the number of nodes, and m, the larger of the number of nodes and edges, what is the running time of this program?

c)   For certain numbers of edges and nodes, this implementation is actually better than the one described in the section. When?

9.4.4*: Suppose that instead of merging lower trees into higher trees in the connected components algorithm of this section, we merge trees with fewer nodes into trees with a larger number of nodes. Is the running time of the connected-components algorithm still $O(m \log n)$?

✦✦ 9.5   Minimal Spanning Trees

There is an important generalization of the connected components problem, in which we are given an undirected graph with edges labeled by numbers (integers or reals). We must not only find the connected components, but for each component we must find a tree connecting the nodes of that component. Moreover, this tree must be *minimal*, meaning that the sum of the edge labels is as small as possible.

Unrooted, unordered trees

The trees talked about here are not quite the same as the trees of Chapter 5. Here, no node is designated the root, and there is no notion of children or of order among the children. Rather, when we speak of "trees" in this section, we mean unrooted, unordered trees, which are just undirected graphs that have no simple cycles.

Spanning tree

A *spanning tree* for an undirected graph G is the nodes of G together with a subset of the edges of G that

1.   Connect the nodes; that is, there is a path between any two nodes using only edges in the spanning tree.

2.   Form an unrooted, unordered tree; that is, there are no (simple) cycles.

If G is a single connected component, then there is always a spanning tree. A *minimal spanning tree* is a spanning tree the sum of whose edge labels is as small as that of any spanning tree for the given graph.

✦   **Example 9.16.** Let graph G be the connected component for the island of Oahu, as in Fig. 9.4 or Fig. 9.10. One possible spanning tree is shown in Fig. 9.22. It is formed by deleting the edges {Maili, Wahiawa} and {Kaneohe, Laie}, and

Weight of a tree

retaining the other five edges. The *weight*, or sum of edge labels, for this tree is 84. As we shall see, that is not a minimum. ✦

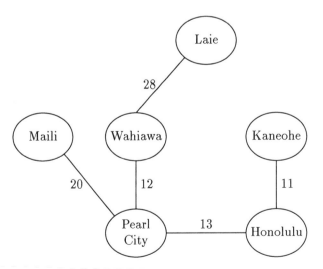

Fig. 9.22. A spanning tree for the island of Oahu.

Rooted and Unrooted Trees

The notion of an unrooted tree should not seem too strange. In fact, we can choose any node of an unrooted tree to be the root. That gives a direction to all edges, away from the root, or from parent to child. Physically, it is as if we picked up the unrooted tree by a node, letting the rest of the tree dangle from the selected node. For example, we could make Pearl City the root of the spanning tree in Fig. 9.22, and it would look like this:

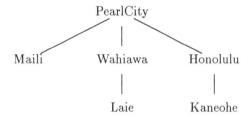

We can order the children of each node if we wish, but the order will be arbitrary, bearing no relation to the original unrooted tree.

Finding a Minimal Spanning Tree

Kruskal's algorithm

There are a number of algorithms to find minimal spanning trees. We shall exhibit one, called *Kruskal's algorithm,* that is a simple extension to the algorithm discussed in the last section for finding connected components. The changes needed are

1. We are required to consider edges in increasing order of their labels. (We happened to choose that order in Example 9.14, but it was not required for connected components.)

2. As we consider edges, if an edge has its ends in different components, then we select that edge for the spanning tree and merge components, as in the algorithm of the previous section. Otherwise, we do not select the edge for the spanning tree, and, of course, we do not merge components.

✦ **Example 9.17.** The Acme Surfboard Wax Company has offices in the thirteen cities shown in Fig. 9.4. It wishes to rent dedicated data transmission lines from the phone company, and we shall suppose that the phone lines run along the roads that are indicated by edges in Fig. 9.4. Between islands, the company must use satellite transmission, and the cost will be proportional to the number of components. However, for the ground transmission lines, the phone company charges by the mile.[5] Thus, we wish to find a minimal spanning tree for each connected component of the graph of Fig. 9.4.

    If we divide the edges by component, then we can run Kruskal's algorithm on

---

[5] This is one possible way to charge for leased telephone lines. One finds a minimal spanning tree connecting the desired sites, and the charge is based on the weight of that tree, regardless of how the phone connections are provided physically.

each component separately. However, if we do not already know the components, then we must consider all the edges together, smallest label first, in the order of Fig. 9.14. As in Section 9.4, we begin with each node in a component by itself.

We first consider the edge {Kaneohe, Honolulu}, the edge with the smallest label. This edge merges these two cities into one component, and because we perform a merge operation, we select that edge for the minimal spanning tree. Edge 2 is {Wahiawa, PearlCity}, and since that edge also merges two components, it is selected for the spanning tree. Likewise, edges 3 and 4, {PearlCity, Honolulu} and {Wahiawa, Maili}, merge components, and are therefore put in the spanning tree.

Edge 5, {Kahului, Keokea}, merges these two cities, and is also accepted for the spanning tree, although this edge will turn out to be part of the spanning tree for the Maui component, rather than the Oahu component as was the case for the four previous edges.

Edge 6, {Maili, PearlCity}, connects two cities that are already in the same component. Thus, this edge is rejected for the spanning tree. Even though we shall have to pick some edges with larger labels, we cannot pick {Maili, PearlCity}, because to do so would form a cycle of the cities Maili, Wahiawa, and Pearl City. We cannot have a cycle in the spanning tree, so one of the three edges must be excluded. As we consider edges in order of label, the last edge of the cycle considered must have the largest label, and is the best choice to exclude.

Edge 7, {Lahaina, Kahului}, and edge 8, {Laie, Kaneohe}, are both accepted for the spanning tree, because they merge components. Edge 9, {Laie, Wahiawa}, is rejected because its ends are in the same component. We accept edges 10 and 11; they form the spanning tree for the "big island" component, and we accept edge 12 to complete the Maui component. Edge 13 is rejected, because it connects Kona and Hilo, which were merged into the same component by edges 10 and 11. The resulting spanning trees of the components are shown in Fig. 9.23. ✦

Why Kruskal's Algorithm Works

We can prove that Kruskal's algorithm produces a spanning tree whose weight is as small as that of any spanning tree for the given graph. Let G be an undirected, connected graph. For convenience, let us add infinitesimal amounts to some labels, if necessary, so that all labels are distinct, and yet the sum of the added infinitesimals is not as great as the difference between two edges of G that have different labels. As a result, G with the new labels will have a unique minimal spanning tree, which will be one of the minimal spanning trees of G with the original weights.

Then, let $e_1, e_2, \ldots, e_m$ be all the edges of G, in order of their labels, smallest first. Note that this order is also the order in which Kruskal's algorithm considers the edges. Let K be the spanning tree for G with the adjusted labels produced by Kruskal's algorithm, and let T be the unique minimal spanning tree for G.

We shall prove that K and T are really the same. If they are different, then there must be at least one edge that is in one but not the other. Let e_i be the first such edge in the ordering of edges; that is, each of $e_1, \ldots, e_{i-1}$ is either in both K and T, or in neither of K and T. There are two cases, depending on whether e_i is in K or is in T. We shall show a contradiction in each case, and thus conclude that e_i does not exist; thus $K = T$, and K is the minimal spanning tree for G.

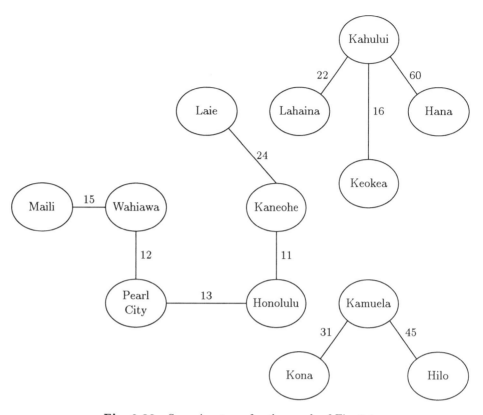

Fig. 9.23. Spanning trees for the graph of Fig. 9.4.

Greed Sometimes Pays

Greedy algorithm

Kruskal's algorithm is a good example of a *greedy algorithm,* in which we make a series of decisions, each doing what seems best at the time. The local decisions are which edge to add to the spanning tree being formed. In each case, we pick the edge with the least label that does not violate the definition of "spanning tree" by completing a cycle. Often, the overall effect of locally optimal decisions is not globally optimum. However, in the case of Kruskal's algorithm, it can be shown that the result is globally optimal; that is, a spanning tree of minimal weight results.

Case 1. Edge e_i is in T but not in K. If Kruskal's algorithm rejects e_i, then e_i must form a cycle with some path P of edges previously selected for K, as suggested in Fig. 9.24. Thus, the edges of P are all found among $e_1, \ldots, e_{i-1}$. However, T and K agree about these edges; that is, if the edges of P are in K, then they are also in T. But since T has e_i as well, P plus e_i form a cycle in T, contradicting our assumption that T was a spanning tree. Thus, it is not possible that e_i is in T but not in K.

Case 2. Edge e_i is in K but not in T. Let e_i connect the nodes u and v. Since T is connected, there must be some acyclic path in T between u and v; call it path Q. Since Q does not use edge e_i, Q plus e_i forms a simple cycle in the graph G.

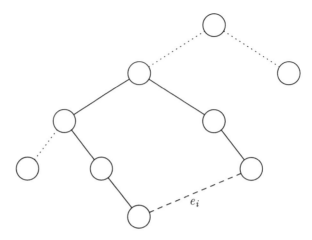

Fig. 9.24. Path P (solid lines) is in T and K; edge e_i is in T only.

There are two subcases, depending on whether or not e_i has a higher label than all the edges on path Q.

a) Edge e_i has the highest label. Then all the edges on Q are among $\{e_1, \ldots, e_{i-1}\}$. Remember that T and K agree on all edges before e_i, and so all the edges of Q are also edges of K. But e_i is also in K, which implies K has a cycle. We thus rule out the possibility that e_i has a higher label than any of the edges of path Q.

b) There is some edge f on path Q that has a higher label than e_i. Suppose f connects nodes w and x. Figure 9.25 shows the situation in tree T. If we remove edge f from T, and add edge e_i, we do not form a cycle, because path Q was broken by the removal of f. The resulting collection of edges has a lower weight than T, because f has a higher label than e_i. We claim the resulting edges still connect all the nodes. To see why, notice that w and x are still connected; there is a path that follows Q from w to u, then follows the edge e_i, then the path Q from v to x. Since $\{w, x\}$ was the only edge removed, if its endpoints are still connected, surely all nodes are connected. Thus, the new set of edges is a spanning tree, and its existence contradicts the assumption that T was minimal.

We have now shown that it is impossible for e_i to be in K but not in T. That rules out the second case. Since it is impossible that e_i is in one of T and K, but not the other, we conclude that K really is the minimal spanning tree T. That is, Kruskal's algorithm always finds a minimal spanning tree.

Running Time of Kruskal's Algorithm

Suppose we run Kruskal's algorithm on a graph of n nodes. As in the previous section, let m be the larger of the number of nodes and the number of edges, but remember that typically the number of edges is the larger. Let us suppose that the graph is represented by adjacency lists, so we can find all the edges in $O(m)$ time.

To begin, we must sort the edges by label, which takes $O(m \log m)$ time, if we use an efficient sorting algorithm such as merge sort. Next, we consider the edges, taking $O(m \log n)$ time to do all the merges and finds, as discussed in the

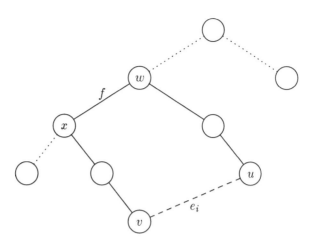

Fig. 9.25. Path Q (solid) is in T.
We can add edge e_i to T and remove the edge f.

previous section. It appears that the total time for Kruskal's algorithm is thus $O\big(m(\log n + \log m)\big)$.

However, notice that $m \leq n^2$, because there are only $n(n-1)/2$ pairs of nodes. Thus, $\log m \leq 2 \log n$, and $m(\log n + \log m) \leq 3m \log n$. Since constant factors can be neglected within a big-oh expression, we conclude that Kruskal's algorithm takes $O(m \log n)$ time.

EXERCISES

9.5.1: Draw the tree of Fig. 9.22 if Wahiawa is selected as the root.

9.5.2: Use Kruskal's algorithm to find minimal spanning trees for each of the components of the graph whose edges and labels are listed in Fig. 9.21 (see the exercises for Section 9.4).

9.5.3**: Prove that if G is a connected, undirected graph of n nodes, and T is a spanning tree for G, then T has $n - 1$ edges. *Hint*: We need to do an induction on n. The hard part is to show that T must have some node v with degree 1; that is, T has exactly one edge containing v. Consider what would happen if for every node u, there were at least two edges of T containing u. By following edges into and out of a sequence of nodes, we would eventually find a cycle. Since T is supposedly a spanning tree, it could not have a cycle, which gives us a contradiction.

9.5.4*: Once we have selected $n - 1$ edges, it is not necessary to consider any more edges for possible inclusion in the spanning tree. Describe a variation of Kruskal's algorithm that does not sort all the edges, but puts them in a priority queue, with the negative of the edge's label as its priority (i.e., shortest edge is selected first by *deleteMax*). Show that if a spanning tree can be found among the first $m/\log m$ edges, then this version of Kruskal's algorithm takes only $O(m)$ time.

9.5.5*: Suppose we find a minimal spanning tree T for a graph G. Let us then add to G the edge $\{u, v\}$ with weight w. Under what circumstances will T be a minimal spanning tree of the new graph?

Euler circuit

9.5.6**: An *Euler circuit* for an undirected graph G is a path that starts and ends at the same node and contains each edge of G exactly once.

a) Show that a connected, undirected graph has an Euler circuit if and only if each node is of even degree.

b) Let G be an undirected graph with m edges in which every node is of even degree. Give an $O(m)$ algorithm to construct an Euler circuit for G.

✦✦ 9.6 Depth-First Search

We shall now describe a graph-exploration method that is useful for directed graphs. In Section 5.4 we discussed the preorder and postorder traversals of trees, where we start at the root and recursively explore the children of each node we visit. We can apply almost the same idea to any directed graph.[6] From any node, we recursively explore its successors.

However, we must be careful if the graph has cycles. If there is a cycle, we can wind up calling the exploration function recursively around the cycle forever. For instance, consider the graph of Fig. 9.26. Starting at node a, we might decide to explore node b next. From b we might explore c first, and from c we could explore b first. That gets us into an infinite recursion, where we alternate exploring from b and c. In fact, it doesn't matter in what order we choose to explore successors of b and c. Either we shall get caught in some other cycle, or we eventually explore c from b and explore b from c, infinitely.

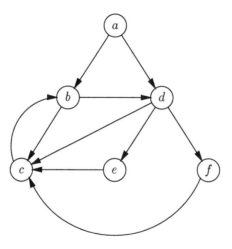

Fig. 9.26. An example directed graph.

There is a simple solution to our problem: We mark nodes as we visit them, and never revisit marked nodes. Then, any node we can reach from our starting node will be reached, but no previously visited node will be revisited. We shall see

---

[6] Notice that a tree can be thought of as a special case of a directed graph, if we regard the arcs of the tree as directed from parent to child. In fact, a tree is always an acyclic graph as well.

that the time taken by this exploration takes time proportional to the number of arcs explored.

The search algorithm is called *depth-first search* because we find ourselves going as far from the initial node (as "deep") as fast as we can. It can be implemented with a simple data structure. Again, let us assume that the type NODE is used to name nodes and that this type is int. We represent arcs by adjacency lists. Since we need a "mark" for each node, which can take on the values VISITED and UNVISITED, we shall create an array of structures to represent the graph. These structures will contain both the mark and the header for the adjacency list.

```
enum MARKTYPE {VISITED, UNVISITED};
typedef struct {
    enum MARKTYPE mark;
    LIST successors;
} GRAPH[MAX];
```

where LIST is an adjacency list, defined in the customary manner:

```
typedef struct CELL *LIST;
struct CELL {
    NODE nodeName;
    LIST next;
};
```

We begin by marking all the nodes UNVISITED. Recursive function dfs(u, G) of Fig. 9.27 works on a node u of some externally defined graph G of type GRAPH.

At line (1) we mark u VISITED, so we don't call dfs on it again. Line (2) initializes p to point to the first cell on the adjacency list for node u. The loop of lines (3) through (7) takes p down the adjacency list, considering each successor, v, of u, in turn.

```
        void dfs(NODE u, GRAPH G)
        {
            LIST p; /* runs down the adjacency list of u */
            NODE v; /* the node in the cell pointed to by p */

(1)         G[u].mark = VISITED;
(2)         p = G[u].successors;
(3)         while (p != NULL) {
(4)             v = p->nodeName;
(5)             if (G[v].mark == UNVISITED)
(6)                 dfs(v, G);
(7)             p = p->next;
            }
        }
```

Fig. 9.27. The recursive depth-first search function.

Line (4) sets v to be the "current" successor of u. At line (5) we test whether v has ever been visited before. If so, we skip the recursive call at line (6) and we move p to the next cell of the adjacency list at line (7). However, if v has never been visited, we start a depth-first search from node v, at line (6). Eventually, we finish the call to dfs(v, G). Then, we execute line (7) to move p down u's adjacency list and go around the loop.

✦ **Example 9.18.** Suppose G is the graph of Fig. 9.26, and, for specificity, assume the nodes on each adjacency list are ordered alphabetically. Initially, all nodes are marked UNVISITED. Let us call dfs(a).[7] Node a is marked VISITED at line (1), and at line (2) we initialize p to point to the first cell on a's adjacency list. At line (4) v is set to b, since b is the node in the first cell. Since b is currently unvisited, the test of line (5) succeeds, and at line (6) we call dfs(b).

Now, we start a new call to dfs, with $u = b$, while the old call with $u = a$ is dormant but still alive. We begin at line (1), marking b VISITED. Since c is the first node on b's adjacency list, c becomes the value of v at line (4). Node c is unvisited, so that we succeed at line (5) and at line (6) we call dfs(c).

A third call to dfs is now alive, and to begin dfs(c), we mark c VISITED and set v to b at line (4), since b is the first, and only, node on c's adjacency list. However, b was already marked VISITED at line (1) of the call to dfs(b), so that we skip line (6) and move p down c's adjacency list at line (7). Since c has no more successors, p becomes NULL, so that the test of line (3) fails, and dfs(c) is finished.

We now return to the call dfs(b). Pointer p is advanced at line (7), and it now points to the second cell of b's adjacency list, which holds node d. We set v to d at line (4), and since d is unvisited, we call dfs(d) at line (6).

For the execution of dfs(d), we mark d VISITED. Then v is first set to c. But c is visited, and so next time around the loop, $v = e$. That leads to the call dfs(e). Node e has only c as a successor, and so after marking e VISITED, dfs(e) returns to dfs(d). We next set $v = f$ at line (4) of dfs(d), and call dfs(f). After marking f VISITED, we find that f also has only c as a successor, and c is visited.

We are now finished with dfs(f). Since f is the last successor of d, we are also finished with dfs(d), and since d is the last successor of b, we are done with dfs(b) as well. That takes us back to dfs(a). Node a has another successor, d, but that node is visited, and so we are done with dfs(a) as well.

Figure 9.28 summarizes the action of dfs on the graph of Fig. 9.26. We show the stack of calls to dfs, with the currently active call at the right. We also indicate the action taken at each step, and we show the value of the local variable v associated with each currently live call, or show that p = NULL, indicating that there is no active value for v. ✦

Constructing a Depth-First Search Tree

Because we mark nodes to avoid visiting them twice, the graph behaves like a tree as we explore it. In fact, we can draw a tree whose parent-child edges are some of the arcs of the graph G being searched. If we are in dfs(u), and a call to dfs(v) results, then we make v a child of u in the tree. The children of u appear, from left to right, in the order in which *dfs* was called on these children. The node upon which the initial call to *dfs* was made is the root. No node can have *dfs* called on it twice, since it is marked VISITED at the first call. Thus, the structure defined is truly a tree. We call the tree a *depth-first search tree* for the given graph.

---

[7] In what follows, we shall omit the second argument of dfs, which is always the graph G.

| dfs(a) | | | | Call dfs(b) |
| $v = b$ | | | | |

| dfs(a) | dfs(b) | | | Call dfs(c) |
| $v = b$ | $v = c$ | | | |

| dfs(a) | dfs(b) | dfs(c) | | Skip; b already visited |
| $v = b$ | $v = c$ | $v = b$ | | |

| dfs(a) | dfs(b) | dfs(c) | | Return |
| $v = b$ | $v = c$ | $p =$NULL | | |

| dfs(a) | dfs(b) | | | Call dfs(d) |
| $v = b$ | $v = d$ | | | |

| dfs(a) | dfs(b) | dfs(d) | | Skip; c already visited |
| $v = b$ | $v = d$ | $v = c$ | | |

| dfs(a) | dfs(b) | dfs(d) | | Call dfs(e) |
| $v = b$ | $v = d$ | $v = e$ | | |

| dfs(a) | dfs(b) | dfs(d) | dfs(e) | Skip; c already visited |
| $v = b$ | $v = d$ | $v = e$ | $v = c$ | |

| dfs(a) | dfs(b) | dfs(d) | dfs(e) | Return |
| $v = b$ | $v = d$ | $v = e$ | $p =$NULL | |

| dfs(a) | dfs(b) | dfs(d) | | Call dfs(f) |
| $v = b$ | $v = d$ | $v = f$ | | |

| dfs(a) | dfs(b) | dfs(d) | dfs(f) | Skip; c already visited |
| $v = b$ | $v = d$ | $v = f$ | $v = c$ | |

| dfs(a) | dfs(b) | dfs(d) | dfs(f) | Return |
| $v = b$ | $v = d$ | $v = f$ | $p =$NULL | |

| dfs(a) | dfs(b) | dfs(d) | | Return |
| $v = b$ | $v = d$ | $p =$NULL | | |

| dfs(a) | dfs(b) | | | Return |
| $v = b$ | $p =$NULL | | | |

| dfs(a) | | | | Skip; d already visited |
| $v = d$ | | | | |

| dfs(a) | | | | Return |
| $p =$NULL | | | | |

Fig. 9.28. Trace of calls made during depth-first search.

✦   **Example 9.19.** The tree for the exploration of the graph in Fig. 9.26 that was summarized in Fig. 9.28 is seen in Fig. 9.29. We show the *tree arcs,* representing the parent-child relationship, as solid lines. Other arcs of the graph are shown as dotted arrows. For the moment, we should ignore the numbers labeling the nodes. ✦

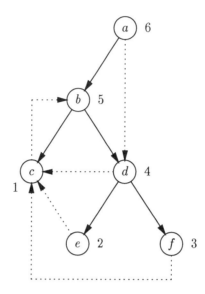

Fig. 9.29. One possible depth-first search tree for the graph of Fig. 9.26.

Classification of Arcs for a Depth-First Search Tree

When we build a depth-first search tree for a graph G, we can classify the arcs of G into four groups. It should be understood that this classification is with respect to a particular depth-first search tree, or equivalently, with respect to the particular order for the nodes in each adjacency list that led to a particular exploration of G. The four kinds of arcs are

1. *Tree arcs,* which are the arcs $u \to v$ such that $\mathtt{dfs(v)}$ is called by $\mathtt{dfs(u)}$.

2. *Forward arcs,* which are arcs $u \to v$ such that v is a proper descendant of u, but not a child of u. For instance, in Fig. 9.29, the arc $a \to d$ is the only forward arc. No tree arc is a forward arc.

3. *Backward arcs,* which are arcs $u \to v$ such that v is an ancestor of u in the tree ($u = v$ is permitted). Arc $c \to b$ is the only example of a backward arc in Fig. 9.29. Any loop, an arc from a node to itself, is classified as backward.

4. *Cross arcs,* which are arcs $u \to v$ such that v is neither an ancestor nor descendant of u. There are three cross arcs in Fig. 9.29: $d \to c$, $e \to c$, and $f \to c$.

Cross arcs go from right to left

In Fig. 9.29, each of the cross arcs go from right to left. It is no coincidence that they do so. Suppose we had in some depth-first search tree a cross arc $u \to v$ such that u was to the left of v. Consider what happens during the call to $\mathtt{dfs(u)}$. By the time we finish $\mathtt{dfs(u)}$, we shall have considered the arc from u to v. If v has not yet been placed in the tree, then it becomes a child of u in the tree. Since

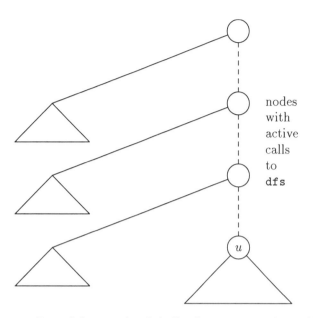

Fig. 9.30. Part of the tree that is built when arc $u \to v$ is considered.

that evidently did not happen (for then v would not be to the right of u), it must be that v is already in the tree when the arc $u \to v$ is considered.

However, Fig. 9.30 shows the parts of the tree that exist while `dfs(u)` is active. Since children are added in left-to-right order, no proper ancestor of node u as yet has a child to the right of u. Thus, v can only be an ancestor of u, a descendant of u, or somewhere to the left of u. Thus, if $u \to v$ is a cross edge, v must be to the left of u, not the right of u as we initially supposed.

The Depth-First Search Forest

We were quite fortunate in Example 9.19 that when we started at node a, we were able to reach all the nodes of the graph of Fig. 9.26. Had we started at any other node, we would not have reached a, and a would not appear in the tree. Thus, the general method of exploring a graph is to construct a sequence of trees. We start at some node u and call `dfs(u)`. If there are nodes not yet visited, we pick one, say v, and call `dfs(v)`. We repeat this process as long as there are nodes not yet assigned to any tree.

When all nodes have been assigned a tree, we list the trees, from left to right, in the order of their construction. This list of trees is called the *depth-first search forest*. In terms of the data types **NODE** and **GRAPH** defined earlier, we can explore an entire externally defined graph G, starting the search on as many roots as necessary by the function of Fig. 9.31. There, we assume that the type **NODE** is `int`, and MAX is the number of nodes in G.

In lines (1) and (2) we initialize all nodes to be **UNVISITED**. Then, in the loop of lines (3) to (5), we consider each node u in turn. When we consider u, if that node has not yet been added to any tree, it will still be marked unvisited when we make the test of line (4). In that case, we call `dfs(u, G)` at line (5) and explore the depth-first search tree with root u. In particular, the first node always becomes the root of a tree. However, if u has already been added to a tree when we perform

```
        void dfsForest(GRAPH G);
        {
            NODE u;

(1)         for (u = 0; u < MAX; u++)
(2)             G[u].mark = UNVISITED;
(3)         for (u = 0; u < MAX; u++)
(4)             if (G[u].mark == UNVISITED)
(5)                 dfs(u, G);
        }
```

Fig. 9.31. Exploring a graph by exploring as many trees as necessary.

the test of line (4), then u will be marked VISITED, and so we do not create a tree with root u.

✦ **Example 9.20.** Suppose we apply the above algorithm to the graph of Fig. 9.26, but let d be the node whose name is 0; that is, d is the first root of a tree for the depth-first spanning forest. We call dfs(d), which constructs the first tree of Fig. 9.32. Now, all nodes but a are visited. As u becomes each of the various nodes in the loop of lines (3) to (5) of Fig. 9.31, the test of line (4) fails except when $u = a$. Then, we create the one-node second tree of Fig. 9.32. Note that both successors of a are marked VISITED when we call dfs(a), and so we do not make any recursive calls from dfs(a). ✦

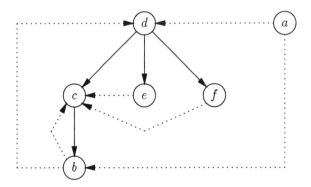

Fig. 9.32. A depth-first search forest.

When we present the nodes of a graph as a depth-first search forest, the notions of forward, backward, and tree arcs apply as before. However, the notion of a cross arc must be extended to include arcs that run from one tree to a tree to its left. Examples of such cross arcs are $a \rightarrow b$ and $a \rightarrow d$ in Fig. 9.32.

The rule that cross arcs always go from right to left continues to hold. The reason is also the same. If there were a cross arc $u \rightarrow v$ that went from one tree to a tree to the right, then consider what happens when we call dfs(u). Since v

The Perfection of Depth-First Search

Regardless of the relationship between the numbers of nodes and arcs, the running time of the depth-first exploration of a graph takes time proportional to the "size" of the graph, that is, the sum of the numbers of nodes and arcs. Thus, depth-first search is, to within a constant factor, as fast as any algorithm that "looks at" the graph.

was not added to the tree being formed at the moment, it must already have been in some tree. But the trees to the right of u have not yet been created, and so v cannot be part of one of them.

Running Time of the Depth-First Search Algorithm

Let G be a graph with n nodes and let m be the larger of the number of nodes and the number of arcs. Then dfsForest of Fig. 9.31 takes $O(m)$ time. The proof of this fact requires a trick. When calculating the time taken by a call dfs(u), we shall not count the time taken by any recursive calls to dfs at line (6) in Fig. 9.27, as Section 3.9 suggested we should. Rather, observe that we call dfs(u) once for each value of u. Thus, if we sum the cost of each call, exclusive of its recursive calls, we get the total time spent in all the calls as a group.

Notice that the while-loop of lines (3) to (7) in Fig. 9.27 can take a variable amount of time, even excluding the time spent in recursive calls to dfs, because the number of successors of node u could be any number from 0 to n. Suppose we let m_u be the out-degree of node u, that is, the number of successors of u. Then the number of times around the while-loop during the execution of dfs(u) is surely m_u. We do not count the execution of dfs(v, G) at line (6) when assessing the running time of dfs(u), and the body of the loop, exclusive of this call, takes $O(1)$ time. Thus, the total time spent in the loop of lines (3) to (7), exclusive of time spent in recursive calls is $O(1 + m_u)$; the additional 1 is needed because m_u might be 0, in which case we still take $O(1)$ time for the test of (3). Since lines (1) and (2) of dfs take $O(1)$ time, we conclude that, neglecting recursive calls, dfs(u) takes time $O(1 + m_u)$ to complete.

Now we observe that during the running of dfsForest, we call dfs(u) exactly once for each value of u. Thus, the total time spent in all these calls is big-oh of the sum of the times spent in each, that is, $O\left(\sum_u (1 + m_u)\right)$. But $\sum_u m_u$ is just the number of arcs in the graph, that is, at most m,[8] since each arc emanates from some one node. The number of nodes is n, so that $\sum_u 1$ is just n. As $n \leq m$, the time taken by all the calls to dfs is thus $O(m)$.

Finally, we must consider the time taken by dfsForest. This program, in Fig. 9.31, consists of two loops, each iterated n times. The bodies of the loops are easily seen to take $O(1)$ time, exclusive of the calls to dfs, and so the cost of the loops is $O(n)$. This time is dominated by the $O(m)$ time of the calls to dfs. Since the time for the dfs calls is already accounted for, we conclude that dfsForest, together with all its calls to dfs, takes $O(m)$ time.

---

[8] In fact, the sum of the m_u's will be exactly m, except in the case that the number of nodes exceeds the number of arcs; recall that m is the larger of the numbers of nodes and arcs.

Postorder Traversals of Directed Graphs

Once we have a depth-first search tree, we could number its nodes in postorder. However, there is an easy way to do the numbering during the search itself. We simply attach the number to a node u as the last thing we do before dfs(u) completes. Then, a node is numbered right after all its children are numbered, just as in a postorder numbering.

```
        int k; /* counts visited nodes */

        void dfs(NODE u, GRAPH G)
        {
            LIST p; /* points to cells of adjacency list of u */
            NODE v; /* the node in the cell pointed to by p */
(1)         G[u].mark = VISITED;
(2)         p = G[u].successors;
(3)         while (p != NULL) {
(4)             v = p->nodeName;
(5)             if (G[v].mark == UNVISITED)
(6)                 dfs(v, G);
(7)             p = p->next;
            }
(8)         ++k;
(9)         G[u].postorder = k;
        }

        void dfsForest(GRAPH G)
        {
            NODE u;

(10)        k = 0;
(11)        for (u = 0; u < MAX; u++)
(12)            G[u].mark = UNVISITED;
(13)        for (u = 0; u < MAX; u++)
(14)            if (G[u].mark == UNVISITED)
(15)                dfs(u, G);
        }
```

Fig. 9.33. Procedure to number the nodes of a directed graph in postorder.

✦ **Example 9.21.** The tree of Fig. 9.29, which we constructed by depth-first search of the graph in Fig. 9.26, has the postorder numbers labeling the nodes. If we examine the trace of Fig. 9.28, we see that the first call to return is dfs(c), and node c is given the number 1. Then, we visit d, then e, and return from the call to e. Therefore, e's number is 2. Similarly, we visit and return from f, which is numbered 3. At that point, we have completed the call on d, which gets number 4. That completes the call to dfs(b), and the number of b is 5. Finally, the original call to a returns, giving a the number 6. Notice that this order is exactly the one we would get if we simply walked the tree in postorder. ✦

We can assign the postorder numbers to the nodes with a few simple modifications to the depth-first search algorithm we have written so far; these changes are summarized in Fig. 9.33.

1.   In the **GRAPH** type, we need an additional field for each node, called `postorder`. For the graph G, we place the postorder number of node u in `G[u].postorder`. This assignment is accomplished at line (9) of Fig. 9.33.

2.   We use a global variable **k** to count nodes in postorder. This variable is defined externally to **dfs** and **dfsForest**. As seen in Fig. 9.33, we initialize k to 0 in line (10) of **dfsForest**, and just before assigning a postorder number, we increment k by 1 at line (8) in **dfs**.

Notice that as a result, when there is more than one tree in the depth-first search forest, the first tree gets the lowest numbers, the next tree gets the next numbers in order, and so on. For example, in Fig. 9.32, a would get the postorder number 6.

Special Properties of Postorder Numbers

The impossibility of cross arcs that go left to right tells us something interesting and useful about the postorder numbers and the four types of arcs in a depth-first presentation of a graph. In Fig. 9.34(a) we see three nodes, u, v, and w, in a depth-first presentation of a graph. Nodes v and w are descendants of u, and w is to the right of v. Figure 9.34(b) shows the duration of activity for the calls to **dfs** for each of these nodes.

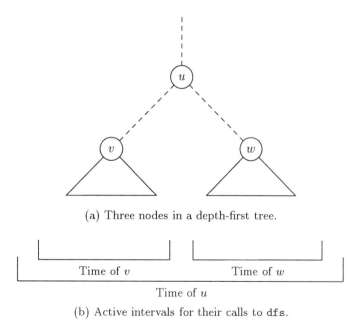

(a) Three nodes in a depth-first tree.

(b) Active intervals for their calls to **dfs**.

Fig. 9.34. Relationship between position in tree and duration of calls.

We can make several observations. First, the call to dfs on a descendant like v is active for only a subinterval of the time during which the call on an ancestor, like u, is active. In particular, the call to dfs(v) terminates before the call to dfs(u) does. Thus, the postorder number of v must be less than the postorder number of u whenever v is a proper descendant of u.

Second, if w is to the right of v, then the call to dfs(w) cannot begin until after the call to dfs(v) terminates. Thus, whenever v is to the left of w, the postorder number of v is less than that of w. Although not shown in Fig. 9.34, the same is true even if v and w are in different trees of the depth-first search forest, with v's tree to the left of w's tree.

We can now consider the relationship between the postorder numbers of u and v for each arc $u \to v$.

1. If $u \to v$ is a tree arc or forward arc, then v is a descendant of u, and so v precedes u in postorder.

2. If $u \to v$ is a cross arc, then we know v is to the left of u, and again v precedes u in postorder.

3. If $u \to v$ is a backward arc and $v \neq u$, then v is a proper ancestor of u, and so v follows u in postorder. However, $v = u$ is possible for a backward arc, since a loop is a backward arc. Thus, in general, for backward arc $u \to v$, we know that the postorder number of v is at least as high as the postorder number of u.

In summary, we see that in postorder, the head of an arc precedes the tail, unless the arc is a backward arc; in which case the tail precedes or equals the head. Thus, we can identify the backward arcs simply by finding those arcs whose tails are equal to or less than their heads in postorder. We shall see a number of applications of this idea in the next section.

EXERCISES

9.6.1: For the tree of Fig. 9.5 (see the exercises for Section 9.2), give two depth-first search trees starting with node a. Give a depth-first search tree starting with node d.

9.6.2*: No matter which node we start with in Fig. 9.5, we wind up with only one tree in the depth-first search forest. Explain briefly why that must be the case for this particular graph.

9.6.3: For each of your trees of Exercise 9.6.1, indicate which of the arcs are tree, forward, backward, and cross arcs.

9.6.4: For each of your trees of Exercise 9.6.1, give the postorder numbers for the nodes.

9.6.5*: Consider the graph with three nodes, a, b, and c, and the two arcs $a \to b$ and $b \to c$. Give all the possible depth-first search forests for this graph, considering all possible starting nodes for each tree. What is the postorder numbering of the nodes for each forest? Are the postorder numbers always the same for this graph?

9.6.6*: Consider the generalization of the graph of Exercise 9.6.5 to a graph with n nodes, $a_1, a_2, \ldots, a_n$, and arcs $a_1 \rightarrow a_2$, $a_2 \rightarrow a_3$, $\ldots$, $a_{n-1} \rightarrow a_n$. Prove by complete induction on n that this graph has 2^{n-1} different depth-first search forests. *Hint*: It helps to remember that $1 + 1 + 2 + 4 + 8 + \cdots + 2^i = 2^{i+1}$, for $i \geq 0$.

9.6.7*: Suppose we start with a graph G and add a new node x that is a predecessor of all other nodes in G. If we run dfsForest of Fig. 9.31 on the new graph, starting at node x, then a single tree results. If we then delete x from this tree, several trees may result. How do these trees relate to the depth-first search forest of the original graph G?

9.6.8**: Suppose we have a directed graph G, from whose representation we have just constructed a depth-first spanning forest F by the algorithm of Fig. 9.31. Let us now add the arc $u \rightarrow v$ to G to form a new graph H, whose representation is exactly that of G, except that node v now appears somewhere on the adjacency list for node u. If we now run Fig. 9.31 on this representation of H, under what circumstances will the same depth-first forest F be constructed? That is, when will the tree arcs for H are exactly the same as the tree arcs for G?

✦✦ 9.7   Some Uses of Depth-First Search

In this section, we see how depth-first search can be used to solve some problems quickly. As previously, we shall here use n to represent the number of nodes of a graph, and we shall use m for the larger of the number of nodes and the number of arcs; in particular, we assume that $n \leq m$ is always true. Each of the algorithms presented takes $O(m)$ time, on a graph represented by adjacency lists. The first algorithm determines whether a directed graph is acyclic. Then for those graphs that are acyclic, we see how to find a topological sort of the nodes (topological sorting was discussed in Section 7.10; we shall review the definitions at the appropriate time). We also show how to compute the transitive closure of a graph (see Section 7.10 again), and how to find connected components of an undirected graph faster than the algorithm given in Section 9.4.

Finding Cycles in a Directed Graph

During a depth-first search of a directed graph G, we can assign a postorder number to all the nodes in $O(m)$ time. Recall from the last section that we discovered the only arcs whose tails are equal to or less than their heads in postorder are the backward arcs. Whenever there is a backward arc, $u \rightarrow v$, in which the postorder number of v is at least as large as the postorder number of u, there must be a cycle in the graph, as suggested by Fig. 9.35. The cycle consists of the arc from u to v, and the path in the tree from v to its descendant u.

The converse is also true; that is, if there is a cycle, then there must be a backward arc. To see why, suppose there is a cycle, say $v_1 \rightarrow v_2 \rightarrow \cdots \rightarrow v_k \rightarrow v_1$, and let the postorder number of node v_i be p_i, for $i = 1, 2, \ldots, k$. If $k = 1$, that is, the cycle is a single arc, then surely $v_1 \rightarrow v_1$ is a backward arc in any depth-first presentation of G.

If $k > 1$, suppose that none of the arcs $v_1 \rightarrow v_2$, $v_2 \rightarrow v_3$, and so on, up to $v_{k-1} \rightarrow v_k$ are backward. Then each head precedes each tail in postorder, and so the postorder numbers $p_1, p_2, \ldots, p_k$ form a decreasing sequence. In particular,

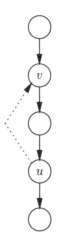

Fig. 9.35. Every backward arc forms a cycle with tree arcs.

$p_k < p_1$. Then consider the arc $v_k \rightarrow v_1$ that completes the cycle. The postorder number of its tail, which is p_k, is less than the postorder number of its head, p_1, and so this arc is a backward arc. That proves there must be some backward arc in any cycle.

As a result, after computing the postorder numbers of all nodes, we simply examine all the arcs, to see if any has a tail less than or equal to its head, in postorder. If so, we have found a backward arc, and the graph is cyclic. If there is no such arc, the graph is acyclic. Figure 9.36 shows a function that tests whether an externally defined graph G is acyclic, using the data structure for graphs described in the previous section. It also makes use of the function **dfsForest** defined in Fig. 9.33 to compute the postorder numbers of the nodes of G.

```
        BOOLEAN testAcyclic(GRAPH G)
        {
            NODE u, v; /* u runs through all the nodes */
            LIST p; /* p points to each cell on the adjacency list
                    for u; v is a node on the adjacency list */

(1)         dfsForest(G);
(2)         for (u = 0; u < MAX; u++) {
(3)             p = G[u].successors;
(4)             while (p != NULL) {
(5)                 v = p->nodeName;
(6)                 if (G[u].postorder <= G[v].postorder)
(7)                     return FALSE;
(8)                 p = p->next;
                }
            }
(9)         return TRUE;
        }
```

Fig. 9.36. Function to determine whether a graph G is acyclic.

After calling `dfsForest` to compute postorder numbers at line (1), we examine each node u in the loop of lines (2) through (8). Pointer p goes down the adjacency list for u, and at line (5), v in turn becomes each successor of u. If at line (6) we find that u equals or precedes v in postorder, then we have found a backward arc $u \rightarrow v$, and we return FALSE at line (7). If we find no such backward arc, we return TRUE at line (9).

Running Time of the Acyclicity Test

As before, let n be the number of nodes of graph G and let m be the larger of the number of nodes and the number of arcs. We already know that the call to `dfsForest` at line (1) of Fig. 9.36 takes $O(m)$ time. Lines (5) to (8), the body of the while-loop, evidently take $O(1)$ time. To get a good bound on the time for the while-loop itself, we must use the trick that was used in the previous section to bound the time of depth-first search. Let m_u be the out-degree of node u. Then we go around the loop of lines (4) to (8) m_u times. Thus, the time spent in lines (4) to (8) is $O(1 + m_u)$.

Line (3) only takes $O(1)$ time, and so the time spent in the for-loop of lines (2) to (8) is $O(\sum_u(1 + m_u))$. As observed in the previous section, the sum of 1 is $O(n)$, and the sum of m_u is m. Since $n \leq m$, the time for the loop of lines (2) to (8) is $O(m)$. That is the same as the time for line (1), and line (9) takes $O(1)$ time. Thus, the entire acyclicity test takes $O(m)$ time. As for depth-first search itself, the time to detect cycles is, to within a constant factor, just the time it takes to look at the entire graph.

Topological Sorting

Suppose we know that a directed graph G is acyclic. As for any graph, we may find a depth-first search forest for G and thereby determine a postorder for the nodes of G. Suppose $(v_1, v_2, \ldots, v_n)$ is a list of the nodes of G in the reverse of postorder; that is, v_1 is the node numbered n in postorder, v_2 is numbered $n-1$, and in general, v_i is the node numbered $n - i + 1$ in postorder.

The order of the nodes on this list has the property that all arcs of G go forward in the order. To see why, suppose $v_i \rightarrow v_j$ is an arc of G. Since G is acyclic, there are no backward arcs. Thus, for every arc, the head precedes the tail. That is, v_j precedes v_i in postorder. But the list is the reverse of postorder, and so v_i precedes v_j on the list. That is, every tail precedes the corresponding head in the list order.

Topological
order

An order for the nodes of a graph G with the property that for every arc of G the tail precedes the head is called a *topological order,* and the process of finding such an order for the nodes is called *topological sorting.* Only acyclic graphs have a topological order, and as we have just seen, we can produce a topological order for an acyclic graph $O(m)$ time, where m is the larger of the number of nodes and arcs, by performing a depth-first search. As we are about to give a node its postorder number, that is, as we complete the call to `dfs` on that node, we push the node onto a stack. When we are done, the stack is a list in which the nodes appear in postorder, with the highest at the top (front). That is the reverse postorder we desire. Since the depth-first search takes $O(m)$ time, and pushing the nodes onto a stack takes only $O(n)$ time, the whole process takes $O(m)$ time.

Applications of Topological Order and Cycle Finding

There are a number of situations in which the algorithms discussed in this section will prove useful. Topological ordering comes in handy when there are constraints on the order in which we do certain tasks, which we represent by nodes. If we draw an arc from u to v whenever we must do task u before v, then a topological order is an order in which we can perform all the tasks. An example in Section 7.10 about putting on shoes and socks illustrated this type of problem.

A similar example is the calling graph of a nonrecursive collection of functions, in which we wish to analyze each function after we have analyzed the functions it calls. As the arcs go from caller to called function, the reverse of a topological order, that is, the postorder itself, is an order in which we can analyze the function, making sure that we only work on a function after we have worked on all the functions it calls.

In other situations, it is sufficient to run the cycle test. For example, a cycle in the graph of task priorities tells us there is no order in which all the tasks can be done, and a cycle in a calling graph tells us there is recursion.

◆ **Example 9.22.** In Fig. 9.37(a) is an acyclic graph, and in Fig. 9.37(b) is the depth-first search forest we get by considering the nodes in alphabetic order. We also show in Fig. 9.37(b) the postorder numbers that we get from this depth-first search. If we list the nodes highest postorder number first, we get the topological order (d, e, c, f, b, a). The reader should check that each of the eight arcs in Fig. 9.37(a) has a tail that precedes its head according to this list. There are, incidentally, three other topological orders for this graph, such as (d, c, e, b, f, a). ◆

The Reachability Problem

A natural question to ask about a directed graph is, given a node u, which nodes can we reach from u by following arcs? We call this set of nodes the *reachable set* for node u. In fact, if we ask this *reachability* question for each node u, then we know for which pairs of nodes (u, v) there is a path from u to v.

Reachable set

The algorithm for solving reachability is simple. If we are interested in node u, we mark all nodes UNVISITED and call dfs(u). We then examine all the nodes again. Those marked VISITED are reachable from u, and the others are not. If we then wish to find the nodes reachable from another node v, we set all the nodes to UNVISITED again and call dfs(v). This process may be repeated for as many nodes as we like.

◆ **Example 9.23.** Consider the graph of Fig. 9.37(a). If we start our depth-first search from node a, we can go nowhere, since there are no arcs out of a. Thus, dfs(a) terminates immediately. Since only a is visited, we conclude that a is the only node reachable from a.

If we start with b, we can reach a, but that is all; the reachable set for b is $\{a, b\}$. Similarly, from c we reach $\{a, b, c, f\}$, from d we reach all the nodes, from e we reach $\{a, b, e, f\}$, and from f we can reach only $\{a, f\}$.

For another example, consider the graph of Fig. 9.26. From a we can reach all the nodes. From any node but a, we can reach all the nodes except a. ◆

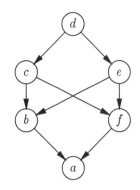

(a) A directed acyclic graph.

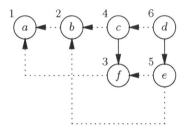

(b) A depth-first search forest.

Fig. 9.37. Topologically sorting an acyclic graph.

Running Time of the Reachability Test

Let us assume we have a directed graph G with n nodes and m arcs. We shall also assume G is represented by the data type **GRAPH** of the previous section. First, suppose we want to find the reachable set for a node u. Initializing the nodes to be **UNVISITED** takes $O(n)$ time. The call to **dfs(u, G)** takes $O(m)$ time, and examining the nodes again to see which are visited takes $O(n)$ time. While we examine the nodes, we could also create a list of those nodes that are reachable from u, still taking only $O(n)$ time. Thus, finding the reachable set for one node takes $O(m)$ time.

Now suppose we want the reachable sets for all n nodes. We may repeat the algorithm n times, once for each node. Thus, the total time is $O(nm)$.

Finding Connected Components by Depth-First Search

In Section 9.4, we gave an algorithm for finding the connected components of an undirected graph with n nodes, and with m equal to the larger of the number of nodes and edges, in $O(m \log n)$ time. The tree structure we used to merge components is of interest in its own right; for example, we used it to help implement Kruskal's minimal spanning tree algorithm. However, we can find connected components more efficiently if we use depth-first search. As we shall see, $O(m)$ time suffices.

The idea is to treat the undirected graph as if it were a directed graph with each edge replaced by arcs in both directions. If we represent the graph by adjacency lists, then we do not even have to make any change to the representation. Now

Transitive Closure and Reflexive-Transitive Closure

Let R be a binary relation on a set S. The reachability problem can be viewed as computing the *reflexive-transitive closure* of R, which is usually denoted R^*. The relation R^* is defined to be the set of pairs (u, v) such that there is a path of length zero or more from node u to node v in the graph represented by R.

Another relation that is very similar is R^+, the *transitive closure* of R, which is defined to be the set of pairs (u, v) such that there is a path of length one or more from u to v in the graph represented by R. The distinction between R^* and R^+ is that (u, u) is always in R^* for every u in S, whereas (u, u) is in R^+ if and only if there is a cycle of length one or more from u to u. To compute R^+ from R^*, we just have to check whether or not each node u has some entering arc from one of its reachable nodes, including itself; if it does not, we remove u from its own reachable set.

---

construct the depth-first search forest for the directed graph. Each tree in the forest is one connected component of the undirected graph.

To see why, first note that the presence of an arc $u \rightarrow v$ in the directed graph indicates that there is an edge $\{u, v\}$. Thus, all the nodes of a tree are connected.

Now we must show the converse, that if two nodes are connected, then they are in the same tree. Suppose there were a path in the undirected graph between two nodes u and v that are in different trees. Say the tree of u was constructed first. Then there is a path in the directed graph from u to v, which tells us that v, and all the nodes on this path, should have been added to the tree with u. Thus, nodes are connected in the undirected graph if and only if they are in the same tree; that is, the trees are the connected components.

♦ **Example 9.24.** Consider the undirected graph of Fig. 9.4 again. One possible depth-first search forest we might construct for this graph is shown in Fig. 9.38. Notice how the three depth-first search trees correspond to the three connected components. ♦

EXERCISES

9.7.1: Find all the topological orders for the graph of Fig. 9.37.

9.7.2*: Suppose R is a partial order on domain D. We can represent R by its graph, where the nodes are the elements of D and there is an arc $u \rightarrow v$ whenever uRv and $u \neq v$. Let $(v_1, v_2, \ldots, v_n)$ be a topological ordering of the graph of R. Let T be the relation defined by $v_i T v_j$ whenever $i \leq j$. Show that

a) T is a total order, and

b)   The pairs in R are a subset of the pairs in T; that is, T is a total order containing the partial order R.

9.7.3: Apply depth-first search to the graph of Fig. 9.21 (after converting it to a symmetric directed graph), to find the connected components.

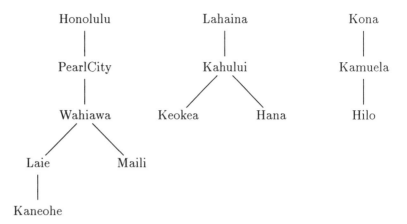

Fig. 9.38. The depth-first search forest divides an undirected graph
into connected components.

9.7.4: Consider the graph with arcs $a \to c$, $b \to a$, $b \to c$, $d \to a$, and $e \to c$.

a)   Test the graph for cycles.
b)   Find all the topological orders for the graph.
c)   Find the reachable set of each node.

9.7.5*: In the next section we shall consider the general problem of finding shortest
paths from a source node s. That is, we want for each node u the length of the
shortest path from s to u if one exists. When we have a directed, acyclic graph, the
problem is easier. Give an algorithm that will compute the length of the shortest
path from node s to each node u (infinity if no such path exists) in a directed,
acyclic graph G. Your algorithm should take $O(m)$ time, where m is the larger of
the number of nodes and arcs of G. Prove that your algorithm has this running
time. *Hint*: Start with a topological sort of G, and visit each node in turn. On
visiting a node u, calculate the shortest distance from s to u in terms of the already
calculated shortest distances to the predecessors of u.

9.7.6*: Give algorithms to compute the following for a directed, acyclic graph G.
Your algorithms should run in time $O(m)$, where m is the larger of the number of
nodes and arcs of G, and you should prove that this running time is all that your
algorithm requires. *Hint*: Adapt the idea of Exercise 9.7.5.

a)   For each node u, find the length of the longest path from u to anywhere.

b)   For each node u, find the length of the longest path to u from anywhere.

c)   For a given source node s and for all nodes u of G, find the length of the *longest*
path from s to u.

d)   For a given source node s and for all nodes u of G, find the length of the longest
path from u to s.

e)   For each node u, find the length of the longest path through u.

✢✦ 9.8 Dijkstra's Algorithm for Finding Shortest Paths

Suppose we have a graph, which could be either directed or undirected, with labels on the arcs (or edges) to represent the "length" of that arc. An example is Fig. 9.4, which showed the distance along certain roads of the Hawaiian Islands. It is quite common to want to know the minimum distance between two nodes; for example, maps often include tables of driving distance as a guide to how far one can travel in a day, or to help determine which of two routes (that go through different intermediate cities) is shorter. A similar kind of problem would associate with each arc the time it takes to travel along that arc, or perhaps the cost of traveling that arc. Then the minimum "distance" between two nodes would correspond to the traveling time or the fare, respectively.

Minimum distance

In general, the *distance* along a path is the sum of the labels of that path. The *minimum distance from node u to node v* is the minimum of the distance of any path from u to v.

✦ **Example 9.25.** Consider the map of Oahu in Fig. 9.10. Suppose we want to find the minimum distance from Maili to Kaneohe. There are several paths we could choose. One useful observation is that, as long as the labels of the arcs are nonnegative, the minimum-distance path need never have a cycle. For we could skip that cycle and find a path between the same two nodes, but with a distance no greater than that of the path with the cycle. Thus, we need only consider

1.   The path through Pearl City and Honolulu.

2.   The path through Wahiawa, Pearl City, and Honolulu.

3.   The path through Wahiawa and Laie.

4.   The path through Pearl City, Wahiawa, and Laie.

The distances of these paths are 44, 51, 67, and 84, respectively. Thus, the minimum distance from Maili to Kaneohe is 44. ✦

Source node

If we wish to find the minimum distance from one given node, called the *source* node, to all the nodes of the graph, one of the most efficient techniques to use is a method called *Dijkstra's algorithm*, the subject of this section. It turns out that if all we want is the distance from one node u to another node v, the best way is to run Dijkstra's algorithm with u as the source node and stop when we deduce the distance to v. If we want to find the minimum distance between every pair of nodes, there is an algorithm that we shall cover in the next section, called Floyd's algorithm, that sometimes is preferable to running Dijkstra's algorithm with every node as a source.

The essence of Dijkstra's algorithm is that we discover the minimum distance from the source to other nodes in the order of those minimum distances, that is, closest nodes first. As Dijkstra's algorithm proceeds, we have a situation like that

Settled node

suggested in Fig. 9.39. In the graph G there are certain nodes that are *settled*, that is, their minimum distance is known; this set always includes s, the source node.

Special path

For the unsettled nodes v, we record the length of the shortest *special path*, which is a path that starts at the source node, travels only through settled nodes, then at the last step jumps out of the settled region to v.

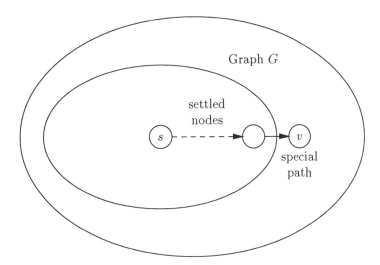

Fig. 9.39. Intermediate stage during the execution of Dijkstra's algorithm.

We maintain a value $dist(u)$ for every node u. If u is a settled node, then $dist(u)$ is the length of the shortest path from the source to u. If u is not settled, then $dist(u)$ is the length of the shortest special path from the source to u. Initially, only the source node s is settled, and $dist(s) = 0$, since the path consisting of s alone surely has distance 0. If there is an arc from s to u, then $dist(u)$ is the label of that arc. Notice that when only s is settled, the only special paths are the arcs out of s, so that $dist(u)$ should be the label of the arc $s \rightarrow u$ if there is one. We shall use a defined constant INFTY, that is intended to be larger than the distance along any path in the graph G. INFTY serves as an "infinite" value and indicates that no special paths have yet been discovered. That is, initially, if there is no arc $s \rightarrow u$, then $dist(u) = $ INFTY.

Now suppose we have some settled and some unsettled nodes, as suggested by Fig. 9.39. We find the node v that is unsettled, but has the smallest $dist$ value of any unsettled node. We "settle" v by

1.   Accepting $dist(v)$ as the minimum distance from s to v.

2.   Adjusting the value of $dist(u)$, for all nodes u that remain unsettled, to account for the fact that v is now settled.

The adjustment required by step (2) is the following. We compare the old value of $dist(u)$ with the sum of $dist(v)$ and label of the arc $v \rightarrow u$, and if the latter sum is smaller, we replace $dist(u)$ by that sum. If there is no arc $v \rightarrow u$, then we do not adjust $dist(u)$.

✦   **Example 9.26.** Consider the map of Oahu in Fig. 9.10. That graph is undirected, but we shall assume edges are arcs in both directions. Let the source be Honolulu. Then initially, only Honolulu is settled and its distance is 0. We can set $dist$(PearlCity) to 13 and $dist$(Kaneohe) to 11, but other cities, having no arc from Honolulu, are given distance INFTY. The situation is shown in the first column of Fig. 9.40. The star on distances indicates that the node is settled.

Among the unsettled nodes, the one with the smallest distance is now Kaneohe,

CITY	ROUND				
	(1)	(2)	(3)	(4)	(5)
Honolulu	0*	0*	0*	0*	0*
PearlCity	13	13	13*	13*	13*
Maili	INFTY	INFTY	33	33	33*
Wahiawa	INFTY	INFTY	25	25*	25*
Laie	INFTY	35	35	35	35
Kaneohe	11	11*	11*	11*	11*

VALUES OF *dist*

Fig. 9.40. Stages in the execution of Dijkstra's algorithm.

and so this node is settled. There are arcs from Kaneohe to Honolulu and Laie. The arc to Honolulu does not help, but the value of $dist$(Kaneohe), which is 11, plus the label of the arc from Kaneohe to Laie, which is 24, totals 35, which is less than "infinity," the current value of $dist$(Laie). Thus, in the second column, we have reduced the distance to Laie to 35. Kaneohe is now settled.

In the next round, the unsettled node with the smallest distance is Pearl City, with a distance of 13. When we make Pearl City settled, we must consider the neighbors of Pearl City, which are Maili and Wahiawa. We reduce the distance to Maili to 33 (the sum of 13 and 20), and we reduce the distance to Wahiawa to 25 (the sum of 13 and 12). The situation is now as in column (3).

Next to be settled is Wahiawa, with a distance of 25, least among the currently unsettled nodes. However, that node does not allow us to reduce the distance to any other node, and so column (4) has the same distances as column (3). Similarly, we next settle Maili, with a distance of 33, but that does not reduce any distances, leaving column (5) the same as column (4). Technically, we have to settle the last node, Laie, but the last node cannot affect any other distances, and so column (5) gives the shortest distances from Honolulu to all six cities. ◆

Why Dijkstra's Algorithm Works

In order to show that Dijkstra's algorithm works, we must assume that the labels of arcs are nonnegative.[9] We shall prove by induction on k that when there are k settled nodes,

a) For each settled node u, $dist(u)$ is the minimum distance from s to u, and the shortest path to u consists only of settled nodes.

b) For each unsettled node u, $dist(u)$ is the minimum distance of any special path from s to u (INFTY if no such path exists).

BASIS. For $k = 1$, s is the only settled node. We initialize $dist(s)$ to 0, which satisfies (a). For every other node u, we initialize $dist(u)$ to be the label of the arc $s \rightarrow u$ if it exists, and INFTY if not. Thus, (b) is satisfied.

---

[9] When labels are allowed to be negative, we can find graphs for which Dijkstra's algorithm gives incorrect answers.

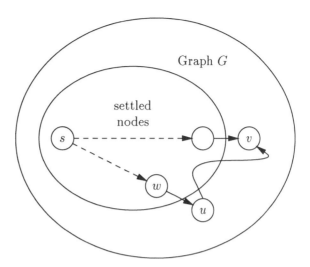

Fig. 9.41. Hypothetical shorter path to v, through w and u.

INDUCTION. Now assume (a) and (b) hold after k nodes have been settled, and let v be the $(k+1)$st node settled. We claim that (a) still holds, because $dist(v)$ is the least distance of any path from s to v. Suppose not. By part (b) of the inductive hypothesis, when k nodes are settled, $dist(v)$ is the minimum distance of any special path to v, and so there must be some shorter nonspecial path to v. As suggested in Fig. 9.41, this path must leave the settled nodes at some node w (which could be s), and go to some unsettled node u. From there, the path could meander in and out of the settled nodes, until it finally arrives at v.

However, v was chosen to be the $(k+1)$st node settled, which means that at this time, $dist(u)$ could not be less than $dist(v)$, or else we would have selected u as the $(k+1)$st node. By (b) of the inductive hypothesis, $dist(u)$ is the minimum length of any special path to u. But the path from s to w to u in Fig. 9.41 is a special path, so that its distance is at least $dist(u)$. Thus, the supposed shorter path from s to v through w and u has a distance that is at least $dist(v)$, because the initial part from s to u already has distance $dist(u)$, and $dist(u) \geq dist(v)$.[10] Thus, (a) holds for $k+1$ nodes, that is, (a) continues to hold when we include v among the settled nodes.

Now we must show that (b) holds when we add v to the settled nodes. Consider some node u that remains unsettled when we add v to the settled nodes. On the shortest special path to u, there must be some penultimate (next-to-last) node; this node could either be v or some other node w. The two possibilities are suggested by Fig. 9.42.

First, suppose the penultimate node is v. Then the length of the path from s to v to u suggested in Fig. 9.42 is $dist(v)$ plus the label of the arc $v \rightarrow u$.

Alternatively, suppose the penultimate node is some other node w. By inductive hypothesis (a), the shortest path from s to w consists only of nodes that were settled prior to v, and therefore, v does not appear on the path. Thus, the length of the shortest special path to u does not change when we add v to the settled nodes.

Now recall that when we settle v, we adjust each $dist(u)$ to be the smaller of

---

[10] Note that the fact that the labels are nonnegative is vital; if not, the portion of the path from u to v could have a negative distance, resulting in a shorter path to v.

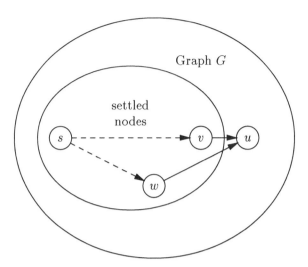

Fig. 9.42. What is the penultimate node on the shortest special path to u?

the old value of $dist(u)$ and $dist(v)$ plus the label of arc $v \rightarrow u$. The former covers the case that some w other than v is the penultimate node, and the latter covers the case that v is the penultimate node. Thus, part (b) also holds, and we have completed the inductive step.

Data Structures for Dijkstra's Algorithm

We shall now present an efficient implementation of Dijkstra's algorithm making use of the balanced partially ordered tree structure of Section 5.9.[11] We use two arrays, one called **graph** to represent the graph, and the other called **potNodes** to represent the partially ordered tree. The intent is that to each graph node u there corresponds a partially ordered tree node a that has priority equal to $dist(u)$. However, unlike Section 5.9, we shall organize the partially ordered tree by least priority rather than greatest. (Alternatively, we could take the priority of a to be $-dist(u)$.) Figure 9.43 illustrates the data structure.

We use **NODE** for the type of graph nodes. As usual, we shall name nodes with integers starting at 0. We shall use the type **POTNODE** for the type of nodes in the partially ordered tree. As in Section 5.9, we shall assume that the nodes of the partially ordered tree are numbered starting at 1 for convenience. Thus, both **NODE** and **POTNODE** are synonyms for **int**.

The data type **GRAPH** is defined to be

```
typedef struct {
    float dist;
    LIST successors;
    POTNODE toPOT;
} GRAPH[MAX];
```

---

[11] Actually, this implementation is only best when the number of arcs is somewhat less than the square of the number of nodes, which is the maximum number of arcs there can be. A simple implementation for the dense case is discussed in the exercises.

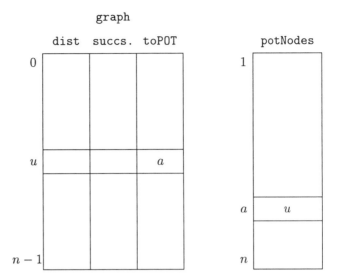

Fig. 9.43. Data structure to represent a graph for Dijkstra's algorithm.

Here, `MAX` is the number of nodes in the graph, and `LIST` is the type of adjacency lists consisting of cells of type `CELL`. Since we need to include labels, which we take to be floating-point numbers, we shall declare as the type `CELL`

```
typedef struct CELL *LIST;
struct CELL {
    NODE nodeName;
    float nodeLabel;
    LIST next;
};
```

We declare the data type `POT` to be an array of graph nodes

```
typedef NODE POT[MAX+1];
```

We can now define the principal data structures:

```
GRAPH graph;
POT potNodes;
POTNODE last;
```

The array of structures `graph` contains the nodes of the graph, the array `potNodes` contains the nodes of the partially ordered tree, and the variable *last* indicates the current end of the partially ordered tree, which resides in `potNodes[1..last]`.

Intuitively, the structure of the partially ordered tree is represented by the positions in the array `potNodes`, as usual for a partially ordered tree. The elements of this array let us tell the priority of a node by referring back to the graph itself. In particular, we place in `potNodes[a]` the index u of the graph node represented. The `dist` field, `graph[u].dist`, gives the priority of node a in the partially ordered tree.

Auxiliary Functions for Dijkstra's Algorithm

We need a number of auxiliary functions to make our implementation work. The most fundamental is the function `swap` that swaps two nodes of the partially ordered tree. The matter is not quite as simple as it was in Section 5.9. Here, the field `toPOT` of `graph` must continue to track the value in the array `potNodes`, as was suggested by Fig. 9.43. That is, if the value `graph[u].toPOT` is a, then it must also be the case that `potNodes[a]` has value u.

The code for `swap` is shown in Fig. 9.44. It takes as arguments a graph `G` and a partially ordered tree `P`, as well as two nodes `a` and `b` of that partially ordered tree. We leave it to the reader to check that the function exchanges the values in entries a and b of the partially ordered tree and also exchanges the `toPOT` fields of the corresponding graph nodes.

```
void swap(POTNODE a, POTNODE b, GRAPH G, POT P)
{
    NODE temp; /* used to swap POT nodes */

    temp = P[b];
    P[b] = P[a];
    P[a] = temp;
    G[P[a]].toPOT = a;
    G[P[b]].toPOT = b;
}
```

Fig. 9.44. Function to swap two nodes of the partially ordered tree.

We shall need to bubble nodes up and down the partially ordered tree, as we did in Section 5.9. The major difference is that here, the value in an element of the array `potNodes` is not the priority. Rather, that value takes us to a node of `graph`, and in the structure for that node we find the field `dist`, which gives us the priority. We therefore need an auxiliary function `priority` that returns `dist` for the appropriate graph node. We shall also assume for this section that smaller priorities rise to the top of the partially ordered tree, rather than larger priorities as in Section 5.9.

Figure 9.45 shows the function `priority` and functions `bubbleUp` and `bubbleDown` that are simple modifications of the functions of the same name in Section 5.9. Each takes a graph `G` and a partially ordered tree `P` as arguments. Function `bubbleDown` also needs an integer `last` that indicates the end of the current partially ordered tree in the array `P`.

Initialization

We shall assume that the adjacency list for each graph node has already been created and that a pointer to the adjacency list for graph node u appears in `graph[u].successors`. We shall also assume that node 0 is the source node. If we take the graph node i to correspond to node $i+1$ of the partially ordered tree, then the array `potNodes` is appropriately initialized as a partially ordered tree. That is, the root of the partially ordered tree represents the source node of the graph, to

```
float priority(POTNODE a, GRAPH G, POT P)
{
    return G[P[a]].dist;
}

void bubbleUp(POTNODE a, GRAPH G, POT P)
{
    if ((a > 1) &&
            (priority(a, G, P) < priority(a/2, G, P))) {
        swap(a, a/2, G, P);
        bubbleUp(a/2, G, P);
    }
}

void bubbleDown(POTNODE a, GRAPH G, POT P, int last)
{
    POTNODE child;

    child = 2*a;
    if (child < last &&
            priority(child+1, G, P) < priority(child, G, P))
        ++child;
    if (child <= last &&
            priority(a, G, P) > priority(child, G, P)) {
        swap(a, child, G, P);
        bubbleDown(child, G, P, last);
    }
}
```

Fig. 9.45. Bubbling nodes up and down the partially ordered tree.

which we give priority 0, and to all other nodes we give priority **INFTY**, our "infinite" defined constant.

As we shall see, on the first round of Dijkstra's algorithm, we select the source node to "settle," which will create the condition we regard as our starting point in the informal introduction, where the source node is settled and **dist[u]** is noninfinite only when there is an arc from the source to u. The initialization function is shown in Fig. 9.46. As with previous functions in this section, **initialize** takes as arguments the graph and the partially ordered tree. It also takes a pointer **pLast** to the integer **last**, so it can initialize it to MAX, the number of nodes in the graph. Recall that **last** will indicate the last position in the array for the partially ordered tree that is currently in use.

Note that the indexes of the partially ordered tree are 1 through MAX, while for the graph, they are 0 through $MAX - 1$. Thus, in lines (3) and (4) of Fig. 9.46, we have to make node i of the graph correspond initially to node $i+1$ of the partially ordered tree.

Implementation of Dijkstra's Algorithm

Figure 9.47 shows the code for Dijkstra's algorithm, using all the functions we

```
      void initialize(GRAPH G, POT P, int *pLast);
      {
            int i; /* we use i as both a graph and a tree node */

(1)         for (i = 0; i < MAX; i++) {
(2)             G[i].dist = INFTY;
(3)             G[i].toPOT = i+1;
(4)             P[i+1] = i;
            }
(5)         G[0].dist = 0;
(6)         (*pLast) = MAX;
      }
```

Fig. 9.46. Initialization for Dijkstra's algorithm.

Initializing with an Exception

Notice that at line (2) of Fig 9.46, we set `dist[1]` to `INFTY`, along with all the other distances. Then at line (5), we correct this distance to 0. That is more efficient than testing each value of i to see if it is the exceptional case. True, we could eliminate line (5) if we replaced line (2) by

```
      if (i == 0)
          G[i].dist = 0;
      else
          G[i].dist = INFTY;
```

but that would not only add to the code, it would increase the running time, since we would have to do n tests and n assignments, instead of $n + 1$ assignments and no tests, as we did in lines (2) and (5) of Fig. 9.46.

have previously written. To execute Dijkstra's algorithm on the graph **graph** with partially ordered tree **potNodes** and with integer **last** to indicate the end of the partially ordered tree, we initialize these variables and then call

```
      Dijkstra(graph, potNodes, &last)
```

The function **Dijkstra** works as follows. At line (1) we call **initialize**. The remainder of the code, lines (2) through (13), is a loop, each iteration of which corresponds to one round of Dijkstra's algorithm, where we pick one node v and settle it. The node v picked at line (3) is always the one whose corresponding tree node is at the root of the partially ordered tree. At line (4), we take v out of the partially ordered tree, by swapping it with the current last node of that tree. Line (5) actually removes v by decrementing **last**. Then line (6) restores the partially ordered tree property by calling **bubbleDown** on the node we just placed at the root. In effect, unsettled nodes appear below *last* and settled nodes are at *last* and above.

At line (7) we begin updating distances to reflect the fact that v is now settled. Pointer p is initialized to the beginning of the adjacency list for node v. Then in the loop of lines (8) to (13), we consider each successor u of v. After setting variable

```
        void Dijkstra(GRAPH G, POT P, int *pLast)
        {
            NODE u, v; /* v is the node we select to settle */
            LIST ps; /* ps runs down the list of successors of v;
                    u is the successor pointed to by ps */

(1)         initialize(G, P, pLast);
(2)         while ((*pLast) > 1) {
(3)             v = P[1];
(4)             swap(1, *pLast, G, P);
(5)             --(*pLast);
(6)             bubbleDown(1, G, P, *pLast);
(7)             ps = G[v].successors;
(8)             while (ps != NULL) {
(9)                 u = ps->nodeName;
(10)                if (G[u].dist > G[v].dist + ps->nodeLabel) {
(11)                    G[u].dist = G[v].dist + ps->nodeLabel;
(12)                    bubbleUp(G[u].toPOT, G, P);
                    }
(13)                ps = ps->next;
                }
            }
        }
```

Fig. 9.47. The main function for Dijkstra's algorithm.

u to one of the successors of v at line (9), we test at line (10) whether the shortest special path to u goes through v. That is the case whenever the old value of $dist(u)$, represented in this data structure by G[u].dist, is greater than the sum of $dist(v)$ plus the label of the arc $v \to u$. If so, then at line (11), we set $dist(u)$ to its new, smaller value, and at line (12) we call bubbleUp, so, if necessary, u can rise in the partially ordered tree to reflect its new priority. The loop completes when at line (13) we move p down the adjacency list of v.

Running Time of Dijkstra's Algorithm

As in previous sections, we shall assume that our graph has n nodes and that m is the larger of the number of arcs and the number of nodes. We shall analyze the running time of each of the functions, in the order they were described. First, swap clearly takes $O(1)$ time, since it consists only of assignment statements. Likewise, priority takes $O(1)$ time.

Function bubbleUp is recursive, but its running time is $O(1)$ plus the time of a recursive call on a node that is half the distance to the root. As we argued in Section 5.9, there are at most $\log n$ calls, each taking $O(1)$ time, for a total of $O(\log n)$ time for bubbleUp. Similarly, bubbleDown takes $O(\log n)$ time.

Function initialize takes $O(n)$ time. That is, the loop of lines (1) to (4) is iterated n times, and its body takes $O(1)$ time per iteration. That gives $O(n)$ time for the loop. Lines (5) and (6) each contribute $O(1)$, which we may neglect.

Now let us turn our attention to function Dijkstra in Fig. 9.47. Let m_v be the out-degree of node v, or equivalently, the length of v's adjacency list. Begin by analyzing the inner loop of lines (8) to (13). Each of lines (9) to (13) take $O(1)$ time, except for line (12), the call to bubbleUp, which we argued takes $O(\log n)$ time. Thus, the body of the loop takes $O(\log n)$ time. The number of times around the loop equals the length of the adjacency list for v, which we referred to as m_v. Thus the running time of the loop of lines (8) through (13) may be taken as $O(1 + m_v \log n)$; the term 1 covers the case where v has no successors, that is, $m_v = 0$, yet we still do the test of line (8).

Now consider the outer loop of lines (2) through (13). We already accounted for lines (8) to (13). Line (6) takes $O(\log n)$ for a call to bubbleDown. The other lines of the body take $O(1)$ each. The body thus takes time $O((1 + m_v) \log n)$.

The outer loop is iterated exactly $n - 1$ times, as last ranges from n down to 2. The term 1 in $1 + m_v$ thus contributes $n - 1$, or $O(n)$. However, the m_v term must be summed over each node v, since all nodes (but the last) are chosen once to be v. Thus, the contribution of m_v summed over all iterations of the outer loop is $O(m)$, since $\sum_v m_v \leq m$. We conclude that the outer loop takes time $O(m \log n)$. The additional time for line (1), the call to initialize, is only $O(n)$, which we may neglect. Our conclusion is that Dijkstra's algorithm takes time $O(m \log n)$, that is, at most a factor of $\log n$ more than the time taken just to look at the nodes and arcs of the graph.

EXERCISES

9.8.1: Find the shortest distance from Detroit to the other cities, according to the graph of Fig. 9.21 (see the exercises for Section 9.4). If a city is unreachable from Detroit, the minimum distance is "infinity."

9.8.2: Sometimes, we wish to count the number of arcs traversed getting from one node to another. For example, we might wish to minimize the number of transfers needed in a plane or bus trip. If we label each arc 1, then a minimum-distance calculation will count arcs. For the graph in Fig. 9.5 (see the exercises for Section 9.2), find the minimum number of arcs needed to reach each node from node a.

9.8.3: In Fig. 9.48(a) are seven species of hominids and their convenient abbreviations. Certain of these species are known to have preceded others because remains have been found in the same place separated by layers indicating that time had elapsed. The table in Fig. 9.48(b) gives triples (x, y, t) that mean species x has been found in the same place as species y, but x appeared t millions of years before y.

a) Draw a directed graph representing the data of Fig. 9.48, with arcs from the earlier species to the later, labeled by the time difference.

b) Run Dijkstra's algorithm on the graph from (a), with AF as the source, to find the shortest time by which each of the other species could have followed AF.

9.8.4*: The implementation of Dijkstra's algorithm that we gave takes $O(m \log n)$ time, which is less than $O(n^2)$ time, except in the case that the number of arcs is close to n^2, its maximum possible number. If m is large, we can devise another implementation, without a priority queue, where we take $O(n)$ time to select the winner at each round, but only $O(m_u)$ time, that is, time proportional to the number of arcs out of the settled node u, to update *dist*. The result is an $O(n^2)$ time algorithm. Develop the ideas suggested here, and write a C program for this implementation of Dijkstra's algorithm.

Australopithecus Afarensis	AF
Australopithecus Africanus	AA
Homo Habilis	HH
Australopithecus Robustus	AR
Homo Erectus	HE
Australopithecus Boisei	AB
Homo Sapiens	HS

(a) Species and abbreviations.

SPECIES 1	SPECIES 2	TIME
AF	HH	1.0
AF	AA	0.8
HH	HE	1.2
HH	AB	0.5
HH	AR	0.3
AA	AB	0.4
AA	AR	0.6
AB	HS	1.7
HE	HS	0.8

(b) Species 1 precedes species 2 by time.

Fig. 9.48. Relationships between hominid species.

9.8.5**: Dijkstra's algorithm does not always work if there are negative labels on some arcs. Give an example of a graph with some negative labels for which Dijkstra's algorithm gives the wrong answer for some minimum distance.

9.8.6**: Let G be a graph for which we have run Dijkstra's algorithm and settled the nodes in some order. Suppose we add to G an arc $u \to v$ with a weight of 0, to form a new graph G'. Under what conditions will Dijkstra's algorithm run on G' settle the nodes in the same order as for G?

9.8.7*: In this section we took the approach of linking the arrays representing the graph G and the partially ordered tree by storing integers that were indices into the other array. Another approach is to use pointers to array elements. Reimplement Dijkstra's algorithm using pointers instead of integer indices.

❖❖ 9.9 Floyd's Algorithm for Shortest Paths

If we want the minimum distances between all pairs of nodes in a graph with n nodes, with nonnegative labels, we can run Dijkstra's algorithm with each of the n nodes as source. Since one run of Dijkstra's algorithm takes $O(m \log n)$ time, where m is the larger of the number of nodes and number of arcs, finding the minimum distances between all pairs of nodes this way takes $O(mn \log n)$ time. Moreover, if m is close to its maximum, n^2, we can use an $O(n^2)$-time implementation of

Dijkstra's algorithm discussed in Exercise 9.8.4, which when run n times gives us an $O(n^3)$-time algorithm to find the minimum distances between each pair of nodes.

There is another algorithm for finding the minimum distances between all pairs of nodes, called *Floyd's algorithm*. This algorithm takes $O(n^3)$ time, and thus is in principle no better than Dijkstra's algorithm, and worse than Dijkstra's algorithm when the number of arcs is much less than n^2. However, Floyd's algorithm works on an adjacency matrix, rather than adjacency lists, and it is conceptually much simpler than Dijkstra's algorithm.

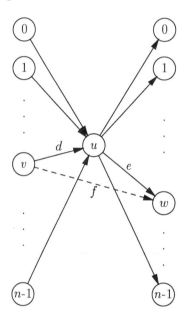

Fig. 9.49. Using node u as a pivot to improve
the distances between some pairs of nodes.

Pivot

The essence of Floyd's algorithm is that we consider in turn each node u of the graph as a *pivot*. When u is the pivot, we try to take advantage of u as an intermediate node between all pairs of nodes, as suggested in Fig. 9.49. For each pair of nodes, say v and w, if the sum of the labels of arcs $v \to u$ and $u \to w$, which is $d + e$ in Fig. 9.49, is less than the current label, f, of the arc from v to w, then we replace f by $d + e$.

A fragment of code implementing Floyd's algorithm is shown in Fig. 9.50. As before, we assume nodes are named by integers starting at 0. We use **NODE** as the type of nodes, but we assume this type is integers or an equivalent enumerated type. We assume there is an $n \times n$ array **arc**, such that **arc[v][w]** is the label of the arc $v \to w$ in the given graph. However, on the diagonal we have **arc[v][v]** = 0 for all nodes v, even if there is an arc $v \to v$. The reason is that the shortest distance from a node to itself is always 0, and we do not wish to follow any arcs at all. If there is no arc from v to w, then we let **arc[v][w]** be **INFTY**, a special value that is much greater than any other label. There is a similar array **dist** that, at the end, holds the minimum distances; **dist[v][w]** will become the minimum distance from node v to node w.

Lines (1) to (3) initialize **dist** to be **arc**. Lines (4) to (8) form a loop in which

```
        NODE u, v, w;

(1)     for (v = 0; v < MAX; v++)
(2)         for (w = 0; w < MAX; w++)
(3)             dist[v][w] = arc[v][w];
(4)     for (u = 0; u < MAX; u++)
(5)         for (v = 0; v < MAX; v++)
(6)             for (w = 0; w < MAX; w++)
(7)                 if (dist[v][u] + dist[u][w] < dist[v][w])
(8)                     dist[v][w] = dist[v][u] + dist[u][w];
```

Fig. 9.50. Floyd's algorithm.

Warshall's Algorithm

Sometimes, we are only interested in telling whether there exists a path between two nodes, rather than what the minimum distance is. If so, we can use an adjacency matrix where the type of elements is BOOLEAN (int), with TRUE (1) indicating the presence of an arc and FALSE (0) its absence. Similarly, the elements of the dist matrix are of type BOOLEAN, with TRUE indicating the existence of a path and FALSE indicating that no path between the two nodes in question is known. The only modification we need to make to Floyd's algorithm is to replace lines (7) and (8) of Fig. 9.50 by

```
(7)     if (dist[v][w] == FALSE)
(8)         dist[v][w] = dist[v][u] && dist[u][w];
```

These lines will set dist[v][w] to TRUE, if it is not already TRUE, whenever both dist[v][u] and dist[u][w] are TRUE.

The resulting algorithm, called *Warshall's algorithm,* computes the reflexive and transitive closure of a graph of n nodes in $O(n^3)$ time. That is never better than the $O(nm)$ time that the method of Section 9.7 takes, where we used depth-first search from each node. However, Warshall's algorithm uses an adjacency matrix rather than lists, and if m is near n^2, it may actually be more efficient than multiple depth-first searches because of the simplicity of Warshall's algorithm.

each node u is taken in turn to be the pivot. For each pivot u, in a double loop on v and w, we consider each pair of nodes. Line (7) tests whether it is shorter to go from v to w through u than directly, and if so, line (8) lowers dist[v][w] to the sum of the distances from v to u and from u to w.

✦ **Example 9.27.** Let us work with the graph of Fig. 9.10 from Section 9.3, using the numbers 0 through 5 for the nodes; 0 is Laie, 1 is Kaneohe, and so on. Figure 9.51 shows the arc matrix, with label INFTY for any pair of nodes that do not have a connecting edge. The arc matrix is also the initial value of the dist matrix.

Note that the graph of Fig. 9.10 is undirected, so the matrix is symmetric; that is, arc[v][w] = arc[v][w]. If the graph were directed, this symmetry might not be present, but Floyd's algorithm takes no advantage of symmetry, and thus works for directed or undirected graphs.

	0	1	2	3	4	5
0	0	24	INFTY	INFTY	INFTY	28
1	24	0	11	INFTY	INFTY	INFTY
2	INFTY	11	0	13	INFTY	INFTY
3	INFTY	INFTY	13	0	20	12
4	INFTY	INFTY	INFTY	20	0	15
5	28	INFTY	INFTY	12	15	0

Fig. 9.51. The `arc` matrix, which is the initial value of the `dist` matrix.

The first pivot is $u = 0$. Since the sum of `INFTY` and anything is `INFTY`, the only pair of nodes v and w, neither of which is u, for which `dist[v][u] + dist[u][w]` is less than `INFTY` is $v = 1$ and $w = 5$, or vice versa.[12] Since `dist[1][5]` is `INFTY` at this time, we replace `dist[1][5]` by the sum of `dist[1][0] + dist[0][5]` which is 52. Similarly, we replace `dist[5][1]` by 52. No other distances can be improved with pivot 0, which leaves the `dist` matrix of Fig. 9.52.

	0	1	2	3	4	5
0	0	24	INFTY	INFTY	INFTY	28
1	24	0	11	INFTY	INFTY	52
2	INFTY	11	0	13	INFTY	INFTY
3	INFTY	INFTY	13	0	20	12
4	INFTY	INFTY	INFTY	20	0	15
5	28	52	INFTY	12	15	0

Fig. 9.52. The matrix `dist` after using 0 as the pivot.

Now we make node 1 the pivot. In the current `dist`, shown in Fig. 9.52, node 1 has noninfinite connections to 0 (distance 24), 2 (distance 11), and 5 (distance 52). We can combine these edges to reduce the distance between nodes 0 and 2 from `INFTY` to $24+11 = 35$. Also, the distance between 2 and 5 is reduced to $11+52 = 63$. Note that 63 is the distance along the path from Honolulu, to Kaneohe, to Laie, to Wahiawa, not the shortest way to get to Wahiawa, but the shortest way that only goes through nodes that have been the pivot so far. Eventually, we shall find the shorter route through Pearl City. The current `dist` matrix is shown in Fig. 9.53.

Now we make 2 be the pivot. Node 2 currently has noninfinite connections to 0 (distance 35), 1 (distance 11), 3 (distance 13), and 5 (distance 63). Among these nodes, the distance between 0 and 3 can be improved to $35 + 13 = 48$, and the

---

[12] If one of v and w is the u, it is easy to see `dist[v][w]` can never be improved by going through u. Thus, we can ignore pairs of the form (v, u) or (u, w) when searching for pairs whose distance is improved by going through the pivot u.

	0	1	2	3	4	5
0	0	24	35	INFTY	INFTY	28
1	24	0	11	INFTY	INFTY	52
2	35	11	0	13	INFTY	63
3	INFTY	INFTY	13	0	20	12
4	INFTY	INFTY	INFTY	20	0	15
5	28	52	63	12	15	0

Fig. 9.53. The matrix dist after using 1 as the pivot.

	0	1	2	3	4	5
0	0	24	35	48	INFTY	28
1	24	0	11	24	INFTY	52
2	35	11	0	13	INFTY	63
3	48	24	13	0	20	12
4	INFTY	INFTY	INFTY	20	0	15
5	28	52	63	12	15	0

Fig. 9.54. The matrix dist after using 2 as the pivot.

distance between 1 and 3 can be improved to $11 + 13 = 24$. Thus, the current dist matrix is shown in Fig. 9.54.

Next, node 3 becomes the pivot. Figure 9.55 shows the current best distance between 3 and each of the other nodes.[13] By traveling through node 3, we can make the following improvements in distances.

1. Between 1 and 5, the distance is reduced to 36.

2. Between 2 and 5, the distance is reduced to 25.

3. Between 0 and 4, the distance is reduced to 68.

4. Between 1 and 4, the distance is reduced to 44.

5. Between 2 and 4, the distance is reduced to 33.

The current dist matrix is shown in Fig. 9.56.

The use of 4 as a pivot does not improve any distances. When 5 is the pivot, we can improve the distance between 0 and 3, since in Fig. 9.56,

dist[0][5] + dist[5][3] = 40

---

[13] The reader should compare Fig. 9.55 with Fig. 9.49. The latter shows how to use a pivot node in the general case of a directed graph, where the arcs in and out of the pivot may have different labels. Fig. 9.55 takes advantage of the symmetry in the example graph, letting us use edges between node 3 and the other nodes to represent both arcs into node 3, as on the left of Fig. 9.49, and arcs out of 3, as on the right of Fig. 9.49.

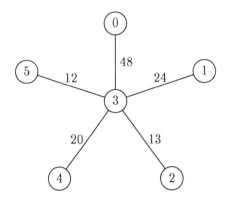

Fig. 9.55. Current best distances to node 4.

	0	1	2	3	4	5
0	0	24	35	48	68	28
1	24	0	11	24	44	36
2	35	11	0	13	33	25
3	48	24	13	0	20	12
4	68	44	33	20	0	15
5	28	36	25	12	15	0

Fig. 9.56. The matrix `dist` after using 3 as the pivot.

	0	1	2	3	4	5
0	0	24	35	40	43	28
1	24	0	11	24	44	36
2	35	11	0	13	33	25
3	40	24	13	0	20	12
4	43	44	33	20	0	15
5	28	36	25	12	15	0

Fig. 9.57. The final `dist` matrix.

which is less than `dist[0][3]`, or 48. In terms of cities, that corresponds to discovering that it is shorter to go from Laie to Pearl City via Wahiawa than via Kaneohe and Honolulu. Similarly, we can improve the distance between 0 and 4 to 43, from 68. The final `dist` matrix is shown in Fig. 9.57. ✦

Why Floyd's Algorithm Works

As we have seen, at any stage during Floyd's algorithm the distance from node v to node w will be the distance of the shortest of those paths that go through only nodes that have been the pivot. Eventually, all nodes get to be the pivot, and `dist[v][w]` holds the minimum distance of all possible paths.

k-path

We define a *k-path* from a node v to a node w to be a path from v to w such that no intermediate node is numbered higher than k. Note that there is no constraint that v or w be k or less.

An important special case is when $k = -1$. Since nodes are assumed numbered starting at 0, a (-1)-path can have no intermediate nodes at all. It can only be either an arc or a single node that is both the beginning and end of a path of length 0.

Figure 9.58 suggests what a k-path looks like, although the end points, v and w, can be above or below k. In that figure, the height of the line represents the numbers of the nodes along the path from v to w.

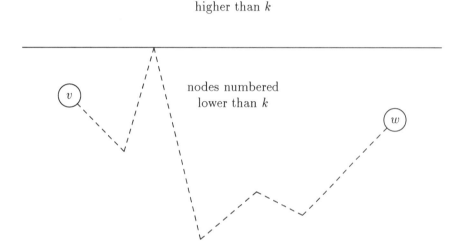

nodes numbered
higher than k

nodes numbered
lower than k

Fig. 9.58. A k-path cannot have nodes higher than k, except (possibly) at the ends.

✦ **Example 9.28.** In Fig. 9.10, the path 0, 1, 2, 3 is a 2-path. The intermediate nodes, 1 and 2, are each 2 or less. This path is also a 3-path, a 4-path, and a 5-path. It is not a 1-path, however, because the intermediate node 2 is greater than 1. Similarly, it is not a 0-path or a (-1)-path. ✦

As we assume nodes are numbered 0 to $n - 1$, a (-1)-path cannot have any intermediate nodes at all, and thus must be an arc or a single node. An $(n-1)$-path is any path at all, since there can be no intermediate node numbered higher than $n - 1$ in any path of a graph with nodes numbered 0 through $n - 1$. We shall prove by induction on k the statement

STATEMENT $S(k)$: If labels of arcs are nonnegative, then just before we set u to $k + 1$ in the loop of lines (4) to (8) of Fig. 9.50, `dist[v][w]` is the length of the shortest k-path from v to w, or **INFTY** if there is no such path.

BASIS. The basis is $k = -1$. We set u to 0 just before we execute the body of the loop for the first time. We have just initialized **dist** to be **arc** in lines (1) to (3). Since the arcs and the paths consisting of a node by itself are the only (-1)-paths, the basis holds.

INDUCTION. Assume $S(k)$, and consider what happens to **dist[v][w]** during the iteration of the loop with $u = k + 1$. Suppose P is a shortest $(k + 1)$-path from v to w. There are two cases, depending on whether P goes through node $k + 1$.

1.   If P is a k-path, that is, P does not actually go through node $k + 1$, then by the inductive hypothesis, **dist[v][w]** already equals the length of P after the kth iteration. We cannot change **dist[u][v]** during the round with $k + 1$ as pivot, because there are no shorter $(k + 1)$-paths.

2.   If P is a $(k + 1)$-path, we can assume that P only goes through node $k + 1$ once, because cycles can never decrease distances (recall we require all labels to be nonnegative). Thus, P is composed of a k-path Q from v to node $k + 1$, followed by a k-path R from node $k + 1$ to w, as suggested in Fig. 9.59. By the inductive hypothesis, **dist[v][k+1]** and **dist[k+1][w]** will be the lengths of paths Q and R, respectively, after the kth iteration.

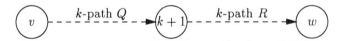

Fig. 9.59. A $(k + 1)$-path P can be broken into two k-paths, Q followed by R.

Let us begin by observing that **dist[v][k+1]** and **dist[k+1][w]** cannot be changed in the $(k + 1)$st iteration. The reason is that all arc labels are nonnegative, and so all lengths of paths are nonnegative; thus the test of line (7) in Fig. 9.50 must fail when u (i.e., node $k + 1$) is one of v or w.

Thus, when we apply the test of line (7) for arbitrary v and w, with $u = k + 1$, the values of **dist[v][k+1]** and **dist[k+1][w]** have not changed since the end of the kth iteration. That is to say, the test of line (7) compares the length of the shortest k-path, with the sum of the lengths of the shortest k-paths from v to $k + 1$ and from $k + 1$ to w. In case (1), where path P does not go through $k + 1$, the former will be the shorter, and in case (2), where P does go through $k + 1$, the latter will be the sum of the lengths of the paths Q and R in Fig. 9.59, and will be the shorter.

We conclude that the $(k + 1)$st iteration sets **dist[v][w]** to the length of the shortest $(k + 1)$-path, for all nodes v and w. That is the statement $S(k + 1)$, and so we conclude the induction.

To finish our proof, we let $k = n - 1$. That is, we know that after finishing all n iterations, **dist[v][w]** is the minimum distance of any $(n - 1)$-path from v to w. But since any path is an $(n - 1)$-path, we have shown that **dist[v][w]** is the minimum distance along any path from v to w.

EXERCISES

9.9.1: Assuming all arcs in Fig. 9.5 (see the exercises for Section 9.2) have label 1, use Floyd's algorithm to find the length of the shortest path between each pair of nodes. Show the distance matrix after pivoting with each node.

9.9.2: Apply Warshall's algorithm to the graph of Fig. 9.5 to compute its reflexive and transitive closure. Show the reachability matrix after pivoting with each node.

9.9.3: Use Floyd's algorithm to find the shortest distances between each pair of cities in the graph of Michigan in Fig. 9.21 (see the exercises for Section 9.4).

9.9.4: Use Floyd's algorithm to find the shortest possible time between each of the hominid species in Fig. 9.48 (see the exercises for Section 9.8).

9.9.5: Sometimes we want to consider only paths of one or more arcs, and exclude single nodes as paths. How can we modify the initialization of the `arc` matrix so that only paths of length 1 or more will be considered when finding the shortest path from a node to itself?

9.9.6*: Find all the acyclic 2-paths in Fig. 9.10.

9.9.7*: Why does Floyd's algorithm not work when there are both positive and negative costs on the arcs?

9.9.8**: Give an algorithm to find the longest acyclic path between two given nodes.

9.9.8**: Suppose we run Floyd's algorithm on a graph G. Then, we lower the label of the arc $u \to v$ to 0, to construct the new graph G'. For what pairs of nodes s and t will `dist[s][t]` be the same at each round when Floyd's algorithm is applied to G and G'?

❖❖ 9.10   An Introduction to Graph Theory

Graph theory is the branch of mathematics concerned with properties of graphs. In the previous sections, we have presented the basic definitions of graph theory, along with some fundamental algorithms that computer scientists have developed to calculate key properties of graphs efficiently. We have seen algorithms for computing shortest paths, spanning trees, and depth-first-search trees. In this section, we shall present a few more important concepts from graph theory.

Complete Graphs

An undirected graph that has an edge between every pair of distinct nodes is called a *complete* graph. The complete graph with n nodes is called K_n. Figure 9.60 shows the complete graphs K_1 through K_4.

The number of edges in K_n is $n(n-1)/2$, or $\binom{n}{2}$. To see why, consider an edge $\{u, v\}$ of K_n. For u we can pick any of the n nodes; for v we can pick any of the remaining $n-1$ nodes. The total number of choices is therefore $n(n-1)$. However, we count each edge twice that way, once as $\{u, v\}$ and a second time as $\{v, u\}$, so that we must divide the total number of choices by 2 to get the correct number of edges.

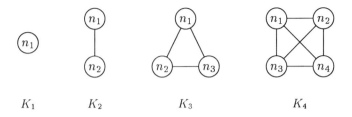

Fig. 9.60. The first four complete graphs.

Complete directed graph

There is also a notion of a complete directed graph. This graph has an arc from every node to every other node, including itself. A complete directed graph with n nodes has n^2 arcs. Figure 9.61 shows the complete directed graph with 3 nodes and 9 arcs.

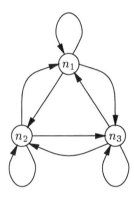

Fig. 9.61. The complete directed graph with three nodes.

Planar Graphs

An undirected graph is said to be *planar* if it is possible to place its nodes on a plane and then draw its edges as continuous lines so that no two edges cross.

◆ Example 9.29. The graph K_4 was drawn in Fig. 9.60 in such a way that its two diagonal edges crossed. However, K_4 is a planar graph, as we can see by the drawing in Fig. 9.62. There, by redrawing one of the diagonals on the outside, we avoid having any two edges cross. We say that Fig. 9.62 is a *plane presentation* of the graph K_4, while the drawing in Fig. 9.60 is a nonplane presentation of K_4. Note that it is permissible to have edges that are not straight lines in a plane presentation. ◆

Plane presentation

Nonplanar graph

In Figure 9.63 we see what are in a sense the two simplest *nonplanar* graphs, that is, graphs that do not have any plane presentation. One is K_5, the complete graph with five nodes. The other is sometimes called $K_{3,3}$; it is formed by taking two groups of three nodes and connecting each node of one group to each node of the other group, but not to nodes of the same group. The reader should try to

Fig. 9.62. A plane presentation of K_4.

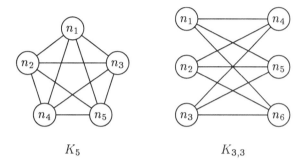

$$K_5 \qquad\qquad K_{3,3}$$

Fig. 9.63. The two simplest nonplanar graphs.

redraw each of these graphs so that no two edges cross, just to get a feel for why they are not planar.

Kuratowski's theorem A famous theorem by Kuratowski states every nonplanar graph contains a "copy" of at least one of these two graphs. We must be a little careful in interpreting the notion of a copy, however, since to see a copy of K_5 or $K_{3,3}$ in an arbitrary nonplanar graph G, we may have to associate some edges in the graphs of Fig. 9.63 with paths in the graph G.

Applications of Planarity

Planarity has considerable importance in computer science. For example, many graphs or similar diagrams need to be presented on a computer screen or on paper. For clarity, it is desirable to make a plane presentation of the graph, or if the graph is not planar, to make as few crossings of edges as possible.

The reader may observe that in Chapter 13 we draw some fairly complex diagrams of circuits, which are really graphs whose nodes are gates and junction points of wires, and whose edges are the wires. Since these circuits are not planar in general, we had to adopt a convention in which wires were allowed to cross without connecting, and a dot signals a connection of wires.

A related application concerns the design of integrated circuits. Integrated circuits, or "chips," embody logical circuits such as those discussed in Chapter 13. They do not require that the logical circuit be inscribed in a plane presentation, but there is a similar limitation that allows us to assign edges to several "levels," often three or four levels. On one level, the graph of the circuit must have a plane presentation; edges are not allowed to cross. However, edges on different levels may cross.

Graph Coloring

Chromatic
number

The problem of *graph coloring* for a graph G is to assign a "color" to each node so that no two nodes that are connected by an edge are assigned the same color. We may then ask how many distinct colors are required to *color* a graph in this sense. The minimum number of colors needed for a graph G is called the *chromatic number* of G, often denoted $\chi(G)$. A graph that can be colored with no more than k colors is called *k-colorable*.

k-colorability

◆ **Example 9.30.** If a graph is complete, then its chromatic number is equal to the number of nodes; that is, $\chi(K_n) = n$. In proof, we cannot color two nodes u and v with the same color, because there is surely an edge between them. Thus, each node requires its own color. K_n is k-colorable for each $k \geq n$, but K_n is not k-colorable if $k < n$. Note that we say, for instance, that K_4 is 5-colorable, even though it is impossible to use all five colors on the four-node graph K_4. However, formally a graph is k-colorable if it can be colored with k or fewer colors, not only if it is colorable with exactly k colors.

As another example, the graph $K_{3,3}$ shown in Fig. 9.63 has chromatic number 2. For example, we can color the three nodes in the group on the left *red* and color the three nodes on the right *blue*. Then all edges go between a *red* and a *blue* node. $K_{3,3}$ is an example of a *bipartite graph*, which is another name for a graph that can be colored with two colors. All such graphs can have their nodes divided into two groups such that no edge runs between members of the same group.

Bipartite graph

As a final example, the chromatic number for the six-node graph of Fig. 9.64 is 4. To see why, note that the node in the center cannot have the same color as any other node, since it is connected to all. Thus, we reserve a color for it, say, *red*. We need at least two other colors for the ring of nodes, since neighbors around the ring cannot get the same color. However, if we try alternating colors — say, *blue* and *green* — as we did in Fig. 9.64, then we run into a problem that the fifth node has both *blue* and *green* neighbors, and therefore needs a fourth color, *yellow*, in our example. ◆

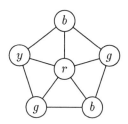

Fig. 9.64. A graph with chromatic number 4.

Applications of Graph Coloring

Finding a good graph coloring is another problem that has many uses in computer science. For example, in our introduction to the first chapter, we considered assigning courses to time slots so that no pair of courses in the same time slot had a student taking both courses. The motivation was to schedule final exams so that no student had to take two exams at the same time. We drew a graph whose nodes were the courses, with an edge between two courses if they had a student in common.

The question of how many time slots we need in which to schedule exams can thus be posed as the question of what is the chromatic number of this graph. All nodes of the same color can be scheduled at the same time since they have no edges between any two of them. Conversely, if we have a schedule that does not cause conflicts for any student, then we can color all the courses scheduled at the same time with the same color, and thus produce a graph coloring with as many colors as there are exam periods.

In Chapter 1 we discussed a heuristic based on finding maximal independent sets to schedule the exams. That is a reasonable heuristic for finding a good coloring of a graph as well. One might expect that one could try all possible colorings for a graph as small as the five-node graph in Fig. 1.1, and indeed that is true. However, the number of possible colorings of a graph grows exponentially with the number of nodes, and it is not feasible to consider all possible colorings for significantly larger graphs, in our search for the least possible number of colors.

Cliques

k-clique

Clique number

A *clique* in an undirected graph G is a set of nodes such that there is in G an edge between every pair of nodes in the set. A clique of k nodes is called a *k-clique*. The size of the largest clique in a graph is called the *clique number* of that graph.

✦   **Example 9.31.** As a simple example, every complete graph K_n is a clique consisting of all n nodes. In fact, K_n has a k-clique for all $k \leq n$, but no k-clique if $k > n$.

The graph of Fig. 9.64 has cliques of size three, but no greater. The 3-cliques are each shown as triangles. There cannot be a 4-clique in this graph, because it would have to include some of the nodes in the ring. Each ring node is connected to only three other nodes, so the 4-clique would have to include some node v on the ring, its neighbors on the ring, and the central node. However, the neighbors of v on the ring do not have an edge between them, so we do not have a 4-clique. ✦

As an example application of cliques, suppose we represented conflicts among courses not as in Fig. 1.1, but rather by putting an edge between two nodes if they *did not have* a student enrolled in both courses. Thus, two courses connected by an edge could have their exams scheduled at the same time. We could then look for Maximal clique   *maximal cliques*, that is, cliques that were not subsets of larger cliques, and schedule the exams for a maximal clique of courses at the same period.

EXERCISES

9.10.1: For the graph of Fig. 9.4,

a)   What is the chromatic number?
b)   What is the clique number?
c)   Give an example of one largest clique.

9.10.2: What are the chromatic numbers of the undirected versions of the graphs shown in (a) Fig. 9.5 and (b) Fig. 9.26? (Treat arcs as edges.)

9.10.3: Figure 9.5 is not presented in a plane manner. Is the graph planar? That is, can you redraw it so there are no crossing edges?

9.10.4*: Three quantities associated with an undirected graph are its degree (maximum number of neighbors of any node), its chromatic number, and its clique number. Derive inequalities that must hold between these quantities. Explain why they must hold.

9.10.5**: Design an algorithm that will take any graph of n nodes, with m the larger of the number of nodes and edges, and in $O(m)$ time will tell whether the graph is bipartite (2-colorable).

9.10.6*: We can generalize the graph of Fig. 9.64 to have a central node and k nodes in a ring, each node connected only to its neighbors around the ring and to the central node. As a function of k, what is the chromatic number of this graph?

9.10.7*: What can you say about the chromatic number of unordered, unrooted trees (as discussed in Section 9.5)?

9.10.8**: Let $K_{i,j}$ be the graph formed by taking a group of i nodes and a group of j nodes and placing an edge from every member of one group to every member of the other group. We observed that if $i = j = 3$, then the resulting graph is not planar. For what values of i and j is the graph $K_{i,j}$ planar?

✦✦ 9.11   Summary of Chapter 9

The table of Fig. 9.65 summarizes the various problems we have addressed in this chapter, the algorithms for solving them, and the running time of the algorithms. In this table, n is the number of nodes in the graph and m is the larger of the number of nodes and the number of arcs/edges. Unless otherwise noted, we assume graphs are represented by adjacency lists.

In addition, we have introduced the reader to most of the key concepts of graph theory. These include

✦   Paths and shortest paths

✦   Spanning trees

✦   Depth-first search trees and forests

✦   Graph coloring and the chromatic number

✦   Cliques and clique numbers

✦   Planar graphs.

PROBLEM	ALGORITHM(S)	RUNNING TIME
Minimal spanning tree	Kruskal's	$O(m \log n)$
Detecting cycles	Depth-first search	$O(m)$
Topological order	Depth-first search	$O(m)$
Single-source reachability	Depth-first search	$O(m)$
Connected components	Depth-first search	$O(m)$
Transitive closure	n depth-first searches	$O(mn)$
Single-source shortest path	Dijkstra's with POT implementation Dijkstra's with implementation of Exercise 9.8.4	$O(m \log n)$ $O(n^2)$
All-pairs shortest path	n uses of Dijkstra with POT implementation n uses of Dijkstra with implementation of Exercise 9.8.4 Floyd's, with adjacency matrix	$O(mn \log n)$ $O(n^3)$ $O(n^3)$

Fig. 9.65. A summary of graph algorithms.

❖❖ 9.12 Bibliographic Notes for Chapter 9

For additional material on graph algorithms, see Aho, Hopcroft, and Ullman [1974, 1983]. Depth-first search was first used to create efficient graph algorithms by Hopcroft and Tarjan [1973]. Dijkstra's algorithm is from Dijkstra [1959], Floyd's algorithm from Floyd [1962], Kruskal's algorithm from Kruskal [1956], and Warshall's algorithm from Warshall [1962].

Berge [1962] covers the mathematical theory of graphs. Lawler [1976], Papadimitriou and Steiglitz [1982], and Tarjan [1983] present advanced graph optimization techniques.

Aho, A. V., J. E. Hopcroft, and J. D. Ullman [1974]. *The Design and Analysis of Computer Algorithms*, Addison-Wesley, Reading, Mass.

Aho, A. V., J. E. Hopcroft, and J. D. Ullman [1983]. *Data Structures and Algorithms*, Addison-Wesley, Reading, Mass.

Berge, C. [1962]. *The Theory of Graphs and its Applications*, Wiley, New York.

Dijkstra, E. W. [1959]. "A note on two problems in connexion with graphs," *Numberische Mathematik* **1**, pp. 269–271.

Floyd, R. W. [1962]. "Algorithm 97: shortest path," *Comm. ACM* **5**:6, pp. 345.

Hopcroft, J. E., and R. E. Tarjan [1973]. "Efficient algorithms for graph manipulation," *Comm. ACM* **16**:6, pp. 372-378.

Kruskal, J. B., Jr. [1956]. "On the shortest spanning subtree of a graph and the traveling salesman problem," *Proc. AMS* **7**:1, pp. 48–50.

Lawler, E. [1976]. *Combinatorial Optimization: Networks and Matroids*, Holt, Rinehart and Winston, New York.

Papadimitriou, C. H., and K. Steiglitz [1982]. *Combinatorial Optimization: Algorithms and Complexity*, Prentice-Hall, Englewood Cliffs, New Jersey.

Tarjan, R. E. [1983]. *Data Structures and Network Algorithms*, SIAM, Philadelphia.

Warshall, S. [1962]. "A theorem on Boolean matrices," *J. ACM* **9**:1, pp. 11-12.

10

Patterns, Automata, and Regular Expressions

❖

A pattern is a set of objects with some recognizable property. One type of pattern is a set of character strings, such as the set of legal C identifiers, each of which is a string of letters, digits, and underscores, beginning with a letter or underscore. Another example would be the set of arrays of 0's and 1's of a given size that a character reader might interpret as representing the same symbol. Figure 10.1 shows three 7 × 7-arrays that might be interpreted as letter A's. The set of all such arrays would constitute the pattern called "A."

```
0 0 0 1 0 0 0        0 0 0 0 0 0 0        0 0 0 1 0 0 0
0 0 1 1 1 0 0        0 0 1 0 0 0 0        0 0 1 0 1 0 0
0 0 1 0 1 0 0        0 0 1 1 0 0 0        0 1 1 0 1 0 0
0 1 1 0 1 1 0        0 1 0 1 0 0 0        0 1 1 1 1 1 0
0 1 1 1 1 1 0        0 1 1 1 0 0 0        1 1 0 0 0 1 1
1 1 0 0 0 1 1        1 0 0 1 1 0 0        1 0 0 0 0 0 1
1 0 0 0 0 0 1        1 0 0 0 1 0 0        0 0 0 0 0 0 0
```

Fig. 10.1. Three instances of the pattern "A."

The two fundamental problems associated with patterns are their definition and their recognition, subjects of this and the next chapter. Recognizing patterns is an integral part of tasks such as optical character recognition, an example of which was suggested by Fig. 10.1. In some applications, pattern recognition is a component of a larger problem. For example, recognizing patterns in programs is an essential part of compiling — that is, the translation of programs from one language, such as C, into another, such as machine language.

There are many other examples of pattern use in computer science. Patterns play a key role in the design of the electronic circuits used to build computers and other digital devices. They are used in text editors to allow us to search for instances of specific words or sets of character strings, such as "the letters **if** followed by any sequence of characters followed by **then**." Most operating systems allow us to use patterns in commands; for example, the UNIX command "`ls *tex`" lists all files whose names end with the three-character sequence "`tex`".

An extensive body of knowledge has developed around the definition and recognition of patterns. This theory is called "automata theory" or "language theory," and its basic definitions and techniques are part of the core of computer science.

✥✥ 10.1 What This Chapter Is About

This chapter deals with patterns consisting of sets of strings. In it, we shall learn:

✦ The "finite automaton" is a graph-based way of specifying patterns. These come in two varieties, deterministic automata (Section 10.2) and nondeterministic automata (Section 10.3).

✦ A deterministic automaton is convertible in a simple way into a program that recognizes its pattern (Section 10.2).

✦ A nondeterministic automaton can be converted to a deterministic automaton recognizing the same pattern by use of the "subset construction" discussed in Section 10.4.

✦ Regular expressions are an algebra for describing the same kinds of patterns that can be described by automata (Sections 10.5 through 10.7).

✦ Regular expressions can be converted to automata (Section 10.8) and vice versa (Section 10.9).

We also discuss string patterns in the next chapter. There we introduce a recursive notation called "context-free grammars" for defining patterns. We shall see that this notation is able to describe patterns not expressible by automata or regular expressions. However, in many cases grammars are not convertible to programs in as simple manner as are automata or regular expressions.

✥✥ 10.2 State Machines and Automata

Programs that search for patterns often have a special structure. We can identify certain positions in the code at which we know something particular about the program's progress toward its goal of finding an instance of a pattern. We call these positions *states*. The overall behavior of the program can be viewed as moving from state to state as it reads its input.

State

To make these ideas more concrete, let us consider a specific pattern-matching problem: "What English words contain the five vowels in order?" To help answer this question, we can use a word list that is found with many operating systems. For example, in the UNIX system one can find such a list in the file **/usr/dict/words**, where the commonly used words of English appear one to a line. In this file, some of the words that contain the vowels in order are

```
abstemious
facetious
sacrilegious
```

Let us write a straightforward C program to examine a character string and decide whether all five vowels appear there in order. Starting at the beginning of the string, the program first searches for an **a**. We shall say it is in "state 0" until it sees an **a**, whereupon it goes into "state 1." In state 1, it looks for an **e**, and when it finds one, it goes into "state 2." It proceeds in this manner, until it reaches "state 4," in which it is looking for a **u**. If it finds a **u**, then the word has all five vowels, in order, and the program can go into an accepting "state 5." It is not necessary to scan the rest of the word, since it already knows that the word qualifies, regardless of what follows the **u**.

We can interpret state i as saying that the program has already encountered the first i vowels, in order, for $i = 0, 1, \ldots, 5$. These six states summarize all that the program needs to remember as it scans the input from left to right. For example, in state 0, while it is looking for an **a**, the program does not need to remember if it has seen an **e**. The reason is that such an **e** is not preceded by any **a**, and so cannot serve as the **e** in the subsequence **aeiou**.

The heart of this pattern-recognition algorithm is the function `findChar(pp,c)` in Fig. 10.2. This function's arguments are `pp` — the address of a pointer to a string of characters — and a desired character c. That is, `pp` is of type "pointer to pointer to character." Function `findChar` searches for the character c, and as a side effect it advances the pointer whose address it is given until that pointer either points past c or to the end of the string. It returns a value of type `BOOLEAN`, which we define to be a synonym for `int`. As discussed in Section 1.6, we expect that the only values for the type `BOOLEAN` will be `TRUE` and `FALSE`, which are defined to be 1 and 0, respectively.

At line (1), `findChar` examines the current character indicated by `pp`. If it is neither the desired character c nor the character `'\0'` that marks the end of a character string in C, then at line (2) we advance the pointer that is pointed to by `pp`. A test at line (3) determines whether we stopped because we exhausted the string. If we did, we return `FALSE`; otherwise, we advance the pointer and return `TRUE`.

Next in Fig. 10.2 is the function `testWord(p)` that tells whether a character string pointed to by `p` has all the vowels in order. The function starts out in state 0, just before line (7). In that state it calls `findChar` at line (7), with second argument `'a'`, to search for the letter **a**. If it finds an **a**, then `findChar` will return `TRUE`. Thus if `findChar` returns `TRUE` at line (7), the program moves to state 1, where at line (8) it makes a similar test for an **e**, scanning the string starting after the first **a**. It thus proceeds through the vowels, until at line (12), if it finds a **u** it returns `TRUE`. If any of the vowels are not found, then control goes to line (13), where `testWord` returns `FALSE`.

The main program of line (14) tests the particular string `"abstemious"`. In practice, we might use `testWord` repeatedly on all the words of a file to find those with all five vowels in order.

Graphs Representing State Machines

We can represent the behavior of a program such as Fig. 10.2 by a graph in which the nodes represent the states of the program. What is perhaps more important, we can design a program by first designing the graph, and then mechanically translating the graph into a program, either by hand, or by using one of a number of programming tools that have been written for that purpose.

```
      #include <stdio.h>

      #define TRUE 1
      #define FALSE 0
      typedef int BOOLEAN;

      BOOLEAN findChar(char **pp, char c)
      {
(1)       while (**pp != c && **pp != '\0')
(2)           (*pp)++;
(3)       if (**pp == '\0')
(4)           return FALSE;
          else {
(5)           (*pp)++;
(6)           return TRUE;
          }
      }

      BOOLEAN testWord(char *p)
      {
          /* state 0 */
(7)       if (findChar(&p, 'a'))
              /* state 1 */
(8)           if (findChar(&p, 'e'))
                  /* state 2 */
(9)               if (findChar(&p, 'i'))
                      /* state 3 */
(10)                  if (findChar(&p, 'o'))
                          /* state 4 */
(11)                      if (findChar(&p, 'u'))
                              /* state 5 */
(12)                          return TRUE;
(13)      return FALSE;
      }

      main()
      {
(14)      printf("%d\n", testWord("abstemious"));
      }
```

Fig. 10.2. Finding words with subsequence aeiou.

The picture representing a program's states is a directed graph, whose arcs are labeled by sets of characters. There is an arc from state s to state t, labeled by the set of characters C, if, when in state s, we go to state t exactly when we see one of **Transition** the characters in set C. The arcs are called *transitions*. If x is one of the characters in set C, which labels the transition from state s to state t, then if we are in state s and receive an x as our next character, we say we "make a transition on x to state t." In the common case that set C is a singleton $\{x\}$, we shall label the arc by x, rather than $\{x\}$.

Accepting state and start state We also label certain of the nodes *accepting states*. When we reach one of these states, we have found our pattern and "accept." Conventionally, accepting states are represented by double circles. Finally, one of the nodes is designated the *start state,* the state in which we begin to recognize the pattern. We indicate the start state by an arrow entering from nowhere. Such a graph is called a *finite automaton* or just *automaton.* We see an example of an automaton in Fig. 10.3.

Automaton

The behavior of an automaton is conceptually simple. We imagine that an automaton receives a list of characters known as the *input sequence.* It begins in the start state, about to read the first character of the input sequence. Depending on that character, it makes a transition, perhaps to the same state, or perhaps to another state. The transition is dictated by the graph of the automaton. The automaton then reads the second character and makes the proper transition, and so on.

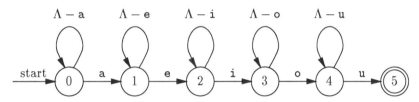

Fig. 10.3. Automaton to recognize sequences of letters that have subsequence `aeiou`.

✦ **Example 10.1.** The automaton corresponding to the function `testWord` of Fig. 10.2 is shown in Fig. 10.3. In this graph, we use a convention that will be followed subsequently; the Greek letter Λ (Lambda) stands for the set of all upper- and lower-case letters. We also use shorthands like $\Lambda - a$ to represent the set of all letters except a.

Node 0 is the start state. On any letter but a, we stay in state 0, but on an a, we go to state 1. Similarly, once we reach state 1, we stay there unless we see an e, in which case we go to state 2. The next states, 3 and 4, similarly are reached when we see an i and then an o. We remain in state 4 unless we see a u, in which case we go to state 5, the lone accepting state. There are no transitions out of state 5, since we do not examine any more of the word being tested, but rather announce success by returning `TRUE`.

It is also worth noting that if we encounter a blank (or any other nonletter) in states 0 through 4, we have no transition. In that case, processing stops, and, since we are not now in an accepting state, we have *rejected* the input. ✦

✦ **Example 10.2.** Our next example is from signal processing. Instead of regarding all characters as potential inputs for an automaton, we shall allow only inputs 0 and 1. The particular automaton we shall design, sometimes called a *bounce filter,* takes a sequence of 0's and 1's as inputs. The object is to "smooth" the sequence by regarding a single 0 surrounded by 1's as "noise," and replacing the 0 by 1. Similarly, one 1 surrounded by 0's will be regarded as noise and replaced by 0.

Bounce filter

As an example of how a bounce filter might be used, we could be scanning a digitized black-white image, line by line. Each line of the image is, in fact, a sequence of 0's and 1's. Since pictures sometimes do have small spots of the wrong color, due, for example, to imperfections in the film or the photography process, it is useful to get rid of such spots, in order to reduce the number of distinct regions in the image and allow us to concentrate on "real" features, rather than spurious ones.

Figure 10.4 is the automaton for our bounce filter. The interpretations of the four states are as follows:

a)   We have just seen a sequence of 0's, at least two in a row.
b)   We have just seen a sequence of 0's followed by a single 1.
c)   We have just seen a sequence of at least two 1's.
d)   We have just seen a sequence of 1's followed by a single 0.

State a is designated the start state, which implies that our automaton will behave as if there were an unseen prefix of 0's prior to the input.

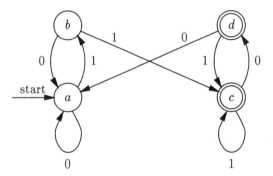

Fig. 10.4. Automaton to eliminate spurious 0's and 1's.

The accepting states are c and d. For this automaton, acceptance has a somewhat different significance from that of the automaton of Fig. 10.3. There, when we reached the accepting state, we said that the whole input was accepted, including characters the automaton had not even read yet.[1] Here, we want an accepting state to say "output a 1," and a nonaccepting state to say "output a 0." Under this interpretation, we shall translate each bit in the input to a bit of the output. Usually, the output will be the same as the input, but sometimes it will differ. For instance, Fig. 10.5 shows the input, states, and their outputs when the input is 0101101.

Input:	0	1	0	1	1	0	1
State:	a	a	b	a	b	c	d	c
Output:	0	0	0	0	0	1	1	1

Fig. 10.5. Simulation of the automaton in Fig. 10.4 on input 0101101.

---

[1] However, we could have modified the automaton to read all letters following the u, by adding a transition from state 5 to itself on all letters.

The Difference Between Automata and Their Programs

Automata are abstractions. As will be clear from Section 10.3, automata render an accept/reject decision on any sequence of input characters by seeing whether there is a path from the start state to some accepting state labeled by that sequence. Thus for example, the action indicated in Fig. 10.5 for the bounce-filter automaton of Fig. 10.4 tells us that the automaton rejects the prefixes ϵ, 0, 01, 010, and 0101, while it accepts 01011, 010110, and 0101101. The automaton of Fig. 10.3 accepts strings like **abstemiou**, but rejects **abstemious**, because there is nowhere to go on the final **s** from state 5.

On the other hand, programs created from automata can use the accept/reject decision in various ways. For example, the program of Fig. 10.2 used the automaton of Fig. 10.3 not to approve of the string that labels the path to the accepting state, but to approve of the entire line of input, that is, **abstemious** instead of **abstemiou**. That is perfectly reasonable, and reflects the way we'd write a program to test for all five vowels in order, regardless of whether we used automata or any other approach. Presumably, as soon as we got to the **u**, our program would print the entire word without examining it further.

The automaton of Fig. 10.4 is used in a more straightforward way. We shall see in Fig. 10.7 a program for the bounce filter that simply translates each accepting state into an action to print a **1**, and translates each rejecting state into an action to print a **0**.

We begin in state a, and since a is nonaccepting, we output 0. It is important to notice that this initial output is not in response to any input, but represents the condition of the automaton when we first turn the device on.

The transition out of state a labeled by input 0 in Fig. 10.4 is to state a itself. Thus the second output is also 0. The second input is 1, and from state a we make a transition on 1 to state b. That state "remembers" that we've seen a single 1, but since b is a nonaccepting state, the output is still 0. On the third input, another 0, we go from state b back to a, and we continue to emit the output 0.

The next two inputs are 1's, which take the automaton first to state b, then to state c. On the first of the two 1's, we find ourselves in state b, which causes output 0; that output turns out to be wrong, because we have in fact started a run of 1's, but we don't know that after reading the fourth input. The effect of our simple design is that all runs, whether of 0's or 1's, are shifted one position to the right, since it takes two bits in a row before the automaton realizes it has seen the beginning of a new run, rather than a "noise" bit. When the fifth input is received, we follow the transition on input 1 from state b to state c. At that point, we make our first 1 output, because c is an accepting state.

The last two inputs are 0 and 1. The 0 takes us from state c to d, so that we can remember that we have seen a single 0. The output from state d is still 1, since that state is accepting. The final 1 takes us back to state c and produces a 1 output. ✦

EXERCISES

10.2.1: Design automata to read strings of 0's and 1's, and

a) Determine if the sequence read so far has even parity (i.e., there have been an even number of 1's). Specifically, the automaton accepts if the string so far has even parity and rejects if it has odd parity.

b) Check that there are no more than two consecutive 1's. That is, accept unless 111 is a substring of the input string read so far.

What is the intuitive meaning of each of your states?

10.2.2: Indicate the sequence of states and the outputs when your automata from Exercise 10.2.1 are given the input 101001101110.

10.2.3*: Design an automaton that reads a word (character string) and tells whether the letters of the word are in sorted order. For example, **adept** and **chilly** have their letters in sorted order; **baby** does not, because an **a** follows the first **b**. The word must be terminated by a blank, so that the automaton will know when it has read all the characters. (Unlike Example 10.1, here we must not accept until we have seen all the characters, that is, until we reach the blank at the end of the word.) How many states do you need? What are their intuitive meanings? How many transitions are there out of each state? How many accepting states are there?

10.2.4: Design an automaton that tells whether a character string is a legal C identifier (letter followed by letters, digits, or underscore) followed by a blank.

10.2.5: Write C programs to implement each of the automata of Exercises 10.2.1 through 10.2.4.

10.2.6: Design an automaton that tells whether a given character string is one of the third-person singular pronouns, **he**, **his**, **him**, **she**, **her**, or **hers**, followed by a blank.

10.2.7*: Convert your automaton from Exercise 10.2.6 into a C function and use it in a program to find all places where the third-person singular pronouns appear as substrings of a given string.

❖❖ 10.3 Deterministic and Nondeterministic Automata

One of the most basic operations using an automaton is to take a sequence of symbols $a_1 a_2 \cdots a_k$ and follow from the start state a path whose arcs have labels that include these symbols in order. That is, for $i = 1, 2, \ldots, k$, a_i is a member of the set S_i that labels the ith arc of the path. Constructing this path and its sequence of states is called *simulating* the automaton on the input sequence $a_1 a_2 \cdots a_k$. This path is said to have the *label* $a_1 a_2 \cdots a_k$; it may also have other labels, of course, since the sets S_i labeling the arcs along the path may each include many characters.

Label of a path

✦ **Example 10.3.** We did one such simulation in Fig. 10.5, where we followed the automaton of Fig. 10.4 on input sequence 0101101. For another example, consider the automaton of Fig. 10.3, which we used to recognize words with subsequence **aeiou**. Consider the character string **adept**.

We start in state 0. There are two transitions out of state 0, one on the set of characters $\Lambda - \mathbf{a}$, and the other on **a** alone. Since the first character in **adept** is **a**,

Terminology for Automaton Inputs

In the examples we shall discuss here, the inputs to an automaton are characters, such as letters and digits, and it is convenient to think of inputs as characters and input sequences as character strings. We shall generally use that terminology here, but we shorten "character string" to just "string" on occasion. However, there are some applications where the inputs on which an automaton makes a transition are chosen from a set more general than the ASCII character set. For instance, a compiler may want to consider a keyword such as `while` to be a single input symbol, which we shall represent by the boldface string **while**. Thus we shall sometimes refer to the individual inputs as "symbols" rather than "characters."

we follow the latter transition, which takes us to state 1. Out of state 1, there are transitions on $\Lambda - $ e and e. Since the second character is d, we must take the former transition, because all letters but e are included in the set $\Lambda - $ e. That leaves us in state 1 again. As the third character is e, we follow the second transition out of state 1, which takes us to state 2. The final two letters of `adept` are both included in the set $\Lambda - $ i, and so our next two transitions are from state 2 to state 2. We thus finish our processing of `adept` in state 2. The sequence of state transitions is shown in Fig. 10.6. Since state 2 is not an accepting state, we do not accept the input `adept`. ◆

Fig. 10.6. Simulation of the automaton in Fig. 10.3 on input `adept`.

Deterministic Automata

The automata discussed in the previous section have an important property. For any state s and any input character x, there is at most one transition out of state s whose label includes x. Such an automaton is said to be *deterministic*.

Simulating a deterministic automaton on a given input sequence is straightforward. In any state s, given the next input character x, we consider each of the labels of the transitions out of s. If we find a transition whose label includes x, then that transition points to the proper next state. If none includes x, then the automaton "dies," and cannot process any more input, just as the automaton of Fig. 10.3 dies after it reaches state 5, because it knows it already has found the subsequence `aeiou`.

It is easy to convert a deterministic automaton into a program. We create a piece of code for each state. The code for state s examines its input and decides which of the transitions out of s, if any, should be followed. If a transition from state s to state t is selected, then the code for state s must arrange for the code of state t to be executed next, perhaps by using a goto-statement.

✦ **Example 10.4.** Let us write a function `bounce()` corresponding to the automaton in Fig. 10.4, the bounce filter. There is a variable x used to read characters from the input. States a, b, c, and d will be represented by labels a, b, c, and d, respectively, and we use label `finis` for the end of the program, which we reach when we encounter a character other than 0 or 1 on the input.

```
void bounce()
{
          char x;

          /* state a */
a:        putchar('0');
          x = getchar();
          if (x == '0') goto a; /* transition to state a */
          if (x == '1') goto b; /* transition to state b */
          goto finis;

          /* state b */
b:        putchar('0');
          x = getchar();
          if (x == '0') goto a; /* transition to state a */
          if (x == '1') goto c; /* transition to state c */
          goto finis;

          /* state c */
c:        putchar('1');
          x = getchar();
          if (x == '0') goto d; /* transition to state d */
          if (x == '1') goto c; /* transition to state c */
          goto finis;

          /* state d */
d:        putchar('1');
          x = getchar();
          if (x == '0') goto a; /* transition to state a */
          if (x == '1') goto c; /* transition to state c */
          goto finis;

finis:    ;

}
```

Fig. 10.7. Function implementing the deterministic automaton of Fig. 10.4.

The code is shown in Fig. 10.7. For instance, in state a we print the character 0, because a is a nonaccepting state. If the input character is 0, we stay in state a, and if the input character is 1, we go to state b. ✦

Disjoint sets

There is nothing in the definition of "automaton" that requires the labels of the transitions out of a given state to be disjoint (sets are *disjoint* if they have no members in common; i.e., their intersection is the empty set). If we have the sort of graph suggested in Fig. 10.8, where on input x there are transitions from state s to states t and u, it is not clear how this automaton could be implemented by a program. That is, when executing the code for state s, if x is found to be the next input character, we are told we must next go to the beginning of the code for state t and also to the beginning of the code for state u. Since the program cannot go to two places at once, it is far from clear how one simulates an automaton with nondisjoint labels on the transitions out of a state.

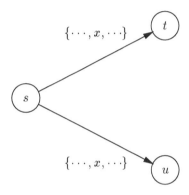

Fig. 10.8. Nondeterministic transition from state s on input x.

Nondeterministic Automata

Nondeterministic automata are allowed (but not required) to have two or more transitions containing the same symbol out of one state. Note that a deterministic automaton is technically a nondeterministic automaton as well, one that happens not to have multiple transitions on one symbol. An "automaton" is in general nondeterministic, but we shall use "nondeterministic automaton" when we want to emphasize that the automaton need not be a deterministic automaton.

Nondeterministic automata are not directly implementable by programs, as we mentioned, but they are useful conceptual tools for a number of applications that we shall discuss. Moreover, by using the "subset construction," to be covered in the next section, it is possible to convert any nondeterministic automaton to a deterministic automaton that accepts the same set of character strings.

Acceptance by Nondeterministic Automata

When we try to simulate a nondeterministic automaton on an input string of characters $a_1 a_2 \cdots a_k$, we may find that this same string labels many paths. It is conventional to say that the nondeterministic automaton *accepts* this input string if at least one of the paths it labels leads to acceptance. Even a single path ending in an accepting state outweighs any number of paths that end at a nonaccepting state.

Nondeterminism and Guessing

A useful way to look at nondeterminism is that it allows an automaton to "guess." If we don't know what to do in a given state on a given input character, we may make several choices of next state. Since any path labeled by a character string leading to an accepting state is interpreted as acceptance, the nondeterministic automaton in effect is given the credit for a right guess, no matter how many wrong guesses it also makes.

✦ **Example 10.5.** The League Against Sexist Speech (LASS) wishes to catch sexist writing that contains the word "man." They not only want to catch constructs such as "ombudsman," but more subtle forms of discrimination such as "maniac" or "emancipate." LASS plans to design a program using an automaton; that program will scan character strings and "accept" when it finds the character string **man** anywhere within the input.

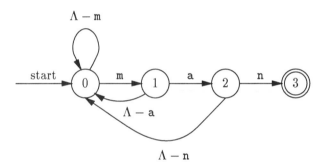

Fig. 10.9. Deterministic automaton that recognizes most, but not all, strings ending in **man**.

One might first try a deterministic automaton like that shown in Fig. 10.9. In this automaton, state 0, the start state, represents the case in which we have not begun to see the letters of "man." State 1 is intended to represent the situation in which we have seen an **m**; in state 2 we have recognized **ma**, and in state 3 we have seen **man**. In states 0, 1, and 2, if we fail to see the hoped-for letter, we go back to state 0 and try again.

However, Fig. 10.9 does not quite work correctly. On an input string such as **command**, it stays in state 0 while reading the **c** and **o**. It goes to state 1 on reading the first **m**, but the second **m** takes it back to state 0, which it does not subsequently leave.

A nondeterministic automaton that correctly recognizes character strings with an embedded **man** is shown in Fig. 10.10. The key innovation is that in state 0 we guess whether an **m** marks the beginning of **man** or not. Since the automaton is nondeterministic, it is allowed to guess both "yes" (represented by the transition from state 0 to state 1) and "no" (represented by the fact that the transition from state 0 to state 0 can be performed on all letters, including **m**) at the same time.

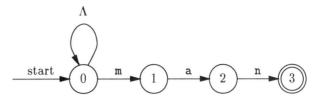

Fig. 10.10. Nondeterministic automaton that recognizes all strings ending in **man**.

Because acceptance by a nondeterministic automaton requires no more than one path to an accepting state, we get the benefit of both guesses.

Figure 10.11 shows the action of the nondeterministic automaton of Fig. 10.10 on input string **command**. In response to the **c** and **o**, the automaton can only stay in state 0. When the first **m** is input, the automaton has the choice of going to state 0 or to state 1, and so it does both. With the second **m**, there is nowhere to go from state 1, and so that branch "dies." However, from state 0, we can again go to either state 0 or 1, and so we do both. When the **a** is input, we can go from state 0 to 0 and from state 1 to 2. Similarly, when **n** is input, we can go from 0 to 0 and from 2 to 3.

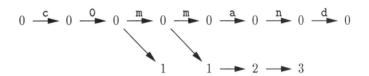

Fig. 10.11. Simulation of nondeterministic automaton of Fig. 10.10 on input string **command**.

Since state 3 is an accepting state, we accept at that point.[2] The fact that we are also in state 0 after seeing **comman** is irrelevant as far as acceptance is concerned. The final transition is on input **d**, from state 0 to 0. Note that state 3 goes nowhere on any input, and so that branch dies.

Also note that the transitions back to state 0, which were present in Fig. 10.9 to handle the case in which the next character of the word **man** was not received, are unnecessary in Fig. 10.10, because in Fig. 10.10 we are not compelled to follow the sequence from state 0 to 1 to 2 to 3 when we see input **man**. Thus, although state 3 looks like it is "dead" and ends computation when we see **man**, we are also in state 0 upon seeing **man**. That state allows us to accept inputs like **manoman** by staying in state 0 during the first **man** and going through states 1, 2, and 3 when the second **man** is read. ✦

---

[2] Notice that the automaton of Fig. 10.10, like that of Fig. 10.3, accepts when it sees the pattern it is looking for, not at the end of the word. When we eventually convert Fig. 10.10 to a deterministic automaton, we can design from it a program that prints the entire word, like the program of Fig. 10.2.

Of course, the design of Fig. 10.10, while appealing, cannot be turned into a program directly. We shall see in the next section how it is possible to turn Fig. 10.10 into a deterministic automaton with only four states. This deterministic automaton, unlike that of Fig. 10.9, will correctly recognize all occurrences of **man**.

While we can convert any nondeterministic automaton into a deterministic one, we are not always as fortunate as we are in the case of Fig. 10.10. In that case, the corresponding deterministic automaton will be seen to have no more states than the nondeterministic automaton, four states for each. There are other nondeterministic automata whose corresponding deterministic automata have many more states. A nondeterministic automaton with n states might be convertible only into a deterministic automaton with 2^n states. The next example happens to be one in which the deterministic automaton has many more states than the nondeterministic one. Consequently, a nondeterministic automaton may be considerably easier to design than a deterministic automaton for the same problem.

Partial anagram

◆ **Example 10.6.** When Peter Ullman, the son of one of the authors, was in fourth grade, he had a teacher who tried to build the students' vocabularies by assigning them "partial anagram" problems. Each week they would be given a word and were asked to find all the words that could be made using one or more of its letters.

One week, when the word was "Washington," the two authors of this book got together and decided to do an exhaustive search to see how many words were possible. Using the file **/usr/dict/words** and a three-step procedure, we found 269 words. Among them were five 7-letter words:

```
agonist
goatish
showing
washing
wasting
```

Since the case of a letter is not significant for this problem, our first step was to translate all upper-case letters in the dictionary into lower case. A program to carry out this task is straightforward.

Our second step was to select the words that contain only characters from the set $S = \{a,g,h,i,n,o,s,t,w\}$, the letters in **washington**. A simple, deterministic automaton can do this task; one is shown in Fig 10.12. The **newline** character is the character that marks the ends of lines in **/usr/dict/words**. In Fig. 10.12, we stay in state 0 as long as we see letters that appear in **washington**. If we encounter any other character besides **newline**, there is no transition, and the automaton can never reach the accepting state 1. If we encounter **newline** after reading only letters in **washington**, then we make the transition from state 0 to state 1, and accept.

The automaton in Fig. 10.12 accepts words such as **hash** that have more occurrences of some letter than are found in the word **washington** itself. Our third and final step, therefore, was to eliminate those words that contain three or more n's or two or more of another of the characters in set S. This task can also be done by an automaton. For example, the automaton in Fig. 10.13 accepts words that have at least two a's. We stay in state 0 until we see an **a**, whereupon we go to state 1. We stay there until we see a second **a**; at that point we go to state 2 and accept. This automaton accepts those words that fail to be partial anagrams of **washington**

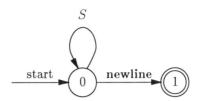

Fig. 10.12. Deterministic automaton that detects words consisting of letters that appear in `washington`.

because they have too many **a**'s. In this case, the words we want are exactly those that never cause the automaton to enter the accepting state 2 at any time during their processing.

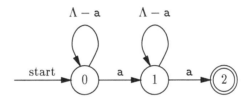

Fig. 10.13. Automaton that accepts if there are two a's.

The automaton of Fig. 10.13 is deterministic. However, it represents only one of nine reasons why a word that is accepted by the automaton of Fig. 10.12 might still not be a partial anagram of `washington`. To accept all the words that have too many instances of a letter in `washington`, we can use the nondeterministic automaton of Fig. 10.14.

Figure 10.14 starts in state 0, and one of its choices on any letter is to remain in state 0. If the input character is any letter in `washington`, then there is another choice; the automaton also guesses that it should transfer to a state whose function it is to remember that one occurrence of this letter has been seen. For instance, on letter **i** we have the choice of going also to state 7. We then remain in state 7 until we see another **i**, whereupon we go to state 8, which is one of the accepting states. Recall that in this automaton, acceptance means that the input string is *not* a partial anagram of `washington`, in this case because it has two **i**'s.

Because there are two **n**'s in `washington`, letter **n** is treated somewhat differently. The automaton can go to state 9 on seeing an **n**, then to state 10 on seeing a second **n**, and then to state 11 on seeing a third **n**, which is where it accepts.

For instance, Fig. 10.15 shows all the states we can enter after reading the input string `shining`. Since we enter accepting state 8 after reading the second **i**, the word `shining` is not a partial anagram of `washington`, even though it is accepted by the automaton of Fig. 10.12 for having only letters that are found in `washington`.

To summarize, our algorithm consisted of three steps:

1.   We first translated all upper-case letters in the dictionary into lower-caser letters.

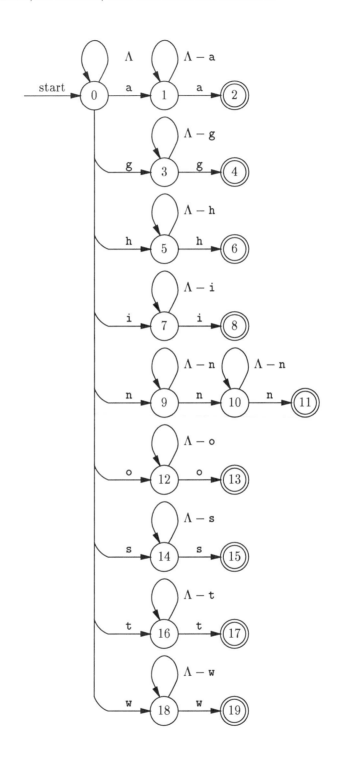

Fig. 10.14. Nondeterministic automaton that detects words with more than one
a, g, h, i, o, s, t, or w, or more than two n's.

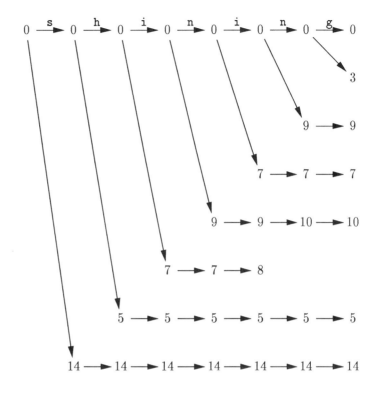

Fig. 10.15. States entered by the nondeterministic automaton of Fig. 10.14 on input string shining.

2. We found all resulting words that are accepted by the automaton of Fig. 10.12 and therefore consist only of letters in washington.

3. We removed from the list created in (2) all those words that are accepted by the nondeterministic automaton of Fig. 10.14.

This algorithm is a straightforward way to find all the partial anagrams of "Washington" in the file /usr/dict/words. Of course, we must find some reasonable way to simulate the nondeterministic automaton of Fig. 10.14, and we shall discuss how that can be done in the next sections. ✦

EXERCISES

10.3.1: Write a C program to implement the algorithm of the deterministic automaton of Fig. 10.9.

10.3.2: Design a deterministic automaton that correctly finds all occurrences of man in a character string. Implement this automaton as a program.

10.3.3: LASS wishes to detect all occurrences of the strings man, son, and father. Design a nondeterministic automaton that will accept whenever it finds the end of any of these three character strings.

10.3.4*: Design a deterministic automaton that solves the same problem as the previous exercise.

Finding Partial Anagrams Without Programming

As an aside, we were able to implement the three-step algorithm in Example 10.6 with almost no programming, using the commands of the UNIX system. For step (1) we used the UNIX command

$$\text{tr A-Z a-z } </usr/dict/words \tag{10.1}$$

to translate from upper to lower case. For step (2) we used the command

$$\text{egrep '\^[aghinostw]*\$'} \tag{10.2}$$

which, roughly, defines an automaton like that of Fig. 10.12. For step (3) we used the command

$$\text{egrep -v 'a.*a|g.*g|h.*h|i.*i|n.*n|o.*o|s.*s|t.*t|w.*w'} \tag{10.3}$$

which specifies something like the automaton of Fig. 10.14. The entire task was done using the three-element pipe

$$\text{(10.1) | (10.2) | (10.3)}$$

That is, the entire command is formed by substituting the text represented by each of the indicated lines. The vertical bar, or "pipe" symbol, makes the input of the command on its left be the input to the command on its right. The **egrep** command is discussed in Section 10.6.

10.3.5: Simulate the automata of Figs. 10.9 and 10.10 on the input string **summand**.

10.3.6: Simulate the automaton of Fig. 10.14 on input strings

a) saint
b) antagonist
c) hashish

Which are accepted?

10.3.7: We can represent an automaton by a relation with attributes State, Input, and Next. The intent is that if (s, x, t) is a tuple, then input symbol x is a label of the transition from state s to state t. If the automaton is deterministic, what is a suitable key for the relation? What if the automaton is nondeterministic?

10.3.8: What data structures would you suggest for representing the relation of the previous exercise, if we only wanted to find the next state(s), given a state and an input symbol?

10.3.9: Represent the automata of

a) Fig. 10.10
b) Fig. 10.9
c) Fig. 10.14

as relations. You may use ellipses to represent the transitions on large sets of letters such as $\Lambda - m$.

❖❖ 10.4   From Nondeterminism to Determinism

In this section we shall see that every nondeterministic automaton can be replaced by a deterministic one. As we have seen, it is sometimes easier to think of a nondeterministic automaton to perform a certain task. However, because we cannot write programs from nondeterministic automata as readily as from deterministic machines, it is quite important that there is an algorithm to transform a nondeterministic automaton into an equivalent deterministic one.

Equivalence of Automata

In the previous sections, we have seen two views of acceptance. In some examples, such as Example 10.1 (words containing the subsequence `aeiou`), we took acceptance to mean that the entire word was accepted, even though we may not have scanned the entire word yet. In others, like the bounce filter of Example 10.2, or the automaton of Fig. 10.12 (words whose letters are all in `washington`), we accepted only when we wanted to signal approval of the exact input that we had seen since we started the automaton. Thus in Example 10.2 we accepted all sequences of inputs that result in a 1 output. In Fig. 10.12, we accepted only when we had seen the **newline** character, and thus knew that the entire word had been seen.

When we talk about the formal behavior of automata, we require only the second interpretation (the input so far is accepted). Formally, suppose A and B are two automata (deterministic or not). We say A and B are *equivalent* if they accept the same set of input strings. Put another way, if $a_1 a_2 \cdots a_k$ is any string of symbols, then the following two conditions hold:

1. If there is a path labeled $a_1 a_2 \cdots a_k$ from the start state of A to some accepting state of A, then there is also a path labeled $a_1 a_2 \cdots a_k$ from the start state of B to some accepting state of B, and

2. If there is a path labeled $a_1 a_2 \cdots a_k$ from the start state of B to some accepting state of B, then there is also a path labeled $a_1 a_2 \cdots a_k$ from the start state of A to some accepting state of A.

❖ **Example 10.7.** Consider the automata of Figs. 10.9 and 10.10. As we noted from Fig. 10.11, the automaton of Fig. 10.10 accepts the input string `comman`, because this sequence of characters labels the path $0 \to 0 \to 0 \to 0 \to 1 \to 2 \to 3$ in Fig. 10.10, and this path goes from the start state to an accepting state. However, in the automaton of Fig. 10.9, which is deterministic, we can check that the only path labeled `comman` is $0 \to 0 \to 0 \to 1 \to 0 \to 0 \to 0$. Thus if Fig. 10.9 is automaton A, and Fig. 10.10 is automaton B, we have a violation of point (2) above, which tells us that these two automata are not equivalent. ❖

The Subset Construction

We shall now see how to "wring the nondeterminism out of an automaton" by constructing an equivalent deterministic automaton. The technique is called the *subset construction,* and its essence is suggested by Figs. 10.11 and 10.15, in which we simulated nondeterministic automata on particular inputs. We notice from these pictures that at any given time, the nondeterministic automaton is in some set of states, and that these states appear in one column of the simulation diagram. That is, after reading some input list $a_1 a_2 \cdots a_k$, the nondeterministic automaton is "in" those states that are reached from the start state along paths labeled $a_1 a_2 \cdots a_k$.

✦ **Example 10.8.** After reading input string `shin`, the automaton illustrated in Fig. 10.15 is in the set of states $\{0, 5, 7, 9, 14\}$. These are the states that appear in the column just after the first **n**. After reading the next **i**, it is in the set of states $\{0, 5, 7, 8, 9, 14\}$, and after reading the following **n**, it is in set of states $\{0, 5, 7, 9, 10, 14\}$. ✦

We now have a clue as to how we can turn a nondeterministic automaton N into a deterministic automaton D. The states of D will each be a set of N's states, and the transitions among D's states will be determined by the transitions of N. To see how the transitions of D are constructed, let S be a state of D and x an input symbol. Since S is a state of D, it consists of states of N. Define the set T to be those states t of automaton N such that there is a state s in S and a transition of N from s to t on a set containing input symbol x. Then in automaton D we put a transition from S to T on symbol x.

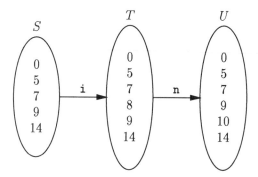

Fig. 10.16. Transitions among deterministic states S, T, and U.

Example 10.8 illustrated transitions from one deterministic state to another on various input symbols. When the current deterministic state is $\{0, 5, 7, 9, 14\}$, and the input symbol is the letter **i**, we saw in that example that the set of next nondeterministic states, according to the nondeterministic automaton of Fig. 10.14, is $T = \{0, 5, 7, 8, 9, 14\}$. From this deterministic state on input symbol **n**, the set of next nondeterministic states U is $\{0, 5, 7, 9, 10, 14\}$. These two deterministic transitions are depicted in Fig. 10.16.

Now we know how to construct a transition between two states of the deterministic automaton D, but we need to determine the exact set of states of D, the start state of D, and the accepting states of D. We construct the states of D by an induction.

BASIS. If the start state of nondeterministic automaton N is s_0, then the start state of deterministic automaton D is $\{s_0\}$, that is, the set containing only s_0.

INDUCTION. Suppose we have established that S, a set of N's states, is a state of D. We consider each possible input character x, in turn. For a given x, we let T be the set of N's states t such that for some state s in S, there is a transition from s to t with a label that includes x. Then set T is a state of D, and there is a transition from S to T on input x.

The accepting states of D are those sets of N's states that include at least one accepting state of N. That makes intuitive sense. If S is a state of D and a set of N's states, then the inputs $a_1 a_2 \cdots a_k$ that take D from its start state to state S also take N from its start state to all of the states in S. If S includes an accepting state, then $a_1 a_2 \cdots a_k$ is accepted by N, and D must also accept. Since D enters only state S on receiving input $a_1 a_2 \cdots a_k$, S must be an accepting state of D.

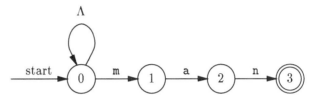

Fig. 10.17. Nondeterministic automaton that recognizes the strings ending in man.

✦ **Example 10.9.** Let us convert the nondeterministic automaton of Fig. 10.10, which we reproduce here as Fig. 10.17, to a deterministic automaton D. We begin with $\{0\}$, which is the start state of D.

The inductive part of the construction requires us to look at each state of D and determine its transitions. For $\{0\}$, we have only to ask where state 0 goes. The answer, which we get by examining Fig. 10.17, is that on any letter except m, state 0 goes only to 0, while on input m, it goes to both 0 and 1. Automaton D therefore needs state $\{0\}$, which it already has, and state $\{0, 1\}$, which we must add. The transitions and states constructed so far for D are shown in Fig. 10.18.

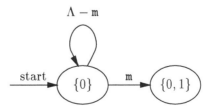

Fig. 10.18. State $\{0\}$ and its transitions.

Next, we must consider the transitions out of $\{0, 1\}$. Examining Fig. 10.17 again, we see that on all inputs except m and a, state 0 goes only to 0, and state 1 goes nowhere. Thus there is a transition from state $\{0, 1\}$ to state $\{0\}$, labeled by all the letters except m and a. On input m, state 1 again goes nowhere, but 0 goes to both 0 and 1. Hence there is a transition from $\{0, 1\}$ to itself, labeled by **m**. Finally, on input **a**, state 0 goes only to itself, but state 1 goes to state 2. Thus there is a transition labeled **a** from state $\{0, 1\}$ to state $\{0, 2\}$. The portion of D constructed so far is shown in Fig. 10.19.

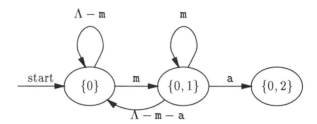

Fig. 10.19. States $\{0\}$ and $\{0, 1\}$ and their transitions.

Now we need to construct the transitions out of state $\{0, 2\}$. On all inputs except **m** and **n**, state 0 goes only to 0, and state 2 goes nowhere, and so there is a transition from $\{0, 2\}$ to $\{0\}$, labeled by all the letters except **m** and **n**. On input **m**, state 2 goes nowhere, and 0 goes to both 0 and 1, and so there is a transition from $\{0, 2\}$ to $\{0, 1\}$ labeled **m**. On input **n**, state 0 goes only to itself and 2 goes to 3. Thus there is a transition labeled **n** from $\{0, 2\}$ to $\{0, 3\}$. This state of D is accepting, since it includes the accepting state of Fig. 10.17, state 3.

Finally, we must supply the transitions out of $\{0, 3\}$. Since state 3 goes nowhere on any input, the transitions out of $\{0, 3\}$ will reflect the transitions out of 0 only, and thus will go to the same states as state $\{0\}$. As the transitions out of $\{0, 3\}$ do not take us to any state of D that we have not already seen, the construction of D is finished. The complete deterministic automaton is shown in Fig. 10.20.

Notice that this deterministic automaton correctly accepts all and only the strings of letters that end in **man**. Intuitively, the automaton will be in state $\{0\}$ whenever the character string so far does not end with any prefix of **man** except the empty string. State $\{0, 1\}$ means that the string seen so far ends in **m**, $\{0, 2\}$ means that it ends in **ma**, and $\{0, 3\}$ means that it ends in **man**. ✦

✦ **Example 10.10.** The nondeterministic automaton of Fig. 10.17 has four states, and its equivalent deterministic automaton of Fig. 10.20 has four states also. It would be nice if all nondeterministic automata converted to small deterministic automata, and many common examples used in compiling of programming languages, for example, do in fact convert to relatively small deterministic automata. Yet there is no guarantee that the deterministic automaton will be small, and a k-state nondeterministic automaton could wind up being converted to a deterministic automaton with as many as 2^k states. That is, the deterministic automaton could have one state for every member of the power set of the set of states of the nondeterministic automaton.

As an example where we get many states, consider the automaton of Fig. 10.14, from the previous section. Since this nondeterministic automaton has 20 states, conceivably the deterministic automaton constructed by the subset construction

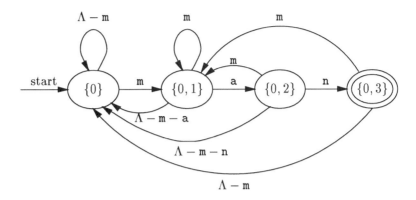

Fig. 10.20. The deterministic automaton D.

A Thought About the Subset Construction

The subset construction is rather tricky to understand. Especially, the idea that states (of the deterministic automaton) can be sets of states (of the nondeterministic automaton) may require some thought and patience to think through. However, this blending of the structured object (the set of states) and the atomic object (a state of the deterministic automaton) into one and the same object is an important concept of computer science. We have seen, and frequently must use, the idea in programs. For example, an argument of a function, say L, apparently atomic, may turn out on closer examination also to be an object with complex structure, for example, a record with fields that connect to other records, thus forming a list. Similarly, the state of D that we called $\{0, 2\}$, for instance, could just as well have been replaced by a simple name, such as "5" or "a," in Fig. 10.20.

could have as many as 2^{20} states or over a million states; these states would be all members of the power set of $\{0, 1, \ldots, 19\}$. It turns out not to be that bad, but there are quite a few states.

We shall not attempt to draw the equivalent deterministic automaton for Fig. 10.14. Rather, let us think about what sets of states we actually need. First, since there is a transition from state 0 to itself on every letter, all sets of states that we actually see will include 0. If the letter **a** has not yet been input, then we cannot get to state 1. However, if we have seen exactly one **a**, we shall be in state 1, no matter what else we have seen. We can make an analogous observation about any of the other letters in **washington**.

If we start Fig. 10.14 in state 0 and feed it a sequence of letters that are a subset of the letters appearing in **washington**, then in addition to being in state 0, we shall also be in some subset of the states 1, 3, 5, 7, 9, 12, 14, 16, and 18. By choosing the input letters properly, we can arrange to be in any of these sets of states. As there are $2^9 = 512$ such sets, there are at least that number of states in the deterministic automaton equivalent to Fig. 10.14.

However, there are even more states, because letter **n** is treated specially in

Fig. 10.14. If we are in state 9, we can also be in state 10, and in fact we shall be in both 9 and 10 if we have seen two **n**'s. Thus, while for the other eight letters we have two choices (e.g., for letter **a**, either include state 1 or don't), for letter **n** we have three choices (include neither of 9 and 10, include 9 only, or include both 9 and 10). Thus there are at least $3 \times 2^8 = 768$ states.

But that is not all. If the input so far ends in one of the letters of **washington**, and we previously saw enough of that letter, then we shall also be in the accepting state corresponding to that letter (e.g., state 2 for **a**). However, we cannot be in two accepting states after the same input. Counting the number of additional sets of states becomes trickier.

Suppose accepting state 2 is a member of the set. Then we know 1 is a member of the set, and of course 0 is a member, but we still have all our options for the states corresponding to the letters other than **a**; that number of sets is 3×2^7, or 384. The same applies if our set includes accepting state 4, 6, 8, 13, 15, 17, or 19; in each case there are 384 sets including that accepting state. The only exception is when accepting state 11 is included (and therefore 9 and 10 are also present). Then, there are only $2^8 = 256$ options. The total number of states in the equivalent deterministic automaton is thus

$$768 + 8 \times 384 + 256 = 4864$$

The first term, 768, counts the sets that have no accepting state. The next term counts the eight cases in which the set includes the accepting state for one of the eight letters other than **n**, and the third term, 256, counts the sets that include state 11. ✦

Why the Subset Construction Works

Clearly, if D is constructed from a nondeterministic automaton N using the subset construction, then D is a deterministic automaton. The reason is that for each input symbol x and each state S of D, we defined a specific state T of D such that the label of the transition from S to T includes x. But how do we know that the automata N and D are equivalent? That is, we need to know that for any input sequence $a_1 a_2 \cdots a_k$, the state S that the automaton D reaches when we

1. Begin at the start state and
2. Follow the path labeled $a_1 a_2 \cdots a_k$

is an accepting state if and only if N accepts $a_1 a_2 \cdots a_k$. Remember that N accepts $a_1 a_2 \cdots a_k$ if and only if there is some path from N's start state, labeled $a_1 a_2 \cdots a_k$, leading to an accepting state of N.

The connection between what D does and what N does is even stronger. If D has a path from its start state to state S labeled $a_1 a_2 \cdots a_k$, then set S, thought of as a set of states of N, is exactly the set of states reached from the start state of N, along some path labeled $a_1 a_2 \cdots a_k$. The relationship is suggested by Fig. 10.21. Since we have defined S to be an accepting state of D exactly when one of the members of S is an accepting state of N, the relationship suggested by Fig. 10.21 is all we need to conclude that either both or neither of D and N accept $a_1 a_2 \cdots a_k$; that is, D and N are equivalent.

We need to prove the relationship of Fig. 10.21; the proof is an induction on k, the length of the input string. The formal statement to be proved by induction on k is that the state $\{s_1, s_2, \ldots, s_n\}$ reached in D by following the path labeled

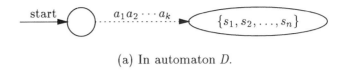

(a) In automaton D.

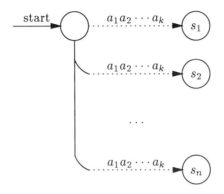

(b) In automaton N.

Fig. 10.21. Relationship between the operation of nondeterministic automaton N and its deterministic counterpart D.

$a_1 a_2 \cdots a_k$ from the start state of D is exactly the set of states of N that are reached from N's start state by following some path labeled $a_1 a_2 \cdots a_k$.

BASIS. Let $k = 0$. A path of length 0 leaves us where we started, that is, in the start state of both automata D and N. Recall that if s_0 is the start state of N, then the start state of D is $\{s_0\}$. Thus the inductive statement holds for $k = 0$.

INDUCTION. Suppose the statement holds for k, and consider an input string

$$a_1 a_2 \cdots a_k a_{k+1}$$

Then the path from the start state of D to state T labeled by $a_1 a_2 \cdots a_k a_{k+1}$ appears as shown in Fig. 10.22; that is, it goes through some state S just before making the last transition to T on input a_{k+1}.

Fig. 10.22. S is the state reached by D just before reaching state T.

We may assume, by the inductive hypothesis, that S is exactly the set of states that automaton N reaches from its start state along paths labeled $a_1 a_2 \cdots a_k$, and we must prove that T is exactly the set of states N reaches from its start state along paths labeled $a_1 a_2 \cdots a_k a_{k+1}$. There are two parts to the proof of this inductive step.

1. We must prove that T does not contain too much; that is, if t is a state of N that is in T, then t is reached by a path labeled $a_1a_2 \cdots a_k a_{k+1}$ from N's start state.

2. We must prove that T contains enough; that is, if t is a state of N reached from the start state along a path labeled $a_1a_2 \cdots a_k a_{k+1}$, then t is in T.

For (1), let t be in T. Then, as suggested by Fig. 10.23, there must be a state s in S that justifies t being in T. That is, there is in N a transition from s to t, and its label includes a_{k+1}. By the inductive hypothesis, since s is in S, there must be a path from the start state of N to s, labeled $a_1a_2 \cdots a_k$. Thus there is a path from the start state of N to t, labeled $a_1a_2 \cdots a_k a_{k+1}$.

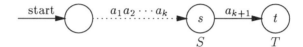

Fig. 10.23. State s in S explains why we put t in T.

Now we must show (2), that if there is a path from the start state of N to t, labeled $a_1a_2 \cdots a_k a_{k+1}$, then t is in T. This path must go through some state s just before making a transition to t on input a_{k+1}. Thus there is a path from the start state of N to s, labeled $a_1a_2 \cdots a_k$. By the inductive hypothesis, s is in set of states S. Since N has a transition from s to t, with a label that includes a_{k+1}, the subset construction applied to set of states S and input symbol a_{k+1}, demands that t be placed in T. Thus t is in T.

Given the inductive hypothesis, we have now shown that T consists of exactly the states of N that are reachable from the start state of N along some path labeled $a_1a_2 \cdots a_k a_{k+1}$. That is the inductive step, and we conclude that the state of the deterministic automaton D reached along the path labeled $a_1a_2 \cdots a_k$ is always the set of N's states reachable along some path with that label. Since the accepting states of D are those that include an accepting state of N, we conclude that D and N accept the same strings; that is, D and N are equivalent, and the subset construction "works."

EXERCISES

10.4.1: Convert your nondeterministic automaton of Exercise 10.3.3 to a deterministic automaton, using the subset construction.

10.4.2: What patterns do the nondeterministic automata of Fig. 10.24(a) to (d) recognize?

10.4.3: Convert the nondeterministic automata of Fig. 10.24(a) to (d) to deterministic finite automata.

Minimization of Automata

One of the issues concerning automata, especially when they are used to design circuits, is how few states are needed to perform a given task. That is, we may ask, given an automaton, whether there is an equivalent automaton with fewer states, and if so, what is the least number of states of any equivalent automaton?

It turns out that if we restrict ourselves to deterministic automata, there is a unique minimum-state deterministic automaton equivalent to any given automaton, and it is fairly easy to find it. The key is to define when two states s and t of a deterministic automaton are *equivalent,* that is, for any input sequence, the paths from s and t labeled by that sequence either both lead to accepting states or neither does. If states s and t are equivalent, then there is no way to tell them apart by feeding inputs to the automaton, and so we can merge s and t into a single state. Actually, we can more easily define when states are not equivalent, as follows.

BASIS. If s is an accepting state and t is not accepting, or vice versa, then s and t are not equivalent.

INDUCTION. If there is some input symbol x such that there are transitions from states s and t on input x to two states that are known not to be equivalent, then s and t are not equivalent.

There are some additional details necessary to make this test work; in particular, we may have to add a "dead state," which is not accepting and has transitions to itself on every input. As a deterministic automaton may have no transition out of a given state on a given symbol, before performing this minimization procedure, we need to add transitions to the dead state from any state, on all inputs for which no other transition exists. We note that there is no similar theory for minimizing nondeterministic automata.

10.4.4*: Some automata have state-input combinations for which there is no transition at all. If state s has no transition on symbol x, we can add a transition from s to a special "dead state" on input x. The dead state is not accepting, and has a transition to itself on every input symbol. Show that adding a "dead state" produces an automaton equivalent to the one with which we started.

10.4.5: Show that if we add a dead state to a deterministic automaton, we can get an equivalent automaton that has paths from the start state labeled by every possible string.

10.4.6*: Show that if we apply the subset construction to a deterministic automaton, we either get the same automaton, with each state s renamed $\{s\}$, or we add a dead state (corresponding to the empty set of states).

10.4.7**: Suppose that we take a deterministic automaton and change every accepting state to nonaccepting and every nonaccepting state to accepting.

a)   How would you describe the language accepted by the new automaton in terms of the language of the old automaton?

Equivalent states (margin note)

Dead state (margin note)

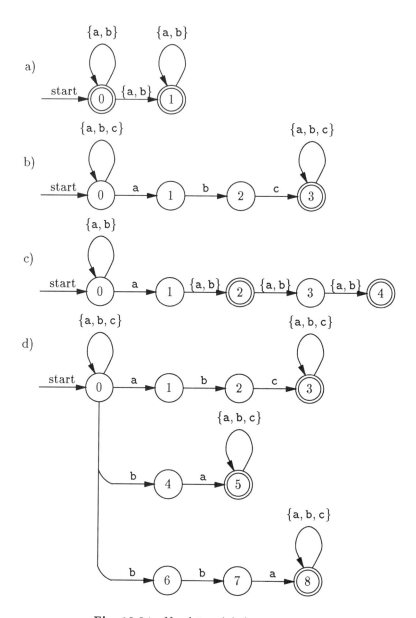

Fig. 10.24. Nondeterministic automata.

b)   Repeat (a) if we first add a dead state to the original automaton.
c)   Repeat (a) if the original automaton is nondeterministic.

✦✦ 10.5 Regular Expressions

An automaton defines a pattern, namely the set of strings labeling paths from the initial state to some accepting state in the graph of the automaton. In this section, we meet *regular expressions*, which are an algebraic way to define patterns. Regular expressions are analogous to the algebra of arithmetic expressions with which we

Notational Convention

We shall continue to use typewriter font for the characters that appear in strings. The regular expression atomic operand for a given character will be denoted by that character in boldface. For instance, **a** is the regular expression corresponding to character **a**. When we need to use a variable, we shall write it in italics. Variables are used to stand for complicated expressions. For instance, we shall use the variable *letter* to stand for "any letter," a set whose regular expression we shall soon meet.

are all familiar, and the relational algebra that we met in Chapter 8. Interestingly, the set of patterns that can be expressed in the regular-expression algebra is exactly the same set of patterns that can be described by automata.

Operands of Regular Expressions

Like all algebras, regular expressions have certain kinds of atomic operands. In the algebra of arithmetic, atomic operands are constants (e.g., integers or reals) or variables whose possible values are constants, and for relational algebra, atomic operands are either fixed relations or variables whose possible values are relations. In the algebra of regular expressions, an atomic operand is one of the following:

1. A character,

2. The symbol ϵ,

3. The symbol $\emptyset$, or

4. A variable whose value can be any pattern defined by a regular expression.

Values of Regular Expressions

Expressions in any algebra have values of a certain type. For arithmetic expressions, values are integers, reals, or whatever type of numbers with which we are working. For relational algebra, the value of an expression is a relation.

For regular expressions, the value of each expression is a pattern consisting of a set of strings often called a *language*. The language denoted by a regular expression E will be referred to as $L(E)$, or the "language of E." The languages of the atomic operands are defined as follows.

Language of a regular expression

1. If **x** is any character, then the regular expression **x** stands for the language $\{\mathbf{x}\}$; that is, $L(\mathbf{x}) = \{\mathbf{x}\}$. Note that this language is a set that contains one string; the string has length 1, and the lone position of that string has the character **x**.

2. $L(\epsilon) = \{\epsilon\}$. The special symbol ϵ as a regular expression denotes the set whose only string is the empty string, or string of length 0.

3. $L(\emptyset) = \emptyset$. The special symbol $\emptyset$ as a regular expression denotes the empty set of strings.

Note that we do not define a value for an atomic operand that is a variable. Such an operand only takes on a value when we replace the variable by a concrete expression, and its value is then whatever value that expression has.

Operators of Regular Expressions

There are three operators used in regular expressions. These can be grouped using parentheses, as in the algebras with which we are familiar. There is an order of precedence and associativity laws that allow us to omit some pairs of parentheses, just as we do in arithmetic expressions. We shall describe the rules regarding parentheses after we examine the operators.

Union

The first, and most familiar, is the *union* operator, which we shall denote $|$.[3] The rule for union is that if R and S are two regular expressions, then $R \mid S$ denotes the union of the languages that R and S denote. That is, $L(R \mid S) = L(R) \cup L(S)$. Recall that $L(R)$ and $L(S)$ are each sets of strings, so the notion of taking their union makes sense.

✦ **Example 10.11.** We know that **a** is a regular expression denoting $\{a\}$, and **b** is a regular expression denoting $\{b\}$. Thus **a** $|$ **b** is a regular expression denoting $\{a, b\}$. That is the set containing the two strings **a** and **b**, each string being of length 1.

Similarly, we can write an expression such as $(\mathbf{a} \mid \mathbf{b}) \mid \mathbf{c}$ to denote the set $\{a, b, c\}$. Since union is an associative operator, that is, it does not matter in what order we group operands when we take the union of three sets, we can omit the parentheses and just write **a** $|$ **b** $|$ **c**. ✦

Concatenation

The second operator for the algebra of regular expressions is called *concatenation*. It is represented by no operator symbol at all, just as multiplication is sometimes written without an operator; for instance, in arithmetic ab denotes the product of a and b. Like union, concatenation is a binary, infix operator. If R and S are regular expressions, then RS is the concatenation of R and S.[4]

$L(RS)$, the language denoted by RS, is formed from the languages $L(R)$ and $L(S)$, as follows. For each string r in $L(R)$ and each string s in $L(S)$, the string rs, the concatenation of strings r and s, is in $L(RS)$. Recall the concatenation of two lists, such as character strings, is formed by taking the elements of the first list, in order, and following them by the elements of the second list, in order.

---

[3] The plus sign $+$ is also commonly used for the union operator in regular expressions; we shall not do so, however.

[4] Technically, we should write RS as $(R)(S)$, to emphasize the fact that R and S are separate expressions and that their parts must not be blended because of precedence rules. The situation is analogous to the fact that if we multiply the arithmetic expression $w + x$ by the arithmetic expression $y + z$, we must write the product as $(w + x)(y + z)$. Note that, because multiplication takes precedence over addition, the product with parentheses omitted, $w + xy + z$, would not be interpreted as the product of $w + x$ and $y + z$. As we shall see, concatenation and union have precedences that make them similar to multiplication and addition, respectively.

Some Tricky Distinctions Among Types

The reader should not be confused by the multiplicity of objects that seem similar, but are actually quite different. For instance, the empty string ϵ is not the same as the empty set $\emptyset$, nor is either the same as the set containing the empty string $\{\epsilon\}$. The first is of type "string" or "list of characters," while the second and third are of type "set of strings."

We should also remember to distinguish between the character **a**, which is of type "character," the string **a** of length 1, which is of type "string," and $\{\mathbf{a}\}$, which as the value of the regular expression **a** is of type "set of strings." Also note that in another context, $\{\mathbf{a}\}$ could be the set containing the character **a**, and we have no notational convention to distinguish the two meanings of $\{\mathbf{a}\}$. However, in the balance of this chapter, $\{\mathbf{a}\}$ will normally have the former interpretation, that is, "set of strings" rather than "set of characters."

✦ **Example 10.12.** Let R be the regular expression **a**, and so $L(R)$ is the set $\{\mathbf{a}\}$. Also let S be the regular expression **b**, so $L(S) = \{\mathbf{b}\}$. Then RS is the expression **ab**. To form $L(RS)$, we need to take every string in $L(R)$ and concatenate it with every string in $L(S)$. In this simple case, both languages $L(R)$ and $L(S)$ are singletons, so we have only one choice from each. We pick **a** from $L(R)$ and **b** from $L(S)$, and concatenate these lists of length 1 to get the string **ab**. Thus $L(RS)$ is $\{\mathbf{ab}\}$. ✦

Example 10.12 can be generalized, in the sense that any string, written in boldface, is a regular expression that denotes the language consisting of one string, the corresponding list of characters. For instance, **then** is a regular expression whose language is $\{\mathtt{then}\}$. We shall see that concatenation is an associative operator, so it doesn't matter how the characters in the regular expression are grouped, and we do not need to use any parentheses.

✦ **Example 10.13.** Now let us look at the concatenation of two regular expressions whose languages are not singleton sets. Let R be the regular expression **a** | (**ab**).[5] The language $L(R)$ is the union of $L(\mathbf{a})$ and $L(\mathbf{ab})$, that is $\{\mathbf{a}, \mathbf{ab}\}$. Let S be the regular expression **c** | (**bc**). Similarly, $L(S) = \{\mathbf{c}, \mathbf{bc}\}$. The regular expression RS is $(\mathbf{a} \mid (\mathbf{ab}))(\mathbf{c} \mid (\mathbf{bc}))$. Note that the parentheses around R and S are required, because of precedence.

	c	bc
a	ac	abc
ab	abc	abbc

Fig. 10.25. Forming the concatenation of $\{a, ab\}$ with $\{c, bc\}$.

---

[5] As we shall see, concatenation takes precedence over union, so the parentheses are redundant.

To discover the strings in $L(RS)$, we pair each of the two strings from $L(R)$ with each of the two strings from $L(S)$. This pairing is suggested in Fig. 10.25. From a in $L(R)$ and c in $L(S)$, we get the string ac. The string abc is obtained in two different ways, either as (a)(bc) or as (ab)(c). Finally, the string abbc is obtained as the concatenation of ab from $L(R)$ and bc from $L(S)$. Thus $L(RS)$ is $\{ac, abc, abbc\}$. ✦

Note that the number of strings in the language $L(RS)$ cannot be greater than the product of the number of strings in $L(R)$ times the number of strings in $L(S)$. In fact, the number of strings in $L(RS)$ is exactly this product, unless there are "coincidences," in which the same string is formed in two or more different ways. Example 10.13 was an instance where the string abc was produced in two ways, and therefore the number of strings in $L(RS)$, which was 3, was one less than the product of the number of strings in the languages of R and S. Similarly, the number of strings in the language $L(R \mid S)$ is no greater than the sum of the number of strings in the languages $L(R)$ and $L(S)$, and can be less only when there are strings in common to $L(R)$ and $L(S)$. As we shall see when we discuss algebraic laws for these operators, there is a close, although not exact, analogy between union and concatenation on one hand, and the arithmetic operators $+$ and $\times$ on the other.

Closure

The third operator is called *Kleene closure* or just *closure*.[6] It is a unary, postfix operator; that is, it takes one operand and it appears after that operand. Closure is denoted by a star, so R^* is the closure of regular expression R. Because the closure operator is of highest precedence, it is often necessary to put parentheses around the R, and write $(R)^*$.

The effect of the closure operator is to say "zero or more occurrences of strings in R." That is, $L(R^*)$ consists of

1. The empty string ϵ, which we can think of as zero occurrences of strings in R.

2. All the strings in $L(R)$; these represent one occurrence of a string in $L(R)$.

3. All the strings in $L(RR)$, the concatenation of $L(R)$ with itself; these represent two occurrences of strings in $L(R)$.

4. All the strings in $L(RRR)$, $L(RRRR)$, and so on, representing three, four, and more occurrences of strings in $L(R)$.

We can informally write

$$R^* = \epsilon \mid R \mid RR \mid RRR \mid \cdots$$

However, we must understand that the expression on the right side of the equals sign is not a regular expression, because it contains an infinite number of occurrences of the union operator. All regular expressions are built from a finite number of occurrences of the three operators.

---

[6] Steven C. Kleene wrote the original paper describing the algebra of regular expressions.

✦ **Example 10.14.** Let $R = \mathbf{a}$. What is $L(R^*)$? Surely ϵ is in this language, as it must be in any closure. The string $\mathbf{a}$, which is the only string in $L(R)$, is in the language, as is $\mathbf{aa}$ from $L(RR)$, $\mathbf{aaa}$ from $L(RRR)$, and so on. That is, $L(\mathbf{a}^*)$ is the set of strings of zero or more $\mathbf{a}$'s, or $\{\epsilon, \mathbf{a}, \mathbf{aa}, \mathbf{aaa}, \ldots\}$. ✦

✦ **Example 10.15.** Now let R be the regular expression $\mathbf{a} \mid \mathbf{b}$, so $L(R) = \{\mathbf{a}, \mathbf{b}\}$, and consider what $L(R^*)$ is. Again, this language contains ϵ, representing zero occurrences of strings from $L(R)$. One occurrence of a string from R gives us $\{\mathbf{a}, \mathbf{b}\}$ for $L(R^*)$. Two occurrences give us the four strings $\{\mathbf{aa}, \mathbf{ab}, \mathbf{ba}, \mathbf{bb}\}$, three occurrences give us the eight strings of length three that consist of $\mathbf{a}$'s and/or $\mathbf{b}$'s, and so on. Thus $L(R^*)$ is all strings of $\mathbf{a}$'s and $\mathbf{b}$'s of any finite length whatsoever. ✦

Precedence of Regular Expression Operators

As we have mentioned informally above, there is a conventional order of precedence for the three operators union, concatenation, and closure. This order is

1.   Closure (highest), then

2.   Concatenation, then

3.   Union (lowest).

Thus when interpreting any expression, we first group the closure operators by finding the shortest expression immediately to the left of a given * that has the form of an expression (i.e., parentheses, if any, are balanced). We may place parentheses around this expression and the *.

Next, we may consider the concatenation operators, from the left. For each, we find the smallest expression immediately to the left and the smallest expression immediately to the right, and we put parentheses around this pair of expressions. Finally, we consider union operators from the left. We find the smallest expression immediately to the left and right of each union, and we place parentheses around this pair of expressions with the union symbol in the middle.

✦ **Example 10.16.** Consider the expression $\mathbf{a} \mid \mathbf{bc}^*\mathbf{d}$. We first consider the *'s. There is only one, and to its left, the smallest expression is $\mathbf{c}$. We may thus group this * with its operand, as $\mathbf{a} \mid \mathbf{b}(\mathbf{c}^*)\mathbf{d}$.

Next, we consider the concatenations in the above expression. There are two, one between the $\mathbf{b}$ and the left parenthesis, and the second between the right parenthesis and the $\mathbf{d}$. Considering the first, we find the expression $\mathbf{b}$ immediately to the left, but to the right we must go until we include the right parenthesis, since expressions must have balanced parentheses. Thus the operands of the first concatenation are $\mathbf{b}$ and $(\mathbf{c}^*)$. We place parentheses around these to get the expression

$$\mathbf{a} \mid \big(\mathbf{b}(\mathbf{c}^*)\big)\mathbf{d}$$

For the second concatenation, the shortest expression immediately to the left is now $\big(\mathbf{b}(\mathbf{c}^*)\big)$, and the shortest expression immediately to the right is $\mathbf{d}$. With parentheses added to group the operands of this concatenation, the expression becomes

$$\mathbf{a} \mid \Big(\big(\mathbf{b}(\mathbf{c}^*)\big)\mathbf{d}\Big)$$

Finally, we must consider the unions. There is only one; its left operand is **a**, and its right operand is the rest of the expression above. Technically, we must place parentheses around the entire expression, yielding

$$\left(\mathbf{a} \mid \left(\left(\mathbf{b}(\mathbf{c}^*)\right)\mathbf{d}\right)\right)$$

but the outer parentheses are redundant. ✦

Additional Examples of Regular Expressions

We close the section with some more complex examples of regular expressions.

✦ **Example 10.17.** We can extend the idea from Example 10.15 to say "strings of any length consisting of symbols $\mathbf{a}_1, \mathbf{a}_2, \ldots, \mathbf{a}_n$" with the regular expression

$$(\mathbf{a}_1 \mid \mathbf{a}_2 \mid \cdots \mid \mathbf{a}_n)^*$$

For instance, we can describe C identifiers as follows. First, define the regular expression

$$letter = \mathbf{A} \mid \mathbf{B} \mid \cdots \mid \mathbf{Z} \mid \mathbf{a} \mid \mathbf{b} \mid \cdots \mid \mathbf{z} \mid {}_-$$

That is, the "letters" in C are the upper- and lowercase letters and the underscore. Similarly define

$$digit = \mathbf{0} \mid \mathbf{1} \mid \cdots \mid \mathbf{9}$$

Then the regular expression

$$letter(letter \mid digit)^*$$

represents all strings of letters, digits, and underscores not beginning with a digit. ✦

✦ **Example 10.18.** Now let us consider a regular expression that is somewhat harder to write: the bounce filter problem discussed in Example 10.2. Recall that we described an automaton that made output 1 whenever the input ended in a sequence of 1's, loosely interpreted. That is, we decided we were in a sequence of 1's as soon as we saw two 1's in a row, but after deciding we were seeing 1's, a single 0 would not dissuade us from that conclusion. Thus the output of the automaton of Example 10.2 is 1 whenever the input ends in a sequence of two 1's, followed by anything, as long as each 0 is either followed immediately by a 1 or is the last input character seen so far. We express this condition by the regular expression

$$(\mathbf{0} \mid \mathbf{1})^*\mathbf{11}(\mathbf{1} \mid \mathbf{01})^*(\epsilon \mid \mathbf{0})$$

To understand this expression, first note that $(\mathbf{0} \mid \mathbf{1})^*$ represents any string of 0's and 1's. These strings must be followed by two 1's, as represented by the expression $\mathbf{11}$. Thus the language of $(\mathbf{0} \mid \mathbf{1})^*\mathbf{11}$ is all strings of 0's and 1's that end (at least) in two 1's.

Next, the expression $(\mathbf{1} \mid \mathbf{01})^*$ represents all strings of 0's and 1's in which all 0's are followed by 1's. That is, the strings in the language for this expression are built by concatenating strings $\mathbf{1}$ and $\mathbf{01}$ in any order and in any quantity. While $\mathbf{1}$ lets us add a 1 to the string being formed at any time, $\mathbf{01}$ forces us to follow any

0 by a 1. Thus the expression $(0 \mid 1)*11(1 \mid 01)*$ represents all strings of 0's and 1's that end in two 1's followed by any sequence in which 0's, if any, are followed immediately by 1's. The final factor, $(\epsilon \mid 0)$, says "an optional 0," that is, the strings just described may be followed by a 0, or not, as we choose. ✦

EXERCISES

10.5.1: In Example 10.13 we considered the regular expression $(a \mid ab)(c \mid bc)$, and saw that its language consisted of the three strings **ac**, **abc**, and **abbc**, that is, an **a** and a **c**, separated by from zero to two **b**'s. Write two other regular expressions that define the same language.

10.5.2: Write regular expressions that define the following languages.

a) The strings for the six C comparison operators, =, <=, <, >=, >, and !=.
b) All strings of 0's and 1's that end in 0.
c) All strings of 0's and 1's with at least one 1.
d) All strings of 0's and 1's with at most one 1.
e) All strings of 0's and 1's such that the third position from the right end is 1.
f) All strings of lower-case letters that are in sorted order.

10.5.3*: Write regular expressions that define the following languages.

a) All strings of **a**'s and **b**'s such that all runs of **a**'s are of even length. That is, strings such as **bbbaabaaaa**, **aaaabb**, and ϵ are in the language; **abbabaa** and **aaa** are not.

b) Strings that represent numbers of type **float** in C.

c) Strings of 0's and 1's having even parity, that is, an even number of 1's. *Hint*: Think of even-parity strings as the concatenation of elementary strings with even parity, either a single 0 or a pair of 1's separated only by 0's.

10.5.4**: Write regular expressions that define the following languages.

a) The set of all C identifiers that are not keywords. If you forget some of the keywords, it is not serious. The point of the exercise is to express strings that are *not* in some reasonably large set of strings.

b) All strings of **a**'s, **b**'s, and **c**'s such that no two consecutive positions are the same character.

c) The set of all strings of two lower-case letters that are not the same. *Hint*: You can "brute-force" this one, but there are 650 pairs of distinct letters. A better idea is to do some grouping. For example, the relatively short expression

$$(a \mid b \mid \cdots \mid m)(n \mid o \mid \cdots \mid z)$$

covers 169 of the 650 pairs.

d) All strings of 0's and 1's that, as a binary number, represent an integer that is a multiple of 3.

10.5.5: Put parentheses in the following regular expressions to indicate the proper grouping of operands according to the precedence of operators union, concatenation, and closure.

a)   **a | bc | de**
b)   **a | b* | (a | b)*a**

10.5.6: Remove redundant parentheses from the following expressions, that is, remove parentheses whose grouping would be implied by the precedence of operators and the fact that union and concatenation are each associative (and therefore, the grouping of adjacent unions or adjacent concatenations is irrelevant).

a)   **(ab)(cd)**
b) $\Big(\mathbf{a} \mid (\mathbf{b(c)}^*)\Big)$
c) $\Big(((\mathbf{a}) \mid \mathbf{b})(\mathbf{c} \mid \mathbf{d})\Big)$

10.5.7*: Describe the languages defined by the following regular expressions.

a) $\emptyset \mid \epsilon$
b) $\epsilon \mathbf{a}$
c) $(\mathbf{a} \mid \mathbf{b})^*$
d) $(\mathbf{a}^*\mathbf{b}^*)^*$
e) $(\mathbf{a}^*\mathbf{ba}^*\mathbf{b})^*\mathbf{a}^*$
f) ϵ^*
g) R^{**}, where R is any regular expression.

✥ 10.6   The UNIX Extensions to Regular Expressions

The UNIX operating system has several commands that use a regular-expression like notation to describe patterns. Even if the reader is not familiar with UNIX or with most of these commands, these notations are useful to know. We find regular expressions used in at least three kinds of commands.

1.   *Editors.* The UNIX editors **ed** and **vi**, as well as most modern text editors, allow the user to scan text for a place where an instance of a given pattern is found. The pattern is specified by a regular expression, although there is no general union operator, just "character classes," which we shall discuss below.

2.   *The pattern-matching program* **grep** *and its cousins.* The UNIX command **grep** scans a file and examines each line. If the line contains a substring that matches the pattern specified by a regular expression, then the line is printed (**grep** stands for "*g*lobally search for *r*egular *e*xpression and *p*rint"). The command **grep** itself allows only a subset of the regular expressions, but the extended command **egrep** allows the full regular expression notation, including some other extensions. The command **awk** allows full regular expression searching, and also treats lines of text as if they were tuples of a relation, thus allowing operations of relational algebra like selection and projection to be performed on files.

3.   *Lexical analysis.* The UNIX command **lex** is useful for writing a piece of a compiler and for many similar tasks. The first thing a compiler must do is partition a program into *tokens,* which are substrings that fit together logically. Examples are identifiers, constants, keywords such as **then**, and operators such as + or <=. Each token type can be specified as a regular expression; for instance, Example 10.17 showed us how to specify the token class "identifier."

Token

The **lex** command allows the user to specify the token classes by regular expressions. It then produces a program that serves as a *lexical analyzer,* that is, a program that partitions its input into tokens.

Character Classes

Often, we need to write a regular expression that denotes a set of characters, or strictly speaking, a set of character strings of length one, each string consisting of a different character in the set. Thus in Example 10.17 we defined the expression *letter* to denote any of the strings consisting of one upper- or lower-case letter, and we defined the expression *digit* to denote any of the strings consisting of a single digit. These expressions tend to be rather long, and UNIX provides some important shorthands.

First, we can enclose any list of characters in square brackets, to stand for the regular expression that is the union of these letters. Such an expression is called a *character class.* For example, the expression [**aghinostw**] denotes the set of letters appearing in the word **washington**, and [**aghinostw**]* denotes the set of strings composed of those letters only.

Second, we do not always have to list all the characters explicitly. Recall that characters are almost invariably coded in ASCII. This code assigns bit strings, which are naturally interpreted as integers, to the various characters, and it does so in a rational way. For instance, the capital letters are assigned consecutive integers. Likewise, the lower-case letters are assigned consecutive integers, and the digits are assigned consecutive integers.

If we put a dash between two characters, we denote not only those characters, but also all the characters whose codes lie between their codes.

◆ **Example 10.19.** We can define the upper- and lower-case letters by [**A-Za-z**]. The first three characters, **A-Z**, represent all the characters whose codes lie between those for **A** and **Z**, that is, all the upper-case letters. The next three characters, **a-z**, similarly denote all the lower-case letters.

Incidentally, because the dash has this special meaning, we must be careful if we want to define a character class including **-**. We must place the dash either first or last in the list. For instance, we could specify the set of four arithmetic operators by [**-+*/**], but it would be an error to write [**+-*/**], because then the range **+-*** would denote all the characters whose codes are between the codes for **+** and *****. ◆

Line Beginning and Ending

Because UNIX commands so frequently deal with single lines of text, the UNIX regular expression notation includes special symbols that denote the beginning and end of a line. The symbol **^** denotes the beginning of a line, and **$** denotes the end of a line.

◆ **Example 10.20.** The automaton of Fig. 10.12 in Section 10.3, started at the beginning of a line, will accept that line exactly when the line consists only of letters in the word **washington**. We can express this pattern as a UNIX regular expression: **^[aghinostw]*$**. In words, the pattern is "the beginning of the line, followed by any sequence of letters from the word **washington**, followed by the end of the line."

Giving Characters Their Literal Meaning

Escape
character

Incidentally, since the characters ^ and $ are given a special meaning in regular expressions, it would seem that we do not have any way to specify these characters themselves in UNIX regular expressions. However, UNIX uses the backslash, \, as an *escape character*. If we precede ^ or $ by a backslash, then the combination of two characters is interpreted as the second character's literal meaning, rather than its special meaning. For instance, \$ represents the character $ within a UNIX regular expression. Likewise, two backslashes are interpreted as a single backslash, without the special meaning of an escape character. The string \\$ in a UNIX regular expression denotes the character backslash followed by the end of the line.

There are a number of other characters that are given special meanings by UNIX in certain situations, and these characters can always be referred to literally, that is, without their special meaning, by preceding them by a backslash. For example, square brackets must be treated this way in regular expressions to avoid interpreting them as character-class delimiters.

As an example of how this regular expression is used, the UNIX command line

```
grep '^[aghinostw]*$' /usr/dict/words
```

will print all the words in the dictionary that consist only of letters from **washington**. UNIX requires, in this case, that the regular expression be written as a quoted string. The effect of the command is that each line of the specified file /usr/dict/words is examined. If it has any substring that is in the set of strings denoted by the regular expression, then the line is printed; otherwise, the line is not printed. Note that the line beginning and ending symbols are essential here. Suppose they were missing. Since the empty string is in the language denoted by the regular expression [aghinostw]*, we would find that every line has a substring (namely ϵ) that is in the language of the regular expression, and thus every line would be printed. ✦

The Wild Card Symbol

The character . in UNIX regular expressions stands for "any character but the newline character."

✦ **Example 10.21.** The regular expression

.*a.*e.*i.*o.*u.*

denotes all strings that contain the vowels, in order. We could use **grep** with this regular expression to scan the dictionary for all words with the vowels in increasing order. However, it is more efficient to omit the .* from the beginning and end, because **grep** searches for the specified pattern as a substring, rather than as the whole line, unless we include the line beginning and ending symbols explicitly. Thus the command

```
grep 'a.*e.*i.*o.*u' /usr/dict/words
```

will find and print all the words that have **aeiou** as a subsequence.

The fact that the dots will match characters other than letters is unimportant, since there are no other characters besides letters and the newline character in the file **/usr/dict/words**. However, if the dot could match the newline character, then this regular expression could allow **grep** to use several lines together to find one occurrence of the vowels in order. It is for examples like this one that the dot is defined not to match the newline character. ✦

Additional Operators

The regular expressions in the UNIX commands **awk** and **egrep** also include some additional operators.

1. Unlike **grep**, the commands **awk** and **egrep** also permit the union operator | in their regular expressions.

2. The unary postfix operators ? and $^+$ do not allow us to define additional languages, but they often make it easier to express languages. If R is a regular expression, then R? stands for $\epsilon \mid R$, that is, an optional R. Thus $L(R?)$ is $L(R) \cup \{\epsilon\}$. R^+ stands for RR^*, or equivalently, "one or more occurrences of words from R." Thus,

$$L(R^+) = L(R) \cup L(RR) \cup L(RRR) \cdots$$

In particular, if ϵ is in $L(R)$, then $L(R^+)$ and $L(R^*)$ denote the same language. If ϵ is not in $L(R)$, then $L(R^+)$ denotes $L(R^*) - \{\epsilon\}$. The operators $^+$ and ? have the same associativity and precedence as *.

✦ **Example 10.22.** Suppose we want to specify by a regular expression real numbers consisting of a nonempty string of digits with one decimal point. It would not be correct to write this expression as [0-9]*\.[0-9]*, because then the string consisting of a dot alone would be considered a real number. One way to write the expression using **egrep** is

[0-9]$^+$\.[0-9]* | \.[0-9]$^+$

Here, the first term of the union covers those numbers that have at least one digit to the left of the decimal point, and the second term covers those numbers that begin with the decimal point, and that therefore must have at least one digit following the decimal point. Note that a backslash is put before the dot so that the dot does not acquire the conventional "wild card" meaning. ✦

✦ **Example 10.23.** We can scan input for all lines whose letters are in strictly increasing alphabetical order with the **egrep** command

egrep '^a?b?c?d?e?f?g?h?i?j?k?l?m?n?o?p?q?r?s?t?u?v?w?x?y?z?$'

That is, we scan each line to see if between the beginning and end of the line there is an optional **a**, and optional **b**, and so on. A line containing the word **adept**, for instance, matches this expression, because the ?'s after **a**, **d**, **e**, **p**, and **t** can be interpreted as "one occurrence," while the other ?'s can be interpreted as "zero occurrences," that is, ϵ. ✦

EXERCISES

10.6.1: Write expressions for the following character classes.

a) All characters that are operators or punctuation symbols in C. Examples are + and parentheses.

b) All the lower-case vowels.

c) All the lower-case consonants.

10.6.2*: If you have UNIX available, write **egrep** programs to examine the file

/usr/dict/words

and find

a) All words that end in **dous**.

b) All words that have only one vowel.

c) All words that have alternating consonants and vowels.

d) All words that have four or more consecutive consonants.

❖❖ 10.7   Algebraic Laws for Regular Expressions

It is possible for two regular expressions to denote the same language, just as two arithmetic expressions can denote the same function of their operands. As an example, the arithmetic expressions $x + y$ and $y + x$ each denote the same function of x and y, because addition is commutative. Similarly, the regular expressions $R \mid S$ and $S \mid R$ denote the same languages, no matter what regular expressions we substitute for R and S; the justification is that union is also a commutative operation.

Often, it is useful to simplify regular expressions. We shall see shortly that, when we construct regular expressions from automata, we often construct a regular expression that is unnecessarily complex. A repertoire of algebraic equivalences may allow us to "simplify" expressions, that is, replace one regular expression by another that involves fewer operands and/or operators, yet that denotes the same language. The process is analogous to what we go through when we manipulate arithmetic expressions to simplify an unwieldy expression. For example, we might multiply two large polynomials and then simplify the result by grouping similar terms. As another example, we simplified expressions of relational algebra in Section 8.9 to allow faster evaluation.

Equivalent regular expressions

Two regular expressions R and S are *equivalent*, written $R \equiv S$, if $L(R) = L(S)$. If so, we say that $R \equiv S$ is an *equivalence*. In what follows, we shall assume that R, S, and T are arbitrary regular expressions, and state our equivalences with these operands.

Proving Equivalences

In this section we prove a number of equivalences involving regular expressions. Recall that an equivalence between two regular expressions is a claim that the languages of these two expressions are equal, no matter what languages we substitute for their variables. We thus prove an equivalence by showing the equality of two languages, that is, two sets of strings. In general, we prove that set S_1 equals set S_2 by proving containment in both directions. That is, we prove $S_1 \subseteq S_2$, and we also prove $S_2 \subseteq S_1$. Both directions are necessary to prove equality of sets.

Ways Union and Concatenation Resemble Plus and Times

In this section, we shall enumerate the most important equivalences involving the regular expression operators union, concatenation, and closure. We begin with the analogy between union and concatenation, on one hand, and addition and multiplication on the other. This analogy is not exact, as we shall see, primarily because concatenation is not commutative, while multiplication is, of course. However, there are many similarities between the two pairs of operations.

To begin, both union and concatenation have identities. The identity for union is $\emptyset$, and for concatenation the identity is ϵ.

1. *Identity for union.* $(\emptyset \mid R) \equiv (R \mid \emptyset) \equiv R$.

2. *Identity for concatenation.* $\epsilon R \equiv R\epsilon \equiv R$.

It should be obvious from the definition of the empty set and union why (1) is true. To see why (2) holds true, if string x is in $L(\epsilon R)$, then x is the concatenation of a string in $L(\epsilon)$ and a string r that is in $L(R)$. But the only string in $L(\epsilon)$ is ϵ itself, and so we know that $x = \epsilon r$. However, the empty string concatenated with any string r is just r itself, and so $x = r$. That is, x is in $L(R)$. Similarly, we can see that if x is in $L(R\epsilon)$, then x is in $L(R)$.

To prove the pair of equivalences (2) we not only have to show that everything in $L(\epsilon R)$ or $L(R\epsilon)$ is in $L(R)$, but we must also show the converse, that everything in $L(R)$ is in $L(\epsilon R)$ and in $L(R\epsilon)$. If r is in $L(R)$, then ϵr is in $L(\epsilon R)$. But $\epsilon r = r$, and so r is in $L(\epsilon R)$. The same reasoning tells us that r is also in $L(R\epsilon)$. We have thus shown that $L(R)$ and $L(\epsilon R)$ are the same language and that $L(R)$ and $L(R\epsilon)$ are the same language, which are the equivalences of (2).

Thus $\emptyset$ is analogous to 0 in arithmetic, and ϵ is analogous to 1. There is another way the analogy holds. $\emptyset$ is an *annihilator* for concatenation; that is,

3. *Annihilator for concatenation.* $\emptyset R \equiv R\emptyset \equiv \emptyset$. In other words, when we concatenate the empty set with anything, we get the empty set. Analogously, 0 is an annihilator for multiplication, since $0 \times x = x \times 0 = 0$.

We can see why (3) is true as follows. In order for there to be some string x in $L(\emptyset R)$, we would have to form x by concatenating a string from $L(\emptyset)$ with a string from $L(R)$. Since there is no string in $L(\emptyset)$, there is no way we can form x. A similar argument shows that $L(R\emptyset)$ must be empty.

The next equivalences are the commutative and associative laws for union that we discussed in Chapter 7.

4. *Commutativity of union.* $(R \mid S) \equiv (S \mid R)$.

5. *Associativity of union.* $\big((R \mid S) \mid T\big) \equiv \big(R \mid (S \mid T)\big)$.

As we mentioned, concatenation is also associative. That is,

6. *Associativity of concatenation.* $\big((RS)T\big) \equiv \big(R(ST)\big)$.

To see why (6) holds true, suppose string x is in $L\big((RS)T\big)$. Then x is the concatenation of some string y in $L(RS)$ and some string t in $L(T)$. Also, y must be the concatenation of some r in $L(R)$ and some s in $L(S)$. Thus $x = yt = rst$. Now consider $L\big(R(ST)\big)$. The string st must be in $L(ST)$, and so rst, which is x, is in $L\big(R(ST)\big)$. Thus every string x in $L\big((RS)T\big)$ is also in $L\big(R(ST)\big)$. A similar argument tells us that every string in $L\big(R(ST)\big)$ must also be in $L\big((RS)T\big)$. Thus these two languages are the same, and the equivalence (6) holds.

Next, we have the distributive laws of concatenation over union, that is,

7. *Left distributivity of concatenation over union.* $\big(R(S \mid T)\big) \equiv (RS \mid RT)$.

8. *Right distributivity of concatenation over union.* $\big((S \mid T)R\big) \equiv (SR \mid TR)$.

Let us see why (7) holds; (8) is similar and is left for an exercise. If x is in

$$L\big(R(S \mid T)\big)$$

then $x = ry$, where r is in $L(R)$ and y is either in $L(S)$ or in $L(T)$, or both. If y is in $L(S)$, then x is in $L(RS)$, and if y is in $L(T)$, then x is in $L(RT)$. In either case, x is in $L(RS \mid RT)$. Thus everything in $L\big(R(S \mid T)\big)$ is in $L(RS \mid RT)$.

We must also prove the converse, that everything in $L(RS \mid RT)$ is in

$$L\big(R(S \mid T)\big)$$

If x is in the former language, then x is either in $L(RS)$ or in $L(RT)$. Suppose x is in $L(RS)$. Then $x = rs$, where r is in $L(R)$ and s is in $L(S)$. Thus s is in $L(S \mid T)$, and therefore x is in $L\big(R(S \mid T)\big)$. Similarly, if x is in $L(RT)$, we can show that x must be in $L\big(R(S \mid T)\big)$. We have now shown containment in both directions, which proves the equivalence (7).

Ways Union and Concatenation Differ from Plus and Times

One reason that union fails to be analogous to addition is the idempotent law. That is, union is idempotent, but addition is not.

9. *Idempotence of union.* $(R \mid R) \equiv R$.

Concatenation also deviates from multiplication in an important way, since concatenation is not commutative, while multiplication of reals or integers is commutative. To see why RS is not in general equivalent to SR, take a simple example such as $R = \mathbf{a}$ and $S = \mathbf{b}$. Then $L(RS) = \{\mathbf{ab}\}$, while $L(SR) = \{\mathbf{ba}\}$, a different set.

Equivalences Involving Closure

There are a number of useful equivalences involving the closure operator.

10. $\emptyset^* \equiv \epsilon$. You may check that both sides denote the language $\{\epsilon\}$.

11. $RR^* \equiv R^*R$. Note that both sides are equivalent to R^+ in the extended notation of Section 10.6.

12. $(RR^* \mid \epsilon) \equiv R^*$. That is, the union of R^+ and the empty string is equivalent to R^*.

EXERCISES

10.7.1: Prove that the right distributive law of concatenation over union, equivalence (8), holds.

10.7.2: The equivalences $\emptyset\emptyset \equiv \emptyset$ and $\epsilon\epsilon \equiv \epsilon$ follow from equivalences already stated, by substitution for variables. Which equivalences do we use?

10.7.3: Prove equivalences (10) through (12).

10.7.4: Prove that

a) $(R \mid R^*) \equiv R^*$
b) $(\epsilon \mid R^*) \equiv R^*$

10.7.5*: Are there examples of particular regular expressions R and S that are "commutative," in the sense that $RS = SR$ for these particular expressions? Give a proof if not, or some examples if so.

10.7.6*: The operand $\emptyset$ is not needed in regular expressions, except that without it, we could not find a regular expression whose language is the empty set. Call a regular expression $\emptyset$-*free* if it has no occurrences of $\emptyset$. Prove by induction on the number of operator occurrences in a $\emptyset$-free regular expression R, that $L(R)$ is not the empty set. *Hint*: The next section gives an example of an induction on the number of operator occurrences of a regular expression.

$\emptyset$-**free regular expression**

10.7.7**: Show by induction on the number of operator occurrences in a regular expression R, that R is equivalent to either the regular expression $\emptyset$, or some $\emptyset$-free regular expression.

❖❖ 10.8   From Regular Expressions to Automata

Remember our initial discussion of automata in Section 10.2, where we observed a close relationship between deterministic automata and programs that used the concept of "state" to distinguish the roles played by different parts of the program. We said then that designing deterministic automata is often a good way to design such programs. However, we also saw that deterministic automata could be hard to design. We saw in Section 10.3 that sometimes nondeterministic automata were easier to design, and that the subset construction allows us to turn any nondeterministic automaton into a deterministic one. Now that we have met regular expressions, we see that often it is even easier to write a regular expression than it is to design a nondeterministic automaton.

Thus, it is good news that there is a way to convert any regular expression into a nondeterministic automaton, and from there we can use the subset construction to convert to a deterministic automaton. In fact, we shall see in the next section that it is also possible to convert any automaton into a regular expression whose

Not All Languages Are Described by Automata

While we have seen many languages that can be described by automata or regular expressions, there are languages that cannot be so described. The intuition is that "automata cannot count." That is, if we feed an automaton with n states a sequence of n of the same symbol, it must twice enter the same state. It then cannot remember exactly how many symbols it has seen. Thus it is not possible, for example, for an automaton to recognize all and only the strings of balanced parentheses. Since regular expressions and automata define the same languages, there is likewise no regular expression whose language is exactly the strings of balanced parentheses. We shall consider the matter of what languages are not definable by automata in the next chapter.

language is exactly the set of strings that the automaton accepts. Thus automata and regular expressions have exactly the same capability to describe languages.

In this section, we need to do a number of things to show how regular expressions are converted to automata.

1. We introduce automata with ϵ-transitions, that is, with arcs labeled ϵ. These arcs are used in paths but do not contribute to the labels of paths. This form of automaton is an intermediate between regular expressions and the automata discussed earlier in this chapter.

2. We show how to convert any regular expression to an automaton with ϵ-transitions that defines the same language.

3. We show how to convert any automaton with ϵ-transitions to an automaton without ϵ-transitions that accepts the same language.

Automata with Epsilon-Transitions

We first extend our notion of automata to allow arcs labeled ϵ. Such automata still accept a string s if and only if there is a path labeled s from the start state to an accepting state. However, note that ϵ, the empty string, is "invisible" in strings, and so when constructing the label for a path we in effect delete all the ϵ's and use only the "real" characters.

♦ **Example 10.24.** Consider the automaton with ϵ-transitions shown in Fig. 10.26. Here, state 0 is the start state, and state 3 is the lone accepting state. One path from state 0 to state 3 is

$$0, 4, 5, 6, 7, 8, 7, 8, 9, 3$$

The labels of the arcs form the sequence

$$\epsilon \, b \, \epsilon \, \epsilon \, c \, \epsilon \, c \, \epsilon \, \epsilon$$

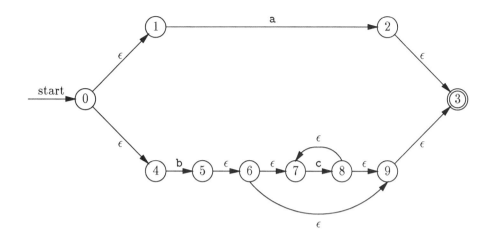

Fig. 10.26. An automaton with ε-transitions for **a | bc***.

When we remember that ε concatenated with any other string is that other string, we see we can "drop out" the ε's to get the string **bcc**, which is the label of the path in question.

You can probably discover that the paths from state 0 to state 3 are labeled by all and only the strings **a**, **b**, **bc**, **bcc**, **bccc**, and so on. A regular expression for this set is **a | bc***, and we shall see that the automaton of Fig. 10.26 is constructed naturally from that expression. ✦

From Expressions to Automata with Epsilon-Transitions

We convert a regular expression to an automaton using an algorithm derived from a complete induction on the number of operator occurrences in the regular expression. The idea is similar to a structural induction on trees that we introduced in Section 5.5, and the correspondence becomes clearer if we represent regular expressions by their expression trees, with atomic operands at the leaves and operators at interior nodes. The statement that we shall prove is:

STATEMENT $S(n)$: If R is a regular expression with n occurrences of operators and no variables as atomic operands, then there is an automaton A with ε-transitions that accepts those strings in $L(R)$ and no others. Moreover, A has

1. Only one accepting state,
2. No arcs into its start state, and
3. No arcs out of its accepting state.

BASIS. If $n = 0$, then R must be an atomic operand, which is either $\emptyset$, ε, or **x** for some symbol **x**. In these three cases, we can design a 2-state automaton that meets the requirements of the statement $S(0)$. These automata are shown in Fig. 10.27.

It is important to understand that we create a new automaton, with states distinct from those of any other automaton, for each occurrence of an operand in the regular expression. For instance, if there were three occurrences of **a** in the expression, we would create three different automata, with six states in all, each similar to Fig. 10.27(c), but with **a** in place of **x**.

The automaton of Fig. 10.27(a) evidently accepts no strings, since you cannot get from the start state to the accepting state; thus its language is $\emptyset$. Figure 10.27(b) is suitable for ϵ, since it accepts the empty string but no other. Figure 10.27(c) is an automaton for accepting only the string **x**. We can create new automata with different values of the symbol **x** as we choose. Note that each of these automata satisfies the three requirements stated above; there is one accepting state, no arcs into the start state and no arcs out of the accepting state.

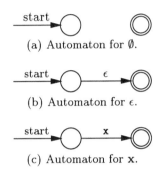

(a) Automaton for $\emptyset$.

(b) Automaton for ϵ.

(c) Automaton for **x**.

Fig. 10.27. Automata for basis cases.

INDUCTION. Now suppose that $S(i)$ is true for all $i \leq n$; that is, for any regular expression R with up to n operator occurrences, there is an automaton satisfying the conditions of the inductive hypothesis and accepting all and only the strings in $L(R)$. Now, let R be a regular expression with $n + 1$ operator occurrences. We focus on the "outermost" operator in R; that is, R can only be of the form $R_1 \mid R_2$, $R_1 R_2$, or $R_1{}^*$, depending on whether union, concatenation, or closure was the last operator used when R was formed.

In any of these three cases, R_1 and R_2 cannot have more than n operators, because there is one operator of R that is not part of either.[7] Thus the inductive hypothesis applies to R_1 and R_2 in all three cases. We can prove $S(n + 1)$ by consideration of these cases in turn.

Case 1. If $R = R_1 \mid R_2$, then we construct the automaton of Fig. 10.28(a). We do so by taking the automata for R_1 and R_2 and adding two new states, one the start state and the other the accepting state. The start state of the automaton for R has ϵ-transitions to the start states of the automata for R_1 and R_2. The accepting states of those two automata have ϵ-transitions to the accepting state of the automaton for R. However, the start and accepting states of the automata for R_1 and R_2 are not start or accepting states in the constructed automaton.

The reason that this construction works is that the only ways to get from the start state to the accepting state in the automaton for R is to follow an ϵ-labeled arc

---

[7] Let us not forget that even though concatenation is represented by juxtaposition, rather than a visible operator symbol, uses of concatenation still count as operator occurrences when deciding how many operator occurrences R has.

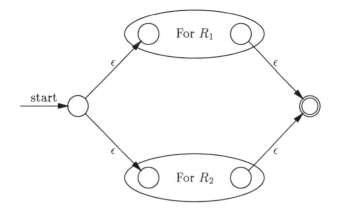

(a) Constructing the automaton for the union of two regular expressions.

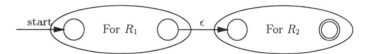

(b) Constructing the automaton for the concatenation of two regular expressions.

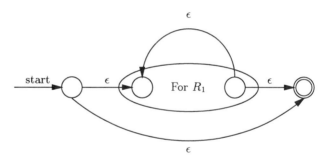

(c) Constructing the automaton for the closure of a regular expression.

Fig. 10.28. Inductive part of the construction of an automaton from a regular expression.

to the start state of the automaton for R_1 or that for R_2. Then, we must follow a path in the chosen automaton to get to its accepting state, and then an ϵ-transition to the accepting state of the automaton for R. This path is labeled by some string s that the automaton we traveled through accepts, because we go from the start state to the accepting state of that automaton. Therefore, s is either in $L(R_1)$ or $L(R_2)$, depending on which automaton we traveled through. Since we only add ϵ's to that path's labels, the automaton of Fig. 10.28(a) also accepts s. Thus the strings accepted are those in $L(R_1) \cup L(R_2)$, which is $L(R_1 \mid R_2)$, or $L(R)$.

Case 2. If $R = R_1 R_2$, then we construct the automaton of Fig. 10.28(b). This automaton has as its start state the start state of the automaton for R_1, and as its accepting state the accepting state of the automaton for R_2. We add an ϵ-transition from the accepting state of the automaton for R_1 to the start state of the automaton for R_2. The accepting state of the first automaton is no longer accepting, and the start state of the second automaton is no longer the start state in the constructed automaton.

The only way to get from the start to the accepting state of Fig. 10.28(b) is

1. Along a path labeled by a string s in $L(R_1)$, to get from the start state to the accepting state of the automaton for R_1, then

2. Along the arc labeled ϵ to the start state of the automaton for R_2, and then

3. Along a path labeled by some string t in $L(R_2)$ to get to the accepting state.

The label of this path is st. Thus the automaton of Fig. 10.28(b) accepts exactly the strings in $L(R_1 R_2)$, or $L(R)$.

Case 3. If $R = R_1{}^*$, we construct the automaton of Fig. 10.28(c). We add to the automaton for R_1 a new start and accepting state. The start state has an ϵ-transition to the accepting state (so string ϵ is accepted), and to the start state of the automaton for R_1. The accepting state of the automaton for R_1 is given an ϵ-transition back to its start state, and one to the accepting state of the automaton for R. The start and accepting states of the automaton for R_1 are not start or accepting in the constructed automaton.

The paths from start to accepting state in Fig. 10.28(c) are either labeled ϵ (if we go directly) or labeled by the concatenation of one or more strings from $L(R_1)$, as we go through the automaton for R_1 and, optionally, around to the start as many times as we like. Note that we do not have to follow the same path through the automaton for R_1 each time around. Thus the labels of the paths through Fig. 10.28(c) are exactly the strings in $L(R_1{}^*)$, which is $L(R)$.

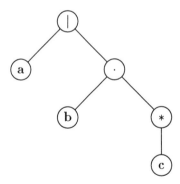

Fig. 10.29. Expression tree for the regular expression **a | bc***.

✦ **Example 10.25.** Let us construct the automaton for the regular expression **a | bc***. An expression tree for this regular expression is shown in Fig. 10.29; it is analogous to the expression trees we discussed in Section 5.2, and it helps us see the order in which the operators are applied to the operands.

There are three leaves, and for each, we construct an instance of the automaton of Fig. 10.27(c). These automata are shown in Fig. 10.30, and we have used the states that are consistent with the automaton of Fig. 10.26, which as we mentioned, is the automaton we shall eventually construct for our regular expression. It should be understood, however, that it is essential for the automata corresponding to the various occurrences of operands to have distinct states. In our example, since each operand is different, we would expect to use different states for each, but even if there were several occurrences of **a**, for example, in the expression, we would create distinct automata for each occurrence.

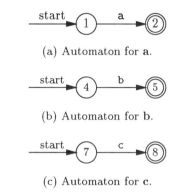

(a) Automaton for **a**.

(b) Automaton for **b**.

(c) Automaton for **c**.

Fig. 10.30. Automata for **a**, **b**, and **c**.

Now we must work up the tree of Fig. 10.29, applying operators and constructing larger automata as we go. The first operator applied is the closure operator, which is applied to operand **c**. We use the construction of Fig. 10.28(c) for the closure. The new states introduced are called 6 and 9, again to be consistent with Fig. 10.26. Fig. 10.31 shows the automaton for the regular expression **c***.

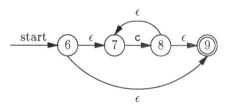

Fig. 10.31. Automaton for **c***.

Next, we apply the concatenation operator to **b** and **c***. We use the construction of Fig. 10.28(b), and the resulting automaton is shown in Fig. 10.32.

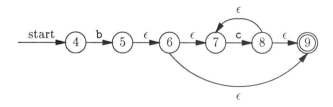

Fig. 10.32. Automaton for **bc***.

Finally, we apply the union operator to **a** and **bc***. The construction used is that of Fig. 10.28(a), and we call the new states introduced 0 and 3. The resulting automaton appeared in Fig. 10.26. ✦

Eliminating Epsilon-Transitions

If we are in any state s of an automaton with ϵ-transitions, we in effect are also in any state that we can get to from s by following a path of arcs labeled ϵ. The reason is that whatever string labels the path we've taken to get to state s, the same string will be the label of the path extended with ϵ-transitions.

✦ **Example 10.26.** In Fig. 10.26, we can get to the state 5 by following a path labeled **b**. From state 5, we can get to states 6, 7, 9, and 3 by following paths of ϵ-labeled arcs. Thus if we are in state 5, we are, in effect, also in these four other states. For instance, since 3 is an accepting state, we can think of 5 as an accepting state as well, since every input string that gets us to state 5 will also get us to state 3, and thus be accepted. ✦

Thus the first question we need to ask is, from each state, what other states can we reach following only ϵ-transitions? We gave an algorithm to answer this question in Section 9.7, when we studied reachability as an application of depth-first search. For the problem at hand, we have only to modify the graph of the finite automaton by removing transitions on anything but ϵ. That is, for each real symbol **x**, we remove all arcs labeled by **x**. Then, we perform a depth-first search of the remaining graph from each node. The nodes visited during the depth-first search from node v is exactly the set of node reachable from v using ϵ-transitions only.

Recall that one depth-first search takes $O(m)$ time, where m is the larger of the number of nodes and arcs of the graph. In this case, there are n depth-first searches to do, if the graph has n nodes, for a total of $O(mn)$ time. However, there are at most two arcs out of any one node in the automata constructed from regular expressions by the algorithm described previously in this section. Thus $m \leq 2n$, and $O(mn)$ is $O(n^2)$ time.

✦ **Example 10.27.** In Fig. 10.33 we see the arcs that remain from Fig. 10.26 when the three arcs labeled by a real symbol, **a**, **b**, or **c**, are deleted. Figure 10.34 is a table giving the reachability information for Fig. 10.33; that is, a 1 in row i and column j means that there is a path of length 0 or more from node i to node j. ✦

Armed with the reachability information, we can construct our equivalent automaton that has no ϵ-transitions. The idea is to bundle into one transition of the new automaton a path of zero or more ϵ-transitions of the old automaton followed by one transition of the old automaton on a real symbol. Every such transition takes us to the second state of one of the automata that were introduced by the basis rule of Fig. 10.27(c), the rule for operands that are real symbols. The reason is that only these states are entered by arcs with real symbols as labels. Thus our new automaton needs only these states and the start state for its own set of states.

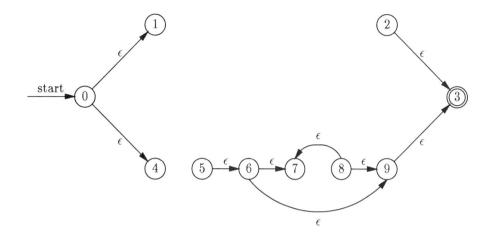

Fig. 10.33. The ϵ-transitions from Fig. 10.26.

	0	1	2	3	4	5	6	7	8	9
0	1	1			1					
1		1								
2			1	1						
3				1						
4					1					
5				1		1	1	1		1
6				1			1	1		1
7								1		
8				1			1	1	1	1
9				1						1

Fig. 10.34. Table of reachability for Fig. 10.33.

Important state   Let us call these states the *important* states.

In the new automaton, there is a transition from important state i to important state j with symbol **x** among its labels if there is some state k such that

1. State k is reachable from state i along a path of zero or more ϵ-transitions. Note that $k = i$ is always permitted.

2. In the old automaton, there is a transition from state k to state j, labeled **x**.

We also must decide which states are accepting states in the new automaton. As we mentioned, when we are in a state, we are effectively in any state it can reach along ϵ-labeled arcs, and so in the new automaton, we shall make state i accepting if there is, in the old automaton, a path of ϵ-labeled arcs from state i to the accepting state of the old automaton. Note that i may itself be the accepting state of the old automaton, which therefore remains accepting in the new automaton.

◆ **Example 10.28.** Let us convert the automaton of Fig. 10.26 to an automaton without ϵ-transitions, accepting the same language. First, the important states are state 0, which is the initial state, and states 2, 5, and 8, because these are entered by arcs labeled by a real symbol.

We shall begin by discovering the transitions for state 0. According to Fig. 10.34, from state 0 we can reach states 0, 1, and 4 along paths of ϵ-labeled arcs. We find a transition on **a** from state 1 to 2 and a transition on **b** from 4 to 5. Thus in the new automaton, there is a transition from 0 to 2 labeled **a** and from 0 to 5 labeled **b**. Notice that we have collapsed the paths $0 \rightarrow 1 \rightarrow 2$ and $0 \rightarrow 4 \rightarrow 5$ of Fig. 10.26 into single transitions with the label of the non-ϵ transition along those paths. As neither state 0, nor the states 1 and 4 that it reaches along ϵ-labeled paths are accepting states, in the new automaton, state 0 is not accepting.

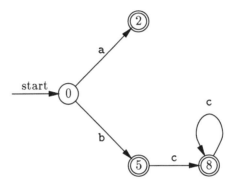

Fig. 10.35. Automaton constructed from Fig. 10.26 by eliminating ϵ-transitions. Note that this automaton accepts all and only the strings in $L(\mathbf{a} \mid \mathbf{bc}^*)$.

Next, consider the transitions out of state 2. Figure 10.34 tells us that from 2 we can reach only itself and 3 via ϵ-transitions, and so we must look for transitions out of states 2 or 3 on real symbols. Finding none, we know that there are no transitions out of state 2 in the new automaton. However, since 3 is accepting, and 2 reaches 3 by ϵ-transitions, we make 2 accepting in the new automaton.

When we consider state 5, Fig. 10.34 tells us to look at states 3, 5, 6, 7, and 9. Among these, only state 7 has a non-ϵ transition out; it is labeled **c** and goes to state 8. Thus in the new automaton, the only transition out of state 5 is a transition on **c** to state 8. We make state 5 accepting in the new automaton, since it reaches accepting state 3 following ϵ-labeled arcs.

Finally, we must look at the transitions out of state 8. By reasoning similar to that for state 5, we conclude that in the new automaton, the only transition out of state 8 is to itself and is labeled **c**. Also, state 8 is accepting in the new automaton.

Figure 10.35 shows the new automaton. Notice that the set of strings it accepts is exactly those strings in $L(\mathbf{a} \mid \mathbf{bc}^*)$, that is, the string **a** (which takes us to state 2), the string **b** (which takes us to state 5), and the strings **bc**, **bcc**, **bccc**, and so on, all of which take us to state 8. The automaton of Fig. 10.35 happens to be deterministic. If it were not, we would have to use the subset construction to convert it to a deterministic automaton, should we wish to design a program that would recognize the strings of the original regular expression. ◆

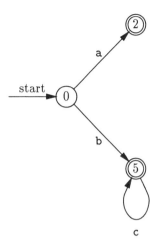

Fig. 10.36. Simpler automaton for the language $L(\mathbf{a} \mid \mathbf{bc}^*)$.

Incidentally, there is a simpler deterministic automaton that accepts the same language as Fig. 10.35. This automaton is shown in Fig. 10.36. In effect, we get the improved automaton by recognizing that states 5 and 8 are equivalent and can be merged. The resulting state is called 5 in Fig. 10.36.

EXERCISES

10.8.1: Construct automata with ϵ-transitions for the following regular expressions.

a)   **aaa** *Hint*: Remember to create a new automaton for each occurrence of operand **a**.

b) $(\mathbf{ab} \mid \mathbf{ac})^*$

c) $(\mathbf{0} \mid \mathbf{1} \mid \mathbf{1}^*)^*$

10.8.2: For each of the automata constructed in Exercise 10.8.1, find the reachable sets of nodes for the graph formed from the ϵ-labeled arcs. Note that you need only construct the reachable states for the start state and the states that have non-ϵ transitions in, when you construct the automaton without ϵ-transitions.

10.8.3: For each of the automata of Exercise 10.8.1, construct an equivalent automaton without ϵ-transitions.

10.8.4: Which of the automata in Exercise 10.8.3 are deterministic? For those that are not, construct an equivalent deterministic automaton.

10.8.5*: For the deterministic automata constructed from Exercises 10.8.3 or Exercise 10.8.4, are there equivalent deterministic automata with fewer states? If so, find minimal ones.

10.8.6*: We can generalize our construction from a regular expression to an automaton with ϵ-transitions to include expressions that use the extended operators of Section 10.7. That statement is true in principle, since each of those extensions is a shorthand for an "ordinary" regular expression, by which we could replace the extended operator. However, we can also incorporate the extended operators directly into our construction. Show how to modify the construction to cover

a) the ? operator (zero or one occurrences)
b) the $^+$ operator (one or more occurrences)
c) character classes.

10.8.7: We can modify the case for concatenation in our algorithm to convert a regular expression into an automaton. In Fig. 10.28(b), we introduced an ϵ-transition from the accepting state of the automaton for R_1 to the initial state of the automaton for R_2. An alternative is to merge the accepting state of R_1 with the initial state of R_2 as shown in Fig. 10.37. Construct an automaton for the regular expression **ab*c** using both the old and the modified algorithms.

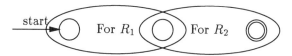

Fig. 10.37. Alternative automaton for the concatenation of two regular expressions.

✦✦ 10.9 From Automata to Regular Expressions

In this section, we shall demonstrate the other half of the equivalence between automata and regular expressions, by showing that for every automaton A there is a regular expression whose language is exactly the set of strings accepted by A. While we generally use the construction of the last section, where we convert "designs" in the form of regular expressions into programs, in the form of deterministic automata, this construction is also interesting and instructive. It completes the proof of the equivalence, in expressive power, of two radically different notations for describing patterns.

Our construction involves the elimination of states, one by one, from an automaton. As we proceed, we replace the labels on the arcs, which are initially sets of characters, by more complicated regular expressions. Initially, if we have label $\{x_1, x_2, \ldots, x_n\}$ on an arc, we replace the label by the regular expression $x_1 \mid x_2 \mid \cdots \mid x_n$, which represents essentially the same set of symbols, although technically the regular expression represents strings of length 1.

In general, we can think of the label of a path as the concatenation of the regular expressions along that path, or as the language defined by the concatenation of those expressions. That view is consistent with our notion of a path labeled by a string. That is, if the arcs of a path are labeled by the regular expressions $R_1, R_2, \ldots, R_n$, in that order, then the path is labeled by w, if and only if string w is in the language $L(R_1 R_2 \cdots R_n)$.

✦ **Example 10.29.** Consider the path $0 \rightarrow 1 \rightarrow 2$ in Fig. 10.38. The regular expressions labeling the arcs are $a \mid b$ and $a \mid b \mid c$, in that order. Thus the set of strings labeling this path are those in the language defined by the regular expression

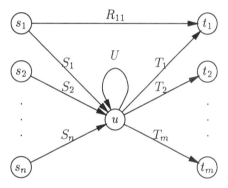

Fig. 10.38. Path with regular expressions as labels. The label of the path is the language of the concatenated regular expressions.

$$(\mathbf{a} \mid \mathbf{b})(\mathbf{a} \mid \mathbf{b} \mid \mathbf{c}),$$

namely, $\{\mathsf{aa}, \mathsf{ab}, \mathsf{ac}, \mathsf{ba}, \mathsf{bb}, \mathsf{bc}\}$. ✦

The State-Elimination Construction

The key step in conversion from an automaton to a regular expression is the elimination of states, which is illustrated in Fig. 10.39. We wish to eliminate state u, but we must keep the regular expression labels of the arcs so that the set of labels of the paths between any two of the remaining states does not change. In Fig. 10.39 the predecessors of state u are $s_1, s_2, \ldots, s_n$, and the successors of u are $t_1, t_2, \ldots, t_m$. Although we have shown the s's and the t's to be disjoint sets of states, there could in fact be some states common to the two groups.

Fig. 10.39. We wish to eliminate state u.

However, if u is a successor of itself, we represent that fact explicitly by an arc labeled U. Should there be no such loop at state u, we can introduce it and give it label $\emptyset$. An arc with label $\emptyset$ is "not there," because any label of a path using that arc will be the concatenation of regular expressions including $\emptyset$. Since $\emptyset$ is the annihilator for concatenation, every such concatenation defines the empty language.

We have also shown explicitly an arc from s_1 to t_1, labeled R_{11}. In general, we suppose that for every $i = 1, 2, \ldots, n$, and for every $j = 1, 2, \ldots, m$, there is an arc from s_i to t_j, labeled by some regular expression R_{ij}. If the arc $s_i \rightarrow t_j$ is actually not present, we can introduce it and give it label $\emptyset$.

Finally, in Fig. 10.39 there is an arc from each s_i to u, labeled by regular expression S_i, and there is an arc from u to each t_j, labeled by regular expression T_j. If we eliminate node u, then these arcs and the arc labeled U in Fig. 10.39 will go away. To preserve the set of strings labeling paths, we must consider each pair s_i and t_j and add to the label of the arc $s_i \rightarrow t_j$ a regular expression that accounts for what is lost.

Before eliminating u, the set of strings labeling the paths from s_i to u, including those going around the loop $u \rightarrow u$ several times, and then from u to t_j, is described by the regular expression $S_i U^* T_j$. That is, a string in $L(S_i)$ gets us from s_i to u; a string in $L(U^*)$ gets us from u to u, following the loop zero, one, or more times. Finally, a string in $L(T_j)$ gets us from u to t_j.

Hence, after eliminating u and all arcs into or out of u, we must replace R_{ij}, the label of the arc $s_i \rightarrow t_j$, by

$$R_{ij} \mid S_i U^* T_j$$

There are a number of useful special cases. First, if $U = \emptyset$, that is, the loop on u is not really there, then $U^* = \emptyset^* = \epsilon$. Since ϵ is the identity under concatenation, $(S_i \epsilon) T_j = S_i T_j$; that is, U has effectively disappeared as it should. Similarly, if $R_{ij} = \emptyset$, meaning that there was formerly no arc from s_i to t_j, then we introduce this arc and give it label $S_i U^* T_j$, or just $S_i T_j$, if $U = \emptyset$. The reason we can do so is that $\emptyset$ is the identity for union, and so $\emptyset \mid S_i U^* T_j = S_i U^* T_j$.

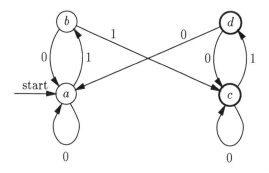

Fig. 10.40. Finite automaton for bounce filter.

✦ **Example 10.30.** Let us consider the bounce filter automaton of Fig. 10.4, which we reproduce here as Fig. 10.40. Suppose we wish to eliminate state b, which thus plays the role of state u in Fig. 10.39. State b has one predecessor, a, and two successors, a and c. There is no loop on b, and so we introduce one, labeled $\emptyset$. There is an arc from a to itself, labeled **0**. Since a is both a predecessor and a successor of b, this arc is needed in the transformation. The only other predecessor-successor pair is a and c. Since there is no arc $a \rightarrow c$, we add one with label $\emptyset$. The diagram of relevant states and arcs is as shown in Fig. 10.41.

For the a–a pair, we replace the label of the arc $a \rightarrow a$ by **0 | 1∅*0**. The term **0** represents the original label of the arc, the **1** is the label of the arc $a \rightarrow b$, $\emptyset$ is the label of the loop $b \rightarrow b$, and the second **0** is the label of the arc $b \rightarrow a$. We can simplify, as described above, to eliminate $\emptyset^*$, leaving us with the expression **0 | 10**. That makes sense. In Fig. 10.40, the paths from a to a, going through b zero or more times, but no other state, have the set of labels {**0**, **10**}.

The pair a–c is handled similarly. We replace the label $\emptyset$ on the arc $a \rightarrow c$ by $\emptyset \mid$ **1∅*1**, which simplifies to **11**. That again makes sense, since in Fig. 10.40, the only path from a to c, via b has label **11**. When we eliminate node b and change the arc labels, Fig. 10.40 becomes Fig. 10.42. Note that in this automaton, some of the arcs have labels that are regular expressions whose languages have strings of

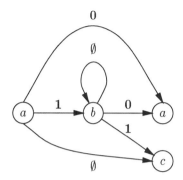

Fig. 10.41. State b, its predecessors, and successors.

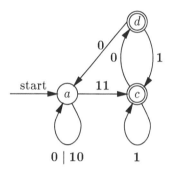

Fig. 10.42. Bounce filter automaton after eliminating state b.

length greater than 1. However, the sets of path labels for the paths among states a, c, and d has not changed from what they were in Fig. 10.40. ♦

Complete Reduction of Automata

To obtain a regular expression that denotes all and only the strings accepted by an automaton A we consider each accepting state t of A in turn. Every string accepted by A is accepted because it labels a path from the start state, s, to some accepting state t. We can develop a regular expression for the strings that get us from s to a particular accepting state t, as follows.

We repeatedly eliminate states of A until only s and t remain. Then, the automaton looks like Fig. 10.43. We have shown all four possible arcs, each with a regular expression as its label. If one or more of the possible arcs does not exist, we may introduce it and label it ∅.

We need to discover what regular expression describes the set of labels of paths that start at s and end at t. One way to express this set of strings is to recognize that each such path gets to t for the first time, and then goes from t to itself, zero or more times, possibly passing through s as it goes. The set of strings that take us to t for the first time is $L(S*U)$. That is, we use strings in $L(S)$ zero or more times, staying in state s as we do, and then we follow a string from $L(U)$. We can stay in state t either by following a string in $L(T)$, which takes us from t to t, or by

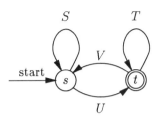

Fig. 10.43. An automaton reduced to two states.

following a string in VS^*U, which takes us to state s, keeps us at s for a while, and then takes us back to t. We can follow zero or more strings from these two groups, in any order, which we can express as $(T \mid VS^*U)^*$. Thus a regular expression for the set of strings that get us from state s to state t is

$$S^*U(T \mid VS^*U)^* \tag{10.4}$$

There is one special case, when the start state s is itself an accepting state. Then, there are strings that are accepted because they take the automaton A from s to s. We eliminate all states but s, leaving an automaton that looks like Fig. 10.44. The set of strings that take A from s to s is $L(S^*)$. Thus we may use S^* as a regular expression to account for the contribution of accepting state s.

Fig. 10.44. Automaton with only the start state.

The complete algorithm for converting an automaton A with start state s to an equivalent regular expression is as follows. For each accepting state t, start with the automaton A and eliminate states until only s and t remain. Of course, we start anew with the original automaton A for each accepting state t.

If $s \neq t$, use formula (10.4) to get a regular expression whose language is the set of strings that take A from s to t. If $s = t$, use S^*, where S is the label of the arc $s \rightarrow s$, as the regular expression. Then, take the union of the regular expressions for each accepting state t. The language of that expression is exactly the set of strings accepted by A.

✦ **Example 10.31.** Let us develop a regular expression for the bounce-filter automaton of Fig. 10.40. As c and d are the accepting states, we need to

1. Eliminate states b and d from Fig. 10.40 to get an automaton involving only a and c.

2. Eliminate states b and c from Fig. 10.40 to get an automaton involving only a and d.

Since in each case we must eliminate state b, Fig. 10.42 has gotten us half way toward both goals. For (1), let us eliminate state d from Fig. 10.42. There is a path labeled **00** from c to a via d, so we need to introduce an arc labeled **00** from c to a. There is a path labeled **01** from c to itself, via d, so we need to add label **01** to the label of the loop at c, and that label becomes **1 | 01**. The resulting automaton is shown in Fig. 10.45.

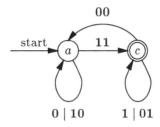

Fig. 10.45. Automaton of Fig. 10.40 reduced to states a and c.

Now for goal (2) we shall again start at Fig. 10.42 and eliminate state c this time. In Fig. 10.42 we can go from state a to state d via c, and the regular expression describing the possible strings is **111*0**.[8] That is, **11** takes us from a to c, **1*** allows us to loop at c zero or more times, and finally **0** takes us from c to d. Thus we introduce an arc labeled **111*0** from a to d. Similarly, in Fig. 10.42 we can go from d to itself, via c, by following strings in **11*0**. Thus this expression becomes the label of a loop at d. The reduced automaton is shown in Fig. 10.46.

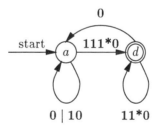

Fig. 10.46. Automaton of Fig. 10.40 reduced to states a and d.

Now we may apply the formula developed in (10.4) to the automata in Figs. 10.45 and 10.46. For Fig. 10.45, we have $S = $ **0 | 10**, $U = $ **11**, $V = $ **00**, and $T = $ **1 | 01**. Thus a regular expression denoting the set of strings that take the automaton of Fig. 10.40 from start state a to accepting state c is

$$(0 \mid 10)\textbf{*}11\big((1 \mid 01) \mid 00(0 \mid 10)\textbf{*}11\big)\textbf{*} \qquad\qquad (10.5)$$

and the expression denoting the strings that take state a to accepting state d is

---

[8] Remember that because * takes precedence over concatenation, **111*0** is parsed as **11(1*)0**, and represents the strings consisting of two or more 1's followed by a 0.

$$(0 \mid 10)\text{*}111\text{*}0\big(11\text{*}0 \mid 0(0 \mid 10)\text{*}111\text{*}0\big)\text{*} \tag{10.6}$$

The expression that denotes the strings accepted by the bounce filter automaton is the union of (10.5) and (10.6), or

$$\Big((0 \mid 10)\text{*}11\big((1 \mid 01) \mid 00(0 \mid 10)\text{*}11\big)\text{*}\Big) \mid$$
$$\Big((0 \mid 10)\text{*}111\text{*}0\big(11\text{*}0 \mid 0(0 \mid 10)\text{*}111\text{*}0\big)\text{*}\Big)$$

There is not much we can do to simplify this expression. There is a common initial factor $(0 \mid 10)\text{*}11$, but little else in common. We can also remove the parentheses around the factor $(1 \mid 01)$ in (10.5), because union is associative. The resulting expression is

$$(0 \mid 10)\text{*}11\Big((1 \mid 01 \mid 00(0 \mid 10)\text{*}11)\text{*} \mid 1\text{*}0\big(11\text{*}0 \mid 0(0 \mid 10)\text{*}111\text{*}0\big)\text{*}\Big)$$

You may recall that we suggested a much simpler regular expression for the same language,

$$(0 \mid 1)\text{*}11(1 \mid 01)\text{*}(\epsilon \mid 0)$$

This difference should remind us that there can be more than one regular expression for the same language, and that the expression we get by converting an automaton to a regular expression is not necessarily the simplest expression for that language. ◆

EXERCISES

10.9.1: Find regular expressions for the automata of

a)   Fig. 10.3
b)   Fig. 10.9
c)   Fig. 10.10
d)   Fig. 10.12
e)   Fig. 10.13
f)   Fig. 10.17
g)   Fig. 10.20

You may wish to use the shorthands of Section 10.6.

10.9.2: Convert the automata of Exercise 10.4.1 to regular expressions.

10.9.3*: Show that another regular expression we could use for the set of strings that get us from state s to state t in Fig. 10.43 is $(S \mid UT\text{*}V)\text{*}UT\text{*}$.

10.9.4: How can you modify the construction of this section so that regular expressions can be generated from automata with ϵ-transitions?

✦✦ 10.10   Summary of Chapter 10

The subset construction of Section 10.4, together with the conversions of Sections 10.8 and 10.9, tell us that three ways to express languages have exactly the same expressive power. That is, the following three statements about a language L are either all true or all false.

1. There is some deterministic automaton that accepts all and only the strings in
    L.

2. There is some (possibly nondeterministic) automaton that accepts all and only
    the strings in L.

3. L is $L(R)$ for some regular expression R.

The subset construction shows that (2) implies (1). Evidently (1) implies (2),
since a deterministic automaton is a special kind of nondeterministic automaton.
We showed that (3) implies (2) in Section 10.8, and we showed (2) implies (3) in
Section 10.9. Thus, all of (1), (2), and (3) are equivalent.

In addition to these equivalences, we should take away a number of important
ideas from Chapter 10.

♦ Deterministic automata can be used as the core of programs that recognize
   many different kinds of patterns in strings.

♦ Regular expressions are often a convenient notation for describing patterns.

♦ There are algebraic laws for regular expressions that make union and concatenation behave in ways similar to $+$ and $\times$, but with some differences.

✦✦ 10.11   Bibliographic Notes for Chapter 10

The reader can learn more about the theory of automata and languages in Hopcroft
and Ullman [1979].

The automaton model for processing strings was first expressed in roughly the
form described here by Huffman [1954], although there were a number of similar
models discussed earlier and concurrently; the history can be found in Hopcroft
and Ullman [1979]. Regular expressions and their equivalence to automata are
from Kleene [1956]. Nondeterministic automata and the subset construction are
from Rabin and Scott [1959]. The construction of nondeterministic automata from
regular expressions that we used in Section 10.8 is from McNaughton and Yamada
[1960], while the construction in the opposite direction, in Section 10.9, is from
Kleene's paper.

The use of regular expressions as a way to describe patterns in strings first
appeared in Ken Thompson's QED system (Thompson [1968]), and the same ideas
later influenced many commands in his UNIX system. There are a number of other
applications of regular expressions in system software, much of which is described
in Aho, Sethi, and Ullman [1986].

Aho, A. V., R. Sethi, and J. D. Ullman [1986]. *Compiler Design: Principles, Techniques, and Tools*, Addison-Wesley, Reading, Mass.

Hopcroft, J. E. and J. D. Ullman [1979]. *Introduction to Automata Theory, Languages, and Computation*, Addison-Wesley, Reading, Mass.

Huffman, D. A. [1954]. "The synthesis of sequential switching machines," *Journal
of the Franklin Institute* **257**:3-4, pp. 161–190 and 275–303.

Kleene, S. C. [1956]. "Representation of events in nerve nets and finite automata," in *Automata Studies* (C. E. Shannon and J. McCarthy, eds.), Princeton University Press.

McNaughton, R. and H. Yamada [1960]. "Regular expressions and state graphs for automata," *IEEE Trans. on Computers* **9**:1, pp. 39–47.

Rabin, M. O. and D. Scott [1959]. "Finite automata and their decision problems," *IBM J. Research and Development* **3**:2, pp. 115-125.

Thompson, K. [1968]. "Regular expression search algorithm," *Comm. ACM* **11**:6, pp. 419–422.

CHAPTER | **11**

❖❖

Recursive Description of Patterns

In the last chapter, we saw two equivalent ways to describe patterns. One was graph-theoretic, using the labels of paths in a kind of graph that we called an "automaton." The other was algebraic, using the regular expression notation. In this chapter, we shall see a third way to describe patterns, using a form of recursive definition called a "context-free grammar" ("grammar" for short).

One important application of grammars is the specification of programming languages. Grammars are a succinct notation for describing the syntax of typical programming languages; we shall see many examples in this chapter. Further, there is mechanical way to turn a grammar for a typical programming language into a "parser," one of the key parts of a compiler for the language. The parser uncovers the structure of the source program, often in the form of an expression tree for each statement in the program.

❖❖ 11.1 What This Chapter Is About

This chapter focuses on the following topics.

✦ Grammars and how grammars are used to define languages (Sections 11.2 and 11.3).

✦ Parse trees, which are tree representations that display the structure of strings according to a given grammar (Section 11.4).

✦ Ambiguity, the problem that arises when a string has two or more distinct parse trees and thus does not have a unique "structure" according to a given grammar (Section 11.5).

✦ A method for turning a grammar into a "parser," which is an algorithm to tell whether a given string is in a language (Sections 11.6 and 11.7).

591

✦ A proof that grammars are more powerful than regular expressions for describing languages (Section 11.8). First, we show that grammars are at least as descriptive as regular expressions by showing how to simulate a regular expression with a grammar. Then we describe a particular language that can be specified by a grammar, but by no regular expression.

❖ 11.2 Context-Free Grammars

Arithmetic expressions can be defined naturally by a recursive definition. The following example illustrates how the definition works. Let us consider arithmetic expressions that involve

1. The four binary operators, $+$, $-$, $*$, and $/$,

2. Parentheses for grouping, and

3. Operands that are numbers.

The usual definition of such expressions is an induction of the following form:

BASIS. A number is an expression.

INDUCTION. If E is an expression, then each of the following is also an expression:

a) (E). That is, we may place parentheses around an expression to get a new expression.

b) $E + E$. That is, two expressions connected by a plus sign is an expression.

c) $E - E$. This and the next two rules are analogous to (2), but use the other operators.

d) $E * E$.

e) E/E.

This induction defines a language, that is, a set of strings. The basis states that any number is in the language. Rule (a) states that if s is a string in the language, then so is the parenthesized string (s); this string is s preceded by a left parenthesis and followed by a right parenthesis. Rules (b) to (e) say that if s and t are two strings in the language, then so are the strings $s+t$, $s-t$, $s*t$, and s/t.

Grammars allow us to write down such rules succinctly and with a precise meaning. As an example, we could write our definition of arithmetic expressions with the grammar shown in Fig. 11.1.

(1) $<Expression>$ → $number$
(2) $<Expression>$ → $($ $<Expression>$ $)$
(3) $<Expression>$ → $<Expression>$ $+$ $<Expression>$
(4) $<Expression>$ → $<Expression>$ $-$ $<Expression>$
(5) $<Expression>$ → $<Expression>$ $*$ $<Expression>$
(6) $<Expression>$ → $<Expression>$ $/$ $<Expression>$

Fig. 11.1. Grammar for simple arithmetic expressions.

The symbols used in Fig. 11.1 require some explanation. The symbol

$<Expression>$

Syntactic category

is called a *syntactic category;* it stands for any string in the language of arithmetic expressions. The symbol → means "can be composed of." For instance, rule (2) in Fig. 11.1 states that an expression can be composed of a left parenthesis followed by any string that is an expression followed by a right parenthesis. Rule (3) states that an expression can be composed of any string that is an expression, the character +, and any other string that is an expression. Rules (4) through (6) are similar to rule (3).

Rule (1) is different because the symbol *number* on the right of the arrow is not intended to be a literal string, but a placeholder for any string that can be interpreted as a number. We shall later show how numbers can be defined grammatically, but for the moment let us imagine that *number* is an abstract symbol, and expressions use this symbol to represent any atomic operand.

The Terminology of Grammars

Metasymbol

There are three kinds of symbols that appear in grammars. The first are "metasymbols," symbols that play special roles and do not stand for themselves. The only example we have seen so far is the symbol →, which is used to separate the syntactic category being defined from a way in which strings of that syntactic category may be composed. The second kind of symbol is a syntactic category, which as we mentioned represents a set of strings being defined. The third kind of symbol is called a *terminal.* Terminals can be characters, such as + or (, or they can be abstract symbols such as *number*, that stand for one or more strings we may wish to define at a later time.

Terminal

Production

A grammar consists of one or more *productions.* Each line of Fig. 11.1 is a production. In general, a production has three parts:

1. A *head,* which is the syntactic category on the left side of the arrow,

Head and body

2. The metasymbol →, and

3. A *body,* consisting of 0 or more syntactic categories and/or terminals on the right side of the arrow.

For instance, in rule (2) of Fig. 11.1, the head is $<Expression>$, and the body consists of three symbols: the terminal (, the syntactic category $<Expression>$, and the terminal).

✦ **Example 11.1.** We can augment the definition of expressions with which we began this section by providing a definition of *number*. We assume that numbers are strings consisting of one or more digits. In the extended regular-expression notation of Section 10.6, we could say

$digit = [0\text{-}9]$
$number = digit^+$

However, we can also express the same idea in grammatical notation. We could write the productions

Notational Conventions

We denote syntactic categories by a name, in italics, surrounded by angular brackets, for example, $<Expression>$. Terminals in productions will either be denoted by a boldface **x** to stand for the string **x** (in analogy with the convention for regular expressions), or by an italicized character string with no angular brackets, for the case that the terminal, like *number*, is an abstract symbol.

We use the metasymbol ϵ to stand for an empty body. Thus, the production $<S> \to \epsilon$ means that the empty string is in the language of syntactic category $<S>$. We sometimes group the bodies for one syntactic category into one production, separating the bodies by the metasymbol |, which we can read as "or." For example, if we have productions

$$<S> \to B_1, <S> \to B_2, \ldots, <S> \to B_n$$

where the B's are each the body of a production for the syntactic category $<S>$, then we can write these productions as

$$<S> \to B_1 \mid B_2 \mid \cdots \mid B_n$$

$$<Digit> \to 0 \mid 1 \mid 2 \mid 3 \mid 4 \mid 5 \mid 6 \mid 7 \mid 8 \mid 9$$

$$<Number> \to <Digit>$$
$$<Number> \to <Number> <Digit>$$

Note that, by our convention regarding the metasymbol |, the first line is short for the ten productions

$$<Digit> \to 0$$
$$<Digit> \to 1$$
$$\cdots$$
$$<Digit> \to 9$$

We could similarly have combined the two productions for $<Number>$ into one line. Note that the first production for $<Number>$ states that a single digit is a number, and the second production states that any number followed by another digit is also a number. These two productions together say that any string of one or more digits is a number.

Figure 11.2 is an expanded grammar for expressions, in which the abstract terminal *number* has been replaced by productions that define the concept. Notice that the grammar has three syntactic categories, $<Expression>$, $<Number>$ and **Start symbol** $<Digit>$. We shall treat the syntactic category $<Expression>$ as the *start symbol*; it generates the strings (in this case, well-formed arithmetic expressions) that we intend to define with the grammar. The other syntactic categories, $<Number>$ and $<Digit>$, stand for auxiliary concepts that are essential, but not the main concept for which the grammar was written. ✦

✦ **Example 11.2.** In Section 2.6 we discussed the notion of strings of balanced parentheses. There, we gave an inductive definition of such strings that resembles, in an informal way, the formal style of writing grammars developed in this section.

Common Grammatical Patterns

Example 11.1 used two productions for $<Number>$ to say that "a number is a string of one or more digits." The pattern used there is a common one. In general, if we have a syntactic category $<X>$, and Y is either a terminal or another syntactic category, the productions

$$<X> \rightarrow <X>Y \mid Y$$

say that any string of one or more Y's is an $<X>$. Adopting the regular expression notation, $<X> = Y^+$. Similarly, the productions

$$<X> \rightarrow <X>Y \mid \epsilon$$

tell us that every string of zero or more Y's is an $<X>$, or $<X> = Y^*$. A slightly more complex, but also common pattern is the pair of productions

$$<X> \rightarrow <X>ZY \mid Y$$

which say that every string of alternating Y's and Z's, beginning and ending with a Y, is an $<X>$. That is, $<X> = Y(ZY)^*$.

Moreover, we can reverse the order of the symbols in the body of the recursive production in any of the three examples above. For instance,

$$<X> \rightarrow Y<X> \mid Y$$

also defines $<X> = Y^+$.

---

(1) $<Digit> \rightarrow 0 \mid 1 \mid 2 \mid 3 \mid 4 \mid 5 \mid 6 \mid 7 \mid 8 \mid 9$

(2) $<Number> \rightarrow <Digit>$
(3) $<Number> \rightarrow <Number> <Digit>$

(4) $<Expression> \rightarrow <Number>$
(5) $<Expression> \rightarrow (<Expression>)$
(6) $<Expression> \rightarrow <Expression> + <Expression>$
(7) $<Expression> \rightarrow <Expression> - <Expression>$
(8) $<Expression> \rightarrow <Expression> * <Expression>$
(9) $<Expression> \rightarrow <Expression> / <Expression>$

Fig. 11.2. Grammar for expressions with numbers defined grammatically.

We defined a syntactic category of "balanced parenthesis strings" that we might call $<Balanced>$. There was a basis rule stating that the empty string is balanced. We can write this rule as a production,

$$<Balanced> \rightarrow \epsilon$$

Then there was an inductive step that said if x and y were balanced strings, then so was $(x)y$. We can write this rule as a production

$$<Balanced> \rightarrow (<Balanced>) <Balanced>$$

Thus, the grammar of Fig. 11.3 may be said to define balanced strings of parenthe-

$$<Balanced> \rightarrow \epsilon$$
$$<Balanced> \rightarrow (<Balanced>) <Balanced>$$

Fig. 11.3. A grammar for balanced parenthesis strings.

ses.

There is another way that strings of balanced parentheses could be defined. If we recall Section 2.6, our original motivation for describing such strings was that they are the subsequences of parentheses that appear within expressions when we delete all but the parentheses. Figure 11.1 gives us a grammar for expressions. Consider what happens if we remove all terminals but the parentheses. Production (1) becomes

$$<Expression> \rightarrow \epsilon$$

Production (2) becomes

$$<Expression> \rightarrow (<Expression>)$$

and productions (3) through (6) all become

$$<Expression> \rightarrow <Expression> <Expression>$$

If we replace the syntactic category $<Expression>$ by a more appropriate name, $<BalancedE>$, we get another grammar for balanced strings of parentheses, shown in Fig. 11.4. These productions are rather natural. They say that

1. The empty string is balanced,

2. If we parenthesize a balanced string, the result is balanced, and

3. The concatenation of balanced strings is balanced.

$$<BalancedE> \rightarrow \epsilon$$
$$<BalancedE> \rightarrow (<BalancedE>)$$
$$<BalancedE> \rightarrow <BalancedE> <BalancedE>$$

Fig. 11.4. A grammar for balanced parenthesis strings
developed from the arithmetic expression grammar.

The grammars of Figs. 11.3 and 11.4 look rather different, but they do define the same set of strings. Perhaps the easiest way to prove that they do is to show that the strings defined by $<BalancedE>$ in Fig. 11.4 are exactly the "profile balanced" strings defined in Section 2.6. There, we proved the same assertion about the strings defined by $<Balanced>$ in Fig. 11.3. ✦

✦ **Example 11.3.** We can also describe the structure of control flow in languages like C grammatically. For a simple example, it helps to imagine that there are abstract terminals *condition* and *simpleStat*. The former stands for a conditional expression. We could replace this terminal by a syntactic category, say $<Condition>$.

The productions for *<Condition>* would resemble those of our expression grammar above, but with logical operators like **&&**, comparison operators like <, and the arithmetic operators.

The terminal *simpleStat* stands for a statement that does not involve nested control structure, such as an assignment, function call, read, write, or jump statement. Again, we could replace this terminal by a syntactic category and the productions to expand it.

We shall use *<Statement>* for our syntactic category of C statements. One way statements can be formed is through the while-construct. That is, if we have a statement to serve as the body of the loop, we can precede it by the keyword **while** and a parenthesized condition to form another statement. The production for this statement-formation rule is

$$<Statement> \; \rightarrow \; \textbf{while} \; (\; condition \;) \; <Statement>$$

Another way to build statements is through selection statements. These statements take two forms, depending on whether or not they have an else-part; they are expressed by the two productions

$$<Statement> \; \rightarrow \; \textbf{if} \; (\; condition \;) \; <Statement>$$
$$<Statement> \; \rightarrow \; \textbf{if} \; (\; condition \;) \; <Statement> \; \textbf{else} \; <Statement>$$

There are other ways to form statements as well, such as for-, repeat-, and case-statements. We shall leave those productions as exercises; they are similar in spirit to what we have seen.

However, one other important formation rule is the block, which is somewhat different from those we have seen. A block is formed by curly braces **{** and **}**, surrounding zero or more statements. To describe blocks, we need an auxiliary syntactic category, which we can call *<StatList>*; it stands for a list of statements. The productions for *<StatList>* are simple:

$$<StatList> \; \rightarrow \; \epsilon$$
$$<StatList> \; \rightarrow \; <StatList> \; <Statement>$$

That is, the first production says that a statement list can be empty. The second production says that if we follow a list of statements by another statement, then we have a list of statements.

Now we can define statements that are blocks as a statement list surrounded by **{** and **}**, that is,

$$<Statement> \; \rightarrow \; \{ \; <StatList> \; \}$$

The productions we have developed, together with the basis production that states that a statement can be a simple statement (assignment, call, input/output, or jump) followed by a semicolon is shown in Fig. 11.5. ✦

EXERCISES

11.2.1: Give a grammar to define the syntactic category *<Identifier>*, for all those strings that are C identifiers. You may find it useful to define some auxiliary syntactic categories like *<Digit>*.

$$<Statement> \rightarrow \textbf{while} \ (\ condition \ ) \ <Statement>$$
$$<Statement> \rightarrow \textbf{if} \ (\ condition \ ) \ <Statement>$$
$$<Statement> \rightarrow \textbf{if} \ (\ condition \ ) \ <Statement> \ \textbf{else} \ <Statement>$$
$$<Statement> \rightarrow \{ \ <StatList> \ \}$$
$$<Statement> \rightarrow simpleStat \ ;$$

$$<StatList> \rightarrow \epsilon$$
$$<StatList> \rightarrow <StatList> \ <Statement>$$

Fig. 11.5. Productions defining some of the statement forms of C.

11.2.2: Arithmetic expressions in C can take identifiers, as well as numbers, as operands. Modify the grammar of Fig. 11.2 so that operands can also be identifiers. Use your grammar from Exercise 11.2.1 to define identifiers.

11.2.3: Numbers can be real numbers, with a decimal point and an optional power of 10, as well as integers. Modify the grammar for expressions in Fig. 11.2, or your grammar from Exercise 11.2.2, to allow reals as operands.

11.2.4*: Operands of C arithmetic expressions can also be expressions involving pointers (the * and & operators), fields of a record structure (the . and -> operators), or array indexing. An index of an array can be any expression.

a)   Write a grammar for the syntactic category $<ArrayRef>$ to define strings consisting of a pair of brackets surrounding an expression. You may use the syntactic category $<Expression>$ as an auxiliary.

b)   Write a grammar for the syntactic category $<Name>$ to define strings that refer to operands. An example of a name, as discussed in Section 1.4, is (*a).b[c][d]. You may use $<ArrayRef>$ as an auxiliary.

c)   Write a grammar for arithmetic expressions that allow names as operands. You may use $<Name>$ as an auxiliary. When you put your productions from (a), (b), and (c) together, do you get a grammar that allows expressions like a[b.c][*d]+e?

11.2.5*: Show that the grammar of Fig. 11.4 generates the profile-balanced strings defined in Section 2.6. *Hint*: Use two inductions on string length similar to the proofs in Section 2.6.

11.2.6*: Sometimes expressions can have two or more kinds of balanced parentheses. For example, C expressions can have both round and square parentheses, and both must be balanced; that is, every (must match a), and every [must match a]. Write a grammar for strings of balanced parentheses of these two types. That is, you must generate all and only the strings of such parentheses that could appear in well-formed C expressions.

11.2.7: To the grammar of Fig. 11.5 add productions that define for-, do-while-, and switch-statements. Use abstract terminals and auxiliary syntactic categories as appropriate.

11.2.8*: Expand the abstract terminal *condition* in Example 11.3 to show the use of logical operators. That is, define a syntactic category $<Condition>$ to take the place of the terminal *condition*. You may use an abstract terminal *comparison* to represent any comparison expression, such as **x+1<y+z**. Then replace *comparison* by a syntactic category *<Comparison>* that expresses arithmetic comparisons in terms of the comparison operators such as < and a syntactic category *<Expression>*. The latter can be defined roughly as in the beginning of Section 11.2, but with additional operators found in C, such as unary minus and **%**.

11.2.9*: Write productions that will define the syntactic category *<SimpleStat>*, to replace the abstract terminal *simpleStat* in Fig. 11.5. You may assume the syntactic category *<Expression>* stands for C arithmetic expressions. Recall that a "simple statement" can be an assignment, function call, or jump, and that, technically, the empty string is also a simple statement.

✦✦ 11.3   Languages from Grammars

A grammar is essentially an inductive definition involving sets of strings. The major departure from the examples of inductive definitions seen in Section 2.6 and many of the examples we had in Section 11.2 is that with grammars it is routine for several syntactic categories to be defined by one grammar. In contrast, our examples of Section 2.6 each defined a single notion. Nonetheless, the way we constructed the set of defined objects in Section 2.6 applies to grammars. For each syntactic category $<S>$ of a grammar, we define a language $L(<S>)$, as follows:

BASIS. Start by assuming that for each syntactic category $<S>$ in the grammar, the language $L(<S>)$ is empty.

INDUCTION. Suppose the grammar has a production $<S> \rightarrow X_1 X_2 \cdots X_n$, where each X_i, for $i = 1, 2, \ldots, n$, is either a syntactic category or a terminal. For each $i = 1, 2, \ldots, n$, select a string s_i for X_i as follows:

1.   If X_i is a terminal, then we may only use X_i as the string s_i.

2.   If X_i is a syntactic category, then select as s_i any string that is already known to be in $L(X_i)$. If several of the X_i's are the same syntactic category, we can pick a different string from $L(X_i)$ for each occurrence.

Then the concatenation $s_1 s_2 \cdots s_n$ of these selected strings is a string in the language $L(<S>)$. Note that if $n = 0$, then we put ϵ in the language.

One systematic way to implement this definition is to make a sequence of rounds through the productions of the grammar. On each round we update the language of each syntactic category using the inductive rule in all possible ways. That is, for each X_i that is a syntactic category, we pick strings from $L(<X_i>)$ in all possible ways.

✦   **Example 11.4.** Let us consider a grammar consisting of some of the productions from Example 11.3, the grammar for some kinds of C statements. To simplify, we shall only use the productions for while-statements, blocks, and simple statements, and the two productions for statement lists. Further, we shall use a shorthand that condenses the strings considerably. The shorthand uses the terminals **w** (*while*), **c** (parenthesized *condition*), and **s** (*simpleStat*). The grammar uses the syntactic category $<S>$ for statements and the syntactic category $<L>$ for statement lists. The productions are shown in Fig. 11.6.

(1) $<S> \rightarrow$ **w c** $<S>$
(2) $<S> \rightarrow$ **{** $<L>$ **}**
(3) $<S> \rightarrow$ **s** ;

(4) $<L> \rightarrow <L> <S>$
(5) $<L> \rightarrow \epsilon$

Fig. 11.6. Simplified grammar for statements.

Let L be the language of strings in the syntactic category $<L>$, and let S be the language of strings in the syntactic category $<S>$. Initially, by the basis rule, both L and S are empty. In the first round, only productions (3) and (5) are useful, because the bodies of all the other productions each have a syntactic category, and we do not yet have any strings in the languages for the syntactic categories. Production (3) lets us infer that **s**; is a string in the language S, and production (5) tells us that ϵ is in language L.

The second round begins with $L = \{\epsilon\}$, and $S = \{$**s**;$\}$. Production (1) now allows us to add **wcs**; to S, since **s**; is already in S. That is, in the body of production (1), terminals **w** and **c** can only stand for themselves, but syntactic category $<S>$ can be replaced by any string in the language S. Since at present, string **s**; is the only member of S, we have but one choice to make, and that choice yields the string **wcs**;.

Production (2) adds string **{}**, since terminals **{** and **}** can only stand for themselves, but syntactic category $<L>$ can stand for any string in language L. At the moment, L has only ϵ.

Since production (3) has a body consisting of a terminal, it will never produce any string other than **s**;, so we can forget this production from now on. Similarly, production (5) will never produce any string other than ϵ, so we can ignore it on this and future rounds.

Finally, production (4) produces string **s**; for L when we replace $<L>$ by ϵ and replace $<S>$ by **s**;. At the end of round 2, the languages are $S = \{$**s**;, **wcs**;, **{}**$\}$, and $L = \{\epsilon,$ **s**;$\}$.

On the next round, we can use productions (1), (2), and (4) to produce new strings. In production (1), we have three choices to substitute for $<S>$, namely **s**;, **wcs**;, and **{}**. The first gives us a string for language S that we already have, but the other two give us new strings **wcwcs**; and **wc{}**.

Production (2) allows us to substitute ϵ or **s**; for $<L>$, giving us old string **{}** and new string **{s;}** for language S. In production (4), we can substitute ϵ or **s**; for $<L>$ and **s**;, **wcs**;, or **{}** for $<S>$, giving us for language L one old string, **s**;, and the five new strings **wcs**;, **{}**, **s;s;**, **s;wcs**;, and **s;{}**.[1]

---

[1] We are being extremely systematic about the way we substitute strings for syntactic categories. We assume that throughout each round, the languages L and S are fixed as they were defined at the end of the previous round. Substitutions are made into each of the production bodies. The bodies are allowed to produce new strings for the syntactic categories of the

The current languages are $S = \{$s;, wcs;, {}, wcwcs;, wc{}, {s;}$\}$, and

$$L = \{\epsilon, \text{ s;, wcs;, {}, s;s;, s;wcs;, s;{}}\}$$

We may proceed in this manner as long as we like. Figure 11.7 summarizes the first three rounds. ◆

	S	L
Round 1:	s;	ϵ
Round 2:	wcs; {}	s;
Round 3:	wcwcs; wc{} {s;}	wcs; {} s;s; s;wcs; s;{}

Fig. 11.7. New strings on first three rounds.

Infinite language

As in Example 11.4, the language defined by a grammar may be infinite. When a language is infinite, we cannot list every string. The best we can do is to *enumerate* the strings by rounds, as we started to do in Example 11.4. Any string in the language will appear on some round, but there is no round at which we shall have produced all the strings. The set of strings that would ever be put into the language of a syntactic category $<S>$ forms the (infinite) language $L(<S>)$.

EXERCISES

11.3.1: What new strings are added on the fourth round in Example 11.4?

11.3.2*: On the ith round of Example 11.4, what is the length of the shortest string that is new for either of the syntactic categories? What is the length of the longest new string for

a) $<S>$
b) $<L>$?

11.3.3: Using the grammar of

a) Fig. 11.3
b) Fig. 11.4

generate strings of balanced parentheses by rounds. Do the two grammars generate the same strings on the same rounds?

---

heads, but we do not use the strings newly constructed from one production in the body of another production on the same round. It doesn't matter. All strings that are going to be generated will eventually be generated on some round, regardless of whether or not we immediately recycle new strings into the bodies or wait for the next round to use the new strings.

11.3.4: Suppose that each production with some syntactic category $<S>$ as its head also has $<S>$ appearing somewhere in its body. Why is $L(<S>)$ empty?

11.3.5*: When generating strings by rounds, as described in this section, the only new strings that can be generated for a syntactic category $<S>$ are found by making a substitution for the syntactic categories of the body of some production for $<S>$, such that *at least one substituted string was newly discovered on the previous round*. Explain why the italicized condition is correct.

11.3.6**: Suppose we want to tell whether a particular string s is in the language of some syntactic category $<S>$.

a) Explain why, if on some round, all the new strings generated for any syntactic category are longer than s, and s has not already been generated for $L(<S>)$, then s cannot ever be put in $L(<S>)$. *Hint*: Use Exercise 11.3.5.

b) Explain why, after some finite number of rounds, we must fail to generate any new strings that are as short as or shorter than s.

c) Use (a) and (b) to develop an algorithm that takes a grammar, one of its syntactic categories $<S>$, and a string of terminals s, and tells whether s is in $L(<S>)$.

❖❖ 11.4   Parse Trees

As we have seen, we can discover that a string s belongs to the language $L(<S>)$, for some syntactic category $<S>$, by the repeated application of productions. We start with some strings derived from basis productions, those that have no syntactic category in the body. We then "apply" productions to strings already derived for the various syntactic categories. Each application involves substituting strings for occurrences of the various syntactic categories in the body of the production, and thereby constructing a string that belongs to the syntactic category of the head. Eventually, we construct the string s by applying a production with $<S>$ at the head.

It is often useful to draw the "proof" that s is in $L(<S>)$ as a tree, which we call a *parse tree*. The nodes of a parse tree are labeled, either by terminals, by syntactic categories, or by the symbol ϵ. The leaves are labeled only by terminals or ϵ, and the interior nodes are labeled only by syntactic categories.

Every interior node v represents the application of a production. That is, there must be some production such that

1. The syntactic category labeling v is the head of the production, and

2. The labels of the children of v, from the left, form the body of the production.

✦ **Example 11.5.** Figure 11.8 is an example of a parse tree, based on the grammar of Fig. 11.2. However, we have abbreviated the syntactic categories $<Expression>$, $<Number>$, and $<Digit>$ to $<E>$, $<N>$, and $<D>$, respectively. The string represented by this parse tree is `3*(2+14)`.

For example, the root and its children represent the production

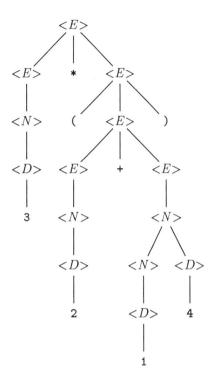

Fig. 11.8. Parse tree for the string $3 * (2 + 14)$ using the grammar from Fig. 11.2.

$$<E> \rightarrow <E> * <E>$$

which is production (6) in Fig. 11.2. The rightmost child of the root and its three children form the production $<E> \rightarrow (<E>)$, or production (5) of Fig. 11.2. ✦

Constructing Parse Trees

Yield of a tree

Each parse tree represents a string of terminals s, which we call the *yield* of the tree. The string s consists of the labels of the leaves of the tree, in left-to-right order. Alternatively, we can find the yield by doing a preorder traversal of the parse tree and listing only the labels that are terminals. For example, the yield of the parse tree in Fig. 11.8 is **3*(2+14)**.

If a tree has one node, that node will be labeled by a terminal or ϵ, because it is a leaf. If the tree has more than one node, then the root will be labeled by a syntactic category, since the root of a tree of two or more nodes is always an interior node. This syntactic category will always include, among its strings, the yield of the tree. The following is an inductive definition of the parse trees for a given grammar.

BASIS. For every terminal of the grammar, say **x**, there is a tree with one node labeled **x**. This tree has yield **x**, of course.

INDUCTION. Suppose we have a production $<S> \rightarrow X_1 X_2 \cdots X_n$, where each of the X_i's is either a terminal or a syntactic category. If $n = 0$, that is, the production

<S>
|
ϵ

Fig. 11.9. Parse tree from production $<S> \to \epsilon$.

is really $<S> \to \epsilon$, then there is a tree like that of Fig. 11.9. The yield is ϵ, and the root is $<S>$; surely string ϵ is in $L(<S>)$, because of this production.

Now suppose $<S> \to X_1 X_2 \cdots X_n$ and $n \geq 1$. We may choose a tree T_i for each X_i, $i = 1, 2, \ldots, n$, as follows:

1.   If X_i is a terminal, we must choose the 1-node tree labeled X_i. If two or more of the X's are the same terminal, then we must choose different one-node trees with the same label for each occurrence of this terminal.

2.   If X_i is a syntactic category, we may choose any parse tree already constructed that has X_i labeling the root. We then construct a tree that looks like Fig. 11.10. That is, we create a root labeled $<S>$, the syntactic category at the head of the production, and we give it as children, the roots of the trees selected for $X_1, X_2, \ldots, X_n$, in order from the left. If two or more of the X's are the same syntactic category, we may choose the same tree for each, but we must make a distinct copy of the tree each time it is selected. We are also permitted to choose different trees for different occurrences of the same syntactic category.

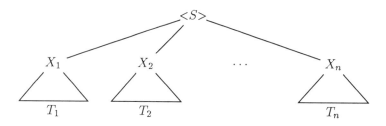

Fig. 11.10. Constructing a parse tree using a production and other parse trees.

Example 11.6. Let us follow the construction of the parse tree in Fig. 11.8, and see how its construction mimics a proof that the string `3*(2+14)` is in $L(<E>)$. First, we can construct a one-node tree for each of the terminals in the tree. Then the group of productions on line (1) of Fig. 11.2 says that each of the ten digits is a string of length 1 belonging to $L(<D>)$. We use four of these productions to create the four trees shown in Fig. 11.11. For instance, we use the production $<D> \to 1$ to create the parse tree in Fig. 11.11(a) as follows. We create a tree with a single node labeled **1** for the symbol **1** in the body. Then we create a node labeled $<D>$ as the root and give it one child, the root (and only node) of the tree selected for **1**.

Our next step is to use production (2) of Fig. 11.2, or $<N> \to <D>$, to discover that digits are numbers. For instance, we may choose the tree of Fig.

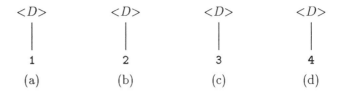

Fig. 11.11. Parse trees constructed using production
$<D> \to 1$ and similar productions.

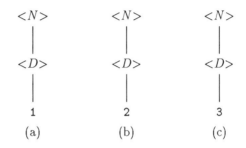

Fig. 11.12. Parse trees constructed using production $<N> \to <D>$.

11.11(a) to substitute for $<D>$ in the body of production (2), and get the tree of Fig. 11.12(a). The other two trees in Fig. 11.12 are produced similarly.

Now we can use production (3), which is $<N> \to <N><D>$. For $<N>$ in the body we shall select the tree of Fig. 11.12(a), and for $<D>$ we select Fig. 11.11(d). We create a new node labeled by $<N>$, for the head, and give it two children, the roots of the two selected trees. The resulting tree is shown in Fig. 11.13. The yield of this tree is the number **14**.

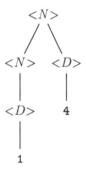

Fig. 11.13. Parse trees constructed using production $<N> \to <N><D>$.

Our next task is to create a tree for the sum **2+14**. First, we use the production (4), or $<E> \to <N>$, to build the parse trees of Fig. 11.14. These trees show that **3**, **2**, and **14** are expressions. The first of these comes from selecting the tree of Fig. 11.12(c) for $<N>$ of the body. The second is obtained by selecting the tree of Fig. 11.12(b) for $<N>$, and the third by selecting the tree of Fig. 11.13.

Then we use production (6), which is $<E> \to <E>+<E>$. For the first $<E>$

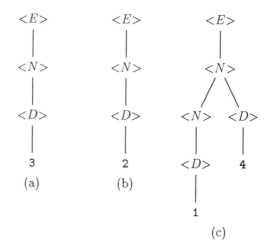

Fig. 11.14. Parse trees constructed using production $<E> \rightarrow <N>$.

in the body we use the tree of Fig. 11.14(b), and for the second $<E>$ in the body we use the tree of Fig. 11.14(c). For the terminal **+** in the body, we use a one-node tree with label **+**. The resulting tree is shown in Fig. 11.15; its yield is **2+14**.

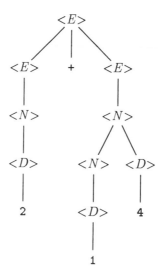

Fig. 11.15. Parse tree constructed using production $<E> \rightarrow <E>+<E>$.

We next use production (5), or $<E> \rightarrow (<E>)$, to construct the parse tree of Fig. 11.16. We have simply selected the parse tree of Fig. 11.15 for the $<E>$ in the body, and we select the obvious one-node trees for the terminal parentheses.

Lastly, we use production (8), which is $<E> \rightarrow <E> * <E>$, to construct the parse tree that we originally showed in Fig. 11.8. For the first $<E>$ in the body, we choose the tree of Fig. 11.14(a), and for the second we choose the tree of Fig. 11.16. ✦

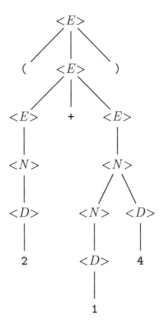

Fig. 11.16. Parse tree constructed using production $<E> \rightarrow (<E>)$.

Why Parse Trees "Work"

The construction of parse trees is very much like the inductive definition of the strings belonging to a syntactic category. We can prove, by two simple inductions, that the yields of the parse trees with root $<S>$ are exactly the strings in $L(<S>)$, for any syntactic category $<S>$. That is,

1.   If T is a parse tree with root labeled $<S>$ and yield s, then string s is in the language $L(<S>)$.

2.   If string s is in $L(<S>)$, then there is a parse tree with yield s and root labeled $<S>$.

This equivalence should be fairly intuitive. Roughly, parse trees are assembled from smaller parse trees in the same way that we assemble long strings from shorter ones, using substitution for syntactic categories in the bodies of productions. We begin with part (1), which we prove by complete induction on the height of tree T.

BASIS. Suppose the height of the parse tree is 1. Then the tree looks like Fig. 11.17, or, in the special case where $n = 0$, like the tree of Fig. 11.9. The only way we can construct such a tree is if there is a production $<S> \rightarrow \mathbf{x_1 x_2} \cdots \mathbf{x_n}$, where each of the $\mathbf{x}$'s is a terminal (if $n = 0$, the production is $<S> \rightarrow \epsilon$). Thus, $\mathbf{x_1 x_2} \cdots \mathbf{x_n}$ is a string in $L(<S>)$.

INDUCTION. Suppose that statement (1) holds for all trees of height k or less. Now consider a tree of height $k + 1$ that looks like Fig. 11.10. Then each of the subtrees T_i, for $i = 1, 2, \ldots, n$, can be of height at most k. For if any one of the subtrees had height $k + 1$ or more, the entire tree would have height at least $k + 2$. Thus, the inductive hypothesis applies to each of the trees T_i.

Fig. 11.17. Parse tree of height 1.

By the inductive hypothesis, if X_i, the root of the subtree T_i, is a syntactic category, then the yield of T_i, say s_i, is in the language $L(X_i)$. If X_i is a terminal, let us define string s_i to be X_i. Then the yield of the entire tree is $s_1 s_2 \cdots s_n$.

We know that $<S> \to X_1 X_2 \cdots X_n$ is a production, by the definition of a parse tree. Suppose that we substitute string s_i for X_i, whenever X_i is a syntactic category. By definition, X_i is s_i if X_i is a terminal. It follows that the substituted body is $s_1 s_2 \cdots s_n$, the same as the yield of the tree. By the inductive rule for the language of $<S>$, we know that $s_1 s_2 \cdots s_n$ is in $L(<S>)$.

Now we must prove statement (2), that every string s in a syntactic category $<S>$ has a parse tree with root $<S>$ and s as yield. To begin, let us note that for each terminal $\mathbf{x}$, there is a parse tree with both root and yield $\mathbf{x}$. Now we use complete induction on the number of times we applied the inductive step (described in Section 11.3) when we deduced that s is in $L(<S>)$.

BASIS. Suppose s requires one application of the inductive step to show that s is in $L(<S>)$. Then there must be a production $<S> \to \mathbf{x}_1 \mathbf{x}_2 \cdots \mathbf{x}_n$, where all the $\mathbf{x}$'s are terminals, and $s = \mathbf{x}_1 \mathbf{x}_2 \cdots \mathbf{x}_n$. We know that there is a one node parse tree labeled $\mathbf{x}_i$ for $i = 1, 2, \ldots, n$. Thus, there is a parse tree with yield s and root labeled $<S>$; this tree looks like Fig. 11.17. In the special case that $n = 0$, we know $s = \epsilon$, and we use the tree of Fig. 11.9 instead.

INDUCTION. Suppose that any string t found to be in the language of any syntactic category $<T>$ by k or fewer applications of the inductive step has a parse tree with t as yield and $<T>$ at the root. Consider a string s that is found to be in the language of syntactic category $<S>$ by $k + 1$ applications of the inductive step. Then there is a production $<S> \to X_1 X_2 \cdots X_n$, and $s = s_1 s_2 \cdots s_n$, where each substring s_i is either

1. X_i, if X_i is a terminal, or

2. Some string known to be in $L(X_i)$ using at most k applications of the inductive rule, if X_i is a syntactic category.

Thus, for each i, we can find a tree T_i, with yield s_i and root labeled X_i. If X_i is a syntactic category, we invoke the inductive hypothesis to claim that T_i exists, and if X_i is a terminal, we do not need the inductive hypothesis to claim that there is a one-node tree labeled X_i. Thus, the tree constructed as in Fig. 11.10 has yield s and root labeled $<S>$, proving the induction step.

Syntax Trees and Expression Trees

Often, trees that look like parse trees are used to represent expressions. For instance, we used *expression trees* as examples throughout Chapter 5. *Syntax tree* is another name for "expression tree." When we have a grammar for expressions such as that of Fig. 11.2, we can convert parse trees to expression trees by making three transformations:

1.   Atomic operands are condensed to a single node labeled by that operand.

2.   Operators are moved from leaves to their parent node. That is, an operator symbol such as + becomes the label of the node above it that was labeled by the "expression" syntactic category.

3.   Interior nodes that remain labeled by "expression" have their label removed.

For instance, the parse tree of Fig. 11.8 is converted to the following expression tree or syntax tree:

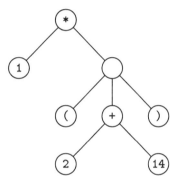

EXERCISES

11.4.1: Find a parse tree for the strings

a)   35+21
b)   123-(4*5)
c)   1*2*(3-4)

according to the grammar of Fig. 11.2. The syntactic category at the root should be $<E>$ in each case.

11.4.2: Using the statement grammar of Fig. 11.6, find parse trees for the following strings:

a)   wcwcs;
b)   {s;}
c)   {s;wcs;}.

The syntactic category at the root should be $<S>$ in each case.

11.4.3: Using the balanced parenthesis grammar of Fig. 11.3, find parse trees for the following strings:

a)   `(()())`
b)   `((()))`
c)   `((())()).`

11.4.4: Find parse trees for the strings of Exercise 11.4.3, using the grammar of Fig. 11.4.

❖❖ 11.5 Ambiguity and the Design of Grammars

Let us consider the grammar for balanced parentheses that we originally showed in Fig. 11.4, with syntactic category $<B>$ abbreviating $<Balanced>$:

$$<B> \rightarrow (<B>) \mid <B><B> \mid \epsilon \qquad (11.1)$$

Suppose we want a parse tree for the string `()()()`. Two such parse trees are shown in Fig. 11.18, one in which the first two pairs of parentheses are grouped first, and the other in which the second two pairs are grouped first.

It should come as no surprise that these two parse trees exist. Once we establish that both `()` and `()()` are balanced strings of parentheses, we can use the production $<B> \rightarrow <B><B>$ with `()` substituting for the first $<B>$ in the body and `()()` substituting for the second, or vice-versa. Either way, the string `()()()` is discovered to be in the syntactic category $<B>$.

Ambiguous grammar

A grammar in which there are two or more parse trees with the same yield and the same syntactic category labeling the root is said to be *ambiguous*. Notice that not every string has to be the yield of several parse trees; it is sufficient that there be even one such string, to make the grammar ambiguous. For example, the string `()()()` is sufficient for us to conclude that the grammar (11.1) is ambiguous. A grammar that is not ambiguous is called *unambiguous*. In an unambiguous grammar, for every string s and syntactic category $<S>$, there is at most one parse tree with yield s and root labeled $<S>$.

An example of an unambiguous grammar is that of Fig. 11.3, which we reproduce here with $<B>$ in place of $<Balanced>$,

$$<B> \rightarrow (<B>)<B> \mid \epsilon \qquad (11.2)$$

A proof that the grammar is unambiguous is rather difficult. In Fig. 11.19 is the unique parse tree for string `()()()`; the fact that this string has a unique parse tree does not prove the grammar (11.2) is unambiguous, of course. We can only prove unambiguity by showing that *every* string in the language has a unique parse tree.

Ambiguity in Expressions

While the grammar of Fig. 11.4 is ambiguous, there is no great harm in its ambiguity, because whether we group several strings of balanced parentheses from the left or the right matters little. When we consider grammars for expressions, such as that of Fig. 11.2 in Section 11.2, some more serious problems can occur. Specifically, some parse trees imply the wrong value for the expression, while others imply the correct value.

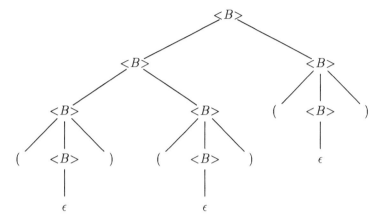

(a) Parse tree that groups from the left.

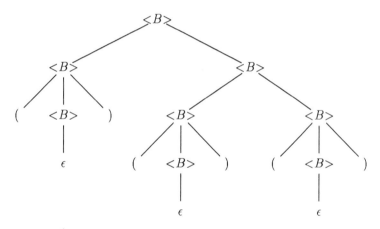

(b) Parse tree that groups from the right.

Fig. 11.18. Two parse trees with the same yield and root.

✦ **Example 11.7.** Let us use the shorthand notation for the expression grammar that was developed in Example 11.5. Then consider the expression 1-2+3. It has two parse trees, depending on whether we group operators from the left or the right. These parse trees are shown in Fig. 11.20(a) and (b).

The tree of Fig. 11.20(a) associates from the left, and therefore groups the operands from the left. That grouping is correct, since we generally group operators at the same precedence from the left; 1-2+3 is conventionally interpreted as (1-2)+3, which has the value 2. If we evaluate the expressions represented by subtrees, working up the tree of Fig. 11.20(a), we first compute $1 - 2 = -1$ at the leftmost child of the root, and then compute $-1 + 3 = 2$ at the root.

On the other hand, Fig. 11.20(b), which associates from the right, groups our expression as 1-(2+3), whose value is -4. This interpretation of the expression is unconventional, however. The value -4 is obtained working up the tree of Fig. 11.20(b), since we evaluate $2 + 3 = 5$ at the rightmost child of the root, and then $1 - 5 = -4$ at the root. ✦

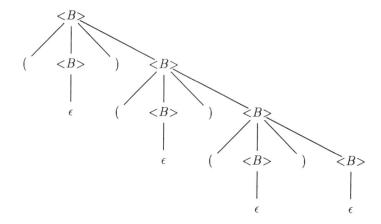

Fig. 11.19. Unique parse tree for the string ( ) ( ) ( ) using the grammar (11.2).

Why Unambiguity Is Important

The parser, which constructs parse trees for programs, is an essential part of a compiler. If a grammar describing a programming language is ambiguous, and if its ambiguities are left unresolved, then for at least some programs there is more than one parse tree. Different parse trees for the same program normally impart different meanings to the program, where "meaning" in this case is the action performed by the machine language program into which the original program is translated. Thus, if the grammar for a program is ambiguous, a compiler cannot properly decide which parse tree to use for certain programs, and thus cannot decide what the machine-language program should do. For this reason, compilers must use specifications that are unambiguous.

Associating operators of equal precedence from the wrong direction can cause problems. We also have problems with operators of different precedence; it is possible to group an operator of low precedence before one of higher precedence, as we see in the next example.

✦ **Example 11.8.** Consider the expression 1+2*3. In Fig. 11.21(a) we see the expression incorrectly grouped from the left, while in Fig. 11.21(b), we have correctly grouped the expression from the right, so that the multiplication gets its operands grouped before the addition. The former grouping yields the erroneous value 9, while the latter grouping produces the conventional value of 7. ✦

Unambiguous Grammars for Expressions

Just as the grammar (11.2) for balanced parentheses can be viewed as an unambiguous version of the grammar (11.1), it is possible to construct an unambiguous version of the expression grammar from Example 11.5. The "trick" is to define three syntactic categories, with intuitive meanings as follows.

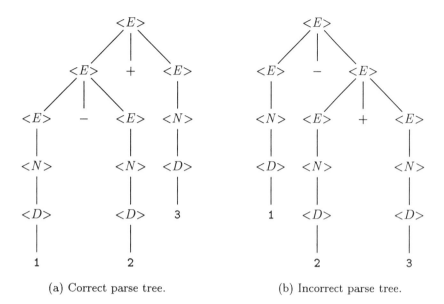

Fig. 11.20. Two parse trees for the expression $1 - 2 + 3$.

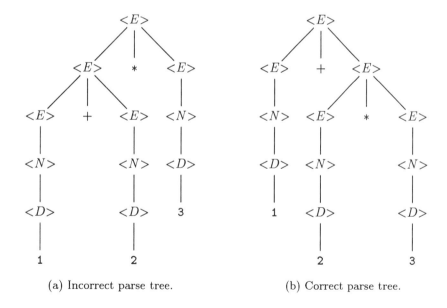

Fig. 11.21. Two parse trees for the expression 1+2*3.

1. *<Factor>* generates expressions that cannot be "pulled apart," that is, a factor is either a single operand or any parenthesized expression.

2. *<Term>* generates a product or quotient of factors. A single factor is a term, and thus is a sequence of factors separated by the operators * or /. Examples of terms are **12** and **12/3*45**.

3. *<Expression>* generates a sum or difference of one or more terms. A single term

is an expression, and thus is a sequence of terms separated by the operators + or −. Examples of expressions are 12, 12/3*45, and 12+3*45−6.

Figure 11.22 is a grammar that expresses the relationship between expressions, terms, and factors. We use shorthands $<E>$, $<T>$, and $<F>$ for $<Expression>$, $<Term>$, and $<Factor>$, respectively.

(1) $<E> \rightarrow <E> + <T> \mid <E> - <T> \mid <T>$

(2) $<T> \rightarrow <T> * <F> \mid <T>/<F> \mid <F>$

(3) $<F> \rightarrow (<E>) \mid <N>$

(4) $<N> \rightarrow <N><D> \mid <D>$

(5) $<D> \rightarrow 0 \mid 1 \mid \cdots \mid 9$

Fig. 11.22. Unambiguous grammar for arithmetic expressions.

For instance, the three productions in line (1) define an expression to be either a smaller expression followed by a + or − and another term, or to be a single term. If we put these ideas together, the productions say that every expression is a term, followed by zero or more pairs, each pair consisting of a + or − and a term. Similarly, line (2) says that a term is either a smaller term followed by * or / and a factor, or it is a single factor. That is, a term is a factor followed by zero or more pairs, each pair consisting of a * or a / and a factor. Line (3) says that factors are either numbers, or expressions surrounded by parentheses. Lines (4) and (5) define numbers and digits as we have done previously.

The fact that in lines (1) and (2) we use productions such as

$$<E> \rightarrow <E> + <T>$$

rather than the seemingly equivalent $<E> \rightarrow <T> + <E>$, forces terms to be grouped from the left. Thus, we shall see that an expression such as 1−2+3 is correctly grouped as (1−2)+3. Likewise, terms such as 1/2*3 are correctly grouped as (1/2)*3, rather than the incorrect 1/(2*3). Figure 11.23 shows the only possible parse tree for the expression 1−2+3 in the grammar of Fig. 11.22. Notice that 1−2 must be grouped as an expression first. If we had grouped 2+3 first, as in Fig. 11.20(b), there would be no way, in the grammar of Fig. 11.22, to attach the 1− to this expression.

The distinction among expressions, terms, and factors enforces the correct grouping of operators at different levels of precedence. For example, the expression 1+2*3 has only the parse tree of Fig. 11.24, which groups the subexpression 2*3 first, like the tree of Fig. 11.21(b) and unlike the incorrect tree of Fig. 11.21(a), which groups 1+2 first.

As for the matter of balanced parentheses, we have not proved that the grammar of Fig. 11.22 is unambiguous. The exercises contain a few more examples that should help convince the reader that this grammar is not only unambiguous, but gives the correct grouping for each expression. We also suggest how the idea of this grammar can be extended to more general families of expressions.

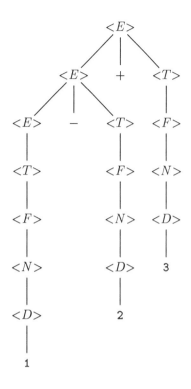

Fig. 11.23. Parse tree for the expression $1 - 2 + 3$ in the unambiguous grammar of Fig. 11.22.

EXERCISES

11.5.1: In the grammar of Fig. 11.22, give the unique parse tree for each of the following expressions:

a) `(1+2)/3`

b) `1*2-3`

c) `(1+2)*(3+4)`

11.5.2*: The expressions of the grammar in Fig. 11.22 have two levels of precedence; + and − at one level, and * and / at a second, higher level. In general, we can handle expressions with k levels of precedence by using $k + 1$ syntactic categories. Modify the grammar of Fig. 11.22 to include the exponentiation operator ^, which is at a level of precedence higher than * and /. As a hint, define a *primary* to be an operand or a parenthesized expression, and redefine a *factor* to be one or more primaries connected by the exponentiation operator. Note that exponentiation groups from the right, not the left, and 2^3^4 means 2^(3^4), rather than (2^3)^4. How do we force grouping from the right among primaries?

11.5.3*: Extend the unambiguous expression grammar to allow the comparison operators, =, <=, and so on, which are all at the same level of precedence and left-associative. Their precedence is below that of + and −.

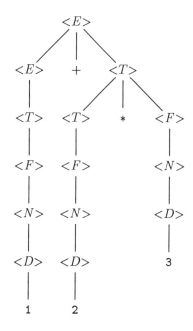

Fig. 11.24. Parse tree for $1 + 2 * 3$ in the unambiguous grammar of Fig. 11.22.

11.5.4: Extend the expression grammar of Fig. 11.22 to include the unary minus sign. Note that this operator is at a higher precedence than the other operators; for instance, -2*-3 is grouped (-2)*(-3).

11.5.5: Extend your grammar of Exercise 11.5.3 to include the logical operators &&, ||, and !. Give && the precedence of *, || the precedence of +, and ! a higher precedence than unary −. && and || are binary operators that group from the left.

11.5.6*: Not every expression has more than one parse tree according to the ambiguous grammar of Fig. 11.2 in Section 11.2. Give several examples of expressions that have unique parse trees according to this grammar. Can you give a rule indicating when an expression will have a unique parse tree?

11.5.7: The following grammar defines the set of strings (other than ϵ) consisting of 0's and 1's only.

$$<String> \rightarrow <String><String> \mid 0 \mid 1$$

In this grammar, how many parse trees does the string 010 have?

11.5.8: Give an unambiguous grammar that defines the same language as the grammar of Exercise 11.5.7.

11.5.9*: How many parse trees does grammar (11.1) have for the empty string? Show three different parse trees for the empty string.

❖❖ 11.6   Constructing Parse Trees

Grammars are like regular expressions, in that both notations describe languages but do not give directly an algorithm for determining whether a string is in the language being defined. For regular expressions, we learned in Chapter 10 how to convert a regular expression first into a nondeterministic automaton and then into a deterministic one; the latter can be implemented directly as a program.

There is a somewhat analogous process for grammars. We cannot, in general, convert a grammar to a deterministic automaton at all; the next section discusses some examples of when that conversion is impossible. However, it is often possible to convert a grammar to a program that, like an automaton, reads the input from beginning to end and renders a decision whether the input string is in the language of the grammar. The most important such technique, called "LR parsing" (the LR stands for left-to-right on the input), is beyond the scope of this book.

Recursive-Descent Parsing

What we shall give instead is a simpler but less powerful parsing technique called "recursive descent," in which the grammar is replaced by a collection of mutually recursive functions, each corresponding to one of the syntactic categories of the grammar. The goal of the function S that corresponds to the syntactic category $<S>$ is to read a sequence of input characters that form a string in the language $L(<S>)$, and to return a pointer to the root of a parse tree for this string.

A production's body can be thought of as a sequence of goals — the terminals and syntactic categories — that must be fulfilled in order to find a string in the syntactic category of the head. For instance, consider the unambiguous grammar for balanced parentheses, which we reproduce here as Fig. 11.25.

$$
\begin{array}{ll}
(1) & <B> \rightarrow \epsilon \\
(2) & <B> \rightarrow (\ <B>\ )\ <B>
\end{array}
$$

Fig. 11.25. Grammar for balanced parentheses.

Production (2) states that one way to find a string of balanced parentheses is to fulfill the following four goals in order.

1.   Find the character (, then

2.   Find a string of balanced parentheses, then

3.   Find the character), and finally

4.   Find another string of balanced parentheses.

In general, a terminal goal is satisfied if we find that this terminal is the next input symbol, but the goal cannot be satisfied if the next input symbol is something else. To tell whether a syntactic category in the body is satisfied, we call a function for that syntactic category.

The arrangement for constructing parse trees according to a grammar is suggested in Fig. 11.26. Suppose we want to determine whether the sequence of terminals $X_1 X_2 \cdots X_n$ is a string in the syntactic category $<S>$, and to find its parse tree if so. Then on the input file we place $X_1 X_2 \cdots X_n$ **ENDM**, where **ENDM** is a special symbol that is not a terminal.[2] We call **ENDM**, the *endmarker,* and its purpose is to indicate that the entire string being examined has been read. For example, in C programs it would be typical to use the end-of-file or end-of-string character for the endmarker.

Endmarker

$$X_1 \qquad X_2 \qquad \cdots \qquad X_n \qquad \text{ENDM}$$
$$\uparrow$$
$$\text{Call } S$$

Fig. 11.26. Initializing the program to discover an $<S>$ on the input.

Input cursor

An *input cursor* marks the terminal to be processed, the *current* terminal. If the input is a string of characters, then the cursor might be a pointer to a character. We start our parsing program by calling the function S for the starting syntactic category $<S>$, with the input cursor at the beginning of the input.

Each time we are working on a production body, and we come to a terminal **a** in the production, we look for the matching terminal **a** at the position indicated by the input cursor. If we find **a**, we advance the input cursor to the next terminal on the input. If the current terminal is something other than **a**, then we fail to match, and we cannot find a parse tree for the input string.

On the other hand, if we are working on a production body and we come to a syntactic category $<T>$, we call the function T for $<T>$. If T "fails," then the entire parse fails, and the input is deemed not to be in the language being parsed. If T succeeds, then it "consumes" some input, but moving the input cursor forward zero or more positions on the input. All input positions, from the position at the time T was called, up to but not including the position at which T leaves the cursor, are consumed. T also returns a tree, which is the parse tree for the consumed input.

When we have succeeded with each of the symbols in a production body, we assemble the parse tree for the portion of the input represented by that production. To do so, we create a new root node, labeled by the head of the production. The root's children are the roots of the trees returned by successful calls to functions for the syntactic categories of the body and leaves created for each of the terminals of the body.

---

[2] In real compilers for programming languages, the entire input might not be placed in a file at once, but terminals would be discovered one at a time by a preprocessor called a "lexical analyzer" that examines the source program one character at a time.

A Recursive-Descent Parser for Balanced Parentheses

Let us consider an extended example of how we might design the recursive function B for the syntactic category $<B>$ of the grammar of Fig. 11.25. B, called at some input position, will consume a string of balanced parentheses starting at that position and leave the input cursor at the position immediately after the balanced string.

The hard part is deciding whether to satisfy the goal of finding a $<B>$ by using production (1), $<B> \rightarrow \epsilon$, which succeeds immediately, or by using production (2), that is,

$$<B> \rightarrow (<B>)<B>$$

The strategy we shall follow is that whenever the next terminal is (, use production (2); whenever the next terminal is) or the endmarker, use production (1).

The function B is given in Fig. 11.27(b). It is preceded by important auxiliary elements in Fig. 11.27(a). These elements include:

1. Definition of a constant **FAILED** to be the value returned by B when that function fails to find a string of balanced parentheses on the input. The value of **FAILED** is the same as **NULL**. The latter value also represents an empty tree. However, the parse tree returned by B could not be empty if B succeeds, so there is no possible ambiguity in this definition of **FAILED**.

2. Definitions of the types **NODE** and **TREE**. A node consists of a label field, which is a character, and pointers to the leftmost child and right sibling. The label may be '**B**' to represent a node labeled B, '**(**' and '**)**' to represent nodes labeled with left- or right-parentheses, respectively, and '**e**' to represent a node labeled ϵ. Unlike the leftmost-child-right-sibling structure of Section 5.3, we have elected to use **TREE** rather than **pNODE** as the type of pointers to nodes since most uses of these pointers here will be as representations of trees.

3. Prototype declarations for three auxiliary functions to be described below and the function B.

4. Two global variables. The first, **parseTree**, holds the parse tree returned by the initial call to B. The second, **nextTerminal**, is the input cursor and points to the current position on the input string of terminals. Note that it is important for **nextTerminal** to be global, so when one call to B returns, the place where it left the input cursor is known to the copy of B that made the call.

5. The function **main**. In this simple demonstration, **main** sets **nextTerminal** to point to the beginning of a particular test string, ()(), and the result of a call to B is placed in **parseTree**.

6. Three auxiliary functions that create tree nodes and, if necessary, combine subtrees to form larger trees. These are:

    a) Function $makeNode0(x)$ creates a node with zero children, that is, a leaf, and labels that leaf with the symbol x. The tree consisting of this one node is returned.

```
#define FAILED NULL

typedef struct NODE *TREE;
struct NODE {
    char label;
    TREE leftmostChild, rightSibling;
};

TREE makeNode0(char x);
TREE makeNode1(char x, TREE t);
TREE makeNode4(char x, TREE t1, TREE t2, TREE t3, TREE t4);
TREE B();

TREE parseTree; /* holds the result of the parse */
char *nextTerminal; /* current position in input string */

void main()
{
    nextTerminal = "()()"; /* in practice, a string
        of terminals would be read from input */
    parseTree = B();
}

TREE makeNode0(char x)
{
    TREE root;

    root = (TREE) malloc(sizeof(struct NODE));
    root->label = x;
    root->leftmostChild = NULL;
    root->rightSibling = NULL;
    return root;
}

TREE makeNode1(char x, TREE t)
{
    TREE root;

    root = makeNode0(x);
    root->leftmostChild = t;
    return root;
}

TREE makeNode4(char x, TREE t1, TREE t2, TREE t3, TREE t4)
{
    TREE root;

    root = makeNode1(x, t1);
    t1->rightSibling = t2;
    t2->rightSibling = t3;
    t3->rightSibling = t4;
    return root;
}
```

Fig. 11.27(a). Auxiliary functions for recursive-descent parser.

```
        TREE B()
        {
(1)         TREE firstB, secondB;

(2)         if(*nextTerminal == '(') /* follow production 2 */ {
(3)             nextTerminal++;
(4)             firstB = B();
(5)             if(firstB != FAILED && *nextTerminal == ')') {
(6)                 nextTerminal++;
(7)                 secondB = B();
(8)                 if(secondB == FAILED)
(9)                     return FAILED;
                    else
(10)                    return makeNode4('B',
                            makeNode0('('),
                            firstB,
                            makeNode0(')'),
                            secondB);
            }
            else /* first call to B failed */
(11)            return FAILED;
        }
        else /* follow production 1 */
(12)        return makeNode1('B', makeNode0('e'));
        }
```

Fig. 11.27(b). Function to construct parse trees for strings of balanced parentheses.

b) Function $makeNode1(x, t)$ creates a node with one child. The label of the new node is x, and the child is the root of the tree t. The tree whose root is the created node is returned. Note that **makeNode1** uses **makeNode0** to create the root node and then makes the root of tree t be the leftmost child of the root. We assume that all leftmost-child and right-sibling pointers are **NULL** initially, as they will be because they are all created by **makeNode0**, which explicitly **NULL**'s them. Thus, it is not mandatory that **makeNode1** to store **NULL** in the **rightSibling** field of the root of t, but it would be a wise safety measure to do so.

c) Function $makeNode4(x, t_1, t_2, t_3, t_4)$ creates a node with four children. The label of the node is x, and the children are the roots of the trees t_1, t_2, t_3, and t_4, from the left. The tree whose root is the created node is returned. Note that **makeNode4** uses **makeNode1** to create a new root and attach t_1 to it, then strings the remaining trees together with right-sibling pointers.

Now we can consider the program of Fig. 11.27(b) line by line. Line (1) is the declaration of two local variables, **firstB** and **secondB**, to hold the parse trees returned by the two calls to B in the case that we elect to try production (2). Line (2) tests if the next terminal on the input is (. If so, we shall look for an instance of the body of production (2), and if not, then we shall assume that production (1) is used, and that ϵ is the balanced string.

At line (3), we increment `nextTerminal`, because the current input (has matched the (in the body of production (2). We now have the input cursor properly positioned for a call to B that will find a balanced string for the first $<B>$ in the body of production (2). That call occurs at line (4), and the tree returned is stored in variable `firstB` to be assembled later into a parse tree for the current call to B.

At line (5) we check that we are still capable of finding a balanced string. That is, we first check that the call to B on line (4) did not fail. Then we test that the current value of `nextTerminal` is). Recall that when B returns, `nextTerminal` points to the next input terminal to be formed into a balanced string. If we are to match the body of production (2), and we have already matched the (and the first $<B>$, then we must next match the), which explains the second part of the test. If either part of the test fails, then the current call to B fails at line (11).

If we pass the test of line (5), then at lines (6) and (7) we advance the input cursor over the right parenthesis just found and call B again, to match the final $<B>$ in production (2). The tree returned is stored temporarily in `secondB`.

If the call to B on line (7) fails, then `secondB` will have value `FAILED`. Line (8) detects this condition, and the current call to B also fails.

Line (10) covers the case in which we have succeeded in finding a balanced string. We return a tree constructed by `makeNode4`. This tree has a root labeled `'B'`, and four children. The first child is a leaf labeled (, constructed by `makeNode0`. The second is the tree we stored in `firstB`, which is the parse tree produced by the call to B at line (4). The third child is a leaf labeled), and the fourth is the parse tree stored in `secondB`, which was returned by the second call to B at line (7).

Line (11) is used only when the test of line (5) fails. Finally, line (12) handles the case where the original test of line (1) fails to find (as the first character. In that case, we assume that production (1) is correct. This production has the body ϵ, and so we consume no input but return a node, created by `makeNode1`, that has the label `B` and one child labeled ϵ.

◆ **Example 11.9.** Suppose we have the terminals ( ) ( ) `ENDM` on the input. Here, `ENDM` stands for the character `'\0'`, which marks the end of character strings in C. The call to B from `main` in Fig. 11.27(a) finds (as the current input, and the test of line (2) succeeds. Thus, `nextTerminal` advances at line (3), and at line (4) a second call to B is made, as suggested by "call 2" in Fig. 11.28.

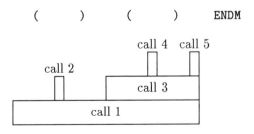

Fig. 11.28. Calls made while processing the input ( ) ( ) `ENDM`.

In call 2, the test of line (2) fails, and we thus return the tree of Fig. 11.29(a) at line (12). Now we return to call 1, where we are at line (5), with) pointed to by **nextTerminal** and the tree of Fig. 11.29(a) in **firstB**. Thus, the test of line (5) succeeds. We advance **nextTerminal** at line (6) and call B at line (7). This is "call 3" in Fig. 11.28.

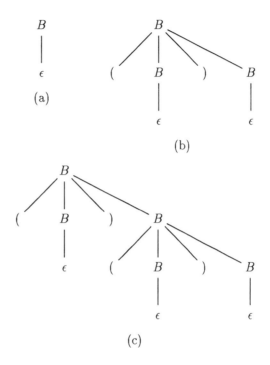

Fig. 11.29. Trees constructed by recursive calls to B.

In call 3 we succeed at line (2), advance **nextTerminal** at line (3), and call B at line (4); this call is "call 4" in Fig. 11.28. As with call 2, call 4 fails the test of line (2) and returns a (distinct) tree like that of Fig. 11.29(a) at line (12).

We now return to call 3, with **nextTerminal** still pointing to), with **firstB** (local to this call of B) holding a tree like Fig. 11.29(a), and with control at line (5). The test succeeds, and we advance **nextTerminal** at line (6), so it now points to **ENDM**. We make the fifth call to B at line (7). This call has its test fail at line (2) and returns another copy of Fig. 11.29(a) at line (12). This tree becomes the value of **secondB** for call 3, and the test of line (8) fails. Thus, at line (10) of call 3, we construct the tree shown in Fig. 11.29(b).

At this point, call 3 returns successfully to call 1 at line (8), with **secondB** of call 1 holding the tree of Fig. 11.29(b). As in call 3, the test of line (8) fails, and at line (10) we construct a tree with a new root node, whose second child is a copy of the tree in Fig. 11.29(a) — this tree was held in **firstB** of call 1 — and whose fourth child is the tree of Fig. 11.29(b). The resulting tree, which is placed in **parseTree** by **main**, is shown in Fig. 11.29(c). ♦

Constructing Recursive-Descent Parsers

Lookahead
symbol

We can generalize the technique used in Fig. 11.27 to many grammars, although not to all grammars. The key requirement is that for each syntactic category $<S>$, if there is more than one production with $<S>$ as the head, then by looking at only the current terminal (often called the *lookahead* symbol), we can decide on the one production for $<S>$ that needs to be tried. For instance, in Fig. 11.27, our decision strategy is to pick the second production, with body $(<B>)<B>$, whenever the lookahead symbol is (, and to pick the first production, with body ϵ, when the lookahead symbol is) or **ENDM**.

It is not possible to tell, in general, whether there is an algorithm for a given grammar that will always make the right decision. For Fig. 11.27, we claimed, but did not prove, that the strategy stated above will work. However, if we have a decision strategy that we believe will work, then for each syntactic category $<S>$, we can design the function S to do the following:

1. Examine the lookahead symbol and decide which production to try. Suppose the chosen production has body $X_1 X_2 \cdots X_n$.

2. For $i = 1, 2, \ldots, n$ do the following with X_i.

   a) If X_i is a terminal, check that the lookahead symbol is X_i. If so, advance the input cursor. If not, then this call to S fails.

   b) If X_i is a syntactic category, such as $<T>$, then call the function T corresponding to this syntactic category. If T returns with failure, then the call to S fails. If T returns successfully, store away the returned tree for use later.

   If we have not failed after considering all the X_i's, then assemble a parse tree to return by creating a new node, with children corresponding to $X_1, X_2, \ldots, X_n$, in order. If X_i is a terminal, then the child for X_i is a newly created leaf with label X_i. If X_i is a syntactic category, then the child for X_i is the root of the tree that was returned when a call to the function for X_i was completed. Figure 11.29 was an example of this tree construction.

   If the syntactic category $<S>$ represents the language whose strings we want to recognize and parse, then we start the parsing process by placing the input cursor at the first input terminal. A call to the function S will cause a parse tree for the input to be constructed if there is one and will return failure if the input is not in the language $L(<S>)$.

EXERCISES

11.6.1: Show the sequence of calls made by the program of Fig. 11.27 on the inputs

a) (())
b) (()())
c) ())(

in each case followed by the endmarker symbol **ENDM**.

11.6.2: Consider the following grammar for numbers.

$$<Number> \rightarrow <Digit><Number> \mid \epsilon$$
$$<Digit> \rightarrow 0 \mid 1 \mid \cdots \mid 9$$

Design a recursive-descent parser for this grammar; that is, write a pair of functions, one for $<Number>$ and the other for $<Digit>$. You may follow the style of Fig. 11.27 and assume that there are functions like $makeNode1$ that return trees with the root having a specified number of children.

11.6.3**: Suppose we had written the productions for $<Number>$ in Exercise 11.6.2 as

$$<Number> \rightarrow <Digit><Number> \mid <Digit>$$

or as

$$<Number> \rightarrow <Number><Digit> \mid \epsilon$$

Would we then be able to design a recursive-descent parser? Why or why not?

(1) $<L> \rightarrow (<E> <T>$
(2) $<T> \rightarrow , <E> <T>$
(3) $<T> \rightarrow)$
(4) $<E> \rightarrow <L>$
(5) $<E> \rightarrow atom$

Fig. 11.30. Grammar for list structures.

11.6.4*: The grammar in Fig. 11.30 defines nonempty lists, which are elements separated by commas and surrounded by parentheses. An element can be either an atom or a list structure. Here, $<E>$ stands for element, $<L>$ for list, and $<T>$ for "tail," that is, either a closing), or pairs of commas and elements ended by). Write a recursive-descent parser for the grammar of Fig. 11.30.

✦✦ 11.7 A Table-Driven Parsing Algorithm

As we have seen in Section 6.7, recursive function calls are normally implemented by a stack of activation records. As the functions in a recursive-descent parser do something very specific, it is possible to replace them by a single function that examines a table and manipulates a stack itself.

Remember that the function S for a syntactic category $<S>$ first decides what production to use, then goes through a sequence of steps, one for each symbol in the body of the selected production. Thus, we can maintain a stack of grammar symbols that roughly corresponds to the stack of activation records. However, both terminals and syntactic categories are placed on the stack. When a syntactic category $<S>$ is on top of the stack, we first determine the correct production. Then we replace $<S>$ by the body of the selected production, with the left end at the top of the stack. When a terminal is at the top of the stack, we make sure it matches the current input symbol. If so, we pop the stack and advance the input cursor.

To see intuitively why this arrangement works, suppose that a recursive-descent parser has just called S, the function for syntactic category $<S>$, and the selected production has body $a<B><C>$. Then there would be four times when this activation record for S is active.

1. When it checks for a on the input,

2. When it makes the call to B,

3. When that call returns and C is called, and

4. When the call to C returns and S is finished.

If, in the table-driven parser, we immediately replace $<S>$ by the symbols of the body, $a<B><C>$ in this example, then the stack will expose these symbols at the same points on the input when control returns to the corresponding activation of S in the recursive-descent parser.

1. The first time, a is exposed, and we check for a on the input, just as function S would.

2. The second time, which occurs immediately afterward, S would call B, but we have $<B>$ at the top of the stack, which will cause the same action.

3. The third time, S calls C, but we find $<C>$ on top of the stack and do the same.

4. The fourth time, S returns, and we find no more of the symbols by which $<S>$ was replaced. Thus, the symbol below the point on the stack that formerly held $<S>$ is now exposed. Analogously, the activation record below S's activation record would receive control in the recursive-descent parser.

Parsing Tables

As an alternative to writing a collection of recursive functions, we can construct a *parsing table*, whose rows correspond to the syntactic categories, and whose columns correspond to the possible lookahead symbols. The entry in the row for syntactic category $<S>$ and lookahead symbol X is the number of the production with head $<S>$ that must be used to expand $<S>$ if the lookahead is X.

Certain entries of the parse table are left blank. Should we find that syntactic category $<S>$ needs to be expanded, and the lookahead is X, but the entry in the row for $<S>$ and the column for X is blank, then the parse has failed. In this case, we can be sure that the input is not in the language.

♦ **Example 11.10.** In Fig. 11.31 we see the parsing table for the grammar of Fig. 11.25, the unambiguous grammar for balanced parentheses. This parsing table is rather simple, because there is only one syntactic category. The table expresses the same strategy that we used in our running example of Section 11.6. Expand by production (2), or $<B> \rightarrow (<B>)<B>$, if the lookahead is (, and expand by production (1), or $<B> \rightarrow \epsilon$, otherwise. We shall see shortly how parsing tables such as this one are used. ♦

	(	)	ENDM
$<B>$	2	1	1

Fig. 11.31. Parsing table for the balanced parentheses grammar.

	w	c	{	}	s	;	ENDM
$<S>$	1		2		3		
$<T>$	4		4	5	4		

Fig. 11.32. Parsing table for the grammar of Fig. 11.33.

(1) $<S> \rightarrow$ **w** **c**$<S>$
(2) $<S> \rightarrow$ **{** $<T>$
(3) $<S> \rightarrow$ **s** **;**

(4) $<T> \rightarrow <S><T>$
(5) $<T> \rightarrow$ **}**

Fig. 11.33. Grammar for simple statements, parsable by recursive descent.

◆   **Example 11.11.** Figure 11.32 is another example of a parsing table. It is for the grammar of Fig. 11.33, which is a variant of the statement grammar of Fig. 11.6.

The grammar of Fig. 11.33 has the form it does so that it can be parsed by recursive descent (or equivalently, by the table-driven parsing algorithm we are describing). To see why this form is necessary, let us consider the productions for $<L>$ in the grammar of Fig. 11.6:

$<L> \rightarrow <L><S> \mid \epsilon$

If the current input is a terminal like **s** that begins a statement, we know that $<L>$ must be expanded at least once by the first production, whose body is $<L><S>$. However, we cannot tell how many times to expand until we examine subsequent inputs and see how many statements there are in the statement list.

Our approach in Fig. 11.33 is to remember that a block consists of a left bracket followed by zero or more statements and a right bracket. Call the zero or more statements and the right bracket the "tail," represented by syntactic category $<T>$. Production (2) in Fig. 11.33 says that a statement can be a left bracket followed by a tail. Productions (4) and (5) say that a tail is either a statement followed by a tail, or just a right bracket.

We can decide whether to expand a $<T>$ by production (4) or (5) quite easily. Production (5) only makes sense if a right bracket is the current input, while production (4) only makes sense if the current input can start a statement. In our simple grammar, the only terminals that start statements are **w**, **{**, and **s**. Thus, we see in Fig. 11.32 that in the row for syntactic category $<T>$ we choose production

(4) on these three lookaheads and choose production (5) on the lookahead }. On other lookaheads, it is impossible that we could have the beginning of a tail, so we leave the entries for other lookaheads blank in the row for $<T>$.

Similarly, the decision for syntactic category $<S>$ is easy. If the lookahead symbol is **w**, then only production (1) could work. If the lookahead is {, then only production (2) is a possible choice, and on lookahead **s**, the only possibility is production (3). On any other lookahead, there is no way that the input could form a statement. These observations explain the row for $<S>$ in Fig. 11.32. ✦

How the Table-Driven Parser Works

Table driver All parsing tables can be used as data by essentially the same program. This *driver* program keeps a stack of grammar symbols, both terminals and syntactic categories. This stack can be thought of as goals that must be satisfied by the remaining input; the goals must be met in order, from the top to the bottom of the stack.

1. We satisfy a terminal goal by finding that terminal as the lookahead symbol of the input. That is, whenever a terminal **x** is on top of the stack, we check that the lookahead is **x**, and if so, we both pop **x** from the stack and read the next input terminal to become the new lookahead symbol.

2. We satisfy a syntactic category goal $<S>$ by consulting the parsing table for the entry in the row for $<S>$ and the column for the lookahead symbol.

   a) If the entry is blank, then we have failed to find a parse tree for the input. The driver program fails.

   b) If the entry contains production i, then we pop $<S>$ from the top of the stack and push each of the symbols in the body of production i onto the stack. The symbols of the body are pushed rightmost first, so that at the end, the first symbol of the body is at the top of the stack, the second symbol is immediately below it, and so on. As a special case, if the body is ϵ, we simply pop $<S>$ off the stack and push nothing.

Suppose we wish to determine whether string s is in $L(<S>)$. In that case, we start our driver with the string s **ENDM** on the input,[3] and read the first terminal as the lookahead symbol. The stack initially only consists of the syntactic category $<S>$.

✦ **Example 11.12.** Let us use the parsing table of Fig. 11.32 on the input

   {w c s ; s ; }ENDM

---

[3] Sometimes the endmarker symbol **ENDM** is needed as a lookahead symbol to tell us that we have reached the end of the input; other times it is only to catch errors. For instance, **ENDM** is needed in Fig. 11.31, because we can always have more parentheses after a balanced string, but it is not needed in Fig. 11.32, as is attested to by the fact that we never put any entries in the column for **ENDM**.

	STACK	LOOKAHEAD	REMAINING INPUT
1)	$<S>$	{	wcs;s;}ENDM
2)	{$<T>$	{	wcs;s;}ENDM
3)	$<T>$	w	cs;s;}ENDM
4)	$<S><T>$	w	cs;s;}ENDM
5)	wc$<S><T>$	w	cs;s;}ENDM
6)	c$<S><T>$	c	s;s;}ENDM
7)	$<S><T>$	s	;s;}ENDM
8)	s;$<T>$	s	;s;}ENDM
9)	;$<T>$	;	s;}ENDM
10)	$<T>$	s	;}ENDM
11)	$<S><T>$	s	;}ENDM
12)	s;$<T>$	s	;}ENDM
13)	;$<T>$	;	}ENDM
14)	$<T>$	}	ENDM
15)	}	}	ENDM
16)	ϵ	ENDM	ϵ

Fig. 11.34. Steps of a table-driven parser using the table of Fig. 11.32.

Figure 11.34 shows the steps taken by the table-driven parser. The stack contents are shown with the top at the left end, so that when we replace a syntactic category at the top of the stack by the body of one of its productions, the body appears in the top positions of the stack, with its symbols in the usual order.

Line (1) of Fig. 11.34 shows the initial situation. As $<S>$ is the syntactic category in which we want to test membership of the string {wcs;s;}, we start with the stack holding only $<S>$. The first symbol of the given string, {, is the lookahead symbol, and the remainder of the string, followed by ENDM is the remaining input.

If we consult the entry in Fig. 11.32 for syntactic category $<S>$ and lookahead {, we see that we must expand $<S>$ by production (2). The body of this production is {$<T>$, and we see that this sequence of two grammar symbols has replaced $<S>$ at the top of the stack when we get to line (2).

Now there is a terminal, {, at the top of the stack. We thus compare it with the lookahead symbol. Since the stack top and the lookahead agree, we pop the stack and advance to the next input symbol, w, which becomes the new lookahead symbol. These changes are reflected in line (3).

Next, with $<T>$ on top of the stack and w the lookahead symbol, we consult Fig. 11.32 and find that the proper action is to expand by production (4). We thus pop $<T>$ off the stack and push $<S><T>$, as seen in line (4). Similarly, the $<S>$ now on top of the stack is replaced by the body of production (1), since that is the action decreed by the row for $<S>$ and the column for lookahead w in Fig. 11.32; that change is reflected in line (5). After lines (5) and (6), the terminals on top of the stack are compared with the current lookahead symbol, and since each matches, they are popped and the input cursor advanced.

The reader is invited to follow lines (7) through (16) and check that each is the proper action to take according to the parsing table. As each terminal, when it gets to the top of the stack, matches the then current lookahead symbol, we do not fail. Thus, the string {wcs;s;} is in the syntactic category $<S>$; that is, it is a statement. ♦

Constructing a Parse Tree

The algorithm described above tells whether a given string is in a given syntactic category, but it doesn't produce the parse tree. There is, however, a simple modification of the algorithm that will also give us a parse tree, when the input string is in the syntactic category with which we initialize the stack. The recursive-descent parser described in the previous section builds its parse trees bottom-up, that is, starting at the leaves and combining them into progressively larger subtrees as function calls return.

For the table-driven parser, it is more convenient to build the parse trees from the top down. That is, we start with the root, and as we choose a production with which to expand the syntactic category at the top of the stack, we simultaneously create children for a node in the tree under construction; these children correspond to the symbols in the body of the selected production. The rules for tree construction are as follows.

1. Initially, the stack contains only some syntactic category, say, $<S>$. We initialize the parse tree to have only one node, labeled $<S>$. The $<S>$ on the stack *corresponds to* the one node of the parse tree being constructed.

2. In general, if the stack consists of symbols $X_1 X_2 \cdots X_n$, with X_1 at the top, then the current parse tree's leaves, taken from left to right, have labels that form a string s of which $X_1 X_2 \cdots X_n$ is a suffix. The last n leaves of the parse tree *correspond to* the symbols on the stack, so that each stack symbol X_i corresponds to a leaf with label X_i.

3. Suppose a syntactic category $<S>$ is on top of the stack, and we choose to replace $<S>$ by the body of a production $<S> \rightarrow Y_1 Y_2 \cdots Y_n$. We find the leaf of the parse tree corresponding to this $<S>$ (it will be the leftmost leaf that has a syntactic category for label), and give it n children, labeled $Y_1, Y_2, \ldots, Y_n$, from the left. In the special case that the body is ϵ, we instead create one child, labeled ϵ.

♦ **Example 11.13.** Let us follow the steps of Fig. 11.34 and construct the parse tree as we go. To begin, at line (1), the stack consists of only $<S>$, and the corresponding tree is the single node shown in Fig. 11.35(a). At line (2) we expanded $<S>$ using the production

$$<S> \rightarrow \{<T>$$

and so we give the leaf of Fig. 11.35(a) two children, labeled { and $<T>$, from the left. The tree for line (2) is shown in Fig. 11.35(b).

Line (3) results in no change in the parse tree, since we match terminals and do not expand a syntactic category. However, at line (4) we expand $<T>$ into $<S><T>$, and so we give the leaf labeled $<T>$ in Fig. 11.35(b) two children with

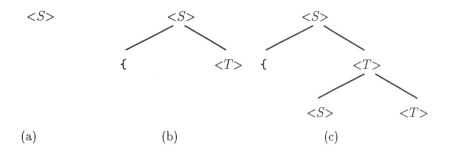

Fig. 11.35. First steps in construction of the parse tree.

these symbols as labels, as shown in Fig. 11.35(c). Then at line (5) the $<S>$ is expanded to **wc**$<S>$, which results in the leaf labeled $<S>$ in Fig. 11.35(c) being given three children. The reader is invited to continue this process. The final parse tree is shown in Fig. 11.36. ✦

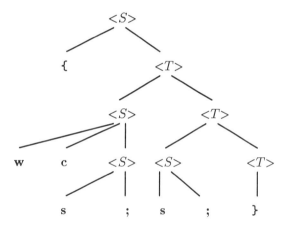

Fig. 11.36. Complete parse tree for the parse of Fig. 11.34.

Making Grammars Parsable

As we have seen, many grammars require modification in order to be parsable by the recursive-descent or table-driven methods we have learned in this section and the previous. While we cannot guarantee that any grammar can be modified so that these methods work, there are several tricks worth learning because they are often effective in making grammars parsable.

Left recursion elimination

The first trick is to *eliminate left recursion*. We pointed out in Example 11.11 how the productions

$$<L> \rightarrow <L><S> \mid \epsilon$$

could not be parsable by these methods because we could not tell how many times to apply the first production. In general, whenever a production for some syntactic category $<X>$ has a body that begins with $<X>$ itself, we are going to get confused as to how many times the production needs to be applied to expand $<X>$. We call this situation *left recursion*. However, we can often rearrange symbols of the body of the offending production so $<X>$ comes later. This step is *left recursion elimination*.

✦ **Example 11.14.** In Example 11.11 discussed above, we can observe that $<L>$ represents zero or more $<S>$'s. We can therefore eliminate the left-recursion by reversing the $<S>$ and $<L>$, as

$$<L> \rightarrow <S><L> \mid \epsilon$$

For another example, consider the productions for numbers:

$$<Number> \rightarrow <Number> <Digit> \mid <Digit>$$

Given a digit as lookahead, we do not know how many times to use the first production to expand $<Number>$. However, we observe that a number is one or more digits, allowing us to reorder the body of the first production, as:

$$<Number> \rightarrow <Digit> <Number> \mid <Digit>$$

This pair of productions eliminates the left recursion. ✦

Left factoring

Unfortunately, the productions of Example 11.14 are still not parsable by our methods. To make them parsable, we need the second trick, which is *left factoring*. When two productions for a syntactic category $<X>$ have bodies that begin with the same symbol C, we cannot tell which production to use, whenever the lookahead is something that could come from that common symbol C.

To *left factor* the productions, we create a new syntactic category $<T>$ that represents the "tail" of either production, that is, the parts of the body that follow C. We then replace the two productions for $<X>$ by a production

$$<X> \rightarrow C <T>$$

and two productions with head $<T>$. These two productions have bodies that are the "tails," that is, whatever follows C in the two productions for $<X>$.

✦ **Example 11.15.** Consider the productions for $<Number>$ that we developed in Example 11.14:

$$<Number> \rightarrow <Digit> <Number> \mid <Digit>$$

These two productions begin with a common symbol, $<Digit>$. We thus cannot tell which to use when the lookahead is a digit. However, we can defer the decision if we left factor them into

$$<Number> \rightarrow <Digit> <Tail>$$
$$<Tail> \rightarrow <Number> \mid \epsilon$$

Here, the two productions for $<Tail>$ allow us to choose the tail of the first production for $<Number>$, which is $<Number>$ itself, or the tail of the second production for $<Number>$, which is ϵ.

Now, when we have to expand $<Number>$ and see a digit as the lookahead, we replace $<Number>$ by $<Digit>$ $<Tail>$, match the digit, and then can choose how to expand tail, seeing what follows that digit. That is, if another digit follows, then we expand by the first choice for $<Tail>$, and if something other than a digit follows, we know we have seen the whole number and replace $<Tail>$ by ϵ. ✦

EXERCISES

11.7.1: Simulate the table-driven parser using the parsing table of Fig. 11.32 on the following input strings:

a) `{s;}`
b) `wc{s;s;}`
c) `{{s;s;}s;}`
d) `{s;s}`

11.7.2: For each of the parses in Exercise 11.7.1 that succeeds, show how the parse tree is constructed during the parse.

11.7.3: Simulate the table-driven parser, using the parsing table of Fig. 11.31, on the input strings of Exercise 11.6.1.

11.7.4: Show the construction of the parse trees during the parses of Exercise 11.7.3.

11.7.5*: The following grammar

(1) $<Statement>$ → **if** ($condition$)
(2) $<Statement>$ → **if** ($condition$) $<Statement>$
(3) $<Statement>$ → $simpleStat$;

represents selection statements in C. It is not parsable by recursive descent (or equivalently, by a table-driven parser), because with lookahead **if**, we cannot tell which of the first two productions to use. Left-factor the grammar to make it parsable by the algorithms of this section and Section 11.6. *Hint*: When you left-factor, you get a new syntactic category with two productions. One has body ϵ; the other has a body that begins with **else**. Evidently, when **else** is a lookahead, the second production can be the choice. For no other lookahead can it be the choice. But, if we examine on what lookaheads it might make sense to expand by the production with body ϵ, we discover that these lookahead symbols include **else**. However, we may arbitrarily decide never to expand to ϵ when the lookahead is **else**. That choice corresponds to the rule that "an **else** matches the previous unmatched **then**." It is thus the "correct" choice. You might wish to find an example of an input where expanding to ϵ with lookahead **else** allows the parser to complete the parse. You will discover that in any such parse, the constructed parse tree matches an **else** with the "wrong" **then**.

11.7.6**: The following grammar

$$<Structure> \rightarrow \textbf{struct } \{ <FieldList> \}$$
$$<FieldList> \rightarrow type \; fieldName \; ; \; <FieldList>$$
$$<FieldList> \rightarrow \epsilon$$

requires some modification in order to be parsable by the methods of this section or the previous. Rewrite the grammar to make it parsable, and construct the parsing table.

✦✦ 11.8 Grammars Versus Regular Expressions

Both grammars and regular expressions are notations for describing languages. We saw in Chapter 10 that the regular expression notation was equivalent to two other notations, deterministic and nondeterministic automata, in the sense that the set of languages describable by each of these notations is the same. Is it possible that grammars are another notation equivalent to the ones we have seen previously?

The answer is "no"; grammars are more powerful than the notations such as regular expressions that we introduced in Chapter 10. We shall demonstrate the expressive power of grammars in two steps. First, we shall show that every language describable by a regular expression is also describable by a grammar. Then we shall exhibit a language that can be described by a grammar, but not by any regular expression.

Simulating Regular Expressions by Grammars

The intuitive idea behind the simulation is that the three operators of regular expressions — union, concatenation, and closure — can each be "simulated" by one or two productions. Formally, we prove the following statement by complete induction on n, the number of operator occurrences in the regular expression R.

STATEMENT For every regular expression R, there is a grammar such that for one of its syntactic categories $<S>$, we have $L(<S>) = L(R)$.

That is, the language denoted by the regular expression is also the language of the syntactic category $<S>$.

BASIS. The basis case is $n = 0$, where the regular expression R has zero operator occurrences. Either R is a single symbol — say, $\textbf{x}$ — or R is ϵ or $\emptyset$. We create a new syntactic category $<S>$. In the first case, where $R = \textbf{x}$, we also create the production $<S> \rightarrow \textbf{x}$. Thus, $L(<S>) = \{\textbf{x}\}$, and $L(R)$ is the same language of one string. If R is ϵ, we similarly create the production $<S> \rightarrow \epsilon$ for $<S>$, and if $R = \emptyset$, we create no production at all for $<S>$. Then $L(<S>)$ is $\{\epsilon\}$ when R is ϵ, and $L(<S>)$ is $\emptyset$ when R is $\emptyset$.

INDUCTION. Suppose the inductive hypothesis holds for regular expressions with n or fewer occurrences of operators. Let R be a regular expression with $n+1$ operator occurrences. There are three cases, depending on whether the last operator applied to build R is union, concatenation, or closure.

1. $R = R_1 \mid R_2$. Since there is one operator occurrence, $\mid$ (union), that is part of neither R_1 nor R_2, we know that neither R_1 nor R_2 have more than n operator occurrences. Thus, the inductive hypothesis applies to each of these, and we can find a grammar G_1 with a syntactic category $<S_1>$, and a grammar G_2 with a syntactic category $<S_2>$, such that $L(<S_1>) = L(R_1)$ and $L(<S_2>) = L(R_2)$. To avoid coincidences when the two grammars are merged, we can assume that as we construct new grammars, we always create syntactic categories with names that appear in no other grammar. As a result, G_1 and G_2 have no syntactic category in common. We create a new syntactic category $<S>$ that appears neither in G_1, in G_2, nor in any other grammar that we may have constructed for other regular expressions. To the productions of G_1 and G_2 we add the two productions

$$<S> \rightarrow <S_1> \mid <S_2>$$

Then the language of $<S>$ consists of all and only the strings in the languages of $<S_1>$ and $<S_2>$. These are $L(R_1)$ and $L(R_2)$, respectively, and so

$$L(<S>) = L(R_1) \cup L(R_2) = L(R)$$

as we desired.

2. $R = R_1 R_2$. As in case (1), suppose there are grammars G_1 and G_2, with syntactic categories $<S_1>$ and $<S_2>$, respectively, such that $L(<S_1>) = L(R_1)$ and $L(<S_2>) = L(R_2)$. Then create a new syntactic category $<S>$ and add the production

$$<S> \rightarrow <S_1><S_2>$$

to the productions of G_1 and G_2. Then $L(<S>) = L(<S_1>)L(<S_2>)$.

3. $R = R_1{}^*$. Let G_1 be a grammar with a syntactic category $<S_1>$ such that $L(<S_1>) = L(R_1)$. Create a new syntactic category $<S>$ and add the productions

$$<S> \rightarrow <S_1><S> \mid \epsilon$$

Then $L(<S>) = L(<S_1>)^*$ because $<S>$ generates strings of zero or more $<S_1>$'s.

✦ **Example 11.16.** Consider the regular expression $\mathbf{a} \mid \mathbf{bc}^*$. We may begin by creating syntactic categories for the three symbols that appear in the expression.[4] Thus, we have the productions

$$<A> \rightarrow \mathbf{a}$$
$$<B> \rightarrow \mathbf{b}$$
$$<C> \rightarrow \mathbf{c}$$

According to the grouping rules for regular expressions, our expression is grouped as $\mathbf{a} \mid (\mathbf{b}(\mathbf{c})^*)$. Thus, we must first create the grammar for $\mathbf{c}^*$. By rule (3) above, we add to the production $<C> \rightarrow \mathbf{c}$, which is the grammar for regular expression $\mathbf{c}$, the productions

---

[4] If one of these symbols appeared two or more times, it would not be necessary to make a new syntactic category for each occurrence; one syntactic category for each symbol would suffice.

$$<D> \rightarrow <C><D> \mid \epsilon$$

Here, syntactic category $<D>$ was chosen arbitrarily, and could have been any category except for $<A>$, $<B>$, and $<C>$, which have already been used. Note that

$$L(<D>) = \left(L(<C>)\right)^* = c^*$$

Now we need a grammar for $\mathbf{bc}^*$. We take the grammar for $\mathbf{b}$, which consists of only the production $<B> \rightarrow \mathbf{b}$, and the grammar for $\mathbf{c}^*$, which is

$$<C> \rightarrow \mathbf{c}$$
$$<D> \rightarrow <C><D> \mid \epsilon$$

We shall create a new syntactic category $<E>$ and add the production

$$<E> \rightarrow <B><D>$$

This production is used because of rule (2) above, for the case of concatenation. Its body has $<B>$ and $<D>$ because these are the syntactic categories for the regular expressions, $\mathbf{b}$ and $\mathbf{c}^*$, respectively. The grammar for $\mathbf{bc}^*$ is thus

$$<E> \rightarrow <B><D>$$
$$<D> \rightarrow <C><D> \mid \epsilon$$
$$<B> \rightarrow \mathbf{b}$$
$$<C> \rightarrow \mathbf{c}$$

and $<E>$ is the syntactic category whose language is the desired one.

Finally, to get a grammar for the entire regular expression, we use rule (1), for union. We invent new syntactic category $<F>$, with productions

$$<F> \rightarrow <A> \mid <E>$$

Note that $<A>$ is the syntactic category for the subexpression $\mathbf{a}$, while $<E>$ is the syntactic category for the subexpression $\mathbf{bc}^*$. The resulting grammar is

$$<F> \rightarrow <A> \mid <E>$$
$$<E> \rightarrow <B><D>$$
$$<D> \rightarrow <C><D> \mid \epsilon$$
$$<A> \rightarrow \mathbf{a}$$
$$<B> \rightarrow \mathbf{b}$$
$$<C> \rightarrow \mathbf{c}$$

and $<F>$ is the syntactic category whose language is that denoted by the given regular expression. ✦

A Language with a Grammar but No Regular Expression

We shall now show that grammars are not only as powerful as regular expressions, but more powerful. We do so by exhibiting a language that has a grammar but has no regular expression. The language, which we shall call E, is the set of strings consisting of one or more 0's followed by an equal number of 1's. That is,

$$E = \{01, 0011, 000111, \ldots\}$$

To describe the strings of E there is a useful notation based on exponents. Let s^n, where s is a string and n is an integer, stand for $ss \cdots s$ (n times), that is, s concatenated with itself n times. Then

$$E = \{0^1 1^1, 0^2 1^2, 0^3 1^3, \ldots\}$$

or using a set-former,

$$E = \{0^n 1^n \mid n \geq 1\}$$

First, let us convince ourselves that we can describe E with a grammar. The following does the job.

(1) $<S> \rightarrow 0<S>1$
(2) $<S> \rightarrow 01$

One use of the basis production (2) tells us that 01 is in $L(<S>)$. On the second round, we can use production (1), with 01 in place of $<S>$ in the body, which yields $0^2 1^2$ for $L(<S>)$. Another application of (1) with $0^2 1^2$ in place of $<S>$ tells us $0^3 1^3$ is in $L(<S>)$, and so on. In general, $0^n 1^n$ requires one use of production (2) followed by $n - 1$ uses of production (1). As there are no other strings we can produce from these productions, we see that $E = L(<S>)$.

A Proof That E Is Not Defined by Any Regular Expression

Now we need to show that E cannot be described by a regular expression. It turns out to be easier to show that E is not described by any deterministic finite automaton. That proof also shows that E has no regular expression, because if E were the language of a regular expression R, we could convert R to an equivalent deterministic finite automaton by the techniques of Section 10.8. That deterministic finite automaton would then define the language E.

Thus, let us suppose that E is the language of some deterministic finite automaton A. Then A has some number of states, say, m states. Consider what happens when A receives inputs $000\cdots$. Let us refer to the initial state of the unknown automaton A by the name s_0. A must have a transition from s_0 on input 0 to some state we shall call s_1. From that state, another 0 takes A to a state we shall call s_2, and so on. In general, after reading i 0's A is in state s_i, as suggested by Fig. 11.37.[5]

Fig. 11.37. Feeding 0's to the automaton A.

Now A was assumed to have exactly m states, and there are $m+1$ states among $s_0, s_1, \ldots, s_m$. Thus, it is not possible that all of these states are different. There must be some distinct integers i and j in the range 0 to m, such that s_i and s_j are really the same state. If we assume that i is the smaller of i and j, then the path of Fig. 11.37 must have at least one loop in it, as suggested by Fig. 11.38. In practice, there could be many more loops and repetitions of states than is suggested by Fig. 11.38. Also notice that i could be 0, in which case the path from s_0 to s_i suggested

---

[5] The reader should remember that we don't really know the names of A's states; we only know that A has m states for some integer m. Thus, the names $s_0, \ldots, s_m$ are not A's names for its states, but rather our names for its states. That is not as odd as it might seem. For example, we routinely do things like create an array s, indexed from 0 to m, and store in $s[i]$ some value, which might be the name of a state of automaton A. We might then, in a program, refer to this state name as $s[i]$, rather than by its own name.

The Pigeonhole Principle

The proof that language E has no deterministic finite automaton used a technique known as the *pigeonhole principle,* which is usually stated as,

> "If $m + 1$ pigeons fly into m pigeonholes, there must be at least one hole with two pigeons."

In this case, the pigeonholes are the states of automaton A, and the pigeons are the m states that A is in after seeing zero, one, two, and up to m 0's.

Notice that m must be finite to apply the pigeonhole principle. The story of the infinite hotel in Section 7.11 tells us that the opposite can hold for infinite sets. There, we saw a hotel with an infinite number of rooms (corresponding to pigeonholes) and a number of guests (corresponding to pigeons) that was one greater than the number of rooms, yet it was possible to accommodate each guest in a room, without putting two guests in the same room.

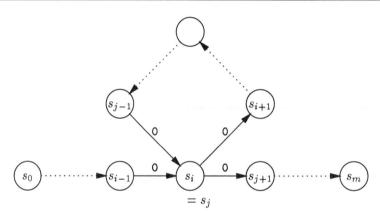

Fig. 11.38. The path of Fig. 11.37 must have a loop.

in Fig. 11.38 is really just a single node. Similarly, s_j could be s_m, in which case the path from s_j to s_m is but a single node.

The implication of Fig. 11.38 is that the automaton A cannot "remember" how many 0's it has seen. If it is in state s_m, it might have seen exactly m 0's, and so it must be that if we start in state m and feed A exactly m 1's, A arrives at an accepting state, as suggested by Fig. 11.39.

However, suppose that we fed A a string of $m + j - i$ 0's. Looking at Fig. 11.38, we see that i 0's take A from s_0 to s_i, which is the same as s_j. We also see that $m - j$ 0's take A from s_j to s_m. Thus, $m - j + i$ 0's take A from s_0 to s_m, as suggested by the upper path in Fig. 11.39.

Hence, $m - j + i$ 0's followed by m 1's takes A from s_0 to an accepting state. Put another way, the string $0^{m-j+i}1^m$ is in the language of A. But since j is greater than i, this string has more 1's than 0's, and is not in the language E. We conclude that A's language is not exactly E, as we had supposed.

As we started by assuming only that E had a deterministic finite automaton and wound up deriving a contradiction, we conclude that our assumption was false; that is, E has no deterministic finite automaton. Thus, E cannot have a regular

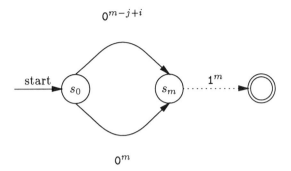

Fig. 11.39. Automaton A cannot tell whether it has seen m 0's or $m - j + i$ 0's.

Languages a Grammar Cannot Define

We might ask whether grammars are the most powerful notation for describing languages. The answer is "not by a long shot." There are simple languages that can be shown not to have a grammar, although the proof technique is beyond the scope of this book. An example of such a language is the set of strings consisting of equal numbers of 0's, 1's, and 2's, in order, that is,

$$\{012, 001122, 000111222, \ldots\}$$

As an example of a more powerful notation for describing languages, consider C itself. For any grammar, and any of its syntactic categories $<S>$, it is possible to write a C program to tell whether a string is in $L(<S>)$. Moreover, a C program to tell whether a string is in the language described above is not hard to write.

Undecidable problems

Yet there are languages that C programs cannot define. There is an elegant theory of "undecidable problems" that can be used to show certain problems cannot be solved by any computer program. The theory of undecidability, with some examples of undecidable problems, is discussed briefly in Section 14.10.

---

expression either.

The language $\{0^n 1^n \mid n \geq 1\}$ is just one of an infinite number of languages that can be specified by a grammar but not by any regular expression. Some examples are offered in the exercises.

EXERCISES

11.8.1: Find grammars that define the languages of the following regular expressions.

a)   (a | b)*a
b)   a* | b* | (ab)*
c)   a*b*c*

11.8.2*: Show that the set of strings of balanced parentheses is not defined by any regular expression. *Hint*: The proof is similar to the proof for the language E above. Suppose that the set of balanced strings had a deterministic finite automaton of m states. Feed this automaton m ('s, and examine the states it enters. Show that the automaton can be "fooled" into accepting a string with unbalanced parentheses.

11.8.3*: Show that the language consisting of strings of the form 0^n10^n, that is, two equal-length runs of 0's separated by a single 1, is not defined by any regular expression.

11.8.4*: One sometimes sees *fallacious* assertions that a language like E of this section is described by a regular expression. The argument is that for each n, 0^n1^n is a regular expression defining the language with one string, 0^n1^n. Thus,

$$01 \mid 0^21^2 \mid 0^31^3 \mid \cdots$$

is a regular expression describing E. What is wrong with this argument?

11.8.5*: Another fallacious argument about languages claims that E has the following finite automaton. The automaton has one state a, which is both the start state and an accepting state. There is a transition from a to itself on symbols 0 and 1. Then surely string 0^i1^i takes state a to itself, and is this accepted. Why does this argument not show that E is the language of a finite automaton?

11.8.6**: Show that each of the following languages cannot be defined by a regular expression.

Palindromes

a) $\{ww^R \mid w$ is a string of a's and b's and w^R is its reversal$\}$

b) $\{0^i \mid i$ is a perfect square$\}$

c) $\{0^i \mid i$ is a prime$\}$

Which of these languages can be defined by a grammar?

❖❖ 11.9 Summary of Chapter 11

After reading this chapter, the reader should be aware of the following points:

✦   How a (context-free) grammar defines a language

✦   How to construct a parse tree to represent the grammatical structure of a string

✦   What ambiguity is and why ambiguous grammars are undesirable in the specification of programming languages

✦   A technique called recursive-descent parsing that can be used to construct parse trees for certain classes of grammars

✦   A table-driven way of implementing recursive-descent parsers

✦   Why grammars are a more powerful notation for describing languages than are regular expressions or finite automata

❖❖ 11.10 Bibliographic Notes for Chapter 11

Context-free grammars were first studied by Chomsky [1956] as a formalism for describing natural languages. Similar formalisms were used to define the syntax of two of the earliest important programming languages, Fortran (Backus et al. [1957]) and Algol 60 (Naur [1963]). As a result, context-free grammars are often referred to as Backus-Naur Form (BNF, for short). The study of context-free grammars through their mathematical properties begins with Bar-Hillel, Perles, and Shamir [1961]. For a more thorough study of context-free grammars and their applications see Hopcroft and Ullman [1979] or Aho, Sethi, and Ullman [1986].

Recursive-descent parsers have been used in many compilers and compiler-writing systems (see Lewis, Rosenkrantz, and Stearns [1974]). Knuth [1965] was the first to identify LR grammars, the largest natural class of grammars that can be deterministically parsed, scanning the input from left to right.

Aho, A. V., R. Sethi, and J. D. Ullman [1986]. *Compiler Design: Principles, Techniques, and Tools*, Addison-Wesley, Reading, Mass.

Backus, J. W. [1957]. "The FORTRAN automatic coding system," *Proc. AFIPS Western Joint Computer Conference*, pp. 188–198, Spartan Books, Baltimore.

Bar-Hillel, Y., M. Perles, and E. Shamir [1961]. "On formal properties of simple phrase structure grammars," *Z. Phonetik, Sprachwissenschaft und Kommunikationsforschung* **14**, pp. 143–172.

Chomsky, N. [1956]. "Three models for the description of language," *IRE Trans. Information Theory* **IT-2**:3, pp. 113–124.

Hopcroft, J. E., and J. D. Ullman [1979]. *Introduction to Automata Theory, Languages, and Computation*, Addison-Wesley, Reading, Mass.

Knuth, D. E. [1965]. "On the translation of languages from left to right," *Information and Control* **8**:6, pp. 607–639.

Lewis, P. M., D. J. Rosenkrantz, and R. E. Stearns [1974]. "Attributed translations," *J. Computer and System Sciences* **9**:3, pp. 279–307.

Naur, P. (ed.) [1963]. "Revised report on the algorithmic language Algol 60," *Comm. ACM* **6**:1, pp. 1–17.

12

❖❖

Propositional Logic

In this chapter, we introduce propositional logic, an algebra whose original purpose, dating back to Aristotle, was to model reasoning. In more recent times, this algebra, like many algebras, has proved useful as a design tool. For example, Chapter 13 shows how propositional logic can be used in computer circuit design. A third use of logic is as a data model for programming languages and systems, such as the language Prolog. Many systems for reasoning by computer, including theorem provers, program verifiers, and applications in the field of artificial intelligence, have been implemented in logic-based programming languages. These languages generally use "predicate logic," a more powerful form of logic that extends the capabilities of propositional logic. We shall meet predicate logic in Chapter 14.

❖❖ 12.1 What This Chapter Is About

Section 12.2 gives an intuitive explanation of what propositional logic is, and why it is useful. The next section, 12,3, introduces an algebra for logical expressions with Boolean-valued operands and with logical operators such as **AND**, **OR**, and **NOT** that operate on Boolean (true/false) values. This algebra is often called *Boolean algebra* after George Boole, the logician who first framed logic as an algebra. We then learn the following ideas.

Boolean algebra

♦ Truth tables are a useful way to represent the meaning of an expression in logic (Section 12.4).

♦ We can convert a truth table to a logical expression for the same logical function (Section 12.5).

♦ The Karnaugh map is a useful tabular technique for simplifying logical expressions (Section 12.6).

♦ There is a rich set of "tautologies," or algebraic laws that can be applied to logical expressions (Sections 12.7 and 12.8).

◆ Certain tautologies of propositional logic allow us to explain such common proof techniques as "proof by contradiction" or "proof by contrapositive" (Section 12.9).

◆ Propositional logic is also amenable to "deduction," that is, the development of proofs by writing a series of lines, each of which either is given or is justified by some previous lines (Section 12.10). This is the mode of proof most of us learned in a plane geometry class in high school.

◆ A powerful technique called "resolution" can help us find proofs quickly (Section 12.11).

❖❖ 12.2   What Is Propositional Logic?

Sam wrote a C program containing the if-statement

$$\text{if (a < b || (a >= b \&\& c == d)) ...} \tag{12.1}$$

Sally points out that the conditional expression in the if-statement could have been written more simply as

$$\text{if (a < b || c == d) ...} \tag{12.2}$$

How did Sally draw this conclusion?

She might have reasoned as follows. Suppose a < b. Then the first of the two OR'ed conditions is true in both statements, so the then-branch is taken in either of the if-statements (12.1) and (12.2).

Now suppose a < b is false. In this case, we can only take the then-branch if the second of the two conditions is true. For statement (12.1), we are asking whether

$$\text{a >= b \&\& c == d}$$

is true. Now a >= b is surely true, since we assume a < b is false. Thus we take the then-branch in (12.1) exactly when c == d is true. For statement (12.2), we clearly take the then-branch exactly when c == d. Thus no matter what the values of a, b, c, and d are, either both or neither of the if-statements cause the then-branch to be followed. We conclude that Sally is right, and the simplified conditional expression can be substituted for the first with no change in what the program does.

Propositional logic is a mathematical model that allows us to reason about the truth or falsehood of logical expressions. We shall define logical expressions formally in the next section, but for the time being we can think of a logical expression as a simplification of a conditional expression such as lines (12.1) or (12.2) above that abstracts away the order of evaluation contraints of the logical operators in C.

Propositions and Truth Values

Notice that our reasoning about the two if-statements above did not depend on what a < b or similar conditions "mean." All we needed to know was that the conditions a < b and a >= b are *complementary*, that is, when one is true the other is false and vice versa. We may therefore replace the statement a < b by a single symbol p, replace a >= b by the expression NOT p, and replace c == d by the symbol q. The symbols p and q are called *propositional variables*, since they can stand for any

Propositional variable

"proposition," that is, any statement that can have one of the *truth values*, true or false.

Logical expressions can contain logical operators such as AND, OR, and NOT. When the values of the operands of the logical operators in a logical expression are known, the value of the expression can be determined using rules such as

1. The expression p AND q is true only when both p and q are true; it is false otherwise.

2. The expression p OR q is true if either p or q, or both are true; it is false otherwise.

3. The expression NOT p is true if p is false, and false if p is true.

The operator NOT has the same meaning as the C operator !. The operators AND and OR are like the C operators && and ||, respectively, but with a technical difference. The C operators are defined to evaluate the second operand only when the first operand does not resolve the matter — that is, when the first operation of && is true or the first operand of || is false. However, this detail is only important when the C expression has side effects. Since there are no "side effects" in the evaluation of logical expressions, we can take AND to be synonymous with the C operator && and take OR to be synonymous with ||.

For example, the condition in Equation (12.1) can be written as the logical expression

$$p \text{ OR } \big((\text{NOT } p) \text{ AND } q\big)$$

and Equation (12.2) can be written as p OR q. Our reasoning about the two if-statements (12.1) and (12.2) showed the general proposition that

$$\Big(p \text{ OR } \big((\text{NOT } p) \text{ AND } q\big)\Big) \equiv (p \text{ OR } q) \tag{12.3}$$

where $\equiv$ means "is equivalent to" or "has the same Boolean value as." That is, no matter what truth values are assigned to the propositional variables p and q, the left-hand side and right-hand side of $\equiv$ are either both true or both false. We discovered that for the equivalence above, both are true when p is true or when q is true, and both are false if p and q are both false. Thus, we have a valid equivalence.

As p and q can be any propositions we like, we can use equivalence (12.3) to simplify many different expressions. For example, we could let p be

```
a == b+1 && c < d
```

while q is a == c || b == c. In that case, the left-hand side of (12.3) is

```
(a == b+1 && c < d) ||                                    (12.4)
   ( !(a == b+1 && c < d) && (a == c || b == c))
```

Note that we placed parentheses around the values of p and q to make sure the resulting expression is grouped properly.

Equivalence (12.3) tells us that (12.4) can be simplified to the right-hand side of (12.3), which is

```
(a == b+1 && c < d) || (a == c || b == c)
```

What Propositional Logic Cannot Do

Propositional logic is a useful tool for reasoning, but it is limited because it cannot see inside propositions and take advantage of relationships among them. For example, Sally once wrote the if-statement

```
if (a < b && a < c && b < c) ...
```

Then Sam pointed out that it was sufficient to write

```
if (a < b && b < c) ...
```

If we let p, q, and r stand for the propositions (a < b), (a < c), and (b < c), respectively, then it looks like Sam said that

$$(p \text{ AND } q \text{ AND } r) \equiv (p \text{ AND } r)$$

This equivalence, however, is not always true. For example, suppose p and r were true, but q were false. Then the right-hand side would be false and the left-hand side true.

It turns out that Sam's simplification is correct, but not for any reason that we can discover using propositional logic. You may recall from Section 7.10 that < is a transitive relation. That is, whenever both p and r, that is, a < b and b < c, are true, it must also be that q, which is a < c, is true.

Predicate logic   In Chapter 14, we shall consider a more powerful model called predicate logic that allows us to attach arguments to propositions. That privilege allows us to exploit special properties of operators like <. (For our purposes, we can think of a predicate as the name for a relation in the set-theoretic sense of Chapters 7 and 8.) For example, we could create a predicate lt to represent operator <, and write p, q, and r as $lt(a,b)$, $lt(a,c)$, and $lt(b,c)$. Then, with suitable laws that expressed the properties of lt, such as transitivity, we could conclude that

$$\big(lt(a,b) \text{ AND } lt(a,c) \text{ AND } lt(b,c)\big) \equiv \big(lt(a,b) \text{ AND } lt(b,c)\big)$$

In fact, the above holds for any predicate lt that obeys the transitive law, not just for the predicate <.

As another example, we could let p be the proposition, "It is sunny," and q the proposition, "Joe takes his umbrella." Then the left-hand side of (12.3) is

"It is sunny, or it is not sunny and Joe takes his umbrella."

while the right-hand side, which says the same thing, is

"It is sunny or Joe takes his umbrella."

❖❖ 12.3   Logical Expressions

As mentioned in the previous section, *logical expressions* are defined recursively as follows.

BASIS. Propositional variables and the logical constants, **TRUE** and **FALSE**, are logical expressions. These are the atomic operands.

INDUCTION. If E and F are logical expressions, then so are

a) E **AND** F. The value of this expression is **TRUE** if both E and F are **TRUE** and **FALSE** otherwise.

b) E **OR** F. The value of this expression is **TRUE** if either E or F or both are **TRUE**, and the value is **FALSE** if both E and F are **FALSE**.

c)   **NOT** E. The value of this expression is **TRUE** if E is **FALSE** and **FALSE** if E is **TRUE**.

That is, logical expressions can be built from the binary infix operators **AND** and **OR**, the unary prefix operator **NOT**. As with other algebras, we need parentheses for grouping, but in some cases we can use the precedence and associativity of operators to eliminate redundant pairs of parentheses, as we do in the conditional expressions of C that involve these logical operators. In the next section, we shall see more logical operators than can appear in logical expressions.

✦   **Example 12.1.** Some examples of logical expressions are:

1.   TRUE

2.   TRUE OR FALSE

3.   NOT p

4. p AND $(q$ OR $r)$

5. $(q$ AND $p)$ OR (NOT $p)$

In these expressions, p, q, and r are propositional variables. ✦

Precedence of Logical Operators

As with expressions of other sorts, we assign a precedence to logical operators, and we can use this precedence to eliminate certain pairs of parentheses. The precedence order for the operators we have seen so far is **NOT** (highest), then **AND**, then **OR** (lowest). Both **AND** and **OR** are normally grouped from the left, although we shall see that they are associative, and that the grouping is therefore irrelevant. **NOT**, being a unary prefix operator, can only group from the right.

✦   **Example 12.2.** NOT NOT p OR q is grouped $($NOT $($NOT $p))$ OR q. NOT p OR q AND r is grouped (NOT $p)$ OR $(q$ AND $r)$. You should observe that there is an analogy between the precedence and associativity of **AND**, **OR**, and **NOT** on one hand, and the arithmetic operators $\times$, $+$, and unary $-$ on the other. For instance, the second of the above expressions can be compared with the arithmetic expression $-p + q \times r$, which has the same grouping, $(-p) + (q \times r)$. ✦

Evaluating Logical Expressions

When all of the propositional variables in a logical expression are assigned truth values, the expression itself acquires a truth value. We can then evaluate a logical expression just as we would an arithmetic expression or a relational expression.

Truth assignment

The process is best seen in terms of the expression tree for an expression, such as that shown in Fig. 12.1 for the expression p AND (q OR r) OR s. Given a *truth assignment,* that is, an assignment of TRUE or FALSE to each variable, we begin at the leaves, which are atomic operands. Each atomic operand is either one of the logical constants TRUE or FALSE, or is a variable that is given one of the values TRUE or FALSE by the truth assignment. We then work up the tree. Once the value of the children of an interior node v are known, we can apply the operator at v to these values and produce a truth value for node v. The truth value at the root is the truth value of the whole expression.

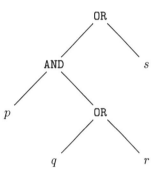

Fig. 12.1. Expression tree for the logical expression p AND (q OR r) OR s.

✦ **Example 12.3.** Suppose we want to evaluate the expression p AND (q OR r) OR s with the truth assignment TRUE, FALSE, TRUE, FALSE, for p, q, r, and s, respectively. We first consider the lowest interior node in Fig. 12.1, which represents the expression q OR r. Since q is FALSE, but r is TRUE, the value of q OR r is TRUE.

We now work on the node with the AND operator. Both its children, representing expressions p and q OR r, have the value TRUE. Thus this node, representing expression p AND (q OR r), also has the value TRUE.

Finally, we work on the root, which has operator OR. Its left child, we just discovered has value TRUE, and its right child, which represents expression s, has value FALSE according to the truth assignment. Since TRUE OR FALSE evaluates to TRUE, the entire expression has value TRUE. ✦

Boolean Functions

The "meaning" of any expression can be described formally as a function from the values of its arguments to a value for the whole expression. For example, the arithmetic expression $x \times (x + y)$ is a function that takes values for x and y (say reals) and returns the value obtained by adding the two arguments and multiplying the sum by the first argument. The behavior is similar to that of a C function declared

```
float foo(float x, float y)
{
    return x*(x+y);
}
```

In Chapter 7 we learned about functions as sets of pairs with a domain and range. We could also represent an arithmetic expression like $x \times (x+y)$ as a function whose domain is pairs of reals and whose range is the reals. This function consists of pairs of the form $((x, y), \; x \times (x + y))$. Note that the first component of each pair is itself a pair, (x, y). This set is infinite; it contains members like $((3, 4), 21)$, or $((10, 12.5), 225)$.

Similarly, a logical expression's meaning is a function that takes truth assignments as arguments and returns either TRUE or FALSE. Such functions are called *Boolean functions.* For example, the logical expression

E: p AND $(p$ OR $q)$

is similar to a C function declared

```
BOOLEAN foo(BOOLEAN p, BOOLEAN q)
{
    return p && (p || q);
}
```

Like arithmetic expressions, Boolean expressions can be thought of as sets of pairs. The first component of each pair is a truth assignment, that is, a tuple giving the truth value of each propositional variable in some specified order. The second component of the pair is the value of the expression for that truth assignment.

Example 12.4. The expression $E = p$ AND $(p$ OR $q)$ can be represented by a function consisting of four members. We shall represent truth values by giving the value for p before the value for q. Then $((\text{TRUE}, \text{FALSE}), \text{TRUE})$ is one of the pairs in the set representing E as a function. It says that when p is true and q is false, p AND $(p$ OR $q)$ is true. We can determine this value by working up the expression tree for E, by the process in Example 12.3. The reader can evaluate E for the other three truth assignments, and thus build the entire Boolean function that E represents. ✦

EXERCISES

12.3.1: Evaluate the following expressions for all possible truth values, to express their Boolean functions as a set-theoretic function.

a) p AND $(p$ OR $q)$

b)   NOT p OR q

c) $(p$ AND $q)$ OR $(\text{NOT } p$ AND NOT $q)$

12.3.2: Write C functions to implement the logical expressions in Exercise 12.3.1.

❖❖ 12.4   Truth Tables

It is convenient to display a Boolean function as a *truth table,* in which the rows correspond to all possible combinations of truth values for the arguments. There is a column for each argument and a column for the value of the function.

p	q	p AND q		p	q	p OR q		p	NOT p
0	0	0		0	0	0		0	1
0	1	0		0	1	1		1	0
1	0	0		1	0	1			
1	1	1		1	1	1			

Fig. 12.2. Truth tables for AND, OR, and NOT.

✦ **Example 12.5.** The truth tables for AND, OR, and NOT are shown in Fig. 12.2. Here, and frequently in this chapter, we shall use the shorthand that 1 stands for TRUE and 0 stands for FALSE. Thus the truth table for AND says that the result is TRUE if and only if both operands are TRUE; the second truth table says that the result of applying the OR operator is TRUE when either of the operands, or both, are TRUE; the third truth table says that the result of applying the NOT operator is TRUE if and only if the operand has the value FALSE. ✦

The Size of Truth Tables

Suppose a Boolean function has k arguments. Then a truth assignment for this function is a list of k elements, each element either TRUE or FALSE. Counting the number of truth assignments for k variables is an example of the assignment-counting problem considered in Section 4.2. That is, we assign one of the two truth values to each of k items, the propositional variables. That is analogous to painting k houses with two choices of color. The number of truth assignments is thus 2^k.

The truth table for a Boolean function of k arguments thus has 2^k rows, one for each truth assignment. For example, if $k = 2$ there are four rows, corresponding to 00, 01, 10, and 11, as we see in the truth tables for AND and OR in Fig. 12.2.

While truth tables involving one, two, or three variables are relatively small, the fact that the number of rows is 2^k for a k-ary function tells us that k does not have to get too big before it becomes unfeasible to draw truth tables. For example, a function with ten arguments has over 1000 rows. In later sections we shall have to contend with the fact that, while truth tables are finite and in principle tell us everything we need to know about a Boolean function, their exponentially growing size often forces us to find other means to understand, evaluate, or compare Boolean functions.

Understanding "Implies"

The meaning of the implication operator $\rightarrow$ may appear unintuitive, since we must get used to the notion that "falsehood implies everything." We should not confuse $\rightarrow$ with causation. That is, $p \rightarrow q$ may be true, yet p does not "cause" q in any sense. For example, let p be "it is raining," and q be "Sue takes her umbrella." We might assert that $p \rightarrow q$ is true. It might even appear that the rain is what caused Sue to take her umbrella. However, it could also be true that Sue is the sort of person who doesn't believe weather forecasts and prefers to carry an umbrella at all times.

Counting the Number of Boolean Functions

While the number of rows in a truth table for a k-argument Boolean function grows exponentially in k, the number of different k-ary Boolean functions grows much faster still. To count the number of k-ary Boolean functions, note that each such function is represented by a truth table with 2^k rows, as we observed. Each row is assigned a value, either **TRUE** or **FALSE**. Thus, the number of different Boolean functions of k arguments is the same as the number of assignments to 2^k items of 2 values. This number is 2^{2^k}. For example, when $k = 2$, there are $2^{2^2} = 16$ functions, and for $k = 5$ there are $2^{2^5} = 2^{32}$, or about four billion functions.

Of the 16 Boolean functions of 2 arguments, we already met two: **AND** and **OR**. Some others are trivial, such as the function that has value 1 no matter what its arguments are. However, there are a number of other functions of two arguments that are useful, and we shall meet them later in this section. We have also seen **NOT**, a useful function of one argument, and one often uses Boolean functions of three or more arguments as well.

Additional Logical Operators

There are four other Boolean functions of two arguments that will prove very useful in what follows.

1. *Implication*, written $\rightarrow$. We write $p \rightarrow q$ to mean that "if p is true, then q is true." The truth table for $\rightarrow$ is shown in Fig. 12.3. Notice that there is only one way $p \rightarrow q$ can be made false: p must be true and q must be false. If p is false, then $p \rightarrow q$ is always true, and if q is true, then $p \rightarrow q$ is always true.

p	q	$p \rightarrow q$
0	0	1
0	1	1
1	0	0
1	1	1

Fig. 12.3. Truth table for "implies."

2. *Equivalence,* written $\equiv$, means "if and only if"; that is, $p \equiv q$ is true when both p and q are true, or when both are false, but not otherwise. Its truth table is shown in Fig. 12.4. Another way of looking at the $\equiv$ operator is that it asserts that the operands on the left and right have the same truth value. That is what we meant in Section 12.2 when we claimed, for example, that $\big(p \text{ OR } (\text{NOT } p \text{ AND } q)\big) \equiv (p \text{ OR } q)$.

3. The NAND, or "not-and," operator applies AND to its operands and then complements the result by applying NOT. We write p NAND q to denote NOT $(p$ AND $q)$.

4. Similarly, the NOR, or "not-or," operator takes the OR of its operands and complements the result; p NOR q denotes NOT $(p$ OR $q)$. The truth tables for NAND and NOR are shown in Fig. 12.4.

p	q	$p \equiv q$	p	q	p NAND q	p	q	p NOR q
0	0	1	0	0	1	0	0	1
0	1	0	0	1	1	0	1	0
1	0	0	1	0	1	1	0	0
1	1	1	1	1	0	1	1	0

Fig. 12.4. Truth tables for equivalence, NAND, and NOR.

Operators with Many Arguments

Some logical operators can take more than two arguments as a natural extension. For example, it is easy to see that AND is associative $[(p$ AND $q)$ AND r is equivalent to p AND $(q$ AND $r)]$. Thus an expression of the form p_1 AND p_2 AND $\cdots$ AND p_k can be grouped in any order; its value will be TRUE exactly when all of $p_1, p_2, \ldots, p_k$ are TRUE. We may thus write this expression as a function of k arguments,

AND $(p_1, p_2, \ldots, p_k)$

Its truth table is suggested in Fig. 12.5. As we see, the result is 1 only when all arguments are 1.

p_1	p_2	$\cdots$	p_{k-1}	p_k	AND $(p_1, p_2, \ldots, p_k)$
0	0	$\cdots$	0	0	0
0	0	$\cdots$	0	1	0
0	0	$\cdots$	1	0	0
0	0	$\cdots$	1	1	0
.	.		.	.	.
.	.		.	.	.
.	.		.	.	.
1	1	$\cdots$	1	0	0
1	1	$\cdots$	1	1	1

Fig. 12.5. Truth table for k-argument AND.

The Significance of Some Operators

The reason that we are especially interested in k-ary AND, OR, NAND, and NOR is that these operators are particularly easy to implement electronically. That is, there are simple means to build "gates," which are electronic circuits that take k inputs and produce the AND, OR, NAND, or NOR of these inputs. While the details of the underlying electronic technologies are beyond the scope of this book, the general idea is to represent 1 and 0, or TRUE and FALSE, by two different voltage levels. Some other operators, such as $\equiv$ or $\rightarrow$, are not that easy to implement electronically, and we generally use several gates of the NAND or NOR type to implement them. The NOT operator, however, can be thought of as either a 1-argument NAND or a 1-argument NOR, and therefore is also "easy" to implement.

Similarly, OR is associative, and we can denote the logical expression p_1 OR p_2 OR $\cdots$ OR p_k as a single Boolean function OR $(p_1, p_2, \ldots, p_k)$. The truth table for this k-ary OR, which we shall not show, has 2^k rows, like the table for k-ary AND. For the OR, however, the first row, where $p_1, p_2, \ldots, p_k$ are all assigned 0, has the value 0; the remaining $2^k - 1$ rows have the value 1.

The binary operators NAND and NOR are commutative, but not associative. Thus the expression without parentheses, p_1 NAND p_2 NAND $\cdots$ NAND p_k, has no intrinsic meaning. When we speak of k-ary NAND, we do not mean any of the possible groupings of

p_1 NAND p_2 NAND $\cdots$ NAND p_k

Rather, we define NAND $(p_1, p_2, \ldots, p_k)$ to be equivalent to the expression

NOT $(p_1$ AND p_2 AND $\cdots$ AND $p_k)$

That is, NAND $(p_1, p_2, \ldots, p_k)$ has value 0 if all of $p_1, p_2, \ldots, p_k$ have value 1, and it has value 1 for all the $2^k - 1$ other combinations of input values.

Similarly, NOR $(p_1, p_2, \ldots, p_k)$ stands for NOT $(p_1$ OR p_2 OR $\cdots$ OR $p_k)$. It has value 1 if $p_1, p_2, \ldots, p_k$ all have value 0; it has value 0 otherwise.

Associativity and Precedence of Logical Operators

The order of precedence we shall use is

1. NOT (highest)
2. NAND
3. NOR
4. AND
5. OR
6. $\rightarrow$
7. $\equiv$ (lowest)

Thus, for example, $p \rightarrow q \equiv$ NOT p OR q is grouped $(p \rightarrow q) \equiv \big((\text{NOT } p) \text{ OR } q\big)$.

As we mentioned earlier, AND and OR are associative and commutative; so is $\equiv$. We shall assume that they group from the left if it is necessary to be specific. The other binary operators listed above are not associative. We shall generally show parentheses around them explicitly to avoid ambiguity, but each of the operators $\rightarrow$, NAND, and NOR will be grouped from the left in strings of two or more of the same operator.

Using Truth Tables to Evaluate Logical Expressions

The truth table is a convenient way to calculate and display the value of an expression E for all possible truth assignments, as long as there are not too many variables in the expression. We begin with columns for each of the variables appearing in E, and follow with columns for the various subexpressions of E, in an order that represents a bottom-up evaluation of the expression tree for E.

When we apply an operator to the columns representing the values of some nodes, we perform an operation on the columns that corresponds to the operator in a simple way. For example, if we wish to take the AND of two columns, we put 1 in those rows that have 1 in both columns, and we put 0's in the other rows. To take the OR of two columns, we put a 1 in those rows where one or both of the columns have 1, and we put 0's elsewhere. To take the NOT of a column, we *complement* the column, putting a 1 where the column has a 0 and vice-versa. As a last example, to apply the operator $\rightarrow$ to two columns, the result has a 0 only where the first has 1 and the second has 0; other rows have 1 in the result.

The rule for some other operators is left for an exercise. In general, we apply an operator to columns by applying that operator, row by row, to the values in that row.

✦ **Example 12.6.** Consider the expression E: $(p \text{ AND } q) \rightarrow (p \text{ OR } r)$. Figure 12.6 shows the truth table for this expression and its subexpressions. Columns (1), (2), and (3) give the values of the variables p, q, and r in all combinations. Column (4) gives the value of subexpression p AND q, which is computed by putting a 1 wherever there is a 1 in both columns (1) and (2). Column (5) shows the value of expression p OR r; it is obtained by putting a 1 in those rows where either column (1) or (3), or both, has a 1. Finally, column (6) represents the whole expression E. It is formed from columns (4) and (5); it has a 1 except in those rows where column (4) has 1 and column (5) has 0. Since there is no such row, column (6) is all 1's, which says that E has the truth value 1 no matter what its arguments are. Such an expression is called a "tautology," as we shall see in Section 12.7. ✦

(1)	(2)	(3)	(4)	(5)	(6)
p	q	r	p AND q	p OR r	E
0	0	0	0	0	1
0	0	1	0	1	1
0	1	0	0	0	1
0	1	1	0	1	1
1	0	0	0	1	1
1	0	1	0	1	1
1	1	0	1	1	1
1	1	1	1	1	1

Fig. 12.6. Truth table for $(p \text{ AND } q) \rightarrow (p \text{ OR } r)$.

Venn Diagrams and Truth Tables

There is a similarity between truth tables and the Venn diagrams for set operations that we discussed in Section 7.3. First, the operation union on sets acts like **OR** on truth values, and intersection of sets acts like **AND**. We shall see in Section 12.8 that these two pairs of operations obey the same algebraic laws. Just as an expression involving k sets as arguments results in a Venn diagram with 2^k regions, a logical expression with k variables results in a truth table with 2^k rows. Further, there is a natural correspondence between the regions and the rows. For example, a logical expression with variables p, q, and r corresponds to a set expression involving sets P, Q, and R. Consider the Venn diagram for these sets:

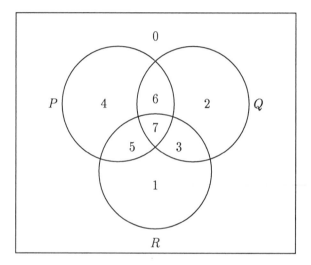

Here, the region 0 corresponds to the set of elements that are in none of P, Q, and R, region 1 corresponds to the elements that are in R, but not in P or Q. In general, if we look at the 3-place binary representation of a region number, say abc, then the elements of the region are in P if $a = 1$, in Q if $b = 1$, and in R if $c = 1$. Thus the region numbered $(abc)_2$ corresponds to the row of the truth table where p, q, and r have truth values a, b, and c, respectively.

When dealing with Venn diagrams, we took the union of two sets of regions to include the regions in either set. In analogy, when we take the **OR** of columns in a truth table, we put 1 in the union of the rows that have 1 in the first column and the rows that have 1 in the second column. Similarly, we intersect sets of regions in a Venn diagram by taking only those regions in both sets, and we take the **AND** of columns by putting a 1 in the intersection of the set of rows that have 1 in the first column and the set of rows with 1 in the second column.

The logical **NOT** operator does not quite correspond to a set operator. However, if we imagine that the union of all the regions is a "universal set," then logical **NOT** corresponds to taking a set of regions and producing the set consisting of the remaining regions of the Venn diagram, that is, subtracting the given set from the universal set.

EXERCISES

12.4.1: Give the rule for computing the (a) `NAND` (b) `NOR` (c) $\equiv$ of two columns of a truth table.

12.4.2: Compute the truth table for the following expressions and their subexpressions.

a) $(p \rightarrow q) \equiv (\text{NOT } p \text{ OR } q)$

b) $p \rightarrow (q \rightarrow (r \text{ OR NOT } p))$

c) $(p \text{ OR } q) \rightarrow (p \text{ AND } q)$

12.4.3*: To what set operator does the logical expression $p \text{ AND NOT } q$ correspond? (See the box comparing Venn diagrams and truth tables.)

12.4.4*: Give examples to show that $\rightarrow$, `NAND`, and `NOR` are not associative.

12.4.5**: A Boolean function f *does not depend on the first argument* if

$$f(\text{TRUE}, x_2, x_3, \ldots, x_k) = f(\text{FALSE}, x_2, x_3, \ldots, x_k)$$

for any truth values $x_2, x_3, \ldots, x_k$. Similarly, we can say f does not depend on its ith argument if the value of f never changes when its ith argument is switched between `TRUE` and `FALSE`. How many Boolean functions of two arguments do not depend on their first or second argument (or both)?

12.4.6*: Construct truth tables for the 16 Boolean functions of two variables. How many of these functions are commutative?

Exclusive or **12.4.7**: The binary *exclusive-or* function, $\oplus$, is defined to have value `TRUE` if and only if exactly one of its arguments are `TRUE`.

a) Draw the truth table for $\oplus$.

b)* Is $\oplus$ commutative? Is it associative?

✦✦ 12.5 From Boolean Functions to Logical Expressions

Now, let us consider the problem of designing a logical expression from a truth table. We start with a truth table as the specification of the logical expression, and our goal is to find an expression with the given truth table. Generally, there is an infinity of different expressions we could use; we usually limit our selection to a particular set of operators, and we often want an expression that is "simplest" in some sense.

This problem is a fundamental one in circuit design. The logical operators in the expression may be taken as the gates of the circuit, and so there is a straightforward translation from a logical expression to an electronic circuit, by a process we shall discuss in the next chapter.

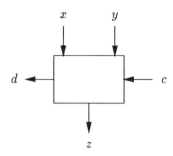

Fig. 12.7. A one-bit adder: $(dz)_2$ is the sum $x + y + c$.

✦ **Example 12.7.** As we saw in Section 1.3, we can design a 32-bit adder out of one-bit adders of the type shown in Fig. 12.7. The one-bit adder sums two input bits x and y, and a carry-in bit c, to produce a carry-out bit d and a sum bit z.

The truth table in Fig. 12.8 tells us the value of the carry-out bit d and the sum-bit z, as a function of x, y, and c for each of the eight combinations of input values. The carry-out bit d is 1 if at least two of x, y, and c have the value 1, and $d = 0$ if only zero or one of the inputs is 1. The sum bit z is 1 if an odd number of x, y, and c are 1, and 0 if not.

	x	y	c	d	z
0)	0	0	0	0	0
1)	0	0	1	0	1
2)	0	1	0	0	1
3)	0	1	1	1	0
4)	1	0	0	0	1
5)	1	0	1	1	0
6)	1	1	0	1	0
7)	1	1	1	1	1

Fig. 12.8. Truth table for the carry-out bit d and the sum-bit z.

We shall present a general way to go from a truth table to a logical expression momentarily. However, given the carry-out function d of Fig. 12.8, we might reason in the following manner to construct a corresponding logical expression.

1.   From rows 3 and 7, d is 1 if both y and c are 1.

2.   From rows 5 and 7, d is 1 if both x and c are 1.

3.   From rows 6 and 7, d is 1 if both x and y are 1.

Condition (1) can be modeled by the logical expression y **AND** c, because y **AND** c is true exactly when both y and c are 1. Similarly, condition (2) can be modeled by x **AND** c, and condition (3) by x **AND** y.

All the rows that have $d = 1$ are included in at least one of these three pairs of rows. Thus we can write a logical expression that is true whenever one or more of the three conditions hold by taking the logical **OR** of these three expressions:

$$(y \text{ AND } c) \text{ OR } (x \text{ AND } c) \text{ OR } (x \text{ AND } y) \qquad\qquad (12.5)$$

The correctness of this expression is checked in Fig. 12.9. The last four columns correspond to the subexpressions y AND c, x AND c, x AND y, and expression (12.5). ✦

x	y	c	y AND c	x AND c	x AND y	d
0	0	0	0	0	0	0
0	0	1	0	0	0	0
0	1	0	0	0	0	0
0	1	1	1	0	0	1
1	0	0	0	0	0	0
1	0	1	0	1	0	1
1	1	0	0	0	1	1
1	1	1	1	1	1	1

Fig. 12.9. Truth table for carry-out expression (12.5) and its subexpressions.

Shorthand Notation

Before proceeding to describe how we build expressions from truth tables, there are some simplifications in notation that will prove helpful.

1. We can represent the **AND** operator by juxtaposition, that is, by no operator at all, just as we often represent multiplication, and as we represented concatenation in Chapter 10.

2. The **OR** operator can be represented by $+$.

3. The **NOT** operator can be represented by an overbar. This convention is especially useful when the **NOT** applies to a single variable, and we shall often write **NOT** p as $\bar{p}$.

✦ **Example 12.8.** The expression p AND q OR r can be written $pq + r$. The expression p AND NOT q OR NOT r can be written $p\bar{q} + \bar{r}$. We can even mix our original notation with the shorthand notation. For example, the expression

$$\big((p \text{ AND } q) \to r\big) \text{ AND } (p \to s)$$

could be written $(pq \to r)$ AND $(p \to s)$ or even as $(pq \to r)(p \to s)$. ✦

One important reason for the new notation is that it allows us to think of AND and OR as if they were multiplication and addition in arithmetic. Thus we can apply such familiar laws as commutativity, associativity, and distributivity, which we shall see in Section 12.8 apply to these logical operators, just as they do to the corresponding arithmetic operators. For example, we shall see that $p(q + r)$ can be replaced by $pq + pr$, and then by $rp + qp$, whether the operators involved are AND and OR, or multiplication and addition.

Product, sum, conjunction, disjunction

Because of this shorthand notation, it is common to refer to the AND of expressions as a *product* and to the OR of expressions as a *sum*. Another name for the

AND of expressions is a *conjunction*, and for the OR of expressions another name is *disjunction*.

Constructing a Logical Expression from a Truth Table

Any Boolean function whatsoever can be represented by a logical expression using the operators AND, OR, and NOT. Finding the simplest expression for a given Boolean function is generally hard. However, we can easily construct *some* expression for and Boolean function. The technique is straightforward. Starting with the truth table for the function, we construct a logical expression of the form

$$m_1 \text{ OR } m_2 \text{ OR } \cdots \text{ OR } m_n$$

Minterm

Each m_i is a term that corresponds to one of the rows of the truth table for which the function has value 1. Thus there are as many terms in the expression as there are 1's in the column for that function. Each of the terms m_i is called a *minterm* and has a special form that we shall describe below.

Literal

To begin our explanation of minterms, a *literal* is an expression that is either a single propositional variable, such as p, or a negated variable, such as NOT p, which we shall often write as $\bar{p}$. If the truth table has k variable columns, then each minterm consists of the logical AND, or "product," of k literals. Let r be a row for which we wish to construct the minterm. If the variable p has the value 1 in row r, then select literal p. If p has value 0 in row r, then select $\bar{p}$ as the literal. The minterm for row r is the product of the literals for each variable. Clearly, the minterm can only have the value 1 if all the variables have the values that appear in row r of the truth table.

Sum of products; disjunctive normal form

Now construct an expression for the function by taking the logical OR, or "sum," of those minterms that correspond to rows with 1 as the value of the function. The resulting expression is in "sum of products" form, or *disjunctive normal form*. The expression is correct, because it has the value 1 exactly when there is a minterm with value 1; this minterm cannot be 1 unless the values of the variables correspond to the row of the truth table for that minterm, and that row has value 1.

✦ **Example 12.9.** Let us construct a sum-of-products expression for the carry-out function d defined by the truth table of Fig. 12.8. The rows with value 1 are numbered 3, 5, 6, and 7. The minterm for row 3, which has $x = 0$, $y = 1$, and $c = 1$, is $\bar{x}$ AND y AND c, which we abbreviate $\bar{x}yc$. Similarly, the minterm for row 5 is $x\bar{y}c$, that for row 6 is $xy\bar{c}$, and that for row 7 is xyc. Thus the desired expression for d is the logical OR of these expressions, which is

$$\bar{x}yc + x\bar{y}c + xy\bar{c} + xyc \tag{12.6}$$

This expression is more complex than (12.5). However, we shall see in the next section how expression (12.5) can be derived.

Similarly, we can construct a logical expression for the sum-bit z by taking the sum of the minterms for rows 1, 2, 4, and 7 to obtain

$$\bar{x}\bar{y}c + \bar{x}y\bar{c} + x\bar{y}\bar{c} + xyc$$

✦

Complete Sets of Operators

The minterm technique for designing sum-of-products expressions like (12.6) shows that the set of logical operators AND, OR, and NOT is a *complete* set, meaning that every Boolean function has an expression using just these operators. It is not hard to show that the NAND operator by itself is complete. We can express the functions AND, OR, and NOT, with NAND alone as follows:

1. $(p \text{ AND } q) \equiv \big((p \text{ NAND } q) \text{ NAND TRUE}\big)$

2. $(p \text{ OR } q) \equiv \big((p \text{ NAND TRUE}) \text{ NAND } (q \text{ NAND TRUE})\big)$

3. $(\text{NOT } p) \equiv (p \text{ NAND TRUE})$

We can convert any sum-of-products expression to one involving only NAND, by substituting the appropriate NAND-expression for each use of AND, OR, and NOT. Similarly, NOR by itself is complete.

An example of a set of operators that is not complete is AND and OR by themselves. For example, they cannot express the function NOT. To see why, note that AND and OR are *monotone*, meaning that when you change any one input from 0 to 1, the output cannot change from 1 to 0. It can be shown by induction on the size of an expression that any expression with operators AND and OR is monotone. But NOT is not monotone, obviously. Hence there is no way to express NOT by AND's and OR's.

Monotone function

p	q	r	a	b
0	0	0	0	1
0	0	1	1	1
0	1	0	0	1
0	1	1	0	0
1	0	0	1	0
1	0	1	1	0
1	1	0	1	0
1	1	1	1	0

Fig. 12.10. Two Boolean functions for exercises.

EXERCISES

12.5.1: Figure 12.10 is a truth table that defines two Boolean functions, a and b, in terms of variables p, q, and r. Write sum-of-products expressions for each of these functions.

12.5.2: Write product-of-sums expressions (see the box on "Product-of-Sums Expressions") for

a) Function a of Fig. 12.10.
b) Function b of Fig. 12.10.
c) Function z of Fig. 12.8.

Product-of-Sums Expressions

Conjunctive
normal form

There is a dual way to convert a truth table into an expression involving AND, OR, and NOT; this time, the expression will be a product (logical AND) of sums (logical OR) of literals. This form is called "product-of-sums," or *conjunctive normal form.*

Maxterm

For each row of a truth table, we can define a *maxterm,* which is the sum of those literals that disagree with the value of one of the argument variables in that row. That is, if the row has value 0 for variable p, then use literal p, and if the value of that row for p is 1, then use $\bar{p}$. The value of the maxterm is thus 1 unless each variable p has the value specified for p by that row.

Thus, if we look at all the rows of the truth table for which the value is 0, and take the logical AND of the maxterms for all those rows, our expression will be 0 exactly when the inputs match one of the rows for which the function is to be 0. It follows that the expression has value 1 for all the other rows, that is, those rows for which the truth table gives the value 1. For example, the rows with value 0 for d in Fig. 12.8 are numbered 0, 1, 2, and 4. The maxterm for row 0 is $x + y + c$, and that for row 1 is $x + y + \bar{c}$, for example. The product-of-sums expression for d is

$$(x + y + c)(x + y + \bar{c})(x + \bar{y} + c)(\bar{x} + y + c)$$

This expression is equivalent to (12.5) and (12.6).

12.5.3**: Which of the following logical operators form a complete set of operators by themselves: (a) $\equiv$ (b) $\rightarrow$ (c) NOR? Prove your answer in each case.

12.5.4**: Of the 16 Boolean functions of two variables, how many are complete by themselves?

12.5.5*: Show that the AND and OR of monotone functions is monotone. Then show that any expression with operators AND and OR only, is monotone.

❖❖ 12.6 Designing Logical Expressions by Karnaugh Maps

In this section, we present a tabular technique for finding sum-of-products expressions for Boolean functions. The expressions produced are often simpler than those constructed in the previous section by the expedient of taking the logical OR of all the necessary minterms in the truth table.

For instance, in Example 12.7 we did an ad hoc design of an expression for the carry-out function of a one-bit adder. We saw that it was possible to use a product of literals that was not a minterm; that is, it was missing literals for some of the variables. For example, we used the product of literals xy to *cover* the sixth and seventh rows of Fig. 12.8, in the sense that xy has value 1 exactly when the variables x, y, and c have the values indicated by one of those two rows.

Similarly, in Example 12.7 we used the expression xc to cover rows 5 and 7, and we used yc to cover rows 3 and 7. Note that row 7 is covered by all three expressions. There is no harm in that. In fact, had we used only the minterms for rows 5 and 3, which are $x\bar{y}c$ and $\bar{x}yc$, respectively, in place of xc and yc, we would have obtained an expression that was correct, but that had two more occurrences of operators than the expression $xy + xc + yc$ obtained in Example 12.7.

The essential concept here is that if we have two minterms differing only by the negation of one variable, such as $xy\bar{c}$ and xyc for rows 6 and 7, respectively, we can combine the two minterms by taking the common literals and dropping the variable in which the terms differ. This observation follows from the general law

$$(pq + \bar{p}q) \equiv q$$

To see this equivalence, note that if q is true, then either pq is true, or $\bar{p}q$ is true, and conversely, when either pq or $\bar{p}q$ is true, then it must be that q is true.

We shall see a technique for verifying such laws in the next section, but, for the moment, we can let the intuitive meaning of our law justify its use. Note also that use of this law is not limited to minterms. We could, for example, let p be any propositional variable and q be any product of literals. Thus we can combine any two products of literals that differ only in one variable (one product has the variable itself and the other its complement), replacing the two products by the one product of the common literals.

Karnaugh Maps

There is a graphical technique for designing sum-of-products expressions from truth tables; the method works well for Boolean functions up to four variables. The idea is to write a truth table as a two-dimensional array called a *Karnaugh map* (pronounced "*car*-no") whose entries, or "points," each represent a row of the truth table. By keeping adjacent the points that represent rows differing in only one variable, we can "see" useful products of literals as certain rectangles, all of whose points have the value 1.

Two-Variable Karnaugh Maps

The simplest Karnaugh maps are for Boolean functions of two variables. The rows correspond to values of one of the variables, and the columns correspond to values of the other. The entries of the map are 0 or 1, depending on whether that combination of values for the two variables makes the function have value 0 or 1. Thus the Karnaugh map is a two-dimensional representation of the truth table for a Boolean function.

✦ **Example 12.10.** In Fig. 12.11 we see the Karnaugh map for the "implies" function, $p \rightarrow q$. There are four points corresponding to the four possible values for p and q. Note that "implies" has value 1 except when $p = 1$ and $q = 0$, and so the only point in the Karnaugh map with value 0 is the entry for $p = 1$ and $q = 0$; all the other points have value 1. ✦

Implicants

An *implicant* for a Boolean function f is a product x of literals for which no assignment of values to the variables of f makes x true and f false. For example, every minterm for which the function f has value 1 is an implicant of f. However, there are other products that can also be implicants, and we shall learn to read these off of the Karnaugh map for f.

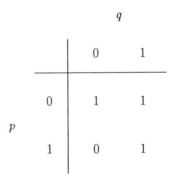

Fig. 12.11. Karnaugh map for $p \to q$.

◆ **Example 12.11.** The minterm pq is an implicant for the "implies" function of Fig. 12.11, because the only assignment of values for p and q that makes pq true, namely $p = 1$ and $q = 1$, also makes the "implies" function true.

As another example, $\bar{p}$ by itself is an implicant for the "implies" function because the two assignments of values for p and q that make $\bar{p}$ true also make $p \to q$ true. These two assignments are $p = 0$, $q = 0$ and $p = 0$, $q = 1$. ◆

Covering points of a Karnaugh map

An implicant is said to *cover* the points for which it has the value 1. A logical expression can be constructed for a Boolean function by taking the OR of a set of implicants that together cover all points for which that function has value 1.

◆ **Example 12.12.** Figure 12.12 shows two implicants in the Karnaugh map for the "implies" function. The larger, which covers two points, corresponds to the single literal, $\bar{p}$. This implicant covers the top two points of the map, both of which have 1's in them. The smaller implicant, pq, covers the point $p = 1$ and $q = 1$. Since these two implicants together cover all the points that have value 1, their sum, $\bar{p} + pq$, is an equivalent expression for $p \to q$; that is, $(p \to q) \equiv (\bar{p} + pq)$. ◆

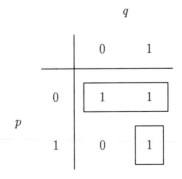

Fig. 12.12. Two implicants $\bar{p}$ and pq in the Karnaugh map for $p \to q$.

Rectangles that correspond to implicants in Karnaugh maps must have a special "look." For the simple maps that come from 2-variable functions, these rectangles can only be

1. Single points,

2. Rows or columns, or

3. The entire map.

A single point in a Karnaugh map corresponds to a minterm, whose expression we can find by taking the product of the literals for each variable appropriate to the row and column of the point. That is, if the point is in the row or column for 0, then we take the negation of the variable corresponding to the row, or column, respectively. If the point is in the row or column for 1, then we take the corresponding variable, unnegated. For instance, the smaller implicant in Fig. 12.12 is in the row for $p = 1$ and the column for $q = 1$, which is the reason that we took the product of the unnegated literals p and q for that implicant.

A row or column in a two-variable Karnaugh map corresponds to a pair of points that agree in one variable and disagree in the other. The corresponding "product" of literals reduces to a single literal. The remaining literal has the variable whose common value the points share. The literal is negated if that common value is 0, and unnegated if the shared value is 1. Thus the larger implicant in Fig. 12.12 — the first row — has points with a common value of p. That value is 0, which justifies the use of the product-of-literals $\bar{p}$ for that implicant.

An implicant consisting of the entire map is a special case. In principle, it corresponds to a product that reduces to the constant 1, or **TRUE**. Clearly, the Karnaugh map for the logical expression **TRUE** has 1's in all points of the map.

Prime Implicants

A *prime implicant* x for a Boolean function f is an implicant for f that ceases to be an implicant for f if any literal in x is deleted. In effect, a prime implicant is an implicant that has as few literals as possible.

Note that the bigger a rectangle is, the fewer literals there are in its product. We would generally prefer to replace a product with many literals by one with fewer literals, which involves fewer occurrences of operators, and thus is "simpler." We are thus motivated to consider only those implicants that are prime, when selecting a set of implicants to cover a map.

Remember that every implicant for a given Karnaugh map consists only of points with 1's. An implicant is a prime implicant because expanding it further by doubling its size would force us to cover a point with value 0.

♦ **Example 12.13.** In Fig. 12.12, the larger implicant $\bar{p}$ is prime, since the only possible larger implicant is the entire map, which cannot be used because it contains a 0. The smaller implicant pq is not prime, since it is contained in the second column, which consists only of 1's, and is therefore an implicant for the "implies" Karnaugh map. Figure 12.13 shows the only possible choice of prime implicants for the "implies" map.[1] They correspond to the products $\bar{p}$ and q, and they give rise to the expression $\bar{p} + q$, which we noted in Section 12.3 was equivalent to $p \rightarrow q$. ♦

---

[1] In general, there may be many sets of prime implicants that cover a given Karnaugh map.

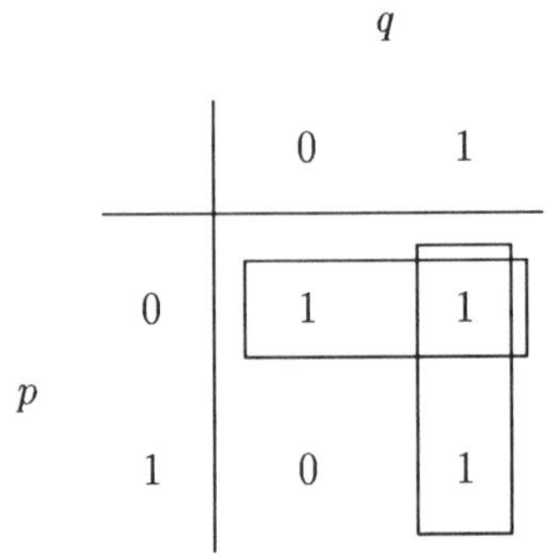

Fig. 12.13. Prime implicants $\bar{p}$ and q for the "implies" function.

Three-Variable Karnaugh Maps

When we have three variables in our truth table, we can use a two-row, four-column map like that shown in Fig. 12.14, which is a map for the carry-out truth table of Fig. 12.8. Notice the unusual order in which the columns correspond to pairs of values for two variables (variables y and c in this example). The reason is that we want adjacent columns to correspond to assignments of truth values that differ in only one variable. Had we chosen the usual order, 00, 01, 10, 11, the middle two columns would differ in both y and c. Note also that the first and last columns are "adjacent," in the sense that they differ only in variable y. Thus, when we select implicants, we can regard the first and last columns as a 2×2 rectangle, and we can regard the first and last points of either row as a 1×2 rectangle.

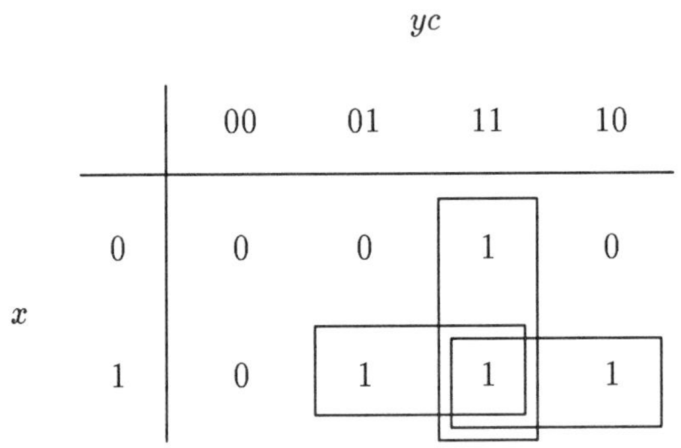

Fig. 12.14. Karnaugh map for the carry-out function with prime implicants xc, yc, and xy.

We need to deduce which rectangles of a three-variable map represent possible implicants. First, a permissible rectangle must correspond to a product of literals. In any product, each variable appears in one of three ways: negated, unnegated, or not at all. When a variable appears negated or unnegated, it cuts in half the number of points in the corresponding implicant, since only points with the proper value for that variable belong in the implicant. Hence, the number of points in an implicant will always be a power of 2. Each permissible implicant is thus a collection of points that, for each variable, either

Reading Implicants from the Karnaugh Map

No matter how many variables are involved, we can take any rectangle that represents an implicant and produce the product of literals that is TRUE for exactly the points in the rectangle. If p is any variable, then

1. If every point in the rectangle has $p = 1$, then p is a literal in the product.

2. If every point in the rectangle has $p = 0$, then $\bar{p}$ is a literal in the product.

3. If the rectangle has points with $p = 0$ and other points with $p = 1$, then the product has no literal with variable p.

a) Includes only points with that variable equal to 0,

b) Includes only points with that variable equal to 1, or

c) Does not discriminate on the basis of the value of that variable.

For three-variable maps, we can enumerate the possible implicants as follows.

1. Any point.

2. Any column.

3. Any pair of horizontally adjacent points, including the end-around case, that is, a pair in columns 1 and 4 of either row.

4. Any row.

5. Any 2×2 square consisting of two adjacent columns, including the end-around case, that is, columns 1 and 4.

6. The entire map.

✦ **Example 12.14.** The three prime implicants for the carry-out function were indicated in Fig. 12.14. We may convert each to a product of literals; see the box "Reading Implicants from the Karnaugh Map." The corresponding products are xc for the leftmost one, yc for the vertical one, and xy for the rightmost one. The sum of these three expressions is the sum-of-products that we obtained informally in Example 12.7; we now see how this expression was obtained. ✦

✦ **Example 12.15.** Figure 12.15 shows the Karnaugh map for the three-variable Boolean function NAND (p, q, r). The prime implicants are

1. The first row, which corresponds to $\bar{p}$.

2. The first two columns, which correspond to $\bar{q}$.

3. Columns 1 and 4, which correspond to $\bar{r}$.

The sum-of-products expression for this map is $\bar{p} + \bar{q} + \bar{r}$. ✦

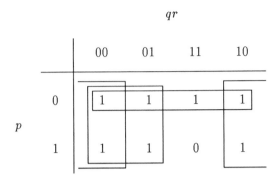

Fig. 12.15. Karnaugh map with prime implicants $\bar{p}$, $\bar{q}$, and $\bar{r}$ for $\mathtt{NAND}(p, q, r)$.

Four-Variable Karnaugh Maps

A four-argument function can be represented by a 4×4 Karnaugh map, in which two variables correspond to the rows, and two variables correspond to the columns. In both the rows and columns, the special order of the values that we used for the columns in three-variable maps must be used, as shown in Fig. 12.16. For four-variable maps, adjacency of both rows and columns must be interpreted in the end-around sense. That is, the top and bottom rows are adjacent, and the left and right columns are adjacent. As an important special case, the four corner points form a 2×2 rectangle; they correspond in Fig. 12.16 to the product of literals $\bar{q}\bar{s}$ (which is not an implicant in Fig. 12.16, because the lower right corner is 0).

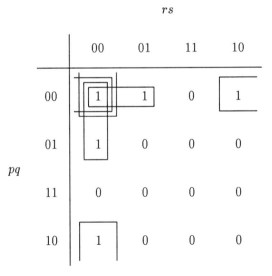

Fig. 12.16. Karnaugh map with prime implicants for the "at most one 1" function.

The rectangles in a four-variable Karnaugh map that correspond to products of literals are as follows:

1.   Any point.

2.   Any two horizontally or vertically adjacent points, including those that are adjacent in the end-around sense.

3.   Any row or column.

4.   Any 2×2 square, including those in the end-around sense, such as two adjacent points in the top row and the two points in the bottom row that are in the same columns. The four corners is, as we mentioned, a special case of a "square" as well.

5.   Any 2×4 or 4×2 rectangle, including those in the end-around sense, such as the first and last columns.

6.   The entire map.

✦   **Example 12.16.** Figure 12.16 shows the Karnaugh map of a Boolean function of four variables, p, q, r, and s, that has the value 1 when at most one of the inputs is 1. There are four prime implicants, all of size 2, and two of them are end-around. The implicant consisting of the first and last points of the top row has points that agree in variables p, q, and s; the common value is 0 for each variable. Thus its product of literals is $\bar{p}\bar{q}\bar{s}$. Similarly, the other implicants have products $\bar{p}\bar{q}\bar{r}$, $\bar{p}\bar{r}\bar{s}$, and $\bar{q}\bar{r}\bar{s}$. The expression for the function is thus

$$\bar{p}\bar{q}\bar{r} + \bar{p}\bar{q}\bar{s} + \bar{p}\bar{r}\bar{s} + \bar{q}\bar{r}\bar{s}$$

✦

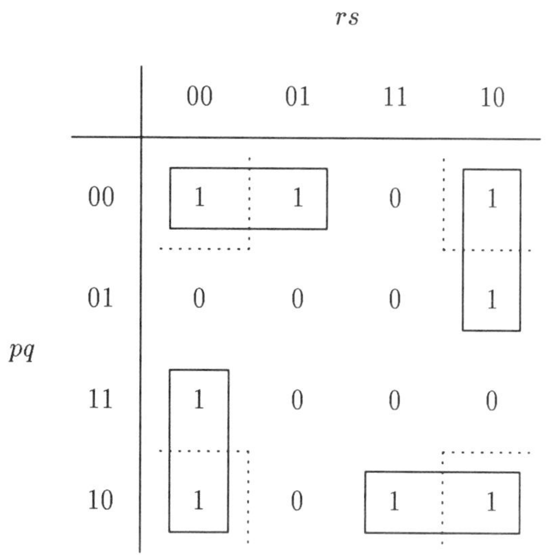

Fig. 12.17.   Karnaugh map with an all-corners prime implicant.

✦ **Example 12.17.** The map of Fig. 12.17 was chosen for the pattern of its 1's, rather than for any significance its function has. It does illustrate an important point. Five prime implicants that together cover all the 1 points are shown, including the all-corners implicant (shown dashed), for which the product of literals expression is $\bar{q}\bar{s}$; the other four prime implicants have products $\bar{p}\bar{q}\bar{r}$, $\bar{p}r\bar{s}$, $p\bar{q}r$, and $p\bar{r}\bar{s}$.

We might think, from the examples seen so far, that to form the logical expression for this map we should take the logical **OR** of all five implicants. However, a moment's reflection tells us that the largest implicant, $\bar{q}\bar{s}$, is superfluous, since all its points are covered by other prime implicants. Moreover, this is the only prime implicant that we have the option to eliminate, since each other prime implicant has a point that only it covers. For example, $\bar{p}\bar{q}\bar{r}$ is the only prime implicant to cover the point in the first row and second column. Thus

$$\bar{p}\bar{q}\bar{r} + \bar{p}r\bar{s} + p\bar{q}r + p\bar{r}\bar{s}$$

is the preferred sum-of-products expression obtained from the map of Fig. 12.17. ✦

EXERCISES

12.6.1: Draw the Karnaugh maps for the following functions of variables p, q, r, and s.

a) The function that is **TRUE** if one, two, or three of p, q, r, and s are **TRUE**, but not if zero or all four are **TRUE**.

b) The function that is **TRUE** if up to two of p, q, r, and s are **TRUE**, but not if three or four are **TRUE**.

c) The function that is **TRUE** if one, three, or four of p, q, r, and s are **TRUE**, but not if zero or two are **TRUE**.

d) The function represented by the logical expression $pqr \rightarrow s$.

e) The function that is **TRUE** if $pqrs$, regarded as a binary number, has value less than ten.

12.6.2: Find the implicants — other than the minterms — for each of your Karnaugh maps from Exercise 12.6.1. Which of them are prime implicants? For each function, find a sum of prime implicants that covers all the 1's of the map. Do you need to use all the prime implicants?

12.6.3: Show that every product in a sum-of-products expression for a Boolean function is an implicant of that function.

Anti-implicant

12.6.4*: One can also construct a product-of-sums expression from a Karnaugh map. We begin by finding rectangles of the types that form implicants, but with all points 0, instead of all points 1. Call such a rectangle an "anti-implicant." We can construct for each anti-implicant a sum of literals that is 1 on all points but those of the anti-implicant. For each variable x, this sum has literal x if the anti-implicant includes only points for which $x = 0$, and it has literal $\bar{x}$ if the anti-implicant has only points for which $x = 1$. Otherwise, the sum does not have a literal involving x. Find all the prime anti-implicants for your Karnaugh maps of Exercise 12.6.1.

12.6.5: Using your answer to Exercise 12.6.4, write product-of-sums expressions for each of the functions of Exercise 12.6.1. Include as few sums as you can.

12.6.6**: How many (a) 1×2 (b) 2×2 (c) 1×4 (d) 2×4 rectangles that form implicants are there in a 4×4 Karnaugh map? Describe their implicants as products of literals, assuming the variables are p, q, r, and s.

✦✦ 12.7 Tautologies

A *tautology* is a logical expression whose value is true regardless of the values of its propositional variables. For a tautology, all the rows of the truth table, or all the points in the Karnaugh map, have the value 1. Simple examples of tautologies are

TRUE
$$p + \bar{p}$$
$$(p + q) \equiv (p + \bar{p}q)$$

Tautologies have many important uses. For example, suppose we have an expression of the form $E_1 \equiv E_2$ that is a tautology. Then, whenever we have an instance of E_1 within any expression, we can replace E_1 by E_2, and the resulting expression will represent the same Boolean function.

Figure 12.18(a) shows the expression tree for a logical expression F containing E_1 as a subexpression. Figure 12.18(b) shows the same expression with E_1 replaced by E_2. If $E_1 \equiv E_2$, the values of the roots of the two trees must be the same, no matter what assignment of truth values is made to the variables. The reason is that we know the nodes marked n in the two trees, which are the roots of the expression trees for E_1 and E_2, must get the same value in both trees, because $E_1 \equiv E_2$. The evaluation of the trees above n will surely yield the same value, proving that the two trees are equivalent. The ability to substitute equivalent expressions for one another is colloquially known as the "substitution of equals for equals." Note that in other algebras, such as those for arithmetic, sets, relations, or regular expressions we also may substitute one expression for another that has the same value.

Substitution of equals for equals

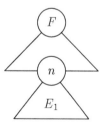
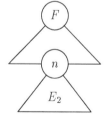

(a) Expression containing E_1 (b) Expression containing E_2

Fig. 12.18. Expression trees showing substitution of equals for equals.

✦ **Example 12.18.** Consider the associative law for the logical operator OR, which can be phrased as the expression

$$\big((p + q) + r\big) \equiv \big(p + (q + r)\big) \tag{12.7}$$

The truth table for the various subexpressions appears in Fig. 12.19. The final column, labeled E, represents the entire expression. Observe that every row has value 1 for E, showing that the expression (12.7) is a tautology. As a result, any time we see an expression of the form $(p + q) + r$, we are free to replace it by $p + (q + r)$. Note that p, q, and r can stand for any expressions, as long as the same expression is used for both occurrences of p, and q and r are likewise treated consistently. ✦

p	q	r	$p + q$	$(p + q) + r$	$q + r$	$p + (q + r)$	E
0	0	0	0	0	0	0	1
0	0	1	0	1	1	1	1
0	1	0	1	1	1	1	1
0	1	1	1	1	1	1	1
1	0	0	1	1	0	1	1
1	0	1	1	1	1	1	1
1	1	0	1	1	1	1	1
1	1	1	1	1	1	1	1

Fig. 12.19. Truth table proving the associative law for OR.

The Substitution Principle

As we pointed out in Example 12.18, when we have a law involving a particular set of propositional variables, the law applies not only as written, but with any substitution of an expression for each variable. The underlying reason is that tautologies remain tautologies when we make any substitution for one or more of its variables. This fact is known as the *substitution principle*.[2] Of course, we must substitute the same expression for each occurrence of a given variable.

✦ **Example 12.19.** The commutative law for the logical operator AND can be verified by showing that the logical expression $pq \equiv qp$ is a tautology. To get some instances of this law, we can perform substitutions on this expression. For example, we could substitute $r + s$ for p and $\bar{r}$ for q to get the equivalence

$$(r + s)(\bar{r}) \equiv (\bar{r})(r + s)$$

Note that we put parentheses around each substituted expression to avoid accidentally changing the grouping of operators because of our operator-precedence conventions. In this case, the parentheses around $r + s$ are essential, but the parentheses around $\bar{r}$ could be omitted.

Some other substitution instances follow. We could replace p by r and not replace q, to get $rq \equiv qr$. We could leave p alone and replace q by the constant expression 1 (TRUE), to get p AND $1 \equiv 1$ AND p. However, we cannot substitute r for the first occurrence of p and substitute a different expression, say $r + s$, for the

---

[2] We should not confuse the substitution principle with the "substitution of equals for equals." The substitution principle applies to tautologies only, while we may substitute equals for equals in any expression.

second. That is, $rq \equiv q(r + s)$ is not a tautology (its value is 0 if $s = q = 1$ and $r = 0$). ◆

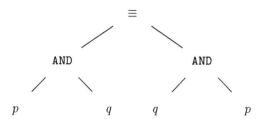

Fig. 12.20. Expression tree for the tautology $pq \equiv qp$.

The reason the substitution principle holds true can be seen if we think about expression trees. Imagine the expression tree for some tautology, such as the one discussed in Example 12.19, which we show in Fig. 12.20. Since the expression is a tautology, we know that, whatever assignment of truth values we make for the propositional variables at the leaves, the value at the root is true (as long as we assign the same value to each leaf that is labeled by a given variable).

Now suppose that we substitute for p an expression with tree T_p and that we substitute for q an expression with tree T_q; in general, we select one tree for each variable of the tautology, and replace all leaves for that variable by the tree selected for that variable.[3] Then we have a new expression tree similar to that suggested by Fig. 12.21. When we make an assignment of truth values for the variables of the new tree, the value of each node that is a root of a tree T_p gets the same value, because the same evaluation steps are performed underneath any such node.

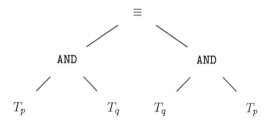

Fig. 12.21. A substitution for the variables of Fig. 12.20.

Once the roots of the trees like T_p and T_q in Fig. 12.21 are evaluated, we have a consistent assignment of values to the variables at the leaves of the original tree, which we illustrated in Fig. 12.20. That is, we take whatever value is computed for the occurrences of T_p, which must all be the same value, and assign it to all

---

[3] As a special case, the tree selected for some variable x can be a single node labeled x, which is the same as making no substitution for x.

the leaves labeled p in the original tree. We do the same for q, and in general, for any variable appearing in the original tree. Since the original tree represents a tautology, we know that evaluating that tree will result in the value **TRUE** at the root. But above the substituted trees, the new and original trees are the same, and so the new tree also produces value **TRUE** at the root. Since the above reasoning holds true no matter what substitution of values we make for the variables of the new tree, we conclude that the expression represented by the new tree is also a tautology.

The Tautology Problem

The tautology problem is to test whether a given logical expression is equivalent to **TRUE**, that is, whether it is a tautology. There is a straightforward way to solve this problem. Construct a truth table with one row for each possible assignment of truth values to the variables of the expression. Create one column for each interior node of the tree, and in a suitable bottom-up order, evaluate each node for each assignment of truth values to the variables. The expression is a tautology if and only if the value of the whole expression is 1 (**TRUE**) for every truth assignment. Example 12.18 illustrated this process.

Running Time of the Tautology Test

If the expression has k variables and n operator occurrences, then the table has 2^k rows, and there are n columns that need to be filled out. We thus expect a straightforward implementation of this algorithm to take $O(2^k n)$ time. That is not long for expressions with two or three variables, and even for, say, 20 variables, we can carry the test out by computer in a few seconds or minutes. However, for 30 variables, there are a billion rows, and it becomes far less feasible to carry out this test, even using a computer. These observations are typical of what happens when one uses an exponential-time algorithm. For small instances, we generally see no problem. But suddenly, as problem instances get larger, we find it is no longer possible to solve the problem, even with the fastest computers, in an amount of time we can afford.

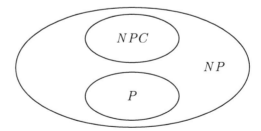

Fig. 12.22. P is the family of problems solvable in polynomial time, NP is the family solvable in nondeterministic polynomial time, and NPC is the family of NP-complete problems.

EXERCISES

12.7.1: Which of the following expressions are tautologies?

Inherent Intractability

The tautology problem, "Is E a tautology," is an important example of a problem that appears to be inherently exponential. That is, if k is the number of variables in expression E, all the known algorithms to solve the tautology problem have a running time that is an exponential function of k.

NP-complete problem

There is a family of problems, called *NP-complete*, which includes many important optimization problems that no one knows how to solve in less than exponential time. Many mathematicians and scientists have worked long and hard trying to find for at least one of these problems an algorithm that runs in less than exponential time, but no such algorithm has yet been found, and so many people now suspect that none exists.

Satisfiability problem

One of the classic NP-complete problems is the *satisfiability problem*: "Is there a truth assignment that makes logical expression E true?" Satisfiability is closely related to the tautology problem, and as with that problem, no significantly better solution to the satisfiability problem is known than cycling through all possible truth assignments.

Either all the NP-complete problems have less-than-exponential time solutions, or none do. The fact that each NP-complete problem appears to require exponential time thus reinforces our belief that all are inherently exponential-time problems. Thus we have strong evidence that the straightforward satisfiability test is about the best we can do.

Incidentally, "NP" stands for "nondeterministic polynomial." "Nondeterministic" informally means "the ability to guess right," as discussed in Section 10.3. A problem can be "solved in nondeterministic polynomial time" if, given a guess at a solution for some instance of size n, we can check that the guess is correct in polynomial time, that is, in time n^c for some constant c.

Satisfiability is an example of such a problem. If someone gave us an assignment of truth values to variables that they claimed, or guessed, made expression E evaluate to 1, we could evaluate E with that assignment to its operands, and check, in time at most quadratic in the length of E, that the expression is satisfiable.

The class of problems that — like satisfiability — can be "solved" by guessing followed by a polynomial time check is called NP. Some problems in NP are actually quite easy, and can be solved without the guessing, still taking only time that is polynomial in the length of the input. However, there are many problems in NP that can be proved to be as hard as any in NP, and these are the NP-complete problems. (Do not confuse "completeness" in this sense, meaning "hardest in the class," with "complete set of operators" meaning "able to express every Boolean function.")

The family of problems solvable in polynomial time with no guessing is often called P. Figure 12.22 shows the relationship between P, NP, and the NP-complete problems. If any NP-complete problem is in P, then $P = NP$, something we doubt very much is the case, because all the known NP-complete problems, and some other problems in NP, appear not to be in P. The tautology problem is not believed to be in NP, but it is as hard or harder than any problem in NP (called an *NP-hard* problem) and if the tautology problem is in P, then $P = NP$.

NP-hard problem

a) $pqr \rightarrow p + q$
b) $\big((p \rightarrow q)(q \rightarrow r)\big) \rightarrow (p \rightarrow r)$
c) $(p \rightarrow q) \rightarrow p$
d) $\big(p \equiv (q + r)\big) \rightarrow (\bar{q} \rightarrow pr)$

12.7.2*: Suppose we had an algorithm to solve the tautology problem for a logical expression. Show how this algorithm could be used to

a)   Determine whether two expressions were equivalent.
b)   Solve the satisfiability problem (see the box on "Inherent Intractability").

❖ 12.8   Some Algebraic Laws for Logical Expressions

In this section, we shall enumerate some useful tautologies. In each case, we shall state the law, leaving the tautology test to be carried out by the reader by constructing the truth table.

Laws of Equivalence

We begin with some observations about how equivalence works. The reader should notice the dual role played by equivalence. It is one of a number of operators that we use in logical expressions. However, it is also a signal that two expressions are "equal," and that one can be substituted for the other. Thus a tautology of the form $E_1 \equiv E_2$ tells us something about E_1 and E_2, namely that either can be substituted for the other within larger expressions, using the principle "equals can be substituted for equals."

Further, we can use equivalences to prove other equivalences. If we have a sequence of expressions $E_1, E_2, \ldots, E_k$, such that each is derived from the previous one by a substitution of equals for equals, then each of these expressions gives the same value when evaluated with the same truth assignment. As a consequence, $E_1 \equiv E_k$ must be a tautology.

12.1. *Reflexivity of equivalence*: $p \equiv p$.

> As with all the laws we state, the principle of substitution applies, and we may replace p by any expression. Thus this law says that any expression is equivalent to itself.

12.2. *Commutative law for equivalence*: $(p \equiv q) \equiv (q \equiv p)$.

> Informally, p is equivalent to q if and only if q is equivalent to p. By the principle of substitution, if any expression E_1 is equivalent to another expression E_2, then E_2 is equivalent to E_1. Thus either of E_1 and E_2 may be substituted for the other.

12.3. *Transitive law for equivalence*: $\big((p \equiv q) \text{ AND } (q \equiv r)\big) \rightarrow (p \equiv r)$.

> Informally, if p is equivalent to q, and q is equivalent to r, then p is equivalent to r. An important consequence of this law is that if we have found both $E_1 \equiv E_2$ and $E_2 \equiv E_3$ to be tautologies, then $E_1 \equiv E_3$ is a tautology.

12.4. *Equivalence of the negations*: $(p \equiv q) \equiv (\bar{p} \equiv \bar{q})$.

> Two expressions are equivalent if and only if their negations are equivalent.

Laws Analogous to Arithmetic

There is an analogy between the arithmetic operators $+$, $\times$, and unary minus on the one hand, and OR, AND, and NOT on the other. Thus the following laws should not be surprising.

12.5. *The commutative law for* AND: $pq \equiv qp$.

Informally, pq is true exactly when qp is true.

12.6. *The associative law for* AND: $p(qr) \equiv (pq)r$.

Informally, we can group the AND of three variables (or expressions) either by taking the AND of the first two initially, or by taking the AND of the last two initially. Moreover, with law 12.5, we can show that the AND of any collection of propositions or expressions can be permuted and grouped any way we wish — the result will be the same.

12.7. *The commutative law for* OR: $(p + q) \equiv (q + p)$.

12.8. *The associative law for* OR: $\big(p + (q + r)\big) \equiv \big((p + q) + r\big)$.

This law and law 12.7 tell us the OR of any set of expressions can be grouped as we like.

12.9. *The distributive law of* AND *over* OR: $p(q + r) \equiv (pq + pr)$.

That is, if we wish to take the AND of p and the OR of two propositions or expressions, we can either take the OR first, or take the AND of p with each expression first; the result will be the same.

12.10. 1 (TRUE) *is the identity for* AND: $(p$ AND $1) \equiv p$.

Notice that $(1$ AND $p) \equiv p$ is also a tautology. We did not need to state it, because it follows from the substitution principle and previous laws. That is, we may substitute simultaneously 1 for p and p for q in 12.5, the commutative law for AND, to get the tautology $(1$ AND $p) \equiv (p$ AND $1)$. Then, an application of 12.3, the transitivity of equivalence, tells us that $(1$ AND $p) \equiv p$.

12.11. 0 (FALSE) *is the identity for* OR: p OR $0 \equiv p$.

Similarly, we can deduce that $(0$ OR $p) \equiv p$, using the same argument as for 12.10.

12.12. 0 *is the annihilator for* AND: $(p$ AND $0) \equiv 0$.[4]

Recall from Section 10.7 that an annihilator for an operator is a constant such that the operator, applied to that constant and any value, produces the annihilator as value. Note that in arithmetic, 0 is an annihilator for $\times$, but $+$ has no annihilator. However, we shall see that 1 is an annihilator for OR.

12.13. *Elimination of double negations*: (NOT NOT p) $\equiv p$.

---

[4] Of course, $(0$ AND $p) \equiv 0$ holds as well. We shall not, in the future, mention all the consequences of the commutative laws.

Exploiting Analogies for Arithmetic and Logical Operators

When we use the shorthand notation for AND and OR, we can often pretend that we are dealing with multiplication and addition, as we use laws 12.5 through 12.12. That is an advantage, since we are quite familiar with the corresponding laws for arithmetic. Thus, for example, the reader should be able to replace $(p + q)(r + s)$ by $pr + ps + qr + qs$ or by $q(s + r) + (r + s)p$ quickly.

What is more difficult, and what requires practice, is applying the laws that are not analogous to arithmetic. Examples are DeMorgan's laws and the distribution of OR over AND. For example, replacing $pq + rs$ by $(p + r)(p + s)(q + r)(q + s)$ is valid, but requires some thought to see how it follows from three applications of 12.14, the distributive law of OR over AND, and commutative and associative laws.

Ways in Which AND and OR Differ from Plus and Times

There are also a number of laws that show the difference between AND and OR on the one hand, and the arithmetic operators $\times$ and $+$ on the other. We enumerate some of them here.

12.14. *The distributive law for* OR *over* AND: $(p + qr) \equiv \big((p + q)(p + r)\big)$.

Just as AND distributes over OR, OR distributes over AND. Note that the analogous arithmetic identity, $x + yz = (x + y)(x + z)$, is false in general.

12.15. 1 *is the annihilator for* OR: $(1 \text{ OR } p) \equiv 1$.

Note that the arithmetic analog $1 + x = 1$ is false in general.

12.16. *Idempotence of* AND: $pp \equiv p$.

Recall that an operator is idempotent if, when applied to two copies of the same value, it produces that value as result.

12.17. *Idempotence of* OR: $p + p \equiv p$.

Note that neither $\times$ nor $+$ is idempotent. That is, neither $x \times x = x$ nor $x + x = x$ is true in general.

12.18 *Subsumption.*

There are two versions of this law, depending on whether we remove a superfluous product or sum.

a) $(p + pq) \equiv p$.

b) $p(p + q) \equiv p$.

Note that if we substitute an arbitrary product of literals for p and another product of literals for q in (a), we are saying that in a sum of products, we can eliminate any product that has a superset of the literals of some other product. The smaller set is said to *subsume* the superset. In part (b) we are saying an analogous thing about a product of sums; we can eliminate a sum that is a superset of the literals of some other sum in the product.

12.19. *Elimination of certain negations.*

    a) $p(\bar{p} + q) \equiv pq$.

    b) $p + \bar{p}q \equiv p + q$.

Notice that (b) is the law that we used in Section 12.2 to explain why Sally's condition could replace Sam's.

DeMorgan's Laws

There are two laws that allow us to push NOT's through an expression of AND's and OR's, resulting in an expression in which all the negations apply to propositional variables. The resulting expression is an AND-OR expression applied to literals. Intuitively, if we negate an expression with AND's and OR's, we can push the negation down the expression tree, "flipping" operators as we go. That is, each AND becomes an OR, and vice versa. Finally, the negations reach the leaves, where they stay, unless they meet a negated literal, in which case we can remove two negations by law 12.13. We must be careful, when we construct the new expression, to place parentheses properly, because the precedence of operators changes when we exchange AND's and OR's.

The basic rules are called "DeMorgan's laws." They are the following two tautologies.

12.20. *DeMorgan's laws.*

    a)   NOT $(pq) \equiv \bar{p} + \bar{q}$.

    b)   NOT $(p + q) \equiv \bar{p}\bar{q}$.

Part (a) says that p and q are not both true exactly when at least one of them is false, and (b) says that neither p nor q is true if and only if they are both false. We can generalize these two laws to allow any number of propositional variables as follows.

    c) $\big(\text{NOT } (p_1 p_2 \cdots p_k)\big) \equiv (\bar{p_1} + \bar{p_2} + \cdots + \bar{p_k})$.

    d) $\big(\text{NOT } (p_1 + p_2 + \cdots + p_k)\big) \equiv (\bar{p_1}\bar{p_2} \cdots \bar{p_k})$.

For example, (d) says that none of some collection of expressions is true if and only if all of them are false.

✦   **Example 12.20.** We have seen in Sections 12.5 and 12.6 how to construct sum-of-products expressions for arbitrary logical expressions. Suppose we start with an arbitrary such expression E, which we may write as $E_1 + E_2 + \cdots + E_k$, where each E_i is the AND of literals. We can construct a product-of-sums expression for NOT E, by starting with

    NOT $(E_1 + E_2 + \cdots + E_k)$

and applying DeMorgan's law (d) to get

$$\big(\text{NOT } (E_1)\big)\big(\text{NOT } (E_2)\big) \cdots \big(\text{NOT } (E_k)\big) \tag{12.8}$$

Now let E_i be the product of literals $X_{i1} X_{i2} \cdots X_{ij_i}$, where each X is either a variable or its negation. Then we can apply (c) to NOT (E_i) to turn it into

$$\bar{X}_{i1} + \bar{X}_{i2} + \cdots + \bar{X}_{ij_i}$$

If some literal X is a negated variable, say $\bar{q}$, then $\bar{X}$ should be replaced by q itself, using law 12.13, which says that double negations can be eliminated. When we make all these changes, (12.8) becomes a product of sums of literals.

For example, $rs + \bar{r}\bar{s}$ is a sum-of-products expression that is true exactly when $r \equiv s$; that is, it can be thought of as a definition of equivalence using AND, OR, and NOT. The following formula, the negation of the one above, is true when r and s are inequivalent, that is, exactly one of r and s is true.

$$\text{NOT } (rs + \bar{r}\bar{s}) \tag{12.9}$$

Now let us apply a substitution to DeMorgan's law (b), in which p is replaced by rs and q is replaced by $\bar{r}\bar{s}$. Then the left-hand side of (b) becomes exactly (12.9), and we know by the principle of substitution that (12.9) is equivalent to the right-hand side of (b) with the same substitution, namely

$$\text{NOT } (rs) \text{ AND NOT } (\bar{r}\bar{s}) \tag{12.10}$$

Now we can apply (a), with the substitution of r for p and s for q, replacing NOT (rs) by $\bar{r} + \bar{s}$. Similarly, (a) tells us that NOT $(\bar{r}\bar{s})$ is equivalent to NOT $(\bar{r})+$ NOT $(\bar{s})$. But NOT $(\bar{r})$ is the same as NOT $\big(\text{NOT } (r)\big)$, which is equivalent to r, since double negations can be eliminated. Similarly, NOT $(\bar{s})$ can be replaced by s. Thus (12.10) is equivalent to $(\bar{r}+\bar{s})(r+s)$. This is a product-of-sums expression for "exactly one of r and s is true." Informally, it says, "At least one of r and s is false and at least one of r and s is true." Evidently, the only way that could happen is for exactly one of r and s to be true. ✦

The Principle of Duality

As we scan the laws of this section, we notice a curious phenomenon. The equivalences seem to come in pairs, in which the roles of AND and OR are interchanged. For example, parts (a) and (b) of law 12.19 are such a pair, and laws 12.9 and 12.14 are such a pair; the latter are the two distributive laws. When the constants 0 and 1 are involved, these two must be interchanged, as in the pair of laws about identities, 12.10 and 12.11.

The explanation for this phenomenon is found in DeMorgan's laws. Suppose we start with a tautology $E_1 \equiv E_2$, where E_1 and E_2 are expressions involving operators AND, OR, and NOT. By law 12.4, NOT $(E_1) \equiv$ NOT (E_2) is also a tautology. Now we apply DeMorgan's laws to push the negations through AND's and OR's. As we do, we "flip" each AND to an OR and vice versa, and we move the negation down to each of the operands. If we meet a NOT operator, we simply move the "traveling" NOT below it, until we come to another AND or OR. The exception occurs when we come to a negated literal, say $\bar{p}$. Then, we combine the traveling NOT with the one already there to leave operand p. As a special case, if a traveling NOT meets a constant, 0 or 1, we negate the constant; that is, (NOT 0) $\equiv$ 1 and (NOT 1) $\equiv$ 0.

✦   **Example 12.21.** Let us consider the tautology 12.19(b). We begin by negating both sides, which gives us the tree of Fig. 12.23(a). Then, we push the negations through the OR's on each side of the equivalence, changing them to AND's; NOT signs appear above each of the arguments of the two OR's, as shown in Fig. 12.23(b). Three of the new NOT's are above variables, and so their travels end. The one that is above an **AND** flips it to an **OR**, and causes **NOT**'s to appear on its two arguments. The right-hand argument becomes **NOT** q, while the left-hand argument, which was **NOT** p, becomes **NOT NOT** p, or simply p. The resulting tree is shown in Fig. 12.23(c).

The tree of Fig. 12.23(c) represents the expression $\bar{p}(p + \bar{q}) \equiv \bar{p}\bar{q}$. To get the expression into the form of law 12.19(a), we must negate the variables. That is, we substitute expression $\bar{p}$ for p and $\bar{q}$ for q. When we eliminate the double negations, we are left with exactly 12.19(a). ◆

Laws Involving Implication

There are several useful tautologies that give us properties of the $\rightarrow$ operator.

12.21. $\big((p \rightarrow q) \text{ AND } (q \rightarrow p)\big) \equiv (p \equiv q)$.

That is, two expressions are equivalent if and only if they each imply the other.

12.22. $(p \equiv q) \rightarrow (p \rightarrow q)$.

The equivalence of two expressions tells us that either one implies the other.

12.23. *Transitivity of implication*: $\big((p \rightarrow q) \text{ AND } (q \rightarrow r)\big) \rightarrow (p \rightarrow r)$.

That is, if p implies q, which implies r, then p implies r.

12.24. It is possible to express implication with **AND** and **OR**. The simplest form is:

a) $(p \rightarrow q) \equiv (\bar{p} + q)$.

We shall see that there are many situations in which we deal with an expression of the form "if this and this and $\cdots$, then that." For example, the programming language Prolog, and many "artificial intelligence" languages depend upon "rules" of that form. These rules are written formally as $(p_1 p_2 \cdots p_n) \rightarrow q$. They may be expressed with only **AND** and **OR**, by the equivalence

b) $(p_1 p_2 \cdots p_n \rightarrow q) \equiv (\bar{p_1} + \bar{p_2} + \cdots + \bar{p_n} + q)$.

That is, both the left-hand and the right-hand sides of the equivalence are true whenever q is true or one or more of the p's are false; both sides are false otherwise.

EXERCISES

12.8.1: Check, by constructing the truth tables, that each of the laws 12.1 to 12.24 are tautologies.

12.8.2: We can substitute expressions for any propositional variable in a tautology and get another tautology. Substitute $x + y$ for p, yz for q, and $\bar{x}$ for r in each of the tautologies 12.1 to 12.24, to get new tautologies. Do not forget to put parentheses around the substituted expressions if needed.

12.8.3: Prove that

a) $p_1 + p_2 + \cdots + p_n$ is equivalent to the sum (logical **OR**) of the p_i's in any order.
b) $p_1 p_2 \cdots p_n$ is equivalent to the product (logical **AND**) of the p_i's in any order.

Hint: A similar result was shown for addition in Section 2.4.

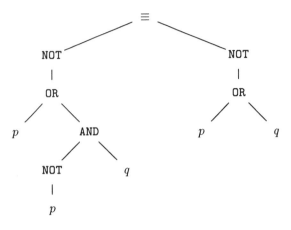

(a) Initial expression tree

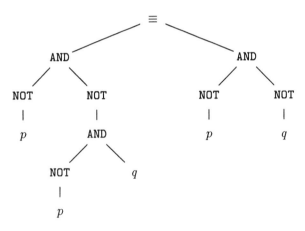

(b) First "pushes" of the negations

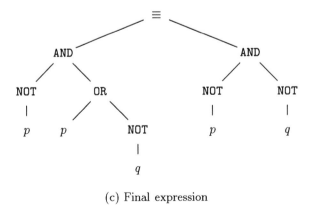

(c) Final expression

Fig. 12.23. Constructing the dual expression.

12.8.4*: Use laws given in this section to transform the first of each pair of expressions into the second. To save effort, you may omit steps that use laws 12.5 through 12.13, which are analogous to arithmetic. For example, commutativity and associativity of AND and OR may be assumed.

a) Transform $pq + rs$ into $(p + r)(p + s)(q + r)(q + s)$.
b) Transform $pq + p\bar{q}r$ into $p(q + r)$.
c) Transform $pq + p\bar{q} + \bar{p}q + \bar{p}\bar{q}$ into 1. (This transformation requires law 12.25 from the next section.)
d) Transform $pq \rightarrow r$ into $(p \rightarrow r) + (q \rightarrow r)$.
e) Transform NOT $(pq \rightarrow r)$ into $pq\bar{r}$.

12.8.5*: Show that the subsumption laws, 12.18(a) and (b), follow from previously given laws, in the sense that it is possible to transform $p + pq$ into p and transform $p(p + q)$ into p using only laws 12.1 through 12.17.

12.8.6: Apply DeMorgan's laws to turn the following expressions into expressions where the only NOT's are applied to propositional variables (i.e., the NOT's appear in literals only).

a) NOT $(pq + \bar{p}r)$
b) NOT (NOT $p + q($NOT $(r + \bar{s})))$

12.8.7*: Prove the generalized DeMorgan's laws 12.20(c) and (d) by induction on k, using the basic laws 12.20(a) and (b). Then, justify the generalized laws informally by describing what the 2^k-row truth tables for each expression and their subexpressions look like.

12.8.8*: Find the pairs of laws in this section that are duals of one another.

12.8.9*: Prove law 12.24(b) by induction on n.

12.8.10*: Show that law 12.24(b) holds by describing the 2^n rows of the truth table for the expression and each of its subexpressions.

12.8.11: Simplify the following by using the subsumption laws and the commutative and associative laws for AND and OR.

a) $w\bar{x} + w\bar{x}y + \bar{z}\bar{x}w$
b) $(w + \bar{x})(w + y + \bar{z})(\bar{w} + \bar{x} + \bar{y})(\bar{x})$

12.8.12*: Show that the arithmetic analogs of laws 12.14 through 12.20 are false, by giving specific numbers for which the analogous equalities to not hold.

12.8.13*: If we start with logical expression whose only operators are AND, OR, and NOT, we can push all the NOT's down the tree until the only NOT's are immediately above propositions; that is, the expression is the AND and OR of literals. Prove that we can do so. *Hint*: Whenever we see a NOT, either it is immediately above another NOT (in which case we can eliminate them both by rule 12.13), or above a proposition (in which case the statement is satisfied), or it is above an AND and OR (in which case we can use DeMorgan's laws to push it down one level). However, a proof that we eventually reach an equivalent expression with all NOT's above propositions cannot proceed by induction on an obvious "size" measure such as the sum of the heights of the nodes labeled NOT. The reason is that when we use DeMorgan's laws to push one NOT down, it is replaced by two NOT's, and this sum might increase. In order to prove that we eventually reach an expression with all **NOT**'s above propositions, you need to find a suitable "size" measure that always decreases when DeMorgan's laws are applied in the direction where a **NOT** is pushed down below an **AND** or **OR**. Find such a size measure and prove the claim.

✥✥ 12.9 Tautologies and Methods of Proof

In the past three sections, we have seen one aspect of logic: its use as a design theory. In Section 12.6 we saw how to use Karnaugh maps to design expressions given a Boolean function, and in Chapter 13 we shall see how this methodology helps design the switching circuits from which computers and other digital devices are built. Sections 12.7 and 12.8 introduced us to tautologies, which can be used to simplify expressions, and therefore serve as another important tool when good expressions must be designed for a given Boolean function.

A second important use of logic will be seen in this section. When people reason or prove statements of mathematics, they use a variety of techniques to further their arguments. Examples of these techniques are

1. Case analysis,
2. Proof of the contrapositive,
3. Proof by contradiction, and
4. Proof by reduction to truth.

In this section we shall define these techniques, showing how each can be used in proofs. We also show how these techniques are justified by certain tautologies of propositional logic.

The Law of Excluded Middle

We begin with several tautologies that represent basic facts about how one reasons.

12.25. *The law of the excluded middle*: $(p + \bar{p}) \equiv 1$ is a tautology.

That is, something is either true or false; there is no middle ground.

✦ **Example 12.22.** As an application of law 12.25, as well as several of the other laws seen so far, we can prove the law $(pq + \bar{p}q) \equiv q$ used in Section 12.6. Begin with

$$(1 \text{ AND } q) \equiv (1 \text{ AND } q)$$

which follows from law 12.1, reflexivity of equivalence, by substituting $1 \text{ AND } q$ for p. Now, by law 12.25, we may replace 1 by $p + \bar{p}$ in the left-hand side above, substituting "equals for equals." Thus

$$((p + \bar{p})q) \equiv (1 \text{ AND } q)$$

is a tautology. On the right-hand side of the equivalence, use law 12.10 to replace $1 \text{ AND } q$ by q. Then, on the left-hand side, we use 12.9, the distributivity of **AND** over **OR**, preceded and followed by law 12.5, the commutativity of **AND**, to show that the left-hand side is equivalent to $pq + \bar{p}q$. Thus we have

$$(pq + \bar{p}q) \equiv q$$

as desired. ✦

A generalization of the law of the excluded middle is a technique of proof called "case analysis," in which we wish to prove an expression E. We take some other expression F and its negation, NOT F, and prove that both F and NOT F imply E. Since F must be either true or false, we can conclude E. The formal basis for case analysis is the following tautology.

12.26. *Case analysis*: $\big((p \to q) \text{ AND } (\bar{p} \to q)\big) \equiv q$.

That is, the two cases occur when p is true and when p is false. If q is implied in both cases, then q must be true. We leave it as an exercise to show that 12.26 follows from 12.25 and other laws we have proved.

12.27. $p\bar{p} \equiv 0$.

A proposition and its negation cannot both be true simultaneously. This law is vital when we make a "proof by contradiction." We discuss this technique of proof shortly, in law 12.29, and also in Section 12.11, when we cover resolution proofs.

Proving the Contrapositive

Sometimes we want to prove an implication, like $p \to q$, but we find it easier to prove $\bar{q} \to \bar{p}$, which is an equivalent expression called the *contrapositive* of $p \to q$. This principle is formalized in the following law.

12.28. *The contrapositive law*: $(p \to q) \equiv (\bar{q} \to \bar{p})$.

✦ **Example 12.23.** Let us consider a simple example of a proof that shows how the contrapositive law may be used. This example also shows the limitations of propositional logic in proofs. Logic takes us part of the way, allowing us to reason about statements without reference to what the statements mean. However, to get a complete proof, we normally have to make some argument that refers to the meaning of our terms. For this example, we need to know what concepts about integers, like "prime," "odd," and "greater than" mean.

We shall consider three propositions about a positive integer x:

a	"$x > 2$"
b	"x is a prime"
c	"x is odd"

The theorem we want to prove is $ab \to c$, that is,

STATEMENT   "If x is greater than 2 and a prime, then x is odd."

We begin by applying some of the laws we have studied to turn the expression $ab \to c$ into an equivalent expression that is more amenable to proof. First, we use law 12.28 to turn it into its contrapositive, $\bar{c} \to$ NOT (ab). Then we use DeMorgan's law 12.20(a) to turn NOT (ab) into $\bar{a} + \bar{b}$. That is, we have transformed the theorem to be proved into $\bar{c} \to (\bar{a} + \bar{b})$. Put another way, we need to prove that

STATEMENT "If x is not odd, then x is not greater than 2 or x is not prime."

We can replace "not odd" by "even," "not greater than 2" by "equal to or less than 2," and "not prime" by "composite." Thus we want to prove

STATEMENT "If x is even, then $x \le 2$ or x is composite."

Now we have gone as far as we can go with propositional logic, and we must start talking about the meaning of our terms. If x is even, then $x = 2y$ for some integer y; that is what it means for x to be even. Since x is assumed through this proof to be a positive integer, y must be 1 or greater.

Now we use case analysis, considering the cases where y is 1, and y is greater than 1, which are the only possibilities, since we just argued that $y \ge 1$. If $y = 1$, then $x = 2$, and so we have proved $x \le 2$. If $y > 1$, then x is the product of two integers, 2 and y, both greater than 1, which means that x is composite. Thus we have shown that if x is even, then either $x \le 2$ (in the case $y = 1$) or x is composite (in the case $y > 1$). ✦

Proof by Contradiction

Frequently, rather than make a "direct" proof of an expression E, we find it easier to start by assuming NOT E and proving from that a *contradiction,* that is, the expression FALSE. The basis for such proofs is the following tautology.

12.29. *Proof by contradiction:* $(\bar{p} \to 0) \equiv p$.

Informally, if starting with $\bar{p}$ we can conclude 0, that is, conclude FALSE or derive a contradiction, then that is the same as proving p. This law actually follows from others we have stated. Start with law 12.24 with $\bar{p}$ in place of p, and 0 in place of q, to get the equivalence

$$(\bar{p} \to 0) \equiv \big(\text{NOT } (\bar{p}) + 0\big)$$

Law 12.13, the elimination of double negatives, lets us replace NOT $(\bar{p})$ by p, and so

$$(\bar{p} \to 0) \equiv (p + 0)$$

Now law 12.11 tells us that $(p + 0) \equiv p$, and so a further substitution gives us

$$(\bar{p} \to 0) \equiv p$$

✦ **Example 12.24.** Let us reconsider the propositions a, b, and c from Example 12.23, which talk about a positive integer x and assert, respectively, that $x > 2$, x is a prime, and x is odd. We want to prove the theorem $ab \rightarrow c$, and so we substitute this expression for p in 12.29. Then $\bar{p} \rightarrow 0$ becomes $(\texttt{NOT}\ (ab \rightarrow c)) \rightarrow 0$.

If we use 12.24 on the first of these implications, we get

$$\Big(\texttt{NOT}\ \big(\texttt{NOT}\ (ab) + c\big)\Big) \rightarrow 0$$

DeMorgan's law applied to the inner **NOT** gives $\big(\texttt{NOT}\ (\bar{a} + \bar{b} + c)\big) \rightarrow 0$. Another use of DeMorgan's law followed by 12.13 twice to eliminate the double negatives turns this expression into $(ab\bar{c}) \rightarrow 0$.

That is as far as propositional logic takes us; now we must reason about integers. We must start with a, b, and $\bar{c}$ and derive a contradiction. In words, we start by assuming that $x > 2$, x is a prime, and x is even, and from these we must derive a contradiction.

Since x is even, we can say $x = 2y$ for some integer y. Since $x > 2$, it must be that $y \geq 2$. But then x, which equals $2y$, is the product of two integers, each greater than 1, and therefore x is composite. Thus we have proven that x is not a prime, that is, the statement $\bar{b}$. Since we were given b, that x is a prime, and we now have $\bar{b}$ as well, we have $b\bar{b}$, which by 12.27 is equivalent to 0, or **FALSE**.

We have thus proved $(\texttt{NOT}\ (ab \rightarrow c)) \rightarrow 0$, which is equivalent to $ab \rightarrow c$ by 12.29. That completes our proof by contradiction. ✦

Equivalence to Truth

Our next proof method allows us to prove an expression to be a tautology by transforming it by substitution of equals for equals until the expression is reduced to 1 (**TRUE**).

12.30. *Proof by equivalence to truth*: $(p \equiv 1) \equiv p$.

✦ **Example 12.25.** The expression $rs \rightarrow r$ says the **AND** of two expressions implies the first of them (and by commutativity of **AND**, also implies the second). We can show that $rs \rightarrow r$ is a tautology by the following sequence of equivalences.

$$
\begin{array}{rcl}
& & rs \rightarrow r \\
1) & \equiv & \texttt{NOT}\ (rs) + r \\
2) & \equiv & (\bar{r} + \bar{s}) + r \\
3) & \equiv & 1 + \bar{s} \\
4) & \equiv & 1
\end{array}
$$

(1) follows by applying law 12.24, the definition of $\rightarrow$ in terms of **AND** and **OR**. (2) is an application of DeMorgan's law. (3) follows when we use 12.7 and 12.8 to reorder terms and then replace $r + \bar{r}$ by 1 according to law 12.25. Finally, (4) is an application of law 12.12, the fact that 1 is an annihilator for **OR**. ✦

EXERCISES

12.9.1: Show that laws 12.25 and 12.27 are duals of each other.

12.9.2*: We would like to prove the theorem "If x is a perfect square and x is even, then x is divisible by 4."

a) Designate propositional variables to stand for the three conditions about x mentioned in the theorem.

b) Write the theorem formally in terms of these propositions.

c) State the contrapositive of your answer to (b), both in terms of your propositional variables and in colloquial terms.

d) Prove the statement from (c). *Hint*: It helps to notice that if x is not divisible by 4, then either x is odd, or $x = 2y$ and y is odd.

12.9.3*: Give a proof by contradiction of the theorem from Exercise 12.9.2.

12.9.4*: Repeat Exercises 12.9.2 and 12.9.3 for the statement "If x^3 is odd, then x is odd" about integers x. (But in 12.9.2(a) there are only two conditions discussed.)

12.9.5*: Prove the following are tautologies by showing they are equivalent to 1 (TRUE).

a) $pq + r + \bar{q}\bar{r} + \bar{p}\bar{r}$

b) $p + \bar{q}\bar{r} + \bar{p}r + q\bar{r}$

12.9.6*: Prove law 12.26, case analysis, by substitution of equals for equals in (instances of) previously proved laws.

12.9.7*: Generalize the case analysis law to the situation where the cases are defined by k propositional variables, which may be true or false in all 2^k combinations. What is the justifying tautology for the case $k = 2$? For general k? Show why this tautology must be true.

✦✦ 12.10 Deduction

We have seen logic as a design theory in Sections 12.6 to 12.8, and as a formalization of proof techniques in Section 12.9. Now, let us see a third side of the picture: the use of logic in *deduction,* that is, in sequences of statements that constitute a complete proof. Deduction should be familiar to the reader from the study of plane geometry in high school, where we learn to start with certain *hypotheses* (the "givens"), and to prove a *conclusion* by a sequence of steps, each of which follows from previous steps by one of a limited number of reasons, called *inference rules.* In this section, we explain what constitutes a deductive proof and give a number of examples.

Hypothesis and conclusion

Inference rule

Unfortunately, discovering a deductive proof for a tautology is difficult. As we mentioned in Section 12.7, it is an example of an "inherently intractable" problem, in the NP-hard class. Thus we cannot expect to find deductive proofs except by luck or by exhaustive search. In Section 12.11, we shall discuss resolution proofs, which appear to be a good heuristic for finding proofs, although in the worst case this technique, like all others, must take exponential time.

What Constitutes a Deductive Proof?

Suppose we are given certain logical expressions $E_1, E_2, \ldots, E_k$ as hypotheses, and we wish to draw a conclusion in the form of another logical expression E. In general, neither the conclusion nor any of the hypotheses will be tautologies, but what we want to show is that

$$(E_1 \text{ AND } E_2 \text{ AND } \cdots \text{ AND } E_k) \to E \qquad (12.11)$$

Applications of Deduction

**Automated
theorem
proving**

In addition to being the stuff of which all proofs in mathematics are ultimately made, deduction or formal proof has many uses in computer science. One application is *automated theorem proving*. There are systems that find proofs of theorems by searching for sequences of steps that proceed from hypotheses to conclusion. Some systems search for proofs on their own, and others work interactively with the user, taking hints and filling in small gaps in the sequence of steps that form a proof. Some believe that these systems will eventually be useful for proving the correctness of programs, although much progress must be made before such facilities are practical.

A second use of deductive proofs is in programming languages that relate deduction to computation. As a very simple example, a robot finding its way through a maze might represent its possible states by a finite set of positions in the centers of hallways. We could draw a graph in which the nodes represent the positions, and an arc $u \rightarrow v$ means that it is possible for the robot to move from position u to position v by a simple move because u and v represent adjacent hallways.

We could also think of the positions as propositions, where u stands for "The robot can reach position u." Then $u \rightarrow v$ can be interpreted not only as an arc, but as a logical implication, that is, "If the robot can reach u, then it can reach v." (Note the "pun"; the arrow can represent an arc or an implication.) A natural question to ask is: "What positions can the robot reach from position a."

We can phrase this question as a deduction if we take the expression a, and all expressions $u \rightarrow v$ for adjacent positions u and v, as hypotheses, and see which propositional variables x we can prove from these hypotheses. In this case, we don't really need a tool as powerful as deduction, because depth-first search works, as discussed in Section 9.7. However, there are many related situations where graph-theoretic methods are not effective, yet the problem can be couched as a deduction and a reasonable solution obtained.

---

is a tautology. That is, we want to show that if we assume $E_1, E_2, \ldots, E_k$ are true, then it follows that E is true.

One way to show (12.11) is to construct its truth table and test whether it has value 1 in each row — the routine test for a tautology. However, that may not be sufficient for two reasons.

1. As we mentioned, tautology testing becomes infeasible if there are too many variables in the expression.

2. More importantly, while tautology testing works for propositional logic, it cannot be used to test tautologies in more complex logical systems, such as predicate logic, discussed in Chapter 14.

We can often show that (12.11) is a tautology by presenting a *deductive proof*. A deductive proof is a sequence of lines, each of which is either a given hypothesis or is constructed from one or more previous lines by a rule of inference. If the last line is E, then we say that we have a proof of E from $E_1, E_2, \ldots, E_k$.

There are many rules of inference we might use. The only requirement is that if an inference rule allows us to write expression F as a line whenever expressions $F_1, F_2, \ldots, F_n$ are lines, then

The Sound of No Hands Clapping

Frequently, we need to understand the limiting case of an operator applied to no operands, as we did in inference rule (a). We asserted that it makes sense to regard the AND of zero expressions (or lines of a proof) as having truth value 1. The motivation is that F_1 AND F_2 AND $\cdots$ AND F_n is true unless there is at least one of the F's that is false. But if $n = 0$, that is, there are no F's, then there is no way the expression could be false, and thus it is natural to take the AND of zero expressions to be 1.

We adopt the convention that whenever we apply an operator to zero operands, the result is the identity for that operator. Thus we expect the OR of zero expressions to be 0, since an OR of expressions is true only if one of the expressions is true; if there are no expressions, then there is no way to make the OR true. Likewise, the sum of zero numbers is taken to be 0, and the product of zero numbers is taken to be 1.

$$(F_1 \text{ AND } F_2 \text{ AND } \cdots \text{ AND } F_n) \to F$$

must be a tautology. For example,

a) Any tautology may be used as a line in a proof, regardless of previous lines. The justification for this rule is that if F is a tautology, then the logical AND of zero lines of the proof implies F. Note that the AND of zero expressions is 1, conventionally, and $1 \to F$ is a tautology when F is a tautology.

Modus ponens b) The rule of *modus ponens* says that if E and $E \to F$ are lines of a proof, then F may be added as a line of the proof. Modus ponens follows from the tautology $\big(p \text{ AND } (p \to q)\big) \to q$; here expression E is substituted for p and F for q. The only subtlety is that we do not need a line with E AND $(E \to F)$, but rather two separate lines, one with E and one with $E \to F$.

c) If E and F are two lines of a proof, then we can add the line E AND F. The justification is that $(p \text{ AND } q) \to (p \text{ AND } q)$ is a tautology; we may substitute any expression E for p and F for q.

d) If we have lines E and $E \equiv F$, then we may add line F. The justification is similar to modus ponens, since $E \equiv F$ implies $E \to F$. That is,

$$\big(p \text{ AND } (p \equiv q)\big) \to q$$

is a tautology, and inference rule (d) is a substituted instance of this tautology.

✦ **Example 12.26.** Suppose we have the following propositional variables, with intuitive meanings as suggested.

r	"It is raining."
u	"Joe brings his umbrella."
w	"Joe gets wet."

We are given the following hypotheses.

$r \to u$	"If it rains, Joe brings his umbrella."
$u \to \bar{w}$	"If Joe has an umbrella, he doesn't get wet."
$\bar{r} \to \bar{w}$	"If it doesn't rain, Joe doesn't get wet."

We are asked to prove $\bar{w}$, that is, Joe never gets wet. In a sense, the matter is trivial, since the reader may check that

$$\big((r \to u) \text{ AND } (u \to \bar{w}) \text{ AND } (\bar{r} \to \bar{w})\big) \to \bar{w}$$

is a tautology. However, it is also possible to prove $\bar{w}$ from the hypotheses, using some of the algebraic laws from Section 12.8 and some of the inference rules just discussed. The approach of finding a proof is the one that we would have to take if we were dealing with a more complex form of logic than propositional calculus or with a logical expression involving many variables. One possible proof, along with the justification for each step, is shown in Fig. 12.24.

The rough idea of the proof is that we use case analysis, considering both the cases where it is raining and it is not raining. By line (5) we have proved that if it is raining, Joe doesn't get wet, and line (6), a given hypothesis, says that if it is not raining Joe doesn't get wet. Lines (7) through (9) combine the two cases to draw the desired conclusion. ✦

1)	$r \to u$	Hypothesis
2)	$u \to \bar{w}$	Hypothesis
3)	$(r \to u) \text{ AND } (u \to \bar{w})$	(c) applied to (1) and (2)
4)	$\big((r \to u) \text{ AND } (u \to \bar{w})\big) \to (r \to \bar{w})$	Substitution into law (12.23)
5)	$r \to \bar{w}$	Modus ponens, with (3) and (4)
6)	$\bar{r} \to \bar{w}$	Hypothesis
7)	$(r \to \bar{w}) \text{ AND } (\bar{r} \to \bar{w})$	(c) applied to (5) and (6)
8)	$\big((r \to \bar{w}) \text{ AND } (\bar{r} \to \bar{w})\big) \equiv \bar{w}$	Substitution into law (12.26)
9)	$\bar{w}$	(d) with (7) and (8)

Fig. 12.24. Example of a deductive proof.

Why a Deductive Proof "Works"

A deductive proof, recall, starts with hypotheses $E_1, E_2, \ldots, E_k$ and adds additional lines (i.e., expressions), each of which is implied by E_1 AND E_2 AND $\cdots$ AND E_k. Each line we add is implied by the AND of zero or more previous lines or is one of the hypotheses. We can show that E_1 AND E_2 AND $\cdots$ AND E_k implies each line of the proof, by induction on the number of lines added so far. To do so, we need two families of tautologies involving implication. The first family is a generalized transitive law for $\to$. For any n:

$$\Big((p \to q_1) \text{ AND } (p \to q_2) \text{ AND } \cdots \text{ AND } (p \to q_n) \tag{12.12}$$
$$\text{AND } \big((q_1 q_2 \cdots q_n) \to r\big)\Big) \to (p \to r)$$

That is, if p implies each of the q_i's, and the q_i's together imply r, then p implies r.

We find that (12.12) is a tautology by the following reasoning. The only way that (12.12) could be false is if $p \rightarrow r$ were false and the left-hand side true. But $p \rightarrow r$ can only be false if p is true and r is false, and so in what follows we shall assume p and $\bar{r}$. We must show that the left-hand side of (12.12) is then false.

If the left-hand side of (12.12) is true, then each of its subexpressions connected by AND is true. For example, $p \rightarrow q_1$ is true. Since we assume p is true, the only way $p \rightarrow q_1$ can be true is if q_1 is true. Similarly, we can conclude that $q_2, \ldots, q_n$ are all true. Thus $q_1 q_2 \cdots q_n \rightarrow r$, must be false, since we assume r is false and we have just discovered that all the q_i's are true.

We started by assuming that (12.12) was false and observed that the right-hand side must therefore be true, and thus p and $\bar{r}$ must be true. We then concluded that the left-hand side of (12.12) is false when p is true and r is false. But if the left-hand side of (12.12) is false, then (12.12) itself is true, and we have a contradiction. Thus (12.12) can never be false and is therefore a tautology.

Note that if $n = 1$ in (12.12), then we have the usual transitive law of $\rightarrow$, which is law 12.23. Also, if $n = 0$, then (12.12) becomes $(1 \rightarrow r) \rightarrow r$, which is a tautology. Recall that when $n = 0$, $q_1 q_2 \cdots q_n$ is conventionally taken to be the identity for AND, which is 1.

We also need a family of tautologies to justify the fact that we can add the hypotheses to the proof. It is a generalization of a tautology discussed in Example 12.25. We claim that for any m and i such that $1 \leq i \leq m$,

$$(p_1 p_2 \cdots p_m) \rightarrow p_i \tag{12.13}$$

is a tautology. That is, the AND of one or more propositions implies any one of them.

The expression (12.13) is a tautology because the only way it could be false is if the left-hand side is true and the right-hand side, p_i, is false. But if p_i is false, then the AND of p_i and other p's is surely false, so the left-hand side of (12.13) is false. But (12.13) is true whenever its left-hand side is false.

Now we can prove that, given

1. Hypotheses $E_1, E_2, \ldots, E_k$, and

2. A set of inference rules such that, whenever they allow us to write a line F, this line is either one of the E_i's, or there is a tautology

   $$(F_1 \text{ AND } F_2 \text{ AND } \cdots \text{ AND } F_n) \rightarrow F$$

   for some set of previous lines $F_1, F_2, \ldots, F_n$,

it must be that $(E_1 \text{ AND } E_2 \text{ AND } \cdots \text{ AND } E_k) \rightarrow F$ is a tautology for each line F. The induction is on the number of lines added to the proof.

BASIS. For a basis, we take zero lines. The statement holds, since it says something about every line F of a proof, and there are no such lines to discuss. That is, our inductive statement is really of the form "if F is a line then $\cdots$," and we know such an if-then statement is true if the condition is false.

INDUCTION. For the induction, suppose that for each previous line G,

$$(E_1 \text{ AND } E_2 \text{ AND } \cdots \text{ AND } E_k) \rightarrow G$$

Deductive Proofs Versus Equational Proofs

The kinds of proofs we saw in Sections 12.8 and 12.9 differ in flavor from the deductive proofs studied in Section 12.10. However, proofs of both kinds involve the creation of a sequence of tautologies, leading to the desired tautology.

In Sections 12.8 and 12.9 we saw equational proofs, where starting with one tautology we made substitutions to derive other tautologies. All the tautologies derived have the form $E \equiv F$ for some expressions E and F. This style of proof is used in high-school trigonometry, for example, where we learn to prove "trigonometric identities."

Deductive proofs also involve discovery of tautologies. The only difference is that each is of the form $E \to F$, where E is the AND of the hypotheses, and F is the line of the proof that we actually right down. The fact that we do not write the full tautology is a notational convenience, not a fundamental distinction. This style of proof should also be familiar from high-school; it is the style of proofs in plane geometry, for example.

---

is a tautology. Let F be the next line added. There are two cases.

Case 1: F is one of the hypotheses. Then $(E_1$ AND E_2 AND $\cdots$ AND $E_k) \to F$ is a tautology because it comes from (12.13) with $m = k$ when we substitute E_j for each p_j, for $j = 1, 2, \ldots, k$.

Case 2: F is added because there is a rule of inference

$$(F_1 \text{ AND } F_2 \text{ AND } \cdots \text{ AND } F_n) \to F$$

where each of the F_j's is one of the previous lines. By the inductive hypothesis,

$$(E_1 \text{ AND } E_2 \text{ AND } \cdots \text{ AND } E_k) \to F_j$$

is a tautology for each j. Thus, if we substitute F_j for q_j in (12.12), substitute

$$E_1 \text{ AND } E_2 \text{ AND } \cdots \text{ AND } E_k$$

for p, and substitute F for r, we know that any substitution of truth values for the variables of the E's and F's makes the left-hand side of (12.12) true. Since (12.12) is a tautology, every assignment of truth values must also make the right-hand side true. But the right-hand side is $(E_1$ AND E_2 AND $\cdots$ AND $E_k) \to F$. We conclude that this expression is true for every assignment of truth values; that is, it is a tautology.

We have now concluded the induction, and we have shown that

$$(E_1 \text{ AND } E_2 \text{ AND } \cdots \text{ AND } E_k) \to F$$

for every line F of the proof. In particular, if the last line of the proof is our goal E, we know $(E_1$ AND E_2 AND $\cdots$ AND $E_k) \to E$.

EXERCISES

12.10.1*: Give proofs of the following conclusions from the following hypotheses. You may use inference rules (a) through (d). For tautologies you may use only the laws stated in Sections 12.8 and 12.9 and tautologies that follow by using instances of these laws to "substitute equals for equals."

a)   Hypotheses: $p \rightarrow q$, $p \rightarrow r$; conclusion: $p \rightarrow qr$.
b)   Hypotheses: $p \rightarrow (q + r)$, $p \rightarrow (q + \bar{r})$; conclusion: $p \rightarrow q$.
c)   Hypotheses: $p \rightarrow q$, $qr \rightarrow s$; conclusion: $pr \rightarrow s$.

12.10.2: Justify why the following is a rule of inference. If $E \rightarrow F$ is a line, and G is any expression whatsoever, then we can add $E \rightarrow (F$ **OR** $G)$ as a line.

✧✧ 12.11   Proofs by Resolution

As we mentioned earlier in this chapter, finding proofs is a hard problem, and since the tautology problem is very likely to be inherently exponential, there is no general way to make finding proofs easy. However, there are many techniques known that for "typical" tautologies appear to help with the exploration needed in the search for a proof. In this section we shall study a useful inference rule, called *resolution,* that is perhaps the most basic of these techniques. Resolution is based on the following tautology.

$$\big((p + q)(\bar{p} + r)\big) \rightarrow (q + r) \tag{12.14}$$

The validity of this rule of inference is easy to check. The only way it could be false is if $q + r$ were false, and the left-hand side were true. If $q + r$ is false, then both q and r are false. Suppose p is true, so that $\bar{p}$ is false. Then $\bar{p} + r$ is false, and the left-hand side of (12.14) must be false. Similarly, if p is false, then $p + q$ is false, which again tells us that the left-hand side is false. Thus it is impossible for the right-hand side to be false while the left-hand side is true, and we conclude that (12.14) is a tautology.

Clause

The usual way resolution is applied is to convert our hypotheses into *clauses,* which are sums (logical **OR**'s) of literals. We convert each of our hypotheses into a product of clauses. Our proof begins with each of these clauses as a line of the proof, and the justification is that each is "given." We then apply the resolution rule to construct additional lines, which will always turn out to be clauses. That is, if q and r in (12.14) are each replaced by any sum of literals, then $q + r$ will also be a sum of literals.

In practice, we shall simplify clauses by removing duplicates. That is, both q and r could include a literal X, in which case we shall remove one copy of X from $q + r$. The justification is found in laws 12.17, 12.7, and 12.8, the idempotence, commutativity, and associativity of **OR**. In general, a useful point of view is that a clause is a set, rather than a list, of literals. The associative and commutative laws allow us to order the literals any way we please, and the idempotent law allows us to eliminate duplicates.

We also eliminate clauses that contain contradictory literals. That is, if both X and $\bar{X}$ are found in one clause, then by laws 12.25, 12.7, 12.8, and 12.15, the clause is equivalent to 1, and there is no need to include it in a proof. That is, by law 12.25, $(X + \bar{X}) \equiv 1$, and by the annihilator law 12.15, 1 OR anything is equivalent to 1.

✦ **Example 12.27.** Consider the clauses $(a + \bar{b} + c)$ and $(\bar{d} + a + b + e)$. We may let b play the role of p in (12.14). Then q is $\bar{d} + a + e$, and r is $a + c$. Notice that we have done some rearrangement to match our clauses with (12.14). First, our second clause has been matched with the first, $p + q$ in (12.14), and our first clause is matched with the second of (12.14). Moreover, the variable that plays the role of p does not appear first in our two clauses, but that is no matter, because the commutative and associative laws for OR justify our rearranging the clauses in any order we choose.

The new clause $q + r$, which may appear as a line in a proof if our two clauses are already in that proof, is $(\bar{d} + a + e + a + c)$. We may simplify this clause by eliminating the duplicate a, leaving $(\bar{d} + a + e + c)$.

As another example, consider the clauses $(a + b)$ and $(\bar{a} + \bar{b})$. We may let a play the roll of p in (12.14); q is b, and r is $\bar{b}$, giving us the new clause $(b + \bar{b})$. That clause is equivalent to 1, and therefore need not be generated. ✦

Putting Logical Expressions in Conjunctive Normal Form

In order to make resolution work, we need to put all hypotheses, and the conclusion, into product-of-sums form, or "conjunctive normal form." There are several approaches that may be taken. Perhaps the simplest is the following.

1. First, we get rid of any operators except AND, OR, and NOT. We replace $E \equiv F$ by $(E \to F)(F \to E)$, by law 12.21. Then, we replace $G \to H$ by

    NOT $(G) + (H)$

    according to law 12.24. NAND and NOR are easily replaced by AND or OR, respectively, followed by NOT. In fact, since AND, OR, and NOT are a complete set of operators, we know that any logical operator whatsoever, including those not introduced in this book, can be replaced by expressions involving only AND, OR, and NOT.

2. Next, apply DeMorgan's laws to push all negations down until they either cancel with other negations by law 12.13 in Section 12.8, or they apply only to propositional variables.

3. Now we apply the distributive law for OR over AND to push all OR's below all AND's. The result is an expression in which there are literals, combined by OR's, which are then combined by AND's; this is a conjunctive normal form expression.

✦ **Example 12.28.** Let us consider the expression

$$p + \Big(q \text{ AND NOT } \big(r \text{ AND } (s \to t) \big) \Big)$$

Note that to balance conciseness and clarity, we are using overbar, $+$, and juxtaposition mixed with their equivalents — NOT, OR, and AND — in this and subsequent expressions.

Step (1) requires us to replace $s \to t$ by $\bar{s} + t$, giving the AND-OR-NOT expression

$$p + \Big(q \text{ AND NOT } \big(r(\bar{s} + t) \big) \Big)$$

In step (2), we must push the first NOT down by DeMorgan's laws. The sequence of steps, in which the NOT reaches the propositional variables is

$$p + \Big(q \big(\bar{r} + \text{ NOT } (\bar{s} + t) \big) \Big)$$
$$p + \Big(q \big(\bar{r} + (\text{NOT } \bar{s})(\bar{t}\ ) \big) \Big)$$
$$p + \Big(q \big(\bar{r} + (s\bar{t}\ ) \big) \Big)$$

Now we apply law 12.14 to push the first OR below the first AND.

$$(p + q) \Big(p + \big(\bar{r} + (s\bar{t}) \big) \Big)$$

Next, we regroup, using law 12.8 of Section 12.8, so that we can push the second and third OR's below the second AND.

$$(p + q) \big((p + \bar{r}) + (s\bar{t}) \big)$$

Finally, we use law 12.14 again, and all OR's are below all AND's. The resulting expression,

$$(p + q)(p + \bar{r} + s)(p + \bar{r} + \bar{t})$$

is in conjunctive normal form. ✦

Inference Using Resolution

We now see the outline of a way to find a proof of E from hypotheses $E_1, E_2, \ldots, E_k$. Convert E and each of $E_1, \ldots, E_k$ into conjunctive normal form expressions F and $F_1, F_2, \ldots, F_k$, respectively. Our proof is a list of clauses, and we start by writing down all the clauses of the hypotheses $F_1, F_2, \ldots, F_k$. We apply the resolution rule to pairs of clauses, and thus we add new clauses as lines of our proof. Then, if we add all the clauses of F to our proof, we have proved F, and we therefore have also proved E.

✦   **Example 12.29.** Suppose we take as our hypothesis the expression

$$(r \to u)(u \to \bar{w})(\bar{r} \to \bar{w})$$

Note that this expression is the AND of the hypotheses used in Example 12.26.[5] Let the desired conclusion be $\bar{w}$, as in Example 12.26. We convert the hypothesis to conjunctive normal form by replacing the $\to$'s according to law 12.24. At this point, the result is already in conjunctive normal form and needs no further manipulation. The desired conclusion, $\bar{w}$, is already in conjunctive normal form, since any single

---

[5]   You should have observed by now that it doesn't matter whether we write many hypotheses or connect them all with AND's and write one hypothesis.

Why Resolution is Effective

In general, the discovery of a proof requires luck or skill to put together the sequence of lines that lead from hypotheses to conclusion. You will by now have noted, while it is easy to check that the proofs given in Sections 12.10 and 12.11 are indeed valid proofs, solving exercises that require the discovery of a proof is much harder. Guessing the sequence of resolutions to perform in order to produce some clause or clauses, as in Example 12.29, is not significantly easier than discovering a proof in general.

However, when we combine resolution with proof by contradiction, as in Example 12.30, we see the magic of resolution. Since our goal clause is 0, the "smallest" clause, we suddenly have a notion of a "direction" in which to search. That is, we try to prove progressively smaller clauses, hoping thereby to prove 0 eventually. Of course, this heuristic does not guarantee success. Sometimes, we must prove some very large clauses before we can start shrinking clauses and eventually prove 0.

Complete proof procedure

In fact, resolution is a *complete* proof procedure for propositional calculus. Whenever $E_1 E_2 \cdots E_k \rightarrow E$ is a tautology, we can derive 0 from $E_1, E_2, \ldots, E_k$ and **NOT** E, expressed in clause form. (Yes, this is a third meaning that logicians give to the word "complete." Recall the others are "a set of operators capable of expressing any logical function," and "a hardest problem within a class of problems," as in "NP-complete".) Again, just because the proof exists doesn't mean it is easy to find the proof.

---

literal is a clause, and a single clause is a product of clauses. Thus we begin with clauses

$$(\bar{r} + u)(\bar{u} + \bar{w})(r + \bar{w})$$

Now, suppose we resolve the first and third clauses, using r in the role of p. The resulting clause is $(u + \bar{w})$. This clause may be resolved with the second clause in the hypothesis, with u in the role of p, to get clause $(\bar{w})$. Since this clause is the desired conclusion, we are done. Figure 12.25 shows the proof as a series of lines, each of which is a clause. ✦

1)	$(\bar{r} + u)$	Hypothesis
2)	$(\bar{u} + \bar{w})$	Hypothesis
3)	$(r + \bar{w})$	Hypothesis
4)	$(u + \bar{w})$	Resolution of (1) and (3)
5)	$(\bar{w})$	Resolution of (2) and (4)

Fig. 12.25. Resolution proof of $\bar{w}$.

Resolution Proofs by Contradiction

The usual way resolution is used as a proof mechanism is somewhat different from that in Example 12.29. Instead of starting with the hypothesis and trying to prove the conclusion, we start with both the hypotheses and the negation of the conclusion and try to derive a clause with no literals. This clause has the value 0, or **FALSE**.

For example, if we have clauses (p) and $(\bar{p})$, we may apply (12.14) with $q = r = 0$, to get the clause 0.

The reason this approach is valid stems from the contradiction law 12.29 of Section 12.9, or $(\bar{p} \to 0) \equiv p$. Here, let p be the statement we want to prove: $(E_1 E_2 \cdots E_k) \to E$, for some hypotheses $E_1, E_2, \ldots, E_k$ and conclusion E. Then $\bar{p}$ is NOT $(E_1 E_2 \cdots E_k \to E)$, or NOT $\big($NOT $(E_1 E_2 \cdots E_k) + E\big)$, using law 12.24. Several applications of DeMorgan's laws tell us that p is equivalent to $E_1 E_2 \cdots E_k \bar{E}$. Thus, to prove p we can instead prove $\bar{p} \to 0$, or $(E_1 E_2 \cdots E_k \bar{E}) \to 0$. That is, we prove that the hypotheses and the negation of the conclusion together imply a contradiction.

✦ **Example 12.30.** Let us reconsider Example 12.29, but start with both the three hypothesis clauses and the negation of the desired conclusion, that is, with clause (w) as well. The resolution proof of 0 is shown in Fig. 12.26. Using the law of contradiction, we can conclude that the hypotheses imply $\bar{w}$, the conclusion. ✦

1)	$(\bar{r} + u)$	Hypothesis
2)	$(\bar{u} + \bar{w})$	Hypothesis
3)	$(r + \bar{w})$	Hypothesis
4)	(w)	Negation of conclusion
5)	$(u + \bar{w})$	Resolution of (1) and (3)
6)	$(\bar{w})$	Resolution of (2) and (5)
7)	0	Resolution of (4) and (6)

Fig. 12.26. Resolution proof by contradiction.

EXERCISES

12.11.1: Use the truth table method to check that expression (12.14) is a tautology.

a	A person has blood type A.
b	A person has blood type B.
c	A person has blood type AB.
o	A person has blood type O.
t	Test T is positive on a person's blood sample.
s	Test S is positive on a person's blood sample.

Fig. 12.27. Propositions for Exercise 12.11.2.

12.11.2: Let the propositions have the intuitive meanings given in Fig. 12.27. Write a clause or product of clauses that express the following ideas.

a) If test T is positive, then that person has blood type A or AB.

b) If test S is positive, then that person has blood type B or AB.

c) If a person has type A, then test T will be positive.

d) If a person has type B, then test S will be positive.

e) If a person has type AB, then both tests T and S will be positive. *Hint*: Note that $(\bar{c} + st)$ is not a clause.

f) A person has type A, B, AB, or O blood.

12.11.3: Use resolution to discover all nontrivial clauses that follow from your clauses in Exercise 12.11.2. You should omit trivial clauses that simplify to 1 (**TRUE**), and also omit a clause C if its literals are a proper superset of the literals of some other clause D.

12.11.4: Give proofs using resolution and proof by contradiction for the implications in Exercise 12.10.1.

✦✦ 12.12 Summary of Chapter 12

In this chapter, we have seen the elements of propositional logic, including:

✦ The principal operators, **AND**, **OR**, **NOT**, $\rightarrow$, $\equiv$, **NAND**, and **NOR**.

✦ The use of truth tables to represent the meaning of a logical expression, including algorithms to construct a truth table from an expression and vice versa.

✦ Some of the many algebraic laws that apply to the logical operators.

We also discussed logic as a design theory, seeing:

✦ How Karnaugh maps help us design simple expressions for logical functions that have up to four variables.

✦ How algebraic laws can be used sometimes to simplify expressions of logic.

Then, we saw that logic helps us express and understand the common proof techniques such as:

✦ Proof by case analysis,

✦ Proof of the contrapositive,

✦ Proof by contradiction, and

✦ Proof by reduction to truth.

Finally, we studied deduction, that is, the construction of line-by-line proofs, seeing:

✦ There are a number of inference rules, such as "modus ponens," that allow us to construct one line of a proof from previous lines.

✦ The resolution technique often helps us find proofs quickly by representing lines of a proof as sums of literals and combining sums in useful ways.

✦ However, there is no known algorithm that is guaranteed to find a proof of an expression in time less than an exponential in the size of the expression.

✦ Moreover, since the tautology problem is "NP-hard," it is strongly believed that no less-than-exponential algorithm for this problem exists.

✦✦ 12.13 Bibliographic Notes for Chapter 12

The study of deduction in logic dates back to Aristotle. Boole [1854] developed the algebra of propositions, and it is from this work that Boolean algebra comes.

Lewis and Papadimitriou [1979] is a somewhat more advanced treatment of logic. Enderton [1972] and Mendelson [1987] are popular treatments of mathematical logic. Manna and Waldinger [1990] present the subject from the point of view of proving correctness of programs.

Genesereth and Nilsson [1987] treat logic from the point of view of applications to artificial intelligence. There, you can find more on the matter of heuristics for discovering proofs, including resolution-like techniques. The original paper on resolution as a method of proof is Robinson [1965].

For more on the theory of intractable problems, read Garey and Johnson [1979]. The concept of NP-completeness is by Cook [1971], and the paper by Karp [1972] made clear the importance of the concept for commonly encountered problems.

Boole, G. [1854]. *An Investigation of the Laws of Thought*, McMillan; reprinted by Dover Press, New York, in 1958.

Cook, S. A. [1971]. "The complexity of theorem proving procedures," *Proc. Third Annual ACM Symposium on the Theory of Computing*, pp. 151–158.

Enderton, H. B. [1972]. *A Mathematical Introduction to Logic*, Academic Press, New York.

Garey, M. R. and D. S Johnson [1979]. *Computers and Intractability: A Guide to the Theory of NP-Completeness*, W. H. Freeman, New York.

Genesereth, M. R. and N. J. Nilsson [1987]. *Logical Foundations for Artificial Intelligence*, Morgan-Kaufmann, San Mateo, Calif.

Karp, R. M. [1972]. "Reducibility among combinatorial problems," in *Complexity of Computer Computations* (R. E. Miller and J. W. Thatcher, eds.), Plenum, New York, pp. 85–103.

Lewis, H. R. and C. H. Papadimitriou [1981]. *Elements of the Theory of Computation*, Prentice-Hall, Englewood Cliffs, New Jersey.

Manna, Z. and R. Waldinger [1990]. *The Logical Basis for Computer Programming* (two volumes), Addison-Wesley, Reading, Mass.

Mendelson, E. [1987]. *Introduction to Mathematical Logic*, Wadsworth and Brooks, Monterey, Calif.

Robinson, J. A. [1965]. "A machine-oriented logic based on the resolution principle," *J. ACM* **12**:1, pp. 23–41.

CHAPTER | 13

❖❖❖

Using Logic
to
Design
Computer Components

In this chapter we shall see that the propositional logic studied in the previous chapter can be used to design *digital* electronic circuits. Such circuits, found in every computer, use two voltage levels ("high" and "low") to represent the binary values 1 and 0. In addition to gaining some appreciation for the design process, we shall see that algorithm-design techniques, such as "divide-and-conquer," can also be applied to hardware. In fact, it is important to realize that the process of designing a digital circuit to perform a given logical function is quite similar in spirit to the process of designing a computer program to perform a given task. The data models differ significantly, and frequently circuits are designed to do many things *in parallel* (at the same time) while common programming languages are designed to execute their steps *sequentially* (one at a time). However, general programming techniques like modularizing a design are as applicable to circuits as they are to programs.

**Parallel and
sequential
operation**

❖❖❖ 13.1 What This Chapter is About

This chapter covers the following concepts from digital circuit design:

✦ The notion of a gate, an electronic circuit that performs a logical operation (Section 13.2).

✦ How gates are organized into circuits (Section 13.3).

✦ Certain kinds of circuits, called combinational, that are an electronic equivalent of logical expressions (Section 13.4).

✦ Physical constraints under which circuits are designed, and what properties circuits must have to produce their answers quickly (Section 13.5).

+ Two interesting examples of circuits: adders and multiplexers. Sections 13.6 and 13.7 show how a fast circuit can be designed for each problem using a divide-and-conquer technique.

+ The memory element as an example of a circuit that remembers its input. In contrast, a combinational circuit cannot remember inputs received in the past (Section 13.8).

❖❖ 13.2 Gates

A *gate* is an electronic device with one or more inputs, each of which can assume either the value 0 or the value 1. As mentioned earlier, the logical values 0 and 1 are generally represented electronically by two different voltage levels, but the physical method of representation need not concern us. A gate usually has one output, which is a function of its inputs, and which is also either 0 or 1.

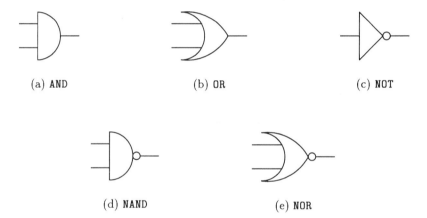

(a) AND   (b) OR   (c) NOT

(d) NAND   (e) NOR

Fig. 13.1. Symbols for gates.

Each gate computes some particular Boolean function. Most electronic "technologies" (ways of manufacturing electronic circuits) favor the construction of gates for certain Boolean functions and not others. In particular, **AND**- and **OR**-gates are usually easy to build, as are **NOT**-gates, which are called *inverters*. **AND**- and **OR**-gates can have any number of inputs, although, as we discuss in Section 13.5, there is usually a practical limitation on how many inputs a gate can have. The output of an **AND**-gate is 1 if all its inputs are 1, and its output is 0 if any one or more of its inputs are 0. Likewise, the output of an **OR**-gate is 1 if one or more of its inputs are 1, and the output is 0 if all inputs are 0. The inverter (**NOT**-gate) has one input; its output is 1 if its input is 0 and 0 if its input is 1.

We also find it easy to implement **NAND**- and **NOR**-gates in most technologies. The **NAND**-gate produces the output 1 unless all its inputs are 1, in which case it produces the output 0. The **NOR**-gate produces the output 1 when all inputs are 0 and produces 0 otherwise. An example of a logical function that is harder to implement electronically is equivalence, which takes two inputs x and y and produces a 1 output if x and y are both 1 or both 0, and a 0 output when exactly

Inverter

one of x and y is 1. However, we can build equivalence circuits out of AND-, OR-, and NOT-gates by implementing a circuit that realizes the logical function $xy + \bar{x}\bar{y}$.

The symbols for the gates we have mentioned are shown in Fig. 13.1. In each case except for the inverter (NOT-gate), we have shown the gate with two inputs. However, we could easily show more than two inputs, by adding additional lines. A one-input AND- or OR-gate is possible, but doesn't really do anything; it just passes its input to the output. A one-input NAND- or NOR-gate is really an inverter.

✦✦ 13.3   Circuits

Circuit inputs and outputs

Gates are combined into circuits by connecting the outputs of some gates to the inputs of others. The circuit as a whole has one or more inputs, each of which can be inputs to various gates within the circuit. The outputs of one or more gates are designated circuit outputs. If there is more than one output, then an order for the output gates must be specified as well.

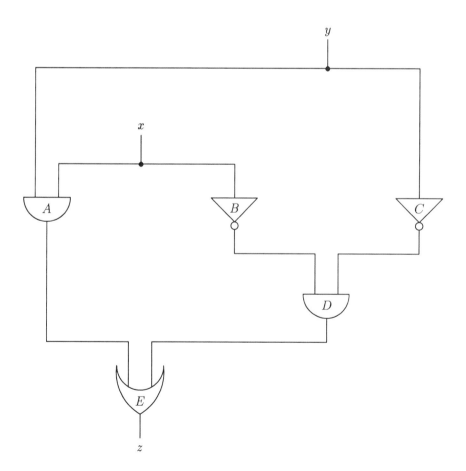

Fig. 13.2. Equivalence circuit: z is the expression $x \equiv y$.

♦ **Example 13.1.** Figure 13.2 shows a circuit that produces as output z, the equivalence function of inputs x and y. Conventionally, we show inputs at the top. Both inputs x and y are fed to gate A, which is an **AND**-gate, and which therefore produces a 1 output when (and only when) $x = y = 1$. Also, x and y are inverted by **NOT**-gates B and C respectively, and the outputs of these inverters are fed to **AND**-gate D. Thus, the output of gate D is 1 if and only if both x and y are 0. Since the outputs of gates A and D are fed to **OR**-gate E, we see that the output of that gate is 1 if and only if either $x = y = 1$ or $x = y = 0$. The table in Fig. 13.3 gives a logical expression for the output of each gate.

Thus, the output z of the circuit, which is the output of gate E, is 1 if and only if the logical expression $xy + \bar{x}\bar{y}$ has value 1. Since this expression is equivalent to the expression $x \equiv y$, we see that the circuit output is the equivalence function of its two inputs. ♦

GATE	OUTPUT OF GATE
A	xy
B	$\bar{x}$
C	$\bar{y}$
D	$\bar{x}\bar{y}$
E	$xy + \bar{x}\bar{y}$

Fig. 13.3. Outputs of gates in Fig. 13.2.

Combinational and Sequential Circuits

There is a close relationship between the logical expressions we can write using a collection of logical operators, such as **AND**, **OR**, and **NOT**, on one hand, and the circuits built from gates that perform the same set of operators, on the other hand. Before proceeding, we must focus our attention on an important class of circuits called *combinational circuits*. These circuits are acyclic, in the sense that the output of a gate cannot reach its input, even through a series of intermediate gates.

We can use our knowledge of graphs to define precisely what we mean by a combinational circuit. First, draw a directed graph whose nodes correspond to the gates of the circuit. Add an arc $u \to v$ if the output of gate u is connected directly to any input of gate v. If the circuit's graph has no cycles, then the circuit is *combinational*; otherwise, it is *sequential*.

♦ **Example 13.2.** In Fig. 13.4 we see the directed graph that comes from the circuit of Fig. 13.2. For example, there is an arc $A \to E$ because the output of gate A is connected to an input of gate E. The graph of Fig. 13.4 clearly has no cycles; in fact, it is a tree with root E, drawn upside-down. Thus, we conclude that the circuit of Fig. 13.2 is combinational.

On the other hand, consider the circuit of Fig. 13.5(a). There, the output of gate A is an input to gate B, and the output of B is an input to A. The graph for this circuit is shown in Fig. 13.5(b). It clearly has a cycle, so that the circuit is sequential.

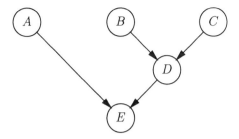

Fig. 13.4. Directed graph constructed from the circuit of Fig. 13.2.

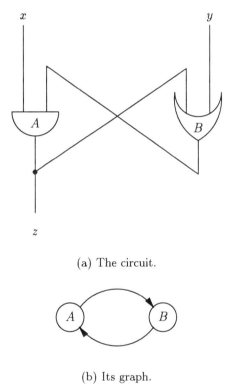

(a) The circuit.

(b) Its graph.

Fig. 13.5. Sequential circuit and its graph.

Suppose inputs x and y to this circuit are both 1. Then the output of B is surely 1, and therefore, both inputs to the **AND**-gate A are 1. Thus, this gate will produce output 1. Now we can let input y become 0, and the output of **OR**-gate B will remain 1, because its other input (the input from the output of A) is 1. Thus, both inputs to A remain 1, and its output is 1 as well.

However, suppose x becomes 0, whether or not y is 0. Then the output of gate A, and therefore the circuit output z, must be 0. We can describe the circuit output z as 1 if, at some time in the past, both x and y were 1 and since then x (but not necessarily y) has remained 1. Figure 13.6 shows the output as a function of time for various input value combinations; the low level represents 0 and the elevated

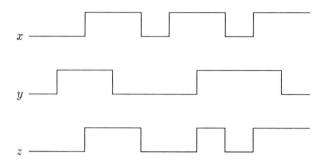

Fig. 13.6. Output as a function of time, for the circuit of Fig. 13.5(a).

Sequential Circuits and Automata

There is a close relationship between the deterministic finite automata that we discussed in Chapter 10 and sequential circuits. While the subject is beyond the scope of this book, given any deterministic automaton, we can design a sequential circuit whose output is 1 exactly when the sequence of inputs of the automaton is accepted. To be more precise, the inputs of the automaton, which may be from any set of characters, must be encoded by the appropriate number of logical inputs (which each take the value 0 or 1); k logical inputs to the circuit can code up to 2^k characters.

level represents 1. ✦

We shall discuss sequential circuits briefly at the end of this chapter. As we just saw in Example 13.2, sequential circuits have the ability to remember important things about the sequence of inputs seen so far, and thus they are needed for key components of computers, such as main memory and registers. Combinational circuits, on the other hand, can compute the values of logical functions, but they must work from a single setting for their inputs, and cannot remember what the inputs were set to previously. Nevertheless, combinational circuits are also vital components of computers. They are needed to add numbers, decode instructions into the electronic signals that cause the computer to perform those instructions, and many other tasks. In the following sections, we shall devote most of our attention to the design of combinational circuits.

EXERCISES

13.3.1: Design circuits that produce the following outputs. You may use any of the gates shown in Fig. 13.1.

Parity function

a) The *parity*, or sum-mod-2, function of inputs x and y that is 1 if and only if exactly one of x and y is 1.

Majority
function

b) The *majority* function of inputs w, x, y, and z that is 1 if and only if three or more of the inputs are 1.

c) The function of inputs w, x, y, and z that is 1 unless all or none of the inputs are 1.

d) The exclusive-or function $\oplus$ discussed in Exercise 12.4.7.

13.3.2*: Suppose the circuit of Fig. 13.5(a) is modified so that both gates A and B are AND-gates, and both inputs x and y are initially 1. As the inputs change, under what circumstances will the output be 1?

13.3.3*: Repeat Exercise 13.3.2 if both gates are OR-gates.

❖ 13.4 Logical Expressions and Circuits

It is relatively simple to build a circuit whose output, as a function of its inputs, is the same as that of a given logical expression. Conversely, given a combinational circuit, we can find a logical expression for each circuit output, as a function of its inputs. The same is not true of a sequential circuit, as we saw in Example 13.2.

From Expressions to Circuits

Given a logical expression with some set of logical operators, we can construct from it a combinational circuit that uses gates with the same set of operators and realizes the same Boolean function. The circuit we construct will always have the form of a tree. We construct the circuit by a structural induction on the expression tree for the expression.

BASIS. If the expression tree is a single node, the expression can only be an input, say x. The "circuit" for this expression will be the circuit input x itself.

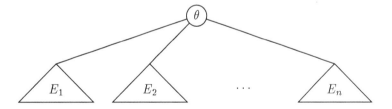

Fig. 13.7. Expression tree for expression $\theta(E_1, E_2, \ldots, E_n)$.

INDUCTION. For the induction, suppose that the expression tree in question is similar to Fig. 13.7. There is some logical operator, which we call θ, at the root; θ might be AND or OR, for example. The root has n subtrees for some n, and the operator θ is applied to the results of these subtrees to produce a result for the whole tree.

Since we are performing a structural induction, we may assume that the inductive hypothesis applies to the subexpressions. Thus, there is a circuit C_1 for expression E_1, circuit C_2 for E_2, and so on.

To build the circuit for E, we take a gate for the operator θ and give it n inputs, one from each of the outputs of the circuits $C_1, C_2, \ldots, C_n$, in that order.

circuit inputs

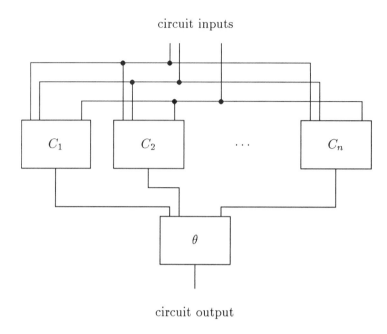

circuit output

Fig. 13.8. The circuit for $\theta(E_1, \ldots, E_n)$ where C_i is the circuit for E_i.

The output of the circuit for E is taken from the θ-gate just introduced. The construction is suggested in Fig. 13.8.

The circuit we have constructed computes the expression in the obvious way. However, there may be circuits producing the same output function with fewer gates or fewer levels. For example, if the given expression is $(x + y)z + (x + y)\bar{w}$, then the circuit we construct will have two occurrences of the subcircuit that realizes the common expression $x + y$. We can redesign the circuit to use just one occurrence of this subcircuit, and feed its output everywhere the common subexpression is used.

There are other more radical transformations that we can make to improve the design of circuits. Circuit design, like the design of efficient algorithms, is an art, and we shall see a few of the important techniques of this art later in this chapter.

From Circuits to Logical Expressions

Now let us consider the inverse problem, constructing a logical expression for an output of a combinational circuit. Since we know that the graph of the circuit is acyclic, we can pick a topological order of its nodes (i.e., of its gates), with the property that if the output of the ith gate in the order feeds an input of the jth gate in the order, then i must be less than j.

✦   **Example 13.3.** One possible topological order of the gates in the circuit of Fig. 13.2 is $ABCDE$, and another is $BCDAE$. However, $ABDCE$ is not a topological order, since gate C feeds gate D, but D appears before C in this sequence. ✦

To build the expression from the circuit, we use an inductive construction. We shall show by induction on i the statement

STATEMENT $S(i)$: For the first i gates in the topological order, there are logical expressions for the output of these gates.

BASIS. The basis will be $i = 0$. Since there are zero gates to consider, there is nothing to prove, so the basis part is done.

INDUCTION. For the induction, look at the ith gate in the topological order. Suppose gate i's inputs are $I_1, I_2, \ldots, I_k$. If I_j is a circuit input, say x, then let the expression E_j for input I_j be x. If input I_j is the output of some other gate, that gate must precede the ith gate in the topological order, which means that we have already constructed some expression E_j for the output of that gate. Let the operator associated with gate i be θ. Then an expression for gate i is $\theta(E_1, E_2, \ldots, E_k)$. In the common case that θ is a binary operator for which infix notation is conventionally used, the expression for gate i can be written $(E_1)\theta(E_2)$. The parentheses are placed there for safety, although depending on the precedence of operators, they may or may not be necessary.

✦ **Example 13.4.** Let us determine the output expression for the circuit in Fig. 13.2, using the topological order $ABCDE$ for the gates. First, we look at AND-gate A. Its two inputs are from the circuit inputs x and y, so that the expression for the output of A is xy.

Gate B is an inverter with input x, so that its output is $\bar{x}$. Similarly, gate C has output expression $\bar{y}$. Now we can work on gate D, which is an AND-gate with inputs taken from the outputs of B and C. Thus, the expression for the output of D is $\bar{x}\bar{y}$. Finally, gate E is an OR-gate, whose inputs are the outputs of A and D. We thus connect the output expressions for these gates by the OR operator, to get the expression $xy + \bar{x}\bar{y}$ as the output expression for gate E. Since E is the only output gate of the circuit, that expression is also the circuit output. Recall that the circuit of Fig. 13.2 was designed to realize the Boolean function $x \equiv y$. It is easy to verify that the expression we derived for gate E is equivalent to $x \equiv y$. ✦

✦ **Example 13.5.** In the previous examples, we have had only one circuit output, and the circuit itself has been a tree. Neither of these conditions holds generally. We shall now take up an important example of the design of a circuit with multiple outputs, and where some gates have their output used as input to several gates. Recall from Chapter 1 that we discussed the use of a *one-bit adder* in building a circuit to add binary numbers. A one-bit adder circuit has two inputs x and y that represent the bits in some particular position of the two numbers being added. It has a third input, c, that represents the carry-in to this position from the position to the right (next lower-order position). The one-bit adder produces as output the following two bits:

One-bit adder

1. The *sum bit z*, which is 1 if an odd number of x, y, and c are 1, and
2. The *carry-out* bit d, which is 1 if two or more of x, y, and c are 1.

Circuit Diagram Convention

When circuits are complicated, as is the circuit in Fig. 13.10, there is a useful convention that helps simplify the drawing. Often, we need to have "wires" (the lines between an output and the input(s) to which it is connected) cross, without implying that they are part of the same wire. Thus, the standard convention for circuits says that wires are not connected unless, at the point of intersection, we place a dot. For example, the vertical line from the circuit input y is not connected to the horizontal lines labeled x or $\bar{x}$, even though it crosses those lines. It is connected to the horizontal line labeled y, because there is a dot at the point of intersection.

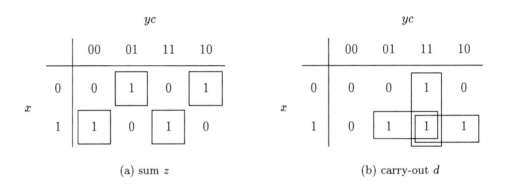

(a) sum z (b) carry-out d

Fig. 13.9. Karnaugh maps for the sum and carry-out functions.

In Fig. 13.9 we see Karnaugh maps for z and d, the sum and carry-out functions of the one-bit adder. Of the eight possible minterms, seven appear in the functions for z or d, and only one, xyc, appears in both.

A systematically designed circuit for the one-bit adder is shown in Fig. 13.10. We begin by taking the circuit inputs and inverting them, using the three inverters at the top. Then we create AND-gates for each of the minterms that we need in one or more outputs. These gates are numbered 1 through 7, and each integer tells us which of its inputs are "true" circuit inputs, x, y, or c, and which are "complemented" inputs, $\bar{x}$, $\bar{y}$, or $\bar{c}$. That is, write the integer as a 3-bit binary number, and regard the bits as representing x, y, and c, in that order. For example, gate 4, or $(100)_2$, has input x true and inputs y and c complemented; that is, it produces the output expression $x\bar{y}\bar{c}$. Notice that there is no gate 0 here, because the minterm $\bar{x}\bar{y}\bar{c}$ is not needed for either output.

Finally, the circuit outputs, z and d, are assembled with OR-gates at the bottom. The OR-gate for z has inputs from the output of each AND-gate whose minterm makes z true, and the inputs to the OR-gate for d are selected similarly.

Let us compute the output expressions for the circuit of Fig. 13.10. The topological order we shall use is the inverters first, then the AND-gates $1, 2, \ldots, 7$, and finally the OR-gates for z and d. First, the three inverters obviously have output expressions $\bar{x}$, $\bar{y}$, and $\bar{c}$. Then we already mentioned how the inputs to the AND-gates were selected and how the expression for the output of each is associated with the

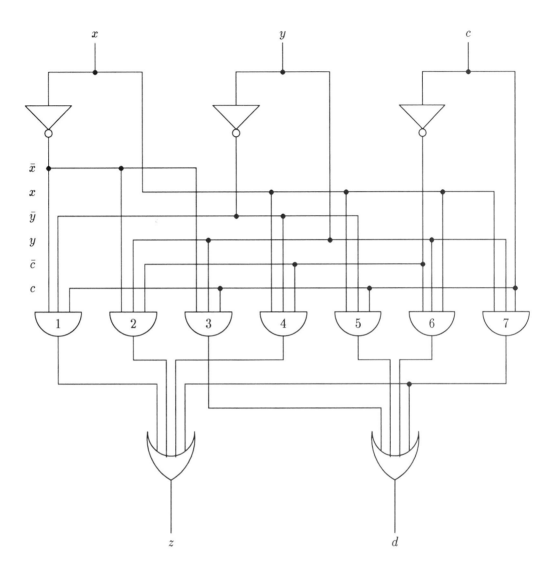

Fig. 13.10. One-bit-adder circuit.

binary representation of the number of the gate. Thus, gate 1 has output expression $\bar{x}\bar{y}c$. Finally, the output of the OR-gate z is the OR of the output expressions for gates 1, 2, 4, and 7, that is

$$\bar{x}\bar{y}c + \bar{x}y\bar{c} + x\bar{y}\bar{c} + xyc$$

Similarly, the output of the OR-gate for d is the OR of the output expressions for gates 3, 5, 6, and 7, which is

$$\bar{x}yc + x\bar{y}c + xy\bar{c} + xyc$$

We leave it as an exercise to show that this expression is equivalent to the expression

$$yc + xc + xy$$

that we would get if we worked from the Karnaugh map for d alone. ✦

EXERCISES

13.4.1: Design circuits for the following Boolean functions. You need not restrict yourself to 2-input gates if you can group three or more operands that are connected by the same operator.

a) $x + y + z$. *Hint*: Think of this expression as $\text{OR}(x, y, z)$.
b) $xy + xz + yz$
c) $x + (\bar{y}\bar{x})(y + z)$

13.4.2: For each of the circuits in Fig. 13.11, compute the logical expression for each gate. What are the expressions for the outputs of the circuits? For circuit (b) construct an equivalent circuit using only **AND**, **OR**, and **NOT** gates.

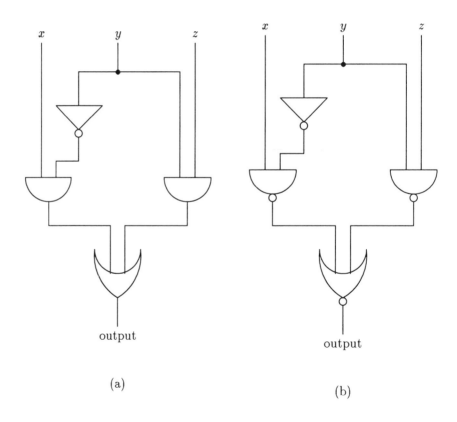

(a)

(b)

Fig. 13.11. Circuits for Exercise 13.4.2.

13.4.3: Prove the following tautologies used in Examples 13.4 and 13.5:

a) $(xy + \bar{x}\bar{y}) \equiv (x \equiv y)$
b) $(\bar{x}yc + x\bar{y}c + xy\bar{c} + xyc) \equiv (yc + xc + xy)$

Chips

Feature size

Micron

Chips generally have several "layers" of material that can be used, in combination, to build gates. Wires can run in any layer, to interconnect the gates; wires on different layers usually can cross without interacting. The "feature size," roughly the minimum width of a wire, is in 1994 usually below half a micron (a *micron* is 0.001 millimeter, or about 0.00004 inches). Gates can be built in an area several microns on a side.

The process by which chips are fabricated is complex. For example, one step might deposit a thin layer of a certain substance, called a *photoresist*, all over a chip. Then a photographic negative of the features desired on a certain layer is used. By shining light or a beam of electrons through the negative, the top layer can be etched away in places where the beam shines through, leaving only the desired circuit pieces.

✦✧✦ 13.5   Some Physical Constraints on Circuits

Integrated circuits

Today, most circuits are built as "chips," or integrated circuits. Large numbers of gates, perhaps as many as millions of gates, and the wires interconnecting them, are constructed out of semiconductor and metallic materials in an area about a centimeter (0.4 inches) on a side. The various "technologies," or methods of constructing integrated circuits, impose a number of constraints on the way efficient circuits can be designed. For example, we mentioned earlier that certain types of gates, such as AND, OR, and NOT, are easier to construct than other kinds.

Circuit Speed

Associated with each gate is a delay, between the time that the inputs become active and the time that the output becomes available. This delay might be only a few nanoseconds (a nanosecond is 10^{-9} seconds), but in a complex circuit, such as the central processing unit of a computer, information propagates through many levels of gates, even during the execution of a single instruction. As modern computers perform instructions in much less than a microsecond (which is 10^{-6} seconds), it is evidently imperative that the number of gates through which a value must propagate be kept to a minimum.

Circuit delay

Thus, for a combinational circuit, the maximum number of gates that lie along any path from an input to an output is analogous to the running time of a program as a figure of merit. That is, if we want our circuits to compute their outputs fast, we must minimize the longest path length in the graph of the circuit. The *delay* of a circuit is the number of gates on the longest path — that is, one plus the length of the path equals the delay. For example, the adder of Fig. 13.10 has delay 3, since the longest paths from input to output go through one of the inverters, then one of the AND-gates, and finally, through one of the OR-gates; there are many paths of length 3.

Notice that, like running time, circuit delay only makes sense as an "order of magnitude" quantity. Different technologies will give us different values of the time that it takes an input of one gate to affect the output of that gate. Thus, if we have two circuits, of delay 10 and 20, respectively, we know that if implemented in the same technology, with all other factors being equal, the first will take half the time of the second. However, if we implement the second circuit in a faster technology, it could beat the first circuit implemented in the original technology.

Size Limitations

The cost of building a circuit is roughly proportional to the number of gates in the circuit, and so we would like to reduce the number of gates. Moreover, the size of a circuit also influences its speed, and small circuits tend to run faster. In general, the more gates a circuit has, the greater the area on a chip that it will consume. There are at least two negative effects of using a large area.

Propagation delay

1.   If the area is large, long wires are needed to connect gates that are located far apart. The longer a wire is, the longer it takes a signal to travel from one end to the other. This *propagation delay* is another source of delay in the circuit, in addition to the time it takes a gate to "compute" its output.

2.   There is a limit to how large chips can be, because the larger they are, the more likely it is that there will be an imperfection that causes the chip to fail. If we have to divide a circuit across several chips, then wires connecting the chips will introduce a severe propagation delay.

Our conclusion is that there is a significant benefit to keeping the number of gates in a circuit low.

Fan-In and Fan-Out Limitations

A third constraint on the design of circuits comes from physical realities. We pay a penalty for gates that have too many inputs or that have their outputs connected to too many other inputs. The number of inputs of a gate is called its *fan-in*, and the number of inputs to which the output of a gate is connected is that gate's *fan-out*. While, in principle, there is no limit on fan-in or fan-out, in practice, gates with large fan-in and/or fan-out will be slower than gates with smaller fan-in and fan-out. Thus, we shall try to design our circuits with limited fan-in and fan-out.

♦   **Example 13.6.** Suppose a particular computer has registers of 32 bits, and we wish to implement, in circuitry, the **COMPARE** machine instruction. One of the things we have to build is a circuit that tests whether a register has all 0's. This test is implemented by an **OR**-gate with 32 inputs, one for each bit of the register. An output of 1 means the register does not hold 0, while an output of 0 means that it does.[1] If we want 1 to mean a positive answer to the question, "Does the register hold 0," then we would complement the output with an inverter, or use a **NOR** gate.

However, a fan-in of 32 is generally much higher than we would like. Suppose we were to limit ourselves to gates with a fan-in of 2. That is probably too low a limit, but will serve for an example. First, how many two-input **OR**-gates do we need to compute the **OR** of n inputs? Clearly, each 2-input gate combines two values into one (its output), and thus reduces by one the number of values we need to compute the **OR** of n inputs. After we have used $n - 1$ gates, we shall be down to

---

[1]   Strictly speaking, this observation is true only in 2's complement notation. In some other notations, there are two ways to represent 0. For example, in sign-and-magnitude, we would test only whether the last 31 bits are 0.

one value, and if we have designed the circuit properly, that one value will be the OR of all n original values. Thus, we need at least 31 gates to compute the OR of 32 bits, $x_1, x_2, \ldots, x_{32}$.

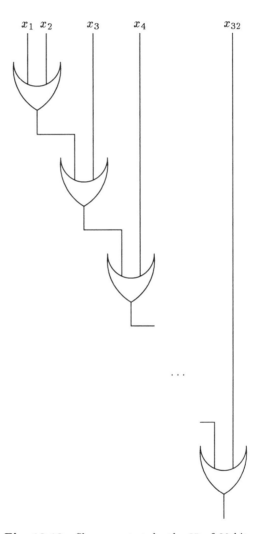

Fig. 13.12. Slow way to take the OR of 32 bits.

A naive way to do this OR is shown in Fig. 13.12. There, we group the bits in a left-associative way. As each gate feeds the next, the graph of the circuit has a path with 31 gates, and the delay of the circuit is 31.

A better way is suggested in Fig. 13.13. A complete binary tree with five levels uses the same 31 gates, but the delay is only 5. We would expect the circuit of Fig. 13.13 therefore to run about six times faster than the circuit of Fig. 13.12. Other factors that influence speed might reduce the factor of six, but even for a "small" number of bits like 32, the clever design is significantly faster than the naive design.

If one doesn't immediately "see" the trick of using a complete binary tree as a circuit, one can obtain the circuit of Fig. 13.13 by applying the divide-and-conquer

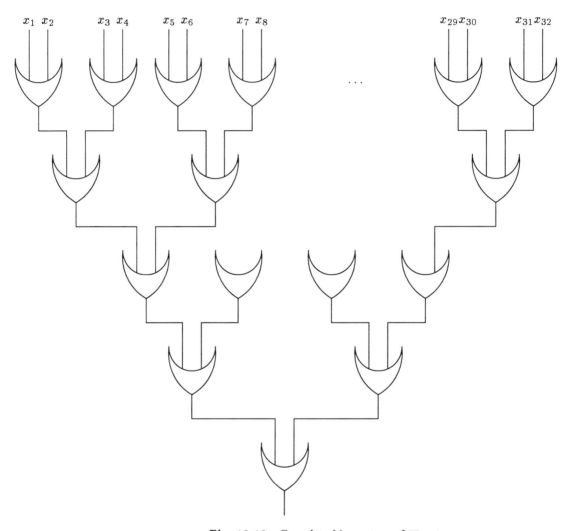

Fig. 13.13. Complete binary tree of OR-gates.

Divide and conquer circuits

paradigm. That is, to take the OR of 2^k bits, we divide the bits into two groups of 2^{k-1} bits each. Circuits for each of the two groups are combined by a final OR-gate, as suggested in Fig. 13.14. Of course, the circuit for the basis case $k = 1$ (i.e., two inputs) is provided not by divide-and-conquer, but by using a single two-input OR-gate. ✦

EXERCISES

13.5.1*: Suppose that we can use OR-gates with fan-in of k, and we wish to take the OR of n inputs, where n is a power of k. What is the minimum possible delay for such a circuit? What would be the delay if we used a naive "cascading" circuit as shown in Fig. 13.12?

13.5.2*: Design divide-and-conquer circuits to perform the following operations. What is the delay of each of your circuits?

a)   Given inputs $x_1, x_2, \ldots, x_n$, produce a 1 output if and only if all inputs are 1.

b)   Given inputs $x_1, x_2, \ldots, x_n$ and $y_1, y_2, \ldots, y_n$, produce a 1 output if and only if each x_i equals y_i, for $i = 1, 2, \ldots, n$. *Hint*: Use the circuit of Fig. 13.2 to test whether two inputs are equal.

13.5.3*: The divide-and-conquer approach of Fig. 13.14 works even when the number of inputs is not a power of two. Then the basis must include sets of two or three inputs; three-input sets are handled by two OR-gates, one feeding the other, assuming we wish to keep strictly to our fan-in limitation of two. What is the delay of such circuits, as a function of the number of inputs?

13.5.4: First-string commandos are ready, willing, and able. Suppose we have n commandos, and circuit inputs r_i, w_i, and a_i indicate, respectively, whether the ith commando, is ready, willing, and able. We only want to send the commando team on a raid if they all are ready, willing, and able. Design a divide-and-conquer circuit to indicate whether we can send the team on a raid.

13.5.5*: Second-string commandos (read Exercise 13.5.4) aren't as professional. We are willing to send them on a raid if each is either ready, willing, or able. In fact, we'll send the team even if at most one of the commandos is neither ready, willing, nor able. Using the same inputs as Exercise 13.5.4, devise a divide-and-conquer circuit that will indicate whether we can send the second-string commando team on a raid.

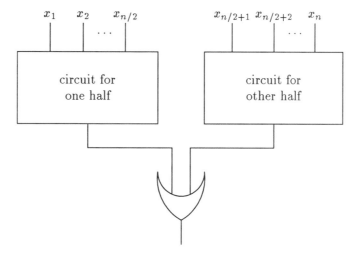

Fig. 13.14. Divide-and-conquer approach to circuit design.

❖ 13.6   A Divide-and-Conquer Addition Circuit

One of the key parts of a computer is a circuit that adds two numbers. While actual microprocessor circuits do more, we shall study the essence of the problem by designing a circuit to add two nonnegative integers. This problem is quite instructive as an example of divide-and-conquer circuit design.

We can build an adder for n-bit numbers from n one-bit adders, connected in one of several ways. Let us suppose that we use the circuit of Fig. 13.10 as a one-bit-adder circuit. This circuit has a delay of 3, which is close to the best we can do.[2] The simplest approach to building an adder circuit is the *ripple-carry adder* which we saw in Section 1.3. In this circuit, an output of each one-bit adder becomes an input of the next one-bit adder, so that adding two n-bit numbers incurs a delay of $3n$. For example, in the case where $n = 32$, the circuit delay is 96.

A Recursive Addition Circuit

We can design an adder circuit with significantly less delay if we use the divide-and-conquer strategy of designing a circuit for $n/2$ bits and using two of them, together with some additional circuitry, to make an n-bit adder. In Example 13.6, we spoke of a divide-and-conquer circuit for taking the OR of many bits, using 2-input OR-gates. That was a particularly simple example of the divide-and-conquer technique, since each of the smaller circuits performed exactly the desired function (OR), and the combination of outputs of the subcircuits was very simple (they were fed to an OR-gate). The two half-size circuits did their work at the same time (in parallel), so their delays did not add.

For the adder, we need to do something more subtle. A naive way to start is to add the left half of the bits (high-order bits) and add the right half of the bits (low-order bits), using identical half-size adder circuits. However, unlike the n-bit OR example, where we could work on the left and right halves independently, it seems that for the adder, the addition for the left half cannot begin until the right half is finished and passes its carry to the rightmost bit in the left half, as suggested in Fig. 13.15. If so, we shall find that the "divide-and-conquer" circuit is actually identical to the ripple-carry adder, and we have not improved the delay at all.

The additional "trick" we need is to realize that we can begin the computation of the left half without knowing the carry out of the right half, provided we compute more than just the sum. We need to answer two questions. First, what would the sum be if there is no carry into the rightmost place in the left half, and second, what would the sum be if there is a carry-in?[3] We can then allow the circuits for the left and right halves to compute their two answers at the same time. Once both have been completed, we can tell whether or not there is a carry from the right half to the left. That tells us which answer is correct, and with three more levels of delay, we can select the correct answer for the left side. Thus, the delay to add n bits will be just three more than the delay to add $n/2$ bits, leading to a circuit of delay $3(1 + \log_2 n)$. That compares very well with the ripple-carry adder for $n = 32$; the divide-and-conquer adder will have delay $3(1 + \log_2 32) = 3(1 + 5) = 18$, compared with 96 for the ripple-carry adder.

---

[2] We can design a more complicated one-bit-adder circuit with delay 2 by complementing all the inputs outside the full adder and computing both the carry and its complement within the full adder.

[3] Note "there is a carry-in" means the carry-in is 1; "no carry-in" means the carry-in is 0.

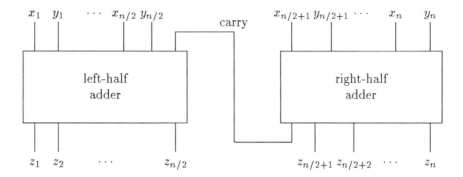

Fig. 13.15. An inefficient divide-and-conquer design for an adder.

n-adder

More precisely, we define an *n-adder* to be a circuit with inputs $x_1, x_2, \ldots, x_n$ and $y_1, y_2, \ldots, y_n$, representing two n-bit integers, and outputs

1. $s_1, s_2, \ldots, s_n$, the n-bit sum (excluding a carry out of the leftmost place, i.e., out of the place belonging to x_1 and y_1) of the inputs, assuming that there is no carry into the rightmost place (the place of x_n and y_n).

2. $t_1, t_2, \ldots, t_n$, the n-bit sum of the inputs, assuming that there is a carry into the rightmost place.

3. p, the *carry-propagate bit*, which is 1 if there is a carry out of the leftmost place, on the assumption that there is a carry into the rightmost place.

4. g, the *carry-generate bit*, which is 1 if there is a carry out of the leftmost place, even if there is no carry into the rightmost place.

Note that $g \rightarrow p$; that is, if g is 1, then p must be 1. However, g can be 0, and p still be 1. For example, if the x's are $1010 \cdots$, and the y's are $0101 \cdots$, then $g = 0$, because when there is no carry in, the sum is all 1's and there is no carry out of the leftmost place. On the other hand, if there is a carry into the rightmost position, then the last n bits of the sum are all 0's, and there is a carry out of the leftmost place; thus $p = 1$.

We shall construct an n-adder recursively, for n a power of 2.

BASIS. Consider the case $n = 1$. Here we have two inputs, x and y, and we need to compute four outputs, s, t, p, and g, given by the logical expressions

$$s = x\bar{y} + \bar{x}y$$
$$t = xy + \bar{x}\bar{y}$$
$$g = xy$$
$$p = x + y$$

To see why these expressions are correct, first assume there is no carry into the one place in question. Then the sum bit, which is 1 if an odd number of x, y, and the carry-in are 1, will be 1 if exactly one of x and y is 1. The expression for s above clearly has that property. Further, with no carry-in, there can only be a

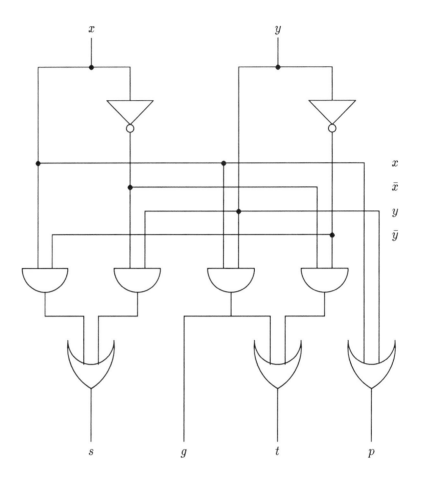

Fig. 13.16. Base case: a 1-adder.

carry-out if both x and y are 1, which explains the expression for g above.

Now suppose that there is a carry-in. Then for an odd number of x, y, and the carry-in to be 1, it must be that both or neither of x and y are 1, explaining the expression for t. Also, there will now be a carry-out if either one or both of x and y are 1, which justifies the expression for p. A circuit for the basis is shown in Fig. 13.16. It is similar in spirit to the full adder of Fig. 13.10, but is actually somewhat simpler, because it has only two inputs instead of three.

INDUCTION. The inductive step is illustrated in Fig. 13.17, where we build a $2n$-adder from two n-adders. A $2n$-adder is composed of two n-adders, followed by two pieces of circuitry labeled **FIX** in Fig. 13.17, to handle two issues:

1. Computing the carry propagate and generate bits for the $2n$-adder

2. Adjusting the left half of the s's and t's to take into account whether or not there is a carry into the left half from the right

First, suppose that there is a carry into the right end of the entire circuit for the

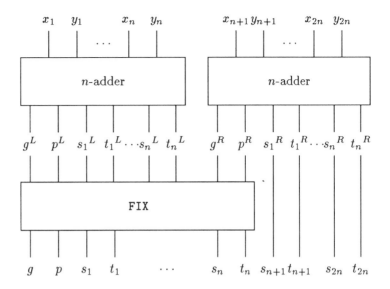

Fig. 13.17. Sketch of the divide-and-conquer adder.

$2n$-adder. Then there will be a carry out at the left end of the entire circuit if either of the following hold:

a)   Both halves of the adder propagate a carry; that is, $p^L p^R$ is true. Note this expression includes the case when the right half generates a carry and the left half propagates it. Then $p^L g^R$ is true, but $g^R \to p^R$, so $(p^L p^R + p^L g^R) \equiv p^L p^R$.

b)   The left half generates a carry; that is, g^L is true. In this case, the existence of a carry-out on the left does not depend on whether or not there is a carry into the right end, or on whether the right half generates a carry.

Thus, the expression for p, the carry-propagate bit for the $2n$-adder, is

$$p = g^L + p^L p^R$$

Now assume there is no carry-in at the right end of the $2n$-adder. Then there is a carry-out at the left end of the $2n$-adder if either

a)   The right half generates a carry and the left half propagates it, or

b)   The left half generates a carry.

Thus, the logical expression for g is

$$g = g^L + p^L g^R$$

Now let us turn our attention to the s_i's and the t_i's. First, the right-half bits are unchanged from the outputs of the right n-adder, because the presence of the left half has no effect on the right half. Thus, $s_{n+i} = s_i{}^R$, and $t_{n+i} = t_i{}^R$, for $i = 1, 2, \ldots, n$.

The left-half bits must be modified, however, to take into account the ways in which the right half can generate a carry. First, suppose that there is no carry-in at the right end of the $2n$-adder. This is the situation that the s_i's are supposed to tell us about, so that we can develop expressions for the s_i's on the left, that is, $s_1, s_2, \ldots, s_n$. Since there is no carry-in for the right half, there is a carry-in for the left half only if a carry is generated by the right half. Thus, if g^R is true, then $s_i = t_i{}^L$ (since the $t_i{}^L$'s tell us about what happens when there is a carry into the left half). If g^R is false, then $s_i = s_i{}^L$ (since the $s_i{}^L$'s tell us what happens when there is no carry into the left half). As a logical expression, we can write

$$s_i = s_i{}^L \bar{g}^R + t_i{}^L g^R$$

for $i = 1, 2, \ldots, n$.

Finally, consider what happens when there is a carry-in at the right end of the $2n$-adder. Now we can address the question of the values for the t_i's on the left as follows. There will be a carry into the left half if the right half propagates a carry, that is, if $p^R = 1$. Thus, t_i takes its value from $t_i{}^L$ if p^R is true and from $s_i{}^L$ if p^R is false. As a logical expression,

$$t_i = s_i{}^L \bar{p}^R + t_i{}^L p^R$$

In summary, the circuits represented by the box labeled **FIX** in Fig. 13.17 compute the following expressions:

$$p = g^L + p^L p^R$$
$$g = g^L + p^L g^R$$
$$s_i = s_i{}^L \bar{g}^R + t_i{}^L g^R, \text{ for } i = 1, 2, \ldots, n$$
$$t_i = s_i{}^L \bar{p}^R + t_i{}^L p^R, \text{ for } i = 1, 2, \ldots, n$$

These expressions can each be realized by a circuit of at most three levels. For example, the last expression needs only the circuit of Fig. 13.18.

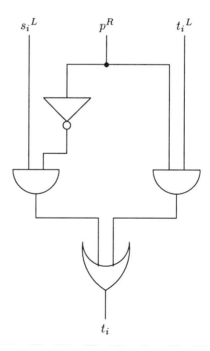

Fig. 13.18. Part of the **FIX** circuitry.

Delay of the Divide-and-Conquer Adder

Let $D(n)$ be the delay of the n-adder we just designed. We can write a recurrence relation for D as follows. For the basis, $n = 1$, examine the basis circuit in Fig. 13.16 and conclude that the delay is 3. Thus, $D(1) = 3$.

Now examine the inductive construction of the circuit in Fig. 13.17. The delay of the circuit is the delay of the n-adders plus the delay of the FIX circuitry. The n-adders have delay $D(n)$. Each of the expressions developed for the FIX circuitry yields a simple circuit with at most three levels. Figure 13.18 is a typical example. Thus, $D(2n)$ is three more than $D(n)$. The recurrence relation for $D(n)$ is thus

$$D(1) = 3$$
$$D(2n) = D(n) + 3$$

The solution, for numbers of bits that are powers of 2, begins $D(1) = 3$, $D(2) = 6$, $D(4) = 9$, $D(8) = 12$, $D(16) = 15$, $D(32) = 18$, and so on. The solution to the recurrence is

$$D(n) = 3(1 + \log_2 n)$$

for n a power of 2, as the reader may check using the methods of Section 3.11. In particular, note that for a 32-bit adder, the delay of 18 is much less than the delay of 96 for the 32-bit ripple-carry adder.

Number of Gates Used by the Divide-and-Conquer Adder

We should also check that the number of gates is reasonable. Let $G(n)$ be the number of gates used in an n-adder circuit. The basis is $G(1) = 9$, as we may see by counting the gates in the circuit of Fig. 13.16. Then we observe that the circuit of Fig. 13.17, the inductive case, has $2G(n)$ gates in the two n-adder subcircuits. To this amount, we must add the number of gates in the FIX circuitry. As we may invert g^R and p^R once, each of the n s_i's and t_i's can be computed with three gates each (two AND's and an OR), or $6n$ gates total. To this quantity we add the two inverters for g^R and p^R, and we must add the two gates each that we need to compute g and p. The total number of gates in the FIX circuitry is thus $6n + 6$. The recurrence for G is hence

$$G(1) = 9$$
$$G(2n) = 2G(n) + 6n + 6$$

Again, our function is defined only when n is a power of 2. The first six values of G are tabulated in Fig. 13.19. For $n = 32$, we see that 954 gates are required. The closed-form expression for $G(n)$ is $3n \log_2 n + 15n - 6$, for n a power of 2, as the reader may show by applying the techniques of Section 3.11.

Actually, we can do with somewhat fewer gates, if all we want is a 32-bit adder. For then, we know that there is no carry-in at the right of the 32nd bit, and so the value of p, and the values of $t_1, t_2, \ldots, t_{32}$ need not be computed at the last stage of the circuit. Similarly, the right-half 16-adder does not need to compute its carry-propagate bit or its 16 t-values; the right-half 8-adder in the right 16-adder does not need to compute its p or t's and so on.

It is interesting to compare the number of gates used by the divide-and-conquer adder with the number of gates used by the ripple-carry adder. The circuit for a full adder that we designed in Fig. 13.10 uses 12 gates. Thus, an n-bit ripple-carry

n	$G(n)$
1	9
2	30
4	78
8	186
16	426
32	954

Fig. 13.19. Numbers of gates used by various n-adders.

adder uses $12n$ gates, and for $n = 32$, this number is 384 (we can save a few gates if we remember that the carry into the rightmost bit is 0).

We see that for the interesting case, $n = 32$, the ripple-carry adder, while much slower, does use fewer than half as many gates as the divide-and-conquer adder. Moreover, the latter's growth rate, $O(n \log n)$, is higher than the growth rate of the ripple-carry adder, $O(n)$, so that the difference in the number of gates gets larger as n grows. However, the ratio is only $O(\log n)$, so that the difference in the number of gates used is not severe. As the difference in the time required by the two classes of circuits is much more significant [$O(n)$ vs. $O(\log n)$], some sort of divide-and-conquer adder is used in essentially all modern computers.

EXERCISES

13.6.1: Draw the divide-and-conquer circuit, as developed in this section, to add 4-bit numbers.

13.6.2: Design circuits similar to Fig. 13.18 to compute the other outputs of the adder in Fig. 13.17, that is, p, g, and the s_i's.

13.6.3**: Design a circuit that takes as input a decimal number, with each digit represented by four inputs that give the binary equivalent of that decimal digit. The output is the equivalent number represented in binary. You may assume that the number of digits is a power of 2 and use a divide-and-conquer approach. *Hint*: What information does the left half circuit (high-order digits) need from the right half (low-order digits)?

13.6.4*: Show that the solution to the recurrence equation

$$D(1) = 3$$
$$D(2n) = D(n) + 3$$

is $D(n) = 3(1 + \log_2 n)$ for n a power of 2.

13.6.5*: Show that the solution to the recurrence equation

$$G(1) = 9$$
$$G(2n) = 2G(n) + 6n + 6$$

is $G(n) = 3n \log_2 n + 15n - 6$ for n a power of 2.

13.6.6**: We observed that if all we want is a 32-bit adder, we do not need all 954 gates as was indicated in Fig. 13.19. The reason is that we can assume there is no carry into the rightmost place of the 32 bits. How many gates do we really need?

❖❖ 13.7 Design of a Multiplexer

Control and data inputs

A *multiplexer*, often abbreviated MUX, is a common form of computer circuit that takes d *control inputs*, say $x_1, x_2, \ldots, x_d$, and 2^d *data inputs*, say $y_0, y_1, \ldots, y_{2^d-1}$, as shown in Fig. 13.20. The output of the MUX is equal to one particular data input, the input $y_{(x_1 x_2 \cdots x_d)_2}$. That is, we treat the control inputs as a binary integer in the range 0 to $2^d - 1$. This integer is the subscript of the data input that we pass to the output.

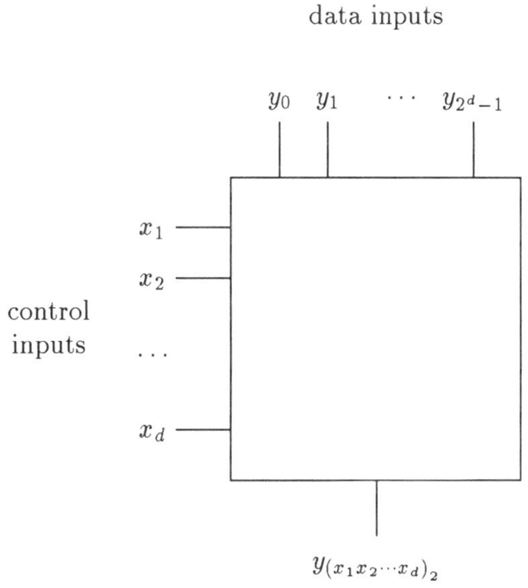

data inputs

Fig. 13.20. A multiplexer circuit schematic.

✦ **Example 13.7.** The circuits computing s_i and t_i in the divide-and-conquer adder are multiplexers with $d = 1$. For instance, the formula for s_i is $s_i{}^L \bar{g}^R + t_i{}^L g^R$ and its circuit schematic is shown in Fig. 13.21. Here, g^R plays the role of the control input x_1, $s_i{}^L$ is the data input y_0, and $t_i{}^L$ is the data input y_1.

As another example, the formula for the output of a MUX with two control inputs, x_1 and x_2, and four data inputs, y_0, y_1, y_2, and y_3, is

$$y_0 \bar{x}_1 \bar{x}_2 + y_1 \bar{x}_1 x_2 + y_2 x_1 \bar{x}_2 + y_3 x_1 x_2$$

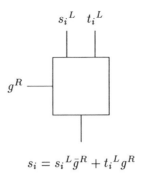

$$s_i = s_i{}^L \bar{g}^R + t_i{}^L g^R$$

Fig. 13.21. A 1-multiplexer.

Notice that there is one term for each data input. The term with data input y_i also has each of the control inputs, either negated or unnegated. We can tell which are negated by writing i as a d-bit binary integer. If the jth position of i in binary has 0, then x_j is negated, and if the jth position has 1, we do not negate x_j. Note that this rule works for any number d of control inputs. ✦

The straightforward design for a multiplexer is a circuit with three levels of gates. At the first level, we compute the negations of the control bits. The next level is a row of AND-gates. The ith gate combines the data input y_i with the appropriate combination of control inputs and negated control inputs. Thus, the output of the ith gate is always 0 unless the control bits are set to the binary representation of i, in which case the output is equal to y_i. The final level is an OR-gate with inputs from each of the AND-gates. As all the AND-gates but one have output 0, the remaining gate, say the ith, which has output y_i, makes the output of the circuit equal to whatever y_i is. An example of this circuit for $d = 2$ is shown in Fig. 13.22.

A Divide-and-Conquer Multiplexer

The circuit of Fig. 13.22 has maximum fan-in 4, which is generally acceptable. However, as d gets larger, the fan-in of the OR-gate, which is 2^d, grows unacceptably. Even the AND-gates, with $d + 1$ inputs each, begin to have uncomfortably large fan-in. Fortunately, there is a divide-and-conquer approach based on splitting the control bits in half, that allows us to build the circuit with gates of fan-in at most 2. Moreover, this circuit uses many fewer gates and is almost as fast as the generalization of Fig. 13.22, provided we require that all circuits be built of gates with the same limit on fan-in.

An inductive construction of a family of multiplexer circuits follows: We call the circuit for a multiplexer with d-control-inputs and 2^d-data-inputs a d-MUX.

BASIS. The basis is a multiplexer circuit for $d = 1$, that is, a 1-MUX, which we show in Fig. 13.23. It consists of four gates, and the fan-in is limited to 2.

INDUCTION. The induction is performed by the circuit in Fig. 13.24, which constructs a $2d$-MUX from $2^d + 1$ copies of d-MUX's. Notice that while we double the number of control inputs, we square the number of data inputs, since $2^{2d} = (2^d)^2$.

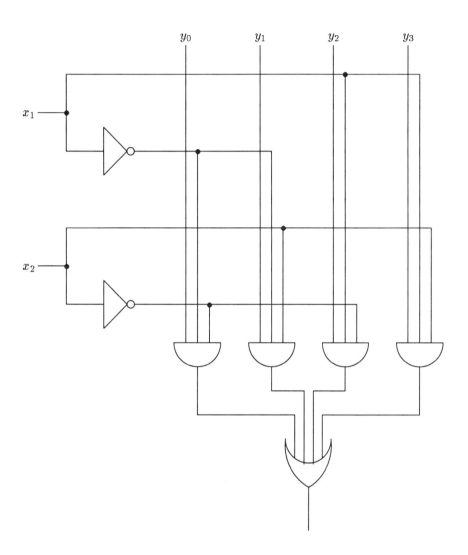

Fig. 13.22. Multiplexer circuit for $d = 2$.

Suppose that the control inputs to the $2d$-MUX call for data input y_i; that is,

$$i = (x_1 x_2 \cdots x_{2d})_2$$

Each d-MUX in the top row of Fig. 13.24 takes a group of 2^d data inputs, starting with some y_j, where j is a multiple of 2^d. Thus, if we use the low-order d control bits, $x_{d+1}, \ldots, x_{2d}$, to control each of these d-MUX's, the selected input is the kth from each group (counting the leftmost in each group as input 0), where

$$k = (x_{d+1} \cdots x_{2d})_2$$

That is, k is the integer represented by the low-order half of the bits.

The data inputs to the bottom d-MUX are the outputs of the top row of d-MUX's, which we just discovered are $y_k, y_{2^d+k}, y_{2 \times 2^d+k}, \ldots, y_{(2^d-1)2^d+k}$. The

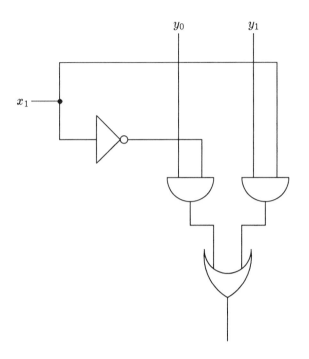

Fig. 13.23. Basis circuit, the multiplexer for $d = 1$.

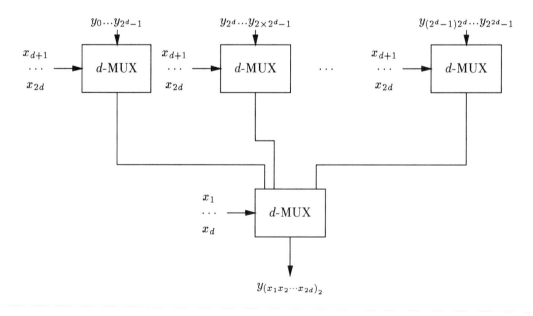

Fig. 13.24. Divide-and-conquer multiplexer.

bottom d-MUX is controlled by $x_1 \cdots x_d$, which represents some integer j in binary; that is, $j = (x_1 \cdots x_d)_2$. The bottom MUX thus selects as its output the jth of its inputs (counting the leftmost as input 0). The selected output is thus y_{j2^d+k}.

We can show that $j2^d + k = i$ as follows. Notice that multiplying j by 2^d has the effect of shifting the binary representation of j left by d places. That is, $j2^d = (x_1 \cdots x_d 0 \cdots 0)_2$, where the string of 0's shown is of length d. Thus, the binary representation of $j2^d + k$ is $(x_1 \cdots x_d x_{d+1} \cdots x_{2d})_2$. That follows because the binary representation of k is $(x_{d+1} \cdots x_{2d})_2$, and there is evidently no carry out of the dth place from the right, when this number is added to the number $j2^d$, which ends in d 0's. We now see that $j2^d + k = i$, because they have the same binary representations. Thus, the $2d$-MUX of Fig. 13.24 correctly selects y_i, where $i = (x_1 \cdots x_{2d})_2$.

Delay of the Divide-and-Conquer MUX

We can calculate the delay of the multiplexer circuit we designed by writing the appropriate recurrence. Let $D(d)$ be the delay of a d-MUX. Inspection of Fig. 13.23 tells us that for $d = 1$, the delay is 3. However, to get a tighter bound, we shall assume that all control inputs are passed through inverters outside the MUX, and not count the level for inverters in Fig. 13.23. We shall then add 1 to the total delay, to account for inversion of all the control inputs, after we determine the delay of the rest of the circuit. Thus, we shall start our recurrence with $D(1) = 2$.

For the induction, we note that the delay through the circuit of Fig. 13.24 is the sum of the delays through any one of the MUX's in the upper row, and the delay through the final MUX. Thus, $D(2d)$ is twice $D(d)$, and we have the recurrence

$$D(1) = 2$$
$$D(2d) = 2D(d)$$

The solution is easy to find. We have $D(2) = 4$, $D(4) = 8$, $D(8) = 16$, and in general, $D(d) = 2d$. Of course, technically this formula only holds when d is a power of 2, but the same idea can be used for an arbitrary number of control bits d. Since we must add 1 to the delay for the inversion of the control inputs, the total delay of the circuit is $2d + 1$.

Now consider the simple multiplexer circuit (an AND for each data input, all feeding one OR-gate). As stated, its delay is 3, independent of d, but we cannot generally build it because the fan-in of the final OR-gate is unrealistic. What happens if we insist on limiting the fan-in to 2? Then the OR-gate, with 2^d inputs, is replaced by a complete binary tree with d levels. Recall that such a tree will have 2^d leaves, exactly the right number. The delay of this tree is d.

We also have to replace the AND-gates with trees of fan-in 2 gates, since in general the AND-gates have $d + 1$ inputs. Recall that when using gates with two inputs, each use of a gate reduces the number of inputs by 1, so that it takes d gates of fan-in 2 to reduce $d + 1$ inputs to one output. If we arrange the gates as a balanced binary tree of AND-gates, we need $\lceil \log_2 d+1 \rceil$ levels. When we add one more level for inverting the control inputs, we have a total delay of $d + 1 + \lceil \log_2(d + 1) \rceil$. This figure compares favorably with the delay $2d + 1$ for the divide-and-conquer MUX, although the difference is not great, as shown in the table of Fig. 13.25.

	DELAY	
d	Divide-and-conquer MUX	Simple MUX
1	3	3
2	5	5
4	9	8
8	17	13
16	33	22

Fig. 13.25. Delay of multiplexer designs.

Gate Count

In this section we compare the number of gates between the simple MUX and the divide-and-conquer MUX. We shall see that the divide-and-conquer MUX has strikingly fewer gates as d increases.

To count the number of gates in the divide-and-conquer MUX, we can temporarily ignore the inverters. We know that each of the d control inputs is inverted once, so that we can just add d to the count at the end. Let $G(d)$ be the number of gates (excluding inverters) used in the d-MUX. Then we can develop a recurrence for G as follows:

BASIS. For the basis case, $d = 1$, there are three gates in the circuit of Fig. 13.23, excluding the inverter. Thus, $G(1) = 3$.

INDUCTION. For the induction, the $2d$-MUX in Fig. 13.24 is built entirely from $2^d + 1$ d-MUX's.

Thus, the recurrence relation is

$$G(1) = 3$$

$$G(2d) = (2^d + 1)G(d)$$

As we saw in Section 3.11, the solution to this recurrence is

$$G(d) = 3(2^d - 1)$$

The first few values of the recurrence are $G(2) = 9$, $G(4) = 45$, and $G(8) = 765$.

Now consider the number of gates used in the simple MUX, converted to use only gates of fan-in 2. As before, we shall ignore the d inverters needed for the control inputs. The final **OR**-gate is replaced by a tree of $2^d - 1$ **OR**-gates. Each of the 2^d **AND**-gates is replaced by a tree of d **AND**-gates. Thus, the total number of gates is $2^d(d + 1) - 1$. This function is greater than the number of gates for the divide-and-conquer MUX, approximately by the ratio $(d + 1)/3$. Figure 13.26 compares the gate counts (excluding the d inverters in each case) for the two kinds of MUX.

	GATE COUNT	
d	Divide-and-conquer MUX	Simple MUX
1	3	3
2	9	11
4	45	79
8	765	2303
16	196,605	1,114,111

Fig. 13.26. Gate count for multiplexer designs (excludes inverters).

More About Divide-and-Conquer

The style of divide-and-conquer algorithm represented by our multiplexer design is a rare, but powerful, form. Most examples of divide-and-conquer split a problem into two parts. Examples are merge sort, the fast adder developed in Section 13.6, and the complete binary tree used to compute the AND or OR of a large number of bits. In the multiplexer, we build a $2d$-MUX from $d + 1$ smaller MUX's. Put another way, a MUX for $n = 2^{2d}$ data inputs is built from $\sqrt{n} + 1$ small MUX's.

EXERCISES

13.7.1: Using the divide-and-conquer technique of this section, construct a

a)   2-MUX
b)   3-MUX

13.7.2*: How would you construct a multiplexer for which the number of data inputs is not a power of two?

One-hot
decoder

13.7.3*: Use the divide-and-conquer technique to design a *one-hot-decoder*. This circuit takes d inputs, $x_1, x_2, \ldots, x_d$ and has 2^d outputs $y_0, y_1, \ldots, y_{2^d-1}$. Exactly one of the outputs will be 1, specifically that y_i such that $i = (x_1, x_2, \ldots, x_d)_2$. What is the delay of your circuit as a function of d? How many gates does it use as a function of d? *Hint*: There are several approaches. One is to design the circuit for d by taking a one-hot-decoder for the first $d - 1$ inputs and splitting each output of that decoder into two outputs based on the last input, x_d. A second is to assume d is a power of 2 and start with two one-hot-decoders, one for the first $d/2$ inputs and the other for the last $d/2$ inputs. Then combine the outputs of these decoders appropriately.

13.7.4*: How does your circuit for Exercise 13.7.3 compare, in delay and number of gates, with the obvious one-hot-decoder formed by creating one AND-gate for each output and feeding to that gate the appropriate inputs and inverted inputs? How does the circuit of Exercise 13.7.3 compare with your circuit of this exercise if you replace AND-gates with large fan-in by trees of 2-input gates?

Majority circuit   **13.7.5***: A *majority circuit* takes $2d - 1$ inputs and has a single output. Its output is 1 if d or more of the inputs are 1. Design a divide-and-conquer majority circuit. What are its delay and gate count as a function of d? *Hint*: Like the adder of Section 13.6, this problem is best solved by a circuit that computes more than we need. In particular, we can design a circuit that takes n inputs and has $n + 1$ outputs, $y_0, y_1, \ldots, y_n$. Output y_i is 1 if exactly i of the inputs are 1. We can then construct the majority circuit inductively by either of the two approaches suggested in Exercise 13.7.3.

13.7.6*: There is a naive majority circuit that is constructed by having one **AND** gate for every set of d inputs. The output of the majority circuit is the **OR** of all these **AND**-gates. How do the delay and gate count of the naive circuit compare with that of the divide-and-conquer circuit of Exercise 13.7.5? What if the gates of the naive circuit are replaced by 2-input gates?

✦✦ 13.8 Memory Elements

Before leaving the topic of logic circuits, let us consider a very important type of circuit that is sequential rather than combinational. A *memory element* is a collection of gates that can remember its last input and produce that input at its output, no matter how long ago that input was given. The main memory of the computer consists of bits that can be stored into and that will hold their value until another value is stored.

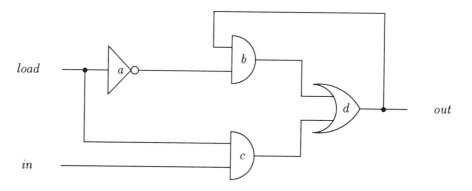

Fig. 13.27. A memory element.

Figure 13.27 is a simple memory element. It is controlled by an input called *load*. Ordinarily, *load* has value 0. In that case, the output of inverter a is 1. Since an **AND**-gate has output 0 whenever one or more of its inputs is 0, the output of **AND**-gate c must be 0 whenever *load* is 0.

If *load* $= 0$ and the output of gate d (which is also the circuit output) is 1, then both inputs to gate b are 1, and so its output is 1. Thus, one of the inputs to **OR**-gate d is 1, and so its output remains 1. On the other hand, suppose the output of d is 0. Then an input to **AND**-gate b is 0, which means that its output is 0. That makes both inputs to d be 0, and so the output remains 0 as long as *load* $= 0$. We conclude that while *load* $= 0$, the circuit output remains what it was.

Real Memory Chips

We should not imagine that Fig. 13.27 represents precisely a typical register bit, but it is not too deceptive. While it also represents a bit of main memory, at least in principle, there are significant differences, and many of the issues in the design of a memory chip involve electronics at a level of detail well beyond the scope of the book.

Because memory chips are used in such great quantities, both in computers and other kinds of hardware, their large-scale production has made feasible some subtle designs for chips storing a million bits or more. To get an idea of the compactness of a memory chip, recall its area is about a square centimeter (10^{-4} square meter). If there are 16 million bits on the chip, then each bit occupies an area equal to 6×10^{-12} square meters, or an area about 2.5 microns on a side (remember, a micron is 10^{-6} meter). If the minimum width of a wire, or the space between wires, is 0.3 micron, that doesn't leave much room for circuitry to build a memory element. To make matters worse, we need not only to store bits, but also to select one of the 16 million bits to receive a value or one of the 16 million to have its value read. The selection circuitry takes up a significant fraction of the space on the chip, leaving even less space for the memory element itself.

Now consider what happens when $load = 1$. The output of inverter a is now 0, so that the output of AND-gate b will be 0 as well. On the other hand, the first input to AND-gate c is 1, so that the output of c will be whatever the input in is. Likewise, as the first input to OR-gate d is 0, the output of d will be the same as the output of c, which in turn is the same as circuit input in. Thus, setting $load$ to 1 causes the circuit output to become whatever in is. When we change $load$ back to 0, that circuit output continues to circulate between gates b and d, as discussed.

We conclude that the circuit of Fig. 13.27 behaves like a memory element, if we interpret "circuit input" as meaning whatever value in has at a time when $load$ is 1. If $load$ is zero, then we say there is no circuit input, regardless of the value of in. By setting $load$ to 1, we can cause the memory element to accept a new value. The element will hold that value as long as $load$ is 0, that is, as long as there is no new circuit input.

EXERCISES

13.8.1: Draw a timing diagram similar to that in Fig. 13.6 for the memory-element circuit shown in Fig. 13.27.

13.8.2: Describe what happens to the behavior of the memory element shown in Fig. 13.27 if an alpha particle hits the inverter and for a short time (but enough time for signals to propagate around the circuit) causes the output of gate a to be the same as its input.

❖❖ 13.9 Summary of Chapter 13

After reading this chapter, the reader should have more familiarity with the circuitry in a computer and how logic can be used to help design this circuitry. In particular, the following points were covered:

✦ What gates are and how they are combined to form circuits

✦ The difference between a combinational circuit and a sequential circuit

✦ How combinational circuits can be designed from logical expressions, and how logical expressions can be used to model combinational circuits

✦ How algorithm-design techniques such as divide-and-conquer can be used to design circuits such as adders and multiplexers

✦ Some of the factors that go into the design of fast circuits

✦ An indication of how a computer stores bits in its electronic circuitry

✦✦ 13.10 Bibliographic Notes for Chapter 13

Shannon [1938] was the first to observe that Boolean algebra can be used to describe the behavior of combinational circuits. For a more comprehensive treatment on the theory and design of combinational circuits, see Friedman and Menon [1975].

Mead and Conway [1980] describe techniques used to construct very large scale integrated circuits. Hennessy and Patterson [1990] discuss computer architecture and the techniques for organizing its circuit elements.

Friedman, A. D., and P. R. Menon [1975]. *Theory and Design of Switching Circuits*, Computer Science Press, New York.

Hennessy, J. L., and D. A. Patterson [1990]. *Computer Architecture: A Quantitative Approach*, Morgan Kaufmann, San Mateo, Calif.

Mead, C., and L. Conway [1980]. *Introduction to VLSI Systems*, Addison-Wesley, Reading, Mass.

Shannon, C. E. [1938]. "Symbolic analysis of relay and switching circuits," *Trans. of AIEE* **57**, pp. 713–723.

❖❖

CHAPTER 14

Predicate Logic

We now turn our attention to a generalization of propositional logic, called "predicate," or "first-order," logic. Predicates are functions of zero or more variables that return Boolean values. Thus predicates can be true sometimes and false sometimes, depending on the values of their arguments. For example, we shall find in predicate logic atomic operands such as $csg(C, S, G)$. Here, csg is the predicate name, and C, S, and G are arguments. We can think of this expression as a representation in logic of the database relation Course-Student-Grade of Fig. 8.1. It returns the value **TRUE** whenever the values of C, S, and G are such that student S got grade G in course C, and it returns **FALSE** otherwise.

Using predicates as atomic operands, instead of propositional variables, gives us a more powerful language than expressions involving only propositions. In fact, predicate logic is expressive enough to form the basis of a number of useful programming languages, such as Prolog (which stands for "*Pro*gramming in *log*ic") and the language SQL that we mentioned in Section 8.7. Predicate logic is also used in reasoning systems or "expert" systems, such as automatic medical diagnosis programs and theorem-proving programs.

❖❖ 14.1 What This Chapter Is About

We introduce predicates in Section 14.2. As we shall see, predicates provide much greater power to express ideas formally than do propositional variables. Much of the development of predicate logic parallels that of propositional logic in Chapter 12, although there are important differences.

✦ Expressions of predicate logic can be built from predicates using the operators of propositional logic (Section 14.3).

✦ "Quantifiers" are operators of predicate logic that have no counterpart in propositional logic (Section 14.4). We can use quantifiers to state that an expression is true for all values of some argument or that there exists at least one value of the argument that makes the expression true.

✦   "Interpretations" for expressions of predicate logic are possible meanings for the predicates and variables (Section 14.5). They are analogous to truth assignments in propositional logic.

✦   Tautologies of predicate logic are expressions that are true for all interpretations. Some tautologies of predicate logic are analogs of tautologies for propositional logic (Section 14.6), while others are not (Section 14.7).

✦   Proofs in predicate logic can be carried out in a manner similar to proofs in propositional logic (Sections 14.8 and 14.9).

In Section 14.10 we discuss some of the implications of predicate logic as to our ability to compute answers to questions. We shall discover the following:

✦   A statement's being a tautology does not mean that it is provable in certain proof systems.

✦   In particular, Gödel's incompleteness theorem tells us that there is a specialized form of predicate logic, dealing with the integers, in which no proof system can provide proofs of every tautology.

✦   Further, Turing's theorem tells us that there are problems we can state but cannot solve by any computer. An example is whether or not a given C program goes into an infinite loop on certain inputs.

✦✦ 14.2   Predicates

A predicate is a generalization of a propositional variable. Recalling Section 12.10, suppose that we have three propositions: r ("It is raining"), u ("Joe takes his umbrella"), and w ("Joe gets wet"). Suppose further that we have three hypotheses, or expressions that we assume are true: $r \rightarrow u$ ("If it rains, then Joe takes his umbrella"), $u \rightarrow \bar{w}$ ("If Joe takes an umbrella, then he doesn't get wet"), and $\bar{r} \rightarrow \bar{w}$ ("If it doesn't rain, Joe doesn't get wet").

What is true for Joe is also true for Mary, and Sue, and Bill, and so on. Thus we might think of the proposition u as u_{Joe}, while w is the proposition w_{Joe}. If we do, we have the hypotheses

$$r \rightarrow u_{Joe}, \ u_{Joe} \rightarrow \bar{w}_{Joe}, \text{ and } \bar{r} \rightarrow \bar{w}_{Joe}$$

If we define the proposition u_{Mary} to mean that Mary takes her umbrella, and w_{Mary} to mean that Mary gets wet, then we have the similar set of hypotheses

$$r \rightarrow u_{Mary}, \ u_{Mary} \rightarrow \bar{w}_{Mary}, \text{ and } \bar{r} \rightarrow \bar{w}_{Mary}$$

We could go on like this, inventing propositions to talk about every individual X we know of and stating the hypotheses that relate the proposition r to the new propositions u_X and w_X, namely,

$$r \rightarrow u_X, \ u_X \rightarrow \bar{w}_X, \text{ and } \bar{r} \rightarrow \bar{w}_X$$

We have now arrived at the notion of a predicate. Instead of an infinite collection of propositions u_X and w_X, we can define symbol u to be a predicate that takes an argument X. The expression $u(X)$ can be interpreted as saying "X takes his or her umbrella." Possibly, for some values of X, $u(X)$ is true, and for other values of X, $u(X)$ is false. Similarly, w can be a predicate; informally $w(X)$ says "X gets wet."

The propositional variable r can also be treated as a predicate with zero arguments. That is, whether it is raining does not depend on the individual X the way u and w do.

We can now write our hypotheses in terms of the predicates as follows:

1. $r \rightarrow u(X)$. (For any individual X, if it is raining, then X takes his or her umbrella.)

2. $u(X) \rightarrow \text{NOT } w(X)$. (No matter who you are, if you take your umbrella, then you won't get wet.)

3. $\text{NOT } r \rightarrow \text{NOT } w(X)$. (If it doesn't rain, then nobody gets wet.)

Atomic Formulas

An *atomic formula* is a predicate with zero or more arguments. For example, $u(X)$ is an atomic formula with predicate u and one argument, here occupied by the variable X. In general, an argument is either a variable or a constant.[1] While, in principle, we must allow any sort of value for a constant, we shall usually imagine that values are integers, reals, or character strings.

Variables and constants

Variables are symbols capable of taking on any constant as value. We should not confuse "variables" in this sense with "propositional variables," as used in Chapter 12. In fact, a propositional variable is equivalent to a predicate with no arguments, and we shall write p for an atomic formula with predicate name p and zero arguments.

Ground atomic formula

An atomic formula all of whose arguments are constants is called a *ground* atomic formula. Nonground atomic formulas can have constants or variables as arguments, but at least one argument must be a variable. Note that any proposition, being an atomic formula with no arguments, has "all arguments constant," and is therefore a ground atomic formula.

Distinguishing Constants From Variables

We shall use the following convention to distinguish constants from variables. A variable name will always begin with an upper-case letter. Constants are represented either by

1. Character strings beginning with a lower-case letter,

2. Numbers, like 12 or 14.3, or

3. Quoted character strings.

---

[1] Predicate logic also allows arguments that are more complicated expressions than single variables or constants. These are important for certain purposes that we do not discuss in this book. Therefore, in this chapter we shall only see variables and constants as arguments of predicates.

Thus, if we want to represent course CS101 by a constant, we could write it as "CS101", for example.[2]

Predicates, like constants, will be represented by character strings beginning with a lower-case letter. There is no possibility that we can confuse a predicate with a constant, since constants can only appear within argument lists in an atomic formula, while predicates cannot appear there.

✦ **Example 14.1.** We might invent a predicate name csg to represent the information contained in the Course-Student-Grade relation discussed in Section 8.2. The atomic formula $csg(C, S, G)$ can be thought of as saying, of variables C, S, and G, that student S took course C and got grade G. Put another way, when we substitute constants c for C, s for S, and g for G, the value of $csg(c, s, g)$ is TRUE if and only if student s took course c and got grade g.

We can also express the particular facts (i.e., tuples) in the relation as ground atomic formulas, by using constants as arguments. For instance, the first tuple of Fig. 8.1 could be expressed as $csg(\text{"CS101"}, 12345, \text{"A"})$, asserting that the student with ID 12345 got an A in CS101. Finally, we can mix constants and variables as arguments, so that we might see an atomic formula like $csg(\text{"CS101"}, S, G)$. This atomic formula is true if variables S and G take on any pair of values (s, g) such that s is a student who took course CS101, and got grade g and false otherwise. ✦

EXERCISES

14.2.1: Identify the following as constants, variables, ground atomic formulas, or nonground atomic formulas, using the conventions of this section.

a)   CS205
b)   cs205
c)   205
d)   "cs205"
e) $p(X, x)$
f) $p(3, 4, 5)$
g)   "$p(3, 4, 5)$"

✦✦ 14.3   Logical Expressions

The notions that we used in Chapter 12 for propositional logic — literals, logical expressions, clauses, and so on — carry over to predicate logic. In the next section we introduce two additional operators to form logical expressions. However, the basic idea behind the construction of logical expressions remains essentially the same in both propositional and predicate logic.

Literals

A *literal* is either an atomic formula or its negation. If there are no variables among the arguments of the atomic formula, then the literal is a *ground* literal.

Ground literal

---

[2] Constants are often called "atoms" in logic. Unfortunately, what we have referred to as "atomic formulas" are also called "atoms" at times. We shall generally avoid the term "atom."

✦ **Example 14.2.** $p(X, a)$ is an atomic formula and a literal. It is not ground because of the argument X, which is a variable by our convention. **NOT** $p(X, a)$ is a literal, but not an atomic formula, and not a ground literal. The expressions $p(a, b)$ and **NOT** $p(a, b)$ are ground literals; only the first is a (ground) atomic formula. ✦

As for propositional logic, we can use an overbar in place of the **NOT** operator. However, the bars become confusing to read when applied to a long expression, and we shall see **NOT** used more frequently in this chapter than in Chapter 12.

Logical Expressions

We can build expressions from atomic formulas just as we built expressions in Section 12.3 from propositional variables. We shall continue to use the operators **AND**, **OR**, **NOT**, $\rightarrow$, and $\equiv$, as well as other logical connectives discussed in Chapter 12. In the next section, we introduce "quantifiers," operators that can be used to construct expressions in predicate logic but have no counterpart in propositional logic.

As with the bar shorthand for **NOT**, we can continue to use the shorthands of juxtaposition (no operator) for **AND** and $+$ for **OR**. However, we use these shorthands infrequently because they tend to make the longer expressions of predicate logic hard to understand.

The following example should give the reader some insight into the meaning of logical expressions. However, note that this discussion is a considerable oversimplification, and we shall have to wait until Section 14.5 to discuss "interpretations" and the meaning that they impart to logical expressions in predicate logic.

✦ **Example 14.3.** Suppose that we have predicates csg and $snap$, which we interpret as the relations Course-Student-Grade and Student-Name-Address-Phone that were introduced in Chapter 8. Suppose also that we want to find the grade of the student named "C. Brown" in course CS101. We could assert the logical expression

$$\big(csg(\text{``CS101''}, S, G) \textbf{ AND } snap(S, \text{``C. Brown''}, A, P)\big) \rightarrow answer(G) \quad (14.1)$$

Here, $answer$ is another predicate, intended to be true of a grade G if G is the grade of some student named "C. Brown" in CS101.

When we "assert" an expression, we mean that its value is **TRUE** no matter what values we substitute for its variables. Informally, an expression such as (14.1) can be interpreted as follows. If we substitute a constant for each of the variables, then each of the atomic formulas becomes a ground atomic formula. We can decide whether a ground atomic formula is true or false by referring either to the "real world," or by looking it up in a relation that lists the true ground atomic formulas with a given predicate. When we substitute 0 or 1 for each of the ground atomic formulas, we can evaluate the expression itself, just as we did for propositional logic expressions in Chapter 12.

In the case of expression (14.1), we can take the tuples in Fig. 8.1 and 8.2(a) to be true. In particular,

$$csg(\text{``CS101''}, 12345, \text{``A''})$$

and

$$snap(12345, \text{``C. Brown''}, \text{``12 Apple St.''}, \text{``555-1234''})$$

are true. Then we can let

$S = 12345$
$G = \text{``A''}$
$A = \text{``12 Apple St.''}$
$P = \text{``555-1234''}$

That makes the left side of (14.1) become 1 **AND** 1, which has the value 1, of course. In principle, we don't know anything about the predicate *answer*. However, we asserted (14.1), which means that whatever values we substitute for its variables, its value is **TRUE**. Since its left side is made **TRUE** by the above substitution, the right side cannot be **FALSE**. Thus we deduce that *answer*("A") is true. ◆

Other Terminology

Clause

We shall use other terms associated with propositional logic as well. In general, when in Chapter 12 we spoke of propositional variables, in this chapter we speak of any atomic formula, including a predicate with zero arguments (i.e., a propositional variable) as a special case. For example, a *clause* is a collection of literals, connected by **OR**'s. Similarly, an expression is said to be in *product-of-sums form* if it is the **AND** of clauses. We may also speak of *sum-of-products form,* where the expression is the **OR** of terms and each such term is the **AND** of literals.

EXERCISES

14.3.1: Write an expression similar to (14.1) for the question "What grade did L. Van Pelt get in PH100?" For what value of its argument is *answer* definitely true, assuming the facts of Figs. 8.1 and 8.2? What substitution for variables did you make to demonstrate the truth of this answer?

14.3.2: Let *cdh* be a predicate that stands for the Course-Day-Hour relation of Fig. 8.2(c), and *cr* a predicate for the Course-Room relation of Fig. 8.2(d). Write an expression similar to (14.1) for the question "Where is C. Brown 9AM Monday morning?" (More precisely, in what room does the course C. Brown is taking on Monday at 9AM meet?) For what value of its argument is *answer* definitely true, assuming the facts of Figs. 8.1 and 8.2? What substitution for variables did you make to demonstrate the truth of this answer?

14.3.3**: Each of the operations of relational algebra discussed in Section 8.7 can be expressed in predicate logic, using an expression like (14.1). For example, (14.1) itself is the equivalent of the relational algebra expression

$$\pi_{\text{Grade}}\left(\sigma_{Course=\text{``CS101''} \textbf{ AND } Name=\text{``C.Brown''}}(CSG \bowtie SNAP)\right)$$

Show how the effect of each of the operations selection, projection, join, union, intersection, and difference can be expressed in predicate logic in the form "expression implies answer." Then translate each of the relational algebra expressions found in the examples of Section 8.7 into logic.

✥✥ 14.4   Quantifiers

Let us return to our example involving the zero-argument predicate r ("It is raining") and the one-argument predicates $u(X)$ ("X takes his umbrella) and $w(X)$ ("X gets wet"). We might wish to assert that "If it rains, then somebody gets wet." Perhaps we could try

$$r \rightarrow w(\text{"Joe"}) \text{ OR } w(\text{"Sally"}) \text{ OR } w(\text{"Sue"}) \text{ OR } w(\text{"Sam"}) \text{ OR } \cdots$$

But this attempt fails because

1.   We can write as an expression the OR of any finite set of expressions, but we cannot write the OR of an infinite set of expressions.

2.   We don't know the complete set of individuals about whom we are speaking.

"There exists"   To express the OR of a collection of expressions formed by substituting every possible value for some variable X, we need an additional way to create expressions of predicate logic. The operator is $\exists$, read "there exists." We use it in expressions such as $(\exists X)w(X)$, or informally, "There exists an individual X such that X gets wet." In general, if E is any logical expression, then $(\exists X)(E)$ is also a logical expression.[3] Its informal meaning is that there is at least one value of X that makes E true. More precisely, for every value of E's other variables, we can find some value of X (not necessarily the same value in all cases) to make E true.

Similarly, we cannot write the infinite AND of expressions like

$$u(\text{"Joe"}) \text{ AND } u(\text{"Sally"}) \text{ AND } u(\text{"Sue"}) \text{ AND } u(\text{"Sam"}) \text{ AND } \cdots$$

"For all"   We instead need a symbol $\forall$ (read "for all") to let us construct the AND of the collection of expressions formed from a given expression by substituting all possible values for a given variable. We write $(\forall X)u(X)$ in this example to mean "for all X, X takes his or her umbrella." In general, for any logical expression E, the expression $(\forall X)(E)$ means that for all possible values of the other variables of E, every constant we may substitute for X makes E true.

Universal and existential quantifiers   The symbols $\forall$ and $\exists$ are called *quantifiers*. We sometimes call $\forall$ the *universal quantifier* and $\exists$ the *existential quantifier*.

✦   **Example 14.4.** The expression $r \rightarrow (\forall X)\big(u(X) \text{ OR } w(X)\big)$ means "If it rains, then for all individuals X, either X takes an umbrella or X gets wet." Note that quantifiers can apply to arbitrary expressions, not just to atomic formulas as was the case in previous examples.

For another example, we can interpret the expression

$$(\forall C)\Big(\big((\exists S)csg(C, S, \text{"A"})\big) \rightarrow \big((\exists T)csg(C, T, \text{"B"})\big)\Big) \tag{14.2}$$

---

[3] The parentheses around the E are sometimes needed and sometimes not, depending on the expression. The matter will be clear when we discuss precedence and associativity of operators later in the section. The parentheses around $\exists X$ are part of the notation and are invariably required.

as saying, "For all courses C, if there exists a student S who gets an A in the course, then there must exist a student T who gets a B." Less formally, "If you give A's, then you also have to give B's."

A third example expression is

$$((\forall X) \text{ NOT } w(X)) \text{ OR } ((\exists Y)w(Y)) \qquad (14.3)$$

Informally, "Either all individuals X stay dry or, at least one individual Y gets wet." Expression (14.3) is different from the other two in this example, in that here we have a tautology — that is, an expression which is true, regardless of the meaning of predicate w. The truth of (14.3) has nothing to do with properties of "wetness." No matter what the set S of values that make predicate w true is, either S is empty (i.e., for all X, $w(X)$ is false) or S is not empty (i.e., there exists a Y for which $w(Y)$ is true). ✦

Recursive Definition of Logical Expressions

As a review, we shall give a recursive definition of the class of logical expressions in predicate logic.

BASIS. Every atomic formula is an expression.

INDUCTION. If E and F are logical expressions, then so are

1. NOT E, E AND F, E OR F, $E \rightarrow F$, and $E \equiv F$. Informally, we may allow other operators of propositional logic, such as NAND, to be used as well.

2. $(\exists X)E$ and $(\forall X)E$, for any variable X. In principle, X need not even appear in E, although in practice such expressions rarely "make sense."

Precedence of Operators

In general, we need to put parentheses around all uses of expressions E and F. However, as with the other algebras we have encountered, it is often possible to remove parentheses because of the precedence of operators. We continue to use the precedence of operators defined in Section 12.4, NOT (highest), AND, OR, $\rightarrow$, and $\equiv$ (lowest). However, quantifiers have highest precedence of all.

✦ **Example 14.5.** $(\exists X)p(X)$ OR $q(X)$ would be grouped

$$((\exists X)p(X)) \text{ OR } q(X)$$

Similarly, the outer pairs of parentheses in (14.3) are redundant, and we could have written

$$(\forall X) \text{ NOT } w(X) \text{ OR } (\exists Y)w(Y)$$

We can also eliminate two pairs of parentheses from (14.2) and write it

$$(\forall C)((\exists S)csg(C, S, \text{"A"}) \rightarrow (\exists T)csg(C, T, \text{"B"}))$$

The pair of parentheses around the entire expression after the $(\forall C)$ is necessary so the "for all C" will apply to the entire expression. ✦

Order of Quantifiers

A common logical mistake is to confuse the order of quantifiers — for example, to think that $(\forall X)(\exists Y)$ means the same as $(\exists Y)(\forall X)$, which it does not. For example, if we informally interpret $loves(X, Y)$ as "X loves Y," then $(\forall X)(\exists Y)loves(X, Y)$ means "Everybody loves somebody," that is, for every individual X there is at least one individual Y that X loves. On the other hand, $(\exists Y)(\forall X)loves(X, Y)$ means that there is some individual Y who is loved by everyone — a very fortunate Y, if such a person exists.

Note that the parentheses around the quantifiers $(\forall X)$ and $(\exists X)$ are not used for grouping, and should be regarded as part of the symbol indicating a quantifier. Also, remember that the quantifiers and NOT are unary, prefix operators, and the only sensible way to group them is from the right.

◆ **Example 14.6.** Thus the expression $(\forall X)$ NOT $(\exists Y)p(X, Y)$ is grouped

$$(\forall X)\Big(\text{NOT }\big((\exists Y)p(X, Y)\big)\Big)$$

and means "For all X there is no Y such that $p(X, Y)$ is true." Put another way, there is no pair of values for X and Y that makes $p(X, Y)$ true. ◆

Bound and Free Variables

Quantifiers interact with the variables that appear in an expression in a subtle way. To address this issue, let us first recall the notion of local and global variables in C. Suppose X is defined as an external variable in a C program, as suggested by Fig. 14.1. Assuming X is not declared in main, the reference to X in main is to the external variable. On the other hand, X is declared in function f as a local (automatic) variable, and all references to X within f are to this local variable.

Local and global variables in C

```
int X;
    ...
main()
{
    ...
    ++X;
    ...
}

void f()
{
    int X;
    ...
}
```

Fig. 14.1. Local and global variables.

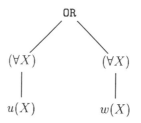

Fig. 14.2. Expression tree for $(\forall X)u(X)$ OR $(\forall X)w(X)$.

There is a close analogy between a declaration of X in a C program on one hand, and a quantifier $(\forall X)$ or $(\exists X)$ on the other. If we have an expression $(\forall X)E$ or $(\exists X)E$, then the quantifier serves to declare X locally for the expression E, as if E were a function and X were declared local to that function.

In what follows, it helps to use the symbol Q to stand for either quantifier. Specifically, we take (QX) to stand for "some quantifier applied to X," that is, either $(\forall X)$ or $(\exists X)$.

If E has a subexpression of the form $(QX)F$, then this subexpression is like a block declared within E that has its own declaration of X. References to X within F refer to the X "declared" by this (QX), while uses of X within E but outside F refer to some other declaration of X — a quantifier either associated with E or with some expression contained within E but enclosing the use of X in question.

✦ **Example 14.7.** Consider the expression

$$(\forall X)u(X) \text{ OR } (\forall X)w(X) \tag{14.4}$$

Informally, "Either everyone takes an umbrella, or everyone gets wet." We might not believe in the truth of this statement, but let us consider it as an example. The expression tree for expression (14.4) is shown in Fig. 14.2. Note that the first quantifier $(\forall X)$ has only the use of X within u as its descendant, while the second $(\forall X)$ has only the use of X within w as a descendant. To tell at which quantifier a use of X is "declared," we have only to trace upwards from the use until we meet a quantifier (QX). Thus the two uses of X refer to different "declarations," and there is no relationship between them. ✦

Note we could have used different variables for the two "declarations" of X in (14.4), perhaps writing $(\forall X)u(X)$ OR $(\forall Y)w(Y)$. In general, we can always rename variables of a predicate logic expression so no one variable appears in two quantifiers. The situation is analogous to a programming language such as C, in which we can rename variables of a program, so that the same name is not used in two declarations. For example, in Fig. 14.1 we could change all instances of the variable name X in the function f to any new variable name Y.

✦ **Example 14.8.** For another example, consider the expression

$$(\forall X)\big(u(X) \text{ OR } (\exists X)w(X)\big)$$

Informally, "For each individual, either that individual takes his umbrella, or there exists some (perhaps other) individual who gets wet." The tree for this expression is shown in Fig. 14.3. Notice that the use of X within w refers to the closest enclosing "declaration" of X, which is the existential quantifier. Put another way, if we travel up the tree from $w(X)$, we meet the existential quantifier before we meet the universal quantifier. However, the use of X within u is not in the "scope" of the existential quantifier. If we proceed upward from $u(X)$, we first meet the universal quantifier. We could rewrite the expression as

$$(\forall X)\big(u(X) \text{ OR } (\exists Y)w(Y)\big)$$

so no variable is quantified more than once. ✦

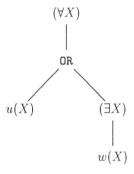

Fig. 14.3. Expression tree for $(\forall X)\big(u(X) \text{ OR } (\exists X)w(X)\big)$.

Bound and free occurrences of variables

We say an occurrence of a variable X within a logical expression E is *bound* by a quantifier (QX) if, in the expression tree for E, that quantifier is the lowest ancestor of this occurrence of X that is a quantifier involving X. If an occurrence of X is not bound by any quantifier, then that occurrence of X is said to be *free*. Thus quantifiers act like "declarations" that are local to the subtree T rooted at the node of the quantifier. They apply everywhere within T, except within a subtree rooted at another quantifier with the same variable. Free variables are like variables global to a function, in that their "declaration," if there is one, occurs somewhere outside the expression in question.

✦ **Example 14.9.** Consider the expression

$$u(X) \text{ OR } (\exists X)w(X)$$

that is, "Either X takes his or her umbrella, or there is some person who gets wet." The tree is shown in Fig. 14.4. As in the previous examples, the two occurrences of X refer to different individuals. The occurrence of X in w is bound to the existential quantifier. However, there is no quantifier for X above the occurrence of X in u, and so this occurrence of X is free in the given expression. This example points up the fact that there can be both free and bound occurrences of the same variable, so that we must talk of "bound occurrences" rather than "bound variables," in some situations. The expressions in Examples 14.7 and 14.8 illustrate that it is also possible for different occurrences of a variable to be bound to different occurrences of quantifiers. ✦

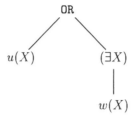

Fig. 14.4. Expression tree for $u(X)$ OR $(\exists X)w(X)$.

EXERCISES

14.4.1: Remove redundant pairs of parentheses from the following expressions.

a) $(\forall X)\Big((\exists Y)\Big(\text{NOT}\,\Big(p(X)\ \text{OR}\ (p(Y)\ \text{AND}\ q(X))\Big)\Big)\Big)$

b) $(\exists X)\Big(\big(\text{NOT}\ p(X)\big)\ \text{AND}\ \big((\exists Y)(p(Y))\ \text{OR}\ \big(\exists X)(q(X,Z))\big)\Big)$

14.4.2: Draw expression trees for the expressions of Exercise 14.4.1. Indicate for each occurrence of a variable to which quantifier, if any, it is bound.

14.4.3: Rewrite the expression of Exercise 14.4.1(b) so that it does not quantify the same variable twice.

14.4.4*: In the box on "Order of Quantifiers," we spoke of a predicate $loves(X, Y)$, and gave it the expected informal interpretation. However, as we shall see in Section 14.5, predicates have no specific interpretation, and we could just as well have taken $loves$ to talk about integers rather than individuals, and for $loves(X, Y)$ to have the informal interpretation that $Y = X + 1$. Under that interpretation, compare the meanings of the expressions $(\forall X)(\exists Y)loves(X, Y)$ and $(\exists Y)(\forall X)loves(X, Y)$. What are their informal interpretations? Which, if either, do you believe?

14.4.5*: Using the csg predicate of our running example, write expressions that assert the following.

a)   C. Brown is an A student (i.e., he gets A's in all his courses).

b)   C. Brown is not an A student.

14.4.6*: Design a grammar that describes the legal expressions of predicate logic. You may use symbolic terminals like $constant$ and $variable$, and you need not avoid redundant parentheses.

✦✦ 14.5 Interpretations

Until now, we have been rather vague about what an expression of predicate logic "means," or how we ascribe a meaning to an expression. We shall approach the subject by first recalling the "meaning" of a propositional logic expression E. That meaning is a function that takes a "truth assignment" (assignment of truth values 0 and 1 to the propositional variables in E) as its argument and produces 0 or 1 as its result. The result is determined by evaluating E with the atomic operands replaced by 0 or 1, according to the given truth assignment. Put another way, the meaning of a logical expression E is a truth table, which gives the value of E (0 or 1) for each truth assignment.

A truth assignment, in turn, is a function that takes propositional variables as arguments and returns 0 or 1 for each. Alternatively, we can see a truth assignment as a table that gives, for each propositional variable, a truth value, 0 or 1. Figure 14.5 suggests the role of these two kinds of functions.

$$p \quad \xrightarrow[assignment]{truth} \quad 0\ or\ 1$$

(a) A truth assignment is a function from predicates to truth values.

$$\begin{matrix} truth \\ assignment \end{matrix} \quad \xrightarrow{meaning} \quad 0\ or\ 1$$

(b) The meaning of an expression is a function from truth assignments to truth values.

Fig. 14.5. The meaning of expressions in propositional logic.

In predicate logic, it is not sufficient to assign a constant 0 or 1 (**TRUE** or **FALSE**) to predicates (unless they have no arguments, in which case they are essentially propositional variables). Rather, the value assigned to a predicate is itself a function that takes values of the predicate's arguments as its own input, and produces 0 or 1 as output.

Domain

More precisely, we must first pick a nonempty *domain* D of values, from which we can select values for the variables. This domain could be anything: integers, reals, or some set of values with no particular name or significance. We assume, however, that the domain includes any constants appearing in the expression itself.

Interpretation for a predicate

Now, let p be a predicate with k arguments. Then an *interpretation for predicate* p is a function that takes as input an assignment of domain elements to each of the k arguments of p and returns 0 or 1 (**TRUE** or **FALSE**). Equivalently, we can see the interpretation of p as a relation with k columns. For each assignment of values to the arguments that makes p true in this interpretation, there is a tuple of the relation.[4]

Interpretation for an expression

Now we can define an *interpretation* for an expression E to be

---

[4] Unlike the relations discussed in Chapter 8, the relation that is the interpretation of a predicate may have an infinite set of tuples.

1.   A nonempty domain D, including any constants appearing in E,

2.   An interpretation for each predicate p appearing in E, and

3.   A value in D for each of the free variables of E, if any.

An interpretation and an "interpretation for a predicate" are illustrated in Fig. 14.6(a) and (b), respectively. Notice that interpretations play the role in predicate logic that is served by truth assignments in propositional logic.

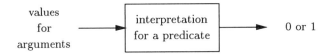

(a) Interpretation for a predicate assigns truth values to
tuples of values for the arguments.

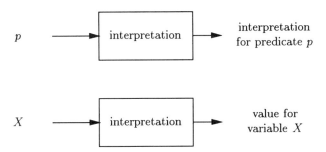

(b) Interpretation assigns a predicate interpretation to each predicate
and a value to each variable (analogous to a truth assignment).

(c) Meaning of an expression assigns a truth value for each interpretation
(analogous to a truth table).

Fig. 14.6. The meaning of expressions in predicate logic.

✦   **Example 14.10.** Consider the following expression of predicate logic:

$$p(X, Y) \rightarrow (\exists Z)\big(p(X, Z) \text{ AND } p(Z, Y)\big) \tag{14.5}$$

One possible interpretation for the predicate p, which we shall call interpretation I_1, is

1.   The domain D is the set of real numbers.

2. $p(U, V)$ is true whenever $U < V$. That is, the interpretation of p is the relation consisting of the infinite set of pairs (U, V) such that U and V are real numbers, and U is less than V.

Then (14.5) states that for any real numbers X and Y, if $X < Y$, then there is some Z lying strictly between X and Y; that is, $X < Z < Y$. For interpretation I_1, (14.5) is always true. If $X < Y$, we can pick $Z = (X + Y)/2$ — that is, the average of X and Y — and we can then be sure that $X < Z$ and $Z < Y$. If $X \geq Y$, then the left-hand side of the implication is false, so surely (14.5) is true.

We can build an infinite number of interpretations for (14.5) based on the interpretation I_1 for predicate p, by picking any real numbers for the free variables X and Y. By what we just said, any of these interpretations for (14.5) will make (14.5) true.

A second possible interpretation, I_2, for p is

1. D is the set of integers.

2. $p(U, V)$ is true if and only if $U < V$.

Now, we claim that (14.5) is true unless $Y = X + 1$. For if Y exceeds X by two or more, then Z can be selected to be $X + 1$. It will then be the case that $X < Z < Y$. If $Y \leq X$, then $p(X, Y)$ is false, and so (14.5) is again true. However, if $Y = X + 1$, then $p(X, Y)$ is true, but there is no integer Z lying strictly between X and Y. Thus for every integer Z, either $p(X, Z)$ or $p(Z, Y)$ will be false, and the right-hand side of the implication — that is, $(\exists Z)\big(p(X, Z) \text{ AND } p(Z, Y)\big)$ — is not true.

We can extend I_2 to an interpretation for (14.5) by assigning integers to the free variables X and Y. The analysis above shows that (14.5) will be true for any such interpretation, except for those in which $Y = X + 1$.

Our third interpretation for p, I_3, is abstract, without a common meaning in mathematics like those possessed by interpretations I_1 and I_2:

1. D is the set of three symbols a, b, c.

2. $p(U, V)$ is true if UV is one of the six pairs

$$aa, ab, ba, bc, cb, cc$$

and false for the other three pairs: ac, bb, and ca.

Then it happens that (14.5) is true for each of the nine pairs XY. In each case, either $p(X, Y)$ is false, or there is a Z that makes the right side of (14.5) true. The nine cases are enumerated in Fig. 14.7. We may extend I_3 to an interpretation for (14.5) in nine ways, by assigning any combination of a, b, and c to the free variables X and Y. Each of these interpretations imparts the value true to (14.5). ◆

Meaning of Expressions

Recall that the meaning of an expression in propositional logic is a function from the truth assignments to truth values 0 and 1, as was illustrated in Fig. 14.5(b). That is, a truth assignment states all that there is to know about the values of the atomic operands of the expression, and the expression then evaluates to 0 or 1. Similarly, in predicate logic, the meaning of an expression is a function that takes an interpretation, which is what we need to evaluate the atomic operands, and returns 0 or 1. This notion of meaning was illustrated in Fig. 14.6(c).

X	Y	Why true
a	a	$Z = a$ or b
a	b	$Z = a$
a	c	$p(a, c)$ false
b	a	$Z = a$
b	b	$p(b, b)$ false
b	c	$Z = c$
c	a	$p(c, a)$ false
c	b	$Z = c$
c	c	$Z = b$ or c

Fig. 14.7. Value of (14.5) under interpretation I_3.

✦ **Example 14.11.** Consider the expression (14.5) from Example 14.10. The free variables of (14.5) are X and Y. If we are given interpretation I_1 of Example 14.10 for p (p is $<$ on reals), and we are given values $X = 3.14$ and $Y = 3.5$, then the value of (14.5) is 1. In fact, with interpretation I_1 for p and any values for X and Y, the expression has value 1, as was discussed in Example 14.10. The same is true of interpretation I_3 for p; any values for X and Y chosen from the domain $\{a, b, c\}$. gives (14.5) the value 1.

On the other hand, if we are given interpretation I_2 (p is $<$ on integers) and values $X = 3$ and $Y = 4$, then (14.5) has value 0 as we discussed in Example 14.10. If we have interpretation I_2 and values $X = 3$ and $Y = 5$ for the free variables, then (14.5) has the value 1. ✦

To complete the definition of "meaning" for an expression, we must formally define how the truth values for atomic operands are translated to a truth value for the expression as a whole. We have been using our intuition previously, based on our understanding of how the logical connectives of propositional logic work and our intuition regarding quantifiers. The formal definition of the value of an expression, given an interpretation I with domain D, is a structural induction on the expression tree for the given logical expression E.

BASIS. If the expression tree is a leaf, then E is an atomic formula $p(X_1, \ldots, X_k)$. The X_i's are all either constants or free variables of expression E. Interpretation I gives us a value for each of the variables, and so we have values for all arguments of p. Likewise, I tells us whether p, with those values as arguments, is true or false. That truth value is the value of the expression E.

INDUCTION. Now, we must assume that we are given an expression E whose expression tree has an operator at the root. There are several cases, depending on what the operator at the root of E is.

First, consider the case where E is of the form E_1 **AND** E_2; that is, the operator at the root is **AND**. The inductive hypothesis may be applied to the subexpressions E_1 and E_2. We can thus evaluate E_1 under interpretation I.[5] Likewise, we can

---

[5] Strictly speaking, we must throw away from I the interpretation for any predicate p that

evaluate E_2 under the interpretation I. If both evaluate to 1, then E evaluates to 1; otherwise, E evaluates to 0.

The induction for other logical operators like OR or NOT is carried out the same way. For OR, we evaluate the two subexpressions and produce value 1 if either subexpression produces value 1; for NOT we evaluate the one subexpression and produce the negation of the value of that expression, and so on for the other operators of propositional logic.

Now suppose E is of the form $(\exists X)E_1$. The root operator is the existential quantifier, and we can apply the inductive hypothesis to the subexpression E_1. The predicates in E_1 all appear in E, and the free variables in E_1 are the free variables of E, plus (possibly) X.[6] Hence, we may construct, for each value v in the domain D, an interpretation for E_1 that is I, with the addition of the assignment of value v to variable X; call this interpretation J_v. We ask, for each value v, whether E_1 is true under interpretation J_v. If there is at least one such value v, then we say that $E = (\exists X)E_1$ is true; otherwise, we say E is false.

Last, suppose that E is of the form $(\forall X)E_1$. Again, the inductive hypothesis applies to E_1. Now we ask whether for every value v in the domain D, E_1 is true under the interpretation J_v. If so, we say E has value 1; if not, E has value 0.

♦ **Example 14.12.** Let us evaluate expression (14.5) with the interpretation I_2 for p ($<$ on the integers) and the values 3 and 7 for free variables X and Y, respectively. The expression tree for (14.5) is shown in Fig. 14.8. We observe that the operator at the root is $\rightarrow$. We did not cover this case explicitly, but the principle should be clear. The entire expression can be written as $E_1 \rightarrow E_2$, where E_1 is $p(X, Y)$, and E_2 is $(\exists Z)(p(X, Z)$ AND $p(Z, Y))$. Because of the meaning of $\rightarrow$, the entire expression (14.5) is true except in the case that E_1 is true and E_2 is false.

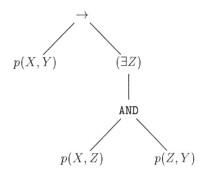

Fig. 14.8. Expression tree for (14.5).

E_1, which is $p(X, Y)$, is easy to evaluate. Since $X = 3$, $Y = 7$, and $p(X, Y)$ is true if and only if $X < Y$, we conclude that E_1 is true. To evaluate E_2 is more

---

appears in E but not E_1. Also, we must drop the value for any free variable that appears in E but not E_1. However, there is no conceptual difficulty if we include in an interpretation additional information that is not used.

[6] Technically, E_1 might not have any free occurrences of X, even though we apply a quantifier involving X to E_1. In that case, the quantifier may as well not be there, but we have not prohibited its presence.

Can we Compute Values of Expressions?

You may be suspicious of our definition as to when an expression E has value 1, in the cases where E is $(\exists X)E_1$ or $(\forall X)E_1$. If domain D is infinite, the test we have proposed, to evaluate E_1 under each interpretation J_v, need not have an algorithm for its execution. Essentially, we are asked to execute function

```
for (each v in D)
    if (E₁ is true under interpretation Jᵥ)
        return TRUE;
return FALSE;
```

for an existential quantifier, and function

```
for (each v in D)
    if (E₁ is false under interpretation Jᵥ)
        return FALSE;
return TRUE;
```

for a universal quantifier.

While the intent of these programs should be apparent, they are not algorithms, since when the domain D is infinite, we go around the loop an infinite number of times. However, although we may not be able to tell whether E is true or false, we are nevertheless offering the correct definition of when E is true; that is, we are ascribing the intended meaning to the quantifiers $\forall$ and $\exists$. In many practical and useful situations, we shall be able to tell whether E is true or false. In other situations, typically involving transformation of expressions into equivalent forms, we shall see that it doesn't matter whether E is true or false. We shall be able to reason that two expressions are equivalent from the definitions of their values, without knowing whether a value v that makes a subexpression like E_1 true exists.

---

difficult. We must consider all possible values of v for Z, to see if there is at least one value that makes $p(X, Z)$ **AND** $p(Z, Y)$ true. For example, if we try $Z = 0$, then $p(Z, Y)$ is true, but $p(X, Z)$ is false, since $X = 3$ is not less than Z.

If we think about the matter, we see that to make $p(X, Z)$ **AND** $p(Z, Y)$ true, we need a value of v such that $3 < v$ [so $p(X, Z)$ will be true] and such that $v < 7$ [so $p(Z, Y)$ will be true]. For example, $v = 4$ makes $p(X, Z)$ **AND** $p(Z, Y)$ true and therefore shows that E_2, or $(\exists Z)\big(p(X, Z)$ **AND** $p(Z, Y)\big)$, is true for the given interpretation.

We now know that both E_1 and E_2 are true. Since $E_1 \to E_2$ is true when both E_1 and E_2 are true, we conclude that (14.5) has value 1 for the interpretation in which predicate p has the interpretation I_2, $X = 3$, and $Y = 7$. ◆

EXERCISES

14.5.1: For each of the following expressions, give one interpretation that makes it true and one interpretation that makes it false.

a) $(\forall X)(\exists Y)(loves(X,Y))$
b) $p(X) \to \mathtt{NOT}\ p(X)$
c) $(\exists X)p(X) \to (\forall X)p(X)$
d) $\bigl(p(X,Y)\ \mathtt{AND}\ p(Y,Z)\bigr) \to p(X,Z)$

14.5.2: Explain why every interpretation makes the expression $p(X) \to p(X)$ true.

✣✣ 14.6 Tautologies

Recall that in propositional logic, we call an expression a tautology if for every truth assignment, the value of the expression is 1. The same idea holds true in predicate logic. An expression E is called a *tautology* if for every interpretation of E, the value of E is 1.

✦ **Example 14.13.** As in propositional logic, it is rare for a "random" expression of predicate logic to be a tautology. For example, the expression (14.5), or

$$p(X,Y) \to (\exists Z)\bigl(p(X,Z)\ \mathtt{AND}\ p(Z,Y)\bigr)$$

which we studied in Example 14.10, is always true under some interpretations for predicate p, but there are interpretations such as I_2 of Example 14.10 — p is $<$ on the integers — for which this expression is not always true (e.g., it is false for $X = 1$ and $Y = 2$). Thus the expression is not a tautology.

An example of a tautology is the expression

$$q(X)\ \mathtt{OR}\ \mathtt{NOT}\ q(X)$$

Here, it does not matter what interpretation we use for predicate q, or what value we assign to the free variable X. If our choice of interpretation makes $q(X)$ true, then the expression is true. If our choice makes $q(X)$ false, then it must make $\mathtt{NOT}\ q(X)$ true, and again the expression is true. ✦

The Substitution Principle

The tautologies of propositional logic are a rich source of tautologies for predicate logic. The principle of substitution, which we introduced in Section 12.7, states that we can take any tautology of propositional logic, make any substitution for the propositional variables, and the result will still be a tautology. This principle still holds true if we allow the substitution of expressions of predicate logic for the propositional variables. For example, the tautology $q(X)\ \mathtt{OR}\ \mathtt{NOT}\ q(X)$, mentioned in Example 14.13, is the substitution of the expression $q(X)$ for propositional variable p in the tautology $p\ \mathtt{OR}\ \mathtt{NOT}\ p$.

The reason the principle of substitution holds true when expressions of predicate logic are substituted for propositional variables is much the same as the reason it holds true when propositional expressions are substituted. When we replace all occurrences of a propositional variable such as p by an expression like $q(X)$, we know that for any interpretation, the value of the substituted expression will be the same wherever it occurs. Since the original expression of propositional logic, into which the substitution is made, is a tautology, it is always true when a consistent substitution of 0 or a consistent substitution of 1 is made for one of its propositional variables.

For example, in the expression $q(X)$ OR NOT $q(X)$, no matter what the interpretation of q or the value of X, $q(X)$ is either true or false. Thus, either the expression becomes 1 OR NOT 1 or it becomes 0 OR NOT 0, both of which evaluate to 1.

Equivalence of Expressions

As in propositional logic, we can define two expressions, E and F, of predicate logic to be equivalent if $E \equiv F$ is a tautology. The "principle of substitution of equals for equals," also introduced in Section 12.7, continues to hold when we have equivalent expressions of predicate logic. That is, if E_1 is equivalent to E_2, then we may substitute E_2 for E_1 in any expression F_1, and the resulting expression F_2 will be equivalent; that is, $F_1 \equiv F_2$.

✦ **Example 14.14.** The commutative law for AND says $(p$ AND $q) \equiv (q$ AND $p)$. We might substitute $p(X)$ for p and $q(Y, Z)$ for q, giving us the tautology of predicate logic

$$\big(p(X) \text{ AND } q(Y, Z)\big) \equiv \big(q(Y, Z) \text{ AND } p(X)\big)$$

Thus the expressions $p(X)$ AND $q(Y, Z)$ and $q(Y, Z)$ AND $p(X)$ are equivalent. Now, if we have an expression like $\big(p(X)$ AND $q(Y, Z)\big)$ OR $q(X, Y)$, we can substitute $q(Y, Z)$ AND $p(X)$ for $p(X)$ AND $q(Y, Z)$, to produce another expression,

$$\big(q(Y, Z) \text{ AND } p(X)\big) \text{ OR } q(X, Y)$$

and know that

$$\Big(\big(p(X) \text{ AND } q(Y, Z)\big) \text{ OR } q(X, Y)\Big) \equiv \Big(\big(q(Y, Z) \text{ AND } p(X)\big) \text{ OR } q(X, Y)\Big)$$

There are more subtle cases of equivalent expressions in predicate logic. Normally, we would expect the equivalent expressions to have the same free variables and predicates, but there are some cases in which the free variables and/or predicates can be different. For example, the expression

$$\big(p(X) \text{ OR NOT } p(X)\big) \equiv \big(q(Y) \text{ OR NOT } q(Y)\big)$$

is a tautology, simply because both sides of the $\equiv$ are tautologies, as we argued in Example 14.13. Thus in the expression $p(X)$ OR NOT $p(X)$ OR $q(X)$ we may substitute $q(Y)$ OR NOT $q(Y)$ for $p(X)$ OR NOT $p(X)$, to deduce the equivalence

$$\big(p(X) \text{ OR NOT } p(X) \text{ OR } q(X)\big) \equiv \big(q(Y) \text{ OR NOT } q(Y) \text{ OR } q(X)\big)$$

Since the left-hand side of the $\equiv$ is a tautology, we can also infer that

$$q(Y) \text{ OR NOT } q(Y) \text{ OR } q(X)$$

is a tautology. ✦

EXERCISES

14.6.1: Explain why each of the following are tautologies. That is, what expression(s) of predicate logic did we substitute into which tautologies of propositional logic?

a) $\big(p(X) \text{ OR } q(Y)\big) \equiv \big(q(Y) \text{ OR } p(X)\big)$

b) $\big(p(X,Y) \text{ AND } p(X,Y)\big) \equiv p(X,Y)$

c) $\big(p(X) \rightarrow \text{FALSE}\big) \equiv \text{NOT } p(X)$

✧ 14.7   Tautologies Involving Quantifiers

Tautologies of predicate logic that involve quantifiers do not have direct counterparts in propositional logic. This section explores these tautologies and shows how they can be used to manipulate expressions. The main result of this section is that we can convert any expression into an equivalent expression with all the quantifiers at the beginning.

Variable Renaming

In C, we can change the name of a local variable, provided we change all uses of that local variable consistently. Analogously, one can change the variable used in a quantifier, provided we also change all occurrences of that variable bound to the quantifier. Also as in C, we must be careful which new variable name we pick, because if we choose a name that is defined outside the function in question, then we may change the meaning of the program, thereby committing a serious error.

Bearing in mind this kind of renaming, we can consider the following type of equivalence and conditions under which it is a tautology.

$$(QX)E \equiv (QY)E' \tag{14.6}$$

where E' is E with all occurrences of X that are bound to the explicitly shown quantifier (QX) replaced by Y. We claim that (14.6) is a tautology, provided no occurrence of Y is free in E. To see why, consider any interpretation I for $(QX)E$ (or equivalently, for $(QY)E'$, since the free variables and predicates of either quantified expression are the same). If I, extended by giving X the value v, makes E true, then I with the value v for Y will make E' true. Conversely, if extending I by using v for X makes E false, then extending I with v for Y makes E' false.

If quantifier Q is $\exists$, then should there be a value v for X that makes E true, there will be a value, namely v, for Y that makes E' true, and conversely. If Q is $\forall$, then all values of X will make E true if and only if all values of Y make E' true. Thus, for either quantifier, $(QX)E$ is true under any given interpretation I if and only if $(QY)E'$ is true under the same interpretation, showing that

$$(QX)E \equiv (QY)E'$$

is a tautology.

✦   **Example 14.15.** Consider the expression

$$((\exists X)p(X,Y)) \text{ OR NOT } ((\exists X)p(X,Y)) \tag{14.7}$$

Making Quantified Variables Unique

Rectified expression

An interesting consequence of (14.6) is that we can always turn any expression E of predicate logic into an equivalent expression in which no two quantifiers use the same variable, and also, no quantifier uses a variable that is also free in E. Such an expression is called *rectified*.

In proof, we may start with the tautology $E \equiv E$. Then, we use (14.6) on the occurrence of E on the right to rename, in turn, each quantified variable by a new variable not used elsewhere in E. The result is an expression $E \equiv E'$, where all quantifiers (QX) of E' involve distinct X's, and these X's do not appear free in E or E'. By the law of transitivity of equivalence for propositional logic, $E \equiv E'$ is a tautology; that is, E and E' are equivalent expressions.

---

which happens to be a tautology. We shall show how to rename one of the two X's, to form another tautology with distinct variables used in the two quantifiers.

If we let E in (14.6) be $p(X, Y)$, and we choose variable Z to play the role of Y in (14.6), then we have the tautology $((\exists X)p(X, Y)) \equiv ((\exists Z)p(Z, Y))$. That is, to construct the expression E' we substitute Z for X in $E = p(X, Y)$, to obtain $p(Z, Y)$. Thus we can substitute "equals for equals," replacing the first occurrence of $(\exists X)p(X, Y)$ in (14.7) by $(\exists Z)p(Z, Y)$, to obtain the expression

$$((\exists Z)p(Z, Y)) \text{ OR NOT } ((\exists X)p(X, Y)).$$

This expression is equivalent to (14.7), and therefore is also a tautology.

Note that we could also replace X in the second half of (14.7) by Z; it doesn't matter whether or not we do so, because the two quantifiers define distinct and unrelated variables, each of which was named X in (14.7). However, we should understand that it is not permissible to replace either occurrence of $\exists X$ by $\exists Y$, because Y is free in each of the subexpressions $p(X, Y)$.

That is, $((\exists X)p(X, Y)) \equiv ((\exists Y)p(Y, Y))$ is not an instance of (14.6) that is a tautology, because Y is free in the expression $p(X, Y)$. To see that it is not a tautology, let p be interpreted as $<$ on integers. Then for any value of the free variable Y, say $Y = 10$, the expression $(\exists X)p(X, Y)$ is true, because we can let $X = 9$, for example. Yet the right side of the equivalence, $(\exists Y)p(Y, Y)$ is false, because no integer is strictly less than itself.

Similarly, it is not permissible to substitute $(\exists Y)p(Y, Y)$ for the first instance of $(\exists X)p(X, Y)$ in (14.7). The resulting expression,

$$((\exists Y)p(Y, Y)) \text{ OR NOT } ((\exists X)p(X, Y)) \tag{14.8}$$

can also be seen not to be a tautology. Again, let the interpretation of p be $<$ on the integers, and let, for instance, the value of the free variable Y be 10. Note that in (14.8), the first two occurrences of Y, in $p(Y, Y)$, are bound occurrences, bound to the quantifier $(\exists Y)$. Only the last occurrence of Y, in $p(X, Y)$, is free. Then $(\exists Y)p(Y, Y)$ is false for this interpretation, because no value of Y is less than itself. On the other hand, $(\exists X)p(X, Y)$ is true when $Y = 10$ (or any other integer, for that matter), and so NOT $((\exists X)p(X, Y))$ is false. As a result, (14.8) is false for this interpretation. ✦

Universal Quantification of Free Variables

An expression with free variables can only be a tautology if the same expression with its free variables universally quantified is a tautology. Formally, for every tautology T and variable X, $(\forall X)T$ is also a tautology. Technically, it does not matter whether or not X appears free in T.

To see why $(\forall X)T$ is a tautology, let $Y_1, \ldots, Y_k$ be the free variables of T; X may or may not be one of them. First, suppose that $X = Y_1$. We need to show that for every interpretation I, $(\forall X)T$ is true. Equivalently, we need to show that for every value v in the domain of I, the interpretation J_v formed from I by giving X the value v makes T true. But T is a tautology, and so every interpretation makes it true.

If X is one of the other free variables Y_i of T, the argument that $(\forall X)T$ is a tautology is essentially the same. If X is none of the Y_i's, then its value doesn't affect the truth or falsehood of T. Thus T is true for all X, simply because T is a tautology.

Closed Expressions

An interesting consequence is that for tautologies, we can assume there are no free variables. We can apply the preceding transformation to universally quantify one free variable at a time. An expression with no free variables is called a *closed* expression.

✦ **Example 14.16.** We know that $p(X,Y)$ OR NOT $p(X,Y)$ is a tautology. We may add universal quantifiers for the free variables X and Y, to get the tautology

$$(\forall X)(\forall Y)\big(p(X,Y) \text{ OR NOT } p(X,Y)\big)$$

✦

Moving Quantifiers Through NOT

There is an infinite version of DeMorgan's law that lets us replace $\forall$ by $\exists$ or vice versa, just as the "normal" DeMorgan's laws allow us to switch between AND and OR, while moving through a NOT. Suppose that we have an expression like

$$\text{NOT } \big((\forall X)p(X)\big)$$

If the domain of values is finite, say $v_1, \ldots, v_n$, then we could think of this expression as NOT $\big(p(v_1) \text{ AND } p(v_2) \text{ AND } \cdots \text{ AND } p(v_n)\big)$. We could then apply DeMorgan's law to rewrite this expression as NOT $p(v_1)$ OR NOT $p(v_2)$ OR $\cdots$ OR NOT $p(v_n)$. On the assumption of a finite domain, this expression is the same as $(\exists X)\big(\text{NOT } p(X)\big)$ — that is, for some value of X, $p(X)$ is false.

In fact, this transformation does not depend on the finiteness of the domain; it holds for every possible interpretation. That is, the following equivalence is a tautology for any expression E.

$$\Big(\text{NOT } \big((\forall X)E\big)\Big) \equiv \big((\exists X)(\text{NOT } E)\big) \tag{14.9}$$

Informally, (14.9) says that E fails to be true for all X exactly when there is some value of X that makes E false.

There is a similar tautology that lets us push a **NOT** inside an existential quantifier.

$$\Big(\text{NOT}\,\big((\exists X)E\big)\Big) \equiv \big((\forall X)(\text{NOT}\ E)\big) \tag{14.10}$$

Informally, there does not exist an X that makes E true exactly when E is false for all X.

✦   **Example 14.17.** Consider the tautology

$$(\forall X)p(X)\ \text{OR}\ \text{NOT}\ \big((\forall X)p(X)\big) \tag{14.11}$$

which we obtain by the principle of substitution from the tautology of propositional logic $p\ \text{OR}\ \text{NOT}\ p$. We may use (14.9) with $E = p(X)$, to replace $\text{NOT}\ \big((\forall X)p(X)\big)$ in (14.11) by $(\exists X)(\text{NOT}\ p(X))$, to yield the tautology

$$(\forall X)p(X)\ \text{OR}\ (\exists X)\big(\text{NOT}\ p(X)\big).$$

That is, either $p(X)$ is true for all X, or there exists some X for which $p(X)$ is false. ✦

Moving Quantifiers Through AND and OR

Laws (14.9) and (14.10), when applied from left to right, have the effect of moving a quantifier outside a negation, "inverting" the quantifier as we do so, that is, swapping $\forall$ for $\exists$ and vice versa. Similarly, we can move quantifiers outside of **AND** or **OR**, but we must be careful not to change the binding of any variable occurrence. Also, we do not invert quantifiers moving through **AND** or **OR**. The expressions of these laws are

$$\big(E\ \text{AND}\ (QX)F\big) \equiv (QX)(E\ \text{AND}\ F) \tag{14.12}$$

$$\big(E\ \text{OR}\ (QX)F\big) \equiv (QX)(E\ \text{OR}\ F) \tag{14.13}$$

where E and F are any expressions, and Q is either quantifier. However, we require that X not be free in E.

Since **AND** and **OR** are commutative, we can also use (14.12) and (14.13) to move quantifiers attached to the left operand of **AND** or **OR**. For example, a form of tautology that follows from (14.12) and the commutativity of **AND** is

$$\big((QX)E\ \text{AND}\ F\big) \equiv (QX)(E\ \text{AND}\ F)$$

Here, we require that X is not free in F.

✦   **Example 14.18.** Let us transform the tautology developed in Example 14.17, that is,

$$(\forall X)p(X)\ \text{OR}\ (\exists X)\big(\text{NOT}\ p(X)\big)$$

so that the quantifiers are outside the expression. First, we need to rename the variable used by one of the two quantifiers. By law (14.6), we can replace the subexpression $(\exists X)$ NOT $p(X)$ by $(\exists Y)$ NOT $p(Y)$, giving us the tautology

$$(\forall X)p(X) \text{ OR } (\exists Y)\big(\text{NOT } p(Y)\big) \tag{14.14}$$

Now we can use (14.13), in its variant form where the quantifier on the left operand of the OR is moved, to take the $\forall$ outside the OR. The resulting expression is

$$(\forall X)\Big(p(X) \text{ OR } (\exists Y)\big(\text{NOT } p(Y)\big)\Big) \tag{14.15}$$

Expression (14.15) differs from (14.14) in form, but not in meaning; (14.15) states that for all values of X, at least one of the following holds:

1. $p(X)$ is true.

2. There is some value of Y that makes $p(Y)$ false.

To see why (14.15) is a tautology, consider some value v for X. If the interpretation under consideration makes $p(v)$ true, then $p(X)$ OR $(\exists Y)\big(\text{NOT } p(Y)\big)$ is true. If $p(v)$ is false, then in this interpretation, (2) must hold. In particular, when $Y = v$, NOT $p(Y)$ is true, and so $(\exists Y)\big(\text{NOT } p(Y)\big)$ is true.

Finally, we can apply (14.13) to move $\exists Y$ outside the OR. The expression that results is

$$(\forall X)(\exists Y)(p(X) \text{ OR NOT } p(Y))$$

This expression also must be a tautology. Informally, it states that for every value of X, there exists some value of Y that makes $p(X)$ OR NOT $p(Y)$ true. To see why, let v be a possible value of X. If $p(v)$ is true in given interpretation I, then surely

$$p(X) \text{ OR NOT } p(Y)$$

is true, regardless of Y. If $p(v)$ is false in interpretation I, then we may pick v for Y, and $(\exists Y)(p(X) \text{ OR NOT } p(Y))$ will be true. ◆

Prenex Form

A consequence of the laws (14.9), (14.10), (14.12), and (14.13) is that, given any expression involving quantifiers and the logical operators AND, OR, and NOT, we can find an equivalent expression that has all its quantifiers on the outside (at the top of the expression tree). That is, we can find an equivalent expression of the form

$$(Q_1 X_1)(Q_2 X_2) \cdots (Q_k X_k)E \tag{14.16}$$

Quantifier-free expression

where $Q_1, \ldots, Q_k$ each stand for one of the quantifiers $\forall$ or $\exists$, and the subexpression E is *quantifier free* — that is, it has no quantifiers. The expression (14.16) is said to be in *prenex form*.

We can transform an expression into prenex form in two steps.

1. Rectify the expression. That is, use law (14.6) to make each of the quantifiers refer to a distinct variable, one that appears neither in another quantifier nor free in the expression.

2. Then, move each quantifier through NOT's by laws (14.9) and (14.10), through AND's by (14.12), and through OR's by (14.13).

Programs in Prenex Form

In principle, we can put a C program in "prenex form," if we rename all local variables so that they are distinct, and then move their declarations into the main program. We generally don't want to do that; we prefer to declare variables locally, so that we don't have to worry, for example, about inventing different names for a variable i used as a loop index in ten different functions. For logical expressions, there is often a reason to put expressions in prenex form, although the matter is beyond the scope of this book.

✦ **Example 14.19.** Examples 14.17 and 14.18 were examples of this process. We started in Example 14.17 with the expression $(\forall X)p(X)$ OR NOT $\big((\forall X)p(X)\big)$. By moving the second $\forall$ through the NOT, we obtained the expression

$$(\forall X)p(X) \text{ OR } (\exists X)\big(\text{NOT } p(X)\big)$$

with which we started in Example 14.18. We then renamed the second use of X, which we could (and should) have done initially. By moving the two quantifiers through the OR, we obtained $(\forall X)(\exists Y)\big(p(X) \text{ OR NOT } p(Y)\big)$, which is in prenex form. ✦

Note that expressions involving logical operators other than AND, OR, and NOT can also be put in prenex form. Every logical operator can be written in terms of AND, OR, and NOT, as we learned in Chapter 12. For example, $E \rightarrow F$ can be replaced by NOT E OR F. If we write each logical operator in terms of AND, OR, and NOT, then we are able to apply the transformation just outlined to find an equivalent expression in prenex form.

Reordering Quantifiers

Our final family of tautologies is derived by noting that in applying a universal quantifier to two variables, the order in which we write the quantifiers does not matter. Similarly, we can write two existential quantifiers in either order. Formally, the following are tautologies.

$$(\forall X)(\forall Y)E \equiv (\forall Y)(\forall X)E \tag{14.17}$$

$$(\exists X)(\exists Y)E \equiv (\exists Y)(\exists X)E \tag{14.18}$$

Note that by (14.17), we can permute any string of $\forall$'s, $(\forall X_1)(\forall X_2)(\cdots)(\forall X_k)$ into whatever order we choose. In effect, (14.17) is the commutative law for $\forall$. Analogous observations hold for law (14.18), which is the commutative law for $\exists$.

EXERCISES

14.7.1: Transform the following expressions into rectified expressions, that is, expressions for which no two quantifier occurrences share the same variable.

a) $(\exists X)\bigg(\big(\text{NOT } p(X)\big) \text{ AND } \big((\exists Y)(p(Y)) \text{ OR } \big((\exists X)(q(X, Z))\big)\big)\bigg)$

b) $(\exists X)\big((\exists X)p(X) \text{ OR } (\exists X)q(X) \text{ OR } r(X)\big)$

14.7.2: Turn the following into closed expressions by universally quantifying each of the free variables. If necessary, rename variables so that no two quantifier occurrences use the same variable.

a) $p(X, Y) \text{ AND } (\exists Y)q(Y)$

b) $(\forall X)\big(p(X, Y) \text{ OR } (\exists X)p(Y, X)\big)$

14.7.3*: Does law (14.12) imply that $p(X, Y) \text{ AND } (\forall X)q(X)$ is equivalent to

$$(\forall X)\big(p(X, Y) \text{ AND } q(X)\big)$$

Explain your answer.

14.7.4: Transform the expressions of Exercise 14.7.1 into prenex form.

14.7.5*: Show how to move quantifiers through an $\rightarrow$ operator. That is, turn the expression $\big((Q_1X)E\big) \rightarrow \big((Q_2Y)F\big)$ into a prenex form expression. What constraints on free variables in E and F do you need?

14.7.6: We can use tautologies (14.9) and (14.10) to move NOT's inside quantifiers as well as to move them outside. Using these laws, plus DeMorgan's laws, we can move all NOT's so they apply directly to atomic formulas. Apply this transformation to the following expressions.

a) $\text{NOT } \big((\forall X)(\exists Y)p(X, Y)\big)$

b) $\text{NOT } \Big((\forall X)\big(p(X) \text{ OR } (\exists Y)q(X, Y)\big)\Big)$

14.7.7*: Is it true that E is a tautology whenever $(\exists X)E$ is a tautology?

❖❖ 14.8 Proofs in Predicate Logic

In this chapter and the next, we shall discuss proofs in predicate logic. We do not, however, extend the resolution method of Section 12.11 to predicate logic, although it can be done. In fact, resolution is extremely important for many systems that use predicate logic. The mechanics of proofs were introduced in Section 12.10. Recall that in a proof of propositional logic we are given some expressions $E_1, E_2, \ldots, E_k$ as hypotheses, or "axioms," and we construct a sequence of expressions (lines) such that each expression either

1. Is one of the E_i's, or

2. Follows from zero or more of the previous expressions by some rule of inference.

Rules of inference must have the property that, whenever we are allowed to add F to the list of expressions because of the presence of $F_1, F_2, \ldots, F_n$ on the list,

$$(F_1 \text{ AND } F_2 \text{ AND } \cdots \text{ AND } F_n) \rightarrow F$$

is a tautology.

Proofs in predicate logic are much the same. Of course, the expressions that are hypotheses and lines of the proof are expressions of predicate logic, not propositional logic. Moreover, it does not make sense to have, in one expression, free variables that bear a relationship to a free variable of the same name in another expression. Thus we shall require that the hypotheses and lines of the proof be closed formulas.

Implicit Universal Quantifiers

However, it is conventional to write expressions in proofs without explicitly showing the outermost universal quantifiers. For example, consider the expression in Example 14.3,

$$\big(csg(\text{``CS101''}, S, G) \text{ AND } snap(S, \text{``C.Brown''}, A, P)\big) \to answer(G) \quad (14.19)$$

Expression (14.19) might be one of the hypotheses in a proof. In Example 14.3, we saw it intuitively as a definition of the predicate $answer$. We might use (14.19) in a proof of, say, $answer(\text{``A''})$ — that is, C. Brown received an A in course CS101.

In Example 14.3 we explained the meaning of (14.19) by saying that for all values of S, G, A, and P, if student S received grade G in CS101 — that is, if $csg(\text{``CS101''}, S, G)$ is true — and student $S$ has name "C. Brown," address $A$, and phone $P$ — that is, if $snap(S, \text{``C.Brown''}, A, P)$ is true — then G is an answer (i.e., $answer(G)$ is true). In that example, we did not have the formal notion of quantifiers. However, now we see that what we really want to assert is

$$(\forall S)(\forall G)(\forall A)(\forall P)\Big(\big((csg(\text{``CS101''}, S, G) \text{ AND } snap(S, \text{``C.Brown''}, A, P)\big)$$
$$\to answer(G)\Big)$$

Because it is frequently necessary to introduce a string of universal quantifiers around an expression, we shall adopt the shorthand notation $(\forall *)E$ to mean a string of quantifiers $(\forall X_1)(\forall X_2)(\cdots)(\forall X_k)E$, where $X_1, X_2, \ldots, X_k$ are all the free variables of expression E. For example, (14.19) could be written

$$(\forall *)\Big(\big(csg(\text{``CS101''}, S, G) \text{ AND } snap(S, \text{``C.Brown''}, A, P)\big) \to answer(G)\Big)$$

However, we shall continue to refer to variables that are free in E as "free" in $(\forall *)E$. This use of the term "free" is strictly incorrect, but is quite useful.

Substitution for Variables as an Inference Rule

In addition to the inference rules discussed in Chapter 12 for propositional logic, such as modus ponens, and substitution of equals for equals in a previous line of the proof, there is an inference rule involving substitution for variables that is quite useful for proofs in predicate logic. If we have asserted an expression E, either as a hypothesis or as a line of a proof, and E' is formed from E by substituting variables or constants for some of the free variables of E, then $E \to E'$ is a tautology, and we may add E' as a line of the proof. It is important to remember that we cannot substitute for bound variables of E, only for the free variables of E.

Formally, we can represent a substitution for variables by a function sub. For each free variable X of E, we may define $sub(X)$ to be some variable or some constant. If we do not specify a value for $sub(X)$, then we shall assume that $sub(X) = X$ is intended. If E is any expression of predicate logic, the expression $sub(E)$ is E with all free occurrences of any variable X replaced by $sub(X)$.

Expressions in Proofs

Remember that when we see an expression E in a proof, it is really short for the expression $(\forall *)E$. Note that $E \equiv (\forall *)E$ is generally not a tautology, and so we are definitely using one expression to stand for a different expression.

It is also helpful to remember that when E appears in a proof, we are not asserting that $(\forall *)E$ is a tautology. Rather, we are asserting that $(\forall *)E$ follows from the hypotheses. That is, if $E_1, E_2, \ldots, E_n$ are the hypotheses, and we correctly write proof line E, then we know

$$\big((\forall *)E_1 \text{ AND } (\forall *)E_2 \text{ AND } \cdots \text{ AND } (\forall *)E_n\big) \rightarrow (\forall *)E$$

is a tautology.

The *law of variable substitution* says that $E \rightarrow sub(E)$ is a tautology. Thus, if E is a line of a proof, we may add $sub(E)$ as a line of the same proof.

♦ **Example 14.20.** Consider the expression (14.19)

$$\big(csg(\text{"CS101"}, S, G) \text{ AND } snap(S, \text{"C.Brown"}, A, P)\big) \rightarrow answer(G)$$

as E. A possible substitution sub is defined by

$$sub(G) = \text{"B"}$$
$$sub(P) = S$$

That is, we substitute the constant "B" for the variable G and we substitute variable S for variable P. The variables S and A remain unchanged. The expression $sub(E)$ is

$$\big(csg(\text{"CS101"}, S, \text{"B"}) \text{ AND } snap(S, \text{"C.Brown"}, A, S)\big) \rightarrow answer(\text{"B"}) \quad (14.20)$$

Informally, (14.20) says that if there is a student S who received a B in CS101, and the student's name is C. Brown, and the student's phone number and student ID are identical, then "B" is an answer.

Notice that (14.20) is a special case of the more general rule expressed by (14.19). That is, (14.20) only infers the correct answer in the case that the grade is B, and C. Brown, by a strange coincidence, has the same student ID and phone number; otherwise (14.20) infers nothing. ♦

♦ **Example 14.21.** The expression

$$p(X, Y) \text{ OR } (\exists Z)q(X, Z) \quad (14.21)$$

has free variables X and Y, and it has bound variable Z. Recall that technically, (14.21) stands for the closed expression $(\forall *)\big(p(X, Y) \text{ OR } (\exists Z)q(X, Z)\big)$, and that here the $(\forall *)$ stands for quantification over the free variables X and Y, that is,

$$(\forall X)(\forall Y)\big(p(X, Y) \text{ OR } (\exists Z)q(X, Z)\big)$$

Substitution as Special-Casing

Example 14.20 is typical, in that whenever we apply a substitution sub to an expression E, what we get is a special case of E. If sub replaces variable X by a constant c, then the expression $sub(E)$ only applies when $X = c$, and not otherwise. If sub makes two variables become the same, then $sub(E)$ only applies in the special case that these two variables have the same value. Nonetheless, substitutions for variables are often exactly what we need to make a proof, because they allow us to apply a general rule in a special case, and they allow us to combine rules to make additional rules. We shall study this form of proof in the next section.

In (14.21), we might substitute $sub(X) = a$, and $sub(Y) = b$, yielding the expression $p(a, b)$ OR $(\exists Z)q(a, Z)$. This expression, which has no free variables because we chose to substitute a constant for each free variable, is easily seen to be a special case of (14.21); it states that either $p(a, b)$ is true or for some value of Z, $q(a, Z)$ is true. Formally,

$$\Big((\forall X)(\forall Y)\big(p(X, Y) \text{ OR } (\exists Z)q(X, Z)\big)\Big) \to \big(p(a, b) \text{ OR } (\exists Z)q(a, Z)\big)$$

is a tautology.

One might wonder what happened to the implied quantifiers in (14.21) when we substituted a and b for X and Y. The answer is that in the resulting expression, $p(a, b)$ OR $(\exists Z)q(a, Z)$, there are no free variables, and so the implied expression $(\forall *)(p(a, b) \text{ OR } (\exists Z)q(a, Z))$ has no prefix of universal quantifiers; that is,

$$p(a, b) \text{ OR } (\exists Z)q(a, Z)$$

stands for itself in this case. We do not replace $(\forall *)$ by $(\forall a)(\forall b)$, which makes no sense, since constants cannot be quantified. ✦

EXERCISES

14.8.1: Prove the following conclusions from hypotheses, using the inference rules discussed in Section 12.10, plus the variable-substitution rule just discussed. Note that you can use as a line of proof any tautology of either propositional or predicate calculus. However, try to restrict your tautologies to the ones enumerated in Sections 12.8, 12.9, and 14.7.

a)   From hypothesis $(\forall X)p(X)$ prove the conclusion $(\forall X)p(X)$ OR $q(Y)$.

b)   From hypothesis $(\exists X)p(X, Y)$ prove the conclusion NOT $\Big((\forall X)\big(\text{NOT } p(X, a)\big)\Big)$.

c)   From the hypotheses $p(X)$ and $p(X) \to q(X)$ prove the conclusion $q(X)$.

✦✦ 14.9   Proofs from Rules and Facts

Perhaps the simplest form of proof in predicate logic involves hypotheses that fall into two classes.

1. *Facts*, which are ground atomic formulas.

2. *Rules*, which are "if-then" expressions. An example is the query (14.19) about C. Brown's grade in CS101,

$$\big(csg(\text{"CS101"}, S, G) \text{ AND } snap(S, \text{"C.Brown"}, A, P)\big) \to answer(G)$$

which we discussed in Example 14.20. Rules consist of the **AND** of one or more atomic formulas on the left-hand side of the implication sign, and one atomic formula on the right-hand side. We assume that any variable appearing in the head also appears somewhere in the body.

Body, head, subgoal

The left-hand side (hypotheses) of a rule is called the *body*, and the right-hand side side is called the *head*. Any one of the atomic formulas of the body is called a *subgoal*. For instance, in (14.19), the rule repeated above, the subgoals are $csg(\text{"CS101"}, S, G)$ and $snap(S, \text{"C.Brown"}, A, P)$. The head is $answer(G)$.

The general idea behind the use of rules is that rules are general principles that we can apply to facts. We try to match the subgoals of the body of a rule to facts that are either given or already proven, by substituting for variables in the rule. When we can do so, the substitution makes the head a ground atomic formula, because we have assumed that each variable of the head appears in the body. We can add this new ground atomic formula to the collection of facts at our disposal for further proofs.

✦ **Example 14.22.** One simple application of proofs from rules and facts is in answering queries as in the relational model discussed in Chapter 8. Each relation corresponds to a predicate symbol, and each tuple in the relation corresponds to a ground atomic formula with that predicate symbol and with arguments equal to the components of the tuple, in order. For example, from the Course-Student-Grade relation of Fig. 8.1, we would get the facts

$$
\begin{array}{ll}
csg(\text{"CS101"}, 12345, \text{"A"}) & csg(\text{"CS101"}, 67890, \text{"B"}) \\
csg(\text{"EE200"}, 12345, \text{"C"}) & csg(\text{"EE200"}, 22222, \text{"B+"}) \\
csg(\text{"CS101"}, 33333, \text{"A--"}) & csg(\text{"PH100"}, 67890, \text{"C+"})
\end{array}
$$

Similarly, from the Student-Name-Address-Phone relation of Fig. 8.2(a), we get the facts

$$
\begin{array}{l}
snap(12345, \text{"C.Brown"}, \text{"12 Apple St."}, 555\text{-}1234) \\
snap(67890, \text{"L.VanPelt"}, \text{"34 Pear Ave."}, 555\text{-}5678) \\
snap(22222, \text{"P.Patty"}, \text{"56 Grape Blvd."}, 555\text{-}9999)
\end{array}
$$

To these facts, we might add the rule (14.19),

$$\big(csg(\text{"CS101"}, S, G) \text{ AND } snap(S, \text{"C.Brown"}, A, P)\big) \to answer(G)$$

to complete the list of hypotheses.

Suppose we want to show that $answer(\text{"A"})$ is true, that is, C. Brown gets an A in CS101. We could begin our proof with all of the facts and the rule, although in this case we only need the rule, the first *csg* fact and the first *snap* fact. That is, the first three lines of the proof are

1. $\big(csg(\text{"CS101"}, S, G) \text{ AND } snap(S, \text{"C.Brown"}, A, P)\big) \to answer(G)$

2. $csg($ "CS101" $, 12345,$ "A" $)$

3. $snap(12345,$ "C.Brown" $,$ "12 Apple St." $, 555\text{-}1234)$

The next step is to combine the second and third lines, using the inference rule that says if E_1 and E_2 are lines of a proof then E_1 **AND** E_2 may be written as a line of the proof. Thus we have line

4. $csg($ "CS101" $, 12345,$ "A" $)$ **AND**
       $snap(12345,$ "C.Brown" $,$ "12 Apple St." $, 555\text{-}1234)$

Next, let us use the law of substitution for free variables to specialize our rule — line (1) — so that it applies to the constants in line (4). That is, we make the substitution

$$sub(S) = \text{"CS101"}$$
$$sub(G) = \text{"A"}$$
$$sub(A) = \text{"12 Apple St."}$$
$$sub(P) = 555\text{-}1234$$

in (1) to obtain the line

5. $\big(csg($ "CS101" $, 12345,$ "A" $)$ **AND**
       $snap(12345,$ "C.Brown" $,$ "12 Apple St." $, 555\text{-}1234)\big)$
                   $\rightarrow answer($ "A" $)$

Finally, modus ponens applied to (4) and (5) gives us the sixth and last line of the proof,

6. $answer($ "A" $)$. ✦

A Simplified Inference Rule

If we look at the proof of Example 14.22, we can observe the following strategy for building a proof from ground atomic formulas and logical rules.

1.   We select a rule to apply and we select a substitution that turns each subgoal into a ground atomic formula that either is a given fact, or is something we have already proved. In Example 14.22, we substituted 12345 for S, and so on. The result appeared as line (4) of Example 14.22.

2.   We create lines of the proof for each of the substituted subgoals, either because they are facts, or by inferring them in some way. This step appeared as lines (2) and (3) in Example 14.22.

3.   We create a line that is the **AND** of the lines corresponding to each of the substituted subgoals. This line is the body of the substituted rule. In Example 14.22, this step appeared as line (5).

4.   We use modus ponens, with the substituted body from (3) and the substituted rule from (1) to infer the substituted head. This step appeared as line (6) in Example 14.22.

We can combine these steps into a single inference rule, as follows. If there is a rule R among the hypotheses and a substitution sub such that in the substituted instance $sub(R)$, each of the subgoals is a line of the proof, then we may add the head of $sub(R)$ as a line of the proof.

Interpreting Rules

Rules, like all expressions that appear in proofs, are implicitly universally quantified. Thus we can read (14.19) as "for all S, G, A, and P, if $csg($"CS101"$, S, G)$ is true, and $snap(S,$ "C.Brown"$, A, P)$ is true, then $answer(G)$ is true." However, we may treat variables that appear in the body, but not in the head, such as S, A, and P, as existentially quantified for the scope of the body. Formally, (14.19) is equivalent to

$$(\forall G)\Big((\exists S)(\exists A)(\exists P)\big(csg(\text{``CS101''}, S, G) \text{ AND } snap(S, \text{``C.Brown''}, A, P)\big)$$
$$\rightarrow answer(G)\Big)$$

That is, for all G, if there exists S, A, and P such that $csg($"CS101"$, S, G)$ and $snap(S,$ "C.Brown"$, A, P)$ are both true, then $answer(G)$ is true.

This phrasing corresponds more closely to the way we think of applying a rule. It suggests that for each value of the variable or variables that appear in the head, we should try to find values of the variables appearing only in the body, that make the body true. If we find such values, then the head is true for the chosen values of its variables.

To see why we can treat variables that are local to the body as existentially quantified, start with a rule of the form $B \rightarrow H$, where B is the body, and H is the head. Let X be one variable that appears only in B. Implicitly, this rule is

$$(\forall *)(B \rightarrow H)$$

and by law (14.17), we can make the quantifier for X be the innermost, writing the expression as $(\forall *)(\forall X)(B \rightarrow H)$. Here, the $(\forall *)$ includes all variables but X. Now we replace the implication by its equivalent expression using NOT and OR, that is, $(\forall *)(\forall X)\big((\text{NOT } B) \text{ OR } H\big)$. Since X does not appear in H, we may apply law (14.13) in reverse, to make the $(\forall X)$ apply to NOT B only, as $(\forall *)\Big(\big((\forall X) \text{ NOT } B\big) \text{ OR } H\Big)$. Next, we use law (14.10) to move the $(\forall X)$ inside the negation, yielding

$$(\forall *)\Big(\big(\text{NOT } (\exists X)(\text{NOT NOT } B)\big) \text{ OR } H\Big)$$

or, after eliminating the double negation, $(\forall *)\Big(\big(\text{NOT } (\exists X)B\big) \text{ OR } H\Big)$. Finally, we restore the implication to get $(\forall *)\Big(\big((\exists X)B\big) \rightarrow H\Big)$.

✦ **Example 14.23.** In Example 14.22, rule R is (14.19), or

$$\big(csg(\text{``CS101''}, S, G) \text{ AND } snap(S, \text{``C.Brown''}, A, P)\big) \rightarrow answer(G)$$

The substitution sub is as given in that example, and the subgoals of $sub(R)$ are lines (2) and (3) in Example 14.22. By the new inference rule, we could write down line (6) of Example 14.22 immediately; we do not need lines (4) and (5). In fact, line (1), the rule R itself, can be omitted from the proof as long as it is a given hypothesis. ✦

✦   **Example 14.24.** For another example of how rules may be applied in proofs, let us consider the Course-Prerequisite relation of Fig. 8.2(b), whose eight facts can be represented by eight ground atomic formulas with predicate cp,

$$cp(\text{``CS101''}, \text{``CS100''}) \qquad cp(\text{``EE200''}, \text{``EE005''})$$
$$cp(\text{``EE200''}, \text{``CS100''}) \qquad cp(\text{``CS120''}, \text{``CS101''})$$
$$cp(\text{``CS121''}, \text{``CS120''}) \qquad cp(\text{``CS205''}, \text{``CS101''})$$
$$cp(\text{``CS206''}, \text{``CS121''}) \qquad cp(\text{``CS206''}, \text{``CS205''})$$

We might wish to define another predicate $before(X, Y)$ that means course Y must be taken before course X. Either Y is a prerequisite of X, a prerequisite of a prerequisite of X, or so on. We can define the notion "before" recursively, by saying

1.   If Y is a prerequisite of X, then Y comes before X.

2.   If X has a prerequisite Z, and Y comes before Z, then Y comes before X.

Rules (1) and (2) can be expressed as rules of predicate logic as follows.

$$cp(X, Y) \rightarrow before(X, Y) \tag{14.22}$$

$$\big(cp(X, Z) \textbf{ AND } before(Z, Y)\big) \rightarrow before(X, Y) \tag{14.23}$$

Let us now explore some of the *before* facts that we can prove with the eight Course-Prerequisite facts given at the beginning of the example, plus rules (14.22) and (14.23). First, we can apply rule (14.22) to turn each of the cp facts into a corresponding *before* fact, yielding

$$before(\text{``CS101''}, \text{``CS100''}) \qquad before(\text{``EE200''}, \text{``EE005''})$$
$$before(\text{``EE200''}, \text{``CS100''}) \qquad before(\text{``CS120''}, \text{``CS101''})$$
$$before(\text{``CS121''}, \text{``CS120''}) \qquad before(\text{``CS205''}, \text{``CS101''})$$
$$before(\text{``CS206''}, \text{``CS121''}) \qquad before(\text{``CS206''}, \text{``CS205''})$$

For example, we may use the substitution

$$sub_1(X) = \text{``CS101''}$$
$$sub_1(Y) = \text{``CS100''}$$

on (14.22) to get the substituted rule instance

$$cp(\text{``CS101''}, \text{``CS100''}) \rightarrow before(\text{``CS101''}, \text{``CS100''})$$

This rule, together with the hypothesis $cp(\text{``CS101''}, \text{``CS100''})$, gives us

$$before(\text{``CS101''}, \text{``CS100''})$$

Now we can use rule (14.23) with the hypothesis $cp(\text{``CS120''}, \text{``CS101''})$ and the fact $before(\text{``CS101''}, \text{``CS100''})$ that we just proved, to prove

$$before(\text{``CS120''}, \text{``CS100''})$$

That is, we apply the substitution

$$sub_2(X) = \text{``CS120''}$$
$$sub_2(Y) = \text{``CS100''}$$
$$sub_2(Z) = \text{``CS101''}$$

to (14.23) to obtain the rule

Paths in a Graph

Example 14.24 deals with a common form of rules that define paths in a directed graph, given the arcs of the graph. Think of the courses as nodes, with an arc $a \to b$ if course b is a prerequisite of course a. Then $before(a, b)$ corresponds to the existence of a path of length 1 or more from a to b. Figure 14.9 shows the graph based on the Course-Prerequisite information from Fig. 11.2(b).

When the graph represents prerequisites, we expect it to be acyclic, because it would not do to have a course that had to be taken before itself. However, even if the graph has cycles, the same sort of logical rules define paths in terms of arcs. We can write these rules

$$arc(X, Y) \to path(X, Y)$$

that is, if there is an arc from node X to node Y, then there is a path from X to Y, and

$$\bigl(arc(X, Z) \text{ AND } path(Z, Y)\bigr) \to path(X, Y)$$

That is, if there is an arc from X to some Z, and a path from Z to Y, then there is a path from X to Y. Notice that these are the same rules as (14.22) and (14.23), with predicate arc in place of cp, and $path$ in place of $before$.

$$\bigl(cp(\text{``CS120''}, \text{``CS101''}) \text{ AND } before(\text{``CS101''}, \text{``CS100''})\bigr)$$
$$\to before(\text{``CS120''}, \text{``CS100''})$$

We then may infer the head of this substituted rule, to prove

$$before(\text{``CS120''}, \text{``CS100''})$$

Similarly, we may apply rule (14.23) to the ground atomic formulas

$$cp(\text{``CS121''}, \text{``CS120''})$$

and $before(\text{``CS120''}, \text{``CS100''})$ to prove $before(\text{``CS121''}, \text{``CS100''})$. Then we use (14.23) on $cp(\text{``CS206''}, \text{``CS121''})$ and $before(\text{``CS121''}, \text{``CS100''})$ to prove

$$before(\text{``CS206''}, \text{``CS100''})$$

There are many other $before$ facts we could prove in a similar manner. ✦

EXERCISES

14.9.1*: We can show that the $before$ predicate of Example 14.24 is the transitive closure of the cp predicate as follows. Suppose there is a sequence of courses $c_1, c_2, \ldots, c_n$, for some $n \geq 2$, and c_1 is a prerequisite of c_2, which is a prerequisite of c_3, and so on; in general, $cp(c_i, c_{i+1})$ is a given fact for $i = 1, 2, \ldots, n-1$. Show that c_1 comes before c_n by showing that $before(c_1, c_i)$ for all $i = 2, 3, \ldots, n$, by induction on i.

14.9.2: Using the rules and facts of Example 14.24, prove the following facts.

a) $before(\text{``CS120''}, \text{``CS100''})$
b) $before(\text{``CS206''}, \text{``CS100''})$

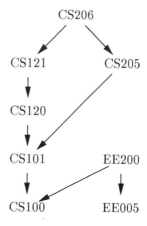

Fig. 14.9. Prerequisite information as a directed graph.

14.9.3: We can speed up the process of following chains of prerequisites by adding to Example 14.24 the rule

$$\bigl(before(X, Z) \ \text{AND} \ before(Z, Y)\bigr) \rightarrow before(X, Y)$$

That is, the first subgoal can be any *before* fact, not just a prerequisite fact. Using this rule, find a shorter proof for Exercise 14.9.2(b).

14.9.4*: How many *before* facts can we prove in Example 14.24?

14.9.5: Let *csg* be a predicate that stands for the Course-Student-Grade relation of Fig. 8.1, *cdh* be a predicate that stands for the Course-Day-Hour relation of Fig. 8.2(c), and *cr* a predicate for the Course-Room relation of Fig. 8.2(d). Let $where(S, D, H, R)$ be a predicate that means student S is in room R at hour H of day D. More precisely, S is taking a course that meets in that room at that time.

a)   Write a rule that defines *where* in terms of *csg*, *cdh*, and *cr*.

b)   If the facts for the predicates *csg*, *cdh*, and *cr* are as given in Figs. 8.1 and 8.2, what *where* facts can you infer? Give a proof of two such facts.

❖❖ 14.10   Truth and Provability

We close our discussion of predicate logic with an introduction to one of the more subtle issues of logic: the distinction between what is provable and what is true. We have seen inference rules that allow us to prove things in either propositional or predicate logic, yet we could not be sure that a given set of rules was complete, in the sense that they allowed us to prove every true statement. We asserted, for instance, that resolution as we presented it in Section 12.11 is complete for propositional logic. A generalized form of resolution, which we do not cover here, is also complete for predicate logic.

Models

However, to understand completeness of a proof-strategy, we need to grasp the notion of "truth." To get at "truth," we need to understand the notion of a *model*. Every kind of logic has a notion of models for a collection of expressions. These models are the interpretations that make the expressions true.

◆ **Example 14.25.** In propositional logic, the interpretations are truth assignments. Consider the expressions $E_1 = p$ AND q and $E_2 = \bar{p}$ OR r. There are eight truth assignments for expressions involving variables p, q, and r, which we may denote by a string of three bits, for the truth values of each of these variables, in order.

The expression E_1 is made true only by those assignments that make both p and q true, that is, by 110 and 111. The expression E_2 is made true by six assignments: 000, 001, 010, 011, 101, and 111. Thus there is only one model for set of expressions $\{E_1, E_2\}$, namely 111, since only this model appears on both lists. ◆

◆ **Example 14.26.** In predicate logic, interpretations are the structures defined in Section 14.5. Let us consider the expression E

$$(\forall X)(\exists Y)p(X, Y)$$

That is, for every value of X there is at least one value of Y for which $p(X, Y)$ is true.

An interpretation makes E true if for every element a of the domain D, there is some element b in D — not necessarily the same b for each a — such that the relation that is the interpretation for predicate p has the pair (a, b) as a member. These interpretations are models of E; other interpretations are not. For example, if domain D is the integers and the interpretation for predicate p makes $p(X, Y)$ true if and only if $X < Y$, then we have a model for expression E. However, the interpretation that has domain D equal to the integers and has the interpretation of p in which $p(X, Y)$ is true if and only if $X = Y^2$, is not a model for expression E. ◆

Entailment

We can now state what it means for an expression E to be true, given a collection of expressions $\{E_1, E_2, \ldots, E_n\}$. We say that $\{E_1, E_2, \ldots, E_n\}$ *entails* expression E if every model M for $\{E_1, E_2, \ldots, E_n\}$ is also a model for E. The *double turnstile* operator $\models$ denotes entailment, as

Double turnstile

$$E_1, E_2, \ldots, E_n \models E$$

The intuition we need is that each interpretation is a possible world. When we say $E_1, E_2, \ldots, E_n \models E$, we are saying that E is true in every possible world where the expressions $E_1, E_2, \ldots, E_n$ are true.

The notion of entailment should be contrasted with the notion of proof. If we have a particular proof system such as resolution in mind, then we can use the *single turnstile* operator $\vdash$ to denote proof in the same way. That is,

Single turnstile

$$E_1, E_2, \ldots, E_n \vdash E$$

means that, for the set of inference rules at hand, there is a proof of E from the hypotheses $E_1, E_2, \ldots, E_n$. Note that $\vdash$ can have different meanings for different proof systems. Also remember that $\models$ and $\vdash$ are not necessarily the same relationship, although we would generally like to have a proof system in which one is true if and only if the other is true.

There is a close connection between tautologies and entailment. In particular, suppose $E_1, E_2, \ldots, E_n \models E$. Then we claim

$$(E_1 \text{ AND } E_2 \text{ AND } \cdots \text{ AND } E_n) \rightarrow E \tag{14.24}$$

is a tautology. Consider some interpretation I. If I makes the left-hand side of (14.24) true, then I is a model of $\{E_1, E_2, \ldots, E_n\}$. Since $E_1, E_2, \ldots, E_n \models E$, interpretation I must also make E true. Thus I makes (14.24) true.

The only other possibility is that I makes the left-hand side of (14.24) false. Then, because an implication is always true when its left-hand side is false, we know (14.24) is again true. Thus (14.24) is a tautology.

Conversely, if (14.24) is a tautology, then we can prove $E_1, E_2, \ldots, E_n \models E$. We leave this proof as an exercise.

Notice that our argument does not depend on whether the expressions involved are of propositional or predicate logic, or some other kind of logic that we have not studied. We only need to know that the tautologies are the expressions made true by every "interpretation" and that a model for an expression or set of expressions is an interpretation making the expression(s) true.

Comparing Provability and Entailment

Consistent proof system

We would like to know that a given proof system allows us to prove everything that is true and nothing that is false. That is, we want the single and double turnstiles to mean the same thing. A proof system is said to be *consistent* if, whenever something can be proved, it is also entailed. That is, $E_1, E_2, \ldots, E_n \vdash E$ implies $E_1, E_2, \ldots, E_n \models E$. For example, we discussed in Section 12.10 why our inference rules for propositional logic were consistent. To be exact, we showed that whenever we started with hypotheses $E_1, E_2, \ldots, E_n$ and wrote a line E in our proof, then $(E_1 \text{ AND } E_2 \text{ AND } \cdots \text{ AND } E_n) \rightarrow E$ was a tautology. By what we argued above, that is the same as saying $E_1, E_2, \ldots, E_n \models E$.

We would also like our proof system to be complete. Then we could prove everything that was entailed by our hypotheses, even if finding that proof was hard. It turns out that the inference rules we gave in Section 12.10, or the resolution rule in Section 12.11 are both complete proof systems. That is, if $E_1, E_2, \ldots, E_n \models E$, then $E_1, E_2, \ldots, E_n \vdash E$ in either of these proof systems. There are also complete proof systems for predicate logic, although we shall not introduce them.

Gödel's Incompleteness Theorem

One of the most striking results of modern mathematics is often seen as a contradiction to what we have just said about there being complete proof systems for predicate logic. This result actually concerns not predicate logic as we have discussed it, but rather a specialization of this logic that lets us talk about integers and the usual operations on integers. In particular, we have to modify predicate logic to introduce predicates for the arithmetic operations, such as

1. $plus(X, Y, Z)$, which we want to be true when and only when $X + Y = Z$,

2. $times(X, Y, Z)$, true exactly when $X \times Y = Z$, and

3. $less(X, Y)$, true exactly when $X < Y$.

Further, we need to restrict the domain in interpretations so that the values appear to be the nonnegative integers. We can do that in one of two ways. One way is to introduce a set of expressions that we assert are true. By selecting these expressions properly, the domain in any interpretation satisfying the expressions must "look like" the integers, and the special predicates such as $plus$ or $less$ must act as would the familiar operations with those names.

◆   **Example 14.27.** We can assert expressions such as

$$plus(X, Y, Z) \to plus(Y, X, Z)$$

which is the commutative law for addition, or

$$\big(less(X, Y) \text{ AND } less(Y, Z)\big) \to less(X, Z)$$

which is the transitive law for $<$. ◆

Perhaps a simpler way to understand the restriction of predicate logic that Gödel's theorem addresses is to suppose that the logic allows only one model, the model in which the domain is the nonnegative integers, and the special predicates are given relations corresponding to their conventional meaning. For instance, we would let the interpretation for predicate $plus$ be

$$\{(a, b, c) \mid a + b = c\}$$

Gödel's theorem states that no matter what consistent proof system one selects, there is some expression E that is true but unprovable! More precisely, if $E_1, E_2, \ldots, E_n$ is a set of expressions all of whose models behave as do the nonnegative integers, then $E_1, E_2, \ldots, E_n \models E$ is true, yet $E_1, E_2, \ldots, E_n \vdash E$ is false. That is, there is no proof of E from $\{E_1, E_2, \ldots, E_n\}$ in our chosen system.

The unprovable expression E may be different for different chosen proof systems. In fact, the selected expression E can be thought of as a way to encode into integers the fact that the expression itself has no proof in the given proof system.

Limits on What a Computer Can Do

An important consequence of Gödel's theorem is that there is a limit on our ability to answer questions about mathematics. If we have a mathematical model as complex as the integers (and many mathematical models are far more complex than integers, as we have seen in this book), then there is no mechanical way we can distinguish true statements from false ones. The best we can do is use some consistent proof system to allow us to search for proofs. If we find one, we are lucky, and we can be sure that the proved statement is true. However, our search may go on forever, without ever finding a proof, even though the statement is true; that is, the statement is entailed by the assumptions we have made to define the mathematical model at hand.

Philosophically, this situation suggests that mathematics will forever remain interesting and challenging. Practically, it suggests that there are limits to what

Undecidability

The logician Alan Turing developed a formal theory of computing in the 1930's considerably before there were any electronic computers to model with his theory. The most important result of this theory is the discovery that certain problems are *undecidable*; no computer whatsoever can answer them.

Turing machine   A centerpiece of the theory is the *Turing machine*, an abstract computer that consists of a finite automaton with an infinite tape divided into squares. In a single move, the Turing machine can read the character on the one square seen by its *tape head*, and based on that character and its current state, replace the character by a different one, change its state, and move the tape head one square left or right. An observed fact is that every real computer, as well as every other mathematical model of what a computing engine should be, can compute exactly what the Turing machine can compute. Thus we take the Turing machine as the standard abstract model of a computer.

However, we do not have to learn the details of what a Turing machine can do in order to appreciate Turing's theory. It suffices to take as a model of a computer a kind of C program that reads character input and has only two possible write statements: `printf("yes\n")` and `printf("no\n")`. Moreover, after making an output of either type, the program must terminate, so that it cannot make a contradictory output later. Understand that a program of this type might, on some inputs, give neither a "yes" nor a "no" response; it might run forever in a loop.

We shall prove that there is no program like D, the "decider" program of Fig. 14.10(a). D supposedly takes as input a program P of the special type above, and says "yes" if P says "yes" when given P itself as input. D says "no" if — when P is given P as input — P either says "no" or P fails to make any decision. As we shall see, it is this requirement that D figure out the occasions when P is never going to render a decision that makes D impossible to write.

However, supposing that D exists, it is a simple matter to write a "complementer" program C, as suggested in Fig. 14.10(b). C is formed from the hypothetical D by changing every statement that prints "no" into one that prints "yes," and vice versa.

Now we ask what happens when C is given itself as input, as suggested in Fig. 14.10(c)? If C says "yes," then as Fig. 14.10(b) reminds us, C is asserting that "C does not say 'yes' on input C." If C says "no," then C is asserting that "C says 'yes' on input C." We now have a contradiction similar to Russell's paradox, where C can say neither "yes" nor "no" truthfully.

The conclusion is that the decider program D does not really exist. That is, the problem solved by D, which is whether a given C program of the restricted type says "yes" or fails to say "yes" (by saying "no" or by saying nothing) when given itself as input, cannot be solved by computer. It is an undecidable problem.

Since Turing's original result, a wide variety of undecidable problems have been discovered. For example, it is undecidable whether a given C program enters an infinite loop on a given input, or whether two C programs produce the same output on the same input.

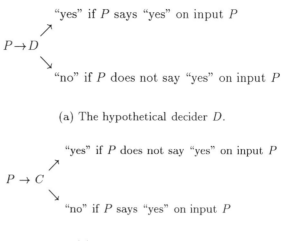

"yes" if P says "yes" on input P

$P \rightarrow D$

"no" if P does not say "yes" on input P

(a) The hypothetical decider D.

"yes" if P does not say "yes" on input P

$P \rightarrow C$

"no" if P says "yes" on input P

(b) The complementer C.

?

$C \rightarrow C$

?

(c) What does C do with itself as input?

Fig. 14.10. Parts of Turing's construction.

we can do with a computer. In particular, we cannot write programs to find proofs in sufficiently complex systems, although we can do so in simple systems, such as propositional logic or even predicate logic without any special predicates or restrictions. The reader should observe the box on "Undecidability," in which a theorem related to Gödel's is discussed. The theory of undecidability allows us to point to specific problems that we can show no computer can solve.

Thus, rather than ending this book on a negative note, the theory of undecidability reminds us that, like mathematics, computer science is destined to challenge the best minds the human race can produce. The student who pursues the subject will learn the art and science that is needed to avoid the undecidable (and the intractable as well). He or she may then join the ranks of those scientists and engineers pushing back the frontiers of what our computing machines can do.

EXERCISES

14.10.1: Let $E_1 = p$, $E_2 = q$, and $E_3 = qr + p\bar{r}$. Describe the models (truth assignments for propositional variables p, q, and r) that make $\{E_1, E_2\}$ true. Describe the models for E_3. Is $E_1, E_2 \models E_3$ true? Why or why not?

14.10.2**: Consider the following expressions of predicate logic.

1. $E_1 = (\forall X)p(X, X)$

2. $E_2 = (\forall X)(\forall Y)\big(p(X, Y) \rightarrow p(Y, X)\big)$

3. $E_3 = (\forall X)(\forall Y)(\forall Z)\Big(\big(p(X, Y) \text{ AND } p(Y, Z)\big) \rightarrow p(X, Z)\Big)$

4. $E_4 = (\forall X)(\forall Y)\big(p(X, Y) \text{ OR } p(Y, X)\big)$

5. $E_5 = (\forall X)(\exists Y)p(X, Y)$

Which of these five expressions are entailed by the other four? In each case, either give an argument about all possible interpretations, to show entailment, or give a particular interpretation that is a model of four of the expressions but not the fifth. *Hint*: Start by imagining that the predicate p represents the arcs of a directed graph, and look at each expression as a property of graphs. The material in Section 7.10 should give some hints either for finding appropriate models in which the domain is the nodes of a certain graph and predicate p the arcs of that graph, or for showing why there must be entailment. Note however, that it is not sufficient to show entailment by insisting that the interpretation be a graph.

14.10.3*: Let S_1 and S_2 be two sets of expressions of predicate logic (or propositional logic — it doesn't matter), and let their corresponding sets of models be M_1 and M_2, respectively.

a)   Show that the set of models for the set of expressions $S_1 \cup S_2$ is $M_1 \cap M_2$.
b)   Is the set of models for set of expressions $S_1 \cap S_2$ always equal to $M_1 \cup M_2$?

14.10.4*: Show that if $(E_1 \text{ AND } E_2 \text{ AND } \cdots \text{ AND } E_n) \rightarrow E$ is a tautology, then $E_1, E_2, \ldots, E_n \models E$.

✦✦ 14.11   Summary of Chapter 14

The reader should have learned the following points from this chapter.

✦   Predicate logic uses atomic formulas, that is, predicates with arguments, as atomic operands and the operators of propositional logic, plus the two quantifiers, "for all" and "there exists."

✦   Variables in an expression of predicate logic are bound by quantifiers in a manner analogous to the binding of variables in a program to declarations.

✦   Instead of the truth assignments of propositional logic, in predicate logic we have a complex structure called an "interpretation." An interpretation consists of a domain of values, relations on that domain for the predicates, and values from the domain for any free variables.

✦   The interpretations that make a set of expressions true are the "models" of that set of expressions.

✦   Tautologies of predicate calculus are those that evaluate to **TRUE** for every interpretation. While many tautologies are obtained by substitution into tautologies of propositional logic, there are also some important tautologies involving quantifiers.

✦ It is possible to put every expression of predicate logic into "prenex form," consisting of a quantifier-free expression to which quantifiers are applied as the last operators.

✦ Proofs in predicate logic can be constructed in a manner similar to proofs in propositional logic.

✦ The substitution of constants for variables in tautologies yields another tautology, and this inference rule is useful in proofs, especially when we work from a database of facts and a collection of rules.

✦ A set of expressions $\{E_1, \ldots, E_n\}$ "entails" an expression E if any model of the former is also a model of the latter. We regard E as "true" given $E_1, \ldots, E_n$ as hypotheses if E is entailed by $E_1, \ldots, E_n$.

✦ Gödel's theorem states that if we take expressions describing number theory (i.e., arithmetic for the nonnegative integers) as hypotheses, then for any proof system, there is some expression that is entailed by the hypotheses but cannot be proved from them.

✦ Turing's theorem describes a formal model of a computer called a "Turing machine" and says that there are problems that cannot be solved by a computer.

✧ 14.12   Bibliographic Notes for Chapter 14

The books on logic, including Enderton [1972], Mendelson [1987], Lewis and Papadimitriou [1981], and Manna and Waldinger [1990] that we cited in Section 12.14, also cover predicate logic.

Gödel's incompleteness theorem appeared in Gödel [1931]. Turing's paper on undecidability is Turing [1936].

Gödel, K. [1931]. "Uber formal unentscheidbare satze der Principia Mathematica und verwander systeme," *Monatschefte fur Mathematik und Physik* **38**, pp. 173–198.

Turing, A. M. [1936]. "On computable numbers with an application to the *entscheidungsproblem*," *Proc. London Math. Soc.* **2**:42, pp. 230–265.

❖ Index